lonely planet

Hawaii

Glenda Bendure
Ned Friary
Sara Benson

LONELY PLANET PUBLICATIONS
Melbourne • Oakland • London • Paris

HAWAIIAN ISLANDS

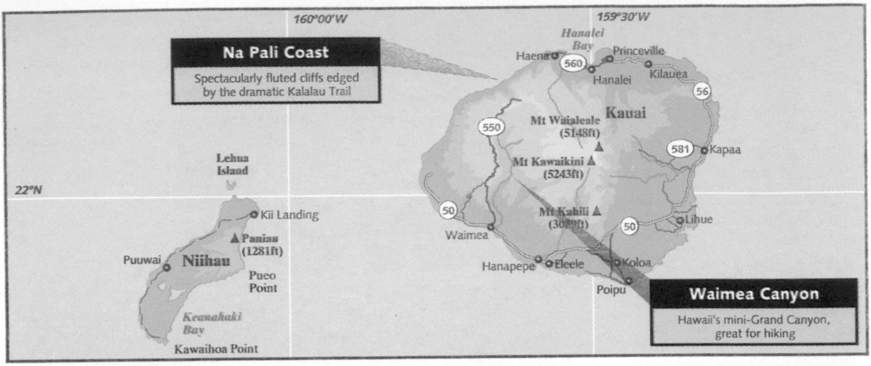

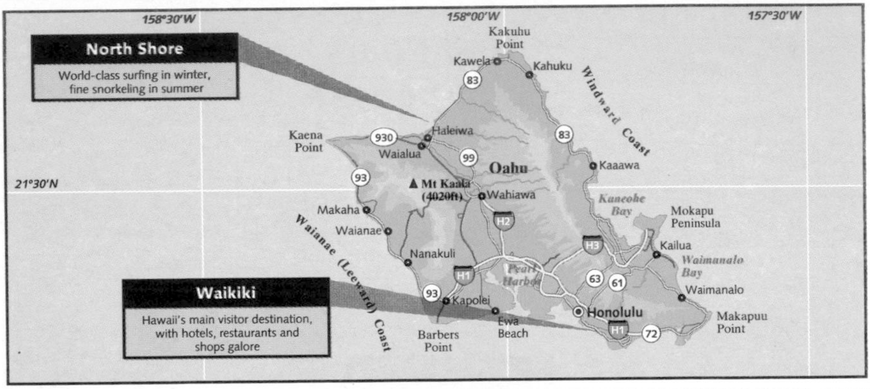

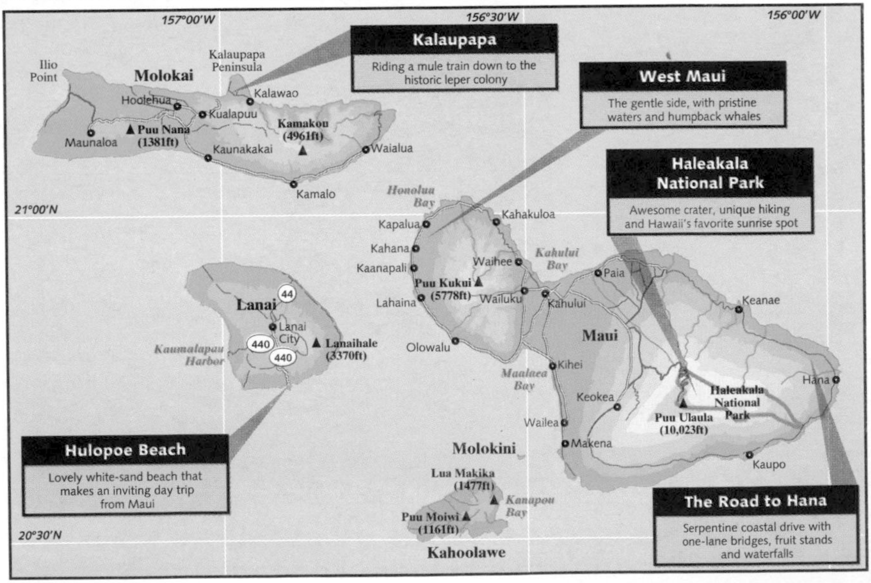

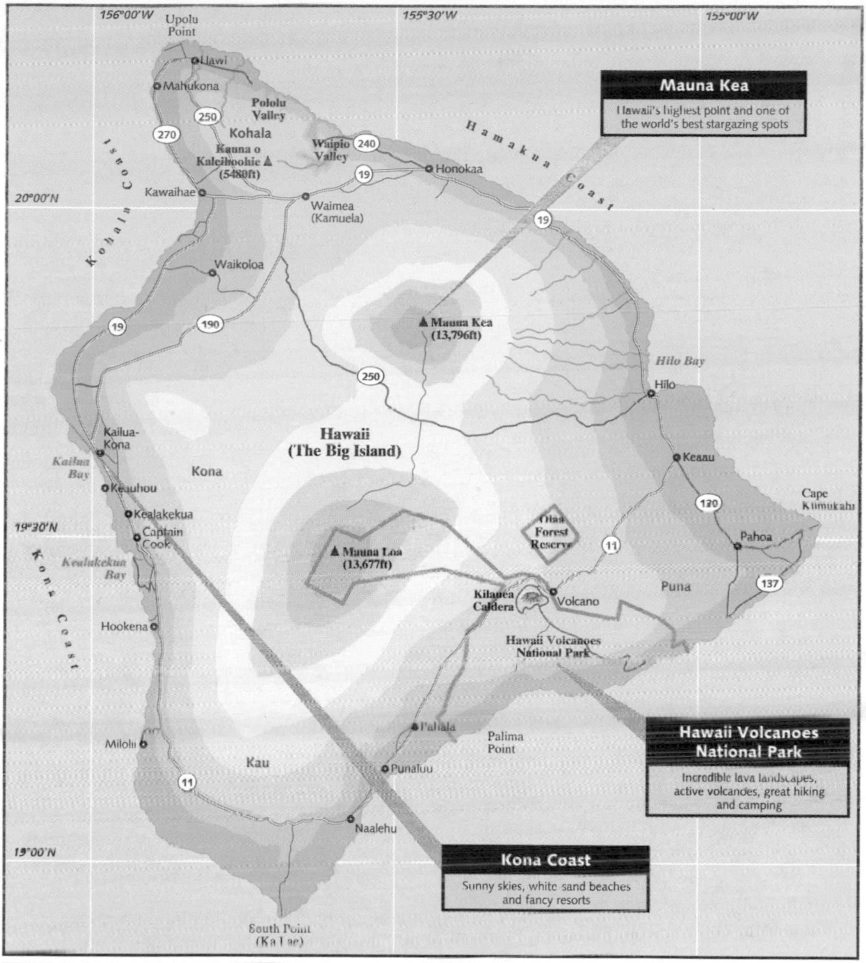

156°00'W
155°30'W
155°00'W
20°00'N
19°30'N
19°00'N
Upolu Point
Hawi
Mahukona
Pololu Valley
Kohala
Kauna o Kaleihoohie
(5480ft)
Waipio Valley
Honokaa
Hamakua Coast
Kawaihae
Waimea (Kamuela)
Kohala Coast
Waikoloa
Mauna Kea
Hawaii's highest point and one of the world's best stargazing spots
Mauna Kea (13,796ft)
Hilo Bay
Hilo
Kailua-Kona
Kailua Bay
Hawaii (The Big Island)
Kona
Keauhou
Kealakekua
Captain Cook
Kealakekua Bay
Kona Coast
Keaau
Cape Kumukahi
Olaa Forest Reserve
Pahoa
Mauna Loa (13,677ft)
Kilauea Caldera
Volcano
Puna
Hookena
Hawaii Volcanoes National Park
Hawaii Volcanoes National Park
Incredible lava landscapes, active volcanoes, great hiking and camping
Pahala
Palima Point
Milolii
Kau
Punaluu
Naalehu
Kona Coast
Sunny skies, white sand beaches and fancy resorts
South Point (Ka Lae)
19
250
270
240
190
11
130
137

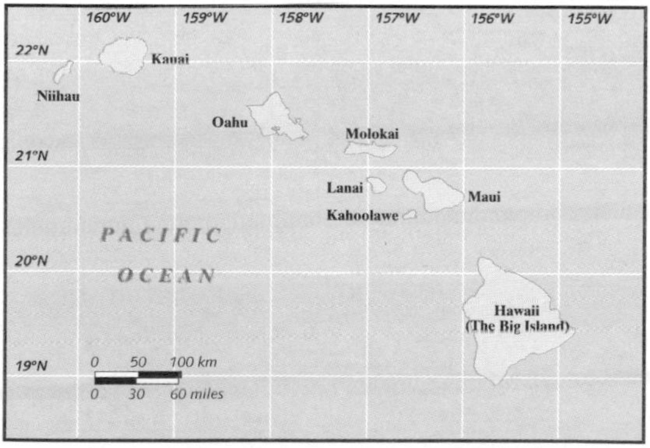

160°W
159°W
158°W
157°W
156°W
155°W
22°N
21°N
20°N
19°N
Kauai
Niihau
Oahu
Molokai
Lanai
Maui
Kahoolawe
PACIFIC OCEAN
Hawaii (The Big Island)
0 50 100 km
0 30 60 miles

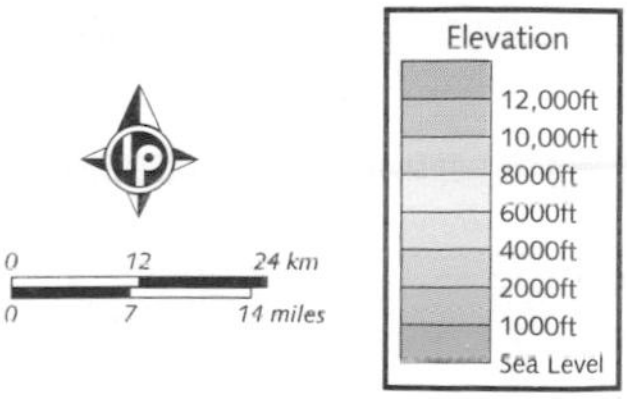

0 12 24 km
0 7 14 miles
Elevation
12,000ft
10,000ft
8000ft
6000ft
4000ft
2000ft
1000ft
Sea Level

Hawaii
6th edition – April 2003
First published – August 1990

Published by
Lonely Planet Publications Pty Ltd ABN. 36 005 607 983
90 Maribyrnong St, Footscray, Victoria 3011, Australia

Lonely Planet Offices
Australia Locked Bag 1, Footscray, Victoria 3011
USA 150 Linden St, Oakland, CA 94607
UK 10a Spring Place, London NW5 3BH
France 1 rue du Dahomey, 75011 Paris

Photographs
Many of the images in this guide are available for licensing from Lonely Planet Images.
w www.lonelyplanetimages.com

Front cover photograph
Plumeria (or frangipani) blossoms (*Plumeri* hybrid), Hawaii
(Greg Vaughn/Getty Images)

ISBN 1 74059 142 9

Printed by SNP SPrint (M) Sdn Bhd
Printed in Malaysia

Contents – Text

Contents – Maps

GETTING AROUND

OAHU

HAWAII (THE BIG ISLAND)

MAUI

MOLOKAI

LANAI

KAHOOLAWE

KAUAI

NIIHAU

NORTHWESTERN HAWAIIAN ISLANDS

HAWAII MAP INDEX

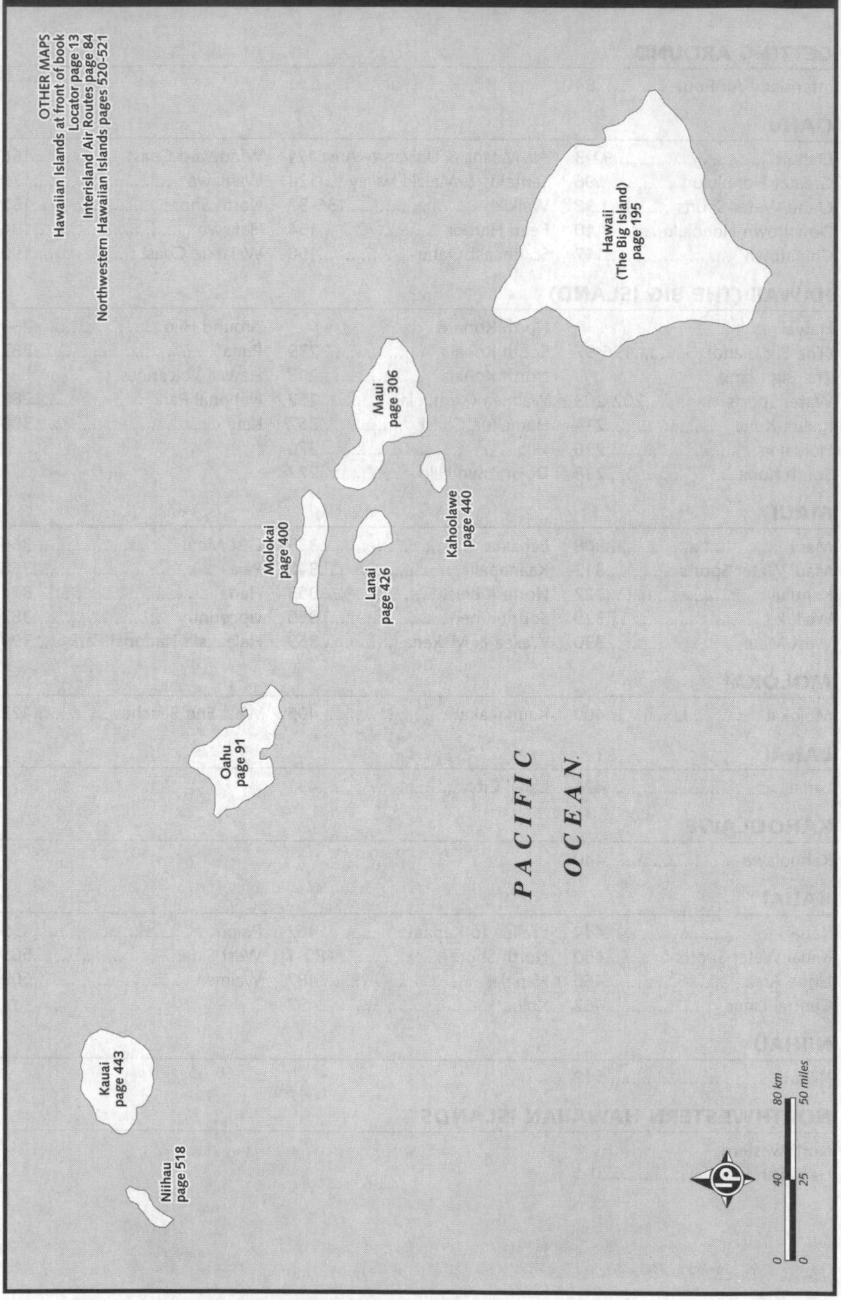

The Authors

Ned Friary & Glenda Bendure

Ned grew up near Boston and studied social thought and political economy at the University of Massachusetts in Amherst. Glenda grew up in California's Mojave Desert and first traveled overseas as a high school American Field Service (AFS) exchange student to India.

After meeting in Santa Cruz, California, where Glenda was completing her university studies, they took to the road and spent several years traveling throughout Asia and the Pacific, with a home base in Japan where Ned taught English and Glenda edited a monthly magazine. On their first trip to Hawaii, they were so taken by the islands that a two-week vacation stretched into a four-month sojourn.

Ned and Glenda have a particular fondness for islands. Over the years they've authored several Lonely Planet books for places as varied as the remote shores of Micronesia, tiny Bermuda and thoroughly modern Denmark. When they're not exploring some distant island, they can often be found hitting the waves back home on Cape Cod.

Sara 'Sam' Benson

Years ago Sara Benson graduated with a liberal arts degree from the University of Chicago and found herself swept away to Maui. She never forgot that taste of wild guava or volcanic mana even as she ran through several jobs as an editor, high school teacher, journalist and corporate hack both in the USA and abroad before signing on with Lonely Planet many moons ago.

FROM THE AUTHORS

Ned Friary & Glenda Bendure Many thanks to the people who helped us on this project: Emilie Travis, wildlife interpreter at Kilauea Point; Curt A Cottrell, Na Ala Hele Trails & Access Program Manager; Allen Tom, Sanctuary Program Manager at Hawaiian Islands Humpback Whale National Marine Sanctuary; Linda Delaney from the Office of Hawaiian Affairs; Jon Giffin of the Division of Forestry & Wildlife; travel consultant Teruo Koike; Honolulu science teacher Ted Brattstrom; and marine biologist Lisa King.

Thanks also to those friends and travelers who shared insights and experiences with us along the way. And last but not least, a hearty aloha to Helen Bendure, Bert Webster and Jim and Barbara Kershner for all their inspiration.

Sara 'Sam' Benson A big thanks to Lonely Planet's Oakland office for lifting me on board this project, especially to all of the cartographers, editors and staff who armed me with anecdotes and professional advice. Special gratitude to Ned Friary, Glenda Bendure and Erin Corrigan for expressing saintly patience.

Mahalo to da max to Lonely Planet author Conner Gorry, and all of the islanders who showed me unstinting aloha. Warmest cheers to little Ip for giving me sanity and a clean, warm and crazy place to call home. Half a decade ago, Blake Macurdy hauled me up out of Haleakala Crater by my backpack straps – thank you.

This Book

Ned and Glenda updated the front-of-the-book chapters and the island chapters of Oahu, Kauai, Niihau, Kahoolawe and the Northwestern Hawaiian Islands.

Sam updated the Maui, Molokai and Lanai chapters of this book. She also updated the Big Island chapter based on work by Conner Gorry and Julie Jares.

FROM THE PUBLISHER

This sixth edition of *Hawaii*, produced at Lonely Planet's Melbourne office, was commissioned by Robert (Bob) Reid and Erin Corrigan, who also developed the title. Editing was coordinated by Rebecca Chau, with maps coordinated by Herman So. Much thanks to project managers Chris Love and Charles Rawlings-Way for keeping things on track. Bethune Carmichael, Peter Cruttenden and Lara Morcombe edited this edition, and design and layout was taken care of by Katie Cason and Cameron Duncan. The cover was designed by Tracey Croom and artwork was provided by Ruth Askevold. Quentin Frayne produced the Language chapter, and Bruce Evans, Victoria Harrison, Sally Morgan and Tamsin Wilson were able to provide some last-minute help.

Thanks

Many thanks to the travelers who used the last edition and wrote to us with helpful hints, useful advice and interesting anecdotes.

Ken Acock, Margaret Terry Adler, Robin Adlerblum, Lael Ambrose, Nate Anderson, Jill Andresevic, Nicola Archer, Connie Baker, Magdalena Balcerek, Christopher Ball, Rolf Ballmoos, Anna Banerji, James G Batol, Jane Battersby, Nano Beivi, Daniel Bleaken, Dorinda & Conrad Boerman, Vincent Boisvert, Walter Bono, Hau Boon Lai, Helan Bottrill, David Bowen, Catherine Breen, Ron Brouwer, Dave Brown, S Bruce Warthman, Alexanderq Brucker, Mike Buckley, Rebecca Buckley, Anne Burgess, Anrea Caloini, Peter Camp-Smith, Gayle M Campbell, Edward & Andrea Canapary, Teresa Carpenter, Katherine Carroll, Kerri Carroll, Elizabeth Cary, Deivy Centeio, Stephen Chase, Yee Cheng, Sumeet Chhibber, Danielle Clode, Matt Collier, Katrina Corcoran, John Cornwell, Peter Cross, James Davis, Mark Davis, Richard Davison, Lanaya Deily, Juli Dent, Andre Desjardins, Osa & Sam Detrick, Ins Dietisheim, Ava Dolan, Debbi Dolan, Mark Domroese, Mildred Dumpel-Tromp, Kylie Duthie, John Dyer, Mike Earnest, Juli & Greg Edward, Louise & Andrew Edwards, Ulrike Eglseder, Jesse Elliott, Diana & Erwin van Engelen, Justin Farley, Marietta Fedder, Pam Feinstein, Wendy Fletcher, Craig Foss, Sheila Freita, Phyllis Frey, Mark Fujiwara, Chirag Gandhi, Tom Ganz, Will Garcher, Carla Garcia, Mary Gentleman, Joel Gerwein, Elizabeth Long Goldman, Annemone Goldschmied, Lori Gonder, James Gordon, Henri Grau, Neil Griggs, John Gropp, Alexander Guenther, Nadine Guitton, Dr Goran Gustafsson, L Guzman, Angela Halse, Anja Hansen, C. Harris, Robert Heath, TS Heaton, Lucy Hein, Lucy & Markus Hein, Nicole Henry, Padraig Heochaidh, Linda & Jack Hibbard, Lori Higa, Eva Himmelberg, Colette Hirata, James Holgate, Nancy & Chuck Hooper, Lee Howard, Simon Huang, Martin Jensen, Stig Jepsen, Brian L Jester, Ruth Johnson, Cheryl Jones, Kelly Jones, Liz Jones, Lloyd Jones, Nancy Kamuda, Shella Keilholz, Sarah Kettley, Teresia Kevin, Derek Kiger, Jim Killebrew, Vanina Killebrew, Min Kim, Olliemarie Kingston, Tom & Marge Kinney, Karen Kissileff, Wayne & Georgina Knapton, John Kosowski, Ann Krumboltz, Larry Kwiatkowski, Frances Kwok, Kay Lamier, Karen Latter, Randy & Rosemary Leach, Grace Lee, Penny Lee, Siri Samantha Lia, Robson Lin, Gavin Lock, Barbara Lohoff, Ana Lopez, Christine Lotter, Aaron Lowe, Teresa Maher, Anne Marie McTrowe, Michael Marquardt, Allegra Marshall, Francine Marshall, Heather Martin, Siobhan Marzluft, Volker Maschmann, Jonathan Masters, Akiko Masuda, Simon McHugh, E McRae, Bruno Medeiros, Rosy Meehan, Bill & Joan Meikle, Harry Melts, Tim Merritt, Russ Michaels, Rita Mihaly, Carolyn Miller, Craig F Miller, Ann Miya, Roz Morris, Keith Mostov, Dan Moulthrop, Franklin Murillo, Bruce & Trish Murray, Chris Murray, Christina Nagel, Stend Narti, Julia Neal, Kelly Nevins, Tim Nevins, Paul Newsome, Peter Nietresta, Anja Niewolik, Ken Norris, Sharron O Laughlin, Kevin P O'Connell, Cynthia O'Keefe, Sharyn & David Olive, Johanna Omelia, Douglas Osborne, Kyle Parker, James Parry, Nort Petrovich, Anna Judith Piller, Bill Pollington, Harriet Potts, Daniel Prall, Thomas Rau, Michael Rausch, Barry Raybould, Beki Ries-Montgomery, Michael Riess, Graham Rivers, Forrest Roberts, Kristen Rogers, Andrea

Rogge, Herwig Rombauts, Dan Sabath, John Sabo, Ralf Schmitz, Michael Schuette, Janna Scopel, Terri Scott, Kimberly Senior, Dawn Sentance, Ali Shanks, Jacob Siboni, Kristie Sills, Jennifer Simmer, Andrew Sinclair, Christos Siopis, Teresa Sivilli, Colette Slover, Catherine Smith, Dawn Smith, Grant Smith, Ken Smith, Michelle Smith, Sue Smith, Eduardo Spaccasassi, Sacha Spector, Geoff Spradley, Carol J Stadum, Matthew Staley, Sandra Starke, Karin Steinkamp, Alexandra Stern, Eric Stevens, Charlie Stokes, Cindy & Kevan Strube, Tim Sturge, Richard Sugiyama, Tammy Svoboda, Giselle Sweet-Escott, Mike Tailor, Steven Taylor, Jeanne Teleia, Carel Ten Horn, Christobel Thomas, Kathleen Thomas, Eric Thomsen, Karen Thomson, Abe Trenk, David Tsai, Mike Tuggle, Judy Uhart, Daphne Uviller, Anne Vaile, Peter Paul van Reenen, Martin & Maggie Varco, Ian & Amanda Vernalls, Judy Vhart, Michael Waldock, Jim R Walker, Anne-Michelle Wand, Catherine Watkins, Mary Wells, Dante Wendlandt, Mary Weremczuk, Jodie Wesley, Keltie White, Karen White Pettigrew, Andreas Wieser, Ken & Arvis Willetts, Ann Wilson-Wilde, Milse Wolbe, Sandra Wolf, Simon Wood, Christopher Wortley, Bart & Hannah Wright, Wynne Wu, Jane Yamashiro, Traci Young, Kathryn Zajkowski, Alberto Zamboni, Erin Zoski

Foreword

ABOUT LONELY PLANET GUIDEBOOKS

The story begins with a classic travel adventure: Tony and Maureen Wheeler's 1972 journey across Europe and Asia to Australia. There was no useful information about the overland trail then, so Tony and Maureen published the first Lonely Planet guidebook to meet a growing need.

From a kitchen table, Lonely Planet has grown to become the largest independent travel publisher in the world, with offices in Melbourne (Australia), Oakland (USA), London (UK) and Paris (France).

Today Lonely Planet guidebooks cover the globe. There is an ever-growing list of books and information in a variety of media. Some things haven't changed. The main aim is still to make it possible for adventurous travelers to get out there – to explore and better understand the world.

At Lonely Planet we believe travelers can make a positive contribution to the countries they visit – if they respect their host communities and spend their money wisely. Since 1986 a percentage of the income from each book has been donated to aid projects and human rights campaigns, and, more recently, to wildlife conservation.

Although inclusion in a guidebook usually implies a recommendation we cannot list every good place. Exclusion does not necessarily imply criticism. In fact there are a number of reasons why we might exclude a place – sometimes it is simply inappropriate to encourage an influx of travelers.

UPDATES & READER FEEDBACK

Things change – prices go up, schedules change, good places go bad and bad places go bankrupt. Nothing stays the same. So, if you find things better or worse, recently opened or long-since closed, please tell us and help make the next edition even more accurate and useful.

Lonely Planet thoroughly updates each guidebook as often as possible – usually every two years, although for some destinations the gap can be longer. Between editions, up-to-date information is available in our free, monthly email bulletin *Comet* (w www.lonelyplanet.com/newsletters). You can also check out the *Thorn Tree* bulletin board and *Postcards* section of our website, which carry unverified, but fascinating, reports from travelers.

Tell us about it! We genuinely value your feedback. A well-traveled team at Lonely Planet reads and acknowledges every email and letter we receive and ensures that every morsel of information finds its way to the relevant authors, editors and cartographers.

Everyone who writes to us will find their name listed in the next edition of the appropriate guidebook. The very best contributions will be rewarded with a free guidebook.

We may edit, reproduce and incorporate your comments in Lonely Planet products such as guidebooks, websites and digital products, so let us know if you don't want your comments reproduced or your name acknowledged.

How to contact Lonely Planet:
Online: e talk2us@lonelyplanet.com.au, w www.lonelyplanet.com
Australia: Locked Bag 1, Footscray, Victoria 3011
UK: 10a Spring Place, London NW5 3BH
USA: 150 Linden St, Oakland, CA 94607

Introduction

Hawaii is an extraordinary place – a touch of magic for some people, a dream destination for others. The very name Hawaii rolls off the tongue like a soft tropical breeze. It conjures up images of hula dancers swaying under tropical palms, tanned surfers barreling their way across the waves and, in the background, the alluring twang of a steel guitar, the perfumed scent of ginger blossoms.

Once you arrive in Hawaii, you'll find that those classic and sometimes cliched images really do hold true. You can while away an evening at a luau, catch a sunset cruise, lounge on a beach chair with a frosty pina colada in hand.

But you'll also find much more. You'll find aloha, Hawaii's renowned spirit of hospitality. A vibrant multiethnic culture. And impossibly beautiful landscapes, from red-hot lava surging into the sea to precipitous hillsides dripping with waterfalls and luxuriant vegetation.

No question about it, Hawaii's natural beauty is awesome. Mark Twain fittingly called it 'the loveliest fleet of islands that lies anchored in any ocean.' Although the Hawaii of today is far more developed than the one Twain explored, it nonetheless remains a gem.

The Hawaiian Islands are high and rugged, lushly green and cut by spectacular gorges and valleys. The islands are ringed with beautiful beaches, ranging from bleached white to jet black, and every single one is open to the public. The terrain is amazingly varied, climbing from lowland deserts to Alpine mountaintops, with everything from barren lava flows to tropical rain forests in between.

Hawaii certainly does have the expected mass tourism, high-rise hotels and crowded beaches. But that's only one side of the picture. You can also find scores of tourist-free areas and secluded beaches to explore. There are small dusty towns with cowhands and rodeos, surfer havens with health food stores and small cafés, and little art communities with galleries and workshops.

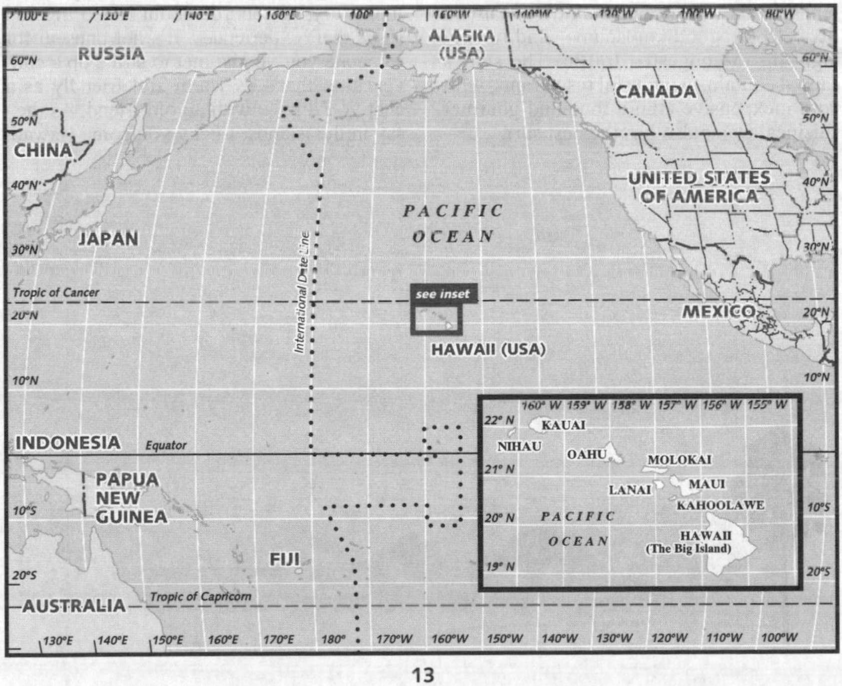

Hawaii boasts some of the world's top surfing and windsurfing spots and has excellent conditions for snorkeling, swimming, diving, kayaking and most other water sports. And it doesn't matter if you're a novice wanting to jump in and get your feet wet for the first time, or an expert looking for some hot competition, you'll find ideal conditions.

There's great beach weather all year round. Hawaii's climate is unusually pleasant for the tropics, as near-constant trade winds prevail. Much of the time the rain falls as short daytime showers that are accompanied by rainbows.

Hawaii's six main islands all feature lovely beaches and splendid scenery. Their leeward coasts are sunny, dry and desert-like, with white sands and turquoise waters. The mountainous windward sides have tropical jungles, cascading waterfalls and pounding surf. The uplands are cool and green, with rolling pastures and small farms. Despite all that the islands have in common, each also has its own unique characteristics.

Oahu is the most developed of the islands, with Waikiki providing nearly half of the tourist accommodations in Hawaii. Honolulu has all the pluses and minuses of urban life, from good museums and lively nightlife to congested traffic. The state's capital contains wonderful restaurants, with both inexpensive ethnic food and gourmet cuisines. Oahu also has the best surf.

Maui is the second largest and second most developed island, but it still boasts plenty of unspoiled places well off the beaten path. The scenic coastal drive to Hana and the sunrise at Haleakala are two of the island's highlights. Maui is also the best island for watching humpback whales.

The Big Island has two things the other islands don't: snow and erupting volcanoes. There's room to move, with enough space for ranchers, astronomers and traditional fishing villages, as well as alternative communities that have settled on the side of lava flows.

Kauai has Hawaii's greenest scenery, a deeply cut canyon resembling a mini-Grand Canyon and the famous razorback cliffs of the Na Pali Coast. The least developed of the four largest islands, it's a mecca for hikers, kayakers and other outdoor enthusiasts.

Molokai, the most Hawaiian of the islands, is rural, slow paced and only lightly visited by tourists. Lanai, the smallest island, has recently reinvented itself, changing from a plantation economy based on pineapples to a luxury resort destination.

Overall, Hawaiians are some of the friendliest folks you'll ever encounter. They love to 'talk story,' to tell you about island life and share their experiences. It's not unusual for someone you've just met to strike up a conversation that's as warm and friendly as a chat you'd have with an old friend. As they say in the islands: Lucky you come Hawaii.

Facts about Hawaii

HISTORY

Hawaii is the northern point of the huge triangle of Pacific Ocean islands known as Polynesia, which means 'many islands.' The other two points of the triangle are Easter Island to the southeast and New Zealand to the southwest.

The exact origins of the original Polynesian settlers remain unknown. Whether they had their roots in Southeast Asia, as has traditionally been thought, or whether they originated in Melanesia, as some archaeologists now believe, is a matter of ongoing debate. Either way, their migratory path apparently took them in an eastwardly direction to settle the southern Polynesian islands of Tonga and Samoa in about 1000 BC. Over the next 1500 years they migrated to the more far-flung areas of Polynesia, with Hawaii being the last area settled.

Archaeological evidence indicates the first Polynesians arrived in Hawaii from the Marquesas Islands between AD 500 and AD 700. Among the links are ancient stone statues found on Hawaii's now-uninhabited Necker Island, which have striking similarities to statues found on the Marquesas Islands.

When the first wave of Tahitians arrived in Hawaii in about AD 1000, they apparently fought and subjugated the Marquesans, who were forced to build temples, irrigation ditches and fishponds for the conquerors.

Hawaiian legends about a tribe of little people called *menehune* may well refer to the Marquesans. Indeed, the word *'menehune'* is very similar to the Tahitian word for 'outcast.'

Ancient Hawaii

The earliest Hawaiians had simple animistic beliefs. Good fishing, a safe journey and a healthy child were all the result of being in tune with the spirits of nature. Offerings to the gods consisted of prayers and a share of the harvest.

Around the 12th century, in a later wave of migration, a powerful Tahitian *kahuna* (priest), Paao, arrived on the Big Island. Convinced that the Hawaiians were too lax in their worship, Paao introduced the concept of offering human sacrifice to the gods and he built the first *luakini heiau*, a type of temple where these sacrifices took place.

Ancient Graffiti

The ancient Hawaiians had no written history, although they did cut petroglyphs into smooth lava rock. Many of these carved pictures are stylized stick figures depicting warriors with spears, barking dogs, birds, canoes and other decipherable images. Some are linear marks, which may have been made to record important events or represent calendars or genealogical charts.

The meanings and purposes behind Hawaiian petroglyphs are mysterious. Some may have been intentionally cryptic, while others might just be random graffiti or the carvings of a budding artist.

Most petroglyphs are found along ancient footpaths and may have been clustered at sites thought to have spiritual power, or *mana*.

The Big Island has the greatest concentration of petroglyphs, with several large fields full of carvings just a few minutes' walk from the main roads.

NED FRIARY

He also established the *kapu* system, a practice of taboos that strictly regulated all social interaction.

*Kapu*s forbade commoners from eating the same food or even walking the same ground as the *alii*, or royalty. A commoner who crossed the shadow of a king could be put to death. *Kapu*s prohibited all women from eating coconuts, bananas, pork and certain varieties of fish.

Paao also decided that Hawaii's blue blood was too diluted and summoned the chief Pili from Kahiki (Tahiti) to establish a new royal lineage. With Pili as chief and Paao as high priest, a new ruling house was formed. Their dynasty was to last 700 years.

King Kamehameha the Great, like all the Big Island chiefs, traced his lineage to Pili. Likewise, Kamehameha's *kahuna nui* (high priest) descended from Paao.

Heiaus The temples erected in ancient Hawaii, called *heiau*s, were built in two basic styles, both constructed of lava rock. One was a simple rectangular enclosure of stone walls built directly on the ground. The other was a more substantial structure built of rocks piled high to form raised terraced platforms. The remains of both types can still be found throughout the islands today.

Inside the *heiau*s were prayer towers, taboo houses and drum houses. These structures were made of native ohia wood, thatched with pili grass (bunchgrass) and tied with cord from the native olona shrub. *Tiki*s, or god images, called *kii*, were carved of wood and placed around the prayer towers.

The *heiau*s were most commonly dedicated to Lono, the god of harvest, or Ku, the god of war. Those built in honor of Ku were called *luakini heiau*s and were the only ones where human sacrifices took place.

*Heiau*s were built on auspicious sites, often perched on cliffs above the coast or in other places thought to have *mana*, or 'spiritual power.' A *heiau*'s significance lay not in the structure itself but in the *mana* of the site. When a *heiau*'s *mana* was gone, it was abandoned.

The *Makahiki*

According to legend, the god Lono rode a rainbow down from the heavens to a breadfruit grove above Hiilawe Falls in the Big Island's Waipio Valley, where he discovered Kaikilani, a beautiful princess, in a paradise-like setting. They fell in love, married, and moved across the island to Kealakekua Bay on the Kona Coast.

When Lono discovered that a chief was lusting after Kaikilani, he became enraged and beat Kaikilani, who, as she lay dying, professed her love for Lono alone. In his grief, Lono traveled restlessly around the island challenging every man he met to a wrestling match and other competitions.

After four months, a still disheartened Lono set sail on a canoe with a tall mast hung with sails made of finely woven Niihau mats.

Fun & Games

Holua racing was ancient Hawaii's most exciting spectator sport. Racers would ride prone on narrow wooden sleds, racing at high speed down steep hills along furrows that had been covered with *pili* grass or ti leaves (the long, shiny leaves of a common native plant) to make the surface smooth. Many of the *holua* slide paths were a mile or two long.

Hawaiians were heavy bettors and often wagered on the *holua* races, as well as on footraces, surfing competitions and many other sports.

Surfing is a Hawaiian creation that was as popular in old Hawaii as it is today. When the waves were up, everyone was out. There were royal surfing grounds and spots for commoners as well. Boards used by commoners were made of breadfruit or koa wood and were about 6ft long. Only the *alii* were free to use the long *olo* boards, which were up to 16ft in length and made of *wiliwili*, the lightest of native woods. The boards were highly prized possessions and were carefully wrapped in tapa (cloth made from pounded bark) and suspended from the ceilings of homes.

Other popular Hawaiian games included *ulu maika*, in which rounded stone discs were rolled between two stakes, somewhat resembling bowling, and *moa pahee*, a similar game using a large wooden dart.

For the more passive, there was *konane*, a strategy game similar to checkers. Indentations were carved into a stone board to hold the pebbles of white coral and black lava that were used as playing pieces.

The huge canoe was laden with so much food that it took 40 men to carry it down to Kealakekua Bay. As he left, Lono pledged to return one day on a floating island covered with trees and full of pigs and chickens.

The Hawaiians remembered Lono each year with a harvest festival, called the *makahiki*, which lasted from October to February. Numerous interisland competitions similar to the Olympics were held, including outrigger canoe races, fishing and surfing tournaments, footraces, wrestling matches and *holua* (sled) racing contests. Even during wartime, fighting would be suspended for the four months of the *makahiki,* so that the games and festivities dedicated to Lono could proceed.

Captain Cook

The Hawaiian Islands were the last of the Polynesian islands to be 'discovered' by the West, mainly because early European explorers who entered the Pacific around the tips of either Africa or South America centered their explorations in the southern hemisphere.

Legendary (or infamous) British explorer Captain James Cook spent the better part of a decade exploring and charting most of the South Pacific before chancing on Hawaii as he sailed from Tahiti in search of a northwest passage to the Atlantic.

On January 18, 1778, Cook spotted the islands of Oahu, Kauai and Niihau. The winds favored Cook's approach toward Kauai, and on January 19, Cook's ships, the *Discovery* and the *Resolution*, sailed into Kauai's Waimea Bay. Cook named the Hawaiian archipelago the Sandwich Islands, in honor of the Earl of Sandwich.

Cook was surprised to find that the islanders showed a strong Tahitian influence in their appearance, language and culture. They sailed out in their canoes to welcome Cook's ships and were eager to trade fish and sweet potatoes for nails. The islanders were not interested in the useless beads and trinkets that Cook had used successfully as barter elsewhere in the Pacific. Metal, which was totally absent from the islands, was the only thing they wanted in exchange.

After two weeks of stocking provisions on Kauai and Niihau, Cook's expedition continued its journey north. Failing to find the fabled passage through the Arctic, Cook sailed back to Hawaii. By coincidence, he arrived on virtually the same date as his first visit the year before.

This time he discovered the remaining Hawaiian Islands. On January 17, 1779, Cook sailed into Kealakekua Bay on the Big Island, where a thousand canoes came out to greet him.

When Cook went ashore the next day, he was met by the high priest and guided to a temple lined with skulls. Everywhere the English captain went, people fell face down on the ground in front of him to the chant of 'Lono.'

As fate would have it, Cook had landed during the *makahiki* festival. The tall masts and white sails of Cook's ships – even the way he had sailed clockwise around the island – all fit the legendary descriptions of how the god Lono would reappear.

Whether the priests actually believed Cook was the reincarnated Lono or whether they just used his appearance to enhance their power and add a little flair to the festivities is unknown. What is clear is that Cook never realized that both of his arrivals to Hawaii had coincided with the *makahiki* festivals – he assumed this was the way things were in everyday Hawaii.

There's little wonder Cook had a favorable impression of the islands. The islanders treated his crew with gracious hospitality. Hawaiian men invited the sailors to boxing matches and other competitions, and the women performed dances for the visitors and readily bedded down with them.

For men who had just spent months roaming inhospitable frozen tundra, this was paradise indeed.

The expedition's skilled artist, John Webber, was allowed to move freely in the villages. Today his detailed drawings of native people, costumes and village life constitute the best visual accounts of life in old Hawaii.

A few weeks after their arrival, the crews had restocked all the supplies needed except firewood. Rather than scour the hillsides for wood, Cook directed his men to haul onboard the temple railings and wooden images from the harborside temple dedicated to Lono. As Cook had been passed off as Lono himself, the priests didn't attempt to stop Cook's men.

On February 4 the English vessels and their crews sailed north out of Kealakekua Bay and headed for Maui. En route they ran into a storm off the northwest coast of the Big Island, where the *Resolution* broke a foremast. Uncertain of finding a safe harbor in Maui, Cook decided to go back to Kealakekua to repair the mast – a decision that would prove to be a fatal mistake.

When Cook arrived back at Kealakekua Bay on February 11, the islanders quickly appeared with the usual provisions to barter. The ruling *alii,* however, seemed upset with the ships' reappearance.

Apparently, the *makahiki* had ended, and not only was Cook's timing inauspicious, but so were the conditions of his return. This time he had arrived in a counterclockwise direction and with a broken sail.

Thievery became a big problem, and after a cutter was stolen, Cook ordered a blockade of Kealakekua Bay and then set off with a party of 11 men to the main village at the northern point of the bay. His intention was to capture the high chief Kalaniopuu and hold him until the boat was returned. This was a tactic that Cook had used elsewhere in the Pacific and one which he saw as reasonable diplomacy.

While Cook was en route to the village, a Hawaiian canoe attempting to sail out of the bay was fired upon by the English sailors. Unbeknownst to Cook's crew, the canoe was transporting a lower chief, Noekema, who was killed in the musket fire.

In the meantime, Cook had reached Kalaniopuu's house, and the chief had agreed to go with him. But as they walked down to the shore, Kalaniopuu's wailing wife ran after him, and the old chief suddenly balked and attempted to get away. In the midst of it all, word of Noekema's death reached the village, where a crowd quickly gathered.

Hoping to prevent bloodshed, Cook let the chief go, but the situation continued to escalate. As Cook was walking toward his boat, he shot at one of the armed Hawaiians who tried to block his way. The pistol misfired and the bullet bounced off the man's chest. The Hawaiians began to throw stones, and Cook ordered his men onshore to fire.

Cook had always assumed, as had been the case on other Pacific islands, that if trouble developed his men could fire a few shots and the natives, upon seeing the blood, would quickly disperse. That assumption proved wrong, however, and the Hawaiians, who were now in an angry frenzy, attacked rather than retreated.

The sailors in the boats fired another round as their captain began to make his way toward them over slippery rocks. Before they could reload, the crowd of Hawaiians moved in and Cook was struck on the head. Stunned by the blow, he staggered into the shallows, where the Hawaiians beat and stabbed him, passing the daggers for others to share in the kill. Four other sailors also died in the battle.

In this freak melee on a shore of the Sandwich Islands, Cook's last discovery, the life of the greatest explorer and navigator of the 18th century came to a bloody end.

Cook's men, shocked by his death, went on a rampage. They burned a village, beheaded two of their victims and rowed across the bay with the heads on poles.

Eventually, Kalaniopuu made a truce and returned those parts of Cook's dismembered body he was able to find. The skull was returned, but it had been stripped of its skin – a common practice bestowed upon great chiefs.

Cook's remains were buried at sea in a military funeral, at which time the Hawaiians placed a *kapu* on the bay and also held ceremonies of their own.

A week after Cook's February 14 death, the two English ships set sail, landing briefly on Oahu, Kauai and Niihau before finally leaving Hawaiian waters on March 15, 1779.

Cook and his crew left the Hawaiians a costly legacy: the iron that was turned into weapons, the introduced diseases that decimated the natives, and the first children of mixed blood. The crew returned home with charts and maps that would allow others to follow in their wake, and in Britain and Europe their stories and drawings were published, stirring the public's keen sense of adventure.

Some of Cook's crew returned to the Pacific, leading their own expeditions. Among them was Captain George Vancouver, who brought the first cattle and horses to Hawaii, and the ill-fated William Bligh, who captained the *Bounty*.

Kamehameha the Great

At the time of Cook's arrival in Hawaii in 1778, the islands were divided into separate warring chiefdoms. Kamehameha the Great, who by 1791 had become sole chief of the Big Island, was to become the first to unite all the Hawaiian Islands under one rule.

In 1795, after conquering Maui and Molokai, Kamehameha successfully invaded Oahu and established his reign there as well.

Kamehameha then made two attempts to invade Kauai, the only island not yet under his control. In 1796 his canoes were caught in a storm at sea and Kamehameha was forced to turn back before ever reaching the island. In 1804, while he was in Oahu again preparing for an invasion of Kauai, his warriors were struck by a deadly outbreak of a feverish disease, probably cholera, and the invasion plans were scrapped. The luck of the draw may have been Kauai's at the time, but Kamehameha's power was too obvious to ignore, so in 1810 Kauai agreed by treaty to accept Kamehameha's overlordship.

The Sandalwood Trade

By the mid-1700s Hawaii was becoming a popular port of call for Yankee traders plying the seas between North America and China.

In the early 1790s American sea captains discovered that Hawaii had great stocks of fragrant sandalwood, worth a premium in China. When the captains showed interest in it, Hawaiian chiefs readily began bargaining the wood away in exchange for foreign weapons.

A lucrative three-way trade developed. From Hawaii, the ships sailed to Canton and traded loads of sandalwood for Chinese silks and porcelain, which were then carried back to New England ports and sold at a high profit. In New England, the ships were reloaded with goods to be traded to the Hawaiians.

Hawaii's forests of sandalwood were so vast at this time that the Chinese name for Hawaii was Tahn Heong Sahn (Sandalwood Mountains).

Trying to maintain the resource, Kamehameha eventually put a *kapu* on all sandalwood forests, giving himself total control over the trade. Even under his relatively shrewd management, most of the profits ended up in the sea captains' fat pockets. Payment for the sandalwood was made in overpriced goods, originally cannons and rifles, and later exotic items such as European furniture.

While Kamehameha was careful not to devastate all his forests or overburden his subjects, his successor, Liholiho, partially lifted the royal *kapu,* allowing island chiefs to get in on the action. The chiefs began purchasing foreign luxuries by signing promissory notes to be paid in future shipments of sandalwood.

To pay off the rising 'debts,' Hawaiian *makaainana* (commoners) were forced into virtual servitude. The men who carted the wood, called *kua leho* (literally, 'calloused backs,' after the thick permanent layer of calluses they developed), were used like packhorses to haul the wood – sandalwood logs were strapped to their backs with bands of ti leaves. It was not uncommon for them to carry heavy loads 20 miles from the interior to ships waiting on the coast. During the height of the trade, missionaries recorded seeing caravans of as many as 3000 men carting wood.

In a few short years after Kamehameha's death, Hawaii's sandalwood forests were exhausted. In a futile attempt to continue the trade, Oahu's Governor Boki, who had heard of vast sandalwood reserves in the New Hebrides (now Vanuatu), set sail in November 1829 with 500 men on an ill conceived expedition to harvest the trees. Boki's ship was lost at sea, and the expedition's other ship, not too surprisingly, received a hostile greeting in New Hebrides.

In August 1830, 20 emaciated survivors sailed back into Honolulu Harbor. Boki had been a popular, if troubled, leader in a rapidly changing Hawaii. Hawaiians grieved in the streets of Honolulu when they heard of Boki's tragedy, and his death marked the end of the sandalwood trade.

End of the Old Religion

King Kamehameha died in 1819 at his Kamakahonu residence on the Big Island. The crown was passed to his son, Liholiho, who was reluctant to be proclaimed Kamehameha II. The real power was passed to Kaahumanu, who had been the favorite of Kamehameha's 21 wives.

Kaahumanu was an ambitious woman, and she was determined to break down the ancient *kapu* system of taboos that restricted her powers. Less than six months after Kamehameha's death, Kaahumanu threw a lavish feast for women of royalty at the sacred Kamakahonu compound. Although one of the most sacred taboos strictly forbade men from eating with women, Kaahumanu forcibly persuaded Liholiho to sit beside her and join in the meal.

It was an otherwise uneventful meal – no angry gods manifested themselves. But in that one act, the old religion was cast aside, along with 600 years of taboos and restrictions. Hawaiians no longer had to fear being put to death for violating the *kapu,* and a flurry of temple-smashing and idol-burning quickly followed.

Those chiefs and *kahuna* who resisted were easily squelched by Liholiho using the powerful army that Kamehameha had left behind. It was the end of an era.

The Missionaries

On April 19, 1820, the brig *Thaddeus* arrived from Boston with the first of the Christian missionaries to Hawaii. By a twist of fate, they landed in Kailua Bay, a stone's throw from Kamakahonu, where Kaahumanu had feasted the overthrow of the old religion six months earlier.

It was a timely arrival for the missionaries. The loss of the Hawaiians' native religion and social structure had left them with a spiritual void into which the Christians zealously stepped.

The *Thaddeus* carried 23 Congregationalists, the first of 12 groups to be sent in the next three decades by the New England–based American Board of Commissioners of Foreign Missions. The leader of this initial group of missionaries was Hiram Bingham.

The missionaries befriended Hawaiian royalty and made inroads quickly. After Queen Kaahumanu became seriously ill, Sybil Bingham, Hiram's wife, nursed her back to health. Shortly after, Kaahumanu showed her gratitude by passing a law forbidding work and travel on the Sabbath.

Up until this time, the Hawaiians had no written language. Using the Roman alphabet, the missionaries established a written Hawaiian language that allowed them to translate the Bible. They taught the Hawaiians to read and write and established the first 'American' high school west of the Rocky Mountains.

With encouragement from the missionaries, the Hawaiians quickly took on Western ways, Western clothing and Western laws.

Liholiho (Kamehameha II)

With Kaahumanu holding the real power, in November 1823 a floundering Liholiho set sail for England with his favorite wife to pay a royal visit to King George – although he failed to inform anyone in England of his plans.

When Liholiho arrived unannounced in London, misfitted in Western clothing and lacking in royal etiquette, the British press roasted him with racist caricatures. He never met King George. While being prepped in the social graces required for an audience with the king, Liholiho and his wife came down with measles. They died in England within a few weeks of each other in July 1824.

The Whalers

Within a year of the missionaries' arrival, whalers began calling on Hawaiian ports. The first were mostly New England Yankees, with a sprinkling of Gay Head Indians and former slaves. As more and more ships arrived, men of all nationalities roamed Hawaiian ports. Most were in their teens or twenties, ripe for adventure.

Towns sprang up with shopkeepers catering to the whalers, and saloons, brothels and hotels boomed. Honolulu and Lahaina became bustling ports of call.

From 1825 to 1870 Hawaii was the whaling center of the Pacific. It was a convenient way station for whalers hunting both the Arctic and Japanese whaling grounds. At its peak, between 500 and 600 whaling ships were pulling into Hawaiian ports each year.

Whaling brought big money to Hawaii, and the dollars spread beyond the whaling towns. Many Maui farmers got their start supplying the whaling ships with potatoes, while Big Island cattle ranches grew with the rising demand for beef, and even the average Hawaiian could earn a little money by turning in sailors who had jumped ship.

The Hawaiians themselves made good whalers, and sea captains gladly paid a $200 bond to the Hawaiian government for each *kanaka* (native Hawaiian) allowed to join their crew. Kamehameha IV even set up his own fleet of whaling ships that flew the Hawaiian flag.

The whaling industry in the Pacific peaked in the mid-19th century, and quickly began to burn itself out. In a few short years, all but the most distant whaling grounds were depleted, with whalers forced to go farther afield to make their kills. By 1860 whale oil prices were dropping as an emerging petroleum industry began to produce a less expensive fuel for lighting.

The last straw for Pacific whaling came in 1871, when an early Arctic storm caught more than 30 ships by surprise, trapping them in ice floes above the Bering Strait. Although more than 1000 seamen were rescued, half of them Hawaiian, the fleet itself was lost.

Sugar Plantations

Ko (sugarcane) arrived in Hawaii with the early Polynesian settlers. While the Hawaiians enjoyed chewing the cane for its juices, they never refined it into sugar.

The first known attempt to produce sugar in Hawaii was in 1802, when a Chinese immigrant in Lanai boiled crushed sugarcane in iron pots. Other Chinese soon set up small sugar mills on the scale of neighborhood bakeries.

In 1835 a young Bostonian, William Hooper, saw bigger opportunities in sugar and set out to establish Hawaii's first sugar plantation. Hooper convinced Honolulu investors Ladd & Company to put up the money for his venture and then worked out a deal with Kamehameha III to lease 980 acres of land on Kauai for $300. His next step was to negotiate with Kauai's *alii* for the right to use Hawaiian laborers.

In the mid-1830s Hawaii was still largely feudalistic. Commoners fished, farmed and lived on land that was under the domain of the local *alii;* in exchange, the commoners worked for the *alii* when needed. Therefore, before Hooper could hire any hands for his plantation, he had to first pay the *alii* a stipend to free the Hawaiians from their traditional work obligations.

The new plantation system, which introduced the concept of growing crops for profit rather than subsistence, marked the advent of capitalism and the introduction of wage labor in Hawaii.

The sugar industry emerged at the same time that whalers began arriving in force. Together, they became the foundation for Hawaii's moneyed economy.

By the 1850s sugar plantations were established on Maui, Oahu and the Big Island, as well as on Kauai.

Sugarcane, a giant grass, only flourishes with abundant water, so plantations were limited to the rainier parts of Hawaii and even then were vulnerable to drought. In 1856 an 11-mile irrigation ditch was dug to bring mountain water to Lihue cane fields, which were suffering from a drought. While this Kauai ditch was intended only as a rescue procedure, its success showed plantation owners the possibilities for irrigating heretofore unsuitable lands.

In the 1870s the 17-mile Hamakua Ditch was dug on Maui, the first of several extensive aqueducts that would carry millions of gallons of water daily from upland rain forests to water-thirsty plantations. These artificial waterways turned dry central plains into drenched cane fields. Today, Hawaii is still crisscrossed with hundreds of miles of working ditches and aqueducts built a century ago.

In addition to the irrigation systems, the sugar companies built flumes and railroads to carry the cane from the fields to the mills. For more than 100 years, sugar formed the backbone of the Hawaiian economy.

Hawaii's Immigrants

While the sugar industry was booming, Hawaii's native population was in decline, largely as the result of diseases that were introduced by foreigners.

To expand their operations, plantation owners began to look overseas for a labor supply. They needed immigrants accustomed to working long days in hot weather – and for whom the low wages would still seem like an opportunity.

In 1852 plantation owners began recruiting laborers from China. In 1868 recruiters went to Japan, and in the 1870s they brought in Portuguese from Madeira and the Azores. After Hawaii's 1898 annexation to the USA resulted in restrictions on Chinese immigration, plantation owners turned to Puerto Ricans and Koreans. Filipinos were the last group of immigrants brought to Hawaii to work the fields; the first wave came in 1906, the last in 1946.

Although these six ethnic groups made up the bulk of the field hands, a number of South Seas islanders, Scots, Scandinavians, Germans, Galicians, Spaniards and Russians all came in turn as well.

Each group brought its own culture, food and religion. Chinese clothing styles mixed with Japanese kimonos and European bonnets. A dozen languages filled the air, and a unique pidgin English developed as a means for the various groups to communicate with one another.

Conditions varied with the ethnic group and the period. At the end of the 19th century, Japanese contract laborers were being paid $15 a month. After annexation, the contracts were considered indentured servitude and were declared illegal under US law. Still, wages as low as a dollar a day were common up until the 1930s.

In all, approximately 350,000 immigrants came to Hawaii to work on the sugar plantations. The continuous flow of immigrant workers was required to replace those who invariably found better options elsewhere. Although some workers came for a set period to save money and return home, others worked out their contracts and then moved off the plantations to farm their own plots or start their own businesses.

Plantation towns like Koloa, Paia and Honokaa grew up around the mills, with barber shops, fish markets, beer halls and bathhouses catering to the workers.

The major immigrant populations – Japanese, Chinese, Filipino and Western European – came to outnumber the native Hawaiians. Together, they created the unique blend of cultures that would continue to characterize Hawaii for generations to come.

Kamehameha III

The last son of Kamehameha the Great, Kamehameha III ruled for 30 years, from 1825 until his death in 1854. In 1840 he introduced Hawaii's first constitution, both to protect his powers and to adjust to changing times. The new constitution established Hawaii's first national legislature and provided for a Supreme Court.

Kamehameha III was also responsible for passing the land act known as the Great Mahele, for establishing religious freedom and giving all male citizens the right to vote.

Hawaii's only 'invasion' by a foreign power took place during Kamehameha III's reign. In 1843 George Paulet, an upstart British commander upset about a petty land deal involving a British national, sailed into Honolulu commanding the British ship *Carysfort* and seized Oahu for six months. In that short period, he Anglicized street names, seized property and began to collect taxes.

To avoid bloodshed, Kamehameha III stood aside as the British flag was raised and the ship's band played 'God Save the Queen.' Queen Victoria herself wasn't flattered. After catching wind of the incident, she dispatched Admiral Richard Thomas to restore Hawaiian independence. Admiral Thomas re-raised the Hawaiian flag at the site of what is today Honolulu's Thomas Square. As the flag was raised, Kamehameha III uttered the words '*Ua mau ke ea o ka aina i ka pono*,' meaning 'The life of the land is perpetuated in righteousness,' which remains Hawaii's official motto.

The Great Mahele

The Great Mahele of 1848, which was introduced under the urging of influential missionaries, permanently altered Hawaiian concepts of land ownership. For the first time, land became a commodity that could be bought and sold.

Through the provisions of the Great Mahele, the king, who had previously owned all land, gave up title to the majority of it. Island chiefs were allowed to purchase some of the lands that they had controlled as fiefdoms for the king. Other lands, which were divided into 3-acre farm plots called *kuleana*, were made available to all Hawaiians. In order to retain their title, chiefs and commoners alike had to pay a tax and register the land.

The chiefs had the option of paying the tax in property, and many did so. Commoners had no choice but to pay the tax in cash. Although the act was intended to turn Hawaii into a country of small farms, in the end only a few thousand Hawaiians carried through with the paperwork and received *kuleana*s.

In 1850 land purchases were opened to foreigners. Unlike the Hawaiians, the Westerners jumped at the opportunity, and before the native islanders could clearly grasp the concept of private land ownership, there was little land left to own.

Within a few decades, the Westerners, who were much more adept at wheeling and dealing in real estate, owned 80% of all privately held lands. Even many of the Hawaiians who had gone through the process of getting their own *kuleana* eventually ended up selling it to the *haole*s (whites) for a fraction of its real value.

Contrary to the picture that the missionaries had painted for Kamehameha III, the Hawaiians suddenly became a landless people, drifting into ghettos in the larger towns. In a bitter twist, many of the missionaries themselves ended up with sizable tracts of land, and more than a few of them left the church to tend their new estates.

Prior to the Great Mahele, Hawaiian commoners had no rights to the land, but they were free to move around and work on the property of any chief. In return for their personal use of the land, they paid the chief in labor or with a percentage of their crops. In this way, they lived off the land. After the Great Mahele, they were simply *off* the land.

Kamehameha IV

Kamehameha IV had a short and rather confusing reign that lasted from 1855 to 1863. He tried to give his rule an element of European regality, à la Queen Victoria, and he and Queen Emma, his consort, established a Hawaiian branch of the Anglican Church of England. He also passed a law mandating all children be given a Christian name along with their Hawaiian name, a statute that stayed on the books until 1967.

Struggles between those wanting to make the monarchy stronger and those wishing to weaken it marked Kamehameha IV's reign.

Kamehameha V

The most significant accomplishment of Kamehameha V, who reigned from 1863 to 1872, was the establishment of a controversial constitution that gave greater power to the king at the expense of elected officials. It also restricted the right to vote.

Kamehameha V, who suffered a severe bout of unrequited love, was the last king from a royal lineage that dated back to the 12th century. From childhood, he was enraptured by Princess Bernice Pauahi, who in the end turned down his proposals, opting instead to marry American Charles Reed Bishop. Jolted by the rejection, Kamehameha V never married, yet he never gave up on the princess. Even on his deathbed, he offered Princess Bernice his kingdom, which she declined.

As the bachelor king left no heirs, his death in December 1872 brought an end to the Kamehameha dynasty. Subsequent kings would be elected by the national legislature.

Lunalilo

King Lunalilo's short reign lasted from 1873 to 1874. His cabinet, made up largely of Americans, was instrumental in paving the way for a treaty of reciprocity with the USA.

Although the USA was the biggest market for Hawaiian sugar, US sugar tariffs ate heavily into profit margins. As a means of eliminating the tariffs, most plantation owners favored the annexation of Hawaii to the USA.

The US government was cool to the idea of annexation, but it warmed to the possibility of establishing a naval base on Oahu. In 1872 General John Schofield was sent to assess Pearl Harbor's strategic value. He was impressed with what he saw – the largest anchorage in the Pacific – and reported his enthusiasm back to Washington.

Although native Hawaiians protested in the streets and the royal troops even staged a little mutiny, there would eventually be a reciprocity agreement that would cede Pearl Harbor to the USA in exchange for duty-free access for Hawaiian sugar.

King Kalakaua

King David Kalakaua, who reigned from 1874 to 1891, was Hawaii's last king. Although known as the 'Merrie Monarch,' he ruled in troubled times.

The first challenge to his reign came on election day. His contender had been the dowager Queen Emma, and when election results were announced, her followers rioted in the streets, requiring Kalakaua to request aid from US and British warships that happened to be in Honolulu Harbor at the time.

Despite the initial turmoil, Kalakaua went on to reign as a great Hawaiian revivalist. He brought back the hula, turning around decades of missionary repression against the 'heathen dance,' and penned the lyrics for the national anthem, 'Hawaii Ponoi,' which is now the state song. He also tried to ensure some self-rule for native Hawaiians, who had become a minority in their own land.

When Kalakaua left for his first trip overseas, scores of Hawaiians came to the waterfront weeping. The last king to leave the islands, Kamehameha II, had come back in a coffin.

While in the USA, Kalakaua met with President Ulysses S Grant and persuaded him to accept Lunalilo's reciprocity treaty, which the US Congress had been resisting.

Kalakaua also managed to postpone the ceding of Pearl Harbor for eight years. He returned to Hawaii a hero – to the business community for the treaty, and to the Hawaiians for simply making it back alive.

The king became a world traveler, visiting India, Egypt, Europe and Southeast Asia. Kalakaua was well aware that Hawaii's days as an independent Polynesian kingdom were numbered. To counter the Western powers that were gaining hold of Hawaii, he made a futile attempt to establish a Polynesian-Pacific empire. On a visit with the emperor of Japan, he even proposed a royal marriage between his niece, Princess Kaiulani, and a Japanese prince, but the Japanese declined.

Visits with other foreign monarchs gave Kalakaua a taste for royal pageantry. He returned home to build Iolani Palace for $360,000, which the business community thought was extravagant. Many influential whites saw the king as a lavish spender, fond of partying and hosting public luaus.

As Kalakaua incurred debts, he became increasingly less popular with the sugar barons, whose businesses were now the backbone of the economy. They formed the Hawaiian League in 1887 and developed their own armies, which stood ready to overthrow Kalakaua. The league presented Kalakaua with a list of demands and forced him to accept a new constitution strictly limiting his powers. The new law of the land also limited suffrage to property owners, which by then excluded the vast majority of Hawaiians.

On July 30, 1889, a group of about 150 Hawaiians attempted to overthrow the new constitution by occupying Iolani Palace. Called the Wilcox Rebellion after its part-Hawaiian leader, it was a confused and futile attempt, and the rebels were forced to surrender.

Kalakaua died in San Francisco in 1891.

Queen Liliuokalani

Kalakaua was succeeded by his sister, Liliuokalani, wife of Oahu governor John O Dominis.

Queen Liliuokalani, who reigned from 1891 to 1893, was even more determined than Kalakaua to increase the power of the monarchy. She charged that the 1887 constitution had illegally been forced upon King Kalakaua; the Hawaii Supreme Court upheld her contention.

In January 1893, as Liliuokalani was preparing to proclaim a new constitution that restored royal powers, a group of armed *haole* businessmen occupied the Supreme Court and declared the monarchy overthrown. They announced a provisional government, led by Sanford Dole, son of a pioneer missionary. A contingent of US sailors came ashore, ostensibly to protect the property of US citizens, but instead the troops marched on the palace and positioned their guns at the queen's residence. Realizing it was futile to oppose US forces, the queen opted to avoid bloodshed and stepped down.

The provisional government immediately appealed to the USA for annexation, while the queen appealed to the USA to restore the monarchy. To Dole's dismay, the timing of events was to the queen's advantage. US president Grover Cleveland, a Democrat, had just replaced a Republican administration and his sentiments clearly favored the queen.

Cleveland sent an envoy, James Blount, to investigate the situation and determine what the US government should do.

In the meantime, Cleveland received Queen Liliuokalani's niece, Princess Kaiulani, who, at the time of the coup, had been in London being prepared for the Hawaiian throne. The beautiful 18-year-old princess eloquently pleaded the monarchy's case. She also made a favorable impression with the American press, which largely caricatured those involved in the coup as dour, greedy buffoons.

Cleveland ordered the US flag be taken down and the queen restored to her throne. However, the provisional government, now firmly in power, turned a deaf ear, declaring that Cleveland was meddling in 'Hawaiian' affairs.

The new government, with Dole as president, inaugurated itself as the Republic of Hawaii on July 4, 1894. Although Cleveland initially favored reversing the situation, he also knew that ousting a government of white Americans and then replacing them with native Hawaiians could well endanger his own political future. Consequently, his subsequent actions were largely limited to rhetoric.

Weary of waiting for outside intervention, in early 1895 a group of Hawaiian royalists attempted a counterrevolution that was easily squashed in a fortnight. Liliuokalani was accused of being a conspirator and placed under arrest.

To humiliate her, the provisional authorities tried her in her own palace and referred to her only as Mrs John O Dominis. She was fined $5000 and sentenced to five years of hard labor, later reduced to nine months of house arrest at the palace.

Liliuokalani spent the rest of her life in her husband's residence, Washington Place, one block from the palace. When she died in November 1917 all of Honolulu came out for the funeral procession. To most islanders, Liliuokalani was still their queen.

Annexation

With the Spanish-American War of 1898, Americans acquired a taste for expansionism.

Along with Pearl Harbor, Hawaii took on a new strategic importance, being midway between the USA and its newly acquired possession, the Philippines. The annexation of Hawaii was passed in the US Congress on July 7, 1898. Hawaii entered the 20th century as a territory of the USA.

In just over a century of Western contact, the native Hawaiian population had been decimated by foreign diseases to which they had no immunity. It began with the venereal disease introduced by Captain Cook's crew in 1778. The whalers followed with cholera and smallpox, and the Chinese immigrants who replaced Hawaiian laborers brought leprosy. By the end of the 19th century, the native Hawaiian population had been reduced from an estimated 300,000 to less than 50,000.

Descendants of the early missionaries had taken over first the land and now the government. Without ever having fought a single battle against a foreign power, Hawaiians had lost their islands to ambitious foreigners. All in all, as far as the native Hawaiians were concerned, the annexation was nothing to celebrate.

The Chinese and Japanese were also uneasy. One of the reasons for the initial reluctance of the US Congress to annex Hawaii had been the racial mix of the islands' population. There were already restrictions on Chinese immigration to the USA, and restrictions on Japanese immigration were expected to follow.

In a rush to avoid a labor shortage, the sugar plantation owners quickly brought 70,000 Japanese immigrants into Hawaii. By the time the immigration wave was over, the Japanese accounted for more than 40% of Hawaii's population.

In the years since the reciprocity treaty with the US, signed in the 1870s, sugar production had increased tenfold. Those who ruled the land ruled the government, and closer ties with the USA didn't change the formula. In 1900 US president McKinley appointed Sanford Dole the first territorial governor.

WWI

Soon after annexation, the US Navy established a huge Pacific headquarters at Pearl Harbor and built Schofield Barracks, the largest US army base anywhere. The military quickly became the leading sector of Oahu's economy.

The islands were relatively untouched by WWI, even though the first German prisoners of war 'captured' by the USA were in Hawaii. They were escorted off the German gunboat *Grier*, which had the misfortune to be docked at Honolulu Harbor when war broke out.

The war affected people in Hawaii in other ways. Heinrich Hackfeld, a German sea captain long settled in the islands, had established Hawaii's most successful merchandise stores, BF Ehler's & Company. He had also developed a real estate empire rooted in sugar, by purchasing Lahaina's Pioneer Mill, among other properties. He lost it all during WWI.

Anti-German sentiments forced Hackfeld to liquidate his holdings, and American Factors (Amfac) took over his properties, renaming the stores Liberty House.

Pineapples & Planes

In the early years of the 20th century, pineapple emerged as Hawaii's second major export crop. James Dole, a cousin of Sanford Dole, purchased the island of Lanai in 1922 and turned it into the world's largest pineapple plantation. Although sugar remained Hawaii's most lucrative crop in export value, the more labor-intensive pineapple eventually surpassed it in terms of employment.

In 1936 Pan American flew the first passenger flights from the US mainland to Hawaii, an aviation milestone that ushered in the transpacific air age. Hawaii was now only hours away from the US West Coast.

WWII

On December 7, 1941, Japanese planes launched a surprise attack on Pearl Harbor, forcing the USA into WWII. Twenty-one US ships were sunk or damaged, along with 347 aircraft. More than 2500 people were killed.

After the smoke cleared, Hawaii was placed under martial law, and Oahu took on the face of a military camp. Already heavily militarized, vast tracts of Hawaii's land were turned over to the US armed forces for expanded military bases, training and weapons testing. Much of that land would never be returned. Throughout the war, Oahu served as the command post for the USA's Pacific operations.

Following the attack on Pearl Harbor, a wave of suspicion landed on the *nisei* (people of Japanese descent) in Hawaii. While sheer numbers prevented the sort of internment practices that took place on the mainland, the Japanese in Hawaii were subject to interrogation, and their religious and civic leaders were sent to mainland internment camps.

Japanese language schools were closed, and many of the teachers were arrested. Posters were hung in restaurants and other public places warning islanders to be careful about speaking carelessly in front of anyone of Japanese ancestry. *Nisei* were dismissed from their posts in the Hawaiian National Guard and prevented from joining the armed services.

Eventually Japanese-Americans were allowed to volunteer for a segregated regiment, although they were kept on the mainland and out of action for much of the war.

During the final stages of the war, when fighting was at its heaviest, the *nisei* were given the chance to form a combat unit. Volunteers were called, and more than 10,000 *nisei* signed up, forming two distinguished Japanese-American regiments. One of these, the 442nd Second Regimental Combat Team, which was sent into action on the European front, became the most decorated fighting unit in US history.

The veterans returned to Hawaii determined not to let the prejudices of the past limit them, and with a renewed conviction that they were entitled to the same opportunities as all other Americans. Many went on to college using the 'GI Bill' (a government programme that paid college expenses for war veterans) and today they account for some of Hawaii's most influential lawyers, judges and civic leaders. Among the veterans of the 442nd is Hawaii's senior US senator, Daniel Inouye, who lost an arm in the fighting.

Unionizing Hawaii

The feisty mainland-based International Longshoremen's and Warehousemen's Union (ILWU) began organizing Hawaiian labor in the 1930s.

Following WWII the ILWU organized an intensive campaign against the 'Big Five' (C Brewer, Castle & Cooke, Alexander & Baldwin, Theo Davies and Amfac), Hawaii's biggest businesses and landholders, all of which had roots in sugar.

The ILWU's six-month waterfront strike in 1949 virtually halted all shipments to and from Hawaii. The union went on to organize plantation strikes that resulted in Hawaii's sugar and pineapple workers becoming the world's highest paid.

The new union movement helped develop a political opposition to the staunchly Republican big landowners, who had maintained a stronghold on the political scene since annexation.

In the 1950s, McCarthyism, the fanatical wave of anti-Communism that had swept the mainland, spilled over to Hawaii. In the fallout, the leader of the ILWU in Hawaii, Jack Hall, was tried and convicted of being a communist.

Postwar Hawaii

WWII brought Hawaii closer to the center stage of American culture and politics.

The prospect of statehood had long been the central topic in Hawaiian politics. Three decades had passed since Hawaii's first delegate to the US Congress, Prince Jonah Kuhio Kalanianaole, introduced the first statehood bill in 1919. The bill had received a cool reception in Washington at that time, and there were mixed feelings in Hawaii as well. However, by the time the war was over, opinion polls showed that two out of three Hawaiian residents favored statehood.

Still, Hawaii was too much of a melting pot for many politicians to support statehood, particularly those from the rigidly segregated southern states. To the overwhelmingly white and largely conservative Congress, Hawaii's multiethnic community

Hawaiian Home Lands

In 1920, under the sponsorship of Prince Jonah Kuhio Kalanianaole, the Territory of Hawaii's congressional delegate, the US Congress passed the Hawaiian Homes Commission Act. The act set aside almost 200,000 acres of land for homesteading by native Hawaiians, who were by this time the most landless ethnic group in Hawaii. Despite this apparently generous gift, the land was but a small fraction of the crown lands that were taken from the Kingdom of Hawaii when the USA annexed the islands in 1898.

Under the legislation, people of at least 50% Hawaiian ancestry were eligible to apply for 99-year leases at $1 a year. Originally, most of the leases were for 40-acre parcels of agricultural land, although more recently residential lots as small as a quarter of an acre have been allocated under the plan.

Hawaii's prime land, already in the hands of the sugar barons, was excluded from the act. Much of what was designated for homesteading was on far more barren turf.

Indeed, the first homesteading village, at Kalanianaole on Molokai, failed when the wells drew brackish waters and destroyed the newly established crops. Still, many Hawaiians were able to make a go of it, settling homesteads on Oahu, the Big Island, Kauai, Maui and Molokai. Presently, there are about 6500 native Hawaiian families living on about 30,000 acres of homestead lands.

Administration of the Hawaiian Home Lands has been riddled with abuse. The majority of the land involved has not been allocated to native Hawaiians but has been leased out to big business, ostensibly as a means of creating an income for the administration of the programme.

In addition, the federal, state and county governments have illegally, and with little or no compensation, taken large tracts of Hawaiian Home Lands for their own use. The Lualualei Naval Reservation alone constitutes one-fifth of all Hawaiian Home Lands on Oahu, where more than 5000 native Hawaiians remain on the waiting list – some for more than 30 years.

was too exotic and foreign to be thought of as 'American.'

Congress was also concerned with the success of Hawaiian labor strikes and the growth of membership in the ILWU. All these factors combined to keep statehood at bay until the end of the 1950s.

Statehood

In March 1959 the US Congress finally passed legislation to make Hawaii a state. On June 27 a plebiscite was held in Hawaii, with more than 90% of the islanders voting for statehood. The island of Niihau was the only precinct to vote against it.

On August 21, 1959, after 61 years of territorial status, Hawaii became the 50th state of the USA.

Hawaiian Sovereignty

Over the past decade, a Hawaiian sovereignty movement, intent on righting some of the wrongs of the past century, has become a strong political force in Hawaii. However, a consensus on what form sovereignty should take has yet to emerge.

Ka Lahui Hawaii, the largest of the many Hawaiian sovereignty groups, has adopted a constitution for a Hawaiian nation within the USA, similar to that of 300 Native American groups on the mainland who have their own tribal governments and lands. Ka Lahui Hawaii wants all Hawaiian Home Lands, as well as the title to much of the crown land taken during annexation, turned over to native Hawaiians. These lands include nearly 1¾ million acres that were held by the Hawaiian kingdom at the time of the 1893 overthrow.

Other native Hawaiian groups are also calling for self-determination. Some favor the restoration of the monarchy, others focus on monetary reparations, but the majority are looking at some form of a nation-within-a-nation model.

One sovereignty demand was addressed in 1993, when US president Bill Clinton signed a resolution apologizing 'to Native Hawaiians for the overthrow of the Kingdom of Hawaii on January 17, 1893, with participation of agents and citizens of the United States, and the deprivation of the rights of Native Hawaiians to self-determination.' The apology went on to 'acknowledge the ramifications of the overthrow' and expressed a commitment to providing 'a proper foundation for reconciliation.'

Ka Lahui introduced state legislation to establish its group as the steward of a new Hawaiian nation, and two other sovereignty bills were also introduced. To sort out the disparity between the three bills, the state legislature established the Hawaiian Sovereignty Advisory Commission to create a mechanism for native Hawaiians to determine what form sovereignty should take.

The commission itself, however, became a source of conflict, as all 20 of the commission members were chosen by the governor, and only 12 of those were selected from nominees submitted by native Hawaiian organizations. Consequently, some groups, such as Ka Lahui and the Nation of Hawaii, refused to participate in the commission.

In the summer of 1996 a commission-sponsored mail-in vote, open to all people of Hawaiian ancestry, was held on the ballot question, 'Shall the Hawaiian People elect delegates to propose a native Hawaiian government?' It was a first-step vote to determine if native Hawaiians wanted to establish a sovereignty process that would be based on electing delegates and holding a convention to chart out their future.

Of the 80,000 ballots mailed to native Hawaiians worldwide, some 30,000 people responded. The initiative passed, with 73% voting yes and 27% against, but in many ways it was a far more divided vote. Some native Hawaiians, including members of Ka Lahui, felt the process was co-opted by the state, which had provided funding for the ballot, and they boycotted the vote. The controversial commission itself disbanded after the vote, and the state declared it would not provide funding for the delegate elections and convention. A nonprofit group, Ha Hawaii, which includes former members of the commission, then spent two years raising funds for that purpose.

In 1999 the Ha Hawaii organized the election of 85 delegates to form a Hawaiian Convention aimed at charting the sovereignty course. However, many groups boycotted this election as well, claiming the Ha Hawaii vote was influenced by the state and the process itself was flawed. Consequently, the voter turnout was only 8.7% – fewer than 9000 of the 102,000 eligible voters participated, and no consensus on a forum for debating sovereignty issues developed.

The focus has since turned to the courts. In February 2000 the US Supreme Court struck down a Hawaii law that had allowed for only persons of native Hawaiian ancestry to vote for trustees of the Office of Hawaiian Affairs, the organization that leads the provision of social and economic benefits to people of Hawaiian ancestry. The ruling had far-reaching ramifications that included nullifying future sovereignty elections.

The conservative Supreme Court ruled that native Hawaiians are a racial group, not a tribe that has a political relationship with the USA, and thus it was discriminatory to disallow non-native residents from voting in such elections.

Native Hawaiians fear that scores of government-funded programmes set up to benefit them, from health care to housing, are now endangered. Hawaii's representatives to the US Congress are trying to counter this situation by creating federal recognition for native Hawaiians as a sovereign people, similar to the status given to most American Indians on the US mainland. A bill to this effect, sponsored by Hawaii's Senator Daniel Akaka, has been introduced to the US Congress. If the bill is enacted it will give federal recognition to native Hawaiians and grant them the right to move ahead with self-government.

Akaka's bill prescribes that the form of native government that emerges must be approved and ratified by the state of Hawaii before it can be certified by the US government. Although attitudes may change as the movement takes shape, polls show that a majority of residents of Hawaii support the concept of Hawaiian sovereignty if it's within the framework of a nation-within-a-nation. Interestingly, support for the sovereignty movement doesn't vary greatly along ethnic lines.

GEOGRAPHY

The Hawaiian Islands stretch 1523 miles in a line from Kure Atoll in the northwest to the Big Island in the southeast. Ka Lae, on the Big Island, is the southernmost point of the USA.

The equator is 1470 miles south of Honolulu, and all the main islands lie south of the tropic of Cancer. Hawaii is on the same latitude as Hong Kong, Bombay and Mexico's Yucatán Peninsula.

Hawaii's eight major islands are, from largest to smallest, Hawaii (the Big Island),

Maui, Oahu, Kauai, Molokai, Lanai, Niihau and Kahoolawe. Together, they have a total land area of 6470 sq miles, which includes 96 small nearshore islands with a combined area of less than 3 sq miles.

The Northwestern Hawaiian Islands lie scattered across a thousand miles of ocean west of Kauai. They consist of 33 islands in 10 clusters with a total land area of just under 5 sq miles.

In total, Hawaii is smaller than Fiji and a bit larger than the US state of Connecticut.

Hawaii's highest mountain is Mauna Kea on the Big Island, which is 13,796ft above sea level. According to the *Guinness Book of Records,* it's the world's highest mountain (33,476ft) when measured from the ocean floor. Mauna Loa, also on the Big Island, is Hawaii's second highest mountain, at 13,677ft.

GEOLOGY

The Hawaiian Islands are the tips of massive mountains, created by a crack in the earth's mantle that has been spewing out molten rock for more than 25 million years. The hot spot is stationary, but the ocean floor is part of the Pacific Plate, which is moving northwest at the rate of about 3 inches a year. (The eastern edge of this plate is California's San Andreas Fault.)

As weak spots in the earth's crust pass over the hot spot, molten lava bursts through as volcanoes, building underwater mountains. Some of them finally emerge above the water as islands.

Every new volcano eventually creeps northward past the hot spot that created it. The farther from the source, the lower the level of volcanic activity; when the volcano reaches a certain distance from the hot spot, it is cut off completely and turns cold.

Once the lava stops, it's a downhill battle. The forces of erosion – wind, rain, waves – slowly wash the mountains away. In addition, the settling of the ocean floor causes the land to gradually recede.

Thus, the once mountainous Northwestern Hawaiian Islands, the oldest in the Hawaiian chain, are now low, flat atolls that in time will be totally submerged.

The Big Island, Hawaii's southernmost island, is still in the birthing process. Its most active volcano, Kilauea, is directly over the hot spot. In its latest eruptive phase, which began in 1983 and still continues, Kilauea has pumped out more than 2 billion cubic yards of lava, making this the largest known volcanic eruption in Hawaii's history.

Less than 30 miles southeast of the Big Island, a new seamount named Loihi has already risen 15,000ft above the ocean floor. The growing mounds of lava are expected to break the ocean surface within 10,000 years – however, if the volcano were to become hyperactive, it could emerge within a century or two.

In 1987 the Woods Hole Oceanographic Institution explored Loihi with *Alvin,* the same deepwater minisub that had discovered the *Titanic* wreck the year before. They measured Loihi's summit to be 3117ft below the surface of the water.

A Fiery Creation

The early Hawaiians were astutely tuned in to geological forces and were well aware of the order in which the islands were created. Their creation story goes something like this:

Pele, the goddess of volcanoes and fire, was born of the marriage of earth and sky. She is both creator and destroyer (not unlike the Hindu god Siva). Her eruptions of molten lava both build the mountains and wreak havoc over everything in their path.

Pele was driven from her home in the northwestern shoals by a jealous older sister, Na Maka o Kahai, goddess of the seas. Pele fled to the southeast and built her home in a crater on Niihau, then on Kauai, and each island in turn. Each time she dug down into the fiery earth deeper than the time before, and each time she was chased away by her sister, the sea.

After being forced from her home on Haleakala on Maui, Pele crossed over to the Big Island. There she built her highest mountains yet and, in their volcanic recesses, made a home far from the reaches of Na Maka o Kahai.

The sea goddess, however, is still never far from Pele's doorstep. She persistently wears away at Pele's home, her waves taking on the lava, eroding it and crushing it into sand.

In time, Pele will again be forced to move on, but for now she makes her home deep in Kilauea, the most active volcano on earth.

Hawaii's volcanoes are shield volcanoes, which form not by explosion but by a slow buildup of layer upon layer of lava. They rise from the sea with gentle slopes and a relatively smooth surface. It's only after aeons of facing the elements that their surfaces become sharply eroded. It's for this reason that the Na Pali cliffs on Kauai, the oldest of the main islands, are the most jagged in Hawaii.

Hawaii's active volcanoes are Kilauea and Mauna Loa, both on the Big Island. The Big Island's Mauna Kea and Hualalai and Maui's Haleakala are dormant, with future eruptions possible. The volcanoes on all the other Hawaiian Islands are considered extinct.

CLIMATE

Overall, Hawaii has great weather. It's balmy and warm, with northeasterly trade winds prevailing most of the year.

Average temperatures differ only about 7°F from winter to summer. Near the coast, daily temperatures average a high of about 83°F and a low of around 68°F.

The rainiest time of the year is from December to March. Not only does winter have about twice the rainfall of summer, but winter storms can also hang around for days. In summer, the rain is more likely to fall as passing showers. This doesn't mean winter is a bad time to go to Hawaii, it just means the weather is more of a gamble.

Rainfall varies even more with location than with season. In places like Kailua-Kona on the Big Island, you can sunbathe on the beach for all but a few days a year. At the same time, you can watch typical afternoon showers pour on the hill slopes just a mile or two inland and know you're well beyond reach.

Hawaii's high volcanic mountains trap the trade winds that blow from the northeast, blocking moisture-laden clouds and bringing abundant rainfall to the windward side of the islands. Hilo, the rainiest city in the USA with 130 inches annually, is on the windward side of the Big Island.

Conversely, the same mountains block the wind and rain from the southwesterly, or leeward, side of the islands, so it's there you'll find the driest, sunniest conditions and the calmest waters. Leeward areas generally receive only 10 to 25 inches of rain a year.

During *kona* (leeward) weather, the winds blow from the south, a shift from the typical

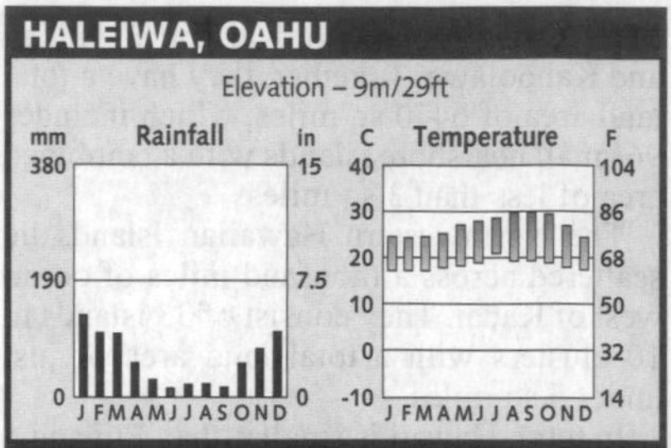

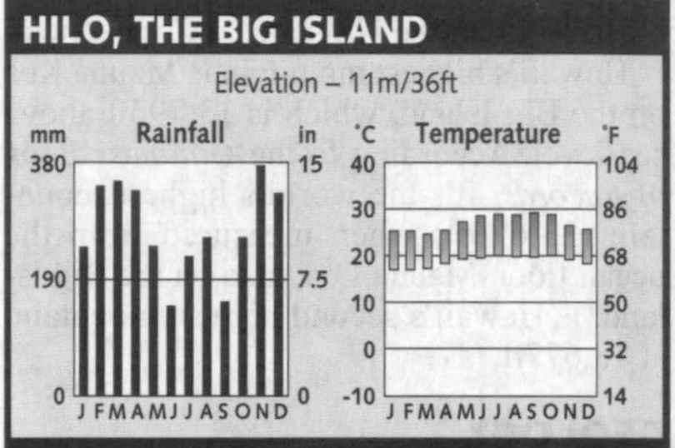

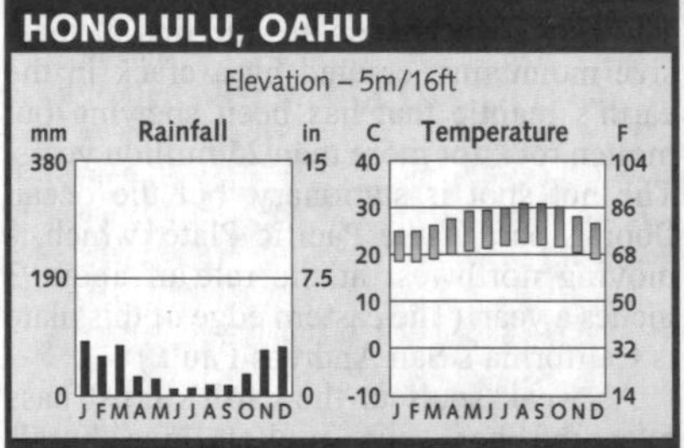

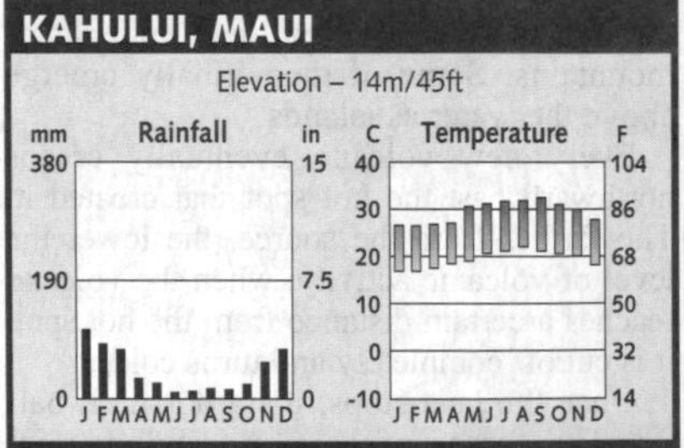

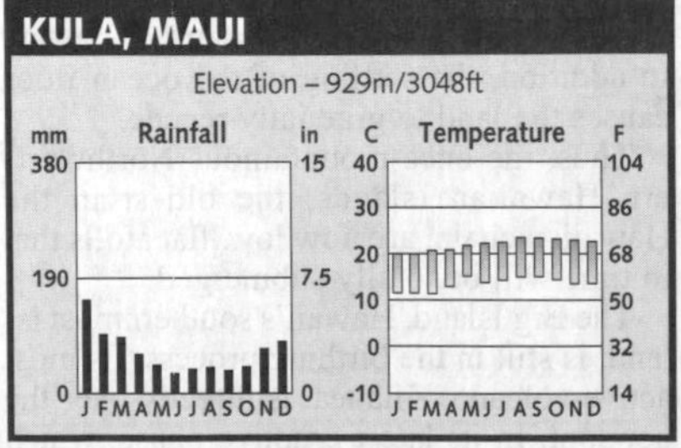

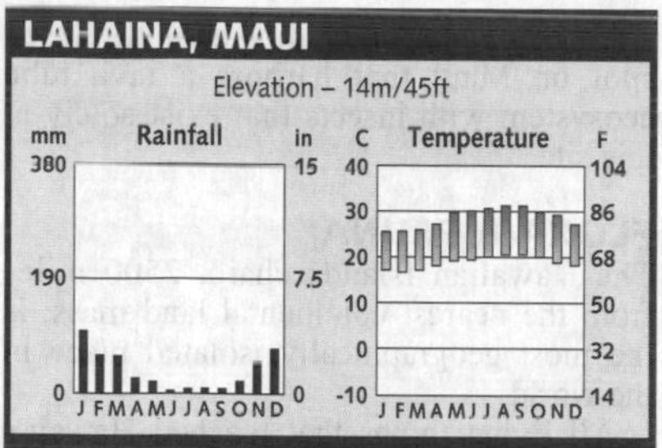

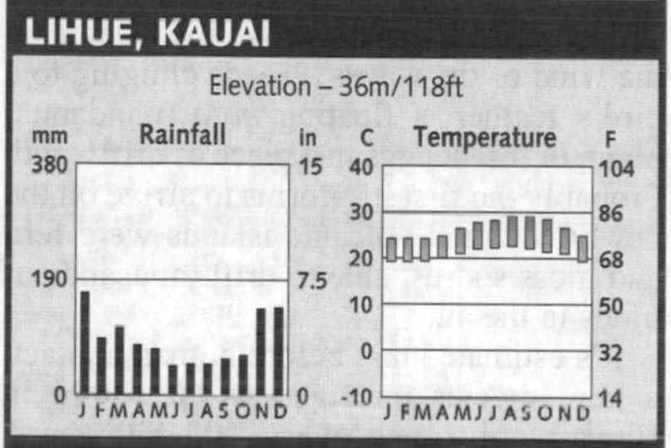

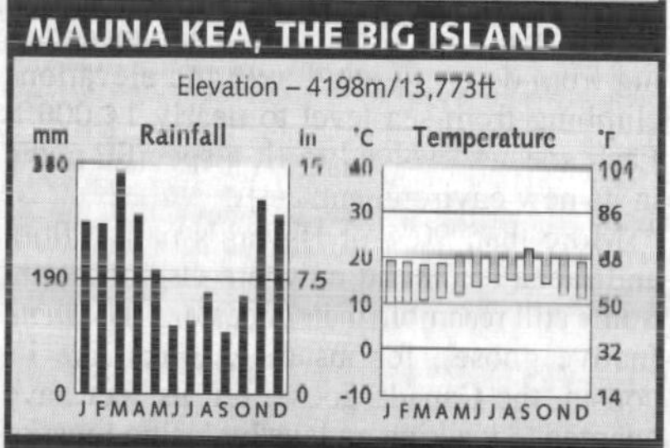

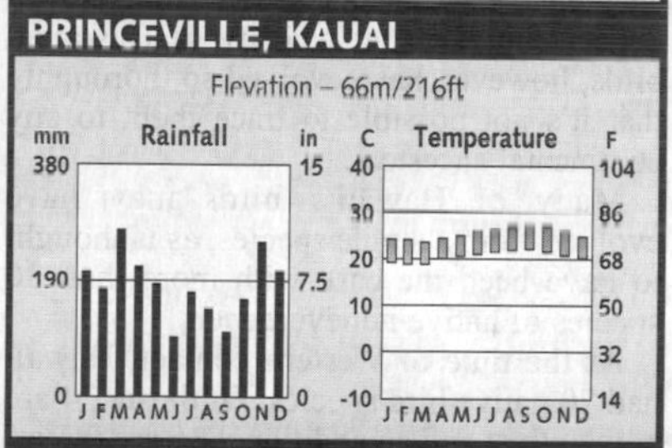

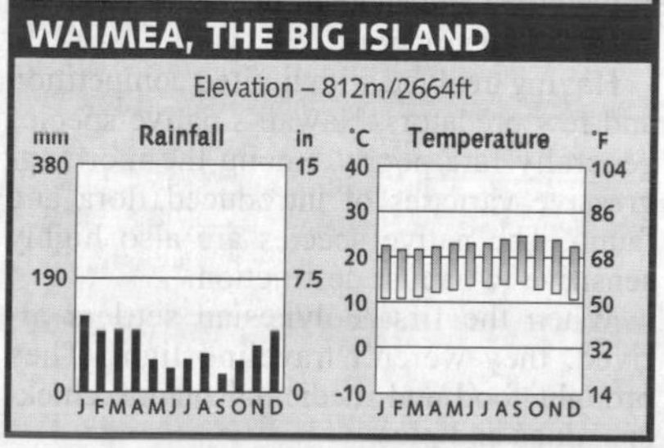

northeast trades. The ocean swell pattern also changes at this time – snorkeling spots suddenly become surfing spots and vice versa. *Kona* storms usually occur in winter and are very unpredictable.

The summits of Mauna Kea and Mauna Loa on the Big Island receive snow each winter, and in some years Haleakala on Maui sports a short-lived snow cover as well. The lowest temperature ever recorded on Mauna Kea, Hawaii's coldest spot, was 11°F, while the highest temperature there was 66°F.

ECOLOGY & ENVIRONMENT

Hawaii's native ecosystems have been greatly stressed by the introduction of exotic flora and fauna species. Erosion caused by free-ranging cattle and goats and the monocrop cultures of sugarcane and pineapple have destroyed native ground covers, resulting in washouts that sweep prime topsoil into the sea and choke nearshore reefs. Tourism-related development has long taken its toll, particularly the proliferation of large resort hotels and golf courses, which commonly are built on fragile coastal lands.

On the plus side, Hawaii has no polluting heavy industry, roadside billboards are not allowed and environmental awareness is more advanced than on much of the US mainland.

There are more than 150 environmental groups in Hawaii, ranging from chapters of international organizations fighting to save the rain forest to neighborhood groups working to protect local beaches from impending development.

One of the broadest based is the Hawaii chapter of the Sierra Club, which has groups on all the main islands. Its activities range from political activism on local environmental issues to weekend outings aimed at eradicating invasive plants from native forests.

The nonprofit Earthjustice Legal Defense Fund, formerly the Sierra Club Legal Defense Fund, is in the forefront, pressing legal challenges against abuses to Hawaii's fragile environment. In conjunction with Greenpeace Hawaii, the group has forced the state of Hawaii to prohibit jet skis in waters used by endangered humpback whales. On behalf of several environmental groups, the Earthjustice Legal Defense Fund filed legal challenges halting a geothermal energy project on the Big Island that would have carved up one of Hawaii's last remaining lowland rain forests.

In still another challenge, the Earthjustice Legal Defense Fund took on both the National Rifle Association and the state to force the removal of introduced mouflon game sheep from the slopes of Mauna Kea on the Big Island. The sheep were found to be the primary cause for the decline of the *palila*, a native honeycreeper. A landmark case, it marked the first time that habitat destruction was successfully defined as the 'taking' (meaning killing, harming or harassing) of an endangered species under the US Endangered Species Act.

The Earthjustice Legal Defense Fund, together with the Center for Marine Conservation and the Sea Turtle Restoration Project, also successfully sued to stop the killing of endangered sea turtles by the longline fishing industry. Most longline ships arrived in Hawaii's waters in the 1990s after depleting fishing stocks in the Atlantic Ocean. Although these operations targeted swordfish or tuna, they laid fishing lines up to 30 miles long, carrying thousands of baited hooks that caught anything that went for the bait, including marine mammals and hundreds of sea turtles. At the time the longline industry was banned in 2001, Earthjustice estimated the population of adult leatherback turtles in the eastern Pacific had dropped from about 250,000 in 1980 to just 3000.

The Nature Conservancy of Hawaii has opted for a different approach: it protects Hawaii's rarest ecosystems by buying up vast tracts of land and working out long-term stewardships with some of Hawaii's biggest landholders. One project included purchasing the Kipahulu Valley on Maui in conjunction with the state and turning the 11,000 acres over to the federal government to become part of Haleakala National Park.

On Molokai, the Nature Conservancy manages the rain forest at Kamakou Preserve and at Pelekunu Valley on the island's wet northeast coast, as well as the wind-swept Moomomi dunes on the dry northwest coast. The group also manages a crater above Hanauma Bay on Oahu, the Waikamoi rain forest on Maui, a native dryland forest in Lanai and a Kauai nesting site for the *ao* (Newell's shearwater), a threatened bird species once thought extinct. In addition, the Nature Conservancy has jurisdiction over a few other areas, including an undisclosed spot on Maui that harbors a lava tube ecosystem with insects that exist solely at this site.

FLORA & FAUNA

The Hawaiian Islands chain, 2500 miles from the nearest continental land mass, is the most geographically isolated place in the world.

All living things that reached Hawaii's shores were carried across the ocean on the wind or the waves – seeds clinging to a bird's feather, a floating *hala* (pandanus) plant, or insect eggs in a piece of driftwood. Probably the first life-forms to arrive on the newly emerged volcanic islands were fern and moss spores, able to drift thousands of miles in the air.

It's estimated that before human contact, a new species managed to take hold in Hawaii only once every 100,000 years. New arrivals found specialized habitats ranging from desert to rain forest and elevations climbing from sea level to nearly 14,000ft. Each species evolved to fit a specific niche in its new environment.

More than 90% of Hawaii's native flora and fauna are found nowhere else on earth. Some still resemble their ancestors. The *nene* (native goose), for instance, looks like its cousin, the Canada goose, but its feet have adapted to walking on lava by losing most of their webbing. The majority of Hawaiian birds, however, have evolved so thoroughly that it's not possible to trace them to any continental ancestors.

Many of Hawaii's birds may have evolved from a single species, as is thought to have been the case with more than 30 species of native honeycreeper.

At the time of Western contact, Hawaii had 70 native bird species. Of those, 24 are now extinct and an additional 36 are threatened with extinction.

Having evolved with limited competition and few predators, Hawaii's native species generally fare poorly among the more aggressive varieties of introduced flora and fauna. The native species are also highly sensitive to habitat destruction.

When the first Polynesian settlers arrived, they weren't traveling light. They brought food and medicinal plants, chickens, dogs and pigs.

The pace of introducing exotic species escalated with the arrival of Westerners, starting with Captain Cook, who dropped off goats and left melon and pumpkin seeds. The next Western visitors left cattle and horses.

Prior to human contact, Hawaii had no land mammals save for monk seals and hoary bats. The introduction of free-ranging pigs, cattle and goats, who all grazed and foraged at will, devastated Hawaii's fragile ecosystems and spelled extinction for many plants.

Some introduced songbirds and game birds spread avian diseases to which native Hawaiian birds had no immunity. Erosion, deforestation and thousands of introduced plants that compete with and choke out native vegetation have all taken their toll.

Today more than 25% of all endangered species in the USA are Hawaiian plants and animals. Of approximately 2400 different native plants, half are either threatened or endangered.

Flora

Because Hawaii's climate varies from dry desert conditions to lush tropical rain forests, you'll find a wide variety of vegetation.

The most prevalent native forest tree is the *ohia lehua*, one of the first plants to colonize old lava flows. Recognizable by its red pom-pom flowers, it grows in barren areas as a shrub and on more fertile land as a tree.

Koa, endemic to Hawaii, is commonly found at higher elevations; it grows up to 100ft high and is unusual in that the young saplings have fernlike compound leaves, while mature trees have flat, crescent-shaped phyllodes. The *kukui* tree, brought by the early Polynesian settlers, has oily nuts that Hawaiians used for candles – hence its common name, the candlenut tree; it's easily identifiable in the forest by its light silver-tinged foliage.

Two trees found along the coast that proved useful in old Hawaii are the *hala*, also called pandanus or screw pine, whose spiny leaves were used for thatching and weaving; and the coconut palm, called *niu*, which thrives in coral sands and produces about 75 coconuts a year.

Kiawe, a non-native tree readily found in dry coastal areas, is a member of the mesquite family that's useful for making charcoal but is a nuisance for beachgoers, as its sharp thorns easily pierce soft sandals.

Common native coastal plants include *pohuehue*, a beach morning glory with pink flowers that's found on the sand just above the high-tide line; and beach *naupaka*, a shrub with oval leaves and a small, white, five-petaled flower that looks as if it's been torn in half. The native *ilima*, with its delicate yellow-orange flowers, can grow at higher elevations but is commonly found along beaches, where it has adapted to harsh winds by growing as a ground cover.

More than 5000 varieties of hibiscus bushes grow in Hawaii; on most, the colorful flowers bloom only for a day. The variety most frequently used in landscape hedges is the red (or Chinese) hibiscus, which was introduced to Hawaii. There are also a number of native hibiscuses, including the *hau* tree, whose flowers open as yellow and change to dark orange as the day goes on. The *kokio keokeo*, a native Hawaiian white hibiscus tree that thrives in moderately moist forests and grows up to 60ft high, is the only Hawaiian hibiscus with a fragrance. The pink butterfly hibiscus, another popular hedge variety, is believed to be a cross between the native white hibiscus and the introduced coral hibiscus.

Hawaii, of course, is abloom with scores of other tropical flowers, most introduced, including blood-red anthuriums, brilliant orange birds-of-paradise, colorful bougainvilleas, red ginger, torch ginger, shell ginger and various heliconias with bright orange and red bracts. There are also hundreds of varieties of orchids, all but four of which are introduced.

Fauna

Hawaiian Monk Seal So named for the cowl-like fold of skin at its neck and for its solitary habits, the Hawaiian monk seal exists only in Hawaii. The Hawaiian name for

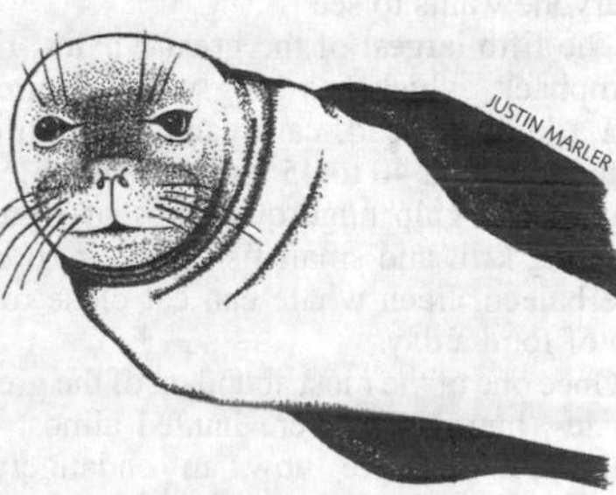

Hawaiian monk seal

the animal is *ilio holo kai*, meaning 'the dog that runs in the sea.'

This species has remained nearly unchanged for 15 million years, though in the past century it has been in danger of dying out completely. Fortunately, conservation efforts, including the translocation of some seals to create a better male-female ratio, appear to be bringing the seals back from the edge of extinction. The Hawaiian monk seal population is currently estimated to be around 1300 seals.

Hawaiian monk seals, which are sensitive to human disruption, breed and give birth primarily in the Northwestern Hawaiian Islands. In recent years, however, sightings of monk seals hauling themselves onto beaches on the main islands – primarily in Kauai, but also on the northern shores of Oahu, Maui and Molokai – have increased.

The annual birth rate for the monk seal pups is between 150 and 175 a year, though because of shark attacks and other predators, the majority fail to reach maturity. Monk seals feed on reef fish, eels, octopus and lobster.

Of the world's two other monk seal species, the Caribbean monk seal is extinct and the Mediterranean monk seal numbers only in the hundreds.

Whales Hawaii's resident whales include the sperm whale, false killer whale, pigmy killer whale, beaked whale, melon-head whale and, most common of all, the pilot whale. The pilot whale is a small whale that often travels in large pods and, like most whales, prefers deep offshore waters.

Several types of migrating whales occasionally pass through Hawaiian waters, including the fin whale, minke whale and right whale. But it is the islands' most frequent visitor – the migrating humpback – that everyone wants to see.

The fifth largest of the great whales, the humpback, which has long white flippers and a knobby head, can reach a length of 45ft and weigh 40 to 45 tons. The toothless humpbacks gulp huge quantities of water, trapping krill and small fish in their filter-like baleen. Each whale can eat close to a ton of food a day.

Once one of the most abundant of the great whales, humpbacks were hunted almost to extinction and are now an endangered species. Around the turn of the 20th century, an estimated 15,000 humpbacks remained. They were still being hunted as late as 1966, when the International Whaling Commission enforced a ban on their slaughter.

The entire population of North Pacific humpbacks is now thought to be about 4000. An estimated two-thirds of those winter in Hawaii, while most of the others migrate to Mexico.

Humpbacks spend the summer feeding in the plankton-rich waters off Alaska, developing a layer of blubber that sustains them through the winter, when the adults go without eating.

Come November, humpbacks begin filtering into Hawaii. During a romantic winter sojourn in the warm tropical waters, the whales mate and give birth. The gestation period is 10 to 12 months.

Mothers stay in shallow waters once their calves are born, apparently as protection from shark attacks. At birth, calves are about 12ft long and weigh 3000 pounds. They are nursed for about six months and can put on 100 pounds a day in the first few weeks.

Humpbacks often put on an amazing acrobatic show – arching dives, breaching and fin splashing. In breaching, humpbacks jump almost clear out of the water and then splash down with tremendous force.

They certainly save the best performances for breeding time. Sometimes several of the bull whales will do a series of crashing breaches to gain the favor of a cow, often bashing into one another, even drawing blood, before the most impressive emerges as the winner.

Luckily for whale watchers, humpbacks are coast-huggers, preferring waters with depths of less than 600ft, which means you can often see them right from the shoreline. They can be found throughout the islands, but their most frequented wintering spot is the shallow area between Maui, Lanai, Molokai and Kahoolawe.

Whales are highly sensitive to human activity and noise and seek out quiet coastal spots. They have abandoned areas where human activities have picked up and seem to have a particular disliking for jet skis.

Humpbacks are protected by US federal law under the Marine Mammal Protection Act and the Endangered Species Act. Coming within 100 yards of a humpback (300 yards in cow or calf waters) is prohibited

> **Official Hawaii**
>
> **State nickname** The Aloha State
> **State flower** *Pua aloalo* (hibiscus)
> **State tree** *Kukui* (candlenut tree)
> **State bird** Nene (Hawaiian goose)
> **State marine mammal** Humpback whale
> **State fish** *Humuhumunukunukuapuaa* (rectangular triggerfish)
> **State motto** *Ua mau ke ea o ka aina i ka pono* (The life of the land is perpetuated in righteousness)
> **State song** 'Hawaii Ponoi' written by King Kalakaua
> **State flag** Designed for King Kamehameha I prior to 1816, it has the UK's Union Jack in the upper left-hand corner. The eight stripes of red, white and blue represent the eight largest islands.
> **State seal** The state seal incorporates the state motto and a heraldic shield flanked by Kamehameha I on one side and the Goddess of Liberty holding the Hawaiian flag on the other. It also has taro and banana leaves, ferns, a phoenix and the statehood year of 1959.

and can result in a $25,000 fine. The rules apply to everyone, including swimmers, kayakers and surfers, and they are strictly enforced – whether violators are aware of the law or not.

Curiously the early Hawaiians seem to have paid little attention to whales – there are no petroglyph drawings of whales and virtually no legends about them.

Dolphins Like whales, dolphins are marine cetaceans and are common in Hawaii. Spinner, bottle-nose, slender-beaked, spotted, striped and rough-toothed varieties can all be found in Hawaiian waters.

Dolphins are nocturnal feeders who often come into calm bays during the day to rest. Although it may seem tempting to swim out and join them, approaching the dolphins can apparently disturb their rest; in addition, it will subject swimmers to a hefty fine under the Marine Mammal Protection Act. This is a current controversy in Hawaii, as swimmers who claim that dolphins enjoy playing in the surf with humans are at odds with federal officials bent on enforcing laws against the harassment of marine mammals.

Incidentally, the mahimahi or 'dolphin' that you may come across on menus in Hawaii is not the marine mammal but a fish.

National Parks

Hawaii has two national parks: Hawaii Volcanoes National Park on the Big Island and Haleakala National Park on Maui. Among the most unique places in the US National Parks system, both Haleakala and Hawaii Volcanoes center on volcanic craters. Both have awesome scenery and include several types of terrain, from sea level to more than 10,000ft, and from barren lava landscapes to lush tropical rain forests. They also have unique flora and fauna and are the main habitat for a number of endangered forest birds, the nene and a host of native flora. The parks offer incredible hikes, some across crater floors, and a variety of camping options. For full details on both parks, see the Big Island and Maui chapters.

The creation of a new national park near La Perouse Bay, Maui, is being considered.

GOVERNMENT & POLITICS

Hawaii has three levels of government: federal, state and county. The seat of state government is in Honolulu.

Hawaii has a typical state government with executive power vested in the governor, who is elected to a four-year term. The present governor, Linda Lingle, was elected in a close race with Democrat Mazie Hirono in 2002. She is only the second Republican to hold the governorship since Hawaii became a state over 40 years ago. She's also Hawaii's first female governor.

The state's lawmaking body is a bicameral legislature. The Senate includes 25 members, elected for four-year terms from the state's 25 senatorial districts. The House of Representatives has 51 members, each elected for a two-year term.

The legislature has a typical Hawaiian casualness. The regular legislative session, which convenes on the third Wednesday of January, meets for a mere 60 days a year. Special sessions of up to 30 days can be convened by the governor, but otherwise, 60 days is it.

Hawaii is divided into four county governments, but unlike the mainland states, it has no municipal government. The city of

Honolulu is part of Honolulu County, which governs all of Oahu; Hawaii County oversees the Big Island; Kauai County governs Kauai and Niihau; and Maui County presides over Maui, Molokai and Lanai.

While the leprosy colony of Kalaupapa on Molokai is called the 'county' of Kalawao, in actuality it has no county government and is under the jurisdiction of the Hawaii State Department of Health.

Each county has a mayor and county council. The counties provide services, such as police and fire protection, that on the mainland are usually assigned to cities. Development issues are usually decided at county level and are the central issue of most mayoral campaigns.

ECONOMY

Tourism is Hawaii's largest industry and accounts for about one-third of the state's income. Hawaii welcomes about 7 million visitors a year. In total they spend about $11 billion in the state, but not all at the same rate.

The second largest sector in the economy is the US military, pumping out $3 billion annually. Hawaii is the most militarized state in the nation. In total, the military has a grip on nearly 250,000 acres of Hawaiian land. The greatest holding is on Oahu, where nearly 25% of the island is controlled by the armed forces and where there are more than 100 installations, from small ridge-top radar stations to Pearl Harbor, the USA's largest naval command center.

Agriculture is the third-largest sector of the economy. Sugar and pineapple, which once formed the backbone of Hawaii's economy, have been scaled back dramatically in recent years. Pineapple production has ceased on Lanai, which until the early 1990s was nicknamed the 'Pineapple Island,' and sugar, which is still being grown on Kauai and Maui, has recently disappeared from the landscape of both the Big Island and Oahu. Today, the two crops account for $125 million in sales, less than half of their value a decade ago.

Meanwhile, diversified crops, defined as all crops except sugar and pineapple, are on the rise and have a combined sales value of nearly $320 million. Of this, Hawaii's farms and nurseries sold nearly $75 million in flowers, while macadamia nuts brought in another $38 million. Other sizable crops include vegetables, tropical fruit, coffee and seed corn.

Hawaii's former agribusiness-based economy is in the midst of change. Hawaii's 'Big Five' companies – Amfac, Castle & Cooke, C Brewer, Theo Davies and Alexander & Baldwin – all had their origins in sugar. The Big Five hold onto their plantations not so much for what's being produced on them but for the potential they hold as future golf courses and condo developments – and bit by bit they're being sold off for those purposes. Some of the biggest buyers have been Japanese developers; more than a third of all Japanese investment in the USA is in Hawaii.

Hawaii's unemployment rate hovers around 5%. The cost of living is 20% higher in Honolulu than in the average US mainland city, while wages are 10% lower. For those stuck in service jobs, the most rapidly growing sector of the economy, it's tough to get by.

Native Hawaiians have the lowest median family income in Hawaii and are at the bottom of most health and welfare indicators, including high school dropout rates, suicide rates and death and major disease statistics. They also make up a disproportionately high percentage of Hawaii's homeless.

POPULATION & PEOPLE

The population of Hawaii is an estimated 1,211,500. Approximately 876,100 people live on Oahu, 148,700 on the Big Island, 117,800 on Maui, 58,300 on Kauai, 7200 on Molokai, 3200 on Lanai and 160 on Niihau.

There is no ethnic majority in Hawaii – everyone belongs to a minority. Some 42% of the population claims 'mixed ethnicity,' with a majority of those having some Hawaiian blood. As for the rest, Caucasians account for approximately 21% of the population, followed by Japanese (18%), Filipinos (12%) and Chinese (4%). There are about 9000 full-blooded Hawaiians, less than 1% of the population.

Hawaii's people are known for their racial harmony. Race is generally not a factor in marriage. Islanders have a fifty-fifty chance of marrying someone of a race different than their own and the majority of children born in Hawaii are *hapa*, or mixed-blood.

EDUCATION

Hawaii is the only US state to have a public education system run entirely by the state. In most other states, county or town education boards set budgetary priorities, but in Hawaii the governor sets the budget for the entire state and local communities have little input.

Compared to other states, Hawaii's public education is dismal. Its teachers, who went on strike in 2002 for the first time in 25 years, are ranked as the lowest paid in the USA when their salaries are adjusted for Hawaii's cost of living. As a result of the strike, starting teachers earn $34,000 (up from $29,000) but that's barely a livable wage in Hawaii and the state has difficulty attracting and keeping qualified teachers.

Many of the public schools, particularly in poor neighborhoods, are rundown, and violence and drugs are problems. Test scores for public school students in all grades are in the bottom 20% when compared with students in the other 49 states.

It is perhaps not surprising that private education is now a thriving alternative to the public school system and Hawaii has the largest percentage of students attending private schools of any US state. Nearly one in five children are now educated in private schools.

The largest of these, the Kamehameha Schools, is for descendants of native Hawaiians only, and is funded by a royal endowment from Princess Bernice Pauahi Bishop. Its approximately 5000 students are provided with an elite education that instills a sense of pride in their Hawaiian heritage.

The Bishop Estate, the private organization that runs Kamehameha Schools, is the largest and richest landholder in Hawaii. Its controversial board of directors, who are politically appointed and paid steep salaries, are often accused of putting their own interests above those of the students. The Kamehameha Schools educates just 2% of native Hawaiians despite that fact that its endowment, valued at well over $1 billion, is capable of providing for far more students.

Some people argue that the private schools, by attracting the brightest and wealthiest students, are partly to blame for the bleak public school conditions, largely because the public schools end up heavily weighted with students from disadvantaged families with little political clout.

Schools in Hawaii operate on a two-semester system; the first semester is from the first week of September to late December, the second from early January to the first week in June.

ARTS

Hula

Hawaii's most distinctive native art form is the hula, a graceful dance that combines facial expressions and body movements to convey stories.

Most ancient hula dances expressed historical events, legendary tales and the accomplishments of the great *alii*. Facial expressions, hand gestures, hip swaying and dance steps were all employed to tell the story. They were performed to rhythmic chants and drum beatings, serving to connect with the world of spirits. Eye movement was very important: if the story was about the sun, the eyes would gaze upward; if about the netherworld, they would gaze downward. One school, the *hula ohelo*, was very sensual, with movements suggesting the act of procreation.

Hula dancers wore tapa cloth, not the grass skirts which were introduced from Micronesia only a hundred years ago.

The Christian missionaries thought this hula dancing all too licentious for their liking and suppressed it. The hula might have been lost forever if not for King Kalakaua, the 'Merrie Monarch,' who revived it in the latter half of the 19th century.

The art of hula has attracted an influx of new students in recent years. Some classes practice in public places, such as school grounds and parks, where visitors are welcome to watch. Although many of the *halau* (hula schools) rely on tuition fees, others receive sponsorship from hotels, shopping centers and county governments, and give weekly public performances in return.

There are numerous island-wide hula competitions. Some of the biggest are the Prince Lot Hula Festival held each July in Oahu; the week-long Merrie Monarch Festival, which begins on Easter Sunday in Hilo; and Ka Molokai Makahiki and Molokai Ka Hula Piko festivals, held respectively in January and May on Molokai, birthplace of the hula.

Music

Contemporary Hawaiian music gives center stage to the guitar, which was first introduced to the islands by Spanish cowboys in the 1830s. The Hawaiians made it uniquely their own, however. In 1889, Joseph Kekuku, a native Hawaiian, designed the steel guitar, one of only two major musical instruments invented in what is now the USA. (The other is the banjo.) The steel guitar is usually played with slack-key tunings and carries the melody throughout the song.

Slack-key guitar, a type of tuning in which some strings are slackened from the conventional tuning to produce a harmonious soulful sound, is also a 19th-century Hawaiian creation and one that has come back into the spotlight in recent times. Some of Hawaii's more renowned slack-key guitar players include Cyril Pahinui, Keola Beamer, Raymond Kane, Dennis Kamakahi and Atta Isaacs Jr, and the late Gabby Pahinui and Sonny Chillingworth.

The ukulele, so strongly identified with Hawaiian music, was actually derived from the braginha, an instrument from Portugal introduced to Hawaii in the 19th century. In the Hawaiian language, the word 'ukulele' means 'jumping flea.'

Both the ukulele and the steel guitar were essential to the lighthearted, romantic music popularized in Hawaii from the 1930s to the 1950s. 'My Little Grass Shack,' 'Lovely Hula Hands' and 'Sweet Leilani' are classic examples. Owing to the 'Hawaii Calls' radio show, which for more than 30 years was broadcast worldwide from the Moana Hotel in Waikiki, this music became instantly recognizable as Hawaiian, conjuring up images of beautiful hula dancers swaying under palm trees in a tropical paradise. Troy Fernandez and Ledward Kaapana are among the present-day masters of the ukulele.

One current sound is Jawaiian, a blending of Hawaiian music and Jamaican reggae. Some of the better-known musicians who emphasize Jawaiian music are Bruddah Waltah, Hoaikane, the Kaau Crater Boys and Kulana.

Other popular contemporary Hawaiian musicians include vocalist-composer Henry Kapono; Hapa, the duo of Kelii Kanealii and Barry Flanagan, who fuse folk, rock and traditional Hawaiian elements; Daniel Ho, an accomplished guitarist and ukulele player who blends Hawaiian sounds with jazz and Asian influences; and Kealii Reichel, a charismatic vocalist and hula dancer known for his Hawaiian ballads and poetic chants.

Visual Arts

Many artists draw inspiration from Hawaii's rich cultural heritage and natural beauty.

The well-known Hawaiian painter Herb Kawainui Kane creates detailed oil paintings focusing on the early Polynesian settlers and King Kamehameha's life. His works are mainly on display in museums and at gallery collections in resorts.

Another notable native Hawaiian artist is Rocky Kaiouliokahihikoloehu Jensen, who does wood sculptures and drawings of Hawaiian gods, ancient chiefs and early Hawaiians, with the aim of creating sacred art in the tradition of *makaku*, or creative artistic *mana*.

Pegge Hopper paints traditional Hawaiian women in relaxed poses using a distinctive graphic design style and bright washes of color. Her work has been widely reproduced on posters and postcards.

Some of Hawaii's most impressive crafts are ceramics, bowls made of native woods and baskets woven of native fibers. The goddess Pele is a source of inspiration for many Big Island artists – some even use molten lava as a sculpting material.

One ancient craft that's been continued in modern times is *lauhala* weaving, which uses the *lau* (leaves) of the *hala* (pandanus) tree. Preparing the leaves for weaving is hard, messy work owing to the razor-sharp spines along the leaf edges and down the center. In old Hawaii, *lauhala* was woven into mats and floor coverings, but today smaller items like hats, place mats and baskets are most common.

Hawaiian quilting is another unique art form. The concept of patchwork quilting was introduced by the early missionaries, but the Hawaiians, who had only recently taken to Western cotton clothing, didn't have a surplus of cloth scraps – and the idea of cutting up new lengths of fabric simply to sew them back together again in small squares seemed absurd. Instead, the Hawaiian women created their own designs using larger cloth pieces, typically with stylized tropical flora on a white background.

A more transitory art form is the creation of the lei. Although the leis most widely worn today by visitors are made of fragrant flowers such as plumeria and tuberose, traditional leis of *mokihana* berries and *maile* leaves were more common in old Hawaii. Both types are still made today.

SOCIETY & CONDUCT

In many ways, contemporary culture in Hawaii resembles contemporary culture in the rest of the USA.

Hawaiians listen to the same pop music and watch the same TV shows as Americans on the mainland. Hawaii has discos and ballroom dancing, rock bands and classical orchestras, junk food and nouvelle cuisine. But the wonderful thing about Hawaii is that the mainland influences largely stand beside, rather than engulf, the culture of the islands.

Not only is traditional Hawaiian culture an integral part of the social fabric but so are the customs of the ethnically diverse immigrants who have made Hawaii their home. Hawaii is more than just a meeting place of East and West; it's also a place where the cultures merge, typically in a manner that brings out the best of both worlds.

The 1970s saw the start of a Hawaiian cultural renaissance that continues today. Hawaiian-language classes are thriving, and there is a concerted effort to reintroduce Hawaiian words into modern speech. Hula classes concentrate more on the nuances of hand movements and facial expressions than on the dramatic hip-shaking that sells dance shows. Many Hawaiian artists and craftspeople are returning to traditional mediums and themes.

Certainly, the tourist centers have long been overrun with packaged Hawaiiana, from plastic leis to theme-park luaus, that practically parodies island culture. But fortunately for the visitor, the growing interest in traditional Hawaiiana is having an impact on the tourist industry, and authentic performances by hula students and contemporary Hawaiian musicians are increasingly easy to find.

The vast majority of people you'll meet in Hawaii are very friendly, helpful and laidback. In general, most people will respond to you in a manner similar to the way you treat them. But Hawaii is not free from prejudice and there are some pockets of resentment against outsiders, particularly against *haoles* (whites) from the US mainland. This can sometimes be expressed as a cold shoulder, but in some areas, especially those that are more isolated, such as the Waianae Coast of Oahu, there can be confrontations. Overall, you need to be sensitive to the mood of people wherever you are.

RELIGION

In the old Hawaiian religion there were four main gods: Ku, Lono, Kane and Kanaloa.

Ku was the ancestor god for all generations of humankind, past, present and future. He presided over all male gods while his wife, Hina, reigned over the female gods. When the sun rose in the morning, it was said to be Ku; when it set in the evening, it was Hina. Like yin and yang, they were responsible for heaven and earth.

Ku had many manifestations, one as the benevolent god of fishing, Ku-ula (Ku of the abundant seas), and others as the god of forests and the god of farming. People prayed to Ku when the harvest was scarce. At a time of drought or other such disaster, a temple would be built to appease Ku.

One of the most fearful of Ku's manifestations was Kukailimoku (Ku, the snatcher of land), the war god whom Kamehameha the Great worshipped. At the temples built for the worship of Kukailimoku, the sacrificial offerings included not only food, pigs and chickens but also human beings.

Lono was the god in charge of the elements, bringing rain and an abundant harvest. He was also the god of fertility and peace.

Kane created the first man out of the dust of the earth and breathed life into him (the Hawaiian word for man is *kane*), and it was from Kane that the Hawaiian chiefs were said to have descended.

Ku, Lono and Kane together created the earth, the moon, the stars and the ocean.

Kanaloa, the fourth major god, was often pitted in struggles against the other three gods. When heaven and earth separated, it was Kanaloa who was placed in charge of the spirits on earth. Forbidden from drinking the intoxicating beverage *kava*, these spirits revolted and along with Kanaloa were driven to the underworld, where Kanaloa became the ruler of the dead.

Below the four main gods, there were 40 lesser gods. The best known was Pele, goddess of volcanoes. Her sister Laka was goddess of the hula, and another sister, Poliahu, was the goddess of snow.

The Hawaiians had gods for all occupations and natural phenomena. There was a god for the tapa maker and a god for the canoe builder, as well as shark gods and mountain gods.

Because some aspects of the ancient Hawaiian religion were so repressive, there was a sort of cultural amnesia after King Kamehameha died and the Christian missionaries stepped in. The Hawaiian religion as it was once known no longer exists. Still, in recent times there's been a revival of some of the spirituality that's entwined with positive aspects of the religion, such as honoring the harvest god Lono during traditional ceremonies like the *makahiki*.

Today, Hawaii's population is religiously diverse. Christianity has the largest following, with Catholicism being the predominant religious denomination in Hawaii. Interestingly, the United Church of Christ, which includes the Congregationalists who initially converted the islands, claim only about half as many members as the Mormons and one-tenth as many as the Catholics.

In addition, Hawaii has about 100 Buddhist temples, scores of Shinto shrines and two dozen Hindu temples. There are also Taoist, Tenrikyo, Jewish and Muslim houses of worship.

Facts for the Visitor

HIGHLIGHTS

Hawaii is a spectacular place with each island offering its own unique highlights.

On Oahu, renowned visitor attractions include Waikiki, Pearl Harbor and the North Shore with its huge winter surf. Honolulu's historic downtown, with the only royal palace in the USA, and the adjacent Chinatown offer a fascinating glimpse of Hawaii's multiethnic society. Other things not to be missed include Kailua's superb beach, the scenic drive around the southeast coast and the view from Diamond Head summit.

On Maui, the must-do's include a trip to Haleakala summit for the sunrise, the serpentine coastal drive to Hana and a visit to historic Lahaina. Maui also has lovely beaches, top-notch windsurfing and excellent winter whale-watching opportunities.

On the Big Island, don't miss Hawaii Volcanoes National Park, with its fascinating landscape of steaming craters and lava flows. Rural Waipio Valley and the cascading Akaka Falls also offer splendid natural scenery. Remnants of ancient Hawaiian culture are plentiful, including *heiaus* (ancient temples) at Puuhonua o Honaunau, which as more widely known as the Place of Refuge, as well as numerous petroglyph fields.

Kauai is certainly a favorite of naturalists and is known for its lush mountainous scenery, especially the Na Pali Coast and Kokee State Park. Both of these locations offer excellent backcountry hiking trails. On Kauai you'll also find the impressive Waimea Canyon, also known as the 'Grand Canyon of the Pacific,' as well as numerous waterways that provide excellent kayaking opportunities.

Molokai's chief attraction is its rural lifestyle and slow pace. Other highlights include Papohaku, the longest beach in Hawaii, a mule trail down to the historic leprosy colony of Kalaupapa, and a shoreline of ancient fishponds.

Lanai promotes its two luxury resorts but it also offers a few off-the-beaten-path sites to explore. Its south coast has a lovely beach, Hulopoe Bay, with fine diving and snorkeling.

PLANNING

When to Go

Hawaii is a great place to visit any time of the year.

Although the busiest tourist season is in winter (December to March), that has more to do with weather *elsewhere,* as many visitors are snowbirds escaping cold winters back home. Essentially the weather in Hawaii is agreeable all year round. It's a bit rainier in the winter and a bit hotter in the summer (June to August), but there are no extremes, and cooling trade winds modify the heat throughout the year.

In terms of cost, spring through fall (April to November) can be a bargain, as some hotel prices drop around April 1 and don't climb back up again until mid-December.

Naturally, certain activities have their peak seasons. For instance, if you're a board surfer, you'll find the biggest waves in winter, whereas if you're a windsurfer, you'll find the best wind conditions in summer.

Maps

The guide booklets handed out by the car rental agencies have simple maps showing the main roads. However, if you really want to explore, a more detailed road map, such as Lonely Planet's *Honolulu & Oahu City Map,* can be invaluable.

Gousha and Rand McNally also publish good Oahu street maps with detailed Honolulu sections. The American Automobile Association (AAA) puts out a good Honolulu road map and an all-Hawaii map, which it distributes free to its members. Nelles maps are also quite good, but can be hard to find.

Recommended is the Ready Mapbook series, which publishes atlas-style books of each of the main islands (Lanai and Molokai are included in the Maui book), with maps covering virtually every road. These atlases, which cost around $10 and are readily available in Hawaii bookstores, are roughly the size of a thick magazine and they're strictly road maps with no topography.

The United States Geological Survey (USGS) publishes topographical maps of Hawaii. Both full-island and detailed sectional maps are available, and there's also an individual USGS map for Hawaii Volcanoes National Park. Maps can be ordered from the **US Geological Survey** *(☎ 800-435-7627, fax 303-202-4693; W earthexplorer.usgs.gov; PO Box 25286, Denver Federal Center, Denver, CO 80225)*. Maps cost $4 to $7 per sheet, plus a $5 mailing fee per order.

USGS maps can also be purchased at several places in Hawaii, including on Kauai at the Kauai Museum in Lihue and the Kokee State Park museum, on Oahu at the **Pacific Map Center** *(☎ 545-3600; 560 N Nimitz, Honolulu)*, and on the Big Island at Hawaii Volcanoes National Park.

Divers and snorkelers should try Franko's Maps ($6.95), a series of laminated, waterproof maps of each island showing snorkeling and diving spots along with pictures of some of the colorful fish found in Hawaiian waters.

What to Bring

Hawaii has balmy weather and a casual attitude toward dress, so for the most part packing is a breeze.

At the lower elevations it's summer all year. Shorts, sandals and a T-shirt or cotton shirt are the standard day dress. If you don't intend spending time at higher elevations, a light jacket or sweater will be the warmest clothing you'll need.

Pack light. You can always pick up something with a tropical Hawaiian print when you get there and dress island-style.

An aloha shirt and lightweight slacks for men, and a cotton dress for women, is pretty much regarded as 'dressing up' on the islands. Only a few of the most exclusive restaurants require anything dressier.

Hawaii does, however, have highland areas (called 'upcountry' on the islands) as well as mountains, and most people get at least as far as these areas. The upcountry can be a good 20°F cooler than the coast, and when the fog blows in and the wind picks up, it gets quite nippy. If you intend to spend any time in the upcountry, plan on another layer of clothing.

The temperature on the mountain summits on the Big Island and Maui can dip below freezing. If you're going to be camping at high elevations, you will need to be prepared for cold weather; a tent, a winter-rated sleeping bag, rain gear and layers of warm clothing are a must.

Camping on the beach is another matter entirely. A very lightweight cotton bag is the most you'll need. Public camping grounds require campers to use tents – a good idea anyway because of mosquitoes.

For hiking, bring footwear with good traction. Many people just wear sneakers, although walking on lava can be tough on the ankles. Serious hikers should consider lugging along their hiking boots.

You won't regret bringing binoculars for watching whales and birds, and a flashlight is useful for exploring caves. Snorkel gear may come in handy too, but you don't need to worry too much about what to bring, as just about anything you forget to pack you can easily buy in Hawaii.

RESPONSIBLE TOURISM

When hiking and camping, be sure to take out everything you bring in; this includes any kind of garbage you create. Parts of Hawaii periodically suffer from drought, so it's important to not waste water. Take short showers and be conservative in your use of towels. Aluminum can recycling is common in Hawaii, and many public places, including beach parks, have separate bins for recycling them.

TOURIST OFFICES

Local Tourist Offices

The main office of the **Hawaii Visitors and Convention Bureau** *(☎ 923-1811, 800-464-2924; e info@hvcb.org; W www.gohawaii.com; 2270 Kalakaua Ave, Suite 801, Waikiki, HI 96815)* will mail you general tourist information on Hawaii.

Tourist offices on Oahu, Maui, Kauai, the Big Island and Molokai can provide information more specific to their islands; phone numbers and addresses are in the individual island chapters.

Tourist Offices Abroad

The following are the addresses for HVCB representatives abroad.

Australia (☎ 02-9955 2619, fax 9955 2171) c/o The Sales Team, Suite 2, Level 2, 34 Burton St, Milsons Point, NSW 2061

Canada (☎ 800-464-2924, W www.gohawaii.com, e info@hvcb.org) 24-hour planning hotline c/o Hawaii Visitors and Convention Bureau

Germany (☎ 61-02 722 411, fax 02 722 409)
c/o American Venture Marketing, Herderstrasse 6–8, 63263 Neu Isenburg
Japan (☎ 03-3201 0430, fax 3201 0433)
Kokusai Bldg, 2nd floor, 3-1-1 Marunouchi, Chiyoda-ku, Tokyo 100-0005
New Zealand (☎ 09-379 3708, fax 309 0725)
c/o Walshes World, Private Bag 92136, 87 Queen St, 2nd floor, Auckland
UK (☎ 020-8941 8116, fax 8941 4011)
Box 208, Sunbury on Thames, Middlesex TW16 5RJ

VISAS & DOCUMENTS

The conditions for entering Hawaii are the same as for entering any state in the USA.

Passport

With the exception of Canadians, who need only proper proof of Canadian citizenship (such as a citizenship card with photo ID or a passport), all foreign visitors must have a valid passport.

Visas

Most foreign visitors to the US need a visa. However, there is a reciprocal visa-waiver programme in which citizens of certain countries may enter the USA for stays of 90 days or less without first obtaining a US visa. Currently these countries are Andorra, Argentina, Australia, Austria, Belgium, Brunei, Denmark, Finland, France, Germany, Iceland, Ireland, Italy, Japan, Liechtenstein, Luxembourg, Monaco, Netherlands, New Zealand, Norway, San Marino, Singapore, Slovenia, Spain, Sweden, Switzerland, the UK and Uruguay.

Under the visa-waiver programme you must have a round-trip ticket that is nonrefundable in the USA and you will not be allowed to extend your stay beyond the 90-day period.

Other travelers will need to obtain a visa from a US consulate or embassy. In most countries the process can be done by mail.

Your passport should be valid for at least six months longer than your intended stay in the USA and you'll need to submit a recent photo (37mm x 37mm) with the application. Documents of financial stability and/or guarantees from a US resident are sometimes required, particularly for those from third world countries.

Visa applicants may be required to 'demonstrate binding obligations' that will ensure their return home. Because of this requirement, those planning to travel through other countries before arriving in the USA are generally better off applying for their US visa while they are still in their home country rather than while on the road.

The validity period for US visitor visas depends on what country you're from. The length of time you'll be allowed to stay in the USA is ultimately determined by US immigration authorities at the port of entry.

If you want to stay in the USA longer than the date stamped on your passport, apply for an extension with the Honolulu office of the **Immigration & Naturalization Service** (☎ *532-3721; 595 Ala Moana Blvd*) before the stamped date.

Travel Insurance

Foreign visitors should be aware that health care in the USA is very expensive. So, it's a good idea to buy travel insurance that covers medical expenses, luggage theft or loss, and cancellations or delays in your travel arrangements.

There is a wide variety of policies available, and the exact coverage depends on the policy you buy, so get your insurer or travel agent to explain the details. Check the small print, since some policies exclude 'dangerous activities,' which can include scuba diving, motorcycling and anything to do with parachutes.

Although you may find a policy that pays doctors or hospitals directly, be aware that many doctors and medical clinics in Hawaii will demand payment at the time of service. If you have to claim later, keep all documentation. Some policies ask you to call (using reverse charges) a center in your home country for an immediate assessment of your problem. Check whether the policy covers ambulances or an emergency flight home.

It's best to purchase travel insurance as early as possible. If you buy it the week before you fly, you might find, for instance, that you're not covered for delays to your flight caused by a strike that may have been in force before you took out the insurance.

Purchasing your ticket with a credit card often provides travel accident insurance and may also give you the right to reclaim your payment if the operator doesn't deliver. Ask your credit card company, or the issuing bank, for details.

Other Documents

All US airlines require passengers to present photo ID as part of the airline check-in procedure.

All foreign visitors (other than Canadians) must bring their passport. US and Canadian citizens may want to bring along a passport as well, in the event they are tempted to extend their travels beyond Hawaii.

All visitors should bring their driver's license and any health insurance or travel insurance cards.

Members of Hostelling International (HI) will be able to take advantage of lower hostel rates at Oahu's HI hostels with their membership cards.

Although Hawaii doesn't offer a lot of student discounts, if you have a student card, bring it along anyway, as flashing it may occasionally win you a discount at museums and other sights.

Members of senior citizen organizations such as the American Association of Retired Persons (AARP) and the Canadian Association of Retired Persons (CARP) can get an occasional hotel or car rental discount by showing their cards.

Members of the American Automobile Association (AAA) or other affiliated automobile clubs can get car rental, airfare and some sightseeing discounts with their membership cards.

Divers should bring their certification cards with them.

Copies

Before you leave home, you should photocopy all important documents (passport data page, credit cards, travel insurance policy, air tickets, driver's license etc). Leave one copy with someone at home and keep another with you, separate from the originals.

It's also a good idea to store details of your vital travel documents in Lonely Planet's free online Travel Vault in case you lose the photocopies or can't really be bothered with them. Your password-protected Travel Vault is accessible online anywhere in the world – just create it at W www.ekno.lonelyplanet.com.

EMBASSIES & CONSULATES

US Embassies

US embassies include the following:

Australia (☎ 02-6214 5600) 21 Moonah Place, Yarralumla, Canberra, ACT 2600

Canada (☎ 613-238 5335) 490 Sussex Dr, Ottawa, Ontario K1N 1G8

France (☎ 01 43 12 22 22) 2 Av Gabriel, 75008 Paris

Germany (☎ 030-8305 0) Neustädtische Kirchstrasse 4-5, 10117 Berlin

Ireland (☎ 01-668 8777) 42 Elgin Rd, Ballsbridge, Dublin 4

Italy (☎ 64 67 41) Via Veneto 119/A, 00187 Rome

Japan (☎ 03-3224 5000) 10–5, Akasaka 1-chome, Minato-ku, Tokyo

Netherlands (☎ 070-310 9209) Lange Voorhout 102, 2514 EJ The Hague

New Zealand (☎ 04-462 6000) 29 Fitzherbert Terrace, PO Box 1190, Thorndon, Wellington

UK (☎ 020-7499 9000) 24/31 Grosvenor Square, London W1A 1AE

Consulates in Hawaii

There are no embassies in Hawaii, but there are several consulates in Honolulu, including the following:

Australia (☎ 524-5050) 1000 Bishop St

Germany (☎ 946-3819) 252 Paoa Place

Italy (☎ 531-2277) 735 Bishop St, Suite 201

Japan (☎ 543-3111) 1742 Nuuanu Ave

Netherlands (☎ 531-6897) 745 Fort St Mall, Suite 702

New Zealand (☎ 547-5117) 900 Richards St, Suite 414

Philippines (☎ 595-6316) 2433 Pali Hwy

CUSTOMS

US Customs allows each person age 21 or older to bring 1 quart of liquor and 200 cigarettes duty-free into the USA. Entry of fresh fruits and plants is restricted and there's a strict quarantine on animals.

MONEY

Currency

The US dollar is the only currency used in Hawaii.

The US dollar is divided into 100 cents. Coins come in denominations of one cent (penny), five cents (nickel), 10 cents (dime), 25 cents (quarter) and 50 cents (half-dollar). Notes come in one-, five-, 10-, 20-, 50- and 100-dollar denominations. Also legal tender but only occasionally seen are a one-dollar coin that the government has tried unsuccessfully to bring into mass circulation and a two-dollar note that is out of favor.

Exchange Rates

At press time, exchange rates were:

country	unit		US dollar
Australia	A$1	=	US$0.54
Canada	C$1	=	US$0.64
euro zone	€1	=	US$0.99
Japan	¥100	=	US$0.86
New Zealand	NZ$1	=	US$0.47
UK	UK£1	=	US$1.57

Exchanging Money

Cash If you're carrying foreign currency, it can be exchanged for US dollars at larger banks throughout Hawaii, such as the ubiquitous Bank of Hawaii.

Traveler's Checks The main benefit of traveler's checks is that they provide protection from theft and loss. Large companies such as American Express and Thomas Cook generally offer efficient replacement policies.

Foreign visitors who carry traveler's checks will find it much easier if the checks are in US dollars. Restaurants, hotels and most stores accept US-dollar traveler's checks as if they're cash, so if that's what you're carrying, odds are you'll never have to use a bank or pay an exchange fee.

Keeping a record of the check numbers and those you have used is vital for replacing lost checks, so keep this information separate from the checks themselves.

For refunds on lost or stolen traveler's checks, call **American Express** (☎ *800-992-3404*) or **Thomas Cook** (☎ *800-287-7362*).

Credit Cards Major credit cards are widely accepted throughout Hawaii, including at car rental agencies and most hotels, restaurants, gas stations, shops and larger grocery stores. Most recreational and tourist activities in Hawaii can also be paid for by credit card. Note, however, that many B&Bs and some condominiums, particularly those handled through rental agencies, do not accept credit cards.

The most commonly accepted cards in Hawaii are Visa, MasterCard and American Express, although JCB, Discover and Diners Club cards are also accepted by a fair number of businesses.

ATMs Automatic teller machines (ATMs) are another handy way to access your money, allowing you to withdraw cash from a bank account back home. The small service charge often works out cheaper than the 1% fee charged for traveler's checks, and there's no need to carry a bundle of checks around.

Major banks such as Bank of Hawaii and First Hawaiian Bank have extensive ATM networks throughout Hawaii that will give cash advances on major credit cards (MasterCard, Visa, American Express, Discover and JCB) and allow cash withdrawals with affiliated ATM cards. Most ATM machines in Hawaii accept bank cards from both the Plus and Cirrus systems, the two largest ATM networks in the USA.

ATMs can be found outside banks, in most large grocery stores, in mall-style shopping centers and in many convenience stores.

International Transfers Transferring money from your home bank will be easier if you've authorized someone back home to access your account. Specify the town, the bank and the branch to which you want your money directed, or ask your home bank to tell you where there's a suitable one, and make sure you get the details right. You can find some of the necessary information on the websites of Hawaii's two largest banks: **Bank of Hawaii** (W *www.boh.com*) and **First Hawaiian Bank** (W *www.fhb.com*).

Costs

How much money you'll need for your visit to Hawaii depends on your traveling style. Some people get by quite cheaply while others rack up huge balances on their American Express card.

An airfare to Hawaii is usually one of the heftier parts of the budget. Fares vary greatly, particularly from the US mainland, so shop around. Interisland flights cost about $60 to $100 one way, depending on how you buy your tickets.

It can be a bit challenging to explore the islands without renting a car, except on Oahu, where there's a good inexpensive bus system. Renting a car usually costs between $150 and $200 a week.

Camping is an alternative to paying for a hotel. Every main island has inexpensive state and county camping grounds and Maui and the Big Island have excellent national parks with free camping.

The main islands each have at least a couple of hostel-style places with dormitory beds for under $20 and either B&Bs or spartan hotels for around $50. For hotels with more standard middle-class amenities expect to pay nearly double that, and if you've got your mind set on a 1st-class beachfront hotel, get ready to pay upwards of $150 a night. For a splurge on a luxury hotel – and Hawaii has some of the world's finest – rates generally begin around $250.

If you're staying awhile, there are ways to cut accommodation costs. Weekly and monthly condo rental rates can beat all but the cheapest hotels. Besides having more space, most condos are turnkey, meaning that they're equipped with virtually everything you'll need, from towels and beach mats to a kitchen stocked with pots and pans. Being able to prepare your own meals in a condo can save a bundle on food costs.

Since much of Hawaii's food is shipped in, grocery prices average 25% higher than on the mainland. Food in neighborhood restaurants is good value in Hawaii, with prices generally as cheap as you'll find on the mainland.

Tipping

Tipping practices are the same as in the rest of the USA. In restaurants, waiters expect a tip of about 15%, while 10% is generally sufficient for taxi drivers, hair stylists and the like. Hotel bellhops are typically tipped $1 or $2 per bag, depending on the weight.

Taxes

Hawaii has a 4.17% state sales tax that is tacked onto virtually everything, including meals, groceries, car rentals and accommodations. An additional 7.24% room tax brings the total tax added to accommodation bills to 11.41%. Another tax targeted at visitors is a $3-a-day 'road use' tax imposed upon all car rentals.

POST & COMMUNICATIONS

Postal Rates

For 1st-class mail sent and delivered within the USA, postage rates are 37¢ for letters up to 1oz (23¢ for each additional ounce) and 23¢ for standard-size postcards. First-class mail between Hawaii and the mainland goes by air and usually takes three to four days.

International airmail rates for letters up to 1oz are 60¢ to Canada or Mexico, 80¢ to other countries. Postcards cost 50¢ to Canada or Mexico, 70¢ to other countries.

Receiving Mail

You can have mail sent to you c/o General Delivery at most post offices in Hawaii. An exception is on Oahu, where all general delivery mail addressed to Honolulu or Waikiki is delivered to the main post office, adjacent to Honolulu International Airport. General delivery mail is usually held for up to 30 days. Most hotels will also hold mail for incoming guests.

Telephone

Pay phones can readily be found in public places such as shopping centers and beach parks. Local calls cost 50¢ at pay phones. Any call made from one point on an island to any other point on that island is a local call. Calls from one island to another are long distance.

To dial direct from one Hawaiian island to another from a pay phone, the rate is $1.40 for the first minute and 15¢ for each additional minute.

Be aware that most hotels add a service charge of around $1 for each local call made from a room phone and most also have hefty surcharges for long-distance calls.

International Calls To make an international call direct from Hawaii, dial ☎ 011 + country code + area code + number. (An exception is to Canada, where you dial ☎ 1 + area code + number.)

Telephone Area Codes

The telephone area code for all of Hawaii is ☎ 808. You don't use the area code when making intraisland calls, but you must use it when calling from one island to another and when calling Hawaii from outside the state. The ☎ 808 area code is not included in telephone numbers given in this book.

All phone numbers listed in this book beginning with ☎ 800, ☎ 877 or ☎ 888 are toll-free calls from the US mainland. The same numbers are sometimes toll-free from Canada as well.

For international operator assistance, dial ☎ 0 (zero). The operator can provide specific rate information and tell you which time periods are the cheapest for calling – these vary with the country being called.

If you're calling Hawaii from abroad, the international country code for the USA is ☎ 1, and all calls to Hawaii are then followed by the area code ☎ 808 and the seven-digit local number.

Phonecards Lonely Planet's ekno global communication service provides low-cost international calls – for local calls you're usually better off with a local phonecard. Ekno also offers free messaging services, email, travel information and an online travel vault, where you can securely store all your important documents. You can join online at **W** www.ekno.lonelyplanet.com, where you will find the local-access numbers for the 24-hour customer-service centre. Once you have joined, always check the ekno website for the latest access numbers for each country and updates on new features.

Fax

You can send and receive faxes through the front desk of most hotels. There are also business centers throughout Hawaii, such as Kinko's, that offer reasonably priced fax services.

Email & Internet Access

One way to stay connected is to travel with your laptop. If you're coming from outside the USA, be sure the power supply is compatible, otherwise you may need to bring along a universal AC adapter and a plug adapter. The telephone socket may be different from that at home as well, so ensure that you have at least a US RJ-11 telephone adapter that works with your modem.

Major Internet service providers such as **America Online** *(AOL;* **W** *www.aol.com)* have dial-in nodes in Hawaii and throughout the USA. If you access your Internet email at home through a smaller ISP, your best option is either to open an account with a global ISP, like AOL, or to rely on public access points to collect your mail.

You can collect mail by opening a free email account such as Yahoo or Hotmail. You can then access your mail on any Internet-connected machine. On the main islands there are cybercafés and business centers, such as Kinko's, that offer inexpensive on-line computer access. Public libraries also have on-line computers, but they typically only have one or two computers, so there's usually a long queue, and you'll need to have a Hawaii library card (see Libraries later in this chapter).

If you're carrying a laptop, you may want to check with your hotel in advance to see if the room comes with a phone jack that can accommodate modem hookups; many hotels now have these data ports in at least some of their rooms.

DIGITAL RESOURCES

There's no better place to start your Web explorations than the **Lonely Planet website** *(**W** www.lonelyplanet.com)*. Here you'll find succinct summaries on traveling to most places on earth, postcards from other travelers and the Thorn Tree bulletin board, where you can ask questions before you go or dispense advice when you get back. You can also find travel news and updates for many of our most popular guidebooks, and the subwwway section links you to the most useful travel resources elsewhere on the Web.

In addition, **W** www.honoluluadvertiser.com, **W** www.planet-hawaii.com and **W** www.alternative-hawaii.com are useful websites that have links to a wealth of Hawaii information.

BOOKS

Numerous books have been written about Hawaii and its people, landscapes, history, culture and unique flora and fauna. The books that follow are just a few of the recommended titles.

Bookstores in Hawaii are all well stocked with Hawaiiana titles, or you can order by mail before you go. The following companies specialize in books on Hawaii, send out catalogs on request and also allow you to shop online.

Bess Press (☎ 734-7159, 800-910-2377, **W** www.besspress.com) 3565 Harding Ave, Honolulu, HI 96816

University of Hawaii Press (☎ 808-956-8255, 888-847-7377, fax 808-988-6052, **W** www.uhpress.hawaii.edu) 2840 Kolowalu St, Honolulu, HI 96822

Lonely Planet

In addition to this book, Lonely Planet publishes separate guidebooks to the islands of Oahu, Maui and the Big Island, with in-depth coverage of those destinations. Lonely Planet's *Diving & Snorkeling Hawaii* is an excellent guide to diving and snorkeling that includes color photos illustrating sites and fish.

Activity Guides

The Beaches of Oahu, *The Beaches of Maui County*, *Beaches of the Big Island* and *Beaches of Kauai and Niihau*, by John Clark, detail each island's coastline and every one of its beaches, including water conditions, shoreline geology and local history.

Surfer's Guide to Hawaii: Hawaii Gets All the Breaks by Greg Ambrose describes the top surfing spots throughout the islands. Light and entertaining, it's packed with everything you need to know about surfing in Hawaii.

Kathy Morey's *Hawaii Trails* (about the Big Island), *Kauai Trails, Maui Trails* and *Oahu Trails* are comprehensive hiking guides with good maps and clear directions.

Hawaiian Hiking Trails by Craig Chisholm is a good statewide hiking guide to Hawaii's best-known trails, all illustrated with a USGS map of the route.

Six Islands on Two Wheels by Tom Koch is a comprehensive guide to cycling in Hawaii. Koch encourages you to bring your own bike to Hawaii and tells you how to outfit it, where to ride and what to expect.

Mountain Biking the Hawaiian Islands by John Alford is an excellent resource for mountain bikers, covering the public trails open to bikers on the islands, with maps and descriptions.

Paddling My Own Canoe by Audrey Sutherland details the author's adventures and ruminations while kayaking solo along the rugged, isolated north shore of Molokai. The book helped popularize wilderness kayaking in Hawaii.

Girl in the Curl: A Century of Women in Surfing by Andrea Gabbard gives long overdue recognition to the role of *wahine* (female) surfers.

Natural History

Hawaii: The Islands of Life has strikingly beautiful photos of the flora, fauna and landscapes being protected by the Nature Conservancy of Hawaii, with text by Gavan Daws.

The Many-Splendored Fishes of Hawaii by Gar Goodson is one of the better of several small, inexpensive fish-identification books, and has good descriptions and 170 color drawings.

Hawaii's Fishes: A Guide for Snorkelers, Divers and Aquarists by John P Hoover, a more expensive and comprehensive field guide, covers more than 230 reef and shore fish of Hawaii, fully illustrated with color photographs.

Hawaii's Birds, by the Hawaii Audubon Society, is the best pocket-size guide to the birds of Hawaii, and has color photos and descriptions of all the native birds and many of the introduced species.

For something more comprehensive, there's *A Field Guide to the Birds of Hawaii & the Tropical Pacific* by H Douglas Pratt.

Trailside Plants of Hawaii's National Parks by Charles H Lamoureux covers common trailside plants and trees in some depth. It's a good book to have if you'll be spending time hiking in the national parks.

Manual of the Flowering Plants of Hawaii by Warren L Wagner, Derral R Herbst and SH Sohmer has in-depth information on Hawaiian flora, including rare and endangered species that have recently been categorized.

Practical Folk Medicine of Hawaii by LR McBride has descriptions of many native medicinal plants and their uses.

History & Culture

Hawaiian Antiquities by David Malo, written in 1838, was the first account of Hawaiian culture written by a Hawaiian. It gives an in-depth history of Hawaii before the arrival of the missionaries.

Shoal of Time by the authoritative historian Gavan Daws is a comprehensive and colorful history covering the period from Captain Cook's 'discovery' of the islands to statehood.

Hawaii's Story by Hawaii's Queen by Queen Liliuokalani, written in 1897, is an autobiographical account of Liliuokalani's life and the circumstances surrounding her 1893 overthrow.

The Betrayal of Liliuokalani: Last Queen of Hawaii, 1838–1917 by Helena G Allen is an insightful account not only of the queen's life but also of missionary activity and foreign encroachment in Hawaii.

Father Damien, the priest who worked in the leprosy colony on Molokai, is the subject of many books, including *Holy Man: Father Damien of Molokai* by Gavan Daws and *Damien the Leper* by John Farrow.

The Kumulipo by Martha Beckwith is a translation of the Hawaiian chant of creation. The chant of 2077 lines begins in the darkness of the spirit world and traces the genealogy of an *alii* (royal) family said to be the ancestors of humankind.

Nana I Ke Kumu (Look to the Source) by Mary Kawena Pukui, EW Haertig and Catherine A Lee is a fascinating two-volume collection of information on Hawaiian cultural practices, social customs and beliefs.

The Legends and Myths of Hawaii is a collection of legends as told by King David Kalakaua. It has a short introduction to Hawaiian culture and history as well.

Keneti by Bob Krauss is a fascinating biography of Kenneth 'Keneti' Emory, the Bishop Museum archaeologist who sailed with writer Jack London, worked with anthropologist Margaret Mead and surfed with Olympian Duke Kahanamoku. Emory, who died in 1992, spent much of his life uncovering the ruins of villages and temples throughout the Pacific, recording them before they disappeared forever.

Legacy of the Landscape by Patrick Vinton Kirch details 50 of the most important Hawaiian archaeological sites, including ancient *heiaus* (stone temples), fishponds and petroglyphs.

Fiction

A Hawaiian Reader, edited by A Grove Day and Carl Stroven, is an excellent anthology with 37 selections, both fiction and nonfiction. It starts with a log entry by Captain James Cook and includes writings from early missionaries as well as Mark Twain, Jack London, Somerset Maugham, David Malo, Martha Beckwith and others. If you only have time to read one book about Hawaii, this inexpensive paperback is a great choice.

Hotel Honolulu, by intrepid travel novelist Paul Theroux, explores the life of a washed-up writer who manages a rundown hotel in Waikiki, with fun pokes at cliched facets of Hawaii.

Talking to the Dead by Sylvia Watanabe is an enjoyable read that portrays a sense of growing up as a second-generation Japanese American in postwar Hawaii.

Another good contemporary read is *Shark Dialogues* by Kiana Davenport, which is part historical novel, part love story and part creation myth written in melodic, transfixing prose.

Hawaii is James Michener's ambitious saga of the islands tracing the Polynesian settlers, the arrival of the missionaries and whalers, the emergence of the sugar barons and the development of Hawaii's multiethnic society.

FILMS

Dozens of feature movies have been filmed in Hawaii and scores of others have used footage of Hawaii as backdrops. One of the few that has insightfully delved into island life is *Picture Bride* (1993), starring Yuki Kudoh, with a cameo by Toshiro Mifune; filmed on Oahu, it depicts the blunt realities of 19th-century Hawaiian plantation life for a Japanese mail-order bride.

Classic movies filmed at least partly on Hawaii include *Song of the Islands* (1942), filmed on the Big Island, starring Betty Grable and Victor Mature; *From Here to Eternity* (1953), filmed in Oahu, starring Burt Lancaster and Deborah Kerr; *Miss Sadie Thompson* (1953), filmed on Kauai, starring Rita Hayworth; *South Pacific* (1958), filmed on Kauai, with Mitzi Gaynor and Rossano Brazzi; *The Old Man and the Sea* (1958), filmed on the Big Island, starring Spencer Tracy; *Blue Hawaii* (1961), filmed on Kauai, starring Elvis Presley and Angela Lansbury; *Hawaii* (1966), filmed on Oahu and Kauai, starring Julie Andrews and Max von Sydow; *Tora! Tora! Tora!* (1970), filmed on Oahu, starring Jason Robards; *King Kong* (1976), filmed on Kauai, with Jessica Lange and Jeff Bridges; and *Raiders of the Lost Ark* (1981), filmed on Kauai, with Harrison Ford.

More recent films that used Hawaii as their base include Steven Spielberg's *Jurassic Park* (1993), and *Jurassic Park III* (2001), filmed in remote valleys on Kauai; Kevin Costner's big washout *Waterworld* (1995), filmed in the waters off the Big Island; *A Very Brady Sequel* (1996), in which the Brady Bunch pops up in Waikiki; *Godzilla* (1998), starring Matthew Broderick, which shot scenes on Oahu's windward coast; and *Molokai: The Story of Father Damien* (1999), starring Peter O'Toole, which was shot on Molokai's Kalaupapa Peninsula. Many of the action scenes from the movie *Pearl Harbor* (2001), starring Ben Affleck, including the mock dogfights, were shot on Oahu.

NEWSPAPERS & MAGAZINES

Hawaii's main paper is the *Honolulu Advertiser*, which is published each morning. The Honolulu paper is sold throughout Hawaii, but the Neighbor Islands also have their own newspapers. The *Hawaii Tribune-Herald* in Hilo, *West Hawaii Today* in Kailua-Kona, the *Maui News* in Wailuku and the *Garden Island* in Lihue are each published at least six times a week.

Several mainland newspapers are also widely available, including *USA Today*, the *Wall Street Journal* and the *Los Angeles Times*. Look for them in the lobbies of larger hotels and in convenience stores. You can get international newspapers at Borders bookstores, which carry an impressively wide selection.

Honolulu and *Hawaii* are the largest general interest magazines about Hawaii. *Honolulu* is geared more toward residents and is published monthly. *Hawaii* has more feature articles aimed at visitors and is published six times a year.

The numerous tourist magazines distributed free on the islands are well worth perusing. They usually have simple maps, a bit of current event information, lots of ads and discount coupons for everything from hamburgers to sunset cruises.

RADIO & TV

Hawaii has about 50 AM and FM radio stations, including some that feature Hawaiian music. Programming varies widely across the dial; for specific details, see the Information sections in the individual island chapters.

On TV you'll find stations representing all the major US networks, as well as cable channels offering tourist information, Japanese-language programmes and more. Almost anything you can watch on the mainland you can watch in Hawaii.

For some local flavor, the evening news on Channel 2 ends with some fine slack-key guitar music by Keola and Kapono Beamer and clips of people waving the *shaka* sign (Hawaiian hand greeting).

PHOTOGRAPHY & VIDEO

Film & Equipment

Both print and slide film are readily available on all the islands. If you're going to be in Hawaii for any length of time, consider having your film developed there, as the high temperature and humidity of the tropics greatly accelerates the deterioration of exposed film. The sooner it's developed, the better the results.

Kodak and Fuji have labs in Honolulu, and island drugstores and camera shops usually send customer orders to those labs. Longs Drugs is one of the cheapest places for both purchasing film and having it developed. All the tourist centers have one-hour print processing shops as well.

Technical Tips

Don't leave your camera in direct sun any longer than necessary. A locked car can heat up like an oven in just a few minutes.

Sand and water are intense reflectors, and in bright light they'll often leave foreground subjects shadowy. You can try compensating by adjusting your f-stop or attaching a polarizing filter, or both, but the most effective technique is to take your beach photos in the gentler light of early morning and late afternoon.

Video Systems

If you purchase videos in Hawaii, make sure they're compatible with your home system. North America uses the NTSC system, which is incompatible with the PAL system used in Europe, Asia and Australia.

TIME

Hawaii does not observe daylight saving time. When it's noon in Hawaii, it's 2pm in Los Angeles, 5pm in New York, 10pm in London, 7am the next day in Tokyo, 8am the next day in Melbourne and 10am the next day in Auckland.

The time difference is one hour greater during those months when other countries are observing daylight saving. For example, from April to October, when it's noon in Hawaii it's 6pm in New York; and from November to March, when it's noon in Hawaii it's 9am in Melbourne.

Hawaii has about 11 hours of daylight in midwinter (December) and almost 13½ hours in midsummer (June). In midwinter, the sun rises at about 7am and sets at about 6pm. In midsummer, it rises before 6am and sets after 7pm.

And then there's 'Hawaiian time,' which is either a slow-down-the-clock pace or a euphemism for being late.

ELECTRICITY

Electricity is 110/120V, 60 cycles. Most outlets accept a flat, two-pronged plug, as elsewhere in the USA, but some grounded outlets also allow you to use items with three-pronged plugs.

WEIGHTS & MEASURES

Hawaii, like other US states, uses the imperial system of measurement. Distances are measured in feet, yards and miles; weights are tallied in ounces, pounds and tons. Those unaccustomed to the US system can consult the metric conversion table on the inside back cover of this book.

LAUNDRY

Many hotels, condominiums and hostels have coin-operated washers and dryers. If there's not one where you're staying, you can find commercial coin-operated laundries on all the islands. The average cost is about $1 to wash a load of clothes and another dollar to dry. Laundry locations are listed in each island chapter.

TOILETS

The sanitation standard is very high in Hawaii. Public toilets are free to use and easy to find – at least in comparison to the US mainland. Virtually every beach park has toilet facilities (also referred to as rest rooms), as do larger shopping centers and most hotel lobbies. Fast-food restaurants are another possibility, though they're generally intended for customers only.

HEALTH

Hawaii is a very healthy place to live and to visit. As it's 2500 miles from the nearest industrial center, there's little air pollution – other than that caused by volcanic activity. Hawaii ranks first of all the 50 US states in life expectancy, which is currently about 76 years for men and 81 years for women.

There are few serious health concerns. The islands are free of most tropical nasties like malaria and cholera, and you can drink water directly out of the tap, although all stream water needs to be boiled or treated.

No immunizations are required to enter Hawaii or any other port in the USA.

There are many poisonous plants in Hawaii, so you should never taste a plant that you cannot positively identify as edible.

If you're new to the heat and humidity, you may find yourself easily fatigued and more susceptible to minor ailments. Acclimatize yourself by slowing down your pace and setting your body clock to the more kicked-back 'Hawaiian time.' Drink plenty of liquids.

If you're planning a long outing or anything strenuous, take enough water and don't push yourself.

Medical Problems & Treatment

Hawaii has 25 acute-care hospitals. While the rural islands of Molokai and Lanai have limited medical facilities, the other islands have fully staffed hospitals with modern facilities. Still, for specialized care and serious illnesses, many islanders have more confidence in Honolulu hospitals than in Neighbor Island facilities.

Dengue Fever This viral infection, which has recently surfaced in Hawaii, is transmitted by mosquitoes and is rapidly becoming one of the top public health problems throughout the tropical Pacific. It spreads when a mosquito bites an infected person and then passes along the virus by biting someone else.

Signs and symptoms of dengue fever include a sudden onset of high fever, severe headaches, joint and muscle pain, nausea and vomiting. A rash of small red spots sometimes appears three or four days after the onset of fever. In the early phase of illness, dengue fever may be mistaken for other infectious diseases, including influenza. Minor bleeding such as nosebleeds may occur in the course of the illness, but this does not mean that you have progressed to the potentially fatal hemorrhagic fever.

You should seek medical help as soon as possible if you think you may be infected. There is no specific treatment for dengue fever. Aspirin should be avoided as it increases the risk of hemorrhaging.

There is no vaccine for dengue fever. The best protection is to avoid mosquito bites at all times by covering up, using insect repellents containing the compound DEET and using mosquito nets.

Leptospirosis Visitors to Hawaii should be aware of leptospirosis, a bacterial disease found in freshwater streams and ponds. The disease is transmitted from animals such as rats, mongooses and wild pigs.

Humans usually pick up leptospirosis when swimming or wading in water contaminated by animal urine; the disease enters the body through the nose, eyes, mouth or cuts to the skin. Leptospirosis can exist in any fresh water, including idyllic-looking waterfalls, because the water may have washed down the slopes through animal habitats.

Because hikers account for many of the cases, the state posts leptospirosis warnings at trailheads. One of the most effective precautions is to avoid unnecessary freshwater crossings, especially if you have open cuts.

Symptoms can occur within two to 20 days after exposure and may include fever, chills, sweating, headaches, muscle pains, vomiting and diarrhea. More severe symptoms include blood in the urine and jaundice. Symptoms may last from a few days to several weeks. Although deaths have been attributed to the disease, they are relatively rare.

Sunburn The closer you get to the equator, the fewer of the sun's rays are blocked out by the atmosphere, so sunburn's always a concern in the tropics. Don't be fooled by what appears to be a hazy overcast day – you can get sunburned surprisingly quickly, even through clouds.

Sunscreen with an SPF (sun protection factor) of 30 is recommended. If you're going into the water, use a water-resistant sunscreen. Snorkelers may want to wear a T-shirt if they plan to be out in the water a long time.

Fair-skinned people can get second-degree burns in the hot Hawaiian sun, and wearing a sun hat is a good idea. The most severe sun is between 10am and 2pm.

Prickly Heat An itchy rash caused by excessive perspiration trapped under the skin, prickly heat usually strikes people who have just arrived in a hot climate and whose pores have not yet opened sufficiently to cope with greater sweating. Keep cool by bathing often or resorting to air-con until you acclimatize.

Heat Exhaustion Dehydration or salt deficiency can cause heat exhaustion. Take time to acclimatize to high temperatures and make sure you get sufficient liquids. Salt deficiency is characterized by fatigue, lethargy, headaches, giddiness and muscle cramps; salt tablets may help. Vomiting or diarrhea can deplete your liquid and salt levels.

Heatstroke This serious, sometimes fatal condition can occur if the body's heat-regulating mechanism breaks down and the body temperature rises to dangerous levels. Long, continuous periods of exposure to high temperatures can leave you vulnerable to heatstroke. Avoid strenuous activity in open sun (such as lengthy hikes or bike rides across lava fields) when you first arrive.

The symptoms of heatstroke include very little perspiration and a high body temperature (102°F to 106°F). Where sweating has ceased, the skin becomes flushed and red. Severe, throbbing headaches and lack of coordination will also occur, and the sufferer may be confused or aggressive. Eventually the victim may become delirious or convulse. Hospitalization is essential, but, in the meantime, you can help by getting heatstroke sufferers out of the sun, removing their clothing, covering them with a wet sheet or towel and then fanning them continually.

Fungal Infections The same climate that produces lush tropical forests also promotes a prolific growth of skin fungi and bacteria. Hot weather fungal infections are most likely to occur between the toes or fingers or in the groin.

To prevent fungal infections, it's essential to keep your skin dry and cool and allow air to circulate. Choose loose cotton clothing rather than artificial fibers, and sandals rather than shoes. If you do get an infection, wash the infected area daily with a disinfectant or medicated soap. Rinse and dry well and then apply an antifungal powder.

Cuts & Scratches Skin punctures and cuts are easily infected in Hawaii's hot and humid climate, and infections can be persistent. Keep any cut or open wound clean and treat it with an antiseptic solution. Keep the area protected, but where possible avoid bandages, which can keep wounds wet.

Coral cuts are even more susceptible to infection because tiny pieces of coral can get embedded in the skin. These cuts are notoriously slow to heal, as the coral releases a weak venom into the wound.

Pesky Creatures Hawaii has no land snakes, but it does have its fair share of annoying mosquitoes as well as centipedes that can give an unpleasant bite. The islands also have bees and ground-nesting wasps, which, like the centipede, generally pose danger only to those who are allergic to their stings. (For information on stinging sea creatures, see Ocean Safety under Dangers & Annoyances later in this chapter.)

This being the tropics, cockroaches are plentiful. Although they don't pose much of a health problem, they do little for the appetite. Condos with kitchens have the most problems.

There are two dangerous arachnids on the islands – the black widow spider and the scorpion – but they're not terribly common.

Ciguatera Poisoning A serious illness, ciguatera is caused by eating fish affected by ciguatoxin, which herbivorous fish can pick up from marine algae. There is no ready way of detecting ciguatoxin, and it's not diminished by cooking. Symptoms usually occur three to five hours after eating.

Ciguatoxin is most common among reef fish (which are not commonly served in restaurants) and hasn't affected Hawaii's deep-sea fish, such as tuna, marlin and mahimahi. The symptoms include nausea; stomach cramps; diarrhea; paralysis; tingling and numbness of the face, fingers and toes; and a reversal of temperature sensations – hot things feel cold and vice versa. Extreme cases can result in unconsciousness and even death. Vomit until your stomach is empty and get immediate medical help.

WOMEN TRAVELERS

Women travelers are no more likely to encounter problems in Hawaii than anywhere else in the USA. Lonely Planet advises everyone – especially women traveling alone – against hitchhiking. If you do thumb a ride, size up the vehicle's occupants carefully and don't hesitate to turn down anyone who makes you feel uncomfortable. If you're camping, opt for popular, well-used camping areas, rather than more remote locales where you might be the only camper; the lesser-used spots sometimes become impromptu drinking hangouts.

GAY & LESBIAN TRAVELERS

Hawaii is as popular a vacation spot for gays and lesbians as it is for straights. The state has strong legislation to protect minorities and a constitutional guarantee of privacy that extends to sexual behavior between consenting adults.

Still, most of the gay scene is very low-key, especially on the Neighbor Islands; public hand-holding and other outward signs of affection between gays is not commonplace. The main gay club scene is on Oahu in Waikiki.

The following sources may be helpful for gay and lesbian visitors.

The volunteer-run **Gay & Lesbian Community Center** (*☎ 951 7000; Ⓦ www.glcc-hawaii.org; Box 22718, Honolulu, HI 96823*) is a good source of information on local issues for gay women and men. The center has support groups, movie nights and a library.

A good website for general information on gay issues is Ⓦ www.gayhawaii.com; it also has links to a variety of gay and lesbian sites that cover items from travel and entertainment to politics.

The monthly gay magazine *Odyssey* (*Ⓦ www.odysseyhawaii.com*), which can be picked up free at gay-friendly businesses throughout Hawaii, covers the gay scene around the islands.

Pacific Ocean Holidays (*☎ 923-2400, 800 735-6600, fax 923-2499; Box 88245, Honolulu, HI 96830*) arranges vacation packages for gay men and women.

DISABLED TRAVELERS

Overall, Hawaii is an accommodating destination for travelers with disabilities.

Waikiki is considered one of the more accessible destinations in the USA for travelers who use wheelchairs. Many of the larger hotels throughout Hawaii have wheelchair-accessible rooms and as more of them renovate their facilities, accessibility improves.

The **Commission on Persons with Disabilities** (*☎ 586-8121; 919 Ala Moana Blvd, Room 101, Honolulu, HI 96814*) distributes

A Glitch in Getting Hitched

Gay marriages in Hawaii? In recent years, it looked as if travelers of all persuasions might be able to tie the knot in Hawaii, as the state took center stage in the movement to legalize same-gender marriages. The debate even took on a national scope, with conservatives in the US Congress taking up legislation to make sure any changes that might be approved in Hawaii didn't spill over into other states.

In December 1996 a Hawaiian judge ruled that state prohibitions against same-sex marriages violated the equal protection clause of Hawaii's constitution, which explicitly bans gender discrimination. In July 1997, Hawaii became the first US state to extend broad rights to domestic partners. To make the law more acceptable to the vocal conservatives who oppose gay marriages, it covers any two adults who cannot legally marry, including not just same-sex couples, but also others such as a mother and adult child or two siblings living together. Those who register are covered under an umbrella of items ranging from medical insurance to survivorship rights.

In the eyes of Hawaii legislators, the domestic partnership law was a compromise, meant to quiet both the pro and con voices in the controversy over gay marriages.

However, in response to the domestic partnership law, conservative members of the state legislature put forth an amendment to Hawaii's state constitution allowing the legislature 'to reserve marriage to opposite-sex couples' only. This amendment was overwhelmingly passed by Hawaii voters in 1998. Progressives challenged the legality of the state constitutional amendment on the grounds that it violated the US Constitution's equal protection clause, but the Hawaii Supreme Court let it stand.

In 2000, Vermont legislators – quietly and free of the national attention that Hawaii received – approved a proposal for civil unions that gave same-sex couples nearly all the benefits, protections and responsibilities that marriages have, making their state the first in the USA to do so.

the *Aloha Guide to Accessibility*, which contains detailed travel tips for people who use wheelchairs. It has general information and covers things like airport access on the major islands. The guide is free whether you request it by mail or get it online at ⓦ www.hawaii.gov/health/dcab.

Accessible Vans of Hawaii (*☎ 871-7785, 800-303-3750; 296 Ahamaha St, Kahului, HI 96732*) books accessible accommodations, rents accessible vans and arranges various activities for disabled travelers on Oahu and Maui.

In the USA, the **Society for the Advancement of Travel for the Handicapped** (*SATH; ☎ 212-447-7284; ⓦ www.sath.org; 347 Fifth Ave, Suite 610, New York, NY 10016*) publishes a quarterly magazine and has various information sheets on travel for the disabled.

SENIOR TRAVELERS

Hawaii is a popular destination for retirees, and lots of senior discounts are available. The applicable age has been creeping lower as well.

For instance, Hawaii's biggest hotel chain, Outrigger, offers across-the-board discounts of 20% to anyone 50 years of age or older, and if you're a member of the American Association of Retired Persons (AARP), they'll usually increase the discount another 5%. Such discounts are available from other hotels as well, so be sure to inquire.

The nonprofit AARP is a good source for travel bargains. For information on joining this advocacy group for Americans 50 years of age and older, contact **AARP** (*☎ 800-424-3410; Membership Center, 3200 E Carson St, Lakewood, CA 90712*).

US citizens who are 62 or older are eligible to purchase a Golden Age Passport for just $10, which allows unlimited lifetime entry into all US national park sites, including those in Hawaii.

Information on Elderhostel study vacations is under Organized Tours in the Getting There & Away chapter.

TRAVEL WITH CHILDREN

Families with children will find lots to do in Hawaii. In addition to beaches and a range of water sports, Hawaii has lots of other outdoor activities and cool sight-seeing attractions for kids of all ages.

Successful travel with young children requires planning and effort. Try not to overdo things; even for adults, packing too much into the time available can cause problems.

Include children in the trip planning; if they've helped to work out where you will be going, they will be much more interested when they get there.

Lonely Planet's *Travel with Children* has lots of valuable tips and interesting anecdotal stories.

USEFUL ORGANIZATIONS

The **Division of State Parks** (☎ *587-0300;* **W** *www.hawaii.gov/dlnr/dsp/dsp.html; PO Box 621, Honolulu, HI 96809)* provides a free brochure on Hawaii's state parks, including camping information and a brief description of each park.

The **Sierra Club** (☎ *538-6616;* **W** *www.hi.sierraclub.org; Box 2577, Honolulu, HI 96803)* offers guided hikes and maintains trails, and is involved in conservation projects throughout Hawaii. Call for recorded information on upcoming hikes. For other information on Sierra Club activities, write or visit the website.

The **Earthjustice Legal Defense Fund** (☎ *599-2436;* **W** *www.earthjustice.org; 223 S King St, 4th floor, Honolulu, HI 96813)* plays a leading role in protecting Hawaii's fragile environment through court action.

The **Nature Conservancy of Hawaii** (☎ *537-4508;* **W** *www.tnc.org; 923 Nuuanu Ave, Honolulu, HI 96817)* protects some of Hawaii's most endangered ecosystems by acquiring land and then arranging long-term stewardships with landowners. The group offers guided hikes into some of its preserves, most notably Kamakou on Molokai and Waikamoi in the Haleakala area on Maui.

The **American Automobile Association** *(AAA;* ☎ *593-2221;* **W** *www.aaa-hawaii.com; 1270 Ala Moana Blvd, Honolulu)*, which has its only Hawaii office in Honolulu, can provide AAA members with information on motoring in Hawaii, including detailed Honolulu and Hawaii road maps. Members are also entitled to discounts on car rentals, air tickets and some hotels and sight-seeing attractions. It provides members with emergency road service and towing (☎ 800-222-4357).

For information on joining AAA on the mainland before arrival in Hawaii, call ☎ 800-564-6222. Membership dues vary by state but average $60 the first year, $45 for subsequent years.

LIBRARIES

Hawaii has a statewide system of public libraries, with nearly 50 branches. Visitors can check out books only after applying for a Hawaii library card; a visitor's card valid for three months costs $10 and can be issued on the spot. As the system is unified, not only can you use the card at all branches, but you can borrow a book at one branch and return it at another branch – even on another island.

Most of the libraries have good Hawaiiana sections, with lots of books on culture, history, flora and fauna. Most also subscribe to Hawaii's daily newspapers as well as a few mainland newspapers such as the *Wall Street Journal* and *USA Today*.

For information on Internet access through Hawaii's public libraries, see Email & Internet Access earlier in this chapter.

DANGERS & ANNOYANCES

Ocean Safety

Drowning is the leading cause of accidental death for visitors. An average of 50 people drown each year in Hawaii.

If you're not familiar with water conditions, ask someone. If there is no lifeguard around, local surfers are generally helpful – they would rather give you the lowdown on water conditions than pull you out later. It's best not to swim alone in any unfamiliar place.

Shorebreaks Waves that break close to or directly on the shore form when ocean swells pass abruptly from deep to shallow waters. If only a couple of feet high, they're generally fine for novice bodysurfers, but if they are any higher they're for experienced bodysurfers only.

Large shorebreaks can hit hard with a slamming downward force. Broken bones, neck injuries, dislocated shoulders and loss of wind are the most common injuries, although anyone wiped out in the water is a potential drowning victim as well.

Rip Currents Rips, or rip currents, are fast-flowing ocean currents moving from shallow nearshore areas out to sea. They are most common in high surf, forming when water from incoming waves builds up near the shore. Essentially the waves are coming in faster than they can flow back out.

Strong Current

Man-O-War

Sharp Coral

High Surf

Dangerous Shorebreak

Waves on Ledge

The water then runs along the shoreline until it finds an escape route out to sea, usually through a channel or out along a point. Swimmers caught up in the current can be taken out to deeper water.

Although rips can be powerful, they usually dissipate 50 to 100 yards offshore. Anyone caught in one should either go with the flow until it loses power or swim parallel to shore to slip out of it. Trying to swim against a rip current can exhaust even the strongest of swimmers.

Undertows Common along steeply sloped beaches, undertows occur where large waves wash back directly into incoming surf. The outflowing water picks up speed as it flows down the slopes. When it hits an incoming wave it pulls under it, creating an undertow. Swimmers caught up in an undertow can be pulled underwater. The most important thing is not to panic. Go with the current until you get beyond the wave.

Rogue Waves Never turn your back on the ocean. Waves don't all come in with equal height or strength. An abnormally high 'rogue wave' can sweep over shoreline ledges such as those circling Hanauma Bay on Oahu or tear up onto beaches such as Lumahai on Kauai. Over the years, numerous people have been swept into the ocean at these beaches.

You need to be particularly cautious during high tide and in stormy weather or high surf.

Some people think rogue waves don't exist because they've never seen one. But that's the point – you don't always see them.

Coral Most coral cuts occur when swimmers are pushed onto the coral by rough waves and surges. It's a good idea to wear diving gloves when snorkeling over shallow reefs. Avoid walking on coral, which can not only cut your feet but also damage the coral.

Jellyfish Take a peek into the water before you plunge in to make sure it's not jellyfish territory. These gelatinous creatures, with saclike bodies and stinging tentacles, are fairly common in Hawaii. You'll most likely see them eight to 10 days after the full moon, when they come into shallow nearshore waters in places such as Waikiki.

Jellyfish are not keen on the sun, and as the day heats up they retreat from shallow waters, so encounters between jellies and beachgoers are most common in the morning. The pain from a sting varies from mild to severe, depending on the variety of jellyfish. Unless you have an allergic reaction to their venom, though, the stings are not dangerous.

Portuguese *Man-of-War* The body of the Portuguese man-of-war consists of a translucent, bluish, bladder-like float, which in Hawaii generally grows to 4 or 5 inches long. Known locally as the 'bluebottle,' it's most often found on the windward coasts, particularly after storms.

The sting of a Portuguese man-of-war is very painful, similar to a bad bee sting except that you're likely to get stung more than once from clusters of long tentacles containing hundreds of stinging cells. Even touching a bluebottle a few hours after it's washed up onshore can result in burning stings.

If you do get stung, quickly remove the tentacles and apply a meat tenderizer containing papain (derived from papaya) to neutralize the toxins – in a pinch, you could use urine as well. For serious reactions, including chest pains or difficulty breathing, seek medical attention immediately.

Fish Stings Encounters with venomous sea creatures in Hawaiian waters are rather rare. You should, however, learn to recognize scorpion fish and lionfish, two related fish that can inject venom through their dorsal spines if touched. Both are sometimes found in quite shallow water.

The Hawaiian lionfish, which grows up to 10 inches long, is strikingly attractive with orange-and-white stripes and feathery appendages that contain poisonous spines; it likes to drift along the reef, particularly at night. The scorpion fish is more drab in appearance, has shorter and less obvious spines, is about six inches in length, and tends to sit immobile on the bottom or on ledges.

The sting from either can cause a sharp burning pain followed by numbness around the area, nausea and headaches. Immediately stick the affected area in water that is as hot as bearable (take care not to unintentionally scald the numb area) and go for medical treatment.

Cone Shells Unless you're sure they're empty, cone shells should be left alone. There's no safe way of picking up a live cone shell, as the animal inside has a long harpoonlike tail that can dart out and reach anywhere on its shell to deliver a painful sting. Soak the wound in hot water and seek medical attention.

A few species, such as the textile cone, whose shell is decorated with brown diamond or triangular shapes, have a venom so toxic that in extreme cases the sting could be fatal.

Sea Urchins The *wana*, or spiny sea urchin, has long brittle spines that can puncture the skin and break off, causing burning and numbness. The spines sometimes inflict a toxin and can cause an infection. You can try to remove the spines with tweezers or by soaking the area in hot water, although more serious cases may require surgical removal.

Eels The *puhi*, or moray eel, is often spotted by snorkelers around reefs and coral heads. The eels constantly open and close their mouths to pump water across their gills, which makes them look far more menacing than they actually are.

Eels don't attack but will protect themselves if they feel cornered by fingers jabbing into the reef holes or crevices they occupy. Eels have sharp teeth and strong jaws which they may clamp if someone sticks a hand in their door.

Sharks More than 35 varieties of sharks are found in Hawaiian waters, including the nonaggressive whale shark and basking shark, which can grow to lengths of 50ft. As Hawaiian waters are abundant with fish, sharks in Hawaii are well fed and most pose little danger to humans.

Sharks are curious and will sometimes investigate divers, although they generally just check things out and continue on their way. If they start to hang around, however, it's probably time for you to go.

Except for the rarely encountered great white shark, the most dangerous shark in Hawaiian waters is the tiger shark, which averages 20ft in length and is identified by vertical bars along its side. The tiger shark is not terribly particular about what it eats and has been known to chomp down on pieces of wood (including surfboards) floating on the ocean.

Should you come face-to-face with a shark, the best thing to do is move casually and quietly away. Don't panic, as sharks are attracted by things that thrash around.

Some aquatic officials suggest thumping an attacking shark on the nose or sticking your fingers into its eyes, which may confuse it long enough to give you time to escape. Some divers who dive in shark waters carry a billy club.

Avoid murky waters. After heavy rains, sharks may come in around river mouths.

Sharks are attracted by blood. Some attacks on humans are related to spearfishing: when a shark is going after a diver's bloody catch, the diver sometimes gets in the way. Sharks are also attracted by shiny things and by anything bright red or yellow, which might influence your choice of swimsuit color.

Unpleasant encounters with sharks are extremely unlikely, however. According to the University of Hawaii Sea Grant College, only about 30 unprovoked shark attacks are known to have occurred in Hawaii between 1900 and 1990; about a third of these were fatal. Nevertheless, in recent years, increasing numbers of both sharks and shark attacks have been reported in Hawaii, with attacks now occurring at a rate of about three per year.

Tsunamis Tidal waves, or tsunamis, are not common in Hawaii but when they do hit they can be severe.

Tsunamis can be generated by earthquakes, typhoons or volcanic eruptions. The largest ever to hit Hawaii was in 1946, the result of an earthquake in the Aleutian Islands. Waves reached a height of about 55ft, entire villages were washed away and 159 people died. Since that time, Hawaii has installed a modern tsunami warning system, which is aired through yellow speakers mounted on telephone poles around the islands. They're tested on the first working day of each month at 11:45am for about one minute.

Although tsunamis traveling across the Pacific can take hours to arrive, others can be caused by earthquakes or volcanic eruptions within Hawaii. For these there may be little warning. Any earthquake strong enough to cause you to grab onto something to keep from falling is a natural tsunami warning. If you're in a low-lying coastal area when one occurs, immediately head for higher ground.

Tsunami inundation maps, which are found in the front of island telephone books, show susceptible areas and safety zones.

Theft & Violence

For the most part, Hawaii is a relatively safe place. But the islands are notorious for rip-offs from parked rental cars. The people who break into these cars are good at what they do; they can pop a trunk or pull out a lock assembly in seconds to get to your loot. What's more, they do it not only when you've left your car in a secluded area to go for a long hike but also in crowded parking lots where you'd expect safety in numbers.

It's certainly best not to leave anything of value in your car any time you walk away from it. If for some reason you feel you must, at least pack things well out of sight *before* you've pulled up to the place where you're going to leave the car.

Other than rip-offs, most hassles encountered by visitors are from drunks. Be tuned in to the vibes on beaches at night and in places where young men hang out to drink.

Overall, violent crime is lower in Hawaii than in most mainland cities. However, there are some pockets of resentment against tourists as well as off-islanders moving in. Oahu tends to be worse than the other islands.

EMERGENCIES

Dial the same **hotline** *(☎ 911)* for police, fire and ambulance emergencies. The inside front covers of island phone books list other vital service agencies, such as poison control, coast guard rescue, and suicide and crisis lines.

If you lose your passport, contact your consulate in Honolulu; a complete list of consulate phone numbers can be found in the Yellow Pages (see also Consulates in Hawaii earlier in this chapter).

For refunds on lost or stolen **American Express** *(☎ 800-992-3404)* or **Thomas Cook** *(☎ 800-287-7362)* traveler's checks, call the hotlines. For any other theft, especially if you intend to file an insurance claim, contact the police to make an incident report.

LEGAL MATTERS

If you are arrested in Hawaii, you have the right to the representation of a lawyer, from the time of your arrest to your trial, and if you can't afford a lawyer, the state will provide one for free. If you do want to hire a lawyer, the **Hawaii State Bar Association** *(☎ 537-9140)* can make referrals; foreign visitors may want to call their consulate for advice.

The minimum drinking age in Hawaii is 21. It's illegal to have open containers of alcohol in motor vehicles, and drinking in public parks or on the beaches is also illegal.

Drunk driving is a serious crime and drivers can incur stiff fines, jail time and penalties if caught. In Hawaii, anyone caught driving with an alcohol blood level of 0.08% or higher is guilty of driving 'under the influence' and will have their driver's license taken away from them on the spot. Further punishment depends upon one's driving record, but if this is a first offense you're still looking at a mandatory 90-day license suspension, alcohol abuse counseling, and possibly two to five days in prison, along with a fine of up to $1000.

As in most places, the possession of marijuana *(pakalolo)* and nonprescription narcotics is illegal in Hawaii. Be aware that US Customs has a zero-tolerance policy for drugs; federal authorities have been known to seize boats after finding even minute quantities of marijuana on board.

For consumer issues, Hawaii's **Department of Commerce & Consumer Affairs** *(☎ 587-1234)* has a handy recorded information line that provides information on your rights regarding refunds and exchanges, timeshare contracts, car rentals and similar topics.

BUSINESS HOURS

While there's a variance of half an hour in either direction, the most common office hours in Hawaii are 8:30am to 4:30pm Monday to Friday. Shops in central areas and malls, as well as large chain stores, are usually open into the evenings and on weekends, and some grocery stores are open 24 hours.

PUBLIC HOLIDAYS & SPECIAL EVENTS

With its multitude of cultures and good year-round weather, Hawaii has a seemingly endless number and variety of holidays, festivals and events. The following list shows just a few of the highlights.

As dates for many events change a bit from year to year, check local newspapers or inquire at one of the tourist offices for exact schedules. Water-sport events are particularly reliant on the weather and the surf, so any schedule is tentative.

January

New Year's Day On New Year's Eve, the night before this national holiday, fireworks displays take place in some of the larger towns and resorts.

Mercedes Championship Held in Maui at Kapalua's Plantation Golf Course near the beginning of January, this event kicks off the PGA tour.

Sony Open in Hawaii This PGA tour golf tournament takes place in Oahu in early January at Oahu's Waialae Country Club.

Chinese New Year Festivities begin at the second new moon after the winter solstice (mid-January to mid-February) with lion dances and strings of firecrackers. Honolulu's Chinatown is the center stage, but there are also events at Wing Ho Temple in Lahaina.

Hula Bowl This classic East versus West college all-star football game is held at Maui's War Memorial Stadium on a Saturday in January.

Ka Molokai Makahiki A modern-day version of the ancient *makahiki* (winter harvest festival) takes place in Kaunakakai on Molokai in mid-January. The weeklong celebration features a tournament of traditional Hawaiian games and sporting events, an outrigger-canoe fishing contest and Hawaiian music and hula dancing.

Martin Luther King Jr Day This national holiday is observed on the third Monday of the month.

Senior Skins Game This senior PGA tour golf tournament takes place in late January at Mauna Lani Resort on the Big Island.

Ala Wai Challenge Canoe Festival Held the third Sunday in January, this outrigger canoe festival takes place along the Ala Wai Canal in Waikiki.

February

NFL Pro Bowl The National Football League's annual all-star game takes place at Oahu's Aloha Stadium near the beginning of the month.

Cherry Blossom Festival This Japanese celebration, which covers the entire month and spills over into March, features tea ceremonies, *mochi* pounding and drumming. Most activities occur on Oahu.

Hawaiian Ladies Open This PGA tour golf tournament takes place in mid-February at Oahu's Kapolei Golf Course.

Presidents Day This national holiday is observed on the third Monday of the month.

Great Aloha Run Honolulu's popular 8.2-mile fun run from Aloha Tower to Aloha Stadium takes place on Presidents Day.

March

Honolulu Festival Held during the second weekend in March, this festival includes plays, street performances, kite making, Japanese dancing and a parade through Waikiki.

St Patrick's Day The March 17 festivities include a parade down Waikiki's Kalakaua Ave.

Prince Kuhio Day On March 26, a state holiday honors Jonah Kuhio Kalanianaole, Hawaii's first delegate to the US Congress. On his native island of Kauai there's a weeklong festival, including canoe races, music and dance.

East Maui Taro Festival Held on the last weekend in March in Hana, Maui, the festivities include hula dancing, outrigger canoe races and traditional Hawaiian food.

Easter This Christian holiday falls in March or April. Many businesses are closed on Good Friday (the Friday before Easter Sunday).

Merrie Monarch Festival Named after King David Kalakaua, this is Hawaii's biggest hula competition and Hawaiiana festival. Held in Hilo on the Big Island, it starts on Easter Sunday and lasts for a week.

April

The Ulupalakua Thing Held on a Saturday in late April at Maui's Tedeschi Vineyards, this fair-like trade show offers the chance to sample food prepared by some of Maui's top chefs, and includes live entertainment.

International Bed Race Held on Oahu, this offbeat wheeled-bed race runs along Kalakaua Ave to Kapiolani Park in late April.

May

May Day Known as Lei Day in Hawaii, the first day of May finds everyone wearing leis. The festivities include lei-making competitions on several islands, and Oahu crowns a lei queen at Kapiolani Park.

Da Kine Classic Held at Maui's Hookipa Beach in early May, this is one of the world's top international windsurfing competitions.

Molokai Ka Hula Piko Held on Molokai in mid-May, this weeklong festival celebrates the birth of the hula, with traditional dance performances, Hawaiian food, cultural demonstrations and visits to sacred sites.

Molokai Challenge Held in late May, this 32-mile kayak race crosses the treacherous Kaiwi Channel, from Kaluakoi Resort on Molokai to Koko Marina, Oahu.

Keauhou–Kona Triathlon Starting at the Big Island's Keauhou Bay, this grueling competition (a half iron man) includes a 56-mile bike race, 13-mile run and 1.2-mile swim. The contest takes place on the last Sunday in May.

Memorial Day The last Monday in May is a national holiday that honors soldiers killed in battle.

50th State Fair Complete with games, rides as well as exhibits, the fair runs for four weekends from late May through June at Oahu's Aloha Stadium.

June

Pan-Pacific Festival Held the first weekend in June, this Japanese-American festival features marching bands, costumed performers and other street entertainment throughout Honolulu and a parade to Kapiolani Park in Waikiki.

King Kamehameha Day This state holiday is celebrated on June 11 or the nearest weekend, with events on all islands. On Oahu, the statue of Kamehameha is ceremoniously draped with leis, and there's a parade from downtown Honolulu to Kapiolani Park. On the Big Island, the Kamehameha statue in the king's hometown of Kapaau is also draped with leis.

Kihoalu This Hawaiian slack-key guitar festival takes place in mid-June at the Maui Arts & Cultural Center.

King Kamehameha Hula Competition This is one of Hawaii's biggest hula contests and is held at the Blaisdell Center in Honolulu near the end of June.

July

Hawaii International Jazz Festival Held over four consecutive nights in mid-July at the Hawaii Theatre in Honolulu, this festival features both local and national jazz performers.

Puuhonua o Honaunau Cultural Festival Held at Puuhonua o Honaunau National Historical Park on the Big Island, this festival includes a reenactment of an ancient Hawaiian royal court, a *hukilau* (net-fishing event), hula and traditional craft displays. It takes place on the weekend closest to July 1.

Independence Day On all the islands, fireworks and festivities mark this national holiday on July 4.

Rodeos Two Hawaiian-style rodeos are held on July 4. One takes place in Waimea on the Big Island and is sponsored by Parker Ranch, Hawaii's largest cattle ranch. The other takes place in Makawao on Maui.

Transpacific Yacht Race In odd-numbered years, sailboats leave southern California on the July 4 weekend and arrive in Honolulu 10 to 14 days later. The race has been held for nearly a century.

Prince Lot Hula Festival Held at Oahu's Moanalua Gardens on the third Saturday of the month, this festival attracts hula competitors from Hawaii's major hula schools.

Kilauea Volcano Wilderness Marathon & Rim Runs This set of contests, held at the end of July at Hawaii Volcanoes National Park on the Big Island, includes a 10-mile run around the rim of Kilauea, a 5.5-mile race into Kilauea Iki Crater and a 26.2-mile marathon through the Kau desert. The event draws an international crowd.

August

Obon This special season, which is celebrated around the islands in July and August, is marked by traditional Japanese dances to honor deceased ancestors. The final event is a floating lantern ceremony at Waikiki's Ala Wai Canal on the evening of August 15.

Ki Hoalu Festival This festival features some of Hawaii's top slack-key guitarists in a free concert at Ala Moana Beach Park.

Hawaiian International Billfish Tournament The world's number-one marlin tournament takes place in Kailua-Kona on the Big Island. It lasts two weeks, usually beginning in early August, and includes a parade and fun events.

Ole Longboard Classic This is Maui's top longboard surfing event, and takes place in mid-August at Launiopoko Beach Park.

Admission Day This state holiday, on the third Friday of August, observes the anniversary of Hawaiian statehood.

September

Labor Day This is a national holiday observed on the first Monday of the month.

Aloha Week This celebration of all things Hawaiian includes parades, cultural events, contests, canoe races and Hawaiian music. Festivities are staggered from mid-September to early October, depending on the island.

Na Wahine o Ke Kai Hawaii's major annual women's outrigger canoe race starts at sunrise at Kaluakoi on Molokai, and ends 40 miles later at Waikiki's Fort DeRussy Beach. It's held near the end of the month.

The Haleakala Run to the Sun Maui's 36.2-mile ultramarathon begins at dawn at sea-level Paia and climbs 10,000ft to the top of Haleakala. It's usually held in late September or early October.

October

Columbus Day This national holiday is observed on the second Monday of the month.

Na Molokai Hoe Hawaii's major men's outrigger canoe race starts shortly after sunrise on Molokai and finishes at Waikiki's Fort DeRussy Beach about five hours later. Teams from Australia, Germany and the US mainland join Hawaiian teams in this annual competition, first held in 1952. It takes place early in the month.

Ironman Triathlon Considered by many to be the ultimate endurance race, this is the triathlon that started it all and remains the world's best known. The 2.4-mile swim, 112-mile bike race and 26.2-mile marathon begins and ends at the Big Island's Kailua Pier on the Saturday in October closest to the full moon.

Princess Kaiulani Commemoration Week Held throughout the third week in October, this event honors Hawaii's last princess with festivities, hula shows and other activities in Waikiki.

Kona Coffee Cultural Festival This week-long event features a parade, a coffee-picking contest and cultural events. It takes place in Kailua-Kona on the Big Island in late October or early November.

Xterra World Championship This off-road triathlon includes a 30km bike ride up the slopes of Haleakala, an 11km trail run and a 1.5km ocean swim. It's held in mid- to late October on Maui.

Aloha Classic World Windsurfing Championship The final event of the Pro Boardsailing Association's world tour features many of the top international competitors. The contest takes place in late October and early November at Maui's Hookipa Beach.

November

Election Day The second Tuesday of the month is a state holiday during election years.

Veterans Day November 11 is a national holiday honoring veterans of the armed services.

PGA Grand Slam of Golf This championship play-off takes place in mid-November in Poipu on Kauai.

Hawaii International Film Festival About 175 films from Pacific Rim and Asian nations are screened in theaters throughout the islands. The festival begins in Oahu in mid-November and continues on the Neighbor Islands the following week.

Ka Hula Lea Festival This statewide hula festival takes place in mid-November in Waikoloa on the Big Island.

The Triple Crown of Surfing These three professional competitions draw the world's top surfers to Oahu's North Shore. The events begin in November and run through December, with the exact dates dependent on when the surf's up.

Thanksgiving This national holiday is celebrated on the fourth Thursday of the month.

December

Pearl Harbor Day In commemoration of the Japanese attack on Oahu, special ceremonies are held at the USS *Arizona* Memorial on December 7.

Bodhi Day The Buddhist Day of Enlightenment is celebrated on the 8th, with ceremonies at Buddhist temples.

Honolulu Marathon The third-largest marathon in the USA is run on the second Sunday of the month along a 26-mile course from the Aloha Tower to Kapiolani Park.

Christmas Day December 25 is a national holiday. Christmas festivals and craft fairs take place on all the islands throughout December.

COURSES

The main venue for courses is the University of Hawaii (UH), which has its main campus at Manoa on Oahu and a smaller campus in Hilo on the Big Island. UH offers both full-time university attendance and summer school courses. For information on UH undergraduate studies, contact the **Admissions & Records Office** *(☎ 956-8975; 2600 Campus Rd, Room 001, Honolulu, HI 96822)*; for information on graduate studies, contact the **Graduate Division** *(☎ 956-8544; Spalding Hall, 2540 Maile Way, Room 354, Honolulu, HI 96822)*.

The summer session consists primarily of two six-week terms. For a catalog, contact the **Summer Session office** *(☎ 956-5666; 2500 Dole St, Krauss Bldg, Room 1001, Honolulu, HI 96822)*.

WORK

US citizens can pursue employment in Hawaii as they would in any other state. Foreign visitors who are in the USA for tourist purposes are not legally allowed to take up employment.

As Hawaii has had a relatively slow economy in the wake of the September 11 attacks on the USA, the job situation is not particularly rosy. Much of the economy is tied to the service industry, with many employees being paid close to the minimum wage. For visitors, the most common work is waiting on tables, and if you're young and energetic there are job possibilities in restaurants and clubs.

If you're hoping to find more serious 'professional' employment, note that Hawaii is considered a tight labor market, with a lack of diversified industries and a relatively immobile labor force. Professional jobs that do open up are generally filled by established Hawaii residents.

A good online resource is **W** www.honolulu advertiser.com, which contains the *Honolulu Advertiser*'s 'help wanted' ads.

For more information on employment in Hawaii, contact the **State Department of Labor & Industrial Relations** *(☎ 586-8700; 830; **W** dlir.state.hi.us; 830 Punchbowl St, Honolulu, HI 96813)*.

ACCOMMODATIONS

Hawaii has a wide variety of accommodations, including B&Bs, hotels and condominiums in all price ranges. There are also a handful of hostels and state park cabins that are quite inexpensive.

In Waikiki, hotels far outnumber condos, while in Kihei and Kona the opposite is true. In most other major tourist destinations in Hawaii, hotels and condos exist in roughly equal numbers.

More than 75,000 hotel and condo rooms cover the state. Oahu, which once had all of Hawaii's visitor accommodations, and until 20 years ago still had 75%, now has only 50% of the accommodations as development continues full speed ahead on the Neighbor Islands.

Some places to stay in Hawaii have different rates for high season and low season (also called peak season and off-season). High season most commonly applies to the winter period (December 15 to March 31). During winter, when demand peaks, those places that offer the best deals, particularly the smaller hotels and condos, typically book up well in advance. During the low season (April to mid-December), cheaper rates are easier to find and getting the room of your choice without advance reservations is far easier.

If you are traveling with children, be aware that some B&Bs and historic inns prohibit children from staying, so it's important to inquire about their policies before making reservations.

Except where noted, the rates given in this book are the same for singles and doubles. Rates do not include the combined room and sales tax of 11.41%, which is added to the price of all accommodations, including B&Bs.

Reservations

A reservation will guarantee you a room on the dates you want, but be aware that most reservations require deposits. Once you have either sent a deposit or guaranteed your booking with a credit card, there may be restrictions on getting a refund if you change your mind.

Many B&Bs, hotels and condominiums will only refund your money if they receive your cancellation a set number of days in advance; three days for a hotel and 30 days for a condominium is typical, but this varies widely. In some instances you'll forfeit your entire deposit, while other places will issue a partial refund. Be sure you understand the cancellation policies and other restrictions before making a deposit.

Camping

Hawaii has numerous public camping grounds but no full-service private camping grounds of the Kampgrounds of America (KOA) type found on the US mainland.

In general, camping in the national parks is better than in the state parks, and the state parks are better choices than the county parks.

Over the years there have been some assaults and numerous thefts targeted at off-island campers. The violence has decreased in most places, though a few camping grounds in rough areas, including the entire Waianae Coast of Oahu, are best avoided. People traveling alone, especially women, need to be particularly cautious.

In terms of theft, the less you look like a tourist, the less likely you are to be targeted; always be careful with your valuables.

Pick your park carefully, especially when you're choosing a county park. Some are well established, with caretakers, and attract other campers, while others are pit stops along the road frequented mostly by drinkers.

For the most part, the farther you are from population centers, the less likely you are to run into hassles. Thieves and drunks aren't big on hiking. Backcountry camping is generally safe on all the islands; your biggest safety concern might be a twisted ankle or an encounter with a wild boar or cross-eyed hunter.

More information on all the following parks can be found in the individual island chapters.

National Parks There are two national parks in Hawaii that allow camping: Haleakala National Park on Maui and Hawaii Volcanoes National Park on the Big Island. These two parks offer some of the finest camping opportunities in Hawaii and also provide spectacular hiking. The parks have both drive-up and wilderness camping areas and getting a space is seldom a problem.

State Parks The five largest islands have state park camping grounds. These range from wilderness areas into which you need to backpack, to developed roadside camp sites. State parks often have caretakers and better security than county parks.

Camping is allowed on Kauai, in Kokee, Na Pali Coast and Polihale State Parks; on Oahu, in Keaiwa Heiau, Malaekahana and Sand Island State Recreation Areas and Kahana Valley State Park; on Molokai, in Palaau State Park; on Maui, in Polipoli Spring State Recreation Area and Waianapanapa State Park; and on the Big Island, in Kalopa State Park and MacKenzie State Recreation Area.

State parks require a permit to camp ($5 per night per site). Developed camping grounds generally have picnic tables, barbecue grills, drinking water, toilets and showers, though the maintenance of the facilities varies greatly.

The maximum length of stay at any one state park is five nights. Another camping permit for the same park will not be issued until 30 days have elapsed.

To apply for a permit, you'll need to be at least 18 years old and provide your address and phone number and, for each camper in the group, an identification number (driver's license, passport or social security number). Applications can be made no more than 30 days before the first camping date. As permits are issued on a first-come, first-served basis, it's best to apply as soon as possible; if you have a change of plans, be sure to cancel so other campers get a chance to use the space.

Camping permits can be obtained from any Division of State Parks office. The main office, **Division of State Parks** (☎ *587-0300; 1151 Punchbowl St, room 131; postal address Box 621, Honolulu, HI 96809; open 8am-3:30pm Mon-Fri)*, handles reservations for all islands. For the locations of other state park offices, see Camping in the individual island chapters.

County Parks All the counties have parks with camping areas, though not all are of equal standard. Some county parks have wonderful white-sand beaches and good facilities, while others are little more than unappealing roadside rest areas that the authorities have turned into 'beach parks' simply by plopping down rest rooms. Just because camping is allowed doesn't mean you'd want to camp there, or even use the beach. For more information on camping at county parks, see the individual island chapters.

Cabins

The state has simple cabins on the Big Island at Kalopa State Park, Hapuna Beach State Park and Mauna Kea State Recreation Area, and on Maui at Polipoli Spring State Recreation Area and Waianapanapa State Park.

In addition to these state-maintained cabins, there are concession-run cabins at Malaekahana State Recreation Area on Oahu and at Kokee State Park on Kauai. For details on staying at these cabins, see the individual island chapters.

Hostels

Hawaii has three hostels associated with **Hostelling International** (HI). Two are on Oahu; one is right in Waikiki and the other is a few miles away near the Honolulu campus of the University of Hawaii. The third is a small hostel near Hawaii Volcanoes National Park on the Big Island.

In addition, a number of private hostel-style places offering inexpensive accommodations have sprung up in recent years. Most are in Waikiki on Oahu, but you'll also find a handful of others on the Neighbor Islands. Rates for a dorm bed are under $20, and more expensive private rooms are often available as well.

B&Bs

Hundreds of B&Bs are scattered around Hawaii. Some are modest spare bedrooms in family households, others are romantic and private hideaways, and a few are full-fledged inns. B&Bs generally begin at around $50, although the average is closer to $75 and the most exclusive properties are $100 to $150. Many require a minimum stay of two or three days, and some give discounts for stays of a week or more. B&Bs vary greatly, but for the most part they offer some of the best lodging bargains in Hawaii.

Because Hawaii state codes place restrictions on serving home-cooked meals, many B&Bs offer a continental breakfast or provide food for guests to cook their own meals. Some places do provide full home-cooked breakfasts – they just don't advertise it.

Keep in mind that Hawaiian B&Bs are small scale – most have only a few guest rooms. Out of consideration for their neighbors and guests, the B&B hosts, who are often not home during the day, discourage unannounced drop-ins. Because of this, some B&Bs do not appear on maps in this book. Same-day reservations are usually hard to get, and even for these you will need to phone in advance – don't just drop in.

In this book, we recommend a number of B&Bs that you can book directly. Many other home-based B&Bs don't handle their own reservations but sign up with B&B reservation services. Some of these agencies book whole houses, condos and studio cottages as well. All require at least part payment in advance and have cancellation penalties. The following are reputable agencies:

Bed & Breakfast Hawaii (☎ 822-7771, 800-733-1632, fax 822-2723; Ⓦ www.bandb-hawaii.com) Box 449, Kapaa, HI 96746. One of the larger statewide services

All Islands Bed & Breakfast (☎ 263-2342, 800-542-0344, fax 263-0308; Ⓦ www.all-islands.com) 463 Iliwahi Loop, Kailua, HI 96734. Books scores of host homes throughout Hawaii

Affordable Paradise Bed & Breakfast (☎ 261-1693, fax 261-7315; Ⓦ www.affordable-paradise.com) 332 Kuukama St, Kailua, HI 96734. Books reasonably priced B&Bs and cottages throughout the islands, with a particularly good selection on Oahu

Condos

Condominiums are individually owned apartments that are fully furnished with everything a visitor needs. Condos are more spacious than hotel rooms, and generally have a living room and full kitchen; many also have washers, dryers, sofa beds and a lanai. Unlike hotels, most condos don't have a daily room-cleaning service.

Although some condo complexes operate similarly to hotels, with a front desk, most condos are booked through rental agents. If you're staying awhile or are traveling with several people, condos almost always work out cheaper than all but the bottom-end hotels. However, most condo units booked through rental agents have a three- to seven-day minimum stay, require deposits and have hefty cancellation fees.

Condos often offer weekly and monthly rates. The general rule is that the weekly rate is six times the daily rate and the monthly is three times the weekly.

As condo rental agencies generally deal with specific destinations, they are listed in the individual island chapters.

Hotels

In Hawaii, as elsewhere, hotels commonly undercut their standard published rates to remain as close to capacity as possible. While some hotels simply offer discounted promotional rates to pick up the slack, a few of the larger chains throw in a free rental car instead. Before booking any hotel, it's worth asking if any specials are available – some places actually have room and car packages for less than the 'standard' room rate!

While a good travel agent at home may know about some of these discounts, many of the best deals are advertised only in Hawaii, and to find them you'll need to pick up a Honolulu newspaper. The travel section of the Sunday *Honolulu Advertiser* is best.

At most hotels the rooms are basically the same, with rates usually corresponding to two variables: the view and the floor. An ocean view often costs 50% to 100% more than a parking lot view, which is sometimes euphemistically called a 'garden view.' And the higher you go, the higher the tariff; the higher floors are generally quieter, especially on busy roads.

The toll-free numbers given in this book are for calls from the US mainland and usually can't be dialed within Hawaii. However, some hotels will accept collect calls from the Neighbor Islands – it never hurts to try.

FOOD

Eating in Hawaii can be a real treat, as the Islands' ethnic diversity has given rise to hundreds of different cuisines. You can find every kind of Japanese food, regional Chinese cuisines, spicy Korean specialities, native Hawaiian dishes and excellent Thai and Vietnamese food.

Although you could spend a bundle eating out, you don't need to, as there are good, cheap neighborhood restaurants to explore on all the islands.

Hawaii also has many restaurants run by renowned chefs that feature gourmet foods of all types, including traditional continental fare. Some of the best restaurants are at the top-end hotels, although a fair number of the more successful chefs have moved on to open their own places.

Many of these 'renegade chefs' specialize in what has been dubbed 'Pacific Rim' or 'Hawaii regional' cuisine, which incorporates fresh island ingredients and borrows liberally from the islands' various ethnic groups. It is marked by creative combinations such as grilled freshwater shrimp with taro chips, wok-charred *ahi* (yellowfin tuna) with island greens, and Peking duck in ginger-*lilikoi* (passion fruit) sauce.

Fresh fish is readily available throughout the islands. Seafood is generally expensive at places catering to tourists, but can be quite reasonable at neighborhood restaurants.

Fruit

Hawaii has an abundance of fruit, including avocado, banana, breadfruit, star fruit, coconut, guava, lychee, mango, papaya, passion fruit and pineapple. Sweet Kau oranges are grown on the Big Island.

Watermelons grown on Molokai are so famous throughout the islands that the airlines had to create special regulations for passengers carrying them out of Molokai to prevent loose melons from bombing their way down the aisles.

Wild fruits can be sometimes be found along trails: these include strawberry guavas, common guavas, thimbleberries, mountain apples, Methley plums and *ohelo* berries.

Hawaiian Food

The traditional Hawaiian feast marking special events is the luau. Local luaus are still commonplace in modern Hawaii for events such as baby christenings. In spirit, these luaus are far more authentic than any of the commercial tourist luaus, but they're family affairs and the short-stay visitor would be lucky indeed to get an invitation to one.

Local Fish

Some of the most popular locally caught fish include:

Hawaiian name	common name
ahi	yellowfin tuna
aku	skipjack tuna
au	swordfish, marlin
kaku	barracuda
mahimahi	a fish called 'dolphin' (not the mammal)
mano	shark
onaga	red snapper
ono	wahoo
opah	moonfish
opakapaka	pink snapper
papio or *ulua*	jack fish
uhu	parrotfish
uku	gray snapper

The main course at a luau is *kalua* pig, which is roasted in a pitlike earthen oven known as an *imu*. The *imu* is readied for cooking by building a fire and heating rocks in the pit. When the rocks are glowing red, layers of moisture-laden banana trunks and green ti leaves are placed over the stones. A pig that has been slit open is filled with some of the hot rocks and laid on top of the bed, and other foods wrapped in ti and banana leaves are placed around it. It's all covered with more ti leaves and a layer of mats and topped off with dirt to seal in the heat, which then bakes and steams the food. Anything cooked in this style is called *kalua*.

The process takes about four to eight hours, depending on the amount of food. A few of the hotel luaus still bake the pig outdoors in this traditional manner and you can often go in the morning and watch them prepare and bury the pig.

Wetland taro is used to make poi, a paste pounded from cooked taro corms. Water is added to make it puddinglike, and its consistency is measured as one-, two- or three-finger poi – which indicates how many fingers are required to bring it from bowl to mouth. Poi is highly nutritious and easily digestible, but it's an acquired taste. It is sometimes fermented to give its flavor more zing.

Laulau is fish, pork and taro wrapped in a ti leaf bundle and steamed. *Lomi* salmon (sometimes called *lomilomi* salmon) is made by marinating thin slices of raw salmon with diced tomatoes and green onions.

Other Hawaiian foods include baked *ulu* (breadfruit), *limu* (seaweed), *opihi* (tiny limpet shells that fishers pick off the reef at low tide) and *pipikaula* (beef jerky). *Haupia*, the standard dessert to a Hawaiian meal, is a stiff pudding made of coconut cream thickened with cornstarch or arrowroot.

In Hawaiian food preparation, ti leaves are indispensable, functioning like a biodegradable version of both aluminum foil and paper plates: food is wrapped in them, cooked in them and served upon them.

Many visitors taste traditional Hawaiian food only at expensive luaus or by sampling a dollop of poi at one of the more adventurous hotel buffet meals. Although Hawaiian food is harder to find than other ethnic foods, a few restaurants throughout the islands serve the real thing, and it's some of the cheapest food in Hawaii.

Local Food

The distinct style of food called 'local' usually refers to a fixed-plate lunch with 'two-scoop rice,' a scoop of macaroni salad and a serving of beef stew, mahimahi or teriyaki chicken, generally scarfed down with chopsticks. A breakfast plate might have Spam, eggs, kimchi and, always, two scoops of rice.

Another popular item is *loco moco*, which consists of rice topped with a hamburger, a fried egg and a generous ladleful of brown gravy.

These local-style meals are the standard fare at diners and lunch wagons. If it's full of starch, fats and gravies, you're probably eating local.

Snacks

Pupu is the word for all kinds of munchies or hors d'oeuvres. Boiled peanuts, soy-flavored rice crackers called *kaki mochi* and sashimi are common *pupu*s.

Poke A local favorite is *poke*, which is raw fish marinated in soy sauce, oil, chili peppers, green onions and seaweed. It comes in many varieties – sesame *ahi* is a particularly delicious one – and all make a nice accompaniment to beer.

Crack Seed A Chinese snack food, crack seed can be sweet, sour, salty or some combination of the three. It's often made from dried fruits, such as plums and apricots, although more exotic ones include sweet-and-sour baby cherry seeds, pickled mangoes and *li hing mui*, one of the sour favorites. Crack-seed shops often sell dried cuttlefish, roasted green peas, candied ginger, beef jerky and rock candy as well.

Shave Ice Similar to mainland snow cones but better, shave ice is made by shaving the ice as fine as powder snow, packing it into a paper cone and drenching with sweet fruit-flavored syrups. Many islanders like the ones with ice cream, sweet adzuki beans or both at the bottom, while kids usually opt for rainbow shave ice, which has colorful stripes of different syrups.

Grocery Stores

You can save money by buying some of your food from grocery stores and preparing your own meals. You don't even have to have

Tropical Treats

Pineapple

Hawaii's number-one fruit crop is the pineapple. Most Hawaiian pineapples are of the smooth cayenne type and weigh a good 5lb.

Pineapples are unique among fruits in that they don't continue to ripen after they're picked. Although they're harvested year-round, the long sunny days of summer produce the sweetest pineapples.

Papaya

Papayas come in several varieties. One of the best of those found in grocery stores is the Solo, a smallish variety with pale strawberry-colored flesh. The flavor of papayas depends largely on where they're grown. Some of the most prized are from the Kapoho area of Puna on the Big Island and the Kahuku area of Oahu. Papayas, which are a good source of calcium and vitamins A and C, are harvested year-round.

Mango

Big old mango trees are abundant in Hawaii, even in remote valleys. The juicy oblong fruits are about 3 inches in diameter and 4 to 6 inches long. The fruits start out green but take on deeper colors as they ripen, usually reddening to an apricot color. Mangoes are a good source of vitamins A and C. Two popular varieties, Pirie and Haden, are less stringy than those usually found in the wild. Mangoes are mainly a summer fruit.

Avocado

Hawaii has three main types of avocado: the West Indian, a smooth-skinned variety that matures in summer and autumn; the rough-skinned Guatemalan, which matures in winter and spring; and the Mexican variety, which has a small fruit and smooth skin. Many of the avocados now in Hawaii are a hybrid of the three. Local avocados tend to be larger and more watery than those grown in California.

Star Fruit

The carambola, or star fruit, is a translucent yellow-green fruit with five ribs like the points of a star. It has a crisp, juicy pulp and can be eaten without being peeled.

Guava

The common guava is a yellow, lime-shaped fruit, about 2 to 3 inches in diameter. It has a moist, pink, seedy flesh, all of which is edible. Guavas can be a little tart but tend to sweeten as they ripen. They're a good source of vitamin C and niacin and can be found along roadsides and trails.

Lilikoi

Passion fruit is a vine with beautiful flowers that grow into small round fruits. The thick skin of the fruit is generally purple or yellow and wrinkles as it ripens. The pulp inside is juicy, seedy and slightly tart. The slimy texture can be a bit of a putoff the first time, but once you taste it you'll be hooked.

Mountain Apple

The mountain apple is a small oval fruit a couple of inches long. The tree is related to the guava, though the fruit is completely different, with a crispy white flesh and a pink skin. The tree bears fruit in the summer and is common along trails.

Ohelo

These berries grow on low shrubs common in lava areas. The *ohelo* is a relative of the cranberry, similar in tartness and size. The fruit is red or yellow and is used in jellies and pies.

Breadfruit

The Hawaiian breadfruit is a large, round, green fruit. It's comparable to potatoes in terms of carbohydrates and is prepared much the same way. In old Hawaii, as in much of the Pacific, breadfruit was one of the traditional staples.

kitchen facilities – most of Hawaii's grocery stores have deli sections with food geared for take-out, with everything from fried chicken and sliced cold cuts to fresh-made *poke* and salads.

One money-saving tip is to get a membership card when you first shop at a supermarket. As is the trend in the rest of the USA, Hawaii's main supermarket chains have initiated a two-tier pricing system. Members get discounted prices, while the rest of the public gets gouged with higher prices – and the difference in the two prices can be significant. Although the chains don't advertise it, short-term visitors can get these free membership cards on the spot simply by asking.

DRINKS

Nonalcoholic Drinks

Tap water is safe to drink, but water from freshwater streams should be boiled.

Cans of Hawaiian-made fruit juices such as guava-orange or passion fruit are stocked at most stores. If you're going for a hike and want to toss a couple of drinks in your daypack, the juices make a good alternative to sodas, as they don't explode when shaken and they taste good even when they're not kept cold.

Alcoholic Drinks

The drinking age in Hawaii is 21. All grocery stores sell liquor, as do most of the smaller food marts. People in their early 20s – or those who look like they are – will need to show a driver's license, passport or similar photo ID to purchase alcohol.

Tedeschi Vineyards, a local winery on Maui, makes a good pineapple wine that is worth a try.

Microbreweries on Oahu, Kauai and the Big Island produce a variety of British- or German-influenced ales and lagers. Although most sell in their own brewpubs only, the Big Island's Kona Brewing Company bottles its ales for sale in grocery stores and restaurants.

And then there are those cool tropical drinks topped with a fruit garnish and paper umbrella – beachside bars are the best place to find them. Three favorites are pina colada, with rum, pineapple juice and cream of coconut; *mai tai,* a mix of rum, grenadine, and lemon and pineapple juices; and Blue Hawaii, a vodka drink colored with blue curacao.

ENTERTAINMENT

Hawaii has an active and varied entertainment scene, and you'll seldom suffer for want of nightlife. Big-name musicians from the mainland like to vacation in Hawaii, and folks like Alicia Keys, Jewel, Janet Jackson, Jimmy Buffett and Sting have included Hawaii in recent tours. They do tend to play where the crowds are, so the best venues for seeing hot stars are on Oahu and Maui.

The four largest islands have community theater productions, occasional film festivals and a variety of cultural events. Oahu and Maui also have symphony orchestras.

You can catch a luau on any of the main islands. Most are big bashy affairs complete with hula dancing and music, tropical drinks and a buffet-style dinner featuring a roasted pig. The majority are held outdoors on the grounds of large resort hotels, which allows the curious to get a sneak preview – if you like what you see, come back and enjoy the fun the next day!

The club scene varies with the island – you'll find the most action in Waikiki, where there are several hot dance spots. Best of the Neighbor Islands for nightlife is Maui, but you can also find decent nightspots on the Big Island and Kauai. If you're heading to Lanai or Molokai, bring a good book!

There's plenty of Hawaiian entertainment as well, including contemporary Hawaiian music, slack-key guitar performances and hula shows. For more detailed information on entertainment, see the individual island chapters.

SPECTATOR SPORTS

In part because of its isolation and relatively low population, Hawaii doesn't have major league sports teams. However, Honolulu's Aloha Stadium hosts a couple of nationally televised football events each winter: the NFL Pro Bowl, an all-star game of the National Football League, and the Hula Bowl, an all-star East versus West college football game. For ticket information, contact the **Aloha Stadium** *(☎ 486-9300)* as far in advance as possible.

Still, some of the most popular spectator sports in Hawaii aren't mainland imports. Surfing, boogie boarding and windsurfing contests attract some of the world's top wave riders and bring out scores of onlookers.

For information on specific sporting events, see Public Holidays & Special Events earlier in this chapter.

SHOPPING

Hawaii has a lot of fine craftspeople, and quality handicrafts can be readily found on all the islands.

Woodworkers use beautifully grained native Hawaiian hardwoods, such as koa, to create calabashes and bowls. Hawaiian bowls are not decorated or ornate, but are shaped to bring out the natural beauty of the wood. The thinner and lighter the bowl, the finer the artistic skill and the greater the value.

There are some excellent island potters, many influenced by Japanese styles and aesthetics. Good *raku* work in particular can be found throughout the islands at reasonable prices.

Lauhala, the leaves of the pandanus tree that were once woven into the mats that Hawaiians slept on, are now woven into place mats, hats and baskets.

Music shops carry recorded traditional and contemporary Hawaiian music. Hula musical instruments such as nose flutes and gourd rattles are uniquely Hawaiian and make interesting gifts.

Niihau shell leis, garlands made from the tiny shells that wash up on the island of Niihau, are one of the most prized Hawaiian souvenirs. Elaborate pieces can cost thousands of dollars.

Hawaii's island-style clothing is colorful and light. The classiest aloha shirts are of lightweight cotton with subdued colors (like those of reverse-fabric prints). Women might want to buy a muumuu, a loose, comfortable, full-length Hawaiian-style dress.

Foods are popular purchases. The standard souvenir is macadamia nuts, either canned or covered in chocolate. Kona coffee, macadamia-nut butters, *lilikoi* or *poha* (gooseberry) preserves and mango chutney all make convenient, compact gift items.

Pineapples are not a great choice in the souvenir department. Not only are they heavy and bulky, but they're likely to be just as cheap at home.

For those who enjoy Japanese food, Hawaii is a good place to pick up ingredients that might be difficult to find back home. Most grocery stores have a wide selection of things such as dried seaweed, *mochi* and *ume* (plums).

Flowers such as orchids, anthuriums and proteas make good gifts if you're flying straight home. Proteas stay fresh for about 10 days and then can be dried. Foreign visitors should check with their airline in advance, however, as there are commonly restrictions against taking agricultural products across international borders.

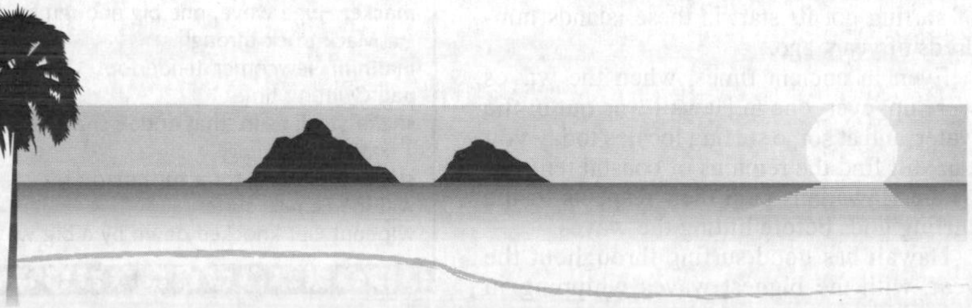

Activities

Only a few activities require planning before you get to Hawaii. Most of the time you can just show up, look around and make an on-the-spot decision.

For information on instruction, equipment rental and specific locations for each activity, see the island chapters.

SWIMMING

Hawaii is endowed with an abundance of lovely beaches and it really would take the better part of a year just to try each one of them once.

The islands have four distinct coastal areas – north shore, south shore, leeward (west) coast and windward (east) coast – each of which has its own peculiar water conditions. The conditions can vary significantly with the season but when it's rough on one side, it's generally calm on another, so you can find good places to swim all year round. As a general rule, the best places to swim in the winter are along the south shores of the islands, and in the summer, the north shores.

Which island has the best beaches is a matter of opinion – many people argue it's Maui, and that island certainly is richly fringed with long sandy strands. The Big Island, on the other hand, with its endless lava coastline, doesn't abound in those mile-long beaches that have made Maui so famous. Instead many of the Big Island's beaches are in small sandy pockets, appearing like little white-sand oases surrounded by a sea of black lava and turquoise water. Some of them are absolutely stunning!

SURFING

Hawaii lies smack in the path of all the major swells that race unimpeded across the Pacific, so it comes as no surprise that the sport of surfing got its start in these islands hundreds of years ago.

Even in ancient times, when the waves were up, everyone in Hawaii was out in the water, and at some surfing locales today you can still find the remains of coastal temples where Hawaiians paid their respects to the surfing gods before hitting the waves.

Hawaii has good surfing throughout the year, with the biggest waves whipping in from November to February along the north shores of the islands. Summer swells, which break along the south shores, are usually not as frequent and not nearly as large as the north-side winter swells.

Oahu's North Shore has Hawaii's top surf action, attracting championship surfers from around the world and hosting big-name surfing competitions. The winter swells at Waimea, Sunset Beach and the Banzai Pipeline can bring in towering 30ft waves, creating the conditions that legends are made of. Waikiki has Oahu's top south-shore surfing.

Though they may be less well known than Oahu's surfing sites, Maui and Kauai also have some very good surfing spots, particularly in winter along their north shores – two of the best spots are Honolua Bay on Maui and Hanalei Bay on Kauai. The Big Island and Molokai are not as notable, but it is possible to surf on both islands.

You'll find a knockout website, Hawaii Surfing News, brimming with everything from surf conditions to upcoming surfing events, at W www.holoholo.org/surfnews.

Surfspeak

Surfers everywhere have their own lingo. Hit the waves in Hawaii, and you're likely to hear some of these terms:

brah Friend, surfing buddy
da kine A great wave, top quality
goofy-footing Surfing with the right foot forward
kaha Traditional Hawaiian term for board surfing
kaha nalu Body surfing
keiki waves Small, gentle waves suitable for kids
macker Huge wave, one big enough to drive a Mack truck through
malihini Newcomer, tenderfoot
pau Quitting time
snake Steal; as in 'that dude's snaking my wave'
stick Local slang for a surfboard
wahine Female surfer
wipeout Get knocked down by a big wave

BODYSURFING & BOOGIE BOARDING

Brennecke's Beach on Kauai and White Sands Beach in Kailua-Kona on the Big Island are top spots for both bodysurfing and boogie boarding. The beaches in Kihei on the south coast of Maui can see some decent conditions when the waves are right. On Oahu, Sandy Beach Park and Makapuu Beach Park are top places for bodysurfing, while the Kapahulu Groin in Waikiki is the domain of boogie boarders.

WINDSURFING

Maui has some of the world's best windsurfing action, with Hookipa Beach near Paia hosting top international windsurfing competitions. Hookipa's death-defying conditions, which include dangerous shorebreaks and razor-sharp coral, are for expert windsurfers only, but tamer spots that are well suited to beginners can be found on other parts of Maui, such as Kihei.

Oahu's Kailua Beach, which is suitable for all levels, attracts the biggest crowd; it offers excellent year-round trade winds and both flat-water and wave conditions in different sections of the bay.

Although Maui and Oahu are by far the top two Hawaiian islands for windsurfing, Kauai also has some fairly good windsurfing spots, most notably Anini Beach on the North Shore, which has conditions good for both beginners and more advanced windsurfers.

Although there are good windsurfing conditions in Hawaii year-round, winter can have flat periods. In general, the best winds are from June to September.

It's possible to rent gear and take lessons on the main islands. Hard-core devotees can arrange package tours that include windsurfing gear rental, accommodations and, in some cases, car rental and airfare.

DIVING

Hawaii's underwater world is spectacular, and there's good year-round diving. Hawaiian waters have excellent visibility, with water temperatures ranging from 72°F to 80°F. Under normal conditions, the leeward shores of the islands have the best diving most months of the year, while the north shores are usually best in the summer.

The marine life around the islands is superb. Almost 700 fish species live in Hawaiian waters, and of these nearly one-third are found nowhere else in the world. Divers often see spinner dolphins, green sea turtles, manta rays and moray eels. Although it's rare for divers to see humpback whales underwater, they do sometimes hear them singing.

Hawaii has underwater caves, canyons, lava tubes, vertical walls and sunken ships. There are all sorts of colorful sponges and corals, including the gemlike black coral.

The four largest islands all have some excellent diving opportunities. Just which island has the best diving? Well, truth be told, no two divers are likely to agree on an answer to that question. And what you're looking for in a dive will make a big difference on where you'll be happiest.

Oahu, for instance, doesn't offer the greatest visibility when compared to the Neighbor Islands, but it has the best selection of wreck dives. The Big Island, on the other hand, has superb visibility and the most dramatic underwater terrain, with beautiful lava formations that are honeycombed with tubes and caverns.

Maui has something the other main islands lack: accessible offshore islands with good coral reefs. Kauai also has excellent diving but weather conditions are much more fickle there, and when the water is rough, which includes most of the winter along Kauai's majestic North Shore, many dive sites are inaccessible.

All of the islands have reputable dive shops. Divers needn't bring anything other than a swimsuit and their diver's certification card.

If you've never dived before, Hawaii is a great place to give it a try. Many of the dive operations offer a short beginner's 'try scuba' course for nondivers, which includes brief instruction followed by a shallow beach or boat dive. For those who want to jump into the sport wholeheartedly, a number of shops also offer full open-water certification courses, which usually take the better part of a week. Oahu, which has the most dive operations of any island, and the Kona Coast of the Big Island are particularly good places for novices to learn the sport.

SNUBA

If you want to get beneath the water's surface but aren't ready for a dive course, snuba offers a combination of snorkeling and diving. Snuba divers breathe through a long air hose attached to an air tank on an inflatable raft that floats on the water's surface. They simply wear a mask and weight belt and can dive down as far as the air hose allows.

All snuba programmes include elementary dive instruction that essentially explains how to clear your face mask and equalize ear pressure. An instructor is in the water with you during the entire dive. Generally, the best snuba experiences are those from boats, as you can get to better dive sites, but snuba from the beach is also available.

Snuba makes for a quick and easy introduction to the underwater world and can certainly whet one's appetite for more serious diving.

SNORKELING

No visitor to Hawaii should miss the opportunity to take a peek into the underwater world. The beauty of snorkeling is that is doesn't require expensive equipment or any particular skill. In many places you don't even have to go underwater to enjoy the sights. With the exception of Molokai, which has a silty shoreline, there are several good snorkeling locations on every island.

Donning a mask and snorkel allows you to turn the beach into a brilliant underwater aquarium. Numerous snorkeling sites throughout Hawaii offer splendid coral gardens and varied and abundant reef fish. Hawaii's nearshore waters harbor some 20 different kinds of butterfly fish alone, as well as large rainbow-colored parrotfish that munch on coral close to shore, red-and-green wrasses, bright yellow tangs, odd-shaped filefish and ballooning puffers, just to name a few.

KAYAKING

Kayaking is becoming increasingly popular in Hawaii, spurred in part by the newer types of stable kayaks that are suitable for beginners.

By far the most popular kayaking destination is Kauai, which offers both navigable rivers leading to scenic natural sights and ocean kayaking along the spectacular Na Pali Coast. In winter, when the surf along the north side of the island gets rough, ocean kayaking moves to Kauai's less spectacular but still pleasant south side.

Ocean kayaking is also picking up in Maui, primarily along that island's southwest coast from Kihei to La Perouse Bay, which is a splendid whale-watching area in winter.

On both Kauai and Maui, you can join guided tours or rent kayaks to head off on your own.

On Oahu, the most popular kayaking spot is the Kailua area, where visitors can rent kayaks right on the beach and paddle across the bay to a deserted island. It's also possible to rent kayaks on Fort DeRussy Beach in Waikiki.

On the Big Island, the main kayaking destination is Kealakekua Bay, a haven for dolphins, a splendid snorkel locale and the site of the monument marking the spot where Captain Cook met his end.

Molokai, whose undeveloped north shore boasts the world's highest sea cliffs, is an overlooked but unsurpassed kayaking destination for those seeking solitude. Suitable for kayaking only in the calm summer months, this part of the island takes about five days to explore and is certainly not for the faint of heart.

FISHING

Hawaii has some of the world's best deep-sea fishing. Popular sport fish include Pacific blue marlin, black marlin, yellowfin tuna, wahoo and mahimahi.

The Kona region of the Big Island holds most of the world records for Pacific blue marlin. Not surprisingly, Kona has Hawaii's biggest charter fishing-boat industry, although charters can be arranged on other islands as well.

In addition to ocean fishing, the state maintains four public freshwater fishing areas: in Kokee on Kauai, in Wahiawa and Nuuanu on Oahu and at Waiakea on the Big Island. Stocked fish include rainbow trout, largemouth and smallmouth bass, bluegill, channel catfish, tilapia and carp. Licenses, which are required for freshwater fishing, are available for nonresidents at $10 a week or $20 a month (free for those 65 and older).

No licenses are required for saltwater fishing when the catch is for private consumption. There are, however, seasons, size limits and other restrictions on taking *ula* (spiny lobster), crab, octopus (*hee* in Hawaiian, and also called *tako* or squid), *opihi* (a kind of limpet), *limu* (seaweed) and certain species of fish. Clams and oysters cannot be taken.

The booklets *Hawaii Fishing Regulations* and *Freshwater Fishing in Hawaii* can be obtained free from the **Division of Aquatic Resources** (*☎ 587-0100; 1151 Punchbowl St, Room 131, Honolulu, HI 96813*). The office also issues licenses.

WHALE WATCHING

Lots of whales can be found in Hawaiian waters, including several resident whale species such as the sperm whale, false killer whale, pilot whale and beaked whale. Nonetheless, it's not these year-round local whales that attract tourists but the migrating humpback whales, which put on phenomenal acrobatic displays, breaching out of the water, slapping their fins and tails on the surface and making grand arching dives.

Approximately two thirds of all the North Pacific's estimated 4000 humpback whales winter in Hawaiian waters, providing visitors with some of the most fantastic whale-watching opportunities to be found anywhere.

Humpbacks begin filtering in to Hawaii around November and some stay as late as May, with most in residence from January to March. They prefer waters with depths of less than 600ft, which means that they come quite close to the shore in Hawaii. At times, they can be spotted off any of the Hawaiian Islands, but the largest numbers congregate in the shallow waters between Maui, Lanai, Molokai and Kahoolawe. The Kona Coast of the Big Island is another favored spot, as is the Penguin Bank, which lies 10 miles west of Molokai.

Whales can often be seen right from the beach, with the best possibilities along the west coast of Maui. To get even closer, take one of the seasonal whale-watching cruises, which depart from all the main islands. Other possibilities for whale watching include kayaking along the shoreline or hopping on either the Maui–Lanai or Maui–Molokai ferries, which cruise past prime humpback territory.

HIKING

Like the islands themselves, the hiking options in Hawaii are incredibly varied, ranging from desert treks to lush rain-forest walks, and from beach strolls to snowy ridgeline trails.

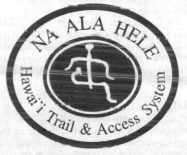

Despite all the development in Hawaii, it's amazing how much land is still in a natural state. There are places where you could walk for days without seeing another soul.

Hikes vary from short family-style nature strolls that can be walked in an hour to backcountry treks that can last several days and require backpacking with your own food, water and gear.

The premier hike in all of Hawaii is on Kauai's Na Pali Coast, where the Kalalau Trail follows an ancient Hawaiian footpath along the edges of the most spectacularly fluted coastal cliffs in Hawaii. The trail winds down into lush valleys where camping is allowed and waterfalls and ruins can be explored.

Na Ala Hele

Of special interest to hikers and naturalists is the work of Na Ala Hele, a group affiliated with Hawaii's Division of Forestry & Wildlife.

Na Ala Hele was established with the task of documenting public access to trails as part of a movement to preserve Hawaii's natural environment and cultural heritage. Throughout the state, the group has negotiated with private landowners and the military to gain access to previously restricted areas and reestablish abandoned trails.

The Na Ala Hele logo signpost – a brown sign that features a yellow hiking petroglyph figure – is marking an increasing number of trailheads as the organization's work continues.

Na Ala Hele is headquartered at the **Division of Forestry & Wildlife** (*🅦 www.hawaiitrails.org; 567 S King St, Suite 132, Honolulu, HI 96813)* The website has maps of the trails, conveniently grouped by island

Hawaii Volcanoes National Park on the Big Island has the distinction of containing both the world's most active volcano and the world's largest mountain mass. The park offers breathtaking hikes down into steaming craters and others that climb the snowcapped summit of Mauna Loa.

At Haleakala National Park on Maui, the volcano is sleepier but equally awe-inspiring, boasting the world's largest crater. Hikes into the caldera can take half a day, while hikes across its floor can take half a week.

There are also hiking trails into ancient valleys, such as Waipio on the Big Island. On Maui and the Big Island you can follow old 'king's trails' along footpaths worn into the lava over hundreds of years by the bare feet of travelers.

Every island has ridgeline trails with panoramic views, as well as trails to secluded beaches and waterfalls. Some islands have trails through nature preserves, where you can observe native plants and birds and enjoy lots of solitude.

Of the organizations that offer guided hikes on the major islands, the most active is the **Sierra Club** (*W www.hi.sierraclub .org*), with branches on Oahu, Maui, Kauai and the Big Island. Local newspapers list hiking schedules.

Safety

A number of Hawaii's hiking trails take you into steep, narrow valleys with gullies that require stream crossings. The capital rule here is that if the water begins to rise, it's not safe to cross, as a flash flood may be imminent. Instead, head for higher ground and wait it out.

Flash floods and falling rocks are the biggest dangers on trails. Be wary of swimming under high waterfalls, as rocks can dislodge from the top, and be careful on the edge of steep cliffs, as cliff-side rock in Hawaii tends to be crumbly.

Darkness sets in soon after sunset in Hawaii, and ridge-top trails are not the place to be caught unprepared in the dark. It's a good idea to carry a flashlight when you're hiking, just in case. Long pants will protect your legs from the overgrown parts of the trail, and sturdy footwear with good traction is advisable on most hikes. Hawaiian trails tend to be quite slippery when wet, so a walking stick always makes a good companion.

Hawaii has no snakes, no poison ivy, no poison oak and few dangers from wild animals. There's a slim possibility of meeting up with a large boar in the backwoods, but they're unlikely to be a problem unless cornered.

RUNNING

Hawaii residents are an outdoor bunch, and running and jogging are popular activities throughout the islands. More than 100 road races, ranging from 'fun runs' to triathlons, are held in Hawaii each year.

Hawaii's biggest race is the Honolulu Marathon, which in recent years has mushroomed into the third-largest marathon in the USA. Held in mid-December, it's an open-entry event, with an estimated half of the 25,000 entrants being first-time marathon runners. For information, send a self-addressed, stamped envelope to **Honolulu Marathon Association** (*☎ 734-7200; W www .honolulumarathon.org; 3435 Waialae Ave, No 208, Honolulu, HI 96816*). You can also download an entry form from its website.

And, of course, there's the world-renowned Ironman Triathlon, held in Kona on the Big Island in October, combining a marathon run with distance swimming and cycling.

Other well-attended races include the Great Aloha Fun Run, an 8.2-mile jaunt held in Honolulu every February; the Oahu Perimeter Relay, a 134-mile relay race around Oahu in late February; and the Kilauea Volcano Wilderness Marathon & Rim Runs, which includes a marathon and shorter races at Hawaii Volcanoes National Park on the Big Island in July.

The comprehensive, bimonthly magazine *Hawaii Race* (*☎ 538-0330; W www.hawaii race.com*) includes upcoming race schedules for all of Hawaii, as well as qualification details and actual entry forms for the major races. It can be picked up free in Hawaii or by annual subscription for $15/24 to addresses within/outside the USA.

MOUNTAIN BIKING

Mountain biking is gaining popularity in Hawaii, and mountain bikes can now be rented on all the main islands. While cycling along roads isn't a problem – other than the shortage of bike lanes – getting off the beaten path is a bit more complicated, since access to public forests and trails is limited.

Ironman Triathlon

The Ironman, the first and foremost of all triathlons, takes place each October on the Big Island's sunny Kona Coast, starting and ending at the pier in Kailua-Kona. The event occurs on the Saturday closest to the full moon, so that all participants will have the amount of light required to safely finish.

It's a grueling, nonstop combination of a 2.4-mile swim, 112-mile bike race and 26.2-mile run that draws the world's top triathletes. Competitors have 17 hours to finish the race, though the top athletes cross the finish line in about half that time. The current men's record, set by Luc Van Lierde of Belgium in 1996, is eight hours and four minutes, while the women's record, set by Paula Newby-Fraser of the USA in 1992, is eight hours and 55 minutes.

The total prize purse is $325,000, with the top male and female finishers receiving $70,000 each.

The Ironman began in 1978 with just 15 participants. The following year, the event was covered by *Sports Illustrated* magazine, which labeled it 'lunatic.' By 1980, the Ironman was drawing enough participants to receive TV coverage on ABC's *Wide World of Sports*, and since that time its popularity has continued to grow by leaps and bounds.

These days, some 50,000 triathletes compete in a couple of dozen worldwide qualifiers in hopes of earning one of the 1500 entry berths in the Ironman event. The athletes who participate in the Ironman represent each US state and Canadian province and approximately 50 other countries.

Harsh Kona conditions make the event the ultimate endurance test, even by triathlon standards. Heat reflected off the lava landscape commonly exceeds 100°F, making dehydration and heat exhaustion major challenges. Many contenders arrive weeks before the race just to acclimatize themselves. On the day of the race, nearly 7000 volunteers line up along the 140-mile course to offer water to passing racers. In all, they hand out some 12,500 gallons of water – more than 8 gallons for each triathlete!

To learn more about the race, including qualifying requirements, visit the Ironman Triathlon World Championship's official website at W www.ironmanlive.com.

On Maui, which just a few years ago had no legally accessible off-road trails, the Maui Mountain Bike Club has worked out an agreement with the state for bike access to some of the hiking trails in Polipoli Spring State Recreation Area and Kula Forest Reserve; in return for access, the club helps maintain the trails.

On the Big Island, which is big on space, the county has designated a number of areas that bikers can use and has funded the publication of a mountain-biking trail map. The routes include the 45-mile Mana Rd loop that circles around Mauna Kea and the 6½-mile beach trail to Pine Trees on the Kona Coast.

On Kauai, the state forestry department has opened 18 of its trails to mountain bikers, including the 13-mile Powerline Trail, a picturesque ridgetop route from Wailua to Princeville, and the Waimea Canyon Trail.

On densely populated Oahu, where mountain bikers are often pitted against hikers, there are fewer options. Bikes have been banned from the Tantalus trails because tire tracks were causing trail erosion but the paved Tantalus Dr, which is also open to vehicles, remains a popular biking route. One excellent Oahu forest trail that is open to mountain bikers is the Maunawili Trail, a scenic 10-mile trek that connects the mountain crest at the Nuuanu Pali Lookout with Waimanalo on the windward coast.

HORSEBACK RIDING

All of the main islands offer horseback riding. Most of the rides go across hillside pastures, offering fine mountain and ocean views. The most unique offering is on Maui, where guides lead horses down a trail of crunchy cinder rock into the depths of Haleakala Crater.

TENNIS

You'll find opportunities to play tennis throughout Hawaii. All of the islands have public county tennis courts that you can use free of charge, but you'll need to bring your own rackets and balls.

You can also play on the grounds of many of the large resort hotels, which have tennis clubs that rent rackets and balls, charge court-time fees and sometimes offer lessons. Some smaller hotels have tennis courts as well, but these are usually reserved for use by their hotel guests. You won't find tennis courts at Waikiki hotels, however, where space is at a premium and virtually every speck of ground that could have held a tennis court has the foundation of a high-rise hotel instead!

GOLF

If you feel like teeing off in paradise, you'll find more than 80 golf courses throughout the islands. These range from county-operated courses with modest fees to some of the top-rated courses in the USA.

Some of the more spectacular courses in Hawaii include the Francis Ii Brown course, sculptured against a jet-black lava flow on the Big Island; Princeville's Prince Course, overlooking scenic Hanalei Bay on Kauai; the mountain-side Koolau Golf Course, which was named the number-one course on Oahu by *Golf Digest*; and the Arnold Palmer–designed Kapalua Bay Course in West Maui, which has a tee on one side of the bay and the green on the other. Little Molokai doesn't have resort-rated courses, but Lanai has two top-notch designer courses: the Manele course overlooking beautiful Hulopoe Bay and the Koele course in the rolling hillsides above Lanai City.

SKYDIVING & GLIDER RIDES

Skydiving and glider rides are offered at Dillingham Airfield on the North Shore of Oahu. With skydiving, you get about an hour of instruction, then you're attached by the hips and shoulders to a skydiver. The two of you jump from a plane at 13,000ft, freefall for a minute, and finish off with a canopy ride that lasts 10 to 15 minutes. Now there's a view you won't soon forget!

The glider rides are tamer but still offer some great bird's-eye views. You go aboard an engineless piloted glider craft, which is towed up by an airplane and then released to slowly, and quietly, glide back to earth.

SAILING CRUISES

There's certainly no lack of options on this one. Scores of sunset sails, dinner cruises and party boats sail out of the main tourist destinations. In the more bustling places, such as Honolulu on Oahu and Lahaina on Maui, there's so much competition that the choices can be mind boggling. If you're finicky, the best bet is to walk along the dock and see which boat strikes your fancy. The most romantic and quietest sails will generally be those that are on catamarans, which operate on wind power.

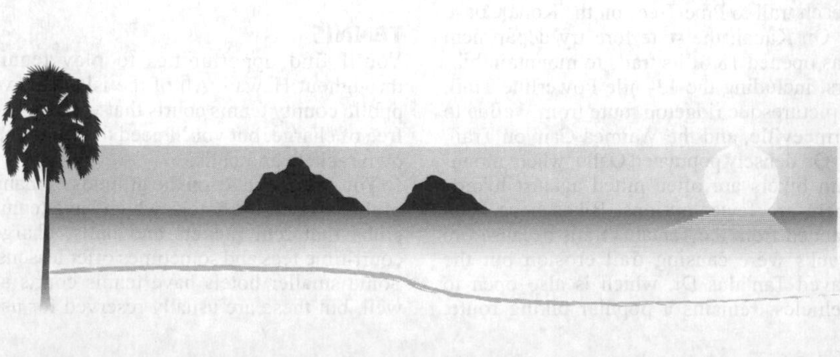

Getting There & Away

AIR

Almost all visitors to Hawaii arrive by air. Hawaii is a major Pacific hub and an intermediate stop on many flights between the US mainland and Asia, Australia, New Zealand and the South Pacific. Passengers on any of these routes are usually allowed to make a stopover in Honolulu. Virtually all international flights, and the majority of domestic flights, arrive at Honolulu international airport. For information on the airport, see Honolulu international airport under Getting There & Away in the Oahu chapter.

Airlines

The following airlines have scheduled flights to Honolulu international airport on Oahu. The seven-digit numbers listed are local Oahu numbers; those that begin with 800 are toll-free numbers.

Air Canada	☎ 800-776-3000
Air New Zealand	☎ 800-262-1234
All Nippon Airways	☎ 800-235-9262
Aloha Airlines	☎ 800-551-1833
America West Airlines	☎ 800-235-9292
American Airlines	☎ 800-223-5436
China Airlines	☎ 955-0088
Continental Airlines	☎ 800-523-3273
Delta Air Lines	☎ 800-221-1212
Garuda Indonesia	☎ 800-342-7832
Hawaiian Airlines	☎ 800-367-5320
Japan Airlines	☎ 521-1441
Korean Air	☎ 800-438-5000
Northwest Airlines	☎ 800-225-2525
Philippine Airlines	☎ 800-435-9725
Qantas Airways	☎ 800-227-4500
Singapore Airlines	☎ 800-742-3333
United Airlines	☎ 800-241-6522

Buying Tickets

Numerous airlines fly to Hawaii and a variety of fares are available. Rather than just walking into the nearest travel agent or airline office, it pays to do a bit of research and shop around first.

You might want to start by perusing the travel sections of magazines and large newspapers such as the *New York Times*, the *San Francisco Chronicle* and the *Los Angeles Times* in the USA; the *Sydney Morning Herald* or Melbourne's *Age* in Australia; and *Time Out* or *TNT* in the UK.

Airfares are constantly in flux. Fares vary with the season you travel, the day of the week you fly, your length of stay and the flexibility the ticket provides for flight changes and refunds. Still, nothing determines fares more than business, and when things are slow, regardless of the season, airlines typically drop fares to fill the empty seats.

The airlines each have their own requirements and restrictions, which also seem to be constantly changing. For the latest deals, browse travel services on the Internet, visit a knowledgeable travel agent or simply start calling the different airlines and comparing ticket prices.

When you call, it's important to ask for the lowest fare, since that's not always the first one the agent will quote you. Each flight has only a limited number of seats available at the cheapest fare. When you make reservations, the agents will generally tell you the best fare that's still available on the date you give them, which may or may not be the cheapest fare that the airline is currently offering. If you make reservations far enough in advance and are a little flexible with dates, you'll usually do better.

Warning

The information in this chapter is particularly vulnerable to change. Prices for international travel are volatile, routes are introduced and canceled, schedules change, special deals come and go, and rules and visa requirements are amended. Airlines and governments seem to take a perverse pleasure in making price structures and regulations as complicated as possible. You should check directly with the airline or a travel agent to make sure you understand how a fare (and any ticket you may buy) works. In addition, the travel industry is highly competitive, and there are many lurks and perks.

The upshot of this is that you should get opinions, quotes and advice from as many airlines and travel agents as possible before you part with your hard-earned cash. The details given in this chapter should be regarded as pointers and are not a substitute for your own careful, up-to-date research.

Round-the-World Tickets Allowing you to fly on the combined routes of two or more airlines, round-the-world (RTW) tickets can be a good deal if you're coming from a great distance and want to visit other parts of the world in addition to Hawaii.

RTW tickets are put together by a combination of two or more airlines and permit you to fly anywhere you want on their route system as long as you travel in one general direction without backtracking. You must usually book the first sector in advance, there may be restrictions on the number of stops permitted, and tickets are usually valid for six months or a year. Most airlines restrict the number of sectors that can be flown within the USA and Canada to three or four, and a few heavily traveled routes (such as Honolulu to Tokyo) are sometimes blacked out all together.

In most cases a 14-day advance purchase is required. After the ticket is purchased, dates can usually be changed without penalty and tickets can be rewritten to add or delete stops for a fee. There's an almost endless variety of airline and destination combinations. Because of Honolulu's central Pacific location, Hawaii can be included on most RTW tickets.

British Airways and Qantas Airways offer a couple of interesting RTW tickets that allow you to combine routes covering the South and central Pacific regions, Asia and Europe. One version, the One World Explorer, is based on the number of continents you visit, requires traveling to a minimum of four continents and allows four stops in each continent visited; extra stops can be added for an additional US$150 each. The One World Explorer costs US$3700 in the USA, A$2999 in Australia and £950 in the UK.

A second, similarly priced British Airways–Qantas ticket is the Global Explorer, which is instead based on the total number of miles flown, allowing 26,000 miles of travel. The main advantage of the Global Explorer is that it allows travel on a couple of additional partner airlines, so you could, for instance, travel from Australia to Johannesburg on South African Airways, something that isn't allowed with the One World Explorer. However, because Qantas has a code-sharing partnership with American Airlines (which means you can book a flight through Qantas, such as New York–Los Angeles, using a Qantas flight number and ticket coupon, but you'll actually fly with American), both of these RTW tickets allow travel within the USA.

Although the British-Qantas RTW tickets are among the most popular and reliable, there are many other airlines teaming up to offer similar deals. A good travel agent can advise you on what's currently available.

Circle Pacific Tickets These tickets allow wide-ranging travel within the Pacific Rim area, including a stop in Hawaii. They're essentially a takeoff on RTW tickets, but, instead of requiring you to continue moving in one general direction, these allow you to circle back around the Pacific Rim. Because you start and end at a city that borders the Pacific, these tickets are most practical for travelers who live in the Pacific region.

Circle Pacific tickets can be with a single carrier or with two airlines linking up to allow stopovers along their Pacific Rim routes. Rather than simply flying from point A to point B, these tickets allow you to swing through much of the Pacific and eastern Asia, taking in a variety of destinations – as long as you keep traveling in the same circular direction.

Circle Pacific routes generally cost around US$2600 when purchased in the USA and A$3000 when purchased in Australia. Some Circle Pacific fares tack on a charge for more than four stopovers, while others, including those offered by Air New Zealand, allow unlimited stops. The Air New Zealand Circle Pacific ticket can make for a good island-hopping itinerary, allowing travel, for instance, from Los Angeles to New Zealand, Australia and a number of south Pacific islands, with a return to the USA via Honolulu.

Another interesting variation is the Circle Micronesia pass with Continental Airlines, which departs from Los Angeles or San Francisco and combines Honolulu with the islands of Micronesia. The price depends on how much of Micronesia you want to see and how far you want to travel. If you only go as far as Guam, for instance, it'll cost you US$1280; if you go to Palau, at the westernmost end of Micronesia, it will cost US$1700. The pass allows for four stops; additional stops can be added for US$50 each.

These Circle Pacific tickets have a seven-day advance purchase requirement and allow a maximum stay of six months.

Discount Fares from Hawaii In Hawaii you'll find discounted fares to virtually any place around the Pacific. Fares vary according to the month, airline and demand, but often you can also find a round-trip fare to Los Angeles or San Francisco for around US$300; to Tokyo for US$450; to Hong Kong for US$500; to Beijing, Saigon or Sydney for US$700; and to Bali for US$750.

If you don't have a destination in mind, you can sometimes find some great on-the-spot deals. The travel pages of the Sunday *Honolulu Advertiser* have scores of ads by travel agencies that advertise discounted overseas fares.

Some of the larger travel agencies that specialize in discount tickets are **King's Travel** (*☎ 593-4481; W www.reallycheapfares.com; 725 Kapiolani Blvd, Honolulu*); **Panda Travel** (*☎ 734-1961; 1017 Kapahulu Ave, Honolulu*); and **Royal Adventure Travel** (*☎ 732-4646; 126 Queen St, Honolulu*).

Travelers with Special Needs

If you have special needs of any sort – you require a vegetarian diet, are taking a baby, or have a medical condition that warrants special consideration – you should let the airline know as soon as possible so they can make arrangements. Remind them when you reconfirm your reservation and again when you check in at the airport. It may also be worth calling several airlines before you book your ticket to find out how each of them handles your particular needs.

Most international airports, including Honolulu international airport, will provide an escorted cart or wheelchair from the check-in desk to the plane when needed, and have ramps, lifts, accessible toilets and reachable phones. Aircraft toilets, on the other hand, are likely to present a problem for some disabled passengers; travelers should discuss this with the airline at an early stage and, if necessary, with their doctor.

As a general rule, children under age two travel for 10% of the standard fare (or free on some airlines) as long as they don't occupy a seat. They don't get a baggage allowance either. 'Skycots,' baby food and diapers should be provided by the airline if requested in advance. Children between ages two and 12 can usually occupy a seat for half to two-thirds of the full fare, and they do get a baggage allowance.

Departure Tax

Taxes and fees for US airports are normally included in the price of tickets when you buy them, whether they're purchased in the USA or abroad.

When you book flights you may notice that those with the fewest connections are often cheaper; that's because airport fees are charged each time you land. Typically, for each US airport you fly into, including connections and stopovers, there's an airport user fee of $2 to $3 tacked on to your ticket price.

There's also an airport security tax, which was enacted after the September 11 terrorist attacks, of $2.50 for each departure you make from a US airport, ostensibly to cover the more thorough screening now given to departing passengers.

Other fees that may be added to the ticket price are a $6 airport departure tax on all passengers traveling from the USA to a foreign destination and a $6.50 North American Free Trade Agreement (Nafta) tax on all passengers entering the USA from a foreign country.

There are no Hawaii-specific taxes to pay when leaving Hawaii.

The US Mainland

Competition is high among airlines flying to Honolulu from the major mainland cities, and at any given time any airline could have the cheapest fare. Sometimes package-tour companies offer the best airfare deals, even if you don't want to buy the whole 'package.' Check with a local travel agent; also see Organized Tours later in this chapter.

Typically, the lowest round-trip fares from the US mainland to Hawaii are about $700 to $1100 from the East Coast and $350 to $650 from the West Coast. For those flying from the East Coast, it may be cheaper to buy two separate tickets – one to the West Coast with a low-fare carrier such as Southwest Airlines, and a separate ticket from the West Coast to Hawaii.

Although conditions vary, the cheapest fares are generally for midweek flights and have advance purchase requirements and other restrictions. These are usually nonrefundable and nonchangeable, at least on the outbound flight (although most airlines make allowances for medical emergencies).

Most mainland flights fly into Honolulu, but there are also direct flights to Maui, Kauai and the Big Island. The service varies with the island. Only one major airline – United – flies straight from the mainland to Kauai, for instance, while several airlines offer service between the mainland and Maui.

The following airlines fly to Honolulu from both the East and West Coasts of the US.

American Airlines	☎ 800-433-7300
Continental Airlines	☎ 800-525-0280
Delta Air Lines	☎ 800-221-1212
Northwest Airlines	☎ 800-225-2525
TWA	☎ 800-221-2000
United Airlines	☎ 800-241-6522

In addition, **Hawaiian Airlines** *(☎ 800-367-5320; W www.hawaiianair.com)* flies to Hawaii from the US West Coast. Hawaiian has nonstop flights to Honolulu from Los Angeles, Seattle, Portland, San Francisco, San Diego and Sacramento. It also has nonstop flights to Maui from Los Angeles, San Francisco and Seattle.

The other interisland airline, **Aloha Airlines** *(☎ 800-367-5250; W www.alohaairlines.com)*, also has several flights between the US West Coast and Hawaii. Aloha offers flights to Honolulu from Las Vegas, Oakland and Orange County. It also flies to Maui from Oakland, Las Vegas and Orange County and to Kona from Oakland and Las Vegas.

And then there's Air Tech's Space-Available FlightPass, which certainly can be the cheapest way to fly between the West Coast and Hawaii. **Air Tech** *(☎ 212-219-7000; W www.airtech.com)* offers super deals by selling standby seats at $119 one way. If you provide the staff with a two- to four-day travel window, they'll get you a seat at a nice price. Currently, flights depart only from Oakland to Honolulu, Lihue, Kona and Maui.

The flight time to Hawaii is about 5½ hours from the West Coast, 11 hours from the East Coast.

Canada

Air Canada offers flights to Honolulu from Vancouver and from other Canadian cities via Vancouver. The cheapest round-trip fares to Honolulu are around C$600 from Vancouver, C$750 from Calgary or Edmonton and C$1200 from Toronto. These fares are for midweek travel, generally allow a maximum stay of either 30 or 60 days and have advance purchase requirements.

Agricultural Inspection

All luggage and carry-on bags leaving Hawaii for the US mainland are checked by an agricultural inspector using an X-ray machine. You cannot take out gardenias, jade vines or roses, even in leis, although most other fresh flowers and foliage are permitted. You can take pineapples and coconuts to the mainland, but most other fresh fruits and vegetables are banned. Other things not allowed to enter mainland states include plants in soil, fresh coffee berries, cactus and sugarcane. Seeds, fruits and plants that have been certified and labeled for export aren't a problem.

Central & South America

Most of the flights to Hawaii from Central and South America go via Houston or Los Angeles, though a few of those from the eastern cities go via New York.

United Airlines has flights from numerous cities in Mexico and Central America, including San José, Guatemala City, Mexico City and Guadalajara. Its lowest round-trip fare from Mexico City to Honolulu is US$900.

The UK & Continental Europe

The most common route to Hawaii from Europe is west via New York, Chicago or Los Angeles. If you're interested in heading east with stops in Asia, it may be cheaper to get a round-the-world ticket instead of returning the same way.

The lowest American Airlines round-trip fares from London, Paris and Frankfurt to Honolulu are usually around US$1200. The best deals are for travel between Monday and Thursday.

United Airlines, Delta Air Lines and Continental Airlines have a similarly priced service to Honolulu from a number of European cities.

You can usually beat the published airline fares at bucket shops and other travel agencies specializing in discount tickets. London is arguably the world's headquarters for bucket shops, and they are well advertised. Two good, reliable agents for cheap tickets in the UK are **Trailfinders** (*☎ 020-7628 7628; Ⓦ www.trailfinders.co.uk; 1 Threadneedle St, London*) and **STA Travel** (*☎ 020-7361 6262; Ⓦ www.statravel.co.uk; 86 Old Brompton Rd, London*).

Australia

Qantas flies to Honolulu from Sydney and Melbourne (via Sydney, but with no change of plane), with round-trip fares ranging from around A$1400 to A$2000, depending on the season. These tickets typically allow a maximum stay of 60 days.

New Zealand

Air New Zealand has Auckland–Honolulu round-trip fares for NZ$1599. These tickets, which have to be purchased at least seven days in advance, allow stays of up to six months; one free stopover is allowed and others are permitted for an additional NZ$100 per stop.

South Pacific Islands

Hawaiian Airlines flies to Honolulu from Tahiti and American Samoa. From American Samoa the round-trip fare starts at US$600. From Tahiti to Honolulu round-trip fares begin at US$725.

For travel from Fiji, Air New Zealand offers a round-trip ticket for US$750. Air New Zealand also flies to Honolulu from Tonga, the Cook Islands and Western Samoa, with round-trip tickets beginning at around US$600 from Western Samoa and US$750 from Tonga and the Cook Islands.

Micronesia

Continental Airlines has nonstop flights from Guam to Honolulu with round-trip fares from US$900.

A more adventurous way to get from Guam, however, would be Continental's island hopper, which stops at the far-flung Micronesian islands of Chuuk, Pohnpei, Kosrae and Majuro before reaching Honolulu. A one-way ticket with free unlimited stopovers is US$730 and there is no advance purchase requirement. If you're coming from Asia, this is a good alternative to a nonstop trans-Pacific flight and a great way to see some of the Pacific's most remote islands without having to spend a lot of money.

Japan

Japan Airlines flies to Honolulu from Tokyo, Osaka, Nagoya, Fukuoka, Hiroshima and Sapporo. Round-trip fares vary a bit with the departing city and the season but, except at busier holiday periods, they're generally around ¥150,000 for a ticket valid for three months.

Fares to Honolulu with Japan's other carrier, All Nippon Airways, are sometimes steeply discounted and can drop to as low as ¥80,000.

Remember that during Japanese holidays, particularly New Year, Golden Week in May, and Obon in August, these fares instantly triple or even quadruple. A few discount travel agencies (mainly in Tokyo, Osaka and Kyoto) offer unbeatable multistop USA tickets for less than ¥100,000.

The American carriers Continental Airlines and Northwest Airlines also have several flights to Honolulu from Japan, with ticket prices that are competitive with those of Japan Airlines.

An interesting alternative, if you're only going one way, is to fly from Japan to Guam (¥74,000) and then pick up a Continental Airlines ticket that allows you to island-hop through much of Micronesia on your way to Honolulu – for around the cost of a direct one-way Japan–Honolulu ticket.

Southeast Asia

There are numerous airlines that fly directly to Hawaii from Southeast Asia.

Northwest Airlines flies to Honolulu from Hong Kong, Bangkok, Manila, Seoul and Singapore. Thai Airways, Korean Air, China Airlines, Singapore Air and Philippine Airlines also offer numerous flights between Southeast Asian cities and Honolulu.

Although there are some seasonal variations, the standard round-trip fares are about US$1000 from Manila, US$1200 from Seoul and Bangkok, US$1400 from Hong Kong and US$1600 from Singapore.

Those fares, however, are the standard published fares, and bucket shops in places such as Bangkok, Singapore and Hong Kong should be able to come up with much better deals – often at around half the price of the standard fares. Remember that a few of these discount agencies are of the hit-and-run variety, so always ask around before you buy. As a minimal precaution against fly-by-night operations, make sure the agency is listed in the phone book.

Also, if you're traveling to the USA from Southeast Asia, you may well find that tickets to the US West Coast are not that much more than tickets to Hawaii, and many allow a free stopover in Honolulu. Consequently, you might want to consider adding the US West Coast on to your Hawaii trip.

SEA

Cruise Ship

In recent years, a handful of cruise ships have begun offering tours that include Hawaii. Many of these trips are referred to as 'repositioning tours,' since they typically visit Hawaii during April, May, September and October on ships that are otherwise used in Alaska during the summer months and in the Caribbean during the winter months.

Because US federal law bans foreign-flagged ships from offering cruises that carry passengers solely between US ports, a foreign port is included on all cruise trips to Hawaii.

Most of these cruises last 10 to 12 days and have fares that start at around US$150 a day per person, based on double occupancy, though discounts and promotions can bring that price down to under US$100 a day. Airfare to and from the departure point is extra.

The typical cruise ship holiday is the ultimate package tour. Other than the effort involved in selecting one, cruises require minimal planning – just pay and show up – and for many people this is a large part of the appeal. Keep in mind that much of your time will be spent at sea, so you'll have notably less time on the islands than someone who flies into Hawaii for a similar time period.

Because cruises cover rooms, meals, entertainment and transportation in one price, they can be relatively good value. While cruises will invariably cost more than lower-end independent travel, they will not necessarily cost more than a conventional package tour that covers airfare and expenses at an upscale resort hotel.

If you've never been on a cruise before, you'll want to ask certain questions before hopping aboard, including: How much time is spent off ship? What is the crew-to-passenger ratio? How big is the ship? What is the size of the room and where is it located? What kind of extra activities and perks, such as free babysitting, are available?

Most travel agents have free cruise-ship brochures, complete with pictures of the ships and cabins. Brochures can also be obtained by contacting the cruise lines directly.

Most Hawaii cruises include stopovers in Honolulu, Maui, Kauai and the Big Island.

Princess Cruises *(☎ 800-568-3262; W www.princess.com)* runs the most cruises and has the most varied trip options. Princess generally offers cruises between Honolulu and Tahiti, or between Honolulu and Vancouver, Canada.

Royal Caribbean Cruise Line *(☎ 800-327-6700; W www.royalcaribbean.com)* typically departs for Honolulu from Ensenada, Mexico, or from Vancouver.

Holland America Cruise Line *(☎ 800-426-0327; W www.hollandamerica.com)* typically departs for Honolulu from San Diego, California, or from Vancouver.

Norwegian Cruise Line *(☎ 800-327-7030; W www.ncl.com)* most commonly goes between Honolulu and Kiribati, but it also has departures from Vancouver and Ensenada, Mexico.

Yacht

Most private yachts weighing anchor in Hawaii do so in Honolulu, though each year a handful of boats also head west from the Big Island to the South Pacific. If you don't have a boat, and you're hoping to get on a crew, your best bet for landing with a skipper is to start poking around the Honolulu ports or the dry dock at Kawaihae on the Big Island in early spring. Experienced crew looking to sail between Hawaii and the US mainland or the US and the South Pacific via Hawaii should try the websites that connect skippers and crews.

Boatcrew.net *(W www.boatcrew.net)* is a well-organized site with a database of boats leaving from various mainland ports. Membership is $10/100 per month/year.

Sailing San Francisco *(W www.sfsailing.com)* lists skippers sailing from the San Francisco Bay Area; a few are long-distance ocean cruisers.

Latitude 38 *(W www.latitude38.com)* has skippers looking for crew to many exotic destinations and lists preferred crew skills (eg, 'have more desire than experience' and 'be willing to bust butt preparing the boat').

ORGANIZED TOURS

There is a slew of package tours available. The basic ones cover just airfare and accommodations, while others add car rentals, sightseeing tours and all sorts of recreational activities.

For those with limited time, package tours can sometimes be the cheapest way to go. As tour consolidators get steeply discounted rates on airfares and hotels, a package tour typically works out cheaper than if you were to book the same flight and hotel separately. Particularly if you are going to Hawaii for a short getaway, package tours can be economical – at times they can be little more than what the airfare alone would cost you.

The costs vary, but one-week tours with airfare and no-frills hotel accommodations usually start around $550 from the US West Coast, $900 from the US East Coast, based on double occupancy. If you want to stay somewhere fancy, the price can easily climb to double that.

Companies with a wide network of offices throughout the USA include **Pleasant Hawaiian Holidays** (W *www.pleasantholidays.com*), **American Express** (W *travel.americanexpress.com*) and **Liberty Travel** (W *www.liberty.com*). Many other companies book package tours, so the best way to see what's being offered in your area may be to just search the Sunday travel section of your newspaper or pick up brochures at a local travel agency. For information on multi-island tours within Hawaii, see the Getting Around chapter.

Specialized Tours

In addition to traditional package tours, some study and environmental tours to Hawaii are available.

Earthwatch International (☎ *800-776-0188, fax 978-461-2332;* W *www.earthwatch.org; 3 Clock Tower Place, Suite 100, PO Box 75, Maynard, MA 01754*) sends volunteers to work on scientific and conservation projects worldwide. Hawaii projects focus on such activities as restoring mountain streams and assisting in humpback whale research. The cost is around US$2000 for programmes that last about two weeks. Meals and accommodations are included, but airfare is not.

Elderhostel (☎ *617-426-8056, 877-426-8056;* W *www.elderhostel.org; 75 Federal St, Boston, MA 02110*) is a nonprofit organization offering educational programmes for those aged 55 or older. The organization has its origins in the youth hostels of Europe and the folk schools of Scandinavia. It offers a full range of ongoing programmes, some on the Big Island in conjunction with the Lyman House Memorial Museum in Hilo and the Volcano Art Center, and others throughout Hawaii affiliated with Hawaii Pacific University. Many programmes focus on Hawaii's people and culture, while others explore the natural environment. The fee is about $650 for one-week programmes, $1300 for two weeks, including accommodations, meals and classes but excluding airfare.

Volunteer Programmes

The **National Park Service** (W *www.nps.gov/volunteer*) has a programme allowing volunteers to work at Hawaii Volcanoes National Park on the Big Island and Haleakala National Park on Maui. Duties may be as varied as staffing information desks, leading guided hikes, trapping predatory animals, monitoring endangered bird and sea turtle species or controlling invasive plants.

Competition is stiff: out of hundreds of applications, only about 25 people can be selected each year. Candidates with a background in natural sciences and a knowledge of first aid are preferred. A three- to six-month (40 hours a week) commitment is required. Volunteers receive no salary or help with airfare, though barracks-style housing and a stipend of $10 a day to help pay for food are provided.

For information, write to **Volunteers In Parks** (*Hawaii Volcanoes National Park;* ☎ *808-985-6092; PO Box 52, Hawaii National Park, HI 96718 • Haleakala National Park; PO Box 369, Makawao, HI 96768*).

The **Student Conservation Association** (☎ *603-543-1700, fax 603-543-1828;* W *www.sca-inc.org; PO Box 550, Charlestown, NH 03603*), sends a handful of people each year to work for three to six months as volunteers at Haleakala National Park in Maui. Positions range from habitat restoration aides to interpretive assistants. Round-trip airfare to Hawaii, a small stipend and accommodations are provided. Anyone over 18 with a high school degree may apply, but preference is generally given to those with a college degree and a background in wildlife, biology or zoology, and experience with IBM-compatible computers and data processing.

Getting Around

AIR

To island-hop around Hawaii, most of the time you'll need to get on a plane, since the only ferries in all of Hawaii are the ones connecting Maui with Lanai and Molokai.

The major airports handling interisland traffic are at Honolulu (on Oahu), Lihue (on Kauai), Kahului (on Maui), and Kona and Hilo (both on the Big Island).

Smaller airports with scheduled commercial flights are Lanai; Molokai (at Hoolehua) and Kalaupapa, both on Molokai; Kapalua West Maui and Hana, both on Maui; and Waimea-Kohala, on the Big Island.

Aloha Airlines and Hawaiian Airlines, the two major interisland carriers, both offer frequent flights in full-bodied jet aircraft between the five major airports.

The smaller airports are served by commuter airlines using prop planes. Island Air, an affiliate of Aloha Airlines, is the largest of the commuter airlines and offers the most extensive schedule.

Airfares

Interisland air travel is competitive in Hawaii and the fares frequently adjust up and down to reflect the competition.

The three largest carriers, Hawaiian Airlines, Aloha Airlines and Island Air, have standard one-way fares of $76 to $105, depending on which flight you catch. The lower-priced fares are usually for flights leaving early in the morning or late in the day.

In addition, there are cheaper promotional deals that come and go. The $55 'flex fare,' for instance, requires a seven-day advance booking and some flexibility on the time of day you fly. Unlike standard tickets, these flex fares are nonrefundable.

Coupons You can save a bundle by using discount coupons instead of purchasing full-fare tickets. The coupons can be used just like tickets. They don't have any advance purchase requirements, and you can make reservations ahead of time before buying them.

INTERISLAND AIR ROUTES

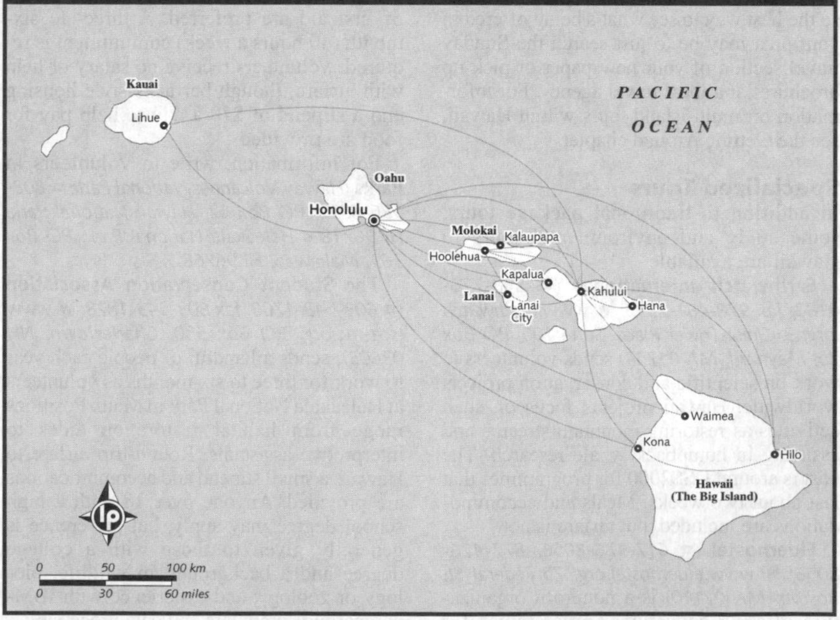

Aloha Airlines offers the best deal at the counter: a $376 book of six unrestricted coupons that can be used on any interisland flight flown by Aloha Airlines. A similar book of six coupons good for flights on both Aloha Airlines and its affiliate Island Air costs $475.

Hawaiian Airlines also sells coupon booklets containing six tickets good for interisland flights between any two destinations it serves. The booklets cost $408 when purchased directly from the airline at the airport ticket counter.

Aloha Airlines' and Hawaiian Airlines' coupon books can be used by any number of people. For example, a couple could use one booklet to make three one-way flights each, or a family of six could use a booklet for a single flight from Honolulu to Maui.

As an alternative to buying the coupon books directly from the airlines, you can buy the coupons individually from discount travel agents around the islands. Prices will vary a bit depending on which travel agency you buy them from, but they are typically priced between $60 and $65.

Hawaiian Airlines also sells its coupons individually for $67 per ticket from Bank of Hawaii ATMs, one of which can be found in the interisland terminal at Honolulu airport (across from Burger King); others can be found around Hawaii at the ubiquitous 7-Eleven stores. You will need to use your PIN number along with your credit card. While these ATM sales have been popular with travelers, some travel agents, who are not keen on losing business, have a less favorable opinion. One Oahu agent tried unsuccessfully to stop the ATM sales, claiming they violated federal banking laws.

Air Passes Aloha Airlines and Hawaiian Airlines offer air passes allowing unlimited air travel for a specified number of consecutive days. You can fly to any destination serviced by the airline as often as you want. The main limitation is that you can fly a maximum of four flights in any one day. Passes are nonrefundable and will not be replaced if lost or stolen.

Aloha Airlines offers a seven-day Island Pass, good for a week of unlimited travel between the Hawaiian Islands on any route offered by Aloha Airlines and Island Air. The cost is $321. Reservations are permitted but not required. You don't need to have a fixed itinerary, and you can buy the pass once you arrive in Hawaii.

Hawaiian Airlines offers a similar pass but allows you to choose between several validity periods ranging from five days to two weeks. The fares for the Hawaiian Airlines passes are $324 for five days, $355 for one week, $419 for 10 days and $479 for two weeks.

Other Discounts Aloha Airlines offers American Automobile Association (AAA) members a 25% discount off the standard ticket fare on all of its interisland flights. Aloha's sister airline, Island Air, offers the same discount on all point-to-point flights (ie, those that don't require a connecting flight). The fare is applicable to AAA cardholders and those traveling with them.

Other schemes come up from time to time, so always ask what promotional fares are currently being offered when you call to make a reservation.

Interisland Airlines

Hawaiian Airlines With more than 150 flights a day, **Hawaiian Airlines** (W *www.hawaiianair.com*), which flies DC-9s, flies to Honolulu, Lihue, Kahului, Kona, Hilo, Molokai and Lanai. Reservation numbers for Hawaiian Airlines are:

Neighbor Islands	☎ 800-882-8811
Oahu	☎ 838-1555
US mainland & Canada	☎ 800-367-5320
American Samoa	☎ 699-1875
Australia	☎ 02-9244 2377
Japan	☎ 03-3214 4774
New Zealand	☎ 09-379 3708
Tahiti	☎ 4215 00
UK	☎ 1753 664406

Aloha Airlines Flying 737s between Honolulu, Lihue, Kahului, Kona and Hilo, **Aloha Airlines** (W *www.alohaairlines.com*) schedules nearly 200 interisland flights a day. Reservation numbers for Aloha Airlines are:

Big Island	☎ 935-5771
Kauai	☎ 245-3691
Maui	☎ 244-9071
Oahu	☎ 484-1111
US mainland & Canada	☎ 800-367-5250
Hong Kong	☎ 852-2826 9118
Osaka	☎ 06-6341 7241
Tokyo	☎ 03-3216 5877
Marshall Islands	☎ 888-477 7010

Island Air Using 18-passenger DeHavilland Dash 6 or 37-passenger Dash 8 aircraft, **Island Air** (W *www.islandair.com)* serves Hawaii's smaller airports. As these prop planes fly lower than jet aircraft, you often get better views. Island Air bookings can also be made through Aloha Airlines.

Island Air has flights to Honolulu, Molokai, Kalaupapa, Kahului, Hana, Kapalua West Maui and Lanai. To some of the more remote sectors, flights are only twice daily, while the more popular routes have around eight flights a day. Reservation numbers for Island Air are:

Neighbor Islands	☎ 800-652-6541
Oahu	☎ 484-2222
US mainland	☎ 800-323-3345

Other Airlines Sometimes consisting of just a single plane, other commuter airlines frequently come and go. Keep in mind that schedules are a bit elastic – if there aren't advance bookings for a flight, the flight is often canceled.

Pacific Wings *(on Maui ☎ 873-0877, from other Hawaiian Islands and the US mainland ☎ 575-4546;* W *www.pacificwings.com)* has scheduled flights between Oahu, Maui, Molokai and Lanai, with charters available to Kauai and the Big Island. Flight frequency varies with the destination, from only once a day to less-trafficked destinations such as Lanai City to dozens of flights in and out of Honolulu each day. Pacific Wings often services airports that other island carriers may not, including Hana and Kapalua on Maui, Waimea on the Big Island and Molokai's Hoolehua airport. Fares vary, but promotional coupons can offer $50 each way to Honolulu, or an unbelievable $50 round trip from Maui to Molokai.

Paragon Air *(on Maui ☎ 244-3356, from other Hawaiian Islands and the US mainland ☎ 800-428-1231;* W *www.paragon-air.com)* flies six-seater prop planes, with flights typically heading out in the morning and coming back in the afternoon. Reservations are required and every seat is a window seat. Special round-trip fares can dip as low as $80 between Maui and most other airports in Maui County, which includes Lanai and Molokai. Otherwise the typical round-trip fare is $110, whether you're flying from Maui to Hana, neighboring Lanai or Kona on the Big Island.

Molokai Air Shuttle *(on Oahu ☎ 545-4988, on Molokai ☎ 567-6847)* flies a five-passenger Piper between Honolulu and Molokai. The flights used to leave on demand when enough people showed up at the airport, but these days you need reservations. Unlike some other airlines, the company charges tourists the same as locals, and offers a round-trip fare of just $65, almost half of any competitor's price. The catch is that you'll need to have your own car (or take a taxi) on the Honolulu side, as Molokai Air Shuttle is located at the back side of the airport, off Lagoon Dr.

BUS

Oahu's excellent island-wide public bus system, called TheBus, makes Oahu the easiest island to get around without a car. You can get almost anywhere on Oahu using TheBus. The schedules are frequent, the service is reliable and the fare is just $1.50 per ride regardless of your destination.

The Big Island has limited public bus service between Kona and Hilo and between Hilo and Hawaii Volcanoes National Park. A couple of other routes serve the Hilo area, but they're geared primarily for commuters and the service is infrequent. While these buses can get you between major towns, they're not practical for short sight-seeing hops.

Kauai has a limited public bus service, operated by the county. It can take visitors between the major island towns and as far north as the village of Hanalei, but it doesn't cover many of the main tourist destinations, such as Waimea Canyon and the lighthouse at Kilauea.

Maui has no county-operated buses. However, a limited private 'shopping shuttle' bus service operates between the Wailea–Kihei area and Kapalua Bay, via Maalaea, Lahaina and Kaanapali. By taking advantage of these inexpensive shuttles, you can get around fairly easily in the heavily touristed areas; however, long-distance routes run infrequently and cost more, and connections are slow. There are also free resort-wide shuttles around Wailea, Kaanapali and Kapalua. There is no public transport to Kahului airport, or around Central Maui, East Maui or the Upcountry.

Molokai has no buses, but there's a mule train!

For detailed information on all of these services, see Getting Around in the individual island chapters.

MOPED & MOTORCYCLE

Motorcycle rentals are not very common in Hawaii, but mopeds are a transportation option in several places. State law requires mopeds to be ridden by one person only and prohibits their use on sidewalks and freeways. Mopeds must always be driven in single file and may not be driven at speeds in excess of 30mph. In Hawaii, all mopeds are limited to a maximum of 2HP (50cc). To drive a moped, you must have a valid driver's license. Hawaiian residents can drive mopeds at age 15, but those with an out-of-state driver's license must be at least 18 years old.

CAR

The minimum age for driving in Hawaii is 18 years, though car rental companies usually have higher age restrictions. If you're under age 25, you should call the car rental agencies in advance to check their policies regarding restrictions and surcharges.

You can legally drive in the state as long as you have a valid driver's license issued by a country that is party to the United Nations Conference on Road & Motor Transport – which covers virtually everyone.

However, car rental companies will generally accept valid foreign driver's licenses only if they're in English. Otherwise, most will require renters to show an international driver's license along with their home license.

Gasoline is about 25% more expensive in Hawaii than on the US mainland, with the price for regular unleaded gasoline averaging about $2 a gallon.

A word of warning: The street addresses on some Hawaiian highways may seem quirky, but there's a pattern to them. You'll often see hyphenated numbers, such as 4-734 Kuhio Hwy. That's because the left side of the number identifies the district breakdown that the post office uses, and the right side identifies the street address within that district. The numbers are in a numerical order – that is, 4-734 comes between 4-732 and 4-736 – but as you drive down the highway, they can throw you because 4-736 may then be followed by 5-002 as a new district starts up.

Road Rules

As with the rest of the USA, driving is on the right-hand side of the road.

Drivers at a red light can turn right after coming to a full stop and yielding to oncoming traffic, unless there's a sign at the intersection prohibiting the turn.

Hawaii requires the use of seat belts for drivers and front-seat passengers. State law also strictly requires the use of child-safety seats for children aged three and under, while four-year-olds must be either in a safety seat or secured by a seat belt. Most of the car rental companies rent child-safety seats, usually for around $5 a day, but they don't always have them on hand so it's advisable to reserve one in advance.

Speed limits are posted and enforced. If you're stopped for speeding, expect to get a ticket, as the police rarely just give warnings. And be aware that cruising unmarked police cars come in the most unlikely models and colors!

Horn honking is considered rude in Hawaii unless required for safety.

Rental

Rental cars are available on all of the islands. With most companies the weekly rate works out far cheaper per day than the straight daily rate. For a small car, the daily rate with unlimited mileage ranges from $30 to $50, while typical weekly rates are $150 to $250. Keep in mind that these are prices with advance reservations; if you haven't booked in advance, you'll typically get stuck paying a higher price.

Rates vary a bit from company to company and within each company depending on season, time of booking and current promotions. If you belong to an automobile club, a frequent-flier programme or a travel

Where's the Highway?

The word 'highway' is used very liberally in Hawaii. Just about every road of any distance gets to be called a highway, including some insignificant secondary roads and even a dirt road or two.

In this book we've given used highway numbers because that's what you'll see on road signs. However, if you're asking for directions, keep in mind that islanders generally refer to roads by name and few pay attention to the route numbers – many wouldn't even be able to tell you the route number of the road on which they live.

club, you'll often be eligible for some sort of discount, so always ask.

One thing to note when renting a car is that rates for midsize and full-size cars are often only a few dollars more per week than the rate for a small car. And because some promotional discounts exclude economy-size cars, at times the lowest rate available may actually be on a larger car.

At any given time any one of the rental companies could be offering the best rates, so you can save money by shopping around. Be sure to ask the agent for the cheapest rate, as the first quote given is not always the lowest.

It's a good idea to make reservations before you visit an island. Walking up to the counter without a reservation will subject you to higher rates, and during busy periods, which can include weekends year-round, cars may be booked out altogether. It can be quite a shock to have planned your Hawaiian vacation around having a car, only to find out when you arrive that none are available!

Another advantage of reservations is that if you have a bottom-line car reserved and none are in the yard when you show up, the upgrade is free.

On daily rentals, most cars are rented on a 24-hour basis, so you could get two days' use by renting at midday and driving around all afternoon, then heading out to explore somewhere else the next morning before the car is due back. Most companies even have an hour's grace period.

In Hawaii, rental rates generally include unlimited mileage, though if you drop off the car at a different location from where you picked it up, there's usually an additional fee and sometimes a mileage charge.

Having a major credit card greatly simplifies the rental process. Without one, some agents simply will not rent vehicles, while others will require prepayment by cash or traveler's checks as well as a deposit of around $300. Some actually do an employment verification and credit check, while others don't do background checks but reserve the right for the station manager to decide whether to rent to you or not. If you intend to rent a car without plastic, it's wise to make your plans well in advance.

You should be aware that many car rental companies are loathe to rent to people who list a camping ground as their address on the island, and a few add 'no camping permitted' to their rental contracts. Most require that you fill in the name and phone number of the place where you're staying.

Most car rental companies officially prohibit use of their cars on dirt roads.

In addition to the rates, you'll be charged a state tax of $3 a day on all car rentals.

Rental Agencies The following are international companies operating in Hawaii whose cars can be booked from offices around the world. The toll-free numbers given are valid from the US mainland.

Alamo (*☎ 800-327-9633; W www.goalamo.com*) has locations at the Kona, Hilo, Kahului and Lihue airports and near the Honolulu and Kapalua West Maui airports.

Avis (*☎ 800-321-3712; W www.avis.com*) is at the main airports on Oahu, Maui, Kauai and the Big Island as well as at four locations around Waikiki. If you're visiting at least two islands, Avis has a multi-island deal that allows you to rent a car at a discounted rate as long as you rent for a minimum of five days on the combined islands.

Budget (*☎ 800-527-0700; W www.budget.com*) is at the main airports on Oahu, Kauai, Molokai, Maui and the Big Island as well as about 35 other locations around Hawaii.

Dollar (*☎ 800-800-4000; W www.dollarcar.com*) is at the airports on Oahu, Kauai, Molokai, Maui and the Big Island as well as numerous locations in Waikiki. It's one of the more liberal agencies for renting to people under the age of 25.

Hertz (*☎ 800-654-3131; W www.hertz.com*) is at the main airports on Oahu, Maui, Kauai and the Big Island as well as the Kapalua West Maui airport.

National (*☎ 800-227-7368; W www.nationalcar.com*) is at the main airports on Oahu, Kauai, Maui and the Big Island and at a couple of locations in Waikiki.

There are a handful of smaller rental agencies in Hawaii as well, but this is one area in which smaller is not necessarily better. For the most part, the big companies offer newer, more reliable cars and fewer hassles.

Insurance Rental companies in Hawaii have liability insurance, which covers people and property that you might hit with their vehicles. Damage to the rental vehicle is not covered. For this, a collision damage waiver

(CDW) is available from car rental agencies, typically for a fee of around $15 a day.

The CDW is not really insurance per se but rather a guarantee that the rental company won't hold you liable for any damages to their car (though even here there are exceptions). If you decline the CDW, you are usually held liable for any damages up to the full value of the car. For recorded information on your legal rights, if damages do occur and you find yourself in a dispute with the rental company, you can call the state **Department of Commerce & Consumer Affairs** (*☎ 808-587-1234 ext 7222*).

If you have collision coverage on your vehicle at home, it might cover damages to car rentals in Hawaii. Check with your insurance company before you make your trip.

Some credit cards, including most 'gold cards' issued by Visa and MasterCard, offer reimbursement coverage for collision damages if you rent the car with that credit card and decline the CDW. If yours doesn't, it may be worth changing to one that does. Check with your credit card company before going on your trip to get the specific details. Be aware that most credit card coverage isn't valid for rentals of more than 15 days or for exotic models, jeeps, vans and 4WD vehicles.

BICYCLE

For the intrepid traveler who doesn't mind blistering heat, strong headwinds and challenging traffic, an adventurous way to get around the Hawaiian Islands is by bicycle.

While it's possible to cycle around all the Hawaiian Islands, when you get away from the coastal routes you'll face some pretty hefty climbs. Because of this, exploring the islands thoroughly by bicycle is an option best suited for well-conditioned cyclists.

Hawaii has been slow to adopt cycle-friendly traits. A few new road projects now include cycle lanes, but such lanes are still relatively rare on the islands. Hawaii's roads also tend to be narrow, and many of the main coastal routes are heavily trafficked.

You'll find places to rent bicycles on all the islands.

If you bring your own bike to Hawaii, you can transport it on interisland flights for $20. The bicycle can be checked at the counter, the same as any baggage, but you'll need to prepare the bike first either by wrapping the handlebars and pedals in foam or by fixing the handlebars to the side and removing the pedals.

For island-specific cycling information, see the Activities and Getting Around sections in the island chapters. See also Mountain Biking in the Activities chapter.

HITCHHIKING

Hitchhiking is never entirely safe in any country in the world, and Lonely Planet doesn't recommend it. Travelers who decide to hitch should understand that they are taking a small but potentially life-threatening risk. People who nevertheless choose to hitch will be safer if they travel in pairs, let someone know where they are planning to go, keep their luggage light and with them at all times, and sit by a door.

BOAT

Ferry

Hawaii's only interisland passenger ferries operate between Maui and Lanai, and between Maui and Molokai. From Maui, the ferries depart from Lahaina Harbor from the public pier in front of the Pioneer Inn. Advance reservations are advised.

Expeditions (*☎ 808-661-3756, 800 695-2624; W www.go-lanai.com*) runs a 24-passenger ferry five times daily between Maui and Lanai. Not only is it much cheaper than flying, but in winter you'll have a fair chance of seeing whales along the way. The boat leaves Lahaina Harbor at 6:45am, 9:15am, 12:45pm, 3:15pm and 5:45pm, depositing passengers an hour later at Manele Bay, a stone's throw from Hulopoe Beach. Return departures from Lanai are at 8am, 10:30am, 2pm, 4:30pm and 6:45pm. The one-way adult/child fare is $25/20. You can buy tickets from the office at the Lahaina pier, or after boarding the boat when coming from Lanai.

Molokai Princess (*☎ 808-667-6165, 800-275-6969; W www.molokaiferry.com*) sails across the thrilling yet rough 'Pakalolo Channel' between Maui and Molokai at least once daily. Commuters regularly stay up on the sun deck, sharing beer and getting drenched by the waves; if you want to stay dry, stash your stuff down below for the 90-minute trip on this 100ft-long vessel. Departures from Lahaina are at 5:15pm daily and 7:30am Monday, Wednesday, Friday and Saturday. The boat leaves Kaunakakai at 5:30am Monday to Saturday, 3:30pm

Sunday, and 2:30pm Monday, Wednesday, Friday and Saturday. The one-way adult/child fare is $42.40/21.20; a book of six one-way coupons costs $185.

Cruise Ship

Norwegian Cruise Line *(☎ 800-327-7030; W www.ncl.com)* is the only company that operates a cruise between the Hawaiian Islands that starts and ends in Hawaii. However, because it's a foreign-registered ship, all cruises also make a jaunt down to Kiribati. The seven-day interisland cruise stops in Kiribati, Maui (Kahului Harbor), Kauai (Nawiliwili Harbor), Hilo and Honolulu. Longer 10- and 11-day itineraries include Kona on the Big Island. Staterooms for the seven-day route start at $800 and top out at $25,000 for an onboard villa.

For information on cruises that begin outside Hawaii, see Cruise Ship in the Getting There & Away chapter.

TAXI

All the main islands have taxis, with the fares based on mileage regardless of the number of passengers. Rates vary, as they're set by each county, but average about $10 per 5 miles.

ORGANIZED TOURS

Day Tours

A number of companies operate half-day and full-day sight-seeing bus tours on each island. Also readily available are specialized adventures, such as whale-watching cruises, bicycle tours down Haleakala, snorkeling trips to Lanai and boat cruises along the Kona Coast, just to mention a few. All of these tours can be booked after arrival in Hawaii. For details, see the Activities and Organized Tours sections of each island chapter.

Overnight Tours

If you want to visit another island while you're in Hawaii but only have a day or two to spare, it might be worth looking into 'overnighters,' which are minitours to the Neighbor Islands that include round-trip airfare, car rental and hotel accommodations.

Rates depend on the accommodations you select, with a one-night package typically starting at $140 per person, based on double occupancy. You can add days for about $65 per person per day.

For those who have an air pass, the same tour companies also sell room and car packages minus the airfare – though the room and car packages offered directly by some hotels may work out cheaper.

The largest companies specializing in overnighters are **Roberts Hawaii** *(on Oahu ☎ 523-9323, from the Neighbor Islands & US mainland ☎ 800-899-9323 W www.robertshawaii.com)* and **Pleasant Island Holidays** *(on Oahu ☎ 922-1515, from the Neighbor Islands ☎ 800-654-4386 W www.pleasantholidays.com)*.

Helicopter Tours

Helicopter tours are readily available from a number of companies on the main islands. They go to some amazing places, with flights over active volcanoes, along towering coastal cliffs and even above inaccessible waterfalls. Prices vary depending on the destination and the length of the flight, with a 30-minute tour averaging about $125 per passenger. Morning flights often have the clearest weather and the smoothest air conditions, but cloudy weather can occur at any time, so keep an eye on the weather forecast.

Before you book a helicopter flight, be ready to make some inquiries. Be aware, for instance, that not every seat in all copters is a window seat. A common configuration is two passengers up front with the pilot, and four people sitting across the back. The two back middle seats simply don't give the photo opportunities proclaimed in the brochures. It's like being a midseat rear passenger on a scenic drive – only there's no getting out at viewpoints! People are usually seated according to weight, so if you're dishing out a lot of money, make sure you know in advance where you'll be sitting.

Oahu

When people think of Hawaii it's often places on Oahu that spring to mind – renowned sightseeing attractions such as Waikiki, Pearl Harbor and Sunset Beach.

Oahu is by far the most developed of the Hawaiian islands and, quite appropriately, has long been nicknamed 'The Gathering Place.' The island is home to nearly 75% of the state's population. It's an urban scene, with highways, high-rises and crowds. If you're looking for a getaway vacation, you'd best continue on to one of the Neighbor Islands.

Still, despite all its development, in terms of scenic beauty Oahu holds its own. It has fluted mountains, aqua-blue bays, and valleys carpeted with pineapple fields.

Oahu has excellent beaches. Hanauma Bay, east of Waikiki, is the most visited snorkeling spot in the islands. The North Shore sees Hawaii's top surfing action, and Kailua (which is on the windward side of the island) has Hawaii's most popular beach for windsurfing.

Honolulu is a modern city with an intriguing blend of Eastern and Western influences. Cultural offerings range from Chinese lantern parades and traditional hula performances to ballet and museums. Honolulu has the only royal palace in the USA, fine city beaches and parks, and some great hilltop views. The city is also a diner's delight, with a wonderful array of ethnic restaurants.

Oahu can be the cheapest Hawaiian island to visit. It's the only one you can get around easily without your own transportation, thanks to the inexpensive, island-wide bus system. Oahu also has some of Hawaii's cheapest accommodations, including several hostels and Ys.

Almost all of Oahu's hotels and tourist facilities are centered in Waikiki. Waikiki resembles a hybrid of Miami Beach and Tokyo, with a population density rivaling the latter. There's a lot happening in Waikiki, but to get a better feel for what Hawaii's all about, you need to step out of it. Be sure to wander through the bustling markets in Honolulu's Chinatown, take a hike along one of the quiet mountain trails of Tantalus and spend some time in the surfer's haven of Haleiwa.

Highlights

- Strolling Waikiki Beach at night, as city lights glisten and the surf laps on the shore
- Visiting the brand-new Hawaii State Art Museum
- Watching the pros ride the waves at the North Shore's Banzai Pipeline
- Reliving history at Pearl Harbor's military memorial
- Windsurfing in the turquoise waters off Kailua Beach

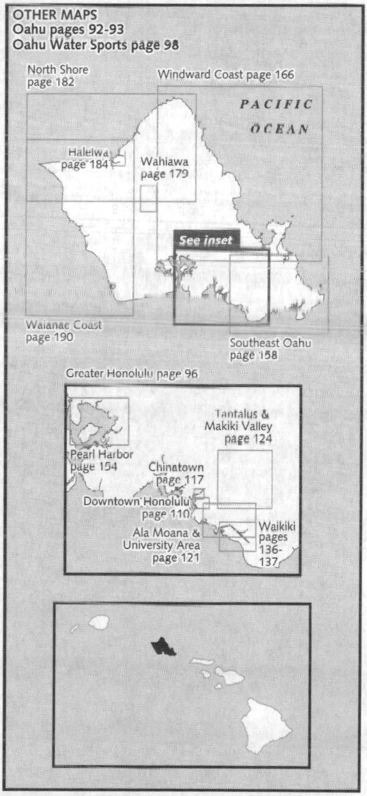

HISTORY

Oahu was the final island conquered by Kamehameha the Great in his campaign to unite Hawaii under his rule.

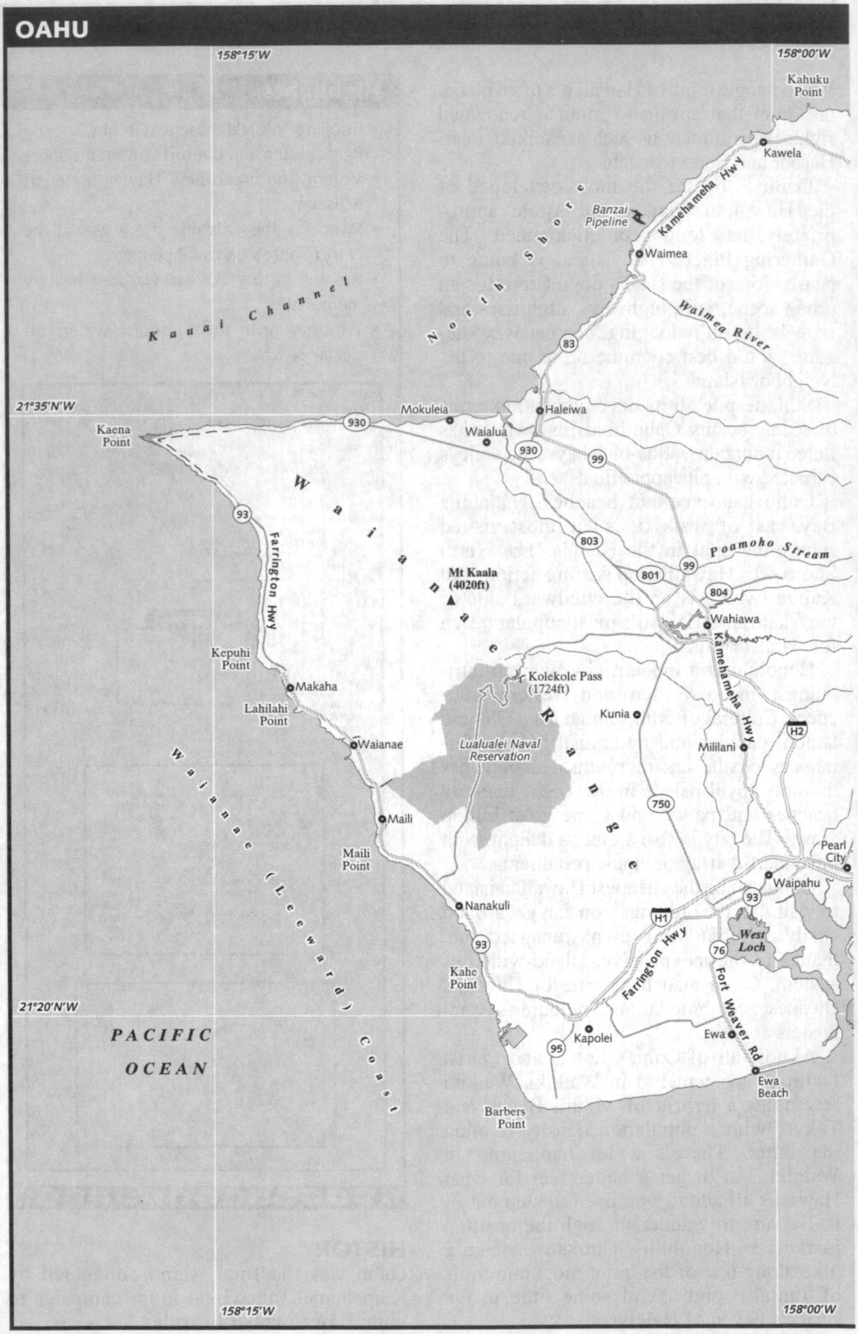
OAHU
158°15'W
158°00'W
Kahuku Point
Kawela
Kamehameha Hwy
Banzai Pipeline
North Shore
Waimea
Waimea River
Kauai Channel
83
21°35'N'W
Mokuleia
Haleiwa
Kaena Point
930
Waialua
99
Waianae Range
93
Farrington Hwy
803
Poamoho Stream
Mt Kaala (4020ft)
801
804
Wahiawa
Kepuhi Point
Kolekole Pass (1724ft)
Makaha
Lahilahi Point
Kunia
H2
Waianae
Lualualei Naval Reservation
Mililani
Waianae (Leeward) Coast
750
Maili
Maili Point
Pearl City
Waipahu
Nanakuli
H1
West Loch
76
Fort Weaver Rd
Kahe Point
21°20'N'W
PACIFIC OCEAN
Kapolei
95
Ewa
Ewa Beach
Barbers Point

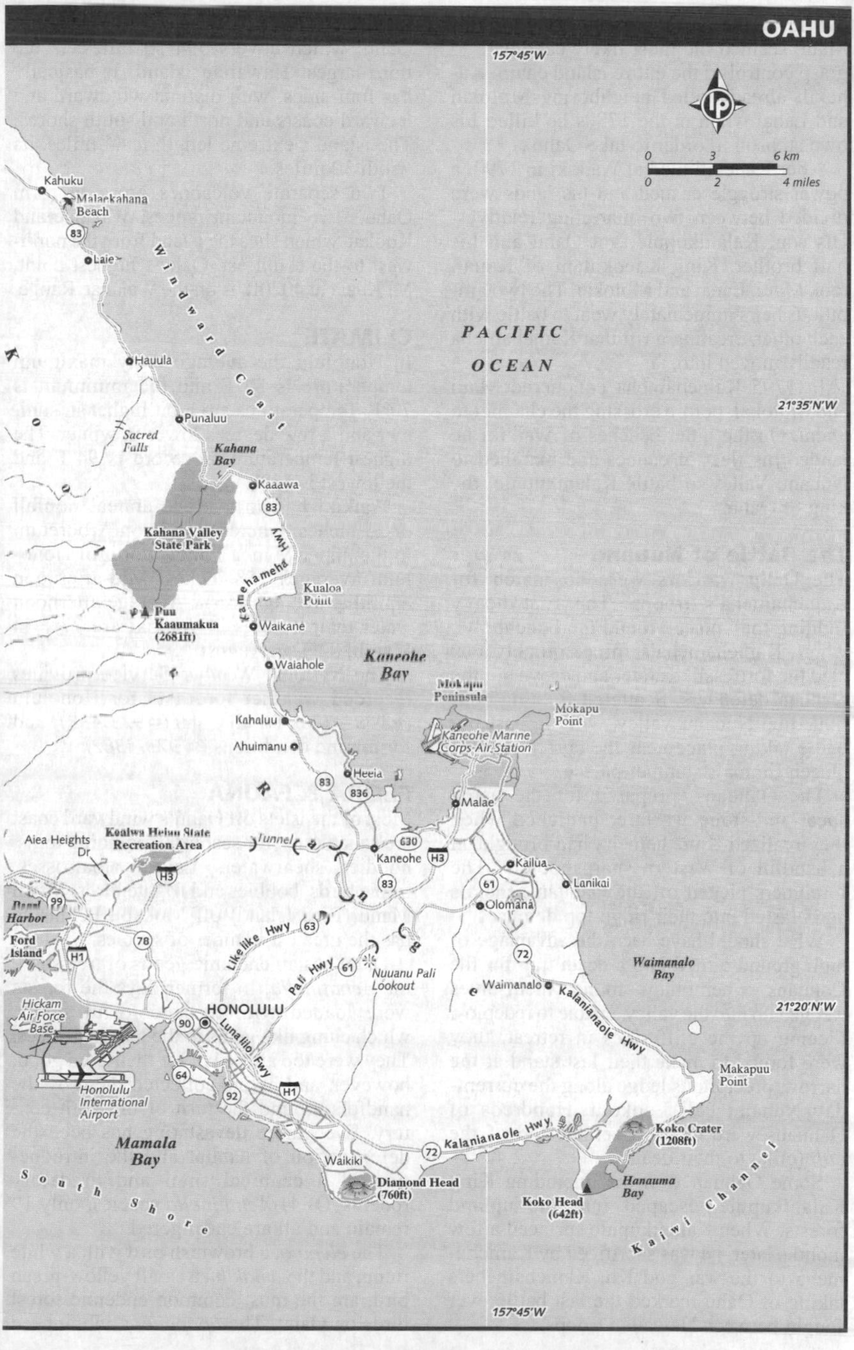
OAHU
157°45'W
0 3 6 km
0 2 4 miles
PACIFIC OCEAN
21°35'N'W
21°20'N'W
Kahuku
Malaekahana Beach
Laie
Windward Coast
Hauula
Punaluu
Sacred Falls
Kahana Bay
Kaaawa
Kahana Valley State Park
Kamehameha Hwy
Kualoa Point
Puu Kaaumakua (2681ft)
Waikane
Waiahole
Kaneohe Bay
Mokapu Peninsula
Mokapu Point
Kaneohe Marine Corps Air Station
Kahaluu
Ahuimanu
Heeia
Malae
Aiea Heights Dr
Keaiwa Heiau State Recreation Area
Tunnel
Kaneohe
Kailua
Lanikai
Olomana
Pearl Harbor
Ford Island
Likelike Hwy
Pali Hwy
Nuuanu Pali Lookout
Waimanalo Bay
Waimanalo
Kalanianaole Hwy
Hickam Air Force Base
HONOLULU
Lunalilo Fwy
Honolulu International Airport
Makapuu Point
Koko Crater (1208ft)
Mamala Bay
Waikiki
Diamond Head (760ft)
Hanauma Bay
Koko Head (642ft)
South Shore
Kaiwi Channel
157°45'W

Prior to that, Kahekili, the aging king of Maui, seemed the most likely candidate to grasp control of the entire island chain. Kahekili already ruled neighboring Molokai and Lanai when in the 1780s he killed his own stepson in order to take Oahu.

After Kahekili died at Waikiki in 1794, a power struggle ensued and his lands were divided between two quarreling relatives. His son, Kalanikupule, got Oahu and his half brother, King Kaeokulani of Kauai, took Maui, Lanai and Molokai. The two ambitious heirs immediately went to battle with each other, creating a rift that Kamehameha readily moved into.

In 1795 Kamehameha conquered Maui and Molokai, before crossing the channel to Oahu. On the quiet beaches of Waikiki he landed his fleet of canoes and marched to Nuuanu Valley to battle Kalanikupule, the king of Oahu.

The Battle of Nuuanu

The Oahu warriors were no match for Kamehameha's troops. The first heavy fighting took place around the Punchbowl, where Kamehameha's forces quickly circled the fortresslike crater and drove out the Oahuan defenders. Scattered fighting continued up Nuuanu Valley, with the last big battle taking place near the current site of Queen Emma's summer palace.

The Oahuans, prepared for the usual spear-and-stone warfare, panicked when they realized Kamehameha had brought in a handful of Western sharpshooters. The foreigners picked off the Oahuan generals and blasted into their ridge-top defenses.

What should have been the advantage of high ground turned into a death trap for the Oahuans when they found themselves wedged up into the valley, unable to redeploy. Fleeing up the cliff sides in retreat, they were forced to make their last stand at the narrow, precipitous ledge along the current-day Nuuanu Pali Lookout. Hundreds of Oahuans were driven over the top of the *pali* (cliff) to their deaths.

Some Oahuan warriors, including King Kalanikupule, escaped into the upland forests. When Kalanikupule surfaced a few months later, he was sacrificed by Kamehameha to the war god Ku. Kamehameha's taking of Oahu marked the last battle ever fought between Hawaiian troops.

GEOGRAPHY

Oahu, which covers 594 sq miles, is the third-largest Hawaiian island. It basically has four sides, with distinct windward and leeward coasts and north and south shores. The island's extreme length is 44 miles, its width 30 miles.

Two separate volcanoes arose to form Oahu's two mountain ranges, Waianae and Koolau, which slice the island from the northwest to the southeast. Oahu's highest point, Mt Kaala at 4020ft, is on the Waianae Range.

CLIMATE

In Honolulu the average daily maximum temperature is 84°F and the minimum is 70°F. Temperatures are a bit higher in summer and a few degrees lower in winter. The highest temperature on record is 94°F and the lowest is 53°F.

Waikiki has an average annual rainfall of 25 inches, whereas the Lyon Arboretum in the upper Manoa Valley, north of Honolulu, averages 158 inches. Mid-afternoon humidity averages 56%. Average afternoon water temperatures in Waikiki are 77°F in March, 82°F in August.

The National Weather Service provides **recorded weather forecasts** for Honolulu *(☎ 973-4380)*, for all Oahu *(☎ 973-4381)* and for marine conditions *(☎ 973-4382)*.

FLORA & FAUNA

Most of the islets off Oahu's windward coast are sanctuaries for seabirds, including terns, noddies, shearwaters, Laysan albatrosses, tropic birds, boobies and frigate birds. Moku Manu (Bird Island) off Mokapu Peninsula has the greatest number of species.

Oahu has an endemic genus of tree snail, the *Achatinella*. In former days the forests were loaded with these colorful snails, which clung like gems to the leaves of trees. They were too attractive for their own good, however, and hikers collected them by the handfuls around the turn of the 20th century. Even more devastating has been the deforestation of habitat and the introduction of a cannibal snail and predatory rodents. Of 41 *Achatinella* species, only 19 remain and all are endangered.

The *elepaio*, a brownish bird with a white rump, and the *amakihi*, a small yellow-green bird, are the most common endemic forest birds on Oahu. The *apapane*, a vibrant red honeycreeper, and the *iiwi*, a bright vermilion bird, are less common.

The only other endemic forest bird, the Oahu creeper, may already be extinct. This small yellowish bird looks somewhat like the *amakihi,* which makes positive identification difficult. The last sighting of the Oahu creeper was in 1985 on the Poamoho Trail.

The most prominent urban birds are pigeons, doves, red-crested cardinals and common mynas. The myna, introduced from India, is a brown, 'spectacled' bird that congregates in noisy flocks. Introduced game birds include pheasants, quails and francolins.

Oahu has wild pigs and goats in its mountain valleys. Brush-tailed rock-wallabies, accidentally released in 1916, reside in the Kalihi Valley. Although rarely seen, the wallabies are of interest to zoologists because they are thought to be an extinct subspecies in their native Australia.

Oahu boasts some excellent botanical gardens. Both Foster Botanical Garden (on the edge of Honolulu's Chinatown), and the Lyon Arboretum (just south of the Manoa Falls, northeast of Honolulu), are home to unique native and exotic species, some of which have disappeared in the wild.

GOVERNMENT

The 'City & County of Honolulu' is the unwieldy name attached to the single political entity governing all of Oahu.

Technically, the City & County of Honolulu also includes the Northwestern Hawaiian Islands, which stretch 1300 miles beyond Kauai to Kure Atoll.

Like Hawaii's other counties, there are no municipal governments. Oahu is administered by a mayor and a nine-member council, elected for four-year terms.

ECONOMY

Oahu's unemployment rate hovers around 5%. Tourism is the largest sector of the economy, accounting for about 30% of Oahu's jobs. It's followed by defense and other government employment, which together account for 22% of all jobs.

Nearly one-fifth of Oahu is still used for agriculture, mainly pineapple production. Sugar production was phased out in 1996. On the North Shore, around Haleiwa and Waialua, coffee trees are being cultivated in former cane fields.

POPULATION & PEOPLE

Oahu's population is 876,000, with Honolulu accounting for nearly half of the total. Other sizable population centers are Pearl City, Kailua, Kaneohe and Kapolei.

Oahu's ethnic breakdown is 20% Japanese, 19% Caucasian, 20% part-Hawaiian (less than 1% pure Hawaiian), 19% mixed ancestry other than part-Hawaiian, 12% Filipino and 5% Chinese, with numerous other Pacific and Asian minorities.

ORIENTATION

Almost all visitors to Oahu land at Honolulu international airport, the only civilian airport on the island. It's on the western outskirts of the Honolulu district, 9 miles west of Waikiki.

H1, the main south-shore freeway, is the key to getting around the island. H1 connects with Hwy 72, which runs around the southeast coast; with the Pali (61) and Likelike (63) Hwys, which lead to the windward coast; with Hwy 93, which leads up the Waianae (leeward) Coast; and with H2, Hwys 99 and 750, which run through the center of the island on the way to the North Shore.

Incidentally, H1 is designated as a US *interstate* freeway – an amusing term to describe a road on an island state in the middle of the Pacific.

Rush hour traffic is heavy heading toward Honolulu in the mornings and away from it in the evenings.

Directions on Oahu are often given by using landmarks, in addition to the Hawaii-wide terms *mauka* (inland) and *makai* (seaward). If someone tells you to go 'Ewa' (a land area west of Honolulu) or 'Diamond Head' (east of Honolulu), it simply means to head in the direction of these areas.

Maps

The free tourist magazines contain simple island maps, but if you plan to explore the island in a rented car or spend time in Honolulu, it's worth picking up a good road map.

The **American Automobile Association** *(AAA; ☎ 593-2221; 1270 Ala Moana Blvd, Honolulu)* puts out a reliable road map of Honolulu and Oahu. Members of AAA, or an affiliated automobile club, can get a free map from the AAA office or from their local affiliate before leaving home. If you're not an AAA member, you can buy a similar

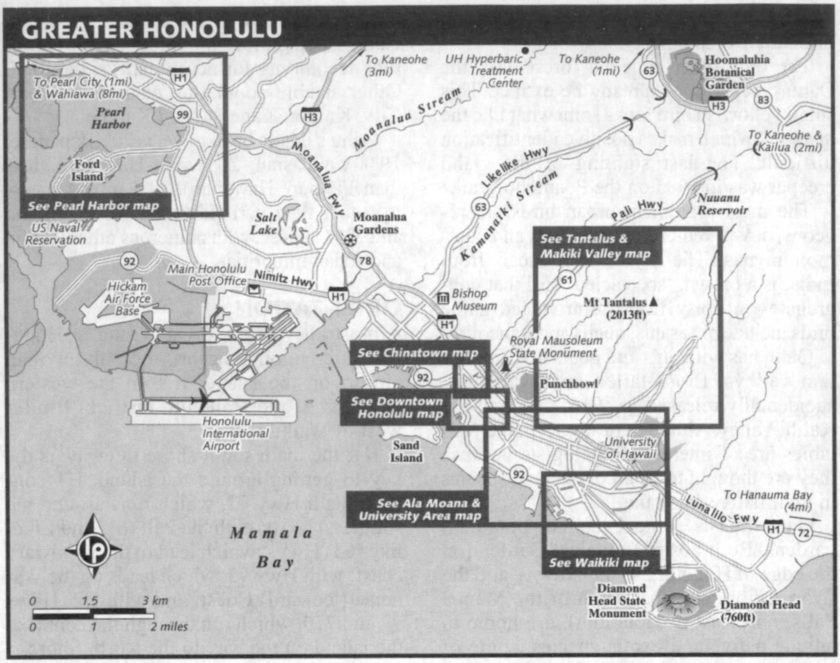

road map published by Rand McNally in convenience stores throughout Oahu.

The most comprehensive map reference – though it has more detail than most visitors will need – is the 200-page *Bryan's Sectional Maps Oahu* atlas, which shows and indexes virtually every street on the island.

INFORMATION

Tourist Offices

The administrative office of the **Hawaii Visitors and Convention Bureau** *(HVCB; ☎ 923-1811, 800-464-2924; ⓔ info@hvcb.org; 2270 Kalakaua Ave, Suite 801, Waikiki, HI 96815)* can mail you general tourist information on Oahu and the rest of Hawaii.

To pick up tourist brochures in person, go to the **HVCB visitor information office** *(☎ 924-0266; 2250 Kalakaua Ave, Suite 502, Waikiki; open 8am-4:30pm Mon-Fri, 8am-noon Sat & Sun)*, which is in the Waikiki Shopping Plaza.

Money

There are nearly 150 banks throughout Oahu, so it's never a problem finding one in the major towns. The **Bank of Hawaii**, Hawaii's largest bank, has a branch at the airport and another in central Waikiki. Elsewhere around Oahu, banks and ATMs can easily be found in central areas and in shopping centers.

Post

There are 35 post offices on Oahu. The **main Honolulu post office** *(3600 Aolele St; open 7:30am-8:30pm Mon-Fri, 8am-4:30pm Sat)* is not in central Honolulu but is at the north side of the airport, opposite the interisland terminal.

All general delivery mail sent to you in Honolulu must be picked up at the main post office. Any mail sent general delivery to the Waikiki post office or other Honolulu branches will either go to the main post office or be returned to the sender. If you're receiving mail in Honolulu, have it addressed to you c/o General Delivery, Main Post Office, 3600 Aolele St, Honolulu, HI 96820-3600.

Newspapers & Magazines

The *Honolulu Advertiser* (ⓦ *www.honoluluadvertiser.com)* and the *Honolulu Star-Bulletin* (ⓦ *www.starbulletin.com)*, which are

Honolulu's two main newspapers, are published daily and have websites that allow you to browse them online.

Oahu also has numerous weekly newspapers, many of which can be picked up free around the island. The most useful of these for visitors is the *Honolulu Weekly* (W *www.honoluluweekly.com*), a progressive paper with an extensive entertainment section.

Numerous free tourist magazines are available at the airport and all around Waikiki. They can be a good source of visitor information, although most of it is paid advertising. *This Week Oahu* and *Spotlight's Oahu Gold* usually have the best discount coupons.

Radio & TV

Oahu has about 30 commercial AM and FM radio stations, as well as three public radio stations. Radio station Da KINE (105.1 FM) plays classic Hawaiian music. Hawaii Public Radio is broadcast by radio stations KHPR (88.1 FM), KKUA (90.7 FM) and KIPO (89.3 FM).

There are a dozen network-affiliated TV stations and numerous cable TV stations. Channels 10 and 11 feature ongoing visitor information and ads geared to tourists.

Bookstores

Oahu has many bookstores with good collections of Hawaiiana books, travel guides and general fiction. National chains such as **Borders, Barnes & Noble** and **Waldenbooks** have shops in the major shopping malls throughout Oahu.

Libraries

Hawaii's statewide library system has its main library, the Hawaii State Library, in downtown Honolulu, next to Iolani Palace. There are 21 other public libraries around Oahu, including ones in Waikiki, Kailua and Kaneohe.

Medical Services & Emergencies

The number for **emergencies** (☎ *911*) should be dialed for all police, fire and ambulance emergencies.

Oahu has several hospitals with 24-hour emergency services, including **Queen's Medical Center** (☎ *538-9011; 1301 Punchbowl St, Honolulu*) and **Straub Clinic & Hospital** (☎ *522-4000; 888 S King St at Ward Ave, Honolulu*). For 24-hour service in Kailua, there's the **Castle Medical Center** (☎ *263-5500; 640 Ulukahiki St*).

Divers with the bends are taken to the **UH Hyperbaric Treatment Center** (☎ *587-3425; 347 N Kuakini St, Honolulu*).

A **suicide and crisis line** (☎ *521-4555*) operates 24 hours a day.

SWIMMING

Oahu is ringed with white-sand beaches, ranging from crowded resort strands to quiet hidden coves. The island has more than 50 beach parks, most with rest rooms and showers; half are patrolled by lifeguards.

The island's four distinct coastal areas have their own peculiar seasonal water conditions. When it's rough on one side, it's generally calm on another, so you can find places to swim year-round.

Oahu's south shore extends from Barbers Point to Makapuu Point and encompasses the most popular beaches on the island, including the extensive white sands of **Waikiki** and **Ala Moana**.

The windward coast extends from Makapuu Point to Kahuku Point. Lovely **Kailua Beach Park**, Oahu's busiest windsurfing spot, also has good swimming conditions and is the best all-around beach on the windward side. Other nice windward beaches are at **Waimanalo Bay** (in the southeast), **Kualoa Point** and **Malaekahana**.

The North Shore extends from Kahuku Point to Kaena Point. Although the North Shore has spectacular waves in winter, it can be as calm as a lake during the summer months. There are attractive sandy strands at **Haleiwa**, **Waimea** and **Sunset Beach**.

The leeward Waianae Coast extends from Kaena Point to Barbers Point. It's the driest, sunniest side of Oahu, with long stretches of white sands. The most popular beach on this side is **Makaha**, which sees big surf in the winter, but has suitable swimming conditions in summer.

SURFING

Oahu has 594 defined surfing sites, nearly twice as many as any of the other Hawaiian islands. In winter, the North Shore gets some of Hawaii's most spectacular surf, with swells reaching 20ft to 30ft. This is the home of **the Banzai Pipeline**, **Sunset Beach** and some of the world's top surfing competitions.

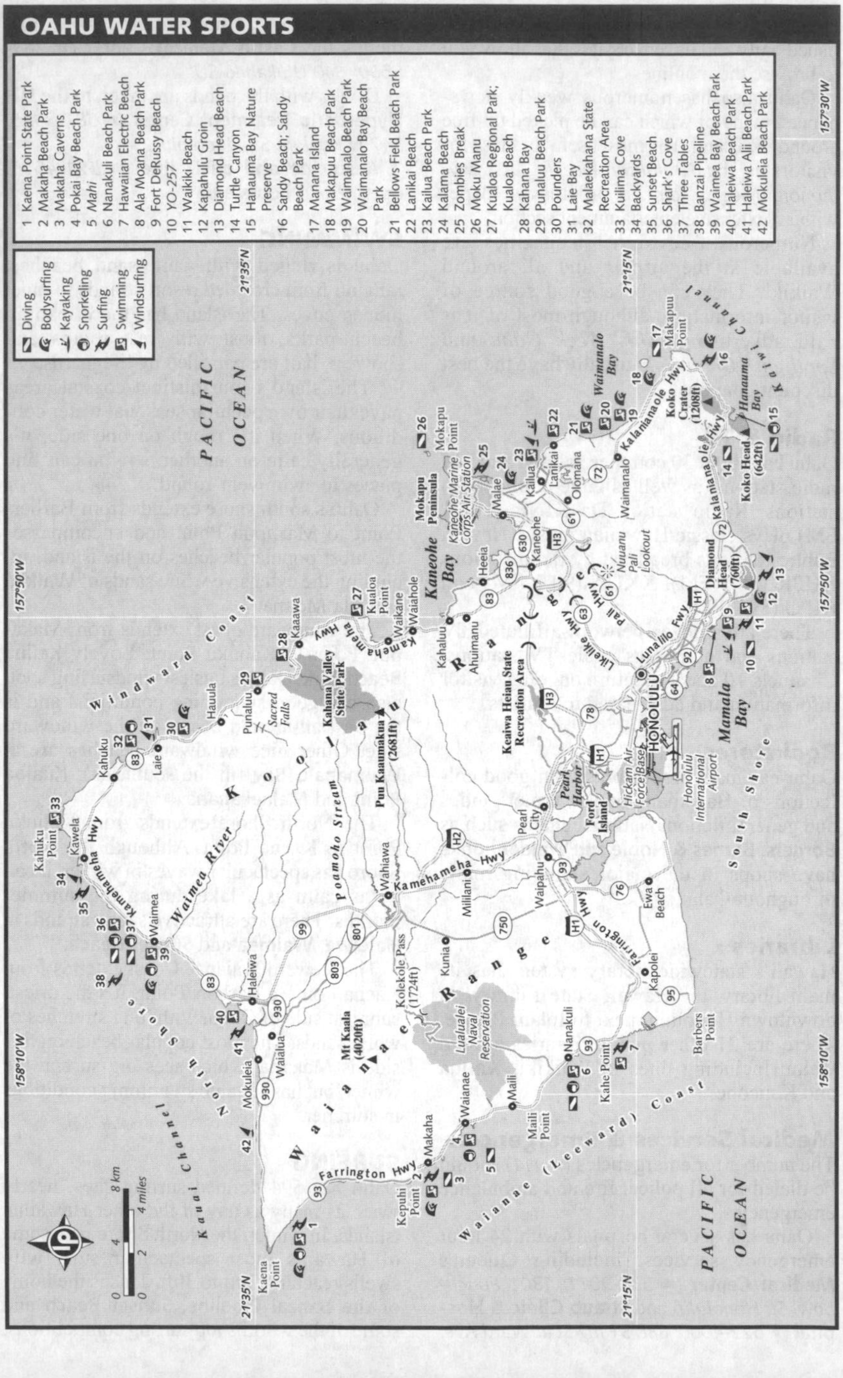
OAHU WATER SPORTS
Diving
Bodysurfing
Kayaking
Snorkeling
Surfing
Swimming
Windsurfing
1 Kaena Point State Park
2 Makaha Beach Park
3 Makaha Caverns
4 Pokai Bay Beach Park
5 Mahi
6 Nanakuli Beach Park
7 Hawaiian Electric Beach
8 Ala Moana Beach Park
9 Fort DeRussy Beach
10 YO-257
11 Waikiki Beach
12 Kapahulu Groin
13 Diamond Head Beach
14 Turtle Canyon
15 Hanauma Bay Nature Preserve
16 Sandy Beach; Sandy Beach Park
17 Manana Island
18 Makapuu Beach Park
19 Waimanalo Beach Park
20 Waimanalo Bay Beach Park
21 Bellows Field Beach Park
22 Lanikai Beach
23 Kailua Beach Park
24 Kalama Beach
25 Zombies Break
26 Moku Manu
27 Kualoa Regional Park; Kualoa Beach
28 Kahana Bay
29 Punaluu Beach Park
30 Pounders
31 Laie Bay
32 Malaekahana State Recreation Area
33 Kuilima Cove
34 Backyards
35 Sunset Beach
36 Shark's Cove
37 Three Tables
38 Banzai Pipeline
39 Waimea Bay Beach Park
40 Haleiwa Beach Park
41 Haleiwa Alii Beach Park
42 Mokuleia Beach Park
PACIFIC OCEAN
PACIFIC OCEAN
Kauai Channel
North Shore
Windward Coast
Waianae (Leeward) Coast
South Shore
Kaiwi Channel
Mamala Bay
Kaneohe Bay
Waimanalo Bay
Hanauma Bay
Waianae Range
Koolau Range
Waimea River
Poamoho Stream
Kaena Point
Kahuku Point
Mokapu Peninsula
Mokapu Point
Makapuu Point
Koko Head (642ft)
Koko Crater (1208ft)
Diamond Head (760ft)
Mt Kaala (4020ft)
Puu Kaaumakua (2681ft)
Kolekole Pass (1724ft)
Kahana Valley State Park
Sacred Falls
Keaiwa Heiau State Recreation Area
Lualualei Naval Reservation
Kaneohe Marine Corps Air Station
Hickam Air Force Base
Honolulu International Airport
Pearl Harbor
Ford Island
Nuuanu Pali Lookout
HONOLULU
Haleiwa
Waialua
Mokuleia
Waimea
Kahuku
Laie
Hauula
Punaluu
Kaaawa
Kualoa
Waikane
Waiahole
Kahaluu
Ahuimanu
Heeia
Kaneohe
Kailua
Lanikai
Olomana
Waimanalo
Wahiawa
Mililani
Pearl City
Waipahu
Kunia
Ewa Beach
Kapolei
Barbers Point
Nanakuli
Kahe Point
Maili
Maili Point
Waianae
Makaha
Kepuhi Point
Kamehameha Hwy
Farrington Hwy
Kalanianaole Hwy
Likelike Hwy
Pali Hwy
Lunalilo Fwy
158°10'W
157°50'W
157°30'W
21°35'N
21°15'N
8 km
4 miles

There's also good winter surfing at **Makaha Beach** on the Waianae Coast.

In summer, when the south shore sees its finest surfing waves, **Waikiki** and **Diamond Head** have some of the best breaks.

Oahu has two telephone services geared to surfers. The **Surf News Network** *(☎ 596-7873)* has a recorded surf line, updated several times a day, reporting winds, wave heights and tides. The **National Weather Service** *(☎ 973-4383)* also provides recorded tide and surf conditions.

The knockout website **Hawaii Surfing News** *(W www.holoholo.org/surfnews)* is brimming with everything from surf conditions to upcoming surfing events.

The county's **Haleiwa Surf Center** *(☎ 637-5051; Haleiwa Alii Beach Park)*, on the North Shore, holds free surfing lessons from 9am to 11am weekends between September and April. Surfboards are provided – all you need to bring is a swimsuit and suntan lotion!

Surf-N-Sea *(☎ 637-9887; 62-595 Kamehameha Ave)*, in Haleiwa (also on the North Shore), rents surfboards for $5 for the first hour, $3.50 each additional hour, or $24 a day. In addition, Surf-N-Sea gives two-hour surfing lessons for $65, including board rental. Surf-N-Sea also sells new and used surfboards.

In Waikiki, surfing lessons can be arranged at the **beach concession stands** at Kuhio Beach Park on Kalakaua Ave. The going rate for a private one-hour lesson is $40; the cost drops to $30 per person if there are two or more people. These Waikiki concession stands also rent surfboards for around $8 an hour or $25 a day.

Planet Surf *(☎ 638-5648; 2570 Kalakaua Ave, Waikiki)*, at the Aston Waikiki Beach Hotel, and **Planet Surf** *(☎ 638-1110)* opposite Pupukea Beach Park in Waimea, rent surfboards for $17 to $20 per 24 hours.

Go Nuts Hawaii *(☎ 926-3367; 159 Kaiulani Ave)*, in Waikiki, also rents surfboards for $17 to $20 per 24 hours.

BODYSURFING & BOOGIE BOARDING

In southeast Oahu, **Waimanalo Beach Park** and the nearby **Bellows Field Beach Park** have gentle shorebreaks good for beginner bodysurfers.

The two hottest (and most dangerous) spots for expert bodysurfers are **Sandy** and **Makapuu Beach Parks** in southeast Oahu. Other top shorebreaks are at **Makaha** on the Waianae Coast, **Waimea Bay** on the North Shore, **Kalama Beach** in Kailua and **Pounders** in Laie on the windward coast.

The most popular boogie-boarding place in Waikiki is at **Kapahulu Groin**.

If you're going to be a lot of boogie boarding, consider buying your own equipment. However, there are plenty of places to rent boards.

The **beach concession stands** on Waikiki Beach charge about $6 an hour, $20 a day for boogie-board rentals.

A less-expensive option, **Planet Surf** rents boogie boards for $10 a day. See its entry under Surfing, earlier, for contact details.

Surf-N-Sea, in Haleiwa, rents boogie boards for $4 for the first hour, $3 for each additional hour. See its entry under Surfing, earlier, for contact details.

Kailua Sailboards & Kayaks *(☎ 262-2555; 130 Kailua Rd)*, in the Kailua Beach Center, rents boogie boards for $12 a half day.

WINDSURFING

Kailua Bay is Oahu's number one windsurfing spot. It has good year-round trade winds and both flat-water and wave conditions in different sections of the bay. Windsurfing shops set up vans at Kailua Beach Park on Monday to Friday and on Saturday mornings, renting boards and giving lessons. It's a great place for beginners to try the sport.

Other good windsurfing spots include **Diamond Head Beach**, for speed and jumps; **Laie Bay**, for open-water cruising; **Mokuleia Beach Park**, for consistent North Shore winds; and **Backyards**, off Sunset Beach, for the island's highest sailable waves. In Waikiki, **Fort DeRussy Beach** is the main windsurfing spot.

Naish Hawaii *(☎ 262-6068, 800-767-6068; 155A Hamakua Dr, Kailua)* – as in windsurfing champion Robbie Naish – has its shop in downtown Kailua, but can deliver equipment to Kailua Beach. Rental rates vary with the board and rig: beginner equipment costs $20 for two hours or $30 for a full day; intermediate and advanced equipment is $35 a half day, $45 a full day. Naish Hawaii gives introductory group lessons for $35 for three hours. For $55 you can get a 1½-hour private lesson that includes an additional two hours of board use.

The other major player is **Kailua Sailboards & Kayaks** *(☎ 262-2555; 130 Kailua Rd)*, which rents beginner equipment for $29 a half day, $39 for a full day or $160 for a week; high-performance boards cost $39 for a half day, $49 for a day or $199 for a week. Three-hour, group beginner lessons cost $49. Kailua Sailboards & Kayaks also offers a package that includes transportation from Waikiki, lessons and gear for $69.

Waikiki Pacific Windsurfing *(☎ 949-8952)*, which you'll find at the Prime Time Sports concession stand on Fort DeRussy Beach, rents windsurfing equipment for $25 an hour or $50 for a half day; add $15 more for an hour-long lesson.

In Haleiwa, **Surf-N-Sea** rents windsurfing equipment at $12 for the first hour and $8 for each additional hour. Two-hour windsurfing lessons are available for $65. See Surfing, earlier, for Surf-N-Sea's contact details.

DIVING

There's a lot of commercial marine activity in the seas around Oahu. Consequently, Oahu's reefs are not as pristine as those of the Neighbor Islands. If you're searching for the most spectacular coral and clearest waters, there are places, such as the Kona side of the Big Island, that easily outshine Oahu.

Nonetheless, there are several reefs in shallow waters around Oahu that make good diving sites. In addition, Oahu offers the best wreck diving in Hawaii.

Top summer dive spots include the caves and ledges at **Three Tables** and **Shark's Cove** on the North Shore and the **Makaha Caverns** on the Waianae Coast. On the south shore, Hanauma Bay has calm diving conditions most of the year and the outer part of the bay has abundant marine life. There are a number of other popular dive spots between Hanauma and Honolulu that provide good winter diving.

Popular wrecks, both of which were deliberately sunk to create artificial reefs, are the **Mahi**, a 165ft naval research ship sunk off Waianae, and **YO-257**, a 110ft navy vessel sunk west of Waikiki. Both of these wrecks are at depths of 60ft to 100ft, have colorful colonies of coral and sponges, and are suitable for intermediate-level divers.

Two-tank dives for certified divers average $90 to $100. The following shops are all five-star PADI operations:

Aaron's Dive Shop (☎ 262-4158, ⓔ aarons@aloha.com) 307 Hahani St, Kailua
Breeze Hawaii Diving Adventure (☎ 735-1857, ⓔ aloha@breezehawaii.com) 3014 Kaimuki Ave, Honolulu
Dive Authority-Honolulu (☎ 596-7234) 333 Ward Ave, Honolulu
Hawaiian Island Aquatics (☎ 622-3483) 1640 Wilikina Dr, Wahiawa
Ocean Concepts (☎ 696-7200, ⓔ ocw@oceanconcepts.com) 85–371 Farrington Hwy, Waianae
South Sea Aquatics (☎ 922-0852, ⓔ ssa@aloha.net) 2155 Kalakaua Ave, Honolulu
See In Sea Scuba (☎ 528-2311, ⓔ info@divehawaii.com) 670 Auhai St, Honolulu
Waikiki Diving Center (☎ 922-2121, ⓔ info@waikikidiving.com) 424 Nahua St, Honolulu

SNORKELING

For snorkeling, **Hanauma Bay** on the south shore is the most frequented year-round spot. In summer, **Pupukea Beach Park**, on the North Shore, provides excellent snorkeling with far less activity than Hanauma.

If you plan on doing a lot of snorkeling, it may be cheaper to buy your own equipment. For those who only want to try it a few times, plenty of places offer rentals by the day or week.

Planet Surf rents snorkel sets for $5 a day, $20 a week. See Surfing, earlier, for Planet Surf's contact details.

Snorkel Bob's *(☎ 735-7944; 702 Kapahulu Ave)*, in Waikiki, rents snorkel sets from $4 to $9 a day, $10 to $30 a week, depending on the quality.

In Haleiwa, **Surf-N-Sea** *(☎ 637-9887; 62-595 Kamehameha Hwy)* rents snorkel sets for $6.50 a half day, $9.50 for 24 hours.

In Kailua, **Kailua Sailboards & Kayaks** *(☎ 262-2555; 130 Kailua Rd)* rents snorkel sets for $12 a day.

If you're going to Hanauma Bay, you can rent snorkel sets at **the beachside concession stand** for $6 a day.

KAYAKING

Kailua Beach, which has a couple of uninhabited nearshore islands that you can paddle to, is the most popular place for kayaking on Oahu.

Busy **Waikiki** is not the most ideal spot for kayaking, although there are kayak rentals available on the beach there as well; stick with the Fort DeRussy Beach area, as it's less crowded than the central Waikiki Beach strip.

With the two Kailua companies listed, you can arrange to pick up your kayak right at the beach.

Twogood Kayaks Hawaii *(☎ 262-5656; 345 Hahani St, Kailua)* rents one-person kayaks for $25/32 per half/full day; two-person kayaks cost $32/42 per half/full day.

Kailua Sailboard & Kayaks *(☎ 262-2555; 130 Kailua Rd, Kailua)* has one- and two-person kayaks at the same rate as Twogood. In addition, it offers a $59 package, which includes transportation from Waikiki, kayak rental and lunch, leaving Waikiki at 8am and returning at 3pm daily.

In Waikiki, **Prime Time Sports** *(☎ 949-8952)* on Fort DeRussy Beach rents one-person kayaks for $10 an hour, two-person kayaks for $20 an hour.

HIKING

The Diamond Head trail that leads three-quarters of a mile from inside the crater of **Diamond Head** up to its summit is the most popular hike on Oahu. It's easy to reach from Waikiki (see Diamond Head under South east Oahu later in this chapter) and ends with a panoramic view of greater Honolulu.

Another nice, short hike is the **Manoa Falls Trail**, just a few miles above Waikiki, where a peaceful path through an abandoned arboretum of lofty trees leads to a waterfall.

The **Tantalus and Makiki Valley area** has the most extensive trail network around Honolulu, with fine views of the city and surrounding valleys. Amazingly, although it's just 2 miles above the city hustle and bustle, this lush forest reserve is unspoiled and offers quiet solitude.

At **Keaiwa Heiau State Park**, northwest of Honolulu, the Aiea Loop Trail leads 4½ miles along a ridge that offers views of Pearl Harbor, Diamond Head and the Koolau Range.

The **Kaena Point Trail** is a scenic coastal hike through a natural area reserve on the westernmost point of Oahu. There are also longer forestry trails in the same area.

On the windward side, you'll find a pleasant hour-long hike out to **Makapuu Point Lighthouse**.

There are also short walks from the **Nuuanu Pali Lookout** (in the Honolulu Watershed Forest Reserve), within **Hoomaluhia Botanical Garden** and along many **beaches**.

For details on these and other hikes, see the respective sections of this chapter.

Guided Hikes

Notices of hiking-club outings are generally listed in the Friday editions of the *Honolulu Star-Bulletin* and *Honolulu Advertiser*.

By joining these outings, you can meet and hike with ecologically minded islanders. Also, the clubs sometimes have permits to go into restricted conservation areas that are otherwise not accessible to individual hikers. Wear sturdy shoes and, on longer hikes, bring lunch and water.

The **Sierra Club** *(☎ 538-6616; W www.hisierraclub/org)* leads hikes and other outings on Saturday and Sunday. These can range from easy 2-mile hikes to strenuous 10-mile treks. Most outings begin at 8am at the Church of the Crossroads, 2510 Bingham St, Honolulu. The hike fee is $3.

The Hawaii Audubon Society *(☎ 528-1432; W hawaii-audubon.50megs.com)* leads bird-watching hikes once a month, usually on a weekend. The suggested donation is $2. Binoculars and a copy of *Hawaii's Birds* are recommended.

Naturalists from the **Hawaii Nature Center** *(☎ 955-0100)*, at the forestry base-yard camp in Makiki, lead hikes on either Saturday or Sunday most weekends. The cost is $8 for nonmembers. Trails range from easy walks, such as the 2½-mile Makiki Loop Trail, to hardy hikes like the 6-mile trek up Mt Kaala, Oahu's highest point. Reservations are required.

RUNNING

Oahuans are big on jogging. It's estimated that Honolulu has more joggers per capita than any other city in the world. **Kapiolani Park and Ala Moana Park** are two favorite jogging spots. There's also a well-beaten 4.8-mile run around Diamond Head crater.

Oahu has about 75 road races each year, from 1-mile fun runs and 5-mile jogs to competitive marathons, biathlons and triathlons. For an annual schedule of running events with times, dates and contact addresses, write to the **Department of Parks & Recreation** *(City & County of Honolulu, 650 S King St, Honolulu, HI 96813)* or view the schedule at W www.co.honolulu.hi.us.

Oahu's best-known race is the **Honolulu Marathon**, which in recent years has mushroomed into the third-largest marathon in the USA. Held in mid-December, it's an open-entry event, with an estimated half of the 25,000 entrants being first-time marathon runners. For information, send a self-addressed, stamped envelope to **Honolulu Marathon Association** *(3435 Waialae Ave, No 208, Honolulu, HI 96816)*. You can download entry forms at W www.honolulumarathon.org.

The Department of Parks & Recreation holds a **Honolulu Marathon Clinic** at 7:30am most Sundays at the Kapiolani Park Bandstand. It's free and open to everyone from beginners to seasoned marathon runners. Runners join groups of their own speed.

CYCLING

It's possible to cycle your way around Oahu, but there's a lot of traffic to contend with, especially in the greater Honolulu area. The state's Department of Transportation publishes a *Bike Oahu* map with possible routes divided into those for novice cyclists, those for experienced cyclists and routes that are not bicycle-friendly. The map can usually be found at the HVCB visitor information center in Waikiki (see Tourist Offices, earlier) and at bike shops.

The Bike Shop, with locations in Honolulu *(☎ 596-0588; 1149 S King St)* as well as Kailua *(☎ 261-1553; 270 Kuulei Rd)*, has good-quality bikes for $16 a day, use of a helmet included.

Planet Surf *(☎ 638-5648; 2570 Kalakaua Ave)*, at the Aston Waikiki Beach Hotel in Waikiki and *(☎ 638-1110)* opposite Pupukea Beach Park in Waimea, rents bikes for $10 a day. **Go Nuts Hawaii** *(☎ 926-3367; 159 Kaiulani Ave)*, in Waikiki, rents bikes for $15 a day. Also in Waikiki are **Blue Sky Rentals** *(☎ 947-0101; 1920 Ala Moana Blvd)* as well as **Coconut Cruisers** *(☎ 924-1646; 2301 Kalakaua Ave)*, at the south side of the Royal Hawaiian Shopping Center; both rent bicycles for $20 a day.

The nonprofit **Hawaii Bicycling League** *(☎ 735-5756; W www.hbl.org)* holds bike rides around Oahu nearly every Saturday and Sunday, ranging from 10-mile jaunts to 60-mile treks. Some outings are restricted to road travel and others include off-road sites. Rides are free and open to the public; the main requisite is that helmets be worn.

HORSEBACK RIDING

Three stables offer horseback riding on the windward side of Oahu.

Correa Trails *(☎ 259-9005; 41-050 Kalanianaole Hwy, Waimanalo)* has one-hour guided trail rides along the Koolau Range (in southeast Oahu), with scenic ocean views, for $50 including transportation from Waikiki.

Kualoa Ranch *(☎ 237-8515; Kamehameha Hwy, Kualoa)*, opposite Kualoa Regional Park, has one-hour trail rides for $35 and 1½-hour rides for $49, going along the foot of the Koolau Range.

Turtle Bay Resort *(☎ 293-8811; 57-091 Kamehameha Hwy, Kahuku)*, in Kahuku, offers 45-minute trail rides for $35 and 1½-hour sunset rides for $65.

TENNIS

Oahu has 182 county tennis courts. If you're staying in Waikiki, the most convenient locations are the 10 lighted courts at **Ala Moana Beach Park**; the 10 unlighted courts at the **Diamond Head Tennis Center**, at the Diamond Head end of Kapiolani Park; and the four lighted **Kapiolani Park** courts, opposite the Waikiki Aquarium. Court time at these 24-hour county facilities is free and on a first-come, first-served basis.

The **Turtle Bay Resort** *(☎ 293-8811)* in Kahuku has 10 courts and charges $12 per person per day, with one-hour playing time guaranteed. The resort also has a pro shop and gives lessons.

GOLF

Oahu has five 18-hole municipal golf courses: **Ala Wai Golf Course** *(☎ 733-7387; Kapahulu Ave)* on the inland side of the Ala Wai Canal, near Waikiki; **Pali Golf Course** *(☎ 266-7612; 45-050 Kamehameha Hwy, Kaneohe)*; **Ted Makalena Golf Course** *(☎ 675-6052; Waipio Point Access Rd, Waipahu)*; **Ewa Villages Golf Course** *(☎ 681-0220; Ewa)*; and **West Loch Golf Course** *(☎ 675-6076; 91-1126 Okupe St, Ewa Beach)*.

Green fees for 18 holes at any of these municipal courses are $42 per person, plus an optional $16 for a gas-powered cart. The reservation system is the same for all municipal courses: call ☎ 296-2000 and key information into the recorded system as prompted. The earliest bookings are taken just three days in advance for visitors and one week in advance for resident golfers.

The Ala Wai Golf Course, which lays claim to being the 'busiest in the world' is the only municipal course near Waikiki. Local golfers who can book earlier in the week usually take all the starting times, leaving none for visitors. However, visiting golfers who don't mind a wait may show up and put their names on the waiting list; as long as the entire golfing party waits at the course, they'll usually get a chance to golf before the day is over. If you come without clubs, you can rent them for $25.

Oahu also has a couple dozen other golf courses, including: private courses restricted to members only; resort courses, charging upwards of $100 to play; and military courses for use by members of the armed services.

SKYDIVING & GLIDING

Skydiving and glider rides are offered at the Dillingham Airfield at Mokuleia on the North Shore. Sometimes there are discounted deals, so always ask about specials and promotions.

For around $200, **Skydive Hawaii** (☎ *637 9700)* will attach you to the hips and shoulders of a skydiver so you can jump together from a plane at 13,000ft, free fall for a minute and finish off with 10 minutes of canopy ride. The whole process, including basic instruction, takes about 1½ hours. Participants must be at least 18 years of age and weigh less than 200lb. Arrangements can also be made to take up experienced skydivers for solo jumps. Planes take off daily, weather permitting.

Glider Rides (☎ *677-3404)* offers 20-minute flights in an engineless piloted glider craft, which is towed by an airplane and then released to slowly glide back to earth. Flights leave daily between 10:30am and 5:30pm, weather permitting. The cost is $100 for one person or $120 for two.

Soar Hawaii (☎ *637-3147)* generally offers the best prices for glider rides, with deals that can be as low as $35 per person for a 20-minute ride. For thrill seekers, it also offers acrobatic rides ($110) that feature barrel rolls, spirals and wingovers – a ride you won't soon forget.

ORGANIZED TOURS

Sightseeing tours by van or bus are offered by **E Noa Tours** (☎ *591-2561)*, **Polynesian Adventure Tours** (☎ *833-3000)* and **Roberts Hawaii** (☎ *539-9400, 800-831-5541)*.

All three companies offer a good variety of tours, including full-day circle-island tours that average $55/30 an adult/child. The circle-island tours typically include Diamond Head crater, the southeast Oahu sights, Byodo-In temple, Sunset Beach, Waimea Falls Park and a drive past the pineapple fields of central Oahu on the return to Waikiki. Some tours include a visit to the Polynesian Cultural Center in Laie instead of the stop at Waimea Falls Park.

There are also several half-day tours that cost about half the price of the circle-island tour. The most popular one includes the main downtown Honolulu sights, Punchbowl crater and the USS *Arizona* Memorial.

Waikiki Trolley

There are a couple of open-air, trolley-style buses that offer services between Waikiki and Honolulu's main tourist sights. Both services run along set routes, with pass-holders free to jump on and off the trolley as often as they like.

The **Rainbow Trolley** (☎ *539-9495)* is both the best value and the simplest service to use. It has 25 stops in all, running from Waikiki in a loop around Kalakaua Ave, past the Honolulu Zoo and along Kuhio Ave and then continuing to the Ala Moana Center, Ward Centre, Iolani Palace, Honolulu Academy of Arts, Chinatown and the Aloha Tower Marketplace. A trolley picks up at each stop about once every 20 minutes from around 8:30am to 10pm daily. It costs $10/18/30 for a one-/two-/four-day pass for adults, $5/8/10 for children under 12 years of age.

The **Waikiki Trolley** (☎ *593-2822)* is pricier and more complicated to use as it has different routes. Its main line, the 'red line,' has about two dozen stops, mostly paralleling the Rainbow Trolley route. It operates every 20 minutes between 8:30am and 4:30pm daily and charges $18/8 for adults/children for a one-day pass.

Cruises

Numerous sunset sails, dinner cruises and party boats leave daily from Kewalo Basin, just west of Ala Moana Beach Park. Rates range from $25 to $100, with dinner cruises averaging about $65. Many provide transport to and from Waikiki and advertise various come-ons and specials; check the free tourist magazines for the latest offers.

Navatek Cruises *(☎ 973-1311)* offers various cruise options aboard a sleek, high-tech catamaran designed to minimize rolling. Of interest are the two-hour whale-watching cruises ($45) that operate from January to April, leaving at 8:30am and again at noon daily. The boat leaves from Pier 6, 350 yards south of Aloha Tower.

A handful of small catamarans depart from Waikiki Beach, including the **Manu Kai** *(☎ 946-7490)*, which docks behind the Duke Kahanamoku statue and charges $10 for one-hour sails. The **Mai Tai** *(☎ 922-5665)*, which departs from Gray's Beach in front of the Sheraton Waikiki, offers 1½-hour sails for $20, longer sunset sails for $30.

Atlantis Submarines *(☎ 973-9811)* has a 65ft, 48-passenger sightseeing submarine that descends to a depth of 100ft. The tour lasts 1¾ hours, including boat transport to and from the sub. About 45 minutes are spent cruising around a ship and two planes that were deliberately sunk to create a dive site. Tours leave from Hilton Hawaiian Village on the hour from 11am to 3pm daily. The cost for adults is $90 for the 11am or 3pm outing, $60 for the others. The cost for children 12 and younger is $40 on all trips.

ACCOMMODATIONS

Some 90% of Oahu's 40,000 visitor rooms are in Waikiki. All but two of Oahu's resort hotels are found in Honolulu.

The Waikiki-Honolulu area contains a wide range of options. The least-expensive places are the two HI-affiliated youth hostels and the handful of private hostel-type lodgings; all of them have dorm beds for under $20. After that, there are rooms at Ys for $30 and a few budget Waikiki hotels that start around $50. Waikiki has lots of mid-range hotels in the $75 to $125 range, as well as high-priced luxury hotels.

To lure customers, some large chains such as Outrigger offer a free rental car if you request it at the time of booking. A few independent hotels occasionally throw in a car as well; it never hurts to ask whenever you book any hotel. If you had planned on renting a car, it can be a tidy savings.

Camping

Camping is allowed at numerous county beach parks, one botanical garden and four state parks.

All county and state camping grounds on Oahu are closed on Wednesday and Thursday nights, ostensibly for maintenance, but also to prevent permanent encampments.

Although thousands of visitors use these camp sites each year without incident, Oahu has more of a reputation for problems than other islands. Rip-offs, especially at roadside and beachfront camping grounds, are not unknown. Camping along the Waianae Coast is not recommended.

State Parks Camping is allowed by permit at Sand Island and Keaiwa Heiau, both in the greater Honolulu area, and at Malaekahana State Recreation Area and Kahana Valley State Park, both on the windward coast.

Keaiwa Heiau is a good choice for an inland park, while the best choice for a coastal state park is the Malaekahana State Recreation Area.

Camping is limited to five nights per month in each park. The cost is $5 per night per site. Permit applications can be made no more than 30 days before the first camping date.

Applications may be made to the **Division of State Parks** *(☎ 587-0300; State Office Building, 1151 Punchbowl St, room 131; postal address Box 621, Honolulu, HI 96809; open 8am-3:30pm Mon-Fri)*.

County Beach Parks Camping is free at several county beach parks, but permits are required.

County camping permits are not available by mail, but can be picked up between 7:45am and 4pm Monday to Friday at the **Department of Parks & Recreation** *(☎ 523-4525; 650 S King St)* in downtown Honolulu in the Honolulu Municipal Building on the corner of King and Alapai Sts.

Permits are also available from satellite city halls, including one at the **Ala Moana Center** *(☎ 973-2600)*, where permits are issued 9am to 4:30pm Monday to Thursday, 9am to 5:45pm Friday, 8am to 4pm Saturday. Other satellite city halls are in Kailua, Kaneohe and Wahiawa.

County camping is allowed from 8am Friday to 8am Wednesday, except at Bellows Field Beach Park, which is open only on weekends.

Backcountry Camping The state forestry division allows backcountry camping along some valley and ridge trails, including in Hauula on the windward coast.

All backcountry camping requires a permit from the **Division of Forestry & Wildlife** *(☎ 587-0166; 1151 Punchbowl St, room 325, Honolulu, HI 96813; open 7:45am-4:15pm Mon-Fri)*. There are no fees.

Camping Supplies **The Bike Shop** *(☎ 596-0588; 1149 S King St, Honolulu)* rents internal-frame backpacks and lightweight, two-person tents. The rate for either item is $35 for up to three days, $70 for a week.

Omar the Tent Man *(☎ 677-8785; 94-158 Leoole St, Waipahu)*, west of Pearl Harbor, rents sleeping bags or external-frame backpacks for $15 for up to three days or $20 per week, and stoves or lanterns for $14 for up to three days, $18 a week. It also rents four-person cabin-tents for $52 for up to three days, $57 a week.

ENTERTAINMENT

Oahu has a lively and varied entertainment scene, ranging from beachside hula shows and traditional Hawaiian music to theater performances and rock concerts. The vast majority of Oahu's entertainment takes place in Waikiki, with central Honolulu being the runner-up venue.

The best place to look for up-to-date entertainment information is in the free *Honolulu Weekly* newspaper and in the Friday edition of the *Honolulu Advertiser*.

More detailed information can be found in the Entertainment sections under specific destinations. For festivals, fairs and sporting events, see the Public Holidays & Special Events section in the Facts for the Visitor chapter.

Luaus

Oahu's two main commercial luaus, **Paradise Cove** *(☎ 973-5828)* and **Germaine's Luau** *(☎ 949-6626)*, are both huge, impersonal affairs held nightly out near the Barbers Point area. Both cost around $50, which includes the bus ride from Waikiki hotels (about one hour each way), a buffet dinner, drinks, a Polynesian show and related hoopla. Children pay about half price.

A pricier, but less crowded, luau is held beachside in Waikiki at the **Royal Hawaiian Hotel** *(☎ 931-7194; 2259 Kalakaua Ave)* on Monday; the cost is $81 for adults, $48 for children aged 5 to 12.

With all luaus, it's best to book in advance, because if a large tour group comes in, they can easily sell out.

SHOPPING

Honolulu is a large, cosmopolitan city with plenty of sophisticated shops selling designer clothing, jewelry and the like. For general crafts, the best deals are usually found at one of the craft shows that are periodically held in city parks (check the newspapers for schedules).

For kitsch souvenirs, there are scores of shops selling fake Polynesian stuff, from Filipino shell hangings and carved coconuts to cheap seashell jewelry and wooden tiki statues. The largest single collection of such shops is at the International Market Place in Waikiki.

In addition, Waikiki has no shortage of swimsuit and T-shirt shops or quick-stop convenience marts. The prolific ABC discount stores are often the cheapest places to buy more mundane items such as beach mats and sunblock, but also have good prices on macadamia nuts, a popular souvenir item.

For local flavor, the **Aloha Stadium Swap Meet** *(☎ 486-1529)*, at Aloha Stadium near Pearl Harbor, has some 1500 vendors and is open from 5am to 3pm on Wednesday, Saturday and Sunday. Private **shuttle buses** *(reservations ☎ 924 9292, 479-3447)* to the flea market pick shoppers up at Waikiki hotels and charge $6 for the round-trip.

Hawaiiana Souvenirs

The **Hula Supply Center** *(☎ 941-5379, 2346 S King St)*, in Ala Moana, sells feather leis, calabash gourds, hula skirts and the like. Although they're intended for Hawaiian musicians and dancers, some of the items would make interesting souvenirs, and prices are reasonable. **Kamaka Hawaii** *(☎ 531-3165; 550 South St, Honolulu)* specializes in handcrafted ukuleles made on Oahu, but expect to pay nearly $500. You can also find ukuleles – imported, but cheaper – at **Hawaiian Ukulele Co** *(☎ 536-3228)* at the Aloha Tower Marketplace, in downtown Honolulu; prices begin around $80.

CDs and cassettes of Hawaiian music also make good souvenirs. You'll find an excellent collection of both classic and contemporary

Hawaiian music at **Borders** (which has a branch at the Ward Centre in Honolulu) and at **Tower Records** *(☎ 941-7774; 611 Keeaumoku)* north of the Ala Moana Center. Both companies allow you to listen to various CDs before you buy.

GETTING THERE & AWAY

The vast majority of flights into Hawaii land at Honolulu international airport, the only commercial airport on Oahu. See the Getting There & Away chapter in the front of this book for information on flights to Oahu.

Honolulu also serves as the hub for the main interisland air carriers and has frequent services to all of the Neighbor Islands. For details on flights to the Neighbor Islands, see the Getting Around chapter in the front of this book.

Honolulu International Airport

This airport *(HNL; ☎ 836-6413)* is modern and has been extensively upgraded and expanded. Although it can be a busy place, it's not particularly difficult to get around.

The airport has all the expected services, including fast-food restaurants, lounges, newsstands, sundry shops, lei stands, gift shops, duty-free shops and a medical clinic with a nurse on duty 24 hours a day.

You'll find a visitor information booth, car-rental counters and hotel courtesy phones in the baggage claim area. A free bus shuttle, called Wiki Wiki, connects the more distant parts of the airport by linking the main terminals with the interisland terminals. It can be picked up in front of the main lobby (on the upper level) and in front of the interisland gates.

If you need to exchange money, Thomas Cook has booths around the airport, including in the international arrival area and the central departure lobby next to the barber shop. On the opposite side of the same barber shop, you'll find an ATM belonging to American Express. If you're in no hurry, you can avoid transaction fees by going to the Bank of Hawaii on the ground level of the terminal, across the street from baggage claim D.

If you arrive early for a flight and are looking for something to do, the free Pacific Aerospace Museum in the main departure lobby has multimedia displays on aviation. There's also an attractive garden on the concourse level.

GETTING AROUND

Oahu is an easy island to get around, whether you travel by public bus or private car.

Traffic in Honolulu can get quite jammed during rush hour, from 7am to 9am and 3pm to 6pm Monday to Friday. Expect heavy traffic in both directions on H1 during this time, as well as when heading toward Honolulu in the morning and away in the late afternoon on the Pali and Likelike Hwys. If you're heading to the airport during rush hour, give yourself plenty of extra time.

To/From the Airport

From the airport you can get to Waikiki by local bus, by airport shuttle services, by taxi or by rental car. A taxi to Waikiki from the airport will cost about $25. The main car rental agencies have booths or courtesy phones in the airport baggage claim area.

The easiest way to drive to Waikiki from the airport is to take Hwy 92, which starts out as Nimitz Hwy and turns into Ala Moana Blvd, before leading directly into Waikiki. Although this route hits more local traffic, it's hard to get lost on it.

If you're into life in the fast lane, connect instead with the H1 Fwy heading east.

On the return to the airport from Waikiki, beware of the poorly marked interchange where H1 and Hwy 78 split; if you're not in the right-hand lane at that point, you could easily end up on Hwy 78. It takes about 20 minutes to get from Waikiki to the airport via H1 *if* you don't hit traffic.

Bus Travel time between the airport and Waikiki on city bus No 19 or 20 is about an hour. The fare is $1.50. The buses run about once every 20 minutes from 5am to 11:15pm Monday to Friday, to 11:45pm on weekends. The bus stops at the roadside median on the terminal's 2nd level, in front of the airline counters. There are two stops; it's best to wait for the bus at the first one, which is in front of Lobby 4. Luggage is limited to what you can hold on your lap or store under your seat, the latter space comparable to the space under an airline seat. For more information on public buses, see the Bus section that follows.

Shuttle A few private companies, such as **Super Shuttle** *(☎ 841-2928, 877-247-8737)*,

Reliable Express (☎ *924-9292)* and **Airport Blue Line** *(☎ 737-7407)*, offer shuttle services between the airport and Waikiki hotels. The ride averages 45 minutes, but can be more or less depending on how many passengers are dropped off before reaching your hotel. Board these buses at the roadside median on the ground level, in front of the baggage claim areas.

The charge is $6 one way or $10 roundtrip. You don't need a reservation from the airport to Waikiki, but you do need to call at least a few hours in advance for the return van to the airport. Shuttles operate from 6am to 10pm.

Bus

Oahu's public bus system, called **TheBus** *(W www.thebus.org)*, is extensive and easy to use. TheBus has about 80 routes, which collectively cover most of Oahu. You can take the bus to watch windsurfers at Kailua or surfers at Sunset Beach, visit Chinatown or the Bishop Museum, snorkel at Hanauma Bay or hike Diamond Head. However, some of the island's prime viewpoints are certainly beyond reach: TheBus doesn't stop at the Nuuanu Pali Lookout, go up to the Tantalus green belt or run as far as Kaena Point on the Waianae Coast.

Buses stop only at marked bus stops. Each bus route can have a few different destinations. The destination is written on the front of the bus next to the number. Buses generally keep the same number when inbound and outbound. For instance, bus No 8 can take you either into the heart of Waikiki or away from it toward Ala Moana – so take note of both the number and the written destination before you jump on.

If you're in doubt, ask the bus driver. They're used to disoriented visitors, and most drivers are patient and helpful.

Overall, the buses are in excellent condition – if anything, they're a bit too modern. Newer buses are air-conditioned, with sealed windows and climate-control that sometimes seem so out of 'control' that drivers wear jackets to ward off the cold! Currently, about half of the buses are equipped with wheelchair lifts and all have bike racks that cyclists can use for free.

Although TheBus is convenient enough, this isn't Tokyo – if you set your watch by the bus here, you'll come up with 'Hawaiian time,' a distinctly laid-back pace. In addition to not getting hung up on schedules, buses can sometimes bottleneck, with one packed bus after another passing right by crowded bus stops. Waiting for the bus anywhere between Ala Moana and Waikiki on a Saturday night can be a particularly memorable experience.

Still, TheBus usually gets you where you want to go, and as long as you don't schedule too much into one day, it's a great deal.

Be Your Own Tour Guide

It's possible to make a cheap day excursion circling the island by bus, beginning at the Ala Moana Center. The No 52 Wahiawa-Circle Island bus goes clockwise up Hwy 99 to Haleiwa and along the North Shore. At the Turtle Bay Resort, on the northern tip of Oahu, it switches signs to No 55 and comes down the windward coast to Kaneohe and down the Pali Hwy back to Ala Moana. The No 55 Kaneohe-Circle Island bus does the same route in reverse. These buses operate every 30 minutes from 5am to around 11pm daily. If you take the circle-island route nonstop, it takes about four hours.

For a shorter excursion from Waikiki, you can make a loop around southeast Oahu by taking bus No 58 to Sea Life Park and then bus No 57 up to Kailua and back into Honolulu. Because you'll need to change buses, ask the driver for a transfer when you first board.

Anytime you get off to explore along the route, you'll need to pay a new $1.50 fare when you reboard.

Fares The one-way fare for all rides is $1.50 for adults, 75¢ for children aged six to 18 and for seniors 65 years and older. Children under the age of six ride free. You can use either coins or $1 bills; bus drivers don't make change.

Transfers, which have a two-hour time limit stamped on them, are given free when more than one bus is required to get to a destination. If needed, ask for one when you board.

Visitor passes, valid for unlimited rides over four consecutive days, cost $15 and can be purchased at any of the ubiquitous ABC Stores.

Monthly bus passes, valid for unlimited rides in a calendar month, cost $27 and can be purchased at satellite city halls, 7-Eleven convenience stores and Foodland and Star supermarkets.

Seniors (65 years and older) and disabled people of any age can buy a $25 bus pass that is valid for unlimited rides during a two-year period. Senior passes are issued at satellite city halls upon presentation of an identification card with a birth date.

Schedules & Information Bus schedules vary with the route; many operate from about 5:30am to 8pm daily, though some main routes, such as those that serve Waikiki, continue until around midnight.

TheBus has a great **telephone service** *(☎ 848-5555; open 5:30am-10pm)*. As long as you know where you are and where you want to go, the staff will tell you not only which bus to catch, but also when the next one will be there. This same number also has a TDD service for the hearing impaired and can provide information on which buses are wheelchair accessible.

You can get printed timetables for individual routes free from any satellite city hall, including the one at the Ala Moana Center. Timetables can also be picked up from the Hawaii State Library, in downtown Honolulu, and from the McDonald's fast-food restaurant on the corner of Liliuokalani Ave and Kalakaua Ave, Waikiki.

When you collect a timetable, be sure to grab one of the free schematic route maps, a handy brochure that maps out routes for the entire island and shows the corresponding bus numbers.

Common Routes Bus Nos 8, 19, 20 and 58 run between Waikiki and the Ala Moana Center, Honolulu's central transfer point. It's hardly worth checking timetables, as one of these buses comes by every few minutes throughout the day. From Ala Moana you can connect with a broad network of buses to points around the island.

Bus Nos 2, 19 and 20 will take you between Waikiki and downtown Honolulu. There's usually a bus every 10 minutes or so.

Bus No 4 runs between Waikiki and the University of Hawaii at Manoa every 10 minutes.

Oahu Driving Times

Although actual driving time may vary depending upon traffic conditions, the average driving times and distances from Waikiki to points of interest around Oahu are as follows:

destination	miles	minutes
Haleiwa	29	50
Hanauma Bay	11	25
Honolulu Airport	9	20
Kaena Point State Park	43	75
Kailua	14	25
Laie	34	60
Makaha Beach	36	60
Nuuanu Pali Lookout	11	20
Sea Life Park	16	35
Sunset Beach	37	65
USS *Arizona* Memorial	12	30
Waimea	34	60
Waipahu	16	30

Car

Budget *(☎ 537-3600)*, **National** *(☎ 831-3800)*, **Hertz** *(☎ 831-3500)*, **Avis** *(☎ 834-5536)* and **Dollar** *(☎ 831-2330)* all have desks at Honolulu international airport and car lots on the airport grounds. **Alamo** *(☎ 833-4585; cnr Nimitz Hwy & Ohohia St)* has its operations outside the airport, about a mile northeast of the airport terminal.

The international car rental companies also have numerous branch locations in Waikiki, many in the lobbies of larger hotels. General rental information and toll-free numbers are in the Getting Around chapter earlier in this book.

Moped

Mopeds are another way of getting around, but they're really best suited to people who already have experience riding in city traffic.

Blue Sky Rentals *(☎ 947-0101; 1920 Ala Moana Blvd)* on the ground floor of Inn on the Park Hotel, is the most reliable place in Waikiki to rent a moped. The rate is $23 for eight hours, $30 for 24 hours.

Taxi

Taxis have meters and charge a flag-down fee of $2.25 to start, and from there fares increase in 30¢ increments at a rate of $2.40 per mile.

There's an extra charge of 40¢ for each suitcase or backpack.

Taxis are readily available at the airport and larger hotels, but are otherwise generally hard to find. To phone for one, try **TheCab** *(☎ 422-2222)*, **Charley's** *(☎ 955-2211)* or **City Taxi** *(☎ 524-2121)*.

Honolulu

In 1793 the English frigate *Butterworth* became the first foreign ship to sail into what is now called Honolulu Harbor. Its captain, William Brown, named the harbor Fair Haven. Ships that followed called it Brown's Harbor. But over time the name Honolulu, which means 'Sheltered Bay,' came to be used for both the harbor and the adjacent seaside district that the Hawaiians had called Kou.

As more and more foreign ships found their way to Honolulu, a harborside village of thatched houses sprouted up and the town became Hawaii's center of trade.

In 1809 Kamehameha I moved his royal court to Honolulu from nearby Waikiki. On what today is the southern end of Bethel St, downtown Honolulu, Kamehameha set up residence to keep an eye on all the trade that moved in and out of the harbor. From there, Hawaiian sandalwood was shipped to Canton in exchange for weapons and luxury goods, which Kamehameha loaded into his harborside warehouses.

In the 1820s whaling ships began pulling into Honolulu for supplies, liquor and women. At the same time, Christian missionaries began coming ashore in order to save souls. Both groups left their mark. Downtown Honolulu has the offices of the 'Big Five' corporations that controlled most of Hawaii's commerce by the end of the 19th century. It is no coincidence that their lists of corporate board members – Alexander, Baldwin, Cooke and Dole – read like rosters from the first mission ships.

The whalers left a different legacy. Hotel St, a line of bars and strip joints a few blocks from the harbor, downtown Honolulu, is still the city's red-light district.

By the early 1900s Honolulu had expanded into a sprawling cosmopolitan city, but the downtown area, extending from the harbor, remains the heart of the city.

Today, Honolulu is the only major city in Hawaii. It has a population of nearly 400,000 and is the state's center of business, culture and politics. It's been the capital of Hawaii since 1845. Honolulu international airport and Honolulu Harbor are Hawaii's two busiest gateways.

Honolulu is home to many people from throughout the Pacific. It's a city of minorities, with no ethnic majority. Honolulu's ethnic diversity can be seen on almost every corner – the sushi shop next door to the Vietnamese bakery, the Catholic church around the block from the Chinese Buddhist temple.

The main federal, state and county offices and the state's highest concentration of historic buildings are found in downtown Honolulu.

DOWNTOWN HONOLULU

Downtown Honolulu is a hodgepodge of past and present, with both sleek high-rises and stately Victorian-era buildings. Architecturally, the area has some striking juxtapositions with a 19th-century royal palace, a modernistic state capitol, a New England missionary church and a Spanish-style city hall all within sight of one another.

The downtown area can be an intriguing area to explore, especially for those keenly interested in Hawaiian history and culture.

If you're heading to the Iolani Palace area from Waikiki, the most frequent and convenient bus is No 2. To go directly to Aloha Tower Marketplace or the Hawaii Maritime Center from Waikiki, take bus No 19 or 20.

Convenient parking lots in front of the Aloha Tower and on Pier 6 adjacent to the Hawaii Maritime Center charge $4 for up to three hours; have your ticket validated at a shop or restaurant and the fee is reduced to $2. There's a flat rate of just $2 all day on weekends.

Information

Money The **First Hawaiian Bank** *(☎ 526-0232; First Hawaiian Center, 999 Bishop St; open 8:30am-4pm Mon-Thur, 8:30am-6pm Fri)* is a convenient downtown bank.

Post The downtown branch of the Honolulu **post office** *(☎ 800-275-8777; 335 Merchant St; open 8am-4:30pm Mon-Fri)* is in the Old Federal Building.

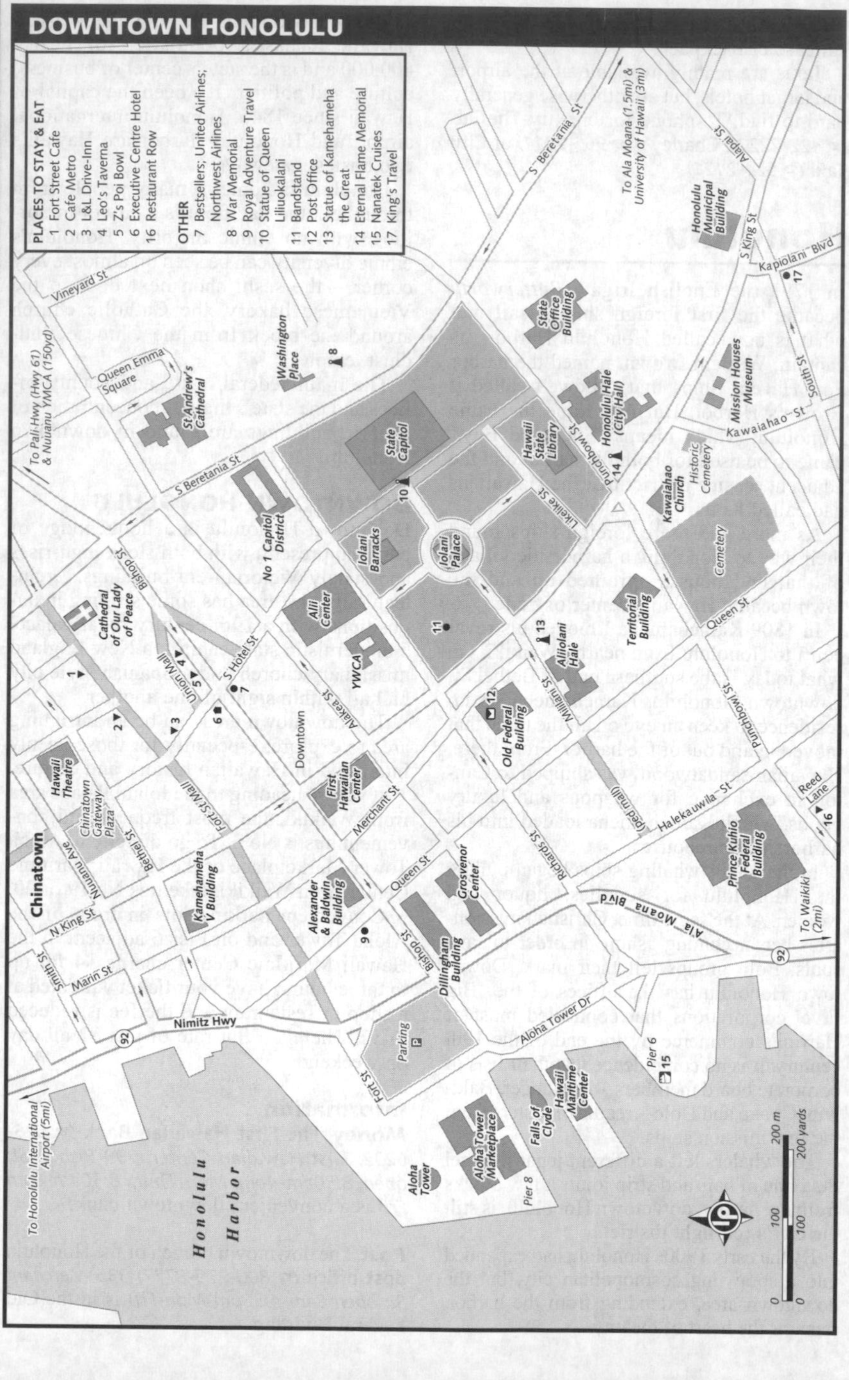
DOWNTOWN HONOLULU
PLACES TO STAY & EAT
1 Fort Street Cafe
2 Cafe Metro
3 L&L Drive-Inn
4 Leo's Taverna
5 Z's Poi Bowl
6 Executive Centre Hotel
16 Restaurant Row
OTHER
7 Bestsellers; United Airlines; Northwest Airlines
8 War Memorial
9 Royal Adventure Travel
10 Statue of Queen Liliuokalani
11 Bandstand
12 Post Office
13 Statue of Kamehameha the Great
14 Eternal Flame Memorial
15 Nanatek Cruises
17 King's Travel
To Pali Hwy (Hwy 61) & Nuuanu YMCA (150yd)
To Ala Moana (1.5mi) & University of Hawaii (3mi)
To Honolulu International Airport (5mi)
To Waikiki (2mi)
Honolulu Harbor
Chinatown
Downtown
Hawaii Theatre
Chinatown Gateway Plaza
Kamehameha V Building
Alexander & Baldwin Building
First Hawaiian Center
YWCA
Alii Center
Cathedral of Our Lady of Peace
No 1 Capitol District
Iolani Barracks
Iolani Palace
State Capitol
Washington Place
St Andrew's Cathedral
Queen Emma Square
State Office Building
Hawaii State Library
Honolulu Hale (City Hall)
Mission Houses Museum
Kawaiahao Church
Historic Cemetery
Cemetery
Honolulu Municipal Building
Territorial Building
Aliiolani Hale
Old Federal Building
Prince Kuhio Federal Building
Grosvenor Center
Dillingham Building
Parking
Aloha Tower
Aloha Tower Marketplace
Falls of Clyde
Hawaii Maritime Center
Pier 6
Pier 8
Nimitz Hwy
Aloha Tower Dr
Ala Moana Blvd
Smith St
Marin St
N King St
Nuuanu Ave
Bethel St
Fort St Mall
Union Mall
Bishop St
S Hotel St
Alakea St
Merchant St
Queen St
Fort St
Richards St
Halekauwila St
Reed Lane
Punchbowl St
Mililani St
Likelike St
S Beretania St
Vineyard St
Kawaiahao St
South St
Kapiolani Blvd
S King St
Alapai St
200 m
200 yards

Bookstores A well-stocked bookstore, **Bestsellers** (*☎ 528-2378; 1001 Bishop St*) has a good selection of travel guides, novels and maps.

Library The central branch of the **Hawaii State Library** (*☎ 586-3500; 478 S King St; open 9am-5pm Mon, Fri & Sat, 9am-8pm Tues & Thur, 10am-5pm Wed*), adjacent to Iolani Palace, has a sunny central courtyard and a good selection of periodicals to browse.

Walking Tour

Downtown Honolulu's most beautiful buildings are all within easy walking distance of each other.

A good starting place is **Iolani Palace**, the area's most pivotal spot, both historically and geographically. At the rear of the palace, en route to the **state capitol**, you'll pass a **statue of Queen Liliuokalani**. You can enter the capitol through the rear, and exit on the S Beretania St side, opposite the **war memorial**.

After turning left on S Beretania St, you'll pass **Washington Place** and **St Andrew's Cathedral**. From there, return to and continue down Richards St past **No 1 Capitol District**, an elegant five-story building erected in 1928 that now houses the **Hawaii State Art Museum**; and the **YWCA**, built in 1927 by Julia Morgan, the renowned architect who designed the William Randolph Hearst San Simeon estate in California.

Turn right on S King St to get to the **First Hawaiian Center**, which has a worthwhile art gallery, and then turn left on Bishop St to pass the **Alexander & Baldwin Building**, c. 1929, whose curious facade incorporates tropical fruit, Hawaiian fish as well as the Chinese characters for prosperity and longevity.

Turn left on Queen St and you'll see the four-story **Dillingham Building**, built in 1929 in Italian Renaissance style, and now mirrored in the sleek reflective glass of the adjacent 30-story **Grosvenor Center** – a study in contrasts.

Head back via Merchant St and proceed south, where you'll see the **Old Federal Building**, a Spanish colonial structure, as well as **Aliiolani Hale** and a **statue of Kamehameha the Great**. Just beyond that is the historic **Kawaiahao Church** and the **Mission Houses Museum**.

As you make your way back to Iolani Palace, take a look at two classic period buildings on Punchbowl St: **Honolulu Hale**, the city hall, and the **Hawaii State Library**, with its grand column facade.

Iolani Palace

Iolani Palace (*☎ 522-0832; tours adult/child $20/5 every 15 minutes; 9am-2:30pm Tues-Sat*) is a must-see sight. There's simply no other place in Hawaii where you can get a more poignant sense of Hawaiian history during that pivotal 19th century, when Hawaiian royalty feasted, the white tax-paying business community steamed, and plots and counterplots simmered. So much happened within the walls of Iolani Palace, happy and sad, by monarchs and by those who overthrew them, that you can almost sense the spirits of those who were once here.

The only royal palace in the USA, Iolani was the residence of King Kalakaua and Queen Kapiolani from 1882 to 1891 and of Queen Liliuokalani, Kalakaua's successor, for two years after that. Following the overthrow of the Hawaiian kingdom in 1893, the palace became the capitol – first for the republic, then for the territory and later for the state of Hawaii.

It wasn't until 1969 that the current state capitol was built and the legislators moved out of their cramped palace quarters. By the time they left, Iolani Palace was in a shambles. A lengthy multimillion-dollar renovation painstakingly restored the palace to its former glory, and in 1978 it opened as a museum. Today, visitors must wear booties over their shoes to protect the highly polished wooden floors.

The **throne room**, decorated in red and gold, features the original thrones of the king and queen and is at the heart of the palace. In addition to celebrations full of pomp and pageantry, it was in the throne room that King Kalakaua danced his favorite Western dances – the polka, the waltz and the Virginia reel – into the wee hours of the morning. Not all the events that took place here were joyous. Two years after she was dethroned by American businessmen, Queen Liliuokalani was brought back to the palace and tried for treason in the throne room. In a move calculated to humiliate the Hawaiian people, she spent nine months as a prisoner in Iolani Palace, her former home.

The interior of the palace can only be seen on a guided tour, which lasts about an hour;

Hawaii's New Treasure

Visitors to Oahu have a new not-to-be-missed highlight: the **Hawaii State Art Museum** (*☎ 808-586-0900; W www.state.hi.us/sfca; 250 S Hotel St; admission free; open 10am-4pm Tues-Sat*). The museum, which opened in November 2002, culminates years of work by artists, cultural organizations and the state government, and showcases the work of artists who have lived in the islands since Hawaii became a state in 1959. Visitors immediately realize that the remarkable scenery and traditions of the state have proved incredibly inspirational for artists.

The collection makes the museum one of the best medium-sized art museums in the United States. And it's not just the works, which range from paintings to photographs to sculpture and more, but the overall design of the museum and the composition of the collection itself which are impressive. Works are displayed around interrelated themes, which include island traditions, social issues, Hawaiian heritage as well as the pure beauty of the land and sea. Labels provide in-depth information on why works were chosen for display, and Hawaii's confluence of Asian, Pacific and American cultures is evident throughout. The curators have done an excellent job of capturing the soul of the islands and the heart of the people. One visitor on opening day said, 'You see a beautiful sculpture and realize you know the artist and then you look at a painting and see your neighbor.'

The building itself is a work of art: it's the old YMCA which was built in 1928 on prime real estate near Iolani Palace and across from the site of the future state capitol. The museum presently occupies the building's 2nd floor; with time it will be expanded to cover all five floors so that a good portion of the state's 5000-work collection can be shown. Sadly, visitors can't take a dip in the inviting courtyard swimming pool, once a refuge for scores of frolicking soldiers and seamen during WWII.

After climbing a grand staircase, visitors see a model of the canoe thought to have brought the first Polynesians to Hawaii. Behind the model is *The Discovery of Hawaii*, a painting by Herb Kawainui Kane that is rapidly gaining iconic status in the state. It shows the awed voyagers on that first canoe as they crest a wave and catch site of an erupting volcano.

A visit to the museum can easily occupy an hour or more, but the sensible admissions policy (it's free!) means that you can pop in after the palace, enjoy a few of the 360 works on display and then save others for another visit. Among the many highlights are the following:

- A series of ink drawings by Huc-Mazelet Luquiens captures the rhythm of life in Hawaii in the 1920s before tourism, the military, changing economics and population growth altered everything.
- A sculpture of shoes left on steps depicts *E Komo Mai*, the Hawaiian spirit of welcome where anybody can remove their footwear and make themselves at home. The artist, George Kahumokio, is best known for his slack-key guitar playing.
- *Ronin Samurai* is part of a 1982 series by Masami Teraoka that uses traditional Japanese painting techniques to take a wry look at tourism. In this work a samurai and geisha are shown snorkeling in Hanauma Bay.
- *Kahoolawe Room* is a jarring painting that is Anne Miura's depiction of what her house on Maui felt like every time a Navy test bomb exploded on nearby Kahoolawe.
- A series of photographs by Mark Hamasaki continue the theme of social comment which doesn't always favor the government. The brutal assault on the land which marked the construction of the H3 highway in the 1980s is presented in stark black and white. The builders of the highway, who hired Hamasaki to record the project, definitely got more than they bargained for.
- Kids of all ages love *Introducing Ruddy Spuddy*, which comically depicts the chaos that hit painter Sally French's household when she unexpectedly inherited a potato farm in California.
- *The Drummer* by Jean Charlot is a masterpiece by the painter who spent many years in the islands before his death in 1979. It shows a local drummer intent on his music in a way that will have you hearing it.

Part of the space is used for rotating special exhibits, so you can always expect a surprise or two.

Ryan Ver Berkmoes

children younger than 5 are not admitted. Because of the palace's high upkeep expenses, the tours aren't cheap, but it's well worth the price to stroll through this unique, history-laden site. Sometimes you can join a tour on the spot, but it's advisable to call ahead for reservations.

Palace Grounds The palace grounds, which are free and are open to the public during daylight hours, have a lengthy history. Before Iolani Palace was built, there was a simpler house on these grounds that was used by King Kamehameha III, who ruled for 30 years (1825–54). In ancient times it was the site of a Hawaiian temple.

The palace ticket window and a gift shop are in the former **barracks** of the Royal Household Guards, a building that looks oddly like the uppermost layer of a medieval fort that's been sliced off and plopped on the ground.

The **domed pavilion** on the grounds was originally built for the coronation of King Kalakaua in 1883 and is still used for the inauguration of governors and for Friday afternoon concerts by the Royal Hawaiian Band.

The **grassy mound** surrounded by a wrought iron fence was the site of a royal tomb until 1865, when the remains of King Kamehameha II and Queen Kamamalu were moved to the Royal Mausoleum in Nuuanu. The huge **banyan tree** between the palace and the state capitol is thought to have been planted by Queen Kapiolani.

Queen Liliuokalani Statue

The statue of Hawaii's last queen stands between Iolani Palace and the capitol. It faces Washington Place, Liliuokalani's home and place of exile for more than 20 years. The bronze statue is holding the Hawaii constitution that Liliuokalani wrote in 1893, in fear of which US businessmen overthrew her; *Aloha Oe*, a popular hymn that she composed; and *Kumulipo*, the Hawaiian chant of creation.

State Capitol

Hawaii's state capitol *(587-0666; 415 S Beretania St)* is not your standard gold dome. Built in the 1960s, it was a grandiose attempt at a 'theme' design.

Its two central legislative chambers are cone-shaped to represent volcanoes; the rotunda is open to let gentle trade winds blow through; the supporting columns represent palm trees; and the whole structure is encircled by a large pool symbolizing the ocean surrounding Hawaii. Visitors are free to walk through the rotunda and peer through viewing windows into the two legislative chambers.

In front of the capitol is a **statue of Father Damien**, the Belgian priest who in 1873 volunteered to work among the lepers of Molokai. He died of the disease 16 years later aged 49. The stylized sculpture was created by Venezuelan artist Marisol Escubar.

Directly opposite the state capitol on S Beretania St is a sculptured eternal torch – a **war memorial** dedicated to soldiers who died in WWII.

Honolulu Academy of Arts

The Honolulu Academy of Arts *(☎ 532-8700; 900 S Beretania St; adult/senior & student/child under 13 $7/4/free; open 10am-4:30pm Tues-Sat, 1pm-5pm Sun)* is an exceptional museum, with solid Asian, European and Pacific art collections. Hawaii's only comprehensive fine arts museum, it houses nearly 40,000 pieces of artwork.

The museum has a predominantly classical facade with some 30 galleries branching off a series of garden courtyards. Don't miss the splendid Asian gallery, with exhibits ranging from serene Buddhas to fierce samurai armor. Considered one of the finest Asian art collections in the USA, it gives almost equal weight to both Chinese and Japanese works of art. Among the highlights is the collection of *Scenes of Kyoto*, painted by the renowned Japanese artist Kano Motohide, and the extensive Ming Dynasty collection. The latter includes pivotal works by Shen Zhou, who is credited with establishing a compositional technique that significantly influenced Ming painting styles.

In 2001, the museum opened the Henry R Luce Pavilion, a striking contemporary wing that added 10,000 sq ft of additional exhibit space. It contains Hawaiiana artifacts and paintings reflecting Hawaiian culture on its upper level and modern art on the ground floor, including works by such modernist luminaries as Henry Moore and Georgia O'Keeffe.

European art of the 19th and 20th centuries is represented in a roomful of paintings by Henri Matisse, Paul Cézanne, Claude Monet,

Paul Gauguin, Vincent van Gogh and Camille Pissarro. There's also a worthwhile collection of 16th- to 18th-century European artists such as Pieter de Hotch, Sir Thomas Lawrence and Carlo Bonavia, and a number of Madonna-and-child oil paintings from 14th-century Italy.

The Pacific art exhibits include ceremonial carvings, war clubs and masks from Papua New Guinea, and body ornaments and navigational stick charts from Micronesia. The museum also exhibits some fine eclectic pieces, ranging from sculptures and miniature figurines from India to fertility figures and even ceremonial carvings from African tribespeople.

There is a gift shop and an appealing lunch café overlooking a fountain courtyard. Bus No 2 from Waikiki stops out front; there's metered parking behind the museum.

Hawaii Maritime Center

The Hawaii Maritime Center *(☎ 536-6373; Pier 7; adult/child over 6/child under 6 $7.50/4.50/free; open 8:30am-5pm daily)*, near the Aloha Tower, is a great place to get a sense of Hawaii's history. The museum covers everything from the arrival of Captain Cook to modern-day windsurfing, with lots of fun tidbits you won't find anywhere else.

Interesting displays on early tourism include a reproduction of a Matson liner stateroom and photos of Waikiki in the days when just the Royal Hawaiian and the Moana hotels shared the shore with Diamond Head. Both hotels were built by Matson in the early 1900s to accommodate the passengers they carried on their cruises. Ironically, Matson sold the hotels off to the Sheraton chain in 1959, just before the jet age and statehood launched sleepy tourism into a booming industry.

The maritime center is also home to the 266ft *Falls of Clyde*, the world's last four-masted, four-rigged ship. Built in 1878, in Glasgow, Scotland, the *Falls* was once used to carry sugar and passengers between Hilo and San Francisco. It was later converted into an oil tanker and eventually stripped down to a barge. A Hawaiian group raised funds to rescue the ship in 1963, just before it was scheduled to be sunk to create a breakwater off Vancouver. The *Falls* was eventually brought to Honolulu and restored, and is now registered as a National Historic Landmark. Visitors can stroll the deck and walk down into the cargo holds.

The center is also home port to the 60ft *Hokulea*, a double-hulled sailing canoe constructed to resemble the type of boat used by Polynesians in their migrations. It has made a number of voyages from Hawaii to the South Pacific, retracing the routes of the early Polynesian seafarers and using only traditional methods of navigation, such as wave patterns and the position of the stars.

Aloha Tower

Built in 1926 at the edge of the downtown district, the 10-story Aloha Tower is a Honolulu landmark that for years was the city's tallest building. In the days when all tourists arrived by ship, this icon of prewar Hawaii – with its four-sided clock tower inscribed with the word 'Aloha' – greeted every visitor. Today, cruise ships still disembark at the terminal beneath the tower. Take a peek through the terminal windows to see colorful murals depicting the Honolulu of bygone days.

The Aloha Tower's top-floor **observation deck** *(☎ 537-9260; Pier 9; admission free; open 9am-sunset daily)* offers a sweeping 360° view of Honolulu's large commercial harbor. Note: the only access to the top is via an elevator that's occasionally out of commission, but you can always take in the view from one of the nearby waterfront restaurants.

Beneath the tower is the Aloha Tower Marketplace, a shopping center with numerous kiosks, stores and eateries.

St Andrew's Cathedral

King Kamehameha IV, who was attracted by the royal trappings of the Church of England, decided to build his own cathedral in Hawaii. He and his consort, Queen Emma, founded the Anglican Church of Hawaii in 1858.

The cathedral's cornerstone was finally laid in 1867 by King Kamehameha V. Kamehameha IV had died four years earlier on St Andrew's Day – hence the church's name.

The architecture of St Andrew's *(☎ 524-2822; cnr Alakea & S Beretania Sts; open 9am-5pm daily)* is French Gothic, and the stone and glass used in the cathedral were shipped from England. Its most striking feature is the impressive window of hand-blown stained glass that forms the western facade and reaches from the floor to the eaves. In the right section of the glass you can see the

Reverend Thomas Staley, the first bishop sent to Hawaii by Queen Victoria, alongside Kamehameha IV and Queen Emma.

Kawaiahao Church

Oahu's oldest church *(cnr Punchbowl & King Sts; admission free; open 8am-4pm daily)* was built on the site where the first missionaries constructed a grass thatch church shortly after their arrival in 1820. The original was an impressive structure that seated 300 people on *lauhala* mats, woven from *hala* (pandanus) leaves.

Still, thatch wasn't quite what the missionaries had in mind, so they designed a more typical New England–style Congregational church with simple Gothic influences. Completed in 1842, the church is made of 14,000 coral slabs that weigh about 1000lb each. Hawaiian divers chiseled these huge blocks of coral out of Honolulu's underwater reef – a task that took four years.

The clock tower was donated by Kamehameha III, and the old clock, installed in 1850, still keeps accurate time. The rear seats of the church, marked by *kahili* (feather staffs) and velvet padding, were for royalty and are still reserved for descendants of royalty today.

The **tomb of King Lunalilo**, the successor to Kamehameha V, is on the church grounds at the main entrance. Lunalilo ruled for only one year before his death in 1874 at the age of 39.

The **cemetery** at the rear of the church is a fun place to poke around and is a bit like a who's who of colonial history. You'll find the gravestones of early missionaries buried alongside other important Westerners of the day, including the infamous Sanford Dole, who after overthrowing Queen Liliuokalani became the first territorial governor of Hawaii.

Mission Houses Museum

Mission Houses Museum *(☎ 531-0481; 553 S King St; tours adult/child $10/6 at 10am, 11am, 1pm and 2pm Tues-Sat)* contains three of the original buildings of the Sandwich Islands Mission headquarters. The houses are authentically furnished with handmade quilts on the beds, settees in the parlor and iron cooking pots in the stone fireplaces.

The first missionaries packed more than their bags when they left Boston – they actually brought a prefabricated wooden house, now called the **Frame House**, around the Horn with them! Designed to withstand cold New England winter winds, the house's small windows instead block out Honolulu's cooling trade winds, keeping the two-story house hot and stuffy. Erected in 1821, it's the oldest wooden structure in Hawaii.

The coral-block **Chamberlain House** was the early mission storeroom, a necessity as Honolulu had few shops in those days. Upstairs are hoop barrels, wooden crates packed with dishes and the desk and quill pen Levi Chamberlain used to work on accounts. Levi was appointed by the mission to buy, store and dole out supplies to the missionary families, who survived on a meager allowance – as the account books on the desk testify.

The **Printing Office** housed a lead-type press that was used to print the Bible in the Hawaiian language. The guided tours take in the whole shebang, and last about an hour.

Aliiolani Hale

Aliiolani Hale (House of Heavenly Kings) was the first major government building constructed by the Hawaiian monarchy. Constructed in 1874, it has housed the Hawaii Supreme Court and was once also home to the state legislature. It was originally designed by Australian architect Thomas Rowe to be a royal palace, although it was never used as such.

It was on the steps of Aliiolani Hale, in January 1893, that Sanford Dole proclaimed the establishment of a provisional government and the overthrow of the Hawaiian monarchy.

A stately **statue of Kamehameha the Great**, cast in Florence, Italy, in the 1880s, stands in front of Aliiolani Hale. Each year on June 11, a state holiday honoring Kamehameha, the statue is ceremoniously draped with layer upon layer of 12ft leis.

Honolulu Hale

City Hall, also known as Honolulu Hale *(☎ 523-2489; 530 S King St)*, is largely of Spanish mission design, with a tiled roof, decorative balconies, arches and pillars. Built in 1927, it bears the initials of CW Dickey, Honolulu's most famous architect of the day. The building, which is on the National Register of Historic Places, has some interesting frescoes and an open-air courtyard that's sometimes used for concerts and art exhibits.

On the lawn out front is an **eternal-flame memorial** erected to honor the victims of the September 11 terrorist attacks on the US mainland.

Washington Place

Washington Place, the governor's official residence, is a large colonial-style building surrounded by stately trees, built in 1846 by US sea captain John Dominis. The captain's son, also named John, became the governor of Oahu and married the Hawaiian princess who later became Queen Liliuokalani. After the queen was dethroned, she lived at Washington Place in exile until her death in 1917.

A plaque near the sidewalk on the left side of Washington Place is inscribed with the words to *Aloha Oe*, the anthem composed by Queen Liliuokalani.

First Hawaiian Center

The First Hawaiian Center, the headquarters of the First Hawaiian Bank, contains a worthwhile **gallery** *(☎ 526-0232; 999 Bishop St; admission free; open 8:30am-4pm Mon-Thur, 8:30am-6pm Fri)*, which is operated in conjunction with the Contemporary Museum. The gallery features quality changing exhibits of modern Hawaiian art.

The building itself, Hawaii's tallest high-rise, has some notable features, including a four-story-high glass wall containing 185 prisms that was designed by the famed New York glass artist Jamie Carpenter.

CHINATOWN

A walk through Chinatown is like a trip to Asia. Although it's predominantly Chinese, it has Vietnamese, Thai and Filipino influences as well.

Chinatown is busy and colorful. It has a lively market that could be right off a back street in Hong Kong; fire-breathing dragons curl their way up the red pillars outside the Bank of Hawaii; and good, cheap ethnic restaurants abound. You can get tattooed, consult with an herbalist, munch on moon cakes or slurp a steaming bowl of Vietnamese soup. There are temples, shrines, noodle factories, antique shops and art galleries to explore.

Chinatown has seen some urban renewal, particularly on its downtown edge. The spiffed-up image includes a new 'entranceway' on the corner of S Hotel & Bethel Sts marked by a small park, two marble lions and a new high-rise complex. However, despite creeping gentrification, Chinatown still has its seamy side. Just a block away on S Hotel St, you'll find darkened doorways advertising 'video peeps' for 25¢ and bawdy nightspots with names like Risqué Theatre and Paradise Lost.

Places to eat in Chinatown are listed near the end of the Honolulu section.

History

Chinese immigrants who had worked off their sugarcane plantation contracts began settling in Chinatown and opening up small businesses around 1860.

In December 1899, the bubonic plague broke out in the area. The 7000 Chinese, Hawaiians and Japanese who made the crowded neighborhood their home were cordoned off and forbidden to leave. As more plague cases arose, the Board of Health decided to conduct controlled burns of infected homes. On January 20, 1900, the fire brigade set fire to a building on the corner of Beretania St and Nuuanu Ave. The wind suddenly picked up and the fire spread out of control, racing toward the waterfront. To make matters worse, police guards stationed inside the plague area attempted to stop quarantined residents from fleeing. Nearly 40 acres of Chinatown burned to the ground on that fateful day.

Not everyone thought the fire was accidental. Just the year before, Chinese immigration into Hawaii had been halted by the US annexation of the islands, and Chinatown

Flower Power

Chinatown herbalists are both physicians and pharmacists, with walls full of small wooden drawers each filled with a different herb. They'll size you up, feel your pulse and listen to you describe your ailments before deciding which drawers to open, mixing herbs and flowers and wrapping them for you to take home and boil together. The object is to balance yin and yang forces. You can find herbalists at the Chinatown Cultural Plaza and along N King and Maunakea Sts.

itself was prime real estate on the edge of the burgeoning downtown district.

Despite the adverse climate, the Chinese held their own and a new Chinatown arose from the ashes.

In the 1940s, thousands of US GIs walked the streets of Chinatown before being shipped off to Iwo Jima and Guadalcanal. Many spent their last days of freedom in Chinatown's brothels, pool halls and tattoo parlors.

Information

The **Bank of Hawaii** (☎ *532-2480; 101 N King St; open 8:30am-4pm Mon-Thur, 8:30am-6pm Fri)* is on the west side of Chinatown.

There's a branch **post office** (☎ *800-275-8777; River St; open 9am-4pm Mon-Fri, 9am-noon Sat)* in the Chinatown Cultural Plaza.

Orientation

Chinatown is immediately north of downtown Honolulu, roughly bounded by Honolulu Harbor, Bethel St, Vineyard Blvd and River St.

Chinatown is full of one-way streets, traffic is thick and parking can be tight, so you may want to take the bus even if you have a car. However, there are parking garages at the Chinatown Gateway Plaza on Nuuanu Ave and in the Hale Pauahi complex on N Beretania St north of Maunakea St. Note that N Hotel St is open to bus traffic only.

To get to Chinatown by bus from Waikiki, you can take bus No 2 to N Hotel St in the center of Chinatown, or bus No 20 to River St on the western edge of Chinatown.

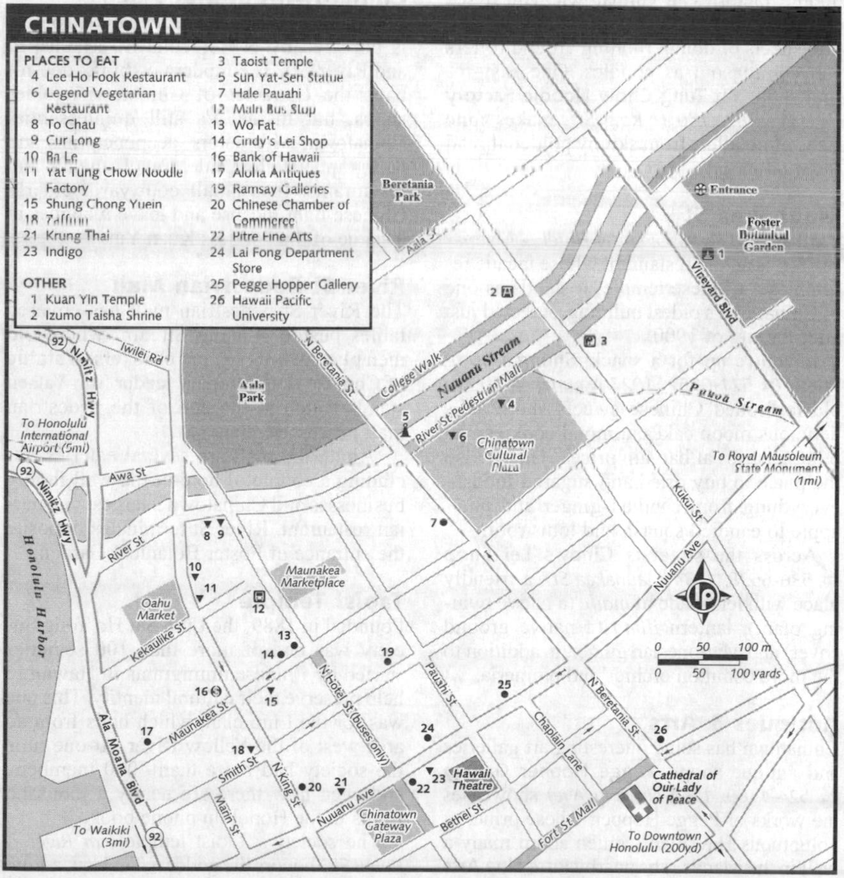

Oahu Market

The heart of Chinatown is Oahu Market *(cnr Kekaulike & N King Sts)*, a lively open-air market.

Everything a Chinese cook needs is on display: pig heads, gingerroot, fresh octopus, quail eggs, slabs of tuna, jasmine rice, long beans and salted jellyfish.

Oahu Market has been an institution since 1904. In 1984, the tenants organized and purchased the market themselves to save it from falling into the hands of developers. Today, it gets a lot of competition from the bustling Maunakea Marketplace, which is newer, larger and has a hot-food section.

Noodle Makers

If you look inside one of the half dozen noodle factories in Chinatown, you'll see clouds of white flour hanging in the air and thin sheets of dough running around rollers and coming out as noodles. One easy-to-find shop, **Yat Tung Chow Noodle Factory** *(☎ 531-7982; 150 N King St)*, makes nine sizes of noodles, from skinny golden thread to fat udon.

Maunakea St

Wo Fat *(☎ 521-5055; cnr N Hotel & Maunakea Sts)* is an old restaurant whose facade resembles a Chinese temple; it stands as one of Chinatown's oldest buildings, erected just after the fire of 1900.

If you're up for a snack, **Shung Chong Yuein** *(☎ 521-0952; 1027 Maunakea St)*, an old-fashioned Chinese sweets shop, sells delicious moon cakes, almond cookies and other pastries at bargain prices. This is also the place to buy dried and sugared foods – everything from candied ginger and pineapple to candied squash and lotus root.

Across the street is **Cindy's Lei Shop** *(☎ 536-6538; 1034 Maunakea St)*, a friendly place with leis made of *maile* (a native twining plant), lantern *ilima* (a native ground cover) and Micronesian ginger, in addition to the more common orchids and plumeria.

Antiques & Arts

Chinatown has some interesting art galleries and antique shops. **Pegge Hopper Gallery** *(☎ 524-1160; 1164 Nuuanu Ave)* showcases the works of Pegge Hopper, whose prints of voluptuous Hawaiian women adorn many a wall in the islands. The nearby **Pitre Fine Arts** *(☎ 521-5773; 1111 Nuuanu Ave)* has a varied collection of interesting contemporary artwork. Also notable is **Ramsay Galleries** *(☎ 537-2787; 1128 Smith St)*, featuring finely detailed pen-and-ink drawings by the artist Ramsay and changing exhibits of high-quality works by other local artists.

For antiques a good place to browse is **Aloha Antiques** *(942 Maunakea St)*, where about 20 vendors sell eclectic collections, including jewelry, Art Deco items, Asian ceramics as well as '50s collectibles. **Lai Fong Department Store** *(1118 Nuuanu Ave)* also sells a variety of antiques and knickknacks, including Chinese silk clothing, Oriental porcelain and old postcards of Hawaii dating back to the first half of the 20th century.

Chinatown Cultural Plaza

This plaza, covering the better part of a block, is bordered by N Beretania St, Maunakea and River Sts. The modern complex doesn't have the character of Chinatown's older shops, but inside it's still quintessential Chinatown, with tailors, acupuncturists and calligraphers alongside travel agents and restaurants. In a small courtyard, elderly Chinese light incense and leave mangoes at a statue of the goddess Kuan Yin.

River St Pedestrian Mall

The River St pedestrian mall has covered tables beside Nuuanu Stream, where old men play mah-jongg and checkers. A **statue** of Chinese revolutionary leader Sun Yatsen stands watch at the end of the pedestrian mall near N Beretania St.

Along the mall are several eateries, including a couple of hole-in-the-wall family businesses and Chinatown's largest vegetarian restaurant. River St terminates opposite the entrance of Foster Botanical Garden.

Taoist Temple

Founded in 1889, the Lum Sai Ho Tong Society was one of more than 100 societies started by Chinese immigrants in Hawaii to help preserve their cultural identity. This one was for the Lum clan, which hails from an area west of the Yellow River. At one time the society had more than 4000 members, and even now there are nearly a thousand Lums in the Honolulu phone book.

The society's Taoist temple *(cnr River & Kukui Sts)* honors the goddess Tin Hau, a Lum child who rescued her father from drowning and was later deified. Many Chinese claim to see her apparition when they travel by boat. The temple is not usually open to the general public, but you can admire the building from the outside.

Izumo Taisha Shrine

The Izumo Taisha Shrine (*☎ 538-7778; 215 N Kukui St; open 9am-5pm daily*), across the river from the Taoist temple, is a small wooden Shinto shrine built by Japanese immigrants in 1923. During WWII, the property was confiscated by the city of Honolulu and wasn't returned to its congregation until 1962.

Incidentally, the 100lb sacks of rice that sit near the altar symbolize good health, while ringing the bell at the shrine entrance is considered an act of purification for those who come to pray.

Foster Botanical Garden

Foster Botanical Garden (*☎ 522-7066; 180 N Vineyard Blvd; adult/child $5/1; open 9am-4pm daily*), at the north side of Chinatown, is Oahu's main botanical garden.

The garden took root in 1850, when German botanist William Hillebrand purchased 5 acres of land from Queen Kalama and planted the trees that now tower in the center of the property. Captain Thomas Foster bought the property in 1867 and continued planting the grounds. In the 1930s, the garden was bequeathed to the city of Honolulu.

Now an impressive 14-acre collection of tropical flora, the garden is laid out according to plant groups, including palms, plumeria and poisonous plants. If you've ever wondered how nutmeg, allspice and cinnamon grow, stroll through the **economic garden**. This section also has black pepper vine that climbs 50ft up a gold tree, a vanilla vine and other herbs and spices.

The **herb garden** was the site of the first Japanese-language school in Oahu. Many Japanese immigrants sent their children here to learn how to read Japanese, hoping to maintain their cultural identity and the option of someday returning to Japan. During the bombing of Pearl Harbor a stray artillery shell exploded in a room full of students. A memorial marks the site.

At the other end of the park, the **wild orchid garden** makes a good place for close-up photography.

Foster Botanical Garden holds many extraordinary plants. For instance, the garden's East African *Gigasiphon macrosiphon*, a tree with white flowers that open in the evening, is thought to be extinct in the wild. It's so rare that it doesn't have a common name.

The native Hawaiian *loulu* palm, taken long ago from Oahu's upper Nuuanu Valley, may also be extinct in the wild. The garden's chicle tree, New Zealand kauri tree and Egyptian doum palm are all reputed to be the largest of their kind in the USA. Oddities include the cannonball tree, the sausage tree and the double coconut palm that's capable of producing a 50lb nut (watch your head!).

Trees are labeled, and a free self-guided tour booklet is available at the entrance. Volunteer guides lead hour-long walking tours at 1pm Monday to Friday, included in the admission price.

Kuan Yin Temple

The Kuan Yin Temple (*☎ 533-6361; 170 N Vineyard Blvd; open during daylight*), near the entrance of Foster Garden, is a bright red Buddhist temple with a green ceramic-tile roof. The ornate interior is richly carved and filled with the sweet, pervasive smell of burning incense.

The temple is dedicated to Kuan Yin Bodhisattva, goddess of mercy, whose statue is the largest in the prayer hall. Devotees burn paper 'money' for prosperity and good luck. Offerings of fresh flowers and fruit are placed at the altar. The large citrus fruit that is stacked pyramid-style is the pomelo, considered a symbol of fertility because of its many seeds.

Honolulu's multiethnic Buddhist community worships at the temple, and respectful visitors are welcome.

Organized Tours

Two organizations offer Chinatown walking tours. Keep in mind, however, that Chinatown is a fun place to poke around on your own, and it can feel a bit touristy being led around in a group. Still, the guides provide a commentary with historical insights and often take you to a few places you're unlikely to walk into otherwise.

With each organization, there's a $5 fee to join the tour, and there's no need for reservations – just show up.

The Hawaii Heritage Center *(☎ 521-2749)* leads walking tours of Chinatown from 9:30am to 11:30am on Friday. Meet on the sidewalk in front of Ramsay Galleries at 1128 Smith St.

The Chinese Chamber of Commerce *(☎ 533-3181; 42 N King St)* leads walking tours of Chinatown from 9:30am to noon on Tuesday for $5. Meet at the chamber office.

ALA MOANA & UNIVERSITY AREA

Ala Moana means 'Path to the Sea.' Ala Moana Blvd (Hwy 92) connects the Nimitz Hwy and the airport with downtown Honolulu and Waikiki. Ala Moana is also the name of a land area just west of Waikiki, which includes Honolulu's largest beach.

Information

Money The **Bank of Hawaii** has branches near the university *(☎ 973-4460; 1010 University Ave)* and at the north side of the Ala Moana Center *(☎ 942-6111; 1441 Kapiolani Blvd)*.

Post There's a branch **post office** *(☎ 800-275-8777; 1450 Ala Moana Blvd; open 8:30am-5pm Mon-Fri, 8:30am-4:15pm Sat)* on the inland side, ground floor, of the Ala Moana Center.

Email & Internet Access A casual cybercafé near the University of Hawaii at Manoa, **Coffee Cove** *(☎ 955-2683; 2600 S King St; open 7am-11pm Mon-Fri, 10am-11pm Sat & Sun)* has Internet access for just $1.25 per 15 minutes.

Bookstores The university area has several good bookstores, including **UH Manoa Campus Bookstore** *(☎ 956-4338; 2465 Campus Rd)* in the Campus Center and **Rainbow Books & Records** *(☎ 955-7994; 1010 University Ave)*, the latter carrying both new and used books.

Ala Moana Center

The Ala Moana Center is Hawaii's biggest shopping center, with some 200 shops. When outer islanders fly to Honolulu to shop, they go to Ala Moana. Tourists wanting to spend the day at a mall usually head here too. Ala Moana Center is Honolulu's major bus transfer point and tens of thousands of passengers transit through daily, so even if you weren't planning to go to the center, you're likely to end up there.

Ala Moana has typical mall anchor stores such as Sears, Macy's and Neiman Marcus as well as lots of specialty shops. A favorite for local color is the **Crack Seed Center**, where you can just scoop from jars full of pickled mangoes, candied ginger, dried cuttlefish and *banzai* (rice crackers, nuts and dried fish) mix.

There are also **airline offices**, a couple of **banks**, a satellite **city hall** where you can get bus schedules, a **supermarket** and a **food court** with scores of ethnic fast-food stalls.

To get to the Ala Moana Center from Waikiki by car, simply head west on Ala Moana Blvd. Bus Nos 8, 19, 20 and 58 connect Waikiki with the Ala Moana Center.

Ala Moana Beach

Ala Moana Beach Park, opposite the Ala Moana Center, is a fine city park with much less hustle and bustle than Waikiki. The park is fronted by a broad, golden-sand beach, nearly a mile long, that's buffered from the traffic noise of Ala Moana Blvd by a spacious, grassy area with shade trees.

This is where Honolulu residents go to jog after work, play volleyball and enjoy weekend picnics. The park has full beach facilities several softball fields, tennis courts, and free parking. It's a very popular park, yet big enough that it never feels crowded.

Ala Moana is a safe place to swim and is a good spot for distance swimmers. However, at low tide the deep channel that runs the length of the beach can be a hazard to poor swimmers who don't realize it's there. A former boat channel, it drops off suddenly to overhead depths. If you want to measure laps, it's 500m between the lifeguard tower at the Waikiki end and the white post in the water midway between the third and fourth lifeguard towers.

The 43-acre peninsula jutting from the east side of the park is the **Aina Moana State Recreation Area**, more commonly known as Magic Island. During the school year, you can often find high-school outrigger-canoe teams practicing here in the late afternoon. There's a nice walk around the perimeter of

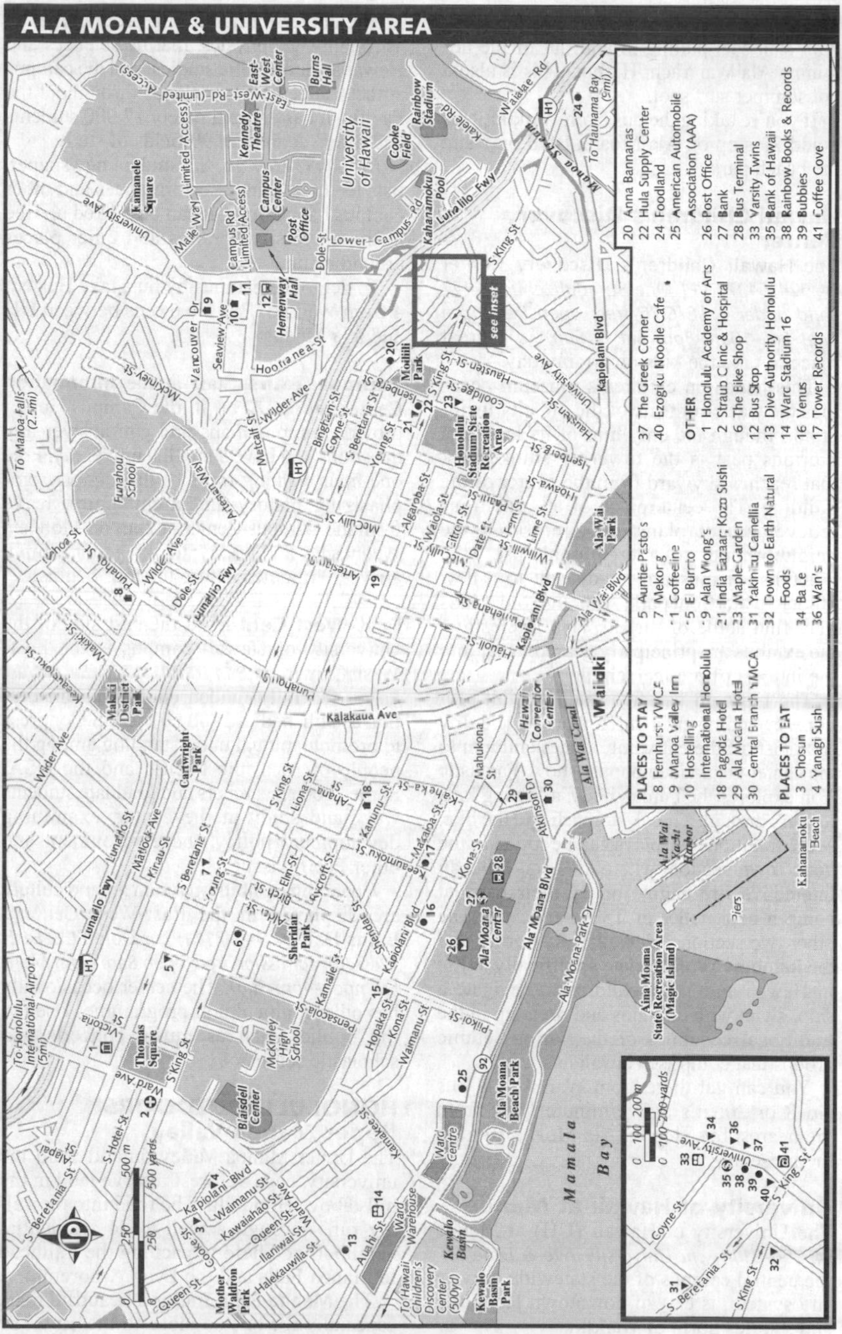
ALA MOANA & UNIVERSITY AREA
PLACES TO STAY
8 Fernhurst YWCA
9 Manoa Valley Inn
10 Hostelling International Honolulu
18 Pagoda Hotel
29 Ala Moana Hotel
30 Central Branch YMCA
PLACES TO EAT
3 Chosun
4 Yanagi Sushi
5 Auntie Pasto's
7 Mekong
11 Coffeeline
15 E Burrito
19 Alan Wong's
21 India Bazaar; Kozo Sushi
23 Maple Garden
31 Yakiniku Camellia
32 Down to Earth Natural Foods
34 Ba Le
36 Wan's
37 The Greek Corner
40 Ezogiku Noodle Cafe
OTHER
1 Honolulu Academy of Arts
2 Straub Clinic & Hospital
6 The Bike Shop
12 Bus Stop
13 Dive Authority Honolulu
14 Ward Stadium 16
16 Venus
17 Tower Records
20 Anna Bananas
22 Hula Supply Center
24 Foodland
25 American Automobile Association (AAA)
26 Post Office
27 Bank
28 Bus Terminal
33 Varsity Twins
35 Bank of Hawaii
38 Rainbow Books & Records
39 Bubbies
41 Coffee Cove

Magic Island, and sunsets can be picturesque, with sailboats pulling in and out of the adjoining Ala Wai Yacht Harbor. This is also a hot summer surf spot.

If you're taking the bus from Waikiki, Nos 8 and 20 stop on Ala Moana Blvd opposite the beach park.

Hawaii Children's Discovery Center

The **Hawaii Children's Discovery Center** *(☎ 524-5437; 111 Ohe St; adult/child 2-17/child under 2 $8/6.75/free; open 9am-1pm Tues-Fri, 10am-3pm Sat & Sun)* is a great place to take the kids on a rainy day.

This hands-on children's museum occupies the waterfront site of the old city incinerator, though the only hint of its less than glorious past is the towering smokestack that reaches skyward from the center of the building. The centerpiece of an ambitious redevelopment plan that's returning the neighborhood to recreational use, the 37,000-sq-ft museum is adjacent to a new 30-acre waterfront park. Although older kids may find some of the displays interesting, the exhibits are principally geared to capture the interest of pre-teen children.

The museum has five main exhibit sections extending over three stories. **The Toy Box**, just off the entry, introduces children to the center via a video puppet show. Fantastic You explores the human body, allowing kids to walk through a mock stomach and the like. More traditional displays can be found in the **Your Town** section, where kids can drive an interactive fire engine or try their hand at being a bank teller or TV interviewer. The other two sections, **Hawaiian Rainbows** and the **Rainbow World**, relate specifically to life in Hawaii and allow children to navigate a ship, swim with dolphins and dress up in the traditional costumes of the various ethnic groups that comprise Hawaiian society.

You can get there from Waikiki via bus No 8 or 20; it's a five-minute walk from the nearest bus stop on Ala Moana Blvd to the museum.

University of Hawaii at Manoa

The University of Hawaii (UH) at Manoa *(☎ 956-8111; cnr University Ave & Dole St)*, the central campus of the statewide university system, is east of downtown Honolulu and 2 miles north of Waikiki.

The university has strong programmes in astronomy, geophysics, marine sciences and Hawaiian and Pacific studies, and the campus attracts students from islands throughout the Pacific. It has approximately 17,000 students and offers degrees in 90 fields of study.

Ka Leo O Hawaii, the student newspaper, lists lectures, music performances and other campus happenings. It can be picked up free at the university libraries and other places around campus.

To get to the campus by bus, take Bus No 4 from Waikiki. Bus No 6 runs between UH and Ala Moana.

Campus Tours Staff at the **Information Center** *(☎ 956-7235)* in the Campus Center provide campus maps and can answer any questions you have about the university. Free one-hour **walking tours** of the campus, emphasizing history and architecture, leave from the Campus Center at 2pm on Monday, Wednesday and Friday; to join a tour, simply arrive 10 minutes before the tour begins.

East-West Center At the east side of the University of Hawaii campus is the East-West Center *(☎ 944-7124; 1777 East-West Rd)*, a federally funded educational institution established in 1960 by the US Congress to promote mutual understanding among the people of Asia, the Pacific and the USA. Some 2000 researchers and graduate students work and study at the center, examining development policy, the environment and other Pacific issues.

Changing exhibits on Asian art and culture are displayed in the East-West Center's **Burns Hall** *(☎ 944-7111; cnr Dole St & East-West Rd; admission free; open 8am-5pm Mon-Fri, noon-4pm Sun)*. The center occasionally has other multicultural programmes open to the public, such as music concerts and scholastic seminars.

HONOLULU OUTDOORS

Upper Manoa Valley

The Upper Manoa Valley, inland from the university, ends at forest reserve land in the hills above Honolulu. The road into the valley runs through a well-to-do residential neighborhood before reaching the trailhead to Manoa Falls and the Lyon Arboretum.

The **Manoa Falls Trail** is a beautiful hike, especially for one so close to the city. The trail runs for three-quarters of a mile above a rocky streambed before ending at the falls. It takes about 30 minutes one way.

Surrounded by lush, damp vegetation, moss-covered stones and tree trunks, you get the feeling you're walking through a thick rain forest a long way from anywhere. The only sounds come from chirping birds and the rushing stream and waterfall. All sorts of trees line the path, including tall *Eucalyptus robusta*, with their soft, spongy, reddish bark; flowering orange African tulip trees; and other lofty varieties that creak like wooden doors in old houses. Many of them were planted by the Lyon Arboretum, which at one time held a lease on the property.

Wild purple orchids and red ginger grow up near the falls, adding to the tranquility found here. The falls are steep and drop about 100ft vertically into a small shallow pool. The pool is not deep enough for swimming, and occasional falling rocks make it inadvisable anyway.

The trail is usually a bit muddy, but not too bad if it hasn't been raining lately. Be careful not to catch your foot in exposed tree roots – they're potential ankle breakers, particularly if you're moving with any speed. The packed clay can be slippery in some steep places, so take your time and enjoy the walk.

About 75ft before Manoa Falls, an inconspicuous trail starts to the left of the chain-link fence. Well worth a little 15-minute side trip, the **Aihualama Trail** offers a broad view of the Manoa Valley, just a short way up the path.

After about five minutes of walking, you'll enter a bamboo forest with some massive old banyan trees. When the wind blows, the forest releases eerie crackling sounds. It's an engaging forest – enchanted or spooky, depending on your mood.

You can return to the Manoa Falls Trail or go on another mile to Pauoa Flats where the trail connects with the Puu Ohia Trail in the Tantalus area.

Lyon Arboretum The **Lyon Arboretum** *(☎ 988-0465; 3860 Manoa Rd; admission $2.50; open 9am-3pm Mon-Sat)* is a great place to go after hiking to Manoa Falls if you want to identify trees and plants you've seen along that trail.

Dr Harold Lyon, after whom the arboretum is named, is credited with introducing 10,000 exotic trees and plants to Hawaii. Approximately half of these are represented in this 193-acre arboretum, which is under the auspices of the University of Hawaii at Manoa. This is not a landscaped tropical flower garden, but a mature and largely wooded arboretum where related species are clustered in a semi-natural state.

Among the plants in the Hawaiian ethnobotanical garden are mountain apple, breadfruit and taro; *ko*, the sugarcane brought by early Polynesian settlers; *kukui* (candlenut tree), which was used to produce lantern oil; and *ti*, which was used for medicinal purposes during ancient times and for making moonshine after Westerners arrived.

A good choice among the arboretum's many short trails is the 20-minute walk up to **Inspiration Point**, which offers a view of the hills that enclose the valley. En route you'll encounter wonderful scents, inviting stone benches and lots of birdsong. The path loops through ferns, bromeliads and magnolias and passes by tall trees, including a bo tree that's a descendant of the tree Gautama Buddha sat under when he received enlightenment.

Helpful staff members at the reception center can provide a map of the garden and information on the arboretum's workshops and children's programmes. Free **guided tours** *(reservations ☎ 988-0465)* are given at 1pm Saturday and 10am Tuesday.

Getting There & Away From Ala Moana Center take the No 5 Manoa Valley bus to the end of the line, which is at the junction of Manoa Rd and Kumuone St. From there, it's a 10-minute walk to the end of Manoa Rd, where the Manoa Falls Trail begins. Lyon Arboretum is at the end of the short drive just to the left of the trailhead.

To get there by car, simply drive to the end of Manoa Rd. There's room to park at the trailhead, but it's not a very secure place, so don't leave anything valuable in the car. Lyon Arboretum has a parking area adjacent to its gardens that's reserved for arboretum visitors only.

Tantalus & Makiki Valley

Just 2 miles from downtown Honolulu, a narrow switchback road cuts its way up the lush green forest reserve land of Tantalus and Makiki Valley. The road climbs up almost to

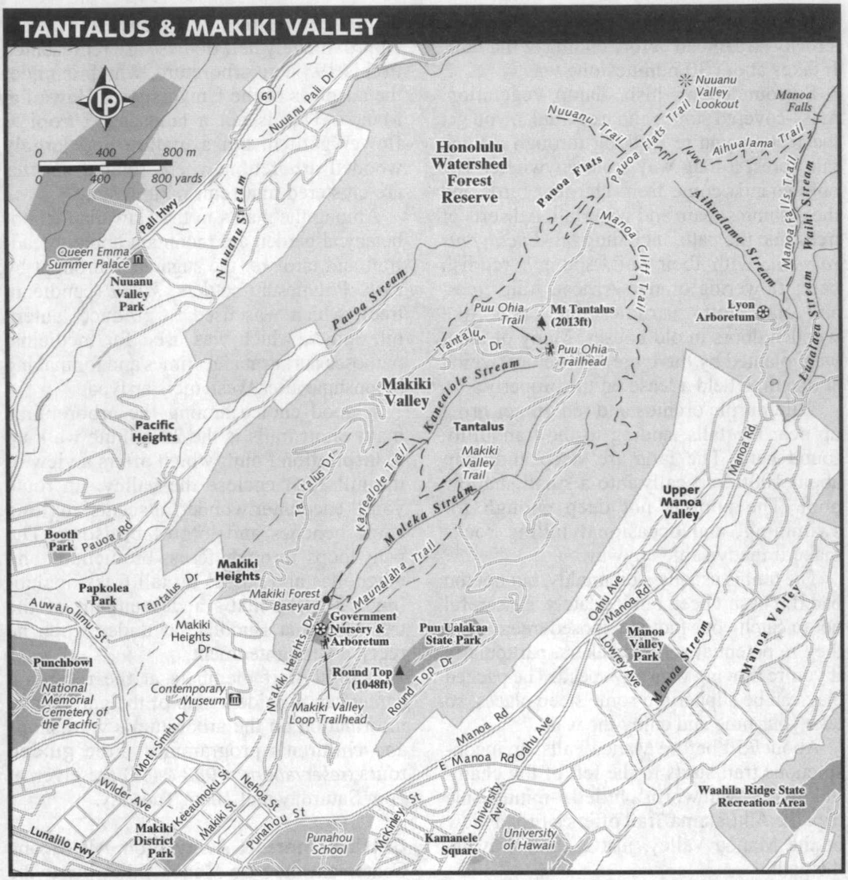

the top of 2013ft Mt Tantalus, with swank mountainside homes tucked in along the way.

Although the road is one continuous loop, the western side is called Tantalus Dr and the eastern side is Round Top Dr. The 8½-mile circuit is Honolulu's finest scenic drive, offering splendid views of the city below.

The route is winding, narrow and steep, but it's in good condition. Among the profusion of dense tropical growth, bamboo, ginger, elephant-ear taro and fragrant eucalyptus trees are easily identified. Vines climb to the top of telephone poles and twist their way across the wires.

A network of hiking trails runs between Tantalus Dr and Round Top Dr and throughout the forest reserve, and there are many trailheads off both roads. The trails are seldom crowded, which seems amazing considering how accessible they are. Perhaps because the drive itself is so nice, the only walking most people do is between their car and the scenic lookouts.

The Makiki Heights area below the forest reserve is one of the most exclusive residential areas in Honolulu and the site of a museum of contemporary art. There's a bus service as far as Makiki Heights, but none around the Tantalus-Round Top loop drive.

Puu Ualakaa State Park From Puu Ualakaa State Park *(open 7am-7:45pm daily summer, 7am-6:45pm daily winter)* you can see an incredible panorama of all Honolulu. The park entrance is 2½ miles up Round Top

Dr from Makiki St. It's half a mile in to the lookout; bear to the left when the road forks.

The sweeping view from the lookout extends from Kahala and Diamond Head on the far left, across Waikiki and downtown Honolulu, to the Waianae Range on the far right. To the southeast is the University of Hawaii at Manoa, easily recognized by its sports stadium; to the southwest you can see clearly into the green mound of Punchbowl crater; the airport is visible on the edge of the coast and Pearl Harbor beyond that.

If you're taking photos, the best time to be here is during the day; however, this is also a fine place to watch evening settle over the city. Arrive 30 minutes before sunset to see the hills before they're in shadow.

Contemporary Museum A delightful modern art museum, the Contemporary Museum (*☎ 526-0232; 2411 Makiki Heights Dr; adult/senior & student/child under 13 $5/3/free; open 10am-4pm Tues-Sat, noon-4pm Sun*) occupies an estate with 3½ acres of gardens.

The estate house was built in 1925 for Mrs Charles Montague Cooke, whose other former home is the present site of the Honolulu Academy of Arts. A fervent patron of the arts and an influential newspaper heiress, she played a founding role in both museums.

The main galleries feature changing exhibits of paintings, sculpture and other contemporary artwork by both national and international artists. A newer building on the lawn holds the museum's most prized piece, a vivid environmental installation by David Hockney based on his sets for *L'Enfant et les Sortilèges*, Ravel's 1925 opera.

Docent-led tours, conducted at 1:30pm, are included in the price of admission. There's a café serving lunch and drinks. The museum, near the intersection of Mott-Smith Dr and Makiki Heights Dr, can be reached by the No 15 bus from downtown Honolulu.

Makiki Valley Loop Trail Three of the Tantalus area hiking trails – Maunalaha Trail, Kanealole Trail and Makiki Valley Trail – can be combined to make the Makiki Valley Loop Trail, a popular 2½-mile hike.

The loop is through a lush and varied tropical forest that starts and ends in Hawaii's first state nursery and arboretum. In this nursery, hundreds of thousands of trees were grown to replace the sandalwood forests that had been leveled in Makiki Valley and elsewhere in Hawaii in the 19th century.

The **Maunalaha Trail** begins at the rest rooms below the parking lot of the Makiki Forest baseyard. It first crosses a bridge, passes taro patches and proceeds to climb the east ridge of Makiki Valley, passing Norfolk pine, bamboo and fragrant allspice and eucalyptus trees. There are some good views along the way.

After three-quarters of a mile, you'll come to a four-way junction, where you'll take the left fork and continue on to the **Makiki Valley Trail**. The trail passes through small gulches and across gentle streams with patches of ginger. Near the Moleka Stream crossing are mountain apple trees (related to allspice and guava), which flower in the spring and fruit in the summer. Edible yellow and strawberry guavas also grow along the trail. There are some fine views of the city below.

The **Kanealole Trail** begins as you cross Kanealole Stream and then follows the stream back to the baseyard, three-quarters of a mile away. The trail leads down through a field of Job's tears; the beadlike bracts of the female flowers of this tall grass are often picked to be strung in leis. Because Kanealole Trail tends to be muddy, be sure to wear shoes with good traction and pick up a walking stick.

To get to the Makiki Forest baseyard, turn left off Makiki St and go half a mile up Makiki Heights Dr. Where the road makes a sharp bend, proceed straight ahead through a green gate into the Makiki Forest Recreation Area and continue until you reach the baseyard. There's a parking lot on the right just before the office.

You can also take the No 15 bus, which runs between downtown and Pacific Heights. Get off near the intersection of Mott-Smith Dr and Makiki Heights Dr and walk down Makiki Heights Dr to the baseyard. It's a mile-long walk between the bus stop and the trailhead.

An alternative is to hike just the Makiki Valley Trail, which you can reach by following Tantalus Dr 2 miles past its intersection with Makiki Heights Dr. As you come around a sharp curve, look for the wooden post marking the trailhead on the right. You can take this route in as far as you want and backtrack out or link up with other trails along the way.

Puu Ohia Trail The Puu Ohia Trail, in conjunction with the Pauoa Flats Trail, leads up to a lookout with a view of Nuuanu reservoir and valley. It's nearly 2 miles one way and makes a hardy hike.

The trailhead is at the very top of Tantalus Dr, 3.6 miles up on the left from its intersection with Makiki Heights Dr. There's a large turnoff opposite the trailhead where you can park.

The Puu Ohia Trail starts up reinforced log steps and leads past ginger, bamboo groves and plenty of beautiful eucalyptus, a fast-growing tree that was planted to protect the watershed. About half a mile up, the trail reaches the top of 2013ft Mt Tantalus (Puu Ohia).

From Mt Tantalus, the trail leads to a service road. Continue on the road to its end, where there's a telephone company building. The trail picks up again behind the left side of the building.

Continue down the trail until it leads into the **Manoa Cliff Trail**, which you'll go left on for a short distance until you come to another intersection, where you'll turn right onto the **Pauoa Flats Trail**. The trail leads down into Pauoa Flats and onward to the lookout. The flats area can be muddy; be careful not to trip on exposed tree roots.

You'll pass two trailheads before reaching the lookout. The first is **Nuuanu Trail**, on the left, which runs three-quarters of a mile along the western side of Upper Pauoa Valley and offers broad views of Honolulu and the Waianae Mountains.

The second is **Aihualama Trail**, a bit further along on the right, which takes you 1¼ miles to Manoa Falls through bamboo groves and under huge old banyan trees. If you were to follow this route, you could then hike down the Manoa Falls Trail, a distance of about a mile, to the end of Manoa Rd and from there catch a bus back to town (see the Upper Manoa Valley section).

Punchbowl

Punchbowl is the bowl-shaped remnant of a long-extinct volcanic crater. At an elevation of 500ft, it sits a mile north of the downtown district and offers a fine view of the city, out to Diamond Head and the Pacific beyond.

The early Hawaiians called the crater Puowaina, the 'hill of human sacrifices.' It's believed there was a *heiau* (ancient stone temple) at the crater and that the slain bodies of *kapu* (taboo) breakers were brought to Punchbowl to be cremated upon the *heiau* altar.

Today it's the site of the 115-acre **National Memorial Cemetery of the Pacific** *(☎ 532-3720; 2177 Puowaina Dr; admission free; open 8am-5:30pm daily Oct-Feb, 8am-6:30pm daily Mar-Sept)*. The remains of Hawaiians sacrificed to appease the gods now share the crater floor with the bodies of more than 25,000 soldiers, more than half of whom were killed in the Pacific during WWII.

The remains of Ernie Pyle, the distinguished war correspondent who covered both world wars and was hit by machine gun fire on Ie Shima during the final days of WWII, lie in section D, grave 109. Five stones to the left, at grave D-1, is the marker for astronaut Ellison Onizuka, the Big Island native who perished in the 1986 *Challenger* space shuttle disaster. Their resting places are marked with the same style of flat granite stone that marks each of the cemetery's graves.

A huge memorial at the rear of the cemetery has eight marble courts representing different Pacific regions. The memorial is inscribed with the names of the 26,289 Americans missing in action from WWII and the Korean War. Two additional half courts have the names of 2489 soldiers missing from the Vietnam War.

For a good view of the city, walk to the lookout, 10 minutes south of the memorial.

If you're driving to Punchbowl, take the H1 to the Pali Hwy. There's a marked exit as you start up the Pali Hwy; watch closely, because it comes up quickly! From there, follow the signs through a series of narrow streets on the short route up to the cemetery.

By bus, take No 2 from Waikiki to downtown Honolulu and get off at Beretania and Alapai Sts, where you transfer to bus No 15. Ask the driver where to get off. It's about a 15-minute walk to Punchbowl from the bus stop.

Royal Mausoleum State Monument

The Royal Mausoleum *(2261 Nuuanu Ave; admission free; open 8am-4:30pm Mon-Fri)* contains the remains of Kings Kamehameha

II, III, IV and V, as well as King David Kalakaua and Queen Liliuokalani, Hawaii's last reigning monarchs. Conspicuously absent are the remains of Kamehameha the Great, the last king to be buried in secret in accordance with Hawaii's old religion.

The original mausoleum building, which is usually locked, is now a chapel; the caskets are in nearby crypts. Other gravestones honor Kamehameha I's British confidant John Young and American Charles Reed Bishop, husband of Princess Bernice Pauahi Bishop.

The Royal Mausoleum is on Nuuanu Ave, just before it meets the Pali Hwy. You can get there by taking the No 4 Nuuanu Dowsett bus from Waikiki.

Bishop Museum

The Bishop Museum *(☎ 847-3511; 1525 Bernice St; adult/child 4-12/child under 4 $15/12/free; open 9am 5pm daily)* is considered the finest Polynesian anthropological museum in the world, although the presentation can be a bit dry.

The main gallery, the **Hawaiian Hall**, has three floors of exhibits that cover the cultural history of Hawaii. The 1st floor, dedicated primarily to pre-Western-contact Hawaii, has a full-sized pili-grass thatched house, carved temple images, shark-toothed war clubs and similar displays.

One of the museum's most impressive holdings is a feather cloak once worn by Kamehameha the Great. It was created entirely of the yellow feathers of the now-extinct *mamo*, a predominately black bird with a yellow upper tail. Some 80,000 *mamos* were caught, plucked and released to create this single cloak. To get a sense of just how few feathers each bird had available for sacrifice, look at the nearby taxidermic *mamo*, to the left of the Queen Liliuokalani exhibit.

The 2nd floor is dedicated to the varied influences of 19th-century Hawaii. Here you will find traditional tapa cloth robes, missionary-inspired quilt work and barter items that Yankee traders brought to the islands; there's also a small whaling exhibit.

The top floor has displays on the various ethnic groups that comprise present-day Hawaii. Like Hawaii itself, it has a bit of everything, including samurai armor, Portuguese festival costumes, Taoist fortune-telling sticks and a Hawaiian ukulele made of coconut shells. To top it off, a 55ft sperm whale skeleton hangs from the ceiling.

The **Kahili Room**, a small gallery off the main hall, features portraits of Hawaiian royalty and a display of *kahili*, the feathered staffs used at coronations and royal funerals. Other exhibits cover the cultures of Polynesia, Micronesia and Melanesia.

The museum's modern wing, the **Castle Building**, has changing natural-history exhibits, some interactive, designed for children. The museum is also home to Oahu's only **planetarium**, which has shows at 11:30am, 1:30pm, 2:30pm and 3:30pm; shows are included in the museum admission price.

The gift shop off the lobby sells books on the Pacific that are not easily found elsewhere, as well as some quality Hawaiian crafts and souvenirs. There's also a snack shop open to 4pm.

To get to the Bishop Museum by bus from Waikiki or downtown Honolulu, take the No 2 School St bus to Kapalama St, and turn right on Bernice St. By car, take exit 20B off the H1, go inland on Houghtailing St and turn left on Bernice St.

PLACES TO STAY – BUDGET

Ala Moana & University Area

Hosteling International Honolulu *(☎ 946-0591, fax 946-5904; ⓔ ayhaloha@lava.net; 2323A Seaview Ave; dorm beds nonmembers/members $17/14; rooms $44/38; office open 8am-noon, 4pm-midnight)* is a small, well-run hostel in a quiet residential neighborhood in the area. It has seven dorm rooms with bunk beds that can accommodate up to 43 travelers, with men and women in separate dorms, and two rooms for couples. If you're not a Hostelling International (HI) member, there's a three-night maximum stay. HI membership is sold on site; the cost is $25 for Americans, $18 for foreign visitors. The hostel has a TV lounge, guest kitchen, laundry room, lockers and bulletin boards with lots of handy information for new arrivals.

Central Branch YMCA *(☎ 941-3344, fax 941-8821; 401 Atkinson Dr; ⓔ centralymca@yahoo.com; singles/doubles $30/41, singles & doubles with bath $53)*, on the east side of the Ala Moana Center, is conveniently located just outside Waikiki. There are 114 rooms in all. The rooms with shared bath, which are available to men only, are small and simple, resembling those in a student dorm. Rooms with private bath, which are a bit nicer but still small and basic, are open to both men and women. Guests receive YMCA privileges, including free use of the sauna, pool and gym. There's a coin laundry, a TV lounge and a snack bar.

Fernhurst YWCA (☎ *941-2231, fax 949-0266;* ⓔ *fernywca@gte.net; 1566 Wilder Ave; bed $15, private room $30)*, about a mile west of the university, has rooms for women only. Although the Y accepts tourists, most guests are local, because Fernhurst provides transitional housing for women in need – and the place can be full for weeks at a time. Each of its 60 rooms has two single beds and two lockable closets. Two rooms share one bathroom. Rates include breakfast and dinner, except on weekends; there are limited kitchen facilities. Advance payment is required and guests must be YWCA members (membership is $30 a year). It costs $20 to rent linen, or you can bring your own. There's a laundry room, TV room and small pool.

Downtown Honolulu

Nuuanu YMCA (☎ *536-3556; 1441 Pali Hwy; rooms per day/week $30/160)*, at the intersection of Pali Hwy and Vineyard Blvd, has mostly long-term tenants, but rents some rooms by the day and week. Accommodations are for men only. Rooms are small and spartan, essentially just a single bed, a desk and a chair. Bathrooms are shared. Guests have access to a TV lounge, the weight room and pool.

PLACES TO STAY – MID-RANGE

Ala Moana & University Area

The **Manoa Valley Inn** (☎ *947-6019, fax 946-6168;* ⓔ *manoavalleyinn@aloha.net; 2001 Vancouver Dr; rooms $99, with bath $140-190)*, located on a quiet side street just near the University of Hawaii at Manoa, is an authentically restored Victorian inn that is on the National Register of Historic Places. The inn's common areas and eight guest rooms are furnished with antiques, and the whole place simply drips with colonial character. The inn is best suited for those who prefer to be outside the main tourist scene. Rates include continental breakfast.

Pagoda Hotel (☎ *941-6611, 800-367-6060, fax 955-5067;* ⓔ *hthcorp@worldnet.att.net; 1525 Rycroft St; rooms/studios $110/115)*, north of the Ala Moana Center, has two sections. The rooms in the hotel itself, which is where you'll find the front desk and lobby, are quiet and have the expected amenities, including air-con, TV and refrigerator. There are also studios with kitchenettes in a nearby apartment complex, but they can feel a bit removed from the main hotel – especially if you're checking in at night. There's nothing distinguished about this hotel, other than a restaurant with a carp pond, but it's an alternative to jumping into the bustling Waikiki scene.

Near the Airport

If you have some dire need to be near Honolulu international airport, there are three hotels outside the airport along a busy highway and beneath flight paths. All provide free 24-hour transport to and from the airport, about 10 minutes away.

Best Western Plaza Hotel (☎ *836-3636, 800-528-1234, fax 834-7406;* ⓔ *plazahotel@aloha.net; 3253 N Nimitz Hwy; rooms $109)* is a modern hotel with 274 pleasant rooms, each with a king or two double beds, TV and refrigerator. This is the most comfortable option near the airport. The only drawback is the noise from the heavy traffic on the overpass adjacent to the front of the hotel – ask for a rear room. The hotel has a pool, lounge and restaurant, and nonsmoking rooms are available. Within walking distance is the Nimitz Mart center, which has a handful of inexpensive fast-food places.

Honolulu Airport Hotel (☎ *836-0661, 800-800-3477, fax 833-1738;* ⓔ *info@honoluluairporthotel.com; 3401 N Nimitz Hwy; rooms $115)* on the corner of Rodgers Blvd, has 308 rooms that are a bit on the small side, but this four-story former Holiday Inn has all the usual amenities, including a lounge, pool and restaurant. Nonsmoking rooms are available. Discounts are common, including a room-and-car deal at the same price as the regular rate.

Pacific Marina Inn (☎ *836-1131, 800-548-8040, fax 833-0851;* ⓔ *pacific_marina_inn_2000@yahoo.com; 2628 Waiwai Loop; rooms $90)* is a mile further east in an industrial area, but on the plus side, it has the least traffic noise. This three-decker motel has small, straightforward rooms with air-con and TV, and the hotel has a pool. There's often an 'airport special' of $65; call from its courtesy phone in the airport's baggage claim area.

PLACES TO STAY – TOP END

Ala Moana

Ala Moana Hotel *(☎ 955-4811, 800-367-6025, fax 944-6839; ⓔ amh.resv@gte.net; 410 Atkinson Dr; rooms $155-225)* looms above the Ala Moana Center, just west of Waikiki. The 1169 rooms, which resemble those of a chain hotel, have TV, air-con, small refrigerators and room safes. The lower rates are for lower-floor city-view rooms, with prices rising as you climb, topping out at ocean-view rooms on the 35th floor. The hotel is popular with business travelers, especially overnighting airline crews.

Downtown Honolulu

The **Executive Centre Hotel** *(☎ 539-3000, 800-922-7866, fax 523-1088; ⓔ res.exc@aston-hotels.com; 1088 Bishop St; rooms $170-250)* is Honolulu's only downtown hotel. Geared for businesspeople, it has 116 suites, each large and comfortable with modern amenities that include three phones, voice mail, two TVs, a refrigerator and a room safe. As the hotel is on the upper floors of a high-rise, most of the rooms have fine city views. The pricier rooms have ocean views and kitchen facilities. There's a fitness center, heated lap pool and a business center with secretarial services and laptop rentals. Rates include continental breakfast and the morning newspaper.

PLACES TO EAT

Honolulu has an incredible variety of restaurants that mirror the city's multiethnic composition, and if you know where to look it can also be quite cheap. The key is to get out of the tourist areas and eat where the locals do.

Ala Moana & the University Area

Not surprisingly, the area around the University of Hawaii at Manoa supports an interesting collection of reasonably priced ethnic restaurants, coffee shops and health food stores. The following places are all within a 10-minute walk of the three-way intersection of S King St, S Beretania St and University Ave.

Bubbies *(1010 University Ave; open noon-midnight Mon-Thur, noon-1am Fri & Sat, noon-11:30pm Sun)*, an ice-cream shop on the corner of Beretania St, is a great place to go if you're up for homemade ice cream ($2.65 single cone) in luscious tropical flavors such as papaya-ginger.

Ba Le *(1019 University Ave; snacks $1-5; open 7am-7:30pm Mon-Sat)*, a branch of a local Vietnamese bakery/café, sells good, inexpensive French rolls, croissants and sandwiches, as well as Vietnamese noodle dishes and salads.

Coffeeline *(cnr University and Seaview Aves; dishes $3-6; open 7am-3:45pm Mon-Fri, 8am-noon Sat)* is a casual student hangout with good coffees and vegetarian food. Proudly serving 'slow food,' Coffeeline offers up vegan soup, 'big hippie' sandwiches, hearty salads and a few hot dishes such as spinach lasagna. Blues and jazz music plays all day and there's a large stack of alternative magazines to browse.

Ezogiku Noodle Cafe *(1010 University Ave; dishes $5-7; open 11am-11pm daily)* serves up steaming bowls of Japanese ramen, curries and fried rice. Nothing memorable, but it's relatively cheap and there's usually some sort of combination deal adding on a free order of *gyoza* (grilled garlic-and-pork-filled dumplings) with lunch orders.

Down to Earth Natural Foods *(☎ 947-7678; 2525 S King St; open 7:30am-9pm daily)* is Honolulu's largest natural foods supermarket. A great place to shop, it carries everything from Indian chapatis to local organic produce. The store also has a vegetarian deli with a salad bar and hot dishes such as tahini tofu balls or vegetable curry for $6 a pound.

Wan's *(1023 University Ave; dishes $6-10; open 10:30am-3:30pm, 5pm-10pm daily)* is a wonderful little family-run Thai restaurant, and as neat as a pin. It has an extensive menu, including many vegetarian dishes. The scrumptious curries come in numerous versions, including Penang and yellow, but if you like things fiery go with the hot-and-spicy red curry, dubbed 'Wan's Evil Thai.'

India Bazaar *(2320 S King St; meals $7; open 11am-7:30pm daily)*, in a shopping plaza, is a small café selling inexpensive Indian food. Plates are dished up with your choice of curried items, either vegetarian or chicken, plus spiced rice. Side orders of pappadams, chapatis and raita cost less than $1.

Kozo Sushi *(2334 S King St; meals $5-7; open 9am-7pm Mon-Sat, 9am-6pm Sun)*, in the same complex as India Bazaar, is a branch of a local chain that specializes in good, inexpensive sushi. You can get set meals or order à la carte. Top choices include the fresh tuna roll and the California *maki*, a crab and avocado roll. Although it's mostly take-out, the shop has a couple of tables where you can sit and eat.

Maple Garden *(☎ 941-6641; 909 Isenberg St; mains $6.50-10; open 11am-2pm, 5:30pm-10pm daily)*, around the corner from S King St, is a popular local Sichuan restaurant with delicious food at reasonable prices. There are scores of vegetarian, beef, pork, chicken, duck and seafood options. House specialties include eggplant in hot garlic sauce, black-bean prawns and smoky Sichuan duck. At lunch there are multi-item plate specials for just $6.

The Greek Corner *(☎ 942-5503; 1025 University Ave; mains $10-12; open 11am-1:30pm Mon-Fri, 5pm-9:30pm daily)* is an inviting eatery with good Greek food, and being near the university, prices are cheaper than they'd be in a trendier part of town. Main dishes, which come with Greek salad, rice and pita bread, include popular standards like lamb kebab, moussaka and stuffed grape leaves. The place has plenty of choices for vegetarians and meat eaters alike.

Yakiniku Camellia *(☎ 946-7595; 2494 S Beretania St; lunch/dinner buffet $10/15.75; open lunch 11am-3pm, dinner 3pm-10pm daily)* offers tasty all-you-can-cook Korean buffets. It's quality food, and if you've worked up an appetite, it's a fine deal. The mainstay is pieces of chicken, pork and beef that you select and grill at your table. Accompanying this are 18 marinated side dishes, miso and seaweed soups, salads and fresh fruit. When selecting *kimchi*, keep in mind that the redder they are, the hotter they are. Everything here is authentic, right down to the vending machine selling Korean-language newspapers.

Old Spaghetti Factory *(1050 Ala Moana Blvd; open 11:30am-2pm & 5pm-10pm Mon-Fri, 11:30am-10:30pm Sat, 4pm-9:30pm Sun)*, in the Ward Warehouse, is hard to beat for cheap eats with a water view. This family-style chain restaurant has an elaborate decor, chock-full of antiques, Tiffany stained glass – even an old streetcar. At lunch you can order spaghetti with tomato sauce ($4.10), with clam sauce ($5) or with meatballs ($6). All meals come with bread and a simple salad. Dishes are about a dollar more at dinner. The food is average, but the price is right, the surroundings interesting and it's a fun place to go with kids.

Mekong *(1295 S Beretania St; appetizers $4-7, mains $7-10; open 11am-2pm Mon-Fri, 5pm-9:30pm daily)* is one of the oldest Thai restaurants in Honolulu. It's a small unpretentious place with a solid reputation for good food and fair prices. The menu includes excellent spring rolls, tasty noodle dishes and a variety of curries in both vegetarian and meat versions.

El Burrito *(550 Piikoi St; dishes $8-10; open 11am-8pm Mon-Thur, 11am-9pm Fri & Sat)*, near the Ala Moana Center, could be a neighborhood restaurant on a back street in Mexico City. This hole-in-the-wall squeezes in about a dozen tables and serves authentic Mexican food: fellow diners are as likely to be chatting in Spanish as English. Expect lines at dinnertime, especially on weekends.

Auntie Pasto's *(1099 S Beretania St; appetizers $5-10, mains $8-12; open 11am-10:30pm Mon-Fri, 4pm-11pm Sat & Sun)* has good Italian food. Pasta is the specialty, with a number of vegetarian varieties such as eggplant parmesan, as well as a full range of seafood and meat choices. Although it's off the tourist track, this popular spot attracts a crowd and you may have to wait for a table – particularly on the weekend.

Chosun *(725 Kapiolani Blvd; meals $6-12; open 11am-11pm daily)* is a good family-run Korean restaurant with a varied menu and reasonable prices. The house specialty is duck, which is prepared in several ways, ranging from *yook gae jang*, a spicy duck soup, to clay-pot roast duck, slow-roasted in a clay pot and stuffed with rice, fruits and nuts.

Pagoda Restaurant *(☎ 941-6611; 1525 Rycroft St; breakfast $4-9, lunch buffet $11, dinner buffet $19-21; breakfast 6:30am-11am Mon-Sat, lunch 11am-2pm Mon-Fri, dinner 4:30pm-9:30pm daily)*, at the Pagoda Hotel, offers a pleasant gardenlike setting bordering a carp pond. The breakfast menu is extensive, there's a lunch buffet of Japanese and American dishes and a fancier dinner buffet with a spread that includes prime rib, crab legs, sashimi, a salad bar and a dessert bar.

Pavilion Cafe *(☎ 532-8734; 900 S Beretania St; dishes $8-13; open 11:30am-2pm Tues-Sat)*, an upscale café in the Honolulu Academy of Arts, has a lovely courtyard setting overlooking the museum's water fountains. The kitchen specializes in gourmet salads and sandwiches, but also makes an innovative pasta of the day. It's a good place to relax and a wonderfully indulging way to support the arts. Reservations are suggested, particularly if there's a special exhibition at the museum.

Yanagi Sushi *(☎ 537-1525; 762 Kapiolani Blvd; à la carte sushi $2-5, meals $10-20; open 11am-2pm daily, 5:30pm-2am Mon-Sat, 5:30pm-10pm Sun)* is one of Honolulu's most popular late-night places. Not only is the sushi here top-rated, but Yanagi also offers a full line of other Japanese dinners prepared to perfection. Ask about the 'late birds' – $8 meal specials available after 10:30pm.

Ward Centre A shopping and restaurant complex, the Ward Centre *(1200 Ala Moana Blvd)* has a couple of top-rated dining spots.

Kaka'ako Kitchen *(meals $6-9; open 7am-10pm Mon-Sat, 7am-5pm Sun)*, at the north west corner of the center, offers fantastic food at bargain prices. A spin-off of the upscale restaurant 3660 On the Rise, Kaka'ako uses the same fresh ingredients and creative flair as its pricier parent operation. Here, however, the food is served plate-lunch style on Styrofoam with brown rice and an organic salad. You can choose from local favorites such as shoyu chicken, or for a bit more, order a gourmet plate such as the sauteed mahimahi (a great choice) or the ginger-sake *ahi* (yellowfin tuna) steak. Eat here at patio tables or take it across the street to Ala Moana Beach for a picnic.

Compadres *(☎ 591-8307; appetizers $5-8, dishes $10-20; open 11am-11pm Mon-Thur, 11am-midnight Fri & Sat, 11am-10pm Sun)*, on the center's upper level, is a bustling Mexican restaurant that draws a crowd and wins plenty of local dining awards. It not only offers the expected enchilada, fajita and taco dishes but also has some interesting cross-cultural fare like spicy peanut Thai quesadillas.

Brew Moon *(☎ 593-0088; snacks $6-9; lunch/dinner $12/18; open 11am-1am daily)*, a stylish, high-energy place, brews its own ales, ranging from a low-calorie 'moonlight' brew to the copper-colored 'Hawaii 5' malt. A fun way to tantalize the taste buds is with the 24oz sampler ($6) of six different ales. Brew Moon serves a wide variety of snacks, including fried calamari, grilled pizzas and sandwiches. Meals such as jambalaya chicken or sauteed fish are available at lunch and dinner.

Kincaid's Fish, Chop & Steak House *(☎ 591-2005; 1050 Ala Moana Blvd; lunch $10-15, dinner $18-30, open 11am-10pm daily)*, in the Ward Warehouse, is a smart upmarket place with good food and a harbor view. A favorite lunch spot for downtown businesspeople, the restaurant specializes in creative seafood dishes and steaks. The best deal is the soup-to-dessert 'early bird' that's available from 5pm to 6pm and offers a choice of several mains for $19.

Downtown Honolulu

There's a cluster of inexpensive restaurants at the north side of the downtown area within easy walking distance of Iolani Palace. As more college students move into this area, the variety of restaurants continues to increase and there are some good choices.

Fort Street Cafe *(1152 Fort St Mall, dishes $4-6; open 7am-7pm Mon-Fri, 7am-4pm Sat)* is usually crowded with students who come here for the cheap Asian plate lunches, Vietnamese *pho* soups and various noodle dishes.

L&L Drive-Inn *(116 S Hotel St; dishes $5; open 8am-6:30pm Mon-Sat)*, offering local-style Chinese fast food, does a bustling business at lunchtime, with items such as sweet and sour pork, broccoli chicken and fried noodles served from steamer trays.

Z's Poi Bowl *(1108 Bishop St; lunch $4-6; open 6:30am-2pm Mon-Fri)*, a little hole-in-the-wall, features take-out plate lunches of traditional Hawaiian food. A typical plate includes selections like *kalua* pig (traditionally baked in an underground oven), *lomi* (raw, diced and marinated salmon), poi and rice.

Leo's Taverna *(1116 Bishop St; dishes $4-8; 8am-6pm Mon-Fri, 10am-3pm Sat)* is a popular Greek restaurant with an extensive menu. Vegetarians can choose from falafels, Greek salad, stuffed grape leaves and the like. For meat eaters, there are kebabs, moussaka and tasty gyros of marinated beef and lamb.

Cafe Metro *(1130 Fort St Mall; meals $6-12; open 9am-6pm Mon-Sat)* is a pleasant café specializing in Tex-Mex fare. You can get such standards as tacos, enchiladas and *chili rellenos* (green chili peppers stuffed with cheese), all served with rice and beans, and it also has salads, shrimp scampi and other items.

Sunset Grill *(☎ 521-4409; cnr Ala Moana Blvd & Punchbowl St; lunch/dinner around $10/20; open 11am-11pm Mon-Fri, 5pm-11pm Sat & Sun)*, in the Restaurant Row complex, offers a varied menu with fresh fish, pastas and grilled meats at dinner and creative salads and sandwiches at lunch. In addition to good food, the restaurant boasts an extensive wine list – including numerous selections by the glass.

Aloha Tower Marketplace This waterfront complex, immediately west of the downtown district, is easily recognized by its landmark clock tower. It boasts some of Honolulu's trendiest seaside restaurants.

Kapono's *(snacks $6-10; open 11am-midnight daily)*, in the marketplace's waterfront courtyard, is not only a happening place for Hawaiian music, but a good spot for a drink and light eats. The menu includes snacks, sandwiches, fried calamari and the like. Happy 'hour' is a daylong event here, running from 11am to 8pm, and featuring $2 draft beers. There's live Hawaiian music from 6pm to 9pm nightly.

Gordon Biersch Brewery Restaurant *(☎ 599-1405; 1st floor; mains $10-23; open 10:30am-10pm Mon-Fri, 10:30am-11pm Sat & Sun)*, on the seaside, is another great spot for a drink. Hawaii's first and most successful microbrewery restaurant, this outpost of the San Francisco brewpub features fresh lagers made according to Germany's centuries-old purity laws. The food is also good: Hawaiian *pupus* (hors d'oeuvres), creative salads, sandwiches and pizzas are available for under $10; the mains include specialty pastas and grilled seafood. There's live entertainment Wednesday to Saturday night.

Big Island Steak House *(☎ 537-4446; lunch specials $7-12, dinner $15-25; open 11am-10pm daily)* is a decent steak restaurant with a fine water view. It specializes in thick, juicy steaks, but also offers grilled fish, baby-back ribs and barbecued chicken.

Chai's Island Bistro *(☎ 585-0011; appetizers $8-12, lunch $12-20, dinner $28-45; open 11am-4pm Mon-Fri, 4pm-10pm daily)* is a spin-off of the popular Singha Thai restaurant in Waikiki. You'll find award-winning Pacific Rim cuisine, with such specialties as crispy duck spring rolls, macadamia-crusted prawns and brandy-glazed Mongolian lamb. It's pricey and there's no water view, but both the food and presentation are winners, and some of Hawaii's top musicians perform nightly at dinner.

Chinatown

For a quintessentially local dining option, head to the food court in the **Maunakea Marketplace** *(N Hotel St; open 7am-3:30pm daily)*. Here you'll find about 20 stalls with mom-and-pop vendors dishing out home-style Chinese, Thai, Vietnamese, Korean and Japanese food. You can get a solid meal for $5 and chow down at tiny wooden tables crowded into the central walkway.

Ba Le *(150 N King St; snacks $1-5; open 6am-5pm Mon-Sat, 6am-3pm Sun)* is another good place for a quick, inexpensive bite. Vegetarian sandwiches – a tangy combo of crunchy carrots, daikon and cilantro – cost just $2.25, while traditional meat sandwiches are a dollar more. For a caffeine jolt, there's sweet, strong French coffee with milk, either hot or cold. It also sells good croissants, shrimp rolls and tapioca puddings.

Krung Thai *(1028 Nuuanu Ave; meals $4-5; open 10:30am-2pm Mon-Fri)* is a good-value Thai eatery on the edge of Chinatown. Lunch, the only meal served, is geared to the business community's 30-minute lunch breaks, with food ready in steamer trays. You can choose from a dozen hot mains, such as broccoli beef, cashew chicken or garlic eggplant, served with rice. There are tables in a rear courtyard where you can sit and enjoy your meal.

To Chau *(1007 River St; open 8am-2:30pm daily)* is a Vietnamese restaurant serving fantastic *pho*, a delicious soup of beef broth, rice noodles and thin slices of beef. It comes with a second plate of fresh basil and hot chili peppers that you add to your liking. A bowl of soup ($4 to $5.20) is a meal in itself, and the shrimp rolls ($3) here are also excellent. The restaurant serves some rice dishes, but just about everybody comes for the soup. It's so popular that even at 10am you may have to line up outside the door for one of the 16 tables. It's well worth the wait.

Cur Long *(1001 River St; dishes $4-7; open 8am-8pm daily)* makes a good alternative if the line at To Chau is too daunting. While this restaurant is relatively large and blandly modern, it too specializes in *pho* and does a good job of it. The menu also includes a few other Vietnamese noodle and rice dishes.

Lee Ho Fook Restaurant *(Chinatown Cultural Plaza; dishes $4-6.50; open 10am-8pm daily)*, on the River St mall, is a hole-in-the-wall family-run place with half a dozen tables and some of the cheapest Chinese food around. Amazingly, there are nearly a hundred items on the menu, from delicious cake noodles to beef in oyster sauce and black-bean shrimp. It's unbeatable value.

Legend Vegetarian Restaurant *(Chinatown Cultural Plaza; dishes $7-12; open 10:30am-2pm, 5:30pm-9pm Thur-Tues)* is a health-oriented Chinese dining spot. It offers some incongruously named dishes (sweet-and-sour vegetarian pork!) that imaginatively use tofu and wheat gluten to duplicate the flavors and textures of meat and seafood. Nonetheless, the restaurant is 100% vegetarian. The menu is not only innovative but extensive as well, and the restaurant packs in a good crowd.

Zaffron *(69 N King St; lunch $8, dinner $13; open 11am-2pm Mon-Sat, 5pm-9pm Wed-Sat)*, at the southwest side of Chinatown, is a good choice if you're looking for home-style Indian food at reasonable prices. This small, family-run restaurant offers a variety of hearty plate lunches and a good dinnertime buffet. You can choose from vegetarian mains, tandoori chicken and meat or fish curries. Each plate lunch includes rice, *nan* and a number of side dishes.

Indigo *(☎ 521-2900; 1121 Nuuanu Ave; appetizers $6-10, dinner $16-26; open 11:30am-2pm Tues-Fri, 6pm-9:30pm Tues-Sat)* has a relaxed, open-air courtyard and good contemporary Asian-Pacific cuisine. Located on the Chinatown-downtown border, behind the Hawaii Theatre, it's a favorite dinner spot for theatergoers. A special treat here is the creative dim sum appetizers, like tempura *ahi* rolls and goat cheese wontons. Dinner features such dishes as mango-glazed ribs and ginger-miso salmon. The gourmet pizzas ($9), which come in vegetarian, Peking duck and spicy chicken varieties, are popular at lunch.

Elsewhere in Honolulu

Hale Vietnam *(1140 12th Ave; mains $6-10; open 11am-10pm daily)*, in the Kaimuki area, well off the beaten path, is a top-notch local favorite with delicious Vietnamese food at moderate prices. A delightful starter is the temple rolls ($4.25), a combination of fresh basil, mint, tofu and yam rolled in rice paper. The yellow curries are also excellent and come in vegetarian, beef and chicken variations. The restaurant is 3 miles northeast of Waikiki; turn south off Waialae Ave onto 12th Ave and go 100 yards.

3660 On the Rise *(☎ 737-1177; 3660 Waialae Ave; appetizers $10, mains $19-26; open 5:30pm-9pm Tues-Sun)* is a trendy restaurant with a loyal Honolulu following. It features 'Euro-Island' cuisine, blending continental and island flavors. Appetizers include escargot, spicy crab cakes and specialty salads. Popular mains include red snapper steamed in a Hawaiian ti leaf, macadamia-nut-crusted lamb and Black Angus garlic steak. The restaurant is 3 miles northeast of Waikiki, on Waialae Ave between 12th and 13th Aves.

Alan Wong's *(☎ 949-2526; 1857 S King St; appetizers $8-12, mains $26-38; open 5pm-10pm daily)*, one of Hawaii's top restaurants, is a high-energy place specializing in upmarket Hawaiian regional cuisine. Chef Wong, who won accolades at the Big Island's exclusive Mauna Lani Resort before striking out on his own, offers a creative menu with an emphasis on fresh local ingredients. Appetizers include the likes of tempura *ahi*, while mains feature fresh seafood such as Wong's signature dish, ginger-crusted onaga (red snapper). Each night there's also a five-course 'tasting menu' ($65). Reservations are recommended.

ENTERTAINMENT

Honolulu has a limited but lively entertainment scene, with most of the action occurring around the university and the Aloha Tower Marketplace. The best place to check updated listings is in the free *Honolulu Weekly*, which is readily found throughout the city.

Theater & Concerts

Honolulu boasts a symphony orchestra, an opera company, ballet troupes, chamber orchestras and numerous community theater groups.

Hawaii Theatre *(☎ 528-0506; 1130 Bethel St)*, in a beautifully restored historic building on the edge of Chinatown, is a major venue for dance, music and theater. Performances range from top contemporary Hawaiian musicians such as Hapa and Hookena to modern dance and film festivals.

Blaisdell Center (*☎ 591-2211; 777 Ward Ave*) presents concerts, Broadway shows and family events, such as the Honolulu Symphony, the Ice Capades, the American Ballet Theatre and occasional big-name rock musicians like Sting.

Academy Theatre (*☎ 532-8768; 900 S Beretania St*), at the Honolulu Academy of Arts, and the **East-West Center** (*☎ 944-7111*), adjacent to the University of Hawaii at Manoa, both present multicultural theater performances and concerts.

Cinemas

Honolulu has several movie theaters showing first-run feature films, including **Ward Stadium 16** (*☎ 594-7000; 1020 Auahi St*), Oahu's biggest theater with 16 screens; and **Restaurant Row 9 Cinemas** (*☎ 526-4171; 500 Ala Moana Blvd*), a nine-screen multiplex at the Restaurant Row complex, downtown.

Varsity Twins (*☎ 973-5833; 1006 University Ave*), a two-screen theater near the University of Hawaii at Manoa, usually shows foreign films, art films and other alternative movies.

Academy Theatre (*☎ 532-8768; 900 S Beretania St*), at the Honolulu Academy of Arts, showcases American independent cinema, foreign films and avant-garde shorts.

Music & Dancing

Anna Bannanas (*☎ 946-5190; 2440 S Beretania St*), not far from the university, is a hot dance place that features blues, ska and reggae bands from 9pm to 2am Thursday to Sunday.

Kapono's (*☎ 536-2161; Aloha Tower Marketplace*) has live music from 9pm to 2am Tuesday to Saturday, featuring jazz, rock and top Hawaiian musicians, including the club's namesake, Henry Kapono.

Gordon Biersch Brewery Restaurant (*☎ 599-4877; Aloha Tower Marketplace*) is a popular waterfront microbrewery with live rhythm and blues, contemporary Hawaiian and soft rock from 9pm to midnight Thursday to Saturday.

Rumours (*☎ 955-4811; 410 Atkinson Dr*), at the Ala Moana Hotel, has dancing to recorded music from 9pm to 4am Thursday to Saturday, with Latin music on Thursday, top 40 music on Friday and hip hop and rhythm and blues on Saturday.

Venus (*☎ 951-8671; 1349 Kapiolani Blvd*), north of the Ala Moana Center, is a popular gay bar with dancing, DJs, and male revues.

Free Entertainment

The **Royal Hawaiian Band** performs from noon to 1pm on Friday (except in August) at the bandstand on the Iolani Palace lawn.

In the **Ala Moana Center**, a courtyard area called Centerstage is the venue for free performances by hula dancers, gospel groups, ballet troupes, local bands and the like. There's something happening almost daily – look for the schedule in the Ala Moana Center's free shopping magazine.

The **Mayor's Office of Culture & Arts** (*☎ 527-5666*) sponsors numerous free performances, art exhibits and musical events, ranging from street musicians in city parks to band concerts in various locales around Honolulu. Call for current events.

Waikiki

There's good reason why Waikiki has become such a holiday mecca. It has a phenomenal seaside location, sunny year-round weather and a plethora of things to do.

Once Hawaii's only tourist destination, Waikiki still accounts for nearly half of the visitor accommodations in the state, with an amazing density of high-rise hotels clustered along an attractive white-sand beach.

Crowded with package tourists from both Japan and North America, Waikiki has 25,000 permanent residents and some 65,000 visitors on any given day, all in an area roughly 1½ miles long and half a mile wide. Waikiki has 450 restaurants, 350 bars and clubs, and more shops than you'd want to count. All in all it boasts some 34,000 hotel and condo rooms.

While the beaches are packed during the day, at night most of the action is along the streets, where window-shoppers, time-share touts and street performers all go about their business. A variety of live music, from mellow Hawaiian to rock, wafts from street-side clubs and hotel lounges.

Waikiki Beach has wonderful orange sunsets, with the sun dropping down between cruising sailboats. The backdrop to Waikiki is scenic Diamond Head, a landmark so dominant that it's used as a directional

Rice Paddies Gave Way to High-Rises

At the beginning of the 19th century, Waikiki was almost entirely wetlands. It had more than 50 acres of fishponds as well as extensive taro patches and rice paddies. Fed by mountain streams from the upland Manoa and Makiki Valleys, Waikiki was one of Oahu's most fertile agricultural areas.

Tourism took root in 1901, when the Moana opened its doors as Waikiki Beach's first real hotel. A tram line was constructed to connect Waikiki to downtown Honolulu, and city folk crowded aboard for the beach. Quickly tiring of the pesky mosquitoes that thrived in the wetlands, these early beachgoers petitioned to have Waikiki's 'swamps' brought under control.

In 1922 the Ala Wai Canal was dug to divert the streams that flowed into Waikiki. Old Hawaii lost out, as farmers had the water drained out from under them. Then, coral rubble was used to fill the ponds, creating what was to become Hawaii's most valuable piece of real estate, and water buffaloes were soon replaced by tourists.

By 1950, Waikiki had 1400 hotel rooms. In those days, surfers could drive their cars to the beach and park on the sand. Then tourism took over in earnest: by 1968 Waikiki had 13,000 hotel rooms and by 1988 that number had more than doubled.

The lack of available land finally halted the boom. In a desperate attempt to squeeze in one more high-rise, St Augustine's Catholic Church, standing on the last speck of uncommercialized property along busy Kalakaua Ave, was nearly sold to a Tokyo developer for $45 million. It took a community uproar and a petition to the Vatican to nullify the deal, so for the time being, what you see here is finally it: simply because nothing else will fit.

marker – islanders say 'go Diamond Head' instead of 'head east.'

Orientation

Waikiki is bounded on two sides by the Ala Wai Canal, on another by the ocean and on the fourth by Kapiolani Park.

Three parallel roads cross Waikiki: Kalakaua Ave, the beach road named after King David Kalakaua; Kuhio Ave, the main drag for Waikiki's buses, which is named after Prince Jonah Kuhio Kalanianaole; and Ala Wai Blvd, which borders the Ala Wai Canal.

City buses are not allowed on Kalakaua Ave, and the traffic on this multilane road is one-way, so it's relatively smooth for driving. However, pedestrians need to be cautious, as cars tend to zoom by at a fairly fast clip.

Walking along the beach is an alternative to using the crowded sidewalks. It's possible to walk the full length of Waikiki along the sand and the seawalls. Although it's rather hot and crowded at midday, it's pleasant at other times. The beach is quite romantic to stroll at night, enhanced by both the city skyline and the surf lapping at the shore.

Information

Tourist Offices The Hawaii Visitors and Convention Bureau's **visitor information office** (*☎ 924-0266; 2250 Kalakaua Ave, Suite 502; open 8am-4:30pm Mon-Fri, 8am-noon Sat & Sun*) is in the Waikiki Shopping Plaza.

Free tourist magazines, such as *This Week Oahu*, *Spotlight's Oahu Gold* and *Best of Oahu*, can readily be found on street corners and in hotel lobbies throughout Waikiki.

Money Waikiki has a **Bank of Hawaii** (*☎ 543-6900; 2220 Kalakaua Ave; open 8:30am-4pm Mon-Thur, 8:30am-6pm Fri*) and a **First Hawaiian Bank** (*☎ 943-4670; 2181 Kalakaua Ave; open 8:30am-4pm Mon-Thur, 8:30am-6pm Fri*), the latter with some interesting Hawaiiana murals by the renowned artist Jean Charlot.

There are ATMs at those banks and at numerous nonbank locations around Waikiki.

Post The Waikiki **post office** (*☎ 973-7515; 330 Saratoga Rd; open 8am-4:30pm Mon, Tues, Thur & Fri, 8am-6pm Wed, 9am-1pm Sat*) is in the center of Waikiki.

Email & Internet Access The **Fishbowl Internet Cafe** (*☎ 922-7565; 2463 Kuhio Ave; open 8am-1am daily*) and **e-c@fe** (*☎ 926-3299; 445 Seaside Ave; open 9am-1am daily*) both offer Internet access for $1 per 10 minutes.

Bookstores Hawaiian books, travel guides and paperback fiction are available at

WAIKIKI

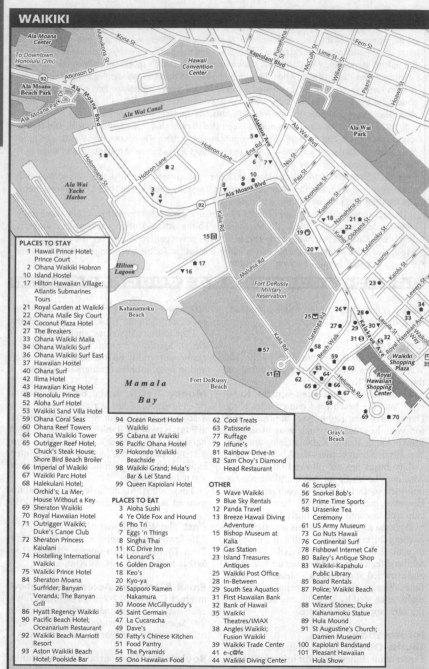

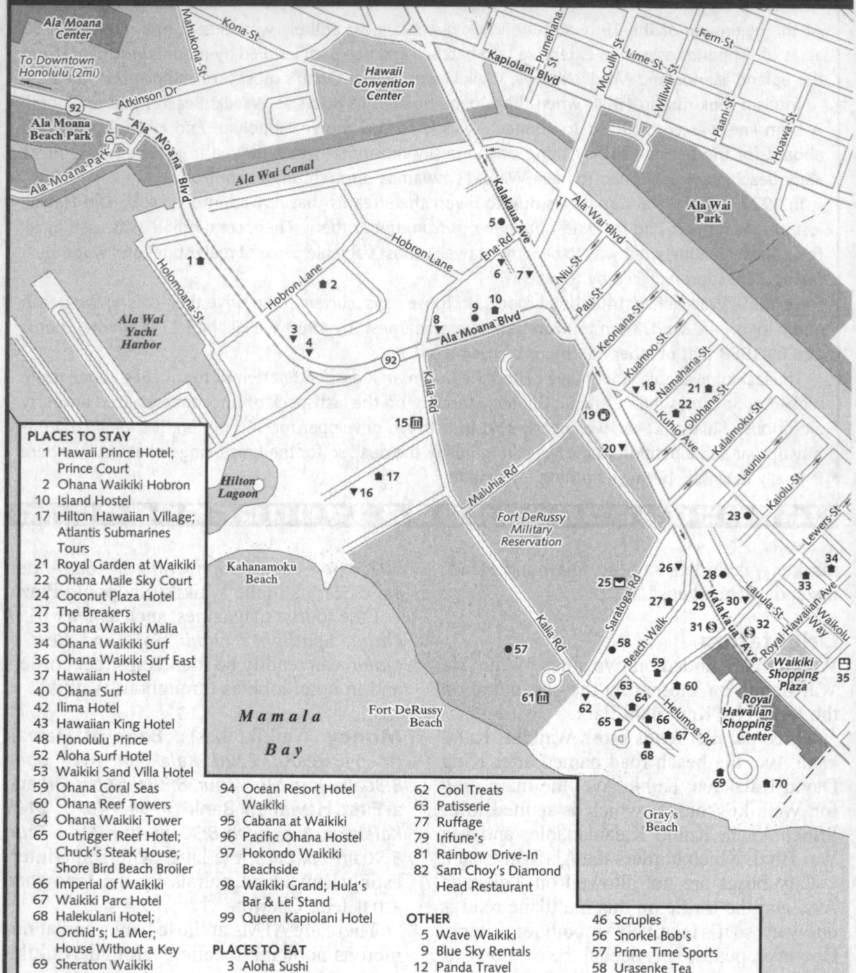

PLACES TO STAY

1 Hawaii Prince Hotel; Prince Court
2 Ohana Waikiki Hobron
10 Island Hostel
17 Hilton Hawaiian Village; Atlantis Submarines Tours
21 Royal Garden at Waikiki
22 Ohana Maile Sky Court
24 Coconut Plaza Hotel
27 The Breakers
33 Ohana Waikiki Malia
34 Ohana Waikiki Surf
36 Ohana Waikiki Surf East
37 Hawaiian Hostel
40 Ohana Surf
42 Ilima Hotel
43 Hawaiian King Hotel
48 Honolulu Prince
52 Aloha Surf Hotel
53 Waikiki Sand Villa Hotel
59 Ohana Coral Seas
60 Ohana Reef Towers
64 Ohana Waikiki Tower
65 Outrigger Reef Hotel; Chuck's Steak House; Shore Bird Beach Broiler
66 Imperial of Waikiki
67 Waikiki Parc Hotel
68 Halekulani Hotel; Orchid's; La Mer; House Without a Key
69 Sheraton Waikiki
70 Royal Hawaiian Hotel
71 Outrigger Waikiki; Duke's Canoe Club
72 Sheraton Princess Kaiulani
74 Hostelling International Waikiki
75 Waikiki Prince Hotel
84 Sheraton Moana Surfrider; Banyan Veranda; The Banyan Grill
86 Hyatt Regency Waikiki
90 Pacific Beach Hotel; Oceanarium Restaurant
92 Waikiki Beach Marriott Resort
93 Aston Waikiki Beach Hotel; Poolside Bar
94 Ocean Resort Hotel Waikiki
95 Cabana at Waikiki
96 Pacific Ohana Hostel
97 Hokondo Waikiki Beachside
98 Waikiki Grand; Hula's Bar & Lei Stand
99 Queen Kapiolani Hotel

PLACES TO EAT

3 Aloha Sushi
4 Ye Olde Fox and Hound
6 Pho Tri
7 Eggs 'n Things
8 Singha Thai
11 KC Drive Inn
14 Leonard's
16 Golden Dragon
18 Keo's
20 Kyo-ya
26 Sapporo Ramen Nakamura
30 Moose McGillycuddy's
45 Saint Germain
47 La Cucaracha
49 Dave's
50 Fatty's Chinese Kitchen
51 Food Pantry
54 The Pyramids
55 Ono Hawaiian Food
62 Cool Treats
63 Patisserie
77 Ruffage
79 Irifune's
81 Rainbow Drive-In
82 Sam Choy's Diamond Head Restaurant

OTHER

5 Wave Waikiki
9 Blue Sky Rentals
12 Panda Travel
13 Breeze Hawaii Diving Adventure
15 Bishop Museum at Kalia
19 Gas Station
23 Island Treasures Antiques
25 Waikiki Post Office
28 In-Between
29 South Sea Aquatics
31 First Hawaiian Bank
32 Bank of Hawaii
35 Waikiki Theatres/IMAX
38 Angles Waikiki; Fusion Waikiki
39 Waikiki Trade Center
41 e-c@fe
44 Waikiki Diving Center
46 Scruples
56 Snorkel Bob's
57 Prime Time Sports
58 Urasenke Tea Ceremony
61 US Army Museum
73 Go Nuts Hawaii
76 Continental Surf
78 Fishbowl Internet Cafe
80 Bailey's Antique Shop
83 Waikiki-Kapahulu Public Library
85 Board Rentals
87 Police; Waikiki Beach Center
88 Wizard Stones; Duke Kahanamoku Statue
89 Hula Mound
91 St Augustine's Church; Damien Museum
100 Kapiolani Bandstand
101 Pleasant Hawaiian Hula Show

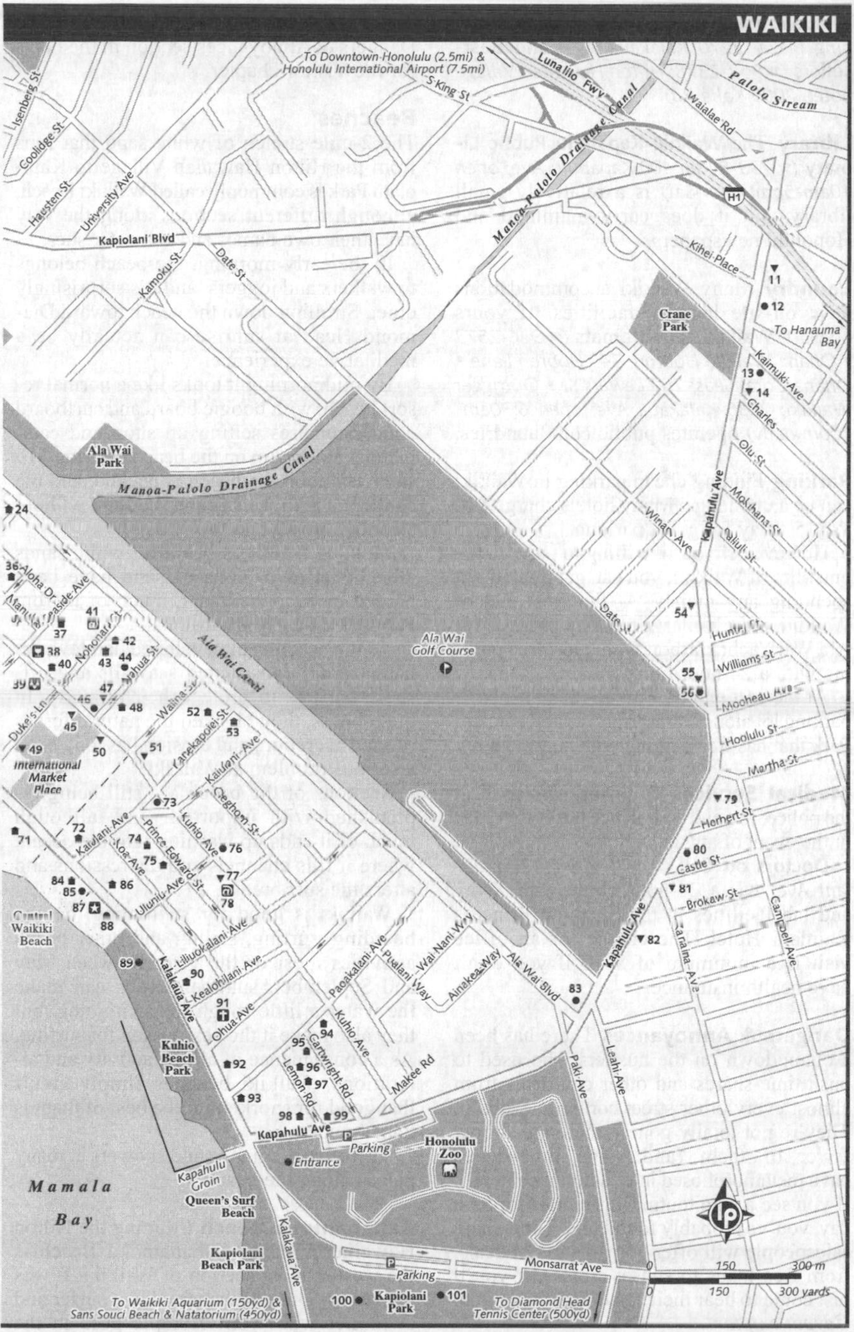
WAIKIKI
To Downtown Honolulu (2.5mi) & Honolulu International Airport (7.5mi)
Lunalilo Fwy
Palolo Stream
S King St
Waialae Rd
Isenberg St
Coolidge St
Hausten St
University Ave
Kapiolani Blvd
Kamoku St
Date St
Manoa-Palolo Drainage Canal
H1
Kihei Place
11
12
Crane Park
To Hanauma Bay
Kaimuki Ave
13
14
Charles
Olu St
Ala Wai Park
Manoa-Palolo Drainage Canal
24
Kapahulu Ave
Mokihana St
Winam Ave
Paliuli St
36
Aloha Dr
Seaside Ave
41
37
Nohonani St
42
38
40
43
44
Ala Wai Canal
Ala Wai Golf Course
Date St
54
Hunter St
Williams St
55
56
Mooheau Ave
39
47
46
48
Walina St
45
Duke's Ln
52
Lauula St
53
Kaiolu St
Kaiulani Ave
49
50
51
Holulu St
International Market Place
Martha St
73
Kuhio Ave
79
Herbert St
71
72
Kaiulani Ave
74
Prince Edward St
Seaside Ave
76
80
Castle St
75
Ulunui St
84
85
86
77
78
81
Brokaw St
87
88
Central Waikiki Beach
Liliuokalani Ave
Campbell Ave
82
Kapahulu Ave
Wai Nani Way
Ainakea Way
Ala Wai Blvd
89
Kealohilani Ave
Paoakalani Ave
Pualani Way
90
Kalakaua Ave
91
Ohua Ave
83
94
Kuhio Ave
95
Cartwright Rd
96
Lemon Rd
97
Makee Rd
Paki Ave
Leahi Ave
Kuhio Beach Park
92
93
98
99
Kapahulu Ave
Parking
Honolulu Zoo
Entrance
Mamala Bay
Kapahulu Groin
Queen's Surf Beach
Kalakaua Ave
Kapiolani Beach Park
Parking
Monsarrat Ave
0
150
300 m
0
150
300 yards
100
Kapiolani Park
101
To Waikiki Aquarium (150yd) & Sans Souci Beach & Natatorium (450yd)
To Diamond Head Tennis Center (500yd)

Waldenbooks *(☎ 922-4154; Waikiki Shopping Plaza, 2270 Kalakaua Ave)* and **Bestsellers** *(☎ 953-2378; Hilton Hawaiian Village hotel, 2005 Kalia Rd).*

Library The **Waikiki-Kapahulu Public Library** *(☎ 733-8488; 400 Kapahulu Ave; open 10am-5pm Mon-Sat)* is a relatively small library, but it does carry mainland and Honolulu newspapers.

Laundry Many Waikiki accommodations have on-site laundry facilities. If yours doesn't, **Waikiki Laundromats** *(☎ 926-2573 • Ohana Waikiki Hobron; 343 Hobron Lane • Ohana Coral Seas; 250 Lewers St • Outrigger Waikiki; 2335 Kalakaua Ave; open 6:30am-10pm daily)* operates public coin laundries.

Parking Finding cheap parking in Waikiki can be a challenge. Many hotels charge $10 to $15 a day for guest parking.

However, if you're willing to park on the outskirts of Waikiki, you can get by without spending any money. At the west end of Waikiki, there's a large public parking lot at Ala Wai Yacht Harbor, which has free parking with a 24-hour limit.

At the east end of Waikiki, there's a large parking lot along Monsarrat Ave at Kapiolani Park that has free parking with no time limit.

Medical Services & Emergencies Call the police, fire and ambulance **hotline** *(☎ 911)* in the event of any emergency.

Doctors on Call *(☎ 971-6000; 120 Kaiulani Ave)* has a 24-hour clinic with X-ray and lab facilities in the Sheraton Princess Kaiulani Hotel. The charge for an office visit is a minimum of $110 if you don't have health insurance.

Dangers & Annoyances There has been a clampdown on the hustlers who used to push time-shares and other con deals from almost every other street corner in Waikiki. They're not totally gone – there are simply fewer of them (and some time-shares have metamorphosed into 'activity centers'). If you see a sign touting car rentals for $5 a day, you've probably found one. Time-share salespeople will offer you all sorts of deals, from free luaus to sunset cruises, if you'll just come to hear their 'no obligation' pitch. *Caveat emptor*.

For information on ocean safety, see the Dangers & Annoyances section in the Facts for the Visitor chapter.

Beaches

The 2-mile stretch of white sand that runs from the Hilton Hawaiian Village to Kapiolani Park is commonly called Waikiki Beach, although different sections along the way have their own names and characteristics.

In the early morning, the beach belongs to walkers and joggers, and it's surprisingly quiet. Strolling down the beach toward Diamond Head at sunrise can actually be a meditative experience.

By midmorning it looks like a normal resort beach, with boogie board and surfboard concessionaires setting up shop and catamarans pulling up on the beach offering $15 sails. By noon the beach is packed, and the challenge is to walk along the sand without stepping on anyone.

Most of Waikiki's beautiful white sands are not its own. Tons of sand have been barged in over the years, much of it from Papohaku Beach on Molokai.

As the beachfront developed, landowners haphazardly constructed seawalls and offshore barriers to protect their property. In the process, they blocked the natural forces of sand accretion, and erosion has long been a serious problem at Waikiki.

Sections of the beach are still being replenished with imported sand, although much of it ends up washing into the ocean, where it fills channels and depressions and alters the surf breaks.

Waikiki is good for swimming, boogie boarding, surfing, sailing and other beach activities most of the year. Between May and September, summer swells can make the water a little rough for swimming, but they also make it the best season for surfing. As a consequence of all the activity and alterations, Waikiki beaches simply aren't that good for snorkeling; the best of them is Sans Souci.

There are lifeguards and showers at many places along the beach.

Kahanamoku Beach Fronting the Hilton Hawaiian Village, Kahanamoku Beach is the westernmost section of Waikiki. It was named for Duke Kahanamoku, a surfer and swimmer who won Olympic gold in the

100m freestyle in 1912 and went on to become a Hawaiian celebrity.

Kahanamoku Beach is protected by a breakwater at one end and a pier at the other, with a coral reef running between the two. It's a calm swimming area with a sandy bottom that slopes gradually.

Fort DeRussy Beach One of the least-crowded Waikiki beaches, Fort DeRussy Beach borders 1800ft of the Fort DeRussy Military Reservation. Like all beaches in Hawaii, it's public; the federal government provides lifeguards and there are showers and other facilities. In addition, you'll find an inviting grassy lawn with palm trees offering some sparse shade, providing an alternative to frying on the sand.

The water is usually calm and good for swimming. When conditions are right, the beach is used by windsurfers, boogie boarders and board surfers. There are two beach huts, open daily, that rent windsurfing equipment, boogie boards, kayaks and snorkel sets.

Gray's Beach Located near the Halekulani Hotel, Gray's Beach was named for a boarding house called Gray's-by-the-Sea that stood on the site in the 1920s. On the same stretch of beach was the original Halekulani, a lovely low-rise mansion that was converted into a hotel in the 1930s. In more recent times, the mansion gave way to the present high-rise hotel.

Because the seawall in front of the Halekulani was built so close to the waterline, the part of the beach fronting the hotel is often totally submerged.

The section of beach that stretches between the Halekulani and the Royal Hawaiian Hotel varies in width from season to season. The waters off the beach are shallow and calm.

Central Waikiki Beach The area between the Royal Hawaiian Hotel and the Waikiki Beach Center is the busiest section of the whole beach and has a nice spread of sand for sunbathing.

Most of the beach has a shallow bottom with a gradual slope. While the swimming's pretty good here, there are also a lot of catamarans, surfers and plenty of other swimmers in the water. Keep your eyes open.

Queen's Surf and Canoe's Surf, Waikiki's best-known surf breaks, are offshore.

Waikiki Beach Center The area opposite the Hyatt Regency Waikiki is the site of the Waikiki Beach Center, which has rest rooms, showers, a police station, surfboard lockers and rental concessions.

The **Wizard Stones of Kapaemahu** – four boulders on the Diamond Head side of the police station – are said to contain the secrets and healing powers of four sorcerers, named Kapaemahu, Kinohi, Kapuni and Kahaloa, who visited from Tahiti in ancient times. Before returning to their homeland, they transferred their powers to these stones.

Just east of the stones is a bronze **statue of Duke Kahanamoku** (1890–1968), Hawaii's most decorated athlete, standing with one of his long-boards. Considered the 'father of modern surfing,' Duke, who lived in Waikiki, gave surfing demonstrations on beaches around the world, from Sydney, Australia, to Rockaway Beach, New York. Many local surfers took issue with the placement of the statue, as Duke is standing with his back to the sea, a position they say he never would have assumed in real life. In response, the city moved the statue as close to the sidewalk as possible, and thus moving it farther from the water.

Kuhio Beach Park This park is marked on its east end by Kapahulu Groin, a walled storm drain with a walkway on top that juts out into the ocean.

A low breakwater seawall runs about 1300ft out from Kapahulu Groin, paralleling the beach. It was built to control sand erosion, and in the process two nearly enclosed swimming pools were formed. Local kids walk out on the breakwater, which is called The Wall, but it can be dangerous to the uninitiated due to a slippery surface and breaking surf.

The pool closest to Kapahulu Groin is best for swimming, with the water near the breakwater reaching depths of 5ft and greater. However, because circulation is limited the water gets murky with a noticeable film of suntan oil. The 'Watch Out Deep Holes' sign refers to holes in the pool's sandy bottom that can be created by swirling currents. Those who can't swim should be cautious in the deeper areas of the pool, as the holes can take waders by surprise.

The park, incidentally, is named after Prince Kuhio, who maintained his residence on this beach. His house was torn down in 1936, 14 years after his death, in order to expand the beach. Between the old-timers who gather each afternoon to play chess and cribbage at Kuhio's sidewalk pavilions and the kids boogie boarding off the Groin, this section of the beach has as much local color as tourist influence.

The city recently spent millions of dollars removing one lane of Kalakaua Ave fronting Kuhio Beach Park and in its place extended the beach and added water fountains, landscaping and a grassy hula mound. All in all, it's a pleasant place to hang out.

Kapahulu Groin This is one of Waikiki's hottest boogie-boarding spots. If the surf's high enough, you're sure to find a few dozen boogie boarders, mostly teenage boys, riding the waves.

The kids ride straight for the wall and then veer away at the last moment, drawing 'oohs' and 'ahs' from the tourists who gather to watch them. Kapahulu Groin is also a great place to catch the sunset.

Kapiolani Beach Park Starting at Kapahulu Groin and extending down to the Natatorium, beyond Waikiki Aquarium, is the Kapiolani Beach Park.

Queen's Surf is the name given to the wide midsection of Kapiolani Beach. The stretch in front of the pavilion is a popular beach with the gay community. It's a pretty decent area for swimming, with a sandy bottom. The beach between Queen's Surf and Kapahulu Groin is shallow and has a lot of broken coral.

Kapiolani Beach Park is a relaxed place with little of the frenzy of activity found in front of the central strip of Waikiki hotels. It's a popular weekend picnicking spot for local families who unload the kids to splash in the water as they line up the barbecue grills.

There are rest rooms and showers at the Queen's Surf pavilion. The surfing area offshore is called Public's and sees some good waves in winter.

Natatorium The Natatorium, at the Diamond Head end of Kapiolani Beach Park, is a 100m-long saltwater swimming pool built after WWI as a memorial for soldiers who died in that war. There were once hopes of hosting an Olympics on Oahu, with this pool as the focal point. In the end, Olympic competitions were never held here, but two Olympic gold medallists – Johnny Weissmuller and Duke Kahanamoku – both trained in this tide-fed pool.

The Natatorium is on the National Register of Historic Places. The city recently spent a hefty $11 million for restoration work on the Natatorium's exterior, but failed to restore the pool to a usable condition; now that the money has run out, it's doubtful that the pool will ever re-open.

Sans Souci Beach Down by the New Otani Kaimana Beach Hotel, Sans Souci is a nice little sandy beach away from the main tourist scene. Despite being off by itself, it too has outdoor showers and a lifeguard station.

Many residents come to Sans Souci to swim their daily laps. A shallow coral reef close to the shore makes for calm, protected waters and provides reasonably good snorkeling. More coral can be found by following the Kapua Channel as it cuts through the reef, although if you swim here beware of currents that can pick up in the channel. Check conditions with the lifeguard before venturing out.

Historic Hotels

Waikiki's two historic hotels, the Royal Hawaiian and the Moana (now the Sheraton Moana Surfrider), both retain their period character and are well worth a visit. These beachside hotels, which are both on the National Register of Historic Places, are a short walk from each other on Kalakaua Ave.

With its pink turrets and Moorish architecture, the **Royal Hawaiian Hotel** is a throwback to the era when Rudolph Valentino was *the* romantic idol and travel to Hawaii was by luxury liner. Inside, the hotel is lovely and airy, with high ceilings and chandeliers and everything in rose colors.

The restored **Sheraton Moana Surfrider** has the aura of an old plantation inn. On the 2nd floor, just up the stairs from the lobby, there's a display of memorabilia from the early hotel days, with scripts from the 'Hawaii Calls' radio show, period photographs and a short video. At 11am and 5pm on Monday, Wednesday and Friday, visitors can join free hour-long historical tours of the Moana; just show up in the lobby, reservations are not necessary.

Fort DeRussy Military Reservation

Fort DeRussy is a US Army post used mainly as a recreation center for the armed forces. This large chunk of Waikiki real estate was acquired by the US Army a few years after Hawaii was annexed to the USA. Prior to that it was swampy marshland and a favorite duck-hunting spot for Hawaiian royalty. The Hale Koa Hotel on the property is open only to military personnel, but there's public access to the beach and the adjacent military museum. The section of Fort DeRussy between Kalia Rd and Kalakaua Ave has public footpaths that provide a shortcut between the two roads.

US Army Museum of Hawaii Battery Randolph, a reinforced concrete building erected in 1911 as a coastal artillery battery, houses the army museum *(☎ 955-9552; admission free, open 10am 4:15pm Tues-Sun)* at Fort DeRussy. The battery once held two formidable 14-inch disappearing guns with an 11 mile range that were designed to recoil down into the concrete walls for reloading after each firing. A 55-ton lead counterweight would then return the carriage to position. When the guns were fired, the entire neighborhood shook.

The battery now exhibits a wide collection of weapons, from Hawaiian shark-tooth clubs to WWII tanks, as well as exhibits on military history as it relates to Hawaii told through dioramas, scale models and period photos. There are historic displays on Kamehameha the Great and on Hawaii's role in WWII.

Bishop Museum at Kalia

This museum *(☎ 947-2458; 2005 Kalia Rd; adult/child $11.95/9.95; open 9am-5pm daily)* in the Hilton Hawaiian Village is intended for people who can't make it over to the main Bishop Museum, on the west side of Honolulu.

Though the Waikiki collection is significantly smaller, it is nonetheless high quality, including Hawaiian artifacts such as stone adzes, hair ornaments, feather capes, a replica pili-grass hut, one of Duke Kahanamoku's 10ft wooden surfboards and some insightful displays on the Hawaiian monarchy, Polynesian migration and the early days of Waikiki tourism.

Oceanarium

The **Pacific Beach Hotel** *(2490 Kalakaua Ave)* houses an impressive three-story 280,000-gallon aquarium that forms the backdrop for two of the hotel restaurants. Even if you're not dining here, you can view the aquarium from the hotel lobby. Divers enter the Oceanarium to feed the tropical fish at noon and 1pm, 6:30pm and 8pm daily.

Damien Museum

St Augustine's Church, off Kalakaua Ave and Ohua Ave, is a quiet little sanctuary in the midst of the hotel district. At the rear of the church a second building houses the modest Damien Museum *(☎ 923-2690; admission free; open 9am-3pm Mon-Fri)*, honoring Father Damien, the Belgian priest famed for his work at the leprosy colony on Molokai. It has a video presentation on the colony, some interesting historical photos and a few of Damien's personal possessions.

Ala Wai Canal

Every day at dawn, people jog and power-walk along the Ala Wai Canal, which forms the northern boundary of Waikiki. Late in the afternoon, outrigger canoe teams paddle along the canal and out to the Ala Wai Yacht Harbor, offering photo opportunities for passersby.

Kapiolani Park

The nearly 200-acre Kapiolani Park, at the Diamond Head end of Waikiki, was a gift from King Kalakaua to the people of Honolulu in 1877. Hawaii's first public park, it was dedicated to Kalakaua's wife, Queen Kapiolani.

In its early days, horse racing and band concerts were the park's big attractions. Although the racetrack is gone, the concerts continue and Kapiolani Park is still the venue for a range of community activities.

The park contains the Waikiki Aquarium, the Honolulu Zoo, Kapiolani Beach Park, the Pleasant Hawaiian Hula Show grounds, the Kapiolani Bandstand and the Waikiki Shell, an outdoor amphitheater that serves as a venue for symphony, jazz and rock concerts. It has sports fields, tennis courts, huge lawns and tall banyan trees.

The Royal Hawaiian Band presents free concerts on Sunday afternoons at the Kapiolani Bandstand. Dance competitions,

Hawaiian music concerts and other activities occur at the bandstand throughout the year.

Waikiki Aquarium This interesting aquarium *(☎ 923-9741; 2777 Kalakaua Ave; adult/child over 13/child under 13 $7/3.50/free; open 9am-5pm daily)* dates to 1904, but had a $3 million makeover just a few years back. It has some fun interactive displays and an impressive shark gallery, where visitors can watch circling reef sharks through a 14ft-wide window.

The aquarium is a great place to identify colorful coral and fish you've seen while snorkeling or diving. Tanks re-create various Hawaiian reef habitats, including those found in a surge zone, a sheltered reef, a deep reef and an ancient reef. There are rare Hawaiian fish with names like the bearded armorhead and the sling-jawed wrasse, along with moray eels, giant groupers and flash-back cuttlefish wavering with pulses of light.

In addition to Hawaiian marine life, you'll find exhibits on other Pacific ecosystems. In 1985 the aquarium was the first to breed the Palauan chambered nautilus in captivity; you can see them, with their unique spiral chambered shells, in the South Pacific section. Also noteworthy are the giant Palauan clams that were raised from dime-sized hatchlings in 1982 and now measure over 2ft, the largest in the USA.

The aquarium also has an outdoor tank with two rare Hawaiian monk seals.

Honolulu Zoo The Honolulu Zoo *(☎ 971-7171; adult/child 6-12 $6/1; open 9am-4:30pm daily)* has been upgraded into a respectable city zoo, with some 300 species spread across 42 acres. A highlight is the naturalized African Savanna section, which has lions, cheetahs, white rhinos, giraffes, zebras, hippos and monkeys. The zoo also has an interesting reptile section, a good selection of tropical birds (including native Hawaiian birds) and a small petting zoo.

Pleasant Hawaiian Hula Show This show *(☎ 945-1851; 2805 Monsarrat Ave; admission free; shows 10am-11am Tues-Thur)*, near the Waikiki Shell, is a staged photo opportunity of hula dancers, ti-leaf skirts and ukuleles. The musicians are a group of older ladies who performed at the Royal Hawaiian Hotel in days gone by.

Art in the Park

Looking for fine art at bargain prices? The best deal for buying paintings directly from island artists is the city sponsored 'Art in the Park' programme, which sets up at the south side of the Honolulu Zoo on Monsarrat Ave in Kapiolani Park. Local artists have been hanging their paintings on the zoo fence each weekend for 30 years.

The artwork is on display 10am to 4pm on weekends and 9am to noon Tuesday. It's an informal open-air event that only takes place when it's not raining. You might just find a great deal here, as many of Hawaii's better painters got their start at the fence.

Once known as the Kodak Hula Show, this is the scene shown on classic postcards where dancers hold up letters forming the words 'Hawaii' and 'Aloha.' The whole thing is quite touristy and heavily nostalgic, but it's entertaining and it's free.

Places to Stay

Waikiki's main beachfront strip, Kalakaua Ave, is lined with high-rise hotels with $200-plus rooms. As is the norm in resort areas, most of these hotels cater to package tourists, driving the prices up for individual travelers.

Better value is generally found at the smaller hostelries on the back streets. There are hotels in the Kuhio Ave area and up near the Ala Wai Canal, which are as nice as some of the beachfront hotels, but half the price. If you don't mind walking 10 minutes to the beach, you can save yourself a bundle.

In many hotels the rooms themselves are the same, with only the views varying; generally the higher the floor, the higher the price. If you're paying extra for a view, you might want to ask to see the room first, as Waikiki certainly doesn't have any truth-in-labeling laws governing when a hotel can call a room 'ocean-view.' While some 'ocean-views' are the real thing, others are merely glimpses of the water as seen through a series of high-rises.

Waikiki has many more hotel rooms than condos. Most of Waikiki's condos are filled with long-term residents and there isn't the proliferation of vacation rental agents as on the Neighbor Islands. The best way to find a condo in Waikiki is to look in the 'Vacation Rentals' section of the daily paper, although the listings can be meager.

Places to Stay – Budget

Hostels In addition to the one HI hostel, there are several private businesses providing hostel-style dormitory accommodations around Waikiki. They all cater to backpackers and draw a fairly international crowd. There are no curfews or other restrictions, except that some of these places, in an effort to avoid taking on local boarders, may require travelers to show a passport or an onward ticket.

The private hostels seem to go through cycles, with standards reflecting changes in management or staffing, which can be frequent. Consequently, if you want to play it safe, consider booking into the HI hostel or a budget hotel for at least the first few nights. Inquire about refund policies before dishing out any money at a private hostel – you can sometimes get a discount on stays of a week or more, but these typically require advance payment and allow no refunds.

Hostelling International Waikiki *(☎ 926-8313, fax 922-3798; ⓔ ayhaloha@lava.net; 2417 Prince Edward St; dorm beds/doubles $17/42; office open 7am-3am)* is a 60-bed hostel on a backstreet a few short blocks from Waikiki Beach. Like other Waikiki hostels, it's in an older, low-rise apartment complex, with the units converted for hostel use mainly by adding extra beds – often in what used to be the living room. In addition to dorms, there are five rooms for couples, each with a small refrigerator and private bath. The maximum stay is seven nights and there's a $3 surcharge if you're not a member; HI membership can be purchased on-site for $25 for Americans, $18 for foreign visitors. Unlike most other HI hostels, there's no dormitory lockout or curfew, and the guest kitchen is accessible all day. You can sometimes get a bed as a walk-in, but at busy times reservations are often necessary two to three weeks in advance.

Hawaiian Hostel *(☎ 924-3303, fax 923-2111; ⓔ info@hawaiianhostel.com; 419 Seaside Ave; bed in 6-bed/2-bed dorm $15/17, rooms $40)* occupies an aging two-story apartment building set back in an alley off Seaside Ave. The digs aren't fancy, but the place has an inviting travelers' atmosphere and cheap rates. In addition to the dorms, there are private rooms that hold up to two people and have a TV and small refrigerator, but share a bath with another room. There's an open-air courtyard, a guest kitchen and laundry facilities. The hostel has a couple of online computers ($3 per 30 minutes) available for guests. It's about a 10-minute walk from Waikiki Beach.

Pacific Ohana Hostel *(☎/fax 921-8111; 2552 Lemon Rd; dorm beds $16.75, semi-private rooms $36, private rooms $50)* is a new hostel that shows promise. It's taken over a small apartment building in its entirety and has done a decent job fixing the rooms up. Dorms have four beds, while the semiprivate rooms have a private bedroom, but require you to pass through the dorm to enter your room or use the shared bath. If you want your own space, consider one of the private rooms, which is essentially a one-bedroom apartment unit with its own kitchen and bath. There's a guest lounge with a kitchen and TV.

Hokondo Waikiki Beachside *(☎ 923-9566, fax 923-7525; ⓔ hokondo@aol.com; 2556 Lemon Rd, Suite B101; dorm beds $20-25, private rooms $55-78)* is another small condo complex that's been converted into hostel-style accommodations, with both dorms and private rooms. The units each have a refrigerator, a stove and a bathroom. It's straightforward, but maintains a higher standard of cleanliness than most of the other private hostels.

Island Hostel *(☎/fax 942-8748; 1946 Ala Moana Blvd; dorm beds $16.75, rooms $50)* occupies part of an older apartment building on the western end of Waikiki. The rooms are small but have TV, hot plates and a bath. The dorms, in particular, can feel a bit confined, but on the plus side sleep only four people. Although it's a bit further from the water than other hostels, it's still within walking distance and the beach at this end of Waikiki is less crowded.

Hotels **Waikiki Prince Hotel** *(☎ 922-1544, fax 924-3712; 2431 Prince Edward St; rooms $50, with kitchenettes $60)* is superb low-end value with 24 units in a six-story building next door to Hostelling International Waikiki. The rooms are simple, but they're cheery and equipped with air-con, TV and bath; for just $10 extra you can opt for one with cooking facilities and a bit more space. On weekly stays, the seventh night is free. It's just a couple of minutes' walk to the beach.

Continental Surf *(☎ 922-2232, 800-922-7866, fax 922-1718; ⓔ continentalsurfhotel@hawaiirr.com; 2426 Kuhio Ave; rooms $59, with kitchenette $68)* has 140 rooms that could benefit from a fresh coat of paint, but are otherwise adequate. All rooms have air-con, cable TV and a refrigerator. Both the standard rooms and kitchenette rooms are the same size. Consequently the rooms with cooking facilities feel a bit squeezed, but if you don't mind giving up the elbow room you'll be able to save money by preparing your own meals. Traffic can be noisy along Kuhio Ave, but by requesting one of the upper-level rooms in this 21-floor hotel, you can avoid most of the noise.

Places to Stay – Mid-Range

Hawaiian King Hotel *(☎ 922-3894, 800-545-1948; ⓔ winston@iav.com; 417 Nohonani St, Suite 409; low season $75-105, high season $95-125)* has 18 pleasant units managed by Patrick Winston. Each has one bedroom with either a queen or two twin beds, a living room, TV, air-con, ceiling fans, lanai and a kitchenette. Although it's an older complex, a lot of money has gone into the units and they have a spiffy decor that's on par with pricier places. There are also a few unrenovated rooms, wearworn but otherwise fine, which can be as low as $49. There's a courtyard pool. Ask about discounts, as Patrick can sometimes fill last-minute vacancies at lower rates. There's a four-day minimum stay.

Honolulu Prince *(☎ 922-1616, 800-922-7866, fax 922-6223; ⓔ info@aston-hotels.com; 317 Nahua St; rooms in low/high season $75/85)*, in the Aston chain, is a reasonable choice for an economy hotel, with full amenities like cable TV, air-con and refrigerators. The lowest-priced rooms are cramped, but for an extra $10 you can get a roomier 'superior,' which has two double beds, a sofa bed and a lanai.

Coconut Plaza Hotel *(☎ 923-8828, 800-882-9696, fax 923-3473; ⓔ info@aston-hotels.com; 450 Lewers St; rooms/studios from $85/100)*, in the Aston chain, is a quiet 80-room hotel near Ala Wai Blvd. Rooms have contemporary decor and full amenities, though they're on the small side. There are often promotions that can cut the above rates by about a third, which then makes this a good budget choice.

Waikiki Sand Villa Hotel *(☎ 922-4744, 800-247-1903, fax 923-2541; ⓔ reserve@waikiki-hotel.com; 2375 Ala Wai Blvd; rooms in low/high season $93/106, studios $156/166)* is on the Ala Wai Canal. This friendly place, popular with young Japanese tourists, has a nice pool and a row of online computers in the lobby available free to hotel guests. The rooms are compact, but most have both a double and a twin bed, and all have a TV, refrigerator and lanai. For the best views, ask for a corner unit. The studios have kitchenettes and can sleep up to four people.

Aloha Surf Hotel *(☎ 923-0222, 800-922-7866, fax 924-7160; ⓦ www.aston-hotels.com; 444 Kanekapolei St; rooms in low/high season $95/110)* has a lively surf theme and has been recently renovated. While the lobby is fun, the rooms in this 200-unit hotel are standard fare and on the small side. Each has a small refrigerator, TV and room safe. There's a small pool.

The Breakers *(☎ 923-3181, 800-426-0494, fax 923-7174; ⓔ thebreakers@aloha.net; 250 Beach Walk, studios $94-100, double/quad suites $135/151)* is an older hotel with 64 units surrounding a courtyard pool. In an area dominated by high-rise hotels, this Polynesian-style place is a throwback to earlier times. The studios are comfortable but unassuming, each with a double bed, a single bed and a kitchenette. Opt for the 2nd-floor units, which have a lanai for just $6 more. The suites are large, with a separate bedroom with a queen bed, a living room, which resembles a studio, with two twin beds and a full kitchen. All units have air-con, TVs and room safes.

Ocean Resort Hotel Waikiki *(☎ 922-3861, 800-367-2317, fax 924-1982; ⓔ res@xoceanresort.com; 175 Paoakalani Ave; standard/deluxe rooms $98/140)*, a former Quality Inn, hosts a fair number of people on low-end package tours. Nonetheless, the 451 rooms have the same amenities as more expensive resort hotels, with air-con, cable TV, refrigerators and room safes. Nonsmoking rooms are available on request, and there are two pools. The deluxe rooms are larger and on higher floors, which are generally quieter. When things are slow, it sometimes offers walk-in rates as low as $60, an unbeatable deal for a hotel of this standard.

Tropical fruit

Shave ice

Blue Hawaii

Ahi (yellowfin tuna) with *limu* (seaweed), green onion and chili

ALL PHOTOGRAPHS BY ANN CECIL

NED FRIARY

USS *Arizona* Memorial, Oahu

ANN CECIL

North Shore welcoming sign, Haleiwa

ERIC WHEATER

Japanese mural, Honolulu

ALISON WRIGHT

Waikiki shoreline

Imperial of Waikiki *(☎ 923-1827, 800-347-2582, fax 923-7848; W www.imperialofwaikiki.com; 205 Lewers St; studios $109, suites from $139)* is a pleasant time-share that rents out unfilled rooms on a space-available basis. It's good value for this neighborhood, directly opposite the exclusive Halekulani Hotel and just a two-minute walk from the beach. Studios have a pull-down double bed, queen sofa bed, microwave and refrigerator. The one-bedroom suites have a kitchenette, a queen bed in the bedroom, and a pull-down bed and queen sofa bed in the living room. There's a pool and a 24-hour front desk.

Queen Kapiolani Hotel *(☎ 922-1941, 800-367-2317, fax 922-2694; e res@queenkapiolani.com; 150 Kapahulu Ave; rooms from $125, with ocean view $175)* is a 19-story hotel at the quieter Diamond Head end of Waikiki. This older hotel has a regal theme: chandeliers, high ceilings and faded paintings of Hawaiian royalty. The standard rooms vary greatly in size, with some very pleasant and others quite cramped. The simplest way to avoid a closet-size space is to request a room with two twin beds instead of a single queen. Ocean-view rooms have lanai with splendid unobstructed views of Diamond Head.

Ilima Hotel *(☎ 923-1877, 800-801-9366, fax 924-8371; e mail@ilima.com; 445 Nohonani St; singles $129-165, doubles $139-175)* is in a less hurried section of Waikiki, about a 10-minute walk from the beach. All 99 units are roomy and bright, with large lanai, two double beds, tasteful rattan furnishings and full kitchens. The rates vary according to the floor, although the rooms themselves are the same. The staff is friendly and there's a small heated pool and fitness room. Popular with business travelers and other return visitors, the Ilima offers free local phone calls and free parking, a rarity in Waikiki.

New Otani Kaimana Beach Hotel *(☎ 923-1555, 800-356-8264, fax 922-9404; e rooms@kaimana.com; 2863 Kalakaua Ave; rooms/studios from $135/160)* is right on Sans Souci Beach on the quieter Diamond Head side of Waikiki. Popular with return visitors, it's a pleasantly low-key place with 125 units. All units have air-con, TV, refrigerators and lanai, and the studios have add-on kitchenettes.

Cabana at Waikiki *(☎ 926-5555, 877-902-2121, fax 926-5566; W www.cabana-waikiki.com; 2551 Cartwright Rd; suites $135-175)* caters to the gay community and is only minutes from Hula's, Waikiki's bustling gay bar. Each of the 15 units has a queen bed, queen sofa bed, full kitchen, lanai, TV and VCR. Rates include continental breakfast, use of an eight-man hot tub, and access to a men's gym.

Aston Waikiki Beach Hotel *(☎ 922-2511, 800-922-7866, fax 923-3656; W www.astonwaikiki.com; 2570 Kalakaua Ave; rooms from $140, with ocean view $245)* has just undergone a $30 million renovation. It looks almost like a reflection of the larger Marriott across the street, and the 713 rooms here are comparable, but less expensive. The best value is the Mauka Tower, an annex off to the side of the main building, where the rates are at the low end and the rooms are larger and quieter than in the main hotel. Ask about discounts that can cut the standard rates by as much as half.

Royal Garden at Waikiki *(☎ 943-0202, 800-367-5666, fax 946-8777; e rghresv@aol.com; 440 Olohana St; rooms $150-250)* is a well-regarded midsize hotel with 220 comfortable rooms. The rooms vary in decor, but all have air-con, TVs, room safes and lanai. The lowest rate is for rooms on the lower floors; as the elevator climbs so do the prices. The hotel has an elegant marble lobby, two swimming pools and an exercise room.

Outrigger & Ohana Hotels Over the years, the **Outrigger** *(☎ 303-369-7777, fax 303-369-9403, toll-free in USA & Canada ☎ 800-688-7444, in Australia, New Zealand, Germany & the UK ☎ 1-800-688-74443; W www.outrigger.com)* chain has snapped up and renovated many of Waikiki's mid-range hotels. It splits its hotels into two categories: Ohana, which includes the more affordable properties, and Outrigger, which covers the high-end hotels. Overall, it's a well-run chain that offers high standards at reasonable prices. At any rate, with one phone call, you can check on the availability of 25% of the hotel rooms in Waikiki!

Ask about promotional deals when making reservations. The Ohana hotels often run a 'SimpleSaver Rate,' which cuts rates as low as $69 – a great deal for hotels of this standard. The Outrigger hotels offer a similar deal called the 'Best Value Rate,' which cuts room prices to about $150. In addition, both Ohana and Outrigger commonly offer a 'Free Ride' programme, which provides a free rental car when you book at the regular room rate; and a 'Fifth Night Free' programme on stays of five nights.

Travelers aged 50 and older, and members of the AAA/CAA auto clubs, are entitled to discounts of about 25% off the regular room rates.

All Ohana and Outrigger rooms have air-con, phones, cable TVs, room safes and refrigerators.

Ohana Maile Sky Court *(☎ 947-2828; 2058 Kuhio Ave; rooms $109, with kitchenette $119)* is one of Ohana's better deals if you don't mind being away from the beach. This 596-unit high-rise hotel has an inviting lobby and a central location convenient to restaurants, shops and entertainment. The rooms are small, but unless you are claustrophobic they're otherwise pleasant.

Ohana Waikiki Surf East *(☎ 923-7671; 422 Royal Hawaiian Ave; studios/suites $129/179)*, a block north of Ohana Waikiki Surf, is a recommendable place if preparing your own meals is a consideration, as there are kitchenettes in all its 102 units. Both the studios and one-bedroom suites are large, and most have a sofa bed, as well as a king or two double beds. The accommodations are superior to many higher-priced Outriggers – the lower price simply reflects the distance from the beach and the fact that the hotel is a converted apartment building with no restaurant or other lobby facilities.

Ohana Waikiki Malia *(☎ 923-7621; 2211 Kuhio Ave; rooms/suites $129/189)* is a 327-room high-rise hotel opposite the Ohana Waikiki Surf. Rooms are comfortable, each with a tiny one-chair lanai and, in most cases, two double beds. Some of the rooms are wheelchair accessible. Upper-floor rooms on the back side are the quietest, and all rooms, regardless of the floor, have the same rate.

Ohana Reef Towers *(☎ 924-8844; 227 Lewers St; rooms $129, with kitchenette $139)* is close to the beach and its 479 rooms are comfortable and well equipped. The kitchenette units not only add cooking facilities, but also have a sofa bed.

Places to Stay – Top End

The following hotels all have the expected 1st-class amenities and in-house restaurants. All are on the beach or across the street from it and all have swimming pools.

Sheraton Princess Kaiulani *(☎ 922-5811, 800-325-3535, fax 923-9912; W www.sheraton-hawaii.com; 120 Kaiulani Ave; rooms from $165)* is the Sheraton's best-value Waikiki property. One of Waikiki's older hotels, it was built in the 1950s by Matson Navigation to help turn Waikiki into a middle-class destination, and from the outside it looks rather like a huge apartment complex. However, the interior is more appealing, and the 1150 rooms are modern and inviting. It's in the busy heart of Waikiki across the street from the beach.

Waikiki Parc Hotel *(☎ 921-7272, 800-422-0450, fax 923-1336; W www.waikikiparc.com; 2233 Helumoa Rd; rooms $190, with ocean view $270)* is another good-value top-end hotel. The Parc has a pleasantly understated elegance. Rooms are average in size, but have nice touches, such as ceramic-tile floors, shuttered lanai doors and bathtubs. The hotel offers various specials, including a three-night 'Parc Sunrise' package that includes free breakfast and parking and costs about 30% less than the regular room rates.

Outrigger Reef Hotel *(☎ 923-3111; 2169 Kalia Rd; rooms $220, with ocean view $350)* is an 883-room hotel right on the beach. The rooms are nice, albeit without any distinct character, and have the usual 1st-class amenities. Wheelchair-accessible rooms are available, and some floors are designated for nonsmokers only.

Outrigger Waikiki *(☎ 923-0711; 2335 Kalakaua Ave; rooms $230, with ocean view $335)* is the chain's other beachfront hotel. This 530-room hotel offers modern amenities and rates that rise with the view. Set on a prime stretch of sand, there's lots of activity here, from beach events to seaside dining.

Waikiki Beach Marriott Resort *(☎ 922-6611, 800-367-5121, fax 921-5222; W www.marriotthotels.com; 2552 Kalakaua Ave; rooms $260, with ocean view $310)* is one of Waikiki's largest hotels, with 1308 rooms in a huge block-long complex opposite the beach. The Marriott recently took over this property and renovated the place, so you can expect everything to be shiny and new. Steep discounts off the standard rates are common.

Sheraton Moana Surfrider *(☎ 922-3111, 800-325-3535, fax 923-0308; W www.sheraton-hawaii.com; 2365 Kalakaua Ave; rooms $265, with ocean view $420)* is a delightful place for those fond of colonial hotels. Built in 1901, the Moana was Hawaii's first beachfront hotel. It's undergone a $50 million historic restoration, authentic right down to the carved columns on the porte-cochere. Despite the modern wings now attached to the main hotel's flanks, the Moana has survived with much of its original character intact. The lobby is open and airy with high plantation-like ceilings and Hawaiian artwork. The rooms in the original building have been restored to their early-19th-century appearance. The furnishings on each floor are made from a different wood, for example, koa on the 5th and cherry on the 6th, and TVs and refrigerators are discreetly hidden behind armoire doors.

Sheraton Waikiki *(☎ 922-4422, 800-325-3535, fax 922-9567; W www.sheraton-hawaii.com; 2255 Kalakaua Ave; rooms $280, with ocean view $450)* is an 1850-room mega-hotel that looms over the historic Royal Hawaiian Hotel. The bustling lobby resembles an exclusive Tokyo shopping center, lined with expensive jewelry stores and boutiques with French names and designer labels.

Hyatt Regency Waikiki *(☎ 921-6026, 800-233-1234, fax 923-7839; W www.hyattwaikiki.com; 2424 Kalakaua Ave; rooms $265, with ocean view $360)* has twin 40-story towers with 1230 rooms. There's a maximum of 18 rooms per floor, so it's quieter and feels more exclusive than other hotels its size. Rooms are pleasantly decorated and the hotel has created a nice little rain forest oasis in the form of a ground-floor atrium resplendent with cascading waterfalls and tropical plants.

Hilton Hawaiian Village *(☎ 949-4321, 800-445-8667, fax 947-7898; W www.hawaiianvillage.hilton.com; 2005 Kalia Rd; rooms $300, with ocean view $405)* is Hawaii's largest hotel, with some 3000 rooms in high-rise towers. The ultimate in mass tourism, it's practically a package-tour city unto itself – all self-contained for people who never want to leave the hotel grounds. It's a busy place, but it maintains a good reputation despite its size. The Hilton is on a nice beach and has some recommendable restaurants.

Halekulani Hotel *(☎ 923-2311, 800-367-2343, fax 926-8004; W www.halekulani.com; 2199 Kalia Rd; rooms $325, with ocean views $440, suites $720)* is widely regarded as Waikiki's premier hotel. The 456 rooms, which are pleasantly subdued rather than posh, have large balconies, marble vanities and personal touches like bathrobes and fresh flowers. The staff are pampering; there are no check-in lines, instead, guests are registered in the privacy of their own room. The Halekulani has received numerous awards and is in the top-10 list of both *Condé Nast Traveler*'s best Pacific Rim Hotels and *Travel & Leisure*'s 'World's Best Service.'

Royal Hawaiian Hotel *(☎ 923-7311, 800-325-3535, fax 924-7098; W www.sheraton-hawaii.com; 2259 Kalakaua Ave; rooms in historic wing from $345, rooms in tower from $550)*, now a Sheraton property, was Waikiki's first luxury hotel. Despite being overshadowed by modern high-rises, the pink, Moorish-style building is still a beautiful place, cool and airy, and loaded with charm. The historic section maintains a classic appeal, with some of the rooms having quiet garden views. This section is easier to book too, as most guests prefer the modern high-rise wing with its ocean views.

Kahala Mandarin Oriental *(☎ 739-8888, 800-367-2525, fax 739-8800; W www.mandarin-oriental.com; 5000 Kahala Ave; rooms $310, with ocean view $500, presidential suite $3650)* is an exclusive luxury hotel in the swank Kahala area, east of Diamond Head. This is where the rich and famous go when they want to avoid the Waikiki scene, a 10-minute drive away. The guest list is Hawaii's most regal and includes Britain's Prince Charles, Spain's King Juan Carlos and the last seven US presidents. The hotel has its own quiet stretch of beach and an enclosed lagoon where dolphins swim just beyond the lanai of the rooms.

Places to Eat – Budget

The **Patisserie** *(2168 Kalia Rd; open 6am-9pm daily)*, in the lobby of the Ohana Edgewater Hotel, has good, inexpensive bakery items. If you want to eat in, there's a small sit-down area where you can get simple breakfast fare and sandwiches for under $5, as well as the usual doughnuts and pastries.

Cool Treats *(2161 Kalia Rd; open 10am-8pm daily)*, a refreshment kiosk on Grey's Beach, sells frosty tropical fruit smoothies and ice-cream cones for around $3.

Dave's *(2330 Kalakaua Ave; open 10am-9pm daily)*, a local favorite in the International Market Place, will satisfy most ice-cream connoisseurs. The ice cream is made on the island and uses organic ingredients and tropical flavors.

Saint Germain *(2301 Kuhio Ave; snacks $5; open 7am-9pm daily)*, a new French bakery, has delicious croissants, as well as soups, salads and hearty sandwiches. The sandwiches are all made fresh to order with your choice of bread, including a nice crispy baguette, and a dozen vegetarian and meat fillings to select from.

Fatty's Chinese Kitchen *(2345 Kuhio Ave; open 10:30am-10:30pm daily)* is a hole-in-the-wall eatery in an alley on the west side of the Miramar hotel. It serves some of the cheapest food to be found in these parts, with rice or chow mein plus one hot main for only $3.50. Add $1 for each additional main. The atmosphere is purely local, with a dozen stools lining a long bar and the cook on the other side chopping away.

Aloha Sushi *(1178 Ala Moana Blvd; open 9am-9pm daily)*, in the Discovery Bay Center, offers an interesting fast-food alternative, selling dozens of varieties of sushi at roughly the same price as a Big Mac. Mix and match them to your taste or order a pre-arranged lunch *bento* – either way you can get a decent take-out meal for around $5.

Eggs 'n Things *(1911 Kalakaua Ave; dishes $3-8; open 11pm-2pm daily)* is a bustling all-nighter. It specializes in breakfast fare, with a variety of waffles, pancakes, crepes and omelettes. The most popular deal is the 'early riser' special of three pancakes and two eggs that's offered from 5am to 9am for just $3.

Ruffage *(☎ 2443 Kuhio Ave; snacks $4-6; open 9am to 7pm Mon-Sat)*, a small health-food store with a snack bar, makes wholesome vegetarian dishes such as tofu omelettes, meat-free burritos, sandwiches and smoothies.

Pho Tri *(478 Ena Rd; soup $6; open 10am-10pm daily)*, a small family-run eatery at the west side of Waikiki, specializes in generous servings of *pho*, a hearty Vietnamese noodle soup spiced with fresh herbs. If you're not in the mood for soup, it also serves some simple, but solid, rice dishes for the same price as the pho.

Moose McGillycuddy's *(310 Lewers St; snacks & mains $6-12; meals served 7:30am-9pm daily)*, perhaps best known as a night-time dance spot, is also a reasonably priced restaurant. A great breakfast deal is the early-bird special (until 11am) of two eggs, bacon and toast for $1.99. Moose also has burgers, salads, Mexican fare and steaks.

Ye Olde Fox and Hound *(1178 Ala Moana Blvd; dishes $4-10; open 10am-11pm daily)* is an English-style pub in the basement of the Discovery Bay Center. If you've got a craving for a Cornish pastie, shepherd's pie or other pub grub, this is the place. It also offers Waikiki's cheapest mug of beer ($1) during its afternoon happy hour, from 2pm to 6pm daily.

Sapporo Ramen Nakamura *(2141 Kalakaua Ave; dishes $7-10; open 11am-midnight daily)* specializes in authentic Japanese ramen in a variety of options, including a delicious version topped with tasty *gyoza*, a grilled garlic-and-pork-filled dumpling. The scene is like a neighborhood eatery in Tokyo, with seating at stools around a small U-shaped bar and fellow diners chatting away in Japanese.

Kapahulu Ave You'll find some great neighborhood restaurants along Kapahulu Ave, the road that starts in Waikiki near the zoo and runs up to the H1 Fwy.

Leonard's *(933 Kapahulu Ave; pastries 65¢-$1; open 6am-9pm daily)*, a Portuguese bakery, is known throughout Honolulu for its *malasadas*, a type of sweet, fried dough rolled in sugar and served warm – like a doughnut without the hole. Try the *haupia malasada*, filled with an addictive coconut cream, and you'll be hooked.

KC Drive Inn *(1029 Kapahulu Ave; snacks $2-5; open 6am-11:30pm daily)*, near the freeway, has been a local favorite since the 1930s. It's known for its Ono Ono malts (a chocolate and peanut-butter blend that tastes like a liquefied Reese's Peanut Butter Cup) and waffle dogs (a hot dog wrapped in a waffle), and also has inexpensive breakfast fare, plate lunches, burgers and *saimin* (Japanese noodle soup) for either eat-in or take-out.

Rainbow Drive-In *(cnr Kapahulu & Kanaina Aves; open 7:30am-9pm daily)* is closer to central Waikiki if you're on foot, and has similar fast food and just as much of a local following.

Ono Hawaiian Food *(726 Kapahulu Ave; meals $8-10; open 11am-7:45pm Mon-Sat)* is *the* place to get traditional Hawaiian food served Hawaiian-style. It's a simple little diner, crowded with aging tables and decorated with sports paraphernalia, but at dinnertime people line up on the sidewalk waiting to get in. A favorite is the *kalua* pig plate, which comes with *lomi* salmon, *pipikaula* beef jerky, *haupia* coconut pudding and either rice or poi. If you're looking to eat local, you can't do better than Ono.

Irifune's *(563 Kapahulu Ave; lunch $7, dinner $10-14; open 11:30am-1:30pm, 5:30pm-9:30pm Tues-Sat)* is a friendly place decorated with Japanese country kitsch. It serves creative food, including a vegetarian *gyoza* stuffed with tofu and cheese ($3.50). Top choice for dinner is the *tataki ahi*, a delicious fresh tuna that's seared lightly on the outside and sashimi-like inside. Or opt for one of the combination dinners that pairs tempura with sashimi and other Japanese favorites. Alcohol is not served, but you can bring your own beer. Although few tourists come up this way, Irifune's is popular with islanders and you may have to wait to be seated at dinner, but it's well worth it.

The Pyramids *(☎ 737-2900; 758 Kapahulu Ave; lunch buffet $9, dinner $13-18; open 11am-2pm & 5.30pm-10pm Mon-Sat, 5pm-9pm Sun)* is an atmospheric Egyptian restaurant with a scrumptious lunch buffet. The buffet features Greek salad, falafels, tahini, tabouleh and *shwarma*, a spiced meat dish cooked on a spit. Dinner is à la carte, with main dishes such as shish kebab, moussaka and marinated lamb. There's belly dancing nightly.

Grocery Stores The best place to get groceries in Waikiki is the **Food Pantry** *(2370 Kuhio Ave)*. Its prices are higher than those of the chain supermarkets, which are all outside Waikiki, but lower than those of Waikiki's numerous convenience stores.

Beyond Waikiki, the easiest supermarket to get to without a car is the **Foodland** at the Ala Moana Center. If you have a car, there's a **Foodland** north of Waikiki close to the eastern intersection of S King and Kapiolani Sts.

Places to Eat – Mid-Range

The Banyan Grill *(☎ 922-3111; 2365 Kalakaua Ave; snacks $5-13; open 3pm-10pm daily)* is an open-air grill in the courtyard between the beach and pool at the upscale Sheraton Moana Surfrider hotel. The chef cooks up your order over a barbecue pit as you sit in a lounge chair and watch. The simple, but tasty, fare includes baby back ribs, teriyaki chicken and grilled shrimp – and the location, beneath the historic hotel's sprawling banyan tree, is particularly engaging. Here you can relax and dine with the rich and famous without breaking the bank.

Shore Bird Beach Broiler *(☎ 922-2887; 2169 Kalia Rd; breakfast buffet $8, dinner $9-20; open 7am-11am & 4:30pm-10pm daily)*, at the Outrigger Reef Hotel, is a fun place with affordable beachfront dining. At one end of this open-air restaurant is a big common grill where you barbecue your own fish, steak or chicken order. Meals come with a buffet bar of salad, chili, rice and fresh fruit. Get seated for dinner before 6pm and you can enjoy the sunset and take advantage of cheaper early-bird prices as well. It's a busy place, so unless you get there early, expect to wait for a table, however, that's scarcely a hardship, as you can hang out on the beach until your name's called. Shore Bird also has a breakfast buffet, but dinner is the real winner here.

Duke's Canoe Club *(☎ 922-2268; 2335 Kalakaua Ave; breakfast & lunch buffet $10, dinner $15-25; open 7am-10pm daily)*, at the Outrigger Waikiki hotel, is the most popular beachfront restaurant in Waikiki. This bustling place takes its name from the late surfing ace Duke Kahanamoku and the outrigger canoe club that was here in earlier days. The breakfast buffet offers omelettes to order, fresh fruit and tasty pastries, while the lunch buffet centers around a salad bar and hot dishes such as chicken and mahimahi. Dinner, which features fresh fish and steaks, includes a grand salad bar with pasta dishes, fruit and muffins. There's live Hawaiian music nightly.

La Cucaracha *(☎ 922-2288; 2310 Kuhio Ave; dishes $8-15; open 2pm-midnight daily)* may come as a surprise – who would expect an authentic family-run Mexican restaurant in the heart of Waikiki? The food is excellent. Dishes, which include rice and beans, range from soft tacos with fresh cilantro and lime to a Mexican-style steak smothered in *salsa verde*. Wash it all down with a potent margarita.

Oceanarium Restaurant *(2490 Kalakaua Ave; breakfast buffet $13, lunch $8, dinner $13-26; open 7am-10pm daily)*, in the Pacific Beach Hotel, has standard hotel fare but a one-of-a-kind view. Its dining room wraps around a stunning three-story aquarium brimming with colorful tropical fish, including some impressive sharks and rays. At breakfast, waffles or French toast cost $7 and there's also a full buffet available. Dinner mains range from pasta to lobster, while lunch features a variety of sandwiches.

Chuck's Steak House *(☎ 923-1228; 2335 Kalakaua Ave; dinner $17-25; open 5pm-10pm daily)*, on the 2nd floor of the Outrigger Waikiki hotel, has a good sunset water view and some good early bird specials. From 5pm to 6pm you can get a teriyaki chicken or grilled mahimahi dinner for $13 and down a few *mai tais* (alcoholic drinks made from rum, grenadine, and lemon and pineapple juices) at just $2.50 each. The regular menu features a variety of steak and seafood choices. All meals come with a simple, but fresh, salad bar, which includes slices of pineapple and melon along with the usual vegies.

Tanaka of Tokyo *(☎ 922-4702; 2250 Kalakaua Ave; lunch $10-15, dinner $16-36; open 11:30am-2pm Mon-Fri, 5:30pm-10pm daily)*, in the Waikiki Shopping Plaza, is a fun place. Its U-shaped teppanyaki tables each have a central grill that's presided over by a chef with 'flying knives,' who cooks and serves meals to the diners at his table. Meals are set courses that include salad, miso soup, rice, an appetizer and dessert. The dinner price is determined by the main selected, with choices ranging from chicken to lobster. Look in the free tourist magazines for coupons that are good for one half-priced meal when two people dine together.

Singha Thai *(☎ 941-2893; 1910 Ala Moana Blvd; mains $12-25; open 4pm-11pm daily)* has award-winning Thai food and a troupe of Thai dancers that performs from 7pm to 9pm nightly. For starters, the shrimp salad and the hot-and-sour *tom yum* soup are tasty house specialties ($10 each). Mains include a variety of spicy curry and noodle dishes as well as some upmarket choices like seared Hawaiian lobster tail in a ginger and chili sauce.

Keo's *(☎ 922-9355; 2028 Kuhio Ave; mains $10-18; open 5pm-11pm daily)*, Waikiki's other top-rated Thai restaurant, also has good food. Keo's has long been a favorite with visiting celebs ranging from Jimmy Carter to Keanu Reeves, but has a loyal local following as well. Owner Keo Sananikone liberally spices the dishes with organically grown herbs from Oahu farms. A house specialty is the Evil Jungle Prince, a spicy curry with basil and coconut milk, that can be ordered in vegetarian, chicken, beef or shrimp versions. The main drawback is that the location, roadside on busy Kuhio Ave, can be noisy.

Places to Eat – Top End

Golden Dragon *(☎ 946-5336; 2005 Kalia Rd; appetizers $7-10, mains $15-30; open 6pm-9:30pm Tues-Sat)*, in the Hilton Hawaiian Village hotel, is a top choice for fine Chinese dining, with both good food and an ocean view. Although the varied menu has some expensive specialties, many dishes, including a tasty Cantonese roast duck and a deliciously crispy lemon chicken, are priced under $20.

Sam Choy's Diamond Head Restaurant *(☎ 732-8645; 449 Kapahulu Ave; meals $20-30; open 5:30pm-9:30pm daily)*, north of the zoo, offers Hawaiian regional cuisine in a contemporary setting. Unlike many other restaurateurs specializing in such fare, Choy serves guests hearty portions and includes both soup and salad with all mains. Among the favorites here are the seafood *laulau* and the crabmeat-stuffed fish. There are a few appetizers on the menu, but because the mains are so generous, most diners forgo the first course.

Prince Court *(☎ 956-1111; 100 Holomoana St; lunch buffet $20, dinner buffet on weekday/weekends $30/39; open 11:30am-2pm Mon-Fri, 5pm-9pm daily)* is a worthy treat. This sleek contemporary restaurant on the 3rd floor of the Hawaii Prince Hotel, offers a fine view of the yacht harbor and wonderful buffets of Asian and Western cuisine. All buffets have hot and cold mains, dim sum, fresh fish, salads and tempting desserts; dinner adds on an array of seafood dishes including crab legs, sashimi and smoked salmon.

Banyan Veranda *(☎ 922-3111; 2365 Kalakaua Ave; 4-course dinner $40; open 5:30pm-9pm daily)*, at the Sheraton Moana Surfrider, has a gem of a setting on the hotel's historic courtyard veranda. The menu, which changes nightly, features French and Pacific Rim influenced dishes. Dinner is accompanied by Hawaiian music and hula dancing. All in all, it makes for a romantic night out.

Orchid's *(☎ 923-2311; buffet $38; open 9:30am-2:30pm)*, at the Halekulani Hotel, has Oahu's best Sunday brunch buffet. The grand spread includes sashimi, sushi, prime rib, smoked salmon, roast suckling pig, an array of salads and fruits and a rich dessert bar. It's a pampering treat, with a fine ocean view, orchid sprays on the tables and a soothing flute and harp duo. It's best to make advance reservations or you may encounter a long wait.

Kyo-ya *(☎ 947-3911; 2057 Kalakaua Ave; lunch $14-20, dinner $30-55; open 11am-1:30pm Mon-Sat, 5:30pm-9pm daily)*, a formal Japanese restaurant with kimono-clad waitresses, has Waikiki's fanciest Japanese cuisine. The menu is extensive, covering eight pages. The specialty here is the *kaiseki* dinner, a traditional Kyoto-style meal that's served with as many as a dozen small courses. Both the setting and food presentation are elegant, and it's a favorite spot among islanders for a special night out.

La Mer *(☎ 923-2311; 2199 Kalia Rd; mains $30-45, 4-course/6-course dinner $80/105; open 6pm-9:30pm daily)*, in the Halekulani Hotel, is regarded by many to be Hawaii's ultimate fine-dining restaurant. It has a neoclassical French menu, with an emphasis on Provençal cuisine and a superb 2nd-floor ocean view. The dining is formal, and men are required to wear jackets (loaners are available). The menu changes daily but typically features items like *ahi* with caviar, bouillabaisse and filet mignon.

Entertainment

Waikiki rocks! It also gyrates, jams, croons, romances and mellows out. There's something here for everyone's taste, whether you're looking for a hot dance club to rock the night away or just want to relax on the beach while listening to Hawaiian music with a tall drink in hand. Waikiki has become *the* main entertainment venue for all of Honolulu, both straight and gay, so you'll never have a problem finding something to do.

For updated schedule information, check the free tourist magazines and the local newspapers.

Hawaiian Music & Hula Waikiki has lots of Hawaiian-style entertainment, from Polynesian shows with beating drums and hula dancers to mellow duos playing slack-key guitar.

You can watch some of Oahu's best hula troupes performing their music and dance for free at a couple of Waikiki venues. The most scenic is the city-sponsored **Kuhio Beach Torch Lighting & Hula Show** *(shows 6:30pm Mon-Thur, 6pm Fri-Sun)* at Kuhio Beach Park's hula mound. Another free hula show takes place at the **International Market Place** *(2330 Kalakaua Ave)* food court from 7:30pm most evenings.

The beachside courtyard at **Duke's Canoe Club** *(☎ 922-2268; 2335 Kalakaua Ave)*, at the Outrigger Waikiki hotel, is Waikiki's most popular venue for contemporary Hawaiian music. There's entertainment from 4pm to 6pm and from 10pm to midnight daily, with the biggest names – including Kapena and Henry Kapono – appearing on weekend afternoons. Great scene – don't miss it.

At the **Banyan Veranda** *(☎ 922-3111; 2365 Kalakaua Ave)*, at the Sheraton Moana Surfrider, you can listen to music beneath the same old banyan tree where 'Hawaii Calls' broadcast its nationwide radio show for four decades beginning in 1935. The performance schedule varies, but typically there's Hawaiian music and a hula dancer from 5:30pm to 8:30pm nightly, followed by classical musicians until 10:30pm.

House Without a Key *(☎ 923-2311; 2199 Kalia Rd)* attracts an older, genteel crowd who gather daily at the Halekulani Hotel's open-air bar for sunset cocktails, Hawaiian music and hula dancing by a former Miss Hawaii.

The **Royal Hawaiian Hotel** *(☎ 931-7194; 2259 Kalakaua Ave; adult/child 5-12 $81/48)* has a beachside luau from 6pm to 8:30pm Monday, which includes a bar, buffet-style dinner and Polynesian show.

Tiny Bubbles

Want a jolt of 1960s nostalgia? If sing-alongs and getting invited on stage to be razzed with jokes sounds like fun, then Don Ho is the way to go. This saucy Honolulu musician has been playing the Waikiki tourist scene since 1962. Sitting behind an organ, he bounces between witty banter, chatting with the audience and singing his classic pop hits like 'Tiny Bubbles' and 'I'll Remember You' – offering a good dose of kitsch in the process.

The show *(☎ 923-3981; Waikiki Beachcomber Hotel, 2300 Kalakaua Ave; admission $32; show 8pm Sun-Thur)* takes place five nights a week, and the admission price includes a cocktail.

Dance Clubs Waikiki's hottest dance club, **Wave Waikiki** *(☎ 941-0424; 1877 Kalakaua Ave; admission $5; open 9pm-4am daily)* has an emphasis on trance, hip hop, funk and alternative music. The minimum age is 21.

Scruples *(☎ 923-9530; 2310 Kuhio Ave; admission $5; open 8pm-4am daily)* is a busy, disco-style, top-40 dance club in the center of Waikiki. The minimum age is 18.

Moose McGillycuddy's *(☎ 923-0751; 310 Lewers St; admission free; open 9pm-1am Mon-Sat)* is a raucous place with live bands; the music is mostly '80s and '90s rock and top 40. The minimum age is 21.

Zanzabar Nightclub *(☎ 924-3939; 2255 Kuhio Ave; admission $5; open 9pm-4am daily)*, in the Waikiki Trade Center, has something happening every night. There's always dancing but the music varies with the night, ranging from techno and trance to top 40. The minimum age is 21.

Bars A good place to linger over a cool tropical drink while soaking up the rays is **The Poolside Bar** *(☎ 921-6264; 2570 Kalakaua Ave)* in the Aston Waikiki Beach Hotel.

Coconut Willy's Bar *(☎ 923-9454; 2330 Kalakaua Ave)*, in the International Market Place, gets a bit loud, but it's a great place to watch people, and there's plenty of night action.

Ye Olde Fox and Hound *(☎ 947-3776; 1178 Ala Moana Blvd)*, an English-style pub in the basement of the Discovery Bay Center, features live sports broadcasts on big-screen TVs and Waikiki's cheapest beer prices.

Harry's Bar *(☎ 923-1234; 2424 Kalakaua Ave)*, in the Hyatt Regency Waikiki, is a fun place that not only mixes up those colorful tropical drinks with little umbrellas but also makes good alcohol-free smoothies. There's usually Hawaiian entertainment in the evening.

Gay Venues On the 2nd floor of the Waikiki Grand hotel, **Hula's Bar & Lei Stand** *(☎ 923-0669; 134 Kapahulu Ave; open 10am-2am daily)* is Waikiki's main gay venue. This open-air bar is a popular place for gays to meet, dance and have a few drinks. It also has an ocean view.

Other gay spots in Waikiki are **Angles Waikiki** *(☎ 926-9766; 2256 Kuhio Ave)*, a nightclub with dancing, a pool table and video games; **Fusion Waikiki** *(☎ 924-2422; 2260 Kuhio Ave)*, which has karaoke and female impersonator shows; and **In-Between** *(☎ 926-7060; 2155 Lauula St)*, a gay karaoke bar open until 2am nightly.

All four of these places welcome both gay men and lesbians, though Hula's and In-Between are frequented predominantly by gay men, while Angles and Fusion tend to have a more mixed crowd.

Cinemas The **Waikiki Theatres** *(☎ 971-5133; Seaside & Kalakaua Aves; admission $7.50)* has three screens showing first-run movies.

IMAX Theatre Waikiki *(☎ 923-4629; 325 Seaside Ave; admission $10)* shows a 40-minute movie of Hawaii's stunning vistas on a 70ft-wide screen, with three-dimensional visual and motion effects that imitate zooming around the islands in a helicopter.

Free Entertainment A pleasant way to pass the evening is to stroll along Waikiki Beach at sunset and sample the outdoor Hawaiian shows that take place at the beachfront hotels. You can wander past the musicians playing at the Sheraton Moana Surfrider's Banyan Veranda, watch bands performing beachside at Duke's Canoe Club, see the poolside performers at the Sheraton Waikiki and so on down the line.

The **Royal Hawaiian Band** performs from 2pm to 3pm Sunday, with the exception of August, at the Kapiolani Park Bandstand. It's a quintessential Hawaiian scene that caps off with the audience joining hands and singing Queen Liliuokalani's *Aloha Oe* in Hawaiian.

The Kapiolani Park Bandstand is also the site of free **Friday Bandstand Concerts** held from 5:30pm to 6:30pm each Friday. A different Hawaiian group performs each week – anything from top-notch slack-key guitar masters to blues and jazz bands.

The **Royal Hawaiian Shopping Center** *(☎ 922-0588; Kalakaua Ave)* offers free events at its fountain courtyard, including a nightly torch lighting ceremony at 6pm that's followed some nights by a 30-minute Polynesian show.

In addition, the shopping center sponsors various daytime activities; all are free and last one hour. Hula lessons are given at 10am Monday and Friday; lei-making lessons are at 11am Monday and Wednesday; and ukulele lessons are at 10am Tuesday and Thursday, and 11:30am Monday, Wednesday and Friday.

To get some exercise while learning about Hawaiian culture, join one of the free **Waikiki Historic Trail** walking tours. These 90-minute walks, led by Native Hawaiian guides, are peppered with interesting historic tidbits on Hawaiian royalty who lived and played in Waikiki in days past. The walks begin at 9am Monday to Friday in front of the Duke Kahanamoku statue at Kuhio Beach Park.

Sunset on the Beach is a free city-sponsored beach party held on Saturday and Sunday evenings at Queen's Surf Beach Hawaiian bands perform on the beach from 4pm and then when darkness falls a huge screen is unscrolled and a movie is shown. Sometimes it's a film with island connections, such as Elvis Presley's *Blue Hawaii* and other nights it's a popular Hollywood flick of the *Star Wars* variety. It's a fun scene!

Other free things to see and do in Waikiki, which are detailed earlier in this chapter, include the Pleasant Hawaiian Hula Show, the Damien Museum, the Oceanarium, the US Army Museum and tours of the historic Sheraton Moana hotel.

And of course don't miss one of the free **hula shows** that are offered nightly (see the earlier Hawaiian Music & Hula section for details).

Shopping

Waikiki has no shortage of souvenir stalls, swimsuit and T-shirt shops, quick-stop convenience marts or fancy boutiques.

You'll never be far from one of the ubiquitous **ABC Discount Marts**, which stand on nearly every other street corner. They're often the cheapest place to pick up vacation necessities, such as beach mats, sunblock and sundry goods.

For cheap souvenirs, there's the **International Market Place** *(☎ 923-9871; 2330 Kalakaua Ave)*, under a sprawling banyan tree in the center of Waikiki, where nearly a hundred stalls sell everything from seashell necklaces and refrigerator magnets to T-shirts and sarongs.

The **Royal Hawaiian Shopping Center** *(☎ 922-0588; Kalakaua Ave)*, Waikiki's biggest shopping center, has dozens of shops selling jewelry and designer clothing. The Royal Hawaiian also has Hawaiian-influenced gift shops, including **Little Hawaiian Craft Shop** *(☎ 926-2662)*, which carries a range of local crafts, from *kukui*-nut key chains and quilt-pattern kits, to high-quality koa bowls.

For antique and used aloha shirts, **Bailey's Antique Shop** *(☎ 734-7628; 517 Kapahulu Ave)* has the island's widest selection. It's a great place to go and look around – almost like a museum.

For eclectic antiques, there's **Island Treasures Antiques** *(☎ 922-8223; 2145 Kuhio Ave)*, which has lots of odds and ends, including jewelry, period glassware, old posters and Asian porcelain.

> **Mellowing Out**
>
> The **Urasenke Foundation of Hawaii** *(☎ 923-3059; 245 Saratoga Rd)* offers tea-ceremony demonstrations on Wednesday and Friday, bringing a rare bit of serenity to busy Saratoga Rd. Students dressed in kimonos perform the ceremony on tatami mats in a formal tea room; for those participating, it can be a meditative experience.
>
> It costs $3 to be served green tea and sweets, or you can watch the ceremony for free. Demonstrations take place at 10am and last about 45 minutes. Reservations are a good idea, but not always essential. Because guests must leave their shoes at the door, the foundation appreciates it if all visitors wear socks.

Pearl Harbor

Pearl Harbor is world famous as the site of the attack that launched the US into WWII. The harbor itself is surrounded by US military bases, but there are also three WWII-related visitor sites that can be intriguing to anyone interested in the history of that era. The best known is the USS *Arizona* Memorial, which should be your first stop. The other two are the USS *Bowfin* Submarine Museum & Park, which is adjacent to the USS *Arizona* Memorial, and the Battleship *Missouri*, where General Douglas MacArthur accepted the Japanese surrender that marked the end of WWII.

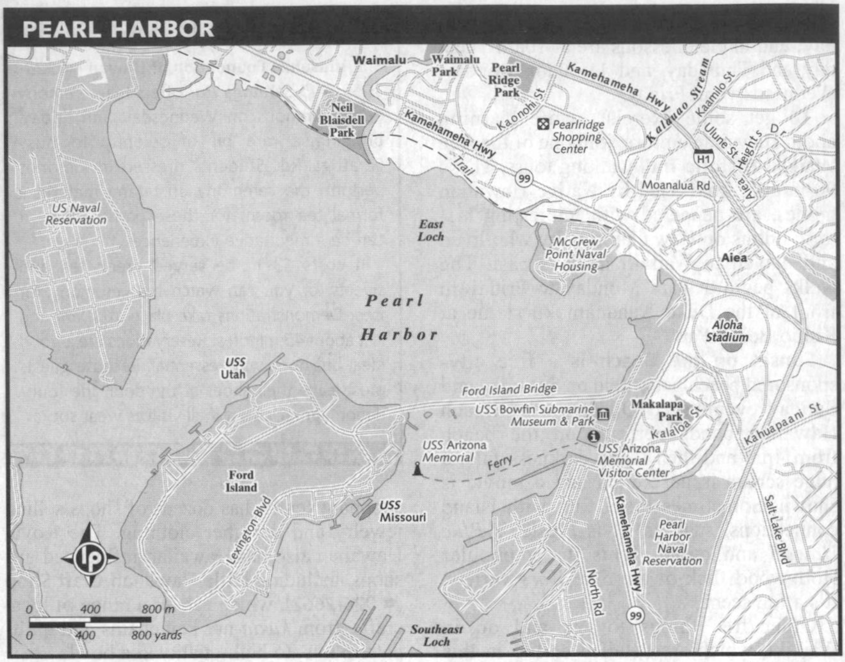

For those looking for a little peace and quiet, the greater Pearl Harbor area also has two low-key sights: Keaiwa Heiau State Park, which holds an ancient medicinal temple and hiking trails, and Hawaii's Plantation Village, which depicts the lifestyle of the various ethnic groups that worked the sugar plantations.

USS *Arizona* Memorial

Over 1.5 million people 'remember Pearl Harbor' each year by visiting the USS *Arizona* Memorial. Operated by the National Park Service, the memorial is Hawaii's most visited attraction.

The **visitor center** (*☎ 422-2771; 24hr recorded information ☎ 422-0561; admission free; open 7:30am-5pm daily; closed Thanksgiving, Christmas & New Year's Day*) encompasses a museum and a theater as well as the offshore memorial at the sunken USS *Arizona*. The park service provides a 75-minute programme that includes a short documentary film on the attack and a boat ride out to the memorial and back.

The 184ft memorial, built in 1962, sits directly over the *Arizona* without touching the sunken ship. The memorial contains the ship's bell and a wall inscribed with the names of those who perished onboard. The average age of the enlisted men on the *Arizona* was just 19 years old.

From the memorial, the battleship is visible 8ft below the surface. The ship rests in about 40ft of water, and even now oozes a gallon or two of oil each day. In the rush to recover from the attack and prepare for war, the navy exercised its option to leave the men in the sunken ship. They remain entombed in its hull, buried at sea.

Pearl Harbor survivors, who act as volunteer historians, are sometimes available to talk with visitors about their experiences on the day of the attack.

There's also a small museum with interesting photos, from both Japanese and US military archives, showing Pearl Harbor before, during and after the attack. One photo is of Harvard-educated Admiral Yamamoto, the brilliant military strategist who planned the attack on Pearl Harbor – even though he personally opposed going to war with the USA. Rather than relish the victory, Yamamoto stated after the attack that he feared

Japan had 'awakened a sleeping giant and filled him with a terrible resolve.'

Weather permitting, programmes run every 15 minutes from 8am to 3pm (from 7:45am in summer) on a first-come, first-served basis. As soon as you arrive, pick up a ticket at the information booth (each person in the party must pick up his or her own ticket); the number printed on the ticket corresponds to the time the tour begins.

Generally, the shortest waits are in the morning, and if you arrive before the crowds, your wait may be less than half an hour; however, waits of a couple of hours are not unknown. The summer months are the busiest, with an average of 4500 people taking the tour daily, and the day's allotment of tickets is sometimes gone by noon.

Admission to everything, including the boat ride, which is provided by the navy, is free. The memorial and all its facilities are accessible to the disabled. There's a snack bar where you can get something simple to eat and a shop selling souvenirs and books.

USS *Bowfin* Submarine Museum & Park

If you have to wait an hour or two for your USS *Arizona* Memorial tour to begin, you might want to stroll over to the adjacent USS *Bowfin* Submarine Museum & Park *(☎ 423-1341; admission to park free, admission to submarine & museum adult/child $8/3; open 8am-5pm daily)*.

The park contains the moored WWII submarine the USS *Bowfin*, as well as the Pacific Submarine Museum, which traces the development of submarines from their early origins to the nuclear age.

Commissioned in May 1943, the *Bowfin* sank 44 ships in the Pacific before the end of the war. Visitors can take a self-guided tour using a 30-minute recorded cassette tape (included in the admission fee) that corresponds with items seen along the walk through the submarine.

There's no charge to enter the park and view the missiles and torpedoes spread around the grounds, look through the periscopes or inspect the Japanese *kaiten*, a suicide torpedo.

The *kaiten* is just what it looks like: a torpedo with a single seat. As the war was closing in on the Japanese homeland, the *kaiten* was developed in a last-ditch effort to ward off an invasion. It was the marine equivalent of the kamikaze pilot and his plane. A volunteer was placed in the torpedo before it was fired. He then piloted it to its target. At least one US ship, the USS *Mississinewa*, was sunk by a *kaiten*. It went down off Ulithi Atoll in November 1944.

Sneak Attack?

On December 7, 1941, a wave of more than 350 Japanese planes attacked Pearl Harbor, home of the US Pacific Fleet.

Some 2335 US soldiers were killed during the two-hour attack. Of those, 1177 died in the battleship USS *Arizona* when it took a direct hit and sank in less than nine minutes. Twenty other US ships were sunk or seriously damaged and 347 airplanes were destroyed that fateful day.

The attack upon Pearl Harbor, which jolted the USA into WWII, caught the US fleet totally by surprise. There had, however, been warnings, some of which were far from subtle.

At 6:40am on December 7, 1941, the USS *Ward* spotted a submarine conning tower approaching the entrance of Pearl Harbor. The *Ward* immediately attacked with depth charges and sank what turned out to be one of five midget Japanese submarines launched to penetrate the harbor.

At 7:02am a radar station on the north shore of Oahu reported planes approaching. Even though they were coming from the west rather than the east, they were assumed to be American planes from the US mainland.

At 7:55am Pearl Harbor was hit. Within minutes the USS *Arizona* went down in a fiery inferno, trapping its crew beneath the surface. It wasn't until 15 minutes after the bombing started that American anti-aircraft guns began to shell the Japanese warplanes.

Battleship *Missouri* Memorial

In 1998, the decommissioned battleship USS *Missouri (☎ 973-2494; adult/child self-guided tour $14/7, group tour $20/13; open 9am-5pm daily)*, nicknamed 'Mighty Mo,' was brought to Ford Island by the nonprofit USS *Missouri* Memorial Association to provide a third element to Pearl Harbor's WWII commemorative sites.

Leave Your Bags Behind

Following the September 11 attacks on New York City, new security measures were enacted at the USS *Arizona* Memorial and the USS *Missouri* Memorial. Visitors now face strict restrictions on what they can bring into these sites.

You are not allowed to bring into the *Arizona* Memorial visitor center, or onto either of the ship tours, any items that allow concealment, and this includes purses, camera bags, fanny packs, backpacks, diaper bags, shopping bags and the like. Also, cameras or video cameras larger than 12 inches are not allowed. It's not that these items are being searched and then allowed in; they simply can't be brought into the sites at all.

If you arrive by bus, there's no place to store your personal items; there are no lockers. If you arrive by car, you could put these items in your trunk, but this is something the park service has advised against in the past because of potential theft from parked cars. So, if you're going to visit these Pearl Harbor sites, plan ahead, and consider securing your items wherever you're staying before heading out.

The 887ft-long *Missouri*, a powerful battleship launched near the end of WWII, served as a flagship during the battles of Iwo Jima and Okinawa. On September 2, 1945, the formal Japanese surrender that ended WWII took place on the battleship's deck. The *Missouri* is now docked just a few hundred yards from the sunken remains of the USS *Arizona*; together, the ships provide a unique set of historical bookends.

A tour of the ship takes approximately two hours. You can poke about the officers' quarters, visit the wardroom that now houses exhibits on the ship's history and walk the deck where General Douglas MacArthur accepted the Japanese surrender. The main advantage of joining a group tour is that it provides access to a 'combat engagement center' where you can watch a simulated naval battle.

It's not possible to drive directly to Ford Island, because it's an active military facility. Instead, a trolley bus shuttles visitors to the *Missouri* from *Bowfin* Park, where the tickets are sold. If you're a history buff the *Missouri* is a worthwhile sight, but if your time or money is more limited visit the *Arizona* Memorial instead.

Getting There & Away

The USS *Arizona* Memorial visitor center and *Bowfin* Park are off Kamehameha Hwy (Hwy 99) on the Pearl Harbor Naval Reservation, just south of the Aloha Stadium. If you're coming from Honolulu, take H1 west to exit 15A (Stadium/*Arizona* Memorial). Make sure you follow the highway signs for the USS *Arizona* Memorial, and not the signs for Pearl Harbor. There's plenty of free parking at the visitor center.

It's easy to get there by public bus. Bus No 42 Ewa Beach is the most direct bus from Waikiki to the visitor center, taking about an hour. Bus No 20 covers the same route, but it makes a stop at the airport, adding about 15 minutes to the travel time.

The private *Arizona* Memorial Shuttle Bus (*☎ 839-0911*) and Hawaii Super Transit (*☎ 841-2989*) both pick up people from Waikiki hotels several times a day, charging $3/5 one way/round-trip for a van ride to the visitor center. The ride takes around 40 minutes.

There are also private boat cruises to Pearl Harbor that leave from Kewalo Basin and cost about $25 – but they don't stop at the visitor center and passengers are not allowed to board the *Arizona* memorial.

HAWAII'S PLANTATION VILLAGE

This village (*☎ 677-0110; 94-695 Waipahu St, Waipahu; adult/child $7/4; open 9am-4pm Mon-Fri, 10am-4pm Sat*), 5 miles northeast of Pearl Harbor, will reward visitors with insights into Hawaii's multiethnic heritage.

The site encompasses 30 homes and buildings set up to re-create a typical plantation village of the early 20th century. The houses are furnished with period pieces illustrating the lifestyles of the eight different ethnic groups – Hawaiian, Japanese, Okinawan, Chinese, Korean, Portuguese, Puerto Rican and Filipino – that worked the sugar plantations. The Chinese cookhouse (c. 1909) was originally on this site, and the Japanese shrine (1914) was moved here; the other structures are replicas authentic to the period.

One-hour guided tours of the village begin on the hour between 9am and 3pm Monday to Friday and from 10am Saturday.

The setting is particularly evocative, as Waipahu was one of Oahu's last plantation towns, and its rusty sugar mill, which operated until 1995, still looms on a knoll directly above this site. While you're waiting for the tour to begin, you can stroll through the small museum off the lobby. All in all, it's a quality, community-based production.

To get there by car, take the H1 Fwy to exit 7, turn left onto Paiwa St, then right onto Waipahu St, continue past the sugar mill and the village is on the left. By bus, No 42 runs between Waikiki and Waipahu every 30 minutes during the day and takes about 1¾ hours.

KEAIWA HEIAU STATE PARK

This 334-acre state park (*☎ 483-2511; Aiea Heights Dr; admission free; open 7am-sunset daily*) in Aiea, 3 miles north-northeast of Pearl Harbor, contains an ancient medicinal temple, camping grounds, picnic facilities and a scenic hiking trail.

At the park entrance is **Keaiwa Heiau**, a 100ft-by-160ft, single-terraced, stone structure built in the 1600s and used by *kahuna lapaau* (herbalist healers). The *kahuna*s used hundreds of medicinal plants and grew many on the grounds surrounding the *heiau*. Among those still found here are *noni* (Indian mulberry), whose pungent yellow fruits were used to treat heart disease; *kukui*, whose nuts were an effective laxative; breadfruit, whose sap soothed chapped skin; and ti leaves, which were wrapped around a sick person to break a fever. Not only did the herbs have medicinal value, but the *heiau* itself was considered to possess life-giving energy. The *kahuna* was able to draw from the powers of both.

Today, people wishing to be healed still place offerings within the *heiau*. The offerings reflect the multiplicity of Hawaii's cultures: rosary beads, New Age crystals and sake cups sit beside flower leis and rocks wrapped in ti leaves.

To get to Keaiwa from Honolulu, head west on Hwy 78 and take the Stadium/Aiea turnoff onto Moanalua Rd. Turn right onto Aiea Heights Dr at the second traffic light. The road winds up through a residential area 2½ miles to the park.

Aiea Loop Trail

The 4½-mile Aiea Loop Trail begins at the top of the park's paved loop road next to the rest rooms and comes back out at the camping ground, about a third of a mile below the start of the trail. The trail starts off in a forest of eucalyptus trees and runs along the ridge. Other trees along the way include ironwood, Norfolk Island pines, edible guava and native *ohia lehua*, which has fluffy red flowers.

Along the trail, there are sweeping vistas of Pearl Harbor, Diamond Head and the Koolau Range. About two-thirds of the way in, the wreckage of a C-47 cargo plane that crashed in 1943 can be spotted through the foliage on the east ridge.

Camping

The park can accommodate 100 campers, in sites that mostly have their own picnic table and barbecue. Sites are not crowded together, but because many are open, there's not a lot of privacy either.

If you're camping in winter, make sure your gear is waterproof, as it rains frequently at this 880ft elevation. The park has rest rooms, showers and drinking water. There's a resident caretaker by the front gate, and the gate is locked at night for security.

As with all Oahu public camping grounds, camping is not permitted on Wednesday and Thursday, and permits must be obtained in advance. For details, see Camping in the Accommodations section at the start of this chapter.

Southeast Oahu

Some of Oahu's finest scenery is along the southeast coast, which curves around the tip of the Koolau Range. Diamond Head, Hanauma Bay and the island's most famous bodysurfing beaches are all just a 20-minute ride from Waikiki.

East of Diamond Head, H1 turns into the Kalanianaole Hwy (Hwy 72), passing the exclusive Kahala residential area, a run of shopping centers and some housing developments that creep into the mountain valleys.

The highway rises and falls as it winds its way around the Koko Head area and Makapuu Point, with beautiful coastal views along the way. The area is geologically fascinating, with boldly stratified rock formations, volcanic craters and lava sea cliffs.

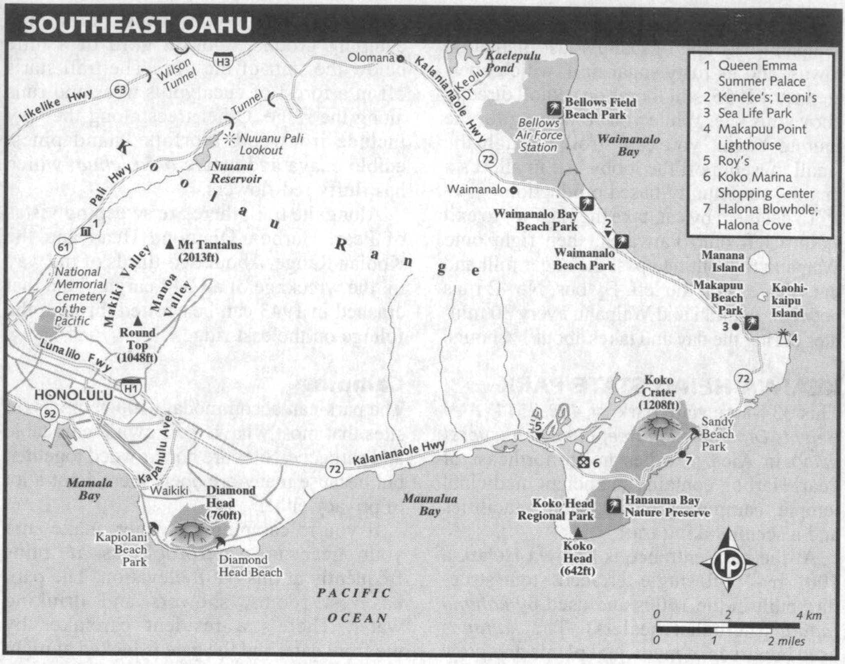

DIAMOND HEAD

Diamond Head *(admission $1; open 6am-6pm daily)* is a tuff cone and crater that was formed by a violent steam explosion deep beneath the earth's surface long after most of Oahu's volcanic activity had stopped. As the backdrop to Waikiki, it's one of the best-known landmarks in the Pacific. The summit is 760ft high.

The Hawaiians called it Leahi and built a *luakini heiau* (temple for human sacrifices) on the top. But ever since 1825, which was when British sailors found calcite crystals sparkling in the sun and mistakenly thought they'd struck it rich, it's been called Diamond Head.

In 1909, the US Army began building Fort Ruger at the edge of the crater. Soldiers built a network of tunnels and topped the rim with cannon emplacements, bunkers and observation posts. Reinforced during WWII, the fort has been a silent sentinel whose guns have never fired.

Diamond Head is a state monument with picnic tables, rest rooms and drinking water. The best reason to visit is to hike the trail to the crater rim for the panoramic view.

Diamond Head Trail

The trail to the summit was built in 1910 to service the military observation stations along the crater rim.

It's a fairly steep hike, with a gain in elevation of 560ft, but it's only three-quarters of a mile to the top and plenty of people of all ages hike up. It takes about an hour to make a round-trip. The trail is open and hot, so you might want to take along something to drink.

As you start up the trail, you can see the summit ahead a bit to the left, at roughly eleven o'clock.

The crater is dry and scrubby with *kiawe* (a relative of the mesquite tree) and koa trees, grasses and wildflowers. The little yellow-orange flowers along the way are native *ilima,* Oahu's official flower.

About 20 minutes up the trail, you enter a long, dark tunnel. Because the tunnel curves you don't see light until you get close to the end. It's a little spooky, but the roof is high enough for you to walk through without bumping your head, there's a hand rail and your eyes should adjust enough to make out shadows in the darkness.

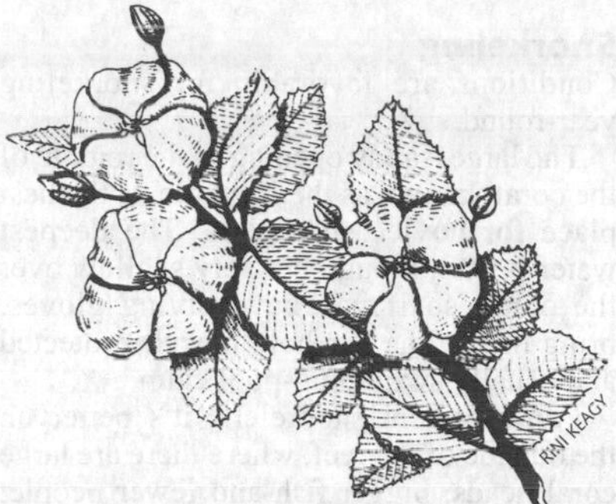

***Ilima*, Oahu's official flower**

Nevertheless, to prevent accidents, the park advises hikers to tote along a flashlight.

The tunnel itself seems like it should be the climax of this long climb, but upon coming out into the light you're immediately faced with a steep 99-step staircase. Persevere! After this there's a shorter tunnel, a narrow spiral staircase inside an unlit bunker and the last of the trail's 271 steps. Be careful when you reach the top – there are some steep drops.

From the top there's a fantastic 360° view taking in the southeast coast to Koko Head and Koko Crater and the leeward coast to Barbers Point and the Waianae Mountains. Below is Kapiolani Park and the Waikiki Shell. You can also see the lighthouse, coral reefs, sailboats and sometimes even surfers waiting for a wave at Diamond Head Beach.

To reach Diamond Head from Waikiki, take bus No 22 or 58, both of which run about twice an hour. It's a 20-minute walk from the bus stop to the trailhead at the parking lot. By car from Waikiki, take Monsarrat Ave to Diamond Head Rd and then take the right turn after Kapiolani Community College into the crater.

Diamond Head Beach

Diamond Head Beach draws both surfers and windsurfers. Conditions are suitable for intermediate to advanced windsurfers, and when the swells are up it's a great place for wave riding. The beach has showers, but no other facilities.

As there's not much to see here unless the wind and surf are up, most people coming this way are touring by car. To get there from Waikiki, follow Kalakaua Ave to Diamond Head Rd. There's a parking lot just beyond the lighthouse. Walk east past the end of the lot and you'll find a paved trail down to the beach. If you don't have your own transport, bus No 14 runs from Waikiki about once an hour.

HANAUMA BAY NATURE PRESERVE

Hanauma *(☎ 396-4229; adult/child $3/free; open 6am-6pm Wed-Mon Nov-Mar, 6am-7pm Wed-Mon Apr-Oct)*, which means 'Curved Bay,' is a wide, sheltered bay of sapphire and turquoise waters set in a rugged volcanic ring.

Once a popular fishing spot, it had nearly been fished out when it was designated a marine life conservation district in 1967. Now that the fish are protected instead of eaten, they swarm in by the thousands.

From the overlook, you view the entire coral reef that stretches across the width of the bay. You're bound to see schools of glittering silver fish, the bright blue flash of parrotfish and perhaps a sea turtle. To see an even more colorful scene, put on a mask, jump in and view it from beneath the surface.

While it's teeming with fish, Hanauma is far from pristine. Arguably, it's being loved to death. With over a million visitors a year, it's often busy and crowded and the heavy use of the bay has taken its toll. The coral on the shallow reef has been damaged by all the action.

Still, efforts are being made to right the wrongs. For your part, be careful not to stand on the reef. Fish feeding by snorkelers, a practice that drew more aggressive fish into the bay, is now banned at Hanauma, resulting in a more natural balance of fish species.

Hanauma is both a county beach park and a state underwater park. It has a snack bar, lifeguards, showers, rest rooms and access for the disabled.

The beachside concession stand, open 8am to 4:30pm daily, rents snorkel sets for $6. You'll need to either hand over $30, a credit card or your car rental keys as a deposit.

Paths lead along low ledges on both sides of the bay; the eastern one goes to the Toilet Bowl, the western one to Witches Brew. When the surf is up, which includes most high-wind days, the paths are gated shut and entry to the ledges is prohibited. At other times you can walk out along the ledges, but you should still be cautious; whenever the tide is high, waves can wash over the ledges, and of course a rogue wave can occur at any time.

More people drown at Hanauma than at any other beach on Oahu. Although the figure is high largely because there are so many visitors at this beach, people drowning in the Toilet Bowl or being swept off the ledges have accounted for a fair number of deaths over the years.

Hanauma Bay is about 10 miles from Waikiki along Hwy 72. The parking lot sometimes fills up by midday, so the earlier you get there the better. It costs $1 per vehicle to enter, but if you're unable to find a space, the fee will be refunded.

Bus No 22, called the Beach Bus, goes to Hanauma Bay (and on to Sea Life Park). On Monday to Friday the first buses leave Waikiki from the corner of Kuhio Ave and Namahana St at 8:15am and 9:15am, with subsequent buses leaving at 55 minutes past the hour until 3:55pm, and then a final bus at 4:25pm. The Beach Bus also stops near the zoo at Monsarrat and Kalakaua Aves, but it often fills to capacity before it reaches that stop. Buses leave Hanauma Bay to return to Waikiki at least once every hour from 11:10am to 5:40pm. On weekends the buses are more frequent (roughly twice an hour), though the schedule is more sporadic.

Toilet Bowl

A 15-minute walk out to the point on the left side of the bay brings you to the Toilet Bowl, a small natural pool in the lava rock. The Toilet Bowl is connected to the sea by an underwater channel, which enables water to surge into the bowl and then flush out from beneath.

People going into the pool for the thrill of it can get quite a ride as it flushes down 4ft to 5ft almost instantly. However, the rock around the bowl is slippery and hard to grip, and getting in is far easier than getting out. It definitely should not be tried alone.

Witches Brew

A 10-minute walk along the right side of the bay will take you to a rocky point. The cove at the southern side of the point is the treacherous Witches Brew, so named for its swirling, turbulent waters.

There's a nice view of Koko Crater from there, and green sand made of olivine can be found along the way.

Snorkeling

Conditions are favorable for snorkeling year-round.

The large, sandy opening in the middle of the coral, known as the Keyhole, is the best place for novice snorkelers. The deepest water is 10ft, though it's very shallow over the coral, so if you have diving gloves, bring them. The Keyhole is well protected and usually swimming-pool calm.

For confident snorkelers, it's better on the outside of the reef, where there are large coral heads, bigger fish and fewer people; to get there follow the directions on the signboard or ask the lifeguard at the southwest end of the beach. Keep in mind that because of the channel current it's generally easier going out than it is getting back in. Don't attempt to swim outside the reef when the water is rough or choppy. Not only will the channel current be strong, but the sand will be stirred up and the visibility poor anyway.

KOKO HEAD REGIONAL PARK

The entire Koko Head area is a county regional park. It includes Hanauma Bay, Koko Head, Halona Blowhole, Sandy Beach and Koko Crater.

Koko Head is backed by Hawaii Kai, an expansive development of condos, houses, shopping centers, a marina and a golf course – all meticulously planned and rather sterile in appearance.

Koko Crater and Koko Head are both tuff cones created about 10,000 years ago in Oahu's last gasp of volcanic activity.

Koko Head

Not to be confused with Koko Crater, Koko Head overlooks and forms the southwest side of Hanauma Bay.

There are two craters atop Koko Head, as well as radar facilities on the 642ft summit. The mile-long summit road is closed to casual visitors.

The Nature Conservancy maintains a preserve inside the shallow Ihiihilauakea Crater, the larger of the two craters. The crater has a unique vernal pool and a rare fern, the *Marsilea villosa*. The site can only be visited with a guide. For information on work parties or weekend excursions to the preserve, call the **Nature Conservancy** *(☎ 537-4508; 923 Nuuanu Ave, Honolulu)*.

ANN CECIL

Diamond Head and Waikiki

ANN CECIL

Surfing contest, Banzai Pipeline, Oahu

GLENDA BENDURE

Duke Kahanamoku statue, Oahu

GLENDA BENDURE

Outrigger canoe, Waikiki

ANDREW SALLMON

Hawaiian hibiscus

ANN CECIL

Yellow hibiscus

NED FRIARY

Tropical bouquet

ALISON WRIGHT

Bromeliad

Halona Blowhole Area

About three-quarters of a mile past Hanauma is a **lookout** with a view of striking coastal rock formations and crashing surf.

A little less than a mile further is the parking lot for the **Halona Blowhole**, where water surges through a submerged tunnel in the rock and spouts up through a hole in the ledge. It's preceded by a gushing sound, created by the air that's being forced out by the rushing water. The action depends on water conditions – sometimes it's barely discernible, while at other times it's a show-stopper.

Down to the right of the parking lot is **Halona Cove**, the little beach where the classic risqué love scene with Burt Lancaster and Deborah Kerr in *From Here to Eternity* was filmed in the 1950s.

Right before the blowhole, a small **stone monument** sits atop Halona Point. It was erected by Japanese fishers to honor those lost at sea.

Sandy Beach

Sandy Beach is one of the most dangerous beaches on the island, if measured in terms of lifeguard rescues and broken necks. It has a punishing shorebreak, a powerful backwash and strong rip currents.

Nevertheless, the shorebreak is extremely popular with bodysurfers who know their stuff. It's equally popular with spectators, who gather to watch the bodysurfers being tossed around in the transparent waves.

Sandy Beach is wide, very long and, yes, sandy. It's frequented by sunbathers, young surfers and admirers of both. When the swells are big, board surfers hit the left side of the beach.

Red flags flown on the beach indicate hazardous water conditions. Even if you don't notice the flags, always check with the lifeguards before entering the water.

Not all the action is in the water. The grassy strip on the inland side of the parking lot is used by people looking skyward for their thrills – it's both a hang-glider landing site and a popular locale for kite-flying.

The park has rest rooms and showers. Bus No 22 stops in front of the beach. **Local Chef** *(open 11am-4pm daily)*, a food wagon, sets up in the parking lot, selling cheap burgers and plate lunches.

Koko Crater

According to Hawaiian legend, Koko Crater is the imprint left by the vagina of Pele's sister Kapo, which was sent here from the Big Island to lure the pig-god Kamapuaa away from Pele.

Inside the crater there's a simple dryland **botanical garden** *(admission free; open 9am-4pm daily)* of plumeria trees, oleander and cacti that's maintained by the county. To get there, take Kealahou St off Hwy 72 opposite the northern end of Sandy Beach. Just over half a mile in, turn left onto the one-lane road to Koko Crater Stables and continue a third of a mile to the garden.

Places to Eat

The Koko Marina Shopping Center, on the corner of Lunalilo Home Rd and Hwy 72, is the main place to eat in this area, with more than a dozen choices ranging from fast food to waterfront dining.

The center's **Whole In One Bagels & Juice Rush** *(open 7am-7pm daily)* has fresh juices, makes a variety of tasty bagels and sells reasonably priced bagel sandwiches. The nearby **Kozo Sushi** *(open 9am-7pm daily)* has good takeaway sushi that's a favorite with locals packing beach picnics – you can get a 15-piece lunch box for just $5. **Yummy Korean BBQ** *(dishes $7; open 10am-7pm daily)* offers tasty barbecued plate lunches, and there are waterfront tables where you can sit and eat. The center also has a **Bubbies** *(open noon-9pm daily)* ice-cream shop selling homemade ice cream.

Roy's *(☎ 396-7697, Hawaii Kai Corporate Plaza, Hwy 72; appetizers $8-10, mains $20-30; open 5:30pm-10pm Mon-Fri, 5pm-10pm Sat & Sun)* is the best upmarket option in Southeast Oahu, if not the entire island. Chef Roy Yamaguchi is a prominent force behind the popularity of Hawaiian regional cuisine, which emphasizes fresh local ingredients and blends European, Polynesian and Asian influences. A superb main dish is the blackened *ahi*, seared outside, rare inside and served with a fiery wasabi sauce. For dessert, the chocolate soufflé is a decadent treat. Roy's is a top choice for a night out – the food is beautifully presented and the service attentive. The restaurant also does a nice job of matching moderately priced wines with its menu. Reservations are advised – request a table with a sunset view.

MAKAPUU POINT

About 1⅓ miles north of Sandy Beach, the 647ft Makapuu Point and its coastal **lighthouse** mark the easternmost point of Oahu. The mile-long service road to the lighthouse is locked to keep out private vehicles, but you're allowed to park off the highway just beyond the gate and walk in from there. Although not difficult, it's an uphill walk and conditions can be hot and windy. There are fine coastal views along the way and at the lighthouse lookout. During the winter, whales are sometimes visible offshore.

Back on the highway, about a third of a mile further along, there's a scenic **roadside lookout** with a view down onto Makapuu Beach, with its aqua-blue waters outlined by white sand and black lava. It's an even more spectacular sight when hang gliders are taking off from the cliffs, which serve as Oahu's top hang-gliding spot.

From the lookout you can see two offshore islands, the larger of which is **Manana Island**, also known as Rabbit Island. This aging volcanic crater is populated by feral rabbits and burrowing wedge-tailed shearwaters. They coexist so closely that the birds and rabbits sometimes even share the same burrows. The island looks vaguely like the head of a rabbit, and if you try hard you may see it, ears folded back. If that doesn't work, you could also try to imagine it as a whale.

In front of it is the smaller **Kaohikaipu Island**, which won't tax the imagination – all it looks is flat.

There's a coral reef between the two islands that divers sometimes explore, but to do so requires a boat.

Makapuu Beach Park

Makapuu Beach is one of the island's top winter bodysurfing spots, with waves reaching 12ft and higher. It also has the island's best shorebreak. As with Sandy Beach, Makapuu is strictly the domain of experienced bodysurfers who can handle rough water conditions and dangerous currents. Surfboards are prohibited.

In summer, when the wave action disappears, the waters can be calm and good for swimming.

The beach is opposite Sea Life Park in a pretty setting, with cliffs in the background and a glimpse of the lighthouse. Two native Hawaiian plants are plentiful – *naupaka* by the beach and yellow-orange *ilima* by the parking lot.

Frigate

Sea Life Park

Hawaii's only marine park is the Sea Life Park (*☎ 259-7933; 41-202 Hwy 72; adult/child 4-12/child under 4 $24/12/free; open 9:30am-5pm daily*).

A highlight is its enormous 300,000-gallon aquarium filled with sea turtles, eels, eagle rays, hammerhead sharks and thousands of colorful reef fish. A spiral ramp circles the 18ft-deep aquarium, allowing you to view the fish from different depths.

There's also the usual theme park entertainment, with shows featuring Atlantic bottlenose dolphins giving choreographed performances. The dolphins tail walk, do the hula and give rides to a 'beautiful island maiden' – it all borders on the kitsch.

The park has a large pool of California sea lions and a smaller pool with harbor seals. Another section has rare Hawaiian monk seals, comprised largely of abandoned pups that have been rescued from the wild; once they reach maturity, they're released back into their natural habitat. The park also has a penguin habitat, a turtle lagoon with green sea turtles and a seabird sanctuary that holds red-footed boobies, albatrosses and great frigate birds.

A $3 parking fee is charged in the main lot; however, if you continue past the ticket booth to the area marked 'additional parking,' there's no fee.

You can visit the park's cafeteria without paying admission, and from there you can also get a free glimpse of the seal and sea lion pools.

Bus Nos 22 (Beach Bus), 57 (Kailua/Sea Life Park) and 58 (Hawaii Kai/Sea Life Park) all stop at the park.

WAIMANALO

Waimanalo Bay has the longest continuous stretch of beach on Oahu: 5½ miles of white sand that stretches from Makapuu Point to Wailea Point. A long coral reef about a mile offshore breaks up the biggest waves, protecting much of the shore.

Waimanalo has three beach parks, all with camping facilities. The setting is scenic, although the area isn't highly regarded for safety.

Waimanalo Beach Park

Waimanalo Beach Park has an attractive beach of soft white sand and the water is excellent for swimming.

This is an in-town county park with a grassy picnic area, rest rooms, changing rooms, showers, ball fields, basketball and volleyball courts and a playground. Camping is allowed in an open area near the road. (For information on obtaining camping permits, see Camping in the Accommodations section earlier in this chapter.)

The park has ironwood trees, but overall it's more open than the other two parks to the north. The scalloped hills of the lower Koolau Range rise up on the inland side of the park, and Manana Island and Makapuu Point are visible to the south. Bus No 57 stops at the park entrance.

Waimanalo Bay Beach Park

This county park, which is about a mile north of Waimanalo Beach Park, has Waimanalo Bay's biggest waves and is very popular with board surfers and bodysurfers.

Locals call the park Sherwood Forest because hoods and car thieves used to hang out there in days past. The park has not totally shaken its reputation, so keep an eye on your belongings.

The park itself is quite appealing, with beachside camp sites shaded with ironwood trees. (For information on obtaining camping permits, see Camping in the Accommodations section near the beginning of this chapter.) There's a lifeguard station, barbecue grills, drinking water, showers and rest rooms.

Bus No 57 stops on the main road in front of the park, and from there it's a third of a mile's walk to the beach and camping ground.

Bellows Field Beach Park

The beach fronting Bellows Air Force Base *(open noon Fri-8am Mon)* is open to civilian beachgoers and campers on weekends only. This long beach has fine sand and a natural setting backed by ironwood trees. The small shorebreak waves are good for beginner bodysurfers and board surfers.

There's a lifeguard, showers, rest rooms and drinking water; the 50 camp sites are set out among the trees. Although it's military property, camping permits are issued through the county Department of Parks & Recreation. For information on obtaining permits, see Camping in the Accommodations section near the beginning of this chapter.

The marked entrance is a quarter of a mile north of Waimanalo Bay Beach Park. Bus No 57 stops in front of the entrance road, and from there it's 1½ miles to the beach.

Places to Eat

Just north of Waimanalo Beach Park, on Hwy 72 near the post office, is **Keneke's** *(lunch $5)*, a local eatery, and **Leoni's**, which

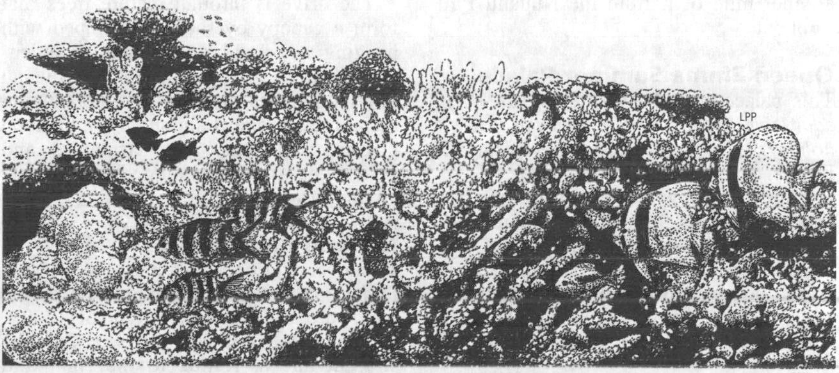

is a bakery that also serves pizzas and subs. There are **food marts** and **fast-food eateries** just south of Waimanalo Bay Beach Park and in a shopping cluster about a mile north of Bellows Field.

PALI HIGHWAY

The Pali Hwy (Hwy 61) runs between Honolulu and Kailua, cutting through the spectacular Koolau Range. It's a scenic little highway, and if it's been raining heavily every fold and crevice in the mountains will have a lacy waterfall streaming down it.

Many Kailua residents commute to work over the Pali, so Honolulu-bound traffic can be heavy in the morning and outbound traffic heavy in the evening. It's less of a problem for visitors, however, as most day-trippers will be traveling against the traffic. Public buses travel the Pali Hwy, but none stop at the Nuuanu Pali Lookout.

Past the 4-mile marker, look up and to the right to see two notches cut about 15ft deep into the crest of the *pali*. These notches are thought to have been dug as cannon emplacements by Kamehameha I.

The original route between Honolulu and windward Oahu was via an ancient footpath that wound its way perilously over these cliffs. In 1845, the path was widened into a horse trail and later into a cobblestone carriage road.

In 1898, the **Old Pali Hwy** (as it's now called) was built following the same route. It was abandoned in the 1950s after tunnels were blasted through the Koolau Range and the present multilane Pali Hwy opened.

You can still drive a loop of the Old Pali Hwy (called Nuuanu Pali Dr) and hike another mile of it from the Nuuanu Pali Lookout.

Queen Emma Summer Palace

This palace *(☎ 595-3167; 2913 Pali Hwy; adult/child $5/1; open 9am-4pm daily; closed holidays)* is a former residence of Queen Emma, the consort of Kamehameha IV.

Emma was three-quarters royal Hawaiian and a quarter English, a granddaughter of the captured British sailor John Young, who became a friend and adviser of Kamehameha I. The house is also known as Hanaiakamalama, the name of John Young's home in Kawaihae on the Big Island, where he served as governor.

After their deaths, the Youngs left the home to Queen Emma, who often slipped away from her formal downtown home to spend time at this cooler retreat. It's a bit like an old Southern plantation house, with a columned porch, high ceilings and louvered windows to catch the breeze.

The home was forgotten after Emma's death in 1885 and was scheduled to be razed in 1915, as the estate was being turned into a public park. The Daughters of Hawaii, a women's group whose members are descendants of early missionaries, rescued it and now run it as a museum.

The house's interior looks much as it did in Queen Emma's day – it's decorated with period furniture collected from five of Emma's homes. Items of particular note include a cathedral-shaped koa cabinet displaying a set of china from Queen Victoria; Emma's necklace of tiger claws, a gift from a maharaja of India; and feather cloaks and capes once worn by Hawaiian royalty.

Queen Emma Summer Palace is at the Pali Hwy's 2-mile marker. By bus, take No 4 Nuuanu Dowsett, which runs about every 15 minutes from Waikiki. Be sure to let the bus driver know in advance where you're going, so you don't miss the stop.

Nuuanu Pali Drive

For a scenic side trip through a shady green forest, turn off the Pali Hwy onto Nuuanu Pali Dr, half a mile past the Queen Emma Summer Palace. The 2-mile road runs parallel to the Pali Hwy and then comes back out to it before the Nuuanu Pali Lookout, so you don't miss anything by taking this side loop – in fact, quite the opposite.

The drive is through mature trees that form a canopy overhead, all draped with hanging vines and wound with philodendrons. The lush vegetation along Nuuanu Pali Dr includes banyan trees with hanging aerial roots, tropical almond trees, bamboo groves, impatiens, angel trumpets and golden cup – a tall climbing vine with large golden flowers.

Nuuanu Pali Lookout

Whatever you do, don't miss the Nuuanu Pali Lookout with its broad view of the windward coast from a height of 1200ft. From the lookout you can see Kaneohe straight ahead, Kailua to the right and

Mokolii Island and the coastal fishpond at Kualoa Park to the far left.

This is windward Oahu – and the winds that funnel through the *pali* are so strong that you can sometimes lean against them. It gets cool enough to appreciate having a jacket.

In 1795, Kamehameha I routed Oahu's warriors up the Nuuanu Trail during his invasion of the island. On these steep cliffs Oahu's warriors made their last stand. Hundreds were thrown to their death over the *pali* by Kamehameha's troops. A hundred years later, during the construction of the Old Pali Hwy, more than 500 skulls were found at the base of the cliffs.

The abandoned Old Pali Hwy winds down from the right of the lookout, ending abruptly at a barrier near the current highway about a mile away. Few people realize the road is here, let alone venture down it. It makes a nice walk and takes about 20 minutes one way. There are good views looking back up at the jagged Koolau Range and out across the valley.

As you get back on the highway, it's easy to miss the sign leading you out of the parking lot, and instinct could send you in the wrong direction. As you drive out of the parking lot, go to the left if you're heading toward Kailua, to the right if heading toward Honolulu.

Windward Coast

Windward Oahu, the island's eastern side, follows the Koolau Range along its entire length. The mountains looming inland are lovely, with scalloped folds and deep valleys. In places, they come so near to the shore that they almost seem to crowd the highway into the ocean.

The windward coast runs from Kahuku Point in the north to Makapuu Point in the south. (For the Waimanalo to Makapuu area, see the Southeast Oahu section.)

The two main towns are Kaneohe and Kailua, both bedroom communities for workers who commute to Honolulu, about 10 miles away.

North of Kaneohe, the windward coast is rural Hawaii, where many Hawaiians toil close to the earth, making a living with small papaya, banana and vegetable farms. The windward side of the island is generally wetter than other parts of the island, and the vegetation is lush and green.

Because the windward coast is exposed to the northeast trade winds, it's a popular area for anything that requires a sail – from windsurfing to yachting.

There are some attractive swimming beaches on the windward coast – notably Kailua, Kualoa and Malaekahana – although many other sections of the coast are too silted for swimming. Swimmers should keep an eye out for stinging Portuguese men-of-war that are sometimes washed in during storms.

Most of the offshore islets that you'll see along this coast have been set aside as bird sanctuaries. These tiny islands are vital habitat for ground-nesting seabirds, which have largely been driven off the populated islands by the introduction of mongooses, cats and other predators.

Two highways cut through the Koolau Range from central Honolulu to the windward coast. The Pali Hwy (Hwy 61) goes straight into Kailua center. The Likelike Hwy (Hwy 63) runs directly into Kaneohe, and, although it doesn't have the scenic stops the Pali Hwy has, it is in some ways more dramatic. Driving away from Kaneohe it feels as if you're heading straight into tall fairy-tale mountains – then you suddenly shoot through a tunnel and emerge on the Honolulu side, the drama gone.

If you're heading both to and from windward Oahu through the Koolau Range, take the Pali Hwy up from Honolulu and the Likelike Hwy back for the best of both. (See the Pali Hwy section for details on that drive.)

KAILUA

In ancient times Kailua (Two Seas) was a place of legends. It was home to a giant that turned into a mountain ridge, the island's first *menehunes* (legendary little people) and numerous Oahuan chiefs. Rich in stream-fed agricultural land, fertile fishing grounds and protected canoe landings, Kailua once served as a political and economic center for the region. The area supported at least three *heiau*s, one of which, Ulupo Heiau, you can still visit today.

Kailua is windward Oahu's largest town, with a population of 36,500. Although the inland section may appear to be little more

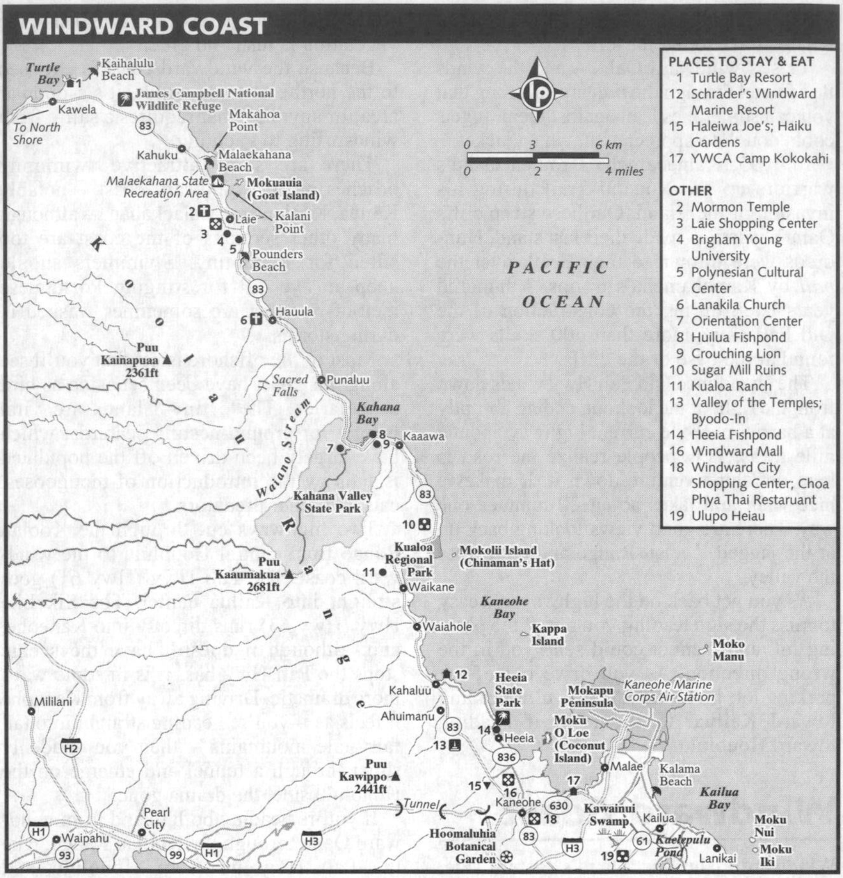

than an average suburban community, Kailua's shoreline is graced with miles and miles of lovely beach – a generous portion of which is public park, and the rest lined with oceanfront homes.

Kailua has long been known as a windsurfing mecca and today it draws increasing numbers of kayakers, too. Considering its size, the town has a fine variety of restaurants. It also has an agreeable mix of locals and visitors, making it a refreshing alternative to over-touristed Waikiki.

Information

Kailua has several banks, including a **Bank of Hawaii** *(☎ 266-4600; 636 Kailua Rd; open 8:30am-4pm Mon-Thur, 8:30am-6pm Fri)* on the town's main road.

The Kailua **post office** *(☎ 266-3996; 335 Hahani St; open 8am-4:30pm Mon-Fri, 8am-2pm Sat)* is in the town center.

Stir Crazy.com *(☎ 261-8804; 45 Hoolai St; open 7am-8pm Mon-Fri, 8am-6pm Sat)* has Internet access for $2.50 per 15 minutes.

Kailua Beach Park

Kailua Beach Park is a stunningly beautiful stretch of glistening white sand at the southeastern end of Kailua Bay. The beach is long and broad with lovely turquoise waters, and the park is popular for long walks, family outings and a full range of water activities.

Kailua Bay is the top **windsurfing** spot in Oahu. Onshore trade winds are predominant and windsurfers can sail at Kailua every month of the year. In different spots around the bay there are different water conditions, some good for jumps and wave surfing, others for flat-water sailing. Two windsurfing companies, **Naish Hawaii** (*☎ 262-6068, 800-767-6068; 155A Hamakua Dr, Kailua)* and **Kailua Sailboards & Kayaks** (*☎ 262-2555; 130 Kailua Rd)*, give lessons and rent boards at the beach park on Monday to Friday and on Saturday mornings.

Kailua Beach has a gently sloping sandy bottom with waters that are generally calm. Swimming is good year-round, but sun bathers should keep in mind that the breezes favored by windsurfers also give rise to blowing sand. The park has rest rooms, showers, lifeguards, a snack shop, a volleyball court and large grassy expanses shaded with ironwood trees.

Kaelepulu Canal divides the park into two sections, although a sandbar sometimes prevents the canal waters from emptying into the bay. Windsurfing activities are centered at the west side of the canal; there's a small boat ramp on the east side.

Kalama Beach, an unimproved beach just north of the park, has gentle waves good for novice bodysurfers. Surfers usually head for the northern end of Kailua Bay at **Kapoho Point** or further still to a break called **Zombies**.

The island offshore, **Popoia Island** (Flat Island), a bird sanctuary where landings are allowed, is a popular place for kayaking.

To get to Kailua Beach Park, take bus No 56 or 57 from Ala Moana Center and transfer to No 70 in Kailua. If you have your own transport, simply stay on Kailua Rd, which begins at the end of the Pali Hwy (Hwy 61) and continues as the main road through town, ending at the beach.

Ulupo Heiau

Ulupo Heiau is a sizable open-platform temple, made of stones piled 30ft high and 140ft long. Its construction is attributed to *menehunes*, the little people who legends say created much of Hawaii's stonework, finishing each project in one night. Fittingly, Ulupo means 'night inspiration.'

In front of the *heiau*, which is thought to have been a *luakini* type used for human sacrifices, is an artist's rendition of how the site probably looked in the 18th century, before Westerners arrived.

If you walk the path across the top of the *heiau*, you get a view of **Kawainui Swamp**, one of Hawaii's largest habitats for endangered waterbirds. Legends say the swamp's ancient fishpond had edible mud at the bottom and was home to a *mo'o*, or lizard spirit.

Ulupo Heiau is a mile south of Kailua Rd. Coming up the Pali Hwy from Honolulu, take Uluoa St, the first left after passing the Hwy 72 junction. Then turn right on Manu Aloha St and right again onto Manuoo St. The *heiau* is behind the YMCA.

Lanikai

If you follow the coastal road as it continues east of Kailua Beach Park, you'll shortly come to Lanikai, an exclusive residential neighborhood. It's fronted by Lanikai Beach, which is an attractive stretch of powdery white sand – at least what's left of it. Much of the sand has washed away as a result of the retaining walls built to protect the homes constructed right on the shore.

The sandy bottom slopes gently and the waters are calm, offering safe swimming conditions similar to those at Kailua. The twin **Mokulua Islands** sit directly offshore.

From Kailua Beach Park, the road turns into the one-way Aalapapa Dr, which comes back around as Mokulua Dr to make a 2½-mile loop. There are 11 narrow beach access walkways off Mokulua Dr. For the best stretches of beach, try the one opposite Kualima Dr or any of the next three.

Places to Stay

Kailua has no hotels, but there are many furnished beachfront cottages, studios and B&B-style rooms in private homes. While the majority are handled by reservation services, the following places can be booked directly with the owners.

Manu Mele Bed & Breakfast (*☎ 262-0016; ⓔ manumele@pixi.com; 153 Kailuana Place; rooms $70-80)* consists of two attractive rooms in the contemporary home of English-born host Carol Isaacs. The largest, the Hibiscus Room, has a king bed, and the smaller, but perfectly suitable, Pikake Room has a queen bed. Each has a private entrance, bathroom, refrigerator, microwave, coffeemaker, air-con, ceiling fan and cable TV. A basket of fruit and baked goods is provided the first morning. The minimum stay is two days. The house has a pool, and a short footpath leads to the beach. Smoking is not allowed in the units.

Paradise Palms Bed & Breakfast *(☎ 254-4234, fax 254-4971; e ppbb@pixi.com; 804 Mokapu Rd; rooms $70-75)* consists of two meticulous studios at the side of Marilyn and Jim Warman's home, at the northwest end of Kailua. The more expensive room has a king bed, the cheaper one a queen bed. Each has a private entrance, bathroom and a kitchenette with refrigerator, microwave and coffeemaker. The units also have cable TV, ceiling fans, air-con and phone. Fresh-baked bread, fruit and coffee are provided upon arrival. Smoking is not allowed. The minimum stay is three days. There's a grocery store and fast-food restaurants just across the street.

Sheffield House *(☎ 262-0721; e rachel@sheffieldhouse.com; 131 Kuulei Rd; rooms $75-95)*, a couple of minutes walk from Kailua Beach, consists of two cozy rental units in the home of Paul and Rachel Sheffield. There's a guest room with a wheelchair-accessible bathroom and a more expensive one-bedroom suite that has a queen bed and a separate sitting area with a queen futon. Each unit has a private entrance, bathroom, TV, microwave, toaster oven, coffeemaker, small refrigerator and ceiling fan. The Sheffields, who have three young children of their own, welcome kids. There's a three-day minimum stay; a basket of pastries, coffee and tea are provided on the first day.

Papaya Paradise Bed & Breakfast *(☎/fax 261-0316; e kailua@compuserve.com; 395 Auwinala Rd; singles & doubles $85, triples $100)* is a 15-minute walk from Kailua Beach. Bob and Jeanette Martz, retired from the army and home most of the time, rent two rooms adjacent to their home. One room has a queen bed and a trundle bed, the other two twin beds; each has a private entrance, bathroom, phone, air-con, ceiling fan and TV. Rates include a continental breakfast, and guests have access to a refrigerator, microwave and swimming pool. Boogie boards and snorkel gear can be borrowed for free. There's usually a three-day minimum stay.

Kailua Tradewinds *(☎ 262-1008; e kailua@compuserve.com; 391 Auwinala Rd; singles & doubles $80, triples $90)*, a vacation rental next door to Papaya Paradise, consists of two studio units at the home of Jona Williams, the Martz's daughter. Breakfast is not provided, but each unit has a refrigerator, microwave and coffeemaker as well as a private entrance, a king bed or two twin beds, TV and phone. One of the units also has a double futon. There's a swimming pool, and beach gear is available for guests to use. The minimum stay is three days.

Akamai Bed & Breakfast *(☎/fax 261-2227, 800-642-5366; e akamai@aloha.net; 172 Kuumele Place; rooms $85)* has two pleasant studio units in a private home about a 10-minute walk from Kailua Beach. Each is modern and comfortable with a refrigerator, microwave, coffeemaker, small bathroom, cable TV and private entrance. Both units have a king bed as well as a sofa bed. The rate includes a fruit basket and breakfast items. There's a laundry room ($1 per load) and a quiet courtyard with a pool. The minimum stay is three days. Smoking is limited to the outdoors.

Hawaii's Hidden Hideaway *(☎ 262-6560, fax 262-6561; e hhhideaway@yahoo.com; 1369 Mokolea Dr; studio/suite $95/135)* consists of three inviting units in an upscale neighborhood just a block from Lanikai Beach. Each has a private entrance, private bath, lanai and kitchenette. There are nice touches, like collections of Hawaiian books perfect for perusing in the evening and free beach gear for guests to borrow. The suite, which has a queen-size canopy bed and a Jacuzzi, would be a fun choice for honeymooners or anyone looking for a romantic getaway. All of the units come stocked with pastries, fruit and coffee. There's a three-day minimum stay. Smoking is not allowed.

Vacation Rentals The rental agents that follow are based in Kailua and they collectively book more than 50 properties.

Affordable Paradise Bed & Breakfast *(☎ 261-1693, fax 261-7315; w www.affordable-paradise.com; 332 Kuukama St, Kailua, HI 96734; rooms/cottages/condos from $45/60/80)* books accommodations in the Kailua area.

All Islands Bed & Breakfast *(☎ 263-2342, 800-542-0344, fax 263-0308; w www.hawaii.rr.com/allislands; 463 Iliwahi Loop, Kailua, HI 96734; rooms $65-75, studios $75-85, cottages $85-95)* also books Kailua-area accommodations.

Pat's Kailua Beach Properties *(☎ 261-1653; fax 261-0893; w www.10kvacationrentals.com/pats; 204 S Kalaheo Ave, Kailua, HI 96734; studios a day/month $70/1700, homes*

$500/12,000) handles a few dozen properties on or near the beach. These range from small studios that can sleep two people to large beachfront houses with five bedrooms that sleep a dozen people.

Places to Eat

Near the Beach *The* place to stop for coffee on the way to the beach is **Kalapawai Market** *(305 S Kalaheo Ave; open 6am-9pm daily)*. You have a choice of fresh brews, with a 12oz cup costing just $1. It also has take-out snacks including good bagels and great sandwiches, as well as a fine selection of wine and beer.

Kailua Beach Restaurant *(130 Kailua Rd; meals $5-7; open 7am-9pm daily)*, in the Kailua Beach Center, is a simple place with good food and cheap prices. Surfers start the morning here with the omelette breakfasts ($3.75), served with bacon and toast, until 10:30am. At other times of the day, the place serves up authentic Chinese food with lots of selections.

Island Snow *(130 Kailua Rd; open 10am-6pm daily)*, also in the Kailua Beach Center, is popular for its shave ice in tropical flavors, such as da-kine lemon and banzai banana.

Buzz's *(☎ 261-4661; 413 Kawailoa Rd; lunch $7-10, dinner $14-24; open 11am-2:30pm & 5pm-10pm daily)*, opposite Kailua Beach Park, has lunches of fresh fish sandwiches, burgers with fries, and Caesar or Thai chicken salads. However, Buzz's is most popular as an evening steak house, serving good, hearty cuts of beef; all dinners include a salad bar. Credit cards are not accepted.

Town Center All of the following eateries are in the town center, within a mile of each other.

Agnes Bake Shop *(46 Hoolai St; open 6am-6pm Tues-Sun)* is a great little bakery that makes whole-grain breads, inexpensive pastries and tempting Portuguese *malasadas*. The *malasadas*, which are served hot, take about 10 minutes to fry up and cost 60¢ each. The shop also sells coffee, tea and Portuguese bean soup, and has half a dozen café tables where you can sit and eat.

Cisco's Cantina *(131 Hekili St; dishes $10; open 11am-10pm Sun-Thur, 11am-11pm Fri & Sat)* is an unpretentious Mexican restaurant that serves generous portions at reasonable prices. In addition to combination plates, you can get a single taco ($6) or enchilada ($8), served with rice and beans.

Boston's North End Pizza *(☎ 263-7757; 29 Hoolai St; pizza $12-18; open 11am-8pm Mon-Fri, 11am-9pm Sat & Sun)* has excellent pizza. In addition to whole pizzas it sells huge slices, each equal to a quarter of a 19-inch pizza, for $3 to $4.75 depending on the toppings. The spinach and fresh garlic version is awesome.

Jaron's *(☎ 261-4600; 201 Hamakua Dr; lunch $7-12, dinner $10-20; open 11am-4pm Mon-Sat, 4pm-9pm Sun-Thur, 4pm-10pm Fri & Sat)* is a reliable favorite with jazzy decor and a varied menu. Lunch choices include a nice blackened *ahi* salad, and a variety of sandwiches served with soup. The dinner menu features pasta, fresh fish and steak dishes, with a green salad included in the price.

Assaggio *(☎ 261-2772; 354 Uluniu St; lunch $7-10, dinner $10-20; open 11:30am-2:30pm & 5pm-9:30pm Tue-Sat)* serves good, moderately priced Italian food in a somewhat upmarket setting. The menu is extensive, with more than 50 pasta, seafood and meat dishes, including the house special chicken Assaggio, a tasty dish brimming with garlic.

Champa Thai *(☎ 263-8281; 306 Kuulei Rd; dishes $7-10; open 11am-2pm Mon-Fri, 5pm-9pm daily)* has the best Thai food on the windward coast. The Penang curry, with coconut milk and shrimp, is a knockout, and it also makes good noodle dishes and Thai salads.

Lucy's Grill *(☎ 230-8188; 33 Aulike St; appetizers $7-12, mains $16-26; open 5pm-10pm Tue-Sat)* has an agreeable ocean theme with surfboards hanging from the walls and a menu featuring seafood. Specialties include fresh fish tacos with papaya salsa, oysters on the half shell and Sichuan-spiced prawns. There are a handful of creative chicken and beef dishes as well. Good food, fun place.

Down To Earth *(201 Hamakua Dr; open 8am-9pm daily)* is a large natural food store with almost everything you could imagine, from bulk granola and organic produce, to vitamins and herbal supplements. For a conventional supermarket, there's a **Safeway** *(200 Hamakua Dr; open 24hr)* nearby.

KANEOHE

Kaneohe is windward Oahu's second largest town, with some 35,000 residents. Kaneohe

Bay, which stretches from Mokapu Peninsula all the way to Kualoa Point, 7 miles north of Kaneohe, is the state's largest bay and reef-sheltered lagoon. Although inshore it's largely silted and not good for swimming, the near-constant trade winds that sweep across the bay are ideal for sailing.

Two highways run north to south through Kaneohe. Kamehameha Hwy (Hwy 836) is closer to the coast and goes by **Heeia State Park**. The Kahekili Hwy, which is more inland, intersects the Likelike Hwy and continues on north past the Byodo-In temple. The highways merge into a single route, Kamehameha Hwy (Hwy 83), a few miles north of Kaneohe.

Kaneohe Marine Corps Air Station occupies the whole of Mokapu Peninsula. The H3 Fwy terminates at its gate.

Hoomaluhia Botanical Garden

The county's youngest and largest botanical garden is Hoomaluhia *(☎ 233-7323; 45-680 Luluku Rd; admission free; open 9am-4pm daily)*, a 400-acre park in the uplands of Kaneohe. The park is planted with groups of trees and shrubs from tropical regions around the world.

It's a peaceful, lush green setting, with a stunning *pali* backdrop. Hoomaluhia is not a landscaped flower garden, but more of a natural preserve. A network of **trails** wind through the park and up to a 32-acre lake (no swimming allowed).

The **visitor center**, although small, has interesting displays on flora and fauna, Hawaiian ethnobotany and the history of the park, which was originally built by the US Army Corps of Engineers as flood protection for the valley below.

The park is at the end of Luluku Rd, which starts 2¼ miles down Kamehameha Hwy from the Pali Hwy. Bus Nos 55 and 56 stop at the Windward City Shopping Center, opposite the start of Luluku Rd. It's 1½ miles up Luluku Rd from the highway to the visitor center and another 1½ miles from the visitor center to the far end of the park – so if you use the bus, expect to do some walking.

Guided two-hour **nature hikes** are held at 10am on Saturday and 1pm on Sunday; you can sometimes join at the last minute, but it's best to call ahead to register.

Camping You're allowed to camp Thursday to Monday nights in Hoomaluhia Park. With a resident caretaker and gates that close at night to noncampers, the park is one of the safest places to camp on Oahu. Like other county camping grounds, there's no fee. You can get a permit in advance at any satellite city hall, or simply go to the park between 9am and 4pm daily to get a permit; if you decide to go straight to the park, call first to be sure space is available. For more information on obtaining camping permits, see Camping in the Accommodations section at the front of this chapter.

Valley of the Temples & Byodo-In

The Valley of the Temples *(☎ 239-8811; adult/child $2/1; open 8am-5pm daily)* is an interdenominational cemetery in a beautiful setting just off the Kahekili Hwy, 1½ miles north of Haiku Rd. For visitors the main attraction is Byodo-In, the 'Temple of Equality,' which is a replica of the 900-year-old temple of the same name in Uji, Japan. This one was dedicated in 1968 to commemorate the 100th anniversary of Japanese immigration to Hawaii.

Byodo-In sits against the Koolau Range. The rich red of the temple against the verdant fluted cliffs is strikingly picturesque, especially when mist settles in on the *pali*.

The temple is meant to symbolize the mythical phoenix. Inside the main hall is a 9ft-tall gold-lacquered Buddha sitting on a lotus. Wild peacocks roam the grounds and hang their tail feathers over the upper temple railings.

Fronting the temple is a carp pond with cruising bullfrogs and cooing doves. The 3-ton brass bell beside the pond is said to bring tranquility and good fortune to those who ring it.

It's all very Japanese, right down to the gift shop selling sake cups, daruma dolls and happy Buddhas. This scene is as close as you'll get to Japan without having to land at Narita.

On the way out, you might want to head up to the hilltop mausoleum with the cross on top for a panoramic view.

No buses go to Byodo-In, but bus No 55 can drop passengers off near the cemetery entrance on Kahekili Hwy. From there, it's two-thirds of a mile to the temple.

Heeia State Park

Heeia State Park is on Kealohi Point, just off Kamehameha Hwy. It has a good view of Heeia Fishpond on the right and Heeia-Kea Harbor on the left.

Before Western contact, stone-walled fishponds, in which fish were raised for royalty, were common along the coast of Oahu. The **Heeia Fishpond** is an impressive survivor that remains largely intact despite the invasive mangrove that grows along its walls and takes root between the rocks.

Coconut Island, just offshore to the southeast of the fishpond, was once a royal playground. It was named for the coconut trees planted there by Princess Bernice Pauahi Bishop. In the 1930s it was the estate of Christian Holmes, heir to the Fleischmann Yeast fortune, who dredged the island, doubling its size to 25 acres. During the war the estate served as an R&R facility. Airbrushed shots of Coconut Island were used in opening scenes for the *Gilligan's Island* TV series. Today the Hawaii Institute of Marine Biology of the University of Hawaii at Manoa occupies a niche on the island, while the rest is privately owned.

Fattening the Fish

The early Hawaiians had a well-developed aquaculture system that used numerous coastal fishponds.

There were essentially two kinds of fishponds. One type was inshore and totally closed off from the sea, although generally close enough to have brackish water. These inshore ponds would be stocked with fry and often had varying salinity levels which the Hawaiians took advantage of by cultivating different varieties of fish in different parts of the pond.

The other kind was a shoreline fishpond, created by building a long stone wall that paralleled the beach and curved back to shore at both ends. For these walled ponds the Hawaiians built *makaha*, or sluice gates, that allowed young fish to swim in but kept fattened fish from swimming back out. The fish in the pond could be easily netted at any time.

Amaama (mullet) and *awa* (milkfish) were the two varieties of fish most commonly raised in these fishponds. Most fishponds were strictly for the *alii* (chief), and commoners were not allowed to eat the fish raised in them.

Although they're no longer in use, the remains of many of those fishponds still dot the coasts of the Hawaiian Islands today.

Places to Stay

YWCA Camp Kokokahi *(☎ 247-2124, fax 247-2125; ⓔ kokokahi@gte.net; 45-035 Kaneohe Bay Dr; tent sites $8, single cabins $25, double cabins per person $16)* is a budget option 1½ miles northeast of Kaneohe center. Although the camp gives priority to groups, it also accepts individual travelers. Accommodations are simple – opt for a tiny cabin all to yourself, get a double cabin with two single beds, or pitch your own tent on the grounds. You can rent linen for $5 per stay if you don't have your own, and guests have access to kitchen, lounge and laundry facilities. Though the camp overlooks Kaneohe Bay, the water is too silted for swimming, but there's a heated pool on the grounds. Two things to keep in mind: the place sometimes fills up completely, so call ahead to make reservations before heading all the way out, and plan on checking in before the office closes at 5pm. Bus No 56 (1¼ hours from Ala Moana Center) stops out front.

Alii Bluffs Windward Bed & Breakfast *(☎ 235-1124, 800-235-1151; ⓔ donm@lava.net; 46-251 Ikiiki St; rooms $60-75)* has two bedrooms in a cozy home filled with Old World furnishings, oil paintings and collectibles. The Victorian Room has one double bed, while the cheaper Circus Room has two twin beds. Each room has a private bathroom. Host Don Munro and his partner De, a retired New York fashion designer, give guests the run of the house. Beach towels and coolers are provided; breakfast and afternoon tea are included in the rates. There's a small pool and a view of Kaneohe Bay.

Schrader's Windward Marine Resort *(☎ 239-5711, 800-735-5711, fax 239-6658; 47-039 Lihikai Dr; 1-bedroom/2-bedroom units from $100/160)* has 57 units in low-rise wooden buildings in a residential neighborhood. Despite the name, the ambience is more like a motel than a resort. So many of the guests are military families that Schrader's provides free transport to the Kaneohe Marine Corps Base. All units have refrigerators, microwaves, TVs, air-con and phones.

Places to Eat

If you're just looking for something quick and cheap, the city's two main shopping centers – the **Windward City Shopping Center** *(45-480 Kaneohe Bay Dr)* and the **Windward Mall** *(46-056 Kamehameha Hwy)* – have lots of inexpensive food options.

Chao Phya Thai Restaurant *(45-480 Kaneohe Bay Dr; dishes $6-9; open 11am-2pm Mon-Sat, 5pm-9pm daily)*, in the Windward City Shopping Center, is a family-run restaurant serving good Thai food, including green papaya salad, *phat thai* (stir-fried rice noodles) and curries. It doesn't serve liquor, but you can bring your own.

Zia's Caffe *(☎ 235-9427; 45-620 Kamehameha Hwy; dishes $7-12; open 11am-10pm Mon-Fri, 4pm-10pm Sat & Sun)*, on Kaneohe's main commercial strip, has good Italian fare at honest prices. There's something for everyone, including mussels marinara, vegetable lasagna, scampi and a delicious shrimp Caesar salad.

Haleiwa Joe's *(☎ 247-6671; 46-336 Haiku Rd; appetizers $6-10, mains $12-20; open 5:30pm-9:30pm Mon-Thur, 5:30pm-10:30pm Fri & Sat)*, at Haiku Gardens, has a romantic, open-air setting with a picturesque view of a lily pond tucked beneath the Koolau Range. The restaurant features excellent Pacific Rim fare, with the likes of *ahi* spring rolls, coconut shrimp tempura and chicken satay, as well as hearty steaks. The gardens are flood-lit at night. You can also drop by Haiku Gardens in the daytime just to stroll around its scenic pond, which takes about 15 minutes. To get there from Kamehameha Hwy, turn west on Haiku Rd just past Windward Mall; after crossing Kahekili Hwy, continue on Haiku Rd a quarter of a mile farther.

WAIAHOLE & WAIKANE

The area north of Kaneohe has a sleepy, local feel to it, with some lovely beaches, interesting hiking opportunities and fine scenery. The Kamehameha Hwy, really just a modest two-lane road, runs the length of the entire coast, doubling as Main St for each of the small towns along the way.

Waiahole and Waikane mark the beginning of rural Oahu. The area is home to family-run orchid nurseries and small coconut, banana, papaya and lemon farms.

Large tracts of Waikane Valley were taken over for military training and target practice during WWII, a use that continued until the 1960s. The government now claims the land has so much live ordnance that it can't be returned to the families it was leased from. This is a source of ongoing contention with local residents, who are upset that much of the inner valley remains off-limits.

KUALOA

Kualoa Regional Park

Kualoa Regional Park, a 153-acre county park on Kualoa Point, is bounded on its southwestern side by Molii Fishpond. From the road southwest of the park the fishpond is visible through the trees as a distinct green line in the bay.

Kualoa is a nice beach park in a scenic setting. The mountains looming precipitously across the road are, appropriately enough, called Pali-ku, meaning 'vertical cliff.' When the mist settles, it looks like a scene from a Chinese watercolor.

The main offshore island is **Mokolii**. In Hawaiian legend, Mokolii is said to be the tail of a nasty lizard or a dog – depending on who's telling the story – that was slain by a god and thrown into the ocean. Following the immigration of Chinese laborers to Hawaii, this conical-shaped island also came to be called Papale Pake, Hawaiian for 'Chinese hat.'

Apua Pond, a 3-acre brackish salt marsh on the point, is a nesting area for the endangered *aeo* (Hawaiian stilt). If you walk down the beach beyond the park, you'll see a bit of **Molii Fishpond**, but it's hard to get a good perspective on it from there. The rock walls are covered with mangrove, *milo* (a native shade tree) and pickleweed.

Sacred Ground

In ancient times, Kualoa was one of the most sacred places on Oahu. When a chief stood on the point, passing canoes lowered their sails in respect. The children of chiefs were brought here to be raised, and it may also have been a place of refuge where *kapu* (taboo) breakers and escaped warriors could seek reprieve from the law. Because of its rich significance to Hawaiians, Kualoa Regional Park is listed in the National Register of Historic Places.

The park is largely open lawn with a few palm trees shading a long, thin strip of beach with shallow waters and safe swimming. It has picnic tables, rest rooms, showers and a lifeguard. Camping is allowed from Friday to Tuesday night, with a permit from the county. For information on obtaining camping permits, see Camping in the Accommodations section near the beginning of this chapter.

Kualoa Ranch

The horses grazing on the green slopes across the road from Kualoa Regional Park belong to Kualoa Ranch (*☎ 237-8515*). Part of the scenic ranch property was used as a backdrop for the movies *Jurassic Park* and *Godzilla*. The ranch offers all sorts of activities, including horseback riding, target shooting and a 'movie set bus tour,' which is popular with Japanese tourists shuttled in from Waikiki.

Back in 1850, Kamehameha III leased about 625 acres of this land for $1300 to Dr Judd, a missionary doctor who became one of the king's advisers. Judd planted the land with sugarcane, built flumes to transport it and imported Chinese laborers to work the fields. His sugar mill trudged along for a few decades but went under just before the reciprocity agreement with the USA opened up mainland sugar markets.

You can still see the remains of the mill's stone stack and a bit of the crumbling walls half a mile north of the beach park, right alongside the road.

KAAAWA

In the Kaaawa area, the road hugs the coast and the *pali* moves right on in, with barely enough space to squeeze a few houses between the base of the cliffs and the road.

Swanzy Beach Park, a narrow neighborhood beach used mainly by fishers, is fronted by a shore wall.

Across the road from the park is a convenience store, a gas station and a postage-stamp-sized post office – pretty much the commercial center of town, such as it is.

Crouching Lion

The crouching lion is a rock formation at the back of the restaurant of the same name, which comes up just north of the 27-mile marker.

In Hawaiian legend, the rock is said to be a demigod from Tahiti who was cemented to the mountain during a jealous struggle between Pele, the volcano goddess, and her sister Hiiaka. When he tried to free himself by pulling into a crouching position, he was turned to stone.

To find him, stand at the **Crouching Lion Inn** sign with your back to the ocean and look straight up to the left of the coconut tree. The figure, which to some people resembles a lion, is on a cliff in the background.

The inn itself is the area's main sit-down restaurant with sandwiches, salads and a few hot plates for $8 to $10 at lunch. Dinners are about double that, although there's usually a cheaper early-bird special.

Continuing north, just past the inn on the right, you get a glimpse of **Huilua Fishpond** on the coast.

KAHANA VALLEY

In old Hawaii the islands were divided into *ahupuaa* – pie-shaped land divisions reaching from the mountains to the sea. They provided everything the Hawaiians needed for subsistence. Kahana Valley, 4 miles long and 2 miles wide, is the only publicly owned *ahupuaa* in Hawaii.

Kahana is a wet valley. Annual rainfall ranges from about 75 inches along the coast to 300 inches in the mountains. Before Westerners arrived, Kahana Valley was planted with wetland taro. Archaeologists have identified the overgrown remnants of more than 130 agricultural terraces and irrigation canals, as well as the remains of a *heiau*, fishing shrines and numerous house sites.

In the early 20th century, the area was planted with sugarcane, which was hauled north to the Kahuku Mill via a small railroad. During WWII, the upper part of Kahana Valley was taken over by the military and used for training soldiers in jungle warfare. In 1965 the state bought Kahana Valley from the Robinson family of Kauai (owners of the island of Niihau) in order to preserve it from development.

About 30 Hawaiian families live in the lower valley. The upper valley remains undeveloped and is mostly used by local hunters who come here on weekends to hunt feral pigs.

While many of Kahana's archaeological sites are deep in the valley and inaccessible, the park's most impressive site, **Huilua**

Fishpond on Kahana Bay, is visible from the main road and can be visited simply by going down to the beach.

Kahana Valley State Park

The entrance to Kahana Valley State Park is a mile north of the Crouching Lion Inn.

When the state purchased Kahana, it also acquired tenants, many of whom had lived in the valley for a long time. Rather than evict a struggling rural population, the state created a plan allowing the 140 residents to stay on the land. The concept is to eventually incorporate the families into a 'living park,' with the residents acting as interpretive guides. The development of the park is a slow process, but after a couple of decades of careful planning and negotiating, the 'living park' concept is inching forward. You'll now find a simple orientation center near the park entrance and tours are being provided to school children and local organizations.

Although there are no tours for individual travelers, you can walk through the valley on your own. The **orientation center** *(☎ 237-7766; open 7:30am-4pm Mon-Fri)* provides a map and has the latest information on trail conditions. Keep in mind that the trails can be slippery when wet, and this is the wettest side of Oahu.

The most accessible of the park trails is the 1¼-mile **Kapaeleele Koa and Keaniani Lookout Trail**, which begins at the orientation center. It goes along the old railroad route, passes a fishing shrine called Kapaeleele Koa and leads to Keaniani Kilo, a lookout that was used in ancient times for spotting schools of fish in the bay. The trail then goes down to the bay and follows the highway back to the park entrance.

If you want to get into the rain forest, there's the **Nakoa Trail**, which makes a 2½-mile loop through tropical vegetation. This trail makes a couple of stream crossings and passes a swimming hole en route. However, the start of the Nakoa Trail is 1¼ miles inland from the orientation center on a rough dirt road, so the total walking distance equals 5 miles.

The park also encompasses **Kahana Bay** with its tree-lined beach and fishpond. The bay is set deep and narrow, and the protected beach provides safe swimming, with a gently sloping sandy bottom.

There are 10 beachside **camp sites** but they're primarily used by island families, so there may be some turf issues for tourists. Camping is allowed with a permit from the state. For more information on obtaining permits, see Camping in the Accommodations section near the beginning of this chapter.

PUNALUU

Punaluu is a scattered little seaside community that doesn't draw much attention from tourists. Nonetheless, it has a couple of low-key places to stay and a decent beach.

At Punaluu Beach Park, there's a long, narrow beach offering fairly good swimming, with an offshore reef that protects the shallow inshore waters in all but stormy weather. Be cautious near the mouth of the Waiono Stream and in the channel leading out from it, as currents are strong when the stream is flowing quickly or when the surf is high.

Places to Stay & Eat

Pat's at Punaluu *(☎ 293-2624; 53-567 Kamehameha Hwy)* is a 136-unit condominium. It's largely residential, older and a bit neglected, but on the plus side, it's on the water with the rooms facing the ocean. There's no front desk, instead rentals are handled by realtors, some of whom post their listings on the condo bulletin board. **Paul Comeau Condo Rentals** *(☎ 467-6215, fax 293-0618; PO Box 589, Kaaawa, HI 96730; studios $80, 1-bedroom/3-bedroom units $100/180)* handles several units at Pat's at Punaluu; all have a three-day minimum.

Punaluu Guesthouse *(☎ 946-0591; 53-504 Kamehameha Hwy; rates per person $22)*, a home in the center of Punaluu, belongs to the owners of Hostelling International Honolulu. Because there are only two rooms and it's a cozy situation, the hostel prescreens potential guests – so if you want to stay at Punaluu Guesthouse, you need to go to the Honolulu hostel first to meet with the staff there and get a referral. There's a shared bath and guests have access to a kitchen.

Ahi's *(☎ 293-5650; 53-146 Kamehameha Hwy; meals $8-15; open 11am-9pm Mon-Sat)*, a third of a mile north of the 25-mile marker, is Punaluu's only restaurant. The specialty is fresh shrimp in a variety of preparations, including shrimp scampi and shrimp tempura.

HAUULA

Hauula is a small, coastal town set against a scenic backdrop of hills and majestic Norfolk pines. There are some good hiking trails in the forest reserve above town.

The main landmark in town is the stone ruins of **Lanakila Church** (c. 1853), which sit perched on a hill opposite Hauula Beach, next to the newer Hauula Congregational Church.

The beach fronting the town is not particularly appealing for swimming, but it occasionally gets waves big enough for local kids to ride. The beach is actually a county park that allows camping, although it's mostly local families that camp there. For information on obtaining camping permits, see Camping in the Accommodations section earlier in this chapter.

Trails

The Division of Forestry & Wildlife maintains two trails in the forest reserve above Hauula. Both trails share the same access point and head into beautiful hills in the lower Koolau Range.

The **Hauula Loop Trail** is a scenic 2½-mile hike that makes a couple of gulch crossings and climbs along a ridge with broad views of the forested interior, the ocean and the town of Hauula. This trail, which forks off to the right shortly after you enter the forest reserve, passes native vegetation such as ohia trees as well as thickly planted groves of shaggy ironwood trees and towering Norfork pines. The hike takes about two hours.

The **Maakua Ridge Trail**, which begins on the left about half a mile after entering the forest reserve, makes a 2½-mile loop that climbs in and out of a couple of gullies and follows the narrow Maakua Ridge. Much of the trail is open and dry, but there are sections that close in, including some thickets of acacia trees that create tunnel effects. There are ridgetop views of the coast and Hauula along the way. The hike takes about 2½ hours.

The signposted trailhead to both hikes is at a bend in Hauula Homestead Rd, about a quarter of a mile up from Kamehameha Hwy. Hauula Homestead Rd is right in town, at the north end of Hauula Beach Park.

Backcountry camping is permitted along the Maakua Ridge Trail. Call the **Division of Forestry & Wildlife** *(☎ 587-0166)* for information, trail maps and the required camping permits.

LAIE

Laie is thought to have been the site of an ancient *puuhonua* – a place where *kapu* breakers and fallen warriors could seek refuge. Today, Laie is the center of the Mormon community in Hawaii.

The first Mormon missionaries to Hawaii arrived in 1850. After an attempt to establish a Hawaiian 'City of Joseph' on the island of Lanai failed amidst a land scandal, the Mormons moved to Laie. In 1865 they purchased 6000 acres of land in the area and slowly expanded their influence.

In 1919 the Mormons constructed a **temple**, a smaller version of the one in Salt Lake City, at the foot of the Koolau Range. This stately temple, at the end of a wide promenade, appears like nothing else on the windward coast. Although there's a visitor center where enthusiastic guides will tell you about Mormonism, tourists are not allowed to enter the temple itself.

Nearby is the Hawaii branch of **Brigham Young University**, with scholarship programmes bringing in students from islands throughout the Pacific.

Information

The **Laie Shopping Center** *(55-510 Kamehameha Hwy)*, about half a mile north of the Polynesian Cultural Center, has a **Bank of Hawaii** *(☎ 293-9238; open 8:30am-4pm Mon-Thur, 8:30am-6pm Fri)* as well as a **post office** *(☎ 293-0337; open 9am-3:30pm Mon-Fri, 9:30am-11:30am Sat)*. The center also has a coin laundry, the **Laie Washerette** *(☎ 293-2821; 55-510 Kamehameha Hwy; open 6am-8pm Mon-Sat)*.

Polynesian Cultural Center

The Polynesian Cultural Center *(PCC; ☎ 293-3333; adult/child 5-11 $35/20; open 12:30pm-9pm Mon-Sat)* is a nonprofit organization belonging to the Mormon Church. The center covers 42 acres and draws about 900,000 tourists a year, more than any other attraction on Oahu, with the exception of the USS *Arizona* Memorial.

The park has seven theme villages representing Samoa, New Zealand, Fiji, Tahiti, Tonga, the Marquesas and Hawaii. The 'villages' contain authentic-looking huts and ceremonial houses, many elaborately built with twisted sennit ropes and hand-carved posts. The huts hold weavings, tapa cloth, feather work and other handicrafts. People of Polynesian descent dressed in native garb demonstrate poi pounding, coconut frond weaving, dances, games and the like.

There's also a replica of an old mission house and a missionary chapel representative of those found throughout Polynesia in the mid-19th century.

Many of the people working here are Pacific Island students from the nearby Brigham Young University, who pay their college expenses with jobs at PCC. The interpreters are amiable and you could easily spend a few hours wandering around chatting or trying to become familiar with a craft or two.

The admission price also includes boat rides along the winding waterway through the park; the Pageant of the Long Canoes, a sort of trumped-up floating talent show at 2:30pm; 45-minute van tours of the Mormon temple grounds and BYU campus; movies at the center's IMAX theater; and the evening Polynesian song and dance show. The Polynesian show, which runs from 7:30pm to 9pm, can be fun – partly authentic, partly Hollywood-style and much like an enthusiastic college production, with elaborate sets and costumes.

There's also a buffet package of $49 for adults and $32 for children that adds on a buffet dinner to all the previously mentioned activities.

Although PCC has many interesting features, it's also very touristy and hard to recommend at the steep admission price.

Beaches

The 1½ miles of beach fronting the town of Laie between Malaekahana State Recreation Area and Laie Point are used by surfers, bodysurfers and windsurfers.

Pounders, half a mile south of the main entrance to PCC, is an excellent bodysurfing beach, but the shorebreak, as the name of the beach implies, can be brutal. There's a strong winter current. The area around the old landing is usually the calmest. Summer swimming is generally good and the beach is sandy.

From **Laie Point** there's a good view of the mountains to the south and of tiny offshore islands. The island to the left with the hole in it is Kukuihoolua, otherwise known as Puka Rock. To get to Laie Point, head seaward on Anemoku St, opposite the Laie Shopping Center, then turn right on Naupaka St and go straight to the end.

Places to Stay & Eat

Laie Inn *(☎ 293-9282, 800-526-4562, fax 293-8115; ⓔ laieinn@hawaii.rr.com; 55-109 Laniloa St; rooms $89)*, right outside the Polynesian Cultural Center, is a two-story motel with 49 rooms surrounding a courtyard swimming pool. Although not special, it's comfortable enough, and each room has a lanai, cable TV, air-con and mini-refrigerator. Rates include a continental breakfast.

Laie Chop Suey *(55-510 Kamehameha Hwy; dishes $5-7; open 10am-8:45pm Mon-Sat)*, in the Laie Shopping Center, is a local-style eatery with standard Chinese fare.

The Laie Shopping Center also has a grocery store and a couple of fast-food chain eateries selling the usual burgers, sandwiches and pizzas.

MALAEKAHANA STATE RECREATION AREA

Malaekahana Beach is a beautiful strand that stretches between Makahoa Point to the north and Kalanai Point to the south. The long, narrow, sandy beach is backed by ironwoods. Swimming is generally good year-round, although there are occasionally strong currents in winter. This popular family beach is also good for many other water activities, including bodysurfing, board surfing and windsurfing. Kalanai Point, the main section of the state park, is less than a mile north of Laie and has picnic tables, barbecue grills, camping, rest rooms and showers.

Mokuauia (Goat Island), a state bird sanctuary just offshore, has a nice sandy cove with good swimming and snorkeling. It's possible to wade over to the island – best when the tide is low and the water's calm, but be sure to ask the lifeguard about water conditions and the advisability of crossing. Be careful of the shallow coral and sea urchins.

You can also snorkel across to Goat Island and off its beaches. Beware of a rip current that's sometimes present off the windward end of the island, where the water is deeper.

Camping

Malaekahana has the best camping grounds at this end of the windward coast. You can pitch a tent in the park's main Kalanai Point section if you have a state park permit; for information on obtaining a permit, see Camping in the Accommodations section earlier in this chapter.

You can also rent a rustic cabin or camp without needing a permit in the Makahoa Point section of the park, which has a separate entrance off Kamehameha Hwy, three-quarters of a mile north of the main park entrance. **Friends of Malaekahana** *(☎ 293-1736; tent sites per person $5, 4-person cabins Mon-Thur/Fri-Sun $55/66, 8-person cabins $66/80)*, a local nonprofit group dedicated to cultural preservation, maintains this end of the park. It's a relatively secure place to stay, with gates locked to vehicles between 7pm and 7am.

KAHUKU

Kahuku is a former sugar town with little wooden cane houses lining the road. The mill in the center of town belonged to the Kahuku Plantation, which produced sugar from 1890 until it closed in 1971. The operation was a relatively small concern, unable to keep up with the increasingly mechanized competition of Hawaii's bigger mills. When the mill shut down, Kahuku's economy skidded into a slump that still lingers today.

A fledgling shopping center now occupies Kahuku's old sugar mill, with small shops ringing the old machinery. The mill's enormous gears, flywheels and pipes have been painted in bright colors to help visitors visualize how a sugar mill works. The steam systems are painted red, the cane-juice systems are light green, hydraulic systems are dark blue and so forth. It looks like something out of *Modern Times* – you can almost imagine Charlie Chaplin caught up in the giant gears.

The center has not been wildly successful, but there's a local plate-lunch eatery, food mart, gas station, post office, bank and a few other shops.

Beaches

The shallow **Kuilima Cove**, also known as Bay View Beach, is fronted by the Turtle Bay Resort, the only hotel in Kahuku. This pleasant white-sand beach, protected by a reef, is one of the area's best swimming spots. It also has a few coral patches that are good for snorkeling. While it's mostly used by resort guests, the cove is open to all.

You can park at one of the free spaces for beachgoers, on the right just before the hotel's guard booth, and walk 10 minutes to the beach.

Kaihalulu Beach is a beautiful, curved, white-sand beach backed by ironwoods. Although a shoreline lava shelf and rocky bottom make the beach poor for swimming, it's good for beachcombing – you can walk east about a mile to Kahuku Point. Local fishers cast throw nets from the shore and pole fish from the point. The dirt road just inland of the beach is also used as a horse trail.

To get to the beach, turn into the Turtle Bay Resort and just before the guard booth turn right into an unmarked parking lot, where there are free spaces for beachgoers. It's a five-minute walk out to the beach; just walk east on the footpath that begins at the field adjacent to the parking lot. There are no facilities.

James Campbell National Wildlife Refuge

This wildlife refuge is a rare freshwater wetlands that provides habitat for Hawaii's four endangered waterbirds – the Hawaiian coot, the Hawaiian stilt, the Hawaiian duck and the Hawaiian gallinule.

During stilt nesting season, normally mid-February to July, the refuge is off-limits to all visitors. The rest of the year, it can be visited only through guided tours, which are provided by refuge staff 4pm to 5:30pm Thursday and 3:30pm to 5pm Saturday. Tours are free, but reservations are required and can be made by calling ☎ 637-6330.

The refuge, which is signposted, is about a mile southeast of the Turtle Bay Resort.

Places to Stay

Turtle Bay Condos *(☎ 293-2800, fax 293-2169; ⓔ trtlbayest@aol.com; PO Box 248, Kahuku, HI 96731; studio $95, with loft $105, 1-bedroom/2-bedroom apartments $115/160)* handles units at Kuilima Estates, a modern condominium complex on the grounds fronting the Turtle Bay Resort. Each unit has a complete kitchen, washer/dryer, TV, phone and lanai. Weekly rates are six times the daily rate; monthly rates are 2½ times the weekly rate. In addition, there's a $50 to $75 cleaning fee for all rentals. The complex has two tennis courts and five pools.

Turtle Bay Resort *(☎ 293-8811, 800-203-3650, fax 293-9147; ⓔ res@turtlebayresort.com; 57-091 Kamehameha Hwy; rooms $139-295)*, perched on Kuilima Point between Turtle Bay and Kuilima Cove, is the only resort hotel on the windward and north shores. Each of the 485 rooms have an ocean view as well as all the expected 1st-class amenities. Turtle Bay is a self-contained resort with a couple of restaurants, two golf courses, two swimming pools, horse stables and 10 tennis courts.

Places to Eat

Giovanni's Shrimp *(open 10:30am-6:30pm daily)*, a truck that parks along the highway just south of the Kahuku Sugar Mill, is the place to go if you like shrimp. Popular with both locals and weekend sightseers from Honolulu, Giovanni's offers a choice of tasty shrimp scampi, lemon-butter grilled shrimp or hot and spicy shrimp. A plate with half a pound of jumbo shrimp and two scoops of rice costs $11. There's a covered picnic area where you can sit and eat.

Turtle Bay Resort has a couple of restaurants offering all-you-can-eat meals and boasting fine ocean views. The lobby-side **Bayview Lounge** *(☎ 293-8811 ext ☎ 6512)* serves a simple evening buffet; some nights it's a pizza and pasta spread, while other nights it's a taco bar or barbecue. The buffet is offered 5:30pm to 8:30pm every night and costs $12 for adults, $8 for children. The hotel's **Sea Tide Room** *(☎ 293-8811 ext 6504)* has an extensive brunch buffet from 10am to 2pm Sunday, which includes fresh shrimps, sushi, meat dishes, omelettes, salads and desserts, all for $22/12.50 an adult/child.

Central Oahu

Central Oahu forms a saddle between the Waianae Mountains on the west and the Koolau Range on the east.

Three routes lead north from Honolulu to Wahiawa, the town smack in the middle of Oahu. The freeway, H2, is the fastest route, whereas Hwy 750, the farthest west, is the most scenic. The least interesting of the options, Hwy 99, catches local traffic as it runs through Mililani, a modern, nondescript residential community.

Most people just zoom up through central Oahu on their way to the North Shore. If your time is limited this isn't a bad idea. There are a few sights along the way, but Wahiawa, the region's commercial center, doesn't really warrant much more than a quick visit anyway.

From Wahiawa two routes, Hwy 803 (Kaukonahua Rd) and Hwy 99 (Kamehameha Hwy), lead down through pineapple country to the North Shore. Hwy 803 is a slightly shorter way to reach Mokuleia than Hwy 99 and about the same distance to Haleiwa. Both are fine scenic roads, and if you're not circling the island, you might as well go up one and down the other.

HIGHWAY 750

Hwy 750 (Kunia Rd) adds a few miles to the drive through central Oahu, but if you have the time it's worth it. Follow H1 to the Kunia/Hwy 750 exit, 3 miles west of where H1 and H2 divide.

After you turn up Hwy 750 the first mile is through creeping suburbia, but then you enter plantation lands. The route runs along the foothills of the Waianae Range and the countryside remains solidly agricultural all the way to Schofield Barracks Military Reservation.

Up the road 2 miles you'll come to a strip of corn fields planted by the Garst Seed Company. Three generations of corn are grown here each year, which makes it possible to develop hybrids of corn seed at triple the rate it would take on the mainland. The little bags placed over each ear of corn prevent them from being cross-pollinated.

A bit further north begins one of the most scenic pineapple fields in Hawaii. There are no buildings and no development – just red earth carpeted with long green strips of pineapples stretching to the edge of the mountains.

From the Hawaii Country Club, just up the road on the right, there's a distant view of Honolulu all the way to Diamond Head.

Kunia

Kunia, a little town in the midst of the pineapple fields, is home to the field workers employed by Del Monte. If you want to see what a current-day plantation village looks like, turn west off Hwy 750 onto

Kunia Dr, which makes a 1¼-mile loop through the town.

Rows of grey-green wooden houses with corrugated tin roofs stand on low stilts. Residents take pride in their little yards, with bougainvillea and other colorful flowers adding a splash of brightness despite the wash of red dust that blows in from the surrounding pineapple fields.

Kunia Dr intersects the highway at about 5½ miles north of the intersection of Hwy 750 and H1 (there's a store and post office near the turnoff) and again at the 6-mile marker.

Kolekole Pass

Kolekole is the gap in the Waianae Mountains that Japanese fighter planes once flew through on their way to bomb Pearl Harbor. The landscape may look familiar, as the flight scene was recreated here 30 years later for the shooting of the popular war film *Tora! Tora! Tora!*

Kolekole Pass, at an elevation of 1724ft, sits above Schofield Barracks Military Reservation. It can be visited as long as the base isn't on some sort of military alert.

Access the pass through Foote Gate, on Hwy 750, a third of a mile south of its intersection with Hwy 99. After passing through the gate, take the first left onto Road A, then the first right onto Lyman Rd. The drive is 5¼ miles up past the barracks, golf course and bayonet assault course. The parking lot is opposite the hilltop with the big white cross that's visible from miles away.

The five-minute walk to the top of the pass ends at a clearing with a view straight down to the Waianae Coast. In Hawaiian mythology, the large, ribbed stone that sits atop the ridge here is said to be the embodiment of a woman named Kolekole who took the form of this stone in order to become the perpetual guardian of the pass. Along the side of the stone are a series of ridges, one of them draining down from a bowl-like depression on the top. Shaped perfectly for a guillotine, the depression has given rise to a more recent 'legend' that Kolekole served as a sacrificial stone for the beheadings of defeated chiefs and warriors. The fact that military bases flank both sides of the pass has no doubt had a little influence on forming this tale.

Just west of the pass the road continues through the Lualualei Naval Reservation down to the Waianae Coast, but you can't take it. The Navy base is a stockyard for nuclear weapons, and there's no public access through that side.

WAHIAWA

Wahiawa, whose name means 'place of noise' in Hawaiian, is a GI town, sitting on the edge of Schofield Barracks Military Reservation, Hawaii's largest army base. Just about every fast-food chain you can think of is found in Wahaiwa's center. Tattoo parlors and pawn shops are the town's main refinements, and if you're looking for a little excitement, there are some rough-and-tumble bars.

To go through town and visit the botanical garden, healing stones and royal birthstones, take Kamehameha Hwy (which is Hwy 80 as it goes through town, although it's Hwy 99 before and after Wahiawa). To make the bypass around Wahiawa, stick with Hwy 99.

Wahiawa Botanical Garden

This botanical garden (☎ *621-7321; 1396 California Ave; admission free; open 9am-4pm daily*) is a mile east of the Kamehameha Hwy.

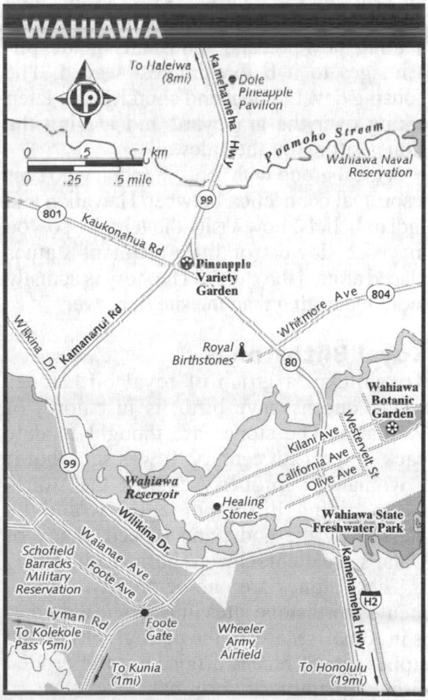

What started out in the 1920s as a site for forestry experiments by the Hawaii Sugar Planters' Association is now a 27-acre county park with shady paths, grand old trees and a wooded ravine.

If you're venturing out of the concrete of Waikiki for the first time, this is a nice place to stop and immerse yourself in a tropical forest. Interesting 70-year-old exotics such as cinnamon, chicle and allspice are grouped in one area. Tree ferns, loulu palms and other Hawaiian natives are in another.

For a description of other plants found here, pick up the free garden brochure at the visitor center.

Healing Stones

Among the odder sights to be labeled with a visitors bureau marker are the 'Healing Stones' that are caged inside a small marble 'temple' next to the Methodist church on California Ave, half a mile west of its intersection with Kamehameha Hwy.

The main stone is thought to have been the gravestone of a powerful Hawaiian chief. Although the chief's original burial place is in a field a mile away, the stone was moved long ago to a graveyard at this site. In the 1920s people thought the stone had healing powers, and thousands made pilgrimages to it before interest waned. The housing development and church came later, taking over the graveyard and leaving the stones sitting on the sidewalk.

A local group with roots in India, who sees a spiritual connection between Hawaiian and Indian beliefs, now visits the temple, so you may see flowers or little elephant statues placed around the stones. The story is actually more interesting than the site, however.

Royal Birthstones

Kukaniloko, a group of royal birthstones where queens gave birth, is just north of Wahiawa. The stones are thought to date back to the 12th century. It was said that if a woman lay properly against the stones while giving birth, her child would be blessed by the gods, and indeed, many of Oahu's great chiefs were born at this site.

These stones are one of only two documented birthstone sites in Hawaii (the other is in Kauai). Many of the petroglyphs on the stones are of recent origin, but the eroded circular patterns are original.

To get to the site from town, go three-quarters of a mile north on Kamehameha Hwy from its intersection with California Ave. Turn left onto the red dirt road directly opposite Whitmore Ave. The stones, marked with a state monument sign, are a quarter of a mile down the road, through a pineapple field, among a stand of eucalyptus and coconut trees. If it's been raining, be aware that the red clay can cake onto car tires, and once back on the paved road, the car may slide as if you're driving on ice.

Pineapple Variety Garden

Del Monte maintains a pineapple demonstration garden in a triangle at the intersection of Hwys 99 and 80.

Smooth cayenne, the commercial variety of pineapple grown in Hawaii, is shown in various growth stages. Each plant produces just two pineapples, with the first one taking nearly two years to reach maturity.

Other commercial varieties of pineapple grown in Australia, the Philippines and Brazil are also on display, as are some varieties of purely decorative bromeliads.

You can pull off to the side of the road and walk through the garden on your own at any time.

Dole Pineapple Pavilion

The Dole Pineapple Pavilion *(☎ 621-8408; 64-1550 Kamehameha Hwy; open 9am-5:30pm daily)* is on Hwy 99, less than a mile north of its intersection with Hwy 80. This touristy complex in the heart of Oahu's pineapple country consists of a bustling gift shop, some simple bromeliad gardens and an expansive hibiscus hedge maze. Dole's processing plant sits across the street, and miles of pineapple fields surround the area.

The gift shop sells pineapple juice, pineapple freezes, pineapple pastries and pineapples boxed to take home. Expect things to be a bit pricey, but the bromeliad gardens are free and it makes a nice opportunity to get out and stretch.

If you feel like getting lost, you can wander through the 'world's largest maze' (adult/child $5/3), which covers nearly 2 acres and contains 1.7 miles of pathways, but truth be told, there's a certain monotony to it. Most people take 15 to 30 minutes to get through.

North Shore

Oahu's North Shore is synonymous with surfing and awesome winter waves. Sunset Beach, the Banzai Pipeline and Waimea Bay are among the world's most famous surf spots and attract top surfers from around the globe.

Other North Shore surf breaks may be less well known, but with names like Himalayas and Avalanche, they're obviously not for neophytes.

It's believed that the earliest Polynesians to arrive on Oahu were drawn to the North Shore by the region's rich fishing grounds, cooling trade winds and moderate rain. The areas that are around Mokuleia, Haleiwa and Waimea all once had sizable Hawaiian settlements and abandoned taro patches still remain in their upland valleys.

By the early 1900s, the Oahu Railroad & Land Company had extended the railroad around Kaena Point and along the entire North Shore, linking the area with Honolulu and bringing in the first beachgoers from the city. Hotels and private beach houses sprang up, but when the railroad stopped running in the 1940s the hotels shut down for good. Sections of abandoned track are still found along many of the beaches.

Waikiki surfers started taking on North Shore waves in the late 1950s and big-time surf competitions followed a few years later. Today, the grandest surfing event of them all is the Triple Crown, consisting of three major surf competitions that take place in early winter, with prize purses reaching six figures.

Before Jumping In...

With the exception of Haleiwa Beach Park, North Shore beaches are notorious for treacherous winter swimming conditions. There are powerful currents along the entire shore. If it doesn't look as calm as a lake, it's probably not safe for swimming or snorkeling.

During the summer, surf conditions along the whole North Shore can mellow right out. Pupukea Beach Park then becomes a prime snorkeling and diving spot, and Waimea Bay, internationally famous for its winter surf, turns into a popular swimming and snorkeling beach.

Surf mania prevails even in the restaurants, which serve up omelettes with names like 'Pumping Surf' and 'Wipe Out.' When the surf's up, half the North Shore population can be found on the beach. On winter weekends, convoys of cars make the trip up from Honolulu to watch surfers ride the waves. If you want to avoid the traffic, simply head up to the North Shore on a weekday.

WAIALUA

Waialua, a former plantation town about a mile west of Haleiwa, is centered around the dusty Waialua Sugar Mill, which closed down in 1996, bringing an end to the last commercial sugar operation on Oahu.

Although the Waialua area remains economically depressed, with many of the surrounding fields overgrown with feral sugarcane, other sections are newly planted with coffee trees – a labor-intensive crop that holds out promise for new jobs. You can see the coffee trees, planted in neat rows, as you come down the slopes into Waialua.

The old sugar mill, which now serves as the coffee operation's headquarters, is chock full of racks where the coffee beans are sorted and dried. You can poke around the place a bit, but there's not much to see, as the visitors center has closed.

As for other sights, this sleepy town has a couple of period buildings, the most interesting being the local watering hole, the Sugar Bar, which occupies the old Bank of Hawaii building down by the mill.

MOKULEIA

The Farrington Highway (Hwy 930) runs west from Thompson Corner to Dillingham Airfield and Mokuleia Beach. (Both this road and the road along the Waianae Coast are called Farrington Hwy, but they don't connect, as each side reaches a dead end about 2½ miles short of Kaena Point.)

Mokuleia Beach is a 6-mile stretch of white sand running from Kaiaka Bay toward Kaena Point. Although some GIs and locals come this way, the beaches don't draw too much of a crowd and the area has sort of a 'boonies' feel to it. The only beach facilities are at Mokuleia Beach Park, and the nearest store is back in Waialua.

Dillingham Airfield is the take-off site for glider rides and skydiving. For details, see Activities earlier in this chapter.

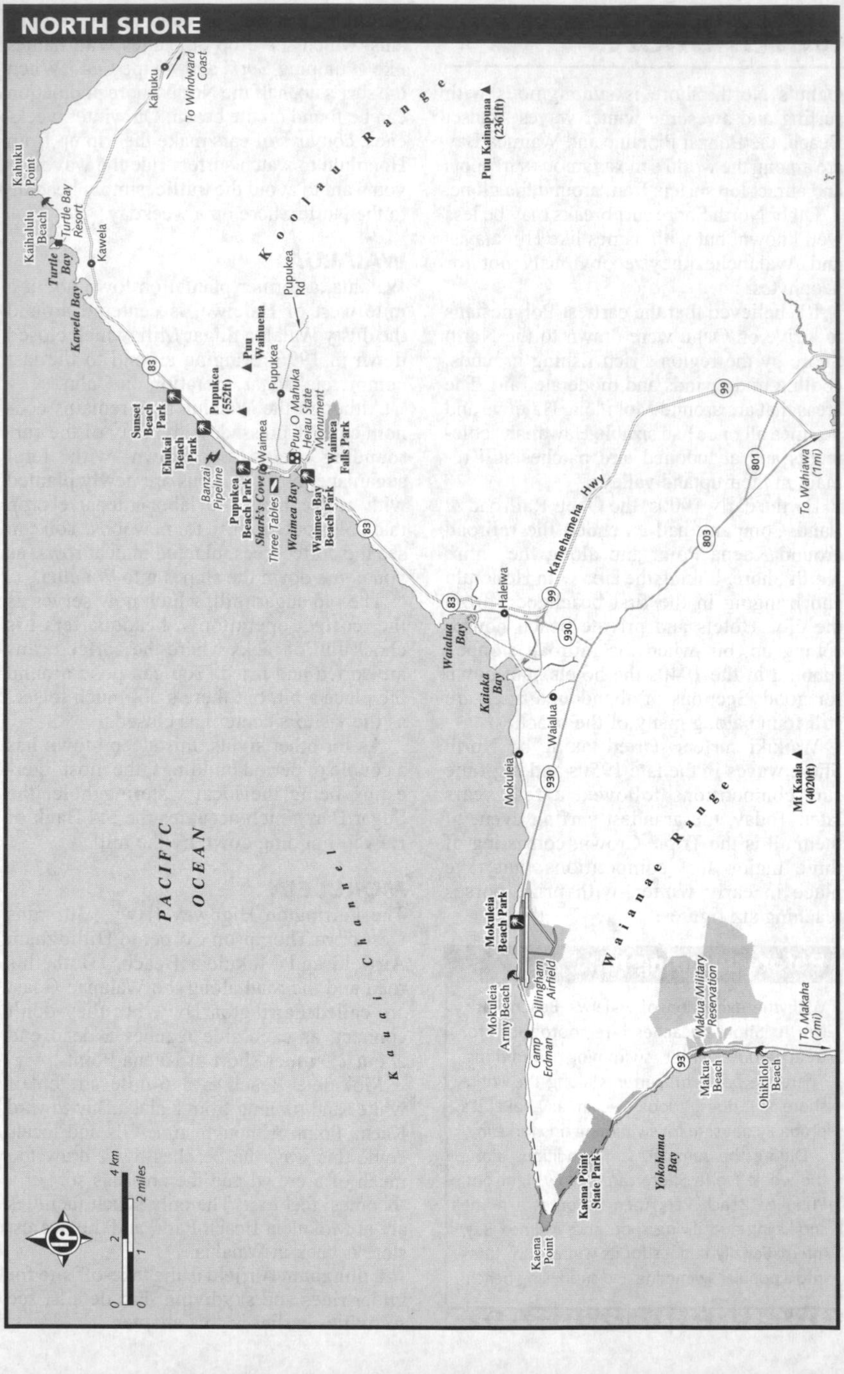
NORTH SHORE
PACIFIC
OCEAN
Kauai Channel
Koolau Range
Waianae Range
Kahuku
To Windward Coast
Kahuku Point
Kaihalulu Beach
Turtle Bay Resort
Turtle Bay
Kawela
Kawela Bay
Puu Kainapuaa (2361ft)
Pupukea Rd
Pupukea
Puu Waihuena
Pupukea (552ft)
Sunset Beach Park
Ehukai Beach Park
Banzai Pipeline
Pupukea Beach Park
Shark's Cove
Waimea
Puu O Mahuka Heiau State Monument
Waimea Falls Park
Three Tables
Waimea Bay
Waimea Bay Beach Park
83
99
801
803
930
93
Kamehameha Hwy
To Wahiawa (1mi)
Haleiwa
Waialua Bay
Kaiaka Bay
Waialua
Mokuleia
Mt Kaala (4020ft)
Mokuleia Beach Park
Mokuleia Army Beach
Dillingham Airfield
Camp Erdman
Makua Military Reservation
Makua Beach
Ohikilolo Beach
To Makaha (2mi)
Yokohama Bay
Kaena Point State Park
Kaena Point
0 2 4 km
0 1 2 miles

Mokuleia Beach Park
Opposite Dillingham Airfield, Mokuleia Beach Park has a large open grassy area with picnic tables, rest rooms and showers. Camping is allowed with a county camping permit. For information on obtaining permits, see Camping in the Accommodations section near the beginning of this chapter.

Mokuleia is sandy but has a lava rock shelf along much of its shoreline. The fairly consistent winds here make it a very popular spot with windsurfers, particularly in spring and autumn. In the winter there are dangerous currents.

Mokuleia Army Beach
Mokuleia Army Beach, opposite the western end of Dillingham Airfield, has the widest stretch of sand on the Mokuleia shore. Once reserved exclusively for military personnel, the beach is now open to the public, although it is no longer maintained and there are no facilities.

The beach is unprotected and has very strong rip currents, especially during winter high surf. Surfing is sometimes good.

Army Beach to Kaena Point
From Army Beach, you can proceed another 1½ miles down the road, passing still more white-sand beaches with aqua-blue waters. You'll usually find someone shore-casting and occasionally a few local people camping.

The terrain is scrub land reaching up to the base of the Waianae Range, while the shoreline is wild and windswept. The area is not only desolate, but can also be a bit trashed, and this is certainly not a must-do drive.

From road's end, it's possible to walk the 2½ miles to Kaena Point along state park lands, but it's more attractive from the other side (for details, see Kaena Point State Park in the Waianae Coast section).

HALEIWA
Haleiwa is the gateway to the North Shore and the main town catering to the multitude of day-trippers who make the circle-island ride.

The 2300 townspeople are a multiethnic mix of families who have lived in Haleiwa for generations as well as more recently arrived surfers, artists and New Age folk.

Most of Haleiwa's shops are along Kamehameha Ave, the main drag through town. Haleiwa has a picturesque boat harbor, bounded on both sides by beach parks. The south side is known for its winter surfing, and the north side is known for the North Shore's safest year-round swimming conditions.

The Anahulu River, which flows out along the boat harbor, is spanned by the Rainbow Bridge, so nicknamed for its distinctive arches. In 1832, John and Ursula Emerson, the first missionaries to the North Shore, built a grass house and missionary school on the riverbank. They called the school Haleiwa, meaning house (*hale*) of the great frigate bird (*iwa*). Over time, the name came to refer to the entire village.

Information
There's a **First Hawaiian Bank** (*☎ 637-5034; 66-135 Kamehameha Ave; open 8:30am-4pm Mon-Thur, 8:30am-6pm Fri*) at the north side of Haleiwa Shopping Plaza.

The Haleiwa **post office** (*☎ 637-1711; 66-437 Kamehameha Ave; open 8am-4pm Mon-Fri, 9am-noon Sat*) is at the south side of town.

The **Coffee Gallery** (*☎ 637-5571; 66-250 Kamehameha Ave; open 8am-8:30pm daily*), in the North Shore Marketplace, has Internet access for $1 per 10 minutes.

North Shore Surf & Cultural Museum
You can get a sense of how integral surfing is to the town's character by visiting the **North Shore Surf & Cultural Museum** (*☎ 637-8888; 66-250 Kamehameha Ave; admission by donation; open most afternoons*), in the North Shore Marketplace, which has a collection of vintage surfboards, period photos and surf

> **Cool Treat**
>
> For many people, the circle-island drive isn't complete without lining up for shave ice at **Matsumoto's** (*66-089 Kamehameha Ave; 8:30am-6pm daily*) tin-roofed general store, in the town center.
>
> Hawaiian shave ice is drenched with sweet syrup like the snow cones found on the US mainland, but it's much better, because the ice is shaved finer. It costs about a dollar for a small shave ice with flavored syrup and $2 for a fancy large one topped with ice cream and sweetened adzuki beans.

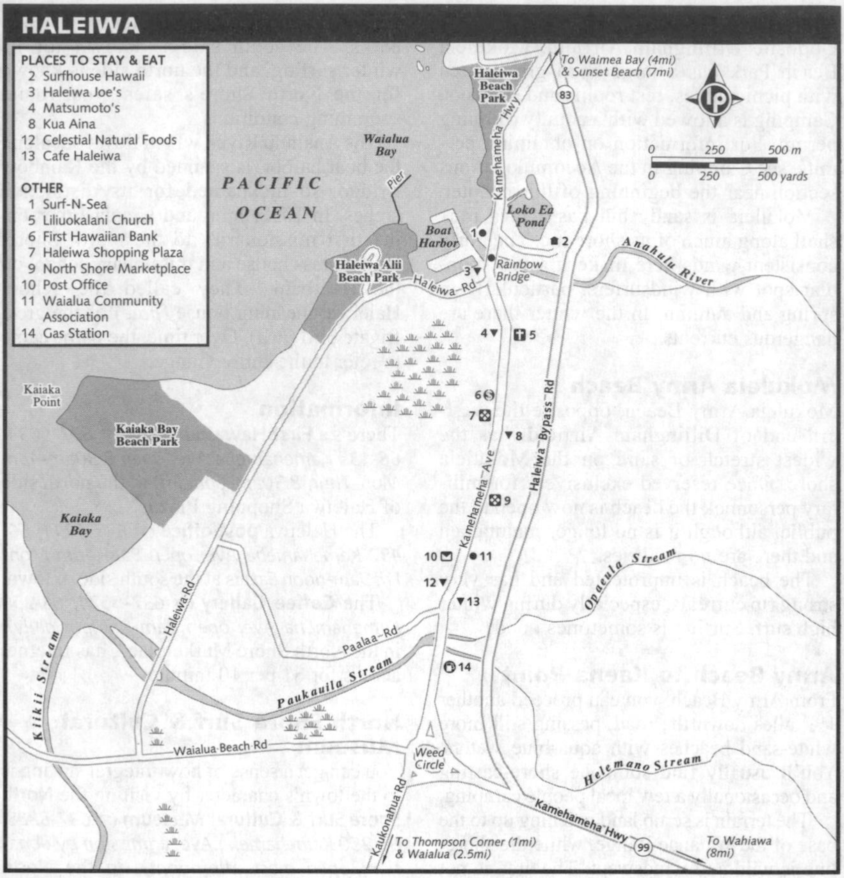

videos. It's run by volunteers, so the hours are flexible. The volunteers are into surfing, of course, so when the surf's up expect the place to be padlocked!

Liliuokalani Church

The Protestant church (*☎ 637-9364; 66-090 Kamehameha Ave*) opposite Matsumoto's takes its name from Queen Liliuokalani, who spent summer on the shores of the Anahulu River and attended services here. Although the church dates from 1832, the current building was constructed in 1961. As late as the 1940s, services were held entirely in Hawaiian.

Of most interest is the unusual seven-dial clock that Queen Liliuokalani gave the church in 1892. The clock shows the hour, day, month and year, as well as the phases of the moon. The queen's 12-letter name replaces the numerals on the clock face. The church is open whenever the minister is in, which is typically in the mornings.

Kaiaka Bay Beach Park

The 53-acre Kaiaka Bay Beach Park is on Kaiaka Bay, about a mile west of town. This is a good place for a picnic, as there are shady ironwood trees, but the in-town beaches are better choices for swimming. Two streams empty out into Kaiaka Bay, muddying up the beach after heavy rainstorms. Kaiaka has rest rooms, picnic tables, showers, and camp sites you can stay at between Friday and Tuesday.

Haleiwa Alii Beach Park

Surfing is king at Haleiwa Alii Beach Park. This attractive park with its generous white-sand beach is the site of several surfing tournaments in the winter, when north swells can bring waves as high as 20ft.

When waves are 5ft and under, lots of younger kids bring their boards out. Any time the waves are 6ft or better, there are also strong currents, and the water conditions are more suited to experienced surfers.

The 20-acre beach park has rest rooms, showers, picnic tables and a lifeguard tower. The shallow areas on the southern side of the beach are the calmest for swimming.

The park's knotty-pine beachfront community building may look familiar. It served as the lifeguard headquarters in the TV series *Baywatch Hawaii*, which used this beach park as its main setting when the show was filmed in Hawaii from 1999 to its demise in 2001.

Haleiwa Beach Park

This park is on the north side of Waialua Bay. As the beach is protected by a shallow shoal and a breakwater, the waters are usually very calm and see little wave action, though north swells occasionally ripple into the bay.

While the beach isn't Haleiwa's most appealing, this 13-acre county park has full beach facilities as well as basketball and volleyball courts, an exercise area and a softball field. It also has a good view of Kaena Point.

Places to Stay

Surfhouse Hawaii *(☎ 637-7146; 🅆 www.surfhouse.com; 62-203 Lokoea Place; single/double tent sites $9/15, dorm beds $15, bungalow $45)* is a backpacker's haven. Situated on 2 acres at the north side of Haleiwa, Surfhouse Hawaii offers three options: eight tent sites in a citrus grove; a simple dormitory-style cabin with six beds; and a private bungalow overlooking its own little garden. All guests have access to kitchen facilities. Some water-sports equipment is available for rent; if you don't have a tent, that can be arranged for a small fee as well. The location, on a side road immediately north of Rainbow Bridge, is within walking distance of both the beach and town center. French is spoken.

Haleiwa's other camping option is at **Kaiaka Bay Beach Park**, where the county allows camping Friday to Tuesday nights. For details on obtaining a permit, see Camping under Accommodations in the Facts for the Visitor chapter.

In addition, people occasionally rent out rooms in their homes. You can often find a couple of room-for-rent notices on the bulletin boards at Celestial Natural Foods and Haleiwa Super Market.

Places to Eat

Cafe Haleiwa *(66-460 Kamehameha Ave; breakfast $3-6, lunch $5-8; open 7am-2pm daily)* is an unpretentious joint with formica tables and walls plastered with surf memorabilia. A popular haunt for both local surfers and day-trippers, it offers good food at cheap prices. A great breakfast choice is the hearty blueberry pancakes ($3.50). Lunch is predominantly sandwiches and Mexican fare.

Coffee Gallery *(66-250 Kamehameha Ave; snacks $2-6; open 8am-8:30pm daily)*, in the North Shore Marketplace, has a mellow setting and good coffees, pastries and sandwiches.

Kua Aina *(66-214 Kamehameha Ave; snacks $4-7; open 11am-8pm daily)* is well-known for grilling up the North Shore's best burgers and fish sandwiches.

Cholo's *(☎ 637-3059; 66-250 Kamehameha Ave; appetizers $3-5, meals $7-11; open 8am-9pm daily)*, in the North Shore Marketplace, has good Mexican food. A great choice is the fresh *ahi* taco, which costs $4 alone or $7 with rice and beans. All the usual Mexican standards and combination plates are available as well.

Haleiwa Joe's *(☎ 637-8005; 66-001 Kamehameha Ave; appetizers $5-10, lunch $8-15, dinner $14-20; open 11:30am-9:30pm daily)* has superb food and a pleasant seaside setting. You can't go wrong ordering the fish, which literally comes right off the boats in the adjacent harbor. Favorites include sashimi, blackened *ahi* and crunchy coconut shrimp. It also serves chicken and steak dishes. Hands down, it's the best upmarket restaurant on the North Shore.

Haleiwa Super Market *(66-197 Kamehameha Ave; open 8am-8pm Mon-Sat, 8:30am-5:30pm Sun)* in the Haleiwa Shopping Plaza is the place for general grocery items, while **Celestial Natural Foods** *(66-443 Kamehameha Ave; open 9am-6:30pm Mon-Sat, 10am-6pm Sun)* carries a good variety of health foods and has a vegetarian deli.

WAIMEA

The Waimea Valley was once heavily settled. The lowlands were terraced in taro, the valley walls dotted with house sites and the ridges topped with *heiaus*. Just about every crop grown in Hawaii thrived in the valley, including a rare pink taro favored by Hawaiian royalty.

Waimea River, now blocked at the beach, originally opened into the bay and was a passage for canoes traveling to villages upstream. The sport of surfing was immensely popular here centuries ago, with the early Hawaiians taking to Waimea's huge waves on their long boards.

When Captain Cook's ships sailed into Waimea to collect water in 1779, shortly after Cook's death on the Big Island, an entry in the ship's log noted that the valley was uncommonly beautiful and picturesque.

However, Western contact wasn't kind to the area. Deforestation above the valley, from logging and the introduction of plantations, contributed to a devastating flood in Waimea in 1894. In addition to water damage, a large quantity of mud washed through the valley, so much so that it permanently altered the shape of Waimea's shore. After the flood, most residents abandoned the valley and resettled elsewhere.

Waimea Bay Beach Park

Waimea Bay is a beautiful, deeply inset bay with turquoise waters and a wide white-sand beach almost 1500ft long. Ancient Hawaiians believed its waters were sacred.

Waimea Bay's mood changes with the seasons; it can be tranquil and as flat as a lake in summer, then savage with incredible surf and the island's meanest rip currents in winter. Waimea boasts Hawaii's biggest surf and holds the record for the highest waves ever ridden in international competition. As at Sunset Beach, the huge north swells bring out crowds of spectators who throng to watch Waimea surfers perform their near-suicidal feats on waves of up to 35ft.

On winter's calmer days the boogie boarders are out in force, but even then sets come in hard and people get pounded. Winter water activities here are not for novices.

Usually the only time the water is calm enough for swimming and snorkeling is from June to September.

Waimea Bay Beach Park is the most popular North Shore beach. There are showers, rest rooms and picnic tables, and a lifeguard is on duty daily.

Pupukea Beach Park

This is a long beach along the highway that includes Three Tables on the left and Shark's Cove on the right. In the middle is Old Quarry, where a wonderful array of jagged rock formations and tide pools are exposed at low tide. This is a very scenic beach, with deep-blue waters, a varied coast and a mix of lava and white sand. The rocks and tide pools are tempting to explore, but be careful – they're razor sharp, and if you slip it's easy to get a deep cut.

The waters off Pupukea Beach are a marine-life conservation district.

There are showers and rest rooms in front of Old Quarry. The beach entrance is opposite an old gas station; bus No 52 stops out front. Snorkel sets and other water sports equipment can be rented from Planet Surf, at the side of the Foodland supermarket.

Three Tables At the western end of the beach, Three Tables gets its name from the ledges rising above the water. In summer when the waters are calm, Three Tables has good snorkeling and diving. It's possible to see some action by snorkeling around the tables, but the best coral and fish as well as some small caves, lava tubes and arches are in deeper water further out. This is a summer-only spot, however. In winter, dangerous rip currents flow between the beach and the tables. Beware of sharp rocks and coral.

Shark's Cove This cove is beautiful both above and below the water's surface. The naming of the cove was done in jest – sharks aren't a particular problem.

In the summer, when the seas are calm, Shark's Cove offers good snorkeling and swimming conditions as well as Oahu's most popular cavern dive. A fair number of beginning divers take lessons here, while the underwater caves will thrill advanced divers.

To get to the caves, swim out of the cove and around to the right. Some of the caves are very deep and labyrinthine, so caution should be used exploring them. There have been a number of drownings in these caves.

The large boulders out on the end of the point to the far right of the cove are said to be followers of Pele, the volcano goddess. As an honor, she gave them immortality by turning them to stone.

Ehukai Beach Park

The main reason people come to Ehukai Beach Park is to watch the pros surf the world-famous **Banzai Pipeline**, a few hundred feet to the left of the park. The Pipeline breaks over a shallow coral reef and can be a death-defying wave to ride.

At Ehukai Beach itself, many board riders and bodysurfers brave a hazardous current to ride the waves. Water conditions mellow out in summer, when it's good for swimming.

The entrance to Ehukai Beach Park is opposite the Sunset Beach Elementary School. The beach has a lifeguard, rest rooms and showers.

Sunset Beach Park

Just south of the 9-mile marker, Sunset Beach Park is a pretty white-sand beach that invites sunbathing, but the main action is in the water. This beach is Oahu's classic winter surf spot, with incredible waves and challenging breaks.

Because of the tremendous surf activity in winter, the slope of the beach becomes increasingly steeper as the season goes on. In the summer, as the sand washes back in, the shoreline begins to smooth out.

Winter swells create powerful rips. Even when the big waves have mellowed in the summer, there's still an along-shore current for swimmers to deal with. The beach has rest rooms, showers and a lifeguard tower.

Backyards, the surf break off Sunset Point at the northern end of the beach, draws a lot of top windsurfers. There's a shallow reef and strong currents to contend with, but Backyards has the island's biggest waves for sailing.

Puu o Mahuka Heiau

Puu o Mahuka Heiau State Monument is a long, low-walled platform temple perched on a bluff above Waimea. The largest *heiau* on Oahu, its construction is attributed to the legendary *menehunes*.

The terraced stone walls are a couple of feet high, although most of the *heiau* is now overgrown. This was an excellent site for a temple, and it's well worth the drive up for the view. It can also be a fine place to watch the sunset.

Walk up above the left side of the *heiau* from the parking lot for a view of Waimea Valley and Waimea Bay. To the west, you can see all the way out along the coast to Kaena Point.

To get to the *heiau*, turn up Pupukea Rd at the Foodland supermarket. The marked turnoff to the *heiau* is about half a mile up the road, and from there it's three-quarters of a mile in. On the drive up there's a good view of Pupukea Beach Park.

Eye for an Eye

In 1792, Captain Vancouver, who had been an officer on one of Captain Cook's vessels a decade earlier, anchored in Waimea Bay. While three of his men were collecting water on shore, they were attacked and killed. It's thought that their bodies were taken up to Puu o Mahuka Heiau on the ridge above the beach and burned as an offering to the gods.

When Vancouver returned a year later demanding justice, the high chief turned over three islanders. Although Vancouver doubted that these particular men had anything to do with the earlier murders, he had come to set an example so he ordered their execution anyway.

Waimea Falls Park

Waimea Falls Park (☎ *638-8511; 59-864 Kamehameha Hwy; adult/child 4-12/child under 4 $24/12/free; open 10am-5:30pm daily*), across from Waimea Bay Beach Park, is a combination botanical garden and cultural theme park.

The main path inside the park, which leads three-quarters of a mile up the Waimea Valley to a waterfall, is flanked by extensive naturalized gardens that are arranged by theme. There are sections of ginger, hibiscus, heliconia, native food plants and medicinal species. In all, they feature some 6000 plant species, including many that are rare and endangered.

The park has several ancient stone platforms and terraces dating back hundreds of years, as well as replicas of thatched buildings similar to those used by the early Hawaiians. Traditional hula dances, Hawaiian games and other demonstrations are held during the day. In addition, several times a day, a cliff diver plunges 60ft into the waterfall pool, thrilling spectators.

Although the valley's natural beauty and ethnobotanical heritage is nicely preserved, the cost of admission is on the steep side. One way to cut the cost is to enter after 3pm (adult/child $14/7). You should still have enough time to catch the last dive show and wander through the gardens, though it will be a bit late for most other activities.

Bus No 52 stops on the highway in front of the park, from where it's a half-mile walk to the park entrance.

Places to Stay

Backpackers *(☎ 638-7838, fax 638-7515; w www.backpackers-hawaii.com; 59-788 Kamehameha Hwy); dorm beds $15-20, rooms $45-65, studios $80-114, cabins $110-200)*, opposite Three Tables, is pretty much a surfers' hangout. A durable place that's been in business for years, it has a few different setups, most of them beach-house casual. The main house has the $15 bunks, while a three-story house behind it has the cheapest rooms. Both houses have shared bathrooms and kitchens. Expect spartan decor and aging furniture, but if you're just looking for a place to crash between waves, this is an option that won't take a deep bite out of your wallet.

A small beachfront building across the road has eight studios with TVs, kitchens and great views. Units on the bottom floor have $20 dorm beds, while those on the top floor are rented as private studios. The third property, a few hundred yards away on the inland side of the road, consists of fully equipped cabins that can sleep four to eight people.

Sharks Cove Rentals *(☎ 779-8535, fax 638-7980; e info@sharkcoverentals.com; 59-672 Kamehameha Hwy; dorm beds $25, rooms $50-60)* consists of two adjacent 3-bedroom houses across from Pupukea Beach Park. One of the houses has a set-up with bunk beds and there's only two people to a room so it's relatively quiet. The other house has three comfortable bedrooms; the more expensive rooms have their own TV and refrigerator. All guests have access to a fully equipped kitchen, a living room with cable TV and a washer and dryer. The place is within easy walking distance of a grocery store.

Ironwoods *(☎ 293-2554, fax 293-2603; 57-531 Kamehameha Hwy; studio per day/week $70/450)*, 2 miles north of Sunset Beach, is a studio in the beachside home of Ann McMann. The studio has a private entrance; a loft bedroom with one king-size bed (or two twin beds) that's reached via a steep ladder staircase; and a downstairs area with a cable TV, a bathroom, a kitchenette and a couch that converts into a single bed. The nightly rate includes a simple breakfast; there's a three-night minimum stay. The unit best suits two people, but three can be squeezed in if it's a family situation. The road is nearby, so expect to hear traffic noise, though it's usually drowned out by the sounds of the sea. The beach is just footsteps from the house. Ann speaks a little German.

Ulu Wehi B&B *(☎/fax 638-8161; e tj4dogs@aol.com; 59-416 Alapio Rd; rooms $85)* is 1½ miles up the hill from Pupukea Beach Park. Tina Jensen and her French husband, Bernie Moriaz, operate a small nursery at their home. They rent out a simple studio unit that has both a double bed and a single bed, a microwave, a refrigerator, a toaster and a coffeepot. The toilet and shower are in a rustic bathhouse in the rear garden. There's a $10 nightly discount on weekly stays. A breakfast that includes tropical fruit from their gardens and homemade baked goods is included. The house has a lovely 75ft lap pool in the backyard and a poolside barbecue that guests are free to use. Smoking is not allowed.

Ke Iki Beach Bungalows *(☎ 638-8229, 866-638-8229; e info@keikibeach.com; 59-579 Ke Iki Rd; streetside 1-bedroom units in low/high season $60/80, beachside 1-bedroom units $130/150, beachside 2-bedroom units $165/195)* consist of 10 renovated apartments fronting a beautiful white-sand beach just north of Pupukea Beach Park. The units are comfortably furnished with a tropical decor of floral prints, rattan chairs and the like. Each unit has a full kitchen, TV and phone, and guests have access to a barbecue, picnic tables and hammocks lazily strung between coconut trees. The location is a gem – the beachside units are right on the sand, the others just a minute's walk from the water.

North Shore Vacation Homes *(☎ 638-7289, 800-678-5263, fax 638-8736; e luckyc@rr.com; 59-229C Ke Nui Rd; 2-bedroom unit in low/high season $145/165, 3-bedroom* *unit in low season $195-220, in high season $225-245)* consists of four pleasant beachside houses sharing a 1-acre lot between Sunset Beach and Turtle Bay. The cheapest unit has two bedrooms, one bath and a living room with a sofa bed, and can accommodate up to four people. The other three units have three bedrooms and two baths and can hold up to six people. Each house has a full kitchen, washer and dryer, cable TV, VCR, phone and a large deck looking out over the ocean. There's typically a seven-night minimum stay, but shorter stays can sometimes be arranged.

In addition, the bulletin board at Pupukea Foodland has notices of roommates wanted and the occasional vacation rental listing, so if you're thinking of staying a while, it's worth taking a look.

Places to Eat

Foodland *(59-720 Kamehameha Hwy; open 6am-10pm daily)*, a supermarket opposite Pupukea Beach Park, has the best grocery prices and selection on the North Shore. It also has a deli selling good, inexpensive fried chicken, perfect for a beachside picnic.

Starbucks *(59-720 Kamehameha Hwy; open 5:30am-8pm daily)*, inside Foodland, sells coffee, brownies, scones and muffins. If you don't want to eat on the premises, you can find cheaper bakery snacks at Foodland itself.

The Hut *(snacks $5-7; open 11am-7pm daily)*, a little white trailer that parks along the highway 100yd north of Foodland, has good burgers, fish sandwiches and chicken teriyaki plates. There are a few tables where you can sit and eat, and a view of the beach across the road.

Sunset Pizza *(☎ 638-8497; 59-176 Kamehameha Hwy; pizza $9-18; open 7am-9pm daily)*, opposite Sunset Beach Park, is a good place for a cheap eat, with $5 meatball subs, $3 pizza slices and whole pizzas made to order.

Waianae Coast

The Waianae (Leeward) Coast is the arid, leeward side of Oahu. In 1793, English captain George Vancouver, the first Westerner to drop anchor here, found a barren wasteland with only a few scattered fishing huts. Just two years later, in 1795, Kamehameha invaded Oahu and the population density along the Waianae Coast swelled with Oahuans who were forced to flee from their homes elsewhere on the island. This isolated western extreme of Oahu became their permanent refuge.

Today, the Waianae Coast still stands separate from the rest of the island. Few tourists come this way – there are no gift shops or sightseeing buses on the Waianae Coast. When you get right down to it, other than watching surfers at Makaha, there aren't a whole lot of sights to see.

The area has a history of resisting development and a reputation for not being receptive to outsiders. In the past, visitors have been the targets of assaults and muggings. There's still a problem with thefts from cars and camp sites, and although things aren't as hostile as they used to be, some locals aren't keen on sharing their space with tourists. Overall, you need to be attuned to the mood of the people.

Farrington Hwy (Hwy 93) runs the length of the leeward coast. There are long stretches of white-sand beaches, some quite attractive, others a bit trashed. In winter, most have treacherous swimming conditions, but at that time they also have some of the island's more challenging surfing. Although the towns themselves are ordinary, the cliffs and valleys cutting into the Waianae Range form a lovely backdrop.

At road's end, there's an undeveloped mile-long beach and a fine nature hike out to scenic Kaena Point.

KAHE POINT

Kahe Point Beach Park, despite its name, does not have a beach, just the rocky cliffs of Kahe Point. The park has running water, picnic tables and rest rooms, but little else to recommend it. The backdrop is punctuated by the smokestacks of the electric power plant across the way.

Hawaiian Electric Beach, a sandy beach north of Kahe Point, is more commonly known as Tracks, the name given to it by beachgoers who used to go there by train before WWII. In the summer this is a fairly calm place to swim, and in the winter it's frequented by surfers. To get there, take the first turnoff after the power plant and drive over the abandoned railroad tracks.

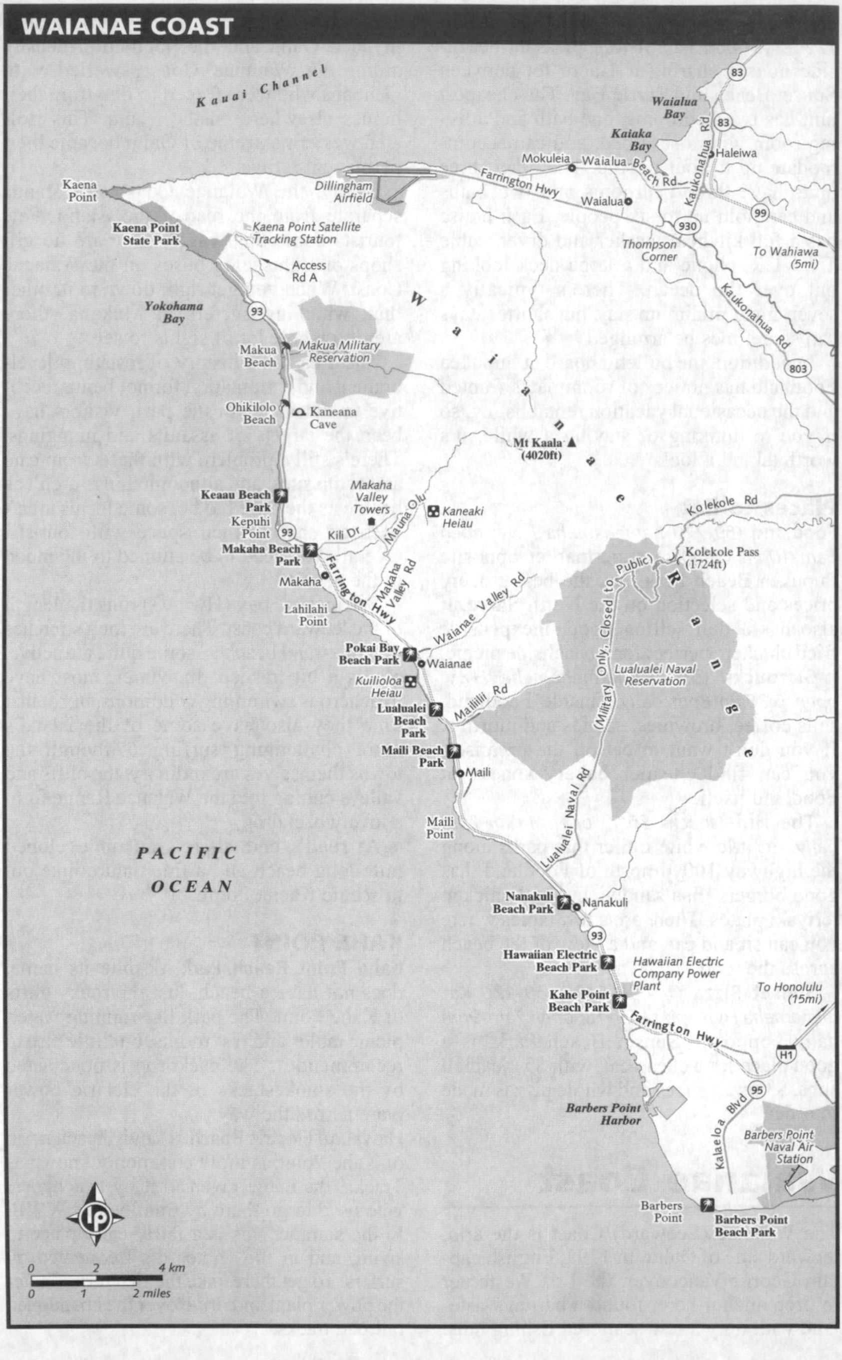
WAIANAE COAST
Kauai Channel
Waialua Bay
Kaiaka Bay
Haleiwa
Mokuleia
Waialua Beach Rd
Kaukonahua Rd
Farrington Hwy
Waialua
Dillingham Airfield
Kaena Point
Kaena Point State Park
Kaena Point Satellite Tracking Station
Access Rd A
Thompson Corner
To Wahiawa (5mi)
Yokohama Bay
Waianae Range
Makua Beach
Makua Military Reservation
Ohikilolo Beach
Kaneana Cave
Mt Kaala (4020ft)
Keaau Beach Park
Kepuhi Point
Makaha Valley Towers
Kaneaki Heiau
Mauna Olu
Kili Dr
Makaha Beach Park
Makaha
Makaha Valley Rd
Kolekole Rd
Kolekole Pass (1724ft)
(Military Only, Closed to Public)
Lahilahi Point
Waianae Valley Rd
Pokai Bay Beach Park
Waianae
Kuilioloa Heiau
Lualualei Naval Reservation
Lualualei Beach Park
Mailiilii Rd
Maili Beach Park
Maili
Maili Point
Lualualei Naval Rd
PACIFIC OCEAN
Nanakuli Beach Park
Nanakuli
Hawaiian Electric Beach Park
Hawaiian Electric Company Power Plant
Kahe Point Beach Park
To Honolulu (15mi)
Barbers Point Harbor
Kalaeloa Blvd
Barbers Point Naval Air Station
Barbers Point
Barbers Point Beach Park
93
83
99
930
803
H1
95
0
2
4 km
0
1
2 miles

NANAKULI

Nanakuli is the biggest town on the Waianae Coast, with 10,800 residents. The site of a Hawaiian Homesteads settlement, Nanakuli has one of the largest native Hawaiian populations on Oahu. The town has supermarkets, a courthouse, a bank and a few fast-food places.

Nanakuli is lined by a broad sandy beach park. There's swimming, snorkeling and diving during the calmer summer season. In winter, high surf can create rip currents and dangerous shorebreaks.

To get to the beach park, turn left at the traffic lights on Nanakuli Ave. This is a community park, with a playground, sports fields, full beach facilities and camp sites. For information on obtaining camping permits, see Camping in the Accommodations section earlier in this chapter.

MAILI

Maili has a long, grassy roadside park with a seemingly endless stretch of white-sand beach. Like other places on this coast, the water conditions are often treacherous in winter, but are usually calm enough for swimming in summer. There's a lifeguard station, a playground, beach facilities and a few coconut palms to provide limited shade.

WAIANAE

Waianae is the second largest town on the Waianae Coast, with a population of 10,500. It has a beach park, a protected boat harbor, a satellite city hall, a police station, supermarkets and lots of fast-food places.

Pokai Bay Beach Park

Protected by Kaneilio Point and a long breakwater, Pokai Bay Beach Park features the calmest year-round swimming on the Waianae Coast. Waves seldom break inside the bay, and the sandy seafloor slopes gently, making the beach a popular spot for families with children.

Snorkeling is fair near the breakwater, where fish gather around the rocks. The bay is also used by local canoe clubs, and you can watch them rowing in the late afternoon. There are showers, rest rooms and picnic tables, and a lifeguard is on duty daily.

Kaneilio Point, which runs along the south side of the bay, is the site of **Kuilioloa Heiau**. Partly destroyed by the army during WWII, this stone temple has been reconstructed by local conservationists.

To get to the beach park and *heiau*, turn onto Lualualei Homestead Rd, heading seaward, at the traffic light immediately north of the Waianae post office.

MAKAHA

Makaha means 'ferocious,' and in days past the valley was notorious for the bandits who waited along the cliffs to ambush passing travelers. Today, Makaha is best known for its world-class surfing. It has a fine beach, a golf course, a few condominiums and Oahu's best-restored *heiau*.

Makaha Beach Park

Makaha Beach is broad, sandy and crescent-shaped, with some of the most daunting winter surf in the islands. Experienced surfers and bodysurfers both hit the waves here.

Over the years Makaha Beach has hosted a number of surf events. In the early 1950s it was the site of Hawaii's first international surfing competition. Although the biggest surfing events have since shifted to Oahu's North Shore, Makaha Beach is still favored by long-boarders. Each March, the beach is the site of the Buffalo Surf Meet, with competitors using old-style surfboards called tankers that can reach 15ft in length.

When the surf's not up, Makaha is a popular swimming beach. When the surf is up, rip currents and a strong shorebreak make swimming hazardous.

In summer the slope of the beach is relatively flat, while in winter the wave action results in a steeper drop. The beach sand is slightly coarse and of calcareous origin, with lots of mollusk-shell fragments. As much as half of it temporarily washes away during winter erosion, but even then Makaha is still an impressive beach.

Snorkeling is good offshore during the calmer summer months. Makaha Caves, out where the waves break farthest offshore, feature underwater caverns, arches and tunnels at depths of 30ft to 50ft. It's a popular leeward diving spot.

Makaha Beach has showers and rest rooms, and lifeguards are on duty daily.

Makaha Valley

For a little loop drive, turn inland from Kili Dr, opposite Makaha Beach Park, where the road skirts up along scalloped green cliffs into Makaha Valley. If you're there at midday, you can visit one of Hawaii's most authentically restored *heiau*s, which sits high in Makaha Valley at the back of a private residential estate.

An estimated 3000 wild peacocks live in the valley, including about two dozen white ones. They can be spotted, or at least heard, throughout the upper valley, and if you visit the *heiau*, it's not unusual to see them performing their courting rituals in the field adjacent to the parking lot.

To get to the *heiau*, take Kili Dr to the Makaha Valley Towers condominium complex and turn right onto Huipu Dr. Half a mile down on the left is Mauna Olu St, which leads a mile into Mauna Olu Estates and up to Kaneaki Heiau.

To get to the Makaha Valley Country Club golf course, stay on Huipu Dr. Makaha Valley Rd, which intersects with Huipu Dr near the golf course, completes the loop, connecting back with the Farrington Hwy.

Kaneaki Heiau Originally a Lono temple, Kaneaki Heiau was dedicated to the god of agriculture. It was later transformed into a *luakini* temple (one dedicated to the war god Ku), and it's thought that Kamehameha used it as a place of worship after he conquered Oahu. Kaneaki Heiau remained in use until the time of Kamehameha's death in 1819.

Restoration, undertaken by the Bishop Museum and completed in 1970, added two prayer towers, a taboo house, drum house, altar and god images. The *heiau* was authentically reconstructed in the traditional manner using ohia tree logs and pili grass shipped over from the Big Island. The immediate setting surrounding the *heiau* remains undisturbed, even though the site is in the midst of a residential estate.

The guard at the Mauna Olu Estates gatehouse usually lets visitors go through to the *heiau*, a three-minute signposted drive past the **gatehouse** *(☎ 695-8174; admission free)*, between the hours of 10am and 2pm Tuesday to Sunday. However, you might want to call in advance, as the guards can be a bit inconsistent in providing access. Also, you'll need to show your rental vehicle contract and driver's license, and there's typically no access if it's raining.

Places to Stay

Makaha doesn't have many accommodations for short-term visitors. There are a handful of condos geared primarily to permanent residents, but none are terribly appealing and they generally require you to stay for at least a week.

Makaha Surfside *(☎ 696-6991, 524-3455; ⓔ riess@lava.net; 85-175 Farrington Hwy; studio/1-bedroom apartments per week $325/425)* is a four-story cinder-block apartment complex a mile south of Makaha Beach. Although it's predominantly residential, some of the 450 units are rented out on a weekly basis. Studios and apartments both have full kitchens. There's nothing special about this place, but it does have a pool.

Makaha Shores *(☎ 696-8415, fax 696-4499; reservations Hawaii Hatfield Realty, 85-833 Farrington Hwy, Suite 201, Waianae, HI 96792; studios per week/month $500/1000)* has a prize location right on the northern end of Makaha Beach, with lanai overlooking the surf. In addition to the studios, there are one-bedroom units that cost about 20% more. Many retired people winter at this condo so it can be tough to book accommodations in the high season. Hawaii Hatfield Realty also handles similarly priced units in **Makaha Valley Towers**, the high-rise complex that's tucked into the valley.

Places to Eat

Makaha Valley Country Club *(84-627 Makaha Valley Rd; dishes $4-8; open 7am-2pm Mon-Fri, 6am-3pm Sat & Sun)*, overlooking the golf course, is a popular lunch spot with a varied menu that includes sandwiches, fried mahimahi and teriyaki beef. Until 10:30am, you can get pancakes, omelettes and similar breakfast fare.

Makaha Drive-In *(84-1150 Farrington Hwy; open 6am-8pm Mon-Sat)*, at the corner of Farrington Hwy and Makaha Valley Rd, serves plate lunches for $5 and burgers and sandwiches for around $2.

There are no places to eat north of Makaha.

NORTH OF MAKAHA

Keaau Beach Park

Keaau Beach Park is another long, open, grassy strip, this time bordering a rocky shore, with camp sites, showers, drinking water, picnic tables and rest rooms. A sandy beach begins at the very northern end of the park, although a rough reef, sharp drop and high seasonal surf make swimming uninviting.

For information on obtaining camping permits, see Camping in the Accommodations section earlier in this chapter.

Driving north along the coast, you'll see low lava sea cliffs, white-sand beaches and patches of *kiawe*. On the inland side, you'll get a glimpse into a run of little valleys.

Kaneana Cave

Kaneana Cave, a massive cave on the right-hand side of the road about 2 miles north of Keaau Beach Park, was once underwater. Its impressive size is the result of wave action that wore away loose rock around an earthquake crack and expanded the cavern over the millennia as the ocean slowly receded.

It's a somewhat uncanny place – often a strong wind gusts near the cave while it's windless just down the road.

Hawaiian *kahuna*s (priests) once performed their rituals inside the cave's inner chamber. Older Hawaiians consider it a sacred place and won't enter for fear it's haunted by the spirits of deceased chiefs. From the collection of broken beer bottles and graffiti inside, it's obvious not everyone shares their sentiments.

From Ohikilolo Beach, below the cave, you can see Kaena Point to the north. Ohikilolo Beach is sometimes called Barking Sands, as the sand is said to make a 'woofing' sound if it's walked on when very dry.

Makua Valley

Scenic Makua Valley opens up wide and grassy, backed by a fan of sharply fluted mountains. Ironically, this very picturesque expanse serves as the ammunition field of the Makua Military Reservation.

The ocean-side road opposite the south end of the reservation leads to a little graveyard shaded by yellow-flowered be-still trees. This is all that remains of the Makua Valley community, forced to evacuate during WWII, when the US military took over the entire valley for bombing practice. War games still take place in the valley, which is fenced off with barbed wire and signs that warn of stray explosives.

Makua Beach, the white-sand beach opposite the military reservation, was a canoe landing in days past. A movie set of Lahaina as it appeared during the 19th century was built on Makua Beach for the 1966 movie *Hawaii*, starring Julie Andrews and Max von Sydow. No trace of the set remains.

> **Nanaue the Shark Man**
>
> Hawaiian legend tells of a child named Nanaue, who was born with an open space between his shoulders. Unknown to his mother, the child's father was the king of sharks in the guise of a man. Nanaue was born half human, half shark. He was human on land, but when he entered the ocean, the opening on his back became a shark's mouth. After a nasty spell in which many villagers were ripped to shreds by a mysterious shark, Nanaue's secret was discovered, and he was forced to swim from island to island as he was hunted down. For a while, he lived near Makua and took his victims into Kaneana Cave via an underwater tunnel.

Satellite Tracking Station

Immediately before the gate to Kaena Point State Park, a road leads up to Kaena Point Satellite Tracking Station, operated by the US Air Force. The tracking station's antennas and domes sit atop the mountains above the point, a couple of them appearing like giant white golf balls perched on the ridge.

There are **hiking trails** above the tracking station, including a 2½-mile ridge trail that leads to Mokuleia Forest Reserve. You'll need to obtain a hiking permit in advance from the **Division of Forestry & Wildlife** (*☎ 587-0166*) to get past the air force's guard station.

KAENA POINT STATE PARK

Kaena Point State Park is an undeveloped 853-acre coastal strip that runs along both sides of Kaena Point, the westernmost point of Oahu.

Until the mid-1940s the Oahu Railroad ran up here from Honolulu and continued around the point, carrying passengers on to Haleiwa on the North Shore.

The attractive mile-long sandy beach on this side of the point is Yokohama Bay, named for the large numbers of Japanese fishers who came here during the railroad days.

Slipping Away

Early Hawaiians believed that when people went into a deep sleep or lost consciousness, their souls would wander. Souls that wandered too far were drawn west to Kaena Point. If they were lucky, they were met here by their *aumakua* (ancestral spirit helper), who led their souls back to their bodies. If unattended, their souls would be forced to leap from Kaena Point into the endless night, never to return.

On clear days, Kauai can be seen from the point. According to legend, it was at Kaena Point that the demigod Maui attempted to cast a huge hook into Kauai and pull it next to Oahu to join the two islands. But the line broke and Kauai slipped away, with just a small piece of it remaining near Oahu. Today, this splintered rock, off the end of Kaena Point, is known as Pohaku o Kauai.

Winter commonly brings huge pounding waves, making Yokohama a popular seasonal surfing and bodysurfing spot. It is, however, best left to the experts because of the submerged rocks, strong rip currents and dangerous shorebreak.

Swimming is pretty much limited to the summer, and then only during calm conditions. When the water's flat, it's possible to snorkel; the best spot with the easiest access is at the south side of the park. Rest rooms, showers and a lifeguard station are also at the south end of the park.

In addition to being a state park, Kaena Point has been designated a natural area reserve because of its unique ecosystem. The extensive dry, windswept coastal dunes that rise above the point are the habitat of many rare native plants. The endangered *Kaena akoko* that grows on the talus slopes is found nowhere else.

More common plants are the beach naupaka, with white flowers that look like they've been torn in half; pau-o-Hiiaka, a vine with blue flowers; and beach morning glory, sometimes found wrapped in the parasite plant *kaunaoa,* which looks like orange plastic fishing line.

Seabirds seen at Kaena Point include shearwaters, boobies and the common noddy – a dark-brown bird with a grayish crown. You can often see schools of spinner dolphins off the beach, and in winter humpback whale sightings are not unusual.

Dirt bikes and 4WD vehicles once created a great deal of disturbance in the dunes, but after Kaena Point became a natural area reserve in 1983, vehicles were restricted and the situation improved. The reserve is once again a nesting site for the rare Laysan albatross, and Hawaii's endangered monk seals occasionally bask in the sun here.

Kaena Point Trail

A 2½-mile (one-way) coastal hike runs from the end of the paved road at Yokohama Bay to Kaena Point, following the old railroad bed. Along the trail are tide pools, sea arches, fine coastal views and the lofty sea cliffs of the Waianae Range. The hike is unshaded (Kaena means 'the heat'), so take plenty of water.

Don't leave anything valuable in your car. Telltale mounds of shattered windshield glass can be found at the road's-end parking area used by most hikers; parking closer to the beach rest rooms or leaving your doors unlocked can decrease the odds of having your car windows smashed.

Hawaii (The Big Island)

The island of Hawaii, aka the Big Island, is nearly twice the size of all the other Hawaiian Islands combined. With climates ranging from tropical to subarctic, the island's geographical variety resembles a minicontinent. Landscapes include one of just about everything: desolate lava flows, lush coastal valleys, high sea cliffs, rolling pastures, deserts and rain forests.

Geologically, it's the youngest Hawaiian island and the only one still growing. Kilauea, the most active volcano on earth, has added 550 acres of coastal land to the island since its latest series of eruptions began in 1983. The Big Island is home to Madame Pele, Hawaiian goddess of volcanoes, and Ku, god of war.

The Big Island has Hawaii's highest mountains, which rise almost 14,000ft above sea level. They make you think of icebergs, not only for their snowcaps but also because their summits are merely the tips of mountain masses rising 32,000ft from the ocean floor.

These giant mountains create a huge barrier that blocks the moist northeasterly trade winds and makes the leeward side of the Big Island the driest region in Hawaii, a perfect testing ground for Ironman triathletes every year. The Kona and Kohala Coasts, on this sunny western side, have the island's finest beaches and water conditions.

The windward east coast on the Hilo side catches the rain and has a predominantly rugged coastline with pounding surf, lush tropical rain forests, deep ravines and majestic waterfalls. Here, forgotten Puna is a riotous district of natural phenomena, where you can soak in volcanic steam vents and witness molten lava dripping into the sea.

Still, the island's most impressive scenery is at Hawaii Volcanoes National Park, which offers excellent hiking and camping in locales that range from tropical beaches to the icy 13,677ft summit of Mauna Loa. You can drive or cycle around the rim of Kilauea's huge caldera, or trek across still-steaming crater floors and wander through giant lava tubes.

The Big Island has Hawaii's best petroglyphs and some of its most important *heiaus* (ancient temples). It also boasts the largest privately owned cattle ranch in the USA and the world's top collection of astronomical observatories. The latter are at the summit of Mauna Kea, Hawaii's highest point at 13,796ft.

Hilo and Kona are the island's two population centers. On the lush, rainy east coast, Hilo is the island's only real city. It is the

Highlights

- Glimpsing a volcano's awesome power
- Gazing at the stars atop Mauna Kea, Hawaii's highest point
- Night diving with luminous manta rays at Kailua Bay
- Descending into Waipio Valley, sacred haven for spirits, kings and rebels
- Touring an ancient temple at Puuhonua o Honaunau or windswept Mookini Heiau

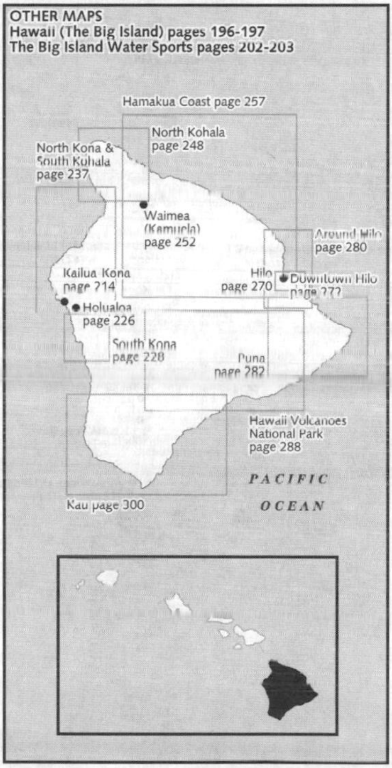

HAWAII (THE BIG ISLAND)

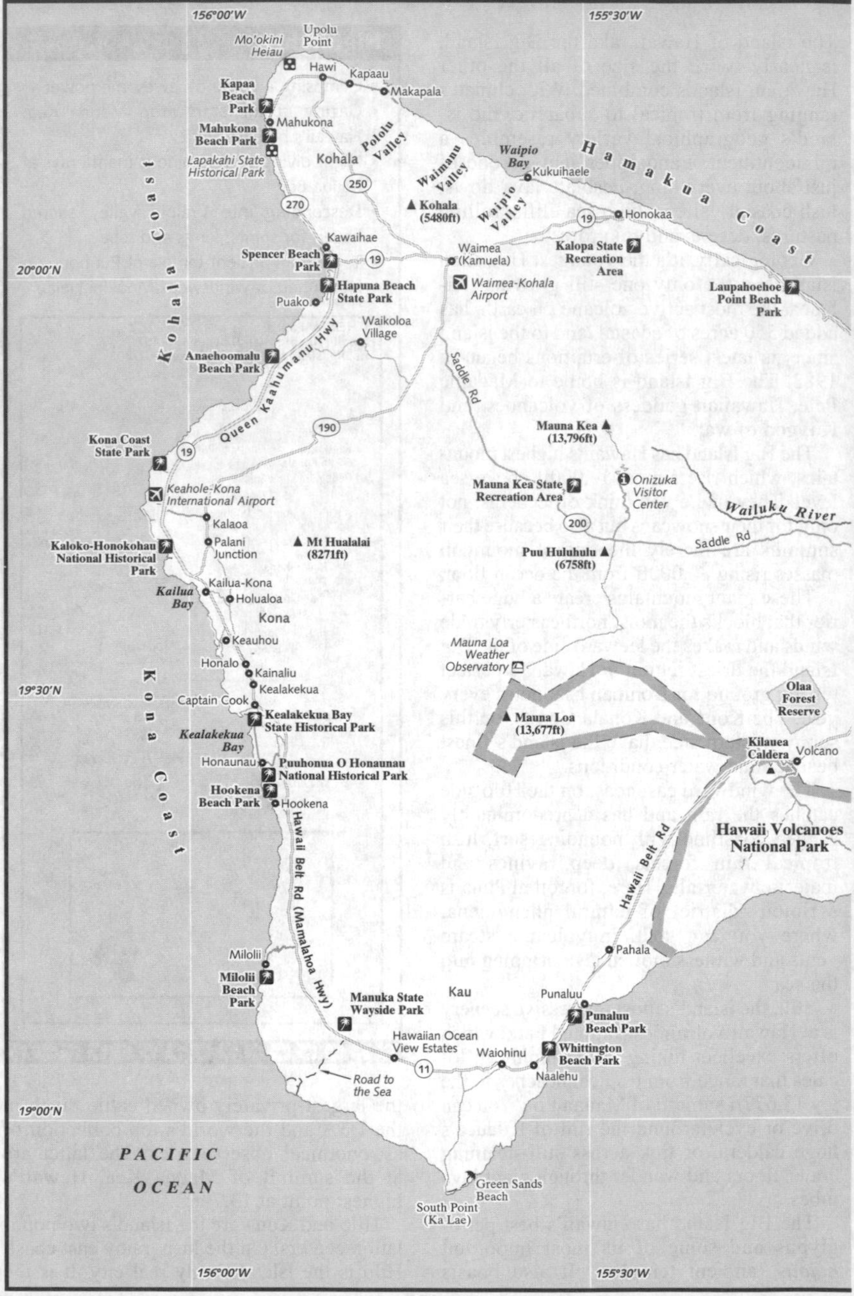

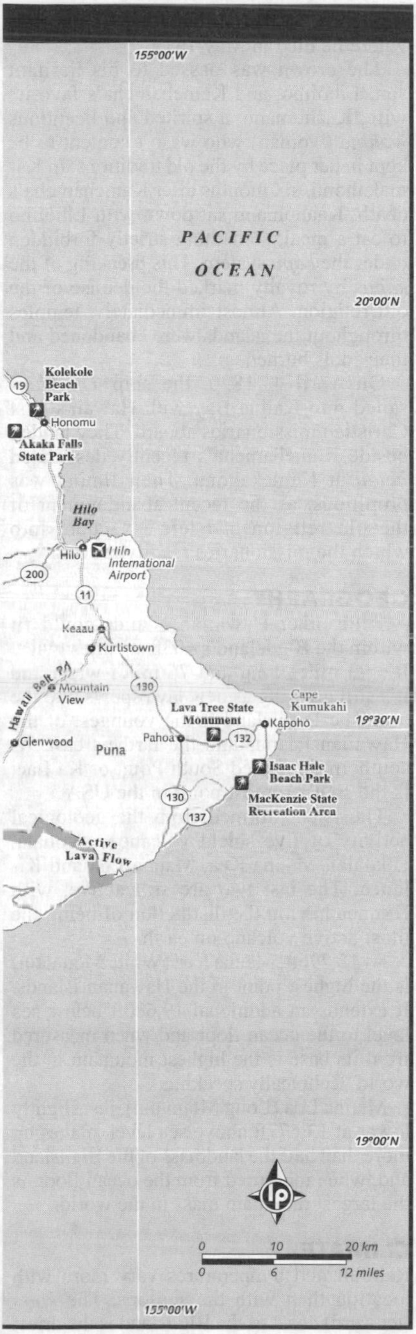

oldest city in Hawaii, and shows its age with character. But it is Kona, on the dry, sunny west coast, that attracts waves of travelers. The Kona region has the lion's share of the island's accommodations and is the focus of most recreational activities, including excellent diving and deep-sea fishing.

The Big Island is big on space, so few places feel crowded. It attracts a lot of adventurous people. It has traditional fishing villages, valleys with taro farmers and wild horses, a 'cowboy country' and alternative folk living off the land.

HISTORY

By and large, the history of the Big Island is the history of Hawaii. Here the first Polynesian settlers alighted between AD 500 and AD 700. This was also where the first *luakini* (temple of human sacrifice) and the *kapu* system of strict taboos regulating all aspects of daily life came into being – both introduced by the Tahitian high priest, Paao, who migrated here in the 12th century. Seven centuries later, the old Hawaiian gods were overthrown and replaced by those of the Christians. English explorer Captain James Cook died on the island in 1779 and Kamehameha the Great, who unified Hawaii, rose to power here in the 18th century.

Kamehameha the Great

Kamehameha the Great was born on the Big Island in 1758. As a young boy, he was brought to Kealakekua Bay to live at the royal court of his uncle, Kalaniopuu, high chief of the island.

Kamehameha became Kalaniopuu's fiercest general, and the chief appointed him guardian of the war god, Kukailimoku, the 'snatcher of land.'

The deity was embodied in a coarsely carved wooden image with a bloody red mouth and a helmet of yellow feathers. Kamehameha carried it into battle with him, and it was said that during the fiercest fighting the image would screech out terrifying battle cries.

Immediately after Kalaniopuu's death in 1782, Kamehameha led his warriors against Kalaniopuu's son, Kiwalao, who had taken the throne. Kiwalao was killed, and Kamehameha emerged as ruler of the Kohala region and one of the ruling chiefs of the Big Island.

Kamehameha's ambitions extended well beyond sharing control of the island. In 1790, with the aid of a captured foreign schooner and two shipwrecked sailors, Isaac Davis and John Young, whom he used as gunners, Kamehameha attacked and conquered the island of Maui.

Shortly after that, Kamehameha was in Molokai preparing for an invasion of Oahu when word reached him that Keoua, chief of the Kau region, was attacking the Hamakua Coast. Keoua boldly pillaged Waipio Valley, which was the most sacred area on the Big Island and the site where Kamehameha had ceremoniously received his war god a decade earlier.

As an angry Kamehameha set sail for home, Keoua's soldiers beat a quick retreat back to Kau. But when the withdrawing troops passed beneath the slopes of Kilauea Crater, the volcano suddenly erupted, and many of the warriors were instantly killed as toxic fumes and ashes swept over them. It is the only known volcanic explosion in the history of Hawaii to have resulted in such mass fatalities. It is possible that casts of the soldiers' footprints, imprinted in volcanic mud and ash, remain on the trail to this day.

In the midst of these power struggles, a prophet from Kauai told Kamehameha that if he built a new *heiau* to honor his war god, Kukailimoku, he would become ruler of all the islands.

Kamehameha did so, completing Puukohola Heiau in Kawaihae in 1791. He then sent word to Keoua that his appearance was requested at the *heiau* for reconciliation. Keoua, well aware that this was a *luakini*, probably knew his fate was sealed, but he sailed to Kawaihae anyway.

Upon landing, Keoua and his party became the *heiau*'s first sacrifices. With Keoua's death, Kamehameha became sole ruler of the Big Island.

Over the next few years, Kamehameha conquered all the islands (except for Kauai, over which he established suzerainty) and named the entire kingdom after his home island, Hawaii.

Losing the Old Religion

Kamehameha the Great established his kingdom's royal court in Lahaina on Maui, but he later returned to his Kamakahonu residence, on the north side of Kailua Bay, where he died in May 1819.

The crown was passed to his hesitant son, Liholiho, and Kamehameha's favorite wife, Kaahumanu, a spirited and licentious *wahine* (woman) who wasn't content to be kept in her place by the old traditions. In Kamakahonu, six months after Kamehameha's death, Kaahumanu sat down with Liholiho to eat a meal, something strictly forbidden under the *kapu* system. This breaking of the *kapu*s by royalty marked the demise of the old religion. Almost immediately, temples throughout the islands were abandoned and their idols burned.

On April 4, 1820, the ship *Thaddeus* sailed into Kailua Bay with Hawaii's first Christian missionaries aboard. They landed beside Kamehameha's recently desecrated *heiau* at Kamakahonu. Their timing was propitious, as the recent abandonment of the old religion had left a vacuum into which the missionaries readily moved.

GEOGRAPHY

All the other Hawaiian islands could fit within the Big Island's 4038 sq miles twice. It's 93 miles long and 76 miles wide, and it's still growing as new lava spews into the sea. The Big Island is the youngest of the Hawaiian Islands and the farthest east. Its southern tip, called South Point or Ka Lae, is the southernmost point in the USA.

The island formed from the geological activity of five shield volcanoes: Kohala, Hualalai, Mauna Kea, Mauna Loa and Kilauea. The last two are still active, with Kilauea having the distinction of being the most active volcano on earth.

At 13,796ft, Mauna Kea (White Mountain) is the highest point in the Hawaiian Islands. It extends an additional 19,680ft below sea level to the ocean floor and when measured from its base is the highest mountain in the world, technically speaking.

Mauna Loa (Long Mountain), just slightly lower at 13,677ft above sea level, makes up more than half the landmass of the Big Island and, when measured from the ocean floor, is the largest mountain mass in the world.

CLIMATE

Rainfall and temperatures vary more with location than with the seasons. The *kona* (leeward) coast of the Big Island is the driest

Vog

'Vog' is a word coined on the Big Island to define the volcanic haze that has been hanging over the island since Kilauea's latest eruptive phase began in 1983. It usually blows toward Kona, and conditions can resemble city smog when the trade winds falter. Vog consists of water vapor, carbon dioxide and significant amounts of sulfur dioxide.

In the early 1990s, an average 275 tons of sulfur dioxide were being emitted from Kilauea daily, causing air quality problems on the Big Island and haze throughout Hawaii. The sulfur dioxide level exceeds standards set by the US Environmental Protection Agency an average of 22 days a year. While this shouldn't present health problems for short-term visitors, scientists are studying the link between vog and respiratory problems for residents.

region in the state. Sun worshippers will strike it rich here. Of course, Hunter S Thompson remarked that 'the Kona Coast in December is as close to hell on earth as a half-bright mammal can get.'

Fortunately, heavenly Hilo and Volcano are only a few hours away. On the windward side of Mauna Kea, near the 2500ft elevation, around 300 inches of rain fall annually. So much rain is squeezed out of the clouds as they rise up Mauna Kea and Mauna Loa that only about 15 inches of precipitation reaches the summits, much of it as snow. Heavy subtropical winter rainstorms in Hilo occasionally bring blizzards to the mountains as low as the 9000ft level.

Average annual rainfall in Volcano, just north of Hawaii Volcanoes National Park, is 160 inches, while along the Kona coast it might be less than 15 inches. Although winter is wetter than summer, location again is the key. In Kona, seasonal rainfall variations are marginal, while in the town of Volcano the rainfall in winter is about twice as much as in summer.

In January, the average daily high temperature is 65°F at Hawaii Volcanoes National Park, 79°F in Hilo and a toasty 81°F in Kailua-Kona. August temperatures rise only 5°F or so. Nighttime lows are about 15°F less.

The **National Weather Service** *(on the Big Island ☎ 961-5582, in Hilo ☎ 935-8555, water conditions ☎ 935-9883)* provides recorded forecasts for the Big Island, Hilo and the vicinity, and for water conditions. **Hawaii Volcanoes National Park** *(☎ 985-6000)* offers recorded information on current volcano eruptions and viewing points.

FLORA & FAUNA

The nene, the endangered goose that is Hawaii's state bird, lives on the upland volcanic slopes. As recently as a hundred years ago, an estimated 25,000 nene lived on the Big Island. Today, there may be under 1000 of the birds left in the wild. With luck, you'll run across these curious and inquisitive creatures at Hawaii Volcanoes National Park.

Other native birds here include the endangered *palila*, a little yellow fellow that survives solely on Mauna Kea's slopes, and the *io* (Hawaiian hawk), which also lives in the uplands. Another endangered bird endemic to the Big Island is the *alala* (Hawaiian crow), which hangs on precariously with a single flock of fewer than a dozen birds. Hakalau Forest Wildlife Refuge outside Waimea harbors the Hawaiian hoary bat and other rare species.

Wild horses roam Waipio Valley, and feral cattle graze on the slopes of Mauna Kea. Wild pigs, goats and sheep – all non-native species – take a toll on the Big Island's environment and are hunted. Still, the most insidious of all introduced species is the mongoose, a commonly seen ferretlike creature whose appetite for native birds and their eggs has led to a drastic decline in endemic avian populations.

Two rare varieties of silversword grow on the Big Island – one on Mauna Kea and the other on Mauna Loa. Related to their better-known Maui cousins, these distant relatives of the sunflower grow off the beaten path.

GOVERNMENT & POLITICS

The Big Island is one county unto itself with an elected mayor and a nine-member council. Hilo is the county seat and political center.

Rivalry is ongoing between old established Hilo and boomtown Kona. The biggest political issue on the island, as elsewhere in Hawaii, is rampant development.

ECONOMY

The Big Island hit the state's highest unemployment rate (5.9%), lowest average income ($23,461) and most residents living below the poverty line (16.6%) in 2001. Yet employment is fairly diversified, with retail trade, government, hotels and construction industries employing about half of the workforce.

Although the last sugar company on Big Island ceased operating in 1996, agriculture is still significant to the economy. The island produces the vast majority of Hawaii's macadamia nuts, coffee and tropical flowers, as well as four-fifths of the state's fruit, including papayas, bananas and oranges. The Big Island has several sizable cattle ranches, which collectively produce most of the beef marketed in the state.

The island's illicit underground agriculture in *pakalolo* (marijuana) has declined greatly as the result of strict police surveillance. But the majority of all marijuana confiscated in Hawaii still comes from the Big Island's Puna and Kau districts.

POPULATION & PEOPLE

The population of the Big Island is approximately 149,000. Hilo holds about a third of the island's population, but the Big Island's demographics are changing rapidly, especially as the Kona Coast development continues at a frantic pace. By 2010, the total island population is projected to jump by one-fifth.

The Big Island's ethnic breakdown is 31% Caucasian, 28% who consider themselves 'mixed race,' 26% Asian and 11% primarily of native Hawaiian descent.

ORIENTATION

The Big Island is divided up into six districts: Kona, Kohala, Waimea, Hilo, Puna and Kau.

The Hawaii Belt Rd circles the island, taking in the main towns and many of the sights. Different segments of the road have different highway numbers and names, but it's easy to follow.

From Kona to Hilo, the northern half of the belt road is 92 miles, and the journey takes over two hours nonstop. The southern Kona–Hilo route is 125 miles and takes approximately three hours.

There are airports in Hilo and Kona. The Hilo airport is right in town. However, most visitors land at Kona airport, which is between the island's main resort areas of Kailua-Kona and Waikoloa.

Maps

General maps of the Big Island are published by Nelles ($5.95) and the University of Hawaii Press ($3.95). If you want to really beat your own path, hefty editions of the *Ready Mapbook* for East and West Hawaii ($9.95 each) are an invaluable resource.

INFORMATION

Tourist Offices

The **Big Island Visitors Bureau** (*☎ 961-5797, 800-464-2924; W www.gohawaii.com; 250 Keawe St, Hilo • ☎ 886-1655; 250 Waikoloa Beach Dr, Waikoloa Beach Resort*) can send you a glossy **vacation planner** (*☎ 800-648-2441*) in advance.

Newspapers & Magazines

West Hawaii Today (*W www.westhawaiitoday.com*), which is the Kona Coast newspaper, and Hilo's **Hawaii Tribune-Herald** (*W www.hilohawaiitribune.com*) are both published daily except Saturday. *West Hawaii Today* has decent international coverage and the daily vog index. Also look for the free *Hawaii Island Journal,* a locally owned, bimonthly paper with entertainment listings.

Free tourist magazines such as *101 Things to Do* and *This Week Big Island* are readily available at the airport, in hotel lobbies and around town. They're good sources of general information and include discount coupons for activities and restaurants island-wide.

Radio & TV

You can find Hawaii National Public Radio (NPR) at 91.1FM. Hawaiian music rules at KAPA 100.3FM in Hilo, 99.1FM in Kona. News, talk radio and sports fans should tune to KPUA 670AM.

Network, public TV and major cable TV stations are relayed from Honolulu. Channel 7 on cable TV features visitor information programmes.

Libraries

There are public libraries in Hilo, Holualoa, Honokaa, Kailua-Kona, Kapaau, Keaau, Kealakekua, Laupahoehoe, Mountain View, Naalehu, Pahala, Pahoa and Waimea.

Emergency

You can call the police, ambulance or fire for **emergencies** (☎ 911). There's also a **24-hour sexual assault hotline** (☎ 935-0677).

The two main hospitals are the **Hilo Medical Center** (☎ 974-6800; Hilo) and the **Kona Coast Community Hospital** (☎ 322-9311; Kealakekua). Waimea has the smaller **North Hawaii Community Hospital** (☎ 885-4444).

ACTIVITIES

Granted, the Big Island doesn't have the wild swells of Oahu's North Shore, or the billowy winds of Maui's Hookipa Beach. But of all the Hawaiian Islands, only one boasts snowboarding in winter, the Ironman Triathlon in fall, the world's clearest stargazing almost every night and live lava flows every day.

The vast majority of recreational activities take place on the west coast. Most of the resorts offer their guests a variety of water activities, including cruises and dive trips. Usually, these are open to the public as well, but only at higher-than-average rates.

Swimming

The Big Island has over 300 miles of shoreline, but it doesn't have the grand expanses of sandy beach you'll find on Maui or Oahu. Instead, most of the Big Island's beaches are sandy pockets bordering bays and coves.

The best swimming spots are on the west coast. Kailua-Kona has a few beaches, although the better ones are farther up the Kona Coast around Waikoloa and South Kohala. Anaehoomalu (A Bay) and Hapuna are both beautiful and easily accessible public beaches. Isolated gems such as paradisiacal Makalawena require a hike (or a 4WD vehicle) to reach but are well worth the effort.

Granted, East Hawaii beaches are not your typical tropical idylls of calm, turquoise waters and powdery white sands. The seas are often rough here and are not for the faint of heart. Still, these windward beaches are mysterious and unique, some with olivine green water and lava black sands, bays teeming with tide pools and ephemeral expanses where you can swim with dolphins or sea turtles. On a few, clothing is optional. The island also has a green crater lake and waterfalls galore.

The county has **public swimming pools** in Honokaa, Hilo, Kapaau, Kealakekua, Laupahochoe and Pahoa. For directions and open swim schedules, call the **Aquatics Division** (☎ 961-8694).

Surfing

Local surfers and boogie boarders do manage to catch waves in a number of places, but many of the island's surf spots have rocky, reef-encrusted shorebreaks and, let's face it, the waves rarely, if ever, get that big. Always check things out thoroughly with locals before heading out.

On the eastern side of the island, check out Pohiki Bay at Isaac Hale Beach Park and, north of Hilo, Honolii Cove and Kolekole Beach Park. Favorite Kona Coast surfing locales are Kahaluu Beach in Keauhou, Banyans (near the banyan tree north of White Sands Beach) and Pine Trees near Wawaloli (OTEC) Beach. White Sands Beach is also one of the best places on the Kona Coast for boogie boarding and bodysurfing.

Windsurfing

The Big Island is not a hot spot for windsurfing. Beginner windsurfers and experienced short-boarders head to Anaehoomalu Bay in Waikoloa, where you can rent equipment and take lessons. When freak winter storm winds are blowing, there's plenty of thrilling chop-hopping on A Bay. Spring trade winds also make for great sailing, but novices are warned off at this time, and rental places may be shuttered.

Diving

The Big Island has excellent diving on the leeward Kona and Kohala Coasts; the best conditions are in spring and summer, but good, calm dive spots can be found year-round. Diving is far more limited on the Hilo side.

Shore dives along the Kona Coast take in steep nearshore drop-offs with lava tubes, caves and diverse marine life. Farther out are about 40 popular boat-dive areas, including an airplane wreck off Keahole Point.

One well-known dive spot is Red Hill, an underwater cinder cone about 10 miles south of Kona. It has beautiful lava formations – including ledges and lots of honeycombed lava tubes nicely lit by streaks of sunlight – as well as coral pinnacles and many brightly colored nudibranchs (types of mollusks).

THE BIG ISLAND WATER SPORTS

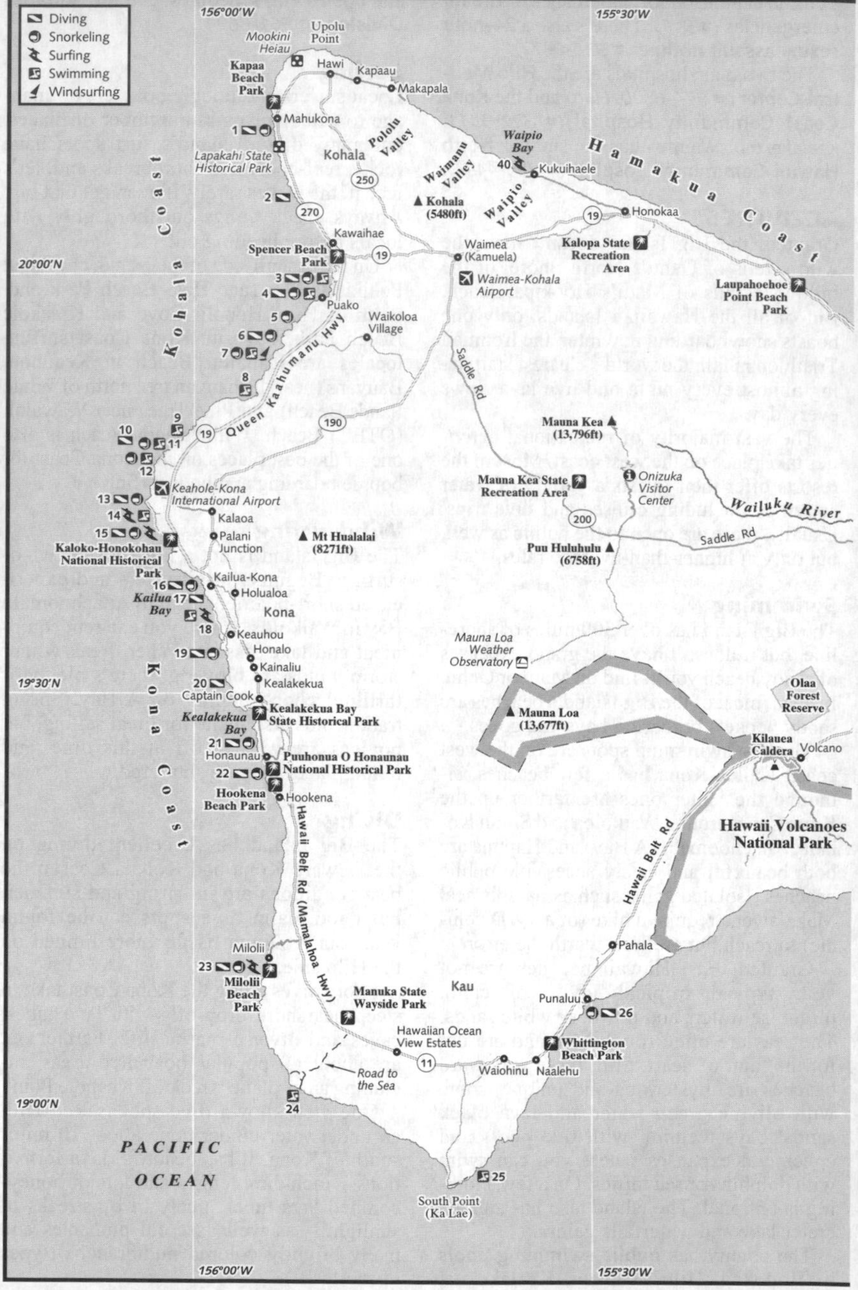

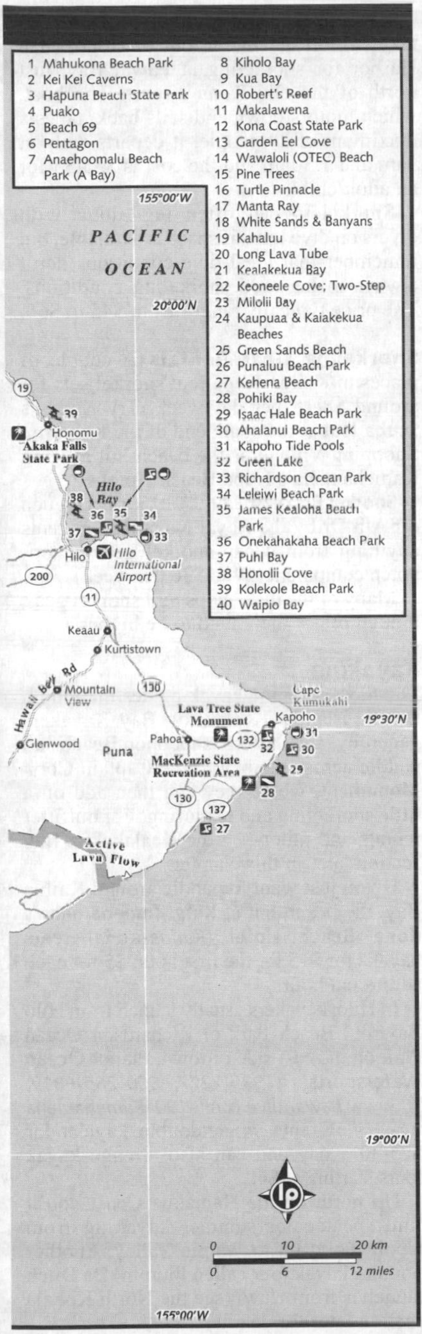

Another good spot is off Kaiwi Point, south of Honokohau Harbor, where sea turtles, large fish and huge eagle rays swim around some respectable drop-offs. Nearby is Suck 'Em Up, a couple of lava tubes you can swim into and let the swell pull you through, like an amusement park ride.

Coral and other marine life flourish in Kealakekua Bay, a protected cove that's calm year-round.

Dive Operations Kona has numerous dive operations. The cost of a two-tank dive averages $75 in the day and $95 at night. Night dives typically focus on viewing manta rays. Introductory dives range from $55 for a one-tank shore dive to around $100 for a two-tank boat dive with several of the dive shops. The larger five-star PADI operations offer certification courses for around $400.

The more established dive operations include the following:

Dive Makai (☎/fax 329-2025, W www.divemakai.com) A personable little operation run by husband-and-wife team Tom Shockley and Lisa Choquette. It has a great word-of-mouth reputation.

Eco-Adventures of Kona (☎ 329-7116, 800-949-3483, W www.eco-adventure.com) 75–5660 Palani Dr, Kailua-Kona. Based at King Kamehameha's Kona Beach Hotel, this is a well-regarded, five-star PADI operation.

Jack's Diving Locker (☎ 329-7585, 800-345-4807, W www.jacksdivinglocker.com) Coconut Grove Marketplace, 75–5819 Alii Dr, Kailua-Kona. This is one of the best outfits for introductory dives, as well as night dives to see the manta rays. Five-star rated by PADI.

Kohala Divers (☎ 882-7774, W www.kohaladivers.com) At the Kawaihae Shopping Center, this is a five-star PADI operation. Guides organize trips up the Kohala Coast.

Kona Coast Divers (☎ 329-8802, W www.konacoastdivers.com) 75–5614 Palani Rd, Kailua-Kona. This one of the largest five-star PADI operations on the island.

Nautilus Dive Center (☎ 935-6939, W www.nautilusdivehilo.com) 382 Kamehameha Ave, Hilo. Nautilus Dive organizes dives and courses in the Hilo area at competitive rates.

Planet Ocean Watersports (☎ 935-7277, 800-265-6819, W www.hawaiidive.com) 100 Kamehameha Ave, Hilo. Planet Ocean offers one-tank shore dives and five-star PADI certification courses.

Sea Paradise Scuba (☎ 322-2500, 800-322-5662, 🅦 www.seaparadise.com) Sea Paradise Scuba is based at Keauhou Bay and tends to head south, often to Red Hill or Kealakekua Bay.

The Kona Aggressor (☎ 329-8182, 800-344-5662, 🅦 www.konaaggressor.com) 74–5588 Pawai Place, Bldg F, Kailua-Kona. This is an 85ft live-aboard dive boat that accommodates up to 10 guests. All-inclusive one-week trips cost $1895 and start each Saturday.

The **Kona Reefers Dive Club** meets on the third Friday of the month and holds shore dives (and sometimes boat dives) open to the public on weekends once a month. Look for announcements in *West Hawaii Today*, or inquire at any of the dive shops.

Snorkeling

Snorkelers will find some sweet spots south of Kailua-Kona. A popular easy-access snorkeling haunt is Kahaluu Beach in Keauhou, which makes a good place for beginners. Two-Step, at the north side of the Place of Refuge, is another terrific drive-up snorkeling spot. There's also beautiful snorkeling in the calm, clear, 30ft-deep waters near Captain Cook's monument at the north end of Kealakekua Bay – however, it takes a hike, horseback ride or boat to reach this area.

Over on the Hilo side, don't miss Puna's Kapoho tide pools.

Snorkeling Cruises The most popular snorkeling cruise is to Kealakekua Bay. Try to book a morning trip, when the ocean is calmer. Prices for the following tours include snorkeling gear, beverages and food.

Fairwind *(☎ 322-2788, 800-677-9461; 🅦 www.fair-wind.com)* makes trips to Kealakekua Bay aboard a 60ft catamaran. The trips leave from Keauhou Bay, which allows for more snorkeling time than other boats. You can choose either a 4½-hour morning tour (adult/child $85/48), or a 3½-hour afternoon tour (adult/child $50/32).

Captain Zodiac *(☎ 329-3199, 800-422-7824; 🅦 www.captainzodiac.com)* offers four-hour tours (adult/child $76/62) aboard bouncy Zodiac rubber rafts, which depart from Honokohau Harbor at 8am and 1pm daily, with pickups possible at the Kailua-Kona and Keauhou piers. Tours include about an hour of snorkeling time at Kealakekua Bay followed by visits to sea caves.

Kamanu Sail and Snorkel *(☎ 329-2021)* takes a 36ft catamaran out of Honokohau Harbor for snorkeling at Pawai Bay, just north of the Old Kona airport. The boat, which motors down and sails back, takes a maximum of 24 people. It departs daily at 9am and 1:30pm and the cost is $55/35 for an adult/child.

Snorkelers can often tag along with divers on dive tours if space is available, but remember that ideal dive conditions don't always make good snorkeling conditions. The price typically ranges from $45 to $65.

Snorkeling Gear Rentals A couple of places in Kailua-Kona rent snorkel sets for around $8/15 per day/week. Try **Morey's Scuba Hut** at the south end of the Kona Inn Shopping Village or the beach hut at King Kamehameha's Kona Beach Hotel.

Snorkel Bob's *(☎ 329-0770)*, with a branch off Alii Dr by the Royal Kona Resort, rents anything from cheap snorkel gear to top-notch equipment ($9 to $36 per week).

Many of the dive shops rent snorkel gear, though prices there tend to be higher.

Kayaking

The most common kayaking destination on the Big Island is Kealakekua Bay. Kayakers generally launch from Napoopoo Beach and paddle across the bay to the Captain Cook Monument, where they can then add on a little snorkeling and exploring. For outfitter rentals and tours, see the Kealakekua Bay section later in this chapter.

If you just want to paddle around Kailua Bay, the beach hut at **King Kamehameha's Kona Beach Hotel** *(Kailua-Kona)* rents kayaks for $15 for the first hour, $5 for each additional hour.

In Hilo, kayakers usually launch from Hilo Bayfront Beach Park or Richardson Ocean Park on the east side of town. **Planet Ocean Watersports** *(☎ 935-7277, 800-265-6819; 🅦 www.hawaiidive.com; 100 Kamehameha Ave, Hilo)* rents single/double kayaks for $25/30 a day and can also arrange kayak tours starting at $40.

Up north on the Hamakua Coast you'll find spectacular summer kayaking from Upolu Point up to Waipio Valley. Another popular kayak tour called Flumin' Da Ditch launches from Hawi (see the North Kohala section later for details).

Fishing

Deep-sea fishing is big on the Kona Coast; this is the world's number-one spot for catching Pacific blue marlin, a spectacular fighting fish with a long swordlike bill. The waters are also rich with *ahi* (yellowfin tuna) and *aku* (bonito or skipjack tuna), swordfish, spearfish and mahimahi. June to August typically sees the biggest hauls for blue marlin, while January to June is the best for striped marlin. Most of the world records for catches of these fish belong to Kona fishers, with at least one marlin weighing 1000lb or more reeled in virtually every year.

You can catch the boats coming in and ogle at the fish weighed at Honokohau Harbor from 11am for the morning charters and around 3pm for the afternoon and full-day charters. Boats flying white flags scored *ahi*, blue flags mean marlin, and inverted flags signify a catch-and-release excursion.

Kona has more than 100 charter fishing boats; many are listed in the *Fishing* freebie that can be picked up at tourist offices and airports. The standard cost for joining an existing party starts at $60 per person for a half-day (four-hour) trip, and your buddies who don't fish can ride along for about $40. Otherwise, if you charter a whole boat, you can take up to six people at a cost of $200 to $425 for half a day, $495 to $750 for a full day, depending upon the boat. Prices include all fishing equipment but not food or drink.

The following centers each book numerous boats: **Charter Services Hawaii** *(☎ 334-1881, 800-567-2650)*; **Fins & Fairways** *(☎ 325-6171; Ⓦ www.fishkona.com)*; **Kona Charter Skippers Association** *(☎ 329-3600, 800-762-7546)*; and **The Charter Desk** *(☎ 329-5735, 888-566-2486)*.

Of the numerous fishing tournaments held in Kona, the granddaddy of them all is the **Hawaiian International Billfish Tournament** *(☎ 329-6155; Ⓦ www.konabillfish.com)*, held in early August and accompanied by a week of festive entertainment.

In addition to ocean fishing, there's a state-maintained public freshwater fishing area at Waiakea in Hilo Bay. Stocked fish include rainbow trout, largemouth and smallmouth bass, channel catfish, tilapia and carp.

No licenses are required for fresh or saltwater fishing, but there are seasons, size limits and other regulations. Contact the **Division of Aquatic Resources** *(in Hilo ☎ 974-6201, in Kona ☎ 327-6226)* for more information.

Hiking

There is excellent hiking all around the Big Island. Some of the best and most varied hikes are inside Hawaii Volcanoes National Park, where trails lead across steaming crater floors, through lush native forests and up to the peak of Mauna Loa.

On the northern tip of the island, steep coastal cliffs and deep valleys reach down from the Kohala Mountains. From the road's end on the northwest side of the range, it's a short hike down to the beach at the bottom of Pololu Valley. On the southeast side, you can take walk down into verdant Waipio Valley or backpack deep into remote Waimanu Valley.

North of Kona, you can hike in from the highway to secluded beaches, or explore portions of ancient footpaths and petroglyph fields. **Na Ala Hele** *(☎ 331-8505; Ⓦ www.hawaiitrails.org)*, a state-sponsored group composed mostly of volunteers, is currently working to reestablish the entire 50-mile historic trail system that once ran between Kailua-Kona and Kawaihae. Mauna Lani Resort and Lapakahi State Park have easy trails, marked with interpretive plaques, around ancient fishponds and through abandoned villages.

South of Kona, a trail leads to the spot where Captain Cook died at Kealakekua Bay. In the center of the island, a strenuous hike leads to the summit of Mauna Kea, while on the slopes below off Saddle Rd, there are short, easy forest trails.

Cycling & Mountain Biking

The Big Island, big on open spaces, long on single tracks and short on tourists, is where mountain biking is fast becoming the hip adventure sport. In addition to established trails, which include the 45-mile Mana Rd loop circling Mauna Kea and the 6½-mile beach trail to Pine Trees on the Kona Coast, there are also miles of 4WD roads to scream through and rocky trails leading to little secret beaches that will surely catch the passing fancy of a cyclist or two.

Several local organizations actively maintain and designate trails, and host weekly rides, including **Big Island Mountain Bike Association** *(BIMBA; ☎ 961-4452;*

(W *www.interpac.net/~mtbike; PO Box 6819, Hilo, HI 96720)* and **People's Advocacy for Trails Hawaii** *(PATH; ☎ 326-9495; W www.hialoha.com/path; PO Box 62, Kailua-Kona, HI 96740)*, which also publishes a free on-line biking guide.

A few operators specialize in cycling tours of the Big Island. **Kona Coast Cycling Tours** *(☎ 327-1133, 877-592-2453; W www.cyclekona.com)* offers half-day ($95) and full-day trips ($145). It also puts together do-it-yourself packages ($18.50) with a detailed map, bibliography and trip log detailing elevation gains and ride distances.

Other well-organized outfitters offering full-fledged vacation packages ($900 to $2300 per person, excluding airfare) that traverse the island include **Backroads** *(☎ 800-462-2848; W www.backroads.com)*, **Bicycle Adventures** *(☎ 800-443-6060; W www.bicycleadventures.com)* and **Odyssey World Cycling Tours** *(☎ 800-433-0528; W www.odyssey2000.com)*. Many of these tour companies offer multisport options that incorporate cycling, hiking, snorkeling and kayaking. Whew.

You can also rent bikes. **Hawaiian Pedals** *(☎ 329-2294; Kona Inn Shopping Village)* rents mountain and hybrid bikes for $20 a day. At affiliated **HP Bike Works** *(☎ 326-2453; W www.hpbikeworks.com; 74-5599 Luhia St)*, higher-end bikes cost $25 a day for front-suspension and road bikes.

Dave's Triathlon Shop *(☎ 329-4522; Kona Square)* rents road bikes for around $25/75 a day/week and bike racks that hold up to three bikes for $5/15. Mountain bikes and hybrids are $15/60 a day/week. The shop also sells and repairs high-caliber equipment.

Horseback Riding

Kings' Trail Rides *(☎ 323-2388; W www.konacowboy.com; Kealakekua)* takes horseback riders down the Captain Cook Trail to Kealakekua Bay for lunch and snorkeling. As the trail is a bit rocky and steep, prior riding experience is preferable. It costs $95.

Kohala Naalapa *(☎ 889-0022; cnr Hwy 250 & Kohala Ranch Rd)* offers 2½-hour trail rides that cross the pastures of Kahua Ranch in Kohala and afford fine views of the coast. The rides depart at 9am and cost $75. A 1½-hour afternoon ride is available in the same area; it leaves at 1pm and costs $55. The Waipio stables are available at ☎ 775-0419.

Paniolo Riding Adventures *(☎ 889-5354; Hwy 250, Kohala)* offers 2½-hour horseback rides for $85 and four-hour rides for $125. Horses are selected according to the rider's experience, but they're all riding horses, not trail horses, and you can canter with the lead wrangler.

Dahana Ranch Roughriders *(☎ 885-0057, 888-399-0057; W www.dahanaranch.com)*, just off the Old Mamalahoa Hwy between Waimea and Honokaa, is owned and operated by native Hawaiians. Horses cross the open range of a working cattle ranch rather than follow trails. Rides are by appointment only; they last 1½ hours ($55) and are open to both novice and experienced riders. Also, with a minimum of four people, a 'city slicker adventure' ($100) can be arranged, during which you'll help drive about 100 head of cattle for around 2½ hours.

For horseback rides in Waipio Valley, see the Waipio section later.

Tennis

From coast to coast, many county parks on the Big Island have municipal tennis courts. These are not sun-cracked concrete and sagging net affairs. Most county courts are well maintained with fresh nets and night lighting. There are even some indoor courts, which may require reservations. Call the **Department of Parks & Recreation** *(☎ 961-8311)* in Hilo for listings of public tennis facilities island-wide.

Many of the larger hotels and resorts allow regular folks (ie, nonguests) to rally on their courts as well. Tennis racket rentals are $3 to $8 per day, with court fees ranging from $5 to $15 per person, per day (with restrictions).

In Kailua-Kona, try the **Royal Kona Resort** *(☎ 329-3111, ext ☎ 7188)* or **Kings Sport & Racquet Club** *(☎ 329-2911; King Kamehameha Kona Beach Hotel)*. And when you're in South Kohala resort land, there's the **Outrigger Waikoloa Beach Hotel Tennis Center** *(☎ 886-6789)*, **Mauna Kea Beach Hotel** *(☎ 882-7222)* and **Orchid at Mauna Lani** *(☎ 885-2000)* courts. In Hilo, head for **Waiakea Racquet Club** *(☎ 961-5499; 400 Hualani St)*.

Most resorts offer private lessons, group lessons and affordable round-robin practice sessions. Rates vary, but expect to drop at least $55 an hour for a private lesson.

Golf

The Big Island has more than a dozen golf courses, including some world-class courses in the Waikoloa area that are laid out on top of lava flows. Environmentalists cringe to see these irrigated oases on the drought-prone leeward coast, however.

The courses that follow are all 18-hole courses, with the exception of the Naniloa Country Club, which has nine holes.

The island's top courses are: **Mauna Kea Golf Course** *(☎ 882-5400)*, near Mauna Kea Beach; **Francis Ii Brown North & South Courses** *(☎ 885-6655; Mauna Lani Resort)*; **Waikoloa Beach & Kings' Courses** *(☎ 886-7778, 877-924-5656)*, both at the Waikoloa Beach Resort; **Hapuna Golf Course** *(☎ 880-3000; Hapuna Beach Prince Hotel)* and the **Four Seasons Hualalai Golf Club** *(☎ 325-8000)*, a PGA-tour course that's open only to members and hotel guests.

Nonguests are charged $185 at the Mauna Lani's Francis Ii courses, $195 at Mauna Kea, $145 at Hapuna and $150 at the two Waikoloa Beach Resort courses. However, you can beat these prices by waiting until midafternoon to tee off – most of the courses then charge at least 50% less. All of the greens fees at these resorts include mandatory carts. Guests staying at the resorts typically get discounts ranging from 20% to 50% off the standard rates.

For the island's most reasonably priced turf, head for the **Hilo Municipal Golf Course** *(☎ 959-7711; 340 Haihai St, Hilo)* which charges $25, plus $15 for a cart. Also try the Volcano and Hilo country clubs.

Skiing & Snowboarding

Skiing in Hawaii is primarily a curiosity event. Snow does fall each winter on the upper slopes of Mauna Kea, though the timing is unpredictable. The ski season usually starts anywhere from early January to late February and can continue for a couple of months.

Skiing Mauna Kea is basically a notch on your novelty belt. The altitude can be tough, and the slopes can have exposed rocks and ice sheets. There are no ski lodges, lifts or trails, although there are some vertical drops of 5000ft.

For a basic run map, click to Ⓦ www.skihawaii.com on-line. Tour operators can provide a full day of skiing or snowboarding for around $250 to $450 per person, or you can simply rent gear for $50. Full rates includes use of ski equipment, transportation to Mauna Kea from Waimea, lunch and a 4WD shuttle service up the mountain after each run.

Racing

The renowned Ironman Triathlon, held in Kailua-Kona each October, combines a 2½-mile ocean swim, 112-mile bike race and 26-mile marathon into one exhaustive endurance race. Some 1500 men and women from 50 countries compete in the Ironman each year, drawing worldwide media coverage. The Ironman usually takes place on the Saturday nearest the full moon, so that late-finishing racers won't have to run along a pitch black highway. It begins and ends near Kailua Pier. Start time is 7am, and top triathletes cross the finish line shortly after 3pm; the other contenders follow throughout the afternoon and evening, with the finish line remaining open to stragglers (kudos!) until midnight. For information on the race, contact **Ironman Triathlon World Championship** *(☎ 329-0063; Ⓦ www.ironmanlive.com; Suite 101, 75-5722 Kuakini Hwy Kailua-Kona, HI 96740)*.

The Kilauea Volcano Wilderness Runs are held at Hawaii Volcanoes National Park in July. There are four separate events: a 10-mile run around the rim of Kilauea Caldera; both a 5-mile run and a 5-mile walk that go down into Kilauea Iki Crater; and a 26-mile marathon through the Kau Desert. For information, contact the **Volcano Art Center** *(☎ 985-8725; Ⓦ www.volcanoartcenter.org; PO Box 106, Hawaii Volcanoes National Park, HI 96718)*.

ORGANIZED TOURS

Roberts Hawaii *(☎ 329-1688, 800-831-5411; Ⓦ www.roberts-hawaii.com)* and **Polynesian Adventure Tours** *(☎ 329-8008, 800-622-3011; Ⓦ www.polyad.com)* offer daylong circle-island bus tours that cost from $55. Both companies pick up passengers at hotels in Waikoloa, Kailua-Kona and Keauhou; the exact time depends on where you're staying, but expect to leave around sunrise and get back around sunset.

Basically, these circle-island tours are a mad dash through Kailua-Kona, Hawaii Volcanoes National Park (focusing on Crater Rim Drive sights), Punaluu black-sand beach, Hilo's Rainbow Falls, the Hamakua Coast and Waimea. Trust us, you'll only get a quick glimpse of most places. More in-depth eight-hour volcano tours (from $45) focus on Hawaii Volcanoes National Park and visit the Kalapana lava flow.

Arnott's Adventure Tours (☎ *969-7097;* 🆆 *www.arnottslodge.com*), at the local Hilo hostel, offers popular backpacker-oriented day tours to Mauna Kea, Waipio Valley and Hawaii Volcanoes National Park. These are geared for active people who prefer to do some hiking and/or swimming during their outings rather than just sitting on a bus. Rates are $48/96 for guests/nonguests.

See the Waipio Valley and Mauna Kea sections later for information about other tours.

Helicopter, Plane & Balloon

The most popular helicopter tours fly over Kilauea Caldera and the live lava flows of the East Rift Zone (ask specifically whether they fly over the active Puu Oo vent or not before booking). Other helicopter tours buzz around the valleys of the Kohala and Hamakua coasts. Expect to pay $120 or more for each 45-minute flight, or up to $350 for a combined two-hour flight.

Tours are canceled during inclement weather, but may fly when it's overcast, which limits visibility. Wait for a sparkling clear day if you can and remember that even if it's sunny in Kona, it may be soupy over Volcano. As it's a competitive market, it's worth checking the free tourist magazines for discount coupons. Call around to compare prices, especially if you're willing to fly standby.

Companies include **Blue Hawaiian Helicopters** (☎ *961-5600, 800-786-2583;* 🆆 *www.bluehawaiian.com*), **Safari Helicopters** (☎ *969-1259, 800-326-3356;* 🆆 *www.safariair.com*), **Sunshine Helicopters** (*in Kona* ☎ *882-1223, in Hilo* ☎ *969-7501, 800-621-3144;* 🆆 *www.sunshinehelicopters.com*) and **Tropical Helicopters** (☎ *961-6810;* 🆆 *www.tropicalhelicopters.com*).

Island Hoppers (☎ *969-2000, 800-538-7590;* 🆆 *www.fly-hawaii.com/above*) has cheaper 50-minute 'flightseeing tours' by small prop plane ($89).

Paradise Balloons (☎ *887-6455;* 🆆 *www.paradiseballoons.com*) offers exhilarating sunrise hot air balloon tours that soar over Mauna Kea, Waimea and the beautiful escarpments of the Kohala Coast (adult/child $240/190).

Whale Watching

Although the best whale watching is off Maui, you can spot whales from the Big Island as well. The season for humpback whales, which are the most popular attraction, usually starts around January and runs to March or April. However, sperm, false killer, dolphin and melon-headed whales – and five dolphin species – can be found in Kona waters year-round.

Marine mammal biologist Dan McSweeney of **Whale Watch** (☎ *322-0028*) leads three-hour whale-watching cruises (adult/child $55/35) leaving from Honokohau Harbor daily. Hydrophones allow passengers to hear whale songs. The tours have a 24-hour nonrefundable cancellation policy.

A couple of the snorkeling tour boats and fishing boats also do whale watches during

Blue whale

humpback season, so it's worth taking a look at listings in the tourist magazines.

Submarine & Glass-Bottom Boats

Atlantis Submarines (☎ *329-6626, 800-548-6262;* W *www.atlantisadventures.net)* gives 45-minute submarine rides that dive down about 100ft in a coral crevice in front of the Royal Kona Resort. The sub has 26 portholes, carries 46 passengers and departs at 10am, 11:30am and 1:30pm. The outing lasts one hour, including the boat ride to and from the sub, and costs $80/42 an adult/child (less for online bookings).

Kailua Bay Charter Company's (☎ *324-1749;* W *www.konaglassbottomboat.com)* 36ft glass-bottom boat is a cheaper option which leaves Kailua Pier at 10am and 2pm daily and circles around Kailua Bay. Trips cost $25/10 per adult/child.

ACCOMMODATIONS

As the island is truly so big, it's worth exploring from a couple of different bases. Most of the island's accommodations are around Kailua-Kona, with the majority of the rooms in condos – though some of these are run like hotels with a front desk and daily rates. If you're planning to stay a week or more, condos are usually a better deal than resort hotels.

If you're on a budget, there are a couple of hostel-style places offering dormitory beds, basic private rooms and sometimes camping. Otherwise, the cheapest digs in the Kona area are *mauka* (inland) of Kailua-Kona at small local hotels in villages such as Holualoa and Captain Cook. The Waikoloa area, which is north of Kailua-Kona, has the island's most expensive beach resorts.

Rainy Hilo doesn't see many visitors, and its lodging choices aren't as numerous as you might expect for a city. But Hilo does have a number of good budget to mid-range options, including a friendly hostel, with two more hostels en route to Hawaii Volcanoes National Park.

In the mountainous uplands, Volcano and Waimea have pleasant B&Bs and a couple of larger places. Other B&Bs and guest houses – from modest bedrooms in family homes to luxurious romantic hideaways – are scattered around the island.

Camping

At first glance, the list of Big Island camping grounds seems to read like some sort of 'Camping Guide to Hell': Laupahoehoe Beach, where a village was washed away in a tidal wave; Halape Beach, where an earthquake sank the shoreline 30ft; and Kamoamoa Beach, which is now buried under a lava flow.

Despite all that, there's really little to worry about. Hawaii's lava isn't the rushing type that sweeps through camping grounds overnight, and tsunami speakers have been set up to warn of approaching tidal waves.

In fact, some of the best and safest camping on the island can be found in Hawaii Volcanoes National Park. See that section later in this chapter for details on the park's two drive-up camping grounds and on trail shelters and tent sites for backcountry hikers. They're all free and rarely full.

State Parks Tent camping is allowed at Kalopa State Recreation Area, which has good facilities and a caretaker, and at MacKenzie State Recreation Area, which is a bit forsaken (many Hawaiians believe powerful spirits dwell in the Mackenzie bluffs, and a camper was murdered there in 1980). Both are free, but permits are required. Primitive shelters (no water) are available at Manuka State Wayside Park in Kau.

There are A-frame shelters at Hapuna Beach and self-contained housekeeping cabins at Kalopa State Recreation Area.

Camping reservations can be made at state park offices on any island. The **Division of State Parks** (☎ *974-6200; Room 204, 75 Aupuni St, PO Box 936, Hilo, HI 96721; open 8am-3:30pm Mon-Fri)* accepts reservations in order of priority – first walk-ins, then requests by mail, then phone requests. The maximum length of stay at any state park is five nights a month.

The cabins and shelters are popular with island families and commonly require booking well in advance. Cancellations do occur, however, and if you're flexible with dates, you might be able to get one without advance reservations.

County Beach Parks The county allows camping at 10 of its beach parks: Kolekole and Laupahoehoe, north of Hilo; Isaac

Hale in Puna; Spencer, Kapaa, Mahukona, Hookena and Milolii, all on the leeward side; and Whittington and Punaluu, both in Kau.

With the exception of Spencer, which is patrolled by a security guard, all of the county parks can be rough and noisy areas, as they're popular among late-night drinkers. Isaac Hale especially isn't recommended for solo women. Remote sites in Kau don't see much traffic, and are sometimes closed during winter storms.

Camping permits are required and can be obtained by mail or in person from the **Department of Parks & Recreation** (*☎ 961-8311; Room 210, 25 Aupuni St, Hilo, HI 96720; open 8:30am-4pm Mon-Fri*), but don't cut it too close to closing time. You can also make reservations by phone through the Hilo office and then pick up the camping permit at **Parks & Recreation** branch offices around the island, including at Kailua-Kona, Captain Cook, Waimea and Naalehu. Of course, the on-line reservation system at **W** www.ehawaii.org is convenient.

Daily camping fees are $5 for adults, $2 for teens and $1 for children 12 and under. Camping is allowed for up to two weeks in each park, except between June and August when it's limited to one week only.

Only Laupahoehoe and Spencer have drinking water. Some county parks have catchment water that can be treated for drinking, while others have brackish water that is unsuitable for drinking but can be used for showers.

Camping Supplies The selection at **Pacific Rent-All** (*☎ 935-2974; 1080 Kilauea Ave, Hilo; open 7am-5pm Mon-Sat, 9am-11am Sun*) is limited and is generally geared more for drive-up camping than backcountry use. However, it rents three-person tents ($23/46 per day/week) and lightweight sleeping bags ($8/24). It also rents Coleman stoves, lanterns, water jugs and other supplies.

Hilo Surplus Store (*☎ 935-6398; 148 Mamo St, Hilo; open 8am-5pm Mon-Sat*) sells camping supplies including rain gear, stoves, sleeping bags, tents and backpacks.

You could also try one of the discount mega-stores, such as Kmart, Wal-Mart and Costco in Kailua-Kona or Wal-Mart and Sears in Hilo.

ENTERTAINMENT

Make no mistake, the Big Island is hurting for nightlife. With so little action, locals often make their own fun. This mostly means raucous raves and full moon parties, a lively DJ scene and decent Mardi Gras and Halloween celebrations. Oftentimes these happenings are spontaneous and with no fixed address, so ask around.

For the latest popular entertainment listings, check *West Hawaii Today,* especially the Friday edition. The biggest after-dark scene centers on the hotels in the Kona and Waikoloa areas. There's plenty of Hawaiian entertainment, including contemporary Hawaiian music, slack-key guitar performances, luaus and hula shows, some of it free. Occasionally these resorts have nightclubs and put on gigs by top-name musicians.

On the opposite side of the island, Hilo and Honokaa have surprisingly sophisticated film and theater communities. In the hinterlands, cock fights (called chicken fights) are technically illegal, but draw crowds of spectators anyway. Big Island rodeos began here near Waimea before they even existed over on the mainland; check **W** www.rodeohawaii.com for details.

SHOPPING

Kona coffee and macadamia nuts are the Big Island's most popular souvenirs. However, 'Kona blend' is only 10% Kona coffee, so if you want the real thing, make sure what you pick up is labeled 100%. Prices change with the market, but as Kona coffee is one of the more expensive gourmet beans, expect prices from $15 a pound.

Lauhala, which are the leaves of the pandanus tree, were once woven into sleeping mats and any manner of household items by ancient Hawaiians; today, master weavers make them into purses, place mats, hats and baskets.

Quite a few local potters are influenced by Japanese styles and aesthetics, and produce fine *raku* work (pottery).

Shops selling local arts and crafts are certainly plentiful. The most notable ones include the Volcano Art Center in Hawaii Volcanoes National Park and the handful of galleries in the hillside village of Holualoa. Drums, nose flutes, gourd rattles as well as other traditional hula instruments are sold in music stores island-wide.

GETTING THERE & AWAY

Air

Most visitors fly into Honolulu first, then connect through to Kona (near Kailua-Kona) or Hilo airport. While there are frequent flights into both, Kona is the busier of the two airports.

Kona gets the bulk of mainland and international flights, as flying directly to Hilo can be prohibitively expensive. If your heart's set on Hilo, it might be cheaper to fly to Kona and travel overland.

Hawaiian Airlines *(☎ 800-882-8811)* and **Aloha Airlines** *(☎ 935-5771)* connect both Big Island airports with the other Hawaiian Islands. **Island Air** *(☎ 800-652-6541)* offers one flight a day from Kona and three flights a day from Hilo to Kapalua/West Maui airport. Other flights go to Honolulu.

For details on international flights, commuter and charter airlines, interisland flight coupons and air passes, see the Getting Around chapter.

Keahole-Kona Airport Kona's international airport *(KOA; ☎ 329-3423)* is on Hwy 19, about 7 miles north of Kailua-Kona. For a relatively busy airport, it's surprisingly casual, and it's all open-air, imparting a tropical feel. There are no jetways and you disembark directly onto the tarmac.

The airport has a visitor information booth, lei stand, restaurant, gift shops, taxi queue, car rental booths and a newsstand.

Hilo Airport Hilo airport *(ITO; ☎ 934-5840/5838)* is off Hwy 11, just under 1 mile south of the Hwy 11 and Hwy 19 intersection. It has the same visitor services as the Keahole-Kona airport.

> **Lava Wasteland?**
>
> Flying into Kona airport can be a shock if you're expecting to see tropical greenery and waving palm trees. Instead, the view from the airplane looks more like a black lava wasteland, as if the island had been paved over in asphalt. Don't panic! This is but one face of the Big Island – and even here, if you look closer, you can catch a glimpse of some fine secluded white-sand beaches squeezed between the lava and the turquoise waters.

Waimea-Kohala Airport The Waimea airport (MUE), off Hwy 190, 1¾ miles south of the intersection of Hwy 19, is mainly used by private planes. The small commuter airline Pacific Wings flies here.

GETTING AROUND

To/From the Airport

At the Hilo and Kona airports, taxis can be picked up curbside, and car rental booths line the road outside the arrival areas. At Waimea-Kohala airport, travelers should call for a taxi in advance. The approximate fare from Kona airport to Kailua-Kona is $20; to Waikoloa it's about $40. From Hilo airport, expect to pay around $15 into downtown Hilo.

Shuttle bus services from the Kona airport pop up from time to time, but they typically charge nearly as much as a taxi. **Speedi Shuttle** *(☎ 329-5433; W www.speedishuttle.com)* charges $17.50 to Kailua-Kona, $30 to the Waikoloa resorts.

Bus

A Big Island bus odyssey just isn't practical, but with a little planning you can get yourself between major towns and attractions.

Hele-On *(☎ 961-8744; office open 7:45am-4:30pm Mon-Fri)*, the county public bus, offers limited island-wide service, but only Monday to Friday. Schedules are available at the Big Island Tourist Bureau and the information kiosk at Hilo's Mooheau bus terminal.

All buses originate from Mooheau terminal, unless otherwise noted.

No 31 Honokaa $3.75, 1¼ hours, six departures to Honokaa, stopping in Laupahoehoe and Paauilo; the first three departures leave from the parking lot just east of the terminal

No 16 Kailua-Kona $6, three hours, one departure at 1:30pm; this bus goes north, stopping all along the Hamakua Coast, and at Waimea's Parker Ranch Center, before reaching the Lanihau Center in Kona; continues to Captain Cook and Honaunau

No 23 Kau $5.25, 2½ hours, one departure at 2:40pm, to Ocean View, stopping in Kurtistown, Volcano, Hawaii Volcanoes National Park, Punaluu, Naalehu and Waiohinu

No 9 Pahoa $2.25, one hour, departures at 2:40pm and 4:45pm, to Pahoa via Keaau

North Kohala-Waikoloa $2.25, 70 minutes, departs Kapaau at 6:20am, goes via Hawi and Mauna Kea–Hapuna–Mauna Lani resorts to the Outrigger and Hilton Waikoloa resorts; northbound bus leaves Waikoloa at 4:15pm

Drivers accept only the exact fare. You can buy a sheet of 10 bus tickets for $6.75; each ticket is valid for 75¢ in fare, so you get a little discount this way and don't have to carry a lot of change. Luggage and backpacks cost $1 extra per piece.

For information on shuttle services around Kailua-Kona and to Keauhou, see Getting Around in the Kailua-Kona section later.

Car & Motorcycle

The following companies have car rental booths at both the Kona and Hilo airports.

Alamo (Kona ☎ 329-8896, Hilo ☎ 961-3343)
Avis (Kona ☎ 327-3000, Hilo ☎ 935-1290)
Budget (Kona ☎ 329-8511, Hilo ☎ 935-6878)
Dollar (Kona ☎ 329-2744, Hilo ☎ 961-6059)
Hertz (Kona ☎ 329-3566, Hilo ☎ 935-2896)
National (Kona ☎ 329-1674, Hilo ☎ 935-0891)
Thrifty (Kona ☎ 329-1339, Hilo ☎ 961-6698)

For more information on the national chains, including toll-free numbers and websites, see the Getting Around chapter.

Harper Car & Truck Rentals *(☎ 969-1478, 800-852-9993; W www.harpershawaii.com; 456 Kalanianaole Ave, Hilo • Kona airport)* is the local car rental agency. Only Harper puts no restrictions on going to Mauna Kea's summit, or most anywhere else on the island, with the exception of Waipio Valley and Green Sands Beach, which are off-limits. Isuzu Troopers, Toyota 4-Runners and Jeep Cherokees all cost $111/665 per day/week. Note that even if you purchase the optional CDW ($20), $5000 is deductible should you damage the vehicle. Motorhome rentals are also available.

Road Distances & Times

destination (from Hilo)	distance (miles)	time (hours)
Hawi	86	2¼
Honokaa	40	1
Kailua-Kona	92	2½
Naalehu	64	1¾
Pahoa	16	½
Volcanoes NP	28	¾
Waikoloa	80	2¼
Waimea	54	1½
Waipio Lookout	50	1¼

destination (from Kailua-Kona)	distance (miles)	time (hours)
Hawi	51	1¼
Hilo	92	2½
Honokaa	61	1½
Naalehu	60	1½
Pahoa	108	3
Volcanoes NP	98	2½
Waikoloa	18	¾
Waimea	43	1
Waipio Lookout	70	1¾

Taxi

The taxi flag-down fee is $2, and it costs $2 per mile after that.

In Hilo, call **Marshall's Taxi** *(☎ 936-2654)* or **Percy's Taxi** *(☎ 969-7060)*. Try **Paradise Taxi & Tours** *(☎ 329-1234)* or **Elsa Taxi** *(☎ 887-6446)* in Kona.

Bicycle

It's possible to cycle around the Big Island, but both sides of the island and their climactic extremes can present challenges. The windward Hilo side is windy and wet, while the western Kona and Kohala coasts seesaw between hot and hellishly hot.

What's more, the terrain is almost never flat, with quick, steep elevation gains that will stretch even stalwart peddlers. There are also very few highway bicycle lanes. However, determined cyclists *do* successfully traverse the island.

Bike shops that rent bicycles also rent safety equipment and car racks, and handle repairs and sales. As Kona is the center of activity for the Ironman Triathlon, a few regional bike shops sell and repair high-caliber equipment; there are also a few worthy outfits in Hilo.

For more on cycling and mountain biking, see the Activities section earlier in this chapter.

Kona

Kona literally means 'leeward.' The Kona Coast refers to the dry, sunny west coast of the Big Island. However, to make matters a little more confusing, the name Kona is also used to refer to Kailua, the largest town on the Kona Coast. The town's name is compounded as Kailua-Kona by the post office and other officialdom to avoid confusion with Kailua on Oahu.

The weather here gives tourists few headaches. It's so consistent on this side of the island that the local paper commonly alternates two forecasts: 'Sunny morning. Afternoon clouds with upslope showers' or 'Sunny morning. Cloudy afternoon with showers over the slopes.' These showers rarely touch the coastline below, however, so Kona is a solid sunshine destination year-round.

KAILUA-KONA

In the 19th century, Kailua-Kona (population 9870) was a favorite retreat for Hawaiian royalty. These days, it's the largest vacation spot on the Big Island. Azure skies and sun, plentiful lodgings, and its central location for exploring the entire Kona Coast are all drawcards.

The setting on the leeward side of Mt Hualalai is pretty. Ancient Hawaiian and early missionary-era historic sites are scattered in and around town. Even though the character is stifled by trinket shops and minimalls, it's still an entertaining place to hang out.

Most of Kailua-Kona's condos are lined up along Alii Dr, the 5-mile coastal road that runs from the town center at Kailua Bay south to Keauhou. This strip sees a lot of power-walkers and joggers, particularly in the early morning hours, but the hottest activity occurs in October when the road serves as the finish line of the world-famous Ironman Triathlon.

Kailua-Kona's biggest disappointment is the lack of fabulous beaches. There are a few swimming, snorkeling and surfing spots, but the island's best beaches are further north up the coast.

Information

Tourist Offices While numerous 'tourist information' booths dot Alii Dr, they primarily house aggressive salespeople who try to lure visitors into listening to timeshare pitches. For useful tourist information, head to concierge and activities desks at the larger hotels in Kailua-Kona.

Money Bank of Hawaii and First Hawaiian Bank both have branches at Lanihau Center on Palani Rd. You'll find ATMs at the banks and at numerous places around town, including the Kona Inn Shopping Village on Alii Dr.

Post & Communications The **post office** *(☎ 331-8307; Lanihau Center, Palani Rd; open 8:30am-4:30pm Mon-Fri, 9:30am-1:30pm Sat)* holds general delivery mail for 10 days.

Zac's Business Center *(☎ 329-0006; North Kona Shopping Center, Kuakini Rd; open 8am-7pm Mon-Fri, 9am-6pm Sat, 10am-4pm Sun)* offers Internet access for $2.75 per 15 minutes, $8 per hour.

Travel Agencies Discounted tickets for interisland travel can be purchased from **Cut Rate Tickets** *(☎ 326-2300; Kona Coast Shopping Center, Palani Rd; open 7am-7pm Mon-Fri, 9am-5pm Sat, 9am-2pm Sun)*.

Bookstores A well-stocked central bookstore, **Middle Earth Bookshoppe** *(☎ 329-2123; Kona Plaza, Alii Dr; open 9am-9pm Mon-Sat, 9am-6pm Sun)* has excellent Hawaiiana and travel sections.

Borders Book & Music Café *(☎ 331-1668, Hwy 19; open 9am-9pm Sun-Thur, 9am-10pm Fri & Sat)* is the area's largest bookseller and also carries a wide selection of US and foreign newspapers.

Bargain Books *(☎ 326-7790; North Kona Shopping Center; open Mon-Sat 10am-9pm, Sun 10am-6pm)* buys, sells and trades new and used books.

Libraries Kona's modern **public library** *(☎ 327-4327; Hualalai Rd; open 10am-8pm Tues, 9am-6pm Wed & Thur, 11am-5pm Fri, 9am-5pm Sat)* sells used paperback books for just 25¢. Advance sign-up for Internet access is required.

Photography Cameras and film can be purchased from **Longs Drugs** *(☎ 261-3030; Lanihau Center, Palani Rd)*, which also offers same-day print processing.

Laundry Most condos have on-site laundry facilities. Coin laundries include **Hele Mai Laundromat** *(☎ 329-3494; North Kona Shopping Center; open 6am-10pm daily)*.

King Kamehameha's Kona Beach Hotel

Kamakahonu, the beach at the north end of Kailua Bay, was the site of the royal

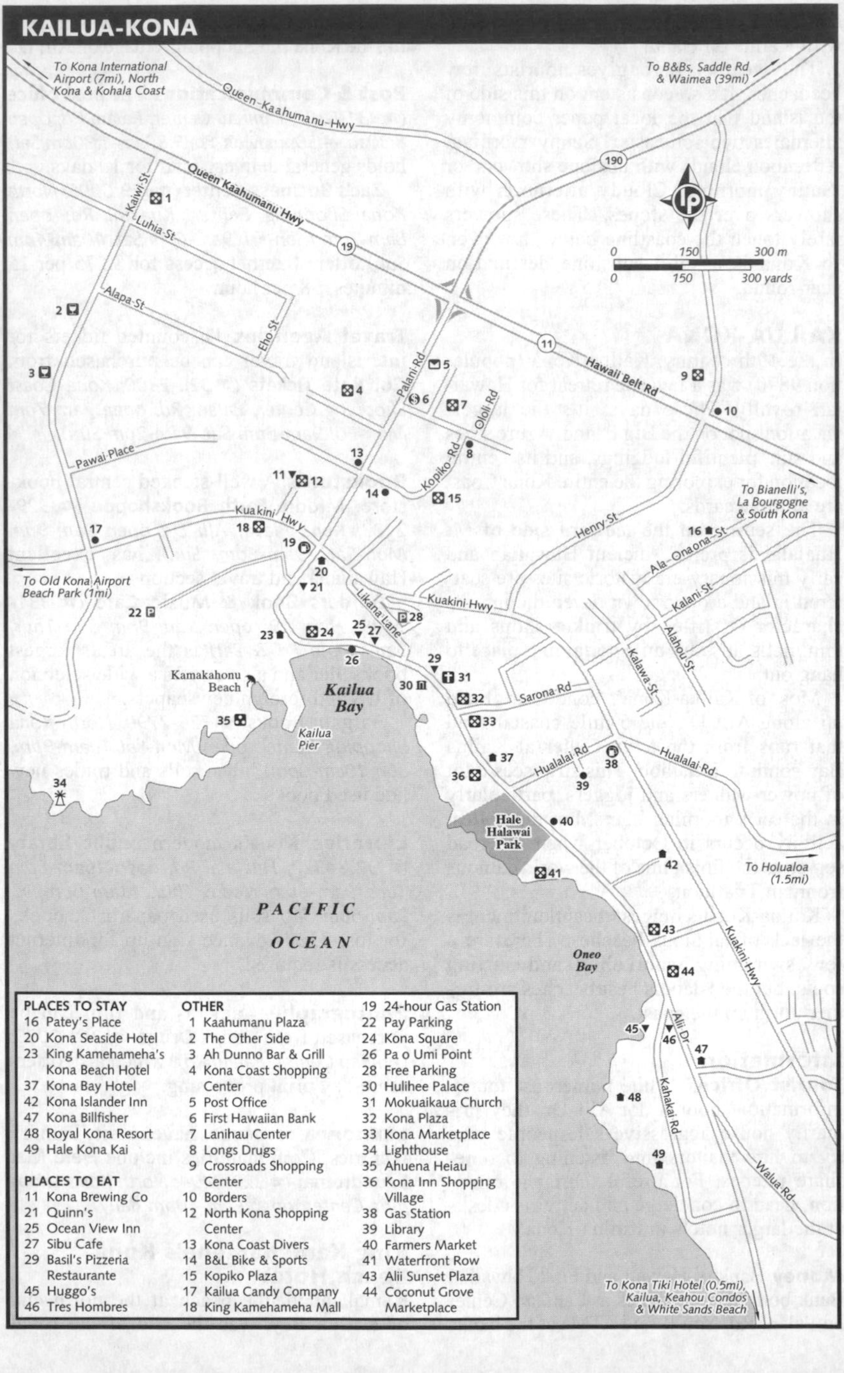
KAILUA-KONA
To Kona International Airport (7mi), North Kona & Kohala Coast
To B&Bs, Saddle Rd & Waimea (39mi)
Queen-Kaahumanu-Hwy
Queen Kaahumanu Hwy
190
19
11
Hawaii Belt Rd
0 150 300 m
0 150 300 yards
Kaiwi-St
Luhia-St
Alapa-St
Eho St
Palani-Rd
Ololi Rd
Kopiko-Rd
Pawai Place
Kuakini Hwy
Likana Lane
Henry-St
Ala-Onaona-St
Kalani St
Alahou St
Kalawa St
Sarona Rd
Hualalai Rd
Alii Dr
Kahakai Rd
Walua Rd
To Bianelli's, La Bourgogne & South Kona
To Old Kona Airport Beach Park (1mi)
To Holualoa (1.5mi)
To Kona Tiki Hotel (0.5mi), Kailua, Keahou Condos & White Sands Beach
Kamakahonu Beach
Kailua Bay
Kailua Pier
Hale Halawai Park
PACIFIC OCEAN
Oneo Bay
PLACES TO STAY
16 Patey's Place
20 Kona Seaside Hotel
23 King Kamehameha's Kona Beach Hotel
37 Kona Bay Hotel
42 Kona Islander Inn
47 Kona Billfisher
48 Royal Kona Resort
49 Hale Kona Kai
PLACES TO EAT
11 Kona Brewing Co
21 Quinn's
25 Ocean View Inn
27 Sibu Cafe
29 Basil's Pizzeria Restaurante
45 Huggo's
46 Tres Hombres
OTHER
1 Kaahumanu Plaza
2 The Other Side
3 Ah Dunno Bar & Grill
4 Kona Coast Shopping Center
5 Post Office
6 First Hawaiian Bank
7 Lanihau Center
8 Longs Drugs
9 Crossroads Shopping Center
10 Borders
12 North Kona Shopping Center
13 Kona Coast Divers
14 B&L Bike & Sports
15 Kopiko Plaza
17 Kailua Candy Company
18 King Kamehameha Mall
19 24-hour Gas Station
22 Pay Parking
24 Kona Square
26 Pa o Umi Point
28 Free Parking
30 Hulihee Palace
31 Mokuaikaua Church
32 Kona Plaza
33 Kona Marketplace
34 Lighthouse
35 Ahuena Heiau
36 Kona Inn Shopping Village
38 Gas Station
39 Library
40 Farmers Market
41 Waterfront Row
43 Alii Sunset Plaza
44 Coconut Grove Marketplace

residence of Kamehameha the Great. Shortly after his death here in 1819, Kamehameha's successors came to Kamakahonu and ended the traditional *kapu* system, sounding a death knell for the old religion.

The ancient sites are now part of the grounds of King Kamehameha's Kona Beach Hotel. A few thatched structures along with carved wooden *kii* (deity images) have been reconstructed above the old stone temple.

The 'beachlet' in front of the hotel is the only downtown swimming spot. Ahuena Heiau, which was once a place of human sacrifice, juts out into the cove and acts as a breakwater, offering protection for swimmers. The waters at Kamakahonu (Eye of the Turtle) are the calmest in Kailua Bay. The hotel's beach hut rents snorkels, kayaks, beach chairs and umbrellas.

Be sure to take a stroll through the sprawling lobby of the hotel, which is full of fascinating displays on various aspects of Hawaiian culture. Ask at the activity desk in the lobby for an in-depth brochure.

The hotel also offers free guided historical tours that visit the indoor displays and take in the hotel's historic grounds. Check at the activity desk for the latest schedule.

Kailua Pier

Kailua Bay was once a major cattle shipping area. Cattle driven down from hillside ranches were stampeded into the water and forced to swim out to waiting steamers, where they were hoisted aboard by sling and shipped to Honolulu slaughterhouses. Kailua Pier was built in 1915.

The pier was long the center of sports fishing on Hawaii, but it simply got too crowded to handle all the action. Now Kona's charter fishing boats use the larger Honokohau Harbor north of town. Kailua Pier is mainly used by dive boats and cruise ship tenders, though its hoist and scales are still put to use for weigh-ins during billfish tournaments.

The tiny patch of sandy beach on the east side of the pier is known as **Kaiakeakua** (Sea of the Gods). It once served as Kamehameha's canoe landing.

Mokuaikaua Church

On April 4, 1820, Hawaii's first Christian missionaries landed at Kailua Bay, stepping out onto a rock that is now one of the footings for the Kailua Pier.

When the missionaries landed, they were unaware that Hawaii's old religion had been abolished on this same spot just a few months before. Their timing couldn't have been more auspicious. Given a favorable reception by Kamehameha's successors, the missionaries established Hawaii's first Christian church on Kailua Bay, a few minutes' walk from Kamehameha's ancient *heiau* and house site.

In 1836, this temporary church was replaced by Mokuaikaua Church *(☎ 329-0655; Alii Dr; admission free)*, a handsome building with walls of lava rock held together by a mortar of sand and coral lime. The posts and beams, hewn with stone adzes and smoothed down with chunks of coral, are made from strong termite-resistant ohia wood, and the pews and pulpit are made of koa, a native hardwood. The steeple tops out at 112ft, making the church the tallest structure in Kailua.

From 9am to 4pm Monday to Saturday, an interpreter is often on site to talk about the church's history. An 8ft model of the brig *Thaddeus*, the ship that brought those first Congregational missionaries to Hawaii, is also on display.

Hulihee Palace

Governor 'John Adams' Kuakini built this modest two-story house in 1838 as his private residence *(☎ 329-1877; 75-5718 Alii Dr; adult/child $5/1; open 9am-4pm Mon-Fri, 10am-4pm Sat & Sun)*. He was also the contractor for Mokuaikaua Church, and both buildings shared the same lava-rock construction. The palace was plastered over inside and out by King Kalakaua in 1885, who had taken to a more polished style after his travels abroad. The palace belonged to a succession of royal owners until the early 1900s, when it was abandoned and fell into disrepair. The Daughters of Hawaii, a group founded in 1903 by daughters of missionaries, took it over and now operate the property as a museum.

The palace is furnished with antiques, many picked up on royal jaunts to Europe. Some of the more Hawaiian pieces include a table inlaid with 25 kinds of native Hawaiian woods, some of which are now extinct, and a number of Kamehameha the Great's personal war spears.

Princess Ruth Keelikolani, who owned the palace in the mid-19th century, preferred to live outside on the palace grounds. After her death, the wooden posts that had supported her grass hut were carved with designs of taro, leis and pineapples and used as posts in one of the beds upstairs.

There's no charge to take a peek at the **fishpond** behind the palace. Although no longer stocked, the pond holds a few colorful tropical fish. Curiously, it also once served as a Queen's Bath and a canoe landing.

Admission includes a 40-minute tour, which provides interesting anecdotes about past royal occupants. The **Kona Historical Society** (*☎ 323-3222; tours $15*), based in Kealakekua, includes palace admission with its historic 75-minute Kailua Village tours at 9:30am and 1:30pm Tuesday and Friday.

Kona Brewing Company

In a warehouse adjacent to the North Kona Shopping Center, the **Kona Brewing Company** (*☎ 334-2739; 75-5629 Kuakini Hwy; open 11am-10pm Mon-Thur, 11am-midnight Fri & Sat, 1pm-9pm Sun*) is the Big Island's first microbrewery. Started in 1994 by a father and son from Oregon, this little family-run operation now ships its brew to the Neighbor Islands. The brewery's mainstay, Pacific Golden Ale, blends traditional pale and honey malts. If you prefer a taste of the islands, try the Lilikoi Wheat, which has a light, passion-fruit accent. These handcrafted ales can be sampled at the conclusion of free brewery tours – conducted at 10:30am and 3pm Monday to Friday. Pints are also served at the brewery's outdoor restaurant.

Old Kona Airport Beach Park

After 1970 the old Kona airport was turned into a state recreation area and beach park. It's easy to overlook, but worth visiting. The beach is much larger than Kailua-Kona beaches and far more peaceful, offering soothing ocean sounds rather than urban traffic noise. It's about 1 mile north of downtown, at the end of the Kuakini Hwy.

The old runway skirts a long sandy beach, but lava rocks run the length of the beach between the sand and the ocean. Although this makes for poor swimming conditions, it's ideal for fishing and exploring tide pools. At low tide, the rocks reveal an intriguing system of little aquarium-like pockets holding tiny sea urchins, crabs and bits of coral. A couple of breaks in the lava,

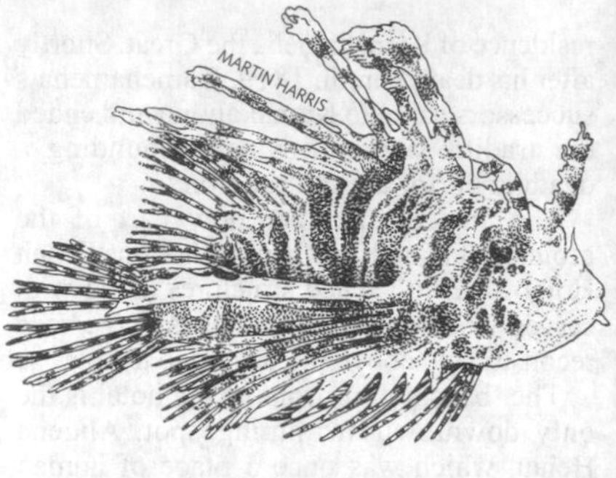

Lionfish

including one in front of the first picnic area, allow entry into the water.

Little **Garden Eel Cove**, which can be reached by a short walk from the north end of the beach, is a good area for scuba divers and confident snorkelers. The reef fish are large and plentiful, and a steep coral wall in deeper waters harbors big moray eels and a wide variety of other sea creatures, such as lionfish and cowries.

When the surf's up, local surfers favor the offshore break. In high surf, though, it's too rough for other water activities.

While this local park is popular with families and picnickers, it's much too big to ever feel crowded. Facilities include rest rooms, showers and covered picnic tables on a lawn dotted with beach heliotrope and short coconut palms. The Kailua-Kona end of the park contains a gym, soccer and softball fields, four outdoor lighted tennis courts and a horseshoe pit. Next to the old runway is a 1-mile-long loop that locals use as a track.

White Sands Beach Park

Though it's known as White Sands, Magic Sands and Disappearing Sands, it's all the same beach, found midway between Kailua-Kona and Keauhou. In winter when the surf is high, the sand can disappear literally overnight, leaving only rocks on the shore. But then the sand magically returns, resulting in a fine white-sand beach.

This is a very popular bodysurfing spot when the rocks aren't exposed. Facilities include bathrooms, showers, picnic tables and a volleyball court. Local kids scramble around the sands and a lifeguard is on duty. Like Kahaluu and many other Kona beaches, it's right next to busy Alii Dr.

THE BIG ISLAND

Special Events

The **Kona Brewers Festival** in early March features more than 50 types of beer. The **Kona Coffee Cultural Festival** fetes Kona's most important industry in early November, with dozens of events from tastings to farm tours.

See also the Special Events section in the Facts for the Visitor chapter.

Places to Stay

Hostel Painted with aquatic murals, friendly **Patey's Place** *(☎ 326-7018, fax 326-7640; ⓔ patey@mail.gte.net; 75-195 Ala-Ona Ona St; dorm beds $19.50, beds in semiprivate rooms $27.50, singles/doubles $35/46; office open 8am-noon & 4pm-10pm)* is the cheapest place to stay in town. It's in a rather congested residential neighborhood a 10-minute walk from the town center. Rooms are worn, but clean. All have ceiling fans, shared baths and shared kitchen access. Amenities include a laundry, bike rental and Internet access. An airport shuttle is also available ($10).

B&Bs Though they lack ocean views, Kona's B&Bs have amiable hosts.

Kiwi Gardens *(☎ 326-1559, fax 329-6618; ⓦ www.kiwigardens.com; 74-4920 Kiwi St; rooms with shared bath $85, master suite $95)* is 3 miles northeast of Kailua-Kona center. Each room in this contemporary home has a fridge. There's a shared guest phone and a large common area with '50s decor, complete with vintage soda fountain and jukebox. Breakfast includes seasonal fruits from the 80 trees in the yard, where guests may spot doves and quail.

Nancy's Hideaway *(☎/fax 325-3132, 866-325-3132; ⓦ www.nancyshideaway.com; 73-1530 Uanani Pl; studio/1-bedroom cottage $95/125)* is rurally set in Kona's up-country, about 6 miles from downtown. Free-standing, immaculate cottages have a private lanai, phones, TVs, VCRs, and are stocked with continental breakfast fixings. Nancy happily dispenses insider advice and she preserves the serenity by discouraging children under 13.

Hotels Most of Kona's hotel options are more convenient than charming.

Kona Tiki Hotel *(☎ 329-1425, fax 327-9402; 75-5968 Alii Dr; rooms $60-65, with kitchenettes $70, plus 3rd person $8)*, a vintage three-story complex squeezed onto a narrow jut of land between the ocean and the road, is a sweet deal. Most of the 15 pleasant rooms have a queen-size and twin bed, and all have a fridge and a breezy oceanfront lanai (the heavenly sound of the surf drowns out traffic noise). Along with personable service, amenities include a small seaside pool, a barbecue grill and complimentary continental breakfast. The hotel is perennially popular with return visitors and books up early. Credit cards are not accepted.

Uncle Billy's **Kona Bay Hotel** *(☎ 329-1393, 800-367-5102, fax 935-7903; ⓔ unclebillys@aloha.net; 75-5739 Alii Dr; rooms $90-100)* is for those who want to be right in the center of town. The older cinder-block buildings lack charm, but the place is relatively inexpensive and the rooms have TV, air-con, refrigerators and phones. There's a pool.

Kona Seaside Hotel *(☎ 329-2455, 800-560-5558, fax 329-6157; ⓦ www.sand-seaside.com; 75-5646 Palani Rd; rooms in old wing $98, in new wing $110-120)*, which attracts an older clientele, has two wings. One's a modern six-story building with private lanai, the older rear poolside wing is simpler and has walls that carry sound, making these rooms less of a good deal. Try booking within Hawaii for a cheaper rate; you don't have to be a Hawaii resident to qualify. Check the Sunday Honolulu newspaper for special packages, such as a free rental car with two nights' stay. For the best deals, call the Honolulu booking desk *(☎ 737 5800)*.

King Kamehameha's Kona Beach Hotel *(☎ 329-2911, 800-367 6060, fax 329-4602; ⓦ www.konabeachhotel.com; 75-5660 Palani Rd; rooms $135-200)*, at Kailua Bay, is on the only beach in town. Located on the site of King Kamehameha's former residence, each of its 460 comfortable rooms possesses two double beds, private lanai, air-con, refrigerator, TV and phone. Other amenities include a pool, lighted tennis courts and free guest parking.

Royal Kona Resort *(☎ 329 3111, 800-774-5662, fax 329-7230; ⓦ www.royalkona.com; 75-5852 Alii Dr; rooms $160-260)*, a former Hilton, has an oceanfront location on the edge of town. Rooms spread across three towers were recently upgraded, and have the expected amenities. Discount deals are available, including a room and rental car package for $125 per day. There's no sandy beach, but guests enjoy a swimming pool, natural saltwater pool and tennis courts. At the waterfront restaurant, the views are far better than the food.

Condos In Kona, condos outnumber hotels many times over. Condos tend to be cheaper than hotels if you're staying awhile and most condo units have fully equipped kitchens. Reservations are recommended in the high season.

Many of Kona's condominiums can be booked through more than one rental agency, and most units are handled by at least one of the following agencies. It's worth shopping around before booking.

Hawaii Resort Management (☎ 329-9393, 800-622-5348, fax 326-4137, W www.konahawaii.com) Suite 105C, 75–5776 Kuakini Hwy
Knutson & Associates (☎ 329-6311, 800-800-6202, fax 326-2178, W www.konahawaiirentals.com) Suite 8, 75–6082 Alii Dr
SunQuest Vacations & Property Management Hawaii (☎ 329-6488, 800-367-5168, Canada ☎ 800-800-5662, fax 329-5480, W www.sunquest-hawaii.com) 77–6435 Kuakini Hwy
Triad Management (☎ 329-6402, 800-345-2823, fax 326-2401) Suite 221, Orchid Bldg, 75–5995 Pottery Terrace, Kuakini Hwy

Most rental agents typically require a three-day minimum stay, but Triad Management requires a five-day minimum stay in the low season and a seven-day minimum in the high season.

Generally speaking, the weekly rate is six times the daily rate and the monthly rate is three times the weekly. However, in the high season, if business is brisk, many places offer only the daily rate, while in the off-season months of April, May and September you might be able to negotiate an even better deal.

If you wait until you arrive in Kona to look for a place, you can sometimes find a good deal under 'Vacation Rentals' in the classified ads of **West Hawaii Today** (*W www.westhawaiitoday.com*). However, this is risky during the high season, when many of the better-value places book up well in advance.

All condos listed here have swimming pools, unless otherwise noted.

Budget Inexpensive condos are plentiful in Kona. Some even have ocean views.

Kona Islander Inn (*☎ 329-3333, 800-622-5348; e kona@konahawaii.com; 75-5776 Kuakini Hwy; high season rates $70-80, low season $35-60*) is an older development downtown. Hawaii Resort Management handles most of the 144 units, and its office is conveniently located at the side of the lobby. Ground-floor units tend to be musty, but others are fixed up nicely. Furnishings vary, but most units have TVs, air-con, kitchenettes, and phones with free local calls. Some units also have VCRs. The complex draws a young, lively crowd and guests often gather around the pool to cook dinner on the barbecue. Cheap rates make it easier to cope with the severely inadequate parking.

Kona Billfisher (*☎ 329-9277; e bilfish@gte.net; 75-5841 Alii Dr; 1-bedroom units $85, 2-bedroom units $110*) tends to have more consistent decor and better upkeep than other moderately priced complexes. The 65 well-outfitted units boast queen-size sofa beds, king-size beds in the bedrooms, both ceiling fans and air-con, plus recently renovated kitchens and lanai. Telephone service is $5 extra. Amenities include laundry, barbecue grills and table tennis. Guests can borrow a VCR. All units are closed for maintenance on the 13th and 14th of each month. It's within walking distance of town.

Alii Villas (*☎ 329-1288; 75-6016 Alii Dr; 1-bedroom units $90*), about a half mile outside town, has an oceanfront pool and an unobstructed view of the sunset. A fair number of seniors enjoy this large restful complex. Though the beige building looks weathered, the 126 units are comfortable. Each unit has a private lanai, cable TV, washer and dryer; most also have a phone and sofa bed. You must book through Knutson & Associates or SunQuest Vacations.

Kona Isle (*75-6100 Alii Dr; rates per week $490-775*) also rents more than a dozen units through **ATR Properties** (*☎ 329-6020, 888-311-6020; e atr@ilhawaii.net*). If the Kona Islander is like the party dorm in college, this complex is comparable to the studious dorm, a reputation that gives the place plenty of repeat business. Amenities include picnic tables, barbecue grills and chaise lounges overlooking the ocean. Units have air-con and microwaves.

Kona Riviera Villa (*☎ 329-1996; 75-6124 Alii Dr; garden-view units high/low season $95/85, oceanfront units $110/100*) is a charming little complex right on the ocean. Each of just 14 comfy units has a full kitchen, a living room, a separate bedroom with a king-size or queen-size bed, ceiling fans and a vanity with a sink. Most have a sofa bed in the living room. The complex also has a coin laundry, brick walkways and a fountain.

Mid-Range Condos in this price range tend to have better amenities, but units can vary tremendously, so ask plenty of questions when booking.

Kona Makai *(75-6026 Alii Dr; 1-bedroom air-con units from $90)*, on the *makai* (seaward) side of the road next to Alii Villas, has one-bedroom units that are fully equipped with everything down to a washer and dryer. Knutson & Associates rents some two-bedroom units. The complex sports an exercise room and tennis courts.

Sea Village *(☎ 329-6488; 75-6002 Alii Dr; 1-bedroom units high season $105-140, low season $90-105)*, about 2 miles outside town, is a 131-unit complex with well-kept grounds that include a tennis court, ocean-side pool and Jacuzzi. Its spacious units have full kitchens. SunQuest Vacations also handles rentals here.

Kona Magic Sands Resort *(77-6452 Alii Dr; studio units $125)* has carefree condos perched by White Sands Beach. About half of the 36 units are handled by Hawaii Resort Management. These are compact studios, but they have full kitchens, TVs, phones, rattan furnishings and oceanfront lanai. Although it's an older building, the units have been upgraded, and it's good value for being right on the water.

Hale Kona Kai *(☎/fax 329-2155, 800-421-3696; 75-5870 Kahakai Rd; 2-person units from $125, extra person $10)* is just beyond the Royal Kona Resort, perfect if you enjoy the sound of the surf (and who doesn't?). Its 22 one-bedroom units aren't brand new, but they're comfortable and have full kitchens and cable TV. All have waterfront lanai with great ocean views; the corner units boast a lovely wraparound lanai. There's a three-day minimum on most units, a $150 security deposit and no holiday check-in.

Kona Reef *(☎ 329-2959, 800-367-5004, fax 329-2762; W www.castleresorts.com; 75-5888 Alii Dr; 1-bedroom units $170-230)* is run like a hotel by Castle Resorts. The tasteful units have the usual amenities, including full kitchens, VCRs, stereos, washers, dryers and private lanai. Rates allow up to four people in a one-bedroom unit, which also has a sofa bed in the living room. It's cheaper by half to book through SunQuest Vacations or Hawaii Resort Management.

Top End Higher rates secure more spacious units and upscale amenities.

Royal Sea-Cliff Resort *(☎ 329-8021, 800-688-7444, fax 326-1887; W www.outrigger.com; 75-6040 Alii Dr; studios $220, 1-bedroom units $250-280, 2-bedroom units $280-325)*, a modern 154-unit complex, has some of Kona's nicest condo units, complete with stylish furnishings, air-con, lanai, modern kitchens, washers and dryers. The complex has tennis courts, freshwater and saltwater pools, a sauna, outdoor lounge areas and covered parking. The Outrigger chain runs the place like a hotel with a front desk. There's no minimum stay. Check the website for various discount schemes.

Places to Eat

Self-Catering Kona has everything from supermarkets to organic health foods. Fresh island fruits, vegetables and flowers are available direct from the growers at the **farmers markets** opposite Waterfront Row *(open 6am-3pm Wed & Fri-Sun)* and at Alii Gardens Market Place *(Alii Dr; open 8am-4pm Wed & Fri-Sun)*, across from Kona Riviera Villa condominiums.

Safeway *(☎ 329-2207; Crossroads Shopping Center; open 24hr)* is Kona's biggest supermarket and has a good bakery, deli and reasonably priced wines. Also try **Sack N Save** *(☎ 326-2729; Lanihau Center, Palani Rd; open 5am-midnight daily)*.

Kona Natural Foods *(☎ 329-2296; Crossroads Shopping Center; open 9am-9pm Mon-Sat, 9am-7pm Sun)*, right next to Safeway, stocks organic wines and produce, along with a good variety of dairy and bulk food products. Its excellent café serves veggie sandwiches and take-out salads from $5. Servers can get testy when closing time looms.

Budget For a cheap meal on the run, try the **French Bakery** *(Kaahumanu Plaza; open 5:30am-3pm Mon-Fri, 5:30am-2pm Sat)* in the industrial area. It makes sticky buns, large muffins and a delicious apple coffee cake ($1.50). The huge Tongan bread ($5), filled with cheese and spinach, can be heated on request. Order it one day in advance.

Island Lava Java *(Alii Sunset Plaza, Alii Dr; snacks $3.75-6.75; open 6am-10pm daily)* is popular for its espresso, sandwiches and good homemade cinnamon rolls, muffins and pies. Both locals and tourists crowd the outdoor tables.

Ocean View Inn *(75-5683 Alii Dr; breakfast $3-6, lunch & dinner $5-11; open 6:30am-2:25pm & 5:15pm-9pm Tues-Sun)*, in the town center, is an unassuming diner, but the best place for cheap local food. You can get Chinese, American and Hawaiian dishes, and it's a good place to try *lomi* salmon (which has been diced and marinated) or a side dish of *poi*, the Hawaiian taro paste.

Ba-Le Kona *(Kona Coast Shopping Center; dishes $3-7; open 10am-9pm Mon-Sat, 11am-7pm Sun)* makes French sandwiches and baked goods right alongside Vietnamese fare. At this brightly lit fast-food gem, a frequent special is Vietnamese crepes made with rice flour, which are then wrapped with lettuce, mint and cilantro and dipped in sauce. It also has hot egg noodle dishes and unusual sandwiches, like pate with steamed pork.

Thai Rin *(Alii Sunset Plaza, Alii Dr; lunch around $8; open lunch 11am-2:30pm Mon-Sat, dinner 5pm-8:30pm daily)* is another worthwhile option. It has curries, *phat thai* (stir-fried rice noodles) and stir-fry dishes, all costing a bit more at dinner.

Manna's *(Crossroads Shopping Center; dishes $5.50-8; open 10am-8:30pm Mon-Sat)*, a Korean barbecue restaurant, packs 'em in, despite the lack of ambience. Manna plates come with four 'veggies' and two scoops of rice. Mains include chicken *katsu* (deep-fried fillets) and charbroiled, marinated short ribs. No credit cards.

Mid-Range If you want a bit of atmosphere, look no further than these eateries.

Bianelli's *(☎ 326-4800; Pines Plaza, Nani Kailua Rd; all-you-can-eat pasta dinners $9.50, pizzas from $10; open 11am-10pm Mon-Fri, 5pm-10pm Sat & Sun)* has filling fare. Because it's a bit off the beaten path on the road toward Holualoa, this bustling Italian trattoria attracts its share of locals. It's not fancy, with plastic checked tablecloths, but it's friendly. Brews from around the world cost from $3.

Kona Brewing Co *(☎ 329-2739; dishes $4-20; open 11am-10pm Mon-Thur, 11am-midnight Fri & Sat, 1pm-9pm Sun)* has an outdoor café with good Greek, spinach and Caesar salads plus creative pizzas. Wash it all down with one of the fresh brews made on site, or opt for the four-beer sampler ($6.50).

Sibu Cafe *(☎ 329-1112; Banyan Court; lunch special Mon-Fri $7; open 11:30am-2:30pm & 5pm-9pm daily)* serves good Indonesian food in a casual café setting. A hearty gado gado salad costs $11.50, and combination plates that offer three dishes (with choices like Balinese chicken, spicy Indian curry or shrimp satay) with brown rice cost $13 at dinner. No credit cards.

Tres Hombres *(☎ 329-2173; Walua Rd; mains $9-15; open 11:30am-9pm daily)* beats Pancho & Lefty's, a busier Mexican joint on Alii Dr, with its fine margaritas and fresh chips. Menu items include steak fajitas, *chile relleno* (Mexican dish of green peppers stuffed with cheese) and fish tacos. Service is attentive, but the restaurant definitely isn't scenic (no ocean views).

Quinn's *(☎ 329-3822; Palini Rd; meals $9-20; open 11am-midnight daily)*, a bar opposite King Kamehameha's Kona Beach Hotel, serves meals in its rear courtyard. The crowd is mostly longtime local residents who come for the consistently good seafood and steak dinners. For the setting, prices aren't cheap – $9 for fish and chips, $20 for an *ahi* dinner – but the portions are large. Burgers, soups and salads are available.

Top End Other high-end restaurants can disappoint in Kona, but all of these places get top marks. Reservations are advised.

Oodles of Noodles *(☎ 329-9222; Crossroads Shopping Center; dishes $10-20; open 8am-9pm daily)* is the trendiest place in town. Run by Amy Ferguson-Ota, former executive chef at one of the Kohala Coast resorts, the restaurant features noodles in all variations – everything from Vietnamese *pho* soup, *phat thai* and Peking duck to grilled chicken fettuccine and a delicious wok-seared *ahi* noodle casserole. The heartwarming menu includes creative salads, appetizers and wines by the glass.

Kona Inn *(☎ 329-4455; mains $15-25; open 11:30am-9:30pm daily, café & bar open 11:30am-11pm)* opened in 1929 as the Big Island's first hotel. It's now a shopping center with a large water-view restaurant of the same name. Steak and seafood dinners are the mainstays, with lighter meals such as calamari sandwiches and chicken Caesar salad for around $10.

Huggo's (☎ *329-1493; 75-5828 Kahakai Rd; dinner $18-30; open 11:30am-2:30pm Mon-Fri, 5:30pm-10pm daily*), near the Royal Kona Resort, is a popular open-air restaurant right on the water's edge – a nice spot for a sunset drink. It attracts the biggest crowd at lunchtime on Tuesday and Thursday, when it features barbecued beef ribs served with baked beans and French bread ($9.50). Steak and fish dishes punctuate the dinner menu.

Cassandra's Greek Taverna (☎ *334-1066; Kona Square; mains $15-30; open 11am-10pm daily*) serves authentic Greek food. Appetizers include Greek salad, hummus, calamari and pickled octopus. For around $15 you can get souvlaki, moussaka or a gyros plate, all served with rice.

La Bourgogne (☎ *329-6711; Kuakini Plaza, Hwy 11 at Lako St; mains $24-32; open 6pm-10pm Tues-Sat*) is about 3 miles south of Kailua-Kona. Despite its location in a mini-mall, with no ocean views, this intimate French restaurant has no trouble filling its dozen or so tables. Consider the roast duck with raspberries and pine nuts or the veal sweetbreads. Staff can help you navigate the extensive wine list.

Entertainment

Bars & Live Music With numerous restaurants, hotels and bars lined up along Alii Dr, Kona has no shortage of sunset views and happy hours.

Huggo's (☎ *329-1493; 75-5828 Kahakai Rd; open 11:30am-2:30pm Mon-Fri, 5:30pm-10pm daily*) has dancing to Top 40, reggae or Hawaiian music from 9pm to at least midnight nightly.

Sam's Hideaway (☎ *326-7267; 75-5725 Alii Dr, Kona Marketplace*) is a loud spot with nightly karaoke. Someone will inevitably stick a mike in your face, so don't come if you're not willing to belt one out.

Hard Rock Cafe (☎ *329-8866; 75-5815 Alii Dr; open 11am-midnight daily*), at the south end of town, plays rock music continuously and music memorabilia covers the walls. The splendid 2nd-floor ocean view is worth something.

LuLu's (☎ *331-2633; Coconut Grove Marketplace; admission free; open 11am-1:30am daily*), next door to the Hard Rock Cafe, boasts 13 TV monitors that plug into sports programmes.

Jakes (☎ *329-7366; Coconut Grove Marketplace; open till 11:30pm Sun-Tues, till 1am Wed-Sat*), in the same building as LuLu's, offers dancing to live music on most nights; Wednesday is Hawaiian with hula dancing, Saturday is for belly dancing.

Kanaka Kava (☎ *327-1660; admission free; open noon-10pm daily*) is another bar in the Coconut Grove Marketplace. Kava is a legal (and traditional) relaxant that's said to 'induce aloha.'

For Hawaiian microbrews, head to **Kona Coast Brewing Co** (☎ *329-4455; café & bar open 11:30am-11pm*).

Escaping the hubbub of Alii Dr, you'll sacrifice an ocean view in favor of bars with more locals than tourists.

Ah Dunno Bar & Grill (☎ *326-2337; 74-5552A Kaiwi St; open till 2am daily*) pulls in sports fans. Come to play pool or listen to live bands Wednesday to Sunday, typically rock and blues.

The Other Side (☎ *329-7226; 74-5484 Kaiwi St; open till 2am daily*) is down the street. This high-ceilinged bar is split in two: The Edge has more disco, while the Other Side concentrates on rock. It's mostly a local crowd that shows up for darts, foosball, pool and an insanely long happy hour from noon to 6pm daily.

Cinemas Showing new releases on 10 screens, **Stadium Cinemas** (☎ *327-0444; Makalapua Shopping Center*) has bargain matinees before 6pm.

Movie rentals are a viable option, as many condos and B&Bs have VCRs. Try **Blockbuster** (☎ *326-7694; Kona Coast Shopping Center; open till 11pm Mon-Thur, midnight Fri-Sun*).

Luaus & Hula Kailua-Kona's big hotels offer lively, albeit hokey, evening luaus.

King Kamehameha's Kona Beach Hotel (☎ *326-4969;* w *www.konabeachhotel.com; 75-5660 Palani Rd; adult/child with dinner $55/21, without dinner $30/14.50; luau 5:30pm-9pm Tues-Thur & Sun*) begins its beachfront luau with a shell-lei greeting, followed by torch lighting, a buffet dinner and a Polynesian dance show. If you stop by around 10am on luau days, you can watch

THE BIG ISLAND

staff members bury the pig in the *imu* (underground oven) – they'll explain it all to you.

The Royal Kona Resort *(☎ 329-3111; 800-774-5662, fax 329-7230; Ⓦ www.royalkona.com; 75-5852 Alii Dr; adult/child with dinner $55/23, without dinner $28/18)* hosts the other luau in town and is also right on the water. However, when we visited, cocktails such as *mai tai* punch (an alcoholic drink made from rum, grenadine, and lemon and pineapple juices) were weak, and the 'all night' open bar only lasted until 7:30pm.

Windjammer Lounge *(☎ 329-3111; Royal Kona Resort, 75-5852 Alii Dr)* puts on a pleasant sunset hula show at 6pm Tuesday to Sunday.

Shopping

The center of Kailua-Kona is thick with small shops selling trinkets, clothing, crafts and other tourist-related goods. The ubiquitous **ABC store** outlets give great discounts on everyday beach essentials. Also visit the outdoor **Alii Gardens Marketplace** *(Alii Dr; open 8am-5pm Wed & Fri-Sun)*, around 1½ miles south of town.

King Kamehameha's Kona Beach Hotel has a **Big Island Outlet** store that features a wide variety of island crafts, food items, T-shirts and oddities like potted *fuku* (Hawaiian-style bonsai trees).

Hula Heaven *(☎ 329-7885; Kona Inn Shopping Village)* warrants a closer look for its more authentic merchandise. The store sells vintage aloha shirts, original clothing and antique maps and prints. Prices are higher.

Mele Kai Music *(☎ 329-1454; Kaahumanu Plaza)* has good selections of Hawaiian music CDs and cassettes.

Kailua Candy Company *(☎ 329-2522; 74-5563 Kaiwi St; gift shop open 8am-6pm Mon-Sat, 8am-4pm Sun)*, in the industrial area, makes delicious homemade chocolates using island fruits and nuts. You can get free samples and take a peek through picture windows at the company's operations.

Getting Around

Bus Between Kailua-Kona and Keauhou, **Alii Shuttle** *(☎ 775-7121)* has several buses in each direction daily, except Sunday (no service). The fare anywhere along this 45-minute route is $2 one way, or you can get a day/week/month pass for $5/20/40. Buses leave the Kona Surf Resort in Keauhou at 8:30am and every 1½ hours thereafter, with the last run at 7pm. Stops include Keauhou Shopping Center, Keauhou Beach Resort, Royal Kona Resort, Kona Inn Shopping Village, King Kamehameha's Kona Beach Hotel and the Lanihau Center. In the southbound direction, buses leave the Lanihau Center every 1½ hours from 9:20am to 6:20pm. Among other things, the shuttle is a good option for getting to Kahaluu Beach Park (next to Keauhou Beach Resort) if you're in Kailua-Kona without a car.

The **Kona Coast Express** *(☎ 331-1582)* makes an 80-minute loop from 7:40am until 8:20pm daily. Stops include the King Kamehameha Hotel with stops at Kona Inn Shopping Village, Coconut Grove Marketplace, Royal Sea Cliff, Casa de Emdeko, Kona by the Sea, Alii Gardens Marketplace, Kona Bali Kai, Keauhou Beach Hotel, Keauhou Shopping Center, Kona Surf Hotel and Keauhou Pier. An all-day pass costs $5.

Parking The center of Kailua-Kona gets congested. Free public parking is available in the lot behind Kona Seaside Hotel, between Likana Lane and the Kuakini Hwy. The Kona Inn Shopping Village provides complimentary parking for patrons in the lot behind the Kona Bay Hotel. Patrons of Kona Marketplace can park for free at the rear of that center. The Coconut Grove Marketplace and Alii Sunset Plaza share an enormous free parking lot out back.

At the north end of Alii Dr, the big parking lot behind King Kamehameha's Kona Beach Hotel offers free parking for the first 15 minutes; it costs $1 per half hour after that. If you purchase something in one of the hotel shops or restaurants, you can get a voucher for free parking.

KEAUHOU

Keauhou is the coastal area immediately south of Kailua-Kona. It starts at Kahaluu Bay and runs south beyond Keauhou Bay and the Kona Surf Resort. Bishop Estate, Hawaii's biggest private landholder, owns the land.

The area was once the site of a major Hawaiian settlement. Although several historical sites can still be explored, they now share their grounds with the planned community comprised of three hotels, nine condo complexes, a shopping center and a 27-hole golf course, all with a country club atmosphere.

Information

The local **post office** *(cnr Alii Dr & Kamehameha III Rd; open 10am-4:30pm Mon-Fri, 10am-3pm Sat)* is at Keauhou Shopping Center. There you'll find a Longs Drugs and another small pharmacy inside **KTA Super Store**, which also has a **Bank of Hawaii** *(open 10am-7pm Mon-Fri, 10am-3pm Sat & Sun)* branch with a 24-hour ATM.

St Peter's Church

St Peter's is Hawaii's most photographed 'quaint church' and is still used for weekend services and weddings. A precious blue and white Catholic spot on the north side of Kahaluu Bay, the church dates back to 1880, though it was moved from White Sands Beach to this site in 1912. Several tidal waves and hurricanes have unsuccessfully attempted to relocate it.

Christians were not the first to deem the site a suitable place to worship the gods. At the north side of the church, you'll find the remains of **Kuemanu Heiau**. Hawaiian royalty, who surfed the waters at the north end of Kahaluu Bay, paid their respects at this temple before hitting the waves.

Locals keep up the surfing tradition here, although high surf usually generates dangerous northward rip currents, and it's not a good spot for beginners.

Kahaluu Beach

Kahaluu (Diving Place) is the island's best easy-access snorkeling spot. The bay is like a big natural aquarium, loaded with colorful marine life. If you haven't tried snorkeling, this is a great place to learn. It's not even necessary to go out over your head to enjoy it! The main drawback is jarring traffic noise from Alii Dr.

Large rainbow parrotfish, schools of silver needlefish, brilliant yellow tangs, butterfly fish and colorful wrasses are among the numerous tropicals easily seen here. The fish are tame enough to eat out of your hand, but if you bring along fish food, you'll be engulfed by frenzied swarms. Go deeper for better coral and fish. At high tide, green sea turtles often swim into the bay to feed.

An ancient breakwater, said to have been built by the *menehune* (legendary 'little people'), is on the reef and protects the bay. Still, when the surf is high, Kahaluu can have strong currents that pull in the direction of the rocks near St Peter's Church, and it's easy to drift away without realizing it. Check your bearings occasionally to make sure you're not being pulled by the current. Before jumping in, take a look at water

THE BIG ISLAND

Green Sea Turtles

Honu or green sea turtles are the most abundant of the three native species of sea turtles found in Hawaiian waters. Because green sea turtles feed on algae that grows in the shallow waters of coastal reefs, they often share beach space with snorkelers. Weighing upward of 200lb at maturity, these gentle giants are a thrill to behold in the water.

The green sea turtle population in Hawaii has been on the increase in recent years, with frequent sightings at places like Kahaluu Beach. The turtles are not permanent residents of the main Hawaiian Islands. About once every four years they return to their ancestral nesting grounds in the remote French Frigate Shoals, 700 miles east of the Big Island, where they mate and nest.

Hawaii's other two native sea turtles are the hawksbill, which is about the same size as the green sea turtle but far rarer, and the leatherback, which weighs up to a ton and is found in deep offshore waters.

LONELY PLANET PUBLICATIONS

condition reports posted on the weathered display board by the picnic pavilion.

A lifeguard is on duty daily, and a snack van sells burgers, sodas and ice cream. Another van rents body boards and silicone snorkel sets ($8 per day); it also sells fish food ($3) and disposable underwater cameras ($14).

The park has a salt-and-pepper beach composed of black lava and white coral sand. Facilities include showers, rest rooms, changing rooms, picnic tables and grills. It's a popular place and often draws a crowd, particularly on weekends, so it's best to get there early. Parking is fairly plentiful.

Keauhou Beach Resort

The grounds of the Keauhou Beach Resort, immediately south of Kahaluu Beach, contain a number of easily explored historical sites. Ask at the front desk for a brochure and site map.

The ruins of Kapuanoni, a **fishing temple**, are on the north side of the hotel. The reconstructed summer **beach house of King Kalakaua** is inland, beside a spring-fed pond once used as a royal bath. You can peek into the simple three-room cottage and see a portrait of the king in his European-style royal dress, a Hawaiian quilt on the bed and *lauhala* (pandanus-leaf) mats on the floor.

Other *heiau* sites are on the south side of the hotel. The remains of the seaside **Keeku Heiau**, just beyond the footbridge that leads to the now defunct Kona Lagoon Hotel, is thought to have been a *luakini*.

The shelf of *pahoehoe* (smooth, ropelike lava) at the south side of the Keauhou Beach Resort holds some interesting **tide pools**, best explored at low tide. The pools contain numerous sea urchins, including spiny and slate pencil types, and small tropical fish.

When the tide is at its very lowest, you can walk out onto a flat lava tongue carved with numerous **petroglyphs**. The site is directly in front of the northern end of the Kona Lagoon Hotel, with most of the petroglyphs about 25ft from the shore. Unless it's low tide, the petroglyphs are submerged and hidden from view.

Keauhou Bay

Keauhou Bay, which has a launch ramp and space for two dozen small boats, is one of the most protected bays on the west coast. If you come by on weekdays in the late afternoon, you can watch the local outrigger canoe club practicing in the bay. There are rest rooms and showers.

In a small clearing just south of the harborside dive shacks, a stone marks the site where Kamehameha III was born in 1814. The young prince was said to have been stillborn and brought back to life by a visiting *kahuna* (priest or spiritual healer).

To get to the bay, turn toward the ocean off Alii Dr onto Kamehameha III Rd. Or drive down Kaleopapa Rd toward Kona Surf Resort, but continue to the end of the road instead of turning into the resort.

Manta Rays

Pacific manta rays are gorgeous, gentle creatures with a wingspan that can measure an impressive 12ft to 14ft. While spotlights off the Kona Surf Hotel used to shine down on the ocean and create a fantastic dinner show of mantas – light attracts plankton and plankton, in turn, attracts mantas – the hotel has long been shuttered.

But don't despair. Several dive outfits offer night dives to see these luminous creatures. Even if you're not a certified diver, you can snorkel at the surface and view the mantas from above. As they cruise around in the surf with their white underbellies flashing against the dark waters, it's hypnotic to watch, and an unforgettable Hawaiian adventure. Remember that mantas make their best showings when there's no moon.

Hawaiian Chocolate Factory

This tiny chocolate factory *(☎ 322-2626; 78-6772 Makenawai St)* is located on Mt Hualalai. It's hard to believe that the sinfully sweet bars of chocolate come from beans that smell like stinky socks. However, the chocolate pods are lovely shades of yellow, gold and fuchsia, and they're harvested every two weeks year-round. The beans are removed by hand from the pods, and the drying process takes up to four weeks.

This is a mom-and-pop operation, and co-owner Bob Cooper offers self-deprecating anecdotes about some of his makeshift equipment while his wife Pam hand-wraps

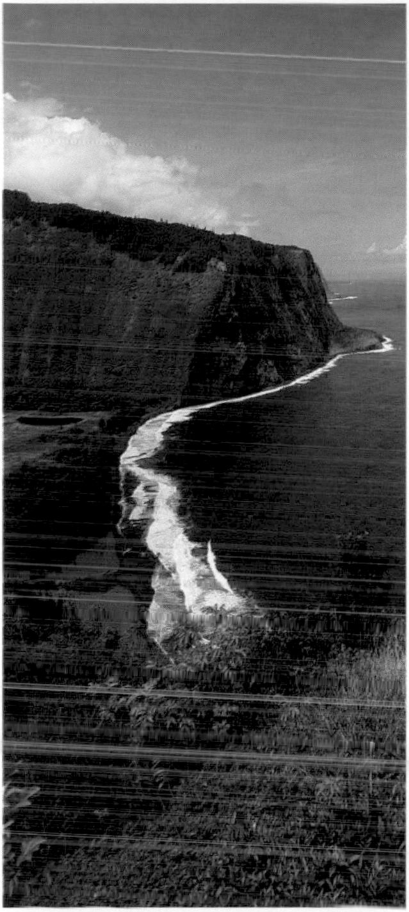

LEE FOSTER

Waipio coastline, the Big Island

MARK PARKES

Lava tube, Kilauea, the Big Island

ANN CECIL

Ti-leaf offering for the fire goddess

ANN CECIL

Coffee 'cherry,' *Arabica typica*

Hilton Waikoloa Village

Puu Hau Kea, on the road to Mauna Loa

Hawaii Volcanoes National Park

the bars in a climate-controlled room. The tours are free but by appointment only.

Places to Stay

Keauhou Resort Condominiums *(☎ 322-9122, 800-367-5286, fax 322-9410; 78-7039 Kamehameha III Rd; 1-bedroom units with garden-view $97, with ocean view $107)* has 48 units with full kitchens, washers and dryers. Although the units are three decades old, most are well maintained, and the property is the cheapest in Keauhou. Add about $25 more for a two-bedroom unit for up to four people. The minimum stay is five days. It's near the golf course and has a pool.

Keauhou Surf & Racquet Club *(☎ 329-3333, 800-622-5348; 78-6800 Alii Dr; 2-bedroom units with golf-course view $150, with ocean view $175)*, a large, modern complex conveniently located near the Keauhou Shopping Center, has three tennis courts, a grass volleyball court and a pool. Not all units have views, but each is spacious and comes equipped with lanai, full kitchen, washer, dryer, TV and VCR. Hawaii Resort Management handles some rentals; Knutson & Associates rates are higher.

The next two Outrigger properties both offer a number of discount schemes, ranging from 25% off for American Automobile Association (AAA) members to fifth-night-free deals. Check Ⓦ www.outrigger.com for details.

Keauhou Beach Resort *(☎ 322-7987, 800-462-6262, fax 322-3117; 78-6740 Alii Dr; rooms with garden view $165-185, with ocean view $205-225)* adjoins Kahaluu Beach Park and has interesting grounds that include historical sites and tide pools. The hotel reopened in the spring of 1999 after a lengthy renovation and is now a member of the Outrigger chain. Spacious, tastefully furnished rooms have minirefrigerators, TVs, lanai and air-con.

Kanaloa at Kona *(☎ 322-9625, 800-688-7444; 78-261 Manukai St; 1-bedroom apartments from $205, 2-bedroom ocean-view units $290)* has 100 condo units with all the standard amenities; oceanfront units have whirlpool spas. There are three pools and two lighted tennis courts.

Other Keauhou condos are largely booked through vacation rental agents. **SunQuest Vacations** *(☎ 329-6488, 800-367-5168, Canada ☎ 800-800-5662, fax 329-5480; Ⓦ www.sunquest-hawaii.com; 77-6435 Kuakini Hwy)* handles units in most of them.

Places to Eat

Royal Thai Café *(Keauhou Shopping Center; dishes $6-10; open 11am-10pm daily)* is dominated by Asian statuary and a large aquarium, but the food holds its own.

Drysdale's Two *(Keauhou Shopping Center; snacks $6-8; open 11am-midnight daily)*, specializing in sandwiches and burgers, is a hot spot for watching sports on TV.

Edward's at Kanaloa *(☎ 322-1434; Kanaloa at Kona, 78-261 Manukai St; mains $20; open 11am-8:30pm Mon-Fri, 8am-8:30pm Sat & Sun)* is oddly situated in a condo complex. This restaurant's truly spectacular sunset view and knowledgeable service draws locals here when they have reason to celebrate. Make early reservations and sip a cocktail before trying the beef tenderloin with creamy port wine and Gorgonzola sauce, or Moroccan spiced chicken on a bed of couscous.

Entertainment

The Keahou Beach Resort's sedate **Verandah Lounge** features jazz on Tuesday nights and mellow Hawaiian music Wednesday to Saturday. Drink prices are reasonable, considering the oceanfront location.

The multiscreen **Keauhou Cinema** *(☎ 324-7200; Keauhou Shopping Center)* shows first-run movies.

Getting Around

Keauhou has a free on-call **shuttle service** *(☎ 322-3500)* that runs around the resort environs between 8am and 4:30pm daily.

HOLUALOA

Holualoa is a sleepy village perched in the hills, 1400ft above Kailua-Kona. The slopes catch afternoon showers, so it's lusher and cooler than on the coast below. It's an enviable location, with a fine view of Kailua Bay's sparkling turquoise waters below.

While Holualoa remains off the beaten path, Kona's relentless development is creeping up this way. Older homes half hidden by jungly gardens are being joined by new houses. An artists' community supports craft shops, galleries and a community art center.

This is pretty much a one-road village, with everything lined up along Hwy 180.

There's a general store, a Japanese cemetery, an elementary school, a couple of churches and a library that's open a few days a week.

From Kailua-Kona, it's a scenic 4 miles up Hualalai Rd to Holualoa. The landscape is bright with poinsettia flowers, coffee bushes and fruit trees of all kinds.

Kona Blue Sky Coffee

More than 400 coffee belt acres on Mt Hualalai's slopes belong to the Twigg-Smith Estate's Kona Blue Sky farm *(☎ 322-1700; 76-973A Hualalai Rd)*, headquartered down the road from Holualoa's gallery row. Visitors are first welcomed with a short video before their tour of the grounds. Then they can see the roasting and packaging that takes place on the premises. The tasting room has requisite free samples of coffee and chocolate-covered beans. Tours, offered between 8:30am and 4pm Monday to Friday, are also free.

Kimura's Lauhala Shop

This **shop** *(☎ 324-0053; cnr Hualalai Rd & Hwy 180; open 9am-5pm Mon-Sat)* sells items woven from *lauhala*, the *lau* (leaf) of the *hala* (pandanus) plant.

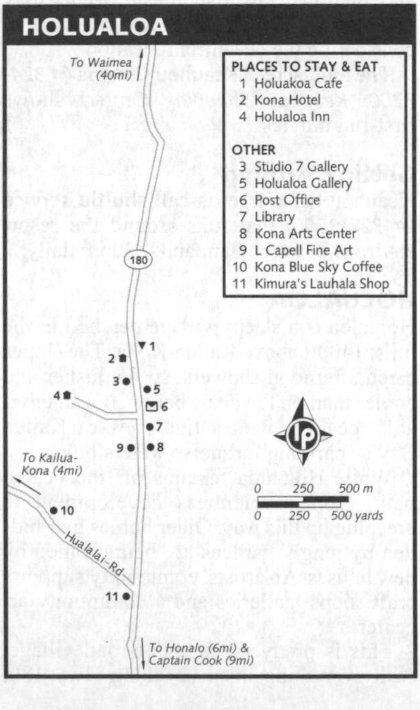

This was once an old plantation store that sold salt and codfish. During the Great Depression of the 1930s, Mrs Kimura started weaving *lauhala* hats and coffee baskets and selling them at the plantations.

Three generations of Kimuras still weave *lauhala* here. Their work is supplemented by the wives of local coffee farmers, who do piecework at home when it's not coffee season. The most common items are place mats, open baskets and hats of a finer weave.

The hardest part, they say, is preparing the *lauhala*, which is messy work, complicated by the sharp spines along the leaf edges. The easy part is the weaving.

Kona Arts Center

The soul of Holualoa is the Kona Arts Center *(Hwy 180; open 10am-3pm Tues-Sat)*, set in a ramshackle former coffee mill with a tin roof and hot-pink doors. Carol Rogers, who's been here since 1965, directs this nonprofit organization and teaches crafts, nurturing the spirit as much as the art. This is a community scene and everyone's welcome to join. For a nominal monthly fee, you can participate in the workshops, which include pottery, batik, tie-dye, basketry, weaving and painting.

Visitors are free to drop in and look around. There's also a small display area with items for sale, including paintings, pottery and baskets made of natural fibers.

Galleries

Visiting galleries is the main thing to do in Holualoa. Most are open 10am to 4pm Tuesday to Saturday.

Studio 7 Gallery *(☎ 324-1335)*, which showcases the artwork of owner Hiroki Morinoue, who works in watercolors, oils, woodblock and sculpture, is a highlight. His wife, Setsuko, is a potter and the gallery's director. The gallery is like a little museum, and the Zen-like setting blends both Hawaiian and Japanese influences, with wooden walkways over lava stones.

Holualoa Gallery *(☎ 322-8484)* sells paintings with a Hawaiiana theme, including a few works by the noted Big Island artist Herb Kawainui Kane, and some creative raku pottery by gallery owner Matt Lovein.

The old Holualoa post office building, opposite the Kona Arts Center, houses **L Capell Fine Art** *(☎ 937-8893)*, whose owner and artist is shifting her focus from representational to more abstract artwork.

Places to Stay & Eat

Kona Hotel *(☎ 324-1155; Hwy 180; singles/doubles $20/26)* is an old local hostelry with high ceilings and some nice views from a bright-pink wooden building in Holualoa center that retains the small-town character (and room rates!) of a bygone era. Rooms are basic with just a bed and dresser, but they're clean; bathrooms are shared and down the hall. With only 11 rooms, the place is often full.

Holualoa Inn *(☎ 324-1121, 800-392-1812, fax 322-2472; ⓔ inn@aloha.net; ⓦ www.konaweb.com/hinn; 76-5932 Mamalahoa Hwy; doubles with bath $175-225)* is perched atop 40 acres of sloping meadows with grand views of the Kona Coast. Built as a getaway by the owner's uncle, chairman of the *Honolulu Advertiser*, the exterior of this 6000-sq-ft contemporary house is all western red cedar, and the interior floors are red eucalyptus from Maui. If you're traveling with more than two people, go for the Bali suite, which has absolutely unbeatable views. Guest amenities include a tiled swimming pool, Jacuzzi, billiard table, rooftop gazebo, living room with fireplace, TV lounge and facilities for preparing light meals. Rates include continental breakfast.

Holuakoa Cafe *(open 6:30am-3pm Mon-Sat)* has good pastries, sandwiches, salads, espresso and herbal teas, plus daily chalkboard specials. Patrons can stretch out in the pleasant courtyard or dine in the inviting hardwood-floored interior.

South Kona

Hwy 11 meanders south from Kailua-Kona through a number of small, upland communities: Honalo, Kainaliu, Captain Cook and Honaunau. Surrounded by coffee farms, macadamia nut groves and fruit trees, these unhurried towns are cooled by frequent afternoon showers, good for both agriculture and overheated mainlanders.

South Kona is short on beaches, but there are a couple of excellent spots for snorkeling and diving. Side roads off Hwy 11 lead to Kealakekua Bay, Puuhonua o Honaunau National Historical Park (commonly called Place of Refuge) and the coastal villages of Hookena and Milolii.

HONALO

Honalo, at the intersection of Hwys 11 and 180, barely qualifies as a village. **Daifukuji Soto Mission**, on the *mauka* side of Hwy 11, is a big Buddhist temple with two altars, gold brocade, large drums and incense burners. As at all Buddhist temples, leave your shoes at the door.

Teshima's Restaurant *(☎ 322-9140; Hwy 11; meals from $7; open 6:30am-1:45pm & 5pm-9pm daily)* is an unpretentious, family-run place serving fresh Japanese food. The best deal is the lunch *teishoku* (set meal) of miso soup, sashimi, sukiyaki, *tsukemono* (pickled vegetables) and rice. The restaurant doesn't accept credit cards and has no liquor license.

In a building out back, Teshima's has 10 **rooms** *(singles/doubles $25/35)* for rent, although most are booked on a monthly basis *($300)*. These small rooms are very basic, each with a double bed and a bath.

KAINALIU

Kainaliu is a little town with positive vibes. Shops such as the Kimura Store, which has been selling traditional fabrics and dry goods here for generations, mingle with the likes of New Age shops and antique, arts and crafts galleries. **Island Books** *(☎ 322-2006; 79-7360 Mamalahoa Hwy)* is a wonderfully well-stocked used bookstore with travel, Hawaiiana, literature and nonfiction titles aplenty.

The focal point is the Aloha Cafe and the adjoining Aloha Theatre, home of the Aloha Community Players. Check the bulletin board for the current performance schedule, which includes anything from indie film screenings to live music and dance.

Aloha Cafe *(☎ 322-3383; Hwy 11; breakfast & lunch $6-13, dinner $14-22; open 8am-3pm & 5pm-9pm daily)* is undoubtedly the best eatery in town, with a distant ocean view from its skinny terrace outside. Choose among vegetarian dishes and fresh fish specials, good salads and sandwiches, fruit smoothies, fresh-squeezed juices, espresso and heavenly cookies.

Evie's Natural Foods *(☎ 322-0739; Hwy 11; items $3-8; open 8am-7pm Mon-Fri, 9am-5pm Sat & Sun)*, south of the Aloha

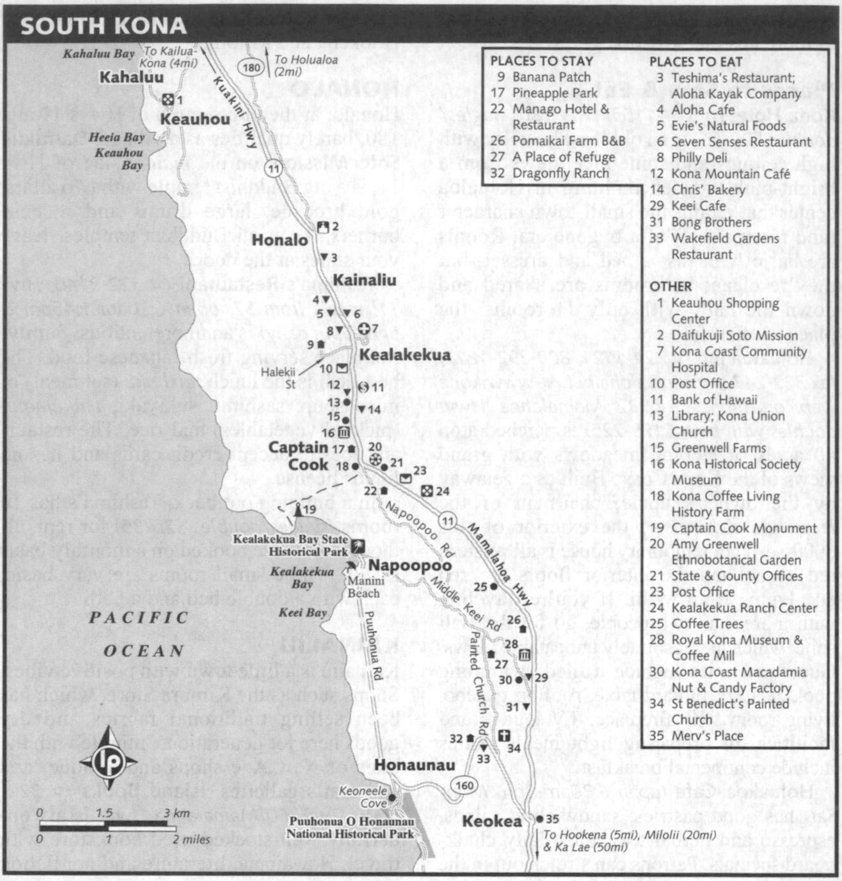

Cafe and also on the *makai* side, sells organic produce, fruit juices, smoothies, salads and sandwiches.

Seven Senses Restaurant *(☎ 322-5083; Hwy 11; dishes $4-10; open 11:30am-2:30pm Mon-Fri)* is a healthy place emphasizing gourmet organic fare. Try the Moroccan chicken wrap, bison burger and various salads, or the hard-to-believe-it's-low-fat chocolate tofu mousse. Funky chalkboards do dual duty as art and there's soothing music, too.

KEALAKEKUA

Kealakekua means 'Path of the Gods,' a name commemorating the series of 40 *heiau* that once ran from Kealakekua Bay north to Kailua-Kona.

Although tiny, this is the commercial center for Kona's hill towns. The Kona Coast's **hospital** *(☎ 322-9311; 79-1019 Haukapila St)* is on the north side of town, a quarter mile inland from Hwy 11. There's a **post office** *(☎ 322-1656; cnr Hwy 11 & Halekii Rd; open 9am-4:30pm Mon-Fri, 9:30am-12:30pm Sat)* and a few banks. Kealakekua's **library** *(☎ 323-7585; open noon-6pm Mon & Wed & Fri, 10am-6pm Tues, noon-7:30pm Thur, 10am-2pm Sat)* offers Internet access. Next door is the coral, mortar and lava-rock **Kona Union Church** (1854).

Kona Historical Society Museum

This stone and mortar building, built in the 1875, was once a general merchandise store and post office. It now houses the historical society's office, archives and a little **museum** (☎ *323-3222; admission by donation $2; open 9am-3pm Mon-Fri*), with quite interesting displays on the area's history, including period photos and other memorabilia. A new **Living History Ranch** focusing on Hawaii from the 1890s to the 1920s will be built on a plot of land next door. Look for them on the *makai* side of Hwy 11, just north of the Kealakekua Grass Shack gift shop.

Greenwell Farms

This farm (☎ *323-2275; Hwy 11; open 8am-5pm Mon-Fri, 8am-4pm Sat*), between the 110-mile and 111-mile markers, has been open for business since the 1850s. Aided by the young volcanic soil of Kona, these hand-picked coffee trees can yield a million pounds of beans annually. Samples, like the quick tours, are free.

Amy Greenwell Ethnobotanical Garden

This garden (☎ *323-3318; admission by donation $4; open 8:30am-5pm Mon-Fri*), south of the 110-mile marker, is full of landscaped walking paths and exotic plants. Bishop Museum placards explain how early Hawaiians took advantage of their limited resources while still showing respect for the *aina* (land). Plants and trees provided their raw materials for food and a variety of useful goods, including medicine, canoes and dye. There are free guided tours at 10am on the second Saturday of each month.

Kona Coffee Living History Farm

Another Kona Historical Society project, this living history farm (☎ *323-2006; adult/child $30/15*) focuses on rural Hawaiian life from the early 1900s to 1945. There are tours on the hour from 9am to 1pm Monday to Friday (and by appointment), which explore the small 1925 homestead house. The costumed interpretive staff demonstrate how early Japanese immigrants to Hawaii lived. Outside, visitors experience the arduous work of coffee picking and witness various aspects of the production process.

Although informative, the entry fee seems steep for what you get. The farm is near the 110-mile marker.

Kona Coffee

Missionaries introduced the first coffee trees to Hawaii in 1827, and by the turn of the 20th century it was an important cash crop throughout the state. However, the erratic rise and fall of coffee prices eventually drove coffee farmers out of business on the other Hawaiian Islands. Only the Big Island's Kona coffee was of high enough quality to sell at a profit during gluts in world markets.

Coffee production in Hawaii had dropped dramatically by 1980, when a rising interest in gourmet coffee sparked sales of the highly aromatic Kona beans. Today, Kona coffee is the most commercially successful coffee grown in the USA. Almost the entire harvest comes from the upland towns of South Kona, from Holualoa in the north to Honaunau in the south. The coffee trees thrive in the rich volcanic soil and under the cloud cover that moves in nearly every afternoon.

A relative of the gardenia, coffee has fragrant white blossoms in the spring. In the summer, the trees have green berries, which turn red as they ripen. The red berries (or 'cherries,' as they're called) don't all ripen at once, so they must be picked by hand several times a season. Harvest season begins in August. Coffee farmers at the lowest elevations may finish by December, while those at the 2000ft level might harvest into March.

Places to Stay

Areca Palms Estate B&B (☎ *323-2276, 800-545-4390, fax 323-3749;* Ⓦ *www.konabedandbreakfast.com; rooms $80-125; reservations 9am-6pm*), formerly Merryman's, is run by Oregon natives. Set in a quiet residential area above Hwy 11, the house resembles an airy cedar lodge, with lots of natural wood, country-style furnishings and exposed-beam ceilings. All rooms have private bath, cable TV and big closets stocked with luxurious robes. The Rose Room has an ocean view. Guests have use of a spacious common living area, guest phone, croquet and a Jacuzzi. Full breakfast is included.

Banana Patch (☎ *322-8888, 800-988-2246, fax 322-7777;* Ⓦ *www.bananabanana.com; rooms $55; 1-bedroom cottages $85-125, 2-bedroom cottages $100-150*), formerly

THE BIG ISLAND

Reggie's Tropical Hideaway, has two vacation rental cottages on a small coffee farm near central Kealakekua, catering to clientele who consider clothing optional. The funky one-bedroom cottage has a full kitchen, deck and Jacuzzi. The two-bedroom cottage has high wooden ceilings, a full kitchen, water bed and lanai, plus a private sundeck with a Jacuzzi.

Places to Eat

Chris' Bakery *(☎ 323-2444; Hwy 11; snacks under $5; open 6am-1pm daily)* has sweetly irresistible offerings.

Kona Mountain Café *(☎ 323-2700; Hwy 11; items $3-10; open 6:30am-6pm Mon-Fri, 8am-5pm Sat, 8am-4pm Sun)* serves stuffed sandwiches, pastries, Kona coffee and espresso. You can eat on the lanai or enjoy the indoor coffeehouse atmosphere.

Philly Deli *(Hwy 11; dishes $5-8; open 7am-5:30pm Mon-Fri, 7am-2pm Sat & Sun)*, an east coast–style spot inside a warehouse, serves reasonably priced eggs, pancakes and other breakfasts. Lunch features sandwiches, burgers and daily specials, such as eggplant Parmesan. Look for signs along the road.

KEALAKEKUA BAY

Over 1 mile wide at its mouth, Kealakekua Bay is a state underwater park and marine life conservation district. Among the protected species here are spinner dolphins that frequently swim into the bay. Fishing is restricted, and the removal of coral and rocks is prohibited.

The north end of the bay has a protected cove with one of the Big Island's premier snorkeling spots. On the bay's southern side is Kealakekua Bay State Historical Park.

Steep sea cliffs prevent land passage between the two ends of the bay. The northern end is accessible only by sea or by a hike along a dirt trail beginning inland near the town of Captain Cook.

Kealakekua Bay State Historical Park

At the end of Napoopoo Rd, 4½ miles from Hwy 11, this busy park's predominant feature is **Hikiau Heiau**, a large platform temple above the beach. The park also has a boat landing, bathrooms, showers and a shack selling soft drinks and souvenirs. Alas, Napoopoo Beach no longer exists, as Hurricane Iniki swept away the sand in 1992, and now only rocks line the shore.

It's forbidden to launch kayaks near the *heiau*, but if you head straight as you drive down Napoopoo Rd instead of veering right toward the *heiau*, you'll find an easy launch spot.

If you keep following Napoopoo Rd to the end and turn left, you can continue south through scrub brush and lava for 4 miles to the Place of Refuge. The road is little more than one lane, but is paved and passable. Be careful if you pull over, as the grasses conceal roadside trenches. Along the road are coastal turnoffs.

Manini Beach faces stunning cliffs, with the Captain Cook monument in plain – albeit distant – sight. Turtles, tangs and other colorful fish are an easy snorkeling option. The best point of entry is to your right just after entering the beach. Evenly spaced palm trees along the shore provide a haven for interesting birds, but don't come for swimming or sunbathing (the beach is rocky). There's a port-a-potty, but no other amenities.

Next, take the second dirt road – if you reach Keei Transfer Station, you've gone to far – and drive on out to **Keei Bay**. If you'd rather not navigate the bumpy road, it's only a 15-minute walk from the paved road. Surfers and kayakers test the waters, but swimming is poor. The short salt-and-pepper beachfront is a virtual forest of coconut trees offering shade. There are no facilities here.

Captain Cook Monument Trail

If you're up for a hardy hike, the trail to the Captain Cook Monument and the cove at the north end of Kealakekua Bay would make even a triathlete sweat. It's not that the trail is particularly steep or uneven, but it is not consistently maintained. At times it's a jungly path through tall elephant grasses, while at other times the trail is kept clear by people who use it for horseback rides to the monument.

To get to the trailhead, turn off Hwy 11 onto Napoopoo Rd and go down about 250 yards, where you'll find a dirt road immediately after the second telephone pole on the right. Start walking down the dirt road and after 200 yards it will fork – stay to the left, which is essentially a continuation of the road you've been walking on. The route is fairly simple and in most places runs between two rock fences on an old Jeep road. When in doubt, stay to the left.

Eventually the coast becomes visible and the trail veers to the left along a broad ledge, goes down the hill and then swings left to the beach. An obelisk **monument** a few minutes' walk to the left marks the spot where Captain Cook was killed at the water's edge.

The **Queen's Bath**, a little lava pool with brackish spring-fed water, lies at the edge of the cove, a few minutes' walk from the monument toward the cliffs. The water is cool and refreshing, and this age-old equivalent of a beach shower is a great way to wash off the salt before hiking back – although the mosquitoes can get a bit testy here.

A few minutes beyond Queen's Bath, the path ends at **Pali-kapu-o-Keoua**, the 'cliffs sacred to the chief Keoua.' The cliffs' numerous caves were the burial places of Hawaiian royalty, and it's speculated that some of Captain Cook's bones were placed here as well. A few lower caves are accessible, but they don't contain anything other than beer cans. The ones higher up are fortunately not as easy to get to and probably still contain bones. All are sacred and should be left undisturbed.

The hike takes about an hour down. It's hot and largely unshaded, and it's a longer uphill climb all the way back. Don't miss the trail's right-hand turn back up onto the lava ledge, as another 4WD road continues straight from the intersection north along the coast. There are no facilities at the bottom of the trail. Be sure to bring your own drinking water and snorkeling gear.

Snorkeling

After working up a sweat hiking, you can slip into the ocean from the rocks on the left side of the cement dock in front of the monument. The water starts out about 5ft deep and gradually deepens to about 30ft. The cove is protected and usually very calm. Visibility is good, and both coral and fish are abundant.

Snorkeling tour boats (see the Activities section earlier in this chapter) pull into the bay in the morning, but they generally don't come ashore, and most leave by lunchtime. Anyway, the cove is big enough so it doesn't feel crowded.

Kayaking

Although there are no longer kayak rental operations at the bay, you can rent kayaks a few miles away in the hillside towns.

Aloha Kayak Company *(☎ 322-2868; Hwy 11)*, opposite Teshima's Restaurant in Honalo, rents single/double kayaks for $25/40 per day, including life vests and a car rack. Snorkel gear costs $5. Ask about guided kayak tours.

Kona Boy *(☎ 323-1234; 79-7491 Hwy 11)*, a half mile north of Kealakekua town, rents single/double kayaks for $25/45. These laid-back guys dispense great advice, but hurry out at closing time to hit the water themselves, so don't be late returning your equipment.

Diving

The aptly named **Long Lava Tube**, just north of Kealakekua Bay, is an intermediate dive site. Lava 'skylights' allow light to penetrate through the ceiling, yet nocturnal species may still be active during the day, and you may see crustaceans, morays and even Spanish dancers. Outside are countless lava formations sheltering critters such as conger eels, Triton's trumpet shells and schooling squirrelfish. Bring your dive light!

CAPTAIN COOK

The town named for the Pacific navigator is on Hwy 11, above the bay where Cook met his end. It's a small, unpretentious town with a few county and state offices, a shopping center, a hotel and a couple of restaurants. The Chevron gas station is open 24 hours.

As you continue south, you'll pass a handful of roadside coffee-tasting rooms that sell locally grown beans and offer freshly brewed samples for free. If you want to inspect some coffee trees close up, with macadamia-nut trees planted just beyond, look for an unmarked pull-off midway between the 107-mile and 108-mile markers, on the *makai* side of the road

Another mile farther south, **Royal Kona Museum & Coffee Mill** *(☎ 328-2511; open 7:45am-5pm daily)* may be more of a gift shop than a museum. There are free coffee samples and a few simple historical exhibits. Out back there's a working coffee operation where you can observe the pulping mill, wash station and drying bins. There's also a walk-through lava tube.

The Final Days of Captain James Cook

Captain James Cook, the first known Westerner to visit Hawaii, sailed into Kealakekua Bay at dawn on January 17, 1779. As fate would have it, he landed during the *makahiki* festival.

Cook's tall masts with white sails – even the way he maneuvered clockwise around the island – appeared to fulfill a prophecy of the return of the god Lono, who was to arrive on a floating island covered with tall trees.

Of course, Cook and his crew were showered with classic Hawaiian *hookipa* (hospitality), with the sharing of food, drink, shelter and, in those days, sex. A high priest performed a series of ceremonies recognizing Cook as the incarnation of the god Lono.

On February 4, the English vessels sailed north out of Kealakekua Bay. Off the northwest coast, however, they ran into a storm, and the *Resolution* broke a foremast. Cook opted to come about, returning to Kealakekua to repair the mast.

When Cook and his crew dropped anchor anew at Kealakekua Bay on February 11, the ruling chiefs considered it a bad portent. Party time was over, the *makahiki* had ended, and Cook's reappearance carried all the wrong signs: he had come into harbor on a counter-clockwise tack and with a busted mast.

After a series of tangled tragedies, Cook and four of his seamen were killed by Hawaiians in a violent struggle at the north end of the bay on February 14. Ironically, the world's greatest navigator was such a poor swimmer that he apparently chose to stumble into an angry crowd rather than swim a few yards out to a waiting boat.

Places to Stay

Pineapple Park *(☎ 323-2224, 877-865-2266; ⓦ www.pineapple-park.com; Hwy 11; camping $12, dorm beds $20, rooms $45-85)*, located next to an exotic fruit stand between the 110-mile and 111-mile markers, primarily draws a European clientele. The hostel has a guest kitchen, laundry facilities and a large common lounge; campers have access to the kitchen and showers. At the bus stop across the street, there's service to Hilo and Kona. For $15 the proprietors offer pickups at Kona airport.

Manago Hotel *(☎ 323-2642, fax 323-3451; Hwy 11; singles/doubles $25/28, motel-style rooms with bath $42-50, tatami rooms $65)* is a family-run hotel that started in 1917 as a restaurant, serving bowls of udon to salespeople on what was once a long journey between Hilo and Kona. Those wanting to stay overnight were charged $1 for a futon on tatami mats. These days, the basic rooms in the original building show their age – spartan furnishings, thin walls and shared baths. A highlight is the unobstructed lanai view of Kealakekua Bay.

Pomaikai Farm B&B *(Lucky Farm; ☎ 328-2112, 800-325-6427, fax 328-2255; ⓦ www.luckyfarm.com; 85-5465 Mamalahoa Hwy; B&B $50-65)*, about 3 miles south of Captain Cook, overlooks Keei Bay. Accommodations include one simple room in the main house, two open-air duplex units behind the house, and a converted coffee barn with an outdoor shower, with all-you-can-eat breakfasts. Guests have access to a common kitchen area with refrigerator, microwave and barbecue grill. Expect some traffic noise.

Cedar House *(☎/fax 328-8829; ⓦ www.cedarhouse-hawaii.com; B&B rooms $70-75, with private bath $85-95)* is perched on a quiet coffee farm 1 mile up from the town center. The house has lots of windows and natural wood, and a deck with a distant ocean view. One of the downstairs rooms has a kitchenette. The helpful hosts speak fluent German, as well as some French and Cantonese.

Places to Eat

A half mile south of the Manago Hotel, **Kealakekua Ranch Center** *(Hwy 11)* has a supermarket, a deli and a few cheap eateries.

Manago Restaurant (*☎ 323-2642; Manago Hotel; meals under $10; open 7am-9am, 11am-2pm & 5pm-7:30pm Tues-Sun*) is a Japanese version of a meat-and-potatoes eatery. It's not health food, but portions are large and the old-style atmosphere is fun. Pork chops are a speciality.

Super J's (*Hwy 11; dishes $6; open 10am-6pm Mon-Sat*) is a Hawaiian take-out find, south of the 107-mile marker. It offers a few menu items, including a *kalua* pig (roasted in an underground oven) plate with cabbage. There are a handful of tables, but few people use them.

HONAUNAU

Honaunau's main attraction is Puuhonua o Honaunau National Historical Park, commonly called the Place of Refuge.

Kona Coast Macadamia Nut & Candy Factory (*☎ 328-8141; Middle Keei Rd; admission free; open 8am-4:30pm Mon-Fri, 8am-4pm Sat, 11am-2pm Sun*) has a little display with a husking machine and a nutcracker. You can try it out, one macadamia nut at a time, and eat the final product. The showroom overlooks the real operation out back, where nuts by the bagful are husked and sorted.

Further south, Hwy 160 connects with Hwy 11 at the store, Merv's Place, then leads down to the Place of Refuge, passing Painted Church Rd and some rural scenery with grazing horses, stone walls and brilliant bougainvillea.

St Benedict's Painted Church

John Berchmans Velghe, a Catholic priest who came to Hawaii from Belgium in 1899, is responsible for the unusual painted interior of this church (*☎ 328-2227; Painted Church Rd*). When Father John arrived, the church was on the coast near the Place of Refuge. One of his first decisions was to move the church 2 miles up the slopes to its present location. It's not clear whether he did this as protection from tsunamis or just in an attempt to rise above – both literally and symbolically – the Place of Refuge and the old gods of 'pagan Hawaii.'

Father John then painted the walls with a series of biblical scenes as an aid in teaching the Bible to natives who couldn't read. He designed the wall behind the altar to resemble the Gothic cathedral in Burgos, Spain. In true Hawaiian style, painted palm leaves look like an extension of the slender columns that support the roof of the church.

This tin-roof church still holds Sunday mass at 7:15am with hymns sung in Hawaiian. Turn north at the 1-mile marker on Hwy 160 and go a quarter mile uphill – a small sign points the way.

Places to Stay

Dragonfly Ranch (*☎ 328-9570, 800-487-2159; w www.dragonflyranch.com; Hwy 160; outdoor lanai cubby $85, rooms/suites/honeymoon suite $100/150/200*), near Painted Church Rd, is a cosmic New Age retreat with a menagerie of pets. The 'soul' proprietor has been running things for over 30 years. Options vary from standard rooms in the main house to an open-air honeymoon suite with a king-size bed on a platform deck without walls; netting keeps out the large but harmless spiders that share the permaculture gardens. Make sure to walk the labyrinth, a maze of rainbow colors behind the house overlooking the sea.

A Place of Refuge (*☎ 328-0604; e crhawaii@kona.net; 83-5440 Painted Church Rd; doubles $65-75*) is a no-frills B&B on a working farm. None of the rooms have TVs, but guests can take in the terrific ocean view from the lanai. Owner Roger Dilts, a part-time Sierra Club activist, lends snorkel gear; also inquire about his kayak. There's no highway noise, but quacking geese make their presence known. Rates include full breakfast, and guests can use the kitchen.

Places to Eat

Bong Brothers (*Hwy 11; closed Sat*), just south of Middle Keei Rd, sells its own coffee as well as organic produce, smoothies and a few deli items. At lunchtime, a vegetarian chef cooks up homemade soups and healthy specials (around $5).

Wakefield Gardens Restaurant (*☎ 328-9930; Hwy 160; dishes $8; open 11am-4pm daily*), just west of Painted Church Rd, has a relaxing open-air dining patio that makes for a pleasant lunch spot. There are sandwiches, salads and plenty of vegetarian options, as well as boxed lunches and yummy homemade pie.

Keei Cafe *(☎ 328-8451; Hwy 11; mains $10-20; open 5:15pm-9pm Tues-Sat)*, at the 106-mile marker, is a simple place with plastic chairs, but it has a credentialed gourmet chef who serves up the area's best dinners. Chalkboard menu specials might include creative vegetarian dishes and delicious fresh *ahi* or *ono* (wahoo, a kind of mackerel).

PUUHONUA O HONAUNAU NATIONAL HISTORICAL PARK

This jaw-droppingly beautiful park *(☎ 328-2288; W www.nps.gov/puho; one-week pass adult/family $3/5; open 7:30am-8pm Sun-Thur, 6am-11pm Fri & Sat)* fronts Honaunau Bay, thus the tongue-twister of a name that simply means 'place of refuge at Honaunau.'

In old Hawaii, breaking any of the many *kapu*s that strictly regulated all daily interactions was thought to anger the gods, who might retaliate with a natural disaster or two. To appease the gods, the offender was hunted down and killed. Commoners who broke a *kapu*, as well as defeated warriors and ordinary criminals, could have their lives spared by reaching the sacred ground of the *puuhonua,* a sanctuary or place of refuge.

This was more of a challenge than it might appear. Since royals and their warriors lived on the grounds immediately surrounding the refuge, *kapu* breakers were forced to swim through open ocean, braving currents and sharks, to get to the *puuhonua.* Once inside the sanctuary, priests performed ceremonies of absolution that apparently placated the gods. *Kapu* breakers could then return home with a clean slate.

Hale o Keawe Heiau, the temple on the point of the cove, was built around 1650. The bones of 23 chiefs were buried there. It's thought that the *mana* (spiritual power) of the chiefs remained in their bones and that this power was added to those who came into the grounds. The *heiau* has been authentically reconstructed. The carved wooden *kii* that stand almost 15ft high beside it are said to embody the ancient gods. Leading up to the *heiau* is a large stone wall built around 1550. This **Great Wall** is more than 1000ft long and 10ft high. The west side of the wall contained the *puuhonua*, and the east side held the royal grounds.

A self-guided walk, detailed in the park brochure, wanders by Hale o Keawe Heiau, two older *heiau*s, a petroglyph, legendary stones, a fishpond, lava tree molds and a few thatched huts and shelters. The canoe on display is hand-carved from koa wood. Also take time to explore the **tide pools** in *pahoehoe* at the south end of the park. The tiny black speckles dotting the shallow pools behind the *heiau* are *pipipi*, a kind of periwinkle. Even better are the pools near the picnic area further south; they harbor coral, black-shelled crabs, small fish and eels, sea hares, and sea urchins with rose-colored spines.

Arrive early in the day for better weather, or risk cloudy afternoon skies in favor of fewer tourists. Twenty-minute orientation talks are usually given at 10am, 10:30am, 11am, 2:30pm, 3pm and 3:30pm daily. A free programme in Hawaiian studies happens monthly in the park's amphitheater, usually at 7:30pm on the first Wednesday of the month. A festival with traditional displays and food, *hukilau* (net fishing) and a 'royal court' is held on the weekend closest to July 1.

1871 Trail

Hiking the 1871 Trail to Kiilae Village takes an enjoyable hour or so. The park office lends out an informative booklet, and the staff will direct you to the nearby trailhead.

On the way to the abandoned village you'll pass a collapsed lava tube and temple ruins before reaching the steep Alahaka Ramp, which once allowed riders on horseback to travel between villages. Halfway up the ramp is Waiu-O-Hina lava tube, which opens to the sea; bring a flashlight if you want to explore it because the floor is rough and jagged rocks jut out overhead.

At the top of the ramp, incredible vistas spread out below. Keep going to the spot where Kiilae Village once stood, then head back to avoid winding up in Hookena.

The trail is tree-lined but not shaded, and it meanders through lava flows, so a morning or late afternoon excursion is advised. Come equipped with water, sunscreen and a hat regardless.

Beaches

Swimming is allowed at shallow **Keoneele Cove** inside the Place of Refuge. The cove was once the royal canoe landing. Snorkeling is best when the tide is rising, as the water

Nasty *Noni*

Unparalleled among traditional restoratives is the *noni* (Indian mulberry), which grows with wild abandon alongside roads. *Noni* is effective against everything from diarrhea to diabetes and tastes bad enough to prove it. While *noni* has received little serious attention from the scientific community so far, Hawaiians have used it topically for generations to treat sores and wounds. *Noni* is even said to be a natural alternative to Viagra.

You'll know the tree by its dark green, waxy leaves; its baseball-sized fruit has alien 'eyes' dimpling its flesh. To prepare *noni*, pick them when they're still hard and just turning white. Wash and put them in a jar just covered with water and set the jar in partial shade to ferment. When the water is nearly evaporated and the *noni* look like decomposing brains, press the pulp through a sieve and transfer to the refrigerator.

Take a tablespoon each morning on an empty stomach. Practitioners maintain the empty stomach directive has nothing to do with *noni*'s flavor, but we wonder. Be sure to consult your own doctor first. Prepared *noni* can be purchased in Big Island health food stores.

is a bit deeper and the tide brings in fish. Sunbathing is discouraged, and visitors are asked not to leave towels or mats on the ground.

Just north of the Place of Refuge is **Two-Step**, a terrific place to snorkel and dive. From the park's parking lot, take the narrow road (marked with a 15mph sign) to the left and go down about 500ft. Snorkelers step off a lava ledge immediately north of the boat ramp into about 10ft of water. It then drops off fairly quickly to about 25ft. Some naturally formed lava steps make it fairly easy to get in and out of the water, but there's no beach here. In winter, high surf can create rough waters.

Visibility is excellent, especially if you come at noon when the sun is directly overhead, with good-sized reef fish and a fine variety of corals close to shore. The predatory 'crown of thorns' starfish can be seen here feasting on live coral polyps. Divers can investigate a ledge a little way out that drops off about 100ft.

HOOKENA

If you have time to explore south Kona, Hookena is a worthwhile detour, and locals are far friendlier than their neighbors in Milolii. Chat them up and they just might invite you to their weekly beachfront potluck dinner.

Hookena was once a bustling village with two churches, a school, courthouse and post office. King Kalakaua sent his friend Robert Louis Stevenson here in 1889 to show him a typical Hawaiian village. Stevenson stayed a week with the town's judge and wrote about Hookena in *Travels in Hawaii*.

In the 1890s, Chinese immigrants began to move into Hookena, setting up shops and restaurants. A tavern and a hotel opened, and the town got rougher and rowdier. In those days, Big Island cattle were shipped from Hookena landing to market in Honolulu. When the circle-island road was built, the steamers stopped coming and people moved away. By the 1920s, the town was all but deserted.

Today Hookena is a tiny fishing community with a small county beach park. The storm-beaten remains of the landing are in front of the toilets. The beach has very soft black sand. There are picnic tables, but no drinking water. **Camping** is allowed with a county permit (see the Accommodations section earlier in this chapter).

The bay is backed by lava sea cliffs, and trees provide shade. When the winter surf is up, local kids with boogie boards hit the waves here. When it's calm, kayakers paddle around and you can snorkel straight out from the landing. It drops off pretty quickly, and there's lots of coral, but don't go too far out or you may encounter strong currents. Pygmy dolphins occasionally come into the bay, sometimes as many as a hundred at once.

The village is just over 2 miles down a narrow road that turns off Hwy 11 between the 101-mile and 102-mile markers.

MILOLII

Milolii means 'fine twist.' Historically, the village was known for its skilled sennit twisters who used bark from the *olona* shrub to make fine cord and highly valued fishnets. Villagers still live close to the sea, and many continue to make a living from it.

While Milolii's one of the most traditional fishing villages in Hawaii, this is more in spirit than in appearance. Old fishing shacks have been replaced with modern homes, and fishers now zip out in motorized boats to do their fishing. The small village consequently holds little of interest to most visitors. Furthermore, Milolii residents generally prefer their isolation and are not enthusiastic about tourists poking around.

The village sits at the edge of an expansive 1926 lava flow that covered the nearby fishing village of Hoopuloa. The turnoff is just south of the 89-mile marker on Hwy 11, then it's 5 miles down a steep but paved single-lane road that cuts across the lava flow, speckled with corrugated tin-roof houses.

Kaimana Guest House & Hostel *(☎ 328-2207; Ⓦ www.kaimanavacations.com; cnr Akahi & Elima Sts; bunks $20, singles/doubles $30/40, cottages $55)* has kayak and snorkel gear for guests. Most travelers don't rest their heads in Milolii, but it is a convenient (and cheap!) stop en route to Volcano.

North Kona

From Kailua-Kona, Hwy 19 (Queen Kaahumanu Hwy) runs north through hot, arid country with a lava landscape. From much of this coast, you can look inland and see Mauna Kea and, to the south of it, Mauna Loa; both are often snowcapped in winter.

Along the road, clumps of brilliant red bougainvillea look striking against the jet-black rock, but otherwise the vegetation is mainly sparse tufts of grass that survive the dry winds. Here and there you'll notice the Big Island's unique version of graffiti – messages spelled out in white coral against a black lava background.

The shoreline from Kailua-Kona to Waikoloa in the South Kohala district was once dotted with tiny fishing villages, but most were wiped out by the tsunami of 1946. Many beautiful secluded beaches and coves lie along this sparsely populated coastline, but they're hidden from the road and accessible only by foot. Once you hike in, you'll find white sands squeezed between a sea of hardened lava and turquoise ocean.

Hwy 19 is flat and straight and easy to zoom along, but it's also a hot spot for radar speed traps, particularly on the stretch between the airport and Kailua. Be aware that the police cruise in anything from Grand Ams to Explorers, so they're tough to spot – but, of course, a blue patrol light on a vehicle rooftop is a dead giveaway.

As part of the Ironman Triathlon route, there are wide, smooth bike lanes bordering both sides of the highway. Cyclists should note that when the air temperature is above 85°F, reflected heat from asphalt and lava can edge the actual temperature above 100°F. No drinking water or services are available along the road.

HONOKOHAU HARBOR

About 2 miles north of Kailua-Kona, Honokohau Harbor was built in 1970 to take some of the burden off Kailua Pier. These days, almost all of Kona's catch comes in here.

If you want to see the charter fishing boats pull up and weigh their catches of marlin and yellowfin tuna, drive straight in, park near the gas station and walk to the dock at the rear of the adjacent building. The best times to see the weigh-ins are generally around 11:30am and 3:30pm.

Accessible by boat off the coast of Honokohau Harbor, **Turtle Pinnacle** is a premier dive site for spotting turtles, which congregate here to clean their shells (small fish feed off the algae and parasites on the turtles' shells). The turtles are accustomed to divers, so they don't shy away from photo opportunities. Other frequent sightings in the water include frogfish, octopuses and pipefish.

Harbor House Restaurant *(dishes $5-10; open 11am-7pm Mon-Sat, 11am-5:30pm Sun)*, in the harbor complex, serves fried shrimp and chips, burgers and frosted mugs of beer ($2 happy hour). There's also a fresh and smoked fish market.

Kaloko-Honokohau National Historical Park

In the developmental stages since 1978 (but who's counting?), this park *(☎ 329-6881; open 8am-3:30pm daily)* covers 1160 acres of fishponds, ancient *heiau* and house sites, burial caves, petroglyphs, a *holua* (sled course), a restored 1-mile segment of the ancient stone footpath called the **King's Trail**, and the entire oceanfront between Kaloko and Honokohau Harbor. There's speculation that the bones of Kamehameha the Great were buried in secret near Kaloko. This, combined with the fact that Aimakapa Fishpond is a habitat for endangered waterbirds, was enough to help squeeze the national park designation through Congress.

On the coast near the north end of the park is **Kaloko Fishpond**. Before the park took over the land from Huehue Ranch, mangrove had invaded the fishpond and spread rapidly, causing native birds to abandon the habitat. The park service eradicated the mangrove in a labor-intensive process that involved cutting and torching the trees, then tearing the new shoots up one by one and burning the roots.

Aimakapa Fishpond, just inland from Honokohau Beach on the park's southern side, is the largest pond on the Kona Coast and another important bird habitat. Like Kaloko, a mangrove invasion required intensive eradication efforts. If you visit this brackish pond, you're likely to see the *aeo* (Hawaiian black necked stilt) and *alaekeokeo* (Hawaiian coot), both endangered native waterbirds that have made a significant return since the pond was cleared.

Kahinihiniula (Queen's Bath) is a brackish spring-fed pool in the middle of a lava flow. Even though it's inland, the water level changes with the tide; at high tide, saltwater seeps in and the water in the pool rises. You can get there by walking inland from the north end of Honokohau Beach. The pool is marked by stone cairns as well as Christmas berries, always a dead giveaway that freshwater is nearby.

While much of the focus within the park is on natural restoration, interpretive trails and a visitor center are in the works. Meanwhile, a ranger is often on hand to answer questions and there are free brochures explaining the cultural and archaeological significance of the site. The entrance is between the 96-mile and 97-mile markers, down a three-quarter-mile-long unpaved road that can be traversed slowly in 2WD vehicles.

Honokohau Beach

This beach, just north of the harbor, is part of the historical park. Take Honokohau Harbor road from Hwy 19, then turn right in front of the marina complex and follow the road a quarter of a mile. Pull off to the right after the dry dock boatyard. The trail begins at a break in the lava wall on the right, near the end of the road. It's a five-minute walk along a well-beaten path to the beach.

The beach itself is composed of large-grained sand – a mix of black lava, white coral and rounded shell fragments. It's not bad for swimming and snorkeling, although the bottom is a bit rocky. For many years, nude sunbathers came in droves, but park rangers now patrol the area and swimsuits are de rigueur. The only facilities are some pit toilets at the end of the trail. Consider bringing insect repellent in case the gnats are feasting.

Places to Eat

In the Kaloko Industrial Park on the *mauka* side of Hwy 19, you'll find a **Costco** (*☎ 334-0770; 73-5600 Maiau St; membership $45; open 11am-8:30pm Mon-Fri, 9:30am-6pm Sat, 10am-6pm Sun*) where members can stock up on cheap bulk groceries, everyday items and discount gas. It's probably worth joining if there are at least two of you and you'll be staying more than a week, or need to buy a big-ticket item.

Sam Choy's (*☎ 326-1545; 73-5576 Kauhola St; meals under $10; open 6am-2pm Mon-Sat, 7am-2pm Sun*), where a mix of locals and tourists come to feast on the famous cuisine of Big Island native Sam Choy, is part of a string of popular restaurants around Hawaii. The setting is casual, with Formica tables and the chef's photos and awards adorning the walls. Try the fried *poke* (marinated raw fish) omelette or a wok rice bowl with meat or veggies, and discover what the fuss is about.

KEAHOLE POINT & WAWALOLI (OTEC) BEACH

At Keahole Point, the seafloor drops steeply just offshore, providing a continuous supply of both cold water from 2000ft depths and warm surface water. Voila! These are ideal conditions for ocean thermal energy conversion (OTEC). The OTEC system operates like a steam turbine, with the difference in temperature between the cold and warm waters providing the energy source. Electricity has been successfully generated at the site, and research continues into ways to make this an economically viable energy resource. If you want to learn more, call for reservations at **public lectures** (*☎ 329-7341, ☎ ext 7; admission $3; held 10am-noon Wed & Thur*) given by the Natural Energy Laboratory of Hawaii.

The turnoff to the state hydroenergy research facility and Wawaloli Beach is 1 mile south of Kona airport between the 94-mile and 95-mile markers. At the beach, where planes drone overhead, there are bathrooms and showers. This windswept lava coastline is rocky and not very good for swimming, although a large, naturally enclosed pool 200 yards south of the bathrooms is deep enough to wade in and great for kids.

The rough dirt road that continues south from the beach leads a half mile to **Pine Trees**, one of the best surfing breaks in the Kona area. Look left as you drive in and you'll see the cluster of trees and a stretch of sand. Spare your rental car unless it's a 4WD.

ONIZUKA SPACE CENTER

The Astronaut Ellison S Onizuka Space Center *(☎ 329-3441; adult/child $3/1; open 8:30am-4:30pm daily)*, opposite the car rental booths at the Kona airport, pays tribute to the Big Island native who perished in the 1986 Challenger space shuttle disaster. The little museum features exhibits and educational films about space and astronauts. Items on display include a moon rock, a NASA space suit and scale models of spacecraft. There's also a space-themed gift shop.

KONA COAST STATE PARK

The attractive sandy beach at Mahaiula Bay is part of a newly established state park *(admission free; closed Wednesday)*. The park has shaded picnic tables, barbecue grills and portable toilets but is otherwise completely undeveloped.

The facilities are at the south side of the beach, but the park's loveliest section is at the north end, about a five-minute walk away. The inshore waters are shallow, and the bottom is gently sloping. Snorkeling and swimming are usually good, but during periods of high surf, which are not infrequent in winter, surfing is the sport of choice on the bay's north side.

The bone-rattling access road starts 2½ miles north of Kona airport, then runs for almost 2 miles across a vast lava flow that's totally devoid of trees and greenery, before depositing you at this little oasis. It's passable in a 2WD car – but go slow!

If you want to explore further, take the walking trail leading north for about 1¼ miles to paradisiacal **Makalawena Beach**. Part of the trail goes through an expanse of lava fields, and the sun reflecting on the black rock will get your blood pumping en route. But the payoff is some fine sand dunes and coves for swimming and snorkeling. Turtles poke their heads up like periscopes above the gentle, idyllic waters. There are no facilities and, during the week, almost no crowds. Weekends are family time.

South of Kona Coast State Park is another hidden treasure called **Makolea Beach**, a small black-sand beach where you probably won't encounter another soul. Just take the easy-to-navigate 'path' along the lava fields; follow the coastline and you can't lose your way (it's actually an easier walk than to Makalawena). This beach lacks shade, and the lava fields and black sand add to the heat, so remember to bring plenty of water. Again, there are no facilities.

KUA BAY

Kua Bay, also known as Maniniowali, has a secluded beach with turquoise waters and gleaming, fine white sands. The beach has a gentle slope, and the waters are inviting for swimmers most of the year and for boogie boarders and bodysurfers in winter.

Conditions are generally calm, but winter storms can generate currents in the bay and can also temporarily clear the beach of its sand. Alas, there are no trees or awnings to provide shade, very little vegetation and no facilities.

The turnoff to the beach is just north of both the 88-mile marker and the grassy 342ft **Puu Kuili**, the highest cinder cone on the seaward side of the highway. Look for the stop sign and gate at the head of the road.

The road is rough and over loose lava stones. Some people do drive down it about a half mile and then park near the roadside, but if you park near the highway it only takes about 15 to 20 minutes to walk in.

At the end of the road, a path crosses the rocks to the south end of the beach. There are no facilities.

KAUPULEHU

After the 1946 tsunami, this fishing village, accessible only by boat, was abandoned until the early 1960s, when a wealthy yachter who had anchored offshore concluded Kaupulehu would be the perfect place for a hideaway hotel.

The Kona Village Resort opened in 1965. It was so isolated it had to build its own airstrip to shuttle in guests – the highway

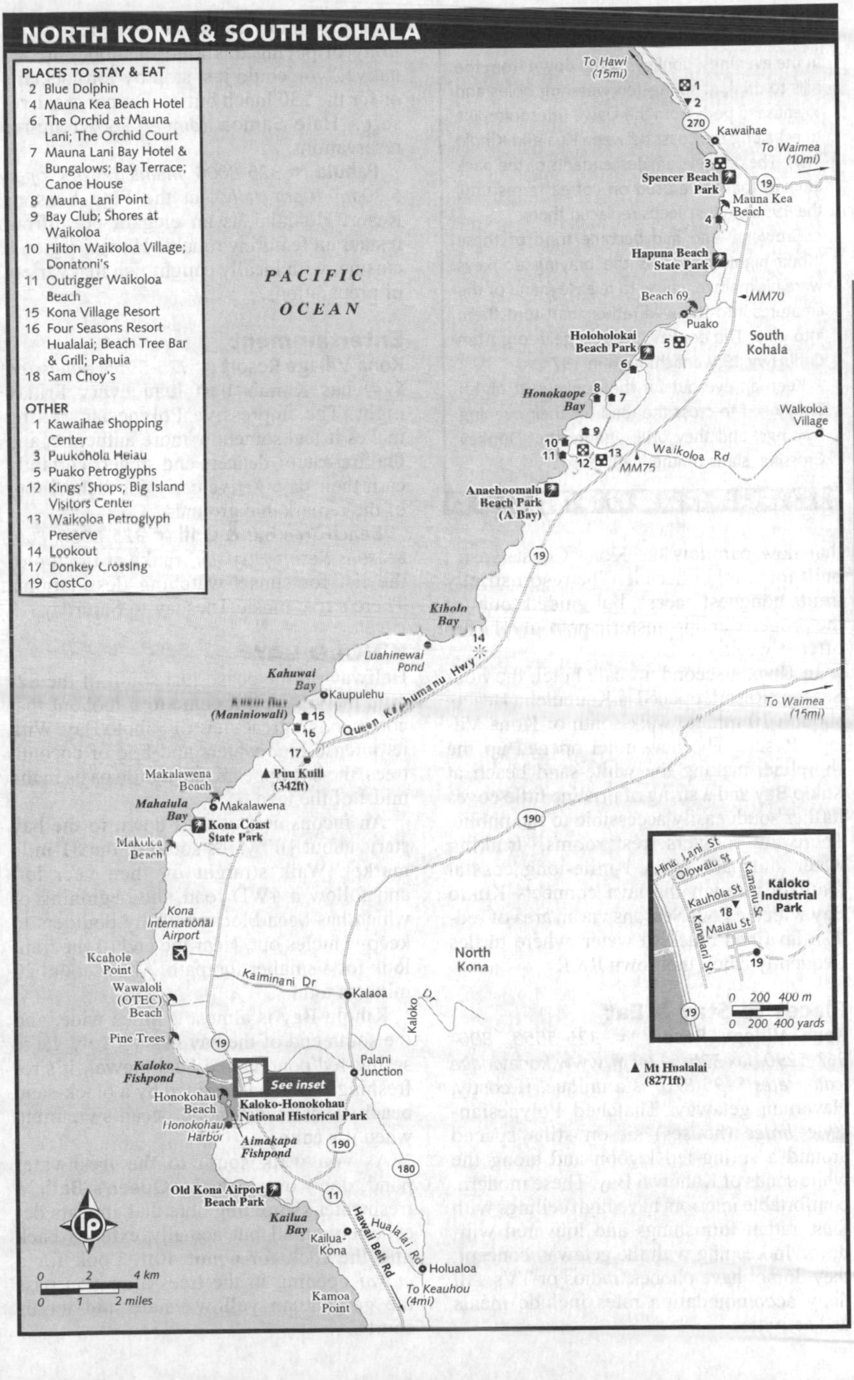
NORTH KONA & SOUTH KOHALA
PLACES TO STAY & EAT
2 Blue Dolphin
4 Mauna Kea Beach Hotel
6 The Orchid at Mauna Lani; The Orchid Court
7 Mauna Lani Bay Hotel & Bungalows; Bay Terrace; Canoe House
8 Mauna Lani Point
9 Bay Club; Shores at Waikoloa
10 Hilton Waikoloa Village; Donatoni's
11 Outrigger Waikoloa Beach
15 Kona Village Resort
16 Four Seasons Resort Hualalai; Beach Tree Bar & Grill; Pahuia
18 Sam Choy's
OTHER
1 Kawaihae Shopping Center
3 Puukohola Heiau
5 Puako Petroglyphs
12 Kings' Shops; Big Island Visitors Center
13 Waikoloa Petroglyph Preserve
14 Lookout
17 Donkey Crossing
19 CostCo
PACIFIC OCEAN
To Hawi (15mi)
270
Kawaihae
To Waimea (10mi)
Spencer Beach Park
19
Mauna Kea Beach
Hapuna Beach State Park
Beach 69
MM70
Puako
South Kohala
Holoholokai Beach Park
Honokaope Bay
Waikoloa Village
Waikoloa Rd
MM75
Anaehoomalu Beach Park (A Bay)
Kiholo Bay
Luahinewai Pond
Kahuwai Bay
Kaupulehu
Kuki'o Bay (Maniniowali)
Queen Kaahumanu Hwy
To Waimea (15mi)
Puu Kuili (342ft)
Makalawena Beach
Mahaiula Bay
Makalawena
Kona Coast State Park
Makalea Beach
190
Kona International Airport
Keahole Point
North Kona
Kaiminani Dr
Wawaloli (OTEC) Beach
Kalaoa
Kaloko Dr
Pine Trees
Kaloko Fishpond
See inset
Palani Junction
Honokohau Beach
Kaloko-Honokohau National Historical Park
Honokohau Harbor
Aimakapa Fishpond
Mt Hualalai (8271ft)
180
Old Kona Airport Beach Park
11
Kailua Bay
Kailua-Kona
Hualalai Rd
Hawaii Belt Rd
Holualoa
To Keauhou (4mi)
Kamoa Point
0 2 4 km
0 1 2 miles
Hina Lani St
Olowalu St
Kamanu St
Kauhola St
Kaloko Industrial Park
Maiau St
Kanalani St
0 200 400 m
0 200 400 yards

Donkey Crossing

In the evenings, donkeys come down from the hills to drink at spring-fed watering holes and to eat seed pods from the *kiawe* (mesquite-like trees) along the coast between Kua and Kiholo Bays. The donkeys are descendants of the pack animals that were used on coffee farms until the 1950s, when Jeeps replaced them.

Growers, who had become fond of these 'Kona nightingales,' as the braying donkeys were nicknamed, chose to release many of the creatures into the wild rather than turn them into glue. The donkeys were largely forgotten until Hwy 19 went through in 1974.

Keep an eye out for the donkeys at night: They need to cross the road for their evening feedings, and they often ignore the 'Donkey Crossing' signs on the highway!

that now parallels the Kona Coast wasn't built for another decade. The resort strictly limits nonguest access, but guided tours of the property and its historic petroglyphs are offered weekly.

In 1996, a second upscale hotel, the Four Seasons Resort, opened at Kaupulehu Beach, about a 10-minute walk south of Kona Village Resort. The new hotel opened up the shoreline, making the white-sand beach at **Kukio Bay** and a string of pristine little coves further south easily accessible to the public. There are showers, rest rooms, drinking water and parking. A 1-mile-long coastal footpath through the lava connects Kukio Bay with the Four Seasons via an area of reddish lava and brackish water, where turtles frequently enjoy their own R&R.

Places to Stay & Eat

Kona Village Resort *(☎ 325-5555, 800-367-5290, fax 325-5124; 🅦 www.konavillage.com; rates $495-870)* is a unique, if costly, Hawaiian getaway. Thatched Polynesian-style *hales* (houses) sit on stilts spaced around a spring-fed lagoon and along the white sands of Kahuwai Bay. These modern, comfortable interiors have high ceilings with fans, rattan furnishings and louvered windows. In keeping with the getaway concept, they do not have phones, radios or TVs. All daily accommodation rates include meals and activities.

If you simply can't get over the obvious irony of paying this kind of money to 'go native,' you could just stop by for cocktails or for the $30 lunch buffet. Dinner at the resort's **Hale Samoa** *(dinner $60)* requires reservations.

Pahuia *(☎ 325-8000; mains $25-48; open 5:30pm-10pm daily)*, at the Four Seasons Resort Hualalai, is an elegant oceanfront restaurant featuring reliable Hawaii regional cuisine, with locally caught fish in a variety of preparations.

Entertainment

Kona Village Resort *(☎ 325-5555; admission $74)* has Kona's best luau every Friday night. The impressive Polynesian setting makes it feel somehow more authentic, and the fire-eaters, dancers and singers certainly earn their pay. Arrive early for a short tour of the remarkable grounds.

Beach Tree Bar & Grill *(☎ 325-8000; Four Seasons Resort Hualalai)* ranks at the top of the list for sunset-watching destinations. There's live music Tuesday to Saturday.

KIHOLO BAY

Halfway up the coast, just south of the 82-mile marker, you'll come to a lookout that commands a great view of Kiholo Bay. With its intense blue waters and line of coconut trees, the bay appears like a little oasis in the midst of the lava.

An inconspicuous trail down to the bay starts about 100 yards south of the 81-mile marker. Walk straight in, then veer left and follow a 4WD road, the beginning of which has been blocked off by boulders to keep vehicles out. Near the end of the trail, look for a smaller footpath. Allow about 20 minutes total.

Kiholo Bay is almost 2 miles wide, and the south end of the bay has a lovely, large spring-fed pond called **Luahinewai**. It's refreshingly cold and fronted by a black-sand beach. There's also good ocean swimming when it's calm.

As you walk south to the freshwater pond, don't overlook the **Queen's Bath**, a freshwater swimming hole that appears deceptively small but actually extends back into the rock for about 40ft. Look for a *makai* opening in the trees after you pass the gargantuan yellow estate and tennis courts.

South Kohala

At Waikoloa you'll enter the South Kohala district. South Kohala was an important area in Hawaiian history, and today's visitors will find ancient trails, *heiau*s, fishponds, and petroglyph sites to explore.

This shoreline stretch of Hwy 19 is also known as the Big Island's Gold Coast, home to swanky resorts and pro golf courses. The resorts have wonderful drive-up beaches, as do nearby beach parks.

WAIKOLOA BEACH RESORT

After crossing into the South Kohala district, a turnoff just south of the 76-mile marker leads to the Outrigger Waikoloa Beach and Hilton Waikoloa Village hotels.

The Kohala branch of the **Big Island Visitors Center** *(☎ 886-1655; Suite B15, 250 Waikoloa Beach Dr; open 8am-4:30pm Mon-Fri)* is in the Kings' Shops complex.

Waikoloa Petroglyph Preserve

As you travel down this road, a lava field etched with impressive petroglyphs is off to the right, immediately before the Kings' Shops complex. If you park at the shopping complex, it's about a five-minute walk along a signposted path to the first of the etchings.

Stay on the path at all times. Do not walk atop the petroglyphs, thereby damaging them irreparably as careless tourists do. Many of the petroglyphs date back to the 16th century; some are graphic (humans, birds, canoes), others cryptic (dots and lines). Later Western influences show in the form of horses and English initials.

Although the footpath through the petroglyphs is called the King's Trail, this section was actually a horse and cattle trail built in the late 19th century. The trail once connected Kailua-Kona with Kawaihae. You can continue on the trail to a historical preserve at the Mauna Lani Resort, about 2 miles away, but it's a hot walk over lava, and a modern-day *kapu* on the trail warns, 'Beyond this point you may be in danger of being struck by a golf ball. Please return as you came.'

Anaehoomalu Beach Park

Often called 'A Bay' by the linguistically challenged, this long, sandy beach, lined with palm trees, curves along an attractive bay.

It's an immaculate beach for an outing if you're staying in Kona, though beaches like Hapuna to the north have more glorious sand. Winter weather can produce rip currents, but the water is usually quite calm. It's popular for swimming and windsurfing.

Both ends of the bay are composed of prehistoric lava flows from Mauna Kea, with *aa* (rough, jagged lava) to the north and smooth *pahoehoe* to the south. The south end of the beach has public facilities, with showers, toilets, changing areas, drinking water and parking.

The north end of the beach, which fronts the Outrigger Waikoloa Beach, has a little fitness area with swing ropes, chin-up bars and a volleyball net. The **beach hut** *(☎ 886-6666, ext ☎ 1)* has the latest on water conditions and rents windsurfing equipment and snorkel sets. It also offers beginner windsurfing and scuba lessons, boat dives, catamaran cruises and rides in a glass-bottom boat.

Anaehoomalu was once the site of royal fishponds, and archaeologists from the Bishop Museum have found evidence here of human habitation dating back more than a thousand years. Two large fishponds lie just beyond the line of coconut trees on the beach. A short footpath starts near the showers and winds by the fishponds, caves, ancient house platforms and a shrine. Interpretive plaques along the way explain the area's history.

There's a good spot for snorkeling at the north end of the beach, directly in front of the sluice gate. Here you'll find coral formations, a fair variety of tropical fish and, with a little luck, sea turtles. If you're not a snorkeler, you can still sometimes see the turtles by simply walking out onto the rock wall that encloses the sluice gate and looking down into the surrounding waters.

Hilton Waikoloa Village

Islanders have nicknamed the 62-acre Hilton Waikoloa Village 'Disneyland.' You won't find serenity at this extravagant development, but there's eye candy. When it opened in 1988 at a cost of $360 million, the hotel billed itself as the world's most expensive resort.

As the hotel had no beach, it built its own, along with a 4-acre saltwater lagoon stocked with tropical fish, a dolphin pool harboring at least a dozen cetaceans, a 'river' with a current for rafting, and sprawling swimming pools with cascading waterfalls. Guests navigate the enormous grounds in canopied boats that cruise artificial canals and on a modernistic tram that looks like something straight out of downtown Tokyo.

Inside you can browse the multimillion-dollar art collection along a 1-mile-long walkway that runs in both directions from the front lobby. Museum-quality pieces include extensive collections from Melanesia, Polynesia and Asia. It's particularly big on Papua New Guinea, with war clubs and spears, spirit boards, carved fighting shields and a partial replica of a ceremonial house.

Park for free at the hotel or walk over from the Outrigger, a quiet 15-minute stroll away along the lava coast.

Places to Stay

Outrigger Waikoloa Beach *(☎ 886-6789, 800-688-7444, fax 800-622-4852; W www.outrigger.com; 69-275 Waikoloa Beach Dr; rooms from $315)* has comfortable rooms with private lanai and a beachside location that's far superior to the Hilton's. The Kings' Shops are within walking distance, so you're not captive to resort prices for all your meals. Outrigger offers numerous promotional discounts via tele-phone or Internet that can save you hundreds of dollars.

Hilton Waikoloa Village *(☎ 885-1234, 800-445-8667, fax 885-2900; W www.hiltonwaikoloavillage.com; 1 Waikoloa Beach Resort; ocean-view rooms $230-540, presidential suite $5500)* mega-hotel has all the usual Hilton amenities and two 18-hole golf courses. Rates vary dramatically depending on the season and the views.

There are two upscale condominium complexes in the area. Each has a pool, but they're both about a 15-minute walk from the beach.

The Shores at Waikoloa *(☎ 885-5001, 800-922-7866; 5460 Waikoloa Beach Dr; 1-bedroom apartments $335, 2-bedroom apartments $390)* is an Aston-managed property. Inquire about discounts for senior and AAA members, as well as fourth-night-free deals.

The Bay Club *(☎ 886-7979, 877-229-2582, fax 886-4538; 5525 Waikoloa Beach Dr; 1-bedroom/2-bedroom units from $300/350)* has a shuttle service to the beach and shopping center.

Places to Eat

The **Kings' Shops** outdoor mall has a small sundries store and a **food pavilion** *(open 9:30am-9:30pm daily)*. Walk through to reach a fish and chips outpost overlooking an artificial lake.

Roy's Waikoloa Bar & Grill *(☎ 886-4321; Kings' Shops; open 11:30am-2pm & 5:30pm-9:30pm daily; mains $22-25)* is a branch of the popular Roy's on Oahu, serving excellent Hawaii regional cuisine. At dinner, expect creative main courses such as rack of lamb in a *lilikoi* (passion fruit) cabernet sauce or blackened *ahi* with pickled ginger.

Big Island Steak House *(☎ 886-8805; Kings' Shops; mains $16-23; open 5pm-10pm daily)* is great for boisterous families who want to escape stuffier resort dining. Sweet macadamia-nut bread arrives soon after you're seated, but save room for sauteed mahimahi served with pineapple salsa or cuts of top sirloin.

Donatoni's *(☎ 885-1234; Hilton Waikoloa Village; mains $24-37; open 6pm-9:30pm Tues-Sat)*, the most highly regarded of the Hilton's fine-dining dinner restaurants, features authentic Italian food. Look for starters like carpaccio, followed by pasta dishes and seafood or steak courses.

Entertainment

Outrigger Waikoloa Beach *(☎ 886-6789; W www.outrigger.com; 69-275 Waikoloa Beach Dr; adult/child $64/32; luau 6pm Sun & Wed)* has a poolside luau with a Hawaiian dinner buffet, an open bar and a Polynesian show. The Outrigger's **Clipper Lounge** serves drinks and *pupus* (snacks) until 11pm nightly.

Hilton Waikoloa Village *(☎ 886-1234; adult/child $58/25; performances 6pm Fri)* presents a 'Legends of the Pacific' dance show. Admission includes a dinner buffet and one cocktail. A guitarist strums from 6pm to 10pm in the Hilton's **Kamuela Provision Company Lounge**.

MAUNA LANI RESORT

After a brief encounter with coconut palms and bright bougainvillea at the highway entrance, visitors turning down Mauna Lani Dr head through a long stretch of lava with virtually no vegetation. Halfway along there's a strikingly green golf course sculpted into the black lava. Mauna Lani Bay Hotel is at the end of the road; The Orchid at Mauna

Lani Hotel and Holoholokai Beach Park are to the north.

Mauna Lani Bay Hotel

The beach in front of the Mauna Lani Bay Hotel is protected, but the water is rather shallow. Snorkelers might want to explore a coral reef beyond the inlet. A less-frequented cove is down by the Beach Club restaurant, a 15-minute walk to the south.

An old coastal foot trail leads about 1 mile farther south to Honokaope Bay, passing a few historical sites, including a fishers' house site and other village remains. The southern end of Honokaope Bay is protected and good for swimming and snorkeling when the seas are calm.

Kalahuipuaa Fishponds

These ancient fishponds are along the beach just south of the Mauna Lani Bay Hotel in a shady grove of coconut palms and shady, native *milo* trees. They are among the few continuously working fishponds in Hawaii.

The ponds are stocked, as they were in ancient times, with *awa* (Hawaiian milkfish). Water circulates from the ocean through traditional *makaha* (sluice gates), which allow small fish to enter but keep mature, fattened catch from leaving. You might notice fish sporadically jumping into the air and slapping down on the water, an exercise that knocks off parasites.

Kalahipuaa Historic Trail

This trail begins on the inland side of the Mauna Lani Bay Hotel, at a marked parking lot opposite the resort's little grocery store. Pick up a free, self-guided trail map from the concierge desk.

The first part of the trail meanders through a former Hawaiian settlement that dates from the 16th century, passing lava tubes once used as cave shelters and a few other archaeological and geological sites marked by interpretive plaques. Keep an eye out for quail, northern and red-crested cardinals, saffron finches and Japanese white-eyes.

The trail then skirts fishponds lined with coconut palms and continues out to the beach, where you'll find a thatched shelter with an outrigger canoe and a historic cottage with a few Hawaiiana items on display. If you continue southwest past the cottage, you can loop around the fishpond and back to your starting point – a round trip of about 1½ miles.

Take a break en route at the attractive cove near the southern tip of the fishpond, where the swimming is good and a lunchtime restaurant offers simple fare.

Holoholokai Beach Park

North of The Orchid at Mauna Lani, this beach has a rocky shoreline composed of coral chunks and lava. It's not a great spot for swimming, but snorkeling is reasonably good when the waters are calm, and winter can bring good surf.

The park has showers, drinking water, rest rooms, picnic tables and grills. For those not picnicking, the main reason for visiting is to walk the trail to the Puako petroglyphs.

Puako Petroglyphs With more than 3000 petroglyphs, the Puako petroglyph preserve has one of the largest collections of ancient lava carvings in Hawaii.

Take Mauna Lani Dr and turn right at the rotary, then right again on the beach road immediately before the grounds of The Orchid. From the inland end of the beach parking lot, a well-marked trail leads three-quarters of a mile to the petroglyphs. The human figures drawn in simple linear forms are some of Hawaii's oldest such drawings. Like all petroglyphs in Hawaii, the meaning of the symbols remains enigmatic.

The aging petroglyphs are fragile, as the ancient lava flow into which they're carved is brittle and cracking. Stepping on the petroglyphs can damage them, so be careful not to. If you want to make rubbings, use the authentically reproduced petroglyphs that have been created for that purpose; they're just a minute's walk down the trail from the parking lot. Bring rice paper and charcoal, or cotton cloth and crayons.

Because of the sharp thorns along the trail, wearing 'rubbah slippah' is unwise – the thorns can easily pierce their soft soles and your feet. The path is only partly shaded.

Places to Stay

Mauna Lani Bay Hotel & Bungalows *(☎ 885-6622, 800-367-2323, fax 885-1484; W www.maunalani.com; 68-1400 Mauna Lani Dr;*

THE BIG ISLAND

mountain-/ocean-view rooms $375/550, 1-bedroom/2-bedroom/3-bedroom villas with kitchen $550/715/910) is one of the finest resort hotels in the islands. This hotel is ritzy but still low-key – a modern open-air structure centered around a breezy atrium that holds waterways, orchid sprays and full-grown coconut trees. A saltwater stream that runs through the hotel and outdoors into the sun holds small black-tipped sharks and a variety of colorful reef fish. Check the website for promotional packages.

Mauna Lani Point *(☎ 667-1666, 800-642-6284, fax 661-1025; W www.classicresorts.com; 50 Nohea Kai Dr; 1-bedroom units from $305, 2-bedroom units $405)* is a luxurious condo complex at the south side of the Mauna Lani Resort.

The Orchid at Mauna Lani *(☎ 885-2000, 800-845-9905, fax 885-5578; W www.orchid-maunalani.com; 1 N Kaniku Dr; garden-/ocean-view rooms from $435/605)*, on Pauoa Bay just north of the Mauna Lani Bay Hotel, is a rather subdued place. Originally part of the Ritz chain, it's now a Sheraton-affiliated property. Inquire about deals for families.

THE BIG ISLAND

Places to Eat

Bay Terrace *(☎ 885-6622; Mauna Lani Bay Hotel; breakfast dishes $8-20, buffet $24; open 6:30am-10:30am daily)* offers a simple but delicious breakfast buffet.

The Orchid Court *(☎ 885-2000; The Orchid at Mauna Lai; breakfast $9-18, buffet $24, dinner $10-28; open 6:30am-11am & 6pm-9:30pm daily)* is a lovely outdoor place with a breakfast buffet. At night it prepares island cuisine like pan-seared *opakapaka* (pink snapper) and fusion pizzas.

Canoe House *(☎ 885-6622; mains $27-50; Mauna Lani Bay Hotel; open 6pm-9pm daily)*, which fronts the beach, is a romantic, open-air dinner restaurant. The menu blends pan-Asian and Hawaiian influences, with an emphasis on seafood. Dishes include grilled lemon-pepper scallops or pancetta-wrapped mahimahi with coconut spinach risotto.

Gallery *(☎ 885-7777; lunch $8-15, dinner $25-30; open 11am-3pm daily, 6pm-8:45pm Tues-Sat)*, at the Mauna Lani resort's golf clubhouse, serves continental and Pacific Rim dishes. The fresh fish is a speciality; try the *onaga* (red snapper) encrusted with macadamia nuts.

Beach Club *(☎ 885-5910; dishes $6-10; open 11am-4pm daily)*, a casual restaurant at the south end of Kaniku Dr overlooking a swimming cove, is a bit easier on the wallet. The menu includes an organic chicken salad and a turkey with avocado sandwich.

Entertainment

Honu Bar *(☎ 885-6622; Mauna Lani Bay Hotel; open until midnight)* offers billiards, cigars and occasional live entertainment. The hotel **atrium** also has live Hawaiian music and hula dancing from 5:30pm to 8:30pm nightly.

The seaside **Ocean Bar** *(The Orchid at Mauna Lani)* has great sunset views from its chaise lounge chairs, while the Orchid's **Polo Bar/Paniolo Lounge** has leather chairs, bookshelves, checkerboards, *pupus* and cigars (you can buy 'em and smoke 'em here).

PUAKO

Puako is a quiet one-road coastal village. To get here, take either the marked turnoff from Hwy 19 or a bumpy side road from Hapuna Beach State Park. **Hoku Loa Church** (1858) is about a half mile beyond the Puako Bay boat ramp. A plain plastered building with a few simple wooden pews, it's still used for Sunday services. The town also has a general store.

Puako is lined with giant **tide pools**, set in the swirls and dips of the *pahoehoe* lava that forms the coastline. Some of the pools are deep enough to shelter live coral and other marine life. Snorkeling can be excellent off Puako, although the surf is usually too rough in winter. A narrow beach of pulverized coral and lava lines much of the shore.

The easiest beach access is at the south end of the village, just 150 yards before the road dead ends. Here a short dirt drive leads out to the water. There is no beach per se, but there is a small cove used for snorkeling and shore diving; be careful of the undertow. A couple of minutes' walk north brings you to a few petroglyphs, a *konane* game board chinked into the lava and tide pools deep enough to cool off in.

Beautiful **Beach 69** has easy access and gentle waves. There's plenty of shade, and boundary trees make it feel like each group of sunbathers has a private little plot. The beach itself has a mix of lava rock and sand. There are no facilities. Turn down Puako Rd between the 70-mile and 71-mile markers, then take the first right turn, and the road quickly becomes one lane. Look for telephone pole #71 on the left-hand side and park. Follow the 'road' to its end and then tramp along the footpath that runs parallel to a wooden fence. And, for those of you with overactive imaginations, telephone pole #71 was once numbered 69, which gave the beach its nickname.

HAPUNA BEACH STATE PARK

The long beautiful stretch of white sand along Hapuna Bay is the Big Island's most popular beach. The park has a landscaped picnic area, showers, pay phones, drinking water and pitiable rest rooms. Lifeguards are on duty daily.

When it's calm, Hapuna affords good swimming, snorkeling and diving. In the winter, it's a hot bodysurfing and boogie-boarding beach. High winter surf can produce strong currents close to the shore and a pounding shorebreak, but waves over 3ft should be left for the experts. Hapuna has had numerous drownings and many of the victims have been tourists unfamiliar with the water conditions.

A tiny cove with a small sandy beach lies about five minutes' walk north of the park. The water is a bit calmer there and, in winter, less sand is kicked up by the waves.

3 Frogs Café *(snacks $2.50-6.50; open 10am-4pm daily)* sells burgers, jumbo sodas and shave ice. A window at the side rents boogie boards or snorkel sets from $5 per half day.

Just up from the beach are six state-owned A-frame **cabins** *(rates $20)* with million-dollar views. Each plywood palace sleeps four people on two platforms (you sleep head to head) and has lights and electricity. They are also surprisingly bug-free. Amenities include shared bathrooms with showers and a cooking pavilion with a stove and fridge. For booking details, see the Accommodations section earlier in this chapter.

MAUNA KEA RESORT

In the early 1960s, Laurance Rockefeller obtained a 99-year lease on the land around Kaunaoa Bay from his friend Richard Smart, owner of Parker Ranch. Five years later, Rockefeller opened Mauna Kea Beach Hotel, the first luxury hotel on the Neighbor Islands. It's at the north side of the bay, just north of the 68-mile marker.

The hotel lobby and grounds have displays of Asian and Pacific artwork, including bronze statues, temple toys and Hawaiian quilts. The north garden holds the most prized possession, a 7th-century pink granite Buddha from a temple in southern India.

Kaunaoa Bay is a gorgeous crescent bay with a white-sand beach that has since come to be known as **Mauna Kea Beach**. It has a gradual slope and fine swimming conditions most of the year. There's good snorkeling on the north side when it's calm. The beach is open to the public, and 30 parking spaces are set aside for beach visitors. If you're having a drink or lunch at the hotel, you can bypass the issue of obtaining a parking pass.

Just north of Mauna Kea Beach is this delightful gem, **Mauumae Beach**, with soft white sand, shady trees and protected waters. Fish don't swim in abundance, but snorkelers do migrate to the south end of the small beach. Enter the Mauna Kea resort, turn right on Kamahoi and cross two wooden bridges. Look for pole #22 on the left and park beside the road. Walk down the five-minute trail to Ala Kahakai post, then turn left. The resort only issues 10 parking passes daily, but beachgoers can also park at nearby Spencer Beach and walk over in 10 minutes on the Ala Kahakai Trail, a shady coastal path.

Mauna Kea Beach Hotel *(☎ 882-7222, 800-882-6060, fax 882-5700; W www.maunakeabeachhotel.com; 62-100 Mauna Kea Beach*

Decadent Sunday Brunch

Everyone should enjoy a leisurely all-you-can-eat buffet brunch at the **Mauna Kea Beach Hotel** *(☎ 882-7222; adult/child $36/18; brunch served 11am-2pm Sun)* at least once. Served in a covered outdoor area overlooking the stellar beach, the buffet is an ostentatious spread including sushi, dim sum, prime rib, lobster bisque, domestic and imported cheeses and a Belgian waffle station, plus the usual array of bacon, eggs, made-to-order omelettes and fresh fruit. Over at the dessert table, you'll think Al Capone just robbed a bakery *and* the local ice-cream shop.

A Hawaiian band performs relaxing music during the meal. The filling fare should render you full for the remainder of the day. Reservations are essential.

Dr; mountain-/ocean-view rooms $350/545) is Kohala's charming grand dame, but it's already showing signs of age after a major renovation in 1995. It has all of the expected resort amenities, including a fitness center, tennis courts and an 18-hole golf course.

If you're spending an evening here, don't miss the luminous **manta rays** at the lookout point between 7pm and 10pm. The resort also hosts a lively Saturday night beachfront **clambake** and a **luau** every Tuesday; each costs $72/36 per adult/child.

SPENCER BEACH PARK

Spencer Beach Park, off Hwy 270 just south of Kawaihae, is a shady place for families with children, as the shallow sandy beach is protected by a reef and by the jetty to the north. If anything, it's a bit too protected – the water tends to get silty. The rocky south end of the beach past the pavilion is better for snorkeling, although entry is not as easy, and kayaking is prohibited.

The park has a lifeguard station, picnic tables, barbecue grills, rest rooms, showers, drinking water and both basketball and volleyball courts. A footpath leads south to Mauumae Beach near the Mauna Kea Resort.

Spencer's **camp sites** are exposed and crowded together, but it's still the best beach north of Kona to sleep under the stars. Campers need a county permit (see the Accommodations section earlier in this chapter).

PUUKOHOLA HEIAU

This national historic site *(☎ 882-7218; admission free; visitor center open 7:30am-4pm daily)*, off to the side of the road that leads down to Spencer Beach, encompasses the last major temple built in Hawaii.

In 1790, after his attempt at a sweeping conquest of the islands was thwarted, King Kamehameha sought the advice of Kapoukahi, a soothsayer from Kauai. Kamehameha was told that if he built a temple to his war god here above Kawaihae Bay, then all of Hawaii would fall to him in battle. Kamehameha immediately began construction of Puukohola Heiau, even laboring alongside his workers.

Completing the *heiau* in 1791, Kamehameha then held a dedication ceremony and invited his last rival on the Big Island, Keoua, the chief of Kau. When Keoua came ashore, he was killed and brought up to the new *luakini* as the first offering to the gods. With Keoua's death, Kamehameha took sole control of the Big Island and then went on to fulfill the soothsayer's prophecy.

Terraced in three steps, Puukohola Heiau was covered with wooden *kii* and thatched structures, including an oracle tower, an altar, a drum house and a shelter for the high priest. After Kamehameha's death in 1819, his son Liholiho and powerful widow Kaahumanu destroyed the *heiau*'s deity images and the temple was abandoned. Today, only the basic rock foundation remains, but it's still an impressive site.

Incidentally, Puukohola means 'Hill of the Whales,' as migrating humpbacks can often be seen offshore during winter.

A two-minute trail to the *heiau* starts at the visitor center, which has a few simple displays and pamphlets. If you arrive after hours, you can park at Spencer Beach Park and walk to the *heiau* along an old entrance road that's now closed to vehicle traffic.

Just beyond Puukohola Heiau are the ruins of **Mailekini Heiau**, which predates Puukohola and was later turned into a fort by Kamehameha. **Hale o Kapuni Heiau**, a third temple dedicated to shark gods, lies submerged just offshore; nearby on land, you can see the stone leaning post where the high chief watched sharks bolt down offerings.

The trail leads across the highway to the site of **John Young's homestead**. Young, a shipwrecked British sailor, served Kamehameha as a military advisor and island governor. Today, all that remains are partial foundations for two of Young's buildings.

KAWAIHAE

Kawaihae has the Big Island's second-largest deepwater commercial harbor. The harbor has fuel tanks, cattle pens and a little local beach park – not really much to attract visitors, most of whom stop in Kawaihae to eat and fuel up on their way to North Kohala.

Makai Hale *(☎ 885-4550, 800-262-9912, fax 885-0559; Ⓦ www.bestbnb.com; singles/doubles $125, additional room for 3rd & 4th person $75)* is just off Hwy 270 and is convenient both for jaunts to Kohala beaches and Waimea. Each room has a private bath and access to a small kitchen area. The deck, with swimming pool and Jacuzzi, offers a postcard view and whale-watching in season.

Cafe Pesto *(☎ 882-1071; Kawaihae Shopping Center, Hwy 270; dishes $8-10, pizzas from $10; open 11am-9pm Sun-Thur, 11am-10pm Fri & Sat)* has a tempting luau pizza with *kalua* pig, sweet onions and pineapple. Also served are excellent calzone, pastas, hot sandwiches and salads.

Blue Dolphin *(☎ 882-7771; Hwy 270; mains from $13; open 5:30pm-9:30pm Fri & Sat; drinks until 11pm)*, south of Kawaihae Shopping Center, has live music on weekends, usually rock and reggae (admission $5). As nightlife is scarce in Kohala, locals (even families!) head here.

North Kohala

The northwest tip of the Big Island is dominated by a central ridge, the Kohala Mountains. The leeward side of the ridge is desertlike. The windward side is lush with coastal cliffs and spectacular hanging valleys.

North Kohala is often bypassed by travelers, but it has a few impressive historical sites, sleepy towns to poke around in and a valley lookout at the end of the road. There are two fully paved routes into the district, an inland road (Hwy 250) and a coastal road (Hwy 270).

Hwy 270 (Akoni Pule Hwy) starts in Kawaihae, takes in the coastal sights of Lapakahi State Historical Park and Mookini Heiau and ends at a lookout above Pololu Valley. A trail runs from there down to the valley floor, but the view alone is worth the drive.

Hwy 250 (Kohala Mountain Rd) runs for 20 miles from Hawi to Waimea. As you head south, the road peaks at 3564ft and Maui rises out of the mist, with the red crater of Haleakala capping the skyline. Mauna Kea and Mauna Loa are visible. Views of the coast and Kawaihae Harbor unfold below, and there's a roadside scenic lookout near the 8-mile marker where you can take it all in. The road then winds through rolling green hills dotted with grazing cattle and descends past neat rows of ironwood trees.

LAPAKAHI STATE HISTORICAL PARK

The park *(admission free; open 8am-4pm daily; closed holidays)* has the feel of a ghost town – which it is. Even the visitors in this desolate spot tend to be few.

This remote fishing village was settled about 600 years ago; as the terrain was rocky and dry, the villagers turned to the sea for their food. Fish were plentiful, and the cove fronting the village provided a safe year-round canoe landing. Eventually some of the villagers moved to the wetter uplands and began to farm, trading their crops for fish with those who had stayed on the coast. In the process, Lapakahi grew into an *ahupuaa*, a wedge-shaped division of land radiating from the mountainous interior out to the sea. When the freshwater table dropped in the 19th century, the village was abandoned.

The park encourages visitors to imagine what life was like centuries ago. A 1-mile-long **loop trail** leads to the remains of stone walls, house sites, canoe sheds and fishing shrines. Displays show how fishers used lift nets to catch *opelu* (scad mackerel), a technique still practiced today, and how the salt used to preserve the fish was dried in stone salt pans. Visitors can try their hands at Hawaiian games, with game pieces and instructions laid out for *oo ihe* (spear throwing), *konane* (Hawaiian checkers) and *ulu maika* (stone bowling).

Lapakahi's waters are part of a marine life conservation district. The fish are so plentiful and the water so clear that you can stand above the shoreline and watch yellow tangs and other colorful fish swim around in the cove below. It is illegal to swim with them, however, and there's no easy beach access.

The park, which is largely unshaded, is just south of the 14-mile marker. Brochures are available at the trailhead. Bring water.

MAHUKONA BEACH PARK

Mahukona Beach Park, 1 mile north of Lapakahi and a half mile off Hwy 270, has an abandoned landing that was once linked by rail to the sugar mills on the north Kohala coast.

The area beyond the landing makes for interesting snorkeling and diving, although it's usually too rough in winter. Entry, via a ladder, is in about 5ft of water. Heading north, it's possible to follow an anchor chain out to a submerged boiler and the remains of a ship in about 25ft of water. Coral lines the bottom and visibility is good when it's calm. You'll find a shower near the ladder where you can rinse off. There is no sandy beach, however.

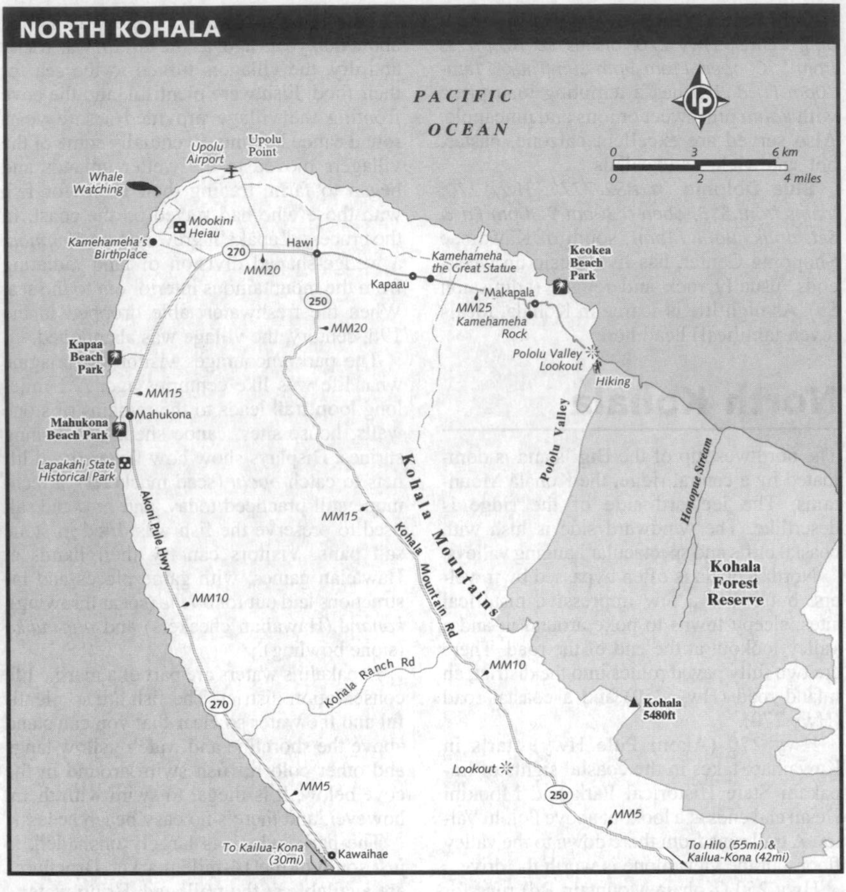

Veer left (south) as you drive in to reach the small, ratty county park. There are rest rooms, but they won't win any prizes for cleanliness. Those planning on **camping** here in the unkempt grassy area should bring their own drinking water, as the park's water is unfit for consumption, and plenty of insect repellent.

For information on camping permits, see the Accommodations section earlier in this chapter, or call **Hisaoka Gym** *(☎ 889-6505; office open 1pm-2pm Mon-Fri)* in Kapaau.

MOOKINI HEIAU

Mookini is a massive temple set atop a grassy knoll on the desolate northern tip of the Big Island. One of the oldest and most historically significant *heiau*s in Hawaii, it commands a clear view out across the ocean to Maui. This eerily windswept site has a sense of timelessness and overarching *mana*.

Chants date Mookini Heiau back to AD 480. This was a *luakini heiau*, where the *alii* (chiefs) offered human sacrifices to the war god Ku. According to legend, it was built in one night with basalt stones gathered in Pololu Valley and passed along a human chain stretching 14 miles.

A *kapu* that once prevented commoners from entering the *heiau* grounds wasn't lifted until recent times, and the site still remains well off the beaten path, even though it has been a national historic landmark since 1963. Because so few people come this way, there's a good chance it will just be you, the wind and the spirits here. Bring along clothes that offer protection from the wind and other elements.

During the winter season, this is a fantastic spot to observe humpback whales; at the northernmost tip of the coast there's an area of freshwater where the massive mammals swim to clean off their barnacles.

The *heiau* is 250ft long, with rock walls reaching 25ft high. The entrance is through the wall on the west side. The long enclosure on the right immediately before the *heiau* entrance was the home of the *mu* who secured sacrificial victims for the *heiau* altar.

A large scallop-shaped altar on the north end of the *heiau* (temple) is thought to have been added by Paao, the Tahitian priest who arrived around the 12th century and introduced human sacrifice to Hawaiian worship. Islanders understandably tried to live a safe distance from Mookini.

The current *kahuna nui* (high priestess), Leimomi Mookini Lum, is the most recent in a long line of Mookini tracing their lineage back to the temple's first high priest. On the third Saturday of each month (except December), she invites Hawaii residents and visitors to the temple to help weed from 9am to noon; bring a lei, work gloves, water, a brown-bag lunch and sunscreen. After visitors have invested their sweat and sense of respect, Leimomi provides an oral history of the *heiau* and answers questions. For information, call ☎ 889-1069 or ☎ 373-8000.

To get here, turn north off Hwy 270 at the 20-mile marker and go 1¾ miles down to Upolu airport. Turn left onto the rutted dirt road that runs parallel to the coast. This road can get very muddy after heavy rains – it's not always passable in a standard car (or even walkable). After 1½ miles you'll come to a fork. The left road leads up to the *heiau*.

Kamehameha's Birthplace

Kamehameha the Great was said to have been born on a stormy winter night in 1758 on this ruggedly desolate coast. According to legend, Kamehameha's mother was told by a *kahuna* that her son would become a destroyer of chiefs and a powerful ruler. The high chief of the island didn't take well to the prophecy, and in a King Herod–like scenario, he ordered the newborn killed. Immediately after birth, the baby was taken to Mookini Heiau for his birth rituals and then into hiding in the nearby mountains. If you continue straight ahead at the fork below the *heiau* for a third of a mile, you'll reach the stone enclosure that marks his birth site.

HAWI

North Kohala's largest town (hah-**vee**) has fewer than 1000 residents, but can be a delightful place to while away a few hours. Although it has a few more storefronts than actual stores, people are being increasingly drawn here by the area's low-key flavor and lower property values.

North Kohala used to be sugar country, and Hawi was the biggest of half a dozen sugar towns. Kohala Sugar Company, which had incorporated all of the mills, closed down its operations in 1975. The park on Hwy 250 in front of the post office is cool and shady with giant banyan trees. Behind the park is the old sugar mill tower, a remnant of the town's former mainstay. You can still see the occasional strip of feral cane among the pastures outside town.

Entering town via Hwy 270, you'll pass the small **visitor center** *(Hwy 270, open 9am-5pm Mon-Fri, weekend hours vary)*, which offers Internet access, a few area

Kohala Ditch

Kohala Ditch is an intricate series of ditches, tunnels and flumes that were built to carry water from the rugged wet interior of the Kohala Forest Reserve out to the Hawi area. The source of the water is the Waikoloa Stream, midway between the Pololu and Waipio Valleys.

The ditch was built in 1906 to irrigate Kohala sugarcane fields. The last Kohala cane was cut in the 1970s, but the ditch continues to be a source of water for Kohala ranches and farms. It was engineered by a sugar baron, John Hind, with the financial backing of Samuel Parker of Parker Ranch. Kohala Ditch runs 22½ miles and was built by Japanese immigrant laborers, who were paid about $1 a day for the hazardous work. More than a dozen of the laborers died during construction.

Much of the ditch runs through 19,000 acres of Kohala land, which the agricultural giant Castle & Cooke sold a few years back to a developer. For guided kayak tours of the ditch, see the Hawi section of this chapter.

brochures and sketch maps. Hawi also has a post office, grocery store, gas station and a few restaurants.

Flumin' da Ditch *(☎ 889-6922, 877-449-6922; Ⓦ www.flumindaditch.com)* offers three-hour kayaking tours of Kohala's historic irrigation system every morning and afternoon for $85/65 per adult/child. Don't expect rapids or whitewater on the journey, but prepare to get soaked. The same company runs Hummer safari tours into the mountain rain forest.

The Landing *(☎ 889-1000; Hwy 270)*, North Kohala's very own day spa, is thriving on massages, body treatments and its kava bar.

Places to Stay

Hawi Hotel *(☎ 889-0419; Ⓦ www.hawihotel.com; 55-514 Hawi Rd; rooms $47-72)*, at the main highway intersection, is a renovated old-style hotel with simple, clean rooms. Over the years, the place has bounced between trying to attract tourists and being given over to long-term boarders. All rooms have baths, but no fans, air-con or telephones.

Cardinals' Haven *(☎ 884-5550, advance reservations ☎ 425-822-3120; doubles/triples $55/60, rooms per week $250; open Nov 20-May 10)*, in the winter home of Peter and Sonja Kamber, enjoys a lovely rural setting 3 miles south of Hawi center. From the yard, you can look across cattle pastures clear out to Maui. It's all quite straightforward, but the guest unit comes with a TV, minikitchenette and sofa bed. Originally from Switzerland, the Kambers speak fluent German and French.

Places to Eat

A **farmers market** *(open 7:30am-1pm Sat)* is held at the park on Hwy 250.

Kohala Health Food *(☎ 889-0277; Hwy 270; open 11am-6pm Mon-Fri, 11am-4:30pm Sat)* sells tea, organic juices and a few packaged natural food items.

Kohala Coffee Mill *(☎ 889-5577; Hwy 270; snacks under $5; open 6:30am-6pm daily)* serves muffins, pastries, natural ice cream and fresh-brewed Kona coffee, not to mention hand-painted coconuts.

Hula La's Mexican Kitchen & Salsa Factory *(Hwy 270; meals under $10; open 10am-8:30pm Mon-Fri, 8am-8:30pm Sat & Sun)* boasts tasty Mexican fare, but only a smattering of tables in close quarters or out on the lanai. No credit cards.

Bamboo *(☎ 889-5555; Hwy 270; lunch/dinner $8/10; open 11am-2:30pm Tues-Sun, 6pm-8:30pm Tues-Sat)* has excellent island food and pleasant tropical decor. Savor the pineapple barbecue chicken, nut-encrusted island fish or Hawaiian stir-fry, and save room for homemade desserts. Occasionally there's live music on weekends. Reservations are recommended.

Aunty's Place *(☎ 889-0899; Hwy 270; meals from $10; open 11am-9pm Mon-Fri, 4pm-9pm Sat, noon-9pm Sun, pizza until 10pm daily)* makes pizzas all day and traditional hearty German dinners at night. While the owner doesn't like to compare her 'housewife cooking' to Waimea's Edelweiss restaurant's 'hotel cooking,' she shouldn't be so modest.

KAPAAU

The Kamehameha the Great statue on the front lawn of the North Kohala Civic Center may look familiar. Its lei-draped and much-photographed twin stands opposite Honolulu's Iolani Palace.

The statue was made in 1880 in Florence, Italy, by American sculptor Thomas Gould. When the ship delivering it sank off the Falkland Islands, a second statue was then cast from the original mold. The duplicate statue arrived in the islands in 1883 and took its place in downtown Honolulu.

Later the sunken statue was recovered from the ocean floor and completed its trip to Hawaii. This original statue was then sent here, to Kamehameha's childhood home, where it now stands watching the traffic trickle along in quiet Kapaau.

The town has a courthouse, police station, library and bank. **Kamehameha Park** boasts a large, modern gymnasium and everything from a ballpark to a swimming pool, all free and open to the public. During the King Kamehameha Day festivities in June, the park hosts a swingin' soiree that includes a parade and Hawaiian dancing, music and food.

Endearing **Kohala Book Shop** *(☎ 889-6400; Hwy 270; open 11am-5pm Tues-Sat)* is not only the biggest and best used bookstore in Hawaii, but also a gathering place for local authors and literary luminaries from abroad.

Immediately around the corner is the colorful home of the Kohala Tong Wo Society, founded in 1886. The building is closed to the public.

Hawaii once had many Chinese societies, providing immigrants with a place to preserve their cultural identity, speak their native language and socialize. This is the last one remaining on the Big Island.

Kalahikiola Church

Protestant missionaries Elias and Ellen Bond, who arrived in Kohala in 1841, built Kalahikiola Church in 1855. The church itself is usually locked, but the detour through lush foliage with chirping birds ain't too shabby. The land and buildings on the drive in are part of the vast Bond estate, proof enough that missionary life wasn't one of total deprivation.

If you want to take a look, turn inland off Hwy 270 onto a narrow road a half mile east of the Kamehameha statue, between the 23-mile and 24-mile markers. The church is a half mile up from the highway.

Kamehameha Rock

Kamehameha Rock is on the right side of the road, about 2 miles east of Kapaau, on a curve just over a small bridge. It's said that Kamehameha carried this rock uphill from the beach below to demonstrate his strength.

When a road crew attempted to move the rock to a different location, they managed to get it up onto a wagon, but the rock stubbornly fell off – a sign that it wanted to stay put. Not wanting to upset Kamehameha's *mana*, the workers left it in place.

Places to Eat

Takata Store *(Hwy 270; open 8am-7pm Mon-Sat, 8am-1pm Sun)*, near the high school, is the largest market in North Kohala. It's stocked with produce, meat and all kinds of other edibles.

Jen's Kohala Cafe *(Hwy 270; dishes $4-7.50; open 10am-5pm daily)*, which is located just opposite the Kamehameha statue, really is the place to eat in town. Jen's has tasty chicken Caesar salads, good chili and a recommendable Greek wrap sandwich with organic greens. Also on the menu are fresh fruit smoothies, deli sandwiches and soups.

MAKAPALA

The little village of Makapala has only a few hundred residents. If you're hiking down to Pololu Valley, the town's little store is the last place to get a drink or snack – if it's open.

Keokea Beach Park is on a scenic rocky coast but isn't a real draw for visitors, as there's no sandy beach and it's not great for water activities. Signs warn about dangerous shorebreaks and strong currents. A protected cove allows for OK swimming. The park has rest rooms, showers, drinking water, picnic pavilions and barbecue grills, but no camping.

The park is about 1 mile in from the highway; take the marked turnoff about 1½ miles before Pololu Valley Lookout. On the way down to the beach, you'll pass an old **Japanese cemetery**. Most of the gravestones are in *kanji* (Japanese script), and a few have filled sake cups in front of them.

Kohala's Guest House *(☎ 889-5606, fax 889-5572; ⓔ svendsen@gte.net; 52-277 Akoni Pule Hwy; studio cottages $59, 2-bedroom & 3-bedroom cottages $110-125)* is near the start of the road down to Keokea Beach Park. Some of these simple, modern cottages sleep up to eight people and have private baths, although smaller ones share facilities. Guests share a fully equipped kitchen and lounge with a stereo, TV and VCR.

POLOLU VALLEY

Hwy 270 ends at a viewpoint that overlooks secluded Pololu Valley, with its scenic backdrop of steeply scalloped coastal cliffs spreading out to the east. The lookout has the kind of strikingly beautiful angle that's rarely experienced without a helicopter tour – some say it's even better than the Waipio Valley Lookout.

Pololu was once thickly planted with wetland taro. Pololu Stream fed the valley, carrying water from the remote, rainy interior to the valley floor. When the Kohala Ditch was built, it siphoned off much of the water and put an end to the taro production. The last islanders left the valley in the 1940s, and the valley slopes are now forest reserve land.

Pololu Valley Trail

The trail from the lookout down to Pololu Valley only takes about 20 minutes to walk. It's steep, but not overly strenuous and you'll be rewarded with lovely vistas throughout.

Be cautious with your footing – much of the trail is packed clay that can be slippery when wet. Some Good Samaritans have provided walking sticks for your assistance, but only use them if the trail feels mucky; the sticks are heavy and they may be more of a hindrance than a help in hot weather.

The black-sand beach fronting the valley stretches for about a half mile and can make an enjoyable stroll. Driftwood collects in great quantities and on rare occasions glass fishing floats get washed up as well. Cattle and horses roam the valley; a gate at the bottom of the trail keeps them in. Surf is usually intimidatingly high in winter, and there can be rip currents year-round. There are no beach facilities.

Organized Tours

Hawaii Forest & Trail *(☎ 331-8505, 800-464-1993; 🅆 www.hawaii-forest.com)* runs operations all over the island, but one of their outposts is at the end of Highway 270 right before the lookout. It offers morning mule rides ($95/85 adult/child) over range land, ridges and to waterfall lookouts, but not into the valley itself.

Mules are used for a few reasons: the sure-footed creatures are steadier than horses and can handle heavier loads. Also, in the early 1900s they helped Japanese laborers build the Kohala Ditch, which you'll see on the tour, so there's a certain symmetry in using them to introduce visitors to the area today.

Waimea (Kamuela)

Waimea has a pretty setting in the foothills of the Kohala Mountains at an elevation of 2670ft. It's cooler than the coast, with more clouds and fog. Afternoon rainbows are common.

Headquartered here is domineering Parker Ranch, Hawaii's largest cattle ranch, which spreads across nearly one-ninth of the Big Island. Almost everything in Waimea is owned, run or leased by Parker Ranch.

Waimea certainly has its *paniolo* (Hawaiian cowboy) influences, but it's also rapidly growing in size and sophistication. It's the main town serving the upscale subdivisions being developed on former ranches in the Kohala Mountains. While many of

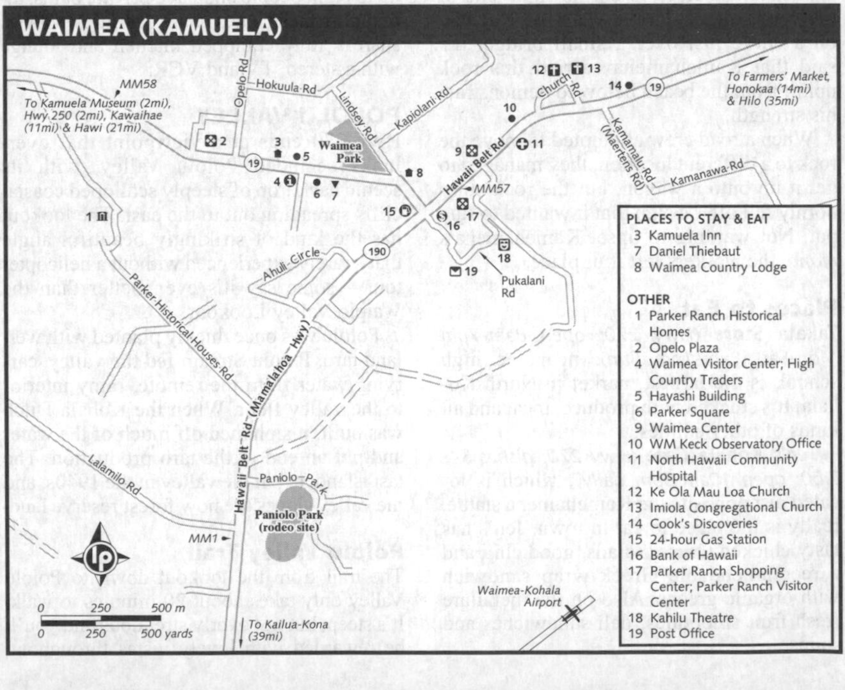

the newcomers are wealthy mainlanders, Waimea is also home to a growing number of international astronomers who work on Mauna Kea.

For most visitors this is just a stopover between Kona and Hilo. Waimea won't wow you with a lot of action or historical sights; the museums are diverting enough and the green pastures truly scenic. The town does have first-rate art galleries and excellent restaurants, some of which have received national kudos.

Orientation & Information

Waimea is also referred to as Kamuela, which is the Hawaiian spelling of Samuel. Although some say the name comes from an early postmaster named Samuel Spencer, most claim it's for Samuel Parker of Parker Ranch fame. Regardless, the result is the same: confusion. Address all Waimea mail to Kamuela.

The **post office** *(☎ 885-6239; 67-1197 Mamalahoa Hwy; open 8am-4:30pm Mon-Fri, 8:30am-10:30am Sat)* is southwest of Parker Ranch Center. The **Waimea Visitor Center** *(☎ 885-6707; 65-1291 Kawaihae Rd, behind High Country Traders; open 8:30am-3:30pm Mon-Fri)* is inside Lindsey House and was built in 1909 by Parker Ranch for a five star employee (those were the days!).

The **WM Keck Observatory office** *(open 8am-4:30pm Mon-Fri)*, in the town center, has a short video and simple displays about the Mauna Kea telescopes, along with information on volcano activities.

Parker Ranch Visitor Center

This small **museum** *(☎ 885-7655, W www.parkerranch.com; Parker Ranch Shopping Center; adult/child $6/4.50; open 9am-5pm daily, last entry 4pm)* has modest exhibits on the ranch's history, including Parker family memorabilia such as portraits, lineage charts, quilts and dishes; cowboy gear, including saddles and branding irons; and some Hawaiian artifacts – stone adzes, lava bowls, poi pounders, and tapa bed covers. That said, other Big Island museums have more extensive and certainly more dynamic Hawaiiana collections.

Perhaps most interesting are the old photos and the 25-minute movie on Parker Ranch, which shows footage of *paniolos* rushing cattle into the sea and lifting them by slings onto the decks of waiting steamers.

A ticket that includes this museum and the Parker Ranch Historical Homes costs $12 for adults, $9.50 for children.

Parker Ranch Historical Homes

These two 19th-century homes *(☎ 885-5433; adult/child $8.50/6; open 10am-5pm daily, last entry 4pm)* are on Hwy 190, less than 1 mile south of the intersection with Hwy 19.

The estate's grand century-old **manor** holds an interesting collection of European art and antique Chinese vases. One room is French provincial, with chandeliers, skylights and master Impressionist paintings. Another room is covered with playbills and photos of actor and Parker descendant Richard (Dick) Smart. Word is that this theatrical eccentric greeted tourists in his bathrobe on more than once occasion before his death in 1992.

Next door is the more modest **Mana Hale**, a re-creation of the original 1840s home built by John Parker in the hills outside Waimea. Parker constructed his home

Parker Ranch

Parker Ranch claims to be the nation's largest privately owned ranch, and some impressive numbers back those words. It has more than 35,000 cattle on 225,000 acres, contained by 850 miles of fence; the ranch produces more than 15 million pounds of beef annually.

Parker Ranch owes its beginnings to John Palmer Parker, a 19-year-old from New England who arrived on the Big Island in 1809 aboard a whaler. He took one look at Hawaii and jumped ship.

Parker soon gained the favor of Kamehameha, who commissioned him to bring the cattle under control. Parker managed to domesticate some of the cattle and butchered others, cutting the herds down to size.

Later, Parker married one of Kamehameha's granddaughters and in the process landed himself a tidy bit of land. He eventually gained control of the entire Waikoloa *ahupuaa* (large land area) clear down to the sea.

Descendants of the Mexican-Spanish cowboys brought over to help round up the cattle still work the ranches today. Indeed, the Hawaiian word for cowboy, *paniolo*, is a corruption of the Spanish word *españoles*.

in essentially the same saltbox style that was popular in his native Massachusetts, except he used koa wood. The original interior was dismantled board by board and rebuilt here. It's now decorated with period furnishings and old photos of the hardy-looking Parker clan.

Church Row

Waimea's first Christian church was a grass hut built in 1830. It was replaced in 1838 by a wooden structure also built using coral stones carved out of the reef. They named it Imiola, which means 'seeking salvation.'

The current **Imiola Congregational Church** *(Sunday services 8:30am & 10:15am)* was constructed in 1857 and restored in 1976. The interior is simple and beautiful; it's built entirely of koa, most of it dating back to the original construction.

In the churchyard is the grave of missionary Lorenzo Lyons, who arrived in 1832 and spent 54 years in Waimea. Lyons wrote many of the hymns, including the popular 'Hawaii Aloha,' that are still sung in Hawaiian here each Sunday. Also in the garden is the church bell, too heavy for the church roof to support.

The green-steepled church next door is the all-Hawaiian **Ke Ola Mau Loa Church**. Buddhists, Baptists and Mormons also have places of worship in this row.

Kamuela Museum

There's a lot of history crammed into this amazingly wonderful museum *(☎ 885-4724; cnr Hwys 19 & 250; adult/child $5/2; open 8am-4pm daily)*.

Formerly operated by a direct descendant of John Parker, the museum is a treasure trove of Hawaiiana: tapa beaters, ancient feather lei, fishhooks made of human bones, a stone knuckle-duster and a dog-toothed death cup. Some items are very rare, and many once belonged to royalty, such as Kamehameha the Great's sacred chair and tables of teak and marble from Iolani Palace.

A quirky collection of non-Hawaiian items ranges from a Tibetan prayer horn to a captured Nazi flag to a piece of rope used on the Apollo 11 mission.

Special Events

Waimea's annual **Fourth of July rodeo**, with cattle roping, bull riding and other hoopla, just celebrated its 40th anniversary. Another whip-cracking rodeo happens every Labor Day weekend, and smaller *paniolo* (Hawaiian cowboy) events occur at other times of the year. The **Aloha Festival Paniolo Parade**, on the weekend near the first day of autumn, honors local cowboys.

Places to Stay

Waimea's reasonably priced accommodation makes it a decent alternative for travelers who prefer upcountry scenery and open spaces.

Kamuela Inn *(☎ 885-4243, 800-555-8968, fax 885-8857; W www.hawaii-bnb.com/kamuela.html; rooms $60-85, suites $90-185)* is a cross between an inn and a small hotel. There are 30 rooms with TV and private bath, but no phones; suites sleep up to four people and have refrigerators and stoves. Free pastries and coffee are provided in the morning.

Waimea Country Lodge *(☎ 885-4100, 800-367-5004, fax 885-6711; W www.castleresorts.com; Lindsey Rd; rooms $90-95, with kitchenette $105)* is a small motel with 21 rooms. All have private baths, phones, TVs and views of the Kohala hills out the back. There can be early morning noise from trucks unloading at the nearby shopping center, however.

Aaah, The Views B&B *(☎ 885-3455, fax 885-4031; W www.beingsintouch.com; 66-1773 Alaneo St; rooms $75-110)* is a cutesy hostelry, just a few minutes west of town. Guests are welcome to use the common kitchen, yoga and meditation rooms, and hammocks on the porch overlooking a stream. The Skylight Room is a romantic alcove, while the Treetop Suite, with its private deck and entrance, can accommodate up to six people. All rooms have cable TV and phones. Discounts are available for longer stays.

Waimea Suite B&B *(☎ 937-2833; e cookshi@aol.com; doubles $125)* is the new venture of knowledgeable local Patti Cook. Two miles east of town off Hwy 19, this two-bedroom apartment faces Mauna Kea and sleeps up to four people. Amenities include a full kitchen stocked with local condiments, dining lanai, cable, TV, VCR, telephone and stereo. If you book directly, you'll receive a $20 gift certificate to her shop, Cook's Discoveries.

Waimea Gardens Cottages *(☎ 885-4550, 800-262-9912, fax 885-0559; ⓔ bestbnbs@aloha.net; doubles $135-150, extra person $15)*, just 2 miles west of town, has two charming cottages with hardwood floors, French doors and a deck. The remodeled unit has a full kitchen, Jacuzzi and private garden, while the newer cottage has a fireplace but more limited cooking facilities. Both come stocked with breakfast items. The owner, Barbara Campbell, also runs **Hawaii's Best Bed & Breakfasts** *(ⓦ www.bestbnb.com)* and can book upscale accommodations around the island, including in Waimea.

Mountain Meadow Ranch *(☎ 775-9376, fax 775-8033; ⓦ www.mountainmeadowranch.com; singles/doubles $70/80, 2-bedroom cottage per day/week $135/800)*, about 11 miles northeast of Waimea off Hwy 19, makes a convenient base for exploring Waipio Valley and the Hamakua Coast. Amiable hosts have set aside the lower level of their redwood home, where there are two bedrooms, a large tiled bathroom, a dry-heat sauna, a TV and VCR in the lounge, and a refrigerator and microwave. Only one party is booked at a time; ie, if you book one bedroom only, the other bedroom won't be rented out during your stay. There's also a pleasant cottage that has two bedrooms, a full kitchen and a living room with a queen-size sofa bed, woodstove, TV and VCR.

Places to Eat

You can buy fresh produce and flowers from the **farmers market** *(open 7am-noon Sat)* at the Hawaiian Home Lands office, at the 55-mile marker on the east side of town.

In Parker Square, look for **Foodland** supermarket and **Waimea Coffee & Co** *(☎ 885-4472; 65-1279 Kawaihae Rd; open 7am-5pm Mon-Fri, 8am-4pm Sat)* for that 100% Kona-grown caffeine jolt. **KTA Super Store** *(☎ 885-8866; 65-1158 Mamalahoa Hwy; open 6:30am-11pm daily)* is at Waimea Center, where you'll also find a health food store, bakery and deli.

Waimea Treats *(☎ 885-2166; Waimea Center; open 10:30am-8pm daily)* serves a rainbow of shave ice and Hawaiian ice-cream flavors

Maha's Café *(☎ 885-0693; Waimea Center; breakfast $3-5, lunch under $10; open 8am-4pm Thur-Mon)* is a cheerful Hawaiian eatery for home-style cooking, such as poi pancakes with coconut syrup or local fish with taro and greens. It's inside Waimea's first frame house, built in 1852; a shop on the side sells Hawaii-made gifts.

Hawaiian Style Café *(☎ 885-4295; Hayashi Bldg; meals $5-10; open 6am-12:45pm Mon-Fri, 4pm-7:30pm Tues-Fri, 7:30am-noon Sun)* will blow your cholesterol level. Inside a funky pink building, the restaurant has an old-style counter with cheap chairs and just three booths. On Friday, the special luau plate is a feast and you gotta love that the chef wears his Spam T-shirt with pride.

Aioli's *(☎ 885-6325; Opelo Plaza; dinner mains $13-21; open 11am-4pm Tues, 11am-8pm Wed & Thur, 11am-9pm Fri & Sat, 8am-2pm Sun)* bakes its own breads, cakes and pastries and at lunch has good sandwiches, salads and soups. Dinners vary from goat cheese enchiladas to fresh seafood and steaks. Aioli's lacks a liquor license, but you can bring your own beer or wine (no corkage fee).

Reservations are recommended for the following places.

Merriman's *(☎ 885-6822; Opelo Plaza; lunch $7-12, mains $17-33; open 11am-1:30pm Mon-Fri, 5:30pm-9pm daily)* draws discerning crowds with its excellent Hawaii regional cuisine. A speciality is the delicious wok-charred *ahi*, blackened on the outside and sashimi-like inside. Chef and owner Peter Merriman pioneered the use of fresh, organically grown and chemical-free products from Big Island farmers and fishers.

Daniel Thiebaut *(☎ 887-2200; 65-1259 Kawaihae Rd; lunch $7-15, dinner mains $20-30; open lunch 11:30am-1:30pm Mon-Fri, dinner 5:30pm-9:30pm daily)* has an elegant plantation-era atmosphere and rattan furniture. Its award-winning French-Asian cuisine features locally grown produce, fish and meat. Salads are recommended, along with the Kona-style fish. Lunch usually comes with a complimentary dessert.

Entertainment

Waimea's entertainment scene is limited, perhaps because cowboys rise at dawn and astronomers work all night!

Kahilu Theatre *(☎ 885-6017; Parker Ranch Center)* stages plays, classical music concerts, dance recitals and other productions.

Koa House Grill *(☎ 885-2088; Waimea Center)* often has live weekend entertainment and raucous karaoke.

Shopping

Reyn's *(☎ 885-4493; Parker Ranch Shopping Center)* is known as the 'Brooks Brothers of the Pacific.' Their signature is Hawaiian fabrics in reverse.

Cook's Discoveries *(☎ 885-3633; 64-1066 Mamalahoa Hwy)*, where almost everything for sale has been made in the islands, stocks gourmet treats, crafty gifts and Hawaiian music CDs and tapes.

Gallery of Great Things *(☎ 885-7706; Parker Square)* is a standout among Waimea's many antiques, art and collectibles galleries. Browse for Hawaiian, Polynesian and Asian art, furnishings and photographs.

Waimea General Store *(☎ 885-4479; Parker Square)* has everything from Hawaiian cookbooks to toys. In a similar vein, **Crackseed, etc** *(☎ 885-6966; Hayashi Bldg)* vends local treats.

Getting There & Away

It's 40 miles from Kailua-Kona along Hwy 190, which becomes Old Mamalahoa Highway in town. It takes about 1½ hours to travel the 55 miles along Hwy 19 to Hilo.

From Kona, the road climbs out of residential areas into a mix of lava flows and dry, grassy rangeland studded with prickly pear cacti. Along the way you'll see a little one-room church, broad distant coastal views, wide-open spaces and tall roadside grasses that have an incredible golden hue in the morning light.

For bus information, see the Getting Around section earlier in this chapter.

AROUND WAIMEA

Waimea to Honokaa

Hwy 19 heads east from Waimea to Honokaa through rolling hills and cattle pastures, with views of Mauna Kea to the south. For a peaceful back road, turn right off Hwy 19 onto the Old Mamalahoa Hwy just west of the 52-mile marker. (If you're coming from Hilo, turn left at the 43-mile marker opposite Tex Drive Inn and then take the next immediate right.)

This 10-mile detour winds through hill country, with small roadside ranches, old wooden fences and grazing horses. This is the part of Hawaii that tourists have yet to discover. Nobody's in a hurry on this road, if they're on it at all. It can make an interesting alternative route for cyclists, although you'll need to be cautious as the road is narrow, winding and hilly.

Mana/Keanakolu Road

To get closer to Mauna Kea for photography or views, drive partway down Mana Rd, which leads around the eastern flank of Mauna Kea. It begins off Hwy 19 at the 55-mile marker on the eastern side of Waimea. After 15 miles, the road becomes Keanakolu Rd and continues about 25 miles to Summit Rd (the road leading up Mauna Kea), near the Humuula Sheep Station.

Only the first part of the Waimea section is paved. The entire road is passable on horseback, on a mountain bike or in a 4WD vehicle, but a couple of dozen cattle gates must be opened and closed along the way. Be aware that it's mostly ranchers and hunters who come this way, and it's a long way from anywhere should you get stuck en route.

Hakalau Forest National Wildlife Refuge This wildlife refuge protects a portion of the state's largest koa-ohia forest, which provides habitat for endangered bird species, including the native hoary bat and Hawaiian hawk.

The Death of David Douglas

The circumstances surrounding the death of famed botanist David Douglas in 1834 are somewhat mysterious, as his gored body was found trapped with an angry bull at the bottom of a pit on the slopes of Mauna Kea. Hunters commonly dug such pits and camouflaged them with underbrush as a means of trapping feral cattle, but the probability of both Douglas and a bull falling into the same hole seemed highly suspicious. Fingers were pointed at Australian Ned Gurney, an escaped convict from Botany Bay who had been hiding out in the area and had been the last person to see Douglas alive.

Hilo authorities, unable to solve the case, packed both Douglas' body and the bull's head in brine and shipped them to Honolulu for further investigation. By the time the body arrived in Oahu, it was so badly decomposed that they hastily buried Douglas' remains at the missionary church and the case was closed.

Puuhonua o Honaunau National Historical Park

ANN CECIL

Puuhonua o Honaunau

LEE FOSTER

Astronomical observatories, Mauna Kea

KARL LEHMANN

Kealakekua Bay State Historical Park

CASEY & ASTRID WITTE MAHANEY

RICHARD CUMMINS

Aloha statue with traditional leis, Honolulu

LEE FOSTER

Traditional mask, Bishop Museum, the Big Island

CLINT LUCAS

Ti-leaf bowls

Only very limited access is allowed into the refuge itself; for information and permits, call the **refuge manager** (☎ *933-6915)* between 8am and 4pm Monday to Friday. The locked entrance is 40 miles up Keanakolu Rd (good 4WDs only, impassable after rains).

There are no facilities and no interpretive signs. An ideal time to visit is during the second week in October, which is National Wildlife Refuge Week, when Hawaiian ornithological experts and rangers are on hand.

David Douglas Memorial A memorial *(Keanakolu Rd)* to David Douglas, the Scottish botanist for whom the Douglas fir tree is named, is about halfway between Waimea and the Saddle Rd. Douglas died in 1834 at this spot.

Hamakua Coast

The Hamakua Coast winds along the island's northeastern shoreline, from the dramatic cliffs of Waipio Valley down 45 miles to Hilo. This is the heart of a defunct Hawaiian sugar industry, and wild cane stalks, some 8ft tall, blow in the trade winds. Streams and waterfalls pulse through gulches on the wet windward slopes of Mauna Kea. From various vantage points, the ocean sparkles deep aquamarine, set brilliantly against green monkeypod crowns and orange African tulip blossoms.

All along its length, the Hawaii Belt Rd (Hwy 19) is an impressive engineering feat spanning lush ravines with a series of

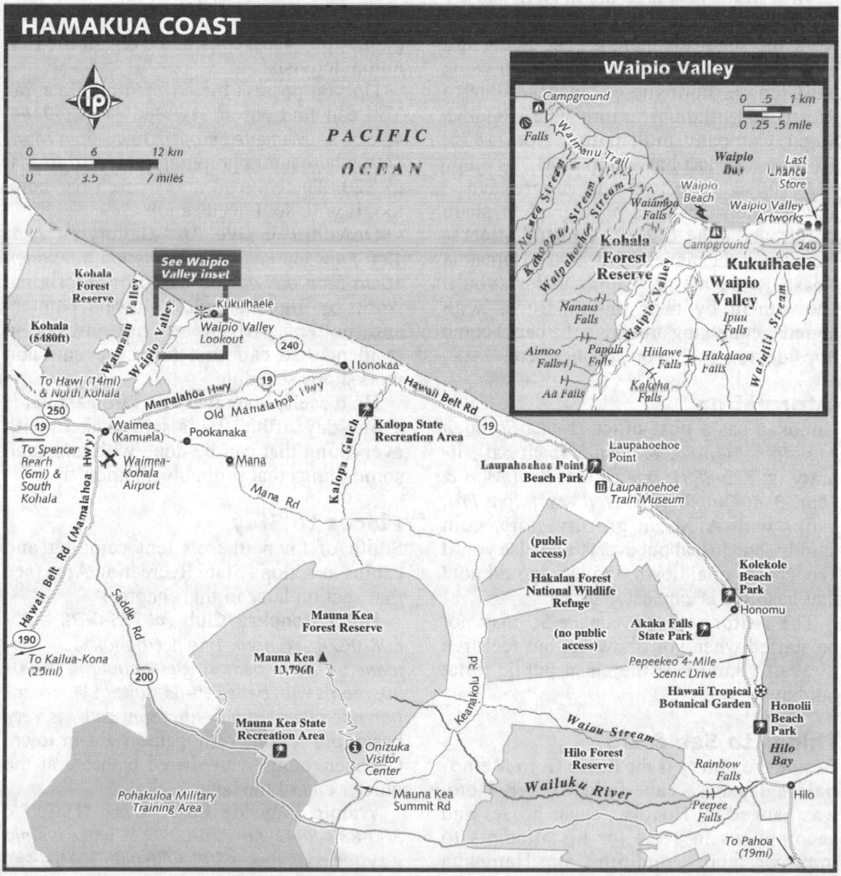

sweeping cantilevered bridges. It's certainly picturesque, with inviting back roads if you have time to dawdle. But even if you're just zipping between Kona and Hilo, at least make time for Waipio Valley Lookout and a hot *malasada* from legendary Tex Drive Inn.

There are many lovely B&Bs along this stretch of coast, but only a few budget places worth recommending. There are, however, camp sites at several public beach parks.

HONOKAA

Like the tides of the Pacific below, Honokaa (population 2185) rises and falls with the times: from cattle and sugar to soldiers and tourists, this town has had to reinvent itself after each crashing wave.

Most of the people living in Honokaa are descendants of immigrants brought here to work the sugar plantations. The Scots and English were the first to arrive; then came the Chinese, Portuguese, Japanese, Puerto Ricans and Filipinos in turn. The Honokaa Sugar Company mill, dating from 1873, processed its last harvest in 1993.

At times reflective and progressive – antique shops and aura photographers share storefronts along historic Mamane Street – Honokaa is the biggest town on the Hamakua Coast. Residents of Waipio Valley (you'll know them by their muddy trucks with hounds scrambling around in the back) come 'topside' to stock up on supplies here.

Information

Honokaa has a **post office** *(Lehua St; open 9am-4pm Mon-Fri, 8:15am-9:45am Sat)*, **library** *(☎ 775-8881; open 11am-7pm Mon & Thur, 9am-5pm Tues & Wed, 9am-3pm Fri)*, banks with ATMs, a grocery store, coin laundry and just about everything else you'd expect in a small town. Drivers should note that gasoline is expensive here.

The **visitor center** *(Mamane St)* may not be staffed when you show up, but feel free to avail yourself of the clean public toilet out back.

Things to See & Do

Beside the library is the **Katsu Goto Memorial**. A Japanese cane-field worker, Goto, was hanged by Honokaa sugar bosses and accomplices in 1889 for his attempts to improve labor conditions on Hamakua plantations. He's considered one of the first union activists.

Taro

Do you possess the coveted purple aura? You can find out at **Starseed** *(☎ 775-9344; 45-3551A Mamane St; open 10am-5pm Mon-Sat)*, where aura photographs cost from $10 to $20. There's also an espresso bar here, too, if your soul needs a jolt.

Downhill at **Live Arts Gallery** *(☎ 775-1240; 45-368 Lehua St; admission free; open 10am-5pm daily)*, you can browse original works by Big Island glass blowers, painters and potters. Artists are not always in residence, so call first for the events and workshops schedule.

Held each November, the **Taro Festival** is a one-day affair that's jam-packed with everything that can be done with taro (and some things that probably shouldn't!).

Places to Stay

South of town, there's tent camping and cabins at Kalopa State Recreation Area (see that section later in this chapter).

Hotel Honokaa Club *(☎ 775-0678, 800-808-0678; Ⓦ home1gte.net/honokaac/; Mamane St; dorm beds/singles/doubles $15/20/30, rooms with bath $45-65, suites $80; reception open 9am-1pm & 4pm-8pm daily)* is very basic, but it's the only game right in town. Cheaper rooms with shared bath are at the quieter end of the hotel.

Waipio Wayside B&B *(☎/fax 775-0275, 800-833-8849, fax 775-0275; Ⓦ www.waipiowayside.com; rooms $95, with bath $115-145)*,

A Hard Nut to Crack

Hawaii's first macadamia trees were planted in Honokaa in 1881 by William Purvis, a sugar plantation manager who brought seedlings from Australia. For 40 years the trees were grown in Hawaii, as in Australia, mainly for ornamental purposes, as the nut shells were once considered too hard to crack.

Hawaii's first large-scale commercial macadamia orchard was planted in Honokaa in 1924. Macadamia nuts have proven to be one of the most commercially viable agricultural crops in Hawaii. They are high in fat, protein and carbohydrates and are an excellent source of several essential vitamins and minerals.

heading toward Waipio Valley, is a 1932 plantation house nestled in a macadamia-nut orchard. There are five rooms, each cozy in their own way – antique furnishings, sprays of flowers, plush linens and bath goodies. Relax in the garden gazebo, on the sprawling lanai or swing in a hammock. Rates include a breakfast of Big Island fruit and coffee.

Places to Eat

Tex Drive Inn *(Hwy 19; open 6am-8:30pm daily)* is reason enough to make the drive between Hilo and Kona. Its famous *malasadas* (Portuguese pastries made of sweet fried dough, rolled in sugar and served warm) cost 75¢ plain. For $1 you can get a delicious filling of flavor, perhaps papaya-pineapple or hot pepper jelly. Oh yes, it also serves superb sandwiches, fresh fish burgers and plate lunches.

In town, stock up on groceries at **TKS Supermarket** *(cnr Mamane & Lehua Sts)* or **Taro Junction Natural Foods** *(Mamane St; open 10am-5:30pm Mon-Fri, 9am-5pm Sat)* west of the hotel. The **farmers market** *(open 6am-3pm Sat)* sets up further west, near Honokaa Trading Company.

New Moon Café *(Mamane St; dishes $3.50-5.50; open 9am-4pm Mon-Fri, 9am-1pm Sat)*, behind Taro Junction Natural Foods, has a mellow patio and occasional live music. Try the decked-out taro burger with an impressive side salad or chill by sipping some kava.

Simply Natural *(Mamame St; dishes $3.50-6.50; open 9am-4pm daily)*, east of the post office intersection, is the place to sate your breakfast cravings for banana taro pancakes, omelettes and smoothies. It also serves lunch. There's a **bakery** *(closed Sun)* next door, where local old-timers and farmers mingle over coffee and sweets.

Jolene's Kau Kau Korner *(☎ 775-9498; 45-3625 Mamane St; lunch $4.50-8; open lunch only Mon-Fri)* ensures the local beef industry is well-represented on its menu, but there are also mushroom burgers. If you've always wanted to try a Hawaiian plate lunch, take this opportunity.

Café Il Mundo *(☎ 775-7711; 45-3626A Mamane St; sandwiches $5-8, pizzas $9-17; open 11am-8pm daily)* does dreamy sandwiches, soups and salads, with fresh pizza slices available before 5pm.

Entertainment

Honokaa People's Theater *(☎ 775-0000; Mamane St; adult/senior/child $6/4/3)*, in a historic building dating from 1930, shows movies each weekend. It also hosts jazz, classical and Hawaiian performing artists during the **Hamakua Music Festival** *(W www.hamakuamusicfestival.com)* in October and November.

Shopping

Honokaa Trading Company *(☎ 775-0808; Mamane St)* is chock-a-block with aloha wear, antiques, used books and all manner of hand-selected Hawaiiana.

Trop Ag Hawaii *(☎ 775-9730; 45-3610 Mamane St)* are purveyors of delicious Hamakua coffee beans. **Hamakua Coffee Roasters**, at the Live Arts Gallery, rivals neighboring Kona farms.

KUKUIHAELE

Outside Honokaa, about 7 miles toward Waipio Valley, a loop road off Hwy 240 leads right down to the tiny village of Kukuihaele. Its name means 'traveling light' in Hawaiian, referring to ghostly night marchers who are said to pass through here carrying torches on their way to Waipio.

There's not much to Kukuihaele. Its 'commercial center' consists of the Last Chance Store and Waipio Valley Artworks gallery and bookshop. Kukuihaele is also the jumping-off point for tour operators into Waipio Valley.

Places to Stay

Many lovely B&Bs are off on village side roads.

Hale Kukui Orchard Retreat *(☎ 775-7130; w www.halekukui.com; studio $95, 2-bedroom units $160, cottages $160)* offers tranquil cottages secluded in an orchard, some with spectacular views. Each cottage has a lanai and guests are welcome to harvest as much of the dozen varieties of fruit grown here as they can eat. The apartment has a Jacuzzi, while the luxury cottage has a full kitchen.

Cliff House Hawaii *(☎ 775-0005, 800-492-4746; w www.cliffhousehawaii.com; 2-bedroom house with kitchen $175)*, gorgeously set on 40 private acres, has huge windows and a wraparound lanai, providing unforgettable views of the sapphire waters and cliffs of Waipio.

Waipio Ridge Vacation Rental *(☎ 775-0603; e rlasko3343@aol.com; PO Box 5039, Kukuihaele, HI 96727; 1-bedroom cottage doubles per day/week $85/450, trailer $75/350)*, almost teetering on a cliff above the valley, is another option. If the view of a lifetime doesn't make you dizzy, the riot of aloha and tribal decor will. The cottage has a queen-size bed and a sofa bed, fully equipped kitchen, TV and VCR. Also on the property is a funky Airstream trailer with a kitchenette and outdoor shower.

Places to Eat

Last Chance Store *(☎ 775-9222; open 9am-3:30pm Mon-Sat)*, in the village, is just that, as no food or supplies are available in Waipio Valley. This small grocery store has snacks, canned chili, beer, water and wine.

Waipio Valley Artworks *(☎ 775-0958, 800-492-4746; open 8am-5pm daily)* sells Tropical Dreams ice cream, muffins, inexpensive sandwiches and coffee.

Luckily, Honokaa is just up the road, where most people go to eat and get provisions.

WAIPIO VALLEY

Hwy 240 ends abruptly at the edge of cliffs overlooking Waipio Valley. If you catch it on a day when it's not hazy, the view is glorious. Everything is lush, a mix of tangled jungle, flowering plants, taro patches and waterfalls. You'll also glimpse the rugged coastal cliffs stretching out to the northwest, and, on the clearest days, you'll see the dark outlines of Maui in the distance.

The largest and southernmost of the seven spectacular amphitheater valleys on the windward side of the Kohala Mountains, Waipio is 1 mile wide at the coast and nearly 6 miles deep. Some near-vertical *pali* (cliffs) wrapped around the valley reach heights of 2000ft. The place readily pulses with *mana,* beckoning travelers to venture down.

The mouth of the valley is fronted by a black-sand beach, which is divided in two by Waipio Stream. There are two hotels tucked in the valley. Otherwise you can camp in Waipio or Waimanu Valley beyond.

Many of the valley's 50 or so residents have taro patches, and you may see farmers knee-deep in the muddy ponds. Other Waipio crops include lotus root, avocados, breadfruit, oranges, limes and *pakalolo* (marijuana). You'll also find *kukui* (candlenut) and mahogany trees, Turk's cap hibiscus and *noni* (mulberries).

History

Waipio means 'curving water,' and the valley is often referred to as the Valley of the Kings. In ancient times, it was the political and religious center of Hawaii and home to the highest *alii*. Umi, the Big Island's ruling chief in the early 16th century, is credited with laying out Waipio's taro fields, many of which are still in production today. Waipio is also the site where Kamehameha the Great received the statue of his fearsome war god, Kukailimoku.

According to oral histories, at least 10,000 people – and possibly many times that number – lived in this fertile valley before the arrival of Westerners. Waipio's sacred status is evidenced by the site of a number of important *heiau*. The most sacred, Pakaalana, was also the site of one of the island's two major *puuhonua*. It's hidden among the trees on the southern end of the beach.

In 1823, William Ellis, the first missionary to visit Waipio Valley, guessed the population to be about 1300. Later in that century, immigrants, mainly Chinese, began to settle in Waipio. At one time, the valley had schools, restaurants and churches, as well as a hotel, post office and jail.

In 1946, Hawaii's most devastating tsunami slammed great waves far back into the valley. Coincidentally or not, no-one in this sacred place perished (every valley resident was also spared during the great

1979 flood). But, afterwards, most people resettled 'topside' and Waipio has been sparsely populated ever since.

Hiking

From the lookout at the end of Hwy 240, you can see the switchback trail that leads to Waimanu Valley on the opposite cliff face. The lookout has rest rooms, but no potable water.

From beside the lookout, a 1-mile-long paved road leads down from beside the lookout into Waipio Valley. It's so steep (25% grade) that only hikers and 4WD vehicles are allowed. Tour companies make the run, but the hike to the valley floor and back is not as terribly difficult as it looks. It only takes about 30 minutes down, 45 minutes back up, and it's shady most of the way. Nevertheless, you'll work up a sweat, so carry plenty of water.

Hiilawe Falls From the bottom of the hill, if you detour five or ten minutes to the left, you may see wild horses grazing along the stream here. It's a beautiful Hawaiian tableau, with precipitous cliffs as a backdrop. Walk until you get a distant view of **Hiilawe Falls**, which is Hawaii's highest free-fall waterfall – a sheer drop of more than 1000ft. Hiking to the falls is possible but challenging, as there's no real trail. It's mainly a lot of bushwhacking. Only goats will make it to the falls in the heart of the rainy season.

Keep in mind that many valley residents who are tolerant of visitors trekking down to visit the beach aren't keen on them exploring the valley interior – there are a lot of 'Private Property' and 'Kapu – No Trespassing' signs, and the farther back in the valley you go, the scarier the dogs become.

Waipio Beach If you turn right at the bottom of the hill, it's only a 10-minute walk to Waipio Beach, but tack on an extra 10 minutes and a pound of mud if it has rained recently. The beach is lined with graceful ironwood trees serving as a barrier against the winds that sometimes whip through here. Surfers catch wave action at Waipio, but mind the rip currents, and, if the sea seems too rough, it is. Rogue waves and a treacherous undertow are features of the roiling ocean here. When it's calm, Waipio Beach is sublime and you might encounter spinner dolphins.

Walk along the beach toward the stream mouth for a good view of **Kaluahine Falls**, which cascade down the cliffs to the east. Getting to them is easier said than done, as the intervening coast is made up of loose, ankle-twisting lava. High surf breaking over the uppermost rocks can be very dangerous.

Local lore has it that night marchers periodically come down from the upper valley to the beach and march to Lua o Milu, a hidden entrance to the netherworld.

Waimanu Valley The switchback trail leading up the northwest cliff face is an ancient Hawaiian footpath. Although it looks arduous, it really isn't all that bad unless you're carrying a heavy load or it's high noon and the sun is blazing. It's used by hunters as well as hikers – you might even come across old-timers on donkeys heading for the backwoods to hunt wild boar. Water is available at numerous gulches and must be boiled or treated before drinking.

Doing part of the trail makes a nice day hike from Waipio, taking about 1½ hours from the floor of Waipio Valley to the third gulch, where there are little pools and a small waterfall. The trail continues up and down a series of ravines to Waimanu Valley, traveling about 8 miles in all from Waipio Valley. Over the last mile, the trail drops sheerly over loose scree and slippery leaves, with frequent washouts and dangerously deep ravines off to one side. If you are carrying a heavy pack or are not an expert hiker, there's no shame in turning back here. There's a basic overnight trail shelter just over half an hour back up the trail, before its final descent into Waimanu Valley. Because of the numerous climbs, allot about seven hours (though gung-ho Hawaiians have been known to do it in four!). Hoofing it all the way to Waimanu Valley and back in a day is unrealistic.

Like a miniature version of Waipio without tourists, Waimanu is another deep valley with steep walls, waterfalls, a lush valley floor and a black-sand beach. On any given day, you'll bask alone among all this stunning beauty.

Waimanu Valley once had a sizable Hawaiian settlement and contains many ruins, including house and *heiau* terraces, stone enclosures and old taro ponds. In the early 19th century, Waimanu was inhabited by an estimated 200 people, but, by the turn of the 20th century, only three families remained. Since the 1946 tsunami, the valley has been abandoned.

Because the valley represents an unaltered Hawaiian freshwater ecosystem, Waimanu has been set aside as a national estuarine sanctuary, and the removal of any plant or aquatic life (except for freshwater prawns and ocean fish) is forbidden.

Dangers & Annoyances The winter rainy season is hardly the optimum time to hike. During heavy rains, streams in Waipio Valley can swell to impassable, usually for just a few hours at a time. It's dangerous to attempt crossing swollen streams if the water reaches above your knees. Flash floods are possible.

If you're planning to hike to Waimanu Valley, heavy rains can make that route hazardous as well. There are a few creeks that cross the trail, as well as a stream in Waimanu Valley, all of which can become impassable torrents after rainstorms. These need to be treated as life-threatening obstacles; be patient and wait for the water to subside.

If you decide it's essential to cross (if it's late in the day, for example), look for a wide, relatively shallow stretch of the stream rather than a bend. Before stepping out from the bank, unclip your chest strap and belt buckle. This makes it easier to slip out of your backpack and swim to safety if you lose your balance and are swept away. Use a walking pole, grasped in both hands, on the upstream side as a third leg, or go arm in arm with a companion, clasping at the wrist, and cross side-on to the flow, taking short steps.

Don't drink from *any* creeks or streams without first boiling or treating the water. Because feral animals roam the area, take precautions against leptospirosis (see the Health section in the Facts for the Visitor chapter).

Organized Tours

Most tours require advance reservations. **Waipio Valley Shuttle** *(☎ 775-7121)* essentially runs 4WD taxi tours, although the driver does point out waterfalls, identify plants and throw in a bit of history. The 90-minute tours depart between 9am and 3pm Monday to Saturday and cost $40/20 per adult/child.

Waipio Valley Wagon Tours *(☎ 775-9518)* offers a one-hour jaunt in an open mule-drawn wagon that carts visitors over rutted roads and over rocky streams. Departures are at 9:30am and 11:30am, 1:30pm and 3:30pm Monday to Saturday and cost $40/20 per adult/child.

Waipio Ridge Stables *(☎ 775-1007, 877-757-1414; W www.topofwaipio.com)* follows the usual valley floor route, with a longer trot out to Hiilawe Falls that ends with a picnic and a swim at a hidden waterfall. The tour costs from $75 to $145.

Places to Stay

Bishop Estate, which owns most of Waipio Valley, allows **camping** at four primitive sites inland from Waipio Beach. There are no toilets (campers are required to bring chemical toilets) and no potable water. The maximum stay is four days, and you must apply for a permit at least two weeks in advance, even earlier for weekend dates and in summer. Each camper is required to sign a liability waiver, but the permits are free. Obtain permits in advance through the **Bishop Estate** *(☎ 322-5300, fax 322-9446; Suite 232, 78-6831 Alii Dr, Kailua-Kona, HI 96740; office open 7:30am-4:30pm daily)*, which you'll find in the Keauhou Shopping Center, in Keauhou just south of Kailua-Kona.

Backcountry camping in Waimanu Valley, which is managed by the state, is allowed by free permit for up to six nights. Facilities include fire pits and a couple of composting outhouses. Reservations are taken no more than 30 days in advance by the **Division of Forestry & Wildlife** *(☎ 974-4221; 19 E Kawili St, PO Box 4849, Hilo, HI 96720; open 7:45am-4:30pm Mon-Fri)*. With at least two weeks' advance notice, you can have the permit mailed to you. Otherwise, pick it up during office hours either at the forestry office in Hilo or the state tree nursery on Hwy 190 in Waimea.

KALOPA STATE RECREATION AREA

A few miles southeast of Honokaa and about 3 miles *mauka* from the marked Hwy 19 turnoff, Kalopa, at an elevation of 2000ft, is cooler and wetter than the coast, averaging about 90 inches of rain a year. Not many folks make it out to this 100-acre swatch of native rain forest.

A nature trail, beginning near the cabins, loops for three-quarters of a mile through old ohia forest, where some of the trees measure more than 3ft in diameter. The woods are inhabited by the *elepaio*, an easily spotted native forest bird about the size of a sparrow. It's brown and white and makes a loud whistle.

A longer hiking trail heads into the adjoining forest reserve. Begin trekking along Robusta Lane, on the left between the caretaker's house and the camping ground. It's about a third of a mile to the edge of Kalopa Gulch through a thick forest of tall eucalyptus trees. The gulch was formed aeons ago by the erosive movement of melting glaciers that originated at Mauna Kea. The trail continues along the rim of the gulch for another mile, while a number of side trails along the way branch off and head west back into the recreation area.

Although the air takes on a nighttime chill here, **tent camping** *(free)* is in a grassy area surrounded by tall trees. You may even have it all to yourself. There are bathrooms and covered picnic pavilions with electricity, running water and barbecue grills – the works! **Simple group cabins** *($55)* have bunk beds, sheets and towels, plus hot showers and a fully equipped kitchen. Permits are required for the cabins and *technically* for the camp sites as well. For details, see the Accommodations section earlier in this chapter.

LAUPAHOEHOE

Laupahoehoe means 'leaf of pahoehoe lava,' which is appropriate for the flat peninsula-like point that was formed by a feisty Mauna Kea eruption. Lava slithered down a ravine and out into the sea, eventually hardening into **Laupahoehoe Point**. About midway between Honokaa and Hilo, a highway sign marks the steep winding road that leads almost 1½ miles down to the coast. There are views of cliffs on the way down, and after heavy rains, waterfalls spring to life in all directions.

Tragedy hit Laupahoehoe on April 1, 1946, when tsunami waves up to 30ft high wiped out the schoolhouse on the point, killing 20 children and four adults. After the tsunami, the whole town moved uphill. A monument on a hillock above the water lists those who died. Every April there's a community festival with food, music and old-timers who 'talk story.'

Laupahoehoe is a rugged coastal area not suitable for swimming. The surf is usually rough and sometimes crashes up over the rocks and onto the lower parking lot (roll up those windows!). Interisland boats once landed here. Indeed, many of the immigrants who came to work the Hamakua Coast sugarcane fields first set foot on the Big Island at Laupahoehoe.

The county beach park on the point has rest rooms, showers, drinking water, picnic pavilions and electricity, and it's relatively secluded. All this makes it convenient for camping but ideal for late-night partying. For permit information, see the Accommodations section earlier in this chapter.

Back up on the highway, the **Laupahoehoe Train Museum** *(☎ 962-6300; adult/child $3/2; open 9am-4:30pm Mon-Fri, 10am-2pm Sat & Sun)* has all the ephemera, knick-knacks and nostalgia of the bygone Hawaiian railroad era. Knowledgeable docents burst with pride when speaking of the restored length of track, ol' Rusty the switch engine and other pieces of rail history that keep rolling in. Look for the museum between the 25-mile and 26-mile markers.

KOLEKOLE BEACH PARK

Beneath a highway bridge, this grassy park sits at the side of Kolekole Stream, which flows down from Akaka Falls. It has small waterfalls, picnic tables, barbecue pits, rest rooms and showers. Locals sometimes surf and boogie board here, but ocean swimming is dangerous.

Tent camping is allowed with a county permit, but keep in mind the park gets busy with picnicking local families on weekends and in summer. For permit information, see the Accommodations section earlier in this chapter.

Turn inland off Hwy 19 at the south end of the Kolekole Bridge, about three-quarters of a mile south of the 15-mile marker.

HONOMU

Honomu is an old sugar town that might have been forgotten if not for its location on the way to Akaka Falls via Hwy 200. As it is, things are pretty slow here. Among the village's handful of old wooden buildings, you'll find a shop selling vintage glass bottles and a few worthy galleries, mixed in with the tourist claptrap.

Hawaii's Artist Ohana *(☎ 963-5467; open 10:30am-5:30pm Tues-Sat)* has a broad selection of Big Island art and handiwork, including fiber baskets, wooden bowls, pottery, jewelry and paintings.

Places to Stay

Akiko's Buddhist Bed & Breakfast *(☎/fax 963-6422; W www.alternative-hawaii.com/akiko; singles/doubles per day $40/55, per week $265/355, per month $550/750)* is a gem for the spiritually inclined. Spare, clean rooms in this rustic home have either futons or regular beds with shared bath. A self-contained studio on the grounds requires a two-week minimum stay. Silence is observed between 6:30pm and 6am in the main house and guests are welcome to join in Zen meditation daily at 5:30am. Check the website or call about special events at the on-site gallery and yoga classes.

Palms Cliff House *(☎ 963-6076, fax 963-6316; W www.palmscliffhouse.com; B&B rooms $175-375, breakfast for nonguests $25)* has eight unique rooms, perfect for those of you in love. All rooms have plush linens, marble baths and a private lanai with views overlooking Pohakumanu Bay; some also have Jacuzzis and gas fireplaces. Guests can enjoy the garden hot tub and a gourmet breakfast on the lanai. Look for the B&B's sign just after the 13-mile marker, on the *makai* side of the highway.

AKAKA FALLS

To visit the Big Island's most impressive drive-up waterfall, turn onto Hwy 220 between the 13-mile and 14-mile markers.

A quick stroll from the parking lot, the lookout is found along a half mile rain forest loop. The unevenly paved trail passes through dense and varied vegetation, including massive philodendrons, fragrant ginger, dangling heliconia, orchids and gigantic bamboo groves. If you start by going to the right, you'll come first to the 100ft **Kahuna Falls**. It's a pretty waterfall, but kind of wimpy when compared to its neighbor. Up ahead **Akaka Falls** drops a sheer 420ft down a fern-draped cliff. Its mood depends on the weather – sometimes it rushes with a mighty roar, and at other times it gently cascades. With a little luck, you might catch a rainbow winking in the spray.

PEPEEKEO 4-MILE SCENIC DRIVE

Between Honomu and Hilo, there's a 4-mile scenic loop off Hwy 19 between the 7-mile and 8-mile markers that makes for a majestic tropical cruise. At the north end of the drive, **What's Shakin'** *(open 10am-5pm daily)* makes raved-about smoothies.

The road crosses a string of one-lane bridges, over little streams and through lush jungle. In places it's almost canopied with African tulip trees, which drop their orange flowers on the road, and with *lilikoi* (passion fruit), guava and tall mango trees. The fruit can be picked up along the roadside in season. There are also many small paths leading to babbling rivers and the coast. Look for one of these on the right about 2½ miles along, just after the one-lane wooden bridge.

If you crave more scenery, stop by **Hawaii Tropical Botanical Garden** *(☎ 964-5233; W www.hawaiigarden.com; adult/child $15/5; open 9am-5pm daily, last entry 4pm)*, a nonprofit nature preserve with 2000 species of tropical plants and a couple of streams and waterfalls. Buy your ticket at the yellow building on the inland side of the road, then walk down the steep incline to the valley garden at nearby Onomea Bay.

For another quick, pretty hike down to the bay, find the **Na Ala Hele** trailhead on the *makai* side of the road, just north of the botanical garden. After a 10-minute hike down a slippery jungle path, you'll come to a finger of lava jutting into the sea. A spur to the right goes to a couple of small waterfalls and a cove. Otherwise continue straight on and look for a rope tied to an almond tree for low-tide beach access. The mosquitoes here are ravenous, but the views might compensate.

Saddle Road

True to its name, Saddle Rd runs between the island's two highest points, with Mauna Kea to the north and Mauna Loa to the south. The road passes over large lava flows and climbs through a variety of terrains and climates. At sunrise and sunset, there's a gentle glow on the mountains and a light show on the clouds. In the early morning, it's crisp enough to see your breath, and if you take the spur road up to Mauna Kea, you'll reach permafrost.

Although most car rental contracts prohibit travel on Saddle Rd, it's a paved road straight across. It's narrow, but it's no big deal – particularly by island standards. Locals attribute the rental car ban to things like military convoys or evening fog. In truth, the rental agencies just don't want to be responsible for the towing charge ($500 and up) if your car breaks down on Hawaii's most remote road. It's 50 miles long and has no gas stations or other facilities along the way, so be sure to start out with a full tank of gas. Crossing the island this way is a bit shorter than taking the northern route of the Hawaii Belt Rd, but then again Saddle Rd is also a bit slower; time-wise there isn't much difference either way.

To the west, the road starts out in cattle ranch land with rolling grassy hills and planted stands of eucalyptus trees. A gated subdivision called Waikii Ranch has divided more than 2000 acres into million-dollar house lots for wealthy urban cowboys.

After about 10 miles, the land starts getting rougher and the pastures and fences fewer. The military takes over where the cows leave off, and you'll eventually come to the Quonset huts of the Pohakuloa Military Training Area. Most vehicles here are military Jeeps and trucks, although in hunting season you'll come across a fair number of pickup trucks.

MAUNA KEA

Mauna Kea (White Mountain) is Hawaii's highest peak, and its 13,796ft summit has a cluster of astronomical observatory domes, considered the greatest collection of large astronomical telescopes in the world. The freezing temperatures and thin air heighten the singular experience, which makes visitors aware of each labored breath and chilled appendage.

The unmarked Summit Rd, which climbs up Mauna Kea, begins off Saddle Rd at the 28-mile marker opposite a hunters' check station. Nearby is a 20-minute hiking trail up Puu Huluhulu (Shaggy Hill), a *kipuka* (oasis) created more than 10,000 years ago.

Summit Rd starts off passing through open range with grazing cattle, which were brought to Hawaii in 1793 by Captain Vancouver. It's easy to spot Eurasian skylarks in the grass, and if you're lucky you might see the *io*, a Hawaiian hawk, hovering overhead. Both birds make their home on the grassy mountain slopes, which are also home to the nene, as well as the *palila*, a small yellow honeycreeper that lives nowhere else in the world. Mouflon (mountain sheep) and feral goats roam freely. Silversword, a distant relative of the sunflower, is also found at this high elevation.

Environmental protection is paramount here exactly because the mountain is the exclusive home for numerous plants, birds and insects. One of the more predominant invasive plants here is mullen, which has soft woolly leaves and shoots up a tall stalk. In spring, the stalks get so loaded down with flowers that they bend over from the weight of what look like big yellow helmets. Mullen is not a native plant but was inadvertently brought in by ranchers as a freeloading weed in grass seed.

It's a well-paved road 6¼ miles (plus a few thousand feet in elevation) up to the Onizuka visitor center. If you've got a small car with a standard transmission, it's probably going to labor a bit. Surprisingly, you don't really get closer views of Mauna Kea's peaks by driving up to the visitor center. The peaks actually look higher and the views are broader from Saddle Rd. But you'll find other stunning vistas from Summit Rd, such as majestic clouds spread out like a soft feather bed below you. Mauna Kea doesn't appear as a single main peak but rather a jumble of peaks, some black, some red-brown, some seasonally snowcapped.

For information on snowboarding and skiing on Mauna Kea, see the Activities section earlier in this chapter.

Onizuka Visitor Center

Officially the Onizuka Center for International Astronomy, the center *(☎ 961-2180; W www.ifa.hawaii.edu; open 9am-noon & 1pm-5pm & 6pm-10pm Mon-Fri, 9am-10pm Sat & Sun)* was named for Ellison Onizuka, a Big Island native and one of the astronauts who perished in the 1986 Challenger space shuttle disaster. Hours are subject to change, so it's a good idea to call ahead. The visitor center is approximately one hour's drive from Hilo, Waimea or Waikoloa, and about two hours from Kailua-Kona.

You can watch a somewhat dated hour-long video on Mauna Kea's observatories, narrated by backyard astronomer Johnny Carson. The center also has photo displays of the observatories, information on discoveries made from the summit, computer-driven astronomy programmes and exhibits of the mountain's history, ecology and geology. If no-one minds, pick out another of the volcano videos to watch while you acclimatize, preferably with a steaming cup of hot chocolate, instant noodles or freeze-dried astronaut food, all sold here.

Across from the visitor center, a 10-minute uphill hike on a well-trodden trail crests a cinder cone and offers glorious sunset views.

Stargazing Programme Every evening from 6pm to 10pm, the visitor center offers an absolutely free astronomy programme with a talk about Mauna Kea and stargazing (weather permitting) using a Meade LX-200 16-inch telescope and both a 14-inch and an 11-inch Celestron telescope. You'll get a chance to view planets, galaxies, star clusters, supernova remnants and planetary nebulae. The staff point out Hawaiian constellations and welcome *keiki* (children). Call to double-check any programme schedule changes, as the drive is too long to be disappointed. Wear warm clothing, too, as night temperatures can sometimes dip to around freezing in winter and into the 40s (°F) in summer.

Summit Tours More than 100,000 tourists visit Mauna Kea annually, and most pass through the visitor center, which offers Mauna Kea summit tours on Saturday and Sunday. The tours visit one or two of the summit telescopes, most commonly the University of Hawaii's 88-inch telescope. The tour is free, but you need to provide your own 4WD transportation to the summit. If you're lucky, you might be able to catch a ride with someone from the visitor center, but you can't count on it. Pregnant women and children under 16 are not allowed due to high-altitude health hazards.

Check-in is at 1pm inside the visitor center, where the first hour is spent watching videos about astronomy on Mauna Kea as you acclimatize. Tours usually last until 5pm and are subject to cancellation at any time when there's inclement weather at the summit. While you're touring the observatories at the summit, don't expect to warm up, as indoor temperatures are kept near freezing to simulate the nighttime temperatures outside.

Summit Observatories

The summit of Mauna Kea has the greatest collection of state-of-the-art optical/infrared submillimeter and radio telescopes on earth and superior conditions for viewing the heavens.

Not only are the Hawaiian Islands isolated, but Mauna Kea is one of the most secluded places in Hawaii. At almost 14,000ft, the summit is above 40% of the earth's atmosphere and 90% of its water vapor. The air is typically clear, dry and stable. It's also relatively free of dust and smog. Only the Andes Mountains match Mauna Kea for cloudless nights, although air turbulence in the Andes makes viewing more difficult.

The University of Hawaii (UH) holds the lease on Mauna Kea from the 12,000ft level to the summit. The university built the summit's first telescope in 1968 with a 24-inch mirror. The telescope sizes have been increasing by leaps and bounds ever since. UH receives observing time at each telescope as one of the lease provisions. Currently 10 telescopes are in operation and one more is in the making.

The **UK Infrared Telescope** *(UKIRT)*, with its 150-inch mirror, was the world's largest infrared telescope until the early 1990s. It can be operated via computers and satellite relays from England's Royal Observatory. The **NASA Infrared Telescope** has measured the heat of volcanoes on Io, one of Jupiter's moons. Io's most active volcano is named after the Hawaiian goddess Pele.

The **WM Keck Observatory** *(W www2.keck.Hawaii.edu:3636)*, a joint project of the California Institute of Technology (Caltech) and the University of California, houses the world's largest and most powerful optical/infrared telescope. Keck featured a breakthrough in telescope design. Previously, the sheer weight of the glass mirrors was a limiting factor in telescope construction. The Keck telescope has a unique honeycomb design with 36 hexagonal mirror segments, each 6ft across, that function as a single piece of glass.

In January 1996, the 390-inch Keck I telescope discovered the most distant galaxy ever observed, at 14 billion light-years away. The discovery of this 'new galaxy,' in the constellation Virgo, has brought into question the very age of the universe itself, because the stars making up the galaxy seemingly predate the 'big bang' that is thought to have created the universe.

A replica of the first telescope, Keck II, became operational in October 1996. The two interchangeable telescopes can function as one – 'like a pair of binoculars searching the sky' – allowing them to study the cores of elliptical galaxies. The cost for the twin Keck observatories, each weighing 300 tons and reaching a height of 8 stories, was approximately $200 million.

The **Keck Visitor Gallery** *(admission free; open 10am-4pm Mon-Fri)* has an informative display, a 12-minute video screening, public bathrooms and a viewing area inside the Keck I dome. Just 150 yards west is Japan's **Subaru Telescope**, which opened in 1999 after a decade of construction. Its $300 million price tag makes this the most expensive observatory yet constructed, and its 22-ton mirror, reaching 27ft in diameter, is the largest optical mirror in existence. The telescope is named for the constellation Pleiades.

Driving to the Summit

Visitors may go up to the summit in daytime, but vehicle headlights are not allowed between sunset and sunrise because they interfere with astronomical observation. What you'll see is mainly the outside of the observatory buildings, where the scientists are at work, although both the University of Hawaii's 88-inch telescope and the WM Keck Observatory have visitor centers.

The road to the summit is paved only as far as Hale Pohaku, the buildings just above the Onizuka visitor center where scientists reside. After 5 miles of gravel, the road becomes pavement again for the final 4½ miles to the top. Travelers en route to the summit should stop first at the Onizuka center for at least 30 minutes to acclimatize before continuing on.

The road from the Onizuka center to the summit is suitable for 4WD vehicles only; although people occasionally go up in standard cars, this is not recommended due to life-threatening problems that can occur with poor traction on the slopes. Harper Car & Truck Rentals is the only car rental company that allows its 4WD Jeeps to be driven to the summit.

The drive takes about 30 minutes. You should drive in low gear and loosen the gas cap to prevent vapor lock. The upper road can be covered with ice during winter. Be particularly careful on the way down and watch out for loose cinder. Driving when the angle of the sun is low – in the hour after sunrise or before sunset – can create blinding conditions that make it difficult to see the road and oncoming cars.

About 4½ miles up is an area called **Moon Valley**, where the Apollo astronauts rehearsed with their lunar rover before their journey to the real moonscape. After another mile, look to the left for a narrow ridge with two caves and black stones. That's **Keanakakoi**, an ancient adze quarry. From this spot, high-quality basalt was quarried to make tools and weapons that were traded throughout the islands. For people interested in archaeology, it's an impressive site. As this is a protected area, nothing should be removed.

Dimming the Light

You might notice, as you tour around the Big Island, that the streetlights have an unusual orange glow. In order to provide Mauna Kea astronomers with the best viewing conditions possible, streetlights on the island have been converted to low-impact sodium. Rather than using the full iridescent spectrum, these orange lights use only a few wavelengths, which the telescopes can be adjusted to remove.

Hiking to the Summit

The daunting 6-mile **Mauna Kea summit trail** starts near the end of the paved road above the Onizuka visitor center. Instead of continuing on the main 4WD road, take the road to the left, then park at the visitor center and walk about 200 yards to the trailhead. Marked with wooden posts, painted metal stakes and stone cairns, the steep trail starts out roughly parallel to the summit road, then diverges around cinder cones. The 'summit' trail actually ends below Millimeter Valley at the impromptu parking area for Lake Waiau. You'll need to walk over another mile uphill along the paved road to reach the true summit, found behind the University of Hawaii telescopes. Maps are available at the visitor center.

Get an early start if you're braving this climb and give yourself the maximum number of daylight hours; most people need

Puu Poliahu

Just below Mauna Kea summit is the Puu Poliahu, home of the goddess of snow.

According to legend, Poliahu is more beautiful than her sister Pele. During catfights over men, Pele would erupt Mauna Kea, then Poliahu would pack it over with ice and snow. Then an angry Pele would erupt again. Back and forth they would go. Interestingly, the legend is metaphorically correct. As recently as 10,000 years ago, there were volcanic eruptions up through glacial ice caps here.

Because of its spiritual significance, the hill is off-limits to astronomical domes, so you won't find observatories here.

at least five hours to reach the summit, slightly less for the return trip (about 10 hours total). Dress in layers of warm clothing and bring plenty of water; also remember to lather on the sunscreen. Starting from 9200ft, the trail climbs almost 4600ft. High altitude, steep grades and brisk weather all make the hike quite strenuous. Don't even attempt it in inclement weather.

Walking on cinders adds difficulty, but there are incredible vistas and strange moon-like landscapes en route to the highest peak. The trail passes through the **Mauna Kea Ice Age Natural Area Reserve**. There was once a Pleistocene glacier here, and scratchings on rocks from the glacial moraine can still be seen. The ancient adze quarry, Keanakakoi, is two-thirds of the way up at 12,400ft. Lake Waiau is still another mile above.

If you walk back down Mauna Kea along the paved road instead of the trail, you'll not only save time but your chances of getting a lift part of the way are fairly good. You might be tempted to hitch a ride up from the Onizuka visitor center and then walk down. But if you haven't spent the previous night on the mountain, there's a serious danger of your not having enough time to acclimatize. Moreover, the trail's steep grade and crumbling cinders can make it most unnerving to walk down, especially as daylight fades and afternoon clouds roll in.

Lake Waiau

This unique alpine lake, sitting inside the Puu Waiau cinder cone in a barren and treeless setting, is rather mysterious. At 13,020ft, it's also the third-highest lake in the USA.

Lake Waiau's strangely green waters are no more than 10ft deep and set on porous cinder in desert conditions of less than 15 inches of rainfall annually. It's fed by permafrost and meltwater from winter snows, which elsewhere on Mauna Kea quickly evaporates. The lake has no freshwater springs and yet it's never dry. Hawaiians used to bring umbilical cords of their babies here and place them in the lake to give their children the strength of the mountain.

The trailhead to Lake Waiau starts from the hairpin turn just before the road's final ascent to the summit observatories; look for a 10mph sign and an impromptu parking area at the side of the road. It takes about 20 minutes to walk to the lake, depending on your fitness level and acclimatization. At the first trail intersection, take the right fork; continuing straight downhill brings you to the ancient adze quarry, Keanakakoi, about a 30-minute walk.

Organized Tours

Paradise Safaris *(☎ 322-2366, 888-322-2366; W www.maunakea.com)* has been leading sunset tours of Mauna Kea summit for almost two decades, including stargazing from the company's own portable telescope. Pickups are in Kailua-Kona, Waikoloa or Waimea. Tours cost $144; however, discounts are available on the Internet for bookings two weeks in advance.

Mauna Kea Summit & Stars Adventure *(☎ 331-8505, 800-464-1993; W www.hawaii-forest.com)* hosts a gourmet dinner at a Parker Ranch outpost before its sunset Mauna Kea summit and stargazing tours ($145). Pickups are in Kailua-Kona and Waikoloa.

Arnott's Lodge *(☎ 969-7097, fax 961-9638; W www.arnottslodge.com; 98 Apanande Rd, Hilo)* offers sunset tours, stargazing tours and a daytime outing to Mauna Kea. Each tour costs $48/96 for guests/nonguests.

MAUNA LOA'S NORTHERN FLANK

The road to Mauna Loa starts just east of Summit Rd and climbs 18 miles up the northern flank of Mauna Loa to a weather station at 11,150ft. There are no visitor facilities or even bathrooms at the weather station.

The narrow road is gently sloping and passable in a standard car. As it's a winding, nearly single-lane drive with some blind spots, give yourself about 45 minutes to drive up. It might be wise to loosen your gas cap before you start in order to avoid vapor lock problems. Park in the lot below the weather station; the equipment used to measure atmospheric conditions is highly sensitive to vehicle exhaust.

The summit and domes of Mauna Kea are visible from here, and when conditions are just right you can glimpse the 'Mauna Kea shadow' at sunset. It's a curious phenomenon in which Mauna Kea sometimes casts a blue-purple shadow behind itself in the sky.

Observatory Trail

The weather station is the trailhead for the steep and difficult Observatory Trail. If you haven't been staying in the mountains, altitude sickness is very likely. Anyone who is not in top shape shouldn't even consider it. Overnight hikers need to register in advance with the Kilauea Visitor Center in Hawaii Volcanoes National Park (see Backcountry Hiking & Camping under Hawaii Volcanoes National Park later in this chapter).

After about 4 miles, the trail connects up with the Mauna Loa Trail, which starts down in the main section of the national park. From the trail junction, it's just over 2½ miles around the caldera's western side to Mauna Loa summit at 13,677ft, or about 2 miles along the caldera's eastern side to Mauna Loa cabin at 13,250ft. All told, the hike to the cabin takes at least four to six hours.

Mauna Loa to Hilo

Heading eastward from the hunters' check station at the foot of Summit Rd, the Saddle Rd terrain gradually becomes ohia-fern forest, shrubby at first, but getting thicker and taller as Hilo gets closer. This section of road has been upgraded and the ride onward to Hilo is a fairly good one, but be cautious of oncoming drivers who hog the center of the road to cut curves.

Kipuka 21 is an oasis of dense plant growth that supports numerous bird species, including the *apapane*, *amakihi* and *iiwi* (a bright red forest bird). You may also glimpse the endangered *akepa* (Hawaiian creeper) in these parts. Park on the right side of the road about two-tenths of a mile beyond the 21-mile marker, from where you'll have to pick your way over the *aa* lava flow for a short, unmarked distance to reach the *kipuka*.

About 4 miles outside Hilo, Akolea Rd leads off to the left and connects in 2 miles to Waianuenue Ave, which passes Peepee Falls, Boiling Pots and Rainbow Falls. Alternatively, if you stay on Saddle Rd, you'll soon come to Kaumana Caves. See Around Hilo later in this chapter for details.

Hilo

Lazing along a crescent-shaped bay dotted with outrigger canoes and palm trees, Hilo is the county capital (population 47,000) and the island's commercial center, not to mention Hawaii's second largest port. But before it puffs up in your mind's eye like an irate blowfish, consider that most folks call it 'old Hilo town,' befitting its pace; original wood facades with corrugated eaves make up the waterfront business district.

For natural beauty, Hilo beats Kona hands down any day – so long as you catch the sun. Measurable rain falls on 278 days every year, leading to the saying that, 'In Hilo, people don't tan, they rust.' Copious rainfall means gushing waterfalls, lush valley gardens, verdant thickets of orchids and tropical fruits aplenty. When it's clear, you'll see the astronomy observatories at op Mauna Kea outlined like meringue peaks against the blue sky, drawing the heavens closer to earth and the summit closer to Hilo.

Heavy rains serve to keep both developers and tourists at bay. Not for lack of trying, resorts have never really been able to make a go of it here on the windward side. The 'rainiest city in the US' just can't compete with the sun-drenched beaches of the Kona coast, making Hilo one of Hawaii's best-kept secrets. It allows easy access to Hawaii Volcanoes National Park, is more affordable than the Kona Coast and has a diverse cultural scene.

Hilo has had a precarious history, making the town a survivor. Natural forces have long been a threat to the city – tidal waves from one side, lava from the other. Two devastating tsunamis hit Hilo in the post-WWII era, and as recently as 1984 a lava flow from

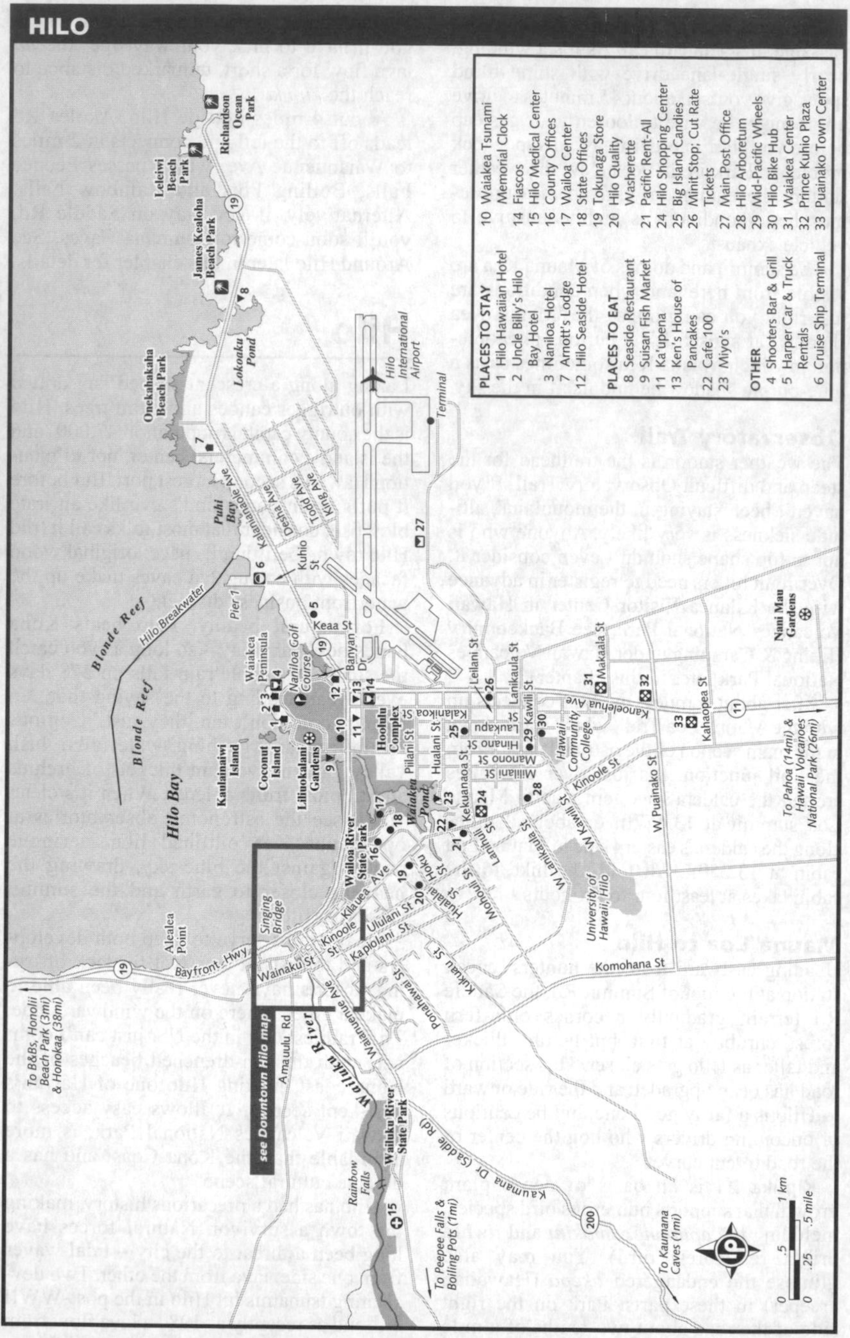
HILO
PLACES TO STAY
1 Hilo Hawaiian Hotel
2 Uncle Billy's Hilo Bay Hotel
3 Naniloa Hotel
7 Arnott's Lodge
12 Hilo Seaside Hotel
PLACES TO EAT
8 Seaside Restaurant
9 Suisan Fish Market
11 Ka'upena
13 Ken's House of Pancakes
22 Cafe 100
23 Miyo's
OTHER
4 Shooters Bar & Grill
5 Harper Car & Truck Rentals
6 Cruise Ship Terminal
10 Waiakea Tsunami Memorial Clock
14 Fiascos
15 Hilo Medical Center
16 County Offices
17 Wailoa Center
18 State Offices
19 Tokunaga Store
20 Hilo Quality Washerette
21 Pacific Rent-All
24 Hilo Shopping Center
25 Big Island Candies
26 Minit Stop; Cut Rate Tickets
27 Main Post Office
28 Hilo Arboretum
29 Mid-Pacific Wheels
30 Hilo Bike Hub
31 Waiakea Center
32 Prince Kuhio Plaza
33 Puainako Town Center
Hilo Bay
Blonde Reef
Hilo Breakwater
Coconut Island
Liliuokalani Gardens
Waiakea Peninsula
Naniloa Golf Course
Wailoa River State Park
Waiakea Pond
Hoolulu Complex
Puhi Bay
Onekahakaha Beach Park
Lokoaku Pond
James Kealoha Beach Park
Leleiwi Beach Park
Richardson Ocean Park
Hilo International Airport
Terminal
Alealea Point
Singing Bridge
Wailuku River
Wailuku River State Park
Rainbow Falls
University of Hawai'i Hilo
Hawai'i Community College
Nani Mau Gardens
see Downtown Hilo map
To B&Bs, Honoli Beach Park (3mi) & Honokaa (38mi)
To Peepee Falls & Boiling Pots (1mi)
To Kaumana Caves (1mi)
To Pahoa (14mi) & Hawaii Volcanoes National Park (26mi)
Kaumana Dr (Saddle Rd)
Bayfront Hwy
Kamehameha Ave
Kanoelehua Ave
Komohana St
Kinoole St
W Puainako St
Kilauea Ave
0 .25 .5 mile
0 .5 1 km

Mauna Loa volcano stopped short just 8 miles above town.

Residents of Japanese, Korean, Filipino, Portuguese, Puerto Rican, Hawaiian and Caucasian descent all live together pretty harmoniously. Alongside this ethnic melange, an alternative community has taken root, with liberal-minded mainlanders having been attracted by Hilo's cheap rents, laidback pace and gorgeous scenery since the 1970s. The town is a 'pedestrian heaven,' with distances that aren't too onerous, drivers that are courteous, and inviting back streets for strolling.

Information

The **Big Island Visitors Bureau** *(☎ 961-5797; cnr Haili & Keawe Sts; open 8am-4:30pm Mon-Fri)* is helpful. The **Bank of Hawaii** *(120 Pauahi • 417 E Kawili)* has a couple of branches with 24-hour ATMs. There are numerous other banks around town.

Hilo has two post offices. The **main post office** *(☎ 933-3019; open 8am-4:30pm Mon-Fri, 8:30am-12:30pm Sat)*, where general delivery mail is held, is on the airport access road. More convenient is the downtown **post office** *(☎ 933-3014; 154 Waianuenue Ave; open 8am-4pm Mon-Fri, 12:30pm-2pm Sat)*, in the federal building.

Behind the Minit Stop gas station, **Cut Rate Tickets** *(☎ 969-1944; Hwy 11 & Leilani St; open 8am-7pm Mon-Fri, 9am-5pm Sat, 9am-2pm Sun)* sells interisland air coupons.

Beach Dog Rental & Sales *(☎ 961-5207; 62 Kinoole St; open 10am-7pm Mon-Fri, 10am-2pm Sat)* charges $2 per 20 minutes for fast Internet connections. Also available are printers, scanners and free coffee.

For shipping services and packing supplies, visit **PostNet** *(☎ 959-0066; Prince Kuhio Plaza; open 9am-7pm Mon-Fri, 9am-4pm Sat, 10am-4pm Sun)*, which also offers photocopying and Internet access.

The **public library** *(☎ 933-8888; 300 Waianuenue Ave; open 10am-5pm Mon-Tues, 9am-7pm Wed-Thur, 9am-5pm Fri, 9am-4pm Sat)* has Internet terminals and an awesome selection of Hawaiian volumes, CDs and rental movies.

Specializing in maps, out-of-print books and Hawaiiana titles, **Basically Books** *(☎ 961-0144, 800-903-6277; W www.basicallybooks.com; 160 Kamehameha Ave)* also carries general travel guides and United States Geological Survey (USGS) topographic maps.

Borders Books & Music Café *(☎ 933-1410; Waiakea Center; open 9am-9pm Sun-Thur, 9am-10pm Fri & Sat)* sells Hawaii guides, international newspapers, magazines and CDs.

Hilo Quality Washerette *(210 Hoku St; open 6am-10pm daily)* is directly behind the 7-Eleven on Kinoole St.

The hospital, **Hilo Medical Center** *(information ☎ 974-4700, emergency room ☎ 974-6800; 1190 Waianuenue Ave)*, is near Rainbow Falls.

THE BIG ISLAND

DOWNTOWN HILO

Downtown Hilo is a quaint mishmash of classic buildings from the early 1900s, many on the National Register of Historic Places, and aging wooden storefronts to poke around.

If you wander a little farther afield, you can explore the backstreets, where there are little Japanese restaurants with faded *kanji* signs, barbershops with hand-pumped chairs and old pool halls.

Lyman House Memorial Museum

A great place to spend a rainy afternoon, this museum *(☎ 935-5021; W www.lymanmuseum.org; 276 Haili St; adult/senior/child $7/5/3; open 9am-4:30pm Mon-Sat)* will teach you all about ancient Hawaiian life, how adzes were made of volcanic clinker and *kukui* nuts were skewered on coconut-frond spines as candles. You can wander past displays of feather lei, tapa cloth and a house made of *pili* (bunchgrass), as the mysteries of *mana*, *kahuna* and *awa* (kava) are revealed.

Afterwards, through the lava tube you go, escorted by the sights and sounds of volcanic eruptions, curtains of fire and molten lava. Science exhibits take you through Hawaii's geologic history, from the first volcanic cone that broke the sea's surface to modern-day Loihi Seamount, with artifacts of spatter, olivine, Pele's tears and fine strands of Pele's hair.

Elsewhere find the museum's world-class collection of minerals and computers linked to Mauna Kea summit astronomical observatories. Upstairs the different lifestyles of those who came as indentured immigrants and stayed on to form Hawaii's multiethnic society are all given their due. Displays include costumes, cultural artifacts and insightful interpretive plaques. From Portugal there's a braguinha, the forerunner of the ukulele.

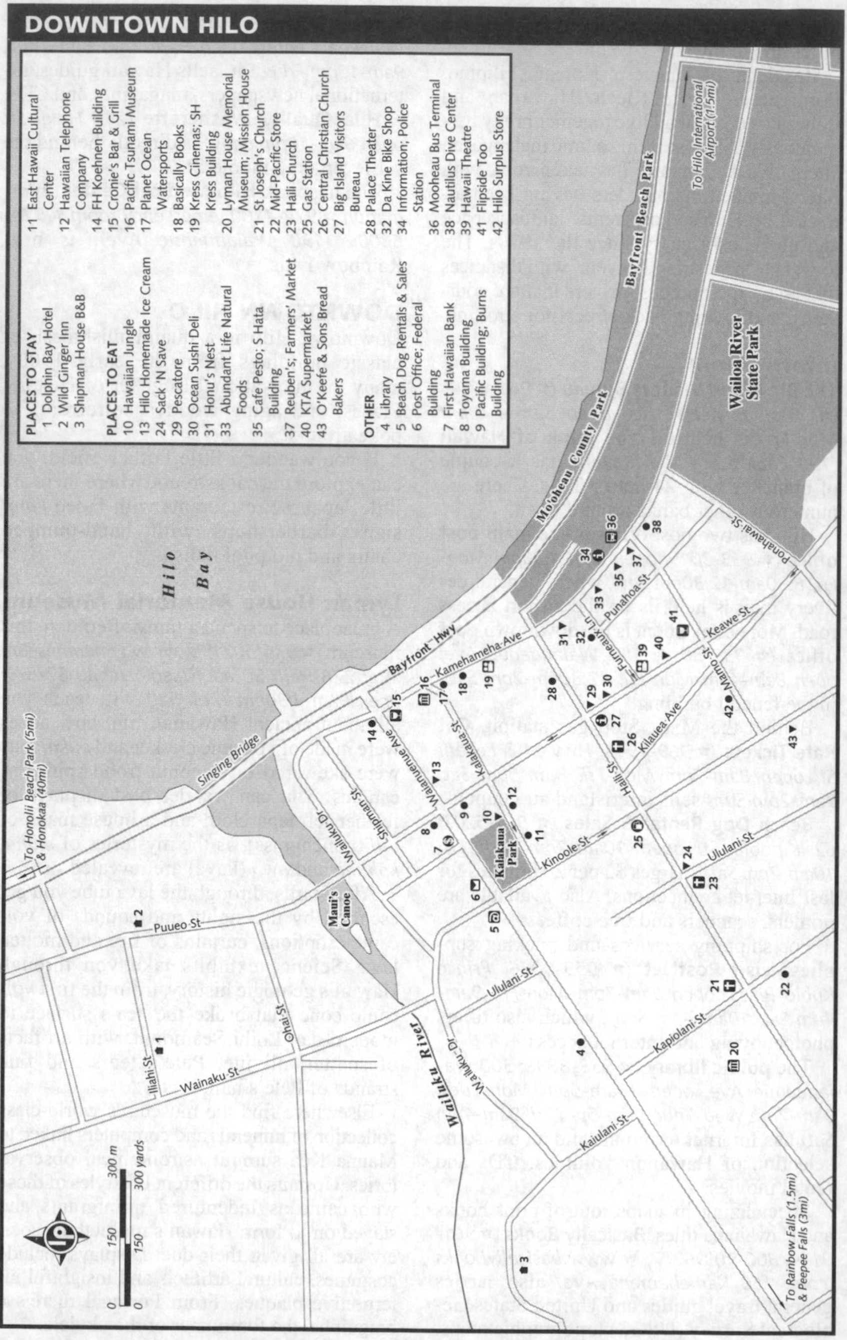
DOWNTOWN HILO
PLACES TO STAY
1 Dolphin Bay Hotel
2 Wild Ginger Inn
3 Shipman House B&B
PLACES TO EAT
10 Hawaiian Jungle
13 Hilo Homemade Ice Cream
24 Sack 'N Save
29 Pescatore
30 Ocean Sushi Deli
31 Honu's Nest
33 Abundant Life Natural Foods
35 Cafe Pesto; S Hata Building
37 Reuben's; Farmers' Market
40 KTA Supermarket
43 O'Keefe & Sons Bread Bakers
OTHER
4 Library
5 Beach Dog Rentals & Sales
6 Post Office; Federal Building
7 First Hawaiian Bank
8 Toyama Building
9 Pacific Building; Burns Building
11 East Hawaii Cultural Center
12 Hawaiian Telephone Company
14 FH Koehnen Building
15 Cronie's Bar & Grill
16 Pacific Tsunami Museum
17 Planet Ocean Watersports
18 Basically Books
19 Kress Cinemas; SH Kress Building
20 Lyman House Memorial Museum; Mission House
21 St Joseph's Church
22 Mid-Pacific Store
23 Haili Church
25 Gas Station
26 Central Christian Church
27 Big Island Visitors Bureau
28 Palace Theater
32 Da Kine Bike Shop
34 Information; Police Station
36 Mooheau Bus Terminal
38 Nautilus Dive Center
39 Hawaii Theatre
41 Flipside Too
42 Hilo Surplus Store
Hilo Bay
Bayfront Beach Park
Mo'oheau County Park
Wailoa River State Park
To Hilo International Airport (1.5mi)
To Honolii Beach Park (5mi) & Honokaa (40mi)
To Rainbow Falls (1.5mi) & Peepee Falls (3mi)
Singing Bridge
Maui's Canoe
Kalakaua Park
Wailuku River
Bayfront Hwy
Kamehameha Ave
Waianuenue Ave
Kalakaua St
Keawe St
Punahoa St
Ponahawai St
Kilauea Ave
Kinoole St
Ululani St
Kapiolani St
Kaiulani St
Wainaku St
Pueo St
Ohai St
Iliahi St
Shipman St
Wailuku Dr
Furneaux Ln
Haili St
Mamo St
0 150 300 m
0 150 300 yards

Adjacent to the museum is the **Mission House**, built by the Reverend David Lyman and his wife, Sarah, in 1839. The two missionaries had seven children of their own and in the attic boarded a number of island boys who attended their church school. The house has many of the original furnishings, including Sarah Lyman's melodeon, rocking chair, china and quilts. Docent-led tours leave hourly throughout the day and are included with museum admission.

Pacific Tsunami Museum

This modern multimedia museum *(☎ 935-0926; W www.tsunami.org; 130 Kamehameha Ave; adult/senior/student $5/4/2; open 9am-4pm Mon-Sat)* captures the destructive horror and triumphant survival left in the wake of Pacific Ocean tsunami. The docents are superbly informed, probably because some are tsunami survivors themselves.

Tsunamis have killed more Hawaiians than all other natural disasters combined, and this museum covers the entire Pacific region. Oral histories and documentary pieces, including those about the David Douglas murder and Mark Twain's shipwreck, are projected on videos and inside a minitheater built in an old bank vault. Computers are available for those who want to know more about these gigantic 'harbor waves.'

The building itself, completed in 1930 and designed by CW Dickey, is also a survivor. Both the 1946 and 1960 tsunamis failed to wash it away. Look up at the tsunami-cam on the roof of the building, which projects live surf images online 24/7/365.

Kalakaua Park

Kalakaua Park is a quiet downtown respite with a statue of 19th-century King David Kalakaua (the 'Merrie Monarch') sitting beneath the shade of a majestic banyan tree. The taro leaf by the King's side symbolizes his connection with the land, while the *ipu* (hula drum) on his right stands for the traditional Hawaiian cultural arts that he helped to revive.

There is also a Korean War veterans memorial, a reflecting pool filled with lilies as well as a time capsule that was sealed on the last total solar eclipse (July 11, 1991) and is due to be opened on the next one (May 3, 2106).

Notable Buildings

On Waianuenue Ave, check out the refurbished **F Koehnen Building**, typical of Hilo's early 20th century bay-front architecture. Just east on Kamehameha Ave is the **SH Kress** building, with pastel Art Deco accents, now a first-run movie theater.

Walking up Kalakaua St across Keawe St, look north to the elegant **Pacific Building** (1922) and the **Burns Building**, next door. Across Waianuenue Ave is the **Toyama Building** (1908), recently painstakingly restored to show off its jester fringe and rose windows. The neoclassical **federal building**, opposite Kalakaua Park on Waianuenue Ave, was built in 1919 with high columns and a Spanish-tile roof.

Back on Kalakaua St, the **East Hawaii Cultural Center** *(☎ 961-5771; W www.lastplace.com/EXHIBITS/EHCC; admission by donation $2; open 10am-4pm Mon-Sat)* was the Hilo police station until 1975. Its hipped roof, covered lanai and other features were common to 19th-century island homes. Gallery openings, plays and performances, Hawaiian-language and cultural classes are held here.

Next door to the cultural center is the jewel in Hilo's architectural crown, the **Hawaiian Telephone Company** building, designed by renowned Honolulu architect CW Dickey in the 1920s. It's of Spanish-mission influence with handsome tile work and a high-hipped roof. Note the metalwork details on the windows, painted panels underneath eaves and the copper drainspout with floral catchment.

Also downtown, the **S Hata Building** (1912) at 308 Kamehameha Ave is a fine example of Renaissance revival architecture that was expropriated from its original Japanese owners by the US government during WWII.

Churches

Haili St was once called **Church Street** for the churches lined up along it. Catholic **St Joseph's Church** *(cnr Haili & Kapiolani Sts)* is a pink paean of Spanish-mission design echoing Southern California. Built in 1919, it has stained-glass windows and trumpeting angels. **Haili Church** *(211 Haili St)* was built in 1859 and looks as if it were airlifted straight out of the New England countryside. Services are held in Hawaiian and English. Downhill toward the bay, the Victorian-style

Central Christian Church *(cnr Kilauea Ave & Haili St)* was built by Portuguese immigrants in the early 1900s.

Naha & Pinao Stones

On the front lawn of the Hilo library are the Naha and Pinao Stones. The **Pinao Stone** was an entrance pillar to an old Hawaiian *heiau*. The **Naha Stone**, from the same temple grounds, is estimated at 2½ tons. According to Hawaiian legend, anyone who had the strength to budge the stone would also have the strength to conquer and unite all the Hawaiian Islands. Kamehameha the Great reputedly met the challenge, overturning the stone in his youth.

Maui's Canoe

At the north end of Keawe St just beyond Wailuku Dr is the Puueo St Bridge, which crosses over the Wailuku River. The large rock in the river upstream on the left is known as Maui's Canoe. Legend has it that the demigod Maui paddled his canoe with such speed across the ocean that he crash-landed here and the canoe turned to stone. Ever the devoted son, Maui was rushing to save his mother, Hina, from a water monster who was trying to drown her by damming the river and flooding her cave beneath Rainbow Falls.

Wailoa River State Park

Wailoa River State Park can be reached from Pauahi St. The Wailoa River flows through the park, and most of **Waiakea Pond** is within the park boundaries. This spring-fed estuarine pond supports saltwater and brackish-water fish species, mostly mullet. There's a boat launch ramp near the mouth of the river for motorless boats. Fishing licenses are not required, but regulations must be followed (see Activities earlier in this chapter).

The park has two **memorials**, one dedicated to the tsunami victims and the other, an eternal flame, dedicated to the area's Vietnam War dead. The **Wailoa Center** *(☎ 944-0416; admission free; open 8:30am-4:30pm Mon, Tues, Thur & Fri, noon-4:30pm Wed, 9am-3pm Sat)* is an eclectic state-run art gallery with interesting photographs of tsunami damage collected downstairs. Hula, Hawaiian-language and quilting courses are occasionally offered. It's best to arrive early, as the gallery staff sometimes lock up by 4pm.

Banyan Drive

Banyan Dr is lined with large, sprawling banyan trees that were planted in the 1930s by royalty and celebrities. If you look closely, you'll find plaques beneath the trees identifying the arborists – Babe Ruth, Amelia Earhart and Cecil B DeMille among them. The road wraps around the edge of Waiakea Peninsula, which juts into Hilo Bay.

The road skirts the 9-hole **Naniloa Country Club Golf Course** *(☎ 935-3000; $20/25 weekdays/weekends)* and Hilo's bay-front hotels. Close by at Kamehameha Ave near Manono St, time stands still at the **Waiakea Tsunami Memorial Clock**. The clock is stuck on 1:05, the exact moment in the predawn hours of May 23, 1960, when Hilo's last major tsunami swept ashore.

Liliuokalani Gardens

Hilo's 30-acre Japanese garden, named for Hawaii's last queen, is filled with koi ponds, patches of bamboo, little arched bridges and a heartbreakingly beautiful little teahouse, all boarded up and unused. Many of the lanterns and pagodas were donated by Japanese regional governments and sister cities in honor of the 100th anniversary of Japanese immigration to Hawaii. The 2 miles of paths here are perfect for a sunset stroll or early morning jog.

Coconut Island

Connected to land by a footbridge, Coconut Island protrudes into the bay opposite Liliuokalani Gardens. The island is a county park with picnic tables and swimming, but it's most popular as a recreational fishing spot.

In ancient times, Coconut Island was called Moku Ola (Island of Life) in part due to the powers of a healing stone on the island that was used by *kahuna* to cure the sick. Moku Ola also had pure spring water, which was said to bring good health, and a birthing stone that instilled *mana* in the children born on the island.

The **Merrie Monarch Festival** (see Special Events in the Facts for the Visitor chapter) has its opening ceremonies here.

Hilo Arboretum

Established in 1920, this shady arboretum *(W Kawili St; admission free; open 8am-3pm Mon-Fri)* has a 20-acre spread of over 1000 species of trees, including some 12 types of

Little Tokyo & Big Tsunamis

On April 1, 1946, Hilo Bay was inundated by a tsunami that had raced across the Pacific from an earthquake epicenter in the Aleutian Islands. It struck at 6:54am without warning.

Fifty-foot waves jumped the seawall and swept over the city. They ripped the first line of buildings from their foundations, carrying them inland and smashing them into the rows behind. As the waves pulled back, they sucked splintered debris and a number of people out to sea.

By 7am the town was littered with shattered buildings. The ground was not visible through the pile of rubble. Throughout Hawaii the tsunami killed 159 people and caused $25 million in property damage. The hardest hit was Hilo, with 96 fatalities.

Hilo's bay-front 'Little Tokyo' bore the brunt of the storm. Shinmachi, which means 'new town' in Japanese, was rebuilt on the same spot.

Fourteen years later, on May 23, 1960, an earthquake off the coast of Chile triggered a tsunami that sped toward Hilo at 440mph. A series of three waves washed up in succession, each one sweeping farther into the city.

Although the tsunami warning speakers roared this time, many people didn't take them seriously. The tiny tsunamis of the 1950s had been relatively harmless, and some people actually went down to the beach to watch the waves.

Those along the shore were swept inland, while others farther up were dragged out into the bay. A few lucky people who managed to grab hold of floating debris were rescued at sea. In the end, this tsunami caused 61 deaths and property damage of over $20 million.

Once more the Shinmachi area was leveled, but this time, instead of being redeveloped, the low-lying bay-front property was turned into parks and the survivors were relocated to higher ground.

palms and infinite varieties of fruit trees, including fig, tamarind, star fruit, breadfruit, pineapple, guava and mangosteen. Ask at the on-site Division of Forestry & Wildlife office to borrow a laminated field guide to the numbered plants. They also issue free fruit picking permits, and visitors are allowed to harvest one sack each.

Beaches

Make no mistake: Hilo is not a beach town. Though there are some decent pockets for snorkeling, catching a break or watching the sunrise along **Kalanianaole Ave**, a 4-mile-long coastal road on the eastern side of Hilo. All of these beaches can get fairly rough with rip currents and surf, so assess conditions carefully before venturing out.

About 1½ miles east of the intersection of Hwys 11 and 19, **Puhi Bay** is a good beginner dive site. If you enter from the grassy outcropping on the eastern side, you'll come to an interesting reef, 'Tetsu's Ledge,' at 30ft. These teeth-rattling cold waters aren't much for swimming, however.

Further east, **Onekahakaha Beach Park**, a quarter of a mile north of Kalanianaole Ave, has rest rooms, showers and a picnic area. A broad sandy-bottomed pool here is formed by a large boulder enclosure. As the water's just 1ft or 2ft deep in most places, it's popular with families with young children. On the Hilo side, an unprotected cove attracts snorkelers on calm days, but mind the seaward current. Swimmers and snorkelers are cautioned not to venture beyond the breakwater at any time.

James Kealoha Beach Park is a roadside county park known locally as 'Four-Mile Beach' because of the distance between the park and the downtown post office. There are showers and rest rooms. For swimming and snorkeling, most people head for the sheltered eastern side of the park, which is protected by an island and a breakwater. It's generally calm there, with clean, clear water and pockets of white sand. The west side of the park is open ocean and much rougher. Locals sometimes net fish here and it's a popular winter surfing spot, although there are strong rip currents.

Almost another mile eastward, **Leleiwi Beach Park** is a good dive site, but the entrance is a bit trickier than at Puhi Bay. The best place to enter is to the left of the third pavilion, where the wall jogs toward the ocean. From there, walk to the level area beyond the gap in the wall.

Richardson Ocean Park, just before the end of the road, has a small black-sand beach fronting Hilo's most popular **snorkeling site**. When the waves get bumpy, it's also boogie boarding territory. On the Hilo side, the bay tends to be colder due to subsurface freshwater springs. The water is warmer and the snorkeling better on the eastern side of the park, which also has a lava shoreline for exploring. There are rest rooms, showers, picnic tables and a lifeguard.

Places to Stay

People don't come to Hilo to hang around a pool but to visit the sights and then head on. Consequently, there are no self-contained beach resorts and the 'vacation rental' condo market that's so common on the Kona Coast is virtually nonexistent here.

Budget Arnott's Lodge *(☎ 969-7097, fax 961-9638; W www.arnottslodge.com; 98 Apapane Rd; tent sites $9, dorm beds/singles/doubles $17/37/47, doubles with bath $57, 2-bedroom units $120)* is the place to connect with other travelers, if you don't mind being on the outskirts of town. There are sex-segregated dorms, wheelchair-accessible portions, camping in the front yard and a slew of private rooms. Amenities at this clean, friendly hostel include a TV and VCR room, free local calls, Internet access and coin laundry. Guests can hop cheap daily shuttles into town or rent bicycles ($10 per day). Adventure island tours cost $48/96 for guests/nonguests. Free airport pickups are available (until 8pm). If you're driving, head east of Hwy 11 on Kalanianaole Ave about 1½ miles, then turn left onto Keokea Loop Rd. The lodge is about 100 yards down the road.

Wild Ginger Inn *(☎ 935-5556, 800-882-1887; W www.wildgingerinn.com; 100 Puueo St; dorm beds $19, rooms $45, with bath $60-90)* is a colorful place amid exuberant gardens with a meandering creek. The rooms have private baths and either a double or two twin beds; most have a small refrigerator and the suites have sitting rooms, kitchenettes and views. Laundry, Internet access and bike rentals are available. Breakfast is included and there are discounts for stays of three nights or more.

Dolphin Bay Hotel *(☎ 935-1466, fax 935-1523; W www.dolphinbayhilo.com; 333 Iliahi St; studios $66-80, 1-bedroom/2-bedroom units $89/99)* is on a hill just above downtown. This family-run hotel is filled with aloha. All 18 apartment-like units have full kitchens, TVs and bathrooms, most with sunken bathtubs. Fresh-picked fruit from the backyard is available, along with free morning coffee. This is one of Hilo's most popular hotels, so reservations are advised. Good weekly rates are available.

Lihi Kai *(☎ 935-7865; 30 Kahoa Rd; rooms $55-60)* is a laid-back B&B in Amy Gamble Lannan's home, perched on a cliff directly above Hilo Bay. Amenities include a small heated swimming pool and a living room with a wonderful ocean view.

Our Place Papaikou's B&B *(☎/fax 964-5250; W www.ourplacebandb.com; rooms $60-80)* has just two sweet rooms in an exposed-beam home beside Kaieie Stream in Papaikou, 6 miles north of Hilo. The smaller room shares a bath, while the master bedroom has a king bed and private bath. Guests share the garden lanai and a grand living room with a fireplace, library and piano. Rates include breakfast.

Mid-Range These places offer more amenities but less character.

Uncle Billy's Hilo Bay Hotel *(☎ 935-0861, on the Big Island ☎ 800-442-5841, in the US & Canada ☎ 800-367-5102, fax 935-7903; W www.unclebilly.com; 87 Banyan Dr; standard/oceanfront rooms $85/105)* is a Hawaiian-owned hotel with a tattered Polynesian theme. Standard rooms are pricey for what you get, although oceanfront rooms are much nicer. You can save over 25% if you book via the Internet, and there are other discount schemes available.

Hale Kai B&B *(☎ 935-6330, fax 935-8439; W www.interpac.net/~halekai; 111 Honolii Pali; ocean-facing rooms $90-100, suites with kitchenette $110)*, off Hwy 19 near the 5-mile marker north of Hilo, is a well-appointed contemporary B&B with fine views across Hilo Bay. All guests have use of a swimming pool and hot tub overlooking the sea.

Hilo Seaside Hotel *(☎ 935-0821, 800-560-5557, fax 969-9195; W www.hiloseasidehotel.com; 126 Banyan Dr; rooms $100-130)* is a complex of two-story motel-style buildings. All rooms have air-con and ceiling fans, TVs, louvered windows and refrigerators. Avoid those around the swimming pool and the noisy street-side Hukilau wing. Better rooms in the deluxe ocean wing have balconies overlooking a carp pond. Inquire about promotional discounts and Internet deals.

Top End You won't find luxury digs like those that have made the Kona and Kohala coasts famous.

Naniloa Hotel *(☎ 969-3333, 800-367-5360, fax 969-6622; 93 Banyan Dr; rooms $100-140, suites $240)* is popular with Japanese tour groups. Standard rooms in Hilo's only 'skyscraper' have air-con, TVs and phones, but are rather straightforward for the rates, which vary depending on the view. The hotel does feature a full-service spa.

Hilo Hawaiian Hotel *(☎ 935-9361, 800-367-5004, fax 961-9642; W www.castleresorts.com; 71 Banyan Dr; garden-/ocean-view rooms $120/150)*, a sprawling place near Coconut Island, is Hilo's best hotel. Rooms are comfortable, with air-con, TV and phone, and most have private lanai. Garden-view rooms look across the parking lot onto the golf course, while ocean-view rooms overlook Hilo Bay. When booking, ask about adding on a rental car at no extra cost.

Shipman House Bed & Breakfast *(☎/fax 934-8002, 800-627-8447; W www.hilo-hawaii.com; 131 Kaiulani St; rooms $150-180)*, on a knoll above town, is a beautiful Victorian mansion that has been in the Shipman family since 1901. Past visitors at this national historic site have included Queen Liliuokalani and Jack London. All rooms, whether in the main house or the 1910 guest cottage, have baths (with gorgeous tubs), ceiling fans, small refrigerators and tasteful furnishings. The congenial owners have added endearing touches, such as guest kimonos, fresh flowers, a library and a grand piano.

Places to Eat

Self-Catering Hilo has lots of places where you can pick up the raw materials for a great meal.

The **farmers market** *(cnr Mamo St & Kamehameha Ave; open 7am-noon Wed & Sat)* has vendors selling island fruits, veggies and flowers direct from the growers at bargain prices. Don't let anyone coerce you into buying overripe or otherwise bogus product.

Suisan Fish Market *(☎ 935-9349; 85 Lihiwai St; open 8am-5pm Mon-Sat)* is where a century-old morning fish auction was once held. You can, of course, still come here to buy fresh fish. Don't miss the delicious selection of *poke*.

Abundant Life Natural Foods *(☎ 935-7411; 292 Kamehameha Ave; open 8:30am-7pm Mon-Tues & Thur-Fri, 7am-7pm Wed & Sat, 10am-5pm Sun)* has all the quality produce, cheeses, juices and bulk foods you'd expect of a health food store, plus a simple smoothie and sandwich bar.

Island Naturals *(☎ 935-5533; Waiakea Center, 303 Maakala St; open 8:30am-8pm Mon-Sat, 10am-7pm Sun)* also has a deli and smoothie counter. Generally, prices are higher here. Hot-food bar selections include *ahi* with coconut, vegetarian *phat thai* and curries ($6.95 per pound).

O'Keefe & Sons Bread Bakers *(☎ 934-9334; 374 Kinoole St; snacks $3-7; open 6am-5pm Mon-Fri, 6am-3pm Sat)* bakes gorgeous artisan breads, as well as pastries and sandwiches that will make your mouth water.

Hilo Homemade Ice Cream *(☎ 969-9559; 1477 Kalanianaole Ave; open 10:30am-5pm Mon-Sat)* has Hilo's best ice cream, with tasty *poha* (gooseberry), zesty ginger and killer Kona coffee flavors.

Downtown also has a **KTA Supermarket** *(323 Keawe St)*. Puainako Town Center has both a **Sack N Save**, vending coffee and doughnuts from 5am, and a **KTA Superstore** selling 30 types of *poke*.

Budget A thoroughly *loco* (crazy) local experience is **Cafe 100** *(☎ 935-8683; 969 Kilauea Ave; sandwiches $2-3.50, lunch $4-6; open 6:45am-8:30pm Mon-Fri, 6:45am-9:30pm Sat & Sun)*. This legendary drive-in is the original home of the *loco moco* (rice topped with a hamburger, fried egg and a cardiac-arresting amount of brown gravy), now in 17 different varieties.

Kaupena *(1710 Kamehameha Ave; snacks $1.50-7; open 9am-6pm Mon-Sat)* is another local favorite for *ono grinds* (good food). It's the 'home of the foot-long *laulau*,' filled with tender fish and pork wrapped in a ti leaf. Side orders of *poke*, poi or *kalua* pig are also available. Make sure you don't miss the original half-coconut, half-taro pudding.

Kuhio Grille *(☎ 959-2336; dishes $5.50-8.50; open 6am-10pm Sun-Thur, 6am-2pm Fri & Sat)*, which is a casual little eatery, can be found at the north side of Prince Kuhio Plaza. This is the 'home of the one-pound *laulau,'* and a local Hawaiian favorite for poi, *lomi* salmon, saimin and *haupia* (coconut pudding). The menu includes omelettes, burgers and kids specials.

Island Infusion *(☎ 933-9555; dishes $5-7.50; open 10am-9pm Mon-Sat, 10am-8pm Sun)*, in the food court of the Waiakea Center, is another of Hilo's tasty Hawaiian-style eateries.

Ken's House of Pancakes *(☎ 935-8711; 1730 Kamehameha Ave; meals $6-12; open 24 hr)* is the perfect spot after Mauna Kea stargazing. A family-friendly diner, Ken's has hundreds of menu combos, including giant Spam omelettes, macadamia-nut pancakes and milkshakes like ambrosia. Dinners such as *kalua* pig and cabbage come with all the trimmings.

Honu's Nest *(270 Kamehameha Ave; dishes $3-9.50; open lunch Mon-Sat)* faces Hilo bay and serves Japanese comfort food. Grab a colorful *bento* (boxed meal) for the beach or settle in for a bowl of *soba* (buckwheat) noodles. The cooks also make *donburi* (rice bowls), tempura and *teishoku* (set meals) with your choice of chicken, fish, squid or tofu.

Mid-Range For traditional and contemporary Japanese seafood, **Ocean Sushi Deli** *(☎ 961-6625; 239 Keawe St; dishes $1.50-20; open 10am-2:30pm & 4:30pm-9pm Mon-Sat)* is fantastic. Scores of inventive specials include nut rolls made with *ahi,* avocado and *kukui* nuts, and sushi rolls with *poke* and maca-damia nuts. Carnivores, we dare you to try the plantation roll (hamburger, onions and gravy). Vegetarian options are plentiful.

Miyo's *(☎ 935-2273; 400 Hualani St; meals $7.50-10.50; open 11am-2pm daily, 5:30pm-8:30pm Mon-Sat)*, at the back of the Waiakea Villas complex, is a charming Japanese restaurant with a teahouse atmosphere overlooking Waiakea Pond. The country cooking is decent and the prices unbeatable, featuring Hilo homemade ice cream for dessert.

Hawaiian Jungle *(☎ 934-0700; 110 Kalakaua St; lunch $5-7, dinner $7.50-16; open 11am-9pm Mon-Fri, 7am-9pm Sat & Sun)* has tiki torches, lazy ceiling fans and large windows overlooking Kalakaua Park. The wholesome Latin and South American food here includes tamales, *lomo saltado* (the classic Peruvian beef dish) and *papas rellenos* (stuffed potatoes). Drop by on a Friday or Saturday evening when there's live music.

Reuben's *(☎ 961-2552; 336 Kamehameha Ave; combination plates $8-9.50; open 11am-9pm Mon-Fri, noon-9pm Sat)* looks strictly Oaxaca cantina: festively painted cinder block, pinatas galore and folding tables and chairs. The food is just as authentic, with freshly fried chips, salsa that will kick your butt, and a fish taco-and-tamale combination plate not soon to be forgotten.

Top End For a few extra bucks, you can experience Hilo's finest dining, often in lovely settings. You'll need reservations.

Pescatore *(☎ 969-9090; 235 Keawe St; breakfast $4-6, lunch $6-12, dinner $20; open 11am-2pm & 5:30pm-9pm daily, 7:30am-11am Sat & Sun)* has attentive service and excellent Italian seafood and pasta, thrown together with a bit of Little Italy social club atmosphere.

Cafe Pesto *(☎ 969-6640; S Hata Bldg, 308 Kamehameha Ave; lunch $8-12, dinner $10-30; open 11am-9pm Sun-Thur, 11am-10pm Fri & Sat)* is one of the Big Island's star restaurants. Memorable meals of creative Hawaii regional cuisine feature Kona lobster, Kamuela beef and even Pahoa corn. Gourmet wood-fired pizzas and innovative salads are just as delicious.

Seaside Restaurant *(☎ 935-8825; 1790 Kalanianaole Ave; meals $18-24; open 5pm-8:30pm Tues-Thur, 5pm-9pm Fri & Sat)* serves the island's freshest fish in an odd faux-paneled dining room. Outdoor tables sit prettily above the family's aqua-farm pond, however. Everything is delicious; try the rainbow trout, perch or mullet steamed in ti leaves with lemon and onions. All meals include rice, salad, apple pie and coffee. Service and portions are stellar.

Entertainment

Locals and visitors gripe about Hilo's lack of nightlife. Check out the free newspaper *Hawaii Island Journal,* the East Hawaii Cultural Center (see the Notable Buildings section earlier in this chapter) and bulletin boards for goings on about town.

Often recommended, **Fiascos** *(☎ 935-7666; 200 Kanoelehua Ave)* may have country line dancing on Thursday evenings and jazz on Friday – and that's about it.

Uncie Billy's Hilo Bay Hotel *(☎ 329-1393, 800-367-5102, fax 935-7903; 75-5739 Alii Dr; live music & hula show 6pm-7:30pm & 8pm-9:30pm daily)* presents an enthusiastic little hula show during dinnertime at its restaurant, where dishes like something from a low-budget wedding start at $11.

The lounge at the **Hilo Hawaiian Hotel** *(☎ 935-9361, 800-367-5004, fax 961-9642; 71 Banyan Dr)* occasionally has live contemporary Hawaiian music.

Shooters Bar & Grill *(☎ 969-7069; 121 Banyan Dr; open till 3:30am Fri & Sat)*, at the Country Club Condo Hotel, is a sleepy chrome-and-linoleum watering hole by day and a drunken train wreck waiting to happen by night. It has DJs, bands, pub fare, pool tables and pinball.

Cronies Bar & Grill *(☎ 935-5158; 11 Waianuenue Ave; closed Sun)* has an atmosphere about as stimulating as its name, but the live local music and dirt-cheap drink specials are worth checking out.

Flipside Too *(☎ 961-0057; 94 Mamo St)* is the place for anyone who likes dive bars. Sticky floors, a couple of pool tables, darts and shadowy characters are all fixtures. Every third Saturday is 'alternative' night.

For such a humble town, Hilo has an addictive film scene.

Palace Theater *(☎ 934-7777; 38 Haili St; admission $6)* shows foreign films, documentaries and director's cuts. The local intelligentsia comes out of the woodwork for special events including concerts, plays and readings.

Hawaii Theatre *(☎ 969-3939; 291 Keawe St; admission $3-5)* shows rare prints, classic oldies, horror B-movies and foreign films. Admission includes free coffee, and that just rocks.

Kress Cinemas *(Art Deco Kress Bldg, 174 Kamehameha Ave)* is an atmospheric place to take in a little celluloid. It screens standard first-run Hollywood films. So do the movie theaters at **Prince Kuhio Plaza** *(Hwy 11)* and **Walakea Shopping Plaza** *(88 Kanoelehua Ave)*. Matinees and Tuesday bargain screenings cost $5. For schedules at all three, call the **hotline** *(☎ 961-3456)*.

For college sports events, call the **University of Hawaii Athletic Department** *(☎ 974-7520; Hoolulu Complex, Manono St; admission from $5)*.

Clown Princess of Hawaii

Clara Inter was a Hawaiian schoolteacher on a glee club trip to Canada in 1936 when she first performed 'Hilo Hattie (Does the Hilo Hop),' to a delighted Canadian crowd. A year or so later in the Monarch Room at Waikiki's Royal Hawaiian Hotel, Clara approached bandleader (and the song's composer) Don McDiarmid, Sr, and asked him to play it. McDiarmid was uncertain that it would go over well at the ritzy hotel, since it was a 'low class' hula, alluding to Hattie doing a dance that 'no law would allow.'

Well, with a taste of applause and fame already under her muumuu from her Canadian experience, Clara wasn't going to be deterred. She convinced him to do the tune and the rest, as they say, is history. Clara Inter was catapulted to international stardom on the wings of this song (with worldwide tours and appearances in several movies including *Song of the Islands* and *Ma & Pa Kettle in Waikiki*), legally changed her name to Hilo Hattie, and eventually lent it to the now famous chain of Hawaiian stores.

Shopping

Besides its major shopping malls, Hilo also has terrific thrift stores for aloha wear and vintage clothing, many clustered on Kamehameha and Kilauea Aves downtown.

Mid-Pacific Store *(☎ 935-3822; 76 Kapiolani St)* has the best selection, hands down. Bring a fat wallet for the silk and crepe kimonos, genuine *palaka* (checked) shirts and retro swimsuits.

Big Island Candies *(☎ 935-8890; 585 Hinano St; open 8:30am-5pm daily)* offers free cookie samples and coffee as you watch candy being hand-dipped in chocolate.

Tokunaga Store *(☎ 935-6965; 26 Hoku St)* has whatever fishing supplies you may need.

Getting Around

Bus The **Hele-On Bus** *(☎ 961-8744)* has a few intracity routes, all costing 75¢ and operating Monday to Friday only.

The **No 4 Kaumana** bus goes five times a day (the first leaves at 7:35am, the last at 2:20pm) from Mooheau Bus Terminal to Hilo Library then to Hilo Medical Center (and Rainbow Falls). A few buses also stop at Prince Kuhio Plaza, Walmart then Banyan Dr.

The **No 6 Waiakea-Uka** bus goes five times a day (the first leaves at 7:05am, the last at 3:05pm) from Mooheau Bus Terminal. It then stops at Hilo Shopping Center, the University of Hawaii, Prince Kuhio Plaza and Walmart.

For island-wide routes, see Getting Around earlier in this chapter.

Bicycle Getting around town by bike is totally feasible. **Da Kine Bike Shop** *(☎ 934-9861; 12 Furneaux St)* is a friendly place, renting $5-a-day rusty cruisers and $50 pro models. It also offers island cycling tours.

Mid-Pacific Wheels *(☎ 935-6211; 1133-C Manono St; open daily)* rents 21-speed bikes for $15 per day.

Hilo Bike Hub *(☎ 961-4452; 318 E Kawili St)* rents cruisers, rock hoppers as well as full-suspension mountain bikes for $20 to $45 per day. Ask about phenomenal weekly discounts.

AROUND HILO

Rainbow Falls

Rainbow Falls is a quick five-minute drive outside of Hilo and worth it for the massive banyan tree alone. You can get a straight-on view of the falls from the lookout in front of the parking lot. The falls are usually seen as a double drop, with the two streams flowing together before hitting the large pool at the bottom.

Waianuenue, literally 'rainbow seen in water,' is the Hawaiian name for this lovely 80ft cascade ringed by palm, ohia and African tulip trees. The gaping cave beneath the falls is fit for a goddess and is said to have been the home of Hina, mother of Maui. The best time for rainbows appearing is morning, although they're by no means guaranteed, as both the sun and mist need to be accommodating.

For a cool little diversion, take the short loop trail to the left of the falls that continues for about five minutes past a giant banyan tree, which supports a canopy so thick that it blocks the sun and has roots so vast it swallows children. The jungle trail ends at the water's edge; swimmers and rock hoppers can explore upriver for private aquatic delights. Be prepared for voracious mosquitoes.

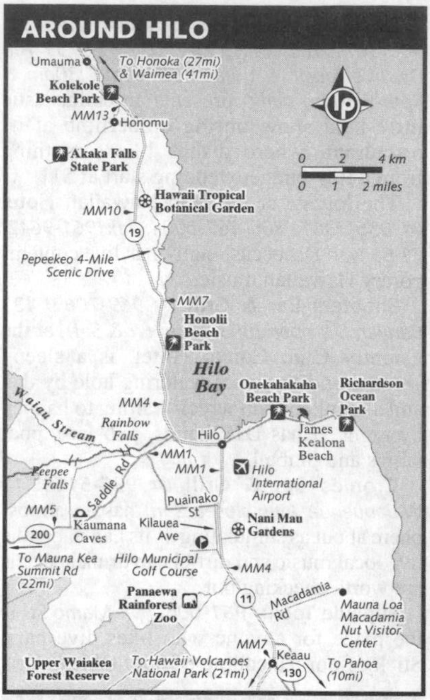

Peepee Falls & Boiling Pots

Up Waianuenue Ave, about 1½ miles past Rainbow Falls, these falls drop over a sheer rock face. As the water cascades downstream over a series of basalt depressions in the river, it swirls and churns into bubbling pools – hence the name Boiling Pots. The viewpoints here are accessible by wheelchair. Locals looking to splash about follow the well-beaten path just beyond the 'No Swimming' sign.

Kaumana Caves

These caves were formed by an 1881 lava flow from Mauna Loa. As the flow subsided, the outer edges of the deep lava stream cooled and crusted over in a tunnel-like effect. The hot molten lava inside then drained out, creating these caves. The caves are wet, mossy and thickly covered with ferns and impatiens. If you have a flashlight, you might want to explore them, although they tend to be quite drippy. They are signposted, about 3 miles up Kaumana Dr (Hwy 200) on the right.

Honolii Beach Park

Honolii Cove is a protected pocket with Hilo's best surfing, and is also popular with boogie boarders. The park has showers and toilets. To get there, take Hwy 19 north out of Hilo. Between the 4-mile and 5-mile markers, make a right onto Nahala and a left onto Kahoa. Join all the other cars parked on the side of the road and head down to the park. For a little variety, you can return to Hwy 19 by following Kahoa downhill onto a one-lane road that winds through enchanting forest.

Nani Mau Gardens

Encompassing more than 20 acres of flowering plants, including a lovely orchid section, these formal gardens *(☎ 959-3500; adult/child $10/6; open 8am-5pm daily)* are another stop on the tour bus headless chicken circuit. Unlike many Hawaiian gardens, this one isn't terribly naturalized or charmingly overgrown. It's about 3 miles south of Hilo. The turnoff from Hwy 11 onto Makalika St is marked with a small sign.

Panaewa Rainforest Zoo

Due to funding cutbacks, Panaewa Rainforest Zoo *(☎ 959-7224; W www.hilozoo.com; admission free; open 9am-4pm daily, petting zoo 1:30pm-2:30pm Sat only)* has seen better days. Free-roaming peacocks have the run of the place. Caged monkeys, reptiles, a pygmy hippo, axis deer and a cross-eyed Bengal tiger from Las Vegas look a bit cramped. You can also see some of Hawaii's endangered birds, such as the nene and the Hawaiian duck, hawk and owl.

To get here, turn off Hwy 11 at W Mamaki St, a few miles south of town, which almost immediately turns into the Stainback Hwy. The zoo is 1 mile further west.

Mauna Loa Macadamia-Nut Visitor Center

C Brewer Co, which owns the Mauna Loa Macadamia Nut operation, produces most of Hawaii's macadamia nuts. The large **visitor center** *(☎ 966-8618; Macadamia Rd; open 8:30am-5:30pm daily)* here caters to tour-bus crowds and is essentially just a gift shop and snack bar. To the side is a working factory, which has an outside walkway with windows that allow visitors to view the large, fast-paced assembly line inside. The little planted area behind the visitor center, with its labeled fruit trees and flowering bushes, is worth walking through if you've come this far.

To get here, turn off Hwy 11 about 5 miles south of Hilo. A 2½-mile access road then cuts across row after row of macadamia trees, as far as the eye can see.

Puna

Pocketed with hidden delights, the Puna district is the easternmost diamond point of the Big Island. Its main attractions all revolve around lava, whether that means black-sand volcanic beaches, lava rock tide pools, ancient forests of lava tree molds or ribbons of red-hot molten stuff born only yesterday. Puna is not known for its beaches, and for the most part waters along the coast here are subject to strong currents and dangerous riptides.

Kilauea's active East Rift Zone slices clear across Puna. The most recent series of eruptions has been spewing lava since 1983. Today Hwy 130 ends abruptly at the 1990 lava flow that buried the former village of Kalapana. A few miles to the southwest, you can see new lava cascading into the sea, creating unstable benches of new land. Not surprisingly, the closer to the rift you get, the cheaper the real estate.

Puna is a maverick district, full of hippies, Hawaiian sovereignty activists and marijuana growers; your typical 'Punatic' may be all of the above. Harvests of Puna butter *pakalolo* (marijuana) have not been stopped by police raids, aerial sprayings or infrared surveillance, making Puna the pot capital of the Big Island. Other crops also take well to lava. Puna is a major producer of anthuriums, grows the best papayas in Hawaii, and raises prize-winning orchids that are often credited to Hilo. Fields of kava and *noni* thrive.

This entire area presents a great opportunity to ditch your guidebook and poke around. Keep in mind that as you cruise around off the beaten path, you may raise a suspicious eye. But that's only because residents are so desperate to keep the district wild, fighting off development every step of the way. Always respect private property and no trespassing signs – you'll see lots of them here.

Orientation

Keaau is the entrance to Puna. Hwy 11 climbs through a few small towns before reaching Hawaii Volcanoes National Park. Hwy 130

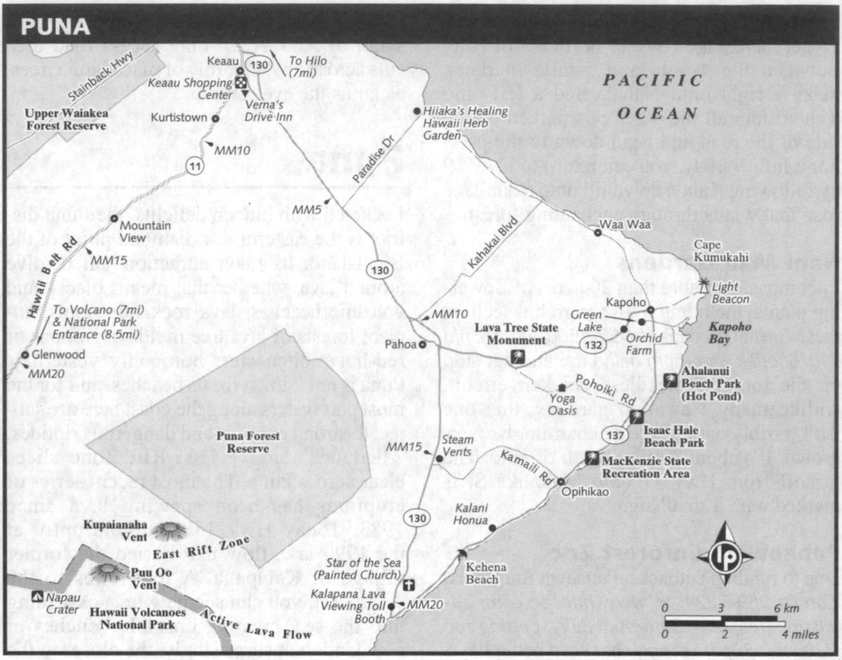

branches off south to Pahoa and continues almost to the coast – but after 21 miles, the road ends at a 1990 lava flow.

KEAAU

Keaau is the small town closest to Hilo. The **library** *(☎ 982-4281; 16-571 Keaau-Pahoa Rd)* usually has an Internet terminal available for walk-ins. The Keaau Shopping Center, off Hwy 11 at the main crossroads, has a post office, launderette and ATM. Across the street is the island's cheapest gas station.

Hiiaka's Healing Hawaiian Herb Garden *(☎ 966-6126; W www.hiiakas.com; 15-1667 2nd St, Hawaiian Paradise Park; admission $10/5 adult/child, with guided tour $15/8; open 1pm-5pm Tues, Thurs & Sat)* is a lovingly tended acre of Hawaiian, Western and Ayurvedic herbs in a sprawling dirt-road subdivision southeast of town. The good-humored herbalist here sells tinctures, teaches workshops and rents out a fully equipped **cottage** *(singles/doubles $50/75)*.

If you're hungry, swing by Keaau Shopping Center. **Keaau Natural Foods** *(☎ 966-8877; open 8:30am-8pm Mon-Fri, 8:30am-7pm Sat, 9am-5pm Sun)* is convenient.

Charley's Bar & Grill *(☎ 966-7589; Keaau Shopping Center; pub grub $5-10; open 11am-midnight Mon & Tues, 11am-2am Wed-Sat, 9am-1am Sun)* serves decent burgers, pizza and ice-cold beers, and has live music, usually Thursday to Saturday nights (admission $3).

Verna's Drive Inn *(snacks $2.50-7.50; open 6am-9pm Mon-Sat, 7:30am-4pm Sun)* is one of five Verna's island-wide, serving the same cholesterol-laden breakfasts and plate lunches.

PAHOA

Deep in Puna's funky heart, Pahoa is a ragamuffin town with raised wooden sidewalks, cowboy architecture and an untamed bohemian edge. It is caught in a wrinkle in time, where alternative vibes left over from the '60s mix with the beeps of ATMs.

Roads in and around Pahoa take many names. For example, the road through town is called Government Main Rd, Old Government Rd, Main St and Pahoa Rd, while it's signposted as Pahoa Village Rd. You'll hear Pahoa Road and Main St most often; addresses are usually written as Government Main Rd.

The town has a **post office** *(☎ 965-1158; open 8:30am-4pm Mon-Fri, 11am-2pm Sat)* and a **public library** *(☎ 965-2171; open 1pm-8pm Mon, 10am-5pm Tues-Thur, 9:30am-4:30pm Fri, 9am-noon Sat)*. In the Pahoa Village Center, **Pahoa Home Video** *(☎ 965-1199)* sells new and used Hawaiiana books, local activity guides and maps.

The weekend **farmers market** *(open from 8am Sat & Sun)* is truly an event. Down some kava here, have your palm read or a massage, buy quality used books and organic goat cheese, or boogie to a local band well into the afternoon. It's best to ask around for the location.

Places to Stay & Eat

Pahoa Orchid Inn *(☎ 965-9664, fax 965-9205; W www.pahoaorchidinn.com; rooms $35-55, with bath $65)* has eight upper-floor rooms in a historic wooden building on Main St. Recently renovated, they are small, but nicely furnished with antiques and arranged around an inner lanai. Most have cable TV and minirefrigerators. Ask about weekly discounts.

Steam Vent Inn *(☎ 965-8800; W www.hawaiivolcanoinn.com; Volcano Ranch, off Hwy 130; bunkhouse bed/room $17/30, suites with bath $75-120)* is perfectly perched on 25 acres, affording ocean views. Main house rooms are sparklingly clean and comfortable, some possessing ocean-facing lanai. Guests share the kitchen, hot tub and volcanic vent steam house. Continental breakfast is complimentary.

As you drive into town, don't miss **Big Island Espresso** *(open 6:30am-noon Mon-Fri, 7am-3pm Sat & Sun)*, a small shack near the post office, for amazing all-natural milkshakes and 75¢ espresso shots.

Pahoa Natural Groceries *(☎ 965-8322; 15-1403 Government Main Rd; open 7:30am-8pm Mon-Sat, 7:30am-6pm Sun)* is a nexus for Pahoa's hippie-and-healthy contingent. Don't miss its toothsome sandwiches and hot-food bar ($5 per pound).

Papa's Cafe *(☎ 965-7100; 15-2950 Government Main Rd; dishes $4.25-6; closed Sun)* is a laid-back café that keeps loose hours. The fabulous falafel, veggie burgers and eclectic fare, with homemade sweets, complement people-watching from the front porch.

Sawasdee Thai Cuisine *(☎ 965-8186; 15-2955 Government Main Rd; dishes $5-12; open noon-8pm Mon-Tues & Thur-Sat)* rises above the pack with unusual curries, many with organic ingredients, locally raised meats and homegrown herbs. Also vying for your attention are fresh salads and sublime appetizers.

Luquin's *(☎ 965-9990; Government Main Rd; meals $6.50-10.50; open 7am-8:30pm daily)* is a Pahoa institution. But can this even be called Mexican food? At least the cocktail bar lets you check out a slice of life, Puna style.

Paolo's Bistro *(☎ 965-7033; Government Main Rd; mains $10-20; open 5:30pm-9pm Tues-Sun)* serves decent Northern Italian fare in an intimate atmosphere, but the waitstaff can get overwhelmed quickly. Save room (and time) for dessert.

Entertainment

Punatix Lounge *(Pahoa Lounge; 15-2929 Government Main Rd; open noon-1am daily)* is a dive with charm. One night it may be packed with drag queens striking a pose, while the next might find local biker club members tattooing each other out back.

Otherwise Pahoa is pretty dead, except when some special event flares up. Full moon parties are just a few of the events that run under the radar. Folks here definitely know what's happening, so ask around.

LAVA TREE STATE MONUMENT

The approach through a tight-knit canopy of monkeypod trees is like a dreamscape. Once inside the park, a 20-minute trail loops through thickets of bamboo and orchids, past 'lava trees' created in 1790, when a rain forest was engulfed in *pahoehoe* from Kilauea's East Rift Zone.

The lava was free-flowing and moved quickly, like a river flooding its banks. As the molten lava ran through the forest, some of it began to congeal around the moisture-laden ohia trunks, while the rest of the flow moved on through and quickly receded. Although the trees themselves burned away, the molds of lava that had formed around them remained.

Now, some 200 years later, there's a ghost forest of lava shells. Some are 10ft high, while others are short enough to look down into, sheltering ferns and frogs within their hollows. Be careful if you walk off the path, as in places the ground is crossed by deep

Puna & Pele

In the Hawaiian language, there are several axioms linking the district of Puna with the goddess Pele. For example, to express anger, someone might say *Ke lauahi maila o Pele ia Puna,* 'Pele is pouring lava out on Puna.'

Equally common on this volatile island are both historic and modern stories of a mysterious woman traveling alone through Puna. Sometimes she's young and attractive, other times she's old and wizened, and often she's seen just before a volcanic eruption. Those who stop and pick her up hitchhiking or show some other kindness are protected from the lava flow.

After the 1960 lava flow destroyed the village of Kapoho, stories circulated about how the lighthouse-keeper in the spared Kapoho lighthouse had offered a meal to an elderly woman who showed up on his doorstep on the eve of the eruption.

cracks, some hidden by new vegetation. It's speculated that one deep fracture, which was caused by an earthquake at the same time as the flow, may have drained much of the lava back into the earth.

To get here, follow Hwy 132 about 2½ miles east of Hwy 130.

KAPOHO

Hwy 132 heads east through orchards of papaya and long rows of vanda orchids to what was once Kapoho, a farming town of about 300 people. The old lighthouse is less than 2 miles down a dirt road east of 'Four Corners,' where Hwys 132 and 137 intersect.

On January 13, 1960, a half-mile-long fountain of fire shot up in the midst of a sugarcane field just above Kapoho. The main flow of liquid *pahoehoe* lava ran toward the ocean but a slower moving offshoot of *aa* lava crept toward the town, burying orchid farms in its path. Two weeks later, the lava entered Kapoho and buried the town. A hot springs resort and nearly 100 homes and businesses disappeared beneath the flow.

Bizarrely, when the river of lava approached the sea at **Cape Kumukahi**, it parted into two flows around the lighthouse, sparing it from destruction. It was later replaced by a modern light protected behind cyclone fencing. Cape Kumukahi, which means 'first beginning' in Hawaiian, is the easternmost point in the state and has some of the verifiably freshest air in the world.

A mile north of Four Corners toward Waa Waa, you can pop in for a three-hour **coconut weaving class** *(admission by donation $5; usually 10am Wed & 11am Sat)* with Bruddah Joe. There's also coastal access at **Orr's Beach** down the road.

RED ROAD (HIGHWAY 137)

Barely above water level, Hwy 137 (Kalapana to Kapoho Beach Rd) is bordered by invasive milo and *hala* trees that look as if they plan to reclaim the road. In a few places, it's so overgrown there's almost a tunnel effect. The highway, nicknamed Red Road for its dust, sometimes floods during winter storms and high surf.

Green Lake

Placid green waters surrounded by breadfruit, guava, avocado and rustling bamboo plants make this freshwater crater lake ideal for swimming (clothing is optional). Park just after the 8-mile marker, opposite Kapoho Beach Rd. Enter through the gate and walk along the road for about five minutes, always bearing right, then take the little path between a garden and a homestead on the right. Beyond the garden, the lake sits prettily at the bottom.

Hale O Naia *(☎ 965-5340; www.hale-o-naia.com; Kapoho Beach Rd; B&B rooms $65-75, suites $125-150)*, a sanctuary in the gated community down Kapoho Beach Rd, is a little slice of paradise. The basic room has a lovely canopy bed, ocean-facing lanai and a private Jacuzzi. There are hammocks and access to kayaks, snorkeling gear and boogie boards.

Kapoho Tide Pools

A mile south of the lighthouse, inside Kapoho Vacationland subdivision, is a sprawling network of tide pools formed in lava basins. To get here, turn off Hwy 137 onto Kapoho Kai Dr, then left at the end on Waiopai Opae, and park near the house festooned with found art objects. Some pools are deep enough for snorkeling (except during low tide). Rich spots are on the windward side, with coral gardens supporting saddle wrasses, moorish idols, butterfly fish, sea urchins and cucumbers.

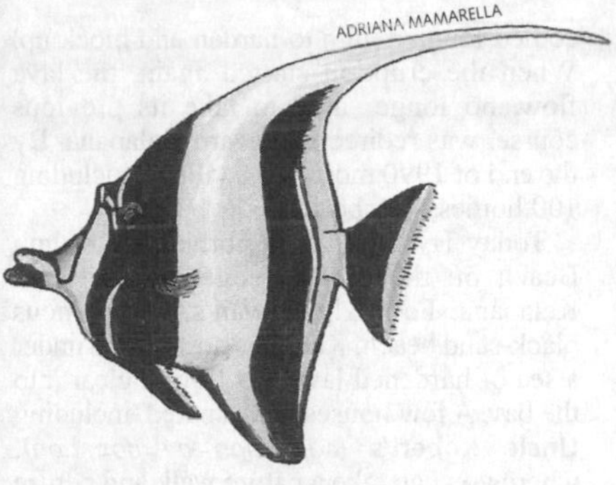

Moorfish idol

Ahalanui Beach Park

Known simply as 'the hot pond' to locals, the star attraction is a thermal spring-fed pool set in lava rock. It's deep enough for swimming, with water temperatures averaging about 90°F. The pool has an inlet to the ocean, which pounds upon the seawall at the *makai* side of the pool, bringing in many tropical fish during high tide and keeping the water clean. Nighttime soaks under the moon and stars are also a possibility.

The park has picnic tables, pit toilets and a lifeguard. There's plenty of parking, but, as always, don't leave valuables in your car.

Isaac Hale Beach Park

This beach at Pohoiki Bay has a chunky lava shoreline. The park also has Puna's only boat ramp. On weekends, there's usually a frenzy of local activity, with family picnics and fishing.

Local kids like to swim near the ramp, which is somewhat protected by a breakwater, and there may be surfers at the south side of the bay. This is also the best place for diving in the district. Enter to the left of the boat ramp, but beware of passing boats.

Soaking fans are in for a treat as there's a small **hot pond** hiding back in the growth along the shore. To reach this 10ft oasis, pick up the beaten path just beyond the house bedecked with 'No Trespassing' signs.

The park has toilets, but no drinking water or showers. **Camping** is allowed, but it's not a very attractive option, as the camping ground is virtually in the parking lot and subject to long-term squatters. For information on county camping permits, see Accommodations earlier in this chapter.

Pohoiki Road

As you veer around the bend to continue following Red Rd, you have the option of staying straight on Pohoiki Rd, a good shortcut to Pahoa town. This is yet another of Puna's shaded, mystical roads that winds through thick forest dotted with papaya orchards and wild *noni*.

Yoga Oasis (*☎ 965-8460, 800-274-4446; W www.yogaoasis.org, 13-683 Pohoiki Rd; singles/doubles $75/95, deluxe tentalow $125/225*) is a 26-acre retreat about 2 miles up from the coast. All rates include daily yoga and an organic breakfast. Rooms and basic tentalows share a spectacular marble bath, while the deluxe model has private facilities and a black bamboo bed. Ask about drop-in yoga classes.

MacKenzie State Recreation Area

Back on Red Rd, you'll find no beach here, only wild 40ft cliffs and dramatically surging surf. Set in a grove of ironwood trees, it is eerily quiet and secluded. Needles underfoot provide a spongy carpet, but also prevent almost anything else from growing here.

Camping is allowed with a state permit, but the facilities (basically picnic tables and latrines) are rundown. Drinking water is unavailable.

Lava Sledding

The most dominant landscape feature in the Kapoho area is the Kapoho Crater, an ancient 420ft cinder cone. The hill is lush green with thick vegetation and has a small crater lake on top of it.

One of its earliest legends goes back to the 14th century. It seems that Kahavari, a young Puna chief, was holding a *holua* (sledding) contest on the slopes of Kapoho Crater. One of the spectators was a woman who stepped forward and challenged the chief to a race. Kahavari tossed the woman an inferior sled and charged down the hill, daring her to overcome him.

Halfway down, he glanced over his shoulder and found her close behind atop a wave of molten lava. It was, of course, the volcano goddess Pele, who chased Kahavari clear out to sea, where he narrowly escaped in a canoe. Everyone and everything in Pele's path was buried in a fiery flood of lava.

Opihikao

The village of Opihikao is marked by a little Congregational church and a couple of houses.

Kalani Honua *(☎ 965-7828, 800-800-6886; Ⓦ www.kalani.com; camp sites from $20, rooms & cottages $105-135, tree house singles/doubles $210/240)*, between the 17-mile and 18-mile markers, is a New Age conference and retreat center. The center conducts tai chi retreats, alternative health workshops, Hawaiian cultural programmes and nature tours, as well as drop-in yoga classes. Its two-story cedar lodges with common kitchens cater to groups, but travelers are welcome if space is available. A day pass for the swimming pool, Jacuzzi, sauna and *watsu* pool (for relaxation stretches) costs $10 for nonguests. The **dining room** serves low-cost, buffet-style vegetarian meals open to anyone who drops by.

Kehena Beach

At the base of a cliff, this black-sand beach was created by a 1955 lava flow. Shaded by coconut and ironwood trees, it's a free-spirited, nude sunbathing spot that attracts a mixed crowd of hippies, Hawaiians, families and seniors. On Sunday it pulsates to the beat of an open drum circle.

Even when it rains in Pahoa, it's usually sunny here. In the morning, it's not unusual for dolphins to venture close to shore. When the water is calm, swimming is usually safe, but mind the currents and undertows. Good, strong swimmers die at Kehena every year, especially in winter. Do not venture beyond the rocky point at the southern end.

Kehena is on Red Rd, immediately south of the 19-mile marker. Look for the little parking lot on the right and you'll see the path down to the beach, a five-minute walk over jagged lava rock. Don't leave any valuables in your car.

Kalapana (Former Village)

For years, the village of Kalapana sat precariously atop Kilauea's restless east rift. When the latest series of eruptions began in 1983, the main lava flow moved down the slope to the west of Kalapana. Much of the early flow passed through a series of lava tubes, which carried the molten lava down to the coast and into the sea. During pauses in the eruption in 1990, the tubes feeding lava to the ocean cooled long enough to harden and block up. When the eruption started again, the lava flow, no longer able to take its previous course, was redirected toward Kalapana. By the end of 1990 most of the village, including 100 homes, was buried.

Today Hwy 137 ends abruptly at Kaimu Beach on the eastern edge of what was Kalapana. Formerly Hawaii's most famous black-sand beach, Kaimu is now buried under a sea of hardened lava that flowed clear into the bay. A few houses were spared, including **Uncle Robert's** *(admission by donation)*, where you can take a nature walk and peruse photos of the devastating volcanic event.

With Uncle Robert's at your back, a 10-minute walk across lava leads to a new **black-sand beach**. You'll need to watch your footing, as there are cracks and thin spots, but it's fairly well-trodden. At the end of the flow, the *pahoehoe* turns to coarse granules and hundreds of baby coconut palms form a natural promenade to the sea. The lonely beach is only an apostrophe of sand.

KALAPANA LAVA FLOW

For the moment, Pele's glory is accessible via a dirt road over the hardened lava beds from the end of Hwy 130 proper, about 1 mile past the intersection with Hwy 137. While the new road has been bad for residents, it's phenomenal for visitors as there's nothing like beholding hot lava hitting the sea, boiling the water and shooting up tall steam plumes. Some nights are more dramatic than others, but always better than anticlimactic daytime viewing. Call the Hawaii Volcanoes National Park **visitor center** *(☎ 985-6000)* about current flow conditions.

From the defunct **toll booth** it's another 2½ miles to where you park your car alongside the road, then another 30-minute walk over lava fields to the viewing area. Bring a flashlight, water and durable shoes. Heed all warning signs, as the lava shelf is fragile and volcanic fumes can be harmful, especially to children, seniors and pregnant women.

HIGHWAY 130

From the edge of the live lava flow at Kalapana, a side road leads up to Hwy 130, which returns to Pahoa. There are a couple of sights along the way.

The 1929 **Star of the Sea** is a little white Catholic church noted for its interior trompe l'oeil murals that create the effect of being in a large cathedral. The style is primitive, but the illusion of depth amazingly effective. The church also has a stained-glass window of Father Damien, who was with the parish before he moved to the leprosy colony on Molokai. Even if it's locked, you're free to walk up and peek at the interior through the front windows. Look for the deconsecrated church, eventually destined to become a community cultural center, alongside the highway at the 20-mile marker.

About 3½ miles south of Pahoa, at the 15-mile marker, a big blue 'Scenic View' highway sign points off into the undergrowth. There's absolutely zilch to view, unless you know what you're looking for: puffs of steam from several low spatter cones signaling a few **natural steam baths**. Follow the well-beaten track for a few minutes, taking the right fork for a two-person sauna with wooden planks. Further back there's a much larger hollow that can accommodate a few people lying down. It can be buggy, with hundreds of voracious cockroaches after dark. Still, it's relaxing and – like many Puna activities – clothing is optional.

HIGHWAY 11 TO VOLCANO

On the way from Keaau to Hawaii Volcanoes National Park, you'll pass through the villages of Kurtistown, Mountain View and Glenwood.

Just after the 12-mile marker, **Dan De Luz's Woods** *(☎ 968-6607; Ahuahu Pl; open 9am-5pm daily)* sells beautiful bowls, platters and furniture made from native sandalwood, koa, mango and banyan trees, all made by a master craftsman. Adjacent **Koa Kaffee** *(☎ 968-1129; open 5am-8pm Wed-Mon, 5am-2pm Tues)* is a little diner cooking up excellent Portuguese bean soup, among other inexpensive dishes.

Pineapple Park Hostel *(☎/fax 968-8170, 800-865-2266; W www.pineapple-park.com; camping $12, dorm beds $20; doubles without/with bath $45/70)* is a soothingly quiet, out-of-the-way option. Amenities include a big guest kitchen, laundry facilities, common room with TV, VCR and a pool table, plus outdoor horseshoes and badminton. Turn left onto South Kulani Rd after the 13-mile marker, then hang a right onto Pohala St, a left on Pikake St and look for the sign on your right.

Mountain View Bakery *(Old Volcano Rd; closed Sun)*, near the 14-mile marker, vends sinful butter rolls (rolls of butter would be more appropriate) and is the 'home of the famous stone cookies' ($4.50 per bag). True to their moniker, these sweeties are rock hard but great with coffee.

In Glenwood, just before the 20-mile marker, **Hirano's Store** has gas and food, but the real reason to pull over here is to see the fuming Puu Oo Vent from the clearing across the way (good luck).

Akatsuka Orchid Gardens *(☎ 967-8234; admission free; open 8:30am-5pm daily)* is a half mile past the 22-mile marker.

Hawaii Volcanoes National Park

Hawaii Volcanoes National Park (HAVO) is unique among US national parks. The huge preserve contains two active volcanoes and terrain ranging from tropical beaches to the subarctic Mauna Loa summit. The centerpiece is steaming Kilauea Caldera, the sunken center of the youngest and most active volcano on earth. Molten lava boils just beneath the surface. It makes a great day hike, or you can drive around the entire rim.

The park's landscape is phenomenal, with dozens of craters and cinder cones, hills piled high with pumice, and hardened oceans of lava (complete with ripples and waves) frozen rock solid on the hillsides. Here and there amid the bone-cracking lava are *kipuka,* rain forests and fern groves that have been spared by lava flows, and other oases that have since grown over them, all protected habitats for native bird species.

The park is one of Hawaii's best places for camping and hiking. It has 140 miles of amazingly varied hiking trails and both drive-up camp sites and backcountry camping. HAVO encompasses about a quarter of a million acres of land – more than the entire island of Molokai – and it's still growing, as lava pouring from Kilauea has added more than 500 acres in the past 15 years.

Kilauea's southeast rift has been active since 1983, destroying everything in its path. The coastal road to Puna was blocked by lava in 1988. The Wahaula Visitor Center on the south coast went under the next year, and

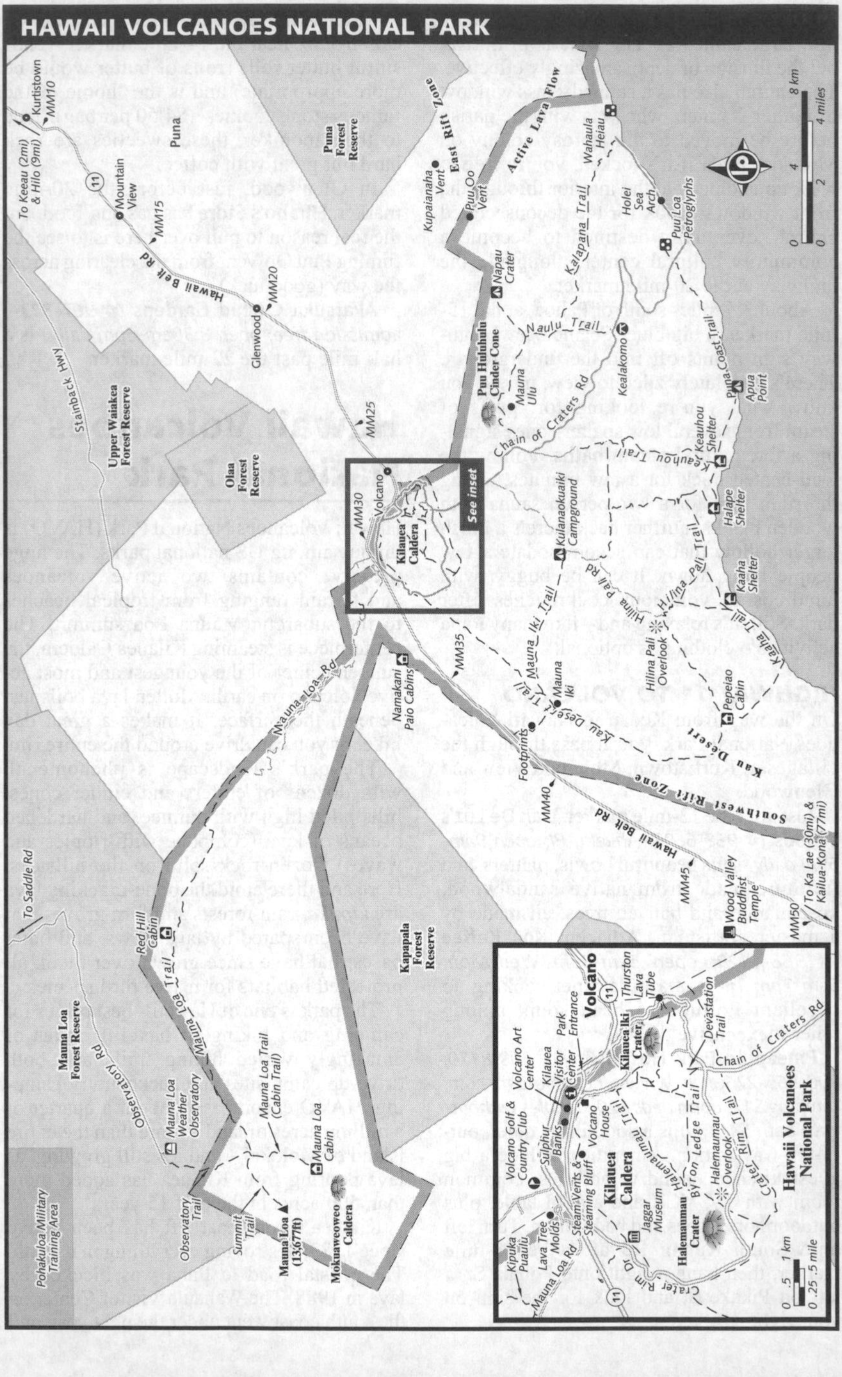
HAWAII VOLCANOES NATIONAL PARK
To Keeau (2mi) & Hilo (9mi)
Kurtistown
MM10
Puna
Mountain View
MM15
Hawaii Belt Rd
MM20
Glenwood
MM25
Stainback Hwy
Upper Waiakea Forest Reserve
Olaa Forest Reserve
Puna Forest Reserve
Kupaianaha Vent
East Rift Zone
Puu Oo Vent
Active Lava Flow
Napau Crater
Kalapana Trail
Wahaula Heiau
Holei Sea Arch
Puu Loa Petroglyphs
Naulu Trail
Puu Huluhulu Cinder Cone
Mauna Ulu
Kealakomo
Chain of Craters Rd
Puna Coast Trail
Apua Point
Keauhou Trail
Keauhou Shelter
Halape Shelter
Hilina Pali Trail
Hilina Pali Rd
Kaaha Shelter
Kaaha Trail
Hilina Pali Overlook
Pepeiao Cabin
Kulanaokuaiki Campground
Mauna Iki Trail
Mauna Iki
Footprints
Kau Desert Trail
Kau Desert
Southwest Rift Zone
Volcano
MM30
Kilauea Caldera
See inset
MM35
MM40
MM45
MM50
Namakani Paio Cabins
Mauna Loa Rd
Wood Valley Buddhist Temple
To Ka Lae (30mi) & Kailua-Kona (77mi)
To Saddle Rd
Red Hill Cabin
Mauna Loa Trail
Kapapala Forest Reserve
Mauna Loa Forest Reserve
Observatory Rd
Mauna Loa Weather Observatory
Mauna Loa Trail (Cabin Trail)
Mauna Loa Cabin
Observatory Trail
Summit Trail
Mokuaweoweo Caldera
Mauna Loa (13,677ft)
Pohakuloa Military Training Area
0 4 8 km
0 2 4 miles
Volcano
Thurston Lava Tube
Park Entrance
Volcano Art Center
Kilauea Visitor Center
Volcano Golf & Country Club
Sulphur Banks
Steam Vents & Steaming Bluff
Volcano House
Kilauea Iki Crater
Devastation Trail
Chain of Craters Rd
Kilauea Caldera
Halemaumau Trail
Byron Ledge Trail
Kipuka Puaulu
Lava Tree Molds
Mauna Loa Rd
Jaggar Museum
Halemaumau Crater
Halemaumau Overlook
Crater Rim Trail
Crater Rim Dr
Hawaii Volcanoes National Park
0 .5 1 km
0 .25 .5 mile

the entire village of Kalapana was buried in 1990. Since that time, the flows have crept farther west, engulfing Kamoamoa Beach in 1994 and later claiming an additional mile of road and most of sacred Wahaula Heiau.

The current series of eruptions, which is the longest in recorded history, has spewed out more than 2.5 billion cubic yards of new lava. Central to the action is the Puu Oo Vent, a smoldering cone in the northeast section of the park. Although many visitors expect to see lava fountains spurting up into the air, this is certainly the exception rather than the rule. Hawaii's shield volcanoes lack the explosive gases of more dramatic volcanoes (eg, Mt St Helens) that spew mud, ash or lava into the air. Here lava mostly oozes and creeps along, while craters huff and puff. In Hawaii, people generally run *to* volcanoes, not away from them. When Pele sends up curtains of fire, Rorschach-type splatterings and flaming lava orbs, cars stream in from all directions.

What you'll be able to see depends on current volcanic activity. From near the end of Chain of Craters Rd, you may see steam clouds billowing and slight ribbons of lava pouring into the sea. Once the sun is down, however, lava tubes on the mountainside glow red in the night sky and lava lakes at the top of vents will be aflame. If the ceiling to a tube collapses, you can see 'skylights': punctures in the earth's surface that reveal the molten lava below.

Orientation

The park's main road is Crater Rim Dr, which circles the moonscape of Kilauea Caldera. You can buzz through the drive-up sites in an hour – and if that's all you have time for, it's unquestionably worth it.

The park's other scenic drive is Chain of Craters Rd, which leads south 20 miles through the volatile East Rift Zone to the coast, ending at the site of the most recent lava activity. Allow about three hours down and back, with stops along the way.

While you can get a good sense of the place in one full day, it would be easy to spend days, if not weeks, exploring this vast and varied park. Escaping the crowds is often as simple as leaving your car in the nearest parking lot. Many of the park sites and shorter trails are even accessible by wheelchair.

Information

The **national park** *(W www.nps.gov/havo; 7-day entry pass per car $10, per person on foot, bicycle or motorcycle $5)* never closes. An annual HAVO pass costs $20. The entrance station also sells annual US National Parks passes ($50).

The park's 24-hour **hotline** *(☎ 985-6000)* tells you what the volcanoes are doing that day and where to best view the action. Updates on eruptions, weather conditions and road closures are available at 530 AM on your radio dial. During periods of prolonged drought, both Mauna Loa Rd and Hilina Pali Rd are subject to closure due to fire-hazard conditions. Drivers should note that the nearest gas is in Volcano town.

Regularly scheduled interpretive programmes include After Dark in the Park, a series of free talks by area experts on cultural, historic and geological matters, usually on Tuesday at 7pm. Annual special events include a Big Island dance and music festival in March, outdoor *hula kahiko* (ancient-style hula) in late May or early June, and a brilliant royal court procession to Halemaumau Crater rim at the end of August.

Climate Get a recorded weather forecast by calling ☎ 961-5582. The park has a wide range of climatic conditions that vary with elevation. Chilly rain, wind and fog typify the moody weather; on any given day, it can change from hot and dry to soaking downpour in a flash. Near Kilauea Caldera, temperatures average 15°F cooler than in Kona. Layer on long pants and a jacket, just in case.

Dangers & Annoyances There have been only two known violent explosions from Kilauea, in 1790 and in 1924. Hawaiian volcanoes are seldom violent, and most of the lava that flows from cracks in the rift zones is slow-moving, giving plenty of warning.

Still, fatalities happen. Most often recent deaths have resulted from unstable collapsing 'benches' of new land and steam explosions at the edge of the active lava flow near the ocean. Other potential hazards include deep cracks in the earth and thin lava crust, which may mask hollows and unstable lava tubes. Stay on marked trails and take all park warning signs seriously.

Another hazard is the toxic cocktail of sulfuric and hydrochloric acid, as well as minute

The Language of Lava

Two of the most important words in the lava lexicon are *aa* and *pahoehoe* (pa-hoy-**hoy**), the two types here on the Big Island. These native Hawaiian terms have been adopted worldwide as lava classification terms.

Aa is the rough, jumbled stuff that wrenches your ankles when you walk on it, making you exclaim ah! ah! It moves so slowly that only the tip of the flow hardens. It's the molten lava pushing from behind that keeps the flow moving, with the hard lava at the front piling up and falling over itself, slowing rolling and clunking its way along.

Pahoehoe is the smooth, ropy blanket that shines red, brown and blue up close, but looks like the charred surface of the moon from afar. *Pahoehoe* refers to the rivers of lava that flow smooth and unbroken. When *pahoehoe* begins to harden, it twists into ropelike coils and swirls, as the outer skin cools and hotter lava underneath continues to move a little. Lava that starts as *pahoehoe* can cool unevenly, lose gas and turn to *aa*. But once *aa*, always *aa*.

glass particles, coming from steam vents. Everyone should take care, but especially those with respiratory and heart conditions, pregnant women and those with infants or young children. High concentrations of fumes hang around Halemaumau Overlook and Sulphur Banks.

The tales are legendary of folks pocketing chunks of Pele's lava, only to sorely regret it later when bad luck strikes them after they return home.

CRATER RIM DRIVE

Crater Rim Dr is a field trip in vulcanology. An amazing 11-mile loop road skirts the rim of Kilauea Caldera and has marked stops at steam vents and smoking crater lookouts.

Natural forces have rerouted the drive more than a few times. Earthquakes in 1975 and 1983 rattled it hard enough to knock sections of road down into the caldera. Quakes come with the territory: there are more than 1200 earthquakes of measurable magnitude on this island every week.

If you take Crater Rim Dr in a counterclockwise direction, you'll start off at the visitor center. Unlike the Chain of Craters Rd, Crater Rim Dr is relatively level, making it a good road for cyclists.

Kilauea Visitor Center

Friendly rangers at the park visitor center *(☎ 985-6017; open 7:45am-5pm daily)* provide updates on volcanic activity and backcountry trail conditions. They have free pamphlets for a few of the park trails, and sell an excellent selection of books and videos on volcanoes, flora and hiking. Ask about guided walks and the fun junior ranger programme for kids.

Inside the center's tiny **theater**, a 25-minute free film on Kilauea Volcano plays on the hour, from 9am to 4pm daily. Footage typically includes flowing rivers of lava and some of the most spectacular lava fountains ever to be caught on film. Commercial videos of recent eruptions run continuously in the center's equally small **museum**, where volcano-related exhibits are due to be upgraded.

Rest rooms, water fountains and pay phones are found outside.

Volcano Art Center

Next door to the visitor center, inside historic 1877 Volcano House lodge, this gallery shop *(☎ 967-7511; W www.volcanoartcenter.org; open 9am-5pm daily)* sells high-quality island pottery, paintings, woodwork, sculpture, jewelry, Hawaiian quilts and more. Many are one-of-a-kind items, and it's worth a visit just to admire the solid workmanship.

The nonprofit arts organization that runs the gallery also puts together craft and cultural workshops, music concerts, plays and dance recitals, all listed in its monthly *Volcano Gazette*.

Sulphur Banks

Next up is Sulphur Banks, where piles of steaming rocks come in Day-Glo colors. This is one of many areas where Kilauea lets off steam, releasing hundreds of tons of sulfuric gases daily. As the steam reaches the surface, it deposits sulfur that crystallizes in fluorescent yellow around the mouths of the vents. The pervasive smell of rotten eggs is from the hydrogen sulfide wafting from the vents. Don't breathe deeply! Other gases in the toxic cocktail include carbon dioxide and sulfur dioxide.

Steam Vents

There are a few nonsulfurous steam vents at the next pull-off, though they're puny compared to the chuffing bluffs nearby. Simple rainwater that sinks into the earth is heated by the hot rocks below and released upward as steam. More interesting is the two-minute walk beyond the vents out to a part of the crater rim aptly called **Steaming Bluff**. The cooler it is, the more steam there'll be. Peek into the cracks and chasms beside the trail here to see *hookupu* (sacred bundles) left for Pele by past visitors.

Jaggar Museum

At this one-room museum *(☎ 985-6049; open 8:30am-5pm daily)*, you'll see real-time seismographs and tiltmeters, a mural of the Hawaiian pantheon and a short history of the museum's founder, Dr Thomas A Jaggar.

It's worth stopping, if only for the fine view of Pele's house, at Halemaumau Crater. Sitting within Kilauea Caldera, it's sometimes referred to as the 'crater within the crater.' Detailed interpretive plaques at the lookout explain the geological workings of volcanoes. When the weather is clear, there's a rapturous view of Mauna Loa to the west, 20 miles away.

Drivers should be careful of the endangered nene that congregate in the parking lot. Feeding them contributes to the road deaths of these endangered birds and is strictly prohibited.

Kilauea Meltdown

The Jaggar Museum, overlooking Kilauea Caldera, is named for Thomas A Jaggar, former head geologist at the Massachusetts Institute of Technology (MIT) and the first scientist to undertake in-depth studies of Kilauea. Jaggar led the group of geologists who lowered the first thermometer into Halemaumau's lava lake in the summer of 1911. It registered 1832°F before melting.

Today the Hawaiian Volcano Observatory, adjacent to the Jaggar Museum, has Kilauea completely wired, making it the most thoroughly studied volcano anywhere in the world. The observatory is not open to casual visitors, but you can view the goings-on at W wwwhvo.wr.usgs.gov.

After leaving the museum, you'll pass the **Southwest Rift**, where you can stop and take a look at the wide fissure slicing across the earth, from caldera summit out to the coast and under the ocean floor.

Halemaumau Overlook

For at least a hundred years (from 1823, when missionary William Ellis first recorded the sight in writing), Halemaumau was a boiling lake of lava, overflowing its banks and then receding.

This fiery lake ensorcelled travelers from all over the world. Some observers compared it to the fires of hell, while others saw primeval creation. Of staring down at it, Mark Twain wrote:

> Circles and serpents and streaks of lightning all twined and wreathed and tied together....I have seen Vesuvius since, but it was a mere toy, a child's volcano, a soup kettle, compared to this.

Of the stink, he quipped. 'The smell of sulfur is strong, but not unpleasant to a sinner.'

In 1924 seeping water touched off a massive steam explosion, causing boulders and mud to rain down and setting off a lightning storm. When it was over, the crater had doubled in size (about 300ft deep by 3000ft wide) and lava activity ceased. The crust has since cooled, although the pungent smell of sulfur persists.

All of the Big Island is Pele's territory, but Halemaumau is the goddess's home. Ceremonial hula is performed in her honor on the crater rim, and throughout the year those wishing to appease Pele leave flowers, bottles of gin and other offerings.

The overlook is at the start of the **Halemaumau Trail**. Although few people who aren't hiking the full trail venture past the overlook, it's an easy half-mile walk to the site of a 1982 lava flow. The spewed lava along the trail has interesting textures and provides an eerie sense of the earth's raw power.

Devastation Trail

Crater Rim Dr continues across the barren Kau Desert and through the fallout area of the 1959 eruption of Kilauea Iki Crater.

The Devastation Trail is a half-mile walk across a former rain forest devastated by cinder and pumice from that eruption. Everything green was wiped out. What remains today are dead ohia trees, stripped bare and sun-bleached white, and some tree molds. You can't keep good flora down, however; ohia trees, *ohelo* berry bushes and ferns have already started colonizing the area anew.

The trail is paved and has parking lots on each end. The prominent cinder cone along the way is Puu Puai (Gushing Hill) formed during the 1959 eruption. The northeast end of the trail looks down into Kilauea Iki Crater.

Chain of Craters Rd intersects Crater Rim Dr opposite the west side parking area for the Devastation Trail.

Thurston Lava Tube

On the east side of the Chain of Craters Rd intersection, Crater Rim Dr passes through the rain forest of native tree ferns and ohia that covers Kilauea's windward slope.

The **Thurston Lava Tube Trail** is an enjoyable 15-minute loop walk that starts out in ohia forest, passes through an impressive lava tube and then enters a fern grove. All the tour buses stop here, so don't expect peace and quiet.

Lava tubes are formed when the outer crust of a river of lava starts to harden but the liquid lava beneath the surface continues to flow on through. After the flow has drained out, the hard shell remains. Dating back perhaps 500 years, Thurston Lava Tube is a grand example – it's tunnel-like and almost big enough to run a train through.

A soundtrack of birdsong accompanies this walk. The *apapane*, a native honeycreeper, is easy to spot. It has a red body, silvery-white underside and flies from flower to flower, taking nectar from the *mamane* (fern) and ohia trees. Feathers from the yellow-and-green *amakihi*, another type of honeycreeper, were once used for Hawaiian royal capes.

Kilauea Iki Crater

When Kilauea Iki (Little Kilauea) burst open in a fiery inferno in November 1959, the whole crater floor turned into a bubbling lake of molten lava. Its fountains reached record heights of 1900ft, lighting the evening sky with a bright orange glow for miles around. At its peak, it gushed out 2 million tons of lava an hour.

From the overlook there's a good view of the 1-mile-wide crater below, used for filming the 2001 remake of *Planet of the Apes*. Crossing the crater is like walking on ice – here, too, there's a lake below the hardened surface, although in this case it's molten magma, not water. Recent plumb tests reveal that the lava is a mere 230ft beneath the surface.

CHAIN OF CRATERS ROAD

Chain of Craters Rd winds 20 miles down the southern slopes of Kilauea Volcano, ending abruptly at the latest East Rift Zone lava flow on the Puna Coast. It's a good paved two-lane road, although there are no services along the way. Allow a few hours round trip to navigate around curves and slow-moving sightseers.

From the road you'll have striking vistas of the coastline far below, and for miles the predominant view is of long fingers of lava reaching down to the sea. In some places the road slices through lava, while elsewhere the lava has won out, paving over the road. You can sometimes find thin filaments of volcanic glass known as Pele's hair in the lava cracks and crevices.

In addition to endless lava expanses, the road takes in an impressive collection of sights, including a handful of craters that you can literally pull up to the rims of and peer into. Some are so new there's no sign of life, while others are thickly forested with *ohia lehua*, wild orchids and chartreuse ferns.

Chain of Craters Rd once connected to Hwys 130 and 137, allowing traffic between the volcano and Hilo via Puna. Lava flows closed the road in 1969, but by 1979 it was back in service, albeit slightly rerouted. Kilauea's active flows cut the link again in 1988 and have since buried a 9-mile stretch of the road.

Ohia lehua

Hilina Pali Road

Hilina Pali Rd starts 2¼ miles down Chain of Craters Rd, passing pit craters of varying size and age, notably the forested **Kokoolau Crater**. From the turnoff, it leads 4 miles to Kulanaokuaiki Campground. It's then another 5 miles to **Hilina Pali Overlook** (2280ft), with a view of the southeast coast.

At the end of the road is the trailhead for the Kau Desert Trail, and for the Kaaha and Hilina Pali Trails that lead down to the coast. They are all hot, dry, backcountry trails.

Mauna Ulu

In 1969, eruptions from Kilauea's east rift began building a new lava shield, which eventually rose 400ft above its surroundings. It was named Mauna Ulu (Growing Mountain). By the time the flow stopped in 1974, it had covered 10,000 acres of parkland and added 200 acres of new land to the coast.

It also buried a 12-mile section of Chain of Craters Rd in lava up to 300ft deep. A half-mile portion of the old road survives, and you can follow it to the lava flow by taking the turnoff on the left, 3½ miles down Chain of Craters Rd. Just beyond this is Mauna Ulu itself.

The **Puu Huluhulu Overlook Trail**, a 3-mile round-trip hike, begins at the parking area, crosses over lava flows from 1974 and climbs to the top of a 150ft cinder cone, where there's a panoramic view that includes Mauna Loa, Mauna Kea, Puu Oo Vent, Kilauea, the East Rift Zone and ocean beyond. This beautiful, moderate hike takes about two hours round trip.

Kealakomo

As you continue down Chain of Craters Rd, you'll be passing over Mauna Ulu's extensive flows. About halfway along the road, at an elevation of 2000ft, is this covered shelter with picnic tables and a superb ocean view. In 1975, a 7.2-magnitude earthquake rocked Kealakomo, dropping the entire shelf 5ft and touching off a tsunami.

After Kealakomo, the road begins to descend along a series of winding switchbacks, some deeply cut through lava flows.

Puu Loa Petroglyphs

The gentle Puu Loa Trail leads for 1 mile to a field of petroglyphs carved into *pahoehoe* lava by early Hawaiians. The site, which is along an ancient trail that once ran between Kau and Puna, has more than 15,000 drawings – perhaps the greatest concentration of petroglyphs in Hawaii. The marked trailhead begins on the Chain of Craters Rd midway between the 16-mile and 17-mile markers.

At the site, stay on the boardwalk at all times – the views of the petroglyphs are quite good, and there's no need to wear them down by trampling over the rocks. **Puu Loa** (Long Hill) at the southeastern edge of the boardwalk, was the place where Hawaiians buried the umbilical cords of their babies in the hope that their children would enjoy longevity. The thousands of dimpled depressions in this petroglyph field may have been pounded out as receptacles for the *piko* (umbilical cords).

Holei Sea Arch

Just before the 19-mile marker, look for the sign marking the Holei Sea Arch. This rugged section of the coast has sharply eroded lava cliffs, called Holei Pali, which are constantly being pounded by crashing surf. The high rock arch carved out of one of the cliffs is impressive, although the wave action of Na Maka O Kahai, goddess of the sea and sister to Pele, has numbered its days.

The End of the Road

Chain of Craters Rd ends abruptly at the coast, where hardened lava flows seal off the road. Park rangers at the basic information station there sell flashlights and water, usually from 1pm to 7pm daily.

In recent times, most of the lava flowing from Kilauea's east rift has come from the Puu Oo Vent. When the molten lava, which is carried downhill in lava tubes, hits the ocean, it boils the water and sends skyward immense acidic steam plumes.

Park rangers try to mark a trail over the hardened lava with small reflectors leading to an observation point that offers a good, though distant, view of the billowing coastal steam cloud. After dark, pulsing surface flows and the steam cloud glow orange. The trail is only about 300 yards, but give yourself about 30 minutes round trip. The walk is over crisp, shiny lava, and you need to watch your footing, as there are sharp jags as well as cracks and holes in the brittle surface. Wear sturdy shoes with good traction.

Go to the Flow

Giving in to visitor demands, the park service somewhat reluctantly allows people to hike from the end of Chain of Craters Rd to the active lava flow.

It's a pretty strenuous trek over hardened lava, and there's no established trail. As the coastline is unstable, hikers should stay about a quarter of a mile inland. The walk eventually leads close to the point where the lava flows dramatically into the sea. Depending on the flow, in all the round-trip hike might take anywhere from twenty minutes to several hours.

The trail is not only unmarked except for temporary reflectors, it's unpatrolled and potentially dangerous. During the day, the black lava reflects the sun's heat and the temperature commonly gets into the high 90s (°F); there's no shade along the way. It's most fascinating to begin late in the afternoon in order to view the orange glow after dark – however, it's inadvisable to be on the trail after sunset without a knowledgeable guide. Arnott's Lodge (see Organized Tours under Mauna Kea earlier) leads guided treks a few days a week.

No matter how you do the hike, you'll need to be prepared. The park service suggests each person carry a minimum of a quart of water, a flashlight with extra batteries, binoculars, a first-aid kit, sunscreen, sturdy boots and long pants.

While the steam plumes are impressive to see from a distance, they are extremely dangerous to view up close. The explosive clash between seawater and 2100°F molten lava can spray scalding water hundreds of feet into the air and can throw chunks of lava up to a half mile inland.

The lava crust itself forms in unstable ledges called lava benches, which can collapse into the ocean without warning. In 1993, a collapsing lava bench sent one islander to his fiery death and burned more than a dozen people in the ensuing steam explosion. In March 1999, the scene almost repeated itself when seven onlookers scattered to safety after a series of explosions began blasting lava bombs into the air and then collapsed the 25-acre lava bench they'd been standing on.

Volcanic activity and viewing conditions are always subject to change, so you should contact the park visitor center for the latest information (☎ 985-6000).

At night a flashlight is required to navigate the ankle-wrenching lava.

MAUNA LOA ROAD

About 2¼ miles west of the visitor center off Hwy 11, this road provides access to the eastern approach of Mauna Loa, the world's most massive active volcano. Mauna Loa has erupted more than 18 times in the past century – the last eruption in March 1984 lasted 21 days. The **Mauna Loa Trail**, a challenging trek which climbs the volcanic slopes, begins at the end of the road after 13½ miles. See Hiking later in this chapter.

At the start of the road there's a turnoff to some **lava tree molds**. These deep, tubelike apertures were formed when a lava flow engulfed the rain forest that stood here. Because the trees were waterlogged, the lava hardened around them instead of burning on contact. As the trees disintegrated, deep holes where the trunks once stood were left in the ground.

A unique sanctuary for native flora and fauna, **Kipuka Puaulu** is about 1½ miles up Mauna Loa Rd. A 1-mile-long loop trail runs through this 100-acre oasis of Hawaiian forest. About 400 years ago, a major lava flow from Mauna Loa's northeast rift covered most of the surrounding area. Pele spared this bit of land when the flow parted, creating an island forest in a sea of lava. In Hawaiian, it's known as a *kipuka*.

Today this is an ecopreserve of rare endemic plants, insects and birds. The lava that surrounds the *kipuka* serves as a protective barrier against invasive foreign species. The young koa trees have fernlike leaves that are replaced with flat, crescent-shaped stalks as the koa matures and rises above the forest floor. The tree provides a habitat for the ferns and climbing peperomia that take root in its moist bark.

Also along the trail you'll hear the songs of several native honeycreepers and pass by a **lava tube** in the dark depths of which a unique species of big-eyed spider was discovered in 1973. A free flora and fauna trail guide is available at the visitor center.

HIKING TRAILS

The park has an extensive network of hiking trails, rising from sea level to over 13,000ft. Trails strike out in a number of directions – across crater floors, down to secluded beaches, through native forests, around the Kau Desert and up to the snowcapped summit of Mauna Loa.

The following hikes range from half-day jaunts to multiday backcountry treks. Remember that except at the cabins and shelters, no drinking water is available anywhere. Trail signs are not reliable, often contradicting each other in distance and direction.

Crater Rim Trail

On the north side of the park, this 11-mile trail skirts the crater rim, while on the south side, it runs outside the paved Crater Rim Dr. You'll actually miss a few of the vehicle road main sights by hiking. But, otherwise, you'll gain. First, by setting off south, you can loop through misty ohia forest down into Kilauea Caldera or Kilauea Iki Crater. Second, you can nosh on *ohelo* berries as birds chirp all around you. Allow five or six hours, with a leisurely lunch break.

Halemaumau Trail

Diagonally across the road from the visitor center are multiple trailhead signs. The first section of the popular Halemaumau Trail briefly threads through a moist ohia forest, with tall ferns and flowering ginger. Then it descends about 500ft to the floor of Kilauea Caldera and strikes out for 3 miles across the surface of the active volcano, pocked with smoking vents.

Shortly after breakfast on April 30, 1982, geologists at the Hawaiian Volcano Observatory watched as their seismographs and tiltmeters went haywire, warning of an imminent eruption. The park service quickly closed off Halemaumau Trail and cleared hikers from the crater floor. Before noon a half-mile fissure broke open in the crater and began spewing out a million cubic meters of lava – and nothing since.

The trail crosses flow after flow, beginning with one from 1974 and continuing over flows from 1885, 1894, 1954, 1971 and 1982, each distinguished by a different shade of black. The trail, which is marked by *ahu* (lava rock cairns), ends about 3½ miles from the visitor center at smoking Halemaumau Overlook (see Crater Rim Dr earlier in this chapter).

The trail is entirely exposed, making it either a hot, dry hike or chillingly damp. Carry water with you as there's none on the way.

Ohelo Berries

Ohelo, a bush about 2ft high with clusters of bright red berries, is one of the early takers to lava. It can be found many places in the park, including near Halemaumau Overlook. These low shrubs are from the heath family, related to blueberries and cranberries. Like their relatives, *ohelo* berries are tart but edible. Unfortunately, they can easily be mistaken for other poisonous varieties of Hawaiian berries, so don't go foraging without a field guide to native flora. In old Hawaii, the berries were said to personify Pele's sister Hiiaka, and were sometimes presented as an offering to Pele.

Kilauea Iki Trail

When Kilauea Iki Crater exploded in 1959, its magnificent lava fountains set a new height record. When the eruption finally settled, a huge expanse of the park southwest of the crater was buried deep in ash. Today, the crater floor is crossed by a popular 4-mile loop hike.

The trail begins near the Thurston Lava Tube parking lot, quickly descending 400ft through fairy-tale ohia forest and then cuts across the 1-mile-wide crater, passing the main smoking vent. The crater floor pulses with steam (and often rainbows), and there's molten lava beneath the hardened surface. Like many trails in the park, the way is delineated with *ahu* (rock cairns). On the crater surface, colorful native fauna stubbornly grows.

Keep to the right to ascend the crater wall on the far side. You'll be on Byron Ledge, the ledge that separates Kilauea Iki from Kilauea Caldera. From there you can connect with the loop trail back to the parking lot or the Byron Ridge and Crater Rim Trails. The former hooks up with Halemaumau Trail after 1 mile.

Footprints Trail

This is the beginning of the Mauna Iki Trail, which leads to a network of trails through the

Kau Desert. The trailhead is between the 37-mile and 38-mile markers on Hwy 11, about 9 miles southwest of Kilauea Visitor Center.

In 1790, a violent and queer steam explosion at Kilauea choked the area in hot, poisonous gases, leaving a blanket of ash several inches thick and wiping out a regiment of warriors who were retreating to Kau after attacking Kamehameha's sacred Waipio Valley. The men were literally stopped in their tracks, suffocated. A shower of hot mud and ashes hardened around them, leaving a permanent cast of their footprints in midsprint.

Two hundred years later, you can still count the toes in a few of the prints – although it takes some imagination these days, as most of the trailside footprints have been seriously damaged by vandals. Every so often erosion exposes more footprints, which are an easy three-quarter-mile hike in from the highway.

Backcountry Trails

Free **hiking shelters** and rustic **cabins** are available along some of the park's backcountry trails. All have pit toilets and limited catchment water that should be treated before drinking. The current level of water at each site is posted on a board at the visitor center. There are also two primitive **camping grounds** that have pit toilets but no shelter or water at Seaside Apua Point along the Puna Coast Trail and Napau Crater camping ground, 3 miles west of the erupting Puu Oo Vent, reached via the Napua Crater Trail.

Before heading out, overnight hikers are required to register for permits, which are free, at the visitor center. Rangers have updates on trail and cabin conditions. Permits are issued on a first-come, first-served basis, beginning no earlier than noon on the day before your intended hike. There's a three-day limit at each backcountry camp site, and each site has a limit of eight to 16 campers.

Trails on the lava flows are unsigned, so bring a compass. Other essential backpacking equipment includes a first-aid kit, a flashlight with extra batteries, a minimum of four quarts of water, an extra stash of food, a mirror (for signaling), cooking stove with fuel (open fires are prohibited), broken-in boots, sunscreen, rain gear and a hat. Note that the desert and coastal trails can make for extremely hot hiking. More information on backcountry hiking, including basic trail maps and hiking books, can be obtained at the visitor center.

On both the Mauna Loa Summit and the Observatory Trails, it's important to acclimatize. Altitude sickness is a danger. Hypothermia from the cold and wind is another hazard. A good windproof jacket, wool sweater, winter-rated sleeping bag and rain gear are all essential. Sunglasses and sunscreen will provide protection from snow glare and the strong rays of the sun that prevail in the thin atmosphere.

Napau Crater Trail Any way you cut it, this is an awesome hike, heading right up to the active Puu Oo Vent, so bring lots of film and binoculars. You can take either the well-marked **Napau Trail** (18-mile round trip, about nine hours) or the **Naulu-Kalapana-Napau** Trail (14½-mile round trip, about seven hours).

The Napau trailhead is at the 3½-mile mark on Chain of Craters Rd, near Mauna Ulu Lava Shield. The trail's first 5 miles follows what was formerly Chain of Craters Rd, before *pahoehoe* lava covered it in 1973–74. There are great examples of pumice and Pele's hair strewn all over the flows.

You'll pass lava trees and the Puu Huluhulu cinder cone before reaching Makaopuhi crater. On clear days the view is religious, with Mauna Loa off to the northwest, Mauna Kea to the north, and fire-breathing Puu Oo Vent straight ahead. At the crater you duck into a cool fern forest where new purple fiddleheads look like staffs from a Dr Seuss musical score. Twenty minutes further along is the Naulu Trail fork, leading to the Kealakomo parking area.

After exiting the fern forest, you'll come to the rock walls of an old depository for *pulu,* the silken clusters encasing the stems of *hapuu* ferns. The ancient Hawaiians used *pulu* to embalm their dead. In modern industrial times, *pulu* was used as mattress ticking and pillow stuffing, until it was discovered *pulu* turns to dust after a few years. Oops!

Ten minutes past the '*pulu* factory' there are fantastic views of the partially collapsed cone. Beyond the junction for the **Napau Crater lookout** is a primitive **camping ground**. Both sites are on a rise that gazes directly on the vent. Hike up past the camp ground toward the toilet, swing around it and follow the almost indistinguishable trail to the floor of the Napau Crater. This new 2-mile stretch heads across the crater right to the base of the mighty Puu Oo Vent.

Mauna Loa Trail The summit trail begins at the end of Mauna Loa Rd, about an hour's drive from the visitor center. Note that this road is occasionally closed owing to drought or eruption activity. This rugged 19-mile trail gradually ascends 6600ft. The high elevation and subarctic conditions make it a serious hike even for those who are fit and well equipped. It takes a minimum of three days, four for proper acclimatization and summit time. Two simple cabins with a dozen or fewer bunks are available on a first-come, first-served basis at Red Hill and Mauna Loa summit. Potable water may be available at both.

At first the trail rises through an ohia forest and above the tree line. After 7½ miles and about four to six hours, you reach Red Hill (Puu Ulaula) at 10,035ft. There are fine views of Mauna Kea to the north and Maui's venerable Haleakala to the northwest.

It's a full day's hike from Red Hill to the summit cabin at 13,250ft. The route is barren, with gaping fissures cleaving the landscape that includes spatter cones. After 9½ miles, you come to Mokuaweoweo Caldera and a fork in the trail. It's another 2 miles along the Cabin Trail to your night's resting place. If you absolutely can't push on, Jaggar's Cave (just beyond the fork) can provide shelter.

The other fork is for the 2½-mile Summit Trail. At 13,677ft, Mauna Loa's summit has a subarctic climate, and temperatures normally drop to freezing every night. Winter snowstorms can last a few days, bringing white-out conditions and snow packs as deep as 9ft. Occasionally, snow falls as low as Red Hill and covers the upper end of the trail. Consult park rangers about weather conditions before setting out, as things can quickly turn nasty.

Kau Desert The Kau Desert Trail network is the most extensive in the park, but so much of it makes for hot, boring and otherwise undesirable hiking. It's best to pick up the trail at the end of Hilina Pali Rd, instead of from Hwy 11. From there, the 5-mile hike to **Pepeiao Cabin** isn't hard, with an elevation gain of fewer than 750ft, but the isolated cabin will offer all the privacy you could ever want. Allow about 4½ hours, longer if you're carrying gear.

Puna Coast Trail This trail starts almost at the end of the Chain of Craters Rd, at about the 19½-mile mark near the Puu Loa Petroglyphs. The entire stretch of this hike is on gorgeous coastal cliffs, but it's also hot. The **Apua Point camping ground** is 6½ miles along a flat, decently marked trail. Remember that this is an endangered turtle nesting ground. Farther west, the Keauhou and Halape **hiking shelters** could be incorporated into a multiday loop that returns via the 7-mile Keauhou Trail. Water is available only at the shelters, not the camping ground.

Fragile Paradise

Halape was an idyllic beachfront camping ground bordered by coconut trees until November 29, 1975, when the strongest earthquake in 100 years shook the Big Island. Just before dawn, rock slides from the upper slopes sent most of the 36 campers running toward the sea, where the coastline suddenly sank. As the beach submerged beneath their feet, a series of tsunami swept the campers up, carrying them first out to sea and then coughing them back on shore. Miraculously, only two people died.

The earthquake left a fine sandy cove inland of the former beach, and despite its turbulent past, Halape is still a lovely spot. Swimming is good in the protected cove, but there are strong currents in the open ocean beyond.

Halape is one of only eight Big Island nesting sites for the endangered hawksbill sea turtle, though they haven't been seen lately. Still, some guidelines to observe include not setting up tents in areas identified as turtle nesting sites, keeping sites clean of food scraps and minimizing the use of night lighting, which can disorient the turtles. Hawksbill turtles also nest at the park's Keauhou and Apua Point backcountry camping areas.

VOLCANO

In the village of Volcano, about 1 mile east of the park, giant fern trees unfurl, ohia trees droop with red, puffy blossoms and the mist dances among sunbeams. No wonder so many artists seclude themselves here.

There's a **post office** *(☎ 967-7611; 19-4030 Old Volcano Rd; open 7:30am-3:30pm Mon-Fri, 11am-noon Sat)* and Internet access at the Lava Rock Cafe. Gas is sold at a couple of pumps beside the café. Tourist and accommodation information is provided at a little shack further west on Old Volcano Rd.

Volcano Golf & Country Club *(☎ 967-7331; Pii Mauna Dr)* has some majestic links sitting beneath Mauna Kea and Mauna Loa volcanoes. It costs $62.50 for the 18-hole green fees and a cart.

PLACES TO STAY

In the Park

The park has two free drive-up camping grounds that are relatively uncrowded outside summer. Sites are first-come, first-served, with a limit of one week at each camping ground. Because of the elevation, nights can be crisp and cool at both.

Kulanaokuaiki Campground *(Hilina Pali Rd)*, about 3½ miles off Chain of Craters Rd, is newer and less developed. It has three camp sites plus toilets, a water catchment system and picnic tables.

Namakani Paio Campground, the park's busiest camping ground, just off Hwy 11, is about 3 miles west of the visitor center. It's a convenient place to stop for the night. Tent sites are in an small meadow that offers little privacy, but is surrounded by fragrant eucalyptus trees. It's about a 1-mile hike to the Jaggar Museum and Crater Rim Trail. There are rest rooms, water, fireplaces and picnic tables.

Namakani Paio Cabins *(bookings at Volcano House ☎ 967-7321; 4-person cabins $40)* are windowless A-frame plywood palaces. Each has a double bed, two single bunks and electric lights, but no power outlets or heating. Bring a sleeping bag to warm you through cold nights. Showers and toilets are shared. Check-in requires refundable deposits for keys ($12) and linen ($20).

Volcano House *(☎ 967-7321, fax 967-8429; annex rooms $85, upper-floor rooms $165-185)* is perched right on the rim of Kilauea Caldera, opposite the visitor center. Although it has an enviable location, not to mention a venerable history, most lower-level rooms look out onto a walkway, and even some of those on the upper floor have only a partial view of the crater. The small rooms have a pleasant character, with koa wood furniture, vintage stationery and, most importantly, heat. There are no TVs, but the hotel has a terrific game library stocking everything from Monopoly to Mankala.

Although the hotel's **dining room** and **snack bar** are your only options for food inside the park, the cafeteria-quality fare is overpriced. Instead, warm yourself by the living room fire, which has been burning for more than 126 years, or order drinks at **Uncle George's Lounge** *(open 4:30pm-9pm daily)*.

In Volcano Town

The village is blooming with places to stay.

Holo Holo Inn *(☎ 967-7950, 800-671-2999, fax 967-8025; W www.enable.org/holoholo; 19-4036 Kalani Honua Rd; beds in 5-bed dorms $15-17; private doubles $40)* is a small, friendly lodge affiliated with Hostelling International. Although the dormitories are clean, they're darkish. The private room has a double bed and two twins. You'll find a shared kitchen, TV room, complimentary coffee and tea, laundry facilities and a sauna. Call for reservations after 4:30pm.

Kulana Artist Sanctuary *(☎ 985-9055; PO Box 190, Volcano, HI 96785; camping/cabins per person $15/20)* is an artists' retreat. Guests share the main house bathroom, kitchen and library, and in the cooperative spirit of the founder's vision, you'll be required to participate in easy caretaking tasks. Unlike some places on the Big Island, Kulana truly lives up to its motto: 'no smoking, alcohol, drugs or drama.' Ask about monthly artist-in-residence rates from $250, plus electricity.

Volcano Inn *(☎ 967-7293, 800-997-2292, fax 985-7349; W www.volcanoinn.com; rooms $55-105, cottages $75-145)* is ensconced in an ohia forest. Cozy, self-contained and heated cedar cottages are tucked away among ferns and loaded with views, plus skylights, stained glass, fireplaces and Hawaiian quilts. You can take breakfast on the lanai or chill in a hammock all afternoon.

Chalet Kilauea Collection *(☎ 967-7786, 800-937-7786, fax 967-8660; W www.volcano-hawaii.com)* has various lodgings spread around town, from affordable rooms with shared bath up to exclusive honeymoon suites. The **Inn at Volcano** *(rooms/suites from $100/300)* is its main B&B property, with rates including afternoon tea. For privacy and creature comforts, try **Volcano Vacation**

Homes *(1-bedroom to 3-bedroom houses $140-380)*, equipped with fireplaces, TV, VCRs and full kitchens. All guests share the inn's garden hot tub. **Volcano B&B** *(rooms with shared bath $50-70)* is a thrifty option, just north of the village center, with a shared kitchen and fireplace.

Volcano Rainforest Retreat *(☎ 985-8696, 800-550-8696; W www.volcanoretreat.com; cottages $85-170)* lets guests tiptoe through the tree ferns and flowers out to three unique cedar cottages. Each harmonizes functional structure with nature. The Forest House is a cedar and redwood octagon; the Sanctuary has a Japanese-style soaking tub. All prices include breakfast and use of the hot tub nestled among the greenery. Reservations are a must.

Kilauea Lodge *(☎ 967-7366, fax 967-7367; W www.kilauealodge.com; B&B rooms/cottages/house from $125/145/175)* has a variety of solid accommodations that have the sort of country comfort you'd expect to find: working fireplaces, high ceilings, quilts and bath tubs. None of the rooms on the main property have TVs or phones, but who needs them with a beautiful garden hot tub?

PLACES TO EAT

It's a long haul from most points in the park out to Volcano town for eats. Pickings are slim at both **Volcano Store** and **Kilauea General Store** on the main road. One or the other is open 5am to 7pm daily.

Volcano Golf and Country Club *(☎ 967-7331; Pii Mauna Dr; breakfast $3.50-6, lunch $7-10; open 8am-2pm Mon-Fri, 6:30am-2pm Sat & Sun)* caters to a local crowd. Things get a little more interesting at lunch, when mahimahi and *kalua* pork are available.

Lava Rock Cafe *(Old Volcano Rd; meals $6-12; open 7:30am-5pm Mon, 7:30am-9pm Tues-Sat, 7:30am-4pm Sun)*, behind Kilauea General Store, is the favored breakfast spot in town, but then again, it's the *only* breakfast spot in town. Steer clear of the saimin and order the French toast with *lilikoi* butter instead.

Thai Thai Restaurant *(19-4084 Old Volcano Rd; dishes $9-13; open 5pm-9pm daily)*, whose owners hail from Thailand, offers tangy curries and noodles with plenty of vegetarian choices. Go wild: it's all fresh, tasty and spicy (if you like) and apportioned generously.

Kilauea Lodge *(☎ 967-7366, fax 967-7367; W www.kilauealodge.com; open from 5:30pm daily)* has a warm country dining room with a stone fireplace and windows looking onto a fern forest. Expect upmarket mains like braised rabbit, venison, parker ranch steaks and fresh fish in papaya-ginger sauce. Reservations are advised.

GETTING THERE & AWAY

Driving nonstop, the national park is 29 miles (45 minutes) from Hilo and 97 miles (2½ hours) from Kailua-Kona.

Kau

The Kau district encompasses the entire southern flank of Mauna Loa, acting as a buffer zone between densely touristed South Kona and the steaming, sulfurous landscape of Hawaii Volcanoes National Park. Note this stretch of Hwy 11 is prone to flooding, washouts and road closures during heavy winter storms. The only other cross island routes are slow Saddle Rd and coastal Hwy 19 between Hilo and Waimea; during the worst storms, even the latter might be closed due to rock slides.

The district is sparsely populated, with only about 5000 people and three real 'towns.' It can be harsh on the eyes, with desertlike expanses of hardened lava, but it must've looked like Eden to the exhausted Polynesian voyagers who first set foot in Hawaii at Ka Lae (South Point). For travelers, exotic beaches are what distinguish this coastline from all others. Kau also has some lush areas in the foothills, where macadamia nuts and most of Hawaii's oranges are grown.

HAWAII VOLCANOES NATIONAL PARK TO PAHALA

Hwy 11 cuts across an 11-mile stretch of the park. From the park's western boundary, it's another 12 miles to Pahala. There's no charge to drive through on the highway or to explore the Mauna Loa side of the park.

Many of the park's longer, more challenging hikes, including the Observatory Trail and the Mauna Loa Summit Trail, are in this section. Between the 37-mile and 38-mile markers, you can access the **Footprints Trail**, which leads to the Mauna Iki Trail

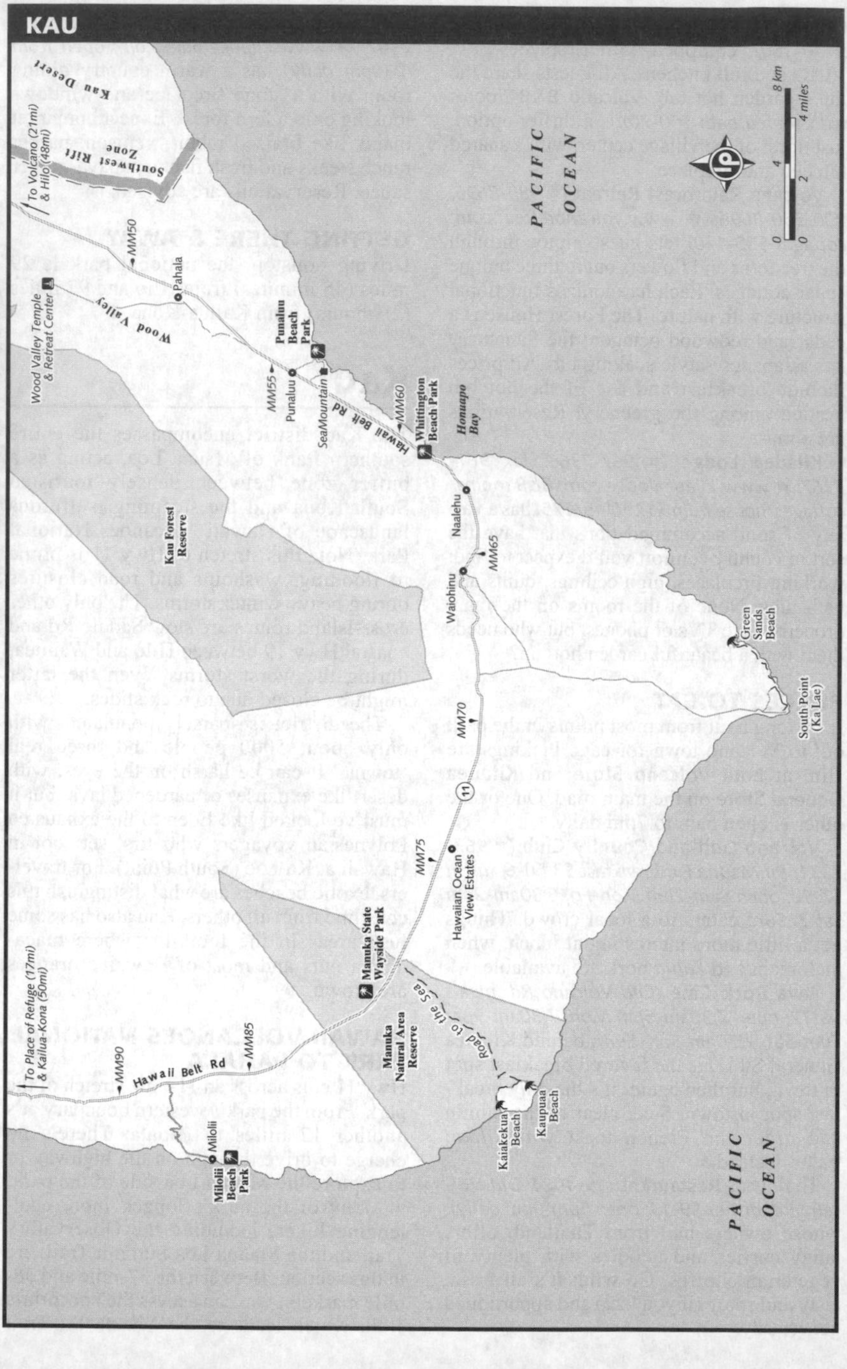
KAU
Kau Desert
Southwest Rift Zone
To Volcano (21mi) & Hilo (48mi)
MM50
Pahala
Wood Valley Temple & Retreat Center
Wood Valley
Punaluu Beach Park
Punaluu
MM55
SeaMountain
MM60
Hawaii Belt Rd
Whittington Beach Park
Honuapo Bay
Kau Forest Reserve
Naalehu
MM65
Waiohinu
Green Sands Beach
South Point (Ka Lae)
MM70
11
MM75
Hawaiian Ocean View Estates
Manuka State Wayside Park
Manuka Natural Area Reserve
Road to the Sea
To Place of Refuge (17mi) & Kailua-Kona (50mi)
MM90
MM85
Hawaii Belt Rd
Miloli
Milolii Beach Park
Kaiakekua Beach
Kaupuaa Beach
PACIFIC OCEAN
PACIFIC OCEAN
0 4 8 km
0 2 4 miles

and a large network of trails through the Kau desert. Kilauea's southwest rift zone runs through this part of the Kau Desert, on the *makai* side of the road. The rift runs for 20 miles, all the way from the Kilauea summit to the coast.

You'll know you're leaving the national park when the signs reading 'Caution: Fault Zones. Watch for Cracks in Road' and 'Caution: Nene Crossing' disappear.

PAHALA

Pahala, on the north side of Hwy 11, is really two hamlets. Kau Agribusiness, which once had 15,000 acres of sugarcane planted for 15 miles in either direction from Pahala, closed its sugar mill in 1996. The company has now introduced groves of macadamia-nut trees on much of the former cane land.

The original sugar town lies down by the old mill, with rickety homes, 'Beware of Dog' signs and junker cars rusting in yards. The northern side of town has modern tract homes, gas stations, a post office, bank with an ATM and **Kau Hospital** *(☎ 928-8331)*.

There are two entrances to Pahala. The southern access is via Maile St, which winds up to the north part of town past the shuttered sugar mill. Alternatively, turn off Hwy 11 at Kamani St, which passes the hospital before heading directly into the commercial part of town. If you bear right onto Pikake just outside of town, it quickly turns into Wood Valley Rd.

Wood Valley

About 4 miles up the slopes from Pahala is the remote Buddhist temple and retreat center of **Nechung Dorje Drayang Ling**. The temple, which enjoys a quiet 25-acre forest setting, was built in the early 20th century by Japanese sugarcane laborers who lived in the valley. In 1975 a Tibetan lama, Nechung Rinpoche, took up residence here, and in 1980 the Dalai Lama visited to dedicate the temple. Since that time, many Tibetan lamas have conducted programmes here and the Dalai Lama himself returned to visit in 1994. In addition to its Buddhist teachings, the center is also used by groups conducting meditation, yoga classes and New Age spiritual programmes. The center can send you a list of upcoming workshops, or check the website at Ⓦ www.nechung.org.

Wood Valley Temple & Retreat Center *(☎ 928-8539, fax 928-6271; dorm beds/singles/doubles $35/50/70)* has a meditation hall with two peaceful guest rooms on the upper floor, as well as simpler rooms and dormitories below. A freestanding guest house with five double rooms is tucked back on the grounds. There's a two-day minimum stay, and all rooms share a bath. Guests must bring their own food, but a kitchen is available. There's a library of books on Buddhist culture, and you're welcome to join the morning services.

The center also produces organic coffee which it sells for $35 per pound – if the old axiom 'you get what you pay for' holds true, this java must deliver enlightenment!

PUNALUU

Punaluu, a small bay with a black-sand beach, was once the site of a major Hawaiian settlement, and in later days it became an important sugar port.

Nowadays it's famous for green turtles that trundle out from the sea to bask in the sun after gorging on *limu* (seaweed). Feel lucky if there isn't a tour bus disgorging breathless honeymooners when you arrive.

Punaluu Beach Park, a county park found just south, has rest rooms, showers, drinking water and a picnic pavilion. Be careful walking about, as the area's black sands are used as nesting sites by hawksbill turtles. Don't approach these gentle giants, as not only are they an endangered species, but they are also very sensitive to human disturbance.

Most days, the swimming leaves a lot to be desired and it's funny to watch *malihini* (newcomers) in tropical swimwear braving the icy, spring-fed waters and strong undertow. Fierce rip currents pull seaward near the pier and there are lots of coconut husks and driftwood floating about.

The most popular section of the beach is the northern pocket, lined with coconut palms and backed by a duck pond. The ruins of the Pahala Sugar Company's old warehouse and pier are a short walk further north. The Kaneeleele Heiau ruins sit on a small rise.

Heading east on Hwy 11, the first Punaluu turnoff is at SeaMountain, Kau's only condo complex. To get to the beach park, take either this turnoff or the next one marked Punaluu Park, less than 1 mile further along.

Places to Stay

There's **camping** at Punaluu Beach park. It's a flat, grassy area overlooking the beach, but with zero privacy. At night, you can drift off to sleep to the sounds of crashing surf. Come daybreak, it's overrun with picnickers. For permit information, see Accommodations earlier in this chapter.

Colony One Condominiums at SeaMountain *(☎ 928-8301, 800-488-8301, fax 928-8008; W www.seamtnhawaii.com; studios $95, 1-bedroom units $120, 2-bedroom units $155)* boasts only a balding golf course with sand patches that are not hazards by design. But, for a spacious condo in the middle of nowhere, it's fairly cheap!

WHITTINGTON BEACH PARK

Not far before Naalehu there's a pull-off with a scenic lookout above Honuapo Bay. From here you can see the cement pilings of the old pier, which was used for shipping sugar and hemp until the 1930s.

The turnoff to Whittington Beach Park is 1 mile beyond the lookout. Although there are tide pools to explore, there's no beach and the ocean is usually too rough for swimming. Endangered green sea turtles can sometimes be seen offshore; apparently they've been frequenting these waters for a long time, as Honuapo means 'caught turtle' in Hawaiian.

Camping is allowed with a county parks permit. It's far enough from the highway to offer a little privacy. The park has rest rooms and sheltered picnic tables, but there's no potable water.

NAALEHU

Sweet little Naalehu's claim to fame is being the southernmost town in the USA. Modest as it is, this is the region's shopping and religious center (2500 souls support six churches) with a grocery store, library, police station, post office, gas station and an ATM.

Naalehu closes up early, so you shouldn't count on getting food or gas here if you're driving back to Kona from Hawaii Volcanoes National Park at night.

Becky's Bed & Breakfast *(☎/fax 929-9690, 866-422-3259; e beckys@hi-inns.com; singles/doubles $70/75)* offers three clean, comfy rooms on the town's main drag. All have private bath and lanai. Breakfast is an all-you-can-eat affair. Guest also have limited kitchen access. Longer stays enjoy a 25% discount.

Naalehu Fruit Stand *(☎ 929-9009; Hwy 11; snacks under $5; open 9am-6pm Mon-Thur, 9am-7pm Fri-Sun)*, a one-stop health food store, bakery and deli, is a quaint destination. The ovens crank out bread in the morning and pizzas to order starting at 11am; macadamia-nut bars and other pastries cost about a dollar. At a few picnic tables out front, you can eat and 'talk story' with the locals.

Punaluu Bakeshop and Visitor's Center *(☎ 929-7343; Hwy 11; open 9am-5pm daily)* is justly renowned, but only for its many flavors of sweet breads and taro rolls, all heavenly and hip-bulging. The onslaught of tourist paraphernalia is relentless, but the public bathrooms (what a find!) are clean.

Shaka Restaurant *(☎ 929-7404; Hwy 11; breakfast & lunch $5-8, dinner $10-15; open 10am-9pm Tues-Sun)* serves full, hearty meals. Breakfast treats include eggs Benedict and French toast made from Punaluu sweet bread, while dinner is a carnivore's delight. They've got a *keiki* menu, full bar and live music most weekends.

WAIOHINU

Before reaching South Point Rd, Hwy 11 winds down into a pretty valley and the sleepy village of Waiohinu, which sits nestled beneath green hills. The town's only claim to fame is the **Mark Twain monkeypod tree**, planted by the author in 1866. The original tree fell in a 1957 hurricane, but hardy new trunks have sprung up and it's once again full grown.

The **Chevron gas station** *(Hwy 11; open 7:30am-7pm daily)* has a convenience store at the side. There's a small **health food store** at Margo's Corner.

Shirakawa Motel *(☎/fax 929-7462; 95-6040 Hwy 11; singles/doubles $30/35, with kitchenette $42)* is a green, weather-beaten motel in the center of town. There are a dozen basic units set beneath verdant hills.

Margo's Corner *(☎ 929-9614; Wakea St; camp sites per person $25, cottage singles/doubles $60/75)* offers bicyclists and backpackers a place to pitch a tent or lay their heads while exploring the Kau area. Rates include a largely organic vegetarian (or vegan) breakfast. The freestanding pentagonal cottage out back has a private bath. Margo's is 2 miles southwest of Waiohinu center, off Kamaoa Rd.

Devastation Day

Kau was the epicenter of the massive 1868 earthquake, the worst Hawaii has ever recorded. For five full days from March 27, the earth was rattled almost continuously by a series of tremors and quakes. Then, on the afternoon of April 2, the earth shook violently in every direction and an inferno broke loose from beneath the surface.

Those fortunate enough to be uphill watched as a rapidly moving river of lava poured down the hillsides and swallowed up everything in its path, including people, homes and cattle. Within minutes, the coast was inundated by tidal waves, and villages near the shore were swept away.

This deadly triple combination of earthquakes, lava flows and tidal waves permanently changed Kau's landscape. Huge cinder cones came crashing down the slopes, one landslide burying an entire village. You can see the 1868 lava flow along the highway 2 miles west of the South Point turnoff. The old village of Kahuku lies beneath it.

Macadamia Meadows B&B *(☎/fax 929-8097, 888-929-8118; w www.macadamiameadows.com; doubles $65-110, 2-bedroom suites $120)* is a half mile south of town, on an 8-acre macadamia farm. This contemporary guest home has open-beam ceiling and large guest rooms with cable TV, private entrances and lanai. There's also a pool and tennis court with ocean views. Continental breakfast features farm-fresh fruit and nuts.

Hobbit House B&B *(☎ 929-9755; w hi-hobbit.com; doubles $170)* is a romantic, whimsical fairy-tale realized. This one-of-a-kind home was built up a steep half-mile 4WD track, set high on a bluff with panoramic ocean views. There are sloping roofs, stained glass and an antique four-poster bed, double Jacuzzi, full kitchen and lanai – and not a straight line in the place!

SOUTH POINT

South Point is the southernmost spot in the USA. In Hawaiian, it's known as Ka Lae, which means simply 'the point.' South Point has rocky coastal cliffs and a turbulent ocean. Incredible as it might seem, it was the site of one of the earliest Hawaiian settlements and may have been where the first Polynesians landed, desperately so by some accounts. Much of the area is now under the jurisdiction of Hawaiian Home Lands. There are no facilities.

From between the 69-mile and 70-mile markers on Hwy 11, one-lane South Point Rd starts out in scattered house sites and macadamia-nut farms, which soon give way to grassy pastures. The winds are bracing here, as evidenced by the trees, some bent almost horizontal with their branches trailing along the ground.

After a few miles, you crest a hill and come upon rows of huge high-tech windmills plopped in a pasture beside the road. With cattle grazing beneath, it's a surreal scene, especially combined with the unearthly whirring sound. Each of these wind turbine generators can produce enough electricity for 100 families. It's thought, theoretically at least, that by using wind energy conversion, the state could produce more than enough electricity to meet its needs – if the controversial Puna geothermal plant didn't already supply enough.

About 4 miles south of the windmills, you'll pass a few abandoned buildings wasting away. Until 1965, this was a Pacific Missile Range station that tracked missiles shot from California to the Marshall Islands in Micronesia.

Ten miles down from the highway, South Point Rd forks. The road to the left goes to Kaulana boat ramp and there may be a sign saying 'Ka Lae Info Center,' which seems to be local slang for 'Sucker!' If you take the right fork, it leads to the craggy coastal cliffs of South Point.

Ka Lae

The confluence of ocean currents just offshore makes this one of Hawaii's most bountiful fishing grounds. Locals fish off the cliff, with some of the bolder ones leaning out over steep lava ledges. Land ruins here include Kalalea Heiau, usually classified as a koa, a small stone pen designed to encourage fish and birds to multiply; look inside for a well-preserved fishing shrine.

An outcropping on the *heiau*'s west side has numerous canoe mooring holes that were drilled long ago into the lava rock. Strong currents would pull the canoes out into deep turbulent waters, where the enterprising ancient Hawaiians could fish, still tethered to the shore, without getting swept out to sea.

The wooden platforms built on the edge of the cliffs have hoists and ladders for the small boats anchored below; you may see a sea turtle or two gliding around in the relatively calm waters below the hoists.

There's a large unprotected *puka* (hole) in the lava directly behind the platforms where you can watch water rage up the sides and recede again with incoming waves. Keep an eye out for it, as it's not obvious until you're almost on top of it.

Walk down past the light beacon and continue along the wall to finally reach the southernmost point in the USA. There are no markers here, no souvenir stands, just crashing surf and lots of wind.

Green Sands Beach

Those who choose the left fork will dead end at a shack. This is neither Ka Lae, nor an info center, but these are just details, right? Here locals charge $5 for 'secure parking' in an impromptu lot. It's foxy (and irksome) in that capitalist way. Legally, shoreline access in Hawaii is by law always free to the public, so they can't charge beachgoers admission, hence the parking ruse. These folks do have the only toilet for miles, which may be priceless for some.

You can walk here from Ka Lae instead by following the shoreline for about 40 minutes. Once you reach the boat ramp near the so-called parking lot, it's another 2½ miles along a rutted dirt road. If you have a high-riding 4WD vehicle, you could consider driving in, but the road is rough and the drive takes about 25 minutes.

It's a gentle and beautiful hike, though windy. Along the way you'll notice pockets of green sand sparkling in the sun. These are semiprecious olivine crystals chipped from the lava cliffs and worn smooth by a relentless and pounding surf. Olivine is a type of volcanic basalt rich in iron, magnesium and silica.

Eventually you'll need to scramble down some cliffs to get to Green Sands Beach. Pick a calm day to visit, as during periods of high surf the entire beach can be flooded. By now, this beautiful small beach is squarely on the beaten path. For a more remote setting, check out the road to the sea (see that section later in this chapter).

HAWAIIAN OCEAN VIEW ESTATES

A few miles before Manuka State Wayside Park, you'll come to the last services for that long stretch of highway up to Honaunau. This is the commercial center, such as it is, for Hawaiian Ocean View Estates (HOVE) and a couple of other isolated south-side subdivisions. You'll find a gas station, post office, hardware store, supermarket and a couple of local eateries.

This area remains one of the last sunny expanses of land in Hawaii to be totally free of resorts. Controversial proposals for large developments occasionally pop up, but so far all have been defeated, to the relief of island environmentalists.

If you want to hide out from civilization for a while, call **Bougainvillea B&B** (*☎/fax 929-7089, 800-688-1763; W www.hi-inns.com/bouga; singles/doubles $65/70)*, which has a swimming pool and hot tub, or **Leilani Bed & Breakfast** (*☎ 939-7452; e leilanibb@aol.com; singles/doubles $45/50, en suite family room $60)*, where the owners lead spelunking tours.

ROAD TO THE SEA

Know that this is *rough* going over lava, ledges, and cracks that threaten to suck you in. Few people venture down this way, and you'll likely have the beaches to yourself. There are 130 words for wind in Hawaiian and you'll most likely experience almost all of them here. Calm days do descend every so often, but most of the time even your inner ears will be exfoliated by flying sand.

Set your odometer when you turn in at the mailboxes between the 79-mile and 80-mile markers. From here it's six long, hard miles over a rudimentary lava track to the black sands at **Kaupuaa**, the smaller of the two beaches. It takes about 45 minutes and is pretty much straight on.

The next beach is reached by turning right at exactly the 5.5 mark. Don't take the right fork at the 5½-mile mark (only a mule could make it up there), and don't take the right-hand fork *beyond* the 5.5 mark or you'll be lost, fast. The track jogs around to the right before heading toward the shore again and the way isn't always readily apparent. Get out and assess the route often; remember that cars sink in sand. Park just before the red *puu* (hill) and walk down to the ocean. If you decide to walk the whole distance, it's only about 1½ miles. Bring as much water as you can carry as it's hot and shadeless, with no potable water.

The reward is a beautiful **green-sand beach**, probably with no-one else around. If you walk to its northern end, you'll come to a lime-colored freshwater pool with a couple of hot pockets.

MANUKA STATE WAYSIDE PARK

The trees and bushes growing at this 13½-acre arboretum include 48 native Hawaiian species and 130 exotics. The park, just north of the 81-mile marker, is in the midst of the 25,500-acre Manuka Natural Area Reserve, which reaches from the slopes of Mauna Loa clear down to the sea. The reserve encompasses a couple of *heiau*s and other ruins. The **Manuka Nature Trail**, a 2-mile interpretive loop that walks across lava flows and through rain forest, begins above the parking lot. A detailed brochure explaining the trail's varied flora can be obtained from the state parks office in Hilo.

Camping is allowed by permit in the three-sided covered shelter near the road, which has space for about five sleeping bags. In a pinch it will serve for an overnight break between Hilo and Kona, but is a bit forlorn with an odd vibe. There are rest rooms and picnic tables, but no drinking water.

Maui

Maui, a demigod with Herculean strength and the trickster cunning of Odysseus, once yanked the Hawaiian islands up out of the sea with a fishhook. He climbed Haleakala volcano and lassoed the sun, refusing to let go until the islands had been rescued from ancient darkness. Today sunseekers still reap the fruits of Maui's mythical labors as they laze along 120 miles of sunshine coast.

'Maui no ka Oi' – Maui is the best! – that's how the saying goes. Maui may not be the biggest island, or where the state capital stands, and it is far away from Waikiki, but if visitors can be judged to vote with their feet, then Maui is the favored son among all of Hawaii's Neighbor Islands. Even endangered humpback whales prefer these warm coastal waters above all others during their winter migrations.

Honeymooners, surfers and hikers all find their own slice of paradise on Maui. And yet there is room for you to secret yourself away in natural ocean baths, secluded waterfalls or at royal volcanic heights. Even in the main tourist urban enclaves – the old whaling town of Lahaina, the Kaanapali and Kapalua resorts, the Kihei strip – there are no super high-rises.

Maui has another, more raw side. Escape is never far away when it takes only a couple of hours to circumnavigate the entire island. Staying in the small towns of Paia, Haiku or Hana is a totally different experience. These settlements sit beneath Haleakala, the massive mountain that provides the scenic backdrop to all of east Maui. Its slopes hold native rain forests, eucalyptus groves, Upcountry farms and open pastures where Hawaiian cowboys still ride.

Haleakala volcano, with a 10,023ft summit, is an extraordinary landscape of spewed red cinders and gray lava hills. Some incredible hiking trails cross the crater floor, and sunrise at the summit is awe inspiring. Haleakala's windward side is lush, wet and rugged. The famed Hana Hwy runs down the full length of it, winding its way above the coast through tropical jungle and past roadside waterfalls. It's arguably the most beautiful coastal road in Hawaii.

Beyond timeless Hana town, the Piilani Hwy takes over and passes by bamboo forests, waterfall pools and the cliffs of Oheo Gulch, then onward for jaw-dropping views up Kaupo Gap and solitary beaches where the ocean roars. Only the dramatic cliffs, lava blowholes and pristine bays of the Kahekili Hwy that snakes around West Maui can compare.

Highlights

- Watching the sunrise atop ancient Haleakala
- Windsurfing with the experts at Hookipa Beach
- Winding along the dramatic sea cliffs of the Hana Hwy
- Cruising through a pod of majestic humpback whales
- Sunning yourself, lizardlike, on Big Beach

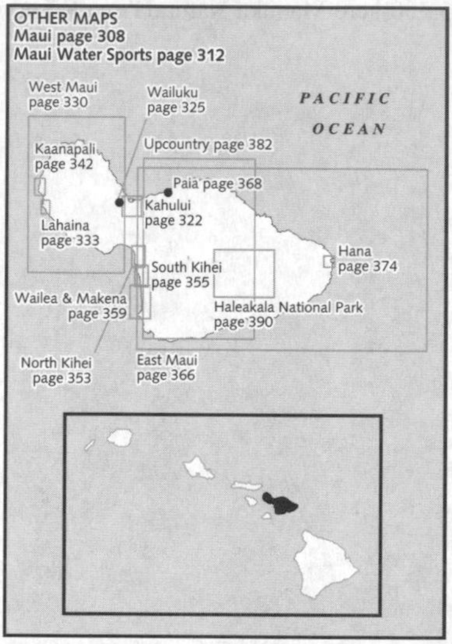

HISTORY

Before Western contact, Maui had three major population centers: the southeast coast around Hana, the Wailuku area and the district of Lele (present-day Lahaina). In the 14th century, Piilani, the chief of the Hana district, conquered the entire island. During his reign, Piilani accomplished some impressive engineering feats. He built Maui's largest temple, Piilanihale Heiau, which still stands today, as well as an extensive island-wide road system. Almost half of Maui's highways still bear his name.

The last of Maui's ruling chiefs was Kahekili. During the 1780s, he was the most powerful chief in Hawaii, bringing both Oahu and Molokai under Maui's rule. In 1790, while Kahekili was in Oahu, Kamehameha the Great launched a bold naval attack on Maui. Using foreign-acquired cannons and the aid of two captured foreign seamen, Isaac Davis and John Young, Kamehameha defeated Maui's warriors in a fierce battle at Iao Valley.

An attack on his own homeland by a Big Island rival forced Kamehameha to withdraw from Maui, but the battles continued over the years. When Kahekili died on Oahu in 1794, his kingdom was divided. In 1795, Kamehameha invaded Maui again, and this time he conquered the entire island and brought it under his rule. In 1800, he halfheartedly established his royal court at Lahaina. It remained the capital of Hawaii until Kamehameha III moved it to Honolulu in 1845.

Whaling Days

Both the whalers and the missionaries reached Lahaina in the early 19th century. They were soon at odds.

Shortly after his arrival in 1823, William Richards, Lahaina's first Protestant missionary, converted Maui's native governor, Hoapili, to Christianity. Under Richards' influence, Hoapili began passing laws against drunkenness and debauchery. But after months at sea, the whalers weren't looking for a prayer service when they pulled into port. To most sailors, there was 'no God west of the Horn.'

In 1826, when English captain William Buckle of the whaler *Daniel* pulled into port, he was outraged to discover Lahaina had a new 'missionary taboo' against womanizing. Buckle's crew came to shore seeking revenge against Richards, but a group of Hawaiian Christians came to Richards' aid and chased the whalers back to their boat.

Following Captain Buckle's purchase of a Hawaiian woman, Richards wrote a letter home reporting the details. It ended up being printed in a prominent New York newspaper and a libel suit soon followed. Richards was summoned to Honolulu to be tried, but he was acquitted by Hawaiian *alii* (chiefs).

The next year, after Governor Hoapili arrested the captain of the *John Palmer* for allowing women to board his ship, the angry crew shot a round of cannonballs at Richards' house. The captain was released, but laws forbidding liaisons between seamen and native women stayed.

After Governor Hoapili's death, laws prohibiting liquor and prostitution were no longer strictly enforced, and whalers began to flock to Lahaina. Soon two-thirds of the whalers coming into Hawaii were landing in Lahaina, which had replaced Honolulu as the favored harbor. In 1846, almost 400 ships pulled into port.

But by the 1860s, the whaling industry started to fizzle. The depletion of the last hunting grounds in the Arctic and the emergence of the petroleum industry spelled the end of the US whaling era. Whaling had been the base of Maui's economy. After the whalers left, Lahaina became all but a ghost town.

Sugar & Tourism

As whaling declined, sugar was on the rise. Two of the first planters were Samuel Alexander and Henry Baldwin, sons of prominent missionaries. In 1870, they began growing sugarcane on 12 acres in Haiku, marking the beginning of Hawaii's biggest sugar corporation.

In 1876, the Alexander & Baldwin company began construction of the Hamakua Ditch, which carried water from the mountainous interior to the Haiku plantations 17 miles away. This system turned Wailuku's dry central plains into green sugar land.

Sugar remained the backbone of the economy until tourism took over in the 1960s. Lahaina became a playground for the international jet set. Instead of sugar, it was sweet sex, drugs and rock 'n' roll that did the trick in the 1970s.

GEOGRAPHY

Maui, the second-largest Hawaiian Island (728 sq miles), arose from the ocean floor as two separate volcanoes. Lava flows and soil erosion eventually built up a flat, valleylike isthmus between the two, providing

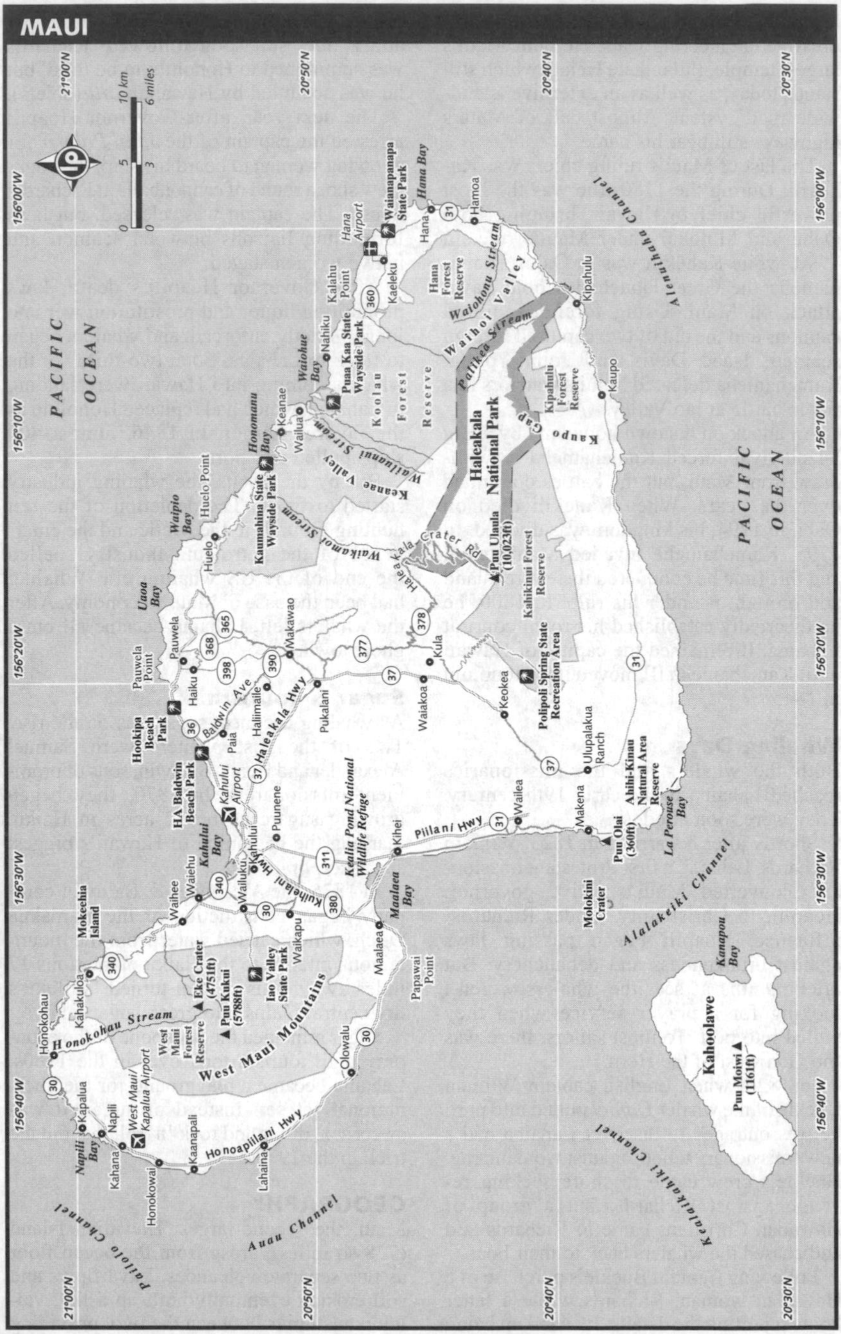
MAUI
PACIFIC OCEAN
PACIFIC OCEAN
21°00'N
20°50'N
20°40'N
20°30'N
156°40'W
156°30'W
156°20'W
156°10'W
156°00'W
0 5 10 km
0 3 6 miles
Pailolo Channel
Auau Channel
Alalakeiki Channel
Kealaikahiki Channel
Alenuihaha Channel
Honokohau
Honokohau Stream
Kahakuloa
Mokeehia Island
Kapalua
Napili Bay
Napili
West Maui/Kapalua Airport
Kahana
Honokowai
Kaanapali
Honoapiilani Hwy
Lahaina
Olowalu
West Maui Mountains
West Maui Forest Reserve
Eke Crater (4751ft)
Puu Kukui (5788ft)
Iao Valley State Park
Waihee
Waiehu
Kahului Bay
Wailuku
Kahului
Waikapu
Maalaea
Maalaea Bay
Papawai Point
Kuihelani Hwy
Kealia Pond National Wildlife Refuge
Kihei
Piilani Hwy
Wailea
Makena
Puu Olai (360ft)
Molokini Crater
Ahihi-Kinau Natural Area Reserve
La Perouse Bay
Ulupalakua Ranch
Kahoolawe
Kanapou Bay
Puu Moiwi (1161ft)
HA Baldwin Beach Park
Kahului Airport
Puunene
Hookipa Beach Park
Baldwin Ave
Pala
Haiku
Halimaile
Haleakala Hwy
Pukalani
Makawao
Pauwela Point
Pauwela
Uaoa Bay
Huelo
Huelo Point
Waipio Bay
Kaumahina State Wayside Park
Honomanu Bay
Keanae
Wailua
Waiohue Bay
Puaa Kaa State Wayside Park
Nahiku
Kalahu Point
Hana Airport
Waianapanapa State Park
Hana Bay
Hana
Hamoa
Kaeleku
Hana Forest Reserve
Koolau Forest Reserve
Waikamoi Stream
Keanae Valley
Wailuanui Stream
Palikea Stream
Waihoi Stream
Waiohonu Stream
Waihoi Valley
Kipahulu
Kipahulu Forest Reserve
Kaupo Gap
Kaupo
Haleakala National Park
Haleakala Crater Rd
Puu Ulaula (10,023ft)
Kahikinui Forest Reserve
Polipoli Spring State Recreation Area
Kula
Waiakoa
Keokea
30
340
380
311
31
36
37
365
368
398
390
377
378
360

a fertile setting for fields of sugarcane and giving Maui the nickname 'The Valley Isle.'

The eastern side of Maui is dominated by Haleakala, which has a summit elevation of 10,023ft and measures 5 miles from sea floor to summit. This younger, larger volcano has a massive craterlike valley containing numerous cinder cones and vents. Haleakala probably last erupted in 1790, which on the geological clock means it could just be snoozing.

The more ancient volcano, now eroded into the West Maui Mountains, has Puu Kukui (5788ft) as its highest point. The rainy northeast sides of both mountain masses are cut with deep ravines and valleys that lead down to the coast. White-sand beaches run along much of the island's western shoreline.

CLIMATE

Maui's *kona* (leeward) west coast is largely dry and sunny. The *koolau* (windward) southeast coast and Kula uplands receive more rain and commonly have intermittent clouds.

Temperatures vary more with elevation than season. The lowest temperature ever recorded at the summit of Haleakala was 14°F, and temperatures hovering around freezing are common on winter nights. The mountain even gets an occasional winter snowcap. Daytime highs vary only about 8°F year-round. Average daily temperatures in August reach 80°F in Lahaina, Kihei or Hana, but only 50°F at Haleakala summit.

Maui gets the most rain between December and March, averaging 15 inches annually along the western coast, 69 inches in Hana. Inside Haleakala crater, conditions range from desert to rain forest. Puu Kukui, which stands just 5 miles from the dry Wailuku plains, holds the US record for annual rainfall – a soggy 739 inches.

For the National Weather Service's recorded forecast of weather conditions on Maui, call ☎ 877-5111. A more extensive marine forecast, including surf conditions, winds and tides, is available by dialing ☎ 877-3477. If you're a board surfer, you'll find the biggest waves in winter; if you're a windsurfer, you'll find the best wind conditions in summer.

FLORA & FAUNA

It's on Maui that you are most likely to see the endangered nene (Hawaiian goose) and the rare silversword plant. Haleakala is the habitat for both. Maui is also the best island for viewing humpback whales.

At least six birds native to Maui are found nowhere else in the world. These are the Maui parrotbill, the Maui creeper, the Maui *akepa* (crested honeycreeper) and the cinnamon-colored *poouli*, all of which are endangered. The *poouli*, quite amazingly, wasn't discovered until 1973, when it was sighted by a group of University of Hawaii students working in a secluded area of the Hana rain forest.

Maui also has feral pigs, goats and game birds, all of which are hunted both for recreational purposes and to control the damage that these introduced species cause to the habitat.

Humpback Whales

After spending their summers in Alaska, more than half of all humpback whales in the North Pacific winter in Hawaii. The peak season for humpbacks is the same as for tourists from cold-weather climates. Some whales arrive as early as November, and a few stay as late as May; most are in residence from January to March.

The largest numbers are found in the shallow waters between Maui, Lanai and Kahoolawe. Humpbacks have tail flukes with distinctive individual markings, making them easy to identify. They can reach lengths of 45ft and weigh up to 45 tons. Despite their size, they often put on an amazing acrobatic show, including arching drives, breaching and fin splashing.

The western coastline of Maui and the eastern shore of Lanai are the chief birthing and nursing grounds for wintering humpbacks. They like to stay in shallow water when they have newborn calves, apparently as a safeguard against shark attacks. Maalaea Bay is a favorite nursing ground. Around Lahaina, where the waters are buzzing with activity, whales generally stay well offshore. The best bet for whale spotting is to go south at least as far as Launiupoko Wayside Park. Maui's finest shoreline whale-watching stretches are from Olowalu to Maalaea Bay and from Keawakapu Beach to Makena Beach.

Humpbacks are highly sensitive to human disturbance and noise. Federal law protects these waters and prohibits boats and swimmers from approaching within 300 yards of the whales, which can result in a $25,000 fine. The rules apply to everyone, including swimmers, kayakers and surfers, and they are strictly enforced – whether violators are aware of the law or not. Some activities, such as jet skiing, are so disruptive that they are banned outright along the southwest coast of Maui from mid-December to mid-April.

GOVERNMENT

Maui County consists of the islands of Maui, Molokai, Lanai and uninhabited Kahoolawe. The county seat is in Wailuku. The county is governed by an elected mayor with a four-year term and nine council members with two-year terms.

ECONOMY

After Oahu, Maui captures the lion's share of Hawaii's tourist industry, accounting for roughly half the visitor accommodations on all the outer islands combined. Numbers, however, don't equate to bargains here. Maui also has the highest room rates in Hawaii, averaging $192 a night, about 25% higher than the state average.

Surprisingly, more land on Maui is used for grazing dairy and beef cattle than for any other purpose. For every acre of sugar, there are 3 acres of ranch land. Both sugar and pineapple harvesting have been drastically scaled back in recent years. *Pakalolo* (marijuana) farming is still a multibillion-dollar industry statewide, with 'Maui Wowie' doing its part.

Kula is one of the state's major flower- and vegetable-producing regions, accounting for more than half of the cabbage, lettuce, onions and potatoes grown in Hawaii and for almost all of the commercially grown proteas and carnations.

Elsewhere the island's high-tech industry is growing. A wealth of scientific research is conducted in various rain forest preserves, marine sanctuaries and atop Haleakala. Maui's unemployment rate is currently 4.5%.

POPULATION & PEOPLE

Maui has a population of 118,000. The Wailuku district, which includes the sister towns of Wailuku and Kahului, is home to half of the island's residents. During the 1990s, the population grew by 30% mostly thanks to immigration from the mainland.

Ethnically, 26% of the population is Caucasian, 16% Filipino and 11% Japanese. About one-quarter of Maui's residents consider themselves to be of 'mixed blood' with some Hawaiian ancestry, but it's estimated that less than 2% are full-blooded Hawaiian.

ORIENTATION

Most visitors to Maui land at the main airport in Kahului.

Be aware that most main roads are called highways whether they're busy four-lane thoroughfares or just quiet country roads. What's more, islanders refer to highways by name, rarely by number. If you ask someone how to find Hwy 36, chances are they aren't going to know – ask for the Hana Hwy instead.

Maps

The best map for getting around the island is the encyclopedic *Ready Mapbook of Maui County*, but admittedly it's bulky. A good lightweight, foldout map is Nelles' *Maui, Molokai & Lanai*. The colorful Franko's Map *Maui, The Valley Isle* (W www.frankosmaps.com) features water sports and is sold at dive shops; it is waterproof and rip resistant.

INFORMATION

Tourist Offices

There are limited visitor information centers in Lahaina (see the West Maui section, later) and Wailuku (central Maui). When all else fails, rely on local word-of-mouth rather than advice from activity desk operators and hotel concierges. For the cyber low-down on Maui, visit W www.infomaui.com or W www.mauivisitor.com.

Post & Communications

The main post office is in Wailuku. The most convenient business center is the 24-hour **Kinko's** (*☎ 871-2000; Dairy Center, 395 Dairy Rd*) in Kahului. Kinko's offers Internet access for 20¢ a minute. Most cybercafés charge less, around $6 per hour, but they tend to be short-lived. Wailuku hostels and a few B&Bs offer free Internet access for guests.

Otherwise there are public library branches in Kahului, Wailuku, Lahaina, Kihei, Makawao and Hana. For information on Internet access through Hawaii's public library systems, see Libraries in the Facts for the Visitor chapter.

Newspapers & Magazines

Maui's main newspaper, the *Maui News* (W *www.mauinews.com)* has good coverage of local and off-island news and comes out daily except Saturday. The alternative free weekly *Maui Time* (W *www.mauitime.com)* has the ultimate lowdown on entertainment, sports and island politics. There are several small community newspapers that focus on local issues, including *Lahaina News* and *Haleakala Times*.

Free tourist magazines such as *This Week Maui* and *101 Things to Do: Maui* are full of ads, discount coupons, simple maps and general sight-seeing information. They're worth picking up at the airport and island hotels and restaurants.

Radio & TV

Maui has numerous radio stations, including KPOA (93.5 FM) and KNUI (900AM), which play Hawaiian music most of the time, and Hawaii NPR (National Public Radio) at 90.7FM.

All the major US mainland TV networks are available on cable. Cable TV Channel 7 has ongoing programmes on Hawaii geared for visitors.

Bookstores

The island's largest bookstore is the mega-chain **Borders** *(☎ 877-6160; Maui Marketplace, 270 Dairy Rd, Kahului; open 9am-10pm Sun-Thur, 9am-11pm Fri & Sat)*. The **Lahaina Book Emporium** *(☎ 661-1399; 505 Front St, Lahaina; open 10am-9pm Mon-Sat, 10am-6pm Sun)* is an impressive independent shop. Also check out the '10¢ bookstore' in Puunene *(☎ 871-6563; open 8am-4pm Mon-Sat)*.

Emergency

There's an **emergency line** *(☎ 911)* for police, ambulance and fire.

Maui Memorial Medical Center *(☎ 244-9056; 221 Mahalani St, Wailuku)* is a large hospital with 24-hour emergency services.

Several clinics offer outpatient services, including **West Maui Healthcare Center** *(☎ 667-9721; Whalers Village, 2435 Kaanapali Pkwy, Kaanapali; open 8am-10pm daily)*. **Planned Parenthood of Hawaii** *(☎ 871-1176; Suite 303, 140 Hoohana St, Kahului)* offers low-cost sexual and reproductive health services. Also see the Kihei, Wailuku and Lahaina sections.

ACTIVITIES

If you're looking for someone honest, drop by **Tom Barefoot's Cashback Tours** *(☎ 888-222-3601;* W *www.tombarefoot.com; 834 Front St, Lahaina)*. This activity booking service keeps extensive files on almost every Maui tour operator. Other activity desks around Lahaina and major resort areas may offer better deals, but not the same guarantees.

Most outdoor equipment rental shops are found in Kahului, near the airport. **Extreme Sports Maui** *(☎ 871-7954, 877-376-6284;* W *www.extremesportsmaui.com; Dairy Center, 397 Dairy Rd)* is an all-purpose, one-stop shop for just about any sport.

Swimming

Maui has endlessly fine beaches. The island's western side is dry and sunny, and water conditions are generally calmer than on the windward northern and eastern coasts.

Most of west and south Maui's best beaches are backed by hotel and condo developments – good if you're looking to stay right at the beach, not so good if you prefer seclusion. Still, there are some gorgeous undeveloped strands, the most notable being Makena's Big and Little Beaches, a short drive south of Kihei.

Those looking for more waters in their pristine natural state should visit the waterfalls and hidden pools along the Hana Hwy, in the Oheo Gulch section of Haleakala National Park, and at the natural ocean baths off the Kahekili Highway, northwest Maui.

Maui County maintains several heated swimming pools open to the public, including **Kahului Pool** *(☎ 270-7110)*, **Kihei Aquatic Center** *(☎ 874-8137)*, **Lahaina Aquatic Center** *(☎ 661-7611)*; Pukalani's **Upcountry Pool** *(☎ 572-1479)* and **Wailuku New Pool** *(☎ 270-7411)*. Call for open swim schedules and directions.

Kayaking

Water conditions on Maui are usually clearest and calmest early in the morning. Favorite kayaking spots are around Kihei (south Maui), near Olowalu and north of Kapalua (west Maui).

South Pacific Kayaks & Outfitters *(☎ 875-4848, 800-776-2326;* W *www.mauikayak.com; Rainbow Mall, 2439 S Kihei Rd, Kihei)* rents single/double kayaks from $30/40 a day. Half-day guided kayak tours include snorkeling

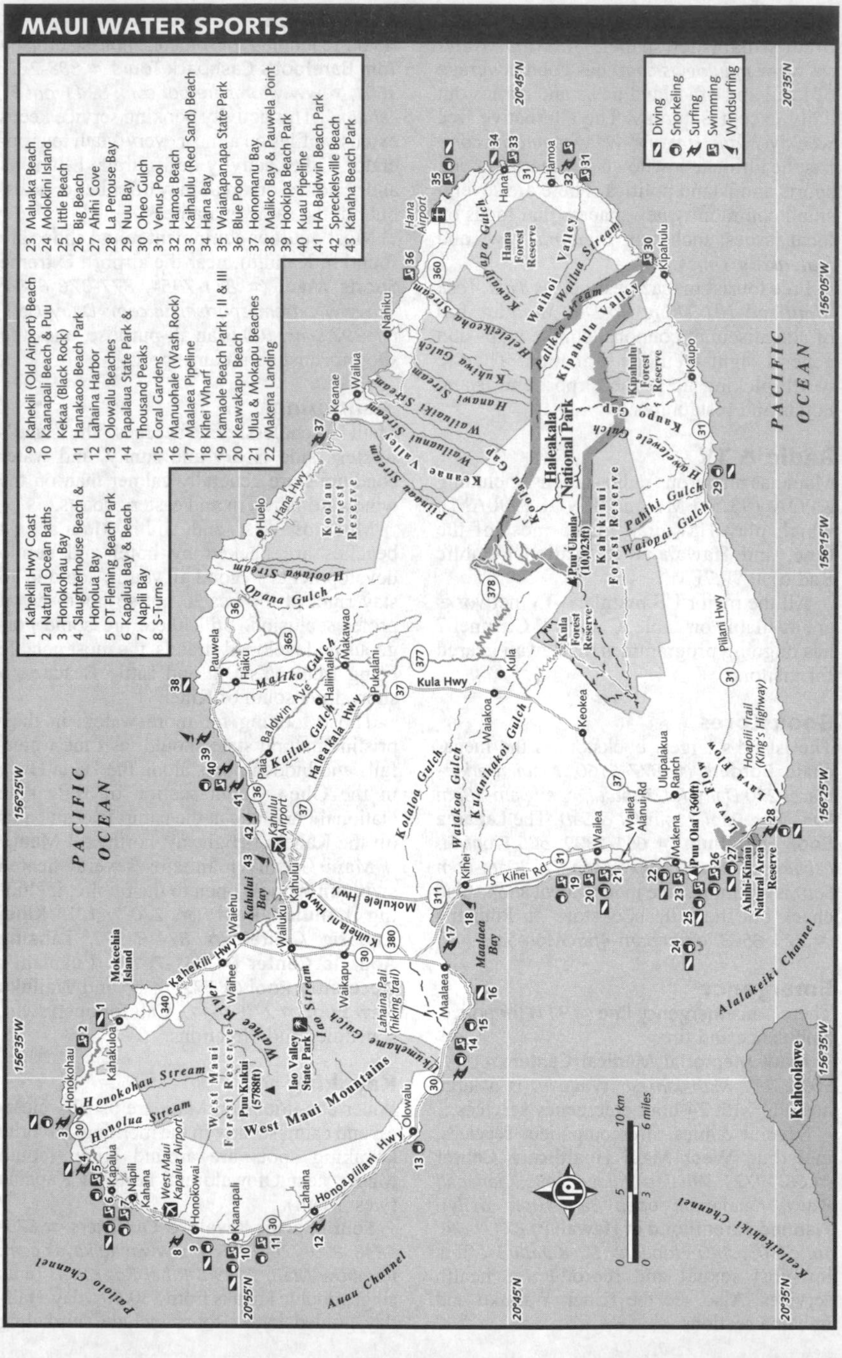
MAUI WATER SPORTS
1 Kahekili Hwy Coast
2 Natural Ocean Baths
3 Honokohau Bay
4 Slaughterhouse Beach & Honolua Bay
5 DT Fleming Beach Park
6 Kapalua Bay & Beach
7 Napili Bay
8 S-Turns
9 Kahekili (Old Airport) Beach
10 Kaanapali Beach & Puu Kekaa (Black Rock)
11 Hanakaoo Beach Park
12 Lahaina Harbor
13 Olowalu Beaches
14 Papalaua State Park & Thousand Peaks
15 Coral Gardens
16 Manuohale (Wash Rock)
17 Maalaea Pipeline
18 Kihei Wharf
19 Kamaole Beach Park I, II & III
20 Keawakapu Beach
21 Ulua & Mokapu Beaches
22 Makena Landing
23 Maluaka Beach
24 Molokini Island
25 Little Beach
26 Big Beach
27 Ahihi Cove
28 La Perouse Bay
29 Nuu Bay
30 Oheo Gulch
31 Venus Pool
32 Hamoa Beach
33 Kaihalulu (Red Sand) Beach
34 Hana Bay
35 Waianapanapa State Park
36 Blue Pool
37 Honomanu Bay
38 Maliko Bay & Pauwela Point
39 Hookipa Beach Park
40 Kuau Pipeline
41 HA Baldwin Beach Park
42 Spreckelsville Beach
43 Kanaha Beach Park
Diving
Snorkeling
Surfing
Swimming
Windsurfing
PACIFIC OCEAN
Haleakala National Park
West Maui Mountains
Kahoolawe
Alalakeiki Channel
Auau Channel
Pailolo Channel
Kealaikahiki Channel

and lunch, and visit La Perouse Bay or west Maui ($55 to $90).

Kelii's Kayak Tours (☎ *888-874-7652;* W *www.mauikayak.info)* offers guided ocean kayak tours ($60 to $100) with stops for snorkeling.

Big Kahuna Adventures (☎ *875-6395;* W *www.bigkahunaadventures.com; Island Surf Bldg, 1993 S Kihei Rd)* offers kayak tours around Makena and outrigger canoe trips from Kihei Cove ($60 to $85).

Kayaks can also be rented from **Duke's Surf & Rental Shop** (☎ *661-1970; 602 Front St, Lahaina)*. Other operations include **Tradewind Kayak** (☎ *879-2247)* and **Hana Bay Kayaks & Outfitters** (☎ *264-9566)*.

Scuba & Snorkeling

Some dive and snorkel boat tours go along the Maui shoreline, but the main destinations are the sunken volcanic crater of Molokini and the island of Lanai. Although a few dive boats take snorkelers, and some snorkeling tours take divers, as a rule you'll be better off going out on a tour that's geared for the activity you're doing.

For snorkeling from the beach, prime spots include Kaanapali's Puu Kekaa (Black Rock); around the rocky points of Wailea and Makena beaches; and, in summer, at Honolua Bay and Slaughterhouse Beach. Also try the ocean coves of Ahihi-Kinau Natural Area Reserve, where you can often spot fish from the shore. Kapalua Bay is generally one of the calmest places for snorkeling year-round.

Lanai also has clear snorkeling waters, but without the crowds. The most common destination is Hulopoe Beach off Manele Bay, although a few boats go around to the northern side of the island. The Cathedrals dive sites offer intriguing grotto formations with caves, arches and connecting passageways.

Molokini, only a few miles off the southwest coast, is Maui's most popular snorkeling tour site. The fish are tame and numerous and the water is clear. Molokini has walls, ledges, white-tipped reef sharks, manta rays, turtles and a wide variety of other marine life for divers. But don't expect pristine conditions – dozens of tour boats crowd the islet every day, and all of the activity has taken a toll on the reef. Some sections have been permanently damaged, largely from dropped and dragged anchors that have carved swaths in the coral.

Molokini

The largely submerged volcanic crater of Molokini lies midway between the islands of Maui and Kahoolawe. Half of the crater rim has eroded away, leaving a crescent moon shape that rises 160ft above the ocean surface.

Legends say that Molokini was created by a jealous Pele, goddess of volcanoes. When one of the goddess's lovers secretly married a *mo'o* (shape-shifting water lizard), an angry Pele chopped the sacred lizard in half, leaving Molokini as its tail and Puu Olai in Makena as its head. Other tales fancifully claim that Molokini, which means 'many ties' in Hawaiian, is an umbilical cord left over from the birth of Kahoolawe.

Today, Molokini draws scores of snorkelers and divers, who come here for its clear waters with abundant fish and coral. Black coral was once prolific in Molokini's deeper waters. However, most of it made its way into Lahaina jewelry stores before Molokini was declared a conservation district in 1977. During WWII, the US navy shelled Molokini for target practice, and live bombs are still occasionally found on the crater floor. (Don't worry, there's no real danger posed to casual divers and snorkelers).

Generally speaking, ocean conditions are calmest and clearest in the morning; afternoon winds may pick up surges and make things murky. **Maui Dive Shop** (☎ *800-542-3483;* W *www.mauidiveshop.com)* branches around the island have a good free map that details the island's best diving and snorkeling spots, as well as waterproof full-color maps and plasticized reef fish identification cards for sale.

Dive Operators Most dive schools offer a range of refresher and advanced certification courses. Beginners should expect to spend four days studying and learning the ropes; small certification classes are best. Book directly, and don't monkey around with activity desks.

Maui Dive Shop (☎ *800-542-3483;* W *www.mauidiveshop.com)*, a five-star PADI operation, offers one-tank introductory dives for $70, two-tank boat dives for $100, and 3½-day certification courses from $300.

MAUI

However, boats take up to 18 people at a time – talk about a cattle call. It has several branches around the island.

Maui Dreams Dive Co *(☎ 874-5332, 888-921-3483; W www.mauidreamsdiveco.com; Island Surf Bldg, 1993 S Kihei Rd, Kihei)* is a family-run, five-star PADI outfit that gets enthusiastic reviews for small group size and personal attention. Discounts might include a night dive for $40, one-tank underwater scooter dive for $80 or certification course for $225.

Ed Robinson's Diving Adventures *(☎ 879-3584, 800-635-1273; W www.mauiscuba.com)*, run by an underwater photographer, caters to certified divers looking for site variety and environmental background talks. Two-tank boat dives cost $105, and two-tank night dives or Lanai dives $125.

Mike Severns *(☎ 879-6596; W www.mikesevernsdiving.com)* literally wrote the book on diving Molokini. Certified divers appreciate the thorough pretrip briefings on marine life, with two-tank dives costing $120. Night charters go out to see coral spawning.

Also check out **Kapalua Dive Company** (see the West Maui section).

Snorkeling Tours & Rentals Countless snorkeling cruises leave for Molokini daily from Maalaea and Lahaina harbors. Boats are usually out from about 7am to noon and charge at least $40 per person, including snacks and snorkeling gear. Competition is strong, so deals and discount coupons are easy to come by.

Pacific Whale Foundation *(☎ 879-8811, 800-942-5311; W www.pacificwhale.org)* offers nonprofit Molokini and Lanai reef tours (from $50) led by experienced marine naturalists. Its 65ft ecoboats are powered by recycled cooking oil! Special deals often lower the rates, or let kids go free.

Trilogy Excursions *(☎ 661-4743, 888-225-6284; W www.sailtrilogy.com)* operates a day tour by catamaran from Lahaina to Lanai's Hulopoe Beach, including breakfast, a barbecue lunch and snorkeling (adult/child $170/85). It also does trips to Molokini ($95). Onboard naturalists and Internet booking discounts somewhat compensate for how busy and crowded the trips are.

Snorkeling gear can be rented at reasonable prices from most dive shops, which may also offer snorkel and dive outings to Lanai, or at inflated prices from hotel beach huts. A few high-profile chains have come-on rates for cheap snorkel gear, but you'll probably want better quality, and prices will rise accordingly. Consider buying your own set from a discount store in Kahului. Many condos provide free snorkel gear for guests.

Surfing

Maui has some unbeatable surfing spots, with peak surfing conditions from November to March. **Hookipa Beach** near Paia has surfing almost year-round, with incredible winter waves. When conditions are right, **Honolua Bay** near the northern tip of west Maui has the island's top action.

The **Maalaea Pipeline**, at the south side of Maalaea Bay, has been described by *Surfer* magazine as one of the world's 10 best fast breaks. Beginners crowd the shores near Lahaina, including along the breakwall.

Surfing lessons typically last 1½ to two hours and cost $50 to $75. Most places guarantee that students of all ages will be surfing at the end of the lesson. Try **Nancy Emerson's School of Surfing** *(☎ 244-7873; W www.surfclinics.com)*, **Goofy Foot Surf School** *(☎ 244-9283; W www.goofyfootsurfschool.com)* and **Surf Dog** *(☎ 250-7873; W www.surfdogmaui.com)* run by a local Maui boy.

Gentler shorebreaks good for **bodysurfing** are HA Baldwin Beach Park in Paia, DT Fleming Beach Park near Kapalua and beaches in the Kihei and Wailea area.

Both surfboards ($15 to $20 per day) and boogie boards ($8/45 per day/week) can be rented at numerous locations around Maui, including many of the windsurfing shops.

Maui Tropix *(☎ 871-8726; 261 Dairy Rd, Kahului)* sells Maui Built surfboards and paraphernalia.

Windsurfing

Maui is a mecca for windsurfers. Some of the world's best windsurfing is at Hookipa Beach near Paia, though it's suitable for experts only. Those who aren't quite there yet head to nearby Spreckelsville Beach or Kanaha Beach in Kahului.

Overall, the island is known for its consistent winds, and windsurfers can find action in any month. Although trade winds can blow at any time of the year and flat spells could also hit anytime, generally the windiest time is June to September and the flattest from December to February.

Parts of the Kihei coast offer slalom sailing in summer. In Maalaea Bay, conditions are good for advanced speed sailing; the winds are usually strong and blow offshore toward Kahoolawe. During the winter, on those occasions when *kona* winds blow, the Maalaea–Kihei area is often the only place windy enough to sail and becomes the main scene for all windsurfers.

Most windsurfing shops are based in Kahului. The following shops sell and rent windsurfing gear and give lessons themselves or through an affiliate that works out of the same shop. Daily rental rates for two sails and a board start around $45; introductory windsurfing classes usually cost $70. The business is very competitive, so if you ask about discounts and let it be known that you're getting quotes from more than one company, you may be offered a better deal.

Hawaiian Island Surf & Sport (☎ 871-4981, 800-231-6958, Ⓦ www.hawaiianisland.com) 415 Dairy Rd, Kahului

Hi-Tech Surf Sports (☎ 877-2111, Ⓦ www.htmaui.com) 425 Koloa St, Kahului

Second Wind Sail, Surf & Kite (☎ 877-7167, 800-936-7787, Ⓦ www.secondwindmaui.com) 111 Hana Hwy, Kahului

Some places will let you use the weekly rate on nonconsecutive days – so you could sail for three days, take a couple of days off and then sail four more days for the same price it would cost to rent the gear for a week straight.

Most of the Kahului shops also sell windsurfing equipment and can book package tours that include accommodations, rental vehicles and windsurfing gear.

Kiteboarding

Kiteboarding is impressive to watch, *!$@ing hard to master. Instructors follow a three-step curriculum, with each lesson lasting one to two hours. First you learn how to fly the giant U-shaped kites, then you practice bodydragging (letting the kite pull you across the water) and finally you step on the modified surfboard.

On Maui all the action centers on Kite Beach, which is the western end of Kanaha Beach Park in Kahului. Check with Maui Kiteboarding Association (Ⓦ *www.maui.net/~hotwind/mka.html)* for the latest guidelines.

Maui Kiteboarding *(☎ 873-0015; Ⓦ www.ksmaui.com; 22 Hana Hwy, Kahului)* has an all-pro staff and offers multilingual and kids' classes. A beginners' course costs $240, with advanced lessons $90 per hour.

Hiking

At Haleakala National Park, some extraordinary trails – from half-day walks to overnight treks – cross the moonscape-like Haleakala Crater. In the Oheo section of the park, which is south of Hana, a trail leads to two impressive waterfalls. The summit Skyline Trail leads down into Polipoli Spring State Recreation Area, which has an extensive trail system in cloud forest.

North of Wailuku are the scenic Waihee Valley Trail and Waihee Ridge Trail, which branch off the Kahekili Hwy. Near Maalaea Bay, the challenging Lahaina Pali trail follows an old footpath through the West Maui Mountains. And, of course, Maui has many white-sand beaches perfect for strolls.

Several pull-offs along the Hana Hwy lead to short nature walks. There's also a historic coastal trail between Waianapanapa State Park and Hana Bay. From La Perouse Bay, on the other side of the island, there's a strenuous coastline hike over a lava footpath. All hikes are detailed in their respective sections.

Sierra Club *(☎ 573-4147; Ⓦ www.hi.sierraclub.org/maui; PO Box 791180, Paia, HI 96779)* outings include hikes on private ranch lands and cleanup days at coastal beaches. Nonmembers usually pay $5 each, and carpooling to trailheads may be available. Other service trips involve helping to rid the island of invasive exotic plants, such as myconia.

The Nature Conservancy *(☎ 572-7849; Ⓦ www.tnc.org/hawaii; PO Box 1716, Makawao, HI 96768)* leads hikes in its exclusive preserves around Haleakala and the West Maui Mountains, about once or twice a month. The suggested donation is $25/15 for nonmembers/members.

Cycling & Mountain Biking

Each morning before dawn, groups of cyclists gather at the top of Haleakala for the thrill of coasting 38 miles down the mountain, with a 10,000ft drop in elevation.

Generally, it's an all-day affair (eight to 10 hours), starting with hotel pickup at around 2:30am, a van ride up the mountain for the sunrise, and about 3½ hours of biking back down. It's not a nonstop cruise, as cyclists must periodically pull over for cars following behind, and the primary exercise is squeezing the brakes – you'll need to pedal only about 400 yards on the entire trip! Keep in mind that the road down Haleakala is narrow and winding with lots of blind curves, and there are no bike lanes.

Pregnant women, children under 12 and those less than 5ft tall are usually not allowed to ride. The going rate before discounts is a steep $115, which includes bike, helmet, transportation and meals. **Maui Downhill** (*☎ 871-2155, 800-535-2453*), **Maui Mountain Cruisers** (*☎ 871-6014, 800-232-6284*) and **Maui Mountain Riders** (*☎ 242-9739, 800-706-7700*) all offer this activity.

Aloha Bicycle Tours (*☎ 249-0911, 800-749-1564*) offers a 33-mile nonsunrise tour ($95) geared for stronger cyclists that begins with a glide down the Haleakala Crater Rd, then takes in various Upcountry sights.

Haleakala Bike Co (*☎ 573-2888, 888-922-2453; W www.bikemaui.com; Haiku Marketplace, 810 Haiku Rd, Haiku*) will rent you a mountain bike with assorted gear, then give you a van ride up to Haleakala from the shop. The cost is $55 in the daytime, $75 in time for the sunrise. If you have your own car, you can rent just a bike and car rack for $35.

For single-track mountain biking, try riding from Skyline Trail in Haleakala National Park down into Polipoli Spring State Recreation Area in the Upcountry, where several other bike trails wind through redwood forests. John Alford's *Mountain Biking the Hawaiian Islands* should be your bible.

Island Biker (*☎ 877-7744; 415 Dairy Rd, Kahului*) rents quality mountain bikes, and carries maps and trail guides.

West Maui Cycles (*☎ 661-9005; 840 Wainee St, Lahaina*) rents street cruisers and mountain bikes.

South Maui Bicycles (*☎ 874-0068; Island Surf Bldg, 1993 S Kihei Rd, Kihei*) rents mountain bikes and off-road cycles.

Hawaii Island Cruzers (*☎ 879-0956; Dolphin Plaza, 2395 S Kihei Rd, Kihei*) rents Schwinn cruisers and mountain bikes.

Haleakala Bike Co (*☎ 575-9575, 888-922-2453; W www.bikemaui.com; Haiku Marketplace, 810 Haiku Rd, Haiku*) rents mountain bikes; long-term rentals are negotiable.

Wheels USA and Kihei Rent A Car also rent older mountain bikes.

Horseback Riding

Maui has lots of ranch land and some of Hawaii's best opportunities for trail rides. The most unusual ride meanders down into Haleakala Crater via Sliding Sands Trail. Still other horse ranches are found near Makena (south Maui), Hana and Oheo Gulch (east Maui) and Keokea (Upcountry).

Pony Express (*☎ 667-2200; W www.ponyexpresstours.com; Haleakala Crater Rd*) is in a eucalyptus grove, 2½ miles up from Hwy 377. The company's half-day and full-day Haleakala Crater rides ($155/190) are open to novice riders and include a picnic lunch on the crater floor. There are also rides across the rolling meadows of Haleakala Ranch, costing from $60. Reservations are required.

Tennis

The county maintains tennis courts at **Lahaina Civic Center** and **Maluuluolele Park** (Lahaina); **Wells Park** and the **War Memorial Complex** (Wailuku); **Kahului Community Center** (Kahului); **Kalama Park** (Kihei); **Hana Ballpark** (Hana); **Eddie Tam Memorial Center** (Makawao); and **Pukalani Community Center** (Pukalani). County courts are free to the public on a first-come, first-served basis and are lit for night play.

Numerous hotels and condos have tennis courts for their guests. At resort clubs in west and south Maui, rates are generally quoted at $15 per person 'per day,' although only the first hour of playing time is guaranteed, after which courts are subject to space availability. Rackets can be rented at all tennis clubs for about $5 a day; some clubs also rent tennis shoes.

Golf

With ocean vistas and volcanic mountains looming above you, golfing just doesn't get much better. Rates at resort courses average $100 to $200, about half that at municipal courses or country clubs. Afternoon wind in some areas can make play difficult, so 'twilight' tee times (usually after 2:30pm) are heavily discounted.

Kapalua and Wailea are the most prestigious places to play, while championship courses found nearby at Kaanapali and Makena are less expensive. You can still enjoy great rounds at the friendly Waiehu municipal course and private country clubs in Kihei, Waikapu, Pukalani and Paia. Pick up the free tourist magazine *Maui Golf Review* for in-depth course profiles. Also see their respective sections.

Club rental and pro shop services are universally available. **Maui Golf Shop** (*☎ 875-4653; 357 Huku Liu Place, Kihei*), behind Tesoro gas station, handles tee-time bookings and rental equipment.

ORGANIZED TOURS

All of the following can easily be booked after arrival, except during the super-peak months of December, July and August. At those times, advance reservations are advised.

Bus & Van

It's possible to catch some of the island's main attractions by joining a half- or full-day tour, although at $40 to $80 per person you'd be better off renting a car.

Most bus and van tours head up Haleakala for the sunrise or down the Hana Hwy. The major operators are **Roberts Hawaii** (*☎ 800-831-5411*) and **Polynesian Adventures** (*☎ 877-4242, 800-622-3011*).

There are also a couple of small local companies offering similar tours, but with more colorful commentary.

Ekahi Tours (*☎ 877-9775, 888-292-2242; W www.ekahi.com*) is a family-run operation that offers free pick-ups around the island. Its unique cultural tour of Kahakuloa village includes a visit to a working taro patch.

Helicopter

Numerous helicopter companies take off from the Kahului heliport for trips around the island. Some cross the channel and tour Molokai's spectacular north shore as well. As helicopters are prohibited from flying over Haleakala, the best volcano lovers can hope for is a peek over the crater rim.

Most companies advertise in the free tourist magazines. Prices are competitive, with many places running perennial specials, such as free use of video cameras. Typical 30-minute tours of the West Maui Mountains cost around $115 and one-hour circle-island tours cost $100. Be aware that not every seat is a window seat; ask about seating policies before making your reservation.

Recommended helicopter companies operating on Maui include **Blue Hawaiian** (*☎ 871-8844, 800-745-2583*), **Alex Air** (*☎ 877-4354, 888-418-8457*) and **Sunshine Helicopters** (*☎ 871-0722, 800-544-2520*).

Cruises

Maui has enough dinner cruises, sunset sails, deep-sea fishing boats and charter sailboats to fill a book. Most leave from Lahaina and Maalaea Bay, although a few depart from south Maui landings. You can get current rates and information from activity booths all around Maui or from the tourist magazines – or just go down to Lahaina Harbor, where the booths and the boats are lined up, and check out the scene for yourself.

Atlantis Submarines (*☎ 667-2224, 800-548-6262; W www.goatlantis.com; Wharf Cinema Center, Lahaina*) operates a 65ft sub in the waters off Lahaina. The sub dives down to a depth of about 130ft to see coral and fish. Tours (adult/child $79/39) leave from Lahaina Harbor via a catamaran from 9am to 1pm daily.

Whale Watching In season, you'll have no trouble finding whale-watching cruises, as they are heavily advertised. Most leave from Maalaea or Lahaina Harbors, though a few leave from Kihei and Kaanapali.

Whale-watching boats range from catamaran sailboats to large cruise vessels. A 2½-hour tour costs $25 to $40 for adults, half-price for children. Some companies have hydrophones to hear whale songs, and some guarantee whale sightings or give another tour free.

Pacific Whale Foundation (*☎ 879-8811, 800-942-5311; W www.pacificwhale.org*) offers a few daily cruises ($21/15 adult/child). You can take a 50ft sailboat from Lahaina and either a 36ft motorboat or a 65ft sailing catamaran from Maalaea, all with onboard naturalists. Proceeds benefit the foundation's marine conservation projects.

Many of the boats that take snorkelers to Molokini in the morning go out whale watching in the afternoon. During the season, there's a good chance of spotting whales on the snorkeling trip to Molokini itself. See Activities earlier in this chapter.

ACCOMMODATIONS

Other than camping, the cheapest places to stay on Maui are the Wailuku hostels. Maui also has some studio-style cottages, vacation rentals and homespun B&Bs charging from around $60, with most of these found in the Haiku–Paia and Hana areas.

Lahaina and Wailuku have excellent historic inns, costing $100 and up. Otherwise condos make up the bulk of mid-range accommodations. Kihei has the highest concentration, but you will also find them all along the West Maui coast. The lower end of this price range is around $75, but it's easy to spend over $100 a night for nothing special. Maui's two biggest resort developments are Kaanapali Beach Resort and Wailea Resort, both of which have luxury hotels and condos.

For advice on condo rentals and contact details for booking agencies, see Accommodations in the Facts for the Visitor chapter. Rates can be substantially lower during the off-season, but even then you'll usually need advance reservations to lock in the best deals.

Camping

Maui has fewer camping options than the other islands. Haleakala National Park, either atop the volcano or at Oheo Gulch beyond Hana, is a good place to camp. In addition to the state and county camping grounds listed here, there's a church-sponsored camping ground at Olowalu (see the West Maui section later in this chapter).

Sports shops in Kahului carry a pathetically limited selection of camping supplies. But they do sell camp-stove fuel canisters, which are not allowed on flights and must be bought on the island.

State Parks Polipoli Spring State Recreation Area and Waianapanapa State Park, the only state parks on Maui with camping areas, both have tent sites and cabins. Permits are required. The maximum length of stay is five consecutive nights per month at each park, and tent camping costs $5.

Polipoli, in Upcountry, has one primitive cabin (closed Tuesday) and a very basic road, which usually requires a 4WD vehicle. Waianapanapa, on the coast near Hana, has 12 housekeeping cabins that are very popular and must be reserved well in advance. Cabins at either park cost $45/55 for up to four/six people.

For camping permits or cabin reservations, contact the **Division of State Parks** *(☎ 984-8109; State Office Bldg, Room 101, 54 S High St, Wailuku, HI 96793; open 8am-3:30pm Mon-Fri)*.

County Parks Maui has only one county park that allows camping: Kanaha Beach Park, just north of Kahukui airport. The sites are directly beneath the flight path, so the airport noise – with flights scheduled from dawn to 11pm – can be annoying. It's also not a very safe area.

Permits cost $3 per day (50¢ for children under 18), and camping is limited to three consecutive nights. Permits are available by mail or in person from the **Department of Parks & Recreation** *(☎ 270-7389; 1580 Kaahumanu Ave, Wailuku, HI 96793)*. The office is in the War Memorial Complex at Baldwin High School in Wailuku.

ENTERTAINMENT

Maui's entertainment scene lags far behind Oahu's. The best source of up-to-date information is Thursday's *Maui News* and the free alternative weekly *Maui Time*.

Maui Arts & Cultural Center (Kahului) has two indoor theaters and a large outdoor amphitheater. **Casanova** (Makawao) sometimes has top-name musicians, and **Hapa's Brew Haus** (Kihei) also has good live music. Otherwise, most of the action is either in Lahaina or Kihei, and at the resort hotels, especially in Kaanapali and Wailea.

Luaus are held regularly in Lahaina, Kaanapali and Wailea, with varying degrees of authenticity (or nil). The **Old Lahaina Luau** (west Maui) foregoes the fire sticks and Tahitian drums in favor of something more traditionally Hawaiian. Free hula shows are offered at many shopping centers, especially in Lahaina and Kaanapali, and performances charitably support local *hula halau* (hula schools).

For Maui's gay community, **Little Beach** in Makena is a daytime meeting spot. There are no gay bars on Maui, but Hapa's and Maui Pizza Café in Kihei and Casanova's in Makawao are gay-friendly evening spots.

SHOPPING

For local arts and crafts, some of the best deals are at **Maui Crafts Guild** (Paia), **Lahaina Arts Society** (Lahaina) and downtown

Makawao galleries. West Maui's **Hawaiian Quilt Collection** *(☎ 800-367-9987; W www.hawaiian-quilts.com)* has stores at the Hyatt Regency in Kaanapali and the Kapalua Shops that offer three-hour introductory Hawaiian quilting classes for about $50, including a starter pillow kit.

Several businesses sell food and flowers, including leis, proteas, papayas, pineapples, Maui onions and husked coconuts, which are agriculturally pre-inspected and delivered to the airport for you to pick up on your way out. Two such places are **Take Home Maui** *(☎ 661-8067; 121 Dickenson St, Lahaina)* and **Airport Flower & Fruit** *(☎ 243-9367, 800-922-9352; W www.mauiexpress.com)*. You can also buy direct from Upcountry farms.

GETTING THERE & AWAY

Maui's discount travel agencies have outlets in Kahului, a short drive from the island's main airport.

Air

For details on international flights, commuter and charter airlines, discounted interisland coupons and air passes, see the Getting Around chapter.

Most domestic and international travelers deplane at **Kahului airport** *(OGG; ☎ 872-3830)*. Even though the main terminal is modern, the open-air plan with a sprinkling of lei and pineapple stands, palm trees waving outside and Hawaiian art immediately make it feel tropical.

There's a small **visitor information desk** *(☎ 872-3893; open 6:30am-10pm daily)* in the baggage claim area. Nearby are courtesy phones for contacting accommodations and ground transportation, plus racks of free tourist magazines and brochures.

Near the gates are a couple of newsstands, snack bars, gift shops, overpriced restaurants and a cocktail lounge. Only a few ATMs are available. There is no baggage storage service, but there is a **lost & found office** *(☎ 872-3821)* on the ground floor corridor. Airport parking costs $7 per day.

Kapalua/West Maui airport *(JHM; ☎ 669-0623)* is a small airport with a 3000ft runway that's serviced by prop planes and commuter aircraft from other Hawaiian Islands. The terminal is off Hwy 30, about midway between Kapalua and Kaanapali, within easy reach of Lahaina.

Hana airport *(HNM; ☎ 248-8208)* has a single terminal and passenger runway mainly used for island-hopping commuter flights. It's off the Hana Hwy, about 3 miles north of Hana town in east Maui.

Ferry

Interisland ferries to Molokai and Lanai depart from Lahaina Harbor. For information on ferry schedules and ticket prices, see the Getting Around chapter.

GETTING AROUND

To/From the Airport

Speedi Shuttle *(☎ 661-6667, 800-977-2605; W www.speedishuttle.com)* has airport transfers on demand, but advance reservations help to speed things along. The price depends on the destination and the size of the group. For example, the cost for two people from Kahului airport is $16 to Wailea, $25 to Kihei and $46 to Lahaina, while a single person pays $13, $22 and $35, respectively. There's a courtesy phone at the baggage claim area – just dial ☎ 65.

Kahului airport taxi dispatchers all have booths near the exit of the baggage claim area. Approximate fares are Wailuku, $13; Kihei, $25; Paia Haiku area, $20 to $30; Lahaina, $45; and Kaanapali, $50.

Taxi fares from Kapalua/West Maui airport average $15 to Kaanapali, $20 to anywhere else along the west Maui coast. Otherwise, many resort hotels offer an airport-shuttle service for a fee.

Bus

Maui has no public bus service, but private lines operate in the west, central and south Maui areas. While they can be used to get away for the day, these buses are geared more to short shopping excursions than sightseeing. All schedules are subject to change.

Akina Aloha Tours *(☎ 879-2828, 800-845-4890; W www.akinatours.com)* operates four routes. All single point-to-point trips on route 2 cost $1; on route 1 or 4, $2; and on route 3, $5. An all-day system-wide pass costs $10. Monthly passes vary from $25 to $65, depending on how many routes are covered.

Along route 1, buses travel an hour-long loop between Kapalua and Kaanapali, stopping at several resorts and condo complexes along the way. The first southbound bus leaves the Ritz-Carlton Kapalua at 9am, arriving at Whalers Village 30 minutes later; the same bus departs the shopping center at 9:40am and returns along the same route to Kapalua. Service is pretty much hourly throughout the day. The last southbound bus from Kapalua is at 8:20pm, while the last northbound bus leaves Whalers Village at 8:55pm.

Route 2 connects the Kaanapali resorts with Lahaina Harbor via the Lahaina Cannery Mall. The first bus leaves the Royal Lahaina Resort in Kaanapali at 8:45am, stopping at Whalers Village ten minutes later and arriving at the Lahaina Harbor flagpole around 9:30am. Buses immediately return to the Royal Lahaina Resort, without making any stops along the way. Service is hourly throughout the day, with the last bus southbound to Lahaina Harbor at 8:45pm.

Buses on express route 3 link Kaanapali and Lahaina with Maalaea Bay and Wailea. The first southbound bus departs Whalers Village at 8:30am, stopping at Lahaina Harbor and Maalaea Harbor Village, before reaching The Shops at Wailea at 9:45am. The bus promptly turns around and follows the same 1¼-hour route back up to Kaanapali. Service is every 2½ hours, with the last northbound bus at 7:45pm and the last southbound departure at 9pm.

Buses along route 4 cover South Maui, namely Kihei, Wailea and Makena. These buses stop at several shopping centers and condos along S Kihei Rd directly opposite the beach parks, plus The Shops at Wailea. The first bus southbound from Suda's Store, north Kihei, leaves at 8am and arrives one hour later at the Maui Prince Hotel in Makena. From the Maui Prince, the first bus northbound is at 7am. Route 4 buses leave every two hours throughout the day, with the last northbound bus at 7pm and the last southbound bus at 8pm.

Akina Tours also offers 'early bird' express shuttles from the Kamaole shopping center in Kihei, leaving at 6:45am and 7:45am for Lahaina Harbor (45 minutes), Whalers Village (one hour) and Kapalua (1¼ hours).

Wailea, Kaanapali and Kapalua all have free resort-wide shuttle services. For Handi-Van paratransit reservations, call ☎ 456-5555.

MAUI

Taxi

Taxi fares are regulated by the county. The minimum flag-down fare is $2.50, and each mile is about $2. Based in Kaanapali, **Classy Taxi** (*☎ 665-0003*) drives 1920s gangster-era limos and a 1933 Rolls Royce. It charges the same rates; reservations are advised.

Car & Moped

Alamo (*☎ 871-6235*), **Avis** (*☎ 871-7575*), **Budget** (*☎ 871-8811*), **Dollar** (*☎ 877-6526*), **Hertz** (*☎ 877-5167*) and **National** (*☎ 871-8851*) all have booths at Kahului airport.

Alamo, Avis, Budget, Dollar and National have offices on Hwy 30 in Kaanapali and will pick up at the Kapalua/West Maui airport. Dollar is the only rental agency serving Hana airport. See the Getting Around chapter for more information on the national chains, including toll-free numbers and websites.

Many local agencies based near Kahului will pick you up free of charge from the airport if you phone in advance, but sometimes only if you're renting the car for longer than a few days. Drivers under age 25 and those without credit cards should expect to pay more.

Word of Mouth (*☎ 877-2436, 800-533-5929;* Ⓦ *www.maui.net/~word; 150 Hana Hwy,*

Driving Times

Average driving times and distances from Kahului are as follows. Naturally these get longer during morning and afternoon rush hours, and on weekends.

destination	mileage	duration (minutes)
Haleakala Summit	36	90
Hana	51	125
Honolua Bay (via Kahekili Hwy)	26	90
Kaanapali	26	50
Kaupo (via Kula)	45	120
Kihei	12	25
La Perouse Bay	21	50
Lahaina	23	40
Maalaea	8	20
Makawao	14	30
Oheo Gulch (via Hana)	61	160
Paia	7	15
Polipoli Springs Camping Ground	24	100
Wailuku	3	15

Kahului) rents old cars by the week for around $110 and newer cars for $125. Daily rates start at $25.

Maui Cruisers *(☎ 249-2319, 877-749-7889, in Canada ☎ 800-488-9083; Ⓦ www.mauicruisers.net; 1270 Piihana Rd, Wailuku)* rents out reliable, used compact cars from $30/150/500 per day/week/month, all inclusive. Here you'll find personable service, honest deals and free racks for surfers.

Wheels USA *(☎ 667-7751, fax 661-8940; 741 Wainee St, Lahaina • ☎ 871-6858; 75 Kaahumanu Ave, Kahului)* rents used compact cars from $25/130 per day/week, Jeeps and dune buggies from $50/250 and mopeds from $36/180.

Kihei Rent A Car *(☎ 879-7257, 800-251-5288; Ⓦ www.kiheirentacar.com; 96 Kio Loop, Kihei)* is family-owned and offers 24-hour roadside assistance. Off-season rates start at $25/125 per day/week.

Some of the windsurf shops can arrange reasonably priced car and van rentals for their customers.

Bicycle

Cyclists on Maui face a number of challenges: narrow roads, heavy traffic, an abundance of hills and mountains, and the same persistent winds that so delight windsurfers. The island's stunning scenery may entice hard-core cyclists, but casual riders hoping to use a bike as a primary source of transportation may well find such conditions daunting. Bicycle lanes are slowly being added in Kihei and from Paia to Kahului.

The full-color *Maui County Bicycle Map* ($6) is available from bicycle shops. Rental rates vary from $15 to $45 per day, $60 to $110 per week, depending on the quality and type of bike. Helmets, locks and even car racks are usually included. See Cycling under the Activities section for bike rental agencies.

Central Maui

Kahului and Wailuku, Maui's two largest communities, flow together to form a single urban sprawl, where island folks live, work and shop. Several major highways crisscross the island's central plain, past waving fields of sugarcane, to Maalaea Bay.

Kahului is the commercial center. The main road, Kaahumanu Ave, is a collection of stores, banks and office buildings and a mile-long strip of shopping centers. Maui's main airport is in Kahului. After landing, most people drive right out of town and don't come back until they're ready to leave. And, with a few exceptions (including discount shopping and sports gear rentals), there's really not much in Kahului for visitors.

Kaahumanu Ave continues west into Wailuku, where it becomes W Main St. Wailuku, the county seat, is the more distinctive and less hurried end of it all. This is an older town with backstreets of curio shops, mom-and-pop stores and hole-in-the-wall ethnic restaurants, plus nearly all of Maui's hostels. You'll pass through here on the way to Iao Valley State Park at least.

KAHULUI

In the 1880s, Kahului became the headquarters of Hawaii's first railroad, which was built to haul sugar from the fields to the refinery and harbor. In 1900, an outbreak of the bubonic plague hit Kahului, and in an attempt to wipe it out, the settlement that had grown up around Kahului Harbor was purposely burned to the ground.

The present-day Kahului is a planned community developed in the 1950s by the Alexander & Baldwin sugar company. It was called 'Dream City' by cane workers, who had long dreamed of moving away from the dusty mill camps into a home of their own. These first tract homes are at the southern end of town.

Kahului Harbor, Maui's deepwater commercial port, services barges, cargo ships and the occasional cruise liner. It's geared for work – there are no charming wharves or sailboats.

Information

Kahului has a **post office** *(☎ 871-2487; 138 S Puunene Ave; open 8:30am-5pm Mon-Fri, 9am-noon Sat)* and a good **public library** *(☎ 873-3097; 90 School St; open 10am-5pm Mon & Thur-Sat, 10am-8pm Tues-Wed)*, offering Internet access.

The 24-hour **Kinko's** *(☎ 871-2000; Dairy Center, 395 Dairy Rd)* offers Internet access for 20¢ per minute, computer rentals, fax transmissions, photocopying and other business services. Other self-service Internet terminals pop up at cafés and fast-food joints around town.

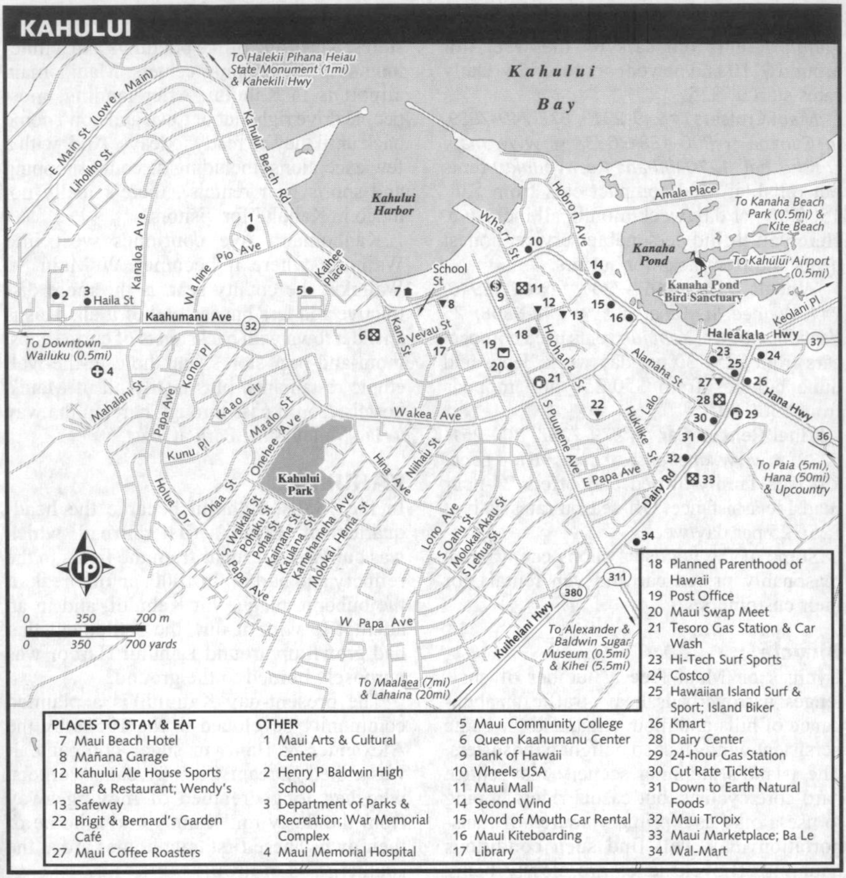

There are two discount travel agencies, both a five-minute drive from the airport, selling air coupons for interisland flights. **Cheap Tickets** *(☎ 242-8094, 800-594-8247; 395 Dairy Rd)* is in the Dairy Center, while **Cut Rate Tickets** *(☎ 871-7300; 333 Dairy Rd; open 7am-7pm Mon-Fri, 9am-5pm Sat, 9am-2pm Sun)* is on the next block.

Borders Books & Music Café *(☎ 877-6160; Maui Marketplace, 270 Dairy Rd; open 9am-10pm Sun-Thur, 9am-11pm Fri & Sat)* carries excellent maps, Hawaiiana and general books, off-island and international newspapers, and all sorts of magazines and CDs.

Kanaha Beach Park

Kanaha is a popular windsurfing and kiteboarding spot, and when the wind is right, it draws a crowd. This beach is the best place in Maui for beginners, and most of the windsurfing shops give their lessons here. That said, boarders can be fiercely territorial, so it's best not to go without a local introduction.

Kanaha is OK for swimming, but most people prefer the cleaner waters of nearby Kihei. You'll find rest rooms, showers and pay phones, as well as picnic tables under the shade of *hau* (hibiscus), ironwood and *kiawe* (thorny) trees. A lifeguard is on duty daily, but that hasn't prevented petty crime and violence on the beach.

The shoreline access sign can be found down by the car rental lots at the airport. From downtown Kahului, take Amala Place, which is the coastal road that starts from the Chevron storage tanks near the east end of Kaahumanu Ave.

Kanaha Pond

Kanaha Pond is a wildlife sanctuary for the endangered black-necked stilt, a wading bird that feeds along the marshy edges of the pond. It's a graceful bird in flight, with long orange legs that trail behind. Even though the stilt population in all Hawaii is estimated at just 1500, the birds can commonly be spotted here.

The pond is a slight respite in the midst of suburbia, beneath the flight path for the airport and just beyond the highway where trucks go barreling along. Access to the pond is on Hwy 396, near the junction of Hwy 36.

An observation deck just beyond the parking lot is a good site for spotting stilts, coots, ducks and black-crowned night herons. Upon entering the sanctuary, if you close the gate behind you and walk in quietly, you should be able to make sightings right there along the shoreline.

It's possible to hike on the service roads in the sanctuary from September to March (when the birds aren't nesting) by obtaining a permit from the **Division of Forestry and Wildlife** *(☎ 984-8100, State Office Bldg, Room 101, 54 S High St, Wailuku)*.

Maui Arts & Cultural Center

The island's home for the arts is Maui Arts & Cultural Center *(MACC; ☎ 242-2787, tour reservations ext ☎ 228, www.mauiarts.org, 1 Cameron Way; gallery admission free; open 11am-5pm Tues-Sun)*, which was built for $32 million dollars on the site of Pa Hula Heiau. Some temple remains can be seen on the free tours given at 11am on Wednesday (reservations required). Art gallery exhibits, which are also open before and after film screenings, change frequently.

Places to Stay

The camping ground at **Kanaha Beach Park** has reopened. However, with flights rumbling overhead from dawn until 11pm and personal safety an issue, you're better off elsewhere. See Accommodations earlier in this chapter.

Kahului's two hotels are on the main commercial strip in an area that hardly conjures up images of vacationing in Hawaii. On an island so small, there is absolutely no need to stay here.

Maui Beach Hotel *(☎ 877-0051, 888-649-3222; 170 Kaahumanu Ave; rooms from $90)*, with a faux-Polynesian lobby and indoor swimming pool, is the better choice.

Places to Eat

You can eat very affordably in Kahului, from organic foods to upmarket global cuisine.

There's a **Safeway** *(Kamehameha Ave)* supermarket and a **Foodland** *(Queen Kaahumanu Center, 275 Kaahumanu Ave)* in town.

Down to Earth Natural Foods *(☎ 877-2661; 305 Dairy Rd; open 7am-9pm Mon-Sat, 8am-8pm Sun)* is a large well-stocked natural foods store with reasonable prices, fresh organic produce and bulk foods. It also has a salad bar, a buffet with a few hot dishes and a vegetarian deli – all for take-out only.

Maui Coffee Roasters *(444 Hana Hwy; snacks $2-7; open 7:30am-6pm Mon-Fri, 8am-5pm Sat, 9am-2:30pm Sun)* sells its coffee of the day for just 50¢ a cup. Locals linger over scones, muffins and sandwiches, not to mention newspapers and chess sets.

Ba Le *(Maui Marketplace, 270 Dairy Rd; snacks $3-7; open 8am-9pm daily)* has good, inexpensive French-Vietnamese fare. You'll find delectable roll sandwiches, flaky croissants, shrimp rolls, plate lunches, Vietnamese *pho* (beef broth, noodles and fresh herbs), soups and noodle dishes, plus a rainbow of tapioca flavors for dessert.

Aloha Grill *(☎ 893-0263; Maui Marketplace, snacks $5-8, open 8am-9pm Mon-Sat, 8am-7pm Sun)* is a miniaturized '50s-style diner and has just six bar stools and a single jukebox. What it lacks in size it makes up for with gourmet burgers and Kahului's largest vegetarian take-out menu. The soda fountain has homemade chocolate, cherry and vanilla cokes.

Brigit & Bernard's Garden Café *(☎ 877-6000; 335 Hoohana St; lunch special $8, mains $9-15; open 10:30am-3pm Mon-Fri, 5pm-9pm Wed-Fri)* is in a shady spot. This caterer's café has a full bar with imported beers and an outdoor garden. The European menu weighs in with heavy dishes like chicken cordon bleu and schnitzel burgers, but there are also healthy salads and light seafood.

Mañana Garage *(☎ 873-0220; 33 Lono Ave; lunch $7-13, dinner $16-26; open 11am-9pm Mon, 11am-10:30pm Tues-Sat)* roves from Cuba and the Caribbean to South America with an impeccable menu including *picadillo* (minced meat) empanadas and guava chicken. Since this Latin-flavored restaurant has been voted everyone's favorite spot, it may be tricky to get evening reservations. On 'amigo Mondays' all seafood dinners are discounted by $10.

Entertainment

First-run movies play at the **Consolidated Theatre Kaahumanu** *(☎ 878-3456; Queen Kaahumanu Center)* and **Wallace Theatres Maui Mall Megaplex** *(☎ 249-2222; 70 E Kaahumanu Ave)*.

Maui Arts & Cultural Center *(MACC; box office ☎ 242-7469; W www.mauiarts.org; 1 Cameron Way)* has two indoor theaters and a large outdoor amphitheater, which are venues for film festivals, community theater, performances by the Maui Symphony Orchestra and Hawaiian cultural organizations. MACC is also one of the hottest places in Hawaii for big-name concerts.

Queen Kaahumanu Center *(☎ 877-4325; 275 Kaahumanu Ave)* hosts free performances by the Old Lahaina Luau at 11:30am on Tuesday and Saturday.

Kahului Ale House Sports Bar & Restaurant *(☎ 877-9001; 355 E Kamehameha Ave; pub menu $5-10; open 11am-2pm daily)*, where Muhammad Ali stares down from posters on the wall, can get a bit rowdy. The big-screen TV, darts and pool are all perks. Live music and DJ nights alternate with karaoke.

Shopping

Kahului has Maui's only discount stores and locally priced shopping malls. For outdoor gear rentals, see the Activities section.

Costco *(☎ 877-5241; 540 Haleakala Hwy)* is a giant wholesale outlet that sells just about everything in bulk, from groceries to batteries. Other everyday supplies and services, including one-hour photo processing and gasoline, are steeply discounted. An annual membership costs $45.

Wal-Mart *(101 Pakaula St)* and **Kmart** *(424 Dairy Rd)* are other discount stores, great for short-term and solo visitors.

There are three major malls nearby. **Queen Kaahumanu Center** is the largest, with a Friday farmers market. **Maui Marketplace** has **The Sports Authority** if you need camping gear. **Maui Mall** is strangely empty, but does have a paper airplane 'museum' and famous **Tasaka Guri Guri** for homemade sweets and exotic sherbets (2 scoops for $1).

Maui Swap Meet *(Puunene Ave; admission 50¢; held 7am-noon Sat)* has a genuine local flavor.

HALEKII-PIHANA HEIAU STATE MONUMENT

Among Maui's most critical historical sites, these two adjoining *heiaus* (temples) sit atop a knoll 2 miles out of Wailuku and have a commanding view of the entire region, clear across the plains of central Maui and up the slopes of Haleakala. The temples were built with stones carried up from Iao Stream.

To get there from Waiehu Beach Rd, turn inland onto Kuhio Place, three-quarters of a mile south of the intersection of Hwys 340 and 330. Then head left onto Hea Place and drive up through the gates. The *heiaus* are less than half a mile from Hwy 340.

Kahekili, the last ruling chief of Maui, lived here, and Keopuolani, wife of Kamehameha I and mother of Kamehamehas II and III, was born at this site. After the decisive battle of Iao in 1790, Kamehameha I came to these *heiaus* to worship his war god Ku, offering what is thought to have been the last human sacrifice on Maui.

Halekii (House of Images), the first *heiau*, has stepped stone walls and a flat grassy top. Watch out for bullhead thorns if you're wearing flip-flops (thongs). *Kii* (deity images) used to sit atop the terraces. The pyramid-like mound of Pihana Heiau is directly ahead, a five-minute walk away. Pihana, which means 'gathering place of supernatural beings,' is fairly overgrown with *kiawe,* wildflowers and weeds. Much larger than Halekii, this *luakini* (temple dedicated to Ku) was once used for human sacrifices. Few people come this way, and doves fly up from the bushes as you approach.

Despite the state monument status, the government has been negligent in protecting the *heiaus*. This is one of the fastest-growing residential areas on Maui, and construction and gravel removal along both sides of the hill have been widespread – so much so that some conservationists are now allowing plants to grow wild to stabilize the lava rock to prevent the *heiau* site from being undermined.

Nevertheless, a certain *mana* (spiritual power) still emanates from the site. To imagine it all through the eyes of the Hawaiians 200 years ago, ignore the industrial warehouses and tract homes and concentrate instead on the wild ocean vistas.

WAILUKU

Wailuku sits beneath the eastern flank of the West Maui Mountains. An ancient religious and political center, one translation of its name means 'waters of slaughter,' after the bloody battles that took place in the surrounding Iao Valley. Kahekili, Maui's last ruling chief, built his royal palace at the valley entrance.

Wailuku is unabashedly local – there's nothing touristy in the whole town. While the central area serves as the county capital, complete with a few midrise government buildings, the backstreets are lined with a colorful hodgepodge of older shops and neighborhood restaurants.

Information

The **Maui Visitors Bureau** *(MVB; ☎ 244-3530; 1727 Wili Pa Loop; open 8am-4:30pm Mon-Fri)* is near the **main post office** *(☎ 244-1653; 250 Imi Kala St; open 8am-4:30pm Mon-Fri, 9am-noon Sat)*. The visitors bureau is essentially an administrative office with a rack of brochures in the lobby; the same brochures are available at the tourist office booth in the airport arrival area.

The hostels have free Internet terminals. **Café Marc Aurel** *(28 N Market St; open 7am-6pm Mon-Fri, 7am-1pm Sat & Sun)* has an Internet terminal with access for $1 per 10 minutes, and **Hale Imua Internet Café** *(☎ 242-1896; Dragon Arts Center)* offers high-speed access for 20¢ per minute or $8 per hour. There's also the **Wailuku public library** *(☎ 243-5766; 251 High St; open 11:30am-8pm Mon & Thur, 10am-5pm Tues-Wed & Fri)*.

Maui Memorial Medical Center *(☎ 244-9056; 221 Mahalani St)* is the island's main hospital and has 24-hour emergency services. **Maui Medical Group** *(☎ 249-8080; 2180 Main St)*, next to Valley Isle Pharmacy, has outpatient clinics.

Bailey House Museum

Built over an earlier royal Hawaiian compound, Bailey House, a five-minute walk up from Kaahumanu Church, was home to the family of missionary Edward Bailey, who came to Wailuku from Boston, Massachusetts, in 1837.

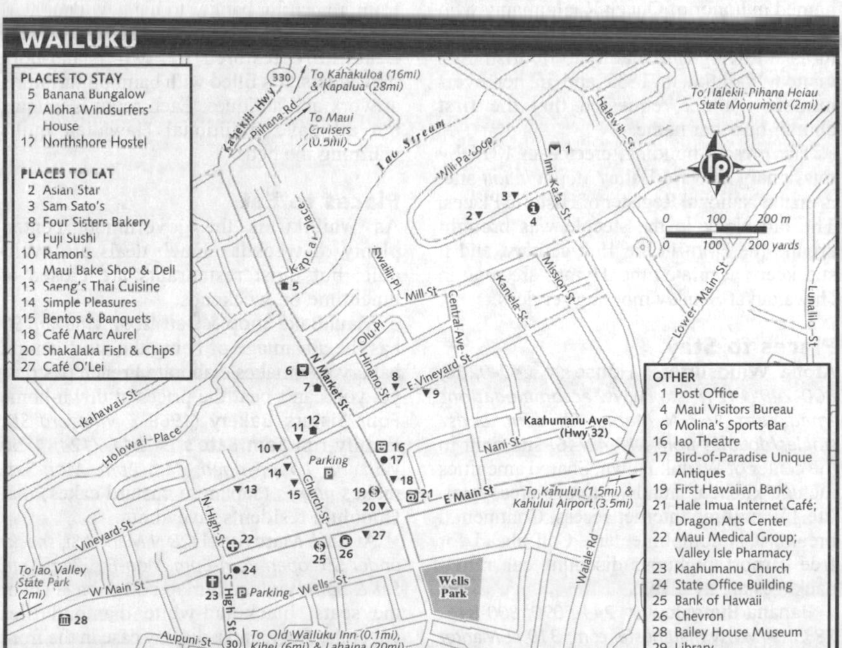

Today this is the headquarters of the Maui Historical Society, which has turned the former mission house into an worthwhile little **museum** (*☎ 244-3326; 2375-A E Main St; adult/child $5/1; open 10am-4pm Mon-Sat*). Inside there's a collection of Hawaiian stone adzes, tapa, bottle gourds, calabashes and the like, as well as period furnishings from the missionary days. Bailey was a painter and engraver, and many of his works are on display.

A highlight is the surfboard used by Olympian Duke Kahanamoku that's above the parking lot at the side of the shed. Compare it to today's sleek fiberglass boards – this six-footer is made of redwood and weighs in at a hefty 150lb!

The downstairs gift shop has quality crafts and a good Hawaiiana book selection. Call ahead to make reservations for docent tours and special programmes, anything from slack-key guitar concerts to Hawaiian herbalism talks.

Kaahumanu Church

Established in 1832, this is the oldest Congregational church in Maui. The church was named in honor of Queen Kaahumanu, who cast aside the old gods and burned temple idols, allowing Christianity to flourish. She visited Wailuku in 1832 and in her ever-humble manner requested that the first church bear her name.

The present building, erected in 1876 by missionary Edward Bailey atop a *heiau* site, is on the National Register of Historic Places. The old clock in the steeple was brought around the Horn in the 19th century, and it still keeps accurate time. Hymns are sung in Hawaiian at Sunday morning services.

MAUI

Places to Stay

Aloha Windsurfers' House (*☎ 249-0206, 800-249-1421; W www.accommodations-maui.com; 167 N Market St; dorm beds/singles/doubles from $17/42/46*) sits right in the center of Wailuku town. Shared amenities include kitchen, laundry, storage area, satellite TV and free Internet access. Continental breakfast is complimentary. Call ahead for free airport pickups; discount car rental packages are available.

Banana Bungalow (*☎ 244-5090, 800-846-7835; W www.mauihostel.com; 310 N Market St; dorm beds/rooms from $17.50/32*) makes shoestring backpackers happy with free Internet access, daily island tours, a backyard Jacuzzi and hammocks. Still, there's plenty not to love, from cramped dormitories to dank private rooms with sagging mattresses. Common amenities include a TV room, group kitchen, coin laundry, a shed for storing windsurfing gear and a daily airport shuttle.

Northshore Hostel (*☎ 242-8999, fax 244-5004; W www.hawaii-hostels.com; 2080 E Vineyard St; dorm beds/singles/doubles $16/29/38*), a funky old building right in the center of Wailuku, is popular with international travelers, with a common kitchen, TV room and free Internet access. While it's certainly not fancy, by Hawaiian standards it's decent budget accommodation. Then again, the management keeps changing hands, so who knows what your experience here will be like.

Molina's Sports Bar (*☎ 244-4100; 197 N Market St*) has utilitarian rooms out back rented by the day, week or month.

Old Wailuku Inn (*☎ 244-5897, 800-305-4899, fax 242-9600; W www.mauiinn.com; 2199 Kahookele St; rooms $120-180*), an elegant 1920s home that was a wedding gift from a wealthy banker to his new daughter-in-law, is shaded by trees and very private. Beautifully restored by two island-born innkeepers, it's filled with bamboo furniture, artwork and antiques. Each room is unique, but all have traditional Hawaiian quilts warming the beds.

Places to Eat

As Wailuku is the government center, plenty of weekday lunch deals are available, but most restaurants are closed at lunchtime on weekends.

Maui Bake Shop & Deli (*2092 Vineyard St*) has the advantage of being the most central bakery and makes elaborate French pastries, yet you can't beat the prices at down-home **Four Sisters Bakery** (*1968 E Vineyard St*). Family-run **Sam Sato's** (*☎ 244-7124; 1750 Wili Pa Loop; open 7am-2pm Mon-Sat*) makes *monja* (Japanese custard cakes) that Honolulu residents rave about.

At **Café Marc Aurel** (*28 N Market St; snacks under $5; open 7am-6pm Mon-Fri, 7am-1pm Sat & Sun*), vintage burlap coffee bags cover the seats, black-and-white diamond tiles cover the floor, and a display case in the front showcases homemade bonbons, memorable fruit scones, slices of quiche and sandwiches. Sip a rich mocha or cappuccino on the outdoor high-backed stools, while regulars look over the newspapers. Ah, delightful.

Simple Pleasures (*☎ 249-0697; 2103 Vineyard St; open 11am-3pm Tues-Sat*), run by friendly foreign chefs, is a basic vegetarian café where you can savor Indian curries, Swedish soups and perhaps *haupia* (coconut) pie or *lilikoi* (passion fruit) and lemon tart for dessert.

Saeng's Thai Cuisine (*☎ 244-1567; 2119 Vineyard St; lunch specials $7, mains $9-12.50; open 11am-2:30pm Mon-Fri, 5pm-9:30pm daily*) has an alluring open-air setting reminiscent of teak Thai houses, plus a wide range of dishes, including excellent curries, savory salads and vegetarian offerings. Best of all, it doesn't hold back on the spiciness.

Bentos & Banquets (*85 Church St; lunch specials $6-8; open 10am-2pm Mon-Fri*) is quite popular with local businesspeople. The menu changes daily, though a few items like roast pork adobo or teriyaki beef are standards.

Also try **Café O'Lei** (*2051 Main St, lunch $5-8*) for gourmet plate lunches and **Shaka-laka Fish & Chips** (*2010 Main St*), which has guava cheesecake.

Fuji Sushi (*1951 E Vineyard St; dishes under $8; open 11am-1pm & 5pm-8:30pm Mon-Sat*) serves up steaming bowls of udon noodles, market-fresh fish and an unusual number of *unagi* (eel) dishes.

Asian Star (*1764 Wili Pa Loop; dishes $6-12; open 10am-9:30pm daily*) is hands-down the island's best Vietnamese restaurant. The extensive menu of classics includes *pho* noodle soup and *banh hoi*, a Vietnamese version of fajitas, with a plate of mint leaves, rice noodles, assorted vegetables and shrimp or tofu, all rolled up with rice-paper wraps. True, the atmosphere here in the industrial loop is minimal, but service is congenial.

Ramon's (*☎ 244-7243; 2101 Vineyard St; dishes $13-20; open 10am-9pm Mon-Fri, 10am-10pm Sat & Sun*) feels like eating at your mother's house – if you happen to be Mexican, that is. Huge portions begin to make up for high prices; try the seafood enchiladas.

Entertainment

Iao Theatre (*☎ 242-6969; N Market St*), built c. 1928, has been restored after years of neglect. Productions by local dramatic groups concentrate mostly on recycled musicals.

Molina's Sports Bar (*☎ 244-4100; 197 N Market St*), near the hostels, has live music and DJ nights. It's the kind of place where you can kick back and spill your beer on the floor without anyone caring.

Shopping

North of Main St, N Market St has a handful of pawnshops, galleries and antique shops, some of them intriguingly cluttered affairs stocking a mishmash of Hawaiiana items. Visit **Bird-of-Paradise Unique Antiques** (*☎ 242-7699; 56 N Market St*).

Dragon Arts Center (*1980 Main St*), a newly restored landmark, houses a few art galleries and import shops.

IAO VALLEY ROAD

In 1790, Kamehameha I attacked Kahului by sea and quickly chased the defending Maui warriors up into precipitous Iao Valley. Those unable to escape over the mountains were slaughtered along the stream. The waters of Iao Stream were so choked with bodies that the area was called Kepaniwai (Dammed Waters).

Today, Iao Valley State Park encompasses much of the upper valley along the stream. Iao Valley Rd leads droves of tourists every day into the park, passing minor sights along the way.

Tropical Gardens of Maui (*☎ 244-3085; adult/child $3/free; open 9am-4:30pm Mon-Sat*), less than a mile from Wailuku, can give you a botany lesson; interpretive plaques here identify many floral species.

Another mile farther, **Kepaniwai County Park** is dedicated to Hawaii's varied ethnic heritage. Around the run-down grounds are a traditional *hale* (Hawaiian house) with a *pili* (grass) roof and a New England–style missionary home. The Asian gardens, which harbor stone pagodas, a carp pond and Chinese pavilion, are nearby. Iao Stream runs through the park and is bordered by picnic shelters with barbecue pits.

Up at the west end of Kepaniwai County Park is the **Hawaii Nature Center** (*☎ 244-6500; 875 Iao Valley Rd; adult/child $6/3.25; open 10am-4pm daily*), a nonprofit educational facility with over two dozen kid-oriented exhibits, some interactive, that identify local birds, explain native stream life and the like. Adults can pick up field guides, natural history books and island maps at the gift shop.

At a bend in the road half a mile after Kepaniwai Country Park, you'll likely see a few cars pulled over and their occupants staring off into Pali Eleele, a gorge on the right. One of the rock formations shows a vague **profile**, weathered by erosion. Some legends associate it with a powerful *kahuna* (priest) who lived here during the 1500s, while others say it bears an uncanny resemblance to John F Kennedy. OK, whatever.

If parking is difficult here, just continue on to Iao Valley State Park, as it's only a couple of minutes' walk from there back to the viewing site.

Iao Valley State Park

Nestled in the mountains, and only 3 miles out of central Wailuku, Iao Valley State Park *(admission free; open 7am-7pm daily)* extends all the way to Puu Kukui (5788ft), Maui's highest and wettest point.

The valley is allegedly named after Iao, the beautiful daughter of Maui. Iao Needle, a rock pinnacle that rises 1200ft from the valley floor, is said to be Iao's clandestine lover, captured by Maui and turned to stone.

Clouds often rise up the valley, forming a shroud around the top of Iao Needle. A stream meanders beneath the needle, and the steep cliffs of the West Maui Mountains form a scenic backdrop. That's why all the tour buses come here. After a two-minute walk from the parking lot, you'll reach a bridge where most people stop to photograph Iao Needle. However, just before the bridge, the walkway that loops downhill by the stream leads to the nicest photo angle – one that captures the stream, bridge and Iao Needle together.

Over the bridge, a short walkway leads up to a sheltered lookout with another fine view of Iao Needle. The all-too-short jaunt will leave most people itching to continue on the closed hiking trail beyond the 'no trespassing' signs.

PUUNENE

Puunene is a working plantation village surrounded by sugarcane fields and built around a mill run by the Hawaiian Commercial & Sugar (C&S) Company. When the mill is in operation, the air hangs heavy with the strange but sweet smell of sugar.

The power plant next to the mill burns residue sugarcane fibers (called bagasse) to run the mill machinery that extracts and refines the sugar. With a capacity of 37,000 kilowatts, it's one of the world's largest biomass power plants. Excess electricity is sold to Maui Electric.

The **Friends of Maui Library** *(☎ 871-6563; open 8am-4pm Mon-Sat)* runs a '10¢ bookstore' behind the mill where stacks of used volumes on any imaginable subject cost a dime each. It's tricky getting here. Head south on Puunene Ave past the mill, then turn left onto Camp Rd 5 and follow the signs around behind the school.

Puunene's main attraction is the excellent **Alexander & Baldwin Sugar Museum** *(☎ 871-8058; cnr Puunene Ave & Hansen Rd; adult/child $5/2; open 9:30am-4:30pm Mon-Sat year-round, 9:30am-4:30pm Sun during Feb, Mar, Jul & Aug)*, opposite the mill. The displays, which explain how sugarcane grows and is harvested, include an elaborate working scale model of a cane-crushing plant.

Most interesting, however, are the images of people. The museum traces how Samuel Alexander and Henry Baldwin gobbled up vast chunks of Hawaiian land, how they fought tooth and nail with an ambitious Claus Spreckels to gain access to Upcountry water, and how they dug the extensive irrigation systems that made large-scale sugarcane plantations a possibility.

Representing the other end of the scale is a turn-of-the-20th-century labor contract from the Japanese Emigration Company stating that the laborer shall be paid $15 a month for working 10 hours a day in the field, 26 days a month (minus $2.50 banked for return passage to Japan). Wives worked equally hard, but were paid less. Illuminating period photos and artifacts of plantation life are also on display.

The museum is in the former home of the mill's superintendent. The curator is an avid photographer and local historian who has worked to restore the machinery found in the gardens, including a cane hauler and a hand ice-shaver.

KEALIA POND NATIONAL WILDLIFE REFUGE

Kealia Pond *(☎ 875-1582; 6-mile marker, Mokulele Hwy)* is a saltwater marsh and bird sanctuary. You can usually spot Hawaiian stilts, an endangered species, wading in the water. The pond is also a habitat for the Hawaiian coot, egrets and herons. In summer, water levels drop, resulting in brackish saltwater (Kealia means 'salt-encrusted place') favored by nesting native bird species. Migratory birds alight here between December and February.

MAALAEA BAY

Maalaea Bay runs along the south side of the isthmus between the twin mountain masses of west and east Maui. Prevailing winds from the north, which funnel between the mountains straight out toward Kahoolawe, create strong midday gusts and some of the best **windsurfing** conditions on Maui.

In winter, when the wind dies down elsewhere, windsurfers still fly along Maalaea Bay. The **Maalaea Pipeline**, south of the harbor, freight-trains right and is the fastest surf break in Hawaii. Summer's southerly swells produce huge tubes.

The bay is fronted by a continuous 3-mile stretch of sandy beach that runs from Maalaea Harbor south to Kihei Wharf. Unfortunately, however, the beach and nearby condos have had problems with theft, car break-ins and other tourist-targeted crimes.

Lahaina Pali Trail

From nearby the bay, this historic 19th-century route zigzags steeply up through *kiawe* and native dryland sandalwood trees. After the first mile it passes into open sun-baked scrub, from where you can see Haleakala and the fertile central plains. Ironwood trees precede the crossing of Kealaloa Ridge (elevation 1600ft), after which you descend through Ukumehame Gulch.

Look out for postcard views of Kahoolawe and Lanai, stray petroglyphs and *paniolo* (cowboy) graffiti. Stay on the footpath all the way down to Papalaua Beach and don't detour onto 4WD roads. The 5½-mile trail should take about three hours, all told. If you haven't arranged to be picked up at Papalaua, you'll have to hitchhike back to your car.

You can hike in either direction, but starting off early from the east side of the mountains keeps you ahead of the blistering sun. Take Hwy 30 to just south of the intersection of Hwy 380 near Maalaea. Look for a trailhead access road around the 5-mile marker and the posted Na Ala Hele sign; note that parking any further inland on this private road is illegal.

Maui Ocean Center

The $20 million state-of-the-art facility Maui Ocean Center *(☎ 270-7000; adult/child $19/13; open 9am-5pm daily, 9am-6pm Jul & Aug)* contains the largest tropical aquarium in the US and some 60 self-paced exhibits of indigenous Hawaiian marine life, proceeding from creatures of the shallowest intertidal waters out into deep ocean life. You could spend hours being hypnotized by the glowing jellyfish tanks and informative audio guide.

The extensive 'living reef' section focuses on the colorful coral and fish you might see while snorkeling in Hawaiian waters. Interpretive displays explain reef formations and identify different types of butterfly fish, wrasses, eels and other tropical fish that are part of the reef ecosystem.

The most dazzling sight is the main aquarium tank, which holds 750,000 gallons of seawater and has a walk-through acrylic tunnel where schools of fish and meandering sharks swim overhead. It's as close as you can get to being underwater without donning dive gear. Elsewhere are interactive displays on whales, sea turtle and stingray tanks, and a small touch pool.

Places to Eat

There are a few scenic mid-range restaurants in the **Maalaea Harbor Village** shopping center adjacent to the museum.

Café O'Lei's Maalaea Grill *(☎ 243-2206; 300 Maalaea Rd; lunch $6-9, dinner mains $13-18; open 10:30am-3pm Mon, 10:30am-9pm Tues-Sun)* lets you enjoy the sea breezes wafting through the harbor-front windows. Fresh seafood and local produce dominate the menu of this Wailuku caterer's new establishment.

West Maui

West Maui rides on the smaller of the island's two volcanoes, but it snares the lion's share of tourists. It encompasses a large oval of land, from Kahului west to the coast and from Honokohau Bay south to Papawai Point. Behind it all, the dramatic West Maui Mountains dominate the landscape, with cliffs casting long shadows over old sugarcane fields.

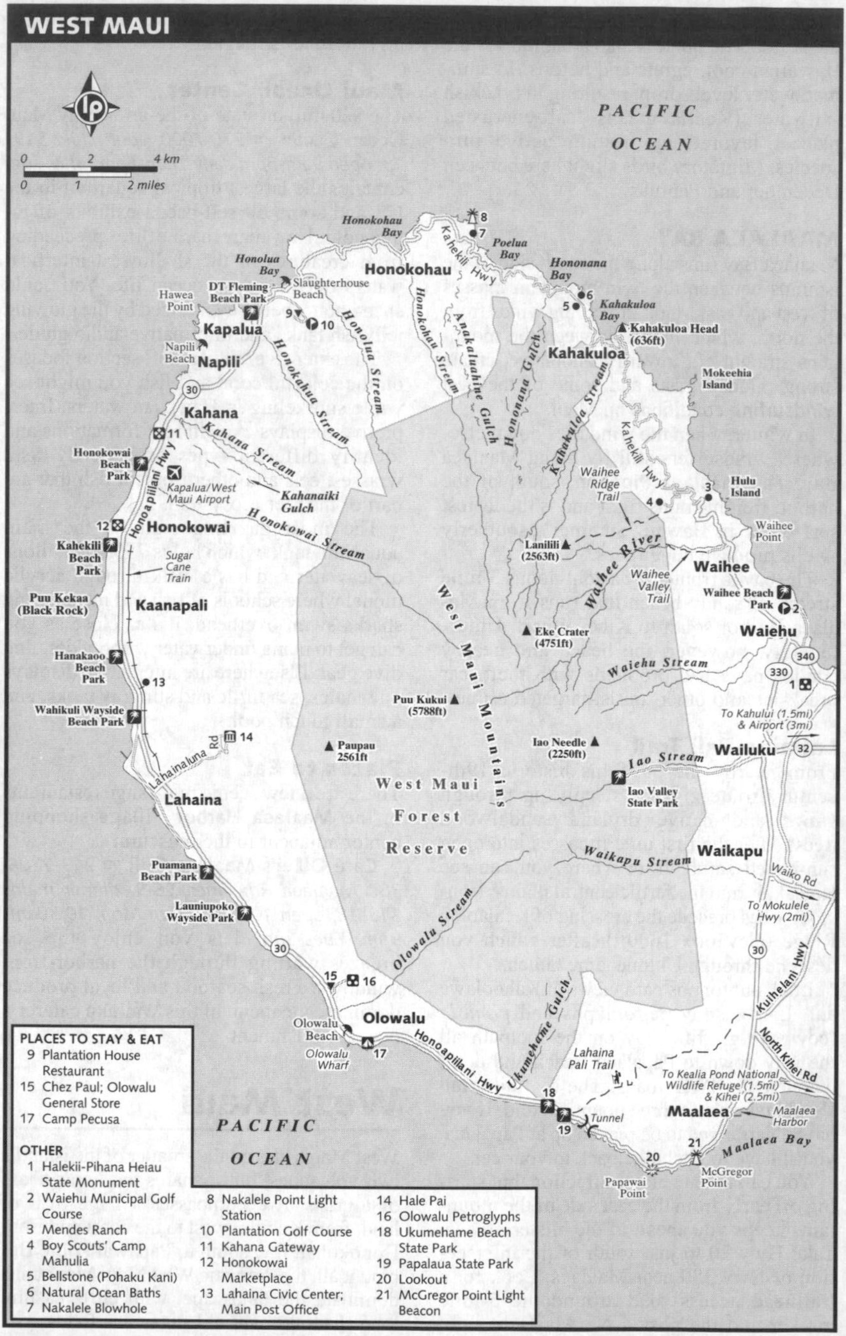
WEST MAUI
0 2 4 km
0 1 2 miles
PACIFIC OCEAN
Honokohau Bay
Poelua Bay
Hononana Bay
Kahakuloa Bay
Honolua Bay
Slaughterhouse Beach
DT Fleming Beach Park
Hawea Point
Kapalua
Napili Beach
Napili
Honokohau
Kahekili Hwy
Honokohau Stream
Honolua Stream
Anakaluahine Gulch
Hononana Gulch
Kahakuloa Stream
Kahakuloa
Kahakuloa Head (636ft)
Mokeehia Island
Hulu Island
Waihee Ridge Trail
Waihee Point
Lanilili (2563ft)
Waihee River
Waihee
Waihee Valley Trail
Waihee Beach Park
Waiehu
Eke Crater (4751ft)
Waiehu Stream
Kahana
Kahana Stream
Honokahua Stream
Honokowai Beach Park
Kapalua/West Maui Airport
Kahanaiki Gulch
Honokowai Stream
Honoapiilani Hwy
Honokowai
Kahekili Beach Park
Sugar Cane Train
Puu Kekaa (Black Rock)
Kaanapali
Hanakaoo Beach Park
Wahikuli Wayside Beach Park
Lahainaluna Rd
Lahaina
West Maui Mountains
Puu Kukui (5788ft)
Paupau 2561ft
West Maui Forest Reserve
Iao Needle (2250ft)
Iao Stream
Iao Valley State Park
To Kahului (1.5mi) & Airport (3mi)
Wailuku
Waikapu Stream
Waikapu
Waiko Rd
To Mokulele Hwy (2mi)
Kuihelani Hwy
North Kihei Rd
Puamana Beach Park
Launiupoko Wayside Park
Olowalu Stream
Olowalu Beach
Olowalu
Olowalu Wharf
Ukumehame Gulch
Lahaina Pali Trail
To Kealia Pond National Wildlife Refuge (1.5mi) & Kihei (2.5mi)
Maalaea
Maalaea Harbor
Maalaea Bay
Tunnel
Papawai Point
McGregor Point
PACIFIC OCEAN
30
330
340
32
PLACES TO STAY & EAT
9 Plantation House Restaurant
15 Chez Paul; Olowalu General Store
17 Camp Pecusa
OTHER
1 Halekii-Pihana Heiau State Monument
2 Waiehu Municipal Golf Course
3 Mendes Ranch
4 Boy Scouts' Camp Mahulia
5 Bellstone (Pohaku Kani)
6 Natural Ocean Baths
7 Nakalele Blowhole
8 Nakalele Point Light Station
10 Plantation Golf Course
11 Kahana Gateway
12 Honokowai Marketplace
13 Lahaina Civic Center; Main Post Office
14 Hale Pai
16 Olowalu Petroglyphs
18 Ukumehame Beach State Park
19 Papalaua State Park
20 Lookout
21 McGregor Point Light Beacon

To many people, west Maui conjures up images of the heavily urbanized strip from Lahaina to the modern beach resorts of Kaanapali north to Kapalua. Nevertheless, a few historic sites survive and it's possible to leave the herds of honeymooners and cruise-ship passengers behind at quieter beaches and along the rugged Kahekili Hwy.

MAALAEA TO LAHAINA

The stretch between Lahaina and Maalaea has pretty mountain scenery, but during winter most people are craning their necks to look seaward as they drive along Honoapiilani Hwy. The popular bumper sticker 'I brake for whales' says it all, as this is a prime whale-watching road. During winter, humpback whales occasionally breach as close as 100 yards from this coast. Forty tons of leviathan suddenly exploding straight up through the water can be a real showstopper! Unfortunately, some drivers hit their brakes and others don't, making for high rear-ender potential.

A couple of inconspicuous roadside lookouts lie just south of the 10-mile marker, but they're both unmarked and difficult to negotiate in heavy traffic. Your best bet is to drive just a little farther to **Papawai Point**, a clearly marked scenic lookout with a parking lot, between the 8- and 9-mile markers. Because the point juts into the waters at the western edge of Maalaea Bay, a favored humpback nursing ground, it's a good whale-sighting spot. Volunteer naturalists staff the lookout in winter; bring your own binoculars.

After the highway tunnel, keep an eye out for the **Lahaina Pali** trailhead past the 10-mile marker (see Maalaea Bay under Central Maui). If traffic is heavy, pull off to the right and either park or wait for a chance to dart across the road to the beaches when traffic clears.

At the 11-mile marker, **Papalaua State Park** has limited facilities and doesn't seem to offer much, except a rich ocean reef far offshore. Dive and snorkel boats anchor offshore at **Coral Gardens**. This reef also creates **Thousand Peaks** toward its west end, with breaks favored by long-boarders and beginning surfers.

Further north at the 12-mile marker is **Ukumehame Beach State Park**. Shaded by ironwood trees, this sandy beach is marginally better for sunbathing or taking a quick dip, but because of the rocky conditions most locals stick with picnicking or fishing.

The Olowalu Massacre

Olowalu Beach was the site of an infamous massacre in 1790. After a skiff was stolen from the US ship *Eleanora* and burned for its iron nails and fittings, Captain Simon Metcalfe retaliated by tricking the Hawaiians into sailing out in their canoes to trade. He then mercilessly gunned them down with his cannons, killing an estimated 100 people. This incident set in motion a chain of karmic events that eventually led to the death of the captain's son Thomas, who was bludgeoned to death by Big Island warriors wielding canoe paddles.

Olowalu

Olowalu, which means 'many hills,' has a lovely setting, with cane fields backed by the West Maui Mountains. There's little to mark it other than Olowalu General Store and a seemingly misplaced French restaurant.

When the water is calm, there's snorkeling between the 13- and 14-mile marker, south of the general store. The coral reef here is large and shallow, and there's a narrow sandy beach to lie on, though be careful of *kiawe* thorns. However, most people find the underwater visibility disappointing.

A dirt access road starting behind the general store leads to the **Olowalu Petroglyphs**. Park near the signposted gate and walk inland along the hot, dusty road for about 15 minutes, always keeping the cinder cone straight ahead of you. As with most of Maui's extant petroglyphs, these figures are carved into the vertical sides of cliffs rather than on *pahoehoe* (smooth, ropy lava) like on the other Hawaiian Islands. Most of the Olowalu figures have been damaged or otherwise covered up by graffiti, but you can still make some out. There is a rickety old viewing platform but no interpretive signs.

Places to Stay & Eat Run by the Episcopal Church, **Camp Pecusa** *(☎ 661-4303; W www.maui.net/~norm/pecusa.html; 800 Olowalu Village Rd; sites per person $6)* has a low-profile 'tent ground' available to individuals on a first-come, first-served basis. It's at the side of a cane field, half a mile south of

Olowalu General Store, on the *makai* (seaward) side of the road. Camping is in the shade and along a beach. The beach is not suitable for swimming, but there's good snorkeling farther out on the reef.

While the camping ground is basic, it does have a solar-heated shower, a couple of outhouses, drinking water and picnic tables. A caretaker lives on the grounds, making this the most secure place in Maui to camp. No alcohol is allowed, and there's a maximum stay of seven nights in any 30-day period. Reservations are not accepted, but space is usually available. Look for the small blue sign, about a half-mile south of the general store.

Chez Paul *(☎ 661-3843; Olowalu Village Rd; mains $22-45; open for dinner daily)*, a fine French seafood restaurant, has been building its stellar reputation since 1968. The interior feels very European, with old-fashioned artwork, white linens and just a dozen tables. French classics are enlivened by Hawaiian touches, perhaps Kona lobster or exotic fruit salsa. Reservations are required.

LAHAINA

Lahaina was once a royal court for Maui chiefs and was the breadbasket, or, more accurately, the breadfruit basket, of West Maui. Its apt name means 'cruel sun,' and the sweltering heat and humidity are more severe here than anywhere else on Maui. The coastal setting and mountain backdrop *are* pretty, however, and it's easy to see why people have been drawn here. There are soft breezes off the water and fine sunset views of Lanai from the Front St seawall.

After Kamehameha I unified the islands, he set up his base in Lahaina, and the capital remained there until 1845. Hawaii's first stone church, missionary school and printing press were all in place in Lahaina by the early 1830s. The whaling years reached their peak in Lahaina in the mid-19th century, with hundreds of ships pulling into port each year. The town took on the whalers' boisterous nature, with hundreds of sick or derelict sailors, who either had been abandoned or jumped ship, roaming the streets. Among the multitudes that landed in Lahaina was Herman Melville, who later penned *Moby Dick*.

These days, Lahaina's streets are jammed with tourists. The old wooden shops that once housed saloons, brothels and provision stores are now crammed with souvenir shops. While there are a few historical sites, Lahaina is abuzz with commercial activity; if you're expecting something quaint and romantic, you may well be disappointed. Chief attractions include homes of missionaries, prisons for sailors and graveyards for both.

Orientation

The focal point of Lahaina is its bustling small-boat harbor, which is backed by the old Pioneer Inn and Banyan Tree Square. Half of Lahaina's sights are clustered in this area, while the other half are scattered around town.

The main drag and tourist strip is Front St, which runs along the shoreline. As you drive north out of town, look for the neon 'JESUS COMING SOON' sign made famous by The Eagles' song 'The Last Resort,' written about the culture of drugs and rock 'n' roll in down-and-out Lahaina during the 1970s.

Information

The **Lahaina Arts Society** *(☎ 667-9193, 866-511-4569; events hotline ☎ 667-9194, 888-310-1117; W www.visitlahaina.com; 648 Wharf St; open 9am-5pm daily)* has a volunteer-staffed information desk inside the old courthouse at Banyan Tree Square.

ATMs are everywhere. Try the **Bank of Hawaii branch** *(☎ 661-8781; open 8:30am-4pm Mon-Thur, 8:30am-6pm Fri; Lahaina Shopping Center)* or **First Hawaiian Bank** *(☎ 661-3655; 215 Papalaua St; open 8:30am-4pm Mon-Thur, 8:30am-6pm Fri)*.

There's often a long wait for a parking space and a longer queue inside the **downtown post office station** *(open 8:15am-4:15pm Mon-Fri; Lahaina Shopping Center)*. The **main post office** *(☎ 661-0904; 1760 Honoapiilani Hwy; open 8:30am-5pm Mon-Fri, 9am-1pm Sat)*, where you pick up mail sent general delivery to Lahaina, is near the Lahaina civic center, a few miles north of town.

The **public library** *(☎ 662-3950; 680 Wharf St; open noon-8pm Tues, 9am-5pm Wed & Thur, 10:30pm-4:30pm Fri & Sat)* has a few Internet terminals. A few eateries around town, including **Karma Cafe** and **Westside Natural Foods & Deli**, also offer limited, and often expensive, online access.

Maui Medical Group *(☎ 249-8080; 130 Prison St)* handles nonemergencies. **Longs Drugs** *(☎ 667-4384)* is at the Lahaina Cannery Mall.

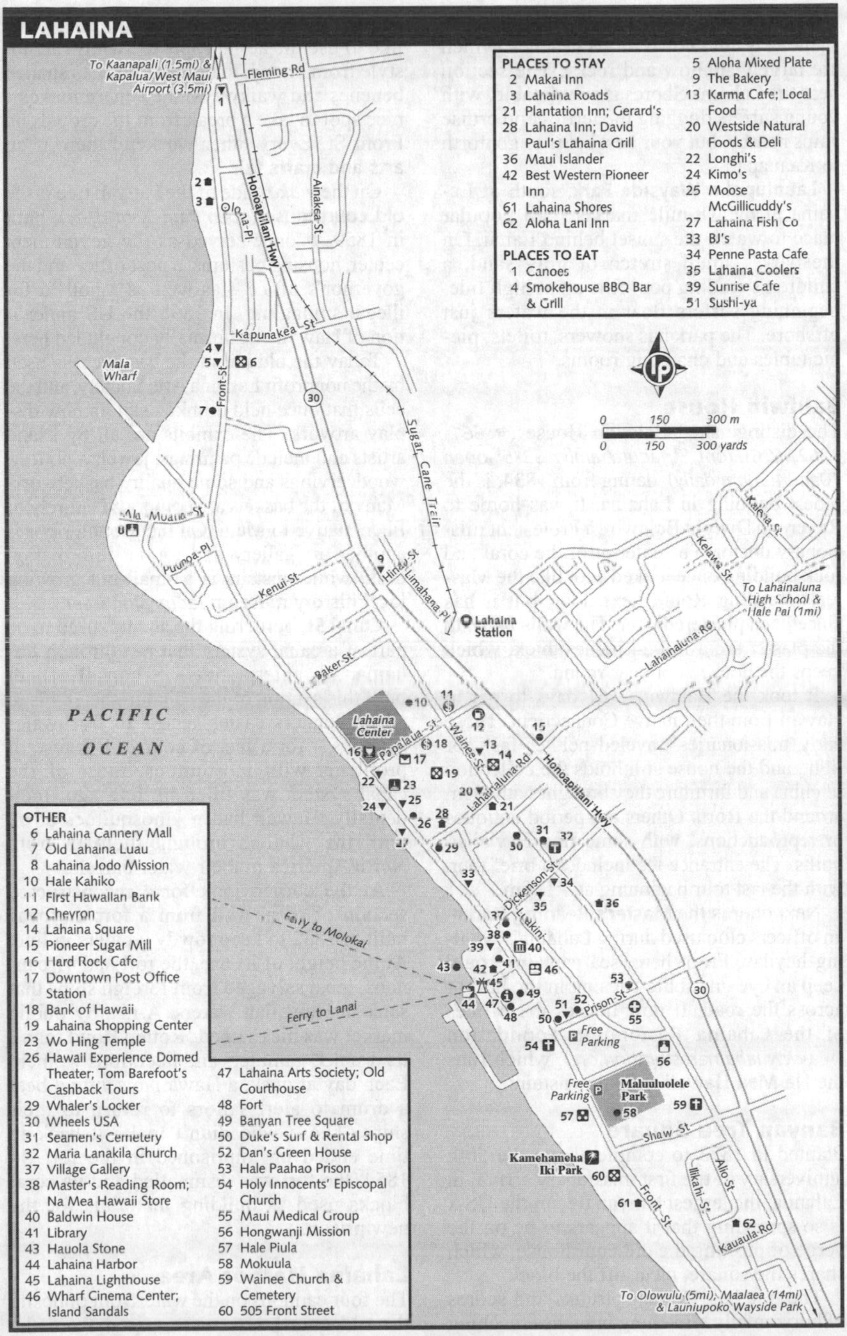
LAHAINA
PLACES TO STAY
2 Makai Inn
3 Lahaina Roads
21 Plantation Inn; Gerard's
28 Lahaina Inn; David Paul's Lahaina Grill
36 Maui Islander
42 Best Western Pioneer Inn
61 Lahaina Shores
62 Aloha Lani Inn
PLACES TO EAT
1 Canoes
4 Smokehouse BBQ Bar & Grill
5 Aloha Mixed Plate
9 The Bakery
13 Karma Cafe; Local Food
20 Westside Natural Foods & Deli
22 Longhi's
24 Kimo's
25 Moose McGillicuddy's
27 Lahaina Fish Co
33 BJ's
34 Penne Pasta Cafe
35 Lahaina Coolers
39 Sunrise Cafe
51 Sushi-ya
OTHER
6 Lahaina Cannery Mall
7 Old Lahaina Luau
8 Lahaina Jodo Mission
10 Hale Kahiko
11 First Hawaiian Bank
12 Chevron
14 Lahaina Square
15 Pioneer Sugar Mill
16 Hard Rock Cafe
17 Downtown Post Office Station
18 Bank of Hawaii
19 Lahaina Shopping Center
23 Wo Hing Temple
26 Hawaii Experience Domed Theater; Tom Barefoot's Cashback Tours
29 Whaler's Locker
30 Wheels USA
31 Seamen's Cemetery
32 Maria Lanakila Church
37 Village Gallery
38 Master's Reading Room; Na Mea Hawaii Store
40 Baldwin House
41 Library
43 Hauola Stone
44 Lahaina Harbor
45 Lahaina Lighthouse
46 Wharf Cinema Center; Island Sandals
47 Lahaina Arts Society; Old Courthouse
48 Fort
49 Banyan Tree Square
50 Duke's Surf & Rental Shop
52 Dan's Green House
53 Hale Paahao Prison
54 Holy Innocents' Episcopal Church
55 Maui Medical Group
56 Hongwanji Mission
57 Hale Piula
58 Mokuula
59 Wainee Church & Cemetery
60 505 Front Street
To Kaanapali (1.5mi) & Kapalua/West Maui Airport (3.5mi)
Fleming Rd
Honoapiilani Hwy
Ainakea St
Olona Pl
Kapunakea St
Front St
Mala Wharf
Sugar Cane Train
Ala Moana St
Puunoa Pl
Kenui St
Hinau St
Limahana Pl
Lahaina Station
Baker St
PACIFIC OCEAN
Lahaina Center
Papalaua St
Wainee St
Lahainaluna Rd
Dickenson St
Lakini
Prison St
Ferry to Molokai
Ferry to Lanai
Free Parking
Maluuluolele Park
Kamehameha Iki Park
Shaw St
Ilikahi St
Alio St
Kauaula Rd
Kalena St
Kelawea St
To Lahainaluna High School & Hale Pai (1mi)
To Olowalu (5mi); Maalaea (14mi) & Launiupoko Wayside Park
0 150 300 m
0 150 300 yards
30

Beaches

Lahaina is not known for its beaches, which are largely shallow and rocky. The section near the Lahaina Shores is swimmable, with young surfers dodging the ferries and cruise ships nearby, but your best bet is to go north to Kaanapali.

Launiupoko Wayside Park, south of Lahaina at the 18-mile marker, is a popular place to watch the sunset behind Lanai. On the park's small stretch of gray sand, a children's wading pool fills up at high tide; beginning surfers float in the waters just offshore. The park has showers, toilets, picnic tables and changing rooms.

Baldwin House

The distinguished Baldwin House *(☎ 661-3262; 696 Front St; adult/family $3/5; open 10am-4:30pm daily)*, dating from 1834, is the oldest building in Lahaina. It was home to Reverend Dwight Baldwin, a Protestant missionary doctor. The exterior of the coral and rock building once looked a lot like the Master's Reading Room next door, but it has since been plastered over. The walls beneath the plaster are a full 24 inches thick, which keeps the house cool year-round.

It took the Baldwins 161 days to get to Hawaii from their native Connecticut. These early missionaries traveled neither fast nor light, and the house still holds the collection of china and furniture they brought with them around the Horn. Others are period antiques or reproductions, with some fine Hawaiian quilts. The entrance fee includes a brief tour, with the last tour beginning at 4:15pm.

Next door is the **Master's Reading Room**, an officers club used during Lahaina's whaling heyday. From here, sea captains could keep an eye on rabble-rousing in the harbor across the road. It now houses the offices of the **Lahaina Restoration Foundation** *(W www.lahainarestoration.org)*, which runs the **Na Mea Hawaii** shop downstairs.

Banyan Tree Square

Planted in 1873 to commemorate the 50th anniversary of the first missionary arrival in Lahaina, the largest banyan tree in the USA is so sprawling that it appears to be on the verge of pushing the old courthouse, which shares the square, clear off the block.

The tree has 16 major trunks and scores of horizontally stretching branches reaching across the better part of an acre. Local kids like to use the aerial roots to swing Tarzan-style from branch to branch. With its shaded benches and walkways, the square makes a nice spot to take a break from the crowds on Front St. Every other weekend there is an **arts and crafts fair**.

On the *makai* side of the banyan tree is the **old courthouse** *(open 9am-5pm daily)*, built in 1859. It once served as the government center, housing customs, a post office and the governor's office – as well as a hotbed for illegal smuggling. In 1898 the US annexation of Hawaii was formally concluded here.

Today the old jail in the basement is used by the nonprofit Lahaina Arts Society, and the cells that once held drunken sailors now display artwork. The exhibits are all by island artists and include paintings, jewelry, pottery, woodcarvings and some quality basketwork. Many of the baskets are composed entirely of fibers native to Maui. On the ground floor is another art gallery and tourist information desk, while upstairs is a small but growing **local history museum** *(admission free)*.

Canal St, bordering the square, used to be part of a canal system that ran through Lahaina. An enterprising US consul officer built this section of the canal in the 1840s to allow whalers easier access to freshwater supplies – for a fee, of course. Because of problems with mosquitoes, most of the canal system was filled in long ago. Incidentally, Hawaii had no mosquitoes at all until the whalers brought them in from North America in their water barrels.

At the corner, look for a reconstructed section of coral wall from a **fort** that was built in 1832 to keep rowdy whalers in line. At the height of its use, the fort had 47 cannons, most salvaged from foreign ships that sank in Hawaiian waters. A nearby public market was nicknamed 'Rotten Row' for all its drunks, gamblers and licentious women. Each day at dusk, a Hawaiian sentinel beat a drum to alert sailors to return to their ships. Those who didn't make it back in time ended up imprisoned in the fort. In 1854, the fort was dismantled and its coral blocks used as building materials for the new prison.

Lahaina Harbor Area

The four cannons on the waterfront opposite the old courthouse were raised from the wreck of a Russian ship that went down in Honolulu Harbor in 1816. Amusingly, they now point directly at Lahaina's crowded small-boat harbor, which is filled with glass-bottom boats, windjammers, sportfishing boats, whale-watchers and sunset sailboats. Booths lining the edge of the harbor sell tickets for most of the cruises, as do the ubiquitous activity booths around town. Interisland ferries dock at the public pier.

The old green-and-white **Pioneer Inn** is the most prominent landmark. It's got a faux whaling-era atmosphere, with swinging doors, ship figureheads and signs warning against womanizing in the rooms. Actually, the two-story Pioneer Inn was built in 1901, long after the whaling boom had passed, but nobody seems to notice or care. Until the 1950s, it was Lahaina's only hotel; Jack London once slept here.

In the same area stands the **Lahaina Lighthouse**, probably the oldest lighthouse in the Pacific. It was commissioned in 1840 to aid whaling ships pulling into Lahaina and was fueled by sperm whale oil. The current structure, which dates from 1905, flashes red with a photoelectrical cell courtesy of the coast guard.

The nearby **Hauola Stone** is a water-worn lava stone on the shoreline. To spot it, look to the right as you face the ocean – it's the middle stone. The Hawaiians believed this flat, seat-shaped stone emitted healing powers to those who sat on it.

Front Street

If you walk north down Front St past the Pioneer Inn and Baldwin House, you'll come to a row of interesting **historical buildings**, which date to the turn of the 20th century. The buildings are best appreciated from the seawall sidewalk or the upstairs lanai of any restaurant.

Wo Hing Temple One of the most unique structures is the Wo Hing Temple (*☎ 661-3262; 858 Front St; admission by donation; open 10am-4:15pm daily*), which opened in 1912 as a meeting hall for the fraternal order of Chee Kung Tong, a Chinese benevolent society.

As Lahaina's ethnic Chinese population declined (with many Chinese-Hawaiians moving to Oahu seeking better business opportunities), so too did the building. It was restored and turned into a museum by the Lahaina Restoration Foundation in 1983. Inside you'll find cultural artifacts and period photos downstairs and a Taoist shrine upstairs.

Whatever you do, don't miss the tin-roof cookhouse out back, which has been set up as a little theater to show fascinating films on old Hawaii shot by inventor Thomas Edison during his visits to the islands in 1898 and 1906.

Wainee Street

Hale Paahao (Stuck-in-Irons House), Lahaina's old **prison** (*admission free*), was built in 1852 by convicts, who dismantled the old harborside fort and carried the stone blocks here to construct these 8ft-high prison walls. Hawaiians could collect bounties by turning in sailors who jumped ship or fooled around with local women.

The prison was restored in 1988 but is already rundown. Inside, one of the whitewashed cells has an authentic-looking 'old seadog' mannequin with a recorded story about 'life in this here calaboose'. In another cell, you'll find a list of offenses and arrests for the year 1855. The top three offenses were drunkenness (330 arrests), adultery and fornication (111) and 'furious riding' (89). Others include profanity, lascivious conduct, aiding deserting sailors and drinking *awa* (kava moonshine). There's

Sperm whale

also a copy of a 16-year-old seaman's diary, vividly describing his time spent in the prison.

The **Seamen's Cemetery** is a few blocks north of the prison, next to **Maria Lanakila Church**, Maui's first Catholic church. It's basically a local cemetery, with only one seaman's tombstone that can be identified. However, historical records indicate that numerous sailors from the whaling era were buried here, including a shipmate of Herman Melville's from the *Acushnet*.

Heading south from the prison, the **Hongwanji Mission** *(551 Wainee St)* is usually locked, but the front doors are glass so you can glance in at the beautiful gilt altar and painted screens. Unlike Buddhist temples in Japan, this one has rows of wooden pews.

Wainee Church *(535 Wainee St)* was built in 1832 as the first stone church in Hawaii. It's gone through a barrage of changes since. The steeple and bell collapsed in 1858. In 1894, the church was torched by royalists because its minister supported the annexation of Hawaii. A second church, built to replace the original, burned to the ground in 1947, and the third was blown away in a storm a few years later. One could get the impression that the old Hawaiian gods didn't take kindly to the house of this foreign deity!

The fourth version, optimistically called Waiola (Waters of Life) Congregational Church, has been standing since 1953. The **cemetery** next door is more interesting than the church. Here lie several notables: Governor Hoapili, who ordered the original church built; Queen Keopuolani, the wife of Kamehameha I; and the Reverend William Richards, Lahaina's first missionary. Some of the old tombstones have interesting inscriptions and photo cameos.

Around Maluuluolele Park

Maluuluolele Park's name means 'the breadfruit shade of Lele' ('Lele' was the ancient name for Lahaina). Today, it has basketball courts, tennis courts, a baseball field and not a hint of its fascinating past.

Maluuluolele Park was once the site of a royal pond containing a legendary *mo'o* (water lizard deity) that visited all the islands of Hawaii to unify the royal bloodlines. An island in the center of the pond called **Mokuula**, which means 'sacred island', was the abode of Maui chiefs and the three Kamehameha kings. It held an ornate burial chamber for royalty, including the tragic Princess Nahienaena who died for love of her brother, King Kamehameha III, in 1836. Polynesian tradition dictated that royal siblings should marry, but missionaries preached against it.

By the 1920s, the island was leveled and the pond filled in. A decade ago, an archaeological study affirmed that the island still lies buried beneath the park.

Friends of Mokuula *(☎ 661-3659; W www.mokuula.com; Suite 234, 505 Front St)* leads historic walking tours of Lahaina as part of its fundraising efforts to create an interpretive center on this historic site.

Across the street, a couple of steps and a grassy building foundation are all that remains of **Hale Piula**, Lahaina's halfhearted attempt at a royal palace in the 1830s. Queen Kaahumanu preferred to sleep in a Hawaiian-style thatched house anyway.

The interior of nearby **Holy Innocents' Episcopal Church** *(561 Front St)* is decorated with a Hawaiiana motif. Paintings on the front of the koa altar depict a fisher in an outrigger canoe and Hawaiian farmers harvesting taro and breadfruit. Above the altar is a Hawaiian Madonna and Child.

Hale Kahiko

At the rear of the **Lahaina Center** *(☎ 667-9216)* is **Hale Kahiko** *(admission free; open 9am-6pm daily)*, which consists of three *pili* houses *(hale)* that replicate a slice of an old Hawaiian village. Despite the irony of being off to the side of a new shopping center's parking lot, the buildings have been constructed in the old manner, using ohia-wood posts and native thatch and fiber lashings.

Each *hale* had a different function; one was used as family sleeping quarters, another used to be a men's eating house (traditional *kapus*, or taboos, forced men and women to eat separately), and the third was a workshop where women made tapa. Covering the landscaped grounds are native plants that Hawaiians used for food or medicinal purposes, including *kukui* (candlenut) and unusual shampoo ginger.

Lahaina Jodo Mission

A large bronze statue of Buddha overlooks the Lahaina Jodo Mission compound, off the north end of Front St, just before the bridge.

With its back to the mountains, the Buddha looks out over the Pacific toward Japan. Nearby is a 90ft pagoda and an enormous temple bell cast in Kyoto; inside are priceless Buddhist paintings by Haijin Iwasaki.

Just to the north is the long **Mala Wharf**, constructed in the 1920s so that interisland ferries could land passengers directly ashore. It never made the grade. Rough seas prevented the ferries from pulling up alongside the pier, forcing them to continue shuttling passengers across the shallows of Lahaina Harbor in small boats. The wharf is now crumbling and closed, though Mala does have a launch ramp for small boats nearby.

Lahainaluna Road

It's hard to think of tourist-jammed Lahaina as a sugar town, but it is. The dusty **Pioneer Sugar Mill**, which straddles Lahainaluna Rd, has been a prominent part of Lahaina for 140 years. Its cane fields once stretched for 17 miles along the coast, but developers are now eager to tear the defunct mill down.

Lahainaluna Seminary, established by Christian missionaries in 1831, was the first US educational institution west of the Rockies, and the alma mater of David Malo. He became Hawaii's first ordained Christian minister and also its first native-rights spokesperson, warning in his early writings that Hawaii was about to be swallowed up by the masses of foreigners arriving on its shores. His book *Mo'olelo Hawaii* (Hawaiian Antiquities) is regarded as the preeminent published account of ancient Hawaiian history and culture.

Lahainaluna is now Lahaina's public high school, considered one of the finest in the state. Malo is buried on the hillside above the school. The school is at the end of Lahainaluna Rd, above the mill. North of the main parking lot, **Hale Pai** *(admission by donation; open 10am-3pm Mon-Fri)* was the site of the first printing press in Hawaii. Although the main purpose of the press was to make the Bible available to Hawaiians, it was also used to produce other works, including the first Hawaiian botany book and, in 1834, Hawaii's first newspaper. You can use a replica of the original Ramage press to handprint your own copy of a page from the first Hawaiian primer. Reprints of amusing 'Temperance Maps' drawn by an early missionary cost only $5.

Places to Stay

The nearest **camping ground** is in Olowalu, 5 miles south of Lahaina. **Patey's Place** *(☎ 667-0999; dorm bed $20, singles/doubles $44/50, with bath & TV $55/60)*, a branch of the Big Island's Kona hostel by the same name, is Lahaina's only hostel. It's very central, and guests share a common kitchen, coin-operated washer and dryer, lockers and snorkeling gear. Call for more information and directions.

B&Bs Usually the minimum stay in a B&B is three days and advance reservations are necessary.

Bambula Inn *(☎ 667-6753, 800-544-5524, fax 667-0979; W www.maui.net/~bambula; garden rooms $80, studio cottages $100-110)* is a white, tropical delight. All accommodations have a private bath, while the studio cottages also have full kitchens. As a bonus, there's snorkel gear to borrow and free sunset cruises on the family sailboat, with whale sightings practically guaranteed during winter. French and German are spoken.

Aloha Lani Inn *(☎ 661-8040, 800-572-5642, fax 661-8045; e melinda@maui.net; W www.maui-vacations.com/aloha; 13 Kauaula Rd; singles/doubles $69/79)*, about a two-minute walk south of Lahaina Shores, is a homey affordable option. Although it's a modest house, guests are free to use the kitchen and enjoy the endless coffee pot. The guest rooms have shared baths and breakfast is not included. The accommodating owner has added pleasant tropical decor, piled the living room with Hawaiiana books and made it all quite cozy.

Old Lahaina House *(☎ 667-4663, 800-847-0761, fax 669-9199; W www.oldlahaina.com; PO Box 10355, Lahaina, HI 96761; rooms $70-115, suites $150-205)*, also just a few minutes south of Lahaina Shores, is a romantic plantation-style house. All rooms have air-con, TV and telephone. The garden shelters a small swimming pool. Except on Sunday, a breakfast of pastries and fruit is included in the rates.

Inns There's no better accommodation than these jewels.

Lahaina Inn *(☎ 661-0577, 800-669-3444, fax 667-9480; W www.lahainainn.com; 127 Lahainaluna Rd; rooms $109-129, suites $159-169)* is a project of owner Rick Ralston's, who spent over $3 million restoring this century-old 12-room hostelry. The rooms are small but delightfully atmospheric, and each has hardwood floors, floral wallpaper, antique furnishings and a lanai. Modern conveniences include air-con, private bath, telephone and piped-in classical music, but no TV. Prices include continental breakfast. Parking costs $5 per night.

Plantation Inn *(☎ 667-9225, 800-433-6815, fax 667-9293; W www.theplantationinn.com; 174 Lahainaluna Rd; rooms $152-202, suites $215-245)* is an elegant two-story Victorian-style inn with hardwood floors, antique furnishings, stained glass and a tiled pool. There are 19 soundproof rooms and suites. It's arguably the classiest place to stay in Lahaina. Prices include a continental breakfast at Gerard's, the renowned restaurant downstairs at the inn.

Condos & Hotels Keep in mind that there is better condo and hotel accommodation just up the coast, starting at Kaanapali.

Best Western Pioneer Inn *(☎ 661-3636, 800-457-5457, fax 667-5708; W www.pioneerinn-maui.com; 658 Wharf St; rooms $100-165)*, a historic two-story hotel, couldn't be more in the middle of the action. Of course, it can be noisy from the traffic, the tourists and the raucous bar, and, sadly, the funky old harbor-front rooms for which the inn was best known are no longer available. Instead, small motel-style rooms face either Front St, Banyan Square or the inn's courtyard. Considering the size of the rooms and the less-than-soundproof walls, the rates are pricey.

Maui Islander *(☎ 667-9766, 800-462-6262, fax 661-3733; W www.ohanahotels.com; 660 Wainee St; rooms/studios/suites $139/159/199)* is a sprawling low-rise hotel with palm trees and retro kitsch appeal. Air-con rooms are nothing special, but the studio apartments have kitchenettes. Promotional deals can knock 30% or more off the rates. There's a pool, a tennis court and a barbecue area, plus discounts for nearby Gold's Gym.

Lahaina Shores *(☎ 661-3339, 800-642-6284, fax 667-1145; W www.lahaina-shores.com; 475 Front St; mountain-view studios $170, 1-bedroom ocean-view units $270)* is a 155-room condo run like a casual seaside resort hotel. It's on the beach next to the 505 Front St shopping center, at the south side of town. Units are spacious and each has a full kitchen and private lanai. The fifth night is usually free, but if you have to pay rack rates, don't bother.

Makai Inn *(☎ 662-3200, fax 661-9027; W www.makaiinn.net; 1415 Front St; rooms $70-105)*, north of the town center, near the Lahaina Cannery Mall, is close to the shopping shuttle bus route. All of the 400-sq-ft units have full kitchens, and some have panoramic ocean views. Although it's a smaller, older condo complex, there's free parking with no minimum stay. Ask about discounts for longer visits.

Klahani Resorts *(☎ 667-2712, 800-669-6284, fax 661-5875; W www.klahani.com; PO Box 11120, Lahaina, HI 96761)* manages condo rentals at the oceanfront **Lahaina Roads** *(1403 Front St)* complex and also at the **Puamana** clubhouse beside Puamana Beach Park, just south of town.

Places to Eat

Like any beach resort town, many eateries are overpriced and sub-par. Happily, there are exceptions.

Budget Lahaina Square, off Wainee St, has a **Foodland** supermarket, a 24-hour **Denny's** restaurant and **Maui Tacos**. In Lahaina Center, **Paniolo Coffee Co** makes strong brews.

Lahaina Cannery Mall, on the northern side of town, has a 24-hour **Safeway** supermarket with take-out salads and a deli. There's also **Ba Le** for Vietnamese food and upmarket **Compadres**, a Mexican chain that serves tacos and margaritas for $2 each on Tuesday.

Westside Natural Foods & Deli *(193 Lahainaluna Rd; open 7:30am-9pm Mon-Sat, 8:30am-8pm Sun)* sells organic produce, yogurt, fresh juice and a variety of bulk trail mixes and granolas. The deli has a salad bar, a few hot vegetarian dishes and café tables.

The Bakery *(991 Limahana Pl; snacks $1.50-6; open 5:30am-3pm Mon-Fri, 5:30am-2pm Sat, 5:30am-noon Sun)* is Lahaina's best bakery. You can get freshly baked artisan breads, tempting sticky buns and huge muffins, plus sandwiches made to order. To get there, turn *mauka* (inland) off Hwy 30 onto Hinau St at Pizza Hut.

Sunrise Cafe *(693-A Front St; open 6am-6pm daily, food served until 3pm)*, steps away from Lahaina harbor, is an artsy little hole-in-the-wall with cinnamon rolls, bagels, pancakes, salads and sandwiches. Sidewalk tables look out toward the ocean.

Sushi-ya *(117 Prison St; meals $5-7.50; open 6am-4pm Mon-Fri)*, opposite a parking lot, is a little hut bursting with a big reputation. The two-scoop plate lunches with macaroni salad are enormous, and you can get saimin and Spam tempura, too.

Karma Cafe *(888 Wainee St; most snacks $3-7.50; open 8am-5pm Mon-Fri)* has Bohemian staff making specialty smoothies and frappe, and a short menu of 'quick grinds' that includes vegetarian dishes. The atmosphere breathes in meditative calm. In the parking lot around back, **Local Food** take-out counter serves inexpensive Hawaiian plate lunches for under $6.

Aloha Mixed Plate *(1285 Front St; dishes $3-7; open 10:30am-10pm daily)* looks like a fast-food joint, but the oceanfront setting and local fare are worthwhile. Around sunset, you'll be able to overhear Old Lahaina Luau's music next door for free!

Mid-Range Looking for a family-friendly Italian kitchen? **Penne Pasta Cafe** *(180 Dickenson St; mains $6-12; open 11am-10pm Mon-Fri, 5pm-9pm Sat & Sun)* has home-baked cheese flatbread, bountiful Caesar salads, pizza and nearly perfect desserts.

Lahaina Coolers *(180 Dickenson St; breakfast & lunch $5-11, dinner $11-18; open 8am-midnight daily)* is where dive masters from local scuba shops hang out. By all accounts, the usual burgers, salads and sandwiches are decently done, with flashier items like papaya salad or vegan eggs Benedict.

Most people dine on Front St, overlooking the lively street scene and the ocean.

BJ's *(730 Front St; mains $6-15; open 11am-late daily)*, a southern California chain restaurant, takes a stab at thick-crust pizza, as well as hot Italian sandwiches, pasta and salads. Until 4pm, a lunch special of a minipizza and salad costs $6.50.

Moose McGillicuddy's *(☎ 667-7758; 844 Front St; breakfast & lunch $6-11, dinner $11-23; open 7:30am-10pm daily)* buzzes with merry vacationers. And you know what? The food ain't half bad. Old license plates, movie posters and other Americana kitsch fill the walls. Seafood dinners are a bit fancier than lunch, but breakfast is your best bet (and don't forget that wake-up cocktail). There are good specials for early birds.

Lahaina Fish Co *(☎ 661-3472; 831 Front St; mains $10-24; open 11am-midnight daily)*, a wooden maritime eatery, concentrates on the essentials, offering a rainbow of fresh fish and a raw bar. Lunch and late-night grill menus are far simpler, serving fish and chips, crab Louie salad and chowder.

Kimo's *(☎ 661-4811; 845 Front St; lunch $7-11, dinner $15-25; open 11am-11pm daily)* is a popular oceanfront restaurant with a sunset view. It's straightforward but elegant enough with a lanai overlooking the ocean; reservations are advised. Skip the unexciting lunch menu and come for seafood and steak dinners accompanied by carrot muffins, sourdough rolls, herbed rice and a Caesar salad.

Smokehouse BBQ Bar & Grill *(☎ 667-7005; 1307 Front St; sandwiches $7-12, platters $13-20; open noon-9pm Mon-Sat, 3pm-9pm Sun)* is far enough north to leave the crowds behind. This local waterfront bar serves a *kiawe*-smoked barbecue with your choice of sides, plus baked beans and cornbread with macadamia-nut butter. Outdoor lanai tables are right on the beach.

Top End Make reservations, especially for tables with a view.

Canoes *(☎ 661-0937; 1450 Front St; mains $21-40, early-bird dinner 5pm-6pm $16; open 5pm-9:30pm daily, cocktails 4pm-10pm)* could make anyone fall in love. The architecture mimics a traditional Hawaiian canoe house, torchlights flicker and waves can be heard crashing across the road; upper-story tables are open to the sea breezes. The menu emphasizes classic Hawaiian seafood and steaks.

Pacific'O *(☎ 667-4341; 505 Front St; lunch $10-15, dinner $20-30; open 11am-4pm & 5:30pm-10pm daily)* is Lahaina's top fine-dining spot, with beachside tables, impeccable service and imaginative contemporary Pacific cuisine. Start off with the signature seafood chowder, then move on to adventurous dinner mains like fresh fish with banana curry and sun-dried fruit chutney. Lunch is a tame affair.

I'o *(☎ 661-8422; 505 Front Street; mains $18-28; open 5:30pm-9pm daily)*, just opposite Pacific'O, is chef David Paul Johnson's venture into nouveau Hawaiian cuisine. The dining room makes postmodern aquarium chic work, and if you dine early, you'll overhear the **Feast at Lele** luau out back. Count on surprising specials, perhaps fresh oysters with star anise–flavored coconut cream or lobster stir-fry with dark cane rum, and long lists of wine and martinis.

David Paul's Lahaina Grill (☎ *667-5117, 800-360-2606; 127 Lahainaluna Rd; mains $26-33; open from 6pm daily*), in the historic Lahaina Inn, is a respected chef-driven restaurant. In an intimate gallery space, a New American menu mixes local produce with tastes from around the continent and the Pacific Rim. House specialities include tequila shrimp with firecracker rice and a trio of duck confit, macadamia nut–smoked duck breast and foie gras with plum sauce.

Gerard's (☎ *661-8939; 174 Lahainaluna Rd; mains $30-40; open 6pm-9pm daily*) serves traditional French country cooking in a romantic candlelight setting at the Plantation Inn. The Gascony-born chef has always supported local farmers and fishers; the seasonal menu changes regularly, but the rack of lamb and homemade sorbet are house standards. Service is stellar.

Entertainment

Front St is the heart of Lahaina's nightlife. Although much of what's happening on the island after dark happens here, as has been the case since the whaling days of yore, Honolulu it ain't. Check listings in Thursday's *Maui News* or the free weekly *Maui Time*.

Happy hour at bars and restaurants is pretty much nightly from about 3pm to 6pm. **Lahaina Coolers** (*180 Dickenson St; open 8am-midnight daily*) also has a late-night happy hour from 10pm until 2am, which is closing time for most bars and clubs. For live entertainment, expect cover charges of $5 to $10 on weekends.

Maui Brews (☎ *667-7794; Lahaina Center*) has a big-screen sports TV in the bar and nightly dancing in the adjacent club, with a mix of DJ nights and live reggae, salsa, island sounds and jazz after 9pm. Both the bar and the club have a good selection of beers on tap, including Hawaiian microbrews.

Hard Rock Café (☎ *667-7400; Lahaina Center*) sometimes catches big-name acts and radio DJs on weekends. There's usually no cover charge, so who's complaining?

Moose McGillicuddy's (☎ *667-7758; 844 Front St; open 7:30am-10pm daily*) has DJs or live music nightly from 9:30pm. Honeymooners, frat boys and everyone else rub shoulders (and just about any other body part you can think of) here.

Pioneer Inn (*658 Wharf St*), a century-old landmark, has a harborside veranda made for people watching. Musicians stroll among the bar tables almost nightly starting around sunset.

Many other Front St restaurants use live music or dancing as bait to lure customers. **Longhi's** (*888 Front St*), which has an interesting koa-wood dance floor, has live rock bands from around 9:30pm on Friday. **BJ's** (*730 Front St; open 11am-late daily*) has live music nightly from 6pm to 8pm; incidentally, this was where the legendary 1970s Blue Max club partied. **Pacific'O** (☎ *667-4341; 505 Front St; open 11am-4pm & 5:30pm-10pm daily*), overlooking the beach, has live jazz from 9pm to midnight on weekends.

Cinemas Lahaina Wharf Cinemas (*Wharf Cinema Center*) and **Front Street Theatres** (*Lahaina Center*) are multiscreen theaters showing first-run movies. For showtimes, call ☎ 249-2222.

Hawaii Experience Domed Theater (☎ *661-8314; 824 Front St; adult/child $7/4; semi-hourly screenings 1pm-9pm daily*) has been showing the same 40-minute film about Hawaii for ages, but on an enormous 180° screen it may be worth it for the aerial photography alone.

Hula & Luaus Old Lahaina Luau (☎ *667-1998, 800-248-5828;* W *www.oldlahainaluau.com; 1251 Front St; adult/child $75/45; luau 5:30pm-8:30pm daily*), on the beach near the Lahaina Cannery Mall, is often voted the most authentic Hawaiian luau on the island. It also runs a Polynesian-style dance show **The Feast at Lele** (☎ *667-5353; 505 Front St; adult/child $90/60*) with a gourmet four-course meal. The luau starts at 5:30pm (April to September) or 6pm (October to March).

There are free **keiki hula shows** at 1pm on Saturday and Sunday at the Lahaina Cannery Mall, which hosts Polynesian dance performances at 7pm on Tuesday and Thursday.

Shopping

Lahaina has numerous arts and crafts galleries, some with high-quality collections and others with mediocre works. 'Art night,' held from 6pm to around 9pm on Friday, is when Lahaina galleries schedule their openings, occasionally with entertainment and hors d'oeuvres.

A good place to start is the **Lahaina Arts Society** *(☎ 667-9193, 866-511-4569; W www.visitlahaina.com; 648 Wharf St; open 9am-5pm daily)*, the **Village Gallery** *(☎ 661-4402, 800-483-8599; 120 Dickenson St)* or the **Village Gallery Contemporary** *(☎ 661-5559; 180 Dickenson Square)*.

Whaler's Locker *(☎ 661-3775; 780 Front St)* offers the best quality and prices of the many, many scrimshaw and netsuke shops on Front St. Amber and shark's teeth are sold.

Island Sandals *(☎ 661-5110; W www.islandsandals.com; 658 Front St)*, tucked around the side of the Wharf Cinema Center, offers quality handmade leather sandals for $125 to $155.

Na Mea Hawaii Store *(☎ 661-3262; 698 Front St)* carries aloha shirts, feathered lei hats, native flora and fauna prints and Hawaiiana books.

Old Lahaina Book Emporium *(☎ 661-1399; 505 Front St; open 10am-9pm Mon-Sat, 10am-6pm Sun)*, Maui's largest independent bookstore, is stacked with all types of new and used volumes, plus vintage Hawaiiana.

Dan's Green House *(☎ 661-8412, 133 Prison St)* sells *fuku-bonsai*, a quasi-bonsai effect created when the roots of the common houseplant *schefflera* (octopus tree) grow around a lava rock. Also for sale are orchids, proteas, coconut-tree sprouts and Hawaiian ti-leaf plants.

Getting Around

Finding a space for your car in Lahaina can be a challenge. Front St has on-street parking, but there's always a line of cruising cars. There's free public parking with a three-hour limit at the south end of Front St. There are also a few private parking lots, averaging $5 per day. Otherwise, park at one of the shopping centers and get your parking ticket validated for free by making a small purchase (suntan oil, bottled water etc).

LAHAINA TO KAANAPALI

On the stretch from Lahaina to Kaanapali, the driving can be aggressive, and traffic often jams up, particularly during morning and late-afternoon rush hours.

Wahikuli Wayside Beach Park, about 2 miles north of Lahaina, occupies a narrow strip of beach between the highway and the ocean. With a gift for prophecy, the Hawaiians named this coastal stretch Wahikuli, or 'noisy place.' The beach is mostly backed by a black-rock retaining wall, though there's a small sandy area. If you don't mind the traffic noise, the swimming conditions are usually fine, and when the water's calm, you can snorkel near the lava outcroppings at the park's south end. There are showers, rest rooms, parking and picnic tables.

Hanakaoo Beach Park is a long sandy beach just south of Kaanapali Beach Resort. It has full facilities and a lifeguard on duty daily. As with all public beach parks, the parking here is free. The beach has a sandy bottom, and water conditions are usually quite safe for swimming. However, southerly swells, which sometimes develop in the summer, can create powerful waves and shorebreaks, while the occasional *kona* storm can kick up rough water conditions in winter.

Gentler shorebreaks are favored by boogie boarders and surfers. You can snorkel down by the second clump of rocks on the south side of the beach park, but it doesn't compare with sites further north. Hanakaoo Beach is also called Canoe Beach, as local canoe clubs store their outriggers here. You can see them paddling up and down the coast in the early mornings and late afternoons.

KAANAPALI

In the late 1950s, Amfac, owner of the Pioneer Sugar Mill, earmarked 600 acres of relatively barren sugarcane land for development as the first resort outside Waikiki. Now Kaanapali is lined with high-rise oceanfront hotels, condominium complexes, two 18-hole golf courses, 40 tennis courts and the Whalers Village shopping center. Despite the opulence of some of its lodgings, the overall development is rather generic – the influence is as much southern Californian as Hawaiian.

Kaanapali boasts 3 miles of sandy beach and pleasant views across Auau Channel to Lanai and Molokai. While Kaanapali is not a 'getaway' in the sense of avoiding the crowds, it has its quieter niches. The north side of Puu Kekaa (Black Rock), for instance, and the condos up around the golf course are less busy than the central beach area.

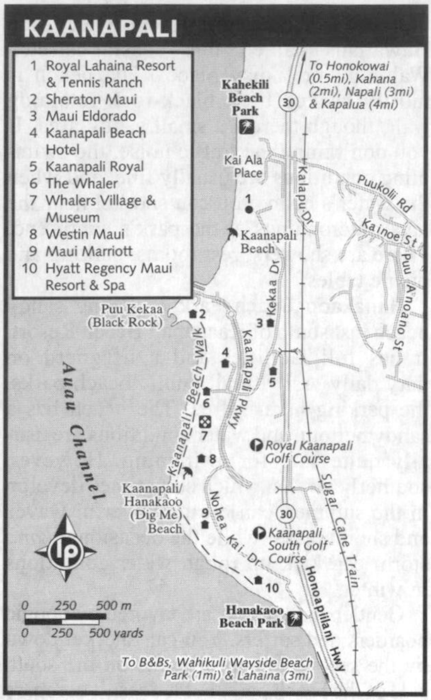

Whalers Village Museum

The high point of any trip to Kaanapali is this small but top-notch **whaling museum** (*☎ 661-4567; Level 3, Whalers Village, 2345 Kaanapali Pkwy; admission free; open 9:30am-10pm daily*). Period photos and detailed interpretive boards sound the depths of whaling history. There are harpoons, whale jawbones and all sorts of scrimshaw, perhaps the only folk art unique to the USA. For a small donation, riveting audio guides are available in four languages.

In the 19th century, whales were considered a 'floating gold mine' of oil, spermaceti, blubber and baleen; prior to the invention of durable plastic, baleen was used for things like corsets and umbrella stays. A lot of the character of the whalers comes through, and you'll get a feel for how rough and dirty the work was. Wages were so low that sailors sometimes owed the ship money by the time they got home and had to sign up for another four-year stint just to pay off the debt.

A film on whales plays continuously next to the museum shop, which sells excellent scrimshaw carvings and audio recordings of New England whaling songs. There's a full-size **sperm whale skeleton** at the front entrance to the shopping center.

Kaanapali Beaches

Kaanapali is really two beaches, with Puu Kekaa (Black Rock) the dividing mark. Officially the stretch north of Black Rock to Honokowai is Kaanapali Beach, while everything south down to the Hyatt is an extension of Hanakaoo Beach Park, here nicknamed 'Dig Me Beach.'

Public beach parking is ridiculously limited; follow the blue shoreline access signs. The Hyatt has free 'self parking' for hotel guests on its south side. Whalers Village offers three hours of public parking with free validation if you spend more than $10 at any of the shops or restaurants. You can also park for free at Kahekili Beach Park and stroll down along the shore.

Kaanapali Hanakaoo Beach Much of the stretch between the Sheraton and the Hyatt can be dangerous, particularly on the point in front of the Marriott, where strong currents sometimes develop. As a general rule, waters are rougher in winter, though actually the worst conditions can occur in early summer if there's a southerly swell.

Be careful in rough surf, as the waves can pick you up and bounce you onto the coral reef that runs from the southern end of the Westin down to the Hyatt, where it's possible to snorkel. Check with the hotel beach huts for the day's water conditions before jumping in.

Puu Kekaa Also known as Black Rock, Puu Kekaa (Kekaa Point) is the rocky lava promontory that protects the beach in front of the Sheraton. This is Kaanapali's safest and best spot for swimming and snorkeling.

You can snorkel along the southern side of Black Rock, where you'll find some nice coral and schools of fish that are used to being fed. The real prize, however, is the horseshoe cove cut into the tip of the rock, where there's more pristine coral, along with abundant tropical fish and the occasional turtle. It's a popular shore-dive spot.

There's often a current to contend with off the point, which can make getting to the cove a little risky, but when it's calm you can swim right around into the horseshoe. Check with the Sheraton beach hut or snorkelers in

Souls Leap

According to traditional Hawaiian beliefs, Puu Kekaa (Black Rock), the westernmost point of Maui, is a place where the spirits of the dead leap into the unknown and are carried to their ancestral homeland.

The rock itself is said to have been created during a scuffle between the demigod Maui and a commoner who questioned Maui's superiority. Maui chased the man to this point, killed him, then froze his body into stone and cast his soul out to sea.

the water for current conditions. If you want to see what the horseshoe cove looks like, you can peer down into it by taking the short footpath from the Sheraton beach to the top of Puu Kekaa.

Kaanapali Beach Walk A mile-long paved beach walk runs between the Hyatt and the Sheraton. In addition to the coastal scenery, both the Hyatt and Westin have some striking garden artwork valued at $2 million each and landscaping worth a detour. If you stroll in the early evening, you'll often be treated to beachside entertainment, most notably in front of Whalers Village and the Marriott, which holds its luau on the oceanfront.

Kahekili Beach Park This beach park at the north side of Kaanapali Beach is dedicated to Kahekili Nui Ahumanu, the last king of Maui. Also called Airport Beach, the park has golden sand and shady palm trees. The waters here are open ocean, but inshore it's usually calm and good for swimming.

If you walk north for about 20 minutes, you'll come to a reef around Honokowai Point, where the clear waters are good for snorkeling when it's calm. Keep your eyes on the shore, though, as currents can be strong.

The beach park has free parking, showers, changing rooms, toilets, a covered picnic pavilion and barbecue grills. To get there from Honoapiilani Hwy, turn west past the 25-mile marker onto Kai Ala Place (opposite Puukolii Rd), then bear right.

Activities

Kaanapali Golf (☎ *661-3691; 2290 Kaanapali Pkwy; green fees & shared cart guests/nonguests $130/150, rates after 2:30pm $75*) has fairways near the highway and the condo complexes. The Tournament North course is slightly less windy than golfing at scenic Kapalua.

Royal Lahaina Tennis Ranch (☎ *667-5200; Royal Lahaina Resort; adult/child under 18 $10/free*) is the largest tennis complex in west Maui, with a 3500-seat stadium and six courts lit for night play. Daily clinics are taught by pros. Passes are also valid at the tennis courts found at the **Maui Marriott Beach & Tennis Club** and the **Sheraton Maui**.

Places to Stay

There are a few B&Bs up in the residential hills between Lahaina and Kaanapali.

House of Fountains (☎ *667-2121, 800-789-6865, fax 667-2120;* W *www.alohahouse.com; 1579 Lokia St; rooms/studios/suites $95/115/145*) has tropical-style accommodations varying from simple rooms to spacious suites, all with air-con, private bath and a full German-style breakfast. Amenities include a guest kitchen, ocean-view sundeck, swimming pool and Jacuzzi. German is spoken.

The GuestHouse B&B (☎ *661-8085, 800-621-8942, fax 661-1896;* W *www.mauiguest house.com; 1620 Ainakea Rd; singles/suites $115/130*) is another modern home, but this time with more tropical Hawaiian touches. It also has a swimming pool. Each large suite has air-con, a telephone, private lanai and its own hot tub or Jacuzzi. Privacy is easy to come by here. Rates include breakfast and free email, laundry facilities, full kitchen access and use of beach gear.

All Kaanapali resort accommodations are either on the beach or within walking distance of it, and all have the expected amenities, including swimming pools. Rooms tend to be boxy, and many are showing their age. Condos farther north along the coast are usually better value.

Kaanapali Royal (☎ *667-7200, 800-676-4112, fax 661-5611;* W *www.kaanapaliroyal.com; 2560 Kekaa Dr; 2-bedroom units from $275*) is a bargain for families. Spacious 2-bedroom units with full kitchen, washer and dryer can sleep up to six people. A heated swimming pool and tennis courts are on-site.

Maui Eldorado (☎ *661-0021, 800-688-7444, fax 667-7039;* W *www.outrigger.com; 2661 Kekaa Dr; studios/1-bedroom units from $195/245*) is a posh low-rise condo complex up the hill from the beach, set on the golf course. Large studios have separate kitchens, as do apartment units. The rack rates are a joke, however. Check the website for discount deals.

For general information on current hotel promotions, visit the Kaanapali resort online (W www.maui.net/~kbra).

Kaanapali Beach Hotel (☎ *661-0011, 800-262-8450, fax 667-5978;* W *www.kbhmaui.com; 2525 Kaanapali Pkwy; rooms/suites from $165/250)* has an enviable beachside location between Whalers Village and Puu Kekaa. While it's an older complex, it's pleasantly low-key and achieves top marks for its Hawaiian hospitality. Free introductory scuba lessons are given daily in the whale-shaped swimming pool.

The Whaler (☎ *661-3484, 800-676-4112, fax 661-8338;* W *www.vacation-maui.com/whaler; 2481 Kaanapali Pkwy; studios $175-205, 1-bedroom-/2-bedroom units from $225/400)*, next to Whalers Village, is a flower-laden high-rise condo complex overlooking a boisterous stretch of beach. It has a $35 check-in fee and parking costs $7. Make sure you get a discount from Whalers Realty, or search the Internet for ads by private condo owners.

Hyatt Regency Maui Resort & Spa (☎ *661-1234, 800-233-1234, fax 667-4497;* W *www.maui.hyatt.com; 200 Nohea Kai Dr; rooms/suites from $275/600)* has priceless artwork, an oceanfront spa and a huge meandering swimming pool with grottoes and a 150ft water slide. Newly renovated rooms have standard Hyatt decor and amenities.

Sheraton Maui (☎ *661-0031, 800-782-9488, fax 661-0458;* W *www.sheraton-hawaii.com; 2605 Kaanapali Pkwy; rooms with garden/ocean view $350/500, suites from $750)* has the prime beach spot, in front of Puu Kekaa. Completely closed down and rebuilt in 1997 to the tune of $150 million, rooms are not quite worth the rates.

Places to Eat

All of the Kaanapali hotels have restaurants, some formal and expensive, others more casual. Your only other option is the Whalers Village shopping center, which has a few fast-food options, mostly in the basement-level **food court**, as well as a café or two.

Hula Grill & Barefoot Bar (☎ *667-6636; appetizers $7-15, mains $10-25; bar open 11am-11pm daily, restaurant 5pm-9:30pm daily)*, which has outdoor dining, a *kiawe* grill and a wood-fired pizza oven, distinguishes itself with the culinary arts of Peter Merriman's Hawaii regional cuisine. Enjoy inventive *pupu*s (hors d'oeuvres) at the sandy beachside bar, or make reservations for the more formal Hula Grill dining room, with heavy-hitters like lobster, fresh fish and steak.

You could easily while away the better part of a morning at one of the resort hotel buffets before hitting the beach.

Swan Court *(Hyatt Regency Maui Resort & Spa; breakfast buffet $20; open 6:30am-11:30am daily)* has a movie-star setting overlooking a swan pond with artificial waterfalls and a Japanese garden.

Kaanapali Mixed Plate Restaurant *(Kaanapali Beach Hotel; buffet for adult/child $9.50/6.50; open 6am-10:45am & 11am-2pm daily)*, is not notable for its culinary delights, but you can certainly eat your fill here of fresh pineapple, eggs, Portuguese sausage, cereals and coffee.

Most lunch options are overpriced. The **Beachfront Market & Pantry** *(Maui Marriott)* does have affordable picnic fixings.

Tropica (☎ *667-2525; Westin Maui, 2365 Kaanapali Pkwy; bar menu $7-15, dinner $17-35, 3-course tasting menu $25; open 5:30pm-9:30pm daily, bar open 3pm-midnight)*, a poolside bar and grill, has a 'fire and ice' menu, ranging from lobster in chili-pepper butter to Hawaiian oysters with cool tropical salsa. Desserts are equally dramatic; the chocolate lava of Pele's Inferno ($9) feeds two.

Teppanyaki Dan *(Sheraton Maui; dinner $20-42; open 6pm-9pm Tues-Sat)* is a Japanese restaurant specializing in *teppanyaki* (a style of cooking over an open grill). Chefs prepare the authentic meals with fresh Hawaiian ingredients right at your table, while you enjoy the restaurant's ocean view. Choose perhaps the steak or Maui lobster with lemongrass essence, finished off with a light citrus or nutty dessert.

Entertainment

Whalers Village (☎ *661-4567; 2435 Kaanapali Pkwy)* has a full calendar of lei making, sand sculpture and other arts classes during the afternoons, then live Hawaiian music, hula and Polynesian dance performances starting at 7pm some nights.

There's often contemporary or Hawaiian music outdoors in the evening at the Whalers Village restaurants, too. **Hula Grill & Barefoot Bar** has sunset Hawaiian music until 8pm daily.

Rusty Harpoon *(☎ 661-3123; Whalers Village)* has even longer happy hours (2pm to 6pm and 10pm to closing) and elevated views over the beach. Patrons come for the pub fare and big-screen satellite TVs.

Many of the Kaanapali hotels feature a variety of entertainment, including dance bands, jazz pianists, Hawaiian music and Polynesian revues. In the courtyard of the **Kaanapali Beach Hotel** there's a free hula show at 6:30pm nightly, followed by Hawaiian music until 9:30pm at the Tiki Terrace.

Sheraton Maui has a torch-lighting and cliff-diving ceremony at sunset nightly, with hula dancing from 6pm to 8pm nightly at its Lagoon Bar.

Hyatt Regency Maui Resort has a torch-lighting ceremony at around 6:15pm daily, followed by Hawaiian music until 9:30pm in the Weeping Banyan Lounge.

Westin Maui *(☎ 667-2525; 2365 Kaanapali Pkwy)* has live Hawaiian entertainment from 5pm to 7pm Monday to Friday, followed by live bands or DJs almost nightly at its poolside bar and grill.

The Kaanapali resort hotel luaus include an *imu* ceremony (when the pig is roasted in an underground oven), open bar, a buffet dinner and Polynesian dance and music show. Just don't expect authenticity. Reservations are required. Most of the shows are held outdoors, so you can get a preview of them by walking along the beach. The best is probably the Hyatt Regency's **Drums of the Pacific** *(nonguests adult/teen/child $75/49/30; open 5:30pm-8pm nightly)*.

Shopping

Whalers Village *(☎ 661-4567; 2435 Kaanapali Pkwy; open 9:30am-10pm daily)* has three levels with more than 50 shops, including upscale clothing stores, souvenir shops, **Waldenbooks**, **Wolf Camera**, antiquarian **Lahaina Printsellers**, **Noa Noa** for Polynesian batik, **Crazy Shirts** and the discount **ABC store**.

Getting Around

A free shuttle runs between the Kaanapali hotels, Whalers Village shopping center, the golf course and the Sugar Cane Train's Kaanapali station approximately every half hour between 9am and 8pm.

Other buses connect Kaanapali with Lahaina, Kapalua, south Maui and the airport; for details, see Getting Around earlier in this chapter.

HONOKAWAI

North of Kaanapali, the road forks. If you want to zip up to the northern beaches, bypassing the condos and resorts, the main road is Honoapiilani Hwy (Hwy 30), which has a bicycle lane. The parallel shoreline road is Lower Honoapiilani Rd, which leads into Honokowai.

To the degree that Kaanapali is a planned community, Honokowai is an unplanned one, consisting mainly of a stretch of assorted condos squeezed between the shoreline and Lower Honoapiilani Rd. The main reason most tourists are here is because the condos are relatively cheap.

Honokowai Beach Park is largely lined with a submerged rock shelf and has poor swimming conditions with shallow water. Most people staying here head to Kaanapali for swimming and snorkeling. Despite the rocky shoreline, the area does have fine views of Molokai and Lanai.

Places to Stay

Most complexes are a bit older and require at least a three-day minimum booking, with surcharges for stays of less than a week.

Hale Maui *(☎ 669-6312, fax 669-1302; W www.maui.net/~halemaui; Lower Honoapiilani Rd, 1-bedroom units $75-95)* has no views and no telephones, but it's right on the beach. Each unit in this mustard-yellow apartment building has a full kitchen. German is spoken.

Honokowai Palms *(☎ 667-2712, 800-669-0795, fax 661-5875; 3666 Lower Honoapiilani Rd; 1-bedroom/2-bedroom units $75)* is a two-story, cinder-block building on the *mauka* side of the road. It's a simple place, but it does have a pool and cheap rates.

Kaleialoha *(☎ 669-8197, 800-222-8688, fax 669-2502; W www.mauicondosoceanfront.com; 3785 Lower Honoapiilani Rd; studios $95, 1-bedroom units $115-125)* has beachfront condos with full kitchens, washers and dryers. Studios face the road. Ask about promotional discounts.

MAUI

Hoyochi Nikko *(☎ 662-0807, 800-487-6002, fax 662-1277; 🅦 www.mauilodging.com/lodging/hoyochi.htm; 3901 Lower Honoapiilani Rd; units $100-165)*, a Maui Lodging property, looks like a traditional Japanese inn, but has average modern interiors. It's almost hidden from the road, with every unit facing the ocean. Each unit has a fully equipped kitchen, washer and dryer; units 202 and 203 have second-bedroom lofts.

Mahina Surf *(☎ 669-6068, 800-367-6086, fax 669-4534; 🅦 www.mahinasurf.com; 4057 Lower Honoapiilani Rd; 1-bedroom/2-bedroom units from $125/155)* borders Kahana. This low-rise complex is nicely set around a large grassy yard with a heated pool. All units are spacious and have kitchens, VCRs, phones and ocean-view lanai. If you're a member of the American Automobile Association (AAA) or the American Association of Retired Persons (AARP), ask for discounts.

Noelani *(☎ 669-8374, 800-367-6030, fax 669-7904; 🅦 www.noelani-condo-resort.com; 4095 Lower Honoapiilani Rd; studio $110, 1-bedroom/2-bedroom/3-bedroom units from $150/210/270)* has aloha atmosphere, plenty of palm trees, two freshwater pools and a startling array of discounts. Each units is right on the beach, with an ocean-facing lanai, full kitchen, sofa bed, phone, TV and VCR; all but the studios have washers and dryers. There are two pools and a Jacuzzi.

MAUI

Places to Eat

For fresh fruits and vegetables, visit the **farmers market** *(held 7am-11:30am Mon, Wed & Fri)* that sets up south of the ABC store, located on Lower Honoapiilani Rd.

Honokowai Okazuya & Deli *(open 10am-2:30pm & 4:30pm-9pm Mon-Sat; dishes $6-10; 3600 Lower Honoapiilani Rd)*, which makes a good chicken Caesar salad and a delicious mahimahi dish with lemon, capers and rice, is a long-running local fave.

Honokowai Marketplace *(3350 Lower Honoapiilani Rd)* has a **Star Market** for groceries and several budget fast-food eateries, including award-winning desserts at **Hula Scoops**. Nearby **Java Jazz & Soup Nutz** is an arty and jazzy café, with strong java to boot. The adjoining kitchen serves a short menu of gourmet soups, sandwiches and pasta, all under $10.

KAHANA

Kahana is the newer high-rise stretch immediately north of Honokowai. It's more upscale, with condo and room rates averaging well above $100. White-sand **Kahana Beach** has reasonable swimming conditions; for snorkeling, a good area is along the rocky outcropping at the north side of the Kahana Sunset condominium complex. However, there's no public access.

The **Kahana Gateway shopping center** *(4405 Honoapiilani Hwy)* has a gas station, a Bank of Hawaii with an ATM, an Internet café and a coin laundry (last wash 8pm daily). The **Kahana Manor** *(4310 Lower Honoapiilani Rd)* has a convenience store, pub and one-hour photo lab.

Places to Stay & Eat

Royal Kahana *(☎ 669-5911, 800-688-7444, fax 669-5950; 🅦 www.outrigger.com; 4365 Lower Honoapiilani Rd; studios with garden/ocean view $210/230, 1-bedroom units $265-290)* is an enormous white high-rise, but the location near the beach and the shopping center is ideal. The units are spacious, modern and comfortable, mostly with full kitchens, private lanai, washers and dryers. Amenities include a heated pool, two tennis courts, a small fitness room and sauna. Visit the website for special packages.

At the Kahana Gateway, **Whalers General Store** *(open 6:30am-11pm daily)* offers a few fast-food items. **Ashley's Internet Café** *(☎ 669-0949)* serves prized ice-cream sundaes, deli sandwiches and local mixed-plate lunches (under $8).

Roy's Kahana Bar & Grill *(☎ 669-6999; mains $16.50-27; open 5:30pm-9:30pm daily)* and **Roy's Nicolina Restaurant***(☎ 669-5000)* are branches of the renowned Roy's in Honolulu. Each features a contemporary Eurasian blend of French techniques with Japanese and Hawaiian culinary traditions. Dominated by a copper exhibition kitchen, the grill has 40ft-high ceilings, koa furniture and artwork; Nicolina, right next door, is quieter. Half of each menu is devoted to Roy's classic dishes, such as Sichuan ribs and Upcountry salads, while another fresh sheet of imaginative daily specials is created by individual head chefs. Dining at either place might be an unforgettable experience – especially after tasting the chocolate souffle.

Fish & Game Brewing House & Rotisserie *(☎ 669-3474; Kahana Gateway; bar menu $5-13, lunch $8-18, dinner $24-35; open 11am-1am daily)* must have mighty chutzpah to open a restaurant anywhere near Roy's. That said, the rotisserie chicken, sandwiches and shellfish flown in from the Pacific northwest all go down well with microbrews at this sports bar with a clubby dining room.

NAPILI

Napili Kai Beach Club, built in 1962, was the first hotel north of Kaanapali. To protect the bay, as well as their investment, Napili Kai organized area landowners and petitioned the county to create a zoning bylaw restricting all Napili Bay buildings to the height of a coconut tree.

Consequently, Napili today is one of the more relaxed niches on the coast. And it's so easy to fall in love with this, Maui's sunniest neighborhood, which thrives on repeat visitors. Most of Napili's condos are on the beach and for the most part are away from the road and the sound of traffic.

Napili Bay has a beautiful, curved, golden-sand beach, with excellent swimming and snorkeling when it's calm. Big waves occasionally make it into the bay in the winter, attracting bodysurfers, but also creating strong rip currents.

Places to Stay & Eat

Most accommodations in Napili require a minimum stay of three to five days.

Hale Napili *(☎ 669-6184, 800-245-2266, fax 665-0066; Ⓦ www.maui.net/~halenapi; 65 Hui Dr; garden/oceanfront studios $110/150, 1-bedroom units $175)* is a well-maintained little condo complex on the beach. The Hawaiian management couldn't be friendlier, so it books up quickly. All rooms have full kitchens, queen and sofa beds, TVs, phones with answering machines, ceiling fans, and lanai. Ask about off-season and promotional discounts.

Napili Shores *(☎ 669-8061, 800-688-7444, fax 669-5407; 5315 Lower Honoapiilani Rd; Ⓦ www.outrigger.com; garden/oceanfront studio $177/233, garden/oceanfront 1-bedroom unit $211/239)* has extremely helpful staff. It's quiet enough to really appreciate the setting. Low-lying buildings stretch down to the beach along a grassy expanse, past a swimming pool and gazebo restaurant. There's also a convenience store here. Check the website for discounts.

Napili Kai Beach Club *(☎ 669-6271, 800-367-5030, fax 669-0086; Ⓦ www.napilikai.com; 5900 Lower Honoapiilani Rd; rooms with/without kitchenette from $220/190, suites with full kitchen $360-760)*, at the northern end of Napili Bay, is a sprawling resort with an oceanfront swimming pool. The staff are friendly – almost pampering. The beautiful units are tasteful, with Polynesian decor and nice touches like Japanese shoji dividers and private lanai. The catch here is the price, but the maximum number of guests per unit is gratifyingly high. Ask about special deals on car rentals.

Sea House Restaurant *(Napili Kai Beach Club; lunch $4-12, dinner mains $18-27; open 8am-10:30am, 11:30am-2pm & 5:30pm-9pm daily)* has an appealing setting and features open-air dining with a sunset view. If only the American cooking could compare (it doesn't). A Friday night dinner buffet (adult/child $35/20) features a hula show by local children; reservations are required.

Napili Plaza *(cnr Napilihau St & Hwy 30)* shopping center has a **grocery store** *(open 6:30am-11pm daily)* and lots of budget eats. Try **The Coffee Store, Maui Tacos**, or **Mama's Ribs Rotisserie** *(open 11am-7pm daily)* for local mixed-plate lunches (under $10).

KAPALUA

The Kapalua resort development has the upscale Kapalua Bay and Ritz-Carlton hotels, some luxury condos, a few restaurants and three golf courses. It's a small, uncrowded development – the most exclusive in northwest Maui – with the finest sushi on the island and beautiful beaches that make it worth the drive.

Kapalua Beach

Kapalua Beach, at Kapalua Bay, is a pretty white-sand crescent beach with a clear view of Molokai across the channel. The long rocky outcroppings at both ends of the bay make Kapalua Beach the safest year-round swimming spot on this coast. There's good snorkeling on the right side of the beach, where you'll find lots of large tangs, butterfly fish, wrasses and orange slate-pencil sea urchins.

Take the paved drive immediately north of Napili Kai Beach Club, which is marked

Bone Rattling

The Honokahua sand dunes just south of Fleming Beach were excavated in 1988 during the construction of the Ritz-Carlton hotel. After skeletal remains were found, an earthshaking controversy broke loose.

The Honokahua burial ground is thought to contain the remains of over 2000 Hawaiians who were returned to their *one hanau* (birth sands) here between AD 950 and the 18th century. Keeping ancestral bones safely undisturbed has long been an important duty for traditional Hawaiians. In ancient times, islanders often went to great lengths to hide said bones inside elaborate burial chambers, lava tubes or underwater grottoes. Some believed that by 'planting' the bones in the ground, their ancestors would nourish them, both spiritually and physically, through crops that sprouted there.

After repeated protests by native Hawaiian activists, construction at Honokahua was eventually halted, the skeletons were reinterred and the hotel site was relocated *mauka* of the seaside graves. But the political momentum didn't stop there. Island burial councils are now overseeing the repatriation of native Hawaiian remains from leading institutions around the world. As for the Ritz-Carlton, it ironically now prides itself on leading 'culturally sensitive' tours of the burial site for guests.

by a blue shoreline access sign, to get to a parking area with about 25 public spaces. A tunnel from the parking lot leads under the Bay Club restaurant to the beach.

Oneloa Beach

This forgotten beach is near the Ritz-Carlton resort, off the lower links of the Ironwoods golf course; turn north at the end of Office Rd to find a few casual parking spots. Most of the beachfront itself is rocky, with strong rip currents and swells. If you walk around the monument (see the boxed text 'Bone Rattling') and out to Makaluapuna Point, you'll reach the spiky lava formations called **Dragon's Teeth**, carved by erosion and sea salt. You can also get here from the west end of DT Fleming Beach Park, but this requires picking your way carefully across fields of light-colored lava.

Activities

Kapalua Dive Company (☎ *662-0872, 877-669-3448, fax 662-0692;* 🅦 *www.kapaluadive.com; tours from $90)* has divers use specially designed kayaks to paddle for about 20 minutes from Kapalua Beach out to Hawea Point, where sea turtles are numerous. Other 'mixed plate' dive packages are available, too.

Kapalua Golf (☎ *669-8044, 877-527-2582; 2000 Village Rd; green fees & cart, resort guests/nonguests from $115/160)* manages the Plantation course, where the PGA Mercedes Championships are held each January, and the Bay and Village courses, both designed by Arnold Palmer.

Kapalua Tennis *(Tennis Garden* ☎ *669-5677, Village Tennis Center* ☎ *665-0112; resort guests/nonguests $10/12, racquet rental $6)* is near the Ritz-Carlton.

Check with the **Kapalua Shops** (☎ *800-527-2582;* 🅦 *www.kapaluamaui.com)* for information on slack-key guitar and hula performances, plus beginning hula and lei-making workshops.

Organized Tours

Maui Pineapple Company, which is the only pineapple canning company operating in the US, opens its fields for **educational tours** (☎ *669-8088; adult $26; 2½hr tours 9:30am & 1pm Mon-Fri)* led by the Kapalua Nature Society. Reservations are required, and you must wear covered shoes (no sandals). Check in 30 minutes in advance at the Kapalua Villas reception center, opposite Honolua Store.

Places to Stay

The **Kapalua Villas** (☎ *669-8088, 800-545-0018, fax 669-5234;* 🅦 *www.kapaluavillas.com; 500 Office Rd; 1-bedroom units $199-279, 2-bedroom units $299-469)* are luxury condos sleeping four to six people each, making them quite a bargain. The Bay Villas are closest to the beach, but the Ridge Villas up on the golf course also have ocean views. Full resort amenities include free tennis. Ask about special promotional packages.

Kapalua Bay Hotel (☎ *669-5656, 800-367-8000, fax 669-4694;* 🅦 *www.kapaluabayhotel.com; 1 Bay Dr; rooms with garden/ocean view from $350/510)* is a stylish complex on the beach. Breathe in the sea breezes on open-air walkways, or recline on tropical cane and koa wood furniture in the lobby. Demonstrations of Hawaiian arts take place daily, with live Hawaiian guitar music every evening in the Lehua Lounge.

Places to Eat

Honolua Store *(Office Rd; lunches $4-6; open until 3pm)* is an old general store that has a cafeteria-style deli serving local food (takeout only) like stew and fried chicken .

Sansei Seafood Restaurant & Sushi Bar *(☎ 669-6286; Kapalua Shops; à la carte dishes $4-19, mains $16-24; open 5:30pm-10pm daily)*, with antique sake bottles and Japanese paper kites all around, lets you feast on innovative, prize-winning hot appetizers, as well as classic sushi and sashimi. No matter where on the island you have to drive from, you won't regret making the pilgrimage here. It has good early-bird discounts.

Plantation House Restaurant *(☎ 669-6299; 2000 Plantation Club Dr; breakfast $5-15, lunch $8-14, dinner $22-30; open 8am-3pm & 5:30pm-9pm daily)*, at the golf course, looks somewhat exclusive but has a fine view across the fairways clear down to the ocean. Best are the breakfast dishes, from Cajun-spiced sashimi eggs Benedict to fresh-picked pineapple in cinnamon sauce. Dinner is a much pricier affair with seafood, duck and steak main courses. Come for sunset cocktails at the **bar**.

NORTHERN BEACHES

Kapalua marks the end of development on the west Maui coast. From there on, it's all rural Hawaii, with golf carts giving way to pickup trucks and old cars with surfboards tied on top. The coast gets more lush and scenically rugged as you go along. Quickly you meet the beginning of the Kahekili Hwy, and it's possible to continue around on this coastal road to the Kahului–Wailuku area of central Maui.

DT Fleming Beach Park

At the north side of Kapalua on Honokohau Bay, this county beach park has rest rooms, picnic facilities and showers. It was named after the Scotsman who first developed the area's pineapple industry. Look for the blue shoreline access sign after the 31-mile marker on the *makai* side of Hwy 30.

The long sandy beach is backed by ironwood trees. The conditions are good for surfing and bodysurfing, with winter providing the biggest waves. The shorebreaks can be tough, however, and this beach is second only to Hookipa near Paia, for injuries.

There's a lifeguard on duty daily. Take notice of the sign warning of dangerous currents – the beach has seen a number of drownings over the years. The reef out on the right is good for snorkeling, but only when it's very calm.

Slaughterhouse Beach & Honolua Bay

About a mile north of Fleming Beach are Slaughterhouse Beach (Mokuleia Bay) and Honolua Bay. The two bays are separated by the narrow Kalaepiha Point and together form the Honolua-Mokuleia Bay Marine Life Conservation District. Fishing is prohibited, as is collecting shells, coral, rocks or sand. In the winter, both bays see heavy surf and sand erosion.

Honolua Bay faces northwest, and when it catches the winter swells, it has some of the best surfing to be found anywhere in the world. Spinner dolphins may be seen offshore.

Slaughterhouse Beach, named for the slaughterhouse that once sat on the cliffs above, is a hot bodysurfing spot during the summer when the rocks aren't exposed. Unlike rocky Honolua, this bay has a white-sand crescent.

In summer, snorkeling is excellent in both bays. Both sides of Honolua Bay have good reefs with lots of different coral formations, while the midsection of the bay has a sandy bottom. Honolua Stream empties into the bay, and it can get quite murky after heavy rains. When it's calm, you can snorkel around Kalaepiha Point from one bay to the other.

To get to Honolua Bay, beachgoers have traditionally parked their cars at a few pull-offs along the road, then scrambled along rough paths down to the beach. However, these paths cross private property. Slaughterhouse Beach, at the 32-mile marker, has limited parking spaces and a concrete stairway leading down to the sea.

KAHEKILI HIGHWAY

The Kahekili Hwy (Hwy 340) curves around the undeveloped northeastern side of the West Maui Mountains. It's ruggedly scenic, with deep ravines, eroded red hills and rock-strewn pastures sloping down to lava sea cliffs and aquamarine ocean. The windy route is pastoral and quiet, with a couple of waterfalls, blowholes and one-lane bridges. You'll likely spot cowhands on horseback and lazy egrets riding the backs of cows.

Like its counterpart to the south (the Piilani Hwy around the southern flank of Haleakala), the Kahekili is either shown as a black hole or an unpaved road on most tourist maps. The 20-mile road, however, is paved its entire length – though much of the drive is very winding and narrow, with blind curves and the occasional sign warning of falling rocks.

Traffic crawls along in both directions, but it's easiest to approach it from the highway's southern end, outside Wailuku. The two-lane road between Honokohau and Kahakuloa is easy going, while the section between Kahakuloa and Waihee is mostly one lane (with two-way traffic) and has a few hair-raising cliff-side sections without shoulders. The posted speed limit on most of the road is 15mph, but in some sections it's a mere 5mph. But taking it slowly is the whole point anyway. Allow at least 1½ hours, not counting stops, and be sure to gas up before starting out.

MAUI

Waiehu & Waihee

Waiehu Beach Rd turns into Kahekili Hwy at the northern end of Wailuku, past the Halekii-Pihana State Heiau Monument, and heads through the little towns of Waiehu and Waihee. Old-fashioned **Waiehu Municipal Golf Course** *(☎ 243-7400; 200 Halewaiu Rd; green fees & club rental $45-50)*, down near the shore, is an easily walkable, no-frills course.

Waihee Valley Trail, also known as Swinging Bridges, is an easy 3½-mile trail leading alongside an irrigation ditch over two rope bridges with cracked wooden planks and groaning cables (fun!) to a gentle stream and, further uphill, an artificial dam pool. Same-day hiking permits are available from **Wailuku Agribusiness** *(☎ 244-9570)* in Waikapu. Several people have been injured or killed in flash floods along this trail, so turn back if it starts to rain. To get here, follow Waihee Valley Rd inland from the 5-mile marker to a T-junction, then turn right and enter the forest.

Just before the 7-mile marker, a side road up to the Boy Scouts' Camp Mahulia is a pretty, winding drive through open pasture. It leads to the start of the **Waihee Ridge Trail**, a seldom-trodden route offering varied scenery and breathtaking views of the interior. The trailhead is a mile up, on the left just before the camp. It's marked with a Na Ala Hele sign and a squeeze-through turnstile through the fence. The well-defined trail is 2¼ miles one way and takes about two hours round-trip. It crosses forest reserve land, and though it's a bit steep, it's a fairly steady climb.

From the three-quarter-mile post, panoramic views open up with a scene that sweeps along the gorge of the Waihee River and deep into the interior valleys. The trail ends at the 2563ft peak of Lanilili, where the ridge-top views from the humble picnic table are similar to those you'd get from a helicopter. If it's cloudy when you arrive, wait a few minutes and it should clear up.

Nearby **Mendes Ranch** *(☎ 244-7320; W www.mendesranch.com; 3530 Kahekili Hwy)* is a working cattle ranch, established in 1941. Horseback trail rides ($85 to $130) to rain forest and sea cliff overlooks may include a barbecue lunch.

Waterfalls, Gardens & Galleries

Back on the highway, you'll pass a **waterfall** on the left, rain permitting. For another view, stop at the pull-off a tenth of a mile north of the 8-mile marker and look down into the ravine below; you'll see a picture-perfect waterfall framed by double pools.

Shortly before reaching the 9-mile marker, a sign marks the driveway up to **Aina Anuhea** *(admission $4)*, a private estate offering a 20-minute walk through petite tropical gardens and a banana patch. The admission price includes a glass of pineapple juice, but it's still not really worth stopping.

Continuing around hairpin turns, the highway gradually levels out atop sea cliffs. Before the 10-mile marker, **Bruce Turnbull Studio & Sculpture Garden** *(☎ 667-2787, 800-781-2787; open by appointment only)* covers the site of an ancient Hawaiian garden. You can catch a glimpse of the sculptor's bronze and wood creations set facing the ocean by peering through the gates.

Just before the 14-mile marker, the lemon-colored **Kaukini Gallery & Gift Shop** *(☎ 244-3371)* is artist-owned and operated. Browse works by dozens of island artists, from watercolorists to koa wood-carvers. A few drinks and snacks are sold.

Kahakuloa Village

Kahakuloa lies at the base of a small green valley with working taro patches and cliffs standing like centurions around the bay.

Up out of the valley, at the northern edge of town, a pull-off provides a good view of the village and the rugged coastline. The rise on the south side of Kahakuloa Bay is **Kahakuloa Head**, 636ft high, another of chief Kahekili's favorite cliff-diving spots.

Although it contains only a few dozen simple homes, Kahakuloa (Tall Lord) has two churches. Opposite the banana-bread stand is the little tin-roof Catholic **St Xavier Mission**, just off the road. The **Protestant church**, sporting a green wooden exterior and red-tile roof, hunkers down on the valley floor further north.

Bellstone & Ocean Baths

As you climb out of the valley, the surrounding terrain is hilly, with rocky cattle pastures punctuated by tall sisal plants. At a number of viewpoints and pull-offs, you can stop and explore. Lush pastures beg you to traipse down the cliffs and out along the rugged coastline.

Pohaku Kani is a large bellstone on the inland side of the road, just past the 16-mile marker. If you hit the bellstone with a rock on the Kahakuloa side where the deepest indentations are, you might be able to get a hollow yet resonant sound.

Just opposite, a couple of vague 4WD tracks lead off toward the coast. If you park and head right (south) to reach an overlook, from there you can plan how to navigate your way down the lava cliffs into the **natural ocean baths** at the ocean's edge. Bordered by lava rock and encrusted with semiprecious olivine minerals, incredibly clear, calm pools sit in the midst of roaring surf. Some have natural steps, but take care not to sit near any blowholes. If the area is covered in silt from recent storm runoffs, or the waves look too high, forget about it.

Nakalele Point From impromptu parking areas between the 39- and 38-mile markers, a brief walk leads out to a **light station** at the end of Nakalele Point. The coastline here has interesting pools, arches and other formations worn out of the rocks by the pounding surf.

Continue walking along the coast (there's no trail) for another 15 minutes until you reach the impressive **Nakalele Blowhole**; if you see only a little sputtering, that's because you haven't found *the* mother of all blowholes yet – so keep going.

When the water is surging, the blowhole is visible from the highway further toward the 40-mile marker. During the winter season, you can sometimes spot humpbacks breaching offshore in this area as well.

As you continue north along the road, Molokai comes into view, and the scenery is very lush on the way to **Honokohau Bay**, the furthest point north on Maui.

South Maui

South Maui offers a mixed plate of aquatic adventures and beaches, all enjoying the sunny, dependably dry conditions off Haleakala's leeward slopes. See the Getting Around section earlier in this chapter for bus routes and fares around south Maui.

KIHEI

Kihei is fringed with sandy beaches its entire length and has near-constant sunshine. The beaches have views of Lanai and Kahoolawe as well as of west Maui, which because of the deep cut of Maalaea Bay looks like a separate island from here. It has long attracted sunbathers, boogie boarders and windsurfers.

Thirty years ago, Kihei was a long stretch of undeveloped beach with *kiawe* trees, a scattering of homes and a church or two. But since the 1970s, developers have pounced on Kihei with such intensity that S Kihei Rd, which runs the full length of Kihei, is now lined with condos, gas stations, shopping centers and fast-food places in such congested disarray that it's the example most often cited by the antidevelopment forces on other Neighbor Islands. To them, Kihei is what no town wants to become.

While Kihei's 'condoville' character does not win any prizes for aesthetics, it has advantages for visitors: the sheer abundance of condos means that Kihei's rates are among the cheapest in Maui, and the nightlife is booming. In addition, the infrastructure has begun to catch up with the rampant commercial growth; bike lanes are being added to S Kihei Rd, and steps have been taken to ameliorate some of the traffic problems.

Piilani Hwy (Hwy 31) runs parallel to and bypasses the start-and-stop traffic of S Kihei Rd. Several crossroads connect the two.

Information

Almost all of the shopping plazas and grocery stores have 24-hour ATMs. **CityBank** *(☎ 891-8586; Kukui Mall, 1819 S Kihei Rd)* charges about the lowest ATM fees. **American Savings Bank** *(☎ 879-1977; Longs Center, 1215 S Kihei Rd; open 9am-6pm Mon-Fri, 9am-1pm Sat)* is open later than most.

There is also a **post office** *(1254 S Kihei Rd; open 8:30am-4:30pm Mon-Fri, 9am-1pm Sat)* in town. Cybercafés are generally expensive; try **Cyber Surf Lounge** *(☎ 879-1090; Azeka Place II)* for high-speed Internet access (10¢ per minute, $3 minimum). Customers can check email for free at **Bubba's Burgers** *(☎ 891-2600; 1945 S Kihei Rd; open 10:30am-9pm daily)*.

Kihei has a modern **public library** *(☎ 875-6833; Waimahaihai St; open noon-8pm Tues, 10am-6pm Wed & Fri, 10am-5pm Thur & Sat)*, directly behind the fire station, with a plaque outside marking an ancient koa (fishing shrine) that once stood here.

Longs Drugs *(☎ 879-2669; Longs Center, 1215 S Kihei Rd)* offers a one-hour photo-processing service and sells affordable film. The Lipoa Center has a **coin laundry** *(40 E Lipoa St; open 8am-8pm daily)* next to Hapa's Brew Haus.

For medical emergencies, the nearest hospital is in Wailuku. **Urgent Care Maui Physicians** *(☎ 879-7781; 1325 S Kihei Rd; open 6am-midnight daily)* accepts walk-in patients.

Kihei Wharf

In 1899, Henry Baldwin built a wharf at the north end of Kihei for landing sugar plantation supplies, around which sprang up a lively workers' camp. Sand accretion eventually made the wharf – which once jutted some 200ft out into the bay – obsolete.

The remains of the wharf, which now extend only about 30ft, are used by local fishing families and *keiki*. It's convenient for catching the sunset if you happen to be at the north end of Kihei.

Keolahou Congregational Hawaiian Church

Doused by ocean spray, this little green-and-white church *(177 S Kihei Rd; worship 9:30am Sun)* was established in 1920. Many of the Tongans living on Maui belong to the congregation.

Captain Vancouver Monument

Captain Cook never set foot on Maui, but one of his enterprising crew members, George Vancouver, did. Opposite Auntie Aloha's Hawaiian Hut, a small **totem pole** commemorates Captain Vancouver's landing on the beach at the small fishing village of Kihei in 1792. In between trips to Hawaii, Vancouver went on to 'discover' British Columbia, a journey now done in the opposite direction by thousands of Canadian tourists who flock to Maui each year.

By all accounts Vancouver was a fairly enlightened explorer. He became an impromptu advisor to Kamehameha the Great, who was so impressed by Vancouver's talk of the British Empire that he adopted the union jack into his royal flag, which still symbolizes the Hawaiian sovereignty movement today.

Hawaiian Islands Humpback National Marine Sanctuary

This humble visitor center at the marine sanctuary headquarters *(☎ 879-2818, 800-831-4888; W www.hihwnms.nos.noaa.gov; 726 S Kihei Rd; open 10am-4pm Mon-Fri)* has simple displays and pamphlets on whales, sea turtles and other endangered marine life, as well as traditional Hawaiian aquaculture.

The center's oceanfront lanai makes a great spot for sighting the humpback whales that frequent the bay during the winter season (December to April); a scope is set up for viewing. Ecology-oriented volunteers staff the facility; free guest lectures are given monthly.

David Malo's Church

Another historic site at the northern end of Kihei is the church built in 1853 by David Malo, a noted philosopher and the first Hawaiian ordained to the Christian ministry, as well as a trusted advisor of Kamehameha III and co-author of Hawaii's first constitution and declaration of rights.

While most of the church was dismantled long ago, a 3ft-high section of the church walls still stands next to a grove of palms beside a small cemetery. Eighteen pews are lined up inside the stone walls, where open-air services are held at 9am on Sunday

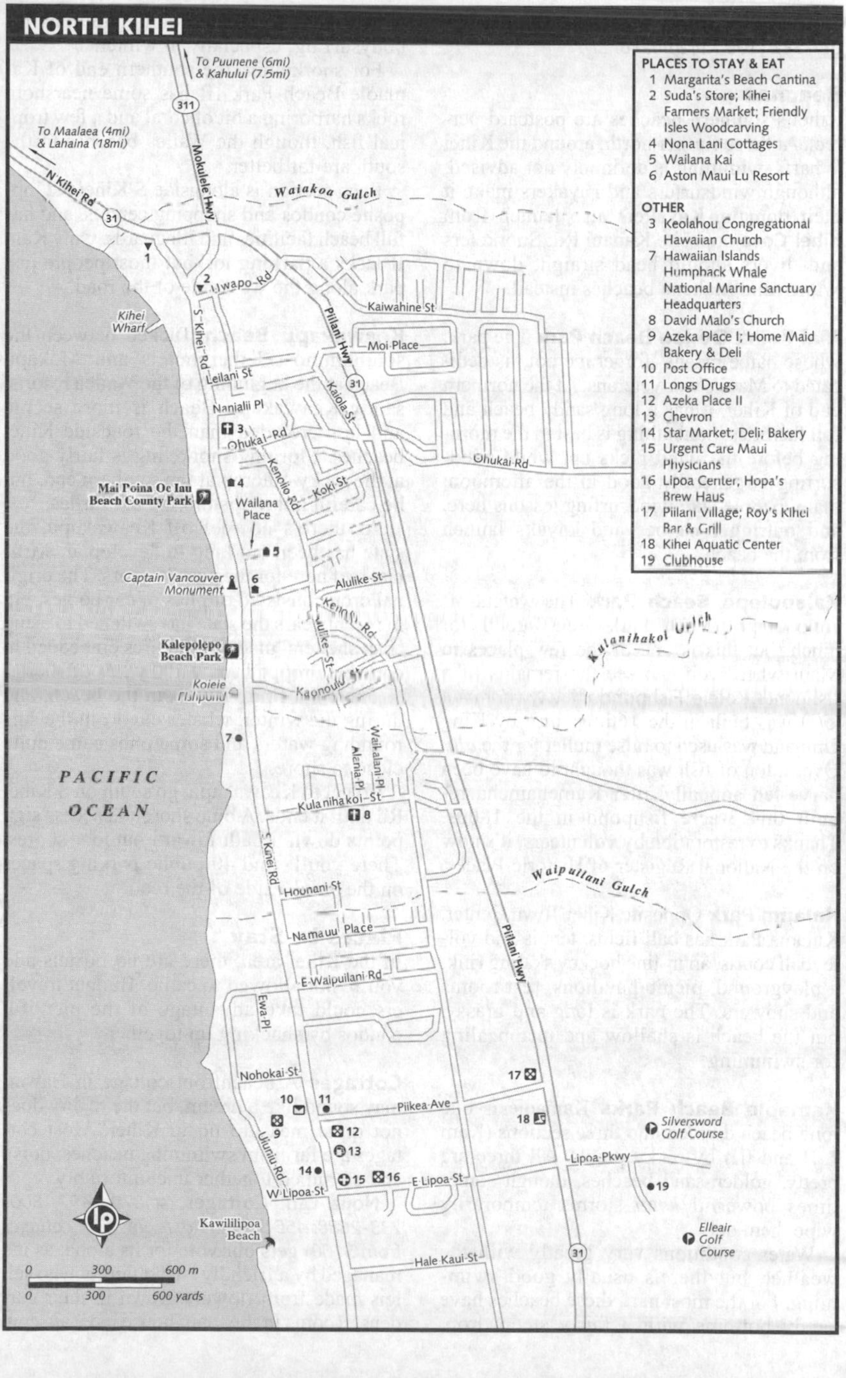
NORTH KIHEI
PLACES TO STAY & EAT
1 Margarita's Beach Cantina
2 Suda's Store; Kihei Farmers Market; Friendly Isles Woodcarving
4 Nona Lani Cottages
5 Wailana Kai
6 Aston Maui Lu Resort
OTHER
3 Keolahou Congregational Hawaiian Church
7 Hawaiian Islands Humphack Whale National Marine Sanctuary Headquarters
8 David Malo's Church
9 Azeka Place I; Home Maid Bakery & Deli
10 Post Office
11 Longs Drugs
12 Azeka Place II
13 Chevron
14 Star Market; Deli; Bakery
15 Urgent Care Maui Physicians
16 Lipoa Center; Hopa's Brew Haus
17 Piilani Village; Roy's Kihei Bar & Grill
18 Kihei Aquatic Center
19 Clubhouse
To Puunene (6mi) & Kahului (7.5mi)
To Maalaea (4mi) & Lahaina (18mi)
N Kihei Rd
Mokulele Hwy
Waiakoa Gulch
Uwapo Rd
Kihei Wharf
S Kihei Rd
Piilani Hwy
Kaiwahine St
Moi Place
Leilani St
Kaiola St
Nanialii Pl
Ohukai Rd
Kenolio Rd
Koki St
Mai Poina Oe Iau Beach County Park
Wailana Place
Captain Vancouver Monument
Alulike St
Keonakai Rd
Kulanihakoi Gulch
Kalepolepo Beach Park
Koieie Fishpond
Kaonoulu St
Waipuilani Gulch
PACIFIC OCEAN
Waiohuli St
Alania Pl
Waikalani Pl
Kulanihakoi St
Hounani St
Namauu Place
E Waipuilani Rd
Ewa Pl
Nohokai St
Piikea Ave
Silversword Golf Course
Lipoa Pkwy
E Lipoa St
W Lipoa St
Uluniu Rd
Kawililipoa Beach
Elleair Golf Course
Hale Kaui St
0 300 600 m
0 300 600 yards
311
31

mornings by **Trinity Episcopal Church-by-the-Sea** *(100 Kulanihakoi St)*.

Beaches

Kihei's southern beaches are postcard perfect. At those further north, around the Kihei Wharf, swimming is definitely not advised, although windsurfers and kayakers make it their domain. Kayakers also launch from **Kihei Cove** opposite Kanani Rd. Snorkelers and divers should head straight down to Wailea and Makena beaches instead.

Mai Poina Oe Iau Beach Park The park, whose name means 'forget me not,' is dedicated to Maui's war veterans. At the northern end of Kihei, it has a long sandy beach and full facilities. Sunbathing is best in the morning before the wind picks up, while windsurfing is generally good in the afternoon; many people take windsurfing lessons here, and outrigger canoes and kayaks launch from the beach.

Kalepolepo Beach Park The waters off Kalepolepo Beach Park aren't good for much, but this is one of the few places in Maui where you can see the remains of a fishpond. **Koieie Fishpond** *(W www.formaui.org)* was built in the 16th century by King Umi and was used to raise mullet for the *alii*. Over a ton of fish was thought to have been harvested annually after Kamehameha rebuilt this 3-acre fishpond in the 1800s. Thanks to restoration by volunteers, it's now on the National Register of Historic Places.

Kalama Park Opposite Kihei Town Center, Kalama Park has ball fields, tennis and volleyball courts, an in-line hockey skating rink, a playground, picnic pavilions, rest rooms and showers. The park is long and grassy, but the beach is shallow and unappealing for swimming.

Kamaole Beach Parks Kamaole is one long beach divided into three sections (Kam I, II and III) by rocky points. All three are pretty, golden-sand beaches, though sometimes powerful *kona* storms temporarily wipe them out.

Water conditions vary greatly with the weather, but there's usually good swimming. For the most part, these beaches have sandy bottoms with a fairly steep drop, which tends to create good conditions for bodysurfing, especially in winter.

For snorkeling, the southern end of Kamaole Beach Park III has some nearshore rocks harboring a bit of coral and a few tropical fish, though the Wailea beaches to the south are far better.

Each section is alongside S Kihei Rd, opposite condos and shopping centers, and has full beach facilities and lifeguards. Only Kam II lacks a parking lot, but most people just park along the west side of the road.

Keawakapu Beach Tucked between the southernmost Kihei hotels and Mokapu Beach at the beginning of the Wailea resorts, sandy Keawakapu Beach is more scenic and less crowded than the roadside Kihei beaches. Morning snorkeling is fairly good at the rocky outcrop at the southern end, but be careful not to disturb the sea turtles.

As there's no reef off Keawakapu, the state has been working to develop an artificial reef here for the past 30 years. The original drop consisted of piles of car bodies, but in recent years the state has switched to using 'fish shelters' made of old tires embedded in concrete dropped some 500 yards offshore.

There's a fine view from the beach, and during the winter, whales cavort in the surrounding waters and sometimes come quite close to shore.

To get to Keawakapu, go south on S Kihei Rd until it ends. A blue shoreline access sign points down a path toward outdoor shores. There you'll find 40 public parking spaces on the *mauka* side of the road.

Places to Stay

In the Kihei area, there are no hostels and you're not allowed to camp. Budget travelers could take advantage of the plentiful condos by shacking up together.

Cottages A beachfront cottage in Hawaii may sound like a dream, but the reality does not quite measure up in Kihei. Most cottages are far from swimming beaches, noisy and crammed together uncomfortably.

Nona Lani Cottages *(☎ 879-2497, 800-733-2688; 455 S Kihei Rd; rooms $75, cottages from $100)* gets our vote for its aloha, as it's managed by a friendly island family who sell leis made from flowers grown in their gardens. Rooms in the main house have air-con,

MAUI

SOUTH KIHEI

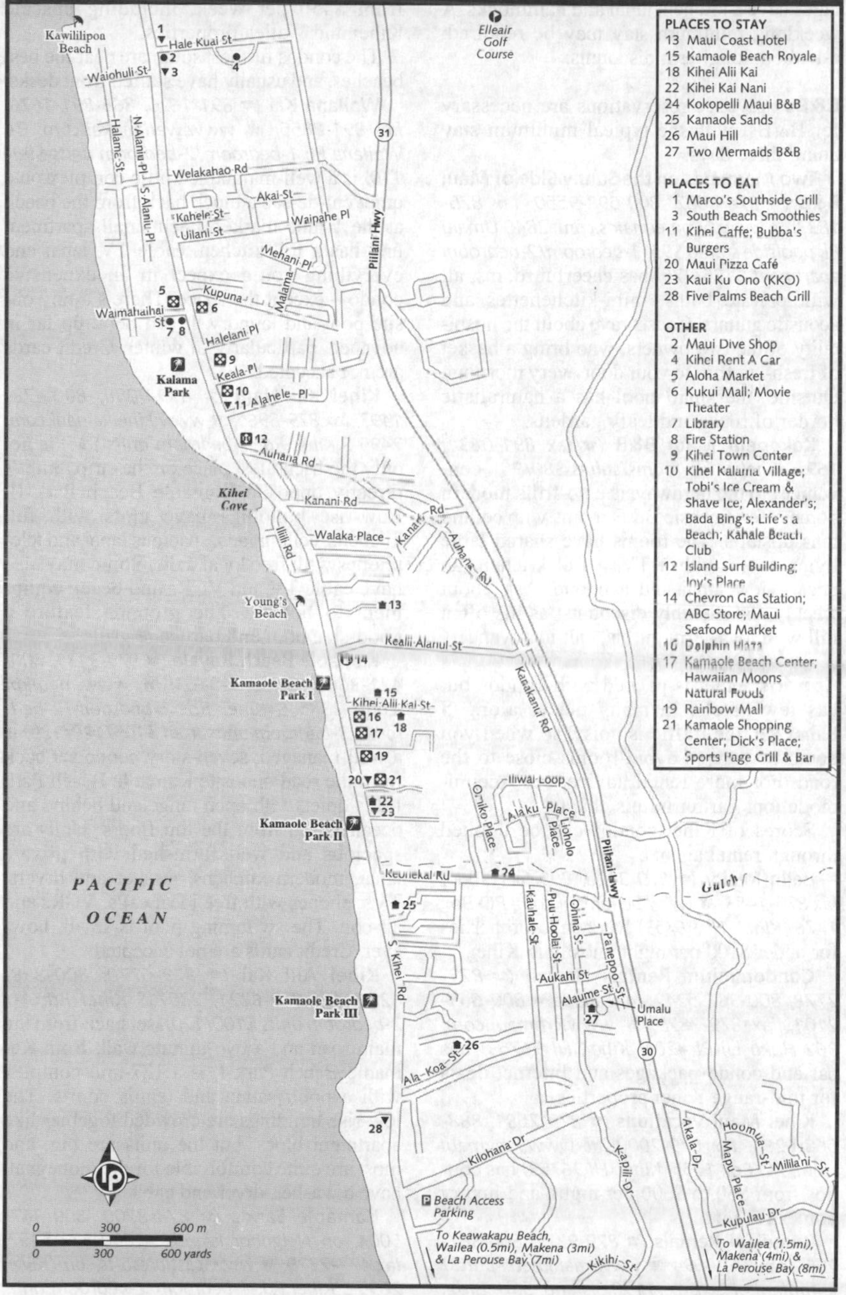

MAUI

private bath and TV. A range of small cottages have a kitchen, lanai and hammocks. A weeklong minimum stay may be required; ask about long-term discounts.

B&Bs Advance reservations are necessary for B&Bs, with the typical minimum stay being three days.

Two Mermaids on the Sunny Side of Maui B&B (☎ *874-8687, 800-598-9550, fax 875-1833;* W *www.twomermaids.com; 2840 Umalu Pl; poolside studio $95, 1-bedroom/2-bedroom apartment $125/175)* has cheerful rooms, all with private baths, mini-kitchenettes and acoustic guitars. Guests rave about the hospitality of the two owners, who bring a basket of fresh-cut fruit to your door every morning. Outside, the small pool has a naturalistic border of rocks and leafy gardens.

Kokopelli Maui B&B (☎*/fax 891-0631; 169 Keonekai Rd; rooms/suites $80/95)*, convenient to the highway, is a no-frills modern home offering basic B&B rooms with ceiling fans upstairs. The rooms have shared large living room with a TV, a full kitchen, an ocean-view lanai and a phone. Ask about weekly and monthly discounts; as it's often full with long-term guests, call in advance.

Condos Kihei is packed with condos but has few hotels. In many places along S Kihei Rd, the traffic is noisy, so when you book, be sure to avoid rooms close to the road. For more rental advice, see Accommodations earlier in this chapter.

Scores of Kihei condos can be booked through rental agents.

Bello Realty (☎ *879-3328, 800-541-3060, fax 875-1483;* W *www.bellomaui.com; PO Box 1776, Kihei, HI 96753)* has condo properties for under $100 per night, mostly in Kihei.

Condominium Rentals Hawaii (☎ *879-2778, 800-367-5242, in Canada* ☎ *800-663-2101, fax 879-7825;* W *www.crhmaui.com; 362 Huku Lii Pl #204, Kihei, HI 96753)* has car and condo packages and Internet deals for mid-range Kihei properties.

Kihei Maui Vacations (☎ *879-7581, 888-568-6284, fax 879-2000;* W *www.kmvmaui.com; PO Box 1055, Kihei, HI 96753)* has condos from $60 to $600 per night, and luxury homes for rent.

Kumulani Rentals (☎ *879-9272, 800-367-2954, fax 874-0094;* W *www.maui.net/~putt3/kumulani; PO Box 1190, Island Surf Bldg, 1993 S Kihei Rd, Kihei, HI 96753)* has condos from $450 per week, including upscale Kihei and Wailea properties.

The condos furthest south are near the best beaches, and usually have staffed front desks.

Wailana Kai (☎ *891-1626, 866-891-1626, fax 891-8855;* W *www.wailanakai.com; 34 Wailana Pl; 1-bedroom/2-bedroom units $90/110)* is a well-maintained little complex on a quiet cul-de-sac a block back from the beach at the 1-mile marker. Each small apartment unit has a full kitchen, cable TV, lanai and everything you'd expect in an expensive condo – except the space. There's a tiny on-site pool and laundry. It can book up far in advance, particularly in winter. Credit cards are not accepted.

Kihei Kai Nani (☎ *879-9088, 800-473-1493, fax 879-8965;* W *www.kiheikainani.com; 2495 S Kihei Rd; 1-bedroom units $95)* is not only the friendliest place on the strip, but it's directly opposite Kamaole Beach Park II. Low-rise buildings have units with full kitchens, ceiling fans, spacious lanai and telephones with free local calls. Some may also have cable TV and VCRs and beach equipment to borrow. The grounds feature a good-size pool and barbecue grills.

Kamaole Beach Royale (☎ *879-3131, 800-421-3661, fax 879-9163;* W *www.mauikbr.com; 2385 S Kihei Rd; 1-bedroom/2-bedroom/3-bedroom units from $105/120/125)* is a well-managed, seven-story condo set back from the road opposite Kamaole Beach Park I. It's quiet, with open rangeland behind and ocean views from the top floors. Units are spacious and well furnished with private lanai, modern kitchens, washer and dryers, TVs, phones with free local calls, VCRs and air-con. The swimming pool is small, however. Credit cards are not accepted.

Kihei Alii Kai (☎ *879-6770, 800-888-6284, fax 879-6221; 2387 S Kihei Rd; 1-/2-bedroom units $100/120)*, set back from the main road and a two-minute walk from Kamaole Beach Park I, is a 127-unit complex with a pool, sauna and tennis courts. The low-rise buildings are crowded together like apartment blocs, but the units are big, and most are quite comfortable for the money; all have a washer, dryer and cable TV.

Kamaole Sands (☎ *874-8700, 800-367-5004, on Neighbor Islands* ☎ *800-272-5257, fax 477-2329;* W *www.castleresorts.com/KSM; 2695 S Kihei Rd; 1-bedroom/2-bedroom units* *from $195/285)* is its own condo city, with four-story buildings set back from the road. Opposite Kamaole Beach Park III, it has a pool, Jacuzzi, tennis courts, landscaped waterfalls and a weekly welcome party with live Hawaiian music. Each spacious unit comes fully equipped with all the modern amenities. Castle Resorts, which handles the front desk, offers promotional deals and Internet booking discounts.

Maui Hill *(☎ 879-6321, 800-922-7866, fax 879-8945; 2881 S Kihei Rd; 1-bedroom/2-bedroom units $205/265)*, regally set on a hillside above Keawakapu Beach Park, has Mediterranean-style villas to prove that condo living can be luxurious. Nothing has been spared outfitting them with full amenities. The weekly *mai tai* parties are a fixture. Look for the retro whale sign pointing uphill from the S Kihei Rd turnoff.

Hotels **Aston Maui Lu Resort** *(☎ 879-5991, 800-922-7866, fax 879-4627; W www.aston-hotels.com; 575 S Kihei Rd; rooms from $130)* has possibly the oldest coconut grove on the island. Unlike many chain resorts, this low-rise complex has a rustic Polynesian feel with all the standard modern amenities and a Maui-shaped pool. Some units front the beach while others are across the road and set back from the highway. Check the website for huge discounts and package deals.

Maui Coast Hotel *(☎ 874-6284, 800-325-4000, fax 875-4731; W www.westcoasthotels.com/mauicoast; 2259 S Kihei Rd, Kihei, HI 96753; rooms/suites from $165/195)* is a modern seven-story hotel. It's set back from the road, so it's quieter than most Kihei condos, and you can enjoy live Hawaiian music nightly at the poolside bar, plus complimentary washers, dryers and tennis courts. Ask about off-season and senior discounts.

Places to Eat

Tasty food with an ocean view is hard to find. Smart travelers may find themselves doing a lot of self-catering in their own condo kitchens. You'll find a **Star Market** supermarket with a deli and bakery south of Azeka Place I, a 24-hour **Foodland** at Kihei Town Center and a **Safeway** at Piilani Village mall.

Kihei Farmers Market *(next to Suda's Store, 61 S Kihei Rd; held 1:30pm-5:30pm Mon, Wed & Fri)* gives away free samples of fruits and vegetables, cheeses, fresh juices and salsas.

Maui Seafood Market *(2349 S Kihei Rd; lunch around $6)*, behind the Chevron gas station, sells fresh fish and hot local plate lunches.

Hawaiian Moons Natural Foods *(☎ 875-4356; Kamaole Beach Center, 2411 S Kihei Rd; salad bar per lb $5; open 8am-8pm Mon-Sat, 8am-6pm Sun)* has an organic produce section, yogurts, juices, trail mix, bulk grains, pineapple-and-coconut muffins, granolas and a few organic wines. It also has a good salad bar, as well as a juice and espresso bar, which closes slightly earlier.

Home Maid Bakery & Deli *(Azeka Place I, 1280 S Kihei Rd; lunches $6; open 6am-4pm daily)*, a humble local bakery, is a mecca for hot *malasadas* (Portuguese doughnuts).

South Beach Smoothies *(1455 S Kihei Rd; snacks under $5; open 8am-4pm Mon-Fri, 9am-2pm Sat)* blends luscious smoothies that are chock-full of fresh fruit for $3.50, including an extra 'side car.' The friendly owner also sells hot dogs and health food snacks.

Tobi's Ice Cream & Shave Ice *(Kihei Kalama Village, 1913 S Kihei Rd; icy delights $3.00-5.25; open 10am-9:30pm daily)* is beloved by *kamaaina* (island folks). Thick, tall milkshakes, 'wild *wahine*' shave ice and tropical smoothies are always mo' bettah here.

Joy's Place *(Island Surf Bldg, 1993 S Kihei Rd; snacks $4-7; open 10am-5pm Mon-Sat, 10am-3pm Sun)*, a small restaurant with a dozen café tables, has home-style food, mostly vegetarian and vegan. You can get organic salads, tortilla-wrapped sandwiches, curried hummus and cheeseless pesto.

Bubba's Burgers *(☎ 891-2600; 1945 S Kihei Rd; snacks $2.75-7.50, open 10:30am-9pm daily)* is the only self-respecting burger joint in town. It swears, 'We cheat tourists, drunks and attorneys,' and charge an outrageous 75¢ for lettuce and tomato because it believes real people shouldn't eat them on their burgers. Try the famous Budweiser beer chili.

Alexander's *(Kihei Kalama Village, 1913 S Kihei Rd; meals $7-10; open 11am-9pm daily)* is a great spot for fish and chips, made with a choice of fresh mahimahi, *ono* (wahoo fish) or *ahi* (yellowfin tuna). Try the sides of hush puppies, fried zucchini and corn bread. The food is prepared for take-out, but there are a few lanai tables where you can eat.

Kihei Caffe *(1945 S Kihei Rd; dishes $5-7; open 5am-3pm daily)*, opposite Kalama Park, is an excellent little breakfast spot, serving Kona coffee, homemade pastries and good karma. Fresh salads and sandwiches are available, as well as tempting banana macadamia-nut pancakes. It's perfect for jet-lagged travelers who wake up *way* too early.

Margarita's Beach Cantina *(☎ 879-5275; Kealia Beach Plaza, 101 N Kihei Rd; mains $11-22; open 11:30am-10pm daily)* has average Mexican food but a great sunset-facing deck overlooking the water. The usual burgers and fajitas are upstaged by all-you-can-eat lobster and prime-rib nights (around $15).

Maui Pizza Café *(☎ 891-2200; 2439 S Kihei Rd; pizza & pasta dishes $8-16; open 11:30am-1am daily)* has a welcoming ambience, and thin-crust pizza is deservedly its signature dish. Order yours piled high with local goodies, perhaps a little *kalua* pig (baked in an underground oven) with Maui onions or scampi in citrus-garlic sauce.

Marco's Southside Grill *(☎ 874-4041; 1445 S Kihei Rd; breakfast $6-10, lunch & dinner $10-26; open 7:30am-10pm daily)* is a posh family-style Italian restaurant done up with Spanish leather chairs, 24-karat beer-tap pulls and white marble. Breakfast is all over the map, but the chocolate-cinnamon French toast comes highly recommended. Later in the day, wood-oven-fired pizzas, hot Italian sandwiches and signature pastas, like vodka rigatoni, are a steal.

Roy's Kihei Bar & Grill *(☎ 891-1120; Piilani Village Mall, 303 Piikea Ave; mains $21-29; open 5:30pm-10pm daily)* is an outpost of famous Hawaiian chef Roy Kahana's mini-empire. As always, the emphasis is on Hawaiian seafood, excellent wine and relaxation.

Kaui Ku Ono *(KKO; 2511 S Kihei Rd; pupus $8-13, mains $10-15; open 8am-midnight daily)* has torchlights blazing nightly and the sun often sets beyond the ocean-facing lanai to the tune of live Hawaiian music. If an inventive *pupu* menu doesn't satisfy your hunger, there's a serious **steakhouse** upstairs.

Five Palms Beach Grill *(☎ 879-2607; Mauna Kai Resort, 2960 S Kihei Rd; breakfast & lunch $10-15, dinner $20-30, 5-course tasting menu $65; open 8am-9:30pm daily)* is an open-air spot, with palm trees waving in the moonlight, for waterfront dining. Dinner brings on heavy hitters such as steak, lobster and market-fresh fish, accented by Molokai sweet potatoes and Maui onions. Everyone raves about the **Sunday champagne brunch** *(rates $20; open 8am-2pm daily)*.

MAUI

Entertainment

The Kukui Mall's **movie theater** *(☎ 878-3456)* features four screens.

Kihei's nightlife scene is second only to Lahaina's, with a couple of bars and DJ clubs staying lively all week long. Admission ($5 to $10) usually only applies on weekends.

Hapa's Brew Haus *(☎ 879-9001; Lipoa Center, 41 E Lipoa St)* is a bar-nightclub that bizarrely serves sushi. On some nights it has a DJ, and on others it offers live music by the likes of local legend Willie K. Look for queer-friendly 'ultra fabulous night' on Tuesday.

Another key triumvirate of places are at **Kihei Kalama Village** *(1945 S Kihei Rd)*, opposite Kalama Beach. DJs from Oahu and the mainland spin at **Bada Bing's** *(☎ 875-0188)*, where $2 drink specials keep things swingin'. **Life's a Beach** *(☎ 891-8010)* is a Bob Marley–lovin' grass shack with live music and DJs. The local watering hole is **Kahale Beach Club** *(☎ 875-7711)*, hidden at the back of the parking lot.

Dick's Place *(☎ 874-8869; Kamaole Shopping Center, 2463 S Kihei Rd)* has a billiards bar that lets you shoot some stick.

Sports Page Grill & Bar *(☎ 879-0602; Kamaole Beach Center, 2411 S Kihei Rd)* has big-screen TVs with sports broadcasts.

A few restaurants also have bars and entertainment. **Maui Pizza Café** has live music, DJs and gay-friendly nights. **Margarita's Beach Cantina** starts happy hour early at 2:30pm, lasting until the sun sets over its oceanfront deck.

Shopping

Kihei overflows with souvenir shops of all sorts. Near the public library, **Aloha Market** is an outdoor collection of stalls selling el cheapo T-shirts, swimwear, island jewelry etc. **Kihei Kalama Village**, opposite Kalama Park, has more of the same.

Friendly Isles Woodcarving *(Suda's Store, 61 S Kihei Rd)* is where you can watch an island woodcarver at work on authentic pieces.

Locals usually shop at **Piilani Village** *(225 Piikea Ave)*, which has Hawaiian and international chain stores. Well-established **Tropical Disc** *(☎ 874-3000; Piilani Village)* has an excellent selection of Hawaiian tunes and headphone setups for previewing popular releases. The hip young staff can help you choose a ukulele, too.

Maui Dive Shop (☎ *879-3388; 1455 S Kihei Rd*), the main outlet of this chain, sells reef walkers, boogie boards, snorkels, fins and wet suits.

ABC Store (☎ *879-2349; 2349 S Kihei Rd*) has liquor, cheap beach mats, suntan lotion and other practical beach items.

WAILEA

The towns of Wailea and Makena, both a world away from the cluttered commercialism of Kihei, lie at the end of the road south of Kihei.

As soon as you enter Wailea, you'll be struck by the contrast with its northern neighbor – everything is green, manicured and precise. As construction ran amok in Kihei, this resort was developed solely by the Alexander & Baldwin sugar company. Makena has followed Wailea's lead, with a luxury hotel and golf course, catering largely to Japanese tourists.

Greenery on Maui's dry side comes with a price tag, however, one that is mostly paid by Upcountry farmers, whose watershed is drained to provide the millions of gallons required by resort guests daily. As one local slogan protests, 'No-one can eat golf balls.' Environmentalists are working to block further non-self-sustainable development.

Wailea's lava-rock coastline is broken by attractive golden-sand beaches that lure swimmers, snorkelers and sunbathers. From Wailea and neighboring Makena, there are good views of Lanai, Kahoolawe and Molokini, and during winter there's superb shoreline whale watching.

Wailea has a few swank hotels on the beach, a number of low-rise condo villas, a shopping center, a trio of golf courses and a tennis club that's been nicknamed 'Wimbledon West.' Bring your platinum credit card, though, if you'd like to dine in a teahouse made of Mt Fuji stones or indulge in the island's grandest spa.

Orientation & Information

If you're heading to Wailea beaches from Lahaina or Kahului, be sure to take the Piilani Hwy (Hwy 31) and not S Kihei Rd. Otherwise the Kihei strip can be a tedious 30 minutes through congested traffic. Wailea's main road is Wailea Alanui Dr, which turns into Makena Alanui Dr after Polo Beach and continues south to Makena.

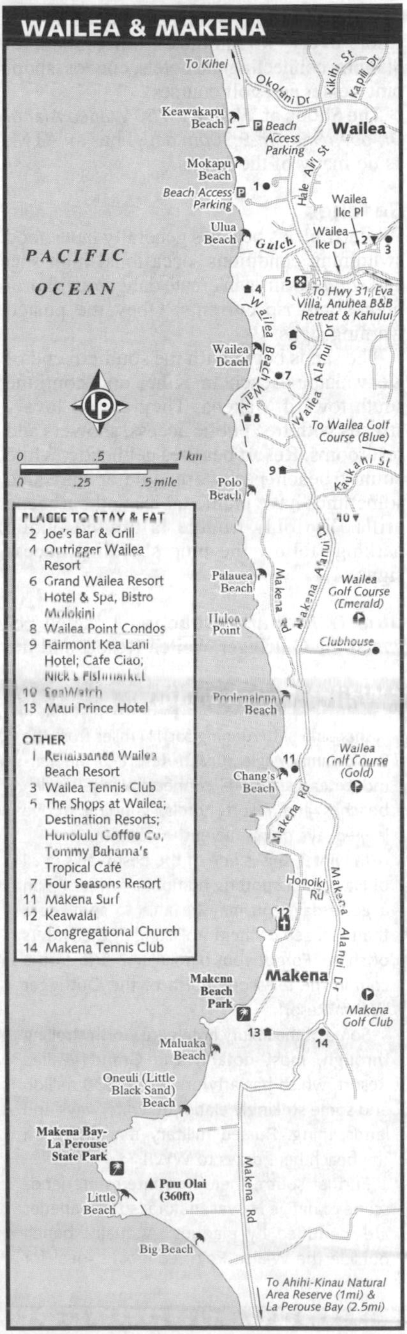

A free **shuttle bus** runs around the Wailea resort every 30 minutes from 6:30am to 8:30pm, connecting the hotels, condos, shopping center and golf courses.

The Shops at Wailea *(3750 Wailea Alanui Dr; open 9:30am-9:30pm daily)* has an ATM, as do many of the hotels.

Beaches

While Wailea's beaches generally have good swimming conditions, occasional high surf and *kona* storms can create dangerous shorebreaks and rip currents. Obey the posted warning signs.

The sands begin with the southern end of Keawakapu Beach in Kihei and continue south toward Makena. They are all lovely strands with free public access, showers and rest rooms. Resort beaches get hectic, while county beach parks are quieter and also sometimes have picnic tables and barbecue grills. The only trouble is limited public parking (follow the blue shoreline access signs).

Ulua & Mokapu Beaches Located between the Outrigger Wailea Resort and the Renaissance Wailea Beach Resort, Ulua Beach is a little gem. The first road south of the Renaissance will take you to the beach parking lot.

There's coral at the rocky outcrop on the right side of Ulua Beach, where it borders its twin, Mokapu Beach. Beginner snorkelers can usually spot long needlefish, schools of goatfish, unicorn tangs and other tropical fish. Snorkeling is best in the morning before the winds pick up. When the surf's up, forget snorkeling – go bodysurfing instead.

Wailea Beach The largest and widest of Wailea's beaches, Wailea slopes gradually, making the inshore waters good for swimming. When the water's calm, there's good snorkeling around the rocky point on the south side of the beach. Divers entering the water at Wailea Beach can follow an offshore reef that runs down to Polo Beach. At times, there's a gentle shorebreak suitable for bodysurfing.

Beach access is from the road running between the Four Seasons Resort and the Grand Wailea Resort Hotel and Spa, both of which front Wailea Beach.

Polo Beach Although fronted by a condo development and the Fairmont Kea Lani Hotel, the south end of Polo beach is seldom crowded.

When there's wave action, boogie boarders and bodysurfers usually find a good shorebreak here. When the waters are calm, the rocks at the north end of the beach are good for snorkeling and spotting a stray turtle or two. At low tide, the lava outcropping at the south end of the beach has some interesting little tide pools that harbor spiny sea urchins and small fish.

To get to Polo Beach, turn down Kaukahi St after the Kea Lani. There's a beach parking lot on the right, near the end of the road.

Palauea Beach Just off Makena Rd, Palauea Beach is a quarter-mile south of Polo Beach. A fair number of people use the beach for surfing and bodysurfing. It's more secluded and less frequented than Polo Beach, but otherwise it's much the same, without the development.

The *kiawe* brushland between the beach and the road is marked private property,

Wailea Beach Walk

A shoreline path running for 1¼ miles from the Renaissance Wailea Beach Resort to the Fairmont Kea Lani Hotel connects all the Wailea beaches and resort hotels, winding above jagged lava points along the oceanfront.

In winter, this is one of the best walks in all of Hawaii for spotting humpback whales – on a good day, you may be able to spot more than a dozen of them frolicking in the waters offshore. Forgot your binoculars? Just drop a coin in the telescope north of the Outrigger Wailea Resort.

Some of the luxury hotels are worth strolling through, most notably the Grand Wailea Resort, which has artwork worth $30 million and some strikingly elaborate waterways and landscaping. Rusted military machinery on the beach here dates to WWII.

Further south, there's an interesting landscape of native Hawaiian flora; some varieties are identified by plaques. A quaint bench outside the Wailea Point condos is ideal for sunset gazing.

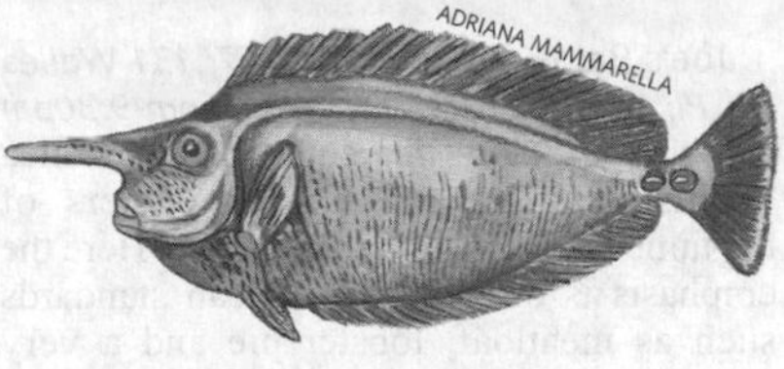

Spotted unicorn

though there are gigantic breaks in the fence where beachgoers cross. You can walk to Palauea Beach from Polo Beach in less than 10 minutes.

Chang's Beach Between the end of the Wailea resort strip and Makena Rd, Chang's Beach is a sandy half-mile-long crescent with too many names, including Paipu Beach, Makena Surf Beach (after the nearest condo complex) and even Love Beach. And yes, it's hard not to love this place.

This beach is not crowded and the shallow, sandy bottom and calm waters make for excellent swimming. There is good snorkeling off both the southern and northern lava points, but be careful not to damage the live coral or disturb the sea turtles. **Haloa Point**, a bit farther north, is a popular scuba-diving spot.

There is one main access point with parking spaces and limited facilities; look for a hand-drawn sign pointing off Wailea Alanui Rd, before the Makena Rd turnoff.

Activities

Wailea Golf Club *(☎ 875-5111, 800-332-1614; 100 Golf Club Dr; green fees & cart $115-160)* has three championship courses. The Emerald is a tropical garden that consistently ranks top, while the Gold is an interesting rugged course taking advantage of volcanic landscapes.

Wailea Tennis Club *(☎ 879-1958, 800-332-1614; 131 Wailea Ike Pl; hourly court rental $28-35)* enforces a dress code. Lessons and equipment rentals are available.

Places to Stay

B&Bs A few B&Bs are found in the exclusive Maui Meadows subdivision, a mile above Wailea Beach on the slopes of Haleakala. Expect at least a three-day minimum stay.

Eva Villa *(☎ 874-6407, 800-884-1885, in Germany ☎ 0800 182 1980; W www.maui.net/~pounder; 85 Kumulani Dr; rooms $115-140)* is inside a private hilltop villa that looks dazzlingly white in the sun. Guests share a swimming pool, Jacuzzi and rooftop sundeck. The gardens also hide a koi pond. The poolside studio and two-bedroom suite have a private bath, while the cottage has a full kitchen, barbecue grill, washer, dryer and wraparound lanai.

Anuhea B&B Health Retreat *(☎ 874-1490, 800-206-4441, fax 874-8587; W www.anuheamaui.com; 3164 Mapu Pl; rooms from $115)* is run by alternative medicine practitioners. Rooms are simple and modern, but most guests will spend more time outdoors in the Jacuzzi, gazebo and gardens. Massage services and off-season discounts are available.

Condos A few of the agencies that are listed in the Kihei section earlier also handle rentals in Wailea.

AA Oceanfront Condominium Rentals *(☎ 879-7288, 800-488-6004, fax 879-7500; W www.makena.com; 2439 S Kihei Rd #102A)* has mostly high-end rentals in Wailea and Makena.

Destination Resorts *(☎ 891-6200, 800-367-5246, fax 874-3554; W www.drhmaui.com; Unit B51, The Shops at Wailea; studios $155, 1-bedroom condos with garden view from $205, 2-bedroom/3-bedroom units $310/600)* books about 300 units in half a dozen complexes around Wailea and Makena. While they aren't cheap (the $50 check-in fee bites), most of the condos are far better value than Wailea's luxury hotels. Ask about car rental and golf packages.

Hotels All of these resorts offer a full range of guest amenities, including jungly swimming pools and free hula classes. The only differences are in style (Polynesian versus Western), attitude and how much luxury you can afford.

Outrigger Wailea Resort *(☎ 879-1922, 800-688-7444, fax 874-8331; W www.outrigger.com; 3700 Wailea Alanui Dr; rooms with garden/mountain/ocean view $325/375/425)*, of all the Wailea resorts, is most in harmony with its Polynesian surrounds. Favored by families and conventioneers, it's an unpretentious, low-key operation that has been recently renovated to the tune of $25 million. The Outrigger chain often offers substantial discounts and promotional packages, especially online. Its one-bedroom condos on the golf course at **The Palms at Wailea** go for much less than a hotel room.

Fairmont Kea Lani Hotel *(☎ 875-4100, 800-659-4100, fax 875-1200; W www.kealani.com; 4100 Wailea Alanui Dr; 1-bedroom suites $325-700, oceanfront villas $1000-1700)* is a luxurious resort with fanciful Moorish-style architecture that resembles something out of *Arabian Nights*. More expensive one-bedroom suites with a private lanai and marble bath sleep for up to four adults, while oceanfront villas come with private plunge pools.

Grand Wailea Resort Hotel & Spa *(☎ 875-1234, 800-888-6100, fax 874-2442; W www.grandwailea.com; 3850 Wailea Alanui Dr; rooms $435)* is the most extravagant resort on Maui. The lobbies are filled with sculptures and artwork, while the grounds are given over to gardens, fountains, a multimillion-dollar mosaic tile pool and a 2000ft-long system of water slides and artificial waterfall grottoes. Some of it has an upscale Hawaiiana motif; all of it is unabashedly opulent. The Grand Suite in the hotel's exclusive Napua Tower is the islands' most expensive night's sleep, setting you back (well, not *you*, perhaps, but setting *someone* back) a cool $10,000. One would hope the bed is comfortable.

Places to Eat

Hotels, the shopping mall or golf clubhouses, are your only choices for places to eat.

Honolulu Coffee Co *(The Shops at Wailea, 2nd level)* has exceptional roasts and budget-minded baked goods.

Cafe Ciao *(Fairmont Kea Lani Hotel; deli open 6:30am-10pm daily)* has a deli shop with pricey but gourmet beach picnic foods for take-out. Best are the thick sandwiches made with artisan breads. Healthy drinks fill the refrigerator.

Bistro Molokini *(Grand Wailea Resort; open 11am-9pm daily)* has reputable *kiawe* wood-fired pizzas for under $20.

Tommy Bahama's Tropical Café *(☎ 875-9983; The Shops at Wailea, 2nd level; lunch $10-14; open 11am-10pm daily)* may cause you to snicker at its obvious faux-tropical commercialism, but the lunch menu is divine, especially the grouper fish, Cayman citrus crab salad (Havana cabana) and pork sandwich with blackberry brandy-barbecue sauce.

Joe's Bar & Grill *(☎ 875-7767; 131 Wailea Ike Pl; mains $18-38; open 5:30pm-9:30pm daily)*, overlooking the courts at the Wailea Tennis Club, is run by the owners of the famed Haliimaile General Store. Here the emphasis is on hearty American standards such as meatloaf, lobster pie and a very popular New York steak. Reserve ahead, or be prepared to wait at the copper-top bar.

SeaWatch *(☎ 875-8080; lunch $8, dinner $24; open 8am-3pm & 5:30pm-9:30pm daily)* is perched on a hillside with a great ocean view and offers both indoor and veranda dining. A breakfast favorite is the crab-cake Benedict, while dinner features the likes of citrus *ponzu* (Japanese-style citrus sauce) pork chops or fresh fish with mango chutney.

Nick's Fishmarket *(Fairmont Kea Lani Hotel; mains $26-45; open 5:30pm daily)* boasts sunset ocean views, torch lighting and an impressive Mediterranean-style dining room, which only enhance its first-class reputation for creative talent and market-fresh fish.

The **Grand Wailea** also has two expensive dinner restaurants, the **Kincha** *(mains $26-53; open 6pm-9pm Thur-Mon)*, which has Japanese haute cuisine and was built with over 800 tons of stone handpicked from Mt Fuji, and **Humuhumunukunukuapuaa** *(mains $22-32; open 5:45pm-9:45pm daily)*, serving seafood and steaks in a Polynesian-style longhouse encircled by a 70,000-gallon saltwater lagoon.

Entertainment

The Wailea hotels often have jazz or live Hawaiian music in their restaurants and lounges. Luaus here do not compare favorably with ones in Lahaina (see West Maui earlier in this chapter).

The Shops at Wailea presents live music on Wednesday, Thursday and Saturday nights, when **Longhi's** restaurant also has a live band until 1:30am.

Shopping

The Shops at Wailea *(3750 Wailea Alanui Dr; open 9:30am-9:30pm daily)*, has discount to high-end chains. Unique shops include Hawaiian jeweler **Na Hoku** *(2nd level)*, specializing in Tahitian black pearls since 1924; **Noa Noa** *(ground level)* for hand-batik Polynesian wear; and **Celebrities** *(2nd level)* gallery with art by the likes of John Lennon and David Bowie. Hawaiian chains include **Crazy Shirts** *(2nd level)* and the discount **ABC Store** *(2nd level)*.

MAKENA

Until recently, Makena was a sleepy and largely overlooked area at the end of the road. In the 19th century, however, it was the busiest settlement this side of Maui. Cattle from Ulupalakua Ranch and other Upcountry pastures were corralled down the mountain to Makena Landing and shipped to market in Honolulu. By the 1920s, interisland boat traffic had shifted to other ports on the island.

In the 1980s, the Seibu Corporation gobbled up 1800 acres of Makena above the old Makena Landing, and developed it into a resort with a golf course, a tennis center, the Maui Prince Hotel and a new road to it all. Is it an improvement over the Hawaiian village once found here, though?

Thankfully, much of Makena remains wild and free. The dominant shoreline feature is Puu Olai, a 360ft cinder hill a mile south of the landing. Just beyond Puu Olai are two knockout beaches at Makena-La Perouse Bay State Park. Big Beach is a huge sweep of glistening sand and a prime sunset-viewing locale with straight-on views of Molokini and Kahoolawe. Little Beach is a secluded cove, still Maui's most popular nude beach.

Makena Bay

To explore the older side of Makena, turn right off Makena Rd after the Makena Surf condo complex and go about a mile to Makena Bay. **Makena Landing** is a local recreational area with boat-launching facilities, showers and toilets. When seas are calm, there's good snorkeling along the rocks at the south side of the landing.

South of the landing is the **Keawalai Congregational Church**, which dates to 1832 and is one of Maui's early missionary churches. The current building was built in 1855 with 3ft-thick walls made of burnt coral rock. A small congregation still meets for Sunday services, which are held at 9:30am in a mix of Hawaiian and English. The church graveyard has a fine bayside view and old tombstones with interesting cameo photographs.

Makena Rd ends shortly after the church at a cul-de-sac on the ocean side of Maui Prince Hotel. Rest rooms and parking are available.

Maluaka Beach

At the southern end of Makena Bay is Maluaka Beach, a beige-sand beach fronting the Maui Prince Hotel. Maluaka is often called Makena Beach, so don't confuse it with Makena Beach Park just north.

The beach, which slopes down from a low sand dune, has a sandy bottom in its center and rocky formations at each end that might provide decent snorkeling. Overall, it's lovely here.

You can park opposite Keawalai Congregational Church and walk through the resort, or drive past the Maui Prince Hotel on Makena Alanui Rd, then take the first road on your right to the tiny beach parking lot, where you'll find rest rooms and a paved sidewalk leading to the beach.

Onelui (Little Black Sand) Beach

South of the Maui Prince Hotel, Makena Rd winds past private villas. Look for the first shoreline access sign and a rutted road leading to this windy, atmospheric salt-and-pepper sand beach. Strong offshore currents make it dangerous for swimming, but sometimes you can spot turtles poking their heads out of the water.

Makena Bay-La Perouse State Park (Little Beach & Big Beach)

Big Beach is the sort of scene that people conjure up when they dream of a Hawaiian beach – beautiful and expansive, with virtually no development on the horizon.

In the late 1960s, it was the site of an alternative-lifestyle encampment that took on the nickname 'Hippie Beach.' The tent city lasted until 1972, when police finally evicted everyone on health code violations. More than a few of Maui's now-graying residents can trace their roots on the island from that crazy time.

The Hawaiian name for Big Beach is Oneloa, literally 'Long Sand.' The golden sands stretch for over half a mile and are as broad as they come, with clear turquoise waters. But the open ocean beyond Big Beach can have powerful rip currents and dangerous shorebreaks during periods of heavy surf. Killer breaks are for experienced bodysurfers only.

The turnoff to the main parking area for Big Beach is exactly a mile past the Maui Prince Hotel. A second parking area lies a quarter mile to the south. You can also park alongside the road and walk in; watch for *kiawe* thorns in the woods behind the beach. As thefts and broken windshields are commonplace in the parking lots, many locals prefer the last option. Your safest bet may be a bit further from the beach, right before the road narrows as it heads toward La Perouse Bay, opposite the **Makena Grill** *(daily specials $6)* food cart.

Little Beach, also known as Puu Olai Beach, is a popular nude beach, despite a rusty old sign and many arrests to the contrary. Citations for nude sunbathing (which is, in fact, illegal) cost a pretty penny. All the uproar over 'nekkid' people here probably has less to do with supposed Hawaiian cultural issues than with the fact that it's one of the few openly gay meeting places on Maui.

Little Beach fronts a sandy cove that usually has a gentle shorebreak ideal for bodysurfing and boogie boarding. Snorkeling along the rocky point is good when the water is calm. The point is hidden by a rocky outcrop that juts out from Puu Olai, the cinder cone that marks the north end of Big Beach. A trail over the rock links the two and takes just a few minutes to walk.

Makena Beach (the collective name for Little Beach and Big Beach) has recently become a state park, which may eventually lead to the addition of full beach facilities, but for now it remains in a natural state except for a couple of pit toilets and picnic tables.

MAUI

Activities

Makena North Golf Course *(☎ 879-3344; 5415 Makena Alanui Dr; green fees & cart $140)* offers a challenging round of championship-caliber golf, although without the prestige of Wailea.

Makena Tennis Club *(☎ 879-8777; 5414 Makena Alanui Dr; courts per hr $18-22, daily clinics $20)* requires advance reservations; bring proper tennis attire.

Places to Stay & Eat

Destination Resorts *(☎ 891-6200, 800-367-5246, fax 874-3554; W www.drhmaui.com; Unit B51, The Shops at Wailea)* handles condo rentals in Makena.

Maui Prince Hotel *(☎ 874-1111, 800-321-6248, fax 879-8763; W www.mauiprincehotel.com; 5400 Makena Alanui Dr; rooms $310-460, suites from $600)* may look like a fortress from the outside, but the interior incorporates a fine sense of Japanese aesthetics. The five-story hotel surrounds a courtyard with waterfalls, running streams, carp ponds and raked rock gardens. All 310 rooms have at least partial ocean views. Special promotions often undercut the rack rates. If you want quiet luxury, this is for you. Its **Molokini Lounge** often has live Hawaiian music and great sunset views to go with cocktails.

Hakone *(Maui Prince Hotel; full dinners $26-45, Mon buffet adult/child $45/25; open 6pm-9pm Mon, 6pm-9:30pm Tues-Sat)* is a refined Japanese restaurant showing Kyoto haute cuisine influences and local Hawaiian flourishes. Try the *rakusen kaiseki* (multicourse chef's tasting menu) with green tea *brulée*.

Prince Court *(Maui Prince Hotel; Sun brunch $40, dinner $24-32; open 6pm-9:30pm daily, Sun brunch seatings 9am, 9:30am, 11:30am & noon)* is a formal dining room specializing in Hawaiian regional cuisine. The five-onion herb bisque is nearly as indulgent as the Sunday champagne brunch.

MAKENA TO LA PEROUSE BAY

Makena Rd continues as a narrow paved road for 3 miles after Big Beach. The road goes through the Ahihi-Kinau Natural Area Reserve before dead-ending at La Perouse Bay. Because the road's narrow and has two-way traffic, it can be a slow drive. Note that this it *not* the road that continues around the island to Kaupo Gap and Hana. To get on that road, you've got to backtrack to Kahului and take Hwy 37 up past Pukalani until it joins the upper Piilani Hwy (see the Upcountry section later).

Ahihi-Kinau Natural Area Reserve

This rugged 2045-acre preserve includes sections of Ahihi Bay and Cape Kinau. Maui's most recent lava flow created most of the cape on its way to the sea at least two centuries ago. The reserve has lava tide pools, coastal lava tubes and all the *aa* (rough, jagged lava) you could ever want to see.

Its distinctive marine life habitat and unique geological features include anchialine pools and *kipuka* ('islands' of land spared but surrounded by lava flows). Fishing and the removal of any flora, fauna or lava is prohibited. The remains of a coastal Hawaiian village – its old sites marked by

The Lost Explorer

In May 1786, the renowned French explorer Jean François de Galaup La Perouse became the first Westerner to land on Maui. La Perouse was a student of the French Enlightenment. His ships carried soldiers and sailors, as well as botanists, astronomers, geographers, zoologists, naturalists and clergy.

As he sailed into the bay that now bears his name, scores of Hawaiian canoes came out to greet him and trade. The admiral visited four villages around Keoneoio, noting especially that the island had 'a burning climate.'

After leaving Hawaii, La Perouse mysteriously disappeared in the Pacific. While no-one knows his fate, some historians speculate that he and his crew were eaten by cannibals in the New Hebrides.

walled and terraced platforms – sit between lava flows at Ahihi Bay.

A little roadside cove just one tenth of a mile south of the first reserve sign offers good snorkeling. It's quite rocky and can be a bit challenging getting in, but the cove has lots of coral and fish. Another trail from the signboard at the southern tip of the preserve, two-tenths of a mile north of Makena Stables, leads *makai* to a series of snorkeling coves, which you'll find if you head north along the coast.

La Perouse Bay

This astounding natural area is steeped in history. The archaeological remains of the early Hawaiian village Keoneoio – mainly *hale* (house) and *heiau* platforms – are scattered among the lava patches. Volunteers patrol the area to discourage car break-ins and educate visitors.

Spinner dolphins come into the bay during the day to rest (they never actually sleep), and can be seen offshore. For expert kayakers, surfers and divers only, the bay offers a real challenge, but the sea life is amazing. However, strong offshore winds put snorkeling and swimming out of the question.

The paved road ends just short of La Perouse Bay. Although it may be possible to drive all the way in on the 4WD road, you're OK parking past where the asphalt ends at **La Perouse Monument** and walking down to the coast. Just before the monument, friendly **Makena Stables** (*☎ 879-0244; 🅆 www.makenastables.com; trail rides $120-195*) leads guided horseback rides on the volcanic slopes; reservations are necessary.

From La Perouse Bay, it's possible to continue on foot along the **King's Hwy (Hoapili) Coastal Trail**. This ancient footpath follows the coastline across jagged barren lava flows, so hiking boots are needed. It's a dry area with no water and little vegetation, and it can get very hot.

The first part of the trail is along the sandy beach at La Perouse Bay. Right after the trail emerges onto the lava fields, it's possible to take a spur trail for three-quarters of a mile down to the light beacon at the tip of Cape Hanamanioa. Alternatively, walk inland to the Na Ala Hele sign and turn right onto the King's Hwy as it climbs up and down through rough *aa* lava inland for the next 2 miles before coming back to the coast to an older lava flow at Kanaio Beach.

East Maui

The famed Hana Hwy runs from old-fashioned Paia to the village of Hana and beyond to the pools of Oheo Gulch. After Hana, the rugged, rewarding Piilani Hwy takes the adventurous around through Kaupo, with its wild volcanic landscape and lonely coastline, back to the Upcountry.

PAIA

Paia is an old sugar town with a fresh coat of paint. As part of the original Alexander & Baldwin sugar plantation, Paia in the early 20th century had a population more than triple its present size. In those days, most of the town's 10,000 residents lived in plantation camps on the cool slopes above the sugar mill.

During the 1950s, many of the town's residents moved to Kahului or Oahu seeking new postwar economic opportunities, shops closed, and Paia began to collect cobwebs. As the Age of Aquarius dawned, hippies seeking paradise found themselves here, followed by windsurfers who began to discover nearby Hookipa Beach in the 1980s. Paia has now been dubbed the 'windsurfing capital of the world,' and has as many international windsurfers as it once had sugarcane workers.

EAST MAUI

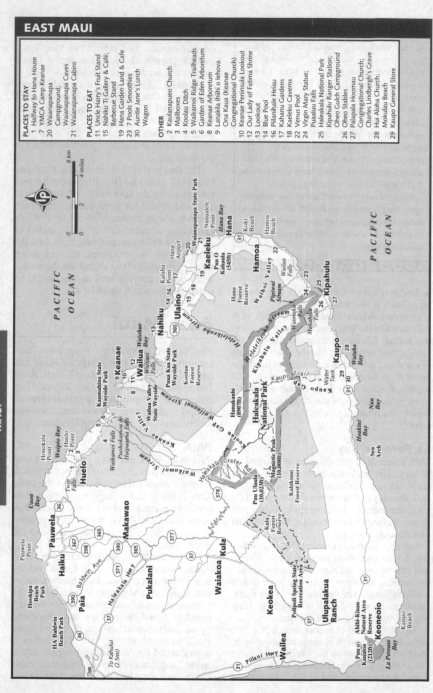

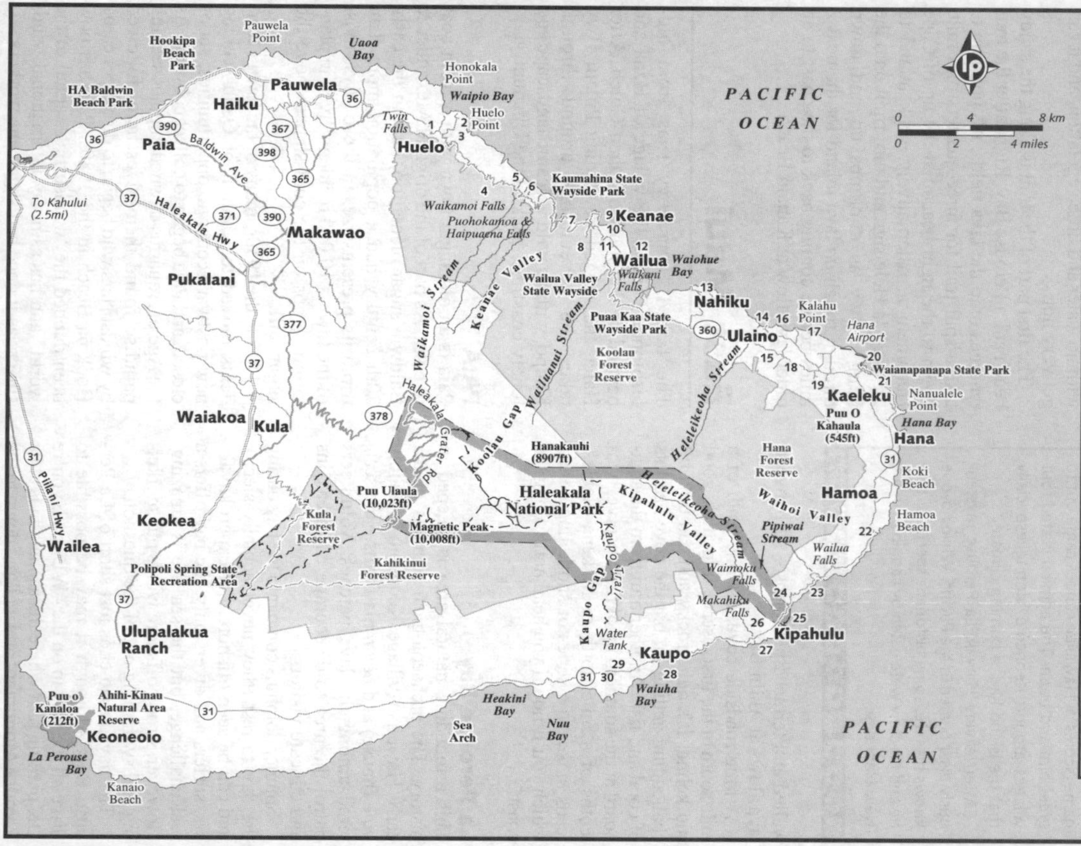

PLACES TO STAY
1 Halfway to Hana House
7 YMCA Camp Keanae
20 Waianapanapa Campground; Waianapanapa Caves
21 Waianapanapa Cabins

PLACES TO EAT
11 Uncle Harry's Fruit Stand
15 Nahiku Ti Gallery & Café; Barbecue Stand
19 Hana Garden Land & Cafe
23 7 Pools Smoothies
30 Auntie Jane's Lunch Wagon

OTHER
2 Kaulanapueo Church
3 Mailboxes
4 Koolau Ditch
5 Waikamoi Ridge Trailheads
6 Garden of Eden Arboretum
8 Keanae Arboretum
9 Lanakila Ihiihi o Iehova Ona Kaua (Keanae Congregational Church)
10 Keanae Peninsula Lookout
12 Our Lady of Fatima Shrine
13 Lookout
14 Blue Pool
16 Piilanihale Heiau
17 Kahanu Gardens
18 Kaeleku Caverns
22 Venus Pool
24 Virgin Mary Statue; Puaaluu Falls
25 Haleakala National Park Kipahulu Ranger Station; Oheo Gulch Campground
26 Oheo Stables
27 Palapala Hoomau Congregational Church; Charles Lindbergh's Grave
28 Hui Aloha Church; Mokulau Beach
29 Kaupo General Store

Many of the old wooden storefronts in town are painted in bright tones of rosy pink, sunshine yellow and sky blue, adding to the town's quirky character. The stores house eclectic galleries, a few surf shops, grocery stores and a variety of tasty restaurants.

Orientation & Information

The Hana Hwy (Hwy 36) runs straight through the center of Paia – this is the last real town before Hana and the last place to gas up your car. Paia is also a link to the Upcountry via Baldwin Ave, passing the old sugar mill. Everything in town is within walking distance.

There's a branch of the **Bank of Hawaii** *(☎ 575-9511; 35 Baldwin Ave; open 8:30am-4pm Mon-Thur, 8:30am-6pm Fri)* and a **post office** *(☎ 579-8866; 120 Baldwin Ave; open 8:30am-4:30pm Mon-Fri, 10:30am-12:30pm Sat)* in town. The **Minit Stop gas station** *(☎ 579-9227; open until 11pm daily)* has an ATM.

There's a **coin laundry** *(Baldwin Ave)* just south of the Vegan Restaurant. **Mana Foods** *(49 Baldwin Ave; open 8:30am-8:30pm daily)* has a good bulletin board, with notices tacked up for everything from rooms for rent to classes in windsurfing or Ashtanga yoga.

Spreckelsville Beach

Spreckelsville Beach, by the golf course between Kahului airport and Paia, is a long stretch of rocky shore composed of sandy strands punctuated with lava outcrops. It's one of the windiest places on the north shore, making it a prime windsurfing spot for beginners, particularly in summer.

To get there, turn toward the ocean on Nonohe Place, which runs along the west side of the Maui Country Club. Turn right where the road ends and look for the blue shoreline access sign.

HA Baldwin Beach Park

HA Baldwin Beach Park, a big county park about a mile west of Paia, has a long sandy beach with good bodysurfing. Swimming and snorkeling may be possible before the afternoon winds pick up. The park also has showers, rest rooms, picnic tables and a well-used baseball and soccer field. A word of caution: crime and drunken nastiness are not unheard of here. Look for the turnoff at the 6-mile marker.

Offshore and closer to Paia town, **Jaws** has become famous for its giant waves where surfers are towed in by wave runners.

Mantokuji Buddhist Mission

Mantokuji, a Buddhist temple built c. 1921 with an ocean view and a massive gong in the yard, is on the Hana side of town. It's fronted by a graveyard with *kanji*-engraved stones, some decorated with tropical flowers. During the summer, the Obon holidays are observed here with religious services and Japanese folk dances.

Hookipa Beach Park

Hookipa, which has long been one of Maui's prime surfing spots, has established itself as Hawaii's premier windsurfing beach. Winter has the biggest waves for board surfers, and summer has the most consistent winds for windsurfers. During shoulder-season weather conditions, the unspoken agreement is that surfers go out in the morning, while windsurfers launch in the afternoon.

Between the strong currents, dangerous shorebreak and razor-sharp coral, this is unquestionably an area for experts. As a spectator venue, it's great, attracting the world's top windsurfers for the Da Kine Classic in May and the Aloha Classic in late fall. Hookipa is just before the 9-mile marker; look for the line of cars on the lookout above the beach. The park has rest rooms, showers and picnic pavilions.

Places to Stay

While Paia has no hostels or hotels, it does have a number of smaller private places to stay. You can also find inexpensive rooms by checking bulletin boards around Paia or by looking in the 'Vacation Rentals' column of the *Maui News* (*W www.mauinews.com*) classifieds.

Most of the booking agencies that rent out beach cottages, vacation homes and B&Bs, both around Paia and in Haiku, require a three-day minimum stay to avoid hefty surcharges.

Hookipa Haven *(☎ 579-8282, 800-398-6284, fax 579-9953; W www.hookipa.com; 62 Baldwin Ave #2A; rooms & studios from $50)* is an established vacation rental service that makes bookings mainly in Paia and the Upcountry. German is spoken.

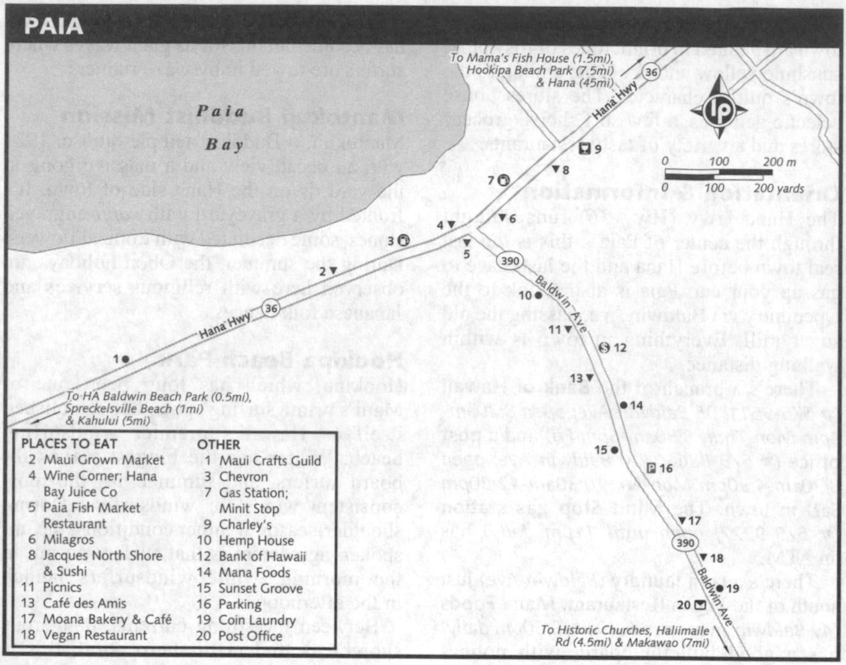

MAUI

Chameleon Vacation Rentals Maui *(☎ 575-9933, 866-575-9933, fax 340-8537; W www.donnachameleon.com; rooms & cottages from $65)*, managed by a friendly, eco-minded booking agent, has everything from oceanfront cottages to rustic cabins in Paia, Haiku and farther along toward Hana.

The Spyglass House *(☎/fax 579-8608, 800-475-6695; W www.spyglassmaui.com; 367 Hana Hwy; rooms $90-150)* is a wonderfully eccentric retreat with porthole windows, bits of stained glass and plenty of hidden nooks and crannies. Set back from the highway beside the ocean, rooms in the original Spyglass House are better furnished than those in the garden. Guests have access to hammocks, a Jacuzzi, barbecue grill and even yoga classes.

Places to Eat

Any excuse for stopping here around mealtime will do, as the food is almost universally wonderful. Nothing better awaits you in Hana, so stock up on picnic supplies and take-out now. Or at least get a tropical smoothie from **Hana Bay Juice Co**, next to the **Wine Corner** *(111 Hana Hwy, cnr Baldwin Ave)* shop.

Mana Foods *(49 Baldwin Ave; open 8:30am-8:30pm daily)* is a large, down-to-earth health food store with a good variety of juices, yogurts, nuts, granolas, cheeses and organic produce. It also offers fresh-baked breads, a salad bar and a few inexpensive take-out hot dishes.

Maui Grown Market *(93 Hana Hwy; picnic lunches $8.50)* offers some unbelievable perks with its picnic baskets. You get a cooler and a Hana Hwy audiotape or CD driving guide to borrow, free coffee or pineapple, and – you're never going to believe this – one of its loveable, well-trained dogs to accompany you on your road trip, if you call at least 24 hours in advance.

Picnics *(30 Baldwin Ave; dishes $5-8, picnic lunches $8.50-13; open 7am-7pm daily)* is a famous deli. Sandwiches include a nice vegetarian spinach nut burger with cheddar cheese ($5.75), as well as more traditional offerings; try the plantation breakfasts or local plate lunches. There's a guide to the Hana Hwy on the back of the take-out menu, and you can get box lunches for the road.

Café des Amis *(42 Baldwin Ave; breakfast & lunch $4-8, dinner $8-12; open 8:30am-8:30pm daily)* is a sunny morning spot, especially for savory or sweet crepes and rich coffee.

Vegan Restaurant *(☎ 579-9144; 115 Baldwin Ave; dishes $3.50-10; open noon-9pm daily)* has only a dozen tables, so arrive early. Who can forget their yummy mashed potatoes or vegan burgers and salads, not to mention a variety of teas and chocolate cake?

Paia Fish Market Restaurant *(2A Baldwin Ave, cnr Hana Hwy; meals $5-15; open 11am-9:30pm daily)* displays its fish in a refrigerated case at the counter. Convivial locals hunker down over fish and chips at wooden tables.

Milagros *(3 Baldwin Ave; lunch $6-10, dinner from $12; open 8am-10pm daily)*, on the opposite corner to the fish market, is a justifiably popular Tex-Mex café with deliciously fresh food and sidewalk dining on a prime people-watching corner. Recommended are the fish tacos served with heavenly salsa.

Moana Bakery & Cafe *(☎ 579-9999; 71 Baldwin Ave; breakfast & lunch $6-10, dinner $8-23; open 8am-9pm daily)*, a soothing spot jointly run by a chef and a French pastry master, features herbs and produce from the café's own garden in its dishes, perhaps spicing some chilled seared *ahi* with Molokai sweet potatoes or Hana Bay crab cakes. At breakfast, choose from malted Belgian waffles or gourmet omelettes.

Jacques North Shore & Sushi *(☎ 579-8844; 120 Hana Hwy; breakfast & lunch $5-8; dinner $10-25; open 8am-midnight daily, bar menu after 9:30pm)* has a pleasant bistro atmosphere and serves Pacific regional dishes with a French accent by Jacques, who once did a stint as the personal chef of the Swedish king. The local favorite is the grilled fresh fish of the day, which is offered nightly, or try the vegan banana curry.

Mama's Fish House *(☎ 579-8488; 799 Poho Pl; dinner $28-35; open 11am-2:30pm & 5pm-9:30pm daily)*, along the Hana Hwy at Kuau Cove, 2 miles east of Paia center near the 8-miles marker (look for the fishing boat on a small rise to your left), has excellent locally caught fish and a pretty ocean view from its coconut grove. Other menu highlights are luau-style set meals, *kalua* pork sandwiches and Maui onion or Kona lobster soup. Lunch is only slightly cheaper than dinner, and make reservations.

Entertainment

Jacques North Shore & Sushi *(☎ 579-8844; 120 Hana Hwy; open 8am-midnight daily, bar menu after 9:30pm)* has the island's longest monkeypod bar and is the most popular place in Paia to have a drink. **Charley's** *(☎ 579-9453; 142 Hana Hwy)* saloon has live music a few days a week and late-night pizza. **Moana Bakery & Cafe** *(☎ 579-9999; 71 Baldwin Ave; open 8am-9pm daily)* has live jazz and flamenco on weekends.

If you want more action, **Casanova**, in Makawao (see the Upcountry section later), is the best bet.

Shopping

Maui Crafts Guild *(☎ 579-9697; 43 Hana Hwy, open 9am 6pm daily)* is a collective of Maui artists and craftspeople who operate the island's best gallery. Located on the *makai* side of the road, as you come into town from Kahului, it sells dyed cloth, woodwork, pottery, natural fiber baskets, beadwork and more. There's also a nice view of the surrounding sugarcane fields from the top floor.

Other notable shops are the **Hemp House** *(16 Baldwin Ave)* for tie-dyed skivvies and **Sunset Groove** *(62 Baldwin Ave)*.

PAIA TO HIGHWAY 360

After Hookipa Beach, fields of sugarcane give way to long rows of pineapples.

After the 10-mile marker, a short gravel road leads down to Maliko Bay with its small boat ramp also used by divers in summer.

Hwy 365, which leads up to Makawao and other Upcountry towns, comes in just after the 16-mile marker. At this point, the Hana Hwy changes numbers from Hwy 36 to Hwy 360 and the mile markers begin again at zero. The road then changes dramatically, slicing through cliffs and becoming more of a mountain road than a highway. Hana is 35 scenic miles away.

THE ROAD TO HANA

The Hana Hwy (Hwy 360) is a cliff-hugger as it winds its way deep into lush valleys and back out above a rugged coastline, snaking around more than 600 twists and turns along the way. Built in 1927 using convict labor, this spectacular coastal drive is also very narrow; in many places, one-lane bridges mark dozens of waterfalls. Some are tiny and Zen-like, others sheer and lacy. The 54 bridges to Hana have 54 poetic Hawaiian names taken from the streams and gulches they cross – names like Heavenly Mist, Burning Star and Reawakening.

The valleys drip with vegetation. African tulip trees add bright splashes of orange to the dense rain forests, bamboo groves and fern-covered hillsides. The road follows the royal trail system constructed by Chief Piilani and completed in the 15th century.

It would take about two hours to drive straight through from Kahului to Hana. But this is not a drive to rush. If you're not staying over in Hana, get an early start to give yourself a full day – or you'll be following the same herd of tourists all day long. Those with time to explore will find short trails to hike, mountain pools to dip in and a couple of historic sites to check out, all just a few minutes beyond the road.

Remember to pull over if local drivers are behind you. They have places to get to and move at a different pace.

Twin Falls

After the 2-mile marker, you'll see a dirt pull-off on your right next to a fruit stand. The fence here is the start of the gentle walk to Twin Falls. If you can't find a place to park, don't worry. There are better waterfalls further down the road.

Places to Stay Only about 5 miles of southeast of Haiku, **Halfway to Hana House** (☎ *572-1176, fax 572-3609; 100 Waipio Rd;* W *www.maui.net/~gailp; B&B studio $85)* is an ocean-view home with herb gardens, bamboo groves, a banana patch and lily pond. The studio has its own private entrance and bath, with chocolate macadamia nuts by your pillow.

The Tea House (☎ *572-5610;* W *www.mauiteahouse.com; PO Box 335, Haiku, HI 96708; 1-bedroom single/double cottages $105/120)*, hidden down near the ocean, is an Asian-style retreat built with recycled walls from a Zen temple in San Francisco. All courtesy of solar power, guests have a small kitchen with fresh herbs, TV, VCR and an open-air bath in a redwood gazebo. There are wild ginger and banana plants, a barbecue grill, and a Tibetan-style stupa on the grounds.

Maluhia Hale (☎ *572-2959;* W *www.maui.net/~djg; PO Box 687, Haiku, HI 96708; suites/cottages $105/115)*, an airy plantation-style house, has a striking cottage with Hawaiian quilts and Chinese porcelain, and a verandah sitting room that can be left open to the elements if the weather is kind. Both the suite and cottage have a kitchenette and private bath.

Huelo

Dirt-packed Huelo Rd, half a mile past the 3-mile marker by the public mailbox stand, leads down to historic **Kaulanapueo Church** (1853), made from coral and stone. The church is likely to be locked, however, so if you're short on time, this one can be easily bypassed. There is no beach access here, as the road dead-ends at gated homes.

Koolau Forest Reserve

After Huelo, the vegetation becomes increasingly lush as the highway snakes along the edge of the Koolau Forest Reserve. Koolau, which means 'windward,' is the windward side of Haleakala and catches the rain clouds. The coast in this area gets 60 to 80 inches of rain a year, while a few miles up on the slopes the annual rainfall is an impressive 200 to 300 inches. The reserve is heavily forested and cut with numerous gulches and streams. From here, there seems to be a one-lane bridge and waterfall around every other bend.

Many of the dirt roads leading inland from the highway are the maintenance roads for the **Koolau Ditch**, which parallels the highway. The century-old system is capable of carrying 450 million gallons of water a day through 75 miles of ditches and tunnels from the rain forest to the dry central plains. If you want to take a closer look, stop at the small pull-off just before the bridge that comes up immediately after the 8-mile marker. Just 100ft above the road you can see a hand-hewn stone-block section of the ditch.

As you leave the village of **Kailua**, you'll notice Norfolk pines up on the hillside, followed by a grove of painted eucalyptus trees with rainbow-colored bark that were introduced from Australia, then you'll see a long stretch of bamboo.

Further on, a half mile past the 9-mile marker, there's a wide turnoff with space for

MAUI

a few cars to park below the **Waikamoi Ridge Trail**. This peaceful 30-minute trail loops through tall trees with wonderful fresh scents. You're welcomed by a sign that reads: 'Quiet. Trees at Work.' The grand reddish trees are *Eucalyptus robusta*. Note the huge climbing philodendron vines wrapped around them – the vines provide an apt illustration of the etymology of 'philodendron,' a Greek word meaning 'lover of trees'! Keep an eye out for occasional metal spikes and tree roots that protrude along the path. From the ridge at the top, there's a good view of the winding Hana Hwy.

Waterfalls & Gardens

Waikamoi Falls is at the bridge just before the 10-mile marker. One waterfall and a pool are near the road. It's possible to walk a short way up to a higher waterfall, but the rocks can be slippery, and the bottom waterfall is prettier anyway.

Past Waikamoi, bamboo grows almost horizontally out from the cliffs, creating a canopy effect over the road. After a half mile is the **Garden of Eden Arboretum** (*☎ 572-9899, 10600 Hana Hwy; admission $5; open 8:30am-2.30pm daily*), designed by a certified arborist. Even if it's a bit of a tourist trap, many people say the verdant nature paths are worth the price of admission.

At the 11-mile marker, near Puohokamoa Bridge and just a few minutes' walk from the road, is **Puohokamoa Falls** – another attractive little waterfall. Because it has more parking space and a couple of picnic tables, Puohokamoa sees more visitors than the other waterfalls.

Haipuaena Falls, half a mile after the 11-mile marker, is a gentle little waterfall with a wonderful pool deep enough for swimming. Most people don't know this one's here, as you can't see the pool from the road. There's space for just one or two cars on the Hana side of the bridge. To reach the falls, walk upstream for a couple of minutes. Wild ginger grows along the path, and ferns hang from the rock wall behind the waterfall, making for quite an idyllic setting.

Shortly after the 12-mile marker, **Kaumahina State Wayside Park** has picnic tables and toilets. A two-minute walk up the hill under the park's tall eucalyptus trees provides a broad ocean vista, with Keanae Peninsula to the southeast.

For the next several miles, the scenery is particularly magnificent, opening up to a new vista as you turn round each bend. If you're on this road after heavy rains, you can expect to see waterfalls galore crashing down the mountains.

Honomanu Bay

Just after crossing the bridge at the 14-mile marker, an inconspicuous and very rough gravel road heads down to **Honomanu Bay** and a rocky black-sand beach used mostly by surfers and fishers. The water's usually too turbulent for swimming, but on very calm days it's possible to kayak here.

Keanae

Keanae is about halfway to Hana. Keanae Valley, which extends down from the Koolau Gap in Haleakala Crater, averages 150 inches of rain a year. Keanae Peninsula was formed by a later eruption of Haleakala that flowed through Koolau Gap down Keanae Valley. Outlined by its black lava shores, the peninsula still wears its birthmark around the edges. It's very flat, like a leaf floating on the water.

Keanae Arboretum, three-quarters of a mile past the 16-mile marker, is unkempt and disappointing. Introduced tropical plants seen here include painted eucalyptus trees and golden-stemmed bamboo. A short paved path leads up past heliconia, ti, banana, guava, breadfruit, ginger and other fragrant plants to dozens of varieties of Hawaiian taro in irrigated patches. However, the garden is often dried out. Swarms of mosquitoes making life miserable.

The road that leads down to **Keanae Peninsula** is just beyond the Keanae Arboretum. Keanae is a quiet little village with colts and goats roaming freely. At the end of the road is a scenic coastline of jagged rock and pounding waves. The rock island down the coast is Mokumana Island, a seabird sanctuary.

Lanakila Ihiihi o Iehova Ona Kaua (Keanae Congregational Church) is an attractive old stone church, built in 1860, about half a mile down. This is one church, made of lava rocks and coral mortar, whose exterior hasn't been covered over with layers of whitewash. A small cemetery is sprinkled with tropical flowers and coconut palm trees.

There's a good view of Keanae village, with its squares of planted taro fed by Keanae Stream, at an unmarked pull-off just past the 17-mile marker. Look for the mailbox under the tsunami speaker. Just before the pull-out, a well-worn steep trail leads down to **Ching's Pond**.

Places to Stay Midway between the 16- and 17-mile markers, **YMCA Camp Keanae** (*☎ 248-8355; e ymcacampkeanae@aol.com; 13375 Hana Hwy; tent sites & dorm beds $15)*, on a knoll overlooking the coast, has guest cabins that can sometimes fill with groups on weekends. Otherwise, the cabins are usually available to individual travelers as hostel-style dorms. The cabins have bunk beds, but you have to bring your own sleeping bag, food and cookware. Kitchen facilities are not available, but the cabins have simple outdoor grills. Advance reservations are required, and there's a three-night limit. Nicer accommodations are also available upon request.

Wailua

Shortly after the Keanae Peninsula Lookout, you'll pass a couple of **fruit stands** along the road selling drinks and snacks. The best one, **Uncle Harry's** *(smoothies $5)*, is run by the family of the late Harry Kunihi Mitchell, a native Hawaiian-rights advocate who wrote the popular 'Mele o Kahoolawe' (Song of Kahoolawe).

MAUI

Take Wailua Rd seaward immediately after Uncle Harry's to get to **Our Lady of Fatima Shrine**. This little white-and-blue chapel, built in 1860, is also known as the Coral Miracle Church. The coral used in the construction came from a freak storm that deposited coral rocks onto a nearby beach. After the church was completed, another rogue storm hit the beach and swept all the leftover piles of coral back into the sea, or so the story goes. The current congregation now uses **St Gabriel's Mission**, the larger and newer church out front.

Wailua Rd dead-ends half a mile down, though you won't want to go that far, as driveways blocked off with logs and milk crates prevent cars from turning around.

Waysides

Back on the Hana Hwy, just before the 19-mile marker, **Wailua Valley State Wayside** lookout comes up on the right. It has a broad view into Keanae Valley, which appears to be a hundred shades of green. You can see a couple of waterfalls, and if it's clear, you can look up at Koolau Gap, a break in the rim of Haleakala Crater.

If you climb up the steps to the right, you can get a good view of Wailua Peninsula, but there's a better view of it at a large paved turnoff a quarter mile down the road.

Halfway between the 22- and 23-mile markers is **Puaa Kaa State Wayside Park**, where a tranquil waterfall empties into a pool before flowing down into a ravine. The park has rest rooms, a pay phone, shaded streamside picnic tables and a pool large enough for swimming.

Before the 29-mile marker is the **Nahiku Ti Gallery & Café**, serving decent coffee and sandwiches. But it's the barbecue stand next door that makes people stop to buy *kalua* pig sandwiches and fresh fried fish. It's probably better than anything you'll get in Hana.

Ulaino Road

Even when it's very dry, you probably won't be able to go the entire 3 miles of Ulaino Rd without a 4WD, but you can usually get as far as the gardens, and then walk in the rest of the way to the Blue Pool.

Opposite the turnoff at the 31-mile marker is **Hana Garden Land & Cafe** *(☎ 248-7340; W www.hanagardenland.com; Kalo Rd)*. The 5-acre grounds boast over 125 varieties of palms, tropical fruit trees, a koi pond and walking paths. A menu emphasizing local produce runs with the motto, 'nothing even close to a hamburger.'

Kaeleku Caverns Until 1999, these caves *(☎ 248-7308; W www.mauicave.com; 1hr tours $29)* were filled with trash and 17,000lb of cow bones. Now you can walk inside lava tubes formed by ancient lava flows. Rain or shine, tours are led through the fragile ecosystem of stalactites and stalagmites; guides will teach you how to 'cave softly.' All gear is provided, including flashlights and hard hats. Reservations are advised.

Kahanu Gardens A 122-acre botanical garden on Kalahu Point, **Kahanu Gardens** *(☎ 248-8912; self-guided tours $10; usually open 10am-2pm Mon-Fri)* is under the jurisdiction of the National Tropical Botanical Garden. This nonprofit group is involved in the propagation and conservation of rare and medicinal plants, and Kahanu Gardens features ethnobotanical collections from Polynesia, Micronesia and Melanesia. Here in one place you'll see *kukui, hala* (pandanus plant), *hau* and the Pacific's largest known collection of *ulu* (breadfruit) cultivars.

The Kahanu grounds are also the site of the astounding **Piilanihale Heiau**, the biggest *heiau* extant in Hawaii, which has a stone platform the size of two football fields. It was built by Piilani, the 14th-century Maui chief who is also credited with the construction of many of the coastal fishponds and taro terraces in the Hana area.

The gardens are about 1½ miles along Ulaino Rd. Admission policies vary; always call ahead to check opening hours.

Blue Pool Past the gardens, Ulaino Rd quickly becomes rough. Major dips in the road pass over two streambeds that clearly call for 4WD vehicles, especially if it has been raining hard recently. The best advice is to park well off to the side of the road before the first streambed and walk the final mile to the coast.

When you get to the water's edge, turn left and strike out across the beach boulders for five minutes or so until you see this paradise on earth. (Unless, of course, things are very dry, in which case you might not see much more than a trickle.)

Waianapanapa State Park

The road into Waianapanapa State Park is immediately after the 32-mile marker, half a mile south of the turnoff to Hana airport. At the T-junction, turn right for the state park cabins, or left if you're heading for the camping ground, picnic pavilions, rest rooms, outdoor showers and water fountains, beach, caves or hiking trails.

The road into the park ends at a parking lot above Pailoa Bay, which is surrounded by a scenic coastline of low rocky cliffs. There's a natural lava arch on the right side of the bay. A short path from the parking lot leads down to the small black-sand beach, which is unprotected and usually has strong rip currents. When it's very calm, the area around the arch is said to be good for snorkeling. Check it out carefully, though, as people have drowned here.

Two impressive lava-tube **caves** are just a five-minute walk from the parking lot along a loop path. On the outside, the caves are covered with ferns and flowering impatiens. Inside, they're dripping wet and cool. Waianapanapa means 'glistening waters,' and should you be tempted to take a dip in the cave pools, the clear mineral waters will leave you feeling squeaky clean.

On certain nights of the year, the waters in the caves turn red. Legend says it's the blood of a princess and her lover who were killed in a fit of rage by the princess's jealous husband after he found them hiding together here. Less romantic types attribute the phenomenon to swarms of tiny bright-red shrimp called *opaeula,* which occasionally emerge from subterranean cracks in the lava.

A **coastal trail** that runs parallel to the ancient King's Hwy leads south about 2 miles from the park to Kainalimu Bay, just north of Hana Bay. Some of the original smooth lava stepping stones are still in place along the trail. Gorgeous coastal views take in endless expanses of cobalt-blue water below craggy black lava outcrops. *Hala* and *naupaka* are the predominant flora along the trail; the *naupaka* has delicate white flowers that look as if they've been torn in half.

Beyond the park cabins, the trail passes blowholes and over a bridge before reaching **heiau ruins** after a three-quarter-mile walk. Just beyond is a small fishing shack. As the trail fades, just keep following the coast over fields of *aa* and *pahoehoe* lava. Once you reach the boulder-strewn beach at Kainalimu Bay, it's about a mile farther to Hana town center.

Places to Stay Tent **camping** is free with a permit; expect wet conditions year-round. Sites are right next to the parking lot, but that isn't a problem once the daytrippers go home. The dozen **housekeeping cabins**, which book up months in advance, are across the park. See Accommodations earlier in this chapter for details on fees and reservations.

HANA

Separated from Kahului by 54 bridges and almost as many miles, the isolated town of Hana has thus far fought off development. The town sits beneath the rainy slopes of Haleakala, surrounded by green pastures and a jagged black coastline. In ancient

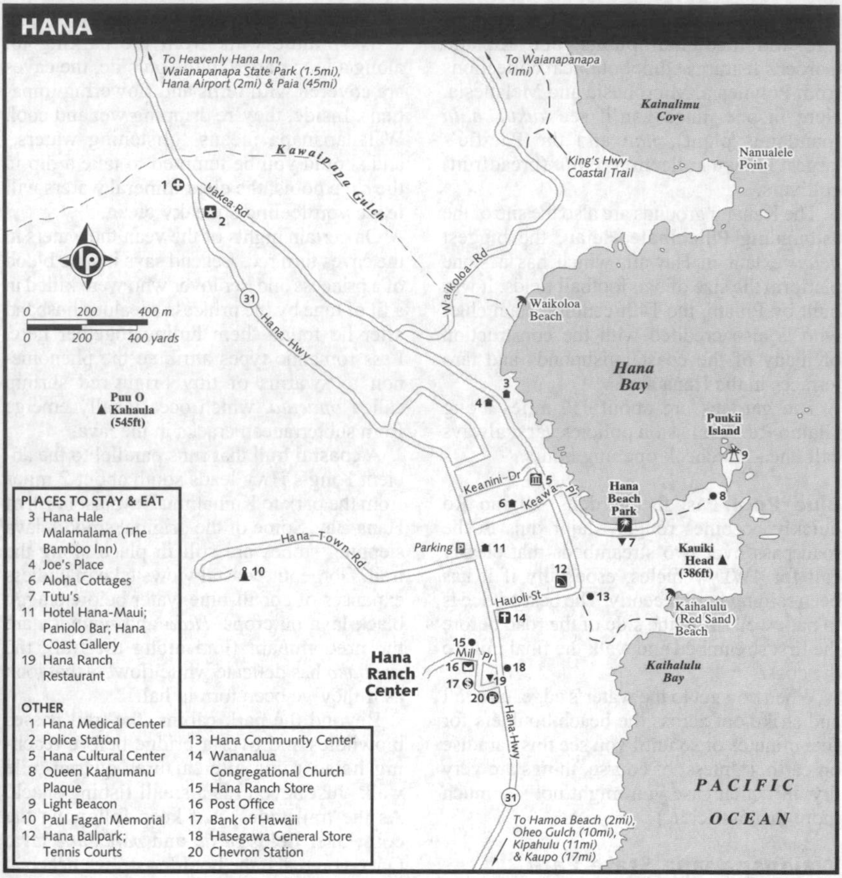

times, it was the royal heart of one of Maui's largest population centers. And even though a line of traffic passes through each day, not many visitors stay on.

Hana is not a grand finale to the magnificent Hana Hwy, and people expecting great things are often disappointed. The simple town itself is sedate. What makes Hana special is more apparent to those who linger here overnight. There's an almost timeless rural character, and though 'Old Hawaii' is an oft-used cliche elsewhere, it's hard not to think of Hana in such terms.

People in Hana cling to their traditional ways. Hana has one of the most Hawaiian communities in the state. Many of its 1900 residents have Hawaiian blood and a strong sense of *ohana* (extended family). If you spend time around here you'll hear the words 'auntie' and 'uncle' a lot.

History

In 1849, a whaler by the name of George Wilfong bought 60 acres of land for planting sugar and changed Hana's landscape for the next century. According to legend, he used spare blubber pots and a team of oxen to squeeze the juice out of the cane. But he couldn't find enough native Hawaiians willing to work on his fledgling plantation.

It wasn't until the Masters and Servants Act of 1850 allowed for the importation of cheap overseas labor that two Danes were able to make a go of it nearby. Chinese, Japanese and Portuguese laborers were brought in to work the new sugarcane fields, and Hana became a booming plantation town. A narrow-gauge railroad connected the fields to the Hana Mill. In the 1940s, Hana could no longer compete with larger sugar operations in central Maui, so the mill shut down.

Enter San Francisco businessman Paul Fagan, the owner of Puu O Hoku Ranch on Molokai, who purchased 14,000 acres in Hana in 1943. Starting with 300 Herefords, Fagan converted the cane fields to ranch land. A few years later, Fagan opened a six-room hotel as a getaway resort called the Kauiki Inn and had his minor-league baseball team, the San Francisco Seals, do spring training here. That's allegedly when visiting sports journalists gave the town its moniker, 'Heavenly Hana'.

Geographically and economically, Hana Ranch and the hotel became the hub of town. Today, Hana Ranch still has a few thousand head of cattle worked by *paniolo* (Hawaiian cowboys). When the cattle are ready for Oahu stockyards, they're trucked all the way up the Hana Hwy to Kahului Harbor. A small community of celebrities, including Carol Burnett and Kris Kristofferson, have long had homes in the Hana area.

Information

Hana Ranch Center is the commercial center of town. It has a **post office** *(open 8am-4:30pm Mon-Fri)*; a tiny **Bank of Hawaii** *(☎ 248-8015; open 3pm-4:30pm Mon-Thur, 3pm-6pm Fri)*; and the **Hana Ranch Store** *(open 7am-7pm daily)*, which sells groceries, liquor and general supplies. Hasegawa General Store has an ATM. There are community bulletin boards outside the post office and the two grocery stores.

Hana closes up early. If you're going to be heading back late, get gas in advance – the **Chevron station**, which has the longest hours, usually closes at 6pm (5:30pm on Sunday).

Things to See & Do

The old 1910 **Hasegawa General Store** *(☎ 248-8231; 5165 Hana Hwy; open 7am-7pm Mon-Sat, 8am-6pm Sun)* burned to the ground in 1990. After a brief hiatus, it relocated under the rusty tin roof of the old theater building in the town center. While some of its character was inevitably lost along with its eclectic inventory, the store is still packed with just about everything from bags of poi and aloha dolls to fishing gear and the record that immortalized the store in song.

The community-run **Hana Cultural Center** *(☎ 248-8622; W www.hookele.com/hccm; admission $2; open 10am-4pm daily)* is a good place to get a sense of Hana's roots. The small museum displays quilts, Hawaiian artifacts, wooden carvings, period photographs and a couple of reconstructed thatched *hale* of the type once found in traditional Hawaiian villages.

The same grounds contain the old Hana district police station and three-bench courthouse, which dates back to 1871. Although it looks like a museum piece, the court is still used a couple of times a month; a judge shows up to hear minor cases such as traffic violations, sparing Hana residents the need to drive all the way to Wailuku.

After Paul Fagan died, his family erected a 1960 **memorial** on Lyon's Hill, which was Fagan's favorite spot for watching the sunset. The huge hilltop cross is now Hana's most dominant landmark. A 15-minute trail up Lyon's Hill starts from opposite the Hotel Hana-Maui.

Wananalua Congregational Church, on the National Register of Historic Places, looks like an ancient Norman church. Built in 1838 with thick walls of lava rock and coral mortar, it replaced the congregation's original grass church. There's a little cemetery at the side with graves randomly laid out rather than lined up in rows. Even at rest, Hana folks like things casual.

The ballpark has public **tennis courts**. Other activities can be arranged through the Hotel Hana-Maui, including one-hour guided horseback rides ($35) along the coast or up into the hills, offered Monday to Saturday. Also make time for the hotel's **Hana Coast Gallery**.

Hana Beach Park

At the southern end of Hana Bay, this black-sand beach has a snack bar, showers, rest rooms, a small boat ramp and picnic tables. Hana folks occasionally come down here with ukuleles, guitars and a few beers for impromptu evening parties.

When water conditions are very calm, snorkeling and diving are good out in the direction of the light beacon. Currents can be strong, and snorkelers shouldn't go beyond the beacon. Surfers head to **Waikoloa Beach**, at the northern end of the bay.

Kauiki Head, the 386ft cinder hill on the south side of Hana Bay, was the site of an ancient fort, and, according to legend, home to the demigod Maui. In 1780, the Maui chief Kahekili successfully fought off a challenge by Big Island chiefs here. The islet at the tip of the point, which now holds a light beacon, is **Puukii**, or 'Image Hill.' The name can be traced to a huge deity image that the great king Umi erected here in the 16th century to ward off invaders.

Queen Kaahumanu, the favorite wife of Kamehameha the Great and one of the most powerful women in Hawaiian history, was born in a cave here in 1768. A crumbly, steep **trail** to a plaque noting the queen's birth starts along the hill at the side of the wharf at Hana Beach Park, passing by a tiny red-sand beach.

Kaihalulu (Red Sand) Beach

On the south side of Kauiki Head, this beach is favored by nude sunbathers. It's a gorgeous little cove with sand eroded from the red cinder hill and beautiful turquoise waters. Although the cove is partly protected by a lava outcrop, the currents can be dangerous if the surf is up. Water drains through a break on the left side, which should be avoided. Your best chance of finding calm waters is in the morning.

The path to the beach is at the end of Uakea Rd beyond the ballpark. It starts across the lawn at the lower side of the Hana Community Center, where a steep 10-minute trail continues down to the beach. The curious can also find an interesting overgrown Japanese cemetery – a remnant of the sugarcane days – along the way.

MAUI

Places to Stay

There are cabins and tent camping at Waianapanapa State Park, just north of Hana, and at Oheo Gulch, about 10 miles south of Hana near Kipahulu. If you plan to camp at Oheo, you'll need to stock up on food and water in Hana.

Most places in town require a two-night minimum stay.

Joe's Place (*☎ 248-7033; 🅦 www.joesrentals.com; Uakea Rd; rooms with/without bath $55/45*) has a handful of small basic rooms that are clean and comfortable enough. Most have two single beds, though a few of them have double beds. Guests have access to a community kitchen, barbecue grills and a TV room.

Aloha Cottages (*☎ 248-8420; Keawa Pl; studios from $62, 2-bedroom cottages $85*), near the Hotel Hana-Maui, is run by the Nakamura family. The studio has twin beds and a hot plate, toaster and fridge, while larger cottages each have a full kitchen, a queen-size bed and two twin beds. All the units are straightforward; none has a phone, but messages are taken.

Tree Houses of Hana, Maui (*☎ 248-7241; 🅔 hanalani@maui.net; PO Box 389, Hana, HI 96713; B&B rooms/tree houses $55/95*) are the real deal, built deep in the jungle with no electricity or running water. Instead, the tree houses have tiki torches, bamboo outhouses with hot showers, hammocks and camp-style kitchens. Guesthouse rooms with ocean views are for the less wild at heart.

Hana Hale Malamalama (*The Bamboo Inn; ☎ 248-7718; 🅦 www.hanahale.com; Uakea Rd; tree house cottage $160, bamboo studio/villa with kitchen $140/185*), centered on a fishpond, is a naturalistic village fully outfitted in bamboo, right down to the outdoor showers. Suites in the main house (called The Bamboo Inn) or the tree house cottage all come with private Jacuzzis, ocean views and timeless serenity.

Heavenly Hana Inn (*☎ 248-8442; 🅦 www.heavenlyhanainn.com; Uakea Rd; 1-bedroom/2-bedroom suites $200/250*) is a landmark *ryokan* (traditional Japanese inn) on the way into town, set back from the 33-mile marker. Every attention has been paid to authentic detail, from gardens down to shoji and rooms for tea and meditation. Each apartment suite is exquisitely tasteful. Deluxe breakfasts must be ordered a week in advance.

Hotel Hana-Maui (*☎ 248-8211, 800-321-4262, fax 248-7202; 🅦 www.hotelhanamaui.com; Hana Hwy; rooms $235-275, cottages $235-655*) is one of Maui's more exclusive getaway hotels, though it's low profile and resembles more of a plantation estate. Everything's very airy and open, with Hawaiian accents from local art to traditional quilt bedspreads. Most rooms are in single-story cottages in rows with bleached hardwood floors, tiled baths, a view over a private garden, and French doors opening to trellised patios. Ask about discount packages.

A couple of vacation rental agencies handle cottages and houses in the Hana area. As the properties can vary greatly in quality and maintenance, get specific details before sending a deposit.

Hana Alii Holidays (*☎ 248-7742, 800-548-0478, fax 248-8595; W hanaalii.com; PO Box 536, Hana, HI 96713*) manages more than a dozen private homes, apartments and cottages. Accommodation ranges from $60 for a studio condo to $295 for a deluxe beachfront cottage.

Hana Plantation Houses (*☎ 248-7868, 800-228-4262, fax 248-8240; W www.hana-maui.com; houses from $72*) rents about a dozen houses with cooking facilities on the lush Hana coast. At the low end, there's a little Japanese-style studio with an efficiency kitchen; at the high end there's a two-bedroom cottage in a garden setting.

Places to Eat

Bring groceries from Kahului or Paia if you plan to stay awhile, as the Hana grocery stores have only a limited selection.

If you're on a budget, skip the Hana Ranch Restaurant. Go instead to **Tutu's** (*dishes under $5; usually open 8am-4pm Mon-Thur*), a Hawaiian fast-food grill at Hana Beach Park, with tables by the bay.

The **Hotel Hana-Maui** (*☎ 248-8211, 800-321-4262, fax 248-7202; W www.hotelhanamaui.com; Hana Hwy; breakfast & lunch $5-16.50, dinner from $25; open 7:30am-10:30am, 11am-2:30pm & 6:15pm-9pm daily*) has a ranch-style dining room with an ocean-view lanai. Small portions and high prices detract from the finely flavored Hawaii regional cuisine, but the aloha atmosphere is rewarding.

Entertainment

There's live Hawaiian music in the hotel's **Paniolo Bar** from 6:30pm to 9pm Thursday to Sunday (admission is free). The restaurant hosts a live hula show put on by local families at 7:30pm Thursday and Saturday.

HANA TO KIPAHULU

From Hana, the road continues on to Kipahulu, passing Oheo Gulch, the southern end of Haleakala National Park. This incredibly lush stretch is perhaps the most beautiful part of the entire drive down from Paia, especially since most of the day-tripper traffic has been left behind.

From Hana to Oheo, the road is narrow and winding. Between the hairpin turns, one-lane bridges and drivers trying to take in all the sights, it's a slow-moving 10 miles (allow at least 45 minutes).

You'll get extra coastal views by detouring along the 1½-mile **Haneoo Rd** loop, which runs past a couple of beaches and ancient shoreline fishponds. The turnoff is just before the 50-mile marker. **Koki Beach** is at the base of a red cinder hill less than half a mile from the start of the loop. Most of Koki's sand washes away in winter, leaving a rocky shoreline. Local surfers who know the coastline sometimes surf here, but rocks and strong currents make it hazardous for newcomers. The offshore rock topped by a few coconut trees is **Alau Island**, a seabird sanctuary. Allegedly the trees were planted by a couple of Hana residents so that they'd have coconut milk to drink while fishing off the island.

A little farther is **Hamoa Beach**, a lovely gray-sand beach that's used by the Hotel Hana-Maui but is accessible to everyone. James Michener once said it was the only beach in the North Pacific that looked as if it actually belonged in the South Pacific. When the surf's up, there's good surfing and bodysurfing, though be aware of rip currents. When seas are calm, swimming in the cove is good. Public access is down the steps below the hotel's bus-stop sign. There are outdoor showers and rest rooms.

Back on the highway just past the 48 mile marker, park near the bridge and then squeeze through the gate, and follow a worn trail along the stream toward the ocean. In five minutes you'll reach the cool, serene **Venus Pool**, protected from rough surf by lava outcroppings.

As you continue south, you'll see waterfalls cascading down the cliffs, orchids growing out of the rocks, and lots of breadfruit and coconut trees. **Paihi Falls**, 3 miles before Oheo at the 45-mile marker, is particularly attractive, with its 100ft drop visible from the road. There's even a statue of the Virgin Mary tucked into a rock face on the *makai* side of the road at **Puaaluu Falls**, past the 43-mile marker. Between the two falls, you'll pass hippie-style **7 Pools Smoothies**.

Oheo Gulch

Oheo Stream dramatically cuts its way through Oheo Gulch in a lovely series of waterfalls and wide pools, each one tumbling into the next one below. Not so long ago, Oheo Gulch was dubbed the 'Seven Sacred Pools' in a tourism promotion scheme. There are actually 24 pools from the ocean all the way up to Waimoku Falls, and they were never sacred. When the sun shines, the pools make good swimming holes. A 2-mile trail runs up the streambed.

A large Hawaiian settlement once spread throughout the Oheo area, and archaeologists have identified the stone remains of more than 700 structures. The early villagers cultivated taro and sweet potatoes in terraced gardens.

One of the expressed intentions of Haleakala National Park (Kipahulu section) is to manage the Oheo area 'to perpetuate traditional Hawaiian farming and *hoonanea*' – a Hawaiian word meaning to pass the time in ease, peace and pleasure. There are no park entrance fees, and it's open 24 hours.

The park's **ranger station** *(☎ 248-7375; open 9am-5pm daily)* has programmes that include occasional Hawaiian-culture demonstrations and short ranger-led walks up into the bamboo forest at 9am daily. A three-hour guided hike to Waimoku Falls is usually offered on Saturday at 9:30am, as long as the weather is accommodating and at least four people want to go. Rest rooms are available near the visitors' parking lot – but drinking water, food and gas are not.

Lower Pools The 20-minute **Kuloa Point Trail** runs from the Oheo Gulch parking lot down to the lower pools and back, passing interpretive signs along the way. The ranger station is near the start of the trail. At the junction with Pipiwai Trail, go right. A few minutes down, you'll come to a broad grassy knoll with a beautiful view of the Hana coast. On a clear day, you can see the Big Island, 30 miles away across Alenuihaha Channel.

The large freshwater pools along the trail are terraced one atop the other and are connected by gentle cascades. They're usually calm and great for swimming, though the water's brisk. The second big pool below the bridge is a favorite. If it's been raining heavily and the water is flowing too high and fast, the pools are closed and signs are posted.

Still, heavy rains falling on the upper slopes can bring a sudden torrent here at any time. If the water starts to rise, get out immediately. People have been swept out to sea from these pools by flash floods. The ocean below is not inviting at all – the water is quite rough, and gray sharks frequent the area.

Actually, most of the injuries that occur here come from falls on slippery rocks. Also hazardous are submerged rocks and ledges in some of the pools; please check carefully before jumping in.

Waterfall Trails On the *makai* side of the ranger station is the **Pipiwai Trail** leading up to Makahiku Falls (half a mile) and Waimoku Falls (2 miles). Or take a shortcut by picking up the trail from the pedestrian crossing across the highway. Allow about three hours round trip. The upper section is muddy, but boardwalks cover some of the worst bits.

Along the path, you'll pass large mango trees and lots of guava before coming to an overlook after about 10 minutes. **Makahiku Falls**, a long bridal-veil waterfall that drops into a deep gorge, is just off to the right. Thick green ferns cover the sides of 200ft basalt cliffs where the fall cascades. The scene is pretty rewarding for such a short walk.

To the left of the overlook, a worn path continues up to the top of the falls, where there's a popular skinny-dipping pool. At around noon the pool is quite enjoyable, but by late afternoon the sun stops hitting it and the mosquitoes move in. Rocks above the falls will keep you from going over the edge as long as the water level isn't high; a cut on one side lets the water plunge over the cliff. But if the water starts to rise, get out immediately – a drop over this sheer 184ft waterfall could obviously be fatal.

Back on the main trail, you walk under guava and banyan trees, cross Palikea Stream (killer mosquitoes thrive here, too) and enter the wonderland of the **Bamboo Forest**, where thick groves bang together musically in the wind. Beyond them is **Waimoku Falls**, a thin, lacy 400ft waterfall dropping down a sheer rock face. When you come out of the first grove, you'll see the waterfall in the distance. The pool under Waimoku Falls was partially filled in by a landslide during a 1976 earthquake, so it's not terribly deep. At any rate, swimming is not recommended because of the real danger of falling rocks.

If you want to take a dip, you'll find better pools to swim in along the way. About

100 yards before Waimoku Falls, you'll cross a little stream. If you go left and walk upstream for 10 minutes (there's not really a trail; just walk alongside the stream), you'll come to an attractive waterfall and a little pool about neck deep. There's also a nice pool in the stream about halfway between Makahiku and Waimoku Falls.

Horseback Riding About another mile southwest, **Oheo Stables** *(☎ 667-2222; W www.maui.net/~ray; 3hr ride $119; departures 10:30am & 11:30am daily)* offers casually paced trail rides to waterfalls within the Kipahulu section of Haleakala National Park. All rides include a 30-minute stop at a waterfall overlook and start off at the horse ranch with a buffet of hot banana muffins, croissants, tree-ripened fruit and coffee.

Places to Stay The national park maintains a **primitive camping ground** about half a mile southeast of the main Oheo Gulch visitors' area. The camping ground is Hawaiian style – free and undeveloped – with just a huge open pasture. There are some incredible places to pitch a tent on grassy cliffs right above the coast and the pounding surf. Not only that, but the camping area is set amid the ruins of an old Hawaiian village, making this quite a powerful place to be under a full moon.

In winter, there are usually only a handful of tents here. It gets quite a few campers in summer, but even then it's generally large enough to handle everyone who shows up. Facilities include pit toilets and a few picnic tables and grills but *no* water. Permits aren't required, though camping is officially limited to three nights each month.

Getting There & Away A lot of people leave the Oheo Gulch area in midafternoon to head back up the Hana Hwy. Some of them, suddenly realizing what a long trek they have ahead, become very impatient drivers.

You might want to consider leaving a little later, which would give you more time to sightsee and enable you to avoid the rush. Getting caught in the dark on the Hana Hwy does have certain advantages. You can see the headlights of oncoming cars around bends that would otherwise be blind, and the traffic is almost nonexistent.

There are no shortcuts back, but sometimes there is another option. From Kipahulu, the Piilani Hwy (don't be misled by the term 'highway' – there's no pavement in places) heads west through Kaupo up to Keokea in Kula. It's usually passable, but not always, and it shouldn't be done in the dark. The Oheo Gulch ranger station can give you the latest information on road conditions. Another option is to drive to the south end of Kipahulu and talk to people coming from the Kaupo direction.

For more details on the drive, see the Piilani Hwy section later in this chapter.

Kipahulu

The village of Kipahulu is less than a mile south of Oheo. At the turn of the 20th century, Kipahulu was one of several sugar plantation villages in the Hana area. It had a working mill from 1890 to 1922. Following the closure of the mill, unsuccessful attempts were made to grow pineapples. Then ranching took hold in the late 1920s.

Today, Kipahulu has both exclusive estates and more modest homes. Fruit stands are set up here and there along the roadside; some are attended by elderly women who string leis and sell bananas, papayas and woven *lauhala* (pandanus-leaf) hats. This is the end of the line for most day visitors who have pushed beyond Hana.

The area was home to aviator hero Charles Lindbergh during the last years of his life. He began visiting in the 1960s, built a cliff-side home in Kipahulu in 1971 and died of cancer here in 1974. Lindbergh is buried in the graveyard of **Palapala Hoomau Congregational Church**. The inscription on his simple grave is taken from Psalm 139. The church itself, with its 26-inch-thick walls and simple wooden pews, dates from 1864. It's known for its window painting of a Polynesian Christ dressed in the red and yellow feather capes worn only by Hawaii's highest chiefs. The churchyard is a peaceful place, with sleepy cats lounging around, waiting for a nice warm car hood to sprawl out on.

Would-be visitors sometimes get the location mixed up with St Paul's Church, which sits on the highway three-quarters of a mile south of Oheo; the dirt drive down to Palapala Hoomau Church is a quarter mile beyond that, on the *makai* side of the road immediately after the 41-mile marker.

PIILANI HIGHWAY

As it continues past Kipahulu, the road changes its name to the Piilani Hwy (Hwy 31), curving along the southern flank of Haleakala. Someday, this may well be a real highway with cars zipping along in both directions. For now, it's an unspoiled adventure. Here you can beat your own path to unnamed beaches and ancient *heiau*s and catch sunset views up Kaupo Gap before heading back to civilization. Signs such as 'Motorists assume risk of damage due to presence of cattle' and 'Narrow winding road, safe speed 10mph' give clues that this is not your standard highway.

The hardest part is finding out if the road is currently open and passable. Many tourist maps mark it as impassable, and car rental agencies say that just being on it is a violation of their contract. But it's almost entirely paved! The stretch between Kaupo and Ulupalakua Ranch has even been upgraded in recent years, even though it may still rattle your bones.

The only tricky section is five unpaved miles after the 39-mile marker leading to the Kaupo area from Kipahulu. Depending on when it was last graded, standard cars can usually make it easily. But after hard rains, streams flow over the road, making passage difficult, if not dangerous. A 4WD vehicle, or at least a high-riding car with a manual transmission, will minimize your chances of bottoming out.

Flash floods sometimes wash away portions of the road, making it impossible to get through until it's repaired. While the best advice about road conditions is though word of mouth from other drivers, you can also call the **Oheo Gulch ranger station** *(☎ 248-7375; open 9am-5pm daily)* or the **county public works department** *(☎ 248-8254; open 6:30am-3pm Mon-Fri)*.

The best way to approach the drive is with an early morning start. Take something to munch and plenty to drink, and check your oil and spare tire. It's a long haul to civilization if you break down, and the tow charge is said to be around $400. From Kipahulu, near Oheo Gulch, to Tedeschi Vineyards (see Upcountry in this chapter), it's 25 rugged miles.

In the Oheo Gulch area, you might find a fruit stand, but drinking water, gas stations and other services are nonexistent beyond Hana. In the early morning or late afternoon, you'll feel like the last soul on earth. Ain't that grand?

Kaupo

As the road winds around from Kipahulu, it skirts the edge of rocky cliffs and the vegetation picks up. First the road is shaded with big mango trees, banyans, bougainvillea and *wiliwili* trees with red tiger-claw blossoms. Then you'll see increasing numbers of *hala* and guava trees as the road bottoms out into gravel.

The village of Kaupo is around the 35-mile marker. Congratulations if you've made it this far in under an hour. However, don't expect a developed village in any sense of the word, as Kaupo is basically a scattered community of *paniolo* – many of them third-generation ranch hands – who work the Kaupo Ranch.

Kaupo Gap is a deep and rugged valley providing the only lowlands on this section of coast. As it was once heavily settled, it has three historic *heiau*s and two churches from the 19th century. While the road curves in and out, it's well worth stopping and looking back for a picturesque view of the church across the bay. There used to be a landing in the bay for shipping Kaupo Ranch cattle, and you can still see steps leading down into the water on a rock jutting out into the ocean.

Loaloa Heiau, the largest temple, is a registered national historical monument. All three *heiau* sites are *mauka* of **Hui Aloha Church**, which is seven-tenths of a mile east of Kaupo General Store. Beside the rocky black-sand Mokulau Beach, this attractive whitewashed church, built in 1859 and restored in 1978, is surrounded by a stone wall and a few windswept trees. The area was an ancient surfing site.

Kaupo General Store *(☎ 248-8054)*, theoretically open from 9:30am to 5pm Monday to Saturday, on the east side of the gap, is 'the only store for 20 miles' and sells snacks, beer and wine. Opening hours can be a bit flexible (to say the least), so it's best not to count on it being open. Further west, **Auntie Jane's Lunch Wagon** commonly sets up in the afternoon, selling organic beef burgers, simple sandwiches and shave ice with healthy doses of aloha.

MAUI

Kaupo to Ulupalakua Ranch

Past town, the views up Kaupo Gap are imbued with *mana* at sunset. Then *makai* of the 31-mile marker, a very rough but short 4WD road passes through a gate and runs down to the ocean at **Nuu Bay**, favored by locals for swimming when the water is calm. Spinner dolphins play offshore sometimes. If you snorkel or dive here, be sure to stay within the protected bay, as strong currents and rip tides inhabit the open ocean beyond.

After another mile, there's a wide turnoff on the *mauka* side of the highway. From here you can walk out to dramatic **Huakini Bay**, where you can sit quietly on smooth boulders and watch the violent surf. As the road continues, it runs in and out of numerous gulches and crosses a few bridges, gradually getting closer to the coast. Striations of lava testify to centuries of volcanic upheaval.

After the 29-mile marker, keep an eye out for a natural lava **sea arch**. Continue driving until it disappears from sight, then spot a turnout on the *makai* side. Park and take the worn footpath down through pastoral green fields to the cliff's edge, where you can see the arch close up and blowholes spout along the coast.

The road continues to rise, finally improving after the 23-mile marker. A few miles south of Ulupalakua Ranch, it crosses an expansive **lava flow**, the same one that covers the La Perouse Bay area (see the South Maui section). Just offshore is the crescent island of Molokini with Kahoolawe beyond. The large grassy hills between here and the sea are volcanic cinder cones. There's such a wide-angle view that the ocean horizon is noticeably curved. Sunsets are bewitching here.

As you approach Tedeschi Vineyards, groves of fragrant eucalyptus trees soon replace drier and scrubbier terrain. It's open rangeland here; cattle graze right beside the road and occasionally mosey across in front of you.

Upcountry

Upcountry, the cool highland area on the western slopes of Haleakala, has some of Maui's finest countryside, with rolling hills, grazing horses and cows in green pastures, all making it look suspiciously like the American West. You have to drive through Upcountry to get to Haleakala National Park, but this salt-of-the-earth region is worth visiting for its own sake because it is *paniolo* country.

From Olinda Rd or the heights of Kula, you can look across the central sugarcane plains to the West Maui Mountains and sea cliffs of the Maui coastline, then onto the Neighbor Islands set against the vast backdrop of the Pacific. Daytime temperatures are cooler in Upcountry than on the coast, and nights can be downright brisk. Peaceful, starry nights cost less up here, with abundant B&Bs.

A fair chunk of the area is occupied by ranches; Haleakala Ranch covers vast spreads to the north, while Ulupalakua Ranch encompasses thousands upon thousands of acres to the south. There are a few small towns near the coast, with the resident population thinning further upland.

Kula, in the navel of Upcountry, boasts rich farmland where most of Maui's vegetables and flowers are grown. On the mountainside above Kula are the delightful cloud forests of Polipoli. Upcountry sight-seeing spots include art galleries, landscaped botanical gardens and protea shops. Makawao, an old *paniolo* town, still hosts a gala Fourth of July rodeo and parade every year.

PAIA TO MAKAWAO

Baldwin Ave (Hwy 390) slowly rolls from Paia up to Makawao, taking a half hour to travel just 7 miles. It starts amid sugarcane fields near the old Paia Sugar Mill, then traverses pineapple fields interspersed with little open patches where cattle graze.

There are two churches along Baldwin Ave. The **Holy Rosary Church & Father Damien Memorial** *(945 Baldwin Rd)*, with its statue garden, comes up first on the right, and **Makawao Union Church** *(1445 Baldwin Ave)*, a stone-block building with stained-glass windows and framed by palm trees, is farther along on the left. **Makawao Union Church**, built in 1916, is on the National Register of Historic Places.

Past Haliimaile Rd just after the 5-mile marker is Kaluanui, the former 9-acre plantation estate of sugar magnates Harry and Ethel Baldwin, which now houses the **Hui Noeau Visual Arts Center** *(☎ 572-6560; W www.huinoeau.com; 2841 Baldwin Ave; admission free; open 10am-4pm Mon-Sat)*. The two-story plantation home with Spanish-style tile

MAUI

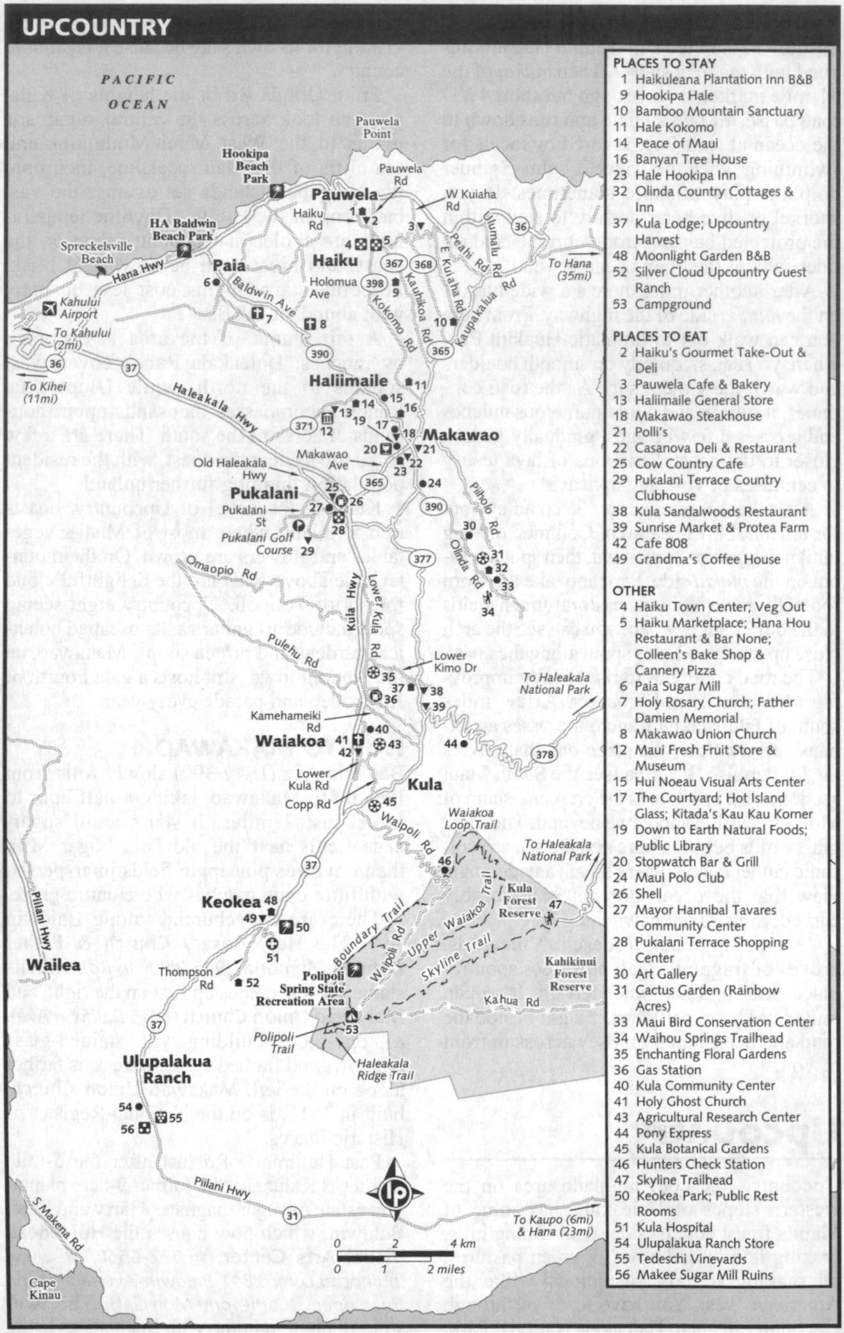
UPCOUNTRY
PACIFIC OCEAN
Pauwela Point
Hookipa Beach Park
Pauwela
Pauwela Rd
W Kuiaha Rd
Haiku Rd
HA Baldwin Beach Park
Spreckelsville Beach
Paia
Haiku
Hana Hwy
Baldwin Ave
Holomua Ave
Kokomo Rd
Kauhikoa Rd
E Kuiaha Rd
Peahi Rd
Ulumalu Rd
Kaupakalua Rd
To Hana (35mi)
Kahului Airport
To Kahului (2mi)
To Kihei (11mi)
Haleakala Hwy
Haliimaile
Makawao
Makawao Ave
Old Haleakala Hwy
Pukalani
Pukalani St
Pukalani Golf Course
Piiholo Rd
Olinda Rd
Omaopio Rd
Pulehu Rd
Kula Hwy
Lower Kula Rd
Lower Kimo Dr
To Haleakala National Park
Kamehameiki Rd
Waiakoa
Lower Kula Rd
Copp Rd
Kula
Waipoli Rd
Waiakoa Loop Trail
To Haleakala National Park
Kula Forest Reserve
Keokea
Boundary Trail
Upper Waiakoa Trail
Skyline Trail
Kahikinui Forest Reserve
Kahua Rd
Thompson Rd
Polipoli Spring State Recreation Area
Polipoli Trail
Haleakala Ridge Trail
Wailea
Piilani Hwy
Ulupalakua Ranch
Piilani Hwy
S Makena Rd
Cape Kinau
To Kaupo (6mi) & Hana (23mi)
0 2 4 km
0 1 2 miles
PLACES TO STAY
1 Haikuleana Plantation Inn B&B
9 Hookipa Hale
10 Bamboo Mountain Sanctuary
11 Hale Kokomo
14 Peace of Maui
16 Banyan Tree House
23 Hale Hookipa Inn
32 Olinda Country Cottages & Inn
37 Kula Lodge; Upcountry Harvest
48 Moonlight Garden B&B
52 Silver Cloud Upcountry Guest Ranch
53 Campground
PLACES TO EAT
2 Haiku's Gourmet Take-Out & Deli
3 Pauwela Cafe & Bakery
13 Haliimaile General Store
18 Makawao Steakhouse
21 Polli's
22 Casanova Deli & Restaurant
25 Cow Country Cafe
29 Pukalani Terrace Country Clubhouse
38 Kula Sandalwoods Restaurant
39 Sunrise Market & Protea Farm
42 Cafe 808
49 Grandma's Coffee House
OTHER
4 Haiku Town Center; Veg Out
5 Haiku Marketplace; Hana Hou Restaurant & Bar None; Colleen's Bake Shop & Cannery Pizza
6 Paia Sugar Mill
7 Holy Rosary Church; Father Damien Memorial
8 Makawao Union Church
12 Maui Fresh Fruit Store & Museum
15 Hui Noeau Visual Arts Center
17 The Courtyard; Hot Island Glass; Kitada's Kau Kau Korner
19 Down to Earth Natural Foods; Public Library
20 Stopwatch Bar & Grill
24 Maui Polo Club
26 Shell
27 Mayor Hannibal Tavares Community Center
28 Pukalani Terrace Shopping Center
30 Art Gallery
31 Cactus Garden (Rainbow Acres)
33 Maui Bird Conservation Center
34 Waihou Springs Trailhead
35 Enchanting Floral Gardens
36 Gas Station
40 Kula Community Center
41 Holy Ghost Church
43 Agricultural Research Center
44 Pony Express
45 Kula Botanical Gardens
46 Hunters Check Station
47 Skyline Trailhead
50 Keokea Park; Public Rest Rooms
51 Kula Hospital
54 Ulupalakua Ranch Store
55 Tedeschi Vineyards
56 Makee Sugar Mill Ruins

roof was designed by famed Honolulu architect CW Dickey in 1917. The nonprofit arts club founded here in the 1930s still offers prestigious classes in printmaking, pottery, woodcarving and a dozen other visual arts. Come visit the galleries, gift shop and extensive grounds, which include reflecting pools, stables turned into art studios and a unique 150-year-old hybrid pine tree.

Haliimaile Road

Haliimaile is a little pineapple town in the middle of plantation fields. Its nearly unpronounceable name (literally, 'fragrant twining shrub') takes after the *maile* plants used for lei making that once covered the area.

To get here, turn right from Baldwin Ave onto Haliimaile Rd, a byway that winds east toward the Haleakala Hwy (Hwy 37). Next door to the old Haliimaile General Store, built c. 1925, is the **Maui Fresh Fruit Store & Museum** *(☎ 573-5129; 870 Haliimaile Rd; admission free; open 10am-6pm Mon-Fri, 9am-5pm Sat)* selling pineapples, local produce and gourmet foodstuffs. At the back are a few photo exhibits and antique objects from the Maui Pineapple Company's sweet century long history.

Places to Stay & Eat Peace Of Maui *(☎ 572-5045, 888-475-5045; W www.peaceofmaui.com; 1290 Haliimaile Rd; singles/doubles $40/45, 1-bedroom cottage with kitchen & bath $75)* is a great down to earth budget option, with astounding sunsets gracing its open fields. Main-house rooms are small, but each has a TV. Guests share the bathrooms, telephone, full kitchen and barbecue grill. The cottage has a deck with a distant ocean view. Breakfast is not included, but the friendly owner provides complimentary homegrown fruit. The property is on a quiet 2-acre homestead at the east side of Haliimaile village. Ask about rental cars and airport pickups.

Haliimaile General Store *(☎ 572-2666; 900 Haliimaile Rd; lunch $9-12, dinner $18-28; open 11am-2:30pm Mon-Fri, 5:30pm-9:30pm daily)*, featuring high ceilings and plantation-era decor, features an exuberant mix of Hawaiian and Asian cooking influences. Stepping through the gracious lanai into this historic venue, spruced up with dramatic flower arrangements and artwork, feels like spring. Lunch plays it safe, with Kula garden salads and meat-loaf sandwiches. Adventurous dinner dishes include tasty Szechuan barbecued salmon flavored with lemongrass. Reservations are advised.

MAKAWAO

Makawao is billed as a *paniolo* town. In the 1800s, it got its start as a ranching town supplying voracious sailors who pulled into Lahaina demanding fresh, red meat. Makawao is still bordered by ranch land, and the false-front wooden buildings in the town center retain an Old West appearance. The town's main event is a big-time rodeo on the Fourth of July, with a parade of *paniolo*s on horseback wearing *palaka*s (checked shirts) and festive leis.

All that aside, Makawao is a town in flux. In the past decade, a sizable amount of alternative culture has seeped in: the health food store has set up down the street from Makawao Feed & Garden, and the gun shops have given way to storefronts specializing in Chinese herbs and yoga. Check the health food store bulletin board – you'll find listings for belly dancing, arts and mantra meditation.

Everything is within a few minutes' walk of the main intersection, where Baldwin Ave (Hwy 390) meets Hwy 365, including the **public library** *(☎ 573-8785; 1159 Makawao Ave; open noon-8pm Mon & Wed, 9:30am-5pm Tues, Thur & Sat)*.

Interesting upscale galleries include those at **The Courtyard** *(3620 Baldwin Ave)*. Most notable here is **Hot Island Glass** *(☎ 572-4527)*, where you can watch glassblowers at work every day until 4:30pm. **Gallery Maui** *(☎ 572-8092)*, down a leafy side lane off Baldwin Ave, had bold and beautiful free-form sculptures, as well as stained glass framed with bamboo. There are also unique clothing boutiques and **Miracles Bookery** *(☎ 572-2317)* in town.

Scenic back roads head out in almost every direction from Makawao. **Olinda Rd** picks up where Baldwin Ave leaves off, drifting up past the Oskie Rice Arena and **Maui Polo Club**, which holds matches on Sunday afternoons in the fall, then further beyond to an **art gallery** *(open 1pm-4pm Tues-Sat)* and **cactus garden** *(open 9am-4pm Tues & Thur)*, also known as Rainbow Acres. Past the 11-mile marker is the Maui Bird Conservation Center (closed to the public), then on the right side of the road is the signposted **Waihou Springs Trailhead**, a quiet half-hour walk through a 20th-century experimental forest. At the top of Olinda Rd, turn left onto Piiholo Rd and wind back down into town.

Places to Stay

The bulletin board at the health food store often has ads for rooms and studios that can be rented on a weekly or monthly basis.

Hale Hookipa Inn *(☎ 572-6698, 877-572-6698; W www.maui-bed-and-breakfast.com; 32 Pakani Pl; rooms $85-105, 2-bedroom suite $145-155)* is a richly historic craftman-style house built in the 1920s. Rooms are furnished with antiques and art, and the most expensive has its own lanai entrance and private bath with a claw-foot tub. The Kona wing suite sleeps up to four people and has its own country kitchen. A continental breakfast buffet is served.

Banyan Tree House *(☎ 572-9021, fax 573-5052; W www.banyantreehouse.com; 3265 Baldwin Ave; cottages $85-110, 3-bedroom home $300)*, where banyan and monkeypod trees cover the grounds of a former plantation manager's house, has four romantic cottages with private bath and lanai. Some offer cooking facilities, a hammock and ocean views. There's also a swimming pool, but no actual tree house.

Olinda Country Cottages & Inn *(☎ 572-1453, 800-932-3435, fax 573-5326; W www.mauibnbcottages.com; 2660 Olinda Rd; rooms/suites $140, cottages $195-245)* is a stately Upcountry home and protea farm perched at the edge of the road. The 'Pineapple Sweet' in the main house has a cheery kitchen and panoramic views. The luxury 'Hidden Cottage' has its own kitchen, washer, dryer, and French doors leading onto an ocean-view deck with a bathtub built for two. Credit cards are not accepted, and there's a two-night minimum stay.

Aloha Cottage *(☎ 573-8500, 888-328-3330, fax 573-8555; W www.alohacottage.com; Olinda Rd; cottage $195-250)*, also called Lotus Blossom or The Thai Treehouse, is built from imported Asian teak and set among groves of rainbow eucalyptus and bamboo. It's a faithful replica of a traditional Thai house, yet with modern extras, such as an open-air tub on a partly screened deck, perfect for honeymoon stargazing. Yoga classes and gourmet meals can be arranged.

Places to Eat

Rodeo General Store *(3661 Baldwin Ave)* sells groceries and supplies.

Down to Earth Natural Foods *(1169 Makawao Ave; open 8am-8pm daily)*, near the library, has organic produce, bulk and packaged foods, a dairy section, juices, sandwiches and a good salad bar with a few hot take-out items sold by the pound.

Kitada's Kau Kau Korner *(Baldwin Ave; open 6:30am-1:30pm Mon-Sat)*, in a funky old building opposite The Courtyard galleries, has been making saimin here for generations. You can slurp down a generously sized bowl for just $3.

Komoda Store & Bakery *(3674 Baldwin Ave; snacks $2-6; open 6:30am-1pm Mon-Sat)*, just south of the main intersection, is a family-run place that bakes tempting cream puffs, cinnamon rolls and other pastries. They're so famous that bakery items typically sell out by noon.

Casanova Deli *(1188 Makawao Ave; dishes around $6; open 8am-6pm Mon-Sat, 8:30am-5pm Sun)*, east of the main intersection, is a popular Italian delicatessen and coffeehouse serving full country breakfasts, giant sandwiches and salads. Strong coffee and tiramisu are prerequisites for lingering at chess tables, while hip locals sit on outdoor stools making gossipy mincemeat of passersby.

Polli's *(☎ 572-7808; 1202 Makawao Ave; breakfast & lunch $6-10, dinner from $12; open 7am-10pm Mon-Sat, 8am-10pm Sun)*, west of the intersection, is a Tex-Mex cantina with a sign, 'Come in and eat, or we'll both starve.' The small bar is bowled over with patrons waiting for tables, where they'll order baby back ribs, 'Makawowie' tacos or vegetarian substitutes.

Casanova Restaurant *(☎ 572-0220; 1188 Makawao Ave; lunch $8-12, dinner from $20; open 11:30am-2:30pm & 5:30pm-9:30pm daily)*, next to the deli, is a decidedly posh place. Hot Italian sandwiches and crispy *kiawe*-fired pizzas make way for island versions of calamari and rigatoni with vodka-tomato sauce at dinner.

Makawao Steakhouse *(☎ 572-8711; 3612 Baldwin Ave; mains $20-30; open 5:30pm-9:30pm daily)* is the last steakhouse standing amidst all this ranchland. Period photographs adorn the old-fashioned pine walls, with surf-and-turf specials and all-you-can-eat nights making it a classic.

KARL LEHMANN

The bronze Buddha, Maui

NED FRIARY

Ukulele player

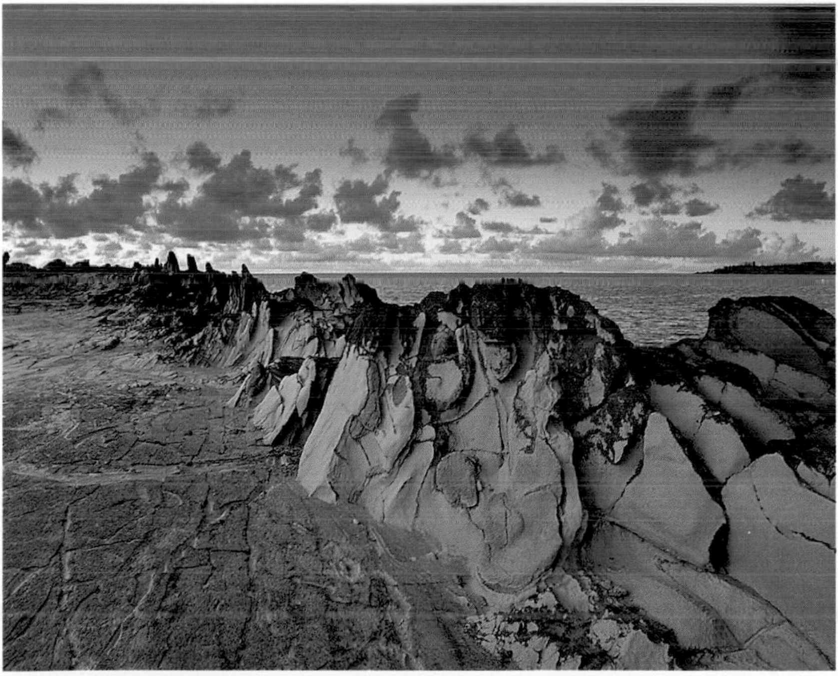
KARL LEHMANN

The Dragon's Teeth, Maui

ANN CECIL

Hula kahiko

JOHN BORTHWICK

Aloha Festival, Oahu

KARL LEHMANN

Traditional Hawaiian drums

Entertainment

Stopwatch Bar & Grill *(☎ 572-1380; 1127 Makawao Ave; open 11am-midnight daily)*, with food served until 8pm or later, is a sports bar that's also good for those looking to fill their stomachs on the cheap. There are DJs and live music some weekends, and admission is usually free.

Casanova *(☎ 572-0220; W www.casanovamaui.com; 1188 Makawao Ave; admission $5-25)* is east Maui's hottest music spot, bringing in mainland performers as well as some of Hawaii's top musicians. DJs spin midweek, followed by live bands – anything from salsa or blues to Jawaiian and Cuban jazz – on weekends. Dress to impress, they say.

HAIKU

A number of roads lead through Haiku, a scattered community that stretches from Makawao down the slopes to the Hana Hwy. Alexander & Baldwin grew their first 12 acres of sugarcane nearby in 1869, and the village once had both a sugar mill and a pineapple cannery. Today, the old cannery houses a few local eateries and quirky shops. The intersection of Haiku and Kokomo Rds marks the center of town.

Modern Haiku is seeing a bit of a revival. Its rural character and its proximity to Makawao and Hookipa have attracted a number of new residents, including windsurfers, artists and New Age folks. The area has some wonderful B&Bs and makes a reasonably convenient base for exploring the whole island.

Places to Stay

Most of these family-run B&Bs require three-day minimum stays. Make reservations well in advance. Others are available through booking agencies in Paia (see the East Maui section earlier in this chapter).

Hookipa Hale *(☎ 575-9357, fax 575-9482; W www.hookipahale.com; 1350 Kauhikoa Rd; rooms & suites $35-60, 2-bedroom cottage $90)* is almost too good to be true: a private country home equipped with a full guest kitchen, an open-air sitting area with twinkling white lights and, most importantly, gracious hosts. Each spacious room has its own TV and a shared telephone line; security deposits are required. There's usually at least a four-day minimum stay.

Hale Kokomo *(☎ 572-5613; e iej@maui.net; W www.bbonline.com/hi/kokomo; 2719 Kokomo Rd; rooms $50-60, suites $80)* is a sprightly Victorian-style house with lush palm ferns in front. It's secluded but only 10 minutes from the beach. Basic, cozy rooms have a shared bathroom and fridge, while suites have their own bathroom (not necessarily attached). All rates include breakfast.

Bamboo Mountain Sanctuary *(☎ 572-4897, fax 572-8848; W www.maui.net/~bamboomt; 1111 Kaupakalua Rd; singles/doubles $55/75, 2-bedroom ocean-view cottage $150)* is a meditative experience. Once sheltering the *zendo* (communal zen meditation hall) of Robert Aitken Roshi's Diamond Sangha, this 20th-century Japanese plantation house has simple, clean rooms. The setting is serene, with verandas overlooking the surrounding forest, and guests have access to a kitchen and a living room with a video library. All are invited to join morning *zazen* (zen meditation). The guesthouse is sometimes closed during retreats.

Haikuleana Plantation Inn B&B *(☎ 575-2890, fax 575-9177; W www.haikuleana.com; 555 Haiku Rd; suites $115)* is a 1870s plantation doctor's home furnished with antiques, vintage Hawaiian maps and artwork. Skip modern rooms in favor of the cedar-paneled Sandwich Islands suite, which comes with its own 18th-century captain's desk. An antique Buddha sits in the garden sanctuary.

Places to Eat & Drink

Pauwela Cafe & Bakery *(375 W Kuiaha Rd; snacks $2-7; open 6am-2pm daily)* is worth a detour off the Hana Hwy for all-day breakfasts, banana bread, kalua pork sandwiches and strong coffee or fresh juice.

Haiku's Gourmet Take-Out & Deli *(771 Haiku Rd; mains $6-12; open 6am-8pm daily)*, in a little house downhill from the old cannery, is another good bakery serving deli salads and plates of gourmet chicken or ribs.

Veg Out *(Haiku Town Center, 810 Kokomo Rd; snacks $3-7; open 10:30am-7:30pm Mon-Fri, 11:30am-6pm Sat & Sun)* shows healthy food just doesn't go out of style in Haiku. This vegetarian kitchen has a long menu, with fresh produce supplied by the Upcountry truck farmers who eat here.

Colleen's Bake Shop & Cannery Pizza *(Haiku Marketplace, 810 Kokomo Rd; sandwiches & salads $5-11, pizza $13-21; bakery* *open 6am-9pm daily; pizzeria open from 4:45pm)* has whole-wheat-crust pizza that some swear by, as long as it's hot and straight out of the oven. You can get slices of the 'virtually vegan' or 'sweet pea' (yes, with green peas) to go.

Hana Hou Restaurant & Bar None *(☎ 575-2661; 810 Haiku Rd; dishes $5-15; open 10am-10pm daily)* is beside the Haiku Marketplace. In Hawaiian pidgin, the name means 'do it again.' Who are we to disagree? For some local grinds, *pupus* or burgers and beer, visit these friendly folks.

PUKALANI

Sunny Pukalani, the biggest Upcountry town with a population of 6000, has nothing to see. It is 2 miles from Makawao along Hwy 365. If you're coming from Kahului, take the Haleakala Hwy (Hwy 37), which climbs for 6 miles through cane fields before heading into town.

A couple of gas stations are on Hwy 37 in the center of town. The Pukalani Terrace Shopping Center, south of the intersection of Hwys 365 and 37, has a coin laundry, **Foodland** supermarket, **post office** *(closed Sun)*, fast-food joints and a bank with an ATM. Less than a mile further west, the very local **Pukalani Country Club** *(☎ 572-1314; W www.pukalanigolf.com; 360 Pukalani St; green fees & cart $51-71)* has sweeping upcountry views.

Places to Eat

Cow Country Cafe *(Upcountry Cafe; 7 Aewa Pl; meals $5-10; open 7am-3pm & 5:30pm-9pm Mon-Sat, brunch 7am-1pm Sun)*, is the place to stop if you're headed downhill from Haleakala after sunrise. Although it's hidden in a little strip mall, the cow signs are easy to spot from the highway. Count on wholesome comfort food, guava shakes, chocolate macadamia-nut desserts and, later in the day, sandwiches made from home-baked bread.

Pukalani Terrace Country Clubhouse *(360 Pukalani St; lunch buffet $9.50; open 6:30am-2pm & 5pm-9pm daily)* is where Pukalanians head when they want ocean views. Take the lunch buffet option or order a complete Hawaiian plate (around $10) with *kalua* pig, *lomi* salmon (raw, diced salmon marinated with tomatoes and onions) and sweet *haupia*.

KULA

The Kula region, perched at an average elevation of 3000ft, is the agricultural heartland of Maui. Crops such as lettuce, tomatoes, carrots, cauliflower and cabbage thrive in Kula's warm days, cool nights and rich volcanic soil. No gourmet cook in Hawaii would be anywhere without sweet Kula onions.

In the 19th century, Portuguese and Chinese immigrants moved in to farm the Kula area after they had worked off their contracts on the sugar plantations. During the Californian gold rush, Hawaiian farmers in Kula shipped so many potatoes off to the miners that the area became known as 'Nu Kaleponi,' the Hawaiian pronunciation for New California.

Kula grows most of Hawaii's proteas, large bright flowers with an unusual flair. Some, like the pincushion varieties, are very delicate, and others have spine-like petals. In spring, you'll find a burst of color right along the roadside as well, as the purple blossoms of the jacaranda tree and the yellow flowers of the gold oak bloom in profusion.

Proteas

The protea family, which is named after the Greek god Proteus who could change shapes at will, comes in more than 1500 different varieties, from macadamia nuts to the showy King Protea, South Africa's national flower.

Originally all proteas were native to South Africa. Their flowers vary from spiky carnations to stalks of tiny flowers held by brightly colored bracts to artichoke blossoms, and they can be as small as a few millimeters or up to 12 inches in diameter.

Hawaiian proteas account for 90% of the world market, with 85 species alone situated solely on the slopes of Haleakala. Proteas thrive on sandy, acidic soil, and the cool nights following warm days in the Upcountry are ideal. Often people along the island's rural highways will set out pots of proteas that you can drive by and pick up, leaving money for them using the honor system. Upcountry nurseries can advise you on how to ship proteas or take them legally through customs. Fresh flowers can last up to three weeks after being cut, and some arrangements dry quite well.

MAUI

Gardens

All of Kula is a garden, but if you want to take a closer look, you can visit several established walk-through botanical gardens. Outside of winter, they may look disappointingly dry.

The University of Hawaii maintains a 20-acre **Agricultural Research Center** (*☎ 878-1213; Mauna Pl; admission free; open 7am-3:30pm Mon-Thur*) above Waiakoa village. It's here that Hawaii's first proteas were established in 1965. You can walk through rows of their colorful descendants, as well as dozens of new hybrids under development. Cuttings are distributed to protea farms across Hawaii, supplying freshly cut flowers to the US mainland, Japan and Europe.

Some sections of the research center garden are used for experiments in plant pathology, but the rest of the garden is open to the public (Friday is the day set aside for pesticide spraying). Call ahead for a personally guided tour. To get here, follow Copp Rd (between the 12- and 13-mile markers on Hwy 37) for a half mile and turn left on Mauna Pl.

Enchanting Floral Gardens (*☎ 878-2531; adult/child $5/1; open 9am-5pm daily*) is sunny, open and orderly, with both tropical and cool weather flowers. It's on Hwy 37 around the 10-mile marker.

Kula Botanical Gardens (*☎ 878-1715; adult/child $4/1; open 9am-4pm daily*) is less appealing, but does have a 'Taboo Garden' of poisonous plants.

Sunrise Market & Protea Farm (*☎ 878-1600, 800-222-2797; Haleakala Crater Rd*), on the way to Haleakala, has a free roadside garden with a small but select group of proteas. **Upcountry Harvest** (*☎ 878-2824, 800-575-6470*), next to Kula Lodge, also sells orchids.

Octagonal Church

The octagonal **Holy Ghost Church** (*☎ 878-1261; Lower Kula Rd; admission by donation; open daily; worship services 5pm Sat, 9:30am Sun*) is a hillside landmark in Waiakoa village. This distinctive white building has a roof that glints silver in the sun and is easily visible from the highway. Built in 1897 by Portuguese immigrants, the church features a beautifully ornate interior that put it on the National Register of Historic Places. If you want to know more, open up the history binder shelved near the guest registry at the back.

Places to Stay

Camp Kula (*☎/fax 876-0000; ⓔ camper@maui.net; PO Box 111, Kula, HI 96790; rooms $35-80*) is a gay-friendly bed and breakfast on seven secluded acres with pretty views of central Maui. There are five guest rooms ranging from a single bed with shared bath to a private suite. All are accessible by wheelchair. Rates include a breakfast of herbal teas, homegrown fruits and baked goodies. Guest can use a fully equipped kitchen and free Internet access.

Kula Lodge (*☎ 878-1535, 800-233-1535, fax 878-2518; ⓦ www.kulalodge.com; studio $110, cottages with lofts $135-165*) is not notably special for the money. All cottages have private decks, but only some have views. There are no TVs or phones. Breakfast is not included.

Places to Eat

Sunrise Market & Protea Farm (*☎ 878-1600, 800-222-2797; Haleakala Crater Rd; open 7:30am-4pm daily*) is a quarter mile up from the intersection of Hwys 378 and 377. You can pick up your post-sunrise java here along with bakery items, wrapped sandwiches and fresh and dried fruits.

Cafe 808 (*Lower Kula Rd, Waiakoa; dishes $3-10; open 6am-8pm daily*), a quarter mile south of the Holy Ghost Church, is a popular local eatery. Its down-home menu is as wide and long as its kitchen. Show up before 11am for banana pancakes, an omelette with home fries or classic *loco moco* (rice topped with hamburger, egg and gravy). The small **Morihara Grocery Store** is across the street.

Kula Lodge (*☎ 878-1535, 800-233-1535, fax 878-2518; ⓦ www.kulalodge.com; breakfast $7-10, lunch $11-18, dinner $18-28; open 6:30am-11:15am, 11:45am-4:15pm & 4:45pm-9pm daily*), less than a mile north of Haleakala Crater Rd, has wraparound windows and a fine view of central Maui and the ocean beyond. Alas, the food in this venerable establishment is less inspired.

Kula Sandalwoods Restaurant (*☎ 878-3523; mains $7-12; open 7am-2pm Mon-Sat, 7am-noon Sun*), just past Kula Lodge on the *mauka* side of Hwy 377, is a family-run place with similar views and more enticing food. Breakfast includes waffles, omelettes and a superb eggs Benedict, while lunch features hearty sandwiches and fresh salads. Choose from terrace or gazebo tables.

POLIPOLI SPRING STATE RECREATION AREA

Polipoli Spring State Recreation Area is high up in Kula Forest Reserve on the western slope of Haleakala. The park is in a coniferous forest and has picnic tables, camping and a network of little-used hiking and mountain biking trails. It's not always possible to get all the way to the park without a 4WD, but it's worth driving even part way up for the view.

Access is via Waipoli Rd, off Hwy 377, just under half a mile before its southern intersection with Hwy 37. Waipoli is a narrow, switchbacking one-lane road through groves of eucalyptus and open rangeland (watch for cattle on the road). Layers of clouds often drift in and out; when they lift, you'll get panoramic views across green rolling hills to the islands of Lanai and Kahoolawe.

Few people venture up this way, and, except for the symphony of bird calls, everything is still. The whole area was planted during the 1930s by the Civilian Conservation Corps (CCC), a Depression-era work programme. Several of the trails pass through old CCC camps and stands of redwood, ash, cypress, cedar and pines. In fact, it all looks somewhat like the northern Californian coast.

When the clouds are heaviest, visibility is measured in inches. The road has some soft shoulders, but the first 6 miles are paved. After the road enters the forest reserve, it reverts to dirt. When it's muddy, the next 4 grinding miles over to the camping ground are not worth trying in a standard car.

Note that only trails above the road are open to mountain bikers. For the Skyline Trail, see the Haleakala National Park section later.

MAUI

Waiakoa Loop Trail

The trailhead for the 3-mile Waiakoa Loop Trail starts at the hunter check station 5 miles up Waipoli Rd, all paved. Walk three-quarters of a mile down the grassy spur road on the left to a gate marking the trail. The hike, which starts out in pine trees, makes a 3-mile loop. You can also connect with the Upper Waiakoa Trail at a junction about a mile up the right side of the loop.

Upper Waiakoa Trail

The Upper Waiakoa Trail is a strenuous 7-mile trail that's been reconstructed in recent years by the Na Ala Hele group. The trail begins off Waiakoa Loop at an elevation of 6000ft, climbs 1800ft, switchbacks and then drops back down again. It's stony terrain, but it's high and open, with good views. Bring plenty of water.

The trail ends on Waipoli Rd between the hunter check station and the camping ground. If you want to start at this end of the trail, keep an eye out for the trail marker for Waohuli Trail, as the Upper Waiakoa Trail begins across the road.

Places to Stay

Tent camping requires a permit from the state, but facilities are limited. There are rest rooms, but no showers or drinking water. Fellow campers are likely to be pig hunters. Otherwise the place can be eerily deserted, not to mention damp. Come properly prepared, as this is cold country; winter temperatures frequently drop below freezing at night.

From the camping ground, which is downhill from the Unit E 'Archery only' sign, it's another half-mile walk down a forest trail to the one housekeeping **cabin**. Unlike the other state cabins, this one has gas lanterns and a wood-burning stove but no electricity or refrigerator.

KEOKEA

Around the turn of the 20th century, Keokea was home mainly to Hakka Chinese who farmed the remote Kula region. The village's green-and-white **St John's Episcopal Church** was built in 1907 to serve the Chinese community. On a clear day, you'll enjoy good views of west Maui and Lanai from the roadside.

Although there's not much to it, Keokea is the last real town before Hana if you're swinging around the southern part of the island. It has a coffee shop, gas pump and a few small stores.

Thompson Ranch *(☎ 878-1910; Thompson Rd)* offers two-hour morning horseback rides ($70).

Places to Stay & Eat

Silver Cloud Upcountry Guest Ranch *(☎ 878-6101, 800-532-1111, fax 878-2132; W www.maui.net/~slvrcld; 1373 Thompson Rd; rooms $85-125, studios $105-145, cottages $160)* is a former ranch turned B&B. It's in a country setting, just over a mile from central Keokea. The atmospheric plantation home has hardwood floors, a fireplace lounge and six guest rooms, all with private baths. The bunkhouse out back has been converted into five small studios, each with a kitchenette and French doors leading to a little porch. A separate honeymoon cottage has a kitchen, claw-foot bathtub, wood-burning stove and covered lanai. Breakfast is included in all rates. Guests share a kitchen, chess sets and hammocks.

Moonlight Garden Bed & Breakfast *(☎ 878-6977, 866-878-6297; Ⓦ www.maui.net/~mauimoon; 213 Kula Hwy; 1-bedroom/2-bedroom cottages $115/125)* consists of two lovely freestanding cottages adjacent to a family home and working farm. The place is quiet and secluded despite being within walking distance of the Keokea village center. Each cottage has a full kitchen, TV, phone, washer and dryer, plus sunset views out to sea; the spacious one-bedroom cottage also features a fireplace, hammock and stargazing deck. The grounds are garden-like with fruit trees and bamboo, and the hosts are friendly and knowledgeable. Credit cards are not accepted, and there's a two-day minimum stay.

Bloom Cottage *(reserve through Hookipa Haven in Paia, East Maui; 2-bedroom cottages $125, 3-bedroom house $150)* is a freestanding saltbox cottage beside the home originally built in the early 1900s for a Kula priest. The cottage has a kitchen, TV, VCR, front porch, and a fireplace to ward off evening chills. Breakfast fixings and laundry facilities are provided. There's a three-night minimum stay.

Grandma's Coffee House *(Hwy 37; dishes $6-8; open 7am-5pm daily)* is where Upcountry folks gravitate for homemade pastries, Kula vegetable salads and fresh dark-roasted Maui coffee. The family that owns Grandma's has been growing coffee beans on the slopes of Haleakala since 1918. If you want to see what coffee trees look like, just walk out to the side porch. They also make picnic lunches if you're headed around the Piilani Hwy to Hana.

ULUPALAKUA RANCH

From Keokea, Hwy 37 winds south through ranch country with good views of Kahoolawe and the little island of Molokini. Even on overcast days, you can often see below the clouds to sunny Kihei on the coast.

In the mid-19th century, Ulupalakua Ranch was a sugar plantation owned by whaling ship captain James Makee. King David Kalakaua, the 'Merrie Monarch,' was a frequent visitor who loved nothing better than to indulge in late-night rounds of poker and champagne. The 25,000-acre ranch has been owned by Pardee Erdman, a petroleum geologist from California, and family, since 1963. It's a working ranch with about 6000 head of cattle, 600 merino sheep and 150 head of Rocky Mountain elk.

Ulupalakua Ranch Store *(open 9am-5pm daily)*, opposite the ranch headquarters 5½ miles south of Keokea, is a small local shop selling cowboy hats, T-shirts, souvenirs and snacks (try the $1 muffins). Be sure to check out the wooden cowboys on the front porch; they were carved by the late artist Reems Mitchell, who lived on the ranch.

Across the way, **Tedeschi Vineyards** *(☎ 878-6058, tastings 9am-5pm daily, tours 10:30am & 1pm daily)*, in the middle of Ulupalakua Ranch, planted its first grapes in 1976. The wines are worth tasting, but only for novelty's sake and because it's all free. Attached to the tasting room and gift shop is a fascinating little **museum** *(admission free)* of ranch history.

Opposite the winery, you can see the remains of the three stacks of the **Makee Sugar Mill**, built in 1878. After this, it's another 25 dusty, bumpy miles to Kaupo along the spectacular Piilani Hwy (see East Maui earlier in this chapter).

Haleakala National Park

In Hawaiian, Haleakala means 'House of the Sun.' Atop this very volcano the prankster demigod Maui lassoed the sun with ropes braided from his sister's hair, and refused to let go even as the sun begged for mercy. Not until the heavenly body agreed to slow its daily race across the sky, and thereby bathe the Hawaiian islands in more hours of glorious sunlight, did Maui release his hold.

The volcano has long been thought of as the island's soul. In ancient times it was a spiritual retreat and battleground for *kahunas*. Other ancient Hawaiians came to quarry lava rock used for making tools, or hid the

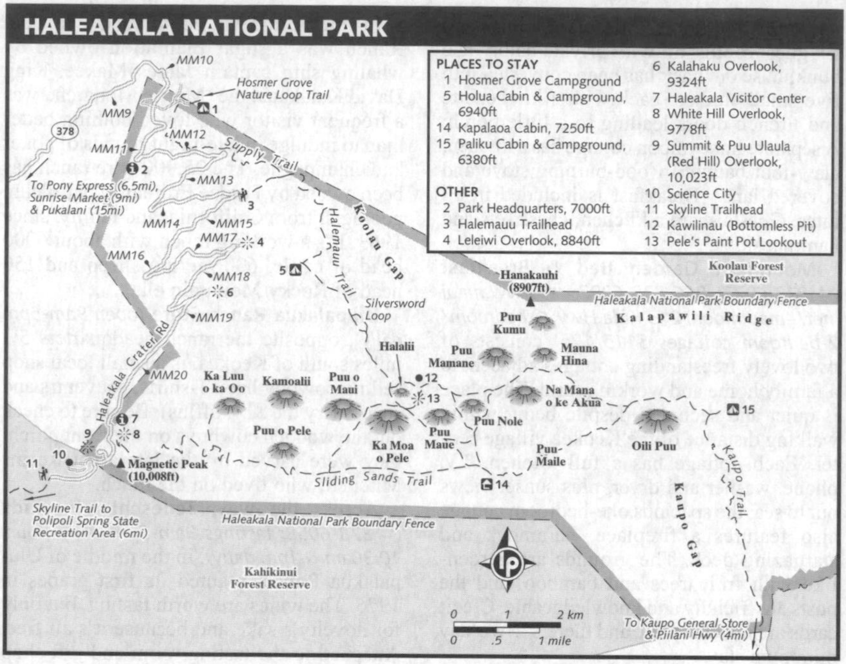

bones of their ancestors and the umbilical cords of newborns deep inside the crater.

Whether it's the lingering *mana* of the gods who once made their home here or the geological forces of the earth, which still release an occasional tremor, Haleakala does emanate a sense of awesome power. Jack London, who sailed to Hawaii in the early 1900s, said Haleakala had 'a message of beauty and wonder for the human soul that cannot be delivered by proxy.'

In its prime, Haleakala probably reached a height of 12,000ft before water erosion began to carve two large river valleys out of the rim. The valley gaps, Koolau Gap on the northwest side and Kaupo Gap on the southeast, are dominant features in the crater wall. Later eruptions have added numerous cinder cones to the floor of Haleakala Crater. The last eruption, over 200 years ago, sent a flow of lava toward Makena and La Perouse Bay. It's likely that, centuries from now, lava will flow once again before Haleakala slips into eternal sleep.

Today Haleakala National Park stretches from the volcano crater down to the pools of Oheo Gulch on the coast south of Hana. There are separate entrances to both sections of the park, but there's no passage between them.

For most visitors, the park revolves around Haleakala Crater, an awesome geological wonder measuring 7½ miles wide, 2½ miles long and 3000ft deep, which means it could swallow the entire isle of Manhattan. The crater resembles the surface of the moon, its seemingly lifeless expanse dotted with high majestic cinder cones. There are unearthly viewpoints all along the crater rim and remarkable hikes trailing across the crater floor, dizzyingly far below.

The requisite pilgrimage to witness the sunrise at the rim of the crater can be an experience that borders on the mystical (see the boxed text 'The Sunrise Experience' later in this chapter). Early morning is usually the best time for viewing the crater. Later in the day, warm air generally forces clouds higher and higher until they pour through the two gaps in the crater's rim and into the crater itself. At sunset, a striking palette of colors reflected over layers of clouds can be nearly as impressive – if it's not completely clouded over.

Information

Haleakala National Park (*W www.nps.gov/hale; 7-day entry pass per car $10, per person on foot, bicycle or motorcycle $5*) never closes, and the pay booth at the park entrance opens well before dawn and stays open late. Annual national park passes ($50) can be purchased at the gate, as can a $20 annual Haleakala pass.

Park headquarters (*☎ 572-4400; open 8am-4pm daily*) are less than a mile up from the park boundary. You can call ahead for recorded information on activities, camping permits and general park conditions. The office has detailed brochures, provides camping permits and sells books on geology and flora and fauna. A few silversword grow in front of the building, and occasionally a pair of nene wander around the parking lot. There is another **visitor center** near the summit.

No food is sold in the park. Bring something to eat, particularly if you're going up for the sunrise; you don't want a growling stomach to rush you all the way back down the mountain before you've had a chance to explore the sights. Bicycles are allowed only on paved roads within the park, so as not to disturb the fragile ecosystem.

It's a good idea to check on **weather conditions** (*☎ 877-5111*) before driving up. It's not uncommon for it to be cloudy at Haleakala when it's clear on the coast. A drizzly sunrise is a particularly disappointing nonevent after getting out of bed at 4am. Always bring warm clothing, as overnight predawn temperatures dip below freezing.

Activities

All park programmes and guided hikes are free. Evening stargazing programmes and full-moon hikes are offered between June and September, when the weather is warm enough. There are also guided walks through Waikamoi Preserve and longer hikes from the summit visitor center.

For bicycle tours and guided horseback rides, see the Activities section near the front of this chapter.

HALEAKALA CRATER ROAD

Haleakala Crater Rd (Hwy 378) twists for 11 miles from Hwy 377 near Kula up to the park entrance, then another 10 miles to Haleakala summit. It's a good paved road, but it's steep and winding. You don't want to rush it, especially when it's dark or foggy. Watch out for cattle wandering freely across the road.

The drive to the summit takes about 1½ hours from Paia or Kahului, two hours from Kihei and a bit longer from Lahaina. If you need gas, fill up the night before, as there are no services on Haleakala Crater Rd. Loosen your gas tank cap about a quarter-turn before starting your ascent to prevent vapor lock.

On your return from the summit, you'll see Maui unfolding below, with sugarcane and pineapple fields creating a patchwork on the valley floor. The highway snakes back and forth, so put your car in low gear to avoid brake failure. Be careful of cyclists.

Hosmer Grove

Hosmer Grove, three-quarters of a mile before park headquarters, has a pleasant half-mile loop trail that begins in the camping ground. The nature walk starts in a forest of introduced trees, then passes into native Hawaiian shrub land. Pick up a trail guide at park headquarters.

The exotics were introduced in 1910 in an effort to develop a lumber industry in Hawaii. They include incense cedar, Norway spruce, Douglas fir, eucalyptus and various pines. Although the trees adapted well enough to grow, they didn't grow fast enough at these elevations to make tree harvesting practical. Thanks to this failure, today there's a park here instead.

Native plants include *akala* (Hawaiian raspberry), *mamane, pilo, kilau* ferns and sandalwood. The *ohelo*, a berry sacred to Pele, and the *pukiawe*, which has red and white berries and evergreen leaves, both help feed the endangered nene.

There are wonderful scents and birdcalls along the trail. The native *iiwi* and *apapane*, both sparrow-size birds with bright red feathers, are fairly common. The *iiwi* has a very loud squeaking call, orange legs and a curved salmon- or yellow-colored bill. The apapane is a fast-moving bird with a black bill, black legs and a white undertail. It feeds on the nectar of ohia flowers, and its wings make a distinctive whirring sound.

Waikamoi Preserve

Waikamoi Preserve is a 5230-acre reserve adjoining Hosmer Grove. It contains native koa and ohia rain forest and is a habitat for

Hawaiian forest birds, including a number of rare and endangered species. The yellow-green Maui creeper and the crested honeycreeper, while both endangered, are more common than some of the others.

The Nature Conservancy (☎ *572-7849*) offers four-hour guided hikes on the second Saturday of each month. The suggested donation is $25 ($15 for members); advance reservations are required. The National Park Service offers free three-hour, 3-mile guided hikes that enter the preserve from Hosmer Grove camping ground at 9am on Mondays and Thursdays. Occasionally hikes are canceled because of the weather conditions, so call ahead.

The Sunrise Experience

Sunrise at Haleakala is an unforgettable experience, one that Mark Twain called the 'sublimest spectacle' he'd ever seen. As you drive up the mountain in the dark, the only sights are twinkling town lights, a sky full of stars, and a distant fishing boat or two on the dark horizon.

About an hour before dawn, the night sky begins to lighten and turn purple-blue, and the stars fade away. Ethereal silhouettes of the mountain ridges appear.

Plan to arrive at the summit about 30 or 40 minutes before the sunrise. The undersides of the clouds lighten up first, accenting the night sky with pale silvery slivers and streaks of pink. About 20 minutes before sunrise, the light intensifies on the horizon in bright oranges and reds, much like a sunset. Turn around for a look at Science City, whose domes turn a blazing pink.

The best photo opportunities occur before the actual sunrise. Every morning is different, but once the sun is up, the silvery lines and the subtleties disappear. If you wake up late or traffic is slow, pull over at one of the lower crater overlooks before first light erupts instead. Everyone comes out for the grand finale, the moment when the disk of the sun appears and everything takes on a fiery glow.

If you don't have a winter jacket or sleeping bag to wrap yourself in, bring a warm blanket from your hotel. This will give you the option of sitting outside in a peaceful spot, say atop White Hill Overlook or partway down Sliding Sands Trail, to take it all in rather than huddling for heat inside the crowded visitor center or summit gazebo.

MAUI

Leleiwi Overlook

Leleiwi Overlook, at an elevation of 8840ft, is just over midway between park headquarters and the summit visitor center. From the parking lot, it's a quick walk out to the overlook, from where you can see the West Maui Mountains and both sides of the isthmus connecting the two sides of Maui. You also get another angle on Haleakala Crater.

In the afternoon, if weather conditions are right, you might see the **Brocken specter**, an optical phenomenon that occurs at high elevations. Essentially, by standing between the sun and the clouds, your image is magnified and projected onto the clouds. The light reflects off tiny droplets of water in the clouds, creating a circular rainbow around your shadow.

Kalahaku Overlook

Kalahaku Overlook, elevation 9324ft, is about a mile above Leleiwi Overlook. The lower section has a fenced enclosure containing lots of silversword, from seedlings to mature plants.

The upper section has an observation deck looking down into Haleakala Crater. With the help of the deck's information plaque, you can clearly identify cinder cones on the crater floor below.

For photography, afternoon light is best. In the early morning, you can get more favorable light by walking a few minutes down an unmarked path to the left of the observation deck.

Haleakala Visitor Center

Almost at the summit, the **visitor center** *(open 6am-3pm daily in summer, 6:30am-3pm in winter)*, on the rim of the crater at 9745ft, is the main sunrise-viewing spot. The center has minor displays on geological and volcanic evolution and a recording explaining what you see on the crater floor 3000ft below. Nature books and postcards are for sale here, and a ranger is usually on duty. There are rest rooms and a pay phone.

Before dawn, the parking lot fills up with tour vans, mountain biking groups, horse trailers and everyone coming to see the sunrise show. Brief natural and cultural history talks are given at the summit visitor center at 9:30am, 10:30am and 11:30am daily. Park rangers also lead a moderately strenuous two-hour hike that goes about a mile down Sliding Sands Trail; meet at the trailhead at 9am on Tuesday and Friday. Guided hikes along the 12-mile Sliding Sands-Halemauu Trail are led once or twice a month.

Summit

The **Puu Ulaula (Red Hill) Overlook**, at 10,023ft, is Maui's highest point. The summit building at the overlook has wraparound windows, and on clear days you can see the Big Island, Lanai, Molokai and even Oahu. **Magnetic Peak**, closer to the crater, has an uncanny ability to mess with your compass.

The summit building is half a mile uphill from the visitor center. Look around the parking lot for 'lava bombs,' hardened molten lava previously expelled from the crater's volcanic vents.

The 37-mile drive from sea level to the summit of Haleakala is said to be the highest elevation gain in the shortest distance anywhere in the world.

Hawaii's State Bird

The native nene is a long-lost cousin of the Canada goose. These birds generally nest in high cliffs surrounded by rugged lava flows with sparse vegetation. Curiously, their feet have adapted to the dry, volcanic landscape by losing most of their webbing.

In 1946 only 50 nene remained alive anywhere in the world. In fact there were no birds left at all inside Haleakala National Park until Boy Scouts carried junior birds back into the crater inside their backpacks! These gentle creatures have now been brought back from the verge of extinction by captive breeding and release programmes.

Currently, Haleakala's nene population is holding steady at about 250. Nene are very friendly and adore hanging out where people do, from the crater floor cabins to park headquarters. Unfortunately, many have been run over by cars. Others have had their return to the wild slowed by food handouts from park visitors, so please don't feed them.

Science City

On the Big Island's Mauna Kea, scientists study the moon. Here at Haleakala, appropriately enough, they study the sun.

Science City, just beyond the summit, is off-limits to visitors. It's under the jurisdiction of the University of Hawaii, which owns some of the domes and leases other land for a variety of private and government research projects. Most recently, the university joined forces with a UK-based educational foundation to break ground for the Faulkes telescope, which will be the world's largest telescope dedicated to public outreach, mostly to remote classrooms.

Department of Defense-related projects here include laser technology related to the 'Star Wars' project, satellite tracking and identification, and a deep-space surveillance system. The newest military telescope, which became operational in 1997 and cost $123 million to build, is capable of identifying a basketball-size object flying in space 20,000 miles away.

HIKING THE CRATER

Hiking the crater floor offers a completely different angle on Haleakala's lunar landscape. Instead of peering down from the rim, you're looking up at the walls and towering cinder cones. It looks so much like a moonscape that US astronauts trained here before going to the moon. Speaking of which, hiking here on full-moon nights is magical.

The sound of cinders crunching underfoot is often the only noise to reach your ears, except for the bark of a *pueo* (Hawaiian owl) and honking of a friendly nene. Ring-necked pheasants are also likely to be startled by your approach and swiftly dart up from the crater floor. The *uau* (dark-rumped petrel), which is an endangered species along with the nene and silversword, nests in the lava rocks after feeding down near the ocean; these seabirds were thought to be extinct until seen again in the crater during the 1970s.

The weather at Haleakala can change suddenly from dry, hot conditions to cold, windswept rain. Although the general rule is sunny in the morning and cloudy in the afternoon, fog and clouds can blow in at any time. No matter what the weather is like at the start of a hike, be prepared for temperatures that can drop into the 50s (°F) during the day and the 30s at night, at any time of year. Hikers without proper clothing risk hypothermia. The climate also changes radically as you walk across the crater floor. In the 4 miles between the Kapalaoa and Paliku cabins, rainfall varies from an annual average of 12 inches to 300 inches. December to May is the wet season.

The 27 miles of trails inside the crater are reliably marked at junctions. To protect the fragile environment, always keep to the center of established trails and do not be tempted off them, even for well-trodden shortcuts through switchbacks. One of the most popular full-day outings is the vigorous 11½-mile hike that starts down Sliding Sands Trail and returns via Halemauu Trail.

With the average elevation on the crater floor at 6700ft, the relatively thin air means that hiking can be quite tiring. The higher elevation also means that sunburn is more likely. Take sunscreen, rain gear, a few layers of clothing, a first-aid kit and plenty of water.

Sliding Sands Trail

Sliding Sands, the summit trail into the crater, starts at the south side of the visitor center parking lot. Most hikers enter the crater this way, although it is possible to do it in the reverse direction, going uphill – just expect slow progress.

Sliding Sands starts out at 9740ft and descends steeply over loose cinders down to the crater floor. The trail leads 9½ miles to the Paliku cabins and camping ground, passing the Kapalaoa cabin at 5¾ miles after roughly four hours. If you hike it after catching the sunrise, you'll walk directly into a gentle warmish wind and the rays of the sun.

The first segment of the trail follows the south wall of the crater. There are great views on the way down, but except for a few shrubs, there's no vegetation in sight. About 2 miles down (a descent of 1400ft), a steep spur trail leads past silversword plants to **Ka Luu o ka Oo** cinder cone, about half a mile north. Four miles down, after an elevation drop of 2500ft, the trail intersects with the first of three spur trails leading north into the cinder desert, which after about 1½ miles meets the Halemauu Trail.

As you strike out across the crater floor for 2 miles to Kapalaoa, verdant ridges rise on your right, eventually giving way to ropy *pahoehoe* lava. From Kapalaoa cabin to Paliku, the descent is gentle and the vegetation gradually increases. Paliku (6380ft) is beneath a sheer cliff at the eastern end of the crater. In contrast to the crater's barren western end, this area receives heavy rainfall, with ohia forests climbing the slopes. This final stretch seems to take an eternity, especially once the rain sets in.

Halemauu Trail

Halemauu Trailhead, 3½ miles above park headquarters and about 6 miles below the summit visitor center, is marked. There's a fair chance you'll find nene in the parking lot, and be careful since many nene have been killed by motorists. If you're camping at Hosmer Grove, you can take the little-known, unexciting **Supply Trail** instead, joining the Halemauu Trail at the crater rim after 2½ miles.

If you're not up for a long hike, even hiking the first mile to the park boundary fence gives a fine view of the crater with Koolau Gap to the east. It's fairly level up to this point. If you continue on the trail and hike down 1400ft and 2 miles of switchbacks,

Camel of the Plant World

The strikingly beautiful silversword *(ahinahina)*, with its pointed silver leaves, is a distant relative of the sunflower. Each of these amazing plants grows for three to 50 years before blooming just once in a lifetime. In its final year, it shoots up a flowering stalk sometimes over 6ft tall. During the summer, that stalk flowers with hundreds of maroon and yellow blossoms. When the flowers go to seed in late autumn, the plant dies.

The silversword, found only in Hawaii, was nearly wiped out in the early 20th century by grazing feral goats and by people who swipe them for souvenirs. It's making a comeback thanks to efforts by the park service staff members. Half of all silverswords today are trampled to death as seedlings, mostly by careless hikers who wander off trails.

Yet the silversword has always been a survivor. After all, it was able to adapt to the barren conditions of its endemic volcanic habitats on Maui and the Big Island. Its shiny leaves have evolved fine silver hairs to reflect the sun's ultraviolet radiation, and the inward curl of these leaves further prevents dehydration. Its shallow expansive root system also collects moisture hiding in the loose volcanic cinders.

then walk another mile across the crater floor to Holua cabin and camping ground, the 8-mile round trip makes for a good workout, but start early before the afternoon clouds roll in and visibility vanishes.

At 6940ft, Holua is one of the lowest areas along this hike, and you'll see impressive views of the crater walls rising a few thousand feet to the west. A few large **lava tubes** here are worth exploring: one up a short, steep cliff behind the cabin, and the other a 15-minute detour further along the trail. If you have energy, push on just another mile to the colorful cinder cones, being sure make a short detour onto the **Silversword Loop**, where you'll see plants in various stages of growth. If you're here in summer, you should be able to see blooms.

The trail continues another 6¼ miles to the Paliku cabin.

Exploring the Cinder Desert

Almost all hiking trails lead to the belly of the beast. There is no way to see this amazing area without backtracking. Three major spur trails connect Sliding Sands Trail, from near Kapalaoa, with the Halemauu Trail between Paliku and Holua. As the trails are not very long, you may even have time to do them all.

The spur trail furthest west takes in many of the crater's most kaleidoscopic cinder cones, and the viewing angle changes with every step. If you prefer stark, black and barren, both of the other spur trails take you through *aa* and *pahoehoe* lava fields, with the one farthest east lying splattered with rust-red cinders.

All three trails end up on the north side of the cinder desert near **Kawilinau**, also known as the Bottomless Pit. Legends say the pit leads down to the sea, though the park service says it's just 65ft deep. You can't really get a good look down the narrow shaft, however. Don't miss taking the short loop trail to sit for a while in the saddle of **Pele's Paint Pot Lookout**, the crater's most jaw-dropping vantage point.

Kaupo Trail

From the Paliku camping ground on the eastern edge of the crater floor, it's possible to continue another 8½ miles down to Kaupo on the southern coast. The first 4 miles of the trail drops 2500ft in elevation before reaching the park boundary. It's a steep rocky trail through rough lava and brushland, but worth coming this far just for the coastal views.

The last 4½ miles pass through Kaupo Ranch property on a rough jeep trail with no shade cover as it descends to the bottom of Kaupo Gap, exiting into a forest where feral pigs snuffle about. Here trail markings become vague, but once you reach the dirt road, it's another 1½ miles to the exit at the east side of the Kaupo General Store.

The 'village' of Kaupo (see the Piilani Hwy section, earlier) is a long way from anywhere, with very little traffic. Still, what traffic there is – largely sightseers braving the circle-island road and locals in pickup trucks – moves slow enough along Kaupo's rough road to start conversation. If you have to walk the final stretch, it's 8 miles to Oheo Gulch camping ground.

This is a strenuous hike, and because of the remoteness and the ankle-twisting conditions, it's not advisable to hike it alone, or even uphill for that matter. According to legend, the demigod Maui used this route as he made his way up into the volcano to harness the sun, but trust us, for mere mortals it's no fun. The National Park Service publishes a Kaupo Trail brochure that people considering the hike should pick up in advance.

Skyline Trail

This otherworldly trail is the major link in a hiking route that begins at 9750ft near the summit of Haleakala and leads down to Polipoli camping ground at 6200ft, a total distance of 8½ miles (about four hours on foot).

The Skyline Trail, a dirt road used to maintain Polipoli Spring State Recreation Area, starts from near Science City in open terrain made up of cinder and craters. After three crunchy miles, it reaches the tree line (at an elevation of 8500ft) and enters native *mamane* forest. In the winter, *mamane* is heavy with clusters of delicate yellow flowers that look like sweet-pea blossoms.

There's solitude on this walk. And if the clouds treat you kindly, you'll have broad views all the way between the barren summit and the dense cloud forest. Eventually the trail meets the main Polipoli access road and merges into Haleakala Ridge Trail, which then connects with Polipoli Trail to the camping ground.

PLACES TO STAY

Accommodations are kept primitive. Backcountry camp sites have pit toilets and limited nonpotable water supplies that are shared with the crater cabins. All water needs to be filtered or chemically treated; conserve it, as water tanks occasionally run dry. Campfires are prohibited, and you must take out all trash. There are no food, electricity or showers available anywhere.

Remember that sleeping at an elevation of 7000ft is nothing like camping on the beach. Without a waterproof tent and a winter-rated sleeping bag, forget about it. In case of genuine emergencies, rangers can sometimes be found at Paliku or Holua ranger cabins – but don't count on it.

Camping

Hosmer Grove has a **drive-up camping ground** immediately after the park entrance, but before the pay booth. It tends to be cloudy and damp, but popular nevertheless. There are picnic tables, grills, toilets and drinking water. Permits are not required, though there's a three-day camping limit per month. It's busier in summer than in winter and is often full on holiday weekends.

Two **backcountry camping grounds** lie inside Haleakala Crater. One is at Holua, 4 miles down the Halemauu Trail at the base of steep cliffs, and the other is at Paliku, below a rain forest ridge at the trail's end. Weather can be unpredictable at both. **Holua** is typically dry after sunrise, until clouds roll back in the late afternoon and make things damp. **Paliku** is in a grassy meadow, with skies overhead alternating between stormy and breathtakingly sunny. Do not camp near the cabins.

Permits are required for crater camping. They are issued at park headquarters on a first-come, first-served basis between 8am and 3pm on the day of the hike. Camping is limited to three nights in the crater each month, with no more than two consecutive nights at either camping ground. Permits can go quickly if large groups show up, a situation that is more likely to occur in summer.

Cabins

Three **rustic cabins** *(1-6 people $40, 7-12 people $80)* lie along trails in the crater. The cabins – one each at Holua, Kapalaoa and Paliku – were built by the CCC in the 1930s, and each has a wood-burning stove, two propane burners, some cooking utensils, 12 bunks with sleeping pads (but no bedding), pit toilets and a limited supply of water and firewood (bring your own fire starter).

Hiking distances to the cabins from the crater rim range from 4 to 10 miles. The driest conditions are at Kapalaoa, in the middle of the cinder desert off the Sliding Sands Trail. Those craving lush rain forest will find Paliku serene. Holua has unparalleled sunrise views. There's a three-day limit, with no more than two consecutive nights in any cabin. Each cabin is rented to only one party at a time.

The problem here is the demand, which is so high the park service actually holds a monthly lottery to award reservations! To enter, your reservation request must be received two months prior to the first day of the month of your proposed stay (eg, requests for cabins on any date in July must arrive before May 1). Your chances increase if you list alternate dates within the same calendar month and if you choose weekdays rather than weekends.

Only written reservation requests *(Haleakala National Park, PO Box 369, Makawao, HI 96768, Attn: CABINS)* are accepted (no phone or fax); include your name, address, phone number, specific dates and cabins, and the number of people in your group. A separate request is needed for each month. Mail early, as postal delivery to Hawaii takes longer than to the US mainland.

If you are selected in the lottery, you will be notified, at which point the fees will have to be paid in full at least three weeks prior to the reservation date. Your permit will be mailed to you, unless you specifically request otherwise. You then need to call or visit the park headquarters with photo ID to pick up the cabin lock combinations. If you plan to start hiking immediately after sunrise, do this in advance since headquarters usually doesn't open until at least 7:30am.

Cancellations occasionally occur, creating last-minute vacancies. You can check for vacancies in person at park headquarters after 8am. Calls regarding cancellations are accepted only between 1pm and 3pm daily, and you'll need to have a credit card available to secure the cabin if there is a vacancy.

Molokai

According to the ancient chants, Molokai was a child of Hina, goddess of the moon and mother to Maui. It is also the most Hawaiian of the main islands, with almost 50% of its population claiming native Hawaiian ancestry. At times Molokai almost seems like some forgotten outpost of the South Pacific, rather than a modern place squeezed between the high-rises of Maui and Oahu.

Only sparsely populated, with a handful of small towns, Molokai is the last stronghold of rural Hawaii, managing to survive in a sort of time warp: no packaged Hawaiiana, no high-rises, more farmers than tourists, and not a single stoplight anywhere on the island. Although the island has garnered a reputation for being wary of outsiders, anyone who shows genuine *aloha aina* (love of the land) will be welcomed. Even newcomers quickly find themselves waving the *shaka* sign (Hawaiian hand greeting) to people on the road who were strangers only yesterday.

If you're looking for lots of action, this isn't the place. Instead, you can sit on the edge of an 800-year-old fishpond and watch the sun rise over distant Haleakala on Maui, then walk along Hawaii's largest beach with barely another soul in sight or take the cliff-side mule trail down to the old leprosy settlement of Kalaupapa. In the evening, you can watch the sun setting behind rustling palms in a royal coconut grove and wind down with mellow guitar music at the quaint Hotel Molokai's oceanfront bar. Ah, paradise.

Highlights

- Tracking the mule trail down to historic Kalaupapa
- Ambling and camping along Molokai's wild, windswept beaches
- Soaking up Kaunakakai's small-town atmosphere
- Reveling along the Kamehameha V Hwy to rural Halawa Valley
- Mountain biking or kayaking around the world's highest sea cliff

HISTORY

For centuries, the battling armies of Maui and Oahu were careful to bypass Molokai. It was the powerful reputations of its *kahuna* (priests, healers and sorcerers) that kept invaders at bay; in fact, they were said to have been able to simply pray their enemies to death. The most famous of these was the prophet Lanikaula, who practiced his arts in the Halawa Valley. His old bones are still hidden in a sacred *kukui* (candlenut) grove on the grounds of Puu o Hoku Ranch (see the East Molokai section later). The island was also an ancient place of refuge for Hawaiians who broke *kapus* (taboos) or were somehow outside the mainstream, and Molokai has a long tradition of transvestitism that continues today.

By the 18th century, magic alone wasn't enough to protect the island from outside influences. Internal dissent among the *alii* (royal chiefs) led Molokai's rulers to align themselves with chiefs from other islands. Oahu, Maui and the Big Island all got involved in the ensuing power struggle.

Eventually the king of Oahu, Peleioholani, established his rule over Molokai. When the daughter he left on Molokai was captured and killed by Molokai chiefs, Peleioholani hastily returned to the island and struck back with a vengeance. Those Molokai chiefs who were unable to flee to Maui were captured and roasted alive. Commoners were tortured.

Oahu continued to rule over Molokai until 1785. Then Maui and the Big Island, which were at war with each other, took alternate turns ruling Molokai for the next decade. In 1795 Kamehameha the Great invaded Molokai with such force that his war canoes were lined up for a full 4 miles along this coast. He quickly brought Molokai under his command and then went on to invade Oahu, the last battle in a campaign that eventually would unite all of the Hawaiian Islands.

The first detailed description of the island was recorded by Captain George Vancouver, a British navigator, who anchored off Molokai in 1792. He guessed Molokai's population at around 10,000. When the missionaries first arrived in the 1830s, they did a more detailed count, estimating 8700 residents. Historically, Molokai's largest settlements were on the rainy south coast of the eastern half of the island, where shallow waters and coastal indentations were ideal for the construction of fishponds, and in the valley wetlands, taro patches flourished.

The missionaries found the densest populations between Kamalo and Waialua, and it is in this area that they established their first missions. Kalaupapa Peninsula held the island's other major settlement, located near the populated North Shore valleys of Halawa, Pelekunu and Wailau. Molokai's central plains and dry western half were barely settled at that time.

Ranching & Agriculture

In the 1850s, Kamehameha V acquired the bulk of Molokai's arable land, forming Molokai Ranch, but overgrazing eventually led to the widespread destruction of native vegetation and fishponds. After his death, the ranch became part of the Bishop Estate, which quickly sold it off to a group of Honolulu businesspeople.

A year later, in 1898, the American Sugar Company, a division of Molokai Ranch, attempted to develop a major sugar plantation in central Molokai. The company built a railroad system to haul the cane, developed harbor facilities and installed a powerful pumping system to draw up water. However, by 1901 the well water used to irrigate the fields had become so saline that the crops failed. The company then moved into honey production on such a big scale that at one point Molokai was the world's largest honey exporter. In the mid-1930s, however, an epidemic wiped out the hives and the industry.

Meanwhile, the ranch continued its efforts to find '*the* crop for Molokai.' Cotton, rice and numerous grain crops all took their turn biting Molokai's red dust. Finally, pineapple took root as the crop most suited to the island's dry, windy conditions. Plantation-scale production began in Hoolehua in 1920. Within 10 years, Molokai's population tripled as immigrants arrived to work the fields.

In the 1970s, competition from overseas brought an end to the pineapple's reign on Molokai. Dole closed down its operation in 1976, and the other island giant, Del Monte, later followed suit. These closures brought hard times and the highest unemployment levels in the state. Then cattle raising, long a mainstay, suddenly collapsed. In a controversial decision in 1985, the state, after finding an incidence of bovine tuberculosis, ordered every head of cattle on Molokai to be destroyed. Molokai Ranch has since restocked some of its herd, but the majority of the 240 smaller cattle owners called it quits.

Molokai Ranch still owns about one-third of Molokai, or more than half of the island's privately held lands. Many locals consider it a thorn in their side, as a number of traditional outdoor activities are restricted on ranch land, to which public access is mostly blocked.

In the 1990s the ranch operated a small wildlife safari park, where many shutterbug tourists snapped pictures of exotic animals and trophy hunters paid $1500 a head to shoot African eland and blackbuck antelope. Rumors abound of how local activists, long resistant to the type of tourist-oriented development that has all but consumed neighboring Maui, made life difficult enough for the ranch that the safari park was shut down. Some of the remaining animals were tragically killed before they could be transported to off-island zoos by an accidental overdose of tranquilizers, just another note in the island's troubled history.

GEOGRAPHY & GEOLOGY

Roughly rectangular in shape, Molokai is Hawaii's fifth-largest island, with a land area of 260 sq miles. The western half is dry and arid, with rolling hills and the gradually sloping range of Maunaloa, capped by Puu Nana (1381ft). The island's highest point, Kamakou (4961ft), is in the middle of the rugged eastern half.

Geologically speaking, Molokai is a union of two separate shield volcanoes that erupted to form two distinct islands. The lofty mountains of eastern Molokai acted like a screen, capturing the clouds. Heavy rainfall and stream erosion then cut deep valleys into its towering north face. Dry western Molokai formed into more modest hills and tableland. Later eruptions spilled lava into the channel that separated the two volcanoes, forming the Hoolehua Plains and creating present-day Molokai.

The Kalaupapa Peninsula, on the north side of Molokai, seems to have been an afterthought by Pele, goddess of volcanoes. An eruption from the then-offshore Kauhako Crater created the flat lava peninsula long after the rest of Molokai had been formed.

Kauhako Crater, at 400ft, is Kalaupapa's highest point.

Molokai's north shore, from Kalaupapa to Halawa, is a wilderness area of coastal mountains and deeply cut valleys. It includes the world's highest sea cliffs, which reach heights of 3300ft with an average gradient of 58°. Hawaii's highest waterfall, Kahiwa Falls (1750ft), drops from these cliffs. The north shore is spectacular, but for the most part its steep slopes and rain forests are impenetrable. The main way to get into the valleys is by boat, but rough winter seas restrict that to the summer season.

CLIMATE

At Kaunakakai, the average daily temperature is 70°F in winter, 78°F in summer. The average annual rainfall is 14 inches.

For recorded weather and marine forecasts by the National Weather Service, call ☎ *552-2477*.

FLORA & FAUNA

The two most dominant tree types on Molokai are *kiawe* in the drier areas and *ohia lehua* in the wetter. Along the banks of streams, which were once heavily cultivated with taro, forests of *kukui* and guava now dominate.

The axis deer that run free in Molokai are descendants of eight deer sent from India in 1868 as a gift to King Kamehameha V. Feral pigs, introduced by the early Polynesian settlers, still roam the upper wetland forests, and feral goats inhabit the steep canyons and valley rims. All three wreak havoc on the environment and are hunted game animals.

Humpback whales spend winters cavorting in the waters between Molokai, Lanai and Maui. In season, look for the whales off Molokai's southeast coast.

Native waterbirds include the common moorhen, Hawaiian coot and black-necked stilt, which are all endangered. Molokai also has five native forest birds, mostly in the undisturbed upland forests, and the Hawaiian owl.

GOVERNMENT

Kalaupapa Peninsula is a quasi-county unto itself, called Kalawao, which is essentially administered by the state Department of Health. The rest of Molokai, along with neighboring Lanai, is swallowed up in the mire of Maui County.

Most administrative decisions affecting Molokai are made on Maui island. Since many community and development issues are also decided at a county level, the island of Maui, with 17 times Molokai's population, has the clout.

In the 1980s, a Maui County committee was appointed to create a community plan to address development issues on Molokai. The committee conducted hearings and surveys on Molokai, and much to the surprise of Molokai residents – who were used to being bullied by Maui's prodevelopment forces – the recommendations put forth in the draft plan were tuned in to their own feelings on growth.

The Molokai Plan called for the preservation of Molokai's rural lifestyle and the maintenance of agriculture as the basis of the island's economy. It also called for all resort development to be limited to the west end and to be low-rise. The Molokai Plan has been widely accepted as the guiding code for land use on Molokai and is referred to whenever there are disputes over development – which is often.

Some critics say that the final compromise draft approved by Maui County officials is too weak to protect key west end archaeological sites and too strong in its support of Molokai Ranch as the key to revitalization. A diversified economy, not a greater reliance on tourism, is what opponents propose. Today you can still pick up on a lot of local anti-development sentiment simply by noticing bumper stickers on Molokai pickup trucks.

ECONOMY

Once Molokai had chronically high unemployment hovering around triple the state average, but its recent jobless rate of 6.5% is only slightly higher than other islands. Many of Molokai's new jobs were created through community-based enterprise, such as school-to-work schemes and training programmes in aquaculture and watershed protection.

Molokai has rich soil, and some feel the island may have the potential to be Hawaii's 'breadbasket.' After pineapple plantations left Molokai in the late 1970s, islanders began to develop small-scale farming more intensely. Significant crops include watermelons, dryland taro, macadamia nuts, sweet

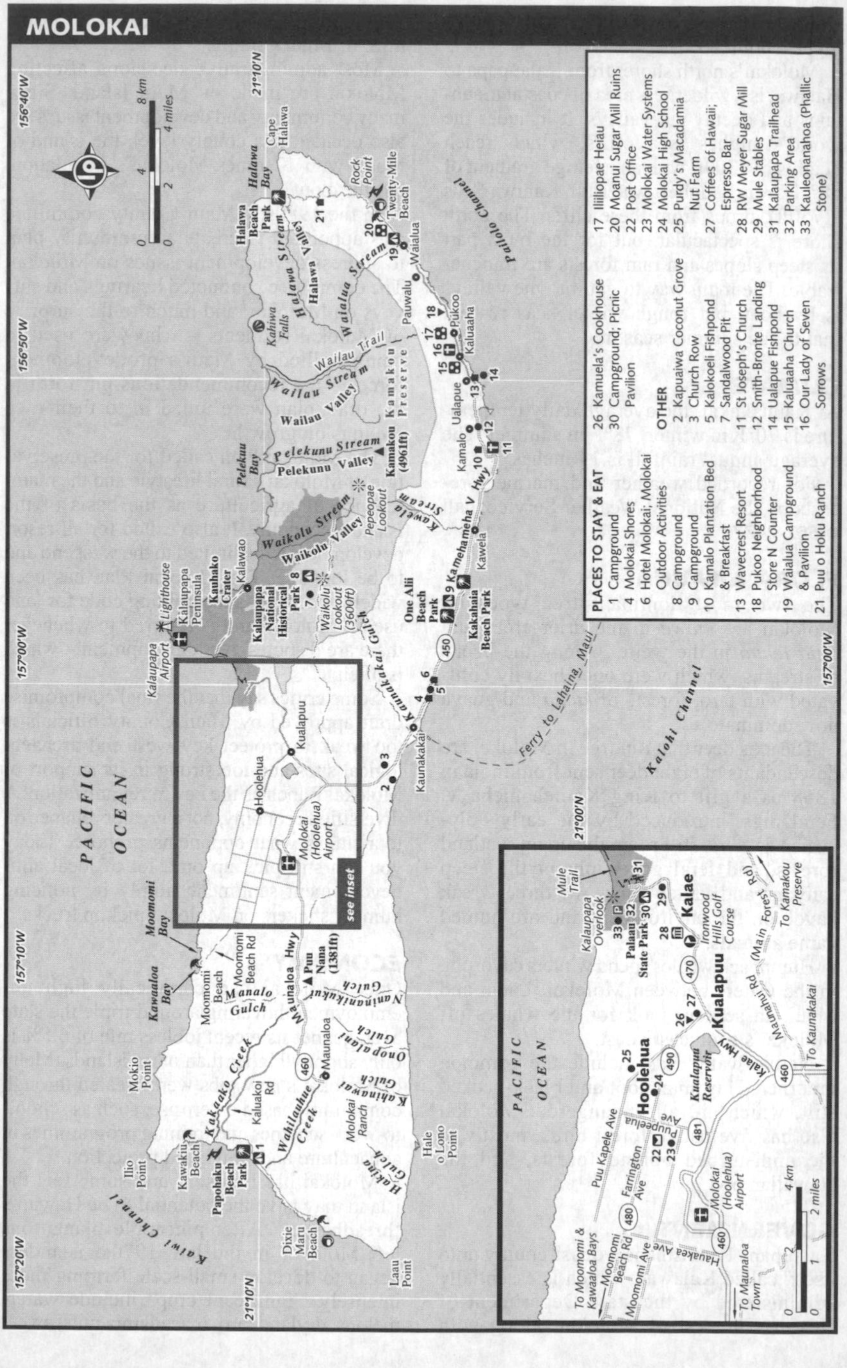
MOLOKAI
PLACES TO STAY & EAT
1 Campground
4 Molokai Shores
6 Hotel Molokai; Molokai Outdoor Activities
8 Campground
9 Campground
10 Kamalo Plantation Bed & Breakfast
13 Wavecrest Resort
18 Pukoo Neighborhood Store N Counter
19 Waialua Campground & Pavilion
21 Puu o Hoku Ranch
26 Kamuela's Cookhouse
30 Campground; Picnic Pavilion
OTHER
2 Kapuaiwa Coconut Grove
3 Church Row
5 Kalokoeli Fishpond
7 Sandalwood Pit
11 St Joseph's Church
12 Smith-Bronte Landing
14 Ualapue Fishpond
15 Kaluaaha Church
16 Our Lady of Seven Sorrows
17 Iliiliopae Heiau
20 Moanui Sugar Mill Ruins
22 Post Office
23 Molokai Water Systems
24 Molokai High School
25 Purdy's Macadamia Nut Farm
27 Coffees of Hawaii; Espresso Bar
28 RW Meyer Sugar Mill
29 Mule Stables
31 Kalaupapa Trailhead
32 Parking Area
33 Kauleonanahoa (Phallic Stone)
PACIFIC OCEAN
Kalohi Channel
Pailolo Channel
Kaiwi Channel
Ferry to Lahaina, Maui
Kalaupapa Peninsula
Kalaupapa National Historical Park
Kamakou Preserve
Kamakou (4961ft)
Halawa Valley
Wailau Valley
Pelekunu Valley
Waikolu Valley
Kaunakakai
Hoolehua
Kualapuu
Kalae
Maunaloa
Molokai (Hoolehua) Airport
Kalaupapa Airport
Papohaku Beach Park
Moomomi Bay
Halawa Bay
Cape Halawa
Laau Point
Ilio Point
see inset

potatoes, seed corn, string beans and onions. In 1991, coffee trees were planted on formerly fallow pineapple fields in Kualapuu and now cover some 600 acres.

POPULATION & PEOPLE

Molokai has a population of 7250. Outside of Niihau, Molokai is the most Hawaiian of the islands, with almost 50% of its people claiming Hawaiian or part-Hawaiian ancestry. This is in part due to the Hawaiian Homes Act of 1921, which awarded 40-acre tracts of land to people with at least 50% Hawaiian ancestry. The purpose of the act was to encourage homesteading among native Hawaiians, who had become the most landless ethnic group in Hawaii. The first settlements under the act were made on Molokai.

Filipino is the next largest ethnic group, followed by Caucasian.

ORIENTATION

Molokai lies midway in the Hawaiian chain, about 25 miles southeast of Oahu and 9 miles northwest of Maui, with Lanai 9 miles directly south. The airport is on the island's flat central plains, more or less in the center of Molokai.

The first thing you see as you drive out of the airport is a sign reading, 'Aloha! Slow Down – This is Molokai.' Hallelujah. At the stop sign, turn right to reach Hwy 460. This one highway is Molokai's main road, stretching from east to west. From Kaunakakai westward, it's called Hwy 460 (Maunaloa Hwy). From Kaunakakai eastward, it's Hwy 450 (Kamehameha V Hwy). East of the airport toward Kaunakakai, Hwy 470 (Kalae Hwy) branches off Hwy 460 and heads up to the Kalaupapa Peninsula overlook.

Maps

The University of Hawaii's joint *Molokai/Lanai* map shows Molokai's topography; it's sold at stores in Kaunakakai. A more user-friendly lightweight fold-out map is Nelles' *Maui, Molokai, Lanai*. The *Ready Mapbook of Maui County*, which includes coverage of Molokai and Lanai, is an invaluable resource for explorers; admittedly, it's bulky.

Molokai is not the place to explore dirt roads just to see what's there. Many dirt paths that seem like they could be roads are just driveways into someone's backyard. As on other islands, there's still a bit of *pakalolo* (marijuana) growing here and there. All in all, folks aren't too keen on outsiders cruising around on their private turf.

On the other hand, if there's a fishpond you want to see and someone's house is between the road and the water, it's usually easy to strike up a conversation and get permission to cross. Molokai people are receptive and friendly to those genuinely interested in Hawaiian ways. If you're lucky, they might even share a little local lore and history with you, particularly the old-timers.

INFORMATION

Central Kaunakakai has the majority of island-wide services, including a tourist information office, banks with ATMs, grocery stores and gas stations. The main post office is also in downtown Kaunakakai; smaller branch post offices are in Hoolehua, Kualapuu, Maunaloa and Kalaupapa.

Molokai's two weekly newspapers, which are both distributed free around the island, provide a glimpse of island life. The *Molokai Advertiser-News* (☎ *558-8253)* is published each Wednesday, while the *Dispatch* (☎ *552-2781)*, with its funny local advice column and events calendar, is published each Thursday. Local and off-island papers can be picked up at the airport and shops in Kaunakakai.

Use the **emergency hotline** (☎ *911)* for police, ambulance and fire emergencies. The **Molokai General Hospital** (☎ *553-5331; 280 Puali St, Kaunakakai)* has 24-hour emergency service.

For special events on Molokai, many of which feature traditional Hawaiian cultural activities, see the Facts for the Visitor chapter.

ACTIVITIES

Molokai has wild ocean waters, rough trails, remote rainforests and a burgeoning number of outdoor adventures. Most rental gear and sports facilities are found at the island's handful of hotels and resorts.

Public tennis facilities at the **Mitchell Pauole Center** *(see the Kaunakakai section later)* are low-cost, as is **Ironwood Hills Golf Club** (☎ *567-6000; Kalae)*, always the course of choice for islanders.

Molokai Outdoor Activities (☎ *553-4477, 877-553-4477;* W *www.molokai-outdoors.com)*, at the Hotel Molokai in Kaunakakai, rents kayaks, snorkel sets, surfboards, fishing poles, tennis rackets and just about anything else you might need. Street cruisers and mountain bike rentals ($15 to $25 per day, $65 to $105 per week) come with free bike racks, helmets and locks.

You can also rent all this equipment, along with golf clubs, fishing spears or camping gear, at competitive rates from **Molokai Rentals and Tours** (*☎ 553-5663, 800-553-9071; W www.molokai-rentals.com*).

The widest variety of organized activities on Molokai are offered by Molokai Ranch; for details, see the West End section later in this chapter. Be forewarned that although the ranch lands are spectacular, from sea cliffs to forest to outback, most activities are priced sky-high, especially for nonguests.

Ocean Sports

Most folks drive to the southeastern end of the island, where the beach around the 20-mile marker offers some of Molokai's best **swimming** and **snorkeling**. Rock Point, not far north of there, and Halawa Bay, at the northern end of the road, are popular **surfing** spots. Closer to Kaunakakai, you may see **windsurfing** offshore, but do not trespass on private land to get to the beaches.

On the west coast, Papohaku Beach is the broadest and longest sandy beach in all of Hawaii, but high winds mean it's not safe for swimming. Just a few miles south is Dixie Maru Beach, with a small protected bay for swimming and snorkeling. If you're looking for something even quieter, Kawakiu Beach is a beautiful crescent beach with fine coastal views and good swimming when seas are calm.

There are other beaches in remote places, but Molokai is about the last place you'd need to torture yourself with washed-out roads or trips through jungle growth simply to get away from it all. You can buy or rent boogie boards, snorkel gear or other equipment from **Molokai Outdoor Activities** (*☎ 553-4477, 877-553-4477; Hotel Molokai*), **Molokai Fish & Dive** (*☎ 553-5926; Ala Malama Ave*) or **Molokai Surf** (*☎ 553-5093; Kamehameha V Hwy*) in Kaunakakai.

Hiking

Molokai offers a few hiking opportunities. The Nature Conservancy's Kamakou Preserve features unique rain forest hikes in the island's rugged interior and out to scenic valley overlooks. The Palaau State Park area has a couple of options. The hike down the mule trail to Kalaupapa not only offers epic views but also provides a way to reach the peninsula without dishing out a lot of money, though permits are required. Back-country trails to waterfalls and remote valleys do exist on the east side of the island and the north shore, but going without being invited by a local guide is inadvisable.

Cycling

If you're up for long hauls and steady uphill climbs, it is possible to cycle around Molokai; pick up a copy of *Mountain Biking the Hawaiian Islands* by John Alford. **Molokai Outdoor Activities** (*☎ 553-4477, 877-553-4477; Hotel Molokai*) rents cruisers and mountain bikes at competitive rates.

Molokai Bicycle (*☎ 553-3931, fax 553-5740, 800-709-2453; W www.bikehawaii.com/molokaibicycle; 80 Mohala St; open 3pm-6pm Tues & Thur, 9am-2pm Sat*) is an expert small Kaunakakai operation renting out road bikes and rigid or front-suspension mountain bikes for $15 to $25 per day, including a helmet, lock and water bottle. Car racks and weekly discounts are also available. The shop hours are limited, but it's possible to make advance arrangements to pick up a bike at other times, including at the airport or ferry dock.

ORGANIZED TOURS

Tours by land or by sea are your two choices. Advance arrangements are always helpful, and often necessary.

Molokai Outdoor Activities (*☎ 553-4477, 877-553-4477; Hotel Molokai*) has a variety of community-run tours by friendly local island residents. For any activity it doesn't offer directly, it can contact someone who does.

Molokai Rentals and Tours (*☎ 553-5663, 800-553-9071; W www.molokai-rentals.com*) is a family-run operation that designs personalized kayaking, hiking, mountain biking and driving tours, with discounts for children.

Driving Tours

Molokai Outdoor Activities offers full and half-day tours almost anywhere around the island, except for Kalaupapa Peninsula. Tours usually need at least four people to go, cost around $125 and may include airport pickups or drop-offs. Choose from the eight-hour Grand Island Tour, or six-hour

East End Cultural Tour, with lunch and snorkeling. It also offers mountain biking tours that coast down from Waikolu Lookout past coffee fields and macadamia-nut farms out to Moomomi Beach, with snorkeling. The guided waterfall hike into Halawa Valley costs $35/20 per adult/child. Other activities may actually be conducted through Molokai Ranch, so ask first.

Molokai Off-Road Tours & Taxi *(☎ 553-3369)* offers 4WD tours, including a 'rain forest adventure' of the interior forests for $50 with a three-person minimum.

Friendly Isle Tours *(☎ 552-2218)* has three-hour island tours, from Kaunakakai through central Molokai out to the west end, for $30 per person. Seven-hour tours, which include a ride through eastern Molokai, cost $50. There's a three-person minimum.

Ocean Tours

If you get at least a few people together, you can get tours tailored to just about any aquatic interest. Prices may be higher than on Maui, but service does tend to be more personable.

Molokai Outdoor Activities offers coastline and sunset kayaking tours for $25 to $50 per person. It can also arrange windsurfing and surfing lessons, snorkel and bodyboarding excursions, sunset cruises, fishing charters and whale-watching trips in season.

Bill Kapuni's Snorkel & Scuba Adventures *(☎ 553-9867)* has a 22ft Boston whaler that can be used for snorkel and dive tours. The cost is $95 for a two-tank dive, $65 for snorkeling. The owner is a PADI dive master who also knows a lot about the craft of building ancient Hawaiian canoes. Whale-watching, sunset, fishing and north shore charters can be arranged.

Molokai Charters *(☎ 553-5852)* offers a $40 two-hour sunset sail and a $50 four-hour sail that includes whale watching in season. There's also a full-day trip to Lanai that includes snorkeling and lunch for $90. All tours leave Kaunakakai aboard Satan's Doll, a 42ft sloop. The boat goes out with a minimum of four people.

Alyce C Sportfishing Charters *(☎ 558-8377)* has a 31ft boat that can be hired for fishing trips, whale-watching jaunts and round-island runs – so long as the weather permits.

ACCOMMODATIONS

Molokai has a total of two hotels, five condo complexes and a handful of B&Bs. For more vacation rental and B&B options, click to Ⓦ www.molokai.com, www.visitmolokai.com or www.molokai-aloha.com; also check with B&B booking agencies listed under Accommodations in the Facts for the Visitor chapter.

Camping

Camping is allowed at Palaau State Park and Waikolu Lookout, at the county beach parks of Papohaku and One Alii, at the Kapuaiwa Coconut Grove in Kaunakakai, and at Waialua Pavilion and Campground in East Molokai.

Most campers take their tents to the west end to Papohaku Beach, although it's very windy there. The less appealing One Alii Beach Park is closer to Kaunakakai, handy for early-morning ferry departures. Isolated, soggy Palaau State Park is near the Kalaupapa trailhead and overlook, and you may have it all to yourself.

State Parks Camping costs $5 per person per night at **Palaau State Park** and at **Waikolu Lookout**, the latter a remote and primitive site just outside Kamakou Preserve. There's a five-day maximum stay at each site.

Permits, which are required, may be obtained at the **Department of Land & Natural Resources office** *(☎ 567-6923; open 7:30am-4pm Mon-Fri)*, in the Molokai Water Systems building, which is just south of the post office on Puupeelua Ave (Hwy 480) in Hoolehua. For Palaau State Park, you can also pick up permits directly from the state park caretaker, whose residence is immediately north of the mule stables on the road to Palaau State Park. Division of State Parks offices on other islands can issue advance permits.

County Parks The **Department of Parks & Recreation** *(☎ 553-3204; open 8am-4pm Mon-Fri)* at the Mitchell Pauole Center in Kaunakakai issues camping permits for Papohaku and One Alii Beach Parks. Permits cost $3 per adult and 50¢ per child (age 17 and under) per night. Permits are limited to three consecutive days; if you want to camp longer, you should return to the county parks office every three days for a new permit.

SHOPPING

Just about every shop in Kaunakakai has an assortment of T-shirts proclaiming Molokai's rural pride, with slogans such as 'Keep Hawaiian Lands in Hawaiian Hands' and 'Molokai Mo' Bettah!' Another local operation is the Big Wind Kite Factory, which sells handmade kites, in Maunaloa.

Molokai-grown coffee is now being commercially harvested, and it can be purchased at the Coffees of Hawaii store in Kualapuu. Or you could take back the same stash islanders do when they leave Molokai: an island-grown watermelon and some fresh-baked Molokai bread from the Kanemitsu Bakery in Kaunakakai.

GETTING THERE & AWAY

If you have time, taking the ferry from Maui is a more sociable experience than flying here. For ferry schedules, commuter airlines, discounted interisland flight coupons and air passes, see the Getting Around chapter. Information on flights to and from Kalaupapa is in the Kalaupapa section later in this chapter.

Molokai (Hoolehua) Airport *(MKK)* contains car rental booths, a snack bar, a liquor lounge, a lei stand, rest rooms, pay phones and a visitor information booth that is occasionally staffed. Molokai newspapers can be picked up free, and off-island papers are for sale.

Island Air *(☎ 800-652-6541)* flies directly to Molokai eight times per day from Honolulu and twice from Kahului, Maui. **Hawaiian Airlines** *(☎ 800-882-8811)* flies nonstop to Molokai every afternoon from Honolulu. Flights to any other island require stopping or even changing planes at Honolulu.

GETTING AROUND

Car & Moped

Renting a car on Molokai is essential if you intend to explore the island thoroughly. Keep in mind that rental vehicles are not allowed to be driven on dirt roads, and there can be restrictions on camping as well.

As there are currently only a few companies operating on Molokai, it's best to book well in advance, especially if you're planning a weekend visit.

Island Kine Auto Rental *(☎ 553-5242, 527-7368, fax 553-3880; W www.molokai-car-rental.com)* rents shiny new compacts from around $30 per day, all inclusive. Trucks and 4WD vehicles are also available. The office is in Kaunakakai, but the staff cheerfully offer pickups at the ferry dock and Molokai airport.

Budget *(☎ 567-6877)* and **Dollar** *(☎ 567-6156)* both base their operations at the airport. See the Getting Around chapter for toll-free reservation numbers and general rental information.

Molokai Outdoor Activities *(☎ 553-4477, 877-553-4477; W www.molokai-outdoors.com)* can arrange car rentals with free racks for bikes, kayaks and surfboards. Yamaha mopeds cost $25 for 24 hours and $125 per week, less if you rent more than one.

There are gas stations in Kaunakakai and Maunaloa.

Taxi

There are no metered taxis on Molokai, but a couple of companies do provide taxi services for set fees. The taxis occasionally meet incoming flights, but to be assured of a ride from the airport, you should make advance reservations.

Molokai Off-Road Tours & Taxi *(☎ 553-3369)* and **Friendly Isle Tours** *(☎ 552-2218)* also offer taxi services and airport transfers, if prearranged, with a three-person minimum. It costs about $10 per person to the Kaluakoi Resort or Molokai Ranch and $12 per person to the Kaunakakai area.

Kaunakakai

In Kaunakakai, if you're down at the beach at night, you may spot what looks like ghosts walking out on the water. There's no need to be spooked – these are actually local fishers who walk far out onto the shallow coastal reef carrying lanterns. The fishing is good at night, when the wind dies down, and lantern light stuns the prey.

Kaunakakai, Molokai's only real town, takes much of its character from what it doesn't have. There's not a single elevator, no neon and no strip malls.

Most of the island's businesses are lined up along Ala Malama Ave, the town's broad main street, where stores have aging wooden false fronts that give Kaunakakai the appearance of an old Wild West town and an almost timeless quality. There are a couple of restaurants, a bakery, a post office,

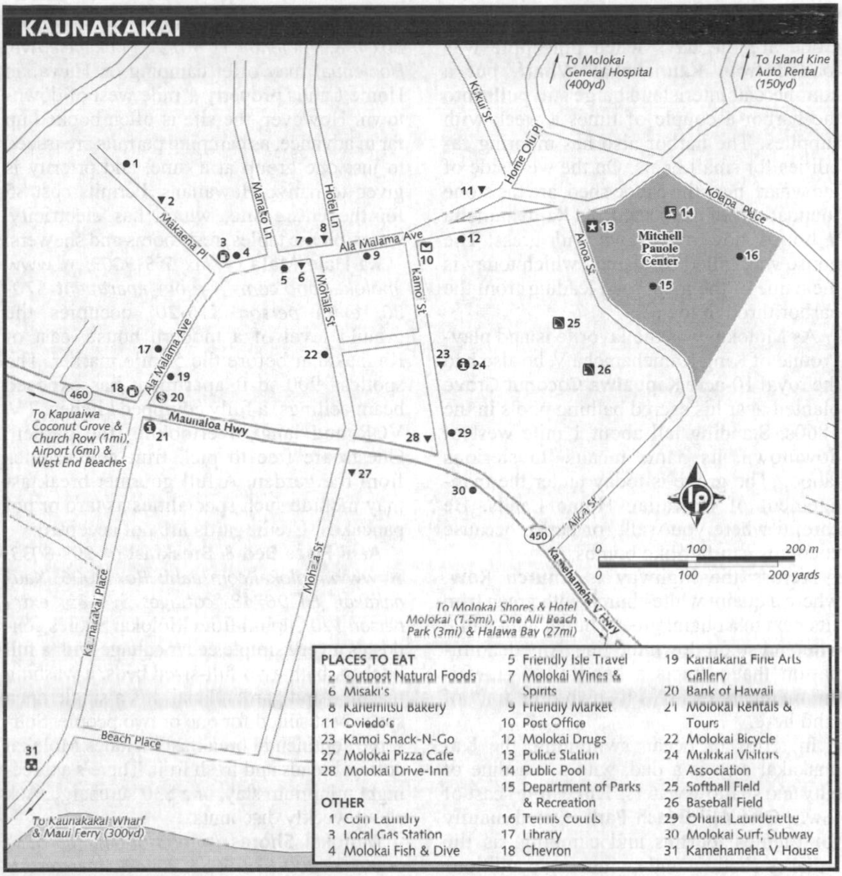

a pharmacy and one of just about everything else a small town needs. The tallest point is still the church steeple.

Information

The **Molokai Visitors Association** *(MVA; ☎ 553-3876, 553-5221, 800-800-6367, Hawaii ☎ 800-553-0404; W www.molokai-hawaii.com; Suite 700, Kamoi Professional Bldg, Kamoi St; open 8:30am-4:30pm Mon-Fri)* can give you brochures and the lowdown on what's happening around the island. **Friendly Isle Travel** *(☎ 553-5357; Ala Malama Ave; open 8am-5pm Mon-Fri)* can assist with travel arrangements.

Banks with 24-hour ATMs are one of Kaunakakai's few concessions to the modern world. The **Bank of Hawaii** *(☎ 553-3273; Ala Malama Ave; open 8:30am-4pm Mon-Thur, 8:30am-6pm Fri)* is the largest. Also around are the **main post office** *(☎ 553-5845; Ala Malama Ave; open 9am-4:30pm Mon-Fri, 9am-11am Sat)* and a good **public library** *(☎ 553-1765; Ala Malama Ave; open 12:30pm-8pm Mon & Wed, 10am-5pm Tues, Thur & Fri)*, where you can browse through off-island newspapers and magazines.

Since Molokai doesn't have a daily newspaper, bulletin boards around Kaunakakai are the prime source of news and announcements. The board next to the Bank of Hawaii is the most extensive.

Ohana Launderette *(open 6am-9pm daily)* is just near the Molokai Drive-Inn. There's another **coin laundry** behind Outpost Natural Foods.

Things to See & Do

Gone are the days when pineapple was loaded from **Kaunakakai Wharf**, but a commercial interisland barge still pulls into the harbor a couple of times a week with supplies. The harbor also has mooring facilities for small boats. On the west side of the wharf, near the canoe shed, are the stone foundations of the oceanfront **Kamehameha V house**, now overgrown with grass. The house was called 'Malama,' which today is the name of the main road leading from the harbor through town.

As Molokai was the favorite island playground of King Kamehameha V, he also had the royal 10-acre **Kapuaiwa Coconut Grove** planted near his sacred bathing pools in the 1860s. Standing tall about 1 mile west of downtown, its name means 'mysterious taboo.' The grove is today under the management of Hawaiian Home Lands. Be careful where you walk (or park), because coconuts can fall like bombs.

Across the highway is **Church Row**, where a quaint white church with green trim sits next to a quaint green church with white trim and so on down the line. Any denomination that attracts a handful of Hawaiian members receives its own little tract of land here.

In terms of ocean swimming, the Kaunakakai area is a dud, with a coastline of silty and shallow waters. Three miles east of town, **One Alii Beach Park** is used mainly for picnics, parties and camping, as the water is shallow and swimming conditions are poor. Two memorials erected in the park commemorate the 19th-century immigration of Japanese citizens to Hawaii.

Kaunakakai Gym *(☎ 553-5141)* at the Mitchell Pauole Center has an indoor swimming pool. Otherwise there are two outdoor **tennis courts** available free to the public. Like everywhere else on Molokai, you're not likely to find a crowd waiting. For outdoor sports shops offering equipment rentals in Kaunakakai, see the Activities section earlier in this chapter.

MOLOKAI

Places to Stay

Camping is allowed at **One Alii Beach Park**, but sites enjoy little privacy thanks to floodlights and late-night carousing. See Accommodations earlier in this chapter for fees and permit details.

Kapuaiwa Coconut Grove *(☎ 567-6296; Box 198, Hoolehua, HI 96729; Puukapele Ave, Hoolehua)* may offer camping on Hawaiian Home Lands property 1 mile west of downtown. However, the site is often booked up far in advance, as camping permits are issued to just one group at a time, and priority is given to native Hawaiians. Permits cost $5 for the entire site, which has electricity, water, picnic tables, rest rooms and showers.

Ka Hale Mala *(☎/fax 553-9009; Ⓦ www.molokai-bnb.com; 4-room apartment $70-80, extra person $15-20)* occupies the ground level of a modern house, east of Kaunakakai before the 5-mile marker. The spotless 900-sq-ft apartment has exposed beam ceilings, a fully equipped kitchen, TV, VCR and lanai overlooking the garden. Guests are free to pick fruit and veggies from the garden. A full gourmet breakfast may include such specialities as taro or poi pancakes. Credit cards are not accepted.

Aahi Place Bed & Breakfast *(☎ 553-8033; Ⓦ www.molokai.com/aahi; Box 2006, Kaunakakai, HI 96748; cottages $75-85, extra person $20)*, uphill from Molokai Shores condos, is a very simple cedar cottage with a full kitchen, bath, two full-sized beds, a washing machine and garden lanai. It's a single open space best suited for one or two people. Self-serve continental breakfast includes Molokai coffee, breads and fresh fruit. There's a three-night minimum stay, or a $30 surcharge. Ask about weekly discounts.

Molokai Shores *(☎ 553-5954, 800-535-0085, fax 800-633-5085; Ⓦ www.marcresorts.com; Kamehameha V Hwy; 1-/2-bedroom oceanfront units $155/199)*, about 1½ miles east of town, belongs to the Marc Resorts chain. Most of the modern condo units are fairly well decorated, and each has a kitchen, sofa bed, cable TV, lanai and ceiling fans. Ask for a unit on the 3rd floor, where rooms have high cathedral ceilings. There's a pool, coin-operated laundry, shuffleboard and barbecue facilities on the premises. Substantial discounts are available for online bookings.

Hotel Molokai *(☎ 553-5347, 800-367-5004, fax 553-5047; Ⓦ www.hotelmolokai.com; standard/oceanfront rooms $82/132, deluxe units with kitchenette $137)*, about 2 miles east of town, has a Polynesian design and a laid-back atmosphere, full of aloha that's perfect for Molokai. Rooms, which are in clusters of two-story buildings, feature private baths, cable TV, phone and modem hookups. Some have kitchenettes and private lanai. If you're sensitive to traffic noise, request a room away from the road; in any unit, rooms on the 2nd floor are generally quieter. There's an oceanfront pool, bar and restaurant, with top-rate sunsets and stargazing from the reef-side beach. For the on-site **Molokai Outdoor Activities** desk, see the Activities section earlier in this chapter.

Places to Eat

Misaki's *(☎ 553-5505; Ala Malama Ave; open 8:30am-8:30pm Mon-Sat, 9am-noon Sun)* and **Friendly Market** *(☎ 553-5595; Ala Malama St; open 8:30am-8:30pm Mon-Fri, 8:30am-6:30pm Sat)* are the island's two major grocery stores.

Outpost Natural Foods *(☎ 553-3377; 70 Makaena Pl; open 9am-6pm Mon-Thur, 9am-4pm Fri, 9am-5pm Sun)* sells health food, including bulk granola, dried fruit, yogurt, vitamins and fresh produce, some of it organic. Fresh juices and deli items are available for take-out, with daily specials including tofu quiche and salad for around $5.

Kanemitsu Bakery *(☎ 553-5855; Ala Malama St; bakery open 5:30am-6:30pm Wed-Mon)* makes *the* Molokai bread that is shipped around the islands, as well as a variety of Danish pastries and doughnuts. The cinnamon apple crisp ($1) is a favorite. Although the restaurant section may look crowded, the food is not up to snuff.

Kamoi Snack-N-Go *(☎ 553-3742; Molokai Professional Bldg, Kamoi St; open 9am-9pm Mon-Sat, noon-9pm Sun)* is a convenience store and sweets shop, scooping up about 30 different flavors of the gourmet, Honolulu-made Dave's ice cream at bargain prices. The tourist office is just next door.

Molokai Drive-Inn *(☎ 553-5655; Kamehameha V Hwy; meals $3-7; open 6am-10pm daily)* is a town landmark that used to be a Dairy Queen, but Molokai wasn't quite ready for a fast-food chain at the time, so the sign came down. It now serves local Hawaiian food, including *loco moco* (Portuguese sausage) and eggs for breakfast, and $5 plate lunches. There are plastic tables inside where you can chow down.

Most of Kaunakakai's other daytime eateries are old-fashioned **lunch counters** on Ala Malama Ave downtown. At Filipino-style **Oviedo's** you can fill up for $5.

Famous Kamuela Cookhouse (see the Kualapuu section later) has a branch, **Kamuela Bar & Grill** *(☎ 553-4286; 93B Ala Malama Street; open daily)*, in Kaunakakai. Locals also flock to the **Molokai Ice House** *(☎ 553-3054; open 6am-7pm Mon-Sat)*, where Hawaiian plate meals are often made from the catch of the day.

Molokai Pizza Cafe *(☎ 553-3288; Kamehameha V Hwy; meals $7.50-15; open 11am-10pm Sun, 10am-10pm Mon-Thur, 10am- 11pm Fri & Sat)* is in a strip mall. Call us crazy, but we didn't think the pizza was all that special. Still, the late hours can be a saving grace and tourists, locals and especially kids keep things jumping. Sub sandwiches, pasta and even the catch of the day are all on the menu.

Hotel Molokai *(☎ 553-5347, 800-367-5004, fax 553-5047; W www.hotelmolokai.com; breakfast & lunch $5-11, dinner $12.50-17.50; open 7am-10am, 11:30pm-1:30pm & 6pm-9pm daily)* is an open-air restaurant that sits right on the beach, with prime sunset views of Lanai and waves lapping at the shore (even splashing onto your table legs). It's the best breakfast spot in town, too. At lunch you can order burgers, teriyaki chicken or mahimahi sandwiches, while at dinner, fresh fish and steaks are under $20. And, oh, the waitstaff – they are absolutely fabulous.

Entertainment

There is very little evening entertainment around Kaunakakai.

Hotel Molokai *(☎ 553-5347, 800-367-5004, fax 553-5047; W www.hotelmolokai.com)* occasionally features local musicians playing mellow Hawaiian guitar, especially on 'aloha Fridays,' at its oceanfront Tiki bar.

Kanemitsu Bakery *(☎ 553-5855; Ala Malama St)* offers true night owls the time-honored tradition of slipping down the alley behind Ala Malama Ave in the wee hours of the morning and knocking on the door to buy hot loaves from the taciturn night-shift baker.

Other than this, the **baseball field** in Kaunakakai is the most active spot on the island. For some local flavor, you could go down and cheer on the Molokai Farmers as they compete against their high school rivals, the Lanai Pinelads.

Shopping

Kamakana Fine Arts Gallery *(☎ 553-8520; Unit 210, Molokai Center, 110 Ala Malama Ave; closed Sun)* represents over 80 Molokai artists at its upstairs gallery. Linger over the handcrafted jewelry, lei, woodcarvings, ukulele, Hawaiian drums, quilts and more.

Molokai Fish & Dive *(☎ 553-5926; Ala Malama Ave)* has the most impressive selection of island T-shirts and postcards. It also stocks water-sports gear, fishing tackle, sunscreen and almost anything else you might need on Molokai.

Molokai Drugs *(☎ 553-5790; Ala Malama Ave; open 8:45am-5:45pm Mon-Sat)*, the local pharmacy, sells film, magazines, maps and Hawaiiana books.

Molokai Wines & Spirits *(Ala Malama Ave; open 9am-10pm daily)* carries a good assortment of imported beers, Hawaiian microbrews and inexpensive wines.

East Molokai

The 27-mile drive from Kaunakakai to Halawa Valley along the Kamehameha V Hwy (Hwy 450) takes about 1½ hours each way. It's a good paved road from start to finish. The road hugs the ocean for much of the drive, with mountains rising up to the north. Although the terrain starts out relatively dry, it becomes lush as you head toward the east end. Check your gas gauge before starting off on the trip, as there are no gas stations after Kaunakakai.

It's all quite pastoral, with small homes tucked into the valleys, horses grazing at the side of the road and silver waterfalls dropping down the mountainsides. The beaches along this stretch are mostly shallow and silted and not particularly good for swimming until you reach the 20-mile marker. The last part of the road is narrow, with lots of hairpin bends and scenic coastal views, as you wind up to a cliff-top view of Halawa Valley.

KAWELA

The **Kakahaia Beach Park**, a grassy roadfront park in Kawela, shortly before the 6-mile marker, has a couple of picnic tables but little other reason to stop. This park is the only part of the **Kakahaia National Wildlife Refuge** open to the public. Most of the 40-acre refuge is inland from the road. It includes marshland, with a dense growth of bulrushes and an inland freshwater fishpond that has been expanded to provide a home for endangered birds such as the Hawaiian stilt and coot.

Fishponds

Along the road to Halawa Valley, look *makai* (seaward) every so often, for Molokai's southeast coast is strung with the largest concentration of ancient fishponds in Hawaii, all evidence of a highly developed system of early aquaculture.

One type of fishpond was inshore and totally closed off from the sea. The other was created by a scallop-shaped stone wall parallel to the beach, which formed a shoreline enclosure. According to legend, fishponds were said to be the work of the menehune, Hawaii's mythical race of little people, who made them appear virtually overnight.

In reality, it took hard labor. Molokai alone once had more than 60 productive shoreline fishponds, constructed from the 13th century onward. Built of lava rock upon the reefs, their slatted sluice gates were set into place and prayed over by kahuna. These sluice gates allowed small fish into the pond, where they were hand-fed with breadfruit and sweet potatoes. Fattened fish were then trapped and easily scooped up with a net.

Many fishponds were strictly for the alii, with commoners forbidden from eating the fish raised in them. The system worked until the mid-1800s, when overgrazing by cattle and sheep resulted in widespread erosion, and the clay that washed down from the mountains choked the ponds. Over the years, efforts have been made to restock a few of the fishponds, mostly with mullet and milkfish. One of the most impressive and easily visited is the Kalokoeli fishpond, behind Molokai Shores condos east of Kaunakakai.

KAMALO

Only two of the four Molokai churches that the island's most famous missionary, Father Damien, built outside of the Kalaupapa Peninsula are still standing, and one of them is **St Joseph's Church** in Kamalo, a small village about 10 miles east of Kaunakakai. This simple, one-room wooden church dating from 1876 has a steeple and bell, five rows of pews and some of the original wavy glass panes. A statue of Damien and a little cemetery are at the side of the church. Only the yellow tsunami warning speaker brings the scene into the 21st century.

Just over three-quarters of a mile after the 11-mile marker, a small sign on the *makai* side of the road notes the **Smith-Bronte Landing**, the site where pilot Ernest Smith and navigator Emory Bronte safely crash-landed their plane at the completion of the world's first civilian flight from the US mainland to Hawaii. The pair left California on July 14, 1927, coming down on Molokai 25 hours and two minutes later. Oahu was the intended destination. A little memorial plaque is set among the *kiawe* trees and grasses, in the spot where they landed.

Kamalo Plantation Bed & Breakfast (*☎/fax 558-8236; W www.molokai.com/kamalo; studio cottage $85, 2 bedroom beach house $140*) is in a fruit orchard opposite St Joseph's Church. Guests of this rural B&B enjoy a breakfast of homemade breads and homegrown fruits. Its grounds feature the stone foundations of an ancient *heiau* (stone temple) and the congenial owners can point out little-known hiking trails in the area. The garden cottage and beach house each have a fully equipped kitchen, barbecue facilities and beach gear, but the latter also has a TV, VCR and extraordinary ocean views. There is a three-night minimum stay.

UALAPUE

A half mile beyond Wavecrest Resort condo development at the 13-mile marker, you'll spot **Ualapue Fishpond** on the *makai* side of the road. It was restored a few years ago and restocked with mullet and milkfish, two species that had been raised there in ancient times. After this, look for the defunct **Ah Ping Store** and its old gas pump at the roadside. This classic building of faded green wood with a red tin roof was a Chinese-owned grocery store in the 1930s.

Wavecrest Resort (*☎ 558-8101, 800-600-4158, fax 553-3867; W www.wavecresthawaii.com; 1-bedroom units per day/month $75/1500*) is a big condo complex with a few units in the rental pool. Others staying here are long-term island residents. The condos vary depending upon the owners' taste, but all are spacious and quiet (maybe too quiet?). Each has separate bedrooms, a roomy living room with a sofa bed, a full kitchen, entertainment center and lanai. Breezes blow right through the oceanfront units, which enjoy great views of Maui and Lanai from the lanai. The resort has a pool, tennis courts, shuffleboard, library and coin laundry. A $40 surcharge applies for stays of less than a week.

KALUAAHA

The village of Kaluaaha is less than 2 miles past Wavecrest. The ruins of **Kaluaaha Church**, Molokai's first Christian church, are a bit off the road and inland but just visible if you keep an eye out. It was built in 1844 by Molokai's first missionary, Harvey R Hitchcock. **Our Lady of Seven Sorrows Church** is a quarter of a mile past the Kaluaaha Church site. The present Our Lady of Sorrows is a 1966 reconstruction of the original wood-frame building, constructed in 1874 by the missionary Father Damien. Sunday mass is celebrated at 7:15am. From the church parking lot, a fine view of an ancient **fishpond** and the hazy high-rise-studded shores of west Maui provide an incongruous backdrop.

ILIILIOPAE HEIAU

Iliiliopae is Molokai's largest and best-known *heiau* on Molokai, and is thought to be the second-largest in all the islands. Over 300ft long and 100ft wide, the *heiau* is about 22ft high on the east side and 11ft high at the other end. The main platform is strikingly level. Historians believed the *heiau* may have originally been three times its current size, reaching out beyond Mapulehu Stream.

Visiting the *heiau* is usually straightforward, but since it is on private property, it's advised that you check with the visitors association in Kaunakakai to see if you need permission in advance.

The turn-off to the *heiau* is on the inland side of the highway, just over half a mile past the 15-mile marker, immediately after Mapulehu Bridge. It starts on a dirt drive on the east side of the creek. After a 10-minute walk, a footpath leads alongside a wall and then off to the left opposite a house, where signs point you into the jungle and across a streambed. The *heiau* is only another two minutes' walk. Watch out for vicious local dogs, though.

Although once a site of human sacrifice, Iliiliopae is today silent except for the chittering

Bloodstones

Legend says that the Iliiliopae Heiau was built in just one night by *menehune* who brought *ililli* (stones) over the mountains from Wailau Valley. In return for their efforts, they were each given one *opae* (shrimp) – hence the temple's name. Myths aside, this may be the oldest religious site extant in Hawaii.

Lono, the god of harvest, and Ku, the god of war, were both worshipped at this *luakini*, where human sacrifices were made, always on the eve of a full moon. Drums were beaten to call all males to the temple where, upon the priest's direction, all fell prone, and the victims to be sacrificed were brought to the platform. Amid chanting and rituals, these victims, always male, were strangled to death and their bodies later burned.

One legend tells of a local man who had lost nine of his 10 sons to sacrifice here. Outraged, he and his only remaining son enlisted the aid of an *aumakua* (ancestral spirit helper), a shark god, who sent a torrent of rain, flooding the *heiau* and washing the priests responsible for the sacrifices into the sea, where they were duly eaten by sharks.

of birds. African tulip trees line the trail to the site, a peaceful place filled with *mana* (power) whose stones still seem to emanate vibrations of a dramatic past. A good place to sit and take it all in is on the north side, up the steps to the right of the *heiau*. That said, keep in mind it is disrespectful to walk across the top of the *heiau*. In doing so you may succumb to heat exhaustion, and perhaps even twist an ankle more easily than you think.

PUKOO

This sleepy backwater was once the seat of local government – complete with a courthouse, jail, wharf and post office – until the plantation folks built Kaunakakai and centered everything there. Now, bit by bit, islanders are beginning to move back to the Pukoo area, and while it's not exactly suburbia, you'll notice a handful of newer homes as the road continues.

Honomuni House (*☎ 558-8383, fax 558-8284; W www.molokai-aloha.com/honomuni; Kamehameha V Hwy; cottage doubles $85, extra adult $10, child free)* is a pleasant guest cottage just beyond the Honomuni Bridge on the *mauka* (inland) side of the highway, before the 18-mile marker, about 1 mile northeast of Pukoo. The garden guest cottage is studio-style, with a fully equipped kitchen, bathroom and outdoor deck and shower. The living room area has a sofa bed, a TV and a small dining table made of wood from the monkeypod tree, which grows on the grounds. Breakfast is not included, but seasonal fruits are provided. Ask about weekly and monthly rates.

Neighborhood Store 'N' Counter (*☎ 558-8498; open 8am-6pm daily, take-out counter closed Wed)*, near the 16-mile marker, is a well-stocked little grocery store, and the only place to get a meal at the east end of the island. Try the fresh fish specials or hearty plate lunches (around $7). There are picnic tables at the side.

WAIALUA

Waialua is a little roadside community just past the 19-mile marker. The attractive little Waialua Congregational Church, which marks the center of the village, was built of stone in 1855. The nearby Waialua Beach is the site of Molokai's *keiki* (child) surf competitions.

Seven-tenths of a mile after the 19-mile marker, begin looking for the remains of a stone chimney, a remnant of the **Moanui Sugar Mill**, which processed sugar from a nearby plantation until the mill burned down in the late 1800s. The ruins are about 50ft inland from the road, just before a stand of tall ironwood trees.

Twenty-Mile Beach, a stretch of white sand, pops up right along the roadside at the 20-mile marker. There are places where you can park just beyond that. During the winter, when other Molokai beaches are rough, this is the area everyone directs you to for swimming and snorkeling. However, when the tide is low, the water is sometimes too shallow for snorkeling inside the reef. Snorkeling is much better beyond the reef, but, unless it's very calm, the currents can be dangerous.

The point of rocks sticking out as the road swings left before the 21-mile marker is called, appropriately enough, **Rock Point**. This is a popular surf spot where local competitions sometimes take place.

Places to Stay

Waialua Campground and Pavilion *(☎ 558-8150, fax 558-8520; e vacate@aloha.net; HC 1, Box 780, Kaunakakai, HI 96748; camp sites per person $15)* is the church's seaside picnic grounds, which are enclosed by a chain-link fence. There's a shower, toilet and picnic tables here. Groups occasionally book the grounds, so you should confirm in advance that space is available.

Dunbar Beachfront Cottages *(☎ 558-8153, 800-673-0520, fax 808-558-8153; w www.molokai-beachfront-cottages.com; 2-bedroom cottages $140)* has two vacation cottages on secluded private beaches in Kainalu, around the 18-mile marker. Each cottage sleeps four people and comes with a fully equipped kitchen, TV, VCR, ceiling fans, laundry, lanai and barbecue grills. A three-night minimum stay is required and there is a $75 cleaning charge.

WAIALUA TO HALAWA

After the 21-mile marker, the road starts to wind upwards. Tall grasses just at the edge seem to be trying to reclaim the road, while ironwood trees and the spindly spikes of sisal plants dot the surrounding hills. It's a good paved road – the only problem is there's not always enough of it. In places, including some cliff-hugging curves, this road is really only wide enough for one car, and you'll need to do some horn tooting. The road levels out just before the 24-mile marker, where there's a view of the small island of Mokuhooniki, a seabird sanctuary.

The fenced grassland in this area is part of Puu O Hoku Ranch, Molokai's second-largest cattle ranch. Founded by Paul Fagan of Hana, Maui, fame, the name means 'where hills and stars meet' – Jimmy Stewart and JFK are among the famous faces who have visited here. A hidden grove of sacred *kukui* trees on the ranch property marks the grave of Lanikaula, a revered 16th-century *kahuna*. Over the years, many islanders claim to have seen the night lanterns of ghost marchers bobbing along near the grove. If you'd like to go **horseback riding** *(☎ 558-8109)* try to call at least 24 hours in advance – it costs $55/75 for a one-hour/two-hour guided trail ride. If you're hungry, drop by the **ranch store** for organic produce.

After passing the 25-mile marker, the jungle closes in, and the scent of eucalyptus fills the air. One and a quarter miles after the 25-mile marker, there's a turnoff with a great panoramic view of Halawa Valley; if the viewpoint is overgrown, just park and walk down the road a little farther to reach a clearing. In the winter, this is also a good place to watch for whales breaching.

There are lots of 'beep as you go' hairpin bends on the one-lane road that leads down to the valley, but the road is in good condition and the incline is reasonably gradual. No worries.

Places to Stay

Puu o Hoku Ranch *(☎ 558-8109, fax 558-8100; w www.puuohoku.com; 2-bedroom cottage/house doubles $125/150, extra guest $10)* rents out a country cottage with a shady lanai, wicker furnishings and a sunny kitchen that makes for a memorable romantic getaway. Weekly rates are discounted.

HALAWA VALLEY

Halawa Valley once had three *heiau*s, two of which are thought to have been used for human sacrifice. Little remains of the sites. In the mid-19th century, the fertile valley had a population of about 500 people and produced most of Molokai's taro as well as many of its melons, gourds and fruits. Taro production declined over the years, coming to an abrupt end in 1946, when a massive tsunami swept up Halawa Valley, wiping out the farms and much of the community. A second tsunami washed the valley clean in 1957. Only a few families now remain in Halawa. Sunday services are still occasionally held in Hawaiian at the valley's little church.

Halawa Beach Park

Halawa Beach was a favored surfing spot for Molokai chiefs and remains so today for local kids. This beach has double coves separated by a rocky outcrop, with the north side a bit more protected than the south. When the water is calm, there's good swimming, but both coves are subject to dangerous rip currents when the surf is heavy. There can also be strong currents whenever Halawa Stream, which empties into the north cove, is flowing heavily.

Halawa Beach Park has rest rooms and running water; the water, which is piped down from the upper valley, does not meet health standards and should be treated before drinking. Although pretty, the place has an eerie, foreboding quality and locals may show some hostility to outsiders. You probably won't want to linger, but if you've come this far, you may as well get out and stretch here before heading back.

Central Molokai

Central Molokai takes in the Hoolehua Plains, which stretch from windswept Moomomi Beach in the west to the former plantation town of Kualapuu. The central part of the island also has forested interiors leading to Kamakou Preserve, a unique rain forest that includes the island's highest mountain. On the north side of central Molokai is Kalaupapa Peninsula, the site of Hawaii's infamous leprosy colony.

The most trodden route in central Molokai is the drive up Hwy 460 from dry grasslands past the Kamakou Preserve mountain road turn-off, which then veers straight onto Hwy 470 alongside the coffee plantation, restored sugar mill museum, mule stables and the trailhead down to Kalaupapa Peninsula. The road ends at Palaau State Park, site of the Kalaupapa Overlook, where you'll find one of the most captivating views on Molokai. It takes about 20 minutes to drive the 10 miles from Kaunakakai, on the southern shore.

KAMAKOU

The mountains that form the spine of Molokai's east side reach up to Kamakou, the island's highest peak, at 4961ft. Hawaiian women used to hike up to the top of Kamakou to bury the afterbirth of their babies. According to folklore, this ritual would lead the newly born children to reach great heights in life. These days, islanders come to the forest to pick foliage for leis as well as to hunt pigs, deer and goats.

The steep mountains here effectively prevent rain clouds from entering Molokai's central plains. Over half of Molokai's water supply comes from these forests. In the 1960s, a 5-mile-long tunnel was bored into the western side of Waikolu Valley. It now carries up to 28 million gallons of water each day down to the Kualapuu Reservoir.

The Nature Conservancy's Kamakou Preserve is a near-pristine rain forest that is home to more than 250 native plants and some of Hawaii's rarest birds. With its mountaintop perch, Kamakou offers some splendid views of the north shore valleys that unfold below. The forest is a treasure.

Kamakou is protected in its wilderness state in part because the rutted dirt road leading to it makes it a challenge to reach. A 4WD is essential. In dry weather, some people do make it as far as the lookout in a car, but if it's been raining at all, it's not advisable to try. In places where the road is narrow, one car that gets stuck can block the whole road. During the rainy season, vehicles leave tracks and the road tends to get progressively more rutted until it's regraded in the summer.

The 10-mile mountain road leading up from the highway to Waikolu Lookout takes about 45 minutes to drive, depending on road conditions. Start the journey by driving north from Kaunakakai on Hwy 460. Turn right three-quarters of a mile after the 3-mile marker, immediately before Manawainui Bridge. The paved road ends shortly at the Kalamaula hunters' check box. Although it starts out fairly smoothly, the road deteriorates as it goes along. Bear left at the first fork, about five minutes' drive up the dirt road, and from there just follow the main road all the way.

The landscape starts off shrubby, dry and dusty, later turning to woods of eucalyptus with patches of cypress and Norfolk pines. Although there's no evidence of it from the road, the Kalamaula area was once heavily settled. It was here that Kamehameha the Great knocked out his two front teeth in grieving the death of a female high chief whom he had come to visit. The trees were planted in the 1930s by the Civilian Conservation Corps (CCC) to stem the erosion and watershed loss caused by the free-range cattle policies of earlier times.

The Molokai Forest Reserve starts about 5½ miles down the main road. A short loop road on the left leads to a former Boy Scout camp that's now used by The Nature Conservancy. After another 1½ miles, there will be an old water tank and reservoir off to the left. Just past this, a sign marked 'Kakalahale' may point to the right. (This is one of several 4WD roads – used by hunters – that lead south to the coast or to Kaunakakai. Once the roads leave forest reserve land, they run across private property, often with closed gates along the way. Ignore them!)

Another 2 miles brings you to the Sandalwood Pit, and 1 mile past that to Waikolu Lookout and Kamakou Preserve.

Sandalwood Pit

The centuries-old **Lua Na Moku Iliahi** (Sandalwood Measuring Pit) is nothing more than a grassy depression on the left side of the road. Today it takes imagination to see the whole picture, as years of water erosion have rounded the sides of the hull-shaped hole. In the early 19th century, shortly after the lucrative sandalwood trade began, the pit was dug to the exact measurements of a 75ft-long ship's hold and filled with fragrant sandalwood logs cleared from the nearby forest.

In the frenzy to make a quick buck to pay for alluring foreign goods, the *alii* forced the *makaainana* (commoners) to abandon their crops and work the forest. When the pit was full, the wood was strapped onto the backs of the laborers, who hauled it down to the harbor for shipment to China. The sea captains made out like bandits, while Hawaii lost its sandalwood forests. After all the mature trees were cut down, the *makaainana* pulled up virtually every new sapling in order to spare their children the misery of another generation of forced harvesting.

Waikolu Lookout

At 3600ft, Waikolu Lookout provides a spectacular view into Waikolu Valley and out to the ocean beyond. Even if you're not able to spend time in Kamakou Preserve, the lookout is a fine destination in itself. Morning is the best time for clear views. If it's been raining recently, you'll be rewarded with numerous waterfalls streaming down the sheer cliff sides. Waikolu means 'three waters' – presumably named for the three drops in the main falls.

A grassy **camping area** is directly opposite the lookout. If you can bear the mist and cold winds that sometimes blow up from the canyon, especially during the afternoon and evening, this could make a base camp for hikes into the preserve. The site has pit toilets but no water supply or other amenities. For information on permits and fees, see the Accommodations section earlier in this chapter.

Kamakou Preserve

In 1982 Molokai Ranch conveyed to The Nature Conservancy of Hawaii the rights to manage the Kamakou Preserve, which starts immediately beyond the Waikolu Lookout. Its 2774 acres of native ecosystems includes cloud forest, bogs, shrub land and habitat for many endangered plants and animals.

Much of the preserve is forested with *ohia lehua*, a native tree with fluffy red blossoms whose nectar is favored by native birds. It is home to two rare avian species that live only on Molokai, the Molokai creeper and Molokai thrush, as well as the bright red *apapane* (Hawaiian honeycreeper), yellow-green *amakihi* and *pueo* (Hawaiian owl). Other treasures include tree ferns, native orchids and silvery lilies.

The road deteriorates quickly from the preserve entrance. Don't even think about driving it without a 4WD. Even with a 4WD, if you're not used to driving in mud and on steep grades, it can be challenging. There are a few spots where it would be easy to flip a vehicle. The Nature Conservancy asks visitors to sign in and out at the preserve entrance. Check out the sign-up sheet, where visitors write short entries on everything from car breakdowns to trail conditions and bird sightings. Occasionally, portions of the preserve are closed. At such times, notices are posted.

Hiking As Kamakou is a rain forest, trails in the preserve can be very muddy. Rain gear is a good idea, and you should bring along an ample supply of drinking water. The **Pepeopae Trail** affords a stunning view of Pelekunu Valley. Along the way, an extensive boardwalk allows hikers to access a nearly undisturbed Hawaiian montane bog, a miniature forest of stunted trees and dwarfed plants, while protecting the fragile ecosystem from being trampled. From the terminus at Pelekunu Valley Overlook, you'll enjoy a view of majestic cliffs, and if it's not too cloudy, you can see down the valley out to the ocean. The area receives about 180 inches of rain each year, making it one of the wettest regions in the Hawaiian Islands.

There are two ways to reach the Pepeopae Trail. The easiest method is to walk from Waikolu Lookout about 2½ miles along the main jeep road to the main trailhead. This is a nice forest walk that takes just over an hour. There are some side roads along the way, but they're largely overgrown and it's obvious which is the main road. You'll eventually come to the 'Pepeopae' sign that marks the start of the trail, which then branches to the left and heads east for 1 mile to the overlook.

The second and far rougher way is to take the **Hanalilolilo Trail**. This trail, which is muddy and poorly defined, begins on the left side of the road about five minutes' walk past the Waikolu Lookout, shortly after entering the preserve. The Hanalilolilo Trail climbs 500ft through a rain forest of moss-covered ohia trees and connects with the Pepeopae Trail after 1½ miles. Turn left on the Pepeopae Trail, and it's about a half-mile walk up to the summit overlooking Pelekunu Valley. Give yourself a good half-day to complete the entire hike back to the entrance.

Guided hikes with **The Nature Conservancy** *(Molokai Preserves ☎ 553-5236, fax 553-9870; W www.nature.org)*, which offer insights into the preserve's history and ecology, are usually conducted on the second Saturday of the month. The cost of $10 for conservancy members and $25 for non-members includes transportation to and from the preserve. Also ask about volunteer workdays if you're seriously interested.

KUALAPUU

Kualapuu is the name of both a 1017ft hill and the village that has grown up north of it. At the base of the hill is the world's largest rubber-lined reservoir, which can hold up to 1.4 billion gallons of water piped in from the rain forests of eastern Molokai. The reservoir is presently the only source of water for both the Hoolehua Plains and the dry west end.

Del Monte set up headquarters here in the 1930s, and Kualapuu developed into a plantation town. The center of Del Monte's activities covered the spread between Kualapuu and the nearby Hoolehua homesteads. When Del Monte decided to phase out its Molokai operations in 1982, the economy came tumbling down; old farm equipment rusted in overgrown pineapple fields for over a decade before the abandoned fields were leased out and replanted them with coffee saplings.

Today the coffee harvest falls between September and January. Stop by **Coffees of Hawaii** *(☎ 567-9241, 800-709-2326; Hwy 490)* for free samples of rich Molokai brews at the company shop, which also sells packaged beans, Hawaiiana books and a few local handicraft items. Walking tours (adult/child $7/3.50) through the coffee fields depart at 9:30am and 11:30am Monday to Friday, weather permitting. The tours last about 45 minutes – a bit less if there aren't many questions for the guide. As nothing on Molokai is exactly bustling, you're required to call ahead and make reservations to let the guides know you're coming.

Kamuela Cookhouse *(☎ 567-9655; Hwy 490; breakfast & lunch $5-10, dinner $8-15; open 6:30am-2:30pm, 8am-2pm Sat & Sun)* is a busy place for such a small town, but that's because it dishes out the best food just about anywhere on Molokai. Breakfasts are filling and so are plate lunches. For sheer indulgence, try a slice of the homemade chocolate macadamia-nut pie or perhaps the *lilikoi*-orange cheesecake.

Espresso Bar *(☎ 567-9241, 800-709-2326; snacks under $5; open 7am-3pm Mon-Fri, 10am-3pm Sat & Sun)* sells bagels and plain sandwiches, plus fresh-ground coffee and espresso (you were expecting something else?).

HOOLEHUA

Hoolehua is the dry plains area that separates eastern and western Molokai. Here, in the 1790s, Kamehameha the Great trained his warriors in a year-long preparation for the invasion of Oahu. Hoolehua was settled as an agricultural community in 1924 as part of the Hawaiian Homes Act, which made public lands available to native Hawaiians. By 1930, more than half of Molokai's ethnic Hawaiian population was living on homesteads.

The first homestead was attempted closer to the coast, at Kalanianaole, but it failed when the well water pumped to irrigate crops turned brackish. Many of those islanders then moved north to Hoolehua, where homesteaders were already planting pineapple, a crop that required little water.

As the two giant pineapple companies established operations in Molokai, homesteaders found it increasingly difficult to market their own pineapples and were eventually compelled to lease their lands to the plantations. Today, there is a reliable water supply and more diversified crops are grown, including coffee, sweet potato, papaya and herbs.

Orientation & Information

Three roads run east to west, with minor crossroads going north to south. Farrington

Ave is Hoolehua's main street, with a fire station, Episcopal church and Molokai's high school. The post office is on Puupeelua Ave (Hwy 480), just south of where it intersects with Farrington Ave. Puukapele Ave leads westward and then merges into another paved road that heads beachward, but the road ends at the Western Space & Missile Center, a radio receiving station for the US air force. Here, a bunch of odd metal towers and wire cables make it look as if grown-up kids have been playing with a giant Erector Set.

Purdy's Macadamia Nut Farm

The Purdy family runs the best little macadamia-nut farm tour *(☎ 567-6601; admission free; open 9:30am-3:30pm Mon-Fri, 10am-2pm Sun)* in all of Hawaii. Unlike tours on the Big Island that focus on processing, Mr Purdy takes you into his orchard and personally explains how the nuts grow. A single macadamia tree can simultaneously be in different stages of progression – with flowers in blossom, tiny nuts just beginning and clusters of mature nuts.

Purdy's 1½ acres of mature trees are nearly 75 years old and grow naturally: no pesticides, herbicides, fertilizers or even pruning. Everything is done in quaint Molokai style: You can crack open macadamia nuts on a stone with a hammer and sample macadamia blossom honey scooped up with slices of fresh coconut. Macadamia nuts (roasted or raw) and honey are for sale.

To get to the farm, turn onto Farrington Ave from Hwy 470. After 1 mile, take a right onto Lihi Pali Ave, just before the high school. The farm is a third of a mile up, on the right.

Mail Home Some Aloha

The postmaster of the Hoolehua **post office** *(☎ 567-6144; open 7:30am-11:30am & 12:30pm-4:30pm Mon-Fri)* stocks baskets of unhusked coconuts that you can address and mail off as a unique (even edible!) 'postcard.' These coconuts, which the postmaster gathers on her own time, are free for this 'post-a-nut' purpose, and she keeps a few felt pens on hand so you can jot down a message on the husk. Priority mail postage for an average-sized coconut to anywhere in the USA costs from $5.

MOOMOMI BEACH

Moomomi Beach, located on the western edge of the Hoolehua Plains, is ecologically unique. Managed by the Nature Conservancy, it stands as one of the few undisturbed coastal sand dune areas left in Hawaii. Among its native grasses and shrubs are at least five endangered plant species that exist nowhere else on earth. It is one of the few places in the populated islands where green sea turtles still find a habitat suitable for breeding. Evidence of an adze quarry and the fossils of a number of long-extinct Hawaiian birds have been unearthed here, preserved over time by Moomomi's arid sands.

Moomomi is not lushly beautiful, but windswept, lonely and wild. In short, totally enchanting and worth the great trouble it takes to find. Follow Farrington Ave west past the intersection with Hwy 480 until the paved road ends. Do not try to take Moomomi Ave instead, unless it has been recently regraded.

From there, it's 2½ miles farther along a red dirt road that is in some areas quite smooth and in others deeply rutted. In places, you may have to skirt the edge of the road and straddle a small gully. It's ordinarily passable in a standard car, although the higher the vehicle the better. Rental car contracts will forbid it, however, and it's definitely best to have a 4WD. After rain, it quickly becomes muddy.

A little over 2 miles after the paved road ends, the road forks. Bear to the right and follow this road half a mile down to the beach.

If it gets too rough, there's a spot halfway down this last stretch where you can pull off to the right and park. If you get lost in the maze of dirt roads, just keep heading toward the sea and look for the picnic pavilion that announces you've found **Moomomi Bay**, with a little sandy beach used by sunbathers. The rocky eastern point that protects the bay provides a perch for fishers. The picnic pavilion, belonging to the Hawaiian Home Lands, has toilets, but bring your own drinking water.

The broad, white-sand beach that people refer to as Moomomi is not here, but at **Kawaaloa Bay**, a 20-minute walk further west. The wind, which picks up steadily each afternoon (brace yourself), blows the sand into interesting ripples and waves. The narrower right side of Kawaaloa Bay is partially sheltered; however, the whole beach can be rough when the surf is up, and swimming is discouraged.

There's a fair chance you'll have Kawaaloa to yourself, but if you don't you can always walk farther on to one of the other sandy coves along the shore. Most of the area that is west of here is open ocean with strong currents. The high hills running inland are actually massive sand dunes. The coastal cliffs, which have been sculptured into jagged abstract designs by wind and water, are made of sand that has petrified due to Moomomi's dry conditions.

Because of the fragile ecology of the dunes, visitors should stay along the beach and on trails only. Visitors are not allowed to take any natural objects, including flora, rocks and coral. Foot access is allowed without a permit via the route described, although visitors with a 4WD vehicle can also get a gate key from the Nature Conservancy and drive directly to Kawaaloa Bay. To do that, a permit application and $25 key deposit are required.

The Nature Conservancy *(Molokai Preserves ☎ 553-5236, fax 553-9870; W www.nature.org)* leads monthly guided hikes of Moomomi, usually on the fourth Saturday of the month. The cost of $10 for conservancy members and $25 for nonmembers includes transportation to and from the preserve. As it's common for hikers to fly over from other islands to join in, the pickup run includes Molokai airport. Reservations are required and spots fill up well in advance.

KALAE

RW Meyer Sugar Mill

Four miles north of Hwy 460 is the sugar mill built by Rudolph W Meyer, an industrious German immigrant. Meyer was on his way to the California gold rush when he dropped by the islands, married a member of Hawaiian royalty and in the process landed a tidy bit of property.

He eventually found his gold in potatoes, which he grew and exported to the Californian miners. He also served as overseer of the Kalaupapa leprosy settlement and as manager of King Kamehameha V's ranch lands.

In the 1850s, Meyer established his own ranch and exported cattle from Palaau village. In one infamous incident, after finding his herd declining, he had all the men of Palaau charged with cattle rustling and sent off to a jailhouse in Honolulu. In 1876, when a new reciprocity treaty gave Hawaiian sugar planters the right to export sugar duty-free to the US, Meyer turned his lands over to sugar and built this mill. It operated for only a decade.

The mill, which is on the National Register of Historic Places, is the last of its kind. A lot of time and money has gone into authentic restorations, including the rebuilding of a 100-year-old steam engine and other rusting machinery abandoned a century ago. The **museum** *(☎ 567-6436; adult/concession $2/1; open 10am-2pm Mon-Sat)* beside the parking lot contains a small display of Molokai's history through period photos, a few Hawaiiana items and a 10-minute video. Meyer and his descendants are buried in a little family plot out back.

Ironwood Hills Golf Course

There are no polo shirts here, just a delightfully casual golf course *(☎ 567-6000; open 7am-5pm daily)*, with crabgrass growing in the sand pits and local golfers who actually look like they're having fun. Originally built by Del Monte for its employees, the course is down the red dirt road at the tree-lined edge of the pasture immediately south of Meyer Sugar Mill. The green fees are $10/15 for 9/18 holes and cart rental is from $7 to $15.

PALAAU STATE PARK

Palaau State Park is at the northern end of Hwy 470. The park's main sight, the Kalaupapa Overlook, is just a couple of minutes' walk from the parking lot. Whether or not you get down to Kalaupapa itself, a visit to the overlook is a must. In the opposite direction, a five-minute trail through a grove of ironwoods leads to a phallic-shaped rock. Both trails are easy to follow. The park has camp sites, picnic areas and lovely stands of paperbark eucalyptus.

Kalaupapa Overlook

The Kalaupapa Overlook provides a scenic overview of the Kalaupapa Peninsula from the edge of a 1600ft cliff. It's like an aerial view without the airplane. Kalaupapa residents use the term 'topside' to refer to all of Molokai outside their peninsula. Seen from the overlook, the reason is obvious. Because of the angle of the sun, the best light for

KARL LEHMANN

Puu Pehe (Sweetheart Rock), Manele Bay, Lanai

KIM GRANT

Wetlands and taro fields, Princeville, Kauai

ANN CECIL

Ancient Hawaiian fishpond, near Kaunakakai, Molokai

Giant frogfish

Green sea turtles

Snorkeling, Oahu

ALL PHOTOGRAPHS BY CASEY & ASTRID WITTE MAHANEY

photography is usually from late morning to mid-afternoon.

The **lighthouse** at the northern end of the peninsula once boasted the most powerful beam in the Pacific. The 700,000-candlepower Fresnel crystal lens cast its light until 1986, when it was taken down and replaced by an electric light beacon.

Interpretive plaques identify the landmarks below and explain Kalaupapa's history as a leprosy colony. The village where all of Kalaupapa's residents live is visible, but Kalawao, the original settlement and site of Father Damien's church and grave, cannot be seen from here.

Kalaupapa means 'flat leaf,' an accurate description of the lava slab peninsula that was created when a low shield volcano poked up out of the sea long after the rest of Molokai had been formed. The dormant Kauhako Crater, visible from the overlook, contains a little lake that's more than 800ft deep.

Hiking There's a vague trail of sorts that continues directly beyond the last plaque at the overlook. Simply follow this trail for 20 minutes or so until it peters out. Few people go this way, and it's very peaceful – if you're lucky, you may even spot deer crossing the trail.

The path, on a carpet of soft ironwood needles, passes through a thickly planted forest of ironwood and eucalyptus, dotted here and there with Norfolk pines. These diagonal rows of trees were planted during a CCC reforestation project in the 1930s. The trees create a canopy over the trail, and, as is generally true under ironwood and eucalyptus trees, there's little undergrowth to obscure the way.

Phallic Rock

Kauleonanahoa, which means 'the penis of Nanahoa,' is Hawaii's premier phallic stone, poking up in a little clearing inside an ironwood grove. Nature has endowed it well, but some say it has also been 'touched up' by human hands. Reputedly women who bring offerings of leis and dollar bills and spend the night here will return home pregnant, but apparently there is no danger in just going to have a look.

Places to Stay

A quarter of a mile before the overlook, the **camping area** is usually quite peaceful, even deserted. It's basically just a field next to a concrete picnic pavilion affording no privacy, especially when local families show up to barbecue and celebrate special occasions. At night, apart from the trickle of passing traffic, the only sounds come from roosters and the braying of mules from the nearby stables. Clouds start gathering in the late afternoon and, by midnight, your tent may well be drenched; the chances of this happening are less likely during the summer dry season, of course. Still, it rains here a lot. There are rest rooms inside the picnic pavilion, but no potable water. Look for the pavilion past the mule stables, which are around the 5-mile marker. For fees and permit information, see the Accommodations section earlier in this chapter.

Kalaupapa Peninsula

Kalaupapa Peninsula seems both strikingly beautiful and strikingly lonely. At the base of majestic and formidable cliffs, it has been a leprosy settlement for more than a century. Now a national historical park managed by the Hawaii Department of Health and the **National Park Service** (**w** *www.nps.gov/kala*), it is unique in that many of the people whose lives are being interpreted are still living on the site.

The trip to the peninsula – accessible only by mule, on foot or by small plane – is one of Molokai's major attractions. It's also a pilgrimage of sorts for admirers of Father Damien (Joseph de Veuster), the Belgian priest who devoted the latter part of his life to helping people with leprosy, before dying of the disease himself.

History

Ancient Hawaiians used Kalaupapa as a refuge when caught in storms at sea. The peninsula held a large settlement at the time of early Western contact, and the area is rich in archaeological sites.

In 1835, doctors in Hawaii diagnosed the state's first case of leprosy, one of many diseases introduced by foreigners. Before modern medicine, leprosy manifested itself in dripping, foul-smelling sores. Eventually, patients experienced loss of sensation and tissue degeneration that could lead to fingers, toes and noses becoming hideously deformed or falling off altogether. Alarmed by the spread of the disease, King Kamehameha V signed into law an act that banished people with leprosy to Kalaupapa Peninsula, beginning in 1865.

Hawaiians called leprosy *mai hookaawale*, which means 'separating sickness,' a disease all the more dreaded because it tore families apart forever. Kalaupapa Peninsula is surrounded on three sides by some of Hawaii's roughest and most shark-infested waters and on the fourth by the world's highest sea cliffs. Some patients arrived in boats whose captains were so terrified of the disease that they would not land, but instead dropped patients overboard into the bay. Those who could, swam to shore.

Once the afflicted arrived on Kalaupapa Peninsula, there was no way out, not even in a casket. The original settlement was in Kalawao, at the wetter eastern end of the peninsula. Early conditions were unspeakably horrible, with the strong stealing rations from the weak and women forced into prostitution or worse. Lifespans were invariably short, and desperate.

Father Damien arrived at Kalaupapa in 1873. He wasn't the first missionary to come, but he was the first to stay. What Damien gave them most of all was a sense of hope. The priest put up more than 300 houses – each little more than four walls, a door and a roof, but still a shelter to those cast here. Damien was a talented carpenter, and some of the solid little churches he had built around Molokai and the Big Island still stand. Damien also nursed the sick, wrapped bandages on oozing sores, hammered coffins and dug graves. On average, he buried one person a day. In 1888, he installed a water pipeline over to the sunny western side of the peninsula, and the settlement moved from Kalawao to where it remains today.

Damien's work inspired others. Brother Joseph Dutton arrived in 1886 and stayed 44 years. In addition to his work with the sick, he was a prolific writer who kept the outside world informed about what was happening in Molokai. Mother Marianne Cope arrived a year before Damien died. She stayed 30 years, helping to establish a girls' home and encouraging patients to live life to the fullest. She is widely considered to be the mother of the hospice movement. Damien died in 1889 at the age of 49. In 1995, he was beatified by Pope John Paul II and is now a candidate for sainthood.

Over the years, some 8000 people have come to the Kalaupapa Peninsula to live out their lives. The same year that Father Damien arrived, a Norwegian scientist named Dr Gerhard Hansen discovered *Mycobacterium leprae,* the bacteria that causes leprosy, thus proving that the disease was not hereditary as previously thought. Even in Damien's day, however, leprosy was one of the least contagious of all communicable diseases: only 4% of human beings are even susceptible to it.

In 1909, a fancy medical facility called the US Leprosy Investigation Station opened at Kalawao. However, the hospital was so out of touch – requiring patients to sign themselves in for two years, live in seclusion and give up all Hawaiian-grown food – that even in the middle of a leprosy colony it attracted only a handful of patients. It closed a few years later.

Since the 1940s, sulfone antibiotics have been used to successfully treat and control leprosy, but the isolation policies in Kalaupapa weren't abandoned until 1969. Today, fewer than 100 patients are living on Kalaupapa Peninsula, the vast majority of them senior citizens. They are of course free to leave, but they choose to stay. When you see this wildly beautiful peninsula for yourself, it's not hard to understand why. Many rightly feel that this is their only home and have long fought against being bought out by the government and displaced from their land.

While the state of Hawaii officially uses the term 'Hansen's Disease' for leprosy, many Kalaupapa residents consider that to be a euphemism that fails to reflect the stigma they have suffered and continue to use the old term 'leprosy.' The degrading appellation 'leper,' however, is offensive to all.

Visiting Kalaupapa

Old state laws that require everyone who enters the settlement to have a 'permit' and be at least 16 years old are no longer a medical necessity, but they continue to be enforced in order to protect the privacy of the patients. There's no actual paper permit. Your reservation with Damien Tours or Molokai Mule Ride acts as your permit. Only guests of Kalaupapa residents are allowed to stay overnight.

On typical tours, the village looks nearly deserted. The sights are mainly cemeteries, churches and memorials. Places where residents go to 'talk story' – the post office, store and hospital – are pointed out, but no stops are made. Visitors are not allowed to photograph the residents. Kalaupapa is a tourist attraction, but its people are not. There are no stores or other public facilities for visitors, but tours do stop at a simple **visitor center** where photographs of the original settlement are on display and books and videos are for sale. Groups then travel across the peninsula to Kalawao.

St Philomena Church (better known as Father Damien's Church) in Kalawao was built in 1872. You can still see where Damien cut open holes in the floor so that the sick who needed to spit could attend church and not be ashamed. The graveyard at the side contains Damien's gravestone and original burial site, although his body was exhumed in 1936 and returned to Belgium. In 1995, his right hand was brought back and reinterred here.

The view from Kalawao is one of the island's finest. You can look out on the *pali* (cliffs) of the northeast coast, each successive cliff side jutting out behind the one in front, each looking more like a shadow in the mist. The **rock island** just offshore is the legendary home of a giant shark. From some angles, it looks like a shark's head coming straight up out of the water, while from other angles it looks like a dorsal fin.

Organized Tours Everyone who comes to the Kalaupapa Peninsula, whether on foot, by mule or by plane, ends up on the school bus with **Damien Tours** *(☎ 567-6171; tours Mon-Sat only)*. Richard Marks, who runs Damien Tours, is a wry storyteller, oral historian and the third generation of his family to live on Kalaupapa. Reservations must be made in advance (call between 4pm and 8pm), and bring your own lunch. The tours ($30) pick up visitors both at the airport and the bottom of the trail.

Getting There & Around

The switchback mule trail down the *pali* is the only land route to the peninsula; the other option for getting to Kalaupapa is by air. No matter how you get there, you cannot wander around by yourself, and must join an organized tour.

Hiking The 3-mile hike along the mule trail takes just over an hour going down, a bit longer going up. It's best to begin hiking by 8am, before the mules start to go down, to avoid walking in fresh dung. The narrow trail is rutted in places and can be slippery and muddy if it's been raining, but otherwise it's not terribly strenuous. The trail starts on the east side of Hwy 470, just north of the mule stables. Don't be intimidated by the 'Unauthorized Persons Keep Out' sign – *if* you have tour reservations, that is.

Mule Rides One of the best-known outings in the islands is the mule ride down the *pali* to Kalaupapa. While the mules move none too quickly – actually, hiking down can be faster – there's a certain thrill in trusting your life to these sure-footed beasts while descending 1600ft on 26 narrow cliff-side switchbacks.

Molokai Mule Ride, Inc *(☎ 553-3876, 800-567-7550, fax 553-5288; W www.muleride.com)* offers rides daily except Sunday. Because the number of saddles is limited, tours can fill up quickly; make reservations well in advance. Tours begin at the mule stables at 8am sharp for a short riding lesson from real *paniolo* (Hawaiian cowboys). At around 8:30am, riders hit the trail, which begins opposite the stables. The mules arrive in Kalaupapa around 10am, and shortly thereafter a bus tour of the peninsula begins. The whole shebang includes lunch and is entirely worth paying $150 a head. Expect to return to the stables at around 3:30pm. Wear loose trousers, close-toed shoes and a windbreaker. Airport transfers are available for $9 per person (two-person minimum).

Air Kalaupapa has a little air strip at the edge of the peninsula and air service via small prop planes. Passengers must first book a tour with Damien Tours before buying air tickets.

For the cheapest airfare, contact **Molokai Air Shuttle** *(☎ 567-6847)*, which offers a 9am flight from the Molokai airport every day but Sunday as long as there are at least two passengers booking the flight. The return flight leaves at 2pm. The cost is $50 round trip.

Pacific Wings *(☎ 873-0877; 888-575-4546)* has flights that leave Honolulu at 8:40am and arrive in Kalaupapa at 9:10am. The return flights leave Kalaupapa at 3:30pm. Fares are $80 each way.

Paragon Air *(on Maui ☎ 244-3356, on the Neighbor Islands & US mainland ☎ 800-428-1231; Ⓦ www.paragon-air.com)* offers flight packages from Maui that include Damien Tours reservations. It costs $210 per person, regardless of whether you depart from Kahului, Kapalua/West Maui or Hana airports.

West End

The Maunaloa Hwy (Hwy 460) heads west, passing Molokai airport, then climbs into the high grassy rangeland of Molokai's arid western side. Hwy 460 is about 17 miles long, and takes a half hour to drive from its start in Kaunakakai to its end at Maunaloa. It's a good paved road all the way, as are the roads to and around Kaluakoi Resort and down to Papohaku and Dixie Maru beaches.

Most other west end roads, however, are privately owned dirt roads that are locked off to the public. Molokai Ranch owns most of the land on this side of the island. Access here is at the whim of the ranch, but either requires special permission or for you to join one of its organized activity tours (or stay as a guest.)

MAUNALOA

The long mountain range that comes into view on the left past the 10-mile marker is Maunaloa, which means 'long mountain.' Its highest point is Puu Nana at 1381ft. In addition to being the site of Hawaii's first hula school and one of the Hawaiian Islands' most important adze quarries, Maunaloa was also once a center of sorcery.

The name Maunaloa not only refers to the mountain range but also to the town at the end of the road. Built in the 1920s by Libby, McNeill & Libby, this little plantation town was the center of the company's pineapple activities on Molokai. Dole, which acquired Libby, McNeill & Libby in 1972, closed down operations in Maunaloa in 1975.

Maunaloa is currently a town in flux. Molokai Ranch, which owns the land that the town sits on, is replacing many of the old plantation-era cottages with modern housing and adding new conveniences, including a business center and movie theater. These days, about 230 people live in the area, most working for the ranch. With 8000 head of cattle, Molokai Ranch is actually the second largest working cattle ranch in the state, although tourists are the main cash crop. For more details on the ranch, see the History section earlier in this chapter.

Molokai Sorcery

According to legend, *kalaipahoa*, or fire gods who roamed the heavens as shooting stars, landed on Maunaloa, where they inhabited a grove of trees. Unsuspecting men who tried to cut down the possessed trees were poisoned upon touching the wood, until at last one of the gods revealed to a *kahuna* the secret of how to cut the trees down. After that, *kahuna* were able to carve the poisoned wood into images that harnessed the force of the gods. During the 17th century it became a powerful sorcery that could be sent off into the night to wreak vengeance upon enemies. It was potent stuff, and none of Molokai's neighbors dared to violate Molokai's sovereignty in those days.

All of Maunaloa's businesses lie along the Maunaloa Hwy, the town's main street. The little rural **post office** *(☎ 552-2852; open 8am-noon & 12:30pm-4:30pm Mon-Fri)* is opposite the grocery store. The village **gas station** *(open 7am-5pm Mon-Fri, 9am-5pm Sat, noon-4pm Sun)* is the only one on the west end.

Molokai Ranch Headquarters & Logo Shop *(see Sheraton Molokai Ranch under Places to Stay later; open 6am-7pm daily)* is on your immediate right after Hwy 460 makes its final turn into town. Step inside for exhibits on ranch history or to make bookings at the activity desk. Activity fees for guests are high, for nonguests even steeper; if things are slow, discounts may be negotiable.

The ranch offers 2½-hour guided horseback rides for $80. The rides cross ranch pasture, providing views of the ocean and Lanai. For the more adventurous, the ranch can also organize a '*paniolo* roundup,' complete with barrel racing, pole vending and cattle herding. Guided hikes led by knowledgeable cultural guides cost $30 to $125. The most fantastic adventures to be had here are on the back of mountain bikes, whether you're racing downhill on a gravity ride or pedaling along the tops of the highest sea cliffs in the world. The instructors are very forgiving; rates vary from $35 to $100. Other ranch activities include kayaking, ocean fishing, archery and special kids' adventures and classes.

Places to Stay

Molokai Ranchhouse (☎ *553-5270;* **W** *www.molokai-ranchhouse.com; 3-bedroom house per day/week from $165/1000)* is a spacious double-decker vacation rental home, complete with fully equipped kitchen, family room, cable TV, laundry and lanai. Everything is done with tasteful island flair, making relaxation paramount.

Sheraton Molokai Ranch (☎ *552-2741, 877-726-4656, fax 552-2773;* **W** *www.sheraton-molokai.com; Maunaloa Hwy; beach/lodge accommodation packages with meals from $170/200)* is a full-service experience, with a $10 per day resort fee entitling guests to free Internet access, faxing and copying; unlimited use of the sauna, pool and gym; and beach gear to borrow. Accommodations are at the lodge hotel or out at remote Kaupoa Beach Village, where each deluxe canvas bungalow has a queen-size bed, solar-powered lights, ceiling fan, shower and lanai. The village has pavilions where chefs prepare buffet style meals, not surprisingly with an emphasis on grilled meats.

A visit to Molokai Ranch is very much a packaged tour. Ranch staff pick up guests at the airport, check them in at the ranch's Maunaloa headquarters and then take them by van along the ranch's red dirt roads to the camp. Although the ranch offers visitors a chance to relax in a remote space and play a bit of *paniolo*, guests generally don't see much of Molokai outside the ranch gates – then again, the ranch does own 54,000 acres, about one-third of the entire island.

Places to Eat

For everyday supplies, **Maunaloa General Store** *(open 8am-6pm Mon-Sat)* also has a reasonable selection of groceries, plus wine and beer.

There's a small **KFC** *(open 11am-8pm Mon-Fri, 11am-9:30pm Sat & Sun)* beside the movie theater, with the usual fried chicken offerings. It's not memorable, but it is the only place in the west end where a whole meal with chicken, potatoes and biscuits costs just $5.

Maunaloa Room (☎ *552-2741, 877-726-4656, fax 552-2773;* **W** *www.sheraton-molokai.com; Maunaloa Hwy; dishes $10-40; open breakfast & dinner daily)* offers more upscale dining, even if the menu is unexciting.

Entertainment

Maunaloa Town Cinemas (☎ *552-2707; Maunaloa Hwy; adult/concession $6/3.50)* shows first-run movies.

At the Sheraton Molokai Ranch's lodge, the **Paniolo Bar** is one of Molokai's only three watering holes. Cocktails and *pupu*s are served in a genteel cowboy atmosphere.

Shopping

Big Wind Kite Factory (☎ *552-2364; 120 Maunaloa Hwy; open 8:30am-5pm Mon-Sat, 10am-2pm Sun)* sells colorful kites in all shapes and styles. Many of the kites with tropical fish and other island-influenced designs are made on-site, and if you're lucky, you can watch the kite makers work.

An extension of the kite factory is the eclectic **gift shop** next door, which has wood carvings from Bali, scrimshaw carvings from Molokai deer, Hawaiiana books and jewelry.

KALUAKOI RESORT

In the 1970s, Molokai Ranch joined with Louisiana Land & Exploration Company to form the Kaluakoi Corporation, which proposed developing western Molokai into a major suburb of Honolulu, complete with a ferry service. The plan called for 30,000 private homes on the heretofore uninhabited west coast. A vocal antigrowth movement boomed quicker than the buildings could, however, and the plan was scrapped.

In its place, a somewhat more modest master plan was drawn up for the development of Kaluakoi Resort. Only 200 of the condo units, one 18-hole golf course and one of the four planned hotels were ever built. Originally owned by the Sheraton, the 290-room hotel never really took off and the occupancy rate was so low that part of it was turned into condos. The house lots have been subdivided, but as yet fewer than 100 houses have been built, mostly exclusive homes scattered along the edge of the beach and up on the bluff.

Later mismanagement by a Japanese corporation effectively ran the resort with its 18-hole golf course into the ground. The greens turned brown, and things looked deserted for a while. Now that may quickly change, however, as Molokai Ranch has bought most of the resort property and reinvolved Sheraton in the project. Visitors today can still have the beaches pretty much to themselves, but that surely won't last.

Turning off Hwy 460 before Maunaloa at the 15-mile marker, a road leads down to the resort and main west end beaches. **Kepuhi Beach** is the white-sand beach in front of the old Kaluakoi Hotel. Swimming conditions are often dangerous here. Not only can there be a tough shorebreak but strong currents can be present even on calm days. During the winter, the surf breaks close to shore, carrying a tremendous amount of sand to and fro. Experienced surfers take to the northern end of the beach.

A five-minute hike up to the top of **Puu o Kaiaka**, a 110ft-high promontory at the south end of Kepuhi Beach, rewards strollers with a nice view of Papohaku Beach. At the top, you'll find the remains of a pulley that was once used to carry cattle down to waiting barges for transport to Oahu slaughterhouses. There was also a 40ft *heiau* on the hilltop until 1967, when the US army bulldozed it. To get to the parking lot, turn off Kaluakoi Rd onto Kaiaka Rd, proceeding a half mile to the road's end.

In the opposite direction, **Make Horse Beach** supposedly takes its name from days past, when wild horses were run off the cliff north of here. *Make* (mah-**kay**) means 'dead' in Hawaiian. This pretty little white-sand beach is more secluded than the one in front of Kaluakoi Hotel. It's a good place for sunbathing, but it's not safe for swimming.

To get here, turn off Kaluakoi Rd onto the road to Paniolo Hale condos and then turn left toward the condo complex. It's best to park just beyond the condos and walk the last quarter of a mile down to the golf course, though some people brave the deeply rutted dirt road to its end, where there's a little spot to park. Once at the golf course, cross a narrow stretch of fairway, and you're on the beach.

Kawakiu Beach, further north along the shoreline, is a broad crescent beach of white sand and bright turquoise waters. To get there, turn off Kaluakoi Rd onto the road to the Paniolo Hale condos, but instead of turning left down to the condos, continue straight toward the golf course. Where the paved road ends, there's space to pull over and park just before crossing the greens. You'll come first to a rocky point at the southern end of the bay. Before descending to the beach, scramble around up here for a scenic view of the coast, south to the sands of Papohaku Beach and north to Ilio Point.

When seas are calm, Kawakiu is generally safe for swimming, although that's more common in summer than winter. When the surf is rough, there are still areas where you can at least get wet. On the southern side of the bay, there's a small, sandy-bottomed wading pool in the rocks. The northern side has an area of flat rocks over which water slides to fill up a shallow shoreline pool.

In 1975, Kawakiu was a focus of Molokai activists, who began demanding access to private, and heretofore forbidden, beaches. The group, Hui Alaloa, marched to Kawakiu from Moomomi in a successful protest that convinced Molokai Ranch to provide public access to this secluded west end beach. On weekends, there are often a few families picnicking under the *kiawe* trees, but at other times you may well have the place to yourself.

Places to Stay & Eat

Many units of the old Kaluakoi Hotel are currently under separate management and are booked as **Kaluakoi Villas** *(☎ 552-2721, 800-525-1470, fax 552-2201; 1131 Kaluakoi Rd)*, where guests enjoy use of the hotel's oceanfront swimming pool. Units each have a private lanai, a TV and a kitchenette with refrigerator, coffeemaker and stove. Ask for a 2nd-floor unit, as these have cathedral ceilings; many offer a peek of the ocean. Standard rates offered by Castle Resorts management are $135 to $150 for studio units, $160 to $190 for one-bedroom units and $240 for an ocean cottage with kitchen. If you surf the Web, you may find independent agents offering individual condo units for less.

The old Kaluakoi Hotel **sundries shop** is open for business, selling wine, beer and a few convenience foods at inflated prices, making a trek up to the **Maunaloa General Store** *(see the Maunaloa section earlier)* pay off when buying supplies or groceries in bulk.

Paniolo Hale *(☎ 552-2731, 800-367-2984, fax 552-2288; W www.paniolohaleresort.com; Lio Place; studios from $115, 1-bedroom units with 2 baths $135, 2-bedroom units $165)* is an airy condominium complex with a pool and barbecue grills. Each spacious condo unit has a kitchen, ceiling fans, TV, washer,

MOLOKAI

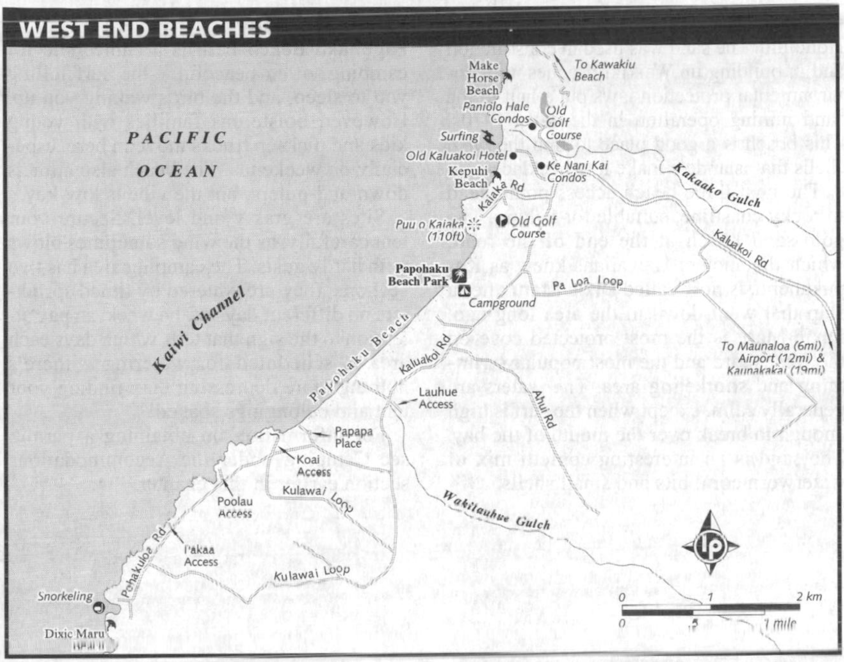

dryer and screened lanai. The minimum stay is usually three nights, especially if you're looking for discounts off the rack rates, which are for garden-view units only. Naturally, ocean views cost more. Check the Web site for special promotions.

Ke Nani Kai (☎ *552-2761, 800-535-0085, fax 800-633-5085;* 🅦 *www.marcresorts.com; off Kepuhi Place; 1-bedroom/2-bedroom units from $155/189)* has condo units that are mostly managed by Marc Resorts. Each has a full kitchen, lanai, washer, dryer and TV; most have a sofa bed in the living room. The units on the 2nd floor have high, exposed-beam ceilings, and the best of them are arguably the nicest on Molokai. Those with ocean views cost up to $30 more, but it's a distant and partial view. Various online discount schemes can cut the rack rates by nearly half. There's a pool and two tennis courts.

WEST END BEACHES

From Molokai's west end beaches, the twinkling lights of Oahu are just 26 miles away. The view is of Diamond Head to the left, Makapuu Point to the right.

Beautiful **Papohaku Beach** lays claim to being Hawaii's largest beach. It's 2½ miles long and vast enough to hold the entire population of Molokai without getting crowded. There's seldom more than a handful of beachgoers, even on sunny days, and at times you can walk the shore without seeing another soul. With soft golden sands gleaming in the sun and wisps of rainbows tossed up in the crashing surf, it's a gorgeous place for barefoot strolling.

So why are so few people there? Well, for one, it can be windy, with gusts of sand continually smacking you in the face. But the main drawback is the water itself, which is usually too treacherous for swimming.

The first access point, which is the most developed of the seven turnoffs from Kaluakoi Rd with parking lots, is **Papohaku Beach Park**, a grassy park with camp sites, indoor *and* outdoor showers, picnic facilities, changing rooms, toilets, water fountains and some thorny *kiawe* trees.

From the third access point, off Papapa Place, there is a broad view of all of Papohaku Beach, stretching north. The large concrete tunnel at the south end of the beach was used to load sand onto barges for shipping to Honolulu. The sand was used in construction and in building up Waikiki beaches until environmental protection laws put a halt to the sand mining operation in the early 1970s. This beach is a good place to find the *puka* shells that islanders make into necklaces.

The next three beach access points lead to rocky coastline, suitable for fishing. The gold-sand beach at the end of the road, which the ancient Hawaiians knew as Kapukahehu, is now called **Dixie Maru** after a ship that went down in the area long ago. Dixie Maru is the most protected cove on the west shore and the most popular **swimming** and **snorkeling** area. The waters are generally calm, except when the surf is high enough to break over the mouth of the bay. The sand is an interesting confetti mix of waterworn coral bits and small shells.

Places to Stay

Papohaku Beach Park is a choice site for camping, often peaceful – the surf lulling you to sleep, and the birds waking you up. However, boisterous families with young kids and pick-up trucks move in here, especially on weekends. The beach also attracts down-and-outers, but the vibe is low-key.

Sites are grassy and level. Secure your tent carefully, as the wind sometimes blows with hardy gusts. The camping area has two sections; they are watered by timed sprinklers on different days of the week, so pay attention to the sign that tells which days each area is scheduled for watering – there's nothing more depressing than finding your tent and belongings soaked!

For information on obtaining a permit, see Camping under the Accommodations section earlier in this chapter.

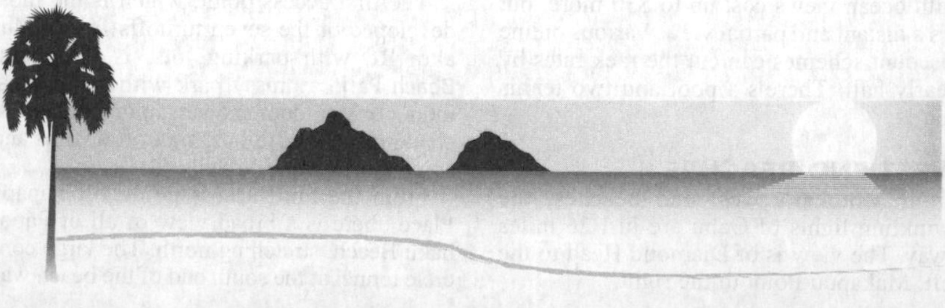

Lanai

Until recently, Lanai was a one-crop, one-company, one-town island. The last two still hold true. For over half a century, Castle & Cooke, the company that owns 98% of Lanai, ran the island as its own private pineapple plantation. For a time, nearly one-fifth of the world's pineapples came from Lanai, but competition from Costa Rican and Philippine pineapples gradually eroded the profitability of the Lanai crop.

Castle & Cooke has today ceased its commercial pineapple operations completely. Instead, CEO David Murdoch has busily tried to turn the boondocks of Lanai into an exclusive tourist destination, opening two luxury resorts (The Lodge at Koele and the Manele Bay Hotel), both with 18-hole golf courses, and building some of the island's first million-dollar vacation homes.

Until the early 1990s, Lanai had only one little hotel; the few visitors who came this way were largely hunters, hikers and independent travelers trying to avoid the tourist scene on the other islands. Now, with its two new resorts, which are among the most expensive ever built in Hawaii, Castle & Cooke is gambling that enough wealthy visitors in search of seclusion will show up to make it all pay off.

On the surface, things haven't altered all that radically yet. The center of Lanai remains Lanai City – not a city at all, but merely a little plantation town of tin-roofed houses and small shops. It's still home to all but a few dozen of Lanai's 3200 residents, most of whom work for the Lanai Company, the nonagricultural subsidiary of Castle & Cooke.

Although Lanai can be interesting to explore, many of the sights are a good distance from town, along rutted dirt roads that require a 4WD vehicle. The island has bright red earth, dry and dusty gullies, white-sand beaches, forested ravines and cool, foggy uplands. It also has some obscure archaeological sites and petroglyphs and the last native dryland forest in Hawaii.

Not surprisingly, visiting can be quite expensive, as the island's only car rental agency and limited accommodations exert a stranglehold over the tourist market. One of the easiest ways to get a glimpse of the island is to take the ferry over from Maui in the morning, snorkel at Hulopoe Bay, and take the boat back in the afternoon, or stay longer and camp overnight on lovely Hulopoe Beach.

Highlights

- Snorkeling and swimming in the pristine waters off Hulopoe Beach
- Diving in the grottoes of the Cathedrals
- Adventuring on Lanai's 4WD roads to shipwrecks and petroglyphs
- Encountering the Garden of the Gods and the Munro Trail

HISTORY

Archaeological studies indicate Lanai was never heavily settled. Villages were relatively small and scattered throughout the island.

Since ancient times, it has been under the rule of its more dominant neighbor, Maui. In 1778, when the Big Island chief Kalaniopuu was routed in a failed attempt to invade Maui, he decided to take his revenge on tiny Lanai and sent warriors under the command of Kamehameha the Great. Kamehameha's troops were brutal. They killed everyone they found and virtually depopulated Lanai.

When English explorer George Vancouver sailed by Lanai in 1792, he saw no villages and noted that the island might at best be only sparsely populated. Treacherous ocean swells, which had already claimed a couple of foreign ships by the 1820s, dissuaded many other would-be visitors from landing.

In 1823, a missionary named William Ellis became the first Westerner to step ashore. He guessed that the island's population was around 2000. Although the early missionaries did not spend a lot of time on Lanai, they still had some influence. They introduced the heretofore unknown concept of adultery to Hawaii, for example, and in the 1830s Maui women accused of that criminal offense were banished to the barren northwestern side of Lanai as punishment, while male offenders were sent to Kahoolawe.

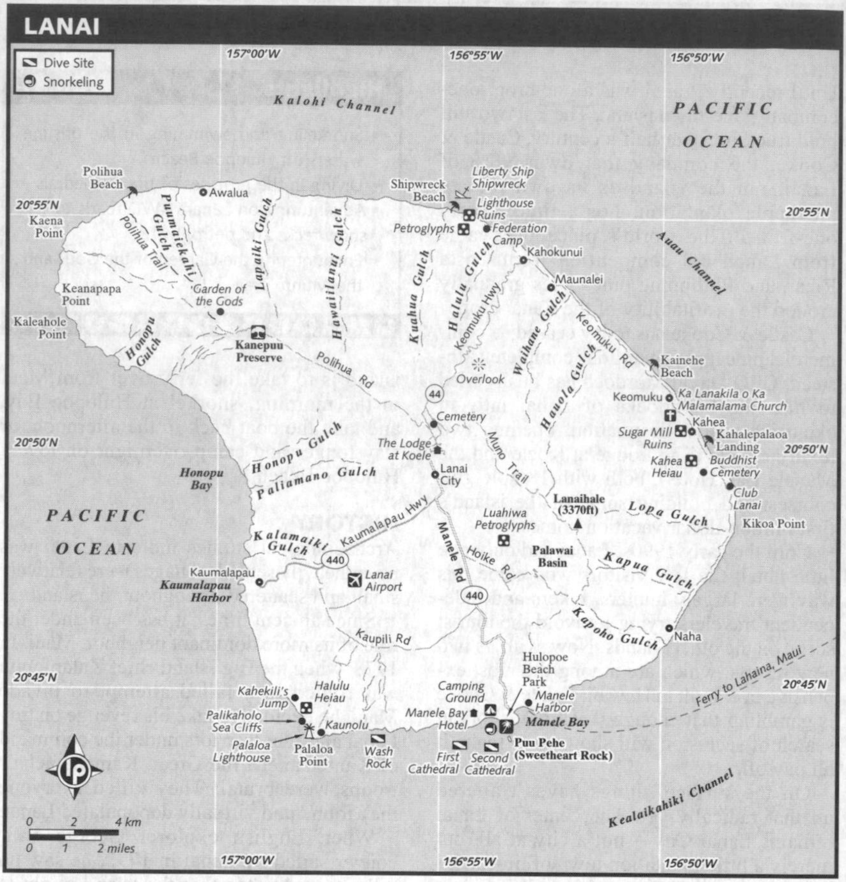

Mormons

In the 1850s, the Mormons moved in and set up a community at Palawai Basin, south of present-day Lanai City. Their intention was to establish a 'City of Joseph' in Hawaii.

The community floundered until 1861, when a new charismatic elder, Walter Gibson, arrived. Mormons from around the islands poured in, as did money to buy Palawai Basin. At the height of it all, there was one Mormon for every Lanaian.

Gibson, a shrewd businessman, handled the financial matters for the community – including the acquisition of land. Things got sticky when it was discovered that he had made the land purchases in his own name, rather than in the church's. In 1864, after refusing to transfer the title of his Lanai holdings to the mother church in Salt Lake City, he was excommunicated by leader Brigham Young.

This apparently suited Gibson just fine. He held onto the prime Lanai real estate he had cornered, and unable to gain title to his property, the Lanai congregation faded away and the 300 or so Mormons left for Laie on Oahu's windward coast, where their church is still based today. Equally calculating in the political arena, Gibson became a friend and confidant of King David Kalakaua in the 1880s and came to hold a number of powerful positions in Kalakaua's cabinet.

Sugar & Cattle

Upon his death, Gibson left the land to his daughter, Talula Lucy. In 1888, she and her

Spirits in the Night

According to legend, Lanai was a land of *akua* (spirits), rumored to be flesh-eaters, and they alone roamed the island until the 15th century.

It was at this time that Kaululaau, the young prince of Maui, lived in what is today the town of Lahaina. He was a mischievous child. After he tore out the breadfruit trees that his father Kaakaleneo had just planted, the elders decided to banish him to uninhabited Lanai, an almost certain death.

Not one to be easily intimidated, Kaululaau learned to trick the evil spirits of Lanai. To avoid being ambushed at night, he convinced the *akua* that he slept in the surf, though when darkness fell he slipped off to the shelter of a cave. Night after night, the *akua* returned to the beach and rushed out to look for the prince in the waves. The longer they searched, the more exhausted they got, until finally the pounding surf overcame them. Kaululaau continued his pranks until all of Lanai's *akua* had either perished or fled to Kahoolawe.

Kaululaau's family had given him up for dead when Mauians noticed a light from a fire across the Auau Channel, which separates Maui and Lanai. When they went over to investigate, they found Kaululaau alive and well, and the island devoid of spirits.

husband, Frederick Hayselden, established the Maunalei Sugar Company. After a landing at Kahalepalaoa on Lanai's east coast was developed, a water-pumping station went up at nearby Keomuku, the surrounding area was planted with sugarcane and the whole shebang was connected by a little railroad.

The sugar days were short-lived, however. By 1901, the pumps were drawing saltwater, the sugarcane had died and the whole enterprise had folded. After the dismal failure with sugar, the land was sold off to ranching interests. In 1910, the newly formed Lanai Company consolidated most of the holdings and established cattle ranching on a large scale. The following year, New Zealander George Munro was hired to manage the ranch, and a landing was established at Manele Bay so that the company could ship cattle to off-island markets.

In 1917, the Baldwin brothers, sons of missionaries from Maui, purchased the Lanai Company. With the exception of a small ranch held by other *haole* (white men) and about 500 acres held by Lanaians, the Baldwins owned the entire island.

Pineapples

In 1922, Jim Dole paid $1.1 million for Lanai, a mere $12 an acre. With the purchase of Lanai, Dole, who had already established pineapple production on Oahu, doubled his holdings of cultivable Hawaiian land.

Dole's Hawaiian Pineapple Company poured millions of dollars into Lanai to turn it into a plantation island. It built the plantation town of Lanai City, dredged Kaumalapau Bay to make it a deepwater harbor, put in roads and water systems, cleared the land and planted pineapples. By the end of the 1920s, production was in full swing.

Dole had marketed his pineapples well and was producing bumper crops – the future looked rosy. Then the Great Depression hit the mainland, and sales plummeted. The newly popular canned pineapples had become an exotic extra, one that most Americans could easily do without in hard times. As company profits plummeted, Castle & Cooke purchased much of the stock and eventually gained a controlling interest in Dole's company; Castle & Cooke has been the dominant force on Lanai ever since.

GEOGRAPHY & GEOLOGY

Lanai is the sixth-largest Hawaiian island. When viewed from Maui, it looks somewhat like the back of a whale rising out of the water; its name means 'hump.' The island is 18 miles long and 13 miles wide, and has an area of 140 sq miles. It lies 9 miles west of Maui and 11 miles south of Molokai.

Lanai was formed by a single volcano, Palawai, now long extinct. The large flat basin of the Palawai crater contains most of its arable land. The terrain and climate are dominated by a ridge running from the northwest to the southeast, which reaches a height of 3370ft on Lanaihale. From there, a series of gulches radiate down to the east coast, ending at a strip of coastal

Sweet Roots

In 1802, a Chinese sandalwood ship carrying Wong Tze-Chun landed on Lanai. An enterprising man, Wong Tze-Chun had brought along granite rollers to crush sugarcane, which had been growing freely on the islands since the arrival of the first Polynesians. Using iron pots, he then boiled the crushed cane down into a sugary syrup. Today, he is commonly credited as the very first person to have attempted commercial sugar production in Hawaii. Although this particular enterprise failed thanks to Lanai's dry soil, this sort of Chinese know-how became the basis for other sugar mills throughout the islands.

flats. On the western side of the ridge you'll find a cool central plateau with Lanai City perched at 1620ft.

The remote southwest coast has sheer sea cliffs, some higher than 1000ft, while the dry and barren northwest portion of the island slopes gently down to the coast.

CLIMATE

Lanai is rather dry. Molokai to the north and Maui to the east draw much of the rain out of the moisture-laden trade winds before they reach Lanai. But even the island's drier areas can get soaked with heavy rainfall during winter storms.

As in the rest of Hawaii, October to April is the rainiest season. Rainfall averages less than 40 inches annually in Lanai City, 10 to 15 inches along most of the coast. The difference is great enough, however, that when it's overcast in Lanai City, chances are that Shipwreck Beach or Manele Bay will be sunny.

Lanai City has a mild climate. Evenings can be brisk, with temperatures commonly dipping down to around 50°F in winter. The highest temperature on record is 88°F. Average temperatures range from 73°F in the summer to 66°F in the winter. For recorded weather forecasts and water conditions, call the **hotline** (☎ *565-6033*).

FLORA & FAUNA

Lanai has suffered the greatest loss of native forests, plants and birds of any of the main Hawaiian islands, thanks to drastic overgrazing. The most noticeable types of vegetation are thorny *kiawe* (a relative of mesquite) trees, common in Lanai's dry coastal areas, and stately Norfolk and Cook Island pines, which abound around Lanai City. There is also a unique native dryland forest, under the protection of the Nature Conservancy.

The island has no mongooses, which eat the eggs of ground-nesting birds, so introduced game birds thrive. Ring-necked pheasants, francolin and chukar partridges, quails, doves and wild turkeys are all common. However, the island has only two endemic birds remaining – the *pueo* (Hawaiian owl) and the *apapane* (native honeycreeper) – and they are scarce.

What Lanai does have is axis deer, descendants of a herd of eight brought to Molokai from India in 1868. The deer were introduced to Lanai in 1920 and are more prolific here than on Molokai, the only other Hawaiian island where they roam free; in fact, there are at least two deer for every person on Lanai. Mouflon sheep were released not long afterward and today inhabit the island's gullies and ridges. Both deer and sheep are hunted.

After a long period of decline, green sea turtles have been making a comeback in recent years, especially along Lanai's remote northeastern shore. The most abundant of the three native turtle species found in Hawaiian waters, the green sea turtle weighs upwards of 200lb at maturity.

GOVERNMENT

Lanai is part of Maui County, but control of the island is largely in the hands of Castle & Cooke, which owns all but 2% of Lanai. Beaches on Lanai, as elsewhere in Hawaii, are in the public domain.

ECONOMY

Although visitors may see 100 acres of high-profile pineapple fields, these small patches are only 'show fields' that produce for the local island market – the last commercial pineapple harvest was in 1992. Some of the former pineapple fields have been given over to forage crops and cattle raising, but the importance of agriculture and ranching is secondary at best.

Lanai's transition from a plantation economy to a tourism-oriented service economy hasn't been entirely smooth. The resorts initially mounted millions of dollars in operating losses, but occupancy rates climbed after the opening of a second golf course. Around that same time, Bill Gates, the Microsoft founder who has become the wealthiest of the world's rich and famous, selected Lanai as the site for his 1995 marriage, creating a publicity shower for the resorts, which have seen a steady growth in visitors despite slowdowns at top-end resorts elsewhere in the Hawaiian Islands.

About 80% of Lanai's 1200 workers are employed by the Lanai Company, mostly in its resort operations. Lanai's unemployment rate sits at 3.5%, which is lower than the statewide average. In the next stage of development, the company intends to build hundreds of luxury homes geared for wealthy, second-home owners who have bypassed Lanai up to now.

POPULATION & PEOPLE

Lanai has seen some dramatic rises and declines in its population. It had dropped well below 200 when Dole arrived in 1922. Filipino immigrants came to the island to work on Dole's pineapple plantation in the mid-20th century.

Lanai's current population has risen to 3000, but that's still less than it was during pineapple's heyday in the 1950s. All but a few dozen of Lanai's residents live in Lanai City. The largest single ethnic group is Filipino (45%), followed by Caucasian (13%), Japanese (8%) and part-Hawaiian (7%).

ORIENTATION

Lanai has only one town, Lanai City, which is in the center of the island. The town is laid out in a sensible grid pattern. Outside Lanai City there are only three paved roads: Keomuku Rd (Hwy 44), which heads northeast toward Shipwreck Beach; Kaumalapau Hwy (Hwy 440), which heads west to the airport and Kaumalapau Harbor; and Manele Rd (also Hwy 440), which flows south toward Manele and Hulopoe Bays.

Maps

As Lanai has so few roads and relatively few visitors, it may come as no surprise that there's no proliferation of road maps. Most will get you lost as often as not.

The University of Hawaii's handy joint *Molokai/Lanai* map shows the topography of Lanai as well as its geographical and archaeological sites. Nelles' *Maui, Molokai & Lanai* map may be less detailed, but it's certainly more user-friendly.

The Lanai Company distributes a simpler foldout map called *The Island of Lanai* that shows Lanai City, the grounds of the two resorts and the island's main roads; it can be picked up free at the hotels. Dollar Rent A Car's *Jeep Safari Drive Guide* has a basic sketch map with off-road directions to major sights, which may come in handy for mountain bikers and hikers. For free copies, stop by Lanai City Service (see Getting Around later in this chapter).

ACTIVITIES

The public recreation complex in Lanai City, which includes **Lanai Gym**, has a 75ft-long pool, a basketball court and a couple of lighted tennis courts.

Anyone looking to do some serious mountain biking on Lanai should buy a copy of *Mountain Biking the Hawaiian Islands* by John Alford. The island offers plenty of dirt roads and trails, from beginner to advanced, but expect challenging hills, strong winds and heat.

Lanai Ecoadventure Centre (☎ *565-7737;* W *www.kayakhawaii.com; 338 8th St; half-day/full-day tours $69/119)*, based in Lanai City, offers kayaking and snorkeling tours and mountain biking adventures along the Munro Trail. It also rents kayaks, snorkel and scuba gear, camping equipment and mountain bikes (from $25 per day).

Cavendish Golf Course, a local nine-hole course on the north side of Lanai City, is the only free golf course in Hawaii and a popular recreation spot for islanders. Anyone can play; simply bring your clubs and begin. There are no dress codes and no fees, though there is a donation box where visitors can make an anonymous offering.

The Lodge at Koele and the Manele Bay Hotel offer a variety of activities, including tennis, horseback riding and scuba diving. Fees are generally quite high, and many activities are limited to hotel guests.

Both resorts also have 18-hole designer golf courses, complete with dress codes and green fees topping out at $200 for nonguests, cart included. The **Challenge at Manele** (☎ *565-2222)* waterfront course was judged brutal but rewarding by Jack Nicklaus.

Muddy Lanai

Most roads on Lanai are dirt roads, many of them built to service the pineapple fields of yesteryear; their conditions vary from good to impassable, largely depending on the weather.

If you rent a 4WD vehicle and plan to travel these roads, ask the rental agency which are currently the best routes to out-of-the-way sights – often there are a few alternatives, and agents know which roads are washed out and which are passable. If you do go off the beaten path and get stuck, it can be a long walk back to town, and you can expect to pay an exorbitant amount in towing and repair fees.

Designed in part by Greg Norman, the **Experience at Koele** *(☎ 565-4653)* sprawls below the mountains. It can prove equally challenging – it once took Nicklaus eight shots just to get off the 17th tee.

GETTING THERE & AWAY

Almost everyone takes the ferry to Lanai – it's possible to spot whales during winter – but you can also fly there. For information on ferry schedules, discounted flight tickets, commuter airlines and air passes, see the Getting Around chapter.

Lanai airport (LNY) is about 3½ miles southwest of Lanai City. **Island Air** *(☎ 800-652-6541)* flies to Lanai from Honolulu six times a day and from Kahului on Maui once daily. **Hawaiian Airlines** *(☎ 800-882-8811)* flies to Lanai nonstop from Honolulu once a day on weekdays, twice daily on weekends, and from Molokai a few times per week. You can also fly between Lanai and any other island, with connections via Honolulu.

GETTING AROUND

Lanai's real adventures start on its 4WD trails, since a standard car will only get you to a few places around the island. Hitching is not easy, except perhaps between Manele Bay and Lanai City, but Lonely Planet can't recommend it because of the potential dangers.

Shuttle

Both resorts have shuttle vans that meet guests at the airport and ferry dock. The same shuttle will also drop guests off at the Hotel Lanai, though officially you're supposed to arrange this in advance. Resort shuttles run about every 30 minutes throughout the day, stopping en route at the Hotel Lanai, and operate late enough for you to catch dinner at either resort and still get back to your own hotel.

Car

Lanai City Service *(☎ 565-7227, 800-533-7808, fax 565-7087; 1036 Lanai Ave, Lanai City)* provides free transfers for car and Jeep rental customers with reservations to its in-town office, an affiliate of Dollar Rent A Car.

Lanai City Service is the only car rental company operating on Lanai. This branch of the Dollar affiliate, unlike those on other islands, requires a one-day deposit to make a booking. Compact cars rent for $60 a day, 4WD Jeep Wranglers about $120, with negotiating discounts nigh impossible.

While there are many dirt roads in fine condition, Lanai City Service restricts all its standard cars to paved roads – only the 4WD Jeeps may be driven on most dirt roads, and even then no additional insurance is available. The Jeeps are usually available on notice, but the cars can be in short supply and sometimes need to be booked more than a week in advance.

Lanai Ecoadventure Centre *(☎ 565-7737; W www.kayakhawaii.com; 338 8th St)* offers 4WD Suburbans from $129 per day.

From time to time, other rental agencies start up, so it's worth asking around.

Taxi

Rabaca's Limousine Service *(☎ 565-6670)* charges $5 per person between the airport and Lanai City and $10 per person between Manele Bay and town, with a two-person minimum. Advance reservations are a good idea; otherwise, you'll have to call to ask if someone is available to come and get you.

Lanai Ecoadventure Centre *(☎ 565-7737)* can arrange a taxi shuttle service if you want to be dropped off at a remote point on the island to explore for the day.

Lanai City

Lanai City is an old plantation town nestled among Norfolk pines, sitting on a cool central plateau beneath the slopes of Lanaihale. Many of the brightly colored houses have

LANAI CITY

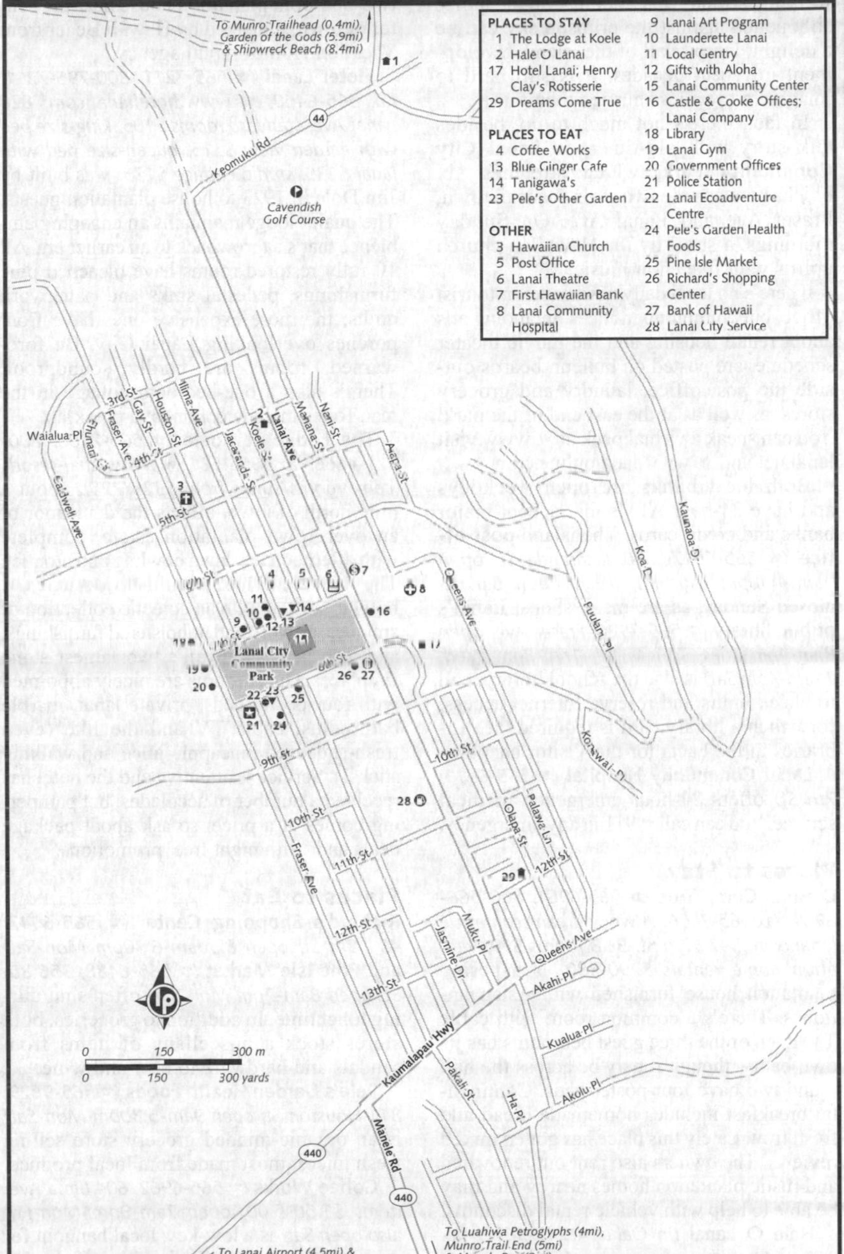
PLACES TO STAY
1 The Lodge at Koele
2 Hale O Lanai
17 Hotel Lanai; Henry Clay's Rotisserie
29 Dreams Come True
PLACES TO EAT
4 Coffee Works
13 Blue Ginger Cafe
14 Tanigawa's
23 Pele's Other Garden
OTHER
3 Hawaiian Church
5 Post Office
6 Lanai Theatre
7 First Hawaiian Bank
8 Lanai Community Hospital
9 Lanai Art Program
10 Launderette Lanai
11 Local Gentry
12 Gifts with Aloha
15 Lanai Community Center
16 Castle & Cooke Offices; Lanai Company
18 Library
19 Lanai Gym
20 Government Offices
21 Police Station
22 Lanai Ecoadventure Centre
24 Pele's Garden Health Foods
25 Pine Isle Market
26 Richard's Shopping Center
27 Bank of Hawaii
28 Lanai City Service
To Munro Trailhead (0.4mi), Garden of the Gods (5.9mi) & Shipwreck Beach (8.4mi)
44
Keomuku Rd
Cavendish Golf Course
3rd St
4th St
5th St
Waialua Pl
Fraser Ave
Gay St
Ilima Ave
Houston St
Jacaranda St
Koele St
Lanai Ave
Manana St
Nani St
Akira St
Ehnani St
Caldwell Ave
Lanai City Community Park
8th St
9th St
10th St
11th St
12th St
13th St
Queens Ave
Koa Ct
Kaunaoa Dr
Puulani Pl
Konawai Pl
Palawa Ln
Olapa St
Jasmine Dr
Nuku Pl
Akahi Pl
Kualua Pl
Akolu Pl
Pakali St
Ha Pl
Kaumalapau Hwy
Manele Rd
440
0 150 300 m
0 150 300 yards
To Luahiwa Petroglyphs (4mi), Munro Trail End (5mi) & Manele Bay (8mi)
To Lanai Airport (4.5mi) & Kaumalapau Harbor (7.5mi)

flowering front gardens. At sunset, just walking around and looking at the pines silhouetted against the crimson sky can be a delight. Despite all of the island development in recent decades, it is still hard to imagine a town less hurried than this.

In fact, there's not much to do, besides talk story with old-timers in **Lanai City Community Park**, which stretches six blocks between the two main roads in town, Fraser Ave and Lanai Ave. On Sunday mornings, a stroll by the **Hawaiian church** uplifts with fine choir music.

There's no local daily newspaper or tourist office, but community notices, including ads about rental housing and the movie theater schedule, are posted on bulletin boards outside the post office, laundry and grocery stores, as well as at the east end of the park. You can sneak a virtual peek at **W** www.visitlanai.net and **W** www.lanaionline.com.

Both local **banks** are open weekdays and have 24-hour ATMs that accept major banks and credit cards. The island **post office** *(☎ 565-6517; 620 Jacaranda St; open 9am-4:30pm Mon-Fri, 10am-noon Sat)* is closed Sunday, as are many shops. Lanai's **public library** *(☎ 565-7920; Fraser Ave; open 8am-4pm Tues, Thur & Fri, 1pm-8pm Wed, 11am-4pm Sat)* is also the school library; call to check hours and reserve Internet access, for which a library card is required (see Libraries in the Facts for the Visitor chapter).

Lanai Community Hospital *(☎ 565-6411; 7th St)* offers 24-hour emergency medical service. You can call ☎ 911 in any emergency.

Places to Stay

Dreams Come True *(☎ 565-6961, 800-566-6961, fax 565-7056; **W** www.dreamscometruelanai.com; 547 12th St; B&B rooms $99, vacation home rentals $290-380)* is a period plantation house furnished with Asian antiques. There's a common room with cable TV. Each of the three guest bedrooms has its own bath – though it may be across the hall – and two have four-poster beds. Continental breakfast includes homemade bread and fresh fruit. Lately this place has gotten mixed reviews. The owners also rent out renovated and rustic plantation homes nearby and may be able to help with vehicle rental discounts.

Hale O Lanai *(in Oahu ☎ 247-3637, fax 235-2644; **W** www.hotspots.hawaii.com/beach rent1.html; 405 Lanai Ave; rooms per night/week from $115/585)* is a simple two-bedroom plantation house near the center of town, managed by Hawaii Beachfront Vacation Homes rental agency.

Hotel Lanai *(☎ 565-7211, 800-795-7211, fax 565-6450; **W** www.hotellanai.com; 828 Lanai Ave; standard rooms $105, king-size bed with garden view $115, queen-size bed with lanai $135, studio cottage $175)* was built by Jim Dole in 1923 to house plantation guests. The quaint lodge maintains an engaging ambience that's a throwback to an earlier era. All 10 fully restored rooms have bleached pine furnishings, pedestal sinks and patchwork quilts; the more expensive ones have front porches overlooking Lanai City. Be forewarned: rooms are hardly soundproof. There's also a one-bedroom cottage in the rear. Rates include continental breakfast.

The Lodge at Koele *(☎ 565-7300, 800-321-4666, fax 565-4561; **W** www.lanai-resorts.com; rooms/suites from $325/725)*, about a mile north of town, affects the demeanor of an overgrown plantation estate, complete with afternoon tea, lawn bowling and croquet. The 'great hall' lobby of this low-rise resort hotel is stuffed with an eclectic collection of antiques, artwork and upholstered furnishings, and also boasts Hawaii's two largest stone fireplaces. Guest rooms are nicely appointed with four-poster beds, private lanai, marble bathrooms, cable TV and the like (even fresh-squeezed pineapple juice and walking sticks!). Service is attentive and the hotel has received a number of accolades, but pampering comes at a price, so ask about package deals and 'fifth night free' promotions.

Places to Eat

Richard's Shopping Center *(☎ 565-6047; 434 8th St; open 8:30am-6:30pm Mon-Sat)* and **Pine Isle Market** *(☎ 565-6488; 356 8th St; open 8am-7pm Mon-Sat)* often shut during lunchtime. In addition to groceries, both stores stock a miscellany of items from sandals and hardware to beer and wine.

Pele's Garden Health Foods *(☎ 565-9629; 811 Houston St; open 9am-5:30pm Mon-Sat)* is an organic-minded grocery store selling fresh juices, most made from local produce.

Coffee Works *(☎ 565-6962; 604 Ilima Ave; items $1.50-5.00; open 7am-9pm Mon-Fri, also open Sat)* is a low-key, local hangout for darn good java and Thai iced coffee, plus homemade croissants, muffins and soups.

Blue Ginger Cafe *(☎ 565-6363; 409 7th St; breakfast & lunch $5-8, dinner $10-15; open 6am-8pm daily)* dishes up three square meals a day. It's an unpretentious little bakery-café with cement floors and plastic chairs. At dinner, daily specials might feature shrimp tempura or fresh mahimahi.

Tanigawa's *(☎ 565-6537; 419 7th St; breakfast & lunch $6; open 6:30am-1pm Thur-Tues)* has the most popular burgers on Lanai – you can get one with the works for a mere $3. At the old-style counter you can sit over coffee and watch the bacon sizzle on the grill.

Pele's Other Garden *(☎ 565-9628, 888-764-3354; cnr 8th St & Houston St; lunch $5-8, dinner $10-16; open 9:30am-3pm & 5pm-9pm Mon-Sat)* is an aromatic combination of an Italian deli, pizzeria and bistro. There are even café tables on the front porch where you can sit and watch the Lanai City traffic trickle by. Picnic baskets are available to go.

Henry Clay's Rotisserie *(☎ 565-4700; mains $19-29; open 5:30pm-9pm daily)*, at the Hotel Lanai, is the island's most bustling dinner spot. Here the chef shows off his New Orleans roots, with memorable dishes such as Creole eggplant angel-hair pasta. The refined dining room has a fireplace, high ceilings and hardwood floors, while gourmet pizzas are available as take-out. The bar stays open until midnight as long as there are customers.

Terrace Dining Room *(breakfast & lunch $10-15, dinner around $30; open 7am-9:30pm daily, high tea 3pm-4:45pm)*, at The Lodge at Koele, is a lobby-side restaurant that overlooks the hotel gardens. Breakfast menu items include blue crab cakes with blood-orange hollandaise and scrambled eggs with lobster and mascarpone cheese. There are lunchtime salads and sandwiches, and dinner features grilled seafood main courses.

Formal Dining Room *(at The Lodge at Koele; mains $40-45; open 6:30pm-9:30pm nightly)* is the most highly rated restaurant on Lanai. Expect à la carte entrees such as seared Hawaiian snapper with gingered crab, corn-and-mushroom risotto, Maine lobster, or venison from Lanai axis deer. While prices are steep, the food and service generally live up to the bill, with muumuu-clad hostesses and candlelight. As the name implies, a jacket is required of men, but one can be borrowed from the front desk.

Entertainment

People go to bed early in Lanai, and there's no real nightlife, although **The Lodge at Koele** usually has mellow Hawaiian music in its lobby every evening from 7pm until 10pm. The hotel also hosts a **visiting artists programme** featuring writers, musicians and famous chefs.

Lanai Theatre *(☎ 565-7500; 7th St; adult/concession $7/4.50)*, the island's cozy little movie theater, shows first-run feature films a few nights per week.

Shopping

Gifts with Aloha *(☎ 565-6589; 363 7th St)* carries locally handcrafted jewelry, wood-carvings, photographic prints and all kinds of island wear, including batik scarves, aloha shirts and Hawaiian-print dresses.

Local Gentry *(☎ 565-9130; 363 7th St)* is a real find, stocking handpicked clothes from around the world. Don't miss the $10 bargain treasure chest.

Lanai Art Program *(☎ 565-7503; 339 7th St)* is a community-run enterprise selling locally made arts and crafts. Hours can be a bit irregular, but you'll often find someone there during the day.

Around Lanai

MANELE ROAD

Heading south out of Lanai City, fully paved Manele Rd (Hwy 440) continues straight past the intersection with Kaumalapau Hwy (also called Hwy 440), which heads west toward the airport and Kaumalapau Harbor.

It takes 25 minutes to drive the 7½ miles to Hulopoe Beach. After about 4 miles, Manele Rd veers to the left, and a mile further, there's a pretty coastal view of both Manele Bay to the left and Hulopoe Bay to the right. The island beyond is Kahoolawe.

Further on, the highway passes the turnoff to the Manele Bay Hotel and rolls downhill to where the ferries from Maui pull in. If you arrive by boat, it's a 10-minute walk from Manele Bay to Hulopoe Beach.

Luahiwa Petroglyphs

Lanai's highest concentration of ancient petroglyphs are carved into dozens of boulders overlooking Palawai Basin. Unfortunately, many of the petroglyphs are quite weathered, although they're still better preserved than those found on Maui. Misguided visitors have further damaged them by trying to re-engrave the petroglyphs with chalk or burning sticks; one can only hope their karma suffers.

It's a little challenging to get to the Luahiwa Petroglyphs. Head south from Lanai City along Manele Rd and look for six taller pine trees on your left. Turn left here onto an unusually wide dirt road, called Hoike Rd, and head for the water tower on the ridge, taking a sharp left after the first mile. Stay on this upper road for at least a half mile until the first boulders are visible near the head of a ravine. Since the trail requires some tight maneuvering here, it might be better to park down below and walk to the petroglyphs.

Manele Harbor

Manele Harbor is a natural crescent-shaped harbor backed by sheer cliffs. Its very protected position not only provides a popular sailboat anchorage, but also makes Lanai one of the easier islands to sail to from Honolulu (although 'easy' is a relative term – the waters can be quite rough).

In the early 20th century, cattle were herded down to Manele Bay for shipment to Honolulu, and you can still see the remains of a cattle chute if you walk around the point at the end of the parking lot. Stone ruins from a Hawaiian fishing village and concrete slabs from the days of cattle ranching are up on the hill above the parking lot, though the ruins are largely overgrown with *kiawe* and *ilima* (a native plant with delicate yellow-orange flowers).

Off the parking lot are rest rooms, showers, drinking water, picnic tables and a little harbormaster's office. Lanai folks like to fish from the stone breakwater that sticks out into the mouth of the bay. Coral is abundant near the cliff sides, where the bottom quickly slopes off to about 40ft. Beyond the bay's western edge, near Puu Pehe rock, is **Cathedrals**, a popular dive site.

Hulopoe Beach

Hulopoe Beach is a gently curving white-sand beach. It's long, broad and protected by a rocky point to the south. The adjacent park has solar-heated outdoor showers, rest rooms with water fountains, picnic tables, pay phones and camp sites.

Just beyond the sandy beach, there's a low lava shelf with tide pools worth exploring and a protected splash pool. Cement steps lead down to the pool from the rocks. It looks as if all the children on Lanai rushed down to scrawl their names in the cement when it was poured in August 1951.

On the north side of the bay, the Manele Bay Hotel sits on a low seaside terrace. Even with the hotel, this is a pretty quiet beach. Generally, the most action occurs when the boats from Maui pull in with snorkelers, who usually head to the left side of Hulopoe Bay, where there are lots of colorful coral and reef fish.

Manele and Hulopoe Bays are part of a marine life conservation district, which prohibits the removal of coral and rocks and restricts many fishing activities. Water activities can be dangerous during *kona* (leeward) storms, when winds produce strong currents and swells.

Puu Pehe Cove

From Hulopoe Beach, a short path leads south to the point where Manele and Hulopoe Bays are parted, this time by a volcanic cinder cone that's sharply eroded on its southerly seaward edge. The lava has rich rust-red colors with swirls of gray and black in fascinating patterns, and its texture is

Sweetheart Rock

According to local lore, an islander named Makakehau once became jealous of his beautiful lover Pehe and he forced her to live in a secluded coastal cave, lest any other young men in the village set eyes on her. One day as he was up in the mountains fetching water, a *kona* storm suddenly blew in and by the time he rushed back down the mountain, powerful waves had swept into the cave, drowning Pehe.

Pehe's lover slipped off with her body at night and carried it out to the top of a nearshore isle, now called Puu Pehe, whereupon he erected a tomb and laid her to rest within. Immersed in grief, he then jumped into the surging waters below and was dashed back onto the rock. The islanders recovered his body, wrapped it in the tapa (bark cloth) shroud they had already prepared for Pehe and buried him in the village.

bubbly and brittle – so brittle that huge chunks of the point have broken off and fallen onto the coastal shelf below. There's also a small sea arch below the point.

Puu Pehe is the name of the cove to the left of the point as well as the sea stack just offshore. This islet has a tomblike formation on top that figures into Hawaiian legend.

Places to Stay

Camping Surprisingly, even with the luxury hotel nearby, **camping** is still allowed at six camp sites just a short stroll from Hulopoe Beach. It can get pretty noisy here, with carousing trucks driving in and out of the parking lot all night long, but the ocean-side setting is lovely. Pick up permits from the **Lanai Company** *(☎ 565-3978; registration fee $5, camp sites per person $5)* inside the Castle & Cooke office building in downtown Lanai City. Sometimes you can get permits without advance reservations if the camping ground's not full, but keep in mind that it's commonly booked up weeks in advance, especially during summer and on weekends throughout the year.

Although it's illegal, Hawaiian families just pitch their tents right on the beach.

Hotels Overlooking Hulopoe Beach, **Manele Bay Hotel** *(☎ 565 7700, 800-321-4666, fax 565-3868; Ⓦ www.manelebayhotel.com; standard rooms $350-395, ocean-view & oceanfront rooms $425-695, suites from $725)* is a Mediterranean-style luxury hotel. Its tropical lobbies are adorned with artwork, antiques and Italian marble floors. The library has leather-bound books and the central lounge has elegant sofas and a grand piano. As might be expected, guest rooms are pleasantly plantation-style, all with four-poster beds, private lanai and marble baths. Guests have a cornucopia of outdoor activities to choose from, or may simply indulge in the spa. Ask about package deals and 'fifth night free' promotions.

Places to Eat

The Manele Bay Hotel is the only dining option outside Lanai City.

Hulopoe Court *(continental/full breakfast buffet $15/22; open 7am-11am daily)* has a sumptuous breakfast buffet. You can also order à la carte, but expect to run up a similar tab. The setting has a bit of everything: high ceilings with showy chandeliers, ornate Chinese vases and a view of the ocean.

The **poolside grill** *(open 11am-5pm daily)* is the main lunch venue, with light eats such as fresh fish sandwiches and a variety of salads. The **Club House** *(open 11am-5pm daily, 5pm-9pm Thur-Mon)* at the hotel golf course has sandwiches, salads, and fish and chips ($10 to $15).

Ihilani Formal Dining Room *(appetizers $20-25, mains $35-45; open 6pm-9:30pm Tues-Sat)* is the hotel's elegant open-air venue, serving fine French-Mediterranean fare. Appetizers include lobster chowder and *ahi* carpaccio, with mains such as fresh fish, Maine lobster and local venison.

Entertainment

The cocktail lounge at The Manele Bay Hotel, **Hale Ahe Ahe**, has live music in the evenings from Tuesday to Saturday.

HIGHWAY 44 & KEOMUKU ROAD

Another well-paved road, the Keomuku Hwy (Hwy 44) heads north past The Lodge at Koele, quickly rising into the cool upland hills, where fog and cloud cover drift above pastures with grazing cattle. Along the way are impromptu overlooks, offering straight-on vistas of the undeveloped southeast shore of Molokai and its tiny islet Mokuhooniki, in great contrast to Maui's Kaanapali high-rises off to your right.

As the road gently slopes down to the coast, the scenery is punctuated by interesting rock formations sitting atop the eroded red earth, similar to those found at Garden of the Gods in northwest Lanai. Farther along, a shipwreck comes into view. After 8 miles, the paved road ends near the coast. To the left, a dirt road leads to Shipwreck Beach, while swerving right onto Keomuku Rd takes you to Keomuku Beach or, for the truly intrepid, all the way to Naha.

Shipwreck Beach

Shipwreck Beach is the name that's been given to 9 miles of Lanai's northeast shore, starting from Kahokunui at the end of Hwy 44 and stretching toward Polihau Beach on the northwest shore. True to its name, there are a couple of shipwrecks here, as well as a coastline that's good for beachcombing.

A low rock shelf lines much of the shore, so the shallow, murky waters are not great for swimming or snorkeling. A lot of driftwood, however, washes up on this windswept beach. Some of the pieces are identifiable as the sun-bleached timbers of shipwrecks – hulls, side planks, perhaps even a gangplank. There are also fishing nets, ropes and the occasional glass float from Japan.

The dirt road that heads left from the highway runs past a series of old wooden beach shacks called Federation Camp, now largely used by fisherfolk. Park here before the sand gets too deep, then walk in for about 10 minutes to the site of a former lighthouse on a lava-rock point, where only the square cement foundations remain.

It's likely to be just you and the driftwood as you walk along, the sand gradually changing colors. In some places, it's a colorful, chunky mixture of rounded shells and bits of rock that look like some sort of beach confetti. Up on the slopes, some of the beach *pohuehue* (morning glory) is entwined with a plant that looks something like yellow-orange fishing line. This is Lanai's official flower, a leafless parasitic vine called *kaunaoa*.

Petroglyphs From the lighthouse foundations, vague trail markings gesture directly inland to a cluster of fragile petroglyphs. A short, rocky path runs through ground cover of flowering pink and yellow lantana and golden *ilima*. The latter is native, while the former was introduced to Hawaii just 50 years ago and has escaped cultivation to become a major pest throughout the islands. The simple figures are etched on large boulders, just off to the right of the path.

Keep your eyes open for wild animals – sightings of mouflon sheep on the inland hills are not uncommon. The males have curled-back horns, and the more dominant ones travel with a harem.

Shipwrecks It's about 15 minutes farther up the beach to a rusting WWII **liberty ship** (cargo ship) that washed up on the reef. You can see the shipwreck clearly from the lighthouse foundations. It's possible to walk another 6 miles all the way to Awalua, but there's not much else to see besides another shipwreck. The hike is windy, hot and dry, although the farther down the beach you go, the prettier it gets.

Keomuku to Naha

Keomuku Beach is the stretch of shore that runs from Kahokunui, at the end of Hwy 44, south to Kahalepalaoa Landing. This uninhabited coast is not particularly attractive, and there's not much to see, other than a few marginal historical sites, scattered groves of coconuts and lots and lots of *kiawe*.

Keomuku Rd, the dirt road that heads right from the highway, is likely to be either dusty or muddy, with deep ruts, though if you catch it after it's been graded, it's not so bad. Still, it is a 4WD road, particularly the stretch beyond the landing. Going the full 12 miles down to Naha, at the end of the road, can take as long as two hours one way when the road is rough, half of that when conditions are better.

Less than a mile down the road, southeast of Hwy 44, is **Maunalei**. An ancient *heiau* (temple) that once sat there was taken apart by Frederick Hayselden, who used its stones to build a cattle fence. Soon after, he lost his shirt in the ill-fated Maunalei Sugar Company – islanders believed it was the temple desecration that had caused the wells to turn salty and kill off the sugarcane Hayselden and his wife had planted.

Another 4 miles further, **Keomuku** was the center of Hayselden's short-lived sugarcane plantation. There's little left to see other than the reconstructed **Ka Lanakila o Ka Malamalama Church**, originally built in 1903 after Maunalei Sugar collapsed. The ruins of a couple of **fishponds** lie along the coast, but they're not easily visible.

Another *heiau* at **Kahea**, 1½ miles south of Keomuku, was also dismantled by Maunalei Sugar Company, this time to build a railroad to transport the sugar to Kahalepalaoa Landing. Kahea, meaning 'red stains,' was a *luakini* (temple), where human sacrifices were made.

Kahalepalaoa Landing, just south of Kahea, has the best beach on this end of the island – a popular destination for day outings from Maui. Just before reaching the fence that tells you this is a private beach, look for a **Buddhist cemetery** on the *mauka* (inland) side of the highway.

From here the road to **Naha** really doesn't offer much more scenery for the effort, but should you want to continue, it's about 4 miles farther. Naha is occasionally used by local fishers but is not a good place for swimming.

NORTHWEST LANAI

Clearly marked by etched rocks reading 'Garden of the Gods,' the well-traveled dirt road into northwest Lanai starts north of Lanai City, just past The Lodge at Koele, reached by turning left between the tennis courts and stables, then following the signs through former pineapple fields. The section of road leading straight through Kanepuu Preserve up to the Garden of the Gods is a fairly good, albeit dusty, route that usually takes about 20 minutes from town. To travel onward to Polihua Beach is another matter, however; the road down to the beach is rocky and narrow and is suitable only for a 4WD. Depending on when the road was last graded, the trip could take anywhere from 20 minutes to an hour.

Kanepuu Preserve

About 5 miles northwest of Lanai City, this diverse native dryland forest is the last of its kind in all of Hawaii. Although Castle & Cooke retains title to the land, it has granted the Nature Conservancy an easement to the 590-acre forest in perpetuity. Native plants here include *iliahi* (Hawaiian sandalwood), *olopua* (olive), *lama* (in the persimmon family), a native gardenia and fragrant vines of *maile*. You'll glimpse many of them on the brief self-guided interpretive walk leading off to your right.

Native dryland forests once covered 80% of Lanai and were also common on the leeward slopes of other Hawaiian islands, but feral goats and cattle made a feast of the foliage. Credit for saving this ecosystem goes to naturalist and former ranch manager George Munro, who fenced hoofed animals out in the 1920s.

Garden of the Gods

There's no garden at the dry Garden of the Gods, but rather a largely barren landscape of strange wind-sculpted rocks in rich shades of ocher, pink and sienna. The colors change with the light, looking pastel in the early morning and late afternoon. How godly the garden appears depends on who's looking. Some people just see rocks, while others find the formations hauntingly beautiful.

Polihua Beach

On the northwestern tip of the island, Polihau is a broad, 1½-mile-long white-sand beach. Although it's gorgeous, strong winds kicking up the sand and insects often make it uncomfortable, and water conditions are treacherous year-round.

Polihua means 'eggs in the bosom' and refers to the green sea turtles that used to nest here en masse. After a long hiatus, the now-endangered turtles are beginning to return. Be careful not to approach or otherwise disturb them, as they are highly sensitive creatures.

MUNRO TRAIL

The completely overhauled Munro Trail is an exhilarating 8½-mile adventure that can be hiked, mountain biked or negotiated in a 4WD vehicle. The trail is named after naturalist George Munro, who planted the trees both here and elsewhere around Lanai in order to provide an island watershed. He selected species that draw moisture from the clouds and fog, both of which are fairly common in the high country (more so in the afternoon than in the morning).

Those making the journey under their own steam should be prepared for steep grades and allow all day. If you're driving and the dirt road has been graded recently, it takes at least three hours. However, be aware that the road can become very muddy (particularly in winter and after heavy rainstorms) and Jeeps often get stuck. It's best to consider this as a fair-weather outing only. Drivers also need to watch out for sheer drops.

To start the trail, head north on Hwy 44, the road to Shipwreck Beach. About a mile past The Lodge at Koele, turn right onto a paved road lined with Norfolk pines, which ends in half a mile at a cemetery with gravestones in Japanese and Pilipino. Mourners have placed sake offerings, pinwheels and toys at some of the burial sites. The **Koloiki Ridge Trail**, a 5-mile hiking nature trail, begins here. Try asking the lodge information desk for a trail map.

Back on the Munro Trail, just follow the signs from the cemetery as it passes through sections planted with eucalyptus and climbs up along the ridge, where the path is draped with ferns and studded with Norfolk pines. Before the Munro Trail was upgraded to a dirt road, it was a footpath. It's along this trail that islanders tried to hide from Kamehameha the Great when he went on a rampage in 1778. Hookio Battleground, where Lanaians made their last stand, is just above Hookio Gulch, about 2½ miles from the start of the trail.

The trail also looks down upon a series of deep ravines that cut across the eastern flank of the mountain, and it passes Lanaihale, which at 3370ft is the highest point on Lanai. On a clear day, you can see all of the inhabited Hawaiian Islands except Kauai and Niihau from various points along the route. Do not stray off the main trail as it descends for 6 miles onto the central plateau. Keep the hills to your left and turn right at the big fork in the road. Once you hit the cattle grate, pavement is not far away. The trail ends back on Manele Rd (Hwy 440).

SOUTHWEST COAST

Kaumalapau Harbor

Kaumalapau, Lanai's commercial harbor, is approximately 7 miles west of Lanai City. Do not confuse Kaumalapau Hwy (Hwy 440), which heads west out of town past the airport access road to the harbor, with Manele Rd (also Hwy 440), which leads south to Manele Bay.

Kaumalapau Harbor was built for shipping pineapples; now that the industry is gone, it's a rather sleepy place. These days, the main traffic here is the cargo boat that arrives weekly from Oahu. You can often find people fishing from the boulder jetty for *awa* (milkfish), a tasty fish that's a common catch in the bay. Scuba divers sometimes use the bay as well, as the deep waters at Kaumalapau are extremely clear. As along most of the southwest coast, Kaumalapau has sheer coastal cliffs.

Kaunolu

This was the site of an early Hawaiian fishing village that was abandoned in the mid-19th century. It was a favorite vacation spot of Kamehameha the Great, who came here to fish the prolific waters of Kaunolu Bay, separated by Kaunolu Gulch.

Kaunolu boasts the greatest concentration of ruins on Lanai, but these days most of the sites are simply too overgrown with *kiawe* to be recognizable. Most of the house foundations sit on the eastern side of the bay. The now obscured **Halulu Heiau**, on the western side, once dominated the whole scene. The temple included a *puuhonua* (place of refuge), where renegade *kapu* (taboo) breakers could be absolved from their death sentences. There are a number of petroglyphs, including some on the southern side of the *heiau*.

Beyond the *heiau* ruins, the Palikaholo sea cliffs rise more than 1000ft. Northwest of the *heiau,* there's a high natural stone wall along the perimeter of the cliff. Look for a break in the wall at the cliff's edge, where there's a sheer 90ft drop. This is **Kahekili's Jump**, named after a high-ranking Hawaiian chief. There's a ledge below it that makes diving into the ocean here a bit death-defying. Apparently, Kamehameha used to amuse himself by making upstart warriors leap from this cliff. More recently, it has been the site of the world-class Red Bull cliff-diving championships.

There are a couple of ways to get to Kaunolu, but all make it nearly impossible to find. Be sure to take lots of water with you and fill up on gas. The easiest way is to follow the Kaumalapau Hwy (Hwy 440) past the airport, turning left at your first opportunity onto a pot-holed dirt road that circles around the south side of the airport. The turnoff to the Kaunolu Trail is usually marked with a painted water pipe, so turn left onto this dirt road, which leads south in the direction of the Palaloa lighthouse. If the road hasn't been washed out by rain recently, you may be able to make it most of the way down with a 4WD vehicle, but odds are you'll have to walk the last mile or so.

Another way to get there is by heading south from Lanai City on Manele Rd (Hwy 440). Three-quarters of a mile past the 9-mile marker, there's a sharp bend in the road. Rather than following the highway left toward Manele Bay, go straight ahead onto an private access road that begins as pavement but soon turns to dirt, then look for the dang water pipe. Either way, you'll end up navigating largely on instinct.

Kahoolawe

Kahoolawe, the uninhabited island 7 miles off the southwest coast of Maui, was used by the US military as a bombing target from WWII until 1990. Although the bombing has now stopped, the island remains off limits because of the stray ammunition that peppers Kahoolawe and its surrounding waters.

Kahoolawe played an important role in Hawaiian history. The channel between Lanai and Kahoolawe, as well as the westernmost point of Kahoolawe itself, is named Kealaikahiki, meaning 'pathway to Tahiti.' When early Polynesian voyagers made the journey between Hawaii and Tahiti, they lined up their canoes at this departure point

More than 500 archaeological sites have been identified on Kahoolawe. They include several *heiaus* (temples) and many koa (native hardwood) shrines and *kuula* (fishing shrine) stones dedicated to the gods of fishers. Puu Moiwi, a large cinder cone in the center of the island, contains one of Hawaii's largest ancient adze quarries.

In 1981 Kahoolawe was added to the National Register of Historic Places as a significant archaeological area. For nearly a decade, the island had the ironic distinction of being the only such historic place that was being used by its government for bombing target practice.

Kahoolawe has now become a symbol of the separation of native Hawaiians from their land and is a focal point in the growing Hawaiian rights movement.

HISTORY

Prisoners & Opium

Since ancient times, Kahoolawe has been under the rule of Maui.

From 1830 to 1848, Kaulana Bay, on the island's northern side, served as a place of exile for Maui men accused of petty crimes. (Female outcasts were sent to Kaena Point on the northwestern tip of Lanai.)

Kahoolawe proved to be less of a 'prison isle' than intended. In 1841, some of the prisoners managed to swim to the Makena area of Maui, where they stole both food and canoes and paddled back with their booty. Later raids included a journey to Lanai, where the men picked up female prisoners and brought them back to Kahoolawe.

Kahoolawe's secluded southwestern side was used for decades by smugglers importing Chinese opium. To avoid detection, they would unload their caches at Hanakanaea Bay (commonly known as Smugglers Bay) on arrival from China and then simply return later in small fishing boats to pick up the illicit goods.

In more recent times, Smugglers Bay was the site of a US military base camp.

Agriculture

Kahoolawe was once a green and forested island. It is now largely barren, and *pili* grass (bunchgrass) and *kiawe* trees (common trees with branches covered in thorns) are the main forces in keeping the dry red soil from blowing away completely.

RC Wyllie, the Scotsman who developed a sugar plantation at Princeville on Kauai, made the first attempt at ranching in 1858. Wyllie leased the entire island of Kahoolawe from the territory of Hawaii, but the sheep he brought over were diseased and the venture failed. Those sheep that survived were left to roam freely, causing serious damage to native plants.

Over the years, the territory granted a series of leases to other ranchers. Cattle were first brought over around 1880, and sheep were also tried again. Land mismanagement was the order of the day.

By the early 1900s feral goats, pigs and sheep had dug up, rooted out and chewed off so much of Kahoolawe's vegetation that the island was largely a dust bowl.

Kahoolawe Ranch

Angus MacPhee, the former manager of Maui's Ulupalakua Ranch, ran Kahoolawe's most successful ranching operation, which lasted from 1918 to 1941.

When MacPhee got his lease from the territorial government in 1918, Kahoolawe was overrun with goats and looked like a wasteland. MacPhee rounded up 13,000 goats, which he sold on Maui, and built a fence across the width of the entire island to keep the remaining goats at one end. He then brought in large redwood tanks to store water and planted grasses and ground cover. Once the land was again green, MacPhee

KAHOOLAWE

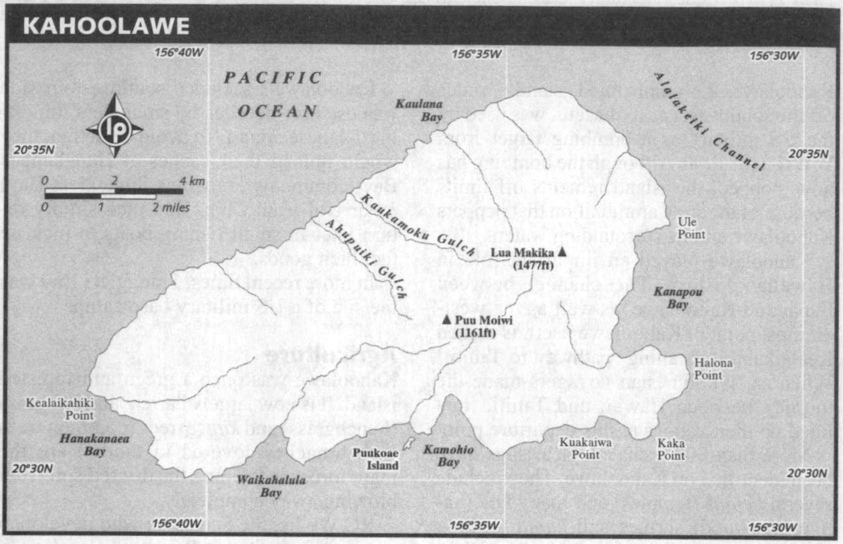

created Kahoolawe Ranch Company in partnership with Harry Baldwin, a sugar plantation owner. Cattle were brought over and raised for the Honolulu market. Ranching Kahoolawe was not easy, but MacPhee, unlike his predecessors, was able to make it profitable.

Inez MacPhee Ashdown, Angus' daughter, has written her story in *Kahoolawe* (Topgallant Publishing Co, Honolulu, 1979). The book includes legends of Kahoolawe, as told to her by native Hawaiians, as well as the ranch's history.

A Bombing Target

In 1939 Kahoolawe Ranch subleased part of the island to the US army for bombing practice and moved the cattle and ranch hands over to Maui.

Following the attack on Pearl Harbor in 1941, the US military took control over all of Kahoolawe and began bombing the entire island. Ranch buildings and water cisterns were used as targets, reducing them to rubble.

Of all the fighting that took place during WWII, Kahoolawe was the most bombed island in the Pacific – even though the 'enemy' never fired upon it.

After the war, civilians were forbidden to return to Kahoolawe; MacPhee was never compensated for his losses.

In 1953 a presidential decree gave the US navy official jurisdiction over Kahoolawe, with the stipulation that when Kahoolawe was no longer 'needed,' the live ammunition would be removed and the island would be returned to the territory of Hawaii.

Kahoolawe Movement

In the mid-1960s Hawaii politicians began petitioning the federal government to cease its military activities and return Kahoolawe to the state of Hawaii. In 1976 a small group of Hawaiians set out in boats and occupied the island in an attempt to attract greater attention to the bombings. There were a series of occupations, some lasting more than a month.

During one of the 1977 crossings, group members George Helm and Kimo Mitchell mysteriously disappeared in the waters off Kahoolawe. Helm had been an inspirational Hawaiian-rights activist, and with his death the Protect Kahoolawe Ohana movement sprang up. Helm's vision of turning Kahoolawe into a sanctuary of Hawaiian culture and identity became widespread among islanders. In June 1977, two group members, Walter Ritte Jr and Richard Sawyer, were tried for trespassing on Kahoolawe and sentenced to six months in jail.

In a letter to President Jimmy Carter asking that the two men be pardoned, Daniel Inouye, US senator from Hawaii, wrote:

It was a form of protest against, what was to them, the unconscionable desecration of the land by the Navy's continued bombing of Kahoolawe. *Aloha aina*, love for the land, is an important part of the Native Hawaiian religion and culture.... Kahoolawe has become a symbol of the resurgence of the Hawaiian people, a movement formulating for many Hawaiians a renewed respect for their culture and their history.

Kahoolawe Today

In 1980 in a court-sanctioned consent decree, the navy reached an agreement with Protect Kahoolawe Ohana that allowed the Ohana regular access to the island. The decree also required the Navy to preserve archaeological sites, eradicate goats and control soil erosion.

Although the bombing continued, the decree restricted the navy from using live munitions on part of the island and from bombing historic sites. In 1982 the Ohana began to go to Kahoolawe to celebrate *makahiki*, the annual observance that honors Lono, god of agriculture and peace.

In 1982, Maui County, of which Kahoolawe is part, adopted a planning document calling for a 20-year phaseout of the military and the development of Kahoolawe as a historical and cultural site, with Protect Kahoolawe Ohana as the steward of the land. The navy refused to recognize the document.

In what many Hawaiians saw as the ultimate insult to their heritage, the US military offered Kahoolawe as a bombing target to foreign nations during biennial Pacific Rim exercises. But in an unanticipated backlash against the military, the exercises brought recognition of what was happening in Kahoolawe into a broader arena. An international movement against the bombing, led by both environmentalist and union groups in New Zealand, Australia, Japan and the UK, resulted in those countries withdrawing from the Kahoolawe exercises. With only the US and Canada willing to participate, the plan was scrapped.

In the late 1980s Hawaii's first native Hawaiian governor, John Waihee, and other state politicians became more outspoken in their demands that Kahoolawe be returned to Hawaiians. In October 1990, as Hawaii's two US senators, Daniel Inouye and Daniel Akaka, were preparing a congressional bill to stop the bombing, President George Bush issued an order to halt military activities. The senators' bill, which became law the next month, required the island to be cleared of munitions and restored to a prewar condition. It also established a federally funded Kahoolawe Conveyance Commission to prepare recommendations on terms for the transfer of the island to the state of Hawaii.

On May 7, 1994, in a ceremony marked by Hawaiian rituals, chants and prayers, the US navy signed over control of Kahoolawe to Governor Waihee and the state of Hawaii. Following the signing, 100 native Hawaiians, dressed in traditional *malos* (loincloths) and *tapa* (bark-cloth) cloaks, went to Kahoolawe to perform sunrise rituals honoring the return of the island. Among the ceremonies was the placing of leis at memorial plaques for Helm and Mitchell.

One enormous obstacle that remains is the cleaning up of live munitions from the island. The federal government has established a $400 million fund for that purpose, but the cleanup now underway will take years to complete. In the meantime, a state entity, the **Kahoolawe Island Reserve Commission** (W *www.state.hi.us/kirc*), has taken over administration of the island and is still in the process of developing a long-term master plan. Proposals for the island's future range from establishing a marine sanctuary to making the island the center for a new Hawaiian nation.

GEOGRAPHY

Kahoolawe is 11 miles long and 6 miles wide, with a land area of 45 sq miles. With the help of a vivid imagination, its shape can be seen as a crouching lion facing eastward.

A ridge runs diagonally across the island, and the terrain is gently sloping. The highest point is the 1477-foot Lua Makika, at the site of the caldera that formed the island. Kahoolawe is a dry, arid island with only 10 to 20 inches of rainfall annually.

Because of the red dust in the air, Kahoolawe often appears to have a pink tinge when viewed from Maui, particularly in the afternoons, when the breezes pick up. At night, it's pitch black.

GETTING THERE & AWAY

There's no public access to the island unless you're a member or guest of **Protect Kahoolawe Ohana** (W *www.kahoolawe.org*). The organization visits the island for a couple of days a month, usually near the full moon, to clean up historic sites and work on revegetation projects, watering plants, pruning dead wood and the like. The Ohana welcomes volunteers, and you can learn more about its projects on its website.

Two weekends every month, offshore waters 20 fathoms (120ft) deep or deeper are open to local fishers, but at all other times boats are prohibited from going within 2 miles of Kahoolawe. As the island and its nearshore waters are still dangerous, because of unexploded ammunition, shoreline access is expected to remain off limits to the public until the cleanup is finally completed, which may still be years away.

Kauai

If you want to revel in some of the lushest scenery on earth, Kauai is an unbeatable destination – the island is so richly green that it's nicknamed 'The Garden Island.' Ever since Elvis made the island famous in *Blue Hawaii*, Kauai has been a prime destination for honeymooners looking for that perfect paradisiacal setting. It's also a perennial favorite of backpackers, who are hot to hit its challenging trails and take advantage of some of the best beachside camping grounds in all of Hawaii.

Kauai is the oldest of the main Hawaiian islands and arose from the sea as a high, smooth island. Over time, heavy rains have eroded deep valleys, while pounding waves and falling sea levels have cut steep cliffs.

The island's central volcanic peak, Mt Waialeale (5148ft), is the wettest place on earth and feeds seven rivers, including Hawaii's only navigable one. A deep north–south rift slices the western end of the island, creating the impressive Waimea Canyon, which is so immense it's commonly dubbed the 'Grand Canyon of the Pacific.'

The North Shore is lush and mountainous, with waterfalls, beautiful beaches and stream-fed valleys. The northwest coast is lined by the steeply fluted Na Pali sea cliffs, Hawaii's foremost hiking destination.

Moviemakers looking for scenery bordering on fantasy have often found it in Kauai. The classic films *South Pacific* and *Raiders of the Lost Ark* were both filmed on Kauai's North Shore. The remote Honopu Valley on the Na Pali Coast was the jungle home of King Kong, while both the Hanapepe and Lawai Valleys served as locations for Steven Spielberg's *Jurassic Park*.

Kauai is the least developed of the four major islands, and most of its interior is made up of mountainous forest reserve. On a plateau below rainy Mt Waialeale sits the Alakai Swamp, where clouds and mist rarely lift, supporting a unique ecosystem where trees grow knee high and rare native birds thrive.

But don't think all of Kauai is thick with rain forest. Kauai's southern and western sides are dry and sunny with long stretches of white-sand beaches that are ideal for sunbathing and water sports.

Highlights

- Trekking along the dramatic cliffs of the Na Pali Coast
- Soaking up rays at Poipu's sunny resorts
- Kayaking down quiet, meandering rivers
- Sighting rare seabirds at Kilauea Point
- Gazing into the deep chasms of Waimea Canyon

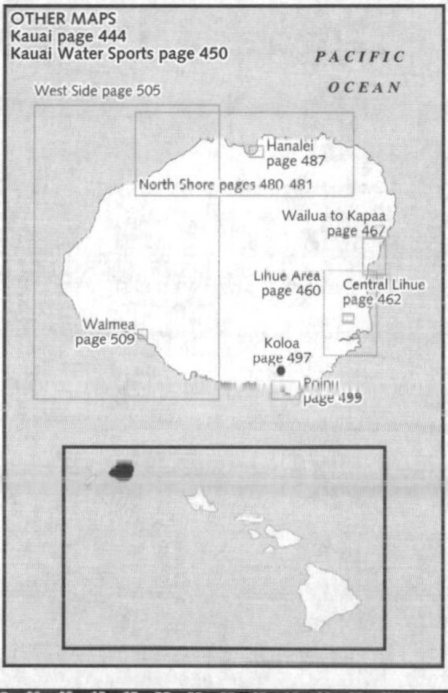

HISTORY

Kauai was probably settled between AD 500 and 700 by Polynesians who migrated from the Marquesas Islands. Archaeological finds, including a type of ring-shaped poi-pounding stone found both in Kauai and the Marquesas, support the connection.

While Hawaiian lore makes no direct references to the Marquesan culture, Kauai is often referred to as the home of a race of little people called *menehune*. Legend after legend tells of happy, Disney-like elves coming down from the mountains to produce great engineering works in stone.

It seems likely that when the first wave of Tahitians arrived in about AD 1000, they conquered and subjugated the Marquesans,

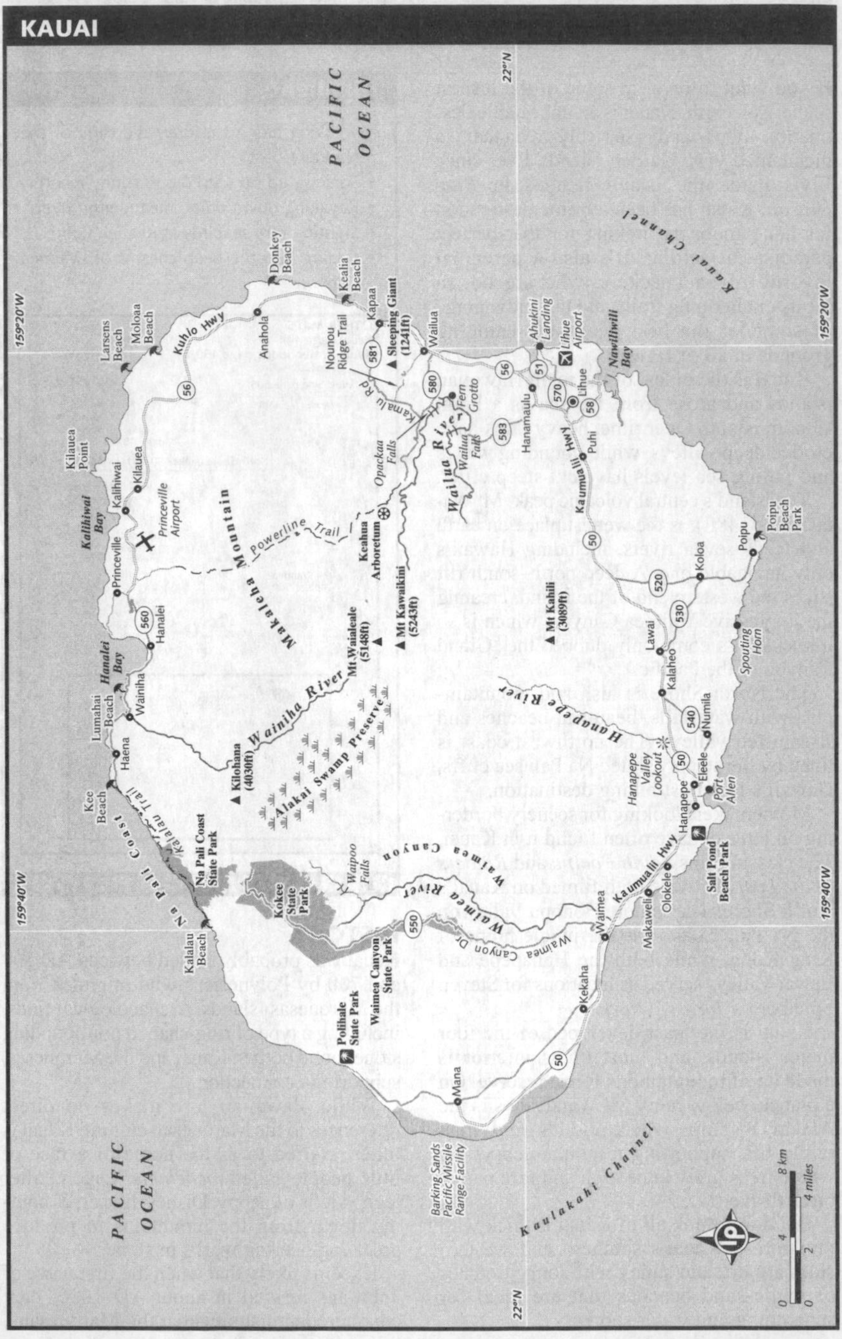
KAUAI
PACIFIC OCEAN
PACIFIC OCEAN
22°N
22°N
159°20'W
159°20'W
159°40'W
159°40'W
Kauai Channel
Kaulakahi Channel
Kilauea Point
Larsens Beach
Moloaa Beach
Kuhio Hwy
Donkey Beach
Kealia Beach
Anahola
Kapaa
Nounou Ridge Trail
Sleeping Giant (1241ft)
Wailua
Kamalu Rd
Fern Grotto
Wailua Falls
Wailua River
Ahukini Landing
Lihue Airport
Lihue
Hanamaulu
Nawiliwili Bay
Kaumualii Hwy
Puhi
Opaekaa Falls
Keahua Arboretum
Kalihiwai Bay
Kalihiwai
Kilauea
Princeville Airport
Princeville
Powerline Trail
Makaleha Mountain
Hanalei
Hanalei Bay
Wainiha
Lumahai Beach
Haena
Kee Beach
Kalalau Trail
Na Pali Coast
Na Pali Coast State Park
Kalalau Beach
Kilohana (4030ft)
Wainiha River
Mt Waialeale (5148ft)
Mt Kawaikini (5243ft)
Mt Kahili (3089ft)
Alakai Swamp Preserve
Waipoo Falls
Waimea Canyon
Kokee State Park
Waimea River
Waimea Canyon Dr
Waimea Canyon State Park
Polihale State Park
Waimea
Kekaha
Mana
Barking Sands Pacific Missile Range Facility
Makaweli
Olokele
Salt Pond Beach Park
Hanapepe
Hanapepe Valley Lookout
Hanapepe River
Port Allen
Eleele
Numila
Kalaheo
Lawai
Koloa
Poipu
Poipu Beach Park
Spouting Horn
56
560
581
580
583
570
51
58
50
520
530
540
550
0 4 8 km
0 2 4 miles

forcing them to build the temples, irrigation ditches and fishponds now attributed to the *menehunes*.

The Tahitian term for 'outcast' is *manahune*. And the diminutive social status the Marquesans had in the eyes of their conquerors may have given rise to tales of a dwarf-size race.

The *menehunes* may have created the temples, but the Tahitian settlers created the legends. While the stonework remains, the true identity of Kauai's 'little people' is lost.

During a subsequent wave of Tahitian migration, around the 12th century, a high chief named Moikeha arrived at Wailua with a fleet of double-hulled canoes. There, inside the royal court, Moikeha was received by Kauai's aging *alii-nui* (high chief), Puna.

Puna gave his daughter to Moikeha in marriage, and upon Puna's death Moikeha became the *alii-nui* of Kauai. Moikeha introduced taro and sweet potatoes to Kauai and sent his son Kila back to Tahiti to fetch the *pahu hula*, a sharkskin drum essential for use in hula temples. This type of drum is still used in hula performances today.

Early Settlements

Kauai is the most isolated of the major islands, lying 72 miles from Oahu, its nearest neighbor. It was never conquered by invaders from another Hawaiian island, and its history is one of autonomy.

Kauai was settled most intensively along river valleys near the coast, such as Wailua, Waimea and Hanalei. Even valleys that were difficult to reach, like Kalalau and Nualolo on the Na Pali Coast, had sizable settlements. When winter seas prevented canoes from landing on the northern shore, trails down precipitous ridges and rope ladders provided access.

When Captain Cook landed on Kauai in 1778 he estimated the island had 50 villages and a total population of about 30,000. Missionaries in the 1820s estimated the population to be closer to 10,000. Historians tend to side with the missionaries and discredit Cook's estimates, but considering the deadly diseases Cook's men left behind, it's possible both were correct.

Kaumualii

Kaumualii was the last chief to reign over an independent Kauai. Although he was a shrewd leader and Kauai's warriors were fierce, it was apparently the power of Kaumualii's *kahunas* (priests) that protected him from the advances of Kamehameha the Great.

In 1796 Kamehameha, who had conquered all the other islands, sailed from Oahu with an armada of war canoes toward Kauai. A mysterious storm suddenly kicked up at sea, compelling him to turn back to Oahu, and he never reached Kauai's shores.

During the next few years, both Kamehameha and Kaumualii continued to prepare for war by gathering foreign weaponry and trying to ally foreign ships to their causes.

In 1804 Kamehameha and his warriors again massed on the shores of Oahu, ready to attack Kauai. However, on the eve of the invasion, an epidemic of what was probably cholera struck the island of Oahu, decimating the would-be invaders and forcing yet another delay.

While Kamehameha's numerically superior forces had Kaumualii unnerved, Kaumualii's uncanny luck had a similar effect on Kamehameha. In 1810 they reached an agreement that recognized Kaumualii as the *alii-nui* of Kauai but ceded the island of Kauai to the Kingdom of Hawaii.

It was essentially a truce, and the plotting continued with Kaumualii never fully accepting Kamehameha's ultimate authority.

Russian Presence

In January 1815 a Russian ship loaded with seal skins was wrecked off the coast near Waimea, and Kaumualii confiscated the cargo. In November, the Russian-American Company sent Georg Anton Schaeffer to retrieve the skins.

When Schaeffer arrived in Hawaii he saw opportunity in the rift between Kaumualii and Kamehameha. In Kauai he exceeded his authority by entering into an agreement with Kaumualii in which he claimed the Russians would provide a ship and military assistance for the invasion of Oahu. In return, Kaumualii offered the Russians half of Oahu plus all the sandalwood on Oahu and Kauai. In September 1816 Hawaiian laborers under Schaeffer's direction began to build forts in Waimea and Hanalei.

Later that year, when Russian naval explorer Otto von Kotzebue visited Hawaii, he informed Kamehameha that the Russian government did not endorse Schaeffer's alliance. Kamehameha, who had become tired of all the scheming, ordered Kaumualii to kick the Russians out or face the consequences. In May 1817 Schaeffer was escorted to his ship and forced to leave Kauai.

The End of a Kingdom

When Kamehameha died in 1819 he was succeeded by his son Liholiho, who didn't trust Kaumualii's loyalties any more than his father had. In 1822 Liholiho set off for Kauai in an 83ft luxury schooner he had purchased from Western traders in exchange for sandalwood.

In Kauai, Liholiho tricked Kaumualii into going out for a cruise. He then kidnapped him and took him to Oahu, where Kaumualii was forced to marry Kamehameha's widow, Kaahumanu. In the grand scheme of royal design, this served to bring Kaumualii into the fold. When Kaumualii passed away in 1824 so too did the Kingdom of Kauai.

GEOGRAPHY

Shaped like a slightly compressed ball, Kauai is 33 miles from east to west and 25 miles from north to south. The highest elevation is Mt Kawaikini, at 5243ft.

The fourth largest of the Hawaiian Islands, Kauai has an area of 558 sq miles.

Kauai arose as a single volcano, of which Mt Waialeale is the eastern rim. Trade winds blow into the deep North Shore valleys, which channel the winds up to the top of Mt Waialeale. Near the mountain's 5148ft summit, cooler temperatures cause the moisture to condense, creating the heaviest rainfall on earth.

CLIMATE

Kauai's temperature varies more with location than season. The average coastal temperatures are 70°F in February and 77°F in August. At Kalalau Beach, the temperature seldom drops below 60°F, while a few thousand feet above, at Kokee State Park, it dips into the 30s during winter nights. Kokee averages a crisp 55°F in February and 65°F in August.

Kauai's average annual rainfall is about 40 inches, but the variances are extreme. Waimea, on the southwest coast, averages 21 inches, while Princeville, in the north, averages 85 inches. And Mt Waialeale in the swampy interior averages a whopping 486 inches, the world record.

Summer trade winds keep the humidity from becoming oppressive and bring in refreshing showers.

Winter is far less predictable. It's quite possible to have fairly continuous downpours for a week at a time in midwinter. Then again, it might be all blue skies and calm seas.

The National Weather Service provides recorded **local weather information** (☎ *245-6001)* and **marine forecasts** *(☎ 245-3564)*.

Hurricane Iniki

On September 11, 1992, Hurricane Iniki, the most powerful storm to strike Hawaii in a century, made a direct hit on Kauai. Packing gusts of 165 miles per hour, Iniki felled thousands of trees and caused serious damage to an estimated 50% of the buildings on Kauai. A combination of powerful gusts and abrupt changes in atmospheric pressure caused some buildings to literally shatter, as if hit by a bomb blast. Although nearly 100 people were injured by flying debris, miraculously only two people were killed.

Even though Kauai is small and lightly populated, the total value of the damage to the island was $1.6 billion. In all, 5000 homes were damaged and 1300 were totally destroyed. Particularly hard hit were Kauai's two main resort areas – Poipu and Princeville – and some beachfront hotels had entire wings washed away by 30ft-high waves. Hotels that did survive were turned into temporary housing for aid workers and Kauai's 8000 newly homeless residents. Tourism was brought to a standstill, and it took years for the hotel industry to bounce back.

As for the natural environment, Kauai is again lushly green, and to the casual eye there's not much to indicate the hurricane ever took place. Nevertheless, some sections of the native *koa* forest have failed to recover and are now overrun by opportunistic exotic plants such as guava, blackberry and banana *poka*. In addition, a couple of Kauai's endangered native bird species have not been spotted on the island since Iniki.

FLORA & FAUNA

Kauai boasts the largest number of native bird species in Hawaii. It is the only major island free of mongoose, which prey upon the eggs of ground-nesting birds.

The greatest concentration of Kauai's native forest bird species can be found in the remote Alakai Swamp. Many of these species are endangered, some having fewer than 100 birds remaining.

The Kauai *oo*, the last of four species of Hawaiian honeyeaters, was thought to be extinct until a nest with two chicks was discovered in Alakai Swamp in 1971. However, the call of the *oo* – that of a single male – was last heard in 1987.

Alakai Swamp is unique in that it has 10 times more native birds than introduced birds. (Elsewhere in Hawaii, introduced birds outnumber the natives many times over.) Not only is the swamp inhospitable to exotic bird species, but due to its high elevation it is also one of the few places in Hawaii where mosquitoes, which transmit avian diseases, do not flourish.

The *ao*, or Newell's shearwater, is a threatened seabird with a call that sounds like a braying donkey. Though it once lived on all major Hawaiian Islands, today the *ao* nests almost exclusively in the mountains of Kauai. This rare species digs earthen burrows and lays just one egg each year. And because it flies only between dusk and dawn, the *ao* often fails to see utility wires strung across its path to the sea. Despite a forestry programme that recovers some of the birds that crash-land, hundreds of *ao* still die in this way each year.

One non-native bird you're apt to see is the *moa*, a jungle fowl that early Polynesian settlers brought to Hawaii. The colorful species of chicken now survives solely on Kauai. Not shy of people, the birds congregate in parking lots looking for handouts.

Hawaii has two native mammals. The hoary bat lives in Kokee State Park, and the Hawaiian monk seal occasionally hauls out on Kauai beaches. You'll never know where the monk seals will show up, but they don't necessarily avoid people – they sometimes appear in such heavily touristed areas as Poipu Beach Park and the Coconut Plantation beach in Wailua. When you observe these endangered creatures, give them a wide berth so as not to disturb them.

Wild pigs, goats and black-tailed deer are non-native mammals that are hunted on the island.

The most common tree in Kauai forests is the *ohia lehua*, which can be identified by its red pom-pom flowers. Koa, *kiawe* and *kukui* (candlenut) are also plentiful, along with guava trees. For more information on Hawaiian vegetation, see the Facts about Hawaii chapter.

GOVERNMENT

Kauai County is composed of the islands of Kauai and Niihau. It's governed by an elected mayor, who serves a four-year term, and a county council, whose seven members serve two-year terms.

ECONOMY

Kauai has a labor force of 30,000 and an unemployment rate of around 7%. The service industry, including hotels, accounts for 42% of all workers. It is followed by wholesale and retail trade at 22%, government at 12% and agriculture at 3%.

Sugar used to be king in the agriculture field, but it's a waning industry. With only one mill still operating, the sugar industry now cultivates about 16,000 acres on Kauai – half of what it was just a decade earlier. Other well-established crops grown commercially are guava, taro and papaya. Attempts to diversify as sugar production declines have resulted in the introduction of new crops, the most important of which is coffee – a crop that now covers some 3400 acres on the west side of Kauai.

POPULATION & PEOPLE

The population of Kauai is 58,300. People of Hawaiian and part-Hawaiian ethnicity make up 23% of Kauai's population. Those of mixed ethnicity other than part-Hawaiian comprise 20%, while Caucasians equal 26%, Filipinos 17% and Japanese 12%.

ORIENTATION

Kauai is roughly circular. A belt road runs three-quarters of the way around the island, from Kee Beach, near Haena in the north, to Polihale in the west.

Travelers arrive at the main airport in Lihue, the county capital, on the east coast. From Lihue, the road runs north past Wailua and Kapaa, continuing up to the Princeville

Resort and Hanalei before ending at the eastern edge of the Na Pali cliffs.

South of Lihue, a side road leads down to the resort beaches at Poipu, while the main road continues west to Waimea. In Waimea, one 'highway' goes west to the arid Barking Sands region and another heads north up Waimea Canyon into Kokee State Park.

Maps

The best foldout road map of the island is *Hawaii, Maui & Kauai* produced by Compass Maps and sold for $4 at bookstores and other stores around the island. That will handle most visitors' needs, but if you want to go all out, the *Ready Mapbook of Kauai* by Odyssey Publishing, a 64-page atlas sold in bookstores for $11, has even more detail, showing virtually every road and alley on Kauai.

For hiking and mountain biking, you can pick up a free foldout topographical map of Kauai at the **Division of Forestry & Wildlife office** *(3060 Eiwa St, room 306, Lihue, HI 96766)*, which shows in detail the island's network of trails. You can also request one by mail; enclose a self-addressed 9-by-12-inch manila envelope with $1.05 postage on it (no checks or cash) for addresses in the USA. For foreign addresses, include enough international reply coupons for a 3½oz letter.

INFORMATION

Tourist Offices

The **Kauai Visitors Bureau** *(☎ 245-3971; Ⓦ www.kauaivisitorsbureau.org; 4334 Rice St, Suite 101, Lihue, HI 96766)* can be visited once you arrive on the island or you can browse its website online anytime.

There's a **hotline** *(☎ 800-262-1400; open 5am-5pm Mon-Fri, 6am-2pm Sat)* that can answer visitor-related questions about Kauai. You can also call this number to request a free 'vacation planning kit.'

Be aware that the tourist office is not affiliated with the various commercial visitor information booths found in busy tourist locales. These commercial ventures are set up to sell activity packages and to lure tourists in to hear time-share sales pitches. Some of these can be quite deceptive – and if you book a tour through the agents and don't attend the time-share sales pitch, you may be charged a fee on your credit card.

Money

The two main banks on the island, the Bank of Hawaii and the First Hawaiian Bank, have branches in all major towns. ATMs can be found in many of the bank branches as well as in most grocery stores.

There are Western Union money transfer stations at Star Market in the Kukui Grove Center in Lihue and at Foodland markets in Waipouli and Princeville.

Newspapers & Magazines

Kauai's main newspaper, the *Garden Island (☎ 245-3681; Ⓦ www.kauaiworld.com; 3137 Kuhio Hwy, Lihue, HI 96766)* publishes daily and is sold at stores throughout the island.

Free tourist magazines such as *This Week Kauai*, *Spotlight's Kauai Gold* and *101 Things to Do* can be picked up at the airport, hotels and major shopping centers. All are loaded with ads and activity information. Also worth picking up is the free *Menu Magazine*, which prints menus of many of Kauai's restaurants.

Kauai Magazine, a full-color quarterly magazine with articles about island life and attractions, is sold in bookstores.

Radio & TV

Kauai has several AM and FM radio stations. Kauai's community radio station, KKCR (90.9 FM and 91.9 FM) typically plays Hawaiian music.

Commercial and public TV stations are relayed from Honolulu, and cable TV is available on Kauai. KVIC, on cable channel 3, is a visitor information channel that shows continuous videos on sightseeing attractions, with ads for restaurants and tourist activities.

Bookstores

Borders *(☎ 246-0862; 4303 Nawiliwili Rd, Lihue)*, at the back of the Kukui Grove Center, is Kauai's biggest bookstore and has comprehensive collections of novels, travel guides, Hawaiiana books, magazines and foreign newspapers.

Waldenbooks *(☎ 822-7749; Kauai Village, Waipouli)* is a smaller store that also contains good travel and Hawaiiana sections. The **Kauai Museum** *(☎ 245-6931; 4428 Rice St, Lihue)* and the **Kokee Museum** *(☎ 335-9975; Kokee State Park)* both have excellent collections of books on Hawaiian flora, fauna, culture and history.

Libraries

You will find public libraries in Lihue, Hanapepe, Kapaa, Koloa, Princeville as well as Waimea.

Emergency

You can reach the police, ambulance and fire services at the **emergency number** *(☎ 911)*.

The main hospital, **Wilcox Memorial Hospital** *(☎ 245-1100; 3420 Kuhio Hwy, Lihue)*, and the smaller **West Kauai Medical Center** *(☎ 338-9431)*, off Waimea Canyon Dr in Waimea, have 24-hour emergency-room services.

SWIMMING

There are respectable beaches all around Kauai (see the Kauai Water Sports map). For swimming conditions, the North Shore is tops in summer and the South Shore in winter.

Hanalei Bay on the North Shore is the island's most popular summer beach, while Poipu, on the South Shore, has a string of beautiful golden-sand beaches that swimmers flock to in winter. Farther to the west, Salt Pond Beach Park is a popular family beach with protected swimming. Farther west again, Kekaha, Barking Sands and Polihale have white-sand beaches, though with open ocean and often treacherous water conditions.

The beaches around Lihue and Kapaa are generally not great for swimming. The safest one is Lydgate Beach Park in Wailua, a large family park with a boulder retaining wall that creates a protected year-round swimming pool.

Many beaches have rough water conditions at various times of the year, so it pays to be cautious. Kauai has an average of nine drownings a year, about half of those on the North Shore between October and May.

Lifeguards are on duty year-round at Salt Pond Beach Park, Poipu Beach Park, Lydgate Beach Park and Hanalei Bay.

In addition to the beaches, the county has free swimming pools open to the public in Kapaa at **Kapaa Beach Park** *(☎ 822-3842)* and in **Waimea** *(☎ 338-1271)* next to the high school.

SURFING

Kauai has 330 named surfing sites, and if you want to know which ones are seeing the best action on any particular day call the **surf hotline** *(☎ 335-3720)*.

Generally, the best surfing is on the north coast in winter, the south coast in summer and the east coast during transitional swells.

Hanalei Bay tends to be a very good spot for North Shore surfing, as well as a good sport for boogie boarding and bodysurfing. Tunnels and Cannons are two other popular North Shore surf spots.

The area around the Sheraton at Poipu Beach is a top summer surf spot. Pakalas, a surf break at the east side of Makaweli, and Majors Bay at Barking Sands are two West Side favorites.

When the breaks are on the East Side, Kealia and the Wailua Bay area opposite Coco Palms can have good surf conditions.

Margo Oberg *(☎ 742-8019)*, a former World Cup surfing champion, gives surfing lessons at Poipu Beach. The cost is \$48 for a 1½-hour class.

Windsurf Kauai *(☎ 828-6838)* offers 1½-hour surfing lessons in winter at Hanalei Bay for \$60.

Nukumoi Beach & Surf Company *(☎ 742-8019)*, near Poipu Beach Park, rents surfboards for \$7.50 an hour, \$25 a day or \$75 a week.

Seasports Divers *(☎ 742-9303)*, at Poipu Plaza in Poipu, rents surfboards for \$20/100 a day/week.

Kayak Kauai *(in Hanalei ☎ 826-9844, in Wailua ☎ 822-9179)* rents soft surfboards for \$15/60 a day/week and fiberglass boards for \$20/80. Surfing lessons cost \$40 per hour.

Hanalei Surf Company *(☎ 826-9000)*, in the Hanalei Center in Hanalei, rents surfboards for \$15/65 a day/week and wetsuit tops for \$4/17.

BOOGIE BOARDING

For boogie boarding, Brennecke's and Shipwreck Beach in Poipu are hot spots, while Hanalei Bay on the North Shore can also see some good action.

Boogie boards can be rented at lots of places. Most of the beach huts at the resort hotels charge about \$5 an hour, while in-town shops are much more reasonable.

Hanalei Surf Company *(☎ 826-9000)*, in the Hanalei Center in Hanalei, rents boogie boards with fins for \$7 a day, \$22 a week. **Pedal & Paddle** *(☎ 826-9069)*, in the Ching Young Village in Hanalei, rents similar equipment at similar prices.

KAUAI WATER SPORTS

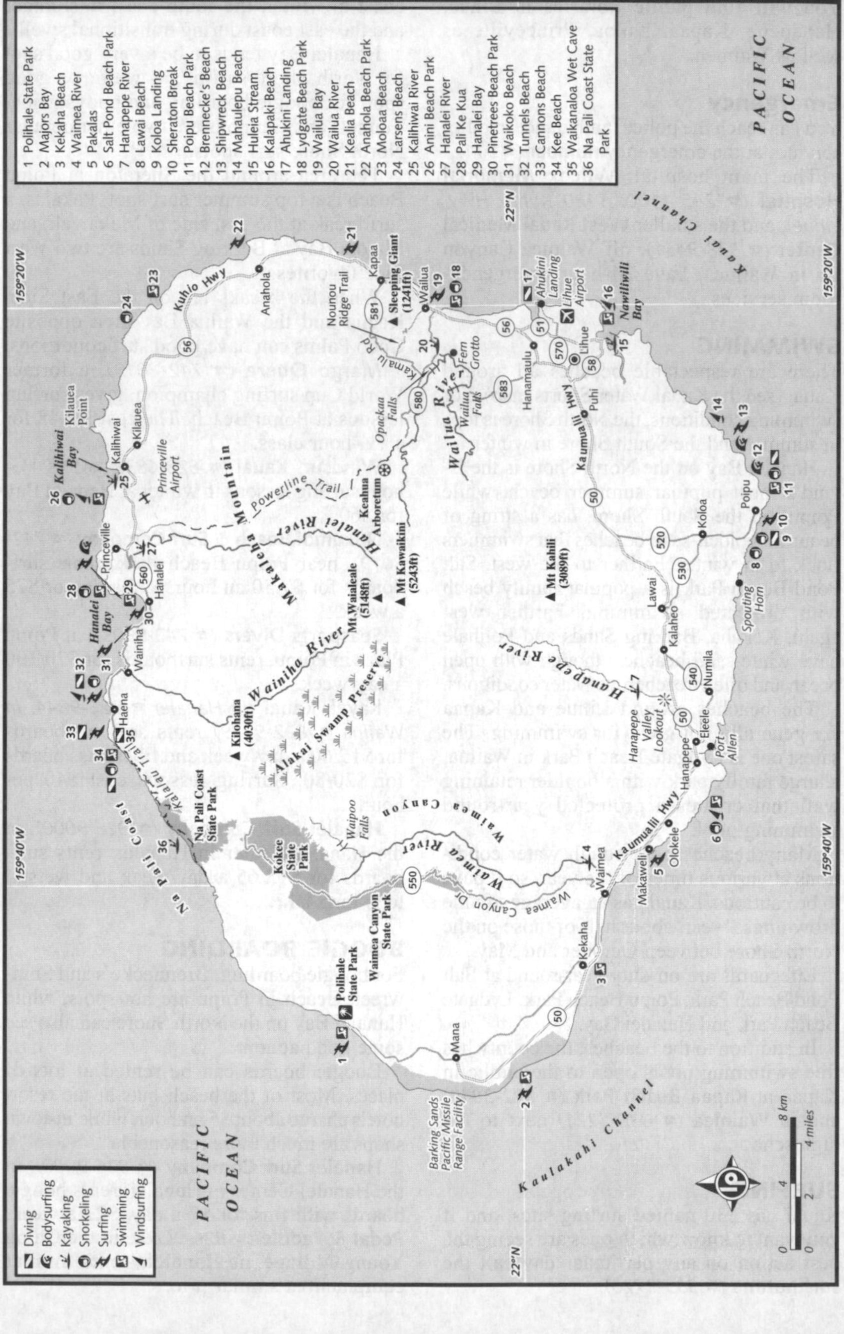

Kayak Kauai *(in Hanalei ☎ 826-9844, in Wailua ☎ 822-9179)* rents boogie boards for $6/24 a day/week.

Nukumoi Beach & Surf Company *(☎ 742-8019)*, conveniently located opposite Poipu Beach Park, rents boogie boards for $5/15 a day/week.

WINDSURFING

Beginner windsurfers usually start off at Anini Beach Park on the North Shore or at Nawiliwili Bay in Lihue. Tunnels Beach in Haena, Mahaulepu Beach on the South Shore and Salt Pond Beach Park in Hanapepe attract more advanced windsurfers, although Anini is also a top-notch place for speed sailing when the wind is up.

At Anini Beach, **Windsurf Kauai** *(☎ 828-6838)* offers lessons for all levels year-round, charging $75 for a three-hour lesson. If you want to sail off on your own, it also rents windsurfing boards with gear for $25 an hour or $50/75 for a half/full day.

DIVING

Popular summer diving spots on the North Shore include Kee Beach, Tunnels Beach and Cannons Beach, all shore dives in the Haena area. Cannons is particularly special; it's a wall dive, with crevices and lava tubes sheltering all sorts of marine life.

Koloa Landing and Poipu Beach Park in Poipu are easy beach dives. On those rare days when *kona* (leeward) winds blow from the south, east-side diving is good and Ahukini Landing becomes a favored site. A number of offshore boat dives are available as well, including dives around Niihau.

Dive shops sometimes give a free introductory scuba lesson at resort hotel pools; for information, check at the hotel beach huts or call the dive shops.

Dive shops offer two-tank dives with equipment for around $85 for shore dives or $100 for boat dives. Most also offer night dives for around $80, introductory dives for beginners for around $100 and certification courses for around $400.

Dive Kauai and Fathom Five Divers are five-star PADI operations.

Four recommendable dive operations are:

Dive Kauai (☎ 822-0452, 800-828-3483, ⓔ email@divekauai.com) 1038 Kuhio Hwy, Kapaa, HI 96746

Fathom Five Divers (☎ 742-6991, 800-972-3078, ⓔ fathom5@fathom-five.com) 3450 Poipu Rd, PO Box 907, Koloa, HI 96756

Seasports Divers (☎ 742-9303, 800-685-5889, ⓔ seasport@pixi.com) Poipu Plaza, Poipu, PO Box 638, Koloa, HI 96756

Sunrise Diving Adventures (☎ 822-7333, 800-695-3483, ⓔ doctrox@aloha.net) 4-1435 Kuhio Hwy, Kapaa, HI 96746

SNUBA

If you really want to slip underwater but don't want to completely load yourself down with dive equipment, you might consider snuba, in which you breathe through an air hose attached to a tank that floats on the water surface.

Snuba Tours of Kauai *(☎ 823-8912)* offers snuba from Lawai Beach in Poipu for $59. The whole thing, including outfitting and orientation, takes 1½ hours; the time in the water is about 45 minutes.

SNORKELING

On the North Shore, Kee Beach has good snorkeling most of the year. Nearby Tunnels Beach offers excellent snorkeling in summer, but be cautious of strong currents.

On the South Shore, the section of Poipu Beach that's just west of Nukumoi Point is one of Kauai's best snorkeling spots for beginners. Another good snorkeling spot in Poipu is Koloa Landing. On the West Side, you can try Salt Pond Beach Park near Hanapepe.

Lots of places rent snorkeling gear. The beach huts at the resort hotels usually charge much higher prices than the in-town shops. A snorkel set at most of the beach huts goes for about $5 an hour.

Hanalei Surf Company *(☎ 826-9000)*, in the Hanalei Center in Hanalei, rents snorkel sets (including corrective masks) for $5/20 a day/week and snorkel vests for $4/17. **Pedal & Paddle** *(☎ 826-9069)*, in the Ching Young Village in Hanalei, also rents snorkel sets for $5/20 a day/week.

Kayak Kauai *(in Hanalei ☎ 826-9844, in Wailua ☎ 822-9179)* rents snorkel sets for $8 a day, $20 a week.

Snorkel Bob's *(in Kapaa ☎ 823-9433; 4-734 Kuhio Hwy, in Koloa ☎ 742-2206; 3236 Poipu Rd)* rents basic snorkel sets for $2.50 a day and good ones for $8.50. Weekly rates range from $9 to $36.

Nukumoi Beach & Surf Company *(☎ 742-8019)*, opposite Poipu Beach Park, rents snorkel sets for $5/15 a day/week.

KAYAKING

With all its waterways, Kauai has some of Hawaii's best kayaking.

The most popular route is up the Wailua River, where you can stop at the Fern Grotto or take a mile-long side hike to a 200ft waterfall. The whole kayak route is about 7 miles round-trip. It has the advantage of being convenient – the launch site, near the mouth of the river, is central, and you can rent a kayak right at the boat ramp. On the downside, this is also the busiest route. On a sunny weekend day, there can be hundreds of people on the Wailua River, mostly kayakers, but also local motorboaters and water-skiers, not to mention the Fern Grotto tour boats with their blaring loudspeaker commentary.

If you prefer a quieter scene, one appealing option is the Hanalei River, which goes through the Hanalei National Wildlife Refuge and meanders into Hanalei Valley. The riverfront is lush and beautiful, in places canopied by overhanging trees. The journey is about 6 miles round-trip, though just how far you'll be able to go depends on the water level in the river, which varies with the rainfall.

Another pleasant kayaking place on the North Shore is the Kalihiwai River up the scenic Kalihiwai Valley, though it's a fairly short route. Other good kayaking spots include the Huleia Stream in the Lihue area and the Hanapepe and Waimea Rivers on the southwest side of the island.

Wailua Kayak & Canoe *(☎ 821-1188)* is right on the water at the Wailua River State Park boat ramp. Single kayaks rent for $25 and double kayaks for $50. If you don't want to set off on your own, there's a five-hour tour that includes the waterfall hike for $75.

Wailua Kayak Adventures *(☎ 822-5795)*, off Hwy 56 behind Coconuts restaurant in Waipouli, will deliver kayaks to the Wailua River. The cost is $25/50 for single/double kayaks, but the staff will sometimes offer discounts.

One way to kayak the Wailua River while avoiding congestion near the river mouth is to rent a kayak from **Kamokila Hawaiian Village** *(☎ 823-0559)*, a sightseeing spot 1½ miles up Hwy 580. The village has its own landing site at a bend in the river, and is within easy paddling distance of the Fern Grotto. The kayak rental fee of $25 per person, using either single or double kayaks, includes admission to the village.

Pedal & Paddle *(☎ 826-9069)*, in the Ching Young Village in Hanalei, rents single/double kayaks for $15/35 a day.

Kayak Kauai *(in Hanalei ☎ 826-9844, in Wailua ☎ 822-9179)* rents single/double kayaks for $26/50 a day. As the Hanalei shop is on the Hanalei River, you can set the boat in the river and paddle right from the shop. In addition to rentals, Kayak Kauai also offers guided tours. A three-hour tour of the Hanalei River costs $60. In summertime, a full-day guided sea-kayaking tour along the Na Pali Coast costs $165.

Outfitters Kauai *(☎ 742-9667)*, at Poipu Plaza in Poipu, rents single kayaks for $35 a day and double kayaks for $50 a day. It also offers guided kayak tours, including an eight-hour South Shore tour from Poipu to Port Allen that operates in the winter and costs $120 and a 12-hour Na Pali Coast tour that operates in the summer and costs $165.

Island Adventures *(☎ 245-9662)* leads 2½-hour guided kayak trips from Nawiliwili Harbor along the Huleia Stream past the Menehune Fishpond and Huleia National Wildlife Refuge. Tours will cost you $49/29 for an adult/child under 12.

Kayak prices typically include paddles, life vests and a car-rack setup when necessary.

FISHING

For deep-sea sport fishing, **True Blue Charters** *(☎ 245-9662)* and **Wild Bill's** *(☎ 822-5963)* take boats out of Nawiliwili Harbor. **Anini Fishing Charters** *(☎ 828-1285)* and **North Shore Charters** *(☎ 828-1379)* are based at Anini Beach.

Kauai has largemouth, smallmouth and peacock bass in some of its private freshwater reservoirs. Two established guide services providing freshwater charters are **JJ's Big Bass Tours** *(☎ 332-9219)* and **Cast & Catch** *(☎ 332-9707)*.

Rainbow trout inhabit several streams and reservoirs in Kokee State Park. The season begins on the first Saturday in August and runs for 16 days, and usually continues on both weekends and holidays through to September. A valid state **freshwater license** *(☎ 274-3344)* is required – see Fishing in the Activities chapter.

HIKING

Kauai has some excellent hikes. The best known is the spectacular 11-mile Kalalau Trail, which hugs the rugged Na Pali Coast.

Kokee State Park is also a hiker's paradise, with the largest concentration of trails on Kauai. Some of these trails lead to splendid cliff-top views of the Na Pali Coast. Others include short nature walks, mountain stream trails and a muddy trek through the unique Alakai Swamp.

South of Kokee, backcountry trails lead down into the picturesque Waimea Canyon, forking into abandoned river valleys.

The Kapaa–Wailua area also offers some pleasant hiking opportunities, including a trail that goes across the chest of the Sleeping Giant mountain. Keahua Arboretum near Wailua is the trailhead for a couple of scenic ridge-top trails, including the Powerline Trail, which goes all the way to Princeville, and the shorter Kuilau Ridge Trail.

These hikes are all detailed in their respective sections.

Guided Hikes

The Kauai division of the **Sierra Club** *(w www.hi.sierraclub.org/kauai/kauai.html; PO Box 3412, Lihue, HI 96766)* offers guided hikes, usually on weekends, that range from strolls up the Sleeping Giant to over-nighters in Waimea Canyon. Advance registration is sometimes required, and a donation of $3 is suggested. You can find the current week's Sierra Club hikes listed in the 'Kauai Times' section of Sunday's *Garden Island* newspaper.

The **Kokee Museum** *(☎ 335-9975)* leads guided hikes on trails in Kokee State Park on weekends in summer, usually departing from the museum around noon. The cost is $3 and reservations are required.

CYCLING & MOUNTAIN BIKING

Mountain biking is growing in popularity on Kauai, and many of the island's forest reserve trails, including the 13-mile Powerline Trail from Keahua Arboretum to Princeville, are open to mountain bikers. The **Division of Forestry & Wildlife** *(☎ 274-3433; 3060 Eiwa St, room 306, Lihue, HI 96766)* has a free leaflet that lists the open trails. The pamphlet should be used in conjunction with the forestry's free topographical map (see the Maps section earlier).

The following companies provide guided group tours for mountain biking.

Kauai Coasters *(☎ 639-2412)* leads cyclists down Waimea Canyon Rd, starting at sunrise from the Kalalau Lookout. The 12-mile ride takes about 1½ hours, mostly coasting downhill. The entire outing lasts about five hours and costs $75.

In addition, **Outfitters Kauai** *(☎ 742-9667)*, located at Poipu Plaza in Poipu, offers a downhill bicycle tour along Waimea Canyon Rd for $80.

You can also just rent a bike and head out on your own, either on mountain trails or on public roads. Bicycle rentals generally include use of a helmet, lock, water bottle and car rack, though some places charge an extra $5 for the car rack.

Kauai Cycle and Tour *(☎ 821-2115; 1379 Kuhio Hwy, Kapaa)* rents 18-speed cruisers for $15/75 a day/week and quality mountain bikes with front suspension for $20/95 a day/week and with full suspension for $35/150. Being a dedicated cycle shop, its bikes tend to be among the best maintained, so if you're near Kapaa this is a good place to do business.

Kayak Kauai *(in Hanalei ☎ 826-9844, in Wailua ☎ 822-9179)* rents mountain bikes for $20/80 a day/week and beach cruisers for $15/60.

Pedal & Paddle *(☎ 826-9069; Ching Young Village, Hanalei)* rents mountain bikes for $20/100 a day/week and beach cruisers for $10/40.

Outfitters Kauai *(☎ 742-9667)*, in the Poipu Plaza, rents beach cruisers for $20 a day, road bikes for $30 and mountain bikes for $30 to $45, with the higher prices for full-suspension models.

HORSEBACK RIDING

CJM Country Stables *(☎ 742-6096)* has some enjoyable rides in the Mahaulepu Beach area. There's a three-hour breakfast ride for $80 and two-hour morning or afternoon rides for $70. A 3½-hour afternoon ride, which includes time for a swim and a picnic on the beach, costs $90. The stables are in Poipu, along the main dirt road 1½ miles east of the Hyatt Regency Kauai.

Princeville Ranch Stables *(☎ 826-6777)*, on Hwy 56 near the Princeville airport, offers a three-hour ride for $110 or a four-hour ride for $120 across ranch lands to a waterfall for a picnic and swim, as well as a 1½-hour ($65) ride along a bluff with ocean views. If you feel more adventurous, there's also a 1½-hour cattle drive for $120.

Silver Falls Ranch (☎ *828-6718*), at the end of Kamookoa Rd in the Kalihiwai area, has a two-hour ranch and rain forest ride for $78 and a three-hour ride that includes swimming at a remote waterfall pool and a picnic lunch for $105.

TENNIS

County tennis courts, which are free and open to the public, are available at the following locations: Wailua Houselots Park and Wailua Homesteads Park, both in Wailua; Hardy St, near the Convention Hall in Lihue; opposite Kauai Community College in Puhi; Kapaa New Park in Kapaa; Knudsen Park in Koloa; Kalawai Park in Kalaheo; and on the corner of Hwys 552 and 50 in Kekaha.

Several hotels have tennis courts available for their guests.

The following places are open to the general public. All rent rackets for around $5.

The **Ala Lani Spa & Tennis Club** (☎ *245-3323*), adjacent to the Kauai Marriott in Lihue, has seven courts. The cost is $20 per court per hour.

The **Kiahuna Tennis Club** (☎ *742-9533; Poipu Rd, Poipu*) has 10 courts and charges $10 per person per hour.

The **Hyatt Regency Kauai** (☎ *742-1234; 1571 Poipu Rd, Poipu*) has four courts and charges $20 per court per hour.

The **Princeville Tennis Club** (☎ *826-3620; 5380 Honoiki Rd, Princeville*) has six courts and charges $15 per person, which allows at least 1½ hours of play.

The **Hanalei Bay Resort Tennis Club** (☎ *826-6522; Princeville*) has eight courts and a full tennis programme, charging $6 per person per hour.

GOLF

Kauai has nine golf courses. Major tournaments are hosted at Princeville's Prince course and at the Poipu Bay Resort. The Kauai Lagoons' Kiele course in Lihue and Princeville's Makai course are also top-rated.

Wailua County Golf Course (☎ *241-6666*), an 18-hole par-72 course off Hwy 56 north of Lihue, is a well-regarded public course that's heavily played. Reservations for morning tee times are taken up to seven days in advance. Greens fees are $32 Monday to Friday and $44 on weekends and holidays. After 2pm, the greens fees drop by half and play is on a first-come, first-served basis. Cart/club rentals cost $14/15.

Kukuiolono Golf Course (☎ *332-9151*), a nine-hole par-36 course on an old estate in Kalaheo, has a grand hilltop view and an earthy appeal. Greens fees are just $7, and pull carts cost a mere $2 more.

Puakea Golf Course (☎ *245-8756*), south of the Kukui Grove Center in Lihue, is Kauai's newest course and has 10 holes. Greens fees are $45, including a cart, and for the same price as 10 holes they'll often let you play the round twice for 20 holes. Club rentals cost $15.

Kauai Lagoons Golf Club (☎ *241-6000*), north of the Kauai Marriott in Lihue, has two 18-hole par-72 courses. The Kiele course charges $130, the Mokihana course $85, with cheaper off-peak rates. Clubs rent for $35.

Kiahuna Golf Club (☎ *742-9595*), an 18-hole par-70 course in Poipu run by the Sports Shinko Group, charges $65 in the early morning, $55 after 11am, cart included. Clubs rent for $20 to $30.

Poipu Bay Resort Golf Course (☎ *742-8711*), an 18-hole par-72 course adjacent to the Hyatt Regency Kauai in Poipu, charges Hyatt guests/nonguests $100/150. Ask about off-peak rates that can cut the standard prices by half. Carts are included in the rate; club rentals cost $40.

Princeville Resort (☎ *826-5070*), on the North Shore, has two championship courses designed by Robert Trent Jones Jr: the 18-hole par-72 Prince, which is Kauai's highest-rated course, and the 27-hole par-72 Makai. Greens and cart fees for the Makai course are $105 for guests staying in Princeville and $125 for nonguests. The fees for the Prince course are $130/175. There are 'matinee discounts' at both courses if you wait until the afternoon to tee off. Club rentals cost $35.

ORGANIZED TOURS

Van

In Kauai, most sightseeing tour prices vary with the pick-up point.

Polynesian Adventure Tours (☎ *246-0122*) offers full-day van tours that include Wailua, Fern Grotto, Koloa, Poipu, Waimea, Waimea Canyon and Kalalau Lookout for $60 with pick-up in Lihue or Wailua, $65 from Poipu or $73 from Princeville. Half-day North Shore tours that take in Hanalei, Haena and Kee Beach cost $33 from Lihue or Wailua, $28 from Princeville or $43 from Poipu. Half-day Waimea Canyon tours cost $39 from Lihue or Wailua, $43 from Poipu or $59 from Princeville. Full-day outings that squeeze in both Waimea Canyon and the North Shore cost $60 from Lihue or Wailua, and $65 from Princeville or Poipu.

TransHawaiian (☎ *245-5108*) and **Roberts Hawaii** (☎ *539-9400*) offer similar tours at comparable prices.

In addition, **Kauai Paradise Tours** (☎ *246-3999*) specializes in tours narrated in German. Full-day sightseeing tours cost from $66 to $88.

Aloha Kauai Tours (☎ *245-6400*) offers tours in 4WD vans that are capable of detouring off the beaten path to take in sights along forest dirt roads. Tours last four to eight hours and cost $60 to $100.

All tour companies offer discounted prices for children.

Helicopter

Many wilderness hikers resent the intrusion of helicopters into otherwise serene areas, and local environmentalists have successfully stopped copter landings on Na Pali Coast beaches. However, these 'Kauai mosquitoes' that are such an irritant to people on the ground no doubt offer some pretty spectacular views as they swoop down into Waimea Canyon, run along the Na Pali Coast and seek out hidden waterfalls.

Several helicopter companies offer flights around Kauai. The free tourist magazines advertise most of them and often have discount coupons.

The going rate is about $130 for a 45-minute 'circle-island tour' that zooms by the main sights. There's usually some sort of 'ultimate splendor' tour that can add on 20 minutes and run up another $50 to $75. Most of the helicopter offices are either in central Lihue, near the corner of Hwy 56 and Ahukini Rd, or at the side of Lihue airport.

Cruises

Like the other islands, Kauai has its fair share of catamaran picnic sails, sunset cruises and the like. It also has something the other islands don't: the spectacular Na Pali Coast.

Several boat companies run cruises down the Na Pali Coast. With its proximity to the Na Pali Coast, Hanalei used to be the most popular departure point. However, because of problems with congestion and pollution concerns, cruises are no longer allowed to depart from the North Shore. Consequently, all cruises to the Na Pali Coast now depart from the western side of Kauai. On the down side, this tends to make the tours both longer and pricier than they have been in the past.

The following cruises offer competitive prices, ranging from about $85 for a four-hour sightseeing tour to about $130 for a daylong outing that includes a snorkeling stop and a light lunch.

Liko Kauai Cruises (☎ *338-0333*), run by a native Niihauan, departs from Kikiaola Harbor in Kekaha, so has the shortest travel time to the Na Pali Coast.

Holo Holo Charters (☎ *246-4656*), **Na Pali Explorer** (☎ *338-9999*) and **Na Pali Eco Adventure** (☎ *826-6804*) depart from Port Allen.

The smoothest rides are generally in the summer. For most of the winter, the seas are too rough on the Na Pali Coast for snorkeling and other nearshore activities, and on some days it's simply too rough for the boats to go out at all. A few companies then switch to the calmer southern shore for snorkeling cruises and whale-watching tours.

ACCOMMODATIONS

Three areas in Kauai – Poipu, Princeville, and the strip from Lihue to Kapaa – contain almost all of the island's hotels and condos.

For the most part, Kauai's beach hotels are a bit expensive. The cheapest begin around $100, although the majority are nearly double that. Condos have a similar price range but tend to be a better deal, particularly if you're traveling in a group.

The best accommodation deals on the island are found in the scattering of B&Bs that have sprung up in recent years. The Wailua area has the greatest concentration of B&Bs, with prices from around $50. Many are in fine homes that are both comfortable and scenically located, a few miles up the slope from the coast. Wailua also makes a good base for exploring, as it's midway between the North Shore and Kokee State Park.

A couple of hostel-style places in Kapaa shore up the bottom end with dorm beds for $20 per person.

Camping

Kauai offers excellent camping. Some camping areas are at lovely drive-up beach parks, some are in dense forest and others are at the end of daylong hikes into remote valleys.

There are camping areas at three state parks, seven county parks and at forest reserve trailside camps in Waimea Canyon and the nearby Kokee area.

State Parks Camping is allowed by permit at Kokee, Polihale and Na Pali Coast State Parks. The cost is $5 per camp site per night at Kokee and Polihale, and $10 per person per night on the Na Pali Coast.

Permits are issued from 8am to 3:30pm Monday to Friday at the **Division of State Parks** (*☎ 274-3444; 3060 Eiwa St, room 306, Lihue, HI 96766*) and at state park offices on other islands. Up to five people may be listed on each permit, but the person applying for the permit must show an ID (such as a driver's license or passport) for each person.

You can also obtain a permit by mail by sending the state park office either a completed official application form or a regular sheet of paper specifying the park(s) at which you want to stay and the exact dates you wish to stay at each park. Along with this application include a photocopy of each camper's ID, with the ID number and birth date clearly readable.

You can apply for a permit as early as a year in advance. During the busy summer period of May to September, Na Pali Coast camp sites are often completely booked up many months ahead, so apply for your permit as far in advance as possible. If you change your mind about camping once you get the permit, be sure to cancel, as otherwise you'll be tying up an empty space and preventing someone else from camping.

At each state park, you may camp for up to five consecutive nights within a 30-day period. At the Na Pali Coast State Park, this means a maximum of five nights on the entire Kalalau Trail, with the additional restriction that you may not spend more than one night at a time in Hanakoa Valley.

County Beach Parks Camping is allowed at Haena, Hanalei, Anini, Anahola, Hanamaulu, Salt Pond and Lucy Wright Parks. The camping areas at Haena, Anini and Salt Pond are all on nice beaches and are good choices. Camping is allowed at Hanalei Beach Park on Friday, Saturday and holidays only.

All county camping grounds have showers and rest rooms, and most have covered picnic pavilions and barbecue grills. There's a typical Hawaiian laissez-faire style to the camping grounds, so don't expect to find numbered sites or caretakers.

Permits, which are required, are $3 per adult per night (no fees for children under 18 or Hawaii residents). There's a limit of seven nights at each camping ground and a limit of 60 days of camping a year.

Permit applications can be made by mail if a completed form and payment are received at the **Division of Parks & Recreation** (*☎ 241-6660; 4444 Rice St, Suite 150, Lihue, HI 96766*) at least one month in advance of your camping date. The blank forms can be downloaded online at W www.kauaigov.org; follow the link to Parks.

Permits can also be obtained in person from 8am to 4:15pm Monday to Friday at the Division of Parks & Recreation office in the Lihue Civic Center, on the corner of Hwys 50 and 56 in central Lihue.

You can also just set up camp and wait for the ranger to come around and collect, but if you do this the fee jumps to $5 per person. Be aware that rangers sometimes wake up campers late at night or as early as 5am to collect fees, and if they determine that the camping area is too full, campers without permits can be asked to move.

The county closes each camping ground one day a week, ostensibly to clean the place up, but also to prevent people from making permanent encampments at the site. Haena and Lucy Wright are closed on Monday; Anini and Salt Pond are closed on Tuesday; Hanamaulu is closed on Wednesday; and Anahola is closed on Thursday. If the closure day happens to coincide with a public holiday, the park will remain open.

Waimea Canyon The Division of Forestry and Wildlife allows backcountry camping at four sites along trails in Waimea Canyon and at two sites (Sugi Grove and Kawaikoi) in the Kokee State Park area. Camping is limited to four nights in the canyon and three nights in the Kokee area within a 30-day period.

Camping permits, which are required and are free, can be picked up in person between 8am and 4pm Monday to Friday at the **forestry office** *(☎ 274-3433; 3060 Eiwa St, room 306, Lihue, HI 96766)*.

You can reserve a permit in advance by phone, but you'll still need to pick up the permit in person, with proper ID, after you arrive on Kauai.

Cabins You can rent cabins in a couple of places on Kauai. The best known are the cabins at Kokee State Park, but also interesting are the cabins at Kahili Mountain Park, a secluded Seventh Day Adventist property north of Koloa. See the relevant sections for more information.

Camping Supplies In Hanalei's Ching Young Village, **Pedal & Paddle** *(☎ 826-9069)* rents two-person tents for $12/35 a day/week, backpacks for $5/20 and sleeping bags, sleeping pads or trail stoves for $3/10 each. The shop also sells the same supplies it rents.

Kayak Kauai *(☎ 826-9844; Hwy 56, Hanalei)* rents two-person tents or backpacks for $8/32 a day/week, camping stoves or sleeping bags for $6/24 and sleeping pads or daypacks for $4/16.

ENTERTAINMENT

OK, let's be honest, no one comes to Kauai for its nighttime entertainment. But that said and done, you can always scratch and find something.

Most of Kauai's entertainment is found at the larger hotels, many of which have live music at least a few nights a week. You can have a frosty tropical drink and listen to live Hawaiian music at resort poolside bars, as well as at some of the trendier waterfront restaurants, like Duke's Canoe Club at the Kauai Marriott in Lihue.

Luaus take place at the Radisson Kauai Beach Resort and Kilohana Plantation in the Lihue area; at Kauai Coconut Beach Resort and Smith's Tropical Paradise in Wailua; at the Hyatt Regency Kauai in Poipu; and at the Princeville Hotel on the North Shore.

If you want to see hula dancing without paying for a luau, there are free hula shows at the Coconut Marketplace in Wailua, the Hyatt Regency Kauai in Poipu and the Poipu Shopping Plaza in Poipu.

For more details on specific venues, see the relevant town sections in this chapter. Check the local paper or the free tourist magazines for the latest entertainment schedules.

Sunshine Markets

For island-grown fruits and vegetables that are both fresher and cheaper than grocery store produce, catch one of the farmers markets, known locally as Sunshine Markets. Not only will you find bargain prices on fruits like papayas, oranges and avocados, but you'll also find items such as passion fruit and guava that aren't sold in supermarkets at all.

The schedule is:

Monday

noon Knudsen Park, Maluhia Rd, Koloa

3pm Kukui Grove Center, Hwy 50, Lihue

Tuesday

2pm Hwy 560, on the western outskirts of Hanalei

3:30pm Kalaheo Neighborhood Center, Papalina Rd, Kalaheo

Wednesday

3pm Kapaa New Park, Olohena Rd, Kapaa

Thursday

3:30pm Hanapepe Town Park, behind the Hanapepe fire station

4:30pm Kilauea Neighborhood Center, Keneke St, Kilauea

Friday

3pm Vidinha Stadium, Hwy 51, Lihue

Saturday

9am Kekaha Neighborhood Center, Elepaio Rd, Kekaha

9am Christ Memorial Episcopal Church, Kolo Rd, Kilauea

Get there early. As a matter of fact, it's best to be there before the starting time, as once the whistle blows there's a big rush and people begin to scoop things up quickly. Depending on the location, it can all wrap up within an hour or so.

SHOPPING

Some popular souvenir items include Niihau shell leis, paintings of Kauai landscapes and island-made products such as coconut soap, macadamia nut cookies and fragrant skin lotions.

The early harvests of Kauai-grown coffee have not been as highly regarded as gourmet Kona coffee on the Big Island, but one new boutique brand, Black Mountain, grown on five acres in Koloa, has recently caught the attention of coffee connoisseurs. America's exclusive department store, Neiman-Marcus, buys most of Black Mountain's harvest, but you can still find it in a few gift shops around the island – it's well worth the search!

Good places to look for locally made arts and crafts include the Kilohana Plantation in Puhi, Ching Young Village in Hanalei, the Kauai Museum in Lihue and shopping centers around the island.

Kauai's largest shopping center, the Kukui Grove Center in Lihue, has a Kauai Products Store that sells a full range of Kauai-made items, from expensive jewelry and koa-wood bowls to papaya-seed dressing and taro chips. The nearby Borders bookstore stocks an excellent selection of Hawaiian music.

GETTING THERE & AWAY

Air

All scheduled passenger flights to Kauai land at **Lihue airport** (*LIH; ☎ 246-1400*).

Hawaiian Airlines (*☎ 245-1813, 800-882-8811*) and **Aloha Airlines** (*☎ 245-3691, 800-241-6522*) have frequent flights connecting Kauai with the other Hawaiian islands. **United Airlines** (*☎ 800-241-6522*) has daily nonstop flights to Lihue from Los Angeles and San Francisco.

Kauai also has a small airport in Princeville on the North Shore, but it no longer has scheduled service.

Lihue airport's modern terminal includes an agricultural inspection station for passengers returning to the mainland, a restaurant, cocktail lounge, flower shop, gift shop and newsstand. You'll find well-stocked racks loaded with activity and accommodations brochures, as well as Kauai's free tourist magazines, in the baggage claim area.

GETTING AROUND

Kauai has a limited public bus service and, while it connects most towns on the island, it's not geared for visitors and won't take you off the beaten path or out to major destinations like Kilauea Point, Waimea Canyon or Kokee State Park. Consequently, renting a car is almost essential for exploring the island in depth.

Kauai's main roads are straightforward and easy to follow. Surprisingly, however, Kauai does have rush-hour traffic jams, especially in central Lihue and on the highway between Lihue and Kapaa. To reduce the rush-hour congestion, from 6am to 8:30am Monday to Friday, orange cones are temporarily set up on Hwy 56 in the Wailua area to create a 'contra-flow' lane; this turns one of the northbound lanes into a southbound lane by reversing the flow of traffic, so that people commuting to Lihue have three lanes open to them instead of the usual two.

To/From the Airport

The public bus does not stop at Lihue airport. Taxis can be picked up curbside in front of the arrival area. Car-rental booths are lined up on the other side of the street, opposite the arrival and departure gates.

Bus

The public bus has two main routes, both originating in the county capital of Lihue and operating an average of eight times a day Monday to Friday and four times a day Saturday. In Lihue, buses can be picked up at the Big Save Supermarket at the northeast side of the Lihue Civic Center.

One route heads north to Hanalei, stopping along the way at the Coconut Marketplace in Wailua, the library in Kapaa, the intersection of Kolo Rd and Hwy 56 in Kilauea and the Princeville Shopping Center before terminating at the Waioli Huiia Church in Hanalei.

The second route runs between Lihue and Kekaha, Kauai's westernmost town, making stops in Kalaheo, Eleele, Hanapepe and Waimea; once a day in each direction, the bus swings down through Koloa and Poipu as well.

None of these buses take very long. The bus from Lihue to either Hanalei or Kekaha takes 1¼ hours, and from Lihue to Kapaa it's just 25 minutes.

In addition to those routes, the service includes a bus that shuttles between Lihue and Kapaa six times a day Monday to Friday, and a local Lihue bus that runs between Lihue's shopping centers once an hour Monday to Friday.

Buses are white with a green sugarcane motif and are marked 'Kauai Bus.'

Destinations are posted in the front window and on the curb side of the bus.

The fare on all routes is $1.50 per ride (75¢ for those over 60 years or under 18 years of age). Have the exact fare ready as drivers are not allowed to make change. There's also a $15 monthly pass. You can get more information on the bus by calling the **information line** *(☎ 241-6410; open 7am-5pm Mon-Sat)*.

If you plan to use the bus extensively, keep in mind that there's no service at all on Sunday or holidays. Carry-on bags have a size limit of 7-by-14-by-22 inches; boogie boards are not allowed and nothing can be stored in the aisles.

You can pick up bus schedules from bus drivers, at public libraries as well as from brochure racks found at the entryway of many supermarkets.

For information on commercial sightseeing bus tours, see Organized Tours earlier in this chapter.

Car & Motorcycle

Budget *(☎ 245-1901)*, **Hertz** *(☎ 245-3356)*, **Avis** *(☎ 245-3512)*, **Alamo** *(☎ 246-0645)*, **Dollar** *(☎ 245-3651)* and **National** *(☎ 245-5636)* have car-rental booths at Lihue airport. For more information, including toll free numbers, see the Getting Around chapter.

Hawaiian Riders *(☎ 822-5409; 4-776 Kuhio Hwy, Waipouli)* rents mopeds for $50 a day and Harley Davidson motorcycles for $119.

Taxi

Taxis charge $2 at flag-fall and then $2 a mile, metered in 25¢ increments. The fare from Lihue airport is about $17 to Coconut Plantation in Wailua, $20 to Kapaa and $30 to Poipu.

Taxi companies include **Akiko's Taxi** *(☎ 822-7588)*, in the Lihue-Kapaa area; **North Shore Cab** *(☎ 639-7829)*, based in Princeville; and **Southshore Cab** *(☎ 742-1525)*, for service on Kauai's south side.

Bicycle

Kauai's roads are generally narrow, shoulders are often nonexistent, and traffic can be a little heavy in places – all safety concerns for cyclists. The hilly terrain is another challenge: expect a hefty workout, especially if you cycle into interior areas. All said and done, a bike can be useful for getting around a limited area, but unless you're a seasoned cyclist accustomed to difficult conditions, don't plan on touring the island extensively by bike.

For details on Mountain Biking as well as a list of bicycle rental shops, see Cycling & Mountain Biking in the earlier Activities section of this chapter.

East Side

The commercial heart of Kauai, the East Side includes the island's largest city, Lihue, as well as Wailua, Waipouli and Kapaa – three small towns with hotels and condo complexes, shopping centers and restaurants. Many visitors to Kauai choose to stay in the relatively inexpensive accommodations of the East Side; its central location makes it a convenient base for exploring the lush river valleys of the North Shore and the sunny beaches to the south.

CENTRAL LIHUE

Lihue, with a population of 6850, is the county capital and the arrival point of virtually all visitors to Kauai. It got its start as a plantation town, and its most impressive building, the old Lihue sugar mill, still sits along Hwy 50 at the south side of town. Once the largest sugar mill in Kauai, it shut down in 2001, ending more than a century of operations.

Still, the loss of the mill hasn't had too much of an impact on Lihue itself, as the backbone of the economy now lies in its office and retail businesses. Virtually all county and state employees work in Lihue and the town is home to the island's main shopping centers. Simply put, if you have business to do in Kauai, you go to Lihue.

Lihue can bustle a bit during the week, but on weekends it's a real sleeper. Although the town is more business than charm, it has some good local restaurants and a worthwhile museum – and that makes Lihue a good destination for lunch and an afternoon of sightseeing.

Information

Kauai Visitors Bureau *(☎ 245-3971; 4334 Rice St, Suite 101; open 8am-4:30pm Mon-Fri)* is in the Watumull Plaza. If you're looking for brochures and other printed tourist information, however, the racks at the airport are better stocked.

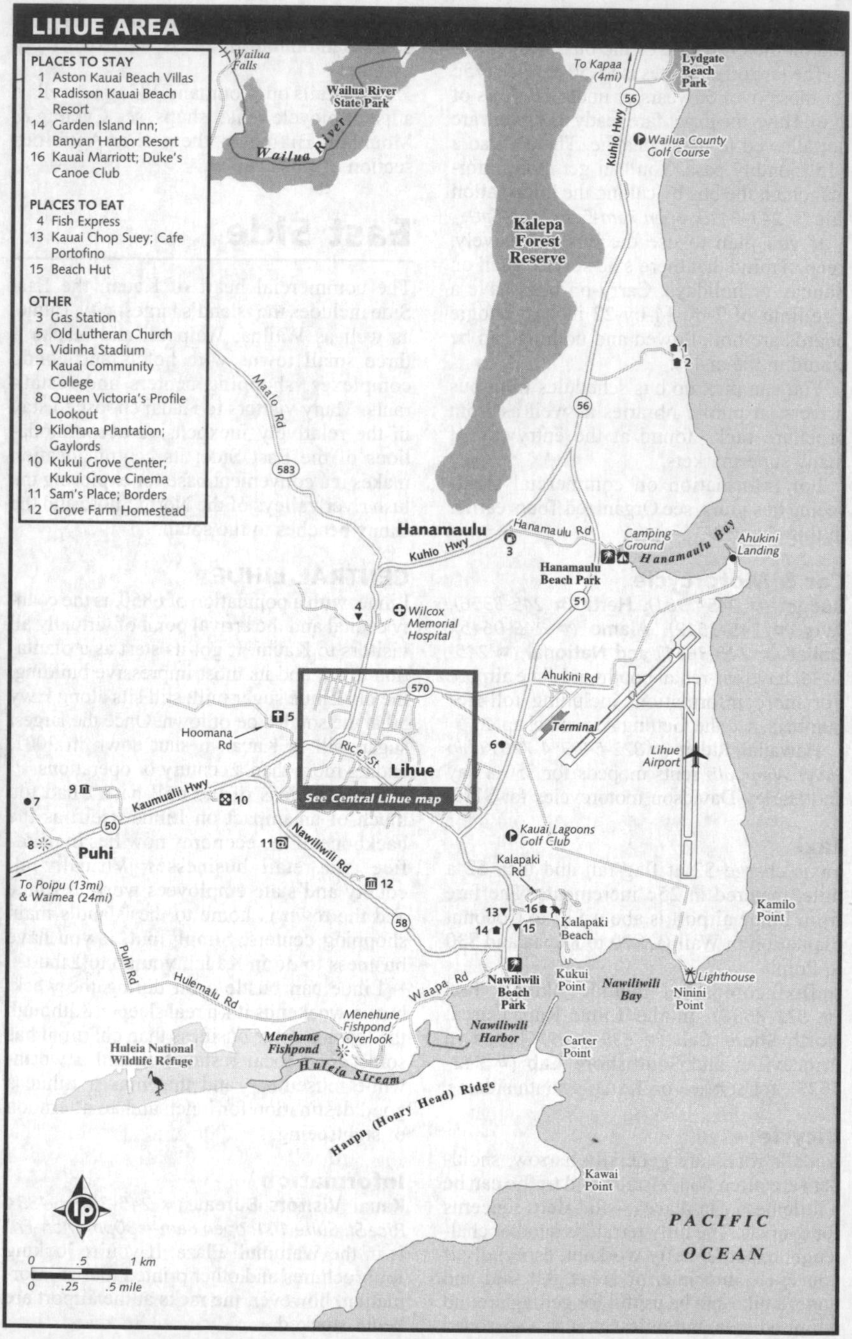
LIHUE AREA
PLACES TO STAY
1 Aston Kauai Beach Villas
2 Radisson Kauai Beach Resort
14 Garden Island Inn; Banyan Harbor Resort
16 Kauai Marriott; Duke's Canoe Club
PLACES TO EAT
4 Fish Express
13 Kauai Chop Suey; Cafe Portofino
15 Beach Hut
OTHER
3 Gas Station
5 Old Lutheran Church
6 Vidinha Stadium
7 Kauai Community College
8 Queen Victoria's Profile Lookout
9 Kilohana Plantation; Gaylords
10 Kukui Grove Center; Kukui Grove Cinema
11 Sam's Place; Borders
12 Grove Farm Homestead
Wailua Falls
Wailua River State Park
Wailua River
To Kapaa (4mi)
Lydgate Beach Park
Kuhio Hwy
Wailua County Golf Course
Kalepa Forest Reserve
Maalo Rd
Hanamaulu
Hanamaulu Rd
Kuhio Hwy
Camping Ground
Hanamaulu Bay
Ahukini Landing
Hanamaulu Beach Park
Wilcox Memorial Hospital
Ahukini Rd
Terminal
Hoomana Rd
Rice St
Lihue
See Central Lihue map
Lihue Airport
Kaumualii Hwy
Puhi
To Poipu (13mi) & Waimea (24mi)
Nawiliwili Rd
Kauai Lagoons Golf Club
Kalapaki Rd
Kalapaki Beach
Kamilo Point
Puhi Rd
Hulemalu Rd
Waapa Rd
Nawiliwili Beach Park
Kukui Point
Nawiliwili Bay
Lighthouse
Ninini Point
Menehune Fishpond Overlook
Menehune Fishpond
Nawiliwili Harbor
Carter Point
Huleia National Wildlife Refuge
Huleia Stream
Haupu (Hoary Head) Ridge
Kawai Point
PACIFIC OCEAN
0 .5 1 km
0 .25 .5 mile

The **Bank of Hawaii** *(☎ 245-6761; 4455 Rice St; open 8:30am-4pm Mon-Thur, 8:30am-6pm Fri, 9am-noon Sat)* is in the town center.

The **post office** *(☎ 800-275-8777; 4441 Rice St; open 8am-4:30pm Mon-Fri, 9am-1pm Sat)* is opposite the Kauai Museum, next to the Bank of Hawaii.

An Internet café in the same building as Borders bookstore, **Sam's Place** *(☎ 245-7332; 4303 Nawiliwili Rd; open 6am-8pm Mon-Sat, 9am-5pm Sun)* charges $2 for the first 10 minutes and $1 for each additional 10 minutes.

Mokihana Travel *(☎ 245-5338; 3016 Umi St, Suite 3)* sells interisland flight tickets at reasonable prices.

The **Lihue Public Library** *(☎ 241-3222; 4344 Hardy St; open 10am-8pm Mon & Wed, 9am-5pm Tues & Thur, 10am-5pm Fri, 9am-1pm Sat)* is a good place to browse local newspapers.

Lihue Laundromat *(4303 Rice St; open 24hr)* is in the Rice Shopping Center in the center of town.

Kauai Museum

A few hours at this museum *(☎ 245-6931; 4428 Rice St; adult/child 13-17/child 6-12 $5/3/1; open 9am-4pm Mon-Fri, 10am-4pm Sat)* will give you an insightful overview of the island's history.

The displays begin with Kauai's volcanic genesis from the ocean floor, then move on to describe the island's unique ecosystems. The 1st floor covers early Hawaii, with displays of hula instruments, poi pounders and tapa-making tools.

Upstairs, the sugarcane workers and missionaries arrive on the scene. A replica of a plantation worker's spartan shack sits opposite the spacious bedroom of an early missionary's house, furnished with a four-poster koa bed and Hawaiian quilts. It is to these folks that Hawaii traces its multiethnic roots and vastly unequal distribution of land and wealth. The displays are accompanied by well-written interpretive presentations of life in old Kauai.

The gift shop has a good selection of Hawaiiana books and a small collection of koa bowls and other handicrafts. If you only want to visit the gift shop, which is inside the museum lobby, you can enter without paying.

If you run out of time before seeing the entire museum, ask for a free reentry pass when you leave.

Old Lutheran Church

From the outside, the oldest Lutheran church in Hawaii is just one more quaint Hawaiian church. From the inside, it tells a far more interesting story.

German immigrants styled their church to resemble the boat that brought them from their homeland to Hawaii in the late 19th century. The floor has been built to slant like the deck of a ship, the balcony resembles a captain's bridge and ship lanterns hang from the ceiling. The current building was actually constructed in 1983, but it's an almost exact replica of the original 1885 church that was leveled by Hurricane Iwa in 1982.

The immigrants themselves now lie at rest in the church cemetery on a knoll overlooking the cane fields in which they toiled.

The church is just a quarter of a mile up Hoomana Rd, which is just west of the intersection of Hwys 56 and 50.

Wailua Falls

Wailua Falls is a strikingly scenic 80ft waterfall just north of Lihue. To get there from Lihue, follow Hwy 56 north and turn left onto Maalo Rd (Hwy 583), a narrow paved road that weaves through sugarcane fields. The road ends at the falls at precisely 3.94 miles – as the highway marker fastidiously proclaims.

Wailua, which means 'two waters,' is usually seen as two falls. However, after heavy rains, it becomes one wide rushing waterfall and you can literally watch fish being thrown out beyond the powerful waters for a flying dive into the pool below.

This is not a waterfall to explore from the top. A sign at the parking lot near a closed path reads, 'Slippery rocks at top of falls. People have been killed.' There are plenty of stories told of people sliding off the rocks, some miraculously grabbing roots and being rescued and others not so lucky.

A third of a mile before the road's end, at a large dirt pull-off, an eroded trail leads to the base of the falls. Because the trail is hazardous, it's not open to the public, but from this pull-off you can get a fine view of a second waterfall, visible to the southeast.

Along the side of the road, keep an eye out for wood roses – bright yellow flowers shaped like morning glories whose seed pods are commonly used in dried floral

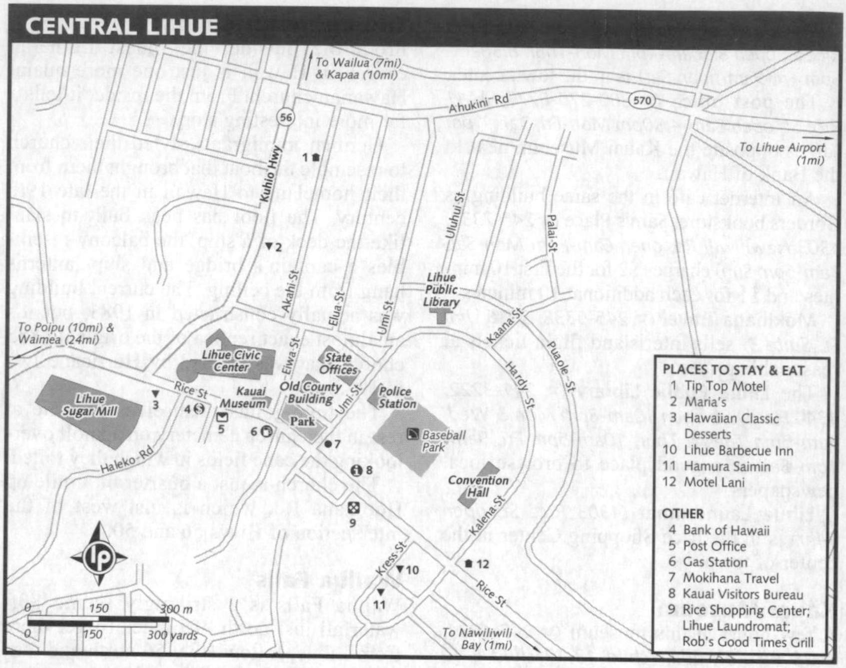

arrangements. The vines bearing the flowers are especially thick around the bridge half a mile south of Wailua Falls.

Hanamaulu

Hanamaulu is a little village between Lihue and Wailua along Hwy 56. It's significant in Hawaiian folklore as the birthplace of Kauai's legendary hero Kawelo, depicted in folktales as a skillful warrior and champion spear thrower. Today, Hanamaulu is a sleepy town with just a few businesses, including a hole-in-the-wall post office and a little doughnut shop that closes each day as soon as the doughnuts are gone.

Three-quarters of a mile from the village center, **Hanamaulu Beach Park** lies at the inside of Hanamaulu Bay, a deep protected bay with a boulder breakwater part way across its mouth. The park has camping grounds with full facilities, but it's more of a local hangout than a visitor destination. The waters are occasionally off limits because of pollution. For information on obtaining a permit to camp, see Camping in the Accommodations section, near the beginning of this chapter.

To get to Hanamaulu Beach Park from Hwy 56, turn *makai* (seaward) onto Hanamaulu Rd at the 7-Eleven. After a quarter mile, turn right onto Hehi Rd. As you enter the park, you'll first go under the highway bridge and then the arched trestle of an abandoned railroad bridge.

Ahukini Landing

If you have some time to kill before your flight, one option is to drive to the end of Hwy 570 to see Ahukini Landing, which is 1½ miles beyond the airport. The road takes you through abandoned cane fields, and crosses a series of narrow-gauge railroad tracks that were once used to bring sugarcane down to the landing. Pretty yellow *ilima* (a native ground cover) and pink chain-of-love flowers grow profusely along the roadside.

Ahukini State Recreation Pier, at the end of the highway, consists largely of cement pillars and the decaying framework of the old pier. A wooden walkway runs out across the pier, providing a prime locale for pole fishing. Across the bay you can see the sands of Hanamaulu Beach Park.

Ninini Point

The lighthouse on Ninini Point stands 100ft above the shore, marking the northern entrance to Nawiliwili Bay. The road down to the lighthouse begins off Hwy 51, a little over half a mile south of the intersection with Hwy 570. Although you'll have to go through a guard gate and cross the Kauai Lagoons Golf Course property to get to the coast, access is free to visitors.

The 2½-mile drive from the gatehouse to the lighthouse passes between the airport fence and the golf course. After 2 miles, the pavement ends and the road continues as dirt; this section is sometimes too rough to pass in a low-slung car, and you may have to hike the last 10 minutes of it.

Not only is there a fine view from the lighthouse, but nearby is one of the few sections of accessible shore in the area. Here, Hawaiians can still fish, pick *opihi* (a kind of mollusk) and gather *limu* (an edible seaweed) as they've done for generations.

Kalapaki Beach

Lihue's best beach is Kalapaki Beach, a wide sandy strand sheltered by points and breakwaters at Nawiliwili Bay. The beach, off Hwy 51, lies in front of the Kauai Marriott, and is often thought of as the Marriott's beach, but it's freely open to the general public as well.

Swimming is usually good, even in the winter, unless storms kick the surf up. The beach hut here rents snorkel gear, surfboards and kayaks.

There's free public beach parking close to the water at the north side of the hotel.

Nawiliwili Beach Park

Nawiliwili Beach Park is largely a parking lot facing an ocean retaining wall. From here, you can look across to the light beacon on Kukui Point, and at the far end of the parking lot you can also see the lighthouse on the more distant Ninini Point.

There's no beach at Nawiliwili Beach Park, but there is a footbridge that crosses Nawiliwili Stream to Kalapaki Beach.

Right at the mouth of the stream under ironwood trees is a simple shelter with a wooden sign reading 'Pine Tree Uptown' – it's an impromptu neighborhood open-air bar of sorts. Old-timers gather here during the day with ice chests of beer to 'talk story' and play music.

Nawiliwili Harbor

Nawiliwili Harbor has both a deepwater port with a large commercial harbor and an adjacent small-boat harbor. Several deep-sea fishing boats are based at the small-boat harbor, which has a picturesque setting backed by the edge of Haupu (Hoary Head) Ridge.

Waapa Rd runs southwest past the harbor and then connects with Hulemalu Rd, which leads up to an overview of the Menehune Fishpond.

Menehune Fishpond Overlook

Half a mile up Hulemalu Rd there's a lookout on the left with a view of Alakoko Fishpond, more commonly called Menehune Fishpond. In the background are the misty cliffs of Haupu Ridge.

The fishpond, created by a stone wall that runs along a bend in Huleia Stream, was said to have been built in one night by Kauai's legendary *menehunes*. The stone wall is now covered by a thick green line of mangrove trees. Morning is the best time for viewing the fishpond as in the afternoon you look into the sun

The **Huleia National Wildlife Refuge** lies along the north side of Huleia Stream. Once planted with taro and rice, the area now provides breeding and feeding grounds for endemic waterbirds. The refuge is not open to the public.

If you continue about a mile past the fishpond overlook and then turn right onto Puhi Rd, you'll arrive at Hwy 50, opposite Kauai Community College.

Grove Farm Homestead

The Grove Farm Homestead Plantation Museum (*☎ 245-3202; Nawiliwili Rd; adult/child under 12 $5/2*), which is 1¾ miles from Waapa Rd, is a preserved farmhouse built in 1864 by George Wilcox, the son of missionaries Abner and Lucy Wilcox. A bit musty and filled with memories, it's a little bit like the house of an elderly aunt. Rocking chairs sit on a covered porch, and one room is lined with bookshelves stuffed with a home library. In one corner, a card table is set up, waiting for a foursome to sit down to a wild game of cribbage.

Two-hour tours begin at 10am and 1pm on Monday, Wednesday and Thursday. Reservations are required, and space sometimes fills up a week or so in advance.

Kilohana Plantation

One and a half miles west of Lihue, Kilohana *(☎ 245-5608; Hwy 50; open 9:30am-9:30pm Mon-Sat, 9:30am-5pm Sun)* is the 1930s sugar plantation estate of Gaylord Parke Wilcox, once head of Grove Farm Homestead. The Tudor-style mansion built by Wilcox was the most distinguished house on Kauai in its day.

The home has been painstakingly restored, with most of the rooms now turned into shops that sell artwork, antiques and handicrafts. It's a nice way to preserve the old estate, and you can have a look around without being charged an admission fee.

Visitors are free to wander through rooms full of antiques. The hallways hold cases of stone poi pounders, koa bowls and a few other Hawaiian artifacts, while Oriental rugs grace the hardwood floors. If you're hungry, you might want to try Gaylord's restaurant (see Places to Eat, later), which occupies the U-shaped courtyard surrounding the lawn.

Many island galleries rent space at Kilohana, giving it one of the widest collections of arts and crafts on Kauai. On the 1st floor, a former cloakroom is now the Hawaiian Collection Room, which sells finely strung Niihau shell leis and scrimshaw.

The upstairs bedrooms have likewise been turned into shops, with displays even in the bathrooms and closets. The works include jewelry, dolls, wood carvings of whales and dolphins, and contemporary paintings by local artists. Behind the main house is Kilohana Clayworks pottery shop, where you can watch potters throwing clay on a wheel.

The 35-acre grounds are still part of a working farm; 20-minute tours in old-fashioned carriages pulled by Clydesdale horses cost $10 for adults and $5 for children under 12, and are available from 11am to 5pm daily.

Queen Victoria's Profile

The rock profile of Queen Victoria, part of Haupu (Hoary Head) Ridge, can be seen from a marked 'scenic view' pull-off in front of Kauai Community College along Hwy 50 in the town of Puhi.

It takes some imagination, but here's how to find it: Position yourself midway in the pull-off facing the mountains to the south. Look across the highway at the telephone pole, then over to the metal light pole in the background to the right. The queen's crowned head is under the arch of the lamp – the crown is the high part at the right, her chin lower and to the left.

Supposedly, she's shaking her thin pointy finger at an imaginary William, saying 'Na, Willy, Willy,' hence the harbor's name.

Who Do You See?

Long before Europeans decided that the vague rock profile on the Haupu Ridge looked like Queen Victoria, the Hawaiians had their own story. They call the rock Hina-i-uka.

Long ago, Peleula, a princess from Oahu, sailed to Kauai to check out rumors that the island had the most handsome men in Hawaii. Hina, a Kauai princess, welcomed her with a royal banquet. At the banquet was Kahili, a young chief from Kilauea, who caught the fancy of both women. To compete for his affections, they danced the hula.

Peleula's dance was stunning. But Hina, who was perfumed with the scent of Kauai's endemic *mokihana* berries, was absolutely mesmerizing, and she became Kahili's lover. The people of Kauai then carved one ridge of the Haupu Mountains into the image of Hina, with her finger up to warn off women from other islands.

Places to Stay

Motel Lani *(☎ 245-2965; 4240 Rice St; standard/deluxe rooms $35/55)* is a family-run place and Lihue's best budget choice, though it sits at a busy intersection. There's a cinder-block building with six rooms that are basic but clean and have private baths, air-con and minirefrigerators. The motel also has a couple of 'deluxe' rooms that are larger and have TVs. There's a two-day minimum stay or a $2 surcharge.

Tip Top Motel *(☎ 245-2333, fax 246-8988; ⓔ tiptop@aloha.net; 3173 Akahi St; rooms $45)* has two dozen rooms in two-story cinder-block buildings. Rooms are basic, with twin beds, air-con and louvered windows, but they do have TV and private baths.

Garden Island Inn *(☎ 245-7227, 800-648-0154; ⓔ info@gardenislandinn.com; 3445 Wilcox Rd; 1st-floor/2nd-floor rooms $65/95)* is an older three-story hotel with 21 rooms that are compact but tidy and modern with

TVs, ceiling fans, minirefrigerators, microwaves and coffeemakers. Rooms on the 2nd floor have air-con and small lanai. The hotel is near an industrial area and at the side of a rather busy road, so expect to hear some traffic noise. On the plus side, it's within walking distance of Kalapaki Beach.

Banyan Harbor Resort *(☎ 245-7333, 800-422-6926, fax 246-4776; ⓔ banyan@aloha.net; 2411 Wilcox Rd; 1-bedroom/2-bedroom units $125/150)* is a large condominium complex adjacent to the Garden Island Inn. It has modern units, each with a full kitchen, a sofa bed in the living room, either one or two compact bedrooms and a washer and dryer. Unlike most places there's no restriction on the number of people in the room. Up to four people could squeeze into the one-bedroom unit, and a family of six might get by in a two-bedroom unit. There's a tennis court and swimming pool.

Radisson Kauai Beach Resort *(☎ 245-1955, 888-245-7717, fax 246-9085; ⓔ info@radissonkauai.com; 4331 Kauai Beach Dr; rooms with mountain view $209, with ocean view $269)*, a few miles north of downtown Lihue, has 345 modern rooms with cushy comforts, data ports, 27-inch TVs and the like. The hotel has the standard design and amenities you'd expect of an upmarket chain, including tennis courts and large, free-form swimming pools.

Aston Kauai Beach Villas *(☎ 245-7711, 800-922-7866; ⓦ www.aston-hotels.com; 4330 Kauai Beach Dr; 1-bedroom/2-bedroom units $230/325, with ocean view $315/385)*, on the same beachfront property as the Radisson, has modern one-bedroom condos for up to four people and two-bedroom units for up to six people. Rates are about 15% cheaper in the low season.

Kauai Marriott *(☎ 245-5050, 800-228-9290, fax 241-6025; ⓔ jogle@hawaiian.net; Kalapaki Beach; rooms with garden view $299, with ocean view $415)* is a 356-room, upmarket hotel with an interesting history. Originally built as the Kauai Surf, the island's first multistory resort spawned a successful campaign to limit the height of new buildings on Kauai. Now, no new hotels can be built taller than a coconut tree. In the late 1980s, the resort was transformed into a luxury hotel with a multimillion-dollar art collection, marble lobbies and acres of artificial lagoons stocked with exotic wildlife. After the devastation of Hurricane Iniki, it reopened as a more scaled-down resort, though it still has a grand pool with spouting fountains, a health spa, tennis courts, a golf course and restaurants. Cheaper promotions are usually available.

Places to Eat

Fish Express *(3343 Kuhio Hwy; open 10am-7pm Mon-Sat, 10am-5pm Sun)*, just south of Wilcox Memorial Hospital, makes superb fresh fish lunches for take-out. From 10am to 3pm Monday to Friday you can get the fish of the day with a choice of several preparations, including grilled with passion-orange sauce or blackened in guava basil, along with rice and green salad for just $7.25. Alternatively opt for a fish sandwich with fries or tasty fish tacos for $6. Outside of lunch hours, you can still buy from the deli case: Generous sashimi trays are $5 and other deli items like tasty *poke* (marinated raw fish) are sold by the pound.

Hamura Saimin *(2956 Kress St; open 10am-10pm daily)*, in central Lihue, serves bowls of freshly made saimin (Japanese noodle soup) for $4 and tasty skewers of barbecued chicken for just a dollar. This little third-generation family-run operation is a throwback to an older Kauai. There are no tables, just a winding saimin bar where visitors and locals rub elbows as they slurp bowls of steaming hot saimin.

Beach Hut *(3474 Rice St; snacks $4-7; open 7am-7pm daily)* is a popular fast-food place near the Kauai Marriott. You order from a window on the ground level and carry your food up to the upper floor, where you can chow down with an ocean view. Pancakes, omelettes and other breakfast standards are available until 10:30am. At lunch, the two hottest items are the bacon-cheddar burger and the fish sandwich.

Kauai Chop Suey *(3501 Rice St; lunch $7, dinner $7-10; open 11am-2pm Tues-Sat, 4:30pm-9pm Tues-Sun)*, in the Harbor Mall, has Kauai's best Cantonese food. The vast menu covers all the standards, with everything from sweet-and-sour chicken to fried tofu with black mushrooms. If you order noodles, opt for the cake noodles, which are delightfully crispy.

Hawaiian Classic Desserts *(4491 Rice St; desserts $3-5, mains $7-10; open 7am-3pm Mon-Sat)*, opposite the Lihue Civic Center, serves more than desserts (though the chocolate decadence cake is a sinful treat). This upmarket café has a quiet open-air deck in the rear where you can enjoy all the usual breakfast options until 11am and hamburgers, sandwiches and a variety of salads at lunch. It's a bit pricey, but if you're not rushed it's a pleasant place to linger.

Lihue Barbecue Inn *(2982 Kress St; meals $7-12; open 11am-2pm Mon-Fri)* packs in a crowd with office workers on their lunch break. This quintessential local eatery, with a line of Formica booths, offers full meals that include soup, a drink, main course and dessert. Mains include everything from hamburgers to fresh fish and barbecued ribs – and the cream pie desserts are second to none.

Maria's *(☎ 246-9122; 3142 Kuhio Hwy; à la carte $4-8, dishes $12-13; open 11am-9pm Mon-Sat)* is a small, cozy place with traditional Mexican fare and cheery service. It serves up burritos, tostados, enchiladas, tacos and quesadillas with varied fillings, and you can order them in more than a dozen set combinations that include rice and beans.

Cafe Portofino *(☎ 245-2121; 3501 Rice St; appetizers $8-10, mains $14-26; open 5pm-10pm daily)*, in the Harbor Mall, serves authentic Italian fare and has collected an impressive number of accolades in recent years. A favorite here is the cheese ravioli in basil cream sauce. A live harpist performs nightly, adding a romantic touch to the dining.

Duke's Canoe Club *(☎ 246-9599; mains $15-25; open 5pm-10pm daily)*, at the Kauai Marriott, is a recommendable beachside restaurant. It has a pleasant atmosphere and a selection of fresh fish with half a dozen different preparations, as well as chicken, pasta and steak dishes. An extensive salad bar is included with all mains. If you come by car, the most convenient place to park is in the lot behind the Beach Hut eatery, where a footbridge crosses the stream to Duke's.

Gaylord's *(☎ 245-9593; lunch $8-11, dinner $19-29; open 11am-3pm Mon-Sat and from 5pm daily)*, at the Kilohana Plantation, enjoys a delightful, open-air estate setting, though the food is more ordinary than the ambience. Lunch features a variety of sandwiches and specialty salads. Dinner ranges from chicken dishes to rack of lamb.

Entertainment

Duke's Canoe Club *(☎ 246-9599)*, at the Kauai Marriott, is a good place to hang out on weekends, when there's live Hawaiian music from 4pm to 6pm Thursday and Friday, and rock music from 9pm to 11pm Friday and Saturday.

Rob's Good Times Grill *(☎ 246-0311; 4303 Rice St)*, in the Rice Shopping Center, attracts a mostly local crowd but is the place to go in Lihue if you want to dance. Music varies with the night. It also has large-screen sports TVs, pool tables and discounted happy-hour drinks.

There are weekly luaus at the **Radisson Kauai Beach Resort** *(☎ 335-5828; 4331 Kauai Beach Dr; adult/child $55/25)* on Monday evenings and at **Kilohana Plantation** *(☎ 245-9593; Hwy 50; adult/child $58/30)* on Tuesday and Thursday evenings.

If you're up for a movie, there's the fourplex **Kukui Grove Cinema** *(☎ 245-5055; 3-2600 Kaumualii Hwy)* in the Kukui Grove Center.

WAILUA

The 3-mile stretch of the Kuhio Hwy (Hwy 56) from Wailua to Kapaa is largely a scattering of shopping centers, restaurants, hotels and condos. Wailua doesn't really have a town center. Most of its sights are clustered around the Wailua River.

Long ago, Wailua was the site of Kauai's royal court, with 'Seven Sacred Heiaus' running from the mouth of the Wailua River up to the top of Mt Waialeale. Six of these *heiau* (temple) sites are located within a mile of the river mouth. Five are visible, while the sixth is abandoned in a field on the northern side of the Wailua River. All date back to the early period of Tahitian settlement and are considered to be of typical construction.

Wailua River State Park is a hodgepodge that includes most of the *heiau* sites, sections of the Wailua River bank, the Fern Grotto, the riverboat basin and a public boat ramp.

The Wailua River, which is estimated at 11¾ miles long, is the only navigable river in Hawaii. Owing to this, it has long been popular with package tourists on riverboat tours, as well as local water-skiers, and in recent years it has become thick with kayakers as well.

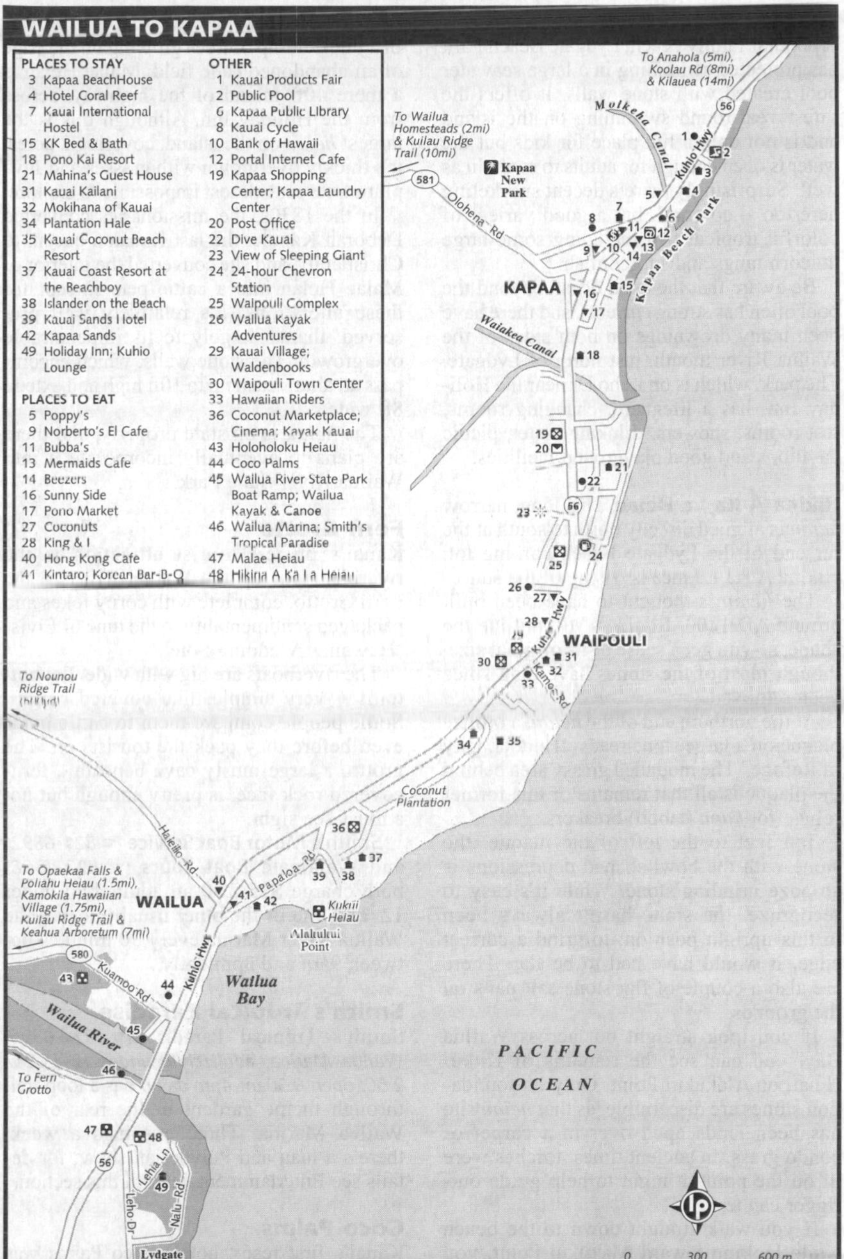
WAILUA TO KAPAA
PLACES TO STAY
3 Kapaa BeachHouse
4 Hotel Coral Reef
7 Kauai International Hostel
15 KK Bed & Bath
18 Pono Kai Resort
21 Mahina's Guest House
31 Kauai Kailani
32 Mokihana of Kauai
34 Plantation Hale
35 Kauai Coconut Beach Resort
37 Kauai Coast Resort at the Beachboy
38 Islander on the Beach
39 Kauai Sands Hotel
42 Kapaa Sands
49 Holiday Inn; Kuhio Lounge
PLACES TO EAT
5 Poppy's
9 Norberto's El Cafe
11 Bubba's
13 Mermaids Cafe
14 Beezers
16 Sunny Side
17 Pono Market
27 Coconuts
28 King & I
40 Hong Kong Cafe
41 Kintaro; Korean Bar-B-Q
OTHER
1 Kauai Products Fair
2 Public Pool
6 Kapaa Public Library
8 Kauai Cycle
10 Bank of Hawaii
12 Portal Internet Cafe
19 Kapaa Shopping Center; Kapaa Laundry Center
20 Post Office
22 Dive Kauai
23 View of Sleeping Giant
24 24-hour Chevron Station
25 Waipouli Complex
26 Wailua Kayak Adventures
29 Kauai Village; Waldenbooks
30 Waipouli Town Center
33 Hawaiian Riders
36 Coconut Marketplace; Cinema; Kayak Kauai
43 Holoholoku Heiau
44 Coco Palms
45 Wailua River State Park Boat Ramp; Wailua Kayak & Canoe
46 Wailua Marina; Smith's Tropical Paradise
47 Malae Heiau
48 Hikina A Ka La Heiau
To Anahola (5mi), Koolau Rd (8mi) & Kilauea (14mi)
To Wailua Homesteads (2mi) & Kuilau Ridge Trail (10mi)
Moikeha Canal
Kuhio Hwy
Kapaa Beach Park
Kapaa New Park
Olohena Rd
KAPAA
Waiakea Canal
WAIPOULI
Kamoa Rd
To Nounou Ridge Trail
Coconut Plantation
Haleilio Rd
Papaloa Rd
To Opaekaa Falls & Poliahu Heiau (1.5mi), Kamokila Hawaiian Village (1.75mi), Kuilau Ridge Trail & Keahua Arboretum (7mi)
WAILUA
Kukuii Heiau
Alakukui Point
Kuamoo Rd
Wailua Bay
Wailua River
To Fern Grotto
Lehia Ln
Leho Dr
Nalu Rd
Lydgate Beach Park
To Lihue (7mi)
PACIFIC OCEAN
0 300 600 m
0 300 600 yards

Lydgate Beach Park

A popular family beach, Lydgate Beach Park has protected swimming in a large seawater pool created with stone walls. It offers the safest year-round swimming on the island and is not only a fun place for kids but the water is deep enough for adults to swim in as well. Surprisingly there's decent snorkeling here too – no coral, but a good variety of colorful tropical fish including some large unicorn tangs and surgeonfish.

Be aware that the open ocean beyond the pool often has strong currents, and there have been many drownings on both sides of the Wailua River mouth, just north of Lydgate. The park, which is on Leho Dr near the Holiday Inn, has a lifeguard, changing rooms, rest rooms, showers, drinking water, picnic pavilions and good playground facilities.

Hikina A Ka La Heiau This long, narrow *heiau* is aligned directly north to south at the far end of the Lydgate Beach parking lot. Hikina A Ka La means 'rising of the sun.'

The *heiau* is thought to have been built around AD 1200. Boulders still outline the shape, so you get a sense of its original size, though most of the stones have long since been removed.

At the northern end of the *heiau*, a bronze plaque on a large stone reads: 'Hauola, City of Refuge.' The mounded grassy area behind the plaque is all that remains of this former refuge for *kapu* (taboo) breakers.

Ten feet to the left of the plaque, the stone with the bowl-shaped depressions is an adze grinding stone. While it's easy to recognize, the stone hasn't always been in this upright position; to grind a correct edge, it would have had to be flat. There are also a couple of flat stone salt pans on the grounds.

If you look straight out across Wailua Bay, you can see the remains of Kukui Heiau on Alakukui Point. Only its foundation stones are discernible, as that *heiau* site has been landscaped over in a carpet of condo grass. In ancient times, torches were lit on the point at night to help guide outrigger canoes.

If you walk straight down to the beach while looking toward Alakukui Point, you may find a few ancient stones with petroglyphs carved into the rock, though they're usually hidden under shifting sands.

Malae Heiau

In a thick clump of trees growing on the edge of an abandoned cane field, Malae Heiau is a mere 40ft inland of the highway, across from the Holiday Inn. Although this is the largest *heiau* on the island, covering 2 acres, it's thickly overgrown with grasses and Java plum trees and almost impossible to explore.

In the 1830s, the missionaries converted Deborah Kapule, the last Kauaian queen, to Christianity, and she converted the interior of Malae Heiau into a cattle pen. Except for these alterations, it's relatively well preserved, thanks largely to its impenetrable overgrowth. The stone walls, which encompass an altar, reach up to 10ft high and extend 8ft wide.

The *heiau* is on state property, and there are plans to eventually incorporate it into Wailua River State Park.

Fern Grotto

Kauai's busiest tourist attraction is the riverboat tour up the Wailua River to the Fern Grotto, complete with corny jokes and packaged sentimentality to the tune of Elvis' 'Hawaiian Wedding Song.'

The riverboats are big with wide, flat bottoms – very simple, like covered barges. Some people compare them to cattle boats even before they pack the tourists on. The grotto, a large musty cave beneath a fern-covered rock face, is pretty enough but not a must-see sight.

Smith's Motor Boat Service *(☎ 821-6892)* and **Waialeale Boat Tours** *(☎ 822-4908)* both charge $15/7.50 an adult/child under 12, and one or the other usually leaves the Wailua River Marina every 30 minutes between 9am and 3pm daily.

Smith's Tropical Paradise

Smith's Tropical Paradise *(☎ 821-6895; Wailua Marina; adult/child under 12 $5.25/2.50; open 8:30am-4pm daily)* has a loop trail through theme gardens at the rear of the Wailua Marina. Three evenings a week, there's a luau and Polynesian show; for details see Entertainment, later in this section.

Coco Palms

Kauai's first resort hotel, Coco Palms was built on the site of Kauai's ancient royal court, in the midst of a historic 45-acre coconut grove. The 'tropical theme' hotel looked a bit like a movie set, with lagoons, thatched cottages and torchlit paths. In fact, the hotel's outdoor chapel was originally built in 1954 for the movie *Sadie Thompson* with Rita Hayworth. The highest-profile wedding that took place at Coco Palms was that of Elvis Presley and Joan Blackman in *Blue Hawaii*, after which thousands of mainland couples flocked to the Coco Palms chapel to take their own wedding vows.

The resort was devastated by Hurricane Iniki and still sits in disrepair, but it remains a Kauai landmark and can be seen from the road.

Highway 580

Also known as Kuamoo Rd, Hwy 580 begins at the traffic light on Hwy 56 at Coco Palms. It passes *heiau*s, historical sites, Opaekaa Falls and Wailua Homesteads before reaching Keahua Arboretum, the starting place for a couple of backcountry trails.

Holoholoku Heiau A *luakini heiau* (a temple used for human sacrifices), Holoholoku is a quarter mile up Hwy 580 on the left. Like all of the Wailua *heiau*s, this one was of enclosure-type construction, with its stone walls built directly on the ground rather than on terraced platforms.

This whole area used to be royal property, and here on the west side of the grounds, against the flat-backed birthstone, queens gave birth to future kings. This stone is marked by a plaque that reads 'Pohaku Hoohanau.' Another stone a few yards away, marked 'Pohaku Piko,' was where the *piko* (umbilical cords) of the babies were left.

Above the temple where Hawaiian royals were born, steps lead to a hilltop cemetery where later-day Japanese laborers lie at rest.

Poliahu Heiau Perched high on a hill overlooking the meandering Wailua River, Poliahu Heiau is named after the snow goddess Poliahu, one of Pele's sisters. This relatively well-preserved *heiau* is thought to have been of the *luakini* type.

Poliahu Heiau is immediately before the Opaekaa Falls lookout, on the opposite side of the road.

Bellstone Immediately south of Poliahu Heiau, on the same side of Hwy 580, look for a 'Falling Rocks' sign that marks a short and rutted dirt drive leading to a bellstone. Because of the road's angle, it's easiest to approach coming downhill from Poliahu.

In old Hawaii, the Wailua River was a naval entrance, and the bellstone at this lookout was thought to have been used by sentries to warn of attacks as well as to ring out announcements of royal births.

There are actually two stones at the end of the drive, one with an all-too-perfect petroglyph whose age is suspect. Archaeologists question just which stone may have been the bellstone. Although you can find depressions in the stones, they may well be the result of modern-day poundings by people trying to check out the resonance for themselves.

A short path down from these rocks leads to a vista of the river, where you can commonly see cattle grazing on the banks below and hear the amplified narration from passing riverboats.

Opaekaa Falls This is a high, broad waterfall that usually flows as a double cascade, though after a heavy rain the two sides often merge. The peaks of the Makaleha Mountains form a scenic backdrop, and white-tailed tropicbirds can often be seen soaring in the valley below the falls.

This is an easy-to-view waterfall, visible from the road. The signposted turnoff to the viewpoint is 1½ miles up Hwy 580 from Wailua. For the best angle, walk up the sidewalk past the parking lot toward the bridge.

Kamokila Hawaiian Village Situated along the shores of the Wailua River, this re-created Hawaiian village *(☎ 823-0559; open 9am-5pm Mon-Sat)* comprises grass huts, an assembly house, a women's house and various other structures that were once common to native communities. This is a small down-home operation run by a Hawaiian family.

A guide describes the function of each building, explains the traditional uses of the native plants that grow on the grounds and does such things as demonstrate the hula, weave ti-leaf bracelets and husk drinking coconuts for guests – all for a $5 donation. The hour-long tour provides a nice sense of aloha that is lost in many larger, mass-produced operations elsewhere.

Kamokila is on the south side of Hwy 580, opposite Opaekaa Falls, at the end of a narrow half-mile-long paved road. You can

KAUAI

also rent kayaks at Kamokila; for details, see Kayaking in the Activities section earlier in this chapter.

Kuilau Ridge Trail For the effort, the Kuilau Ridge Trail is one of the most visually rewarding trails on the island. The marked trailhead is on the right just before Hwy 580 crosses the stream at the Keahua Arboretum, 4 miles up from the junction of Hwys 580 and 581. Don't leave anything of value in your car.

The trail starts up a wide dirt path also used by horses and the occasional renegade dirt biker. Along the way, birdsong emanates from the dense native vegetation, which includes koa trees, *ohia lehua* and thickets of ti. In the upper reaches, the lush, fern-covered hillsides provide broad vistas of the mountains. Guava trees and wild thimbleberries grow along the path.

The hike climbs to a broad ridge offering views into valleys on both sides and clear down to the coast. You can see Kapaa to the east and the island's uninhabited central region to the west. It takes about 40 minutes to walk the 1¼ miles up to a grassy clearing on the ridge-top, where you'll find a couple of picnic tables and a view of Mt Waialeale.

Beyond the clearing, to the right past the picnic area, the Kuilau Ridge Trail continues as a narrow footpath offering even more spectacular views. It ends in about a mile at the Moalepe Trail. If you don't want to go that far, at least walk a little of it, as some of the best vistas are along the next half mile of the trail.

If you go left at the connection with the Moalepe Trail, you'll come to a viewpoint after about 10 minutes. If you go right on Moalepe, you'll come out on Olohena Rd in Wailua Homesteads after about 2¼ miles.

Wailua Homesteads

In the Wailua Homesteads area, on the west side of the Sleeping Giant mountain, the government once offered 160-acre parcels to people willing to work the land. Most early homesteaders used the land to graze cattle, though at one point the Dole Company grew pineapples in the area. Today, Wailua Homesteads is largely a mix of spacious residential lots and pastoral countryside reminiscent of Pennsylvania Dutch farmland.

The main through-road is Hwy 581 (Kamalu Rd), which connects with Hwy 580 at its southern end and with Olohena Rd at its northern end. Together, Kamalu Rd and Olohena Rd form Hwy 581.

Nounou Ridge Trail

The Nounou Ridge Trail climbs up the Sleeping Giant to a summit on the giant's upper chest, affording views of both the east coast and the highland valleys. It's a well-maintained trail that takes 1½ to two hours round-trip. Because the trail is somewhat steep, it provides a hardy workout.

There are two trailheads, both marked. The trail on the western side is a shaded forest trail of tall trees and moss-covered stones. The trail on the eastern side, which is more exposed and a bit longer, begins at a parking lot a mile up Haleilio Rd in the Wailua Houselots neighborhood.

The trail up the western side of the mountain starts on Kamalu Rd (Hwy 581), near house No 1068. Walk through a metal gate marked as a forestry right-of-way and up along a small cattle pasture to the trailhead. If you have a car, note that you can't park at the trailhead, but you can park and access the trail at the end of Lokelani Rd, which is off Kamalu Rd a bit farther north. If you pick up the trail there, it will deposit you on the same pasture but closer to the woods.

This is a wonderful trail to do early in the morning, when it's relatively cool and you can watch the light spread across the valley below. The packed trail can get slippery when wet; look for a walking stick, which hikers sometimes leave near the trailhead.

The eucalyptus trees at the trailhead soon give way to a tall, thick forest of Norfolk pines that were planted in a Civilian Conservation Corps (CCC) reforestation programme during the 1930s. About five minutes into the woods, right after the Norfolk pines begin, there's a fork. Veer left up the path with the large rock beside it.

The trail passes through thick strawberry guava bushes that can grow up to 15ft high; in places, the guava creates a canopied, tunnel-like effect. Strawberry guava has a small red fruit that's eaten whole and is considered the sweetest of any guava.

A few minutes below the summit, the eastern and western trails merge on the ridge. Continue up to the right past some *hala* (pandanus) trees. On the summit is a picnic table shelter that offers protection from the rain. Passing showers can create some incredible valley rainbows. To the west, there's a 180-degree view of Wailua and the Makaleha Mountains.

Below, to the east, you can see Kapaa, Coco Palms and the Wailua River. To the right of the riverboat docks and inland from the Holiday Inn, you can see Malae Heiau as a dark green square in the midst of an abandoned cane field.

If you go south across the picnic area, the trail continues. About five minutes up, there's a rocky area where you can sit and enjoy the view. The ridge continues up the giant's chin. Should it tempt you, size it up carefully. It's sharp, and loose rocks and slides are visible.

Coconut Plantation

Coconut Plantation, on Hwy 56, is the area's main resort development, with four hotels, a condominium and a shopping center. It fronts a half-mile-long beach partially shaded by ironwood trees.

Water activities are restricted due to the low lava shelf that runs along most of the beach and the strong currents that prevail beyond. The best section for swimming is in front of the Kauai Sands Hotel, where there's a break in the lava shelf.

While water conditions are mediocre, the beach makes for good strolling and you can occasionally spot monk seals basking on the shore. The large field between the Kauai Coconut Beach Resort and the Kauai Coast Resort at the Beachboy is popular with golden plovers and other migratory birds.

The resort's shopping center, **Coconut Marketplace**, has numerous boutiques, art galleries and gift shops; all are open 9am to 9pm Monday to Saturday, and 10am to 6pm Sunday.

Places to Stay

B&Bs & Cottages If you don't feel any need to be on the beach, the following Wailua accommodations represent some of the best value on Kauai. The listings in this section are all in the Wailua Homesteads area, about 3 miles from the coast in a rural setting. All are within a mile or so of the intersection of Hwys 581 and 580.

Rosewood B&B *(☎ 822-5216, fax 822-5478; ⓔ rosewood@aloha.net; 872 Kamalu Rd; rooms $40-85, studio cottage $85, 2-bedroom cottage $115)* is a beautifully restored century-old plantation home belonging to Rosemary and Norbert Smith. Upstairs in the home is a stylish guest room with a king bed, a tiled bath with sunken tub, and a mountain view.

Also on the grounds are two attractive cottages. The Victorian Cottage is cheery and spacious with high ceilings, oak floors, ceiling fans, a full kitchen, a master bedroom with a king bed, and an upstairs bedroom with two twin beds. The Thatched Cottage is studio-style with a Hawaiian design that includes coconut fronds on the roof and screened windows all around that open to a garden with birdsong; it has a king bed, kitchenette, ceiling fans, indoor toilet, outdoor hot shower and barbecue grill.

A third building, the Bunkhouse, has three straightforward but certainly comfortable rooms geared for budget travelers. Each has a sink, coffeemaker, microwave, toaster, refrigerator and barbecue grill. All share an indoor toilet and an enclosed outdoor shower set in a garden. Rates are a bargain at $40 for the two smallest rooms – one of which has two single beds and the other a queen – and $50 for the largest, which has a king bed in the loft and a sofa bed on the lower level. All accommodations are nonsmoking. Guests have access to an online computer.

House of Aleva *(☎ 822-4606; 5509 Kuamoo Rd; singles/doubles $40/55)* is a B&B in the home of Ernest and Anita Perry, right on Hwy 580, 2 miles up from Coco Palms. Ernest is a retired merchant seaman and Anita is a retired nurse who reads palms and makes ceramic Hawaiiana sculptures. The two upstairs guest rooms, which share a bath, each have a queen bed as well as a phone, TV, minirefrigerator and microwave. The smaller downstairs room has a twin bed and is rented out as a single room.

Magic Sunrise Hawaii *(☎ 821-9847, fax 823-8542; ⓔ aloha@magicsunrisehawaii.com; 139 Royal Dr; rooms $50-60, cottages $85-100)*, run by a Swiss mother and daughter, has a distinctively New Age flavor and caters mainly to European travelers. It's a delightfully serene place with colorful accommodations decorated with bamboo beds, feather wall hangings, Indian prints and the like. There are a couple of rooms in the main house, a one-bedroom unit with a lanai overlooking the mountains, and a two-bedroom cottage that can comfortably hold up to five people. All guests have access to a kitchen and there's a pool.

Hempey's Garden Island (☎ *822-0478, fax 822-4399;* ⓔ *ph@hawaiianbedandbreakfast.com; 6078 Kolopua Rd; rooms/studios $55/65)* is a B&B in the home of Dan and Patrice Hempey. There are three cozy guest rooms, each with private bath, and a brightly painted studio with a separate entrance and a kitchenette. All guests have access to a kitchen, a sitting room and an online computer. Dan, a lawyer, has been involved in many liberal causes, including rescuing dogs from medical research labs, some of which now live with the Hempeys. Patrice, who hails from Brazil, speaks Portuguese, Spanish, French and Italian.

Inn Paradise (☎ *822-2542;* ⓔ *mcinch@aloha.net; 6381 Makana Rd; units $70-100)* has three units with nice touches like Persian carpets, rattan furnishings and Hawaiiana wall prints. Each has a TV, refrigerator, microwave, toaster, coffeemaker and private entrance. All share a lanai with a view of pasture and mountains. The cheapest, the Prince Kuhio room, has a king bed. The Queen Kapule suite has a king bed and a separate living room with a Murphy bed. The King Kaumualii unit, equipped like a small house, has two bedrooms, one with a king bed, the other with two twins, and a full kitchen; it sleeps up to four people. There's a two-night minimum.

Rainbows End (☎ *823-0066, fax 823-0071;* ⓔ *rainbowsend@lava.net; 6470 Kipapa Rd; rates $115)* is a cute little cottage on a quiet road tucked into a mountain valley. It's small, but homey, with a futon sofa and a small kitchenette in the living room; a bathroom with a claw-foot whirlpool tub; and a comfy bedroom with a queen bed, ceiling fan and stained-glass windows. There's lots of nice touches here, including inlaid mahogany floors, original artwork, and gardens laden with tropical fruits and plants.

Condos & Hotels Part of the Hawaiian-owned Sand & Seaside hotel chain, **Kauai Sands Hotel** (☎ *822-4951, 800-560-5553;* ⓔ *info@sand-seaside.com; 420 Papaloa Rd; rooms $98, with kitchenette $130)* has rooms in a series of two-story buildings that mostly surround the lawn and pool. They're a bit plainer than those in neighboring hotels, but still have all the expected comforts of a resort hotel. In addition, the hotel often offers handsome discounts – the current 'Fun in the Sun' deal cuts rates to as low as $65, depending on how busy the hotel is. All rooms are spacious and have two double beds, air-con, a TV, minirefrigerator and lanai.

Kapaa Sands (☎ *822-4901, 800-222-4901, fax 822-1556;* ⓔ *ksresort@gte.net; 380 Papaloa Rd; studios $117, 2-bedroom units $134, with ocean view $152)* has 20 condo units set up in either duplexes or fourplexes. All have kitchens, lanai, louvered windows to catch the breeze, and at least a partial ocean view. While the complex is an older one, the place has been renovated and the two-bedroom units, which can comfortably accommodate four people, are a relatively good value for two couples traveling together. There's a three-day minimum stay in the low season and a seven-day minimum in winter.

Islander on the Beach (☎ *822-7417, 800-922-7866, fax 822-1947;* ⓔ *info@aston-hotels.com; 484 Kuhio Hwy; rooms with garden view $145, with ocean view $178)* is a pleasant hotel with 195 rooms in half a dozen three-story buildings. Each room has a king bed or two double beds, a refrigerator, coffeemaker, air-con, TV, room safe and lanai. There's a poolside bar.

Kauai Coast Resort at the Beachboy (☎ *822-3441, fax 822-0843;* ⓔ *kbb@aloha.net; 484 Kuhio Hwy; rooms $120, 1-bedroom/2-bedroom condos $185/245)* is a beachfront property that has just been thoroughly renovated. It has both hotel-style rooms with a small refrigerator and coffeemaker and condominium units with full kitchens and a washing machine and dryer. All have stylish furnishings, air-con, lanai, TV and room safe. Amenities include tennis courts, a pool and fitness facilities.

Holiday Inn (☎ *823-6000, 800-823-5111, fax 823-6666;* ⓔ *info@holidayinn-kauai.com; 3-5920 Kuhio Hwy; rooms with garden view $198, with ocean view $231)* is adjacent to Lydgate Beach Park. The hotel's rooms are modern and comfortable, though they vary significantly in size. Request the Pikake Wing, which has larger rooms, each furnished with two queen beds, a big-screen TV, desk and refrigerator. The hotel commonly offers discount schemes, including a perennial 'Great Rate' deal that knocks up to 40%

off the above rates – ask about promotions when booking.

Plantation Hale *(☎ 822-4941, 800-775-4253, fax 822-5599; ⓔ ph@aloha.net; 484 Kuhio Hwy; units $145-165)*, on the highway side of Coconut Plantation, is a member of the Best Western chain. The complex has 160 spacious and modern one-bedroom units, each with either two double beds or one king bed in the bedroom, a queen sofa bed in the living room, a full kitchen, air-con, ceiling fans and two TVs. There are a couple of pools. The rate is the same for up to four people.

Kauai Coconut Beach Resort *(☎ 822-3455, 800-760-8555, fax 822-1830; ⓔ info@kcb.com; 484 Kuhio Hwy; rooms $165, with ocean view $215)*, a former Sheraton, is a 312-room beachside hotel at the quieter north end of Coconut Plantation. The lobby and other common spaces are overdue for renovations, but the rooms are comfortable, with either two doubles or a king bed, TV, room safe, mini-refrigerator, coffeemaker and a tiny lanai. The 4th-floor rooms are the nicest, as they have high ceilings that make the rooms feel a bit larger. There's a pool. Published rates are pricey, but there are a slew of discounts available, and when business slacks off the walk-in rate sometimes drops to just $75.

Places to Eat

The **Coconut Marketplace** *(484 Kuhio Hwy)* has a handful of food kiosks serving inexpensive fare. The best are **Aloha Pizza**, with good, moderately priced calzone and pizza, including a tasty artichoke-garlic version ($6); the **Fish Hut**, with fish and chips ($7); and **Harley's Ribs-N-Chicken**, which has a good Caesar salad with lemon-pepper chicken ($7). The Coconut Marketplace also has a couple of sit-down restaurants and a small convenience store that sells snacks and liquor. All are open from 11am to 8pm, at least.

Hong Kong Cafe *(4-361 Kuhio Hwy; open 10:30am-9:30pm Mon-Fri, 2:30pm-9:30pm Sat & Sun)* is a casual place with inexpensive Chinese food. Plate lunches with items such as lemon chicken, barbecued duck or teriyaki beef are just $4 to $6.

Korean Bar-B-Q *(4-356 Kuhio Hwy; open 10am-9pm Wed-Mon, 4:30pm-9pm Tues)* has good Korean food at honest prices. Combination plates with two scoops of rice and four vegetable side dishes cost $6 with barbecued chicken, or $6.50 with a beef and chicken combination.

Kintaro *(☎ 822-3341; 4-370 Kuhio Hwy; meals $14-20; open 5:30pm-9:30pm Mon-Sat)*, adjacent to Korean Bar-B-Q, is the best Japanese restaurant on the island. It has an excellent sushi bar as well as a fun *teppanyaki* room, where the chef prepares food on an iron grill right at your table – all done with much ado and some impressive knife work. Meals come with soup, rice and tea – so there's nothing that pads up your bill here. Kintaro is simply an unbeatable value for a high-end eatery.

Entertainment

The **Kuhio Lounge** *(☎ 823-6000; 3-5920 Kuhio Hwy)* at the Holiday Inn is a good place for a drink any night, and on Friday nights it becomes the area's hottest dance spot.

Kauai Coconut Beach Resort *(☎ 822-3455; Coconut Plantation; luau adult/child 12-17/child 3-11 $55/33/23)* holds a luau at 6pm nightly, with an open bar, dinner and a Polynesian revue. You can catch a glimpse of the festivities from the hotel parking lot. If you're interested in seeing the *imu* (oven) preparation, you can watch the pig being stuffed with hot rocks and buried at 10:45am.

Smith's Tropical Paradise *(☎ 821-6895; Wailua Marina; luau adult/child 7-13/child 3-6 $56/28.50/18.75)* has a luau with cocktails, dinner and musical show at 5pm on Monday, Wednesday and Friday.

Free hula shows take place at the **Coconut Marketplace** *(☎ 822-3641)* at 5pm daily.

Coconut Marketplace Cinemas *(☎ 821 2324)*, in the Coconut Marketplace, is a two-screen theater showing first-run movies.

WAIPOULI

Waipouli is the mile-long commercial strip between Coconut Plantation and Kapaa. Its biggest draw is its assortment of shopping centers, which are not only the area's largest, but also contain some of Kauai's best places to eat.

In Kauai Village, Waipouli's largest shopping center, you'll find the **Kauai Heritage Center**, which displays handmade wood carvings, feather leis, bamboo nose flutes and other traditional Hawaiian crafts. The center also offers one-day craft workshops for those who would like to learn more.

Information

American Savings Bank *(☎ 822-0529; 4-771 Kuhio Hwy; open 10am-8pm Mon-Fri, 10am-4pm Sat & Sun)* is inside the Foodland supermarket in the Waipouli Town Center.

The Kapaa **post office** *(☎ 800-275-8777; 4-1101 Kuhio Hwy; open 8am-4pm Mon-Fri, 9am-2pm Sat)* is in the Kapaa Shopping Center.

You can wash clothes at **Kapaa Laundry Center** *(☎ 822-3113; 4-1101 Kuhio Hwy; open 7:30am-9:30pm daily)* in the Kapaa Shopping Center.

Sleeping Giant

From a marked viewpoint just north of the Waipouli Complex, look for the outline of the Sleeping Giant atop Nounou Ridge.

According to legend, the friendly giant fell asleep on the hillside after eating too much poi at a luau. When his *menehune* friends needed his help, they tried to awaken him by throwing stones. But the stones bounced from the giant's full belly into his open mouth. As the stones lodged in the giant's throat, he died in his sleep and turned into rock. Now he rests eternally, stretched out on the ridge with his head in Wailua and his feet in Kapaa.

A hiking trail runs across the ridge, connecting Wailua Houselots and Wailua Homesteads (see the earlier Wailua section). At an elevation of 1241ft, the giant's forehead is the highest point on the ridge.

KAUAI

Places to Stay

Mokihana of Kauai *(☎ 822-3971; 796 Kuhio Hwy; rooms $65)* is a time-share complex that rents to nonmembers on the basis of availability. It has 79 studio units on the beach, and while they're quite straightforward they're a real bargain for the money. Each has twin beds, a hot plate, a refrigerator and a lanai with an ocean view. There are no microwaves or ovens in the units, but there are a couple of barbecue grills by the pool.

Kauai Kailani *(rooms $65-75)*, a nearby sister property, has 58 two-bedroom time-share units handled by the front desk at Mokihana. These units have full kitchens, two twin beds in one room and a queen in the other; rates cover up to four people.

You can also make advance reservations for either Mokihana of Kauai or Kauai Kailani through **Hawaii Kailani** *(☎ 360-676-1434, fax 360-676-1435; 1201 11th St, Suite 100, Bellingham, WA 98225)*.

Hale Makani *(☎ 822-5216, fax 822-5478; 321 Makani Rd; house $150)* is a lovely contemporary house in a quiet neighborhood at the base of the Sleeping Giant mountain. With three bedrooms and two baths, it would make a fine choice for a family or small group traveling together. The master bedroom has a king bed, there's a queen bed in the second bedroom and two twins in the third. The house has hardwood floors, cathedral ceilings, a washer, dryer, ceiling fans, a fully equipped kitchen and a living room with a stereo system, TV and VCR. There's a deck in the front with a barbecue grill and an ocean view, and a deck off the master bedroom with a hot tub and mountain view.

Places to Eat

Papaya's Natural Foods *(deli open 9am-7pm daily; store open until 8pm)*, in the Kauai Village shopping center, is an excellent health food store serving wholesome salads, sandwiches and simple meals. Veggie burgers cost $5, while full-meal specials, such as fish tacos with brown rice and salad, are around $8. Although it's take-out style, there are tables in the courtyard where you can relax and eat.

Panda Garden *(dishes $7-12, lunch $6-9; open 10:30am-2pm Thur-Tues, 4pm-9:30pm daily)*, in the Kauai Village shopping center, has Kauai's best Sichuan food. The extensive menu includes vegetarian fare as well as dozens of seafood, duck and meat dishes. In addition to the à la carte menu, there are several four-course dinners to choose from for a reasonable $13 to $16.

King & I *(4-901 Kuhio Hwy; open 4:30pm-9:30pm daily)*, in the Waipouli Plaza, is a friendly family-run Thai restaurant. The green curries, which get their perky color from fresh basil, lime leaves and lemongrass, are delicious. The curries, like most other dishes on the menu, cost $8 for meat varieties and $10 for shrimp or fish. All can be prepared mild, medium or hot. The restaurant also has several vegetarian dishes, including a flavorful eggplant and tofu ($8) prepared in chili oil.

Coconuts *(☎ 823-9777; 4-919 Kuhio Hwy; appetizers $6-10, mains $10-22; open 4pm-10pm Mon-Sat)* is the trendiest new restaurant on this side of the island. It's a lively place that sports a tropical decor and consistently good island-influenced food such as *ahi* tuna with pineapple chutney, *lilikoi*-coconut glazed salmon and Thai curry pasta. Actually, just about everything on the menu will make your mouth water. The only catch is getting a table, since Coconuts only takes reservations for parties of five or more, but if you get here before 6pm you'll beat the crowd.

A Pacific Cafe *(☎ 822-0013; appetizers $8-11, mains $19-25; open 5:30pm-9:30pm daily)*, in Kauai Village, is a bustling, high-energy restaurant serving excellent Pacific Rim cuisine. French chef Jean-Marie Josselin offers a creative menu with dishes like coconut curried soup and sesame-crusted mahimahi in ginger sauce. A Pacific Cafe is a class act, with artful presentation and attentive service – if you're saving one night for a splurge, this is a top choice. Reservations are recommended.

At the opposite end of the gastronomic scale you'll find many fast-food eateries along Kuhio Hwy in Waipouli, including the usual mainland burger and pizza chains.

A good alternative to fast food is the 24-hour **Safeway** supermarket, in Kauai Village, which has a deli counter with fried chicken and salads, a bakery with superb lemon doughnuts and a fish counter with an unbeatable sesame-*ahi poke*. In addition, the store has a good, reasonably priced wine selection – though if you're willing to go with the weekly sale items, the island's best alcohol prices are often found at the adjacent **Longs Drugs**.

KAPAA

Kapaa is an old plantation town with a small commercial center that is half-local, half-tourist oriented. As unimposing as it appears, Kapaa is one of the island's largest towns, with a population of 9500. However, most of the residential area is well inland of the center, and you can walk the main drag in just 10 minutes.

While many of Kapaa's historic buildings were leveled by Hurricane Iniki, most of the reconstruction was in keeping with the town's original character rather than adopting the shopping mall appearance that predominates to the south of Kapaa. Partly because of this appeal the town center (often called Kapaa Town by locals) has attracted new alternative businesses including an Internet café, some good small eateries and a natural food store. Kapaa also has a handful of budget accommodations.

If you're interested in picking up handicrafts, the **Kauai Products Fair**, a crafts fair on the north side of town, has a few dozen stalls where islanders sell pottery, jewelry, batik clothing and the like from Thursday to Sunday.

Information

The **Bank of Hawaii** *(☎ 822-3471; 4-1407 Kuhio Hwy; open 8:30am-4pm Mon-Thur, 8:30am-6pm Fri)* has a branch in the town center.

In the town center, **Portal Internet Cafe** *(☎ 822-7678; 4-1388 Kuhio Hwy)* has several online computers and charges $1 per five minutes, with no minimum.

Bubba's *(☎ 823-0069; 4-1421 Kuhio Hwy)*, a nearby burger joint, allows customers to check their email for free, but there's only one computer so expect a long wait.

Also in the town center is **Kapaa Public Library** *(☎ 821-4422; 4-1464 Kuhio Hwy; open 9am-5pm Mon, Wed & Fri, noon-8pm Tues & Thur)*.

Kapaa Beach Park

This park begins along the north side of Kapaa, where there's a ball field, picnic tables and a public swimming pool. The beach continues south for about a mile; the section fronting the Pono Kai Resort has one of the nicer sandy areas. Along the length of the beach, there's a shoreline foot and bicycle path that follows a former sugarcane rail line and passes over a couple of old bridges. If you're staying in the area, the path makes an appealing alternative to walking along the highway to and from town.

Places to Stay

Kauai International Hostel *(☎ 823-6142; www.hostels.com/kauaihostel; 4532 Lehua St; dorm beds/rooms $20/50)* is a casual, private hostel conveniently located in the center of Kapaa. There are about 30 dorm beds, four to six to a room, and five simple private rooms with double beds. All rooms, including the private ones, have shared bathrooms. The hostel has a common dining room, kitchen, pool table, TV room and coin laundry. This place has been through some ups and downs over the years, and gets mixed reviews, so look it over carefully before plunking down any money in advance.

Kapaa BeachHouse *(☎ 822-3424; Ⓦ www.kauai-blue-lagoon.com; 1552 Kuhio Hwy; singles/doubles $20/35, private rooms $45)* is an aging oceanfront property that's slowly being renovated into a hostel-style guest house. A side project of a local chiropractor, the place has a fine seaside location but it is a work in progress, so don't expect things to be too refined. The dorm has eight bunks, each with a double mattress and a curtain that can be drawn for some privacy. Guests have use of kitchen facilities, a washing machine and an ocean-view deck.

KK Bed & Bath *(☎ 822-7348, 800-615-6211 ext 32; Ⓦ www.kkbedbath.com; 4486 Kauwila St; singles/doubles/triples $35/50/60)* has a convenient location in the town center, just a short walk from the beach. It consists of two identical units in a converted storehouse behind the home of owner Richard Sugiyama. Though Richard refers to them as a budget alternative, the units are comfortable, each with a queen bed, private bath, refrigerator, TV, phone, small table and ceiling fans. A portable barbecue is available, and the place is wheelchair accessible.

Mahina's Guest House *(☎ 823-9364; ⓔ mahinas@hawaiian.net; 4433 Panihi Rd; singles $35-60, doubles $55-80)*, a casual, three-bedroom home near the beach on the south side of Kapaa, provides accommodations for women travelers. One room is shared dorm-style, with two single beds, at $35 per bed. Another room has a queen bed, the third a king bed and the enclosed lanai holds a double bed. Guests share kitchen, bathroom and laundry facilities. Owner Sharon Gonsalves takes efforts to keep allergens low; there are no pets and smoking is not allowed.

Hotel Coral Reef *(☎ 822-4481, 800-843-4659, fax 822-7705; 1516 Kuhio Hwy; rooms $65-99)* is a small, family-run hotel with two sections. The main building has a few rooms with bath, TV and either one queen or a double and twin bed. The rooms in the seaside building are a bit larger and have lanai overlooking the ocean. Complimentary coffee and homemade breads are available at breakfast time in the lobby. There's no pool, but the hotel is right on the beach.

Pono Kai Resort *(☎ 822-9831, 800-535-0085; Ⓦ www.marcresorts.com; 4-1250 Kuhio Hwy; 1-/2-bedroom garden view $145/190, ocean view $190/235)* is a pleasant 219-room beachfront condominium at the south side of Kapaa, within walking distance of the town center. Each of the roomy, well-equipped units has a full kitchen with dishwasher and microwave, and a living room with a queen sofa bed. Additional amenities include air-con, ceiling fans, cable TV and lanai. On the grounds are tennis courts, a pool and a beach.

Places to Eat

The eateries that follow are all within walking distance of each other on Kuhio Hwy (Hwy 56), near its intersection with Olohena Rd.

Pono Market *(4-1300 Kuhio Hwy; open 7am-7pm Mon-Sat)*, a small food store with a deli counter, is the place to get good take-out food and the choices always include traditional Hawaiian fare. Line up with the locals to get generous plate lunches ($6) of teriyaki chicken, sushi, *lomi* (raw, diced salmon marinated with tomatoes and onions) and *poke*. Fresh fruit and vegetables are sold at **Sunny Side**, a large produce stand oppose Pono Market.

Bubba's *(4-1421 Kuhio Hwy; snacks $3-5; open 10:30am-8pm daily)* has chili dogs, fish and chips and a wide range of burgers, including vegetarian and fish burgers.

Poppy's *(4-1495 Kuhio Hwy; snacks $3-6; open 8am-8pm daily)*, at the north side of Kapaa, is a neat little natural food store run by a pair of yoga teachers from Santa Cruz, California. Eat healthy from their vegetarian deli, where you'll find vegan soups, 'fakin-bacon BLT' sandwiches, organic salads and fresh fruit smoothies.

Beezers *(4-1380 Kuhio Hwy; items $3-8; open 11am-10pm daily)* is an old-fashioned ice-cream shop brimming with a nostalgic 1960s decor. Sundaes bear names such as peppermint twist and mustang Sally, and not much else on the menu – which includes hot dogs, pastrami sandwiches and ice-cream sodas – approaches current-day trends.

Mermaids Cafe *(4-1384 Kuhio Hwy; mains $7-10; open 11am-9pm daily)* is a great little owner-run place with top-notch food. It's little more than a kitchen and a handful of sidewalk café tables, but the menu rivals some of Kauai's fanciest restaurants. Dishes include tofu or chicken satay over rice, organic salad with seared *ahi*, and avocado-veggie focaccia sandwiches.

Norberto's El Cafe *(4-1373 Kuhio Hwy; open 5:30pm-9pm Mon-Sat)*, Kauai's original Mexican restaurant, offers hearty portions of decent Mexican fare. Everything is prepared without lard. Full dinner plates include soup, rice and beans for $13 to $16, and miniplates cost a few dollars less. You can wash everything down with margaritas or Mexican brews.

KAPAA TO KILAUEA

The drive north from Kapaa heads through fields of sugarcane, beyond which the jagged peaks of the Anahola Mountains cut their way through the clouds. In the other direction, you'll catch glimpses of bright blue ocean and distant bays.

A couple of scenic lookouts just north of Kapaa offer views. Sunsets can be particularly nice at low tide, when waves break over the shallows and fishers are out with their throw nets.

The long, pretty beach at the 10-mile marker is **Kealia Beach.** During transitional swells, Kealia can become a good place for surfing.

After rainstorms, the beach tends to be heavily littered with tree limbs carried down Kealia Stream, which empties at the south side of the beach.

Donkey Beach

Donkey Beach has long been known as Kauai's main nudist beach. It's frequented largely by gay visitors, though it draws a mixed crowd and is used by both clad and unclad sunbathers. This lovely windswept sandy beach is hidden from the road and takes a little hike to reach.

With the new construction of the Kealia Kai residential development between the road and the shore, the trail to Donkey Beach has recently changed. It is now a straight forward signposted walk with public beach access that's been provided by the new development.

To get to the beach, stop at the paved parking lot at the ocean side of Hwy 56, about halfway between the 11- and 12-mile markers; it's identified with a small sign marked 'Public Shoreline Access.' From there just follow the path down to the beach, which is about a 20-minute walk away.

Despite the fact that the beach is popular with nude sunbathers, nudity is officially illegal on Kauai and the police have on occasion raided the beach and hauled away anyone that they found in the buff. After some unwanted negative publicity following a raid in 2002, the county authorities seem to be backing away from staging further raids, but be aware that this more tolerant policy could again change with the winds.

Speaking of winds, they can be very strong along the coast at Donkey Beach. You'll notice that all the ironwood trees lean away from the shore and those right at the beach are so blown over they almost look like shrubs – that's from the cumulative effect of all those windy days. *Naupaka* and *ilima*, native ground creeping flowers, add a dash of color as they grow in the sand along this otherwise shadeless beach. From October to May, be aware of the high surf that is common here as it creates dangerous rip currents and a powerful shorebreak.

Anahola

Anahola is a small, scattered village, much of it spread out along Anahola Bay. This wide bay, fringed with a nice sandy beach, was an ancient surfing site, and its break is still popular with surfers today.

Anahola Beach Park, a county park on Hawaiian Home Lands, sits at the south side of the bay. To get there, turn off Hwy 56 onto Kukuihale Rd at the 13-mile marker, drive a mile down and then turn onto the dirt beach road. For information on obtaining a permit to camp at the beach park, see Camping under Accommodations, earlier in this chapter.

Anahola's modest commercial center consists of the Anahola post office, a burger stand and a small general store grouped together at the side of Hwy 56, just south of the 14-mile marker.

Places to Eat What may well be the island's best burgers are sold by **Ono Char Burger** *(Hwy 56; snacks $2-7; open 10am-6pm Mon-Sat, 11am-6pm Sun)*. All burgers are a quarter pound and come with lettuce and tomato – a favorite here is the local boy ($5.65), which adds on cheddar cheese, pineapple and teriyaki sauce. The place makes good french fries and onion rings as well, and you can chow down at outdoor picnic tables.

Whalers General Store *(open 6:30am-9:30pm daily)*, next door to the burger stand, has hard-boiled eggs for a quarter, hot dogs for a dollar and cold beer.

Hole in the Mountain

Although the Hole in the Mountain, once an obvious sight, was largely filled in by a landslide, a speck of it is still visible. Slightly north of the 15-mile marker, look back at the mountain, down to the right of the tallest pinnacle, and you'll be able to see a shimmer of light coming through a small opening in the rock face.

Legend says the original hole was created when a giant threw his spear through the mountain, causing the water stored within to gush forth as waterfalls.

Koolau Road

Koolau Rd is a peaceful drive through rich green pastures with white egrets and a smattering of bright wildflowers. Take it as a scenic loop off the highway or as a way to get to Moloaa Beach or Larsens Beach. Both the road and the beaches are well off the tourist track. Neither beach has any facilities.

Koolau Rd connects with Hwy 56 half a mile north of the 16-mile marker and again one-tenth of a mile south of the 20-mile marker.

Moloaa Beach To get to Moloaa Beach from the south, turn right onto Koolau Rd and, after 1¼ miles, turn right onto Moloaa Rd. The road ends three-quarters of a mile down at a few beach houses, but since the road near the beach is narrow, finding a place to park can be quite challenging.

Moloaa is rural, with horses grazing on the hills above the crescent-shaped bay. The northern end of the beach before the rocky outcrop is somewhat protected for swimming, though it's not all that deep. The whole bay can have strong currents when the surf is rough.

Larsens Beach This is a long golden-sand beach, good for solitary strolls and beachcombing. Although it's a bit shallow for swimming, snorkeling can be good when the waters are very calm, which is generally in the summer only. Beware of a current that runs westward along the beach and out through a channel in the reef.

Often the cattle that graze the hills above the beach are the only company you'll encounter. However, if the tide is low, you may well see a few Hawaiian families on the outer edge of the reef collecting an edible seaweed called *limu kohu*. The seaweed found at Larsens is considered to be some of the finest in all of Hawaii.

The turnoff to Larsens Beach is on Koolau Rd, a little more than a mile down from the north intersection of Koolau Rd and Hwy 56, or just over a mile north of the intersection of Moloaa and Koolau Rds. Turn toward the ocean on the dirt road there and then take the immediate left. It's one mile to the parking area and then a five-minute walk downhill to the beach.

North Shore

Kauai's North Shore enjoys an unhurried pace and incredible scenery. Here you'll find deep mountain valleys, rolling pastures, ancient taro fields, white-sand beaches and the rugged Na Pali Coast.

The North Shore is lush and often wet. In winter, that can mean rain for days on end, but in summer it usually means brief showers followed by rainbows. When it's a full-moon, you may even see a moonbow – a rainbow colored with moonbeams.

Rainy days can be almost dreamlike. The tops of the mountains become shrouded in clouds that alternately drift and lift, revealing a series of waterfalls that plunge down the mountainsides.

A drive along the North Shore takes in the seabird sanctuary at Kilauea and a couple of small coastal villages before reaching the resort community of Princeville, with its condos and golf courses.

But it's the area beyond, from Hanalei Bridge to Kee Beach at road's end, that best embodies the North Shore spirit. This is a part of Hawaii that has resisted mass tourism and has stalled development. Its appeal is not in creature comforts but in stunning natural beauty.

KILAUEA

Kilauea is a former sugar plantation town whose main attractions are a picturesque lighthouse and a seabird sanctuary, both at Kilauea Point. The sanctuary is the most visited site on the North Shore and shouldn't be missed.

Kolo Rd, the main turnoff into Kilauea, is a third of a mile beyond the 23-mile marker on Hwy 56. On Kolo Rd, you pass a gas station, a minimart and an Episcopal church, all in quick succession. Kilauea Rd starts opposite the church and ends 2 miles later at Kilauea Point.

Episcopal Church

The little Christ Memorial Episcopal Church attracts attention because of its striking lava-rock architecture. It was built in 1941, but the interesting lava-rock headstones in the churchyard are much older, dating back to when the original Hawaiian Congregational Church stood on this site.

Kilauea Bay

If you're looking for someplace new to explore, you might try Rock Quarry Beach at Kilauea Bay. Also known as Kahili Beach, it's a nice sandy beach and the site of an abandoned rock quarry and steamer landing. This remote beach is mostly used by local fishers, but when the surf is unusually high, surfers also take to these waters. Swimmers should be aware of strong nearshore currents when the surf is up.

Public access is via Wailapa Rd, which begins midway between the 21- and 22-mile markers on Hwy 56. Follow Wailapa Rd north for a half mile beyond Hwy 56 and then turn left on the unmarked dirt road that begins at a bright yellow water valve. The dirt road, which continues for a half mile before ending at the beach, is usually in fairly good shape and passable in a car.

Kilauea Point

A national wildlife refuge, Kilauea Point *(☎ 828-1413; adult/child under 16 $3/free; open 10am-4pm daily, closed federal holidays)* is the northernmost point of the inhabited Hawaiian Islands. Topped by a lighthouse built in 1913, it's picture-postcard material.

Four species of birds come to Kilauea to nest. Most of these birds leave after their young have been reared. Red-footed boobies, the most visible, are abundant on the cliffs to the east of the point, where they build large nests of sticks on the top of the trees. Boobies nest from February to September, with their peak egg laying occurring in spring.

Wedge-tailed shearwaters arrive by April and stay until November, nesting in burrows they dig into Kilauea Point. Another readily spotted species is the red-tailed tropicbird, which nests along the cliff edges from March to October. If you're lucky, you'll spot a pair flying in loops, performing their courtship ritual.

Laysan albatrosses are at Kilauea from about November to July. Some nest on Mokuaeae Rock, straight off the tip of the point. Other albatross nesting sites lie on the grassy clearing to the west of Kilauea Point. If you look out beyond this clearing, you can also see Secret Beach, divided into three scalloped coves by lava fingers.

Great frigate birds nest on the Northwestern Hawaiian Islands, not Kauai, but these aerial pirates visit Kilauea Point to steal food from other birds. Great frigate birds can be spotted circling above Kilauea Point year-round. You won't see the distinctive red throat balloon that the male puffs out to attract females, though, as they're not here for courtship. The frigate birds, which have a wingspan of 7ft and a distinctive forked tail, soar with a mesmerizing grace.

Some of Kauai's estimated 100 nene, the endangered Hawaiian goose that was reintroduced to Kauai in 1982, can also be spotted in the refuge.

While birds are certainly the main attraction at Kilauea Point, with a little luck you may also spot sea turtles swimming in the cove at the base of the cliffs. And during winter, it's not unusual to see whales pass by the point.

Volunteers are usually available to answer questions, and if you want to delve deeper, there's a collection of books on flora and fauna for sale at the visitors center.

Even when the refuge is closed, it's worth driving to the end of Kilauea Rd for the picturesque view of the lighthouse and point.

Guava Kai Plantation

This plantation *(☎ 828-6121; Kuawa Rd; open 9am-5pm daily)* cultivates 480 acres of guava trees that produce juice for Ocean Spray and other juice companies. A visitor center doles out samples of guava juice and sells guava products. There's also a path leading through a garden planted with tropical flowers that makes for a nice short stroll.

NORTH SHORE

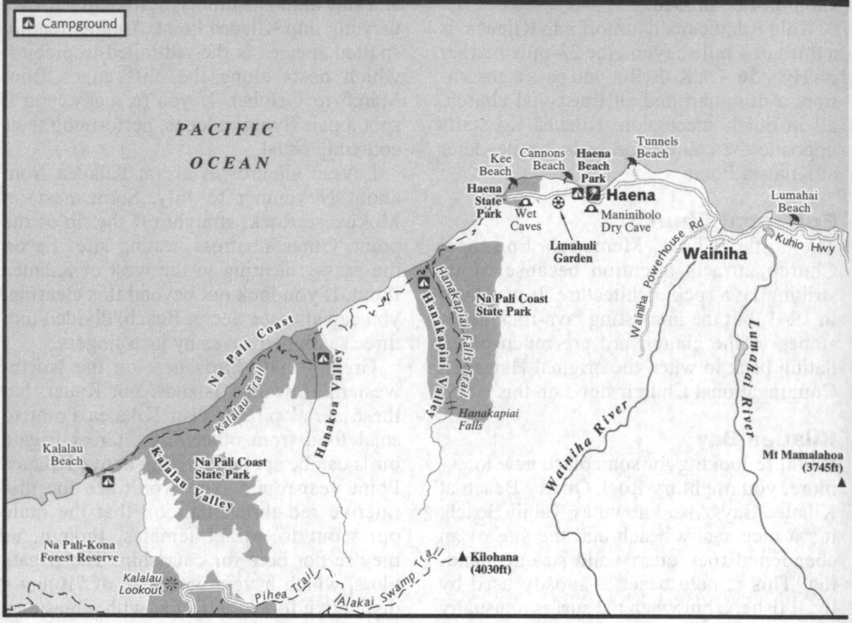

To get there, turn inland onto Kuawa Rd from Hwy 56, just north of the 23-mile marker and a quarter mile south of the Kolo Rd turnoff to Kilauea. The visitor center is about a mile from the highway.

As you go up the road past rows of guava trees, it may seem as if the fruit is too big to be the same guava that grows wild elsewhere on the island – in fact these guava trees are hybrids whose fruit grows to half a pound, twice the normal size.

Places to Stay

Aloha Plantation Kauai *(☎ 828-6872, 877-658-6977; ⓔ alohaplantation@hawaiian.net; 4481 Malulani Rd, Kilauea, HI 96754; rooms $55-65)* is a 1920s plantation house with two guest rooms. It's not fancy but it has plenty of down-home character, the rooms are comfortable and the family that owns the place is friendly. Both rooms have private baths and an old-fashioned Hawaiian decor; the cheaper one has one double bed, the other has two double beds. A breakfast of fresh fruit and pastries is provided and guests have use of a refrigerator and barbecue.

Places to Eat

Farmer's Market *(deli items $4-7; store open 8:30am-8:30pm daily, deli open 10am-2pm)*, a grocery store with a good deli, is in the Kong Lung Center, half a mile up Kilauea Rd from Hwy 56. The deli has hearty sandwiches, homemade soups as well as organic salads at reasonable prices.

Kilauea Bakery & Pau Hana Pizza *(open 6:30am-9pm daily)*, tucked in the back of the Kong Lung Center, sells breakfast pastries, pizza and breads. At lunchtime, you can get a slice of pizza with a salad for $6.25. Whole pizzas cost $8 to $25, depending on the size and toppings. You order everything from the bakery counter, but there are tables on the lawn where you can eat.

Banana Joe's *(open 9am-6pm daily)*, the yellow shack on the inland side of Hwy 56, just north of the Kolo Rd turn-off to Kilauea, is a fun little owner-run place. Joe dishes up a nice fruit frosty ($2.50), made solely of frozen fruit that is squeezed through a processor until it comes out as smooth as ice cream. The papaya and pineapple flavors are the best. You can also buy dried banana strips and fresh fruit grown on the adjacent 6-acre plot.

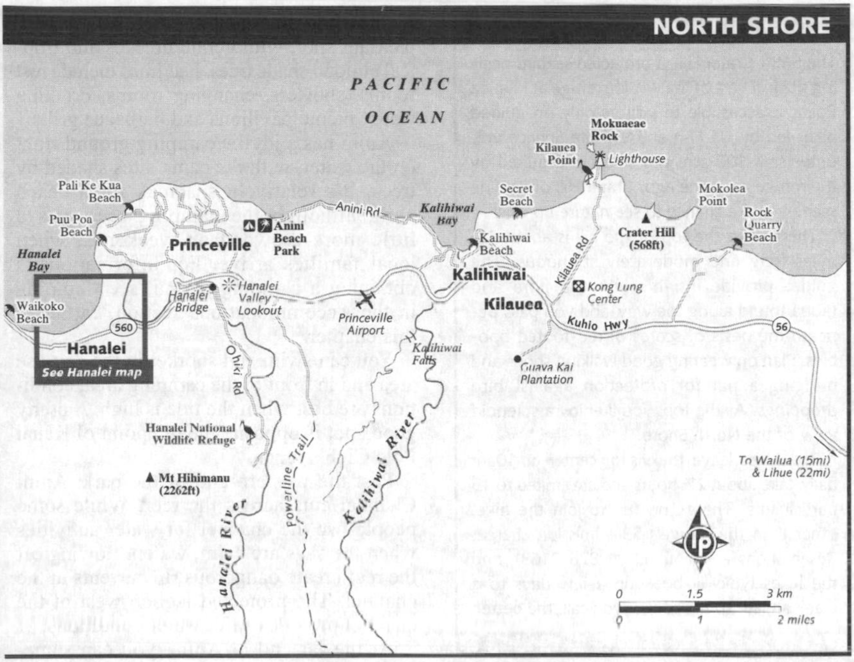

KALIHIWAI

Kalihiwai Rd was a loop road going down past Kalihiwai Beach, connecting with the highway at two points, until the tidal wave of 1957 washed out the Kalihiwai River bridge. The bridge was never rebuilt, and now there are two Kalihiwai Rds, one on each side of the river.

The section of Kalihiwai Rd that is just half a mile west of Kilauea leads down a mile to **Kalihiwai Beach**. At the very end of the road, you can still see the pillars that once supported the bridge. The river empties out into a wide, deep bay. The broad, sandy beach is a popular spot for all kinds of activities, including picnicking, swimming, boogie boarding, bodysurfing and, when the northwest swells roll in, some daredevil surfing along the cliff at the east end of the bay. The river is popular with kayakers. The beach has no facilities.

As you take Kalihiwai Rd back up to the highway, look to the left as soon as you see the 'Narrow Bridge' sign; you'll spot a picturesque waterfall that's partially hidden in a little valley.

Secret Beach

This is a gorgeous golden-sand beach backed by sea cliffs and jungle-like woods. The beach is well off the beaten path, and access to it has changed a number of times over the years, so few visitors discover it. Secret Beach is frequented mostly by Kauai's alternative community, nude sunbathers and the occasional surfer.

To get there, turn down Kalihiwai Rd half mile west of Kilauea and then turn right onto the first dirt road, which is a tenth of a mile from Hwy 56. The road ends at a parking area a third of a mile down. Don't leave anything of value in your car.

The well-defined trail begins from the parking lot along a fence that separates the woods from a horse pasture. After two minutes, it leads downhill through ironwood trees and mixed jungle growth. All in all, the trail only takes about 10 minutes and deposits you at the western end of this long, sandy beach.

While this part of the beach is quite idyllic, if you're up for a stroll or feel the need for even more privacy, you can walk along the beach in the direction of Kilauea Lighthouse.

Crater Hill Hikes

The 568ft Crater Hill, a protected seabird nesting site just east of the wildlife refuge at Kilauea Point, is accessible to visitors only on guided hikes led by US Fish and Wildlife Service volunteers. A 100-acre cliff-side site acquired by the refuge a decade ago, Crater Hill offers fine scenery and a chance to see nature up close.

The trail to the top of the hill is about 1¼ miles long and moderately strenuous. The guides provide insights into the flora and fauna found along the way, and you pass beneath the nests of scores of red-footed boobies. Plan on wearing good walking shoes and bringing a hat for protection against bird droppings. At the top, you'll enjoy a splendid view of the North Shore.

The hikes leave the visitor center at 10am daily, take about 2½ hours and are limited to 15 participants. There's no fee to join the hike, other than the refuge's $3 admission charge. Reservations are required (☎ 828-0168), and the hikes typically book up a few days to a week ahead, so the sooner you call, the better.

The beach has open seas, with high winter surf and dangerous currents prevailing from October to May. In summer, water conditions are much calmer, and swimming and snorkeling can be good.

ANINI

The area known as Anini has a lovely beach fronted by vast reef flats and backed by a beach park. To get there, cross Kalihiwai Bridge, turn onto the second Kalihiwai Rd and then bear left onto Anini Rd. It's about 1½ miles from the highway to the beach.

Over the years, there's been talk of connecting Princeville and Anini by a direct coastal road, but local resistance to the plan has kept the road at bay. For now, Anini's dead-end street means little traffic, keeping this area unhurried and quiet.

Still, Anini is growing, and a number of exclusive homes have been built in recent years, including some by people with Hollywood connections.

Anini Beach Park

Bordering the shoreline for more than a mile, Anini Beach Park is divided into day-use, windsurfing and camping areas. It's a very pleasant spot, with gentle breezes and tropical almond shade trees. Facilities include rest rooms, showers, changing rooms, drinking water, picnic pavilions and barbecue grills.

Anini has a idyllic camping ground right on the water, with the camp sites shaded by trees. It's relatively spacious for a beach park, although the camping area gets a little more crowded on weekends, when local families arrive. For information on obtaining a camping permit, see Camping in the Accommodations section, earlier in this chapter.

You can swim and snorkel in the day-use area and in front of the camping area; conditions are best when the tide is high. A pretty good spot is opposite the midpoint of Kauai Polo Club's fence.

Past the western end of the park, Anini Channel cuts across the reef. While some people use the channel for water activities when the seas are calm, waters flowing off the reef create dangerous rip currents in the channel. The protected lagoon west of the channel provides safer water conditions.

At the far end of Anini, you can sometimes see people walking way out onto the shallow reef of Anini Flats, picking *opihi*, net fishing and catching octopus.

PRINCEVILLE

Kauai's biggest development, Princeville traces its roots to Robert Wyllie, a Scottish doctor who later became foreign minister to Kamehameha IV. In the mid-19th century, Wyllie bought a large coffee plantation in Hanalei and began planting sugar.

When Queen Emma and Kamehameha IV came to visit in 1860, Wyllie named his plantation and surrounding lands Princeville in honor of their young son, Prince Albert. The plantation later became a cattle ranch, and in 1968 ground was broken for the Princeville Resort.

Today, Princeville is a planned community spread over 11,000 acres on a promontory between Anini Beach Park and Hanalei Bay. It has a dozen condo complexes, a luxury hotel, hundreds of private homes, a couple of championship golf courses, restaurants, tennis courts, a shopping center and even its own little airport.

Although Princeville may seem out of place on the North Shore, and it certainly stands in sharp contrast to the free-spirited communities that lay beyond, there's no doubt that its manicured grounds are spacious, the condos are low-rise and the development is uncrowded compared with its counterparts on other islands.

Kuhio Hwy changes from Hwy 56 to Hwy 560 at the 28-mile marker in front of Princeville. The 10-mile stretch from here to Kee Beach at the end of the road is one of the most scenic drives in all of Hawaii.

Information

Princeville Center, the shopping center at the entrance to Princeville, has the main cluster of services for the North Shore, including a small medical clinic, banks, a library and several shops.

The **Bank of Hawaii** *(☎ 826-6761; open 8:30am-4:30pm Mon-Thur, 8:30am-6pm Fri)* is in Princeville Center.

The **post office** *(☎ 800-275-8777; open 10:30am-3:30pm Mon-Fri, 10:30am-12:30pm Sat)* is in Princeville Center across from the Bank of Hawaii.

Akamai Computer Center *(☎ 826-1042; open 10am-5pm Mon-Fri)*, in Princeville Center upstairs from the Bank of Hawaii, has Internet access for $12 an hour.

Also at Princeville Center is the **Princeville Chevron gas station** *(open 6am-10pm Mon-Sat, 6am-9pm Sun)*. If you're driving west toward Kee Beach at the end of the road, this is the last place to buy gas, so check your tank before heading off.

Princeville Hotel

The Princeville Hotel offers a splendid view of Hanalei Bay and the Bali Hai mountains. The luxury hotel was erected amid a great deal of controversy in 1985. Locals, who were miffed at losing one of their favorite sunset spots, nicknamed the bluff-side building 'The Prison.' The original hotel was indeed dark and inward-looking, and it so failed to incorporate its surroundings that the owners closed it down in 1989. Over the next two years, the hotel was gutted and virtually rebuilt. The current Princeville Hotel has a lobby with floor-to-ceiling windows offering 180-degree views of Bali Hai. It also has marble floors, posh furniture, pools of flowing water and a smattering of antiques and artwork, but the real attraction is the view.

Fort Alexander

The site of Fort Alexander, a short-lived Russian fortress (c. 1816), can be found on a grassy knoll at the northwest side of the hotel. The interpretive display, housed in a shelter, points out a couple of stones that were once part of the fort's foundation, but there's little else to see from that era.

Beaches

Princeville is not known for its beaches, but there's a reasonably large one, **Puu Poa Beach**, between the Princeville Hotel and the mouth of the Hanalei River. On the opposite side of the hotel, below the Puu Poa condos, **Pali Ke Kua** (also called Hideaways) is a secluded, sandy pocket of beach that has good swimming and snorkeling when it's calm. High surf, common in winter, can generate dangerous currents at both beaches.

Powerline Trail

In the 1930s, electric transmission lines were run along the mountains, and a 13-mile maintenance route now known as the Powerline Trail was created. There is occasional talk of turning it into a real inland road connecting Princeville to Wailua, but environmental concerns make it unlikely to happen anytime soon.

To get to the trailhead, take the paved road going uphill from Princeville Ranch Stables, a third of a mile after the 27-mile marker on Hwy 56. The pavement ends at a water tank 1¾ miles up; even if you don't plan to hike the trail, the road makes for a pretty drive, offering fine mountain views and glimpses of Hanalei Bay.

The trail continues from the end of the pavement along a rutted 4WD dirt road used mainly by hunters and the power company. It's a full day's walk to its end at the Keahua Arboretum and is recommended only in dry weather.

Places to Stay

Some of Princeville's condo complexes are perched on cliffs and others are by the golf course. While all of the complexes have some units that are vacation rentals, many other units are occupied as year-round housing.

Sometimes you can find residents renting out bedrooms in their condos or homes for about $50 a day. Most people who do this list their rooms on the bulletin board outside the

Foodland supermarket in Princeville Center, though occasionally someone will run an ad in the island newspaper.

Most condo complexes are represented by a number of different rental agents. Agents usually offer cheaper prices than direct bookings at a front desk, but there can be cleaning fees, minimum stays and other restrictions, so get all the details before booking.

The following agents have fairly extensive Princeville rental listings:

Oceanfront Realty (☎ 826-6585, 800-222-5541, fax 826-6478, ⓔ rentals@oceanfrontrealy.com) PO Box 223190, Princeville, HI 96722

Century 21 All Islands (☎ 828-1111, 800-828-1442, fax 828-1113, ⓔ lori@kauai-allislands.com) PO Box 223700, Princeville, HI 96722

North Shore Properties (☎ 826-9622, 800-488-3336, fax 826-1188, ⓔ hnsp@aloha.net) PO Box 607, Hanalei, HI 96714

Sealodge *(1-bedroom units $100)* is one of Princeville's older complexes, and the quarters can be a bit cramped, but it's high on a cliff and many of the 86 units have great sunrise views across the expansive coral reef of Anini. If you leave the windows open, the surf is guaranteed to give you nautical dreams. Units can be booked through the rental agents listed earlier.

Cliffs at Princeville *(☎ 826-6219, 800-622-6219, fax 826-2140; 3811 Edward Rd; units $120-150)* is another older complex, this one with a more ordinary setting, but its units have been refurbished and it remains relatively inexpensive for pricey Princeville. In addition, the units are large, with one bedroom, two bathrooms, front and rear lanai, and all the usual condo amenities. The Cliffs is adjacent to the golf course, and there's a pool.

Pali Ke Kua, a pleasant upscale property near the Princeville Hotel, can be booked through **Marc Resorts** *(☎ 826-9066, 800-535-0085, fax 826-4159; ⓔ marc@aloha.net; 1-bedroom/2-bedroom units $200/240)*, which maintains an office at the complex. The same Marc Resorts office also handles a couple of simpler units for $125 in the nearby **Hale Moi** complex, though most are occupied by long-term residents. Marc offers various discount schemes that can cut rates by as much as 50%, at which times the properties can be a good deal.

Hanalei Bay Resort *(☎ 826-6522, 800-827-4427, fax 826-6680; ⓔ hbr@hawaiian.net; 5380 Honoiki Rd; rooms $185-275, studios $215-240, 1-bedroom condos $350-390)* has both hotel-style rooms and condo units, with the higher priced units having ocean views. The units are pleasant, and the grounds feature a couple of swimming pools (including a large free-form one), eight tennis courts and fine views of Hanalei Bay. Quintus Resorts runs the front desk and handles most of the 280 units here.

Princeville Hotel *(☎ 826-9644, 800-325-3589, fax 826-1166; ⓦ www.princeville.com; 5520 Ka Haku Rd; rooms with garden view $405, with ocean view $615, suites $705-4500)*, a Sheraton property, has 252 luxury rooms with king beds, marble bathrooms and modern amenities that run the gamut from original oil paintings with dimmer-controlled spotlights to liquid-crystal windows between the bedroom and bath that can be turned from opaque to clear with the flick of a switch. All in all, the hotel is an exercise in opulence.

Places to Eat

Foodland supermarket *(open 6am-11pm daily)* in the Princeville Center has a bakery section with inexpensive pastries and a deli with take-out items. The deli's tasty fried chicken breasts are the area's best value at $1.29 – grab a can of fruit juice and you've got yourself a cheap lunch.

Paradise Bar & Grill *(snacks $6-7; open 11am-11pm daily)* is a casual café-style place in the Princeville Center. It specializes in burgers and sandwiches, all served with fries, which come in beef, buffalo, chicken, fish and vegetarian varieties.

Chuck's Steak House *(lunch $5-10, dinner $18-29; open 11:30am-2:30pm Mon-Fri, 6pm-9:30pm daily)*, in the Princeville Center, has standard fare such as burgers, sandwiches and salads at lunch. The dinner menu includes the likes of teriyaki chicken, steaks, prime rib and fish; a salad bar is included with all dinners.

Princeville Restaurant & Bar *(breakfast $6-9, lunch $6-10; open 8am-3pm Mon-Sat, 8am-2pm Sun)*, at the Prince Golf Course a half mile west of the Princeville airport, has a broad view, a country club setting and reasonable prices. At breakfast, which is served until 11am, you can get dishes such as a Belgian waffle topped with fresh fruit and whipped cream or banana macadamia-nut pancakes with bacon. At lunch there are fresh fish sandwiches, good *ahi* salads and a variety of daily specials.

Bali Hai Restaurant (*☎ 826-6522; breakfast & lunch $7-12; dinner appetizers $7-14, mains $17-32; open 7am-11am, 11:30am-2pm & 5:30pm-9:30pm daily*), in the Hanalei Bay Resort, has open-air dining with a wonderful view of Hanalei Bay and the Bali Hai mountains. At breakfast the specialty is the 'taro patch breakfast,' an interesting local combination of two fried eggs, Portuguese sausage, poi pancakes and taro hash browns. Lunch is mainly sandwiches with fries, while dinner features steak, lamb and seafood dishes.

Cafe Hanalei (*☎ 826-2760; breakfast buffet $23; open 6:30am-10:30am Mon-Sat, 6:30am-9:30am Sun*) is the Princeville Hotel's breakfast venue. If you feel like lingering over a buffet, this place offers a striking view of Hanalei Bay, but expect to pay a premium for it. The buffet, which is good but not outstanding, has waffle and omelette stations, pastries, fruit and a few hot dishes such as eggs Benedict and sauteed fish.

La Cascata (*☎ 826-2761; appetizers $8-17, mains $24-35; open 6pm-10pm daily*), also in the Princeville Hotel, has a lovely view of Bali Hai and specializes in upscale Italian food, with pasta, fresh seafood, rack of lamb and beef dishes.

Entertainment

The Living Room (*☎ 826-2764*) at the Princeville Hotel, a lounge with a great view of Hanalei Bay, is a fine place for a sunset drink and also has live entertainment from 7pm to 11pm nightly.

At the Hanalei Bay Resort's **Happy Talk** (*☎ 826-6522*) lounge, there's live jazz from 3pm to 7pm Sunday and Hawaiian music from 6:30pm to 9:30pm on most other nights.

The **Princeville Hotel** (*☎ 826-2788; luau adult/child 6-12 $62.50/30*) stages a luau at 6pm on Monday and Thursday; the cost includes an *imu* ceremony, Hawaiian food and live music and dance.

HANALEI VALLEY

Just beyond Princeville, the **Hanalei Valley Lookout** provides a spectacular bird's-eye view of the valley floor with its meandering river and spread of patchwork taro fields. It's a stunningly beautiful scene, so whatever you do, don't miss it!

The **Hanalei National Wildlife Refuge** encompasses 917 acres of the valley, stretching up both sides of the Hanalei River. The wetland taro farms in the refuge produce two-thirds of Hawaii's commercially grown poi taro, while at the same time serving as habitat for endangered waterbirds.

Prior to Western contact, the valley was planted in taro, but in the mid-1800s rice farming was introduced into Hanalei Valley to feed the Chinese laborers who worked the sugarcane fields. The rice grew so well that by the 1880s it became a major export crop. The demand for rice eventually waned and these days taro once again predominates.

From the lookout, to the lower right you can see the North Shore's first one-lane bridge, which opened in 1912. Visible to the south are the twin peaks of Hihimanu, which in Hawaiian means 'beautiful.'

Hanalei Bridge

The Hanalei Bridge and six other one-lane bridges between the Hanalei River and the end of the road not only link this part of the North Shore to the rest of the island, they also protect it from runaway development.

Big cement trucks and heavy construction equipment are beyond the bridges' limits. Even large package-tour buses are kept at bay.

Over the years, developers have introduced numerous proposals to build a two-lane bridge over the Hanalei River, but North Shore residents have successfully beaten them all down.

While it's not a frequent occurrence, during unusually heavy rains the road between the taro fields and the river can flood and the Hanalei Bridge remains closed until the water subsides.

Rules of the Road

Because there are so many one-lane bridges on the North Shore, there are special rules of the road here. When two cars approach an empty one-lane bridge from opposite directions, the car that reaches the bridge last yields to the entire line-up of approaching cars, rather than alternating one car in each direction.

Ohiki Road

If you want to head into Hanalei Valley, turn left onto Ohiki Rd immediately after the Hanalei Bridge. This scenic drive through the Hanalei National Wildlife Refuge parallels the Hanalei River, starting in taro fields and later passing banana trees, bamboo thickets, *hau* trees, ferns and wild ginger. It dead-ends after 2 miles.

This is a great place for bird watching. From the roadside, you can commonly spot snow-white egrets and night herons as well as some of the endangered waterbirds that reside in the valley, including the Hawaiian coot, the Hawaiian stilt, the Hawaiian duck and the cootlike Hawaiian gallinule with its bright red bill.

For an even closer view of the valley, there's a pleasant little quarter-mile loop trail that takes only 15 minutes to walk and offers a nice panorama. The parking area for the trail is on the left three-quarters of a mile down Ohiki Rd; the signposted trail starts across the road from the parking area.

HANALEI

After the Hanalei Bridge, Kuhio Hwy (Hwy 560) runs parallel to the Hanalei River. The mile before Hanalei village is a pastoral scene of taro patches and grassland. There's no development of any kind and no buildings in sight. Take away the telephone poles and asphalt road, and this is how the area has looked for centuries.

Hanalei, which is backed by lofty mountains and fronted by a lovely bay, has a pleasant low-key village center. The village took a severe battering during Hurricane Iniki, losing many old wooden buildings. Fortunately, most of the reconstruction has been done in a period style matching the original character of the town.

Hanalei is friendly, casual and slow. If you're in a hurry, you're in the wrong place.

Information

There are no banks west of Princeville, but there's a **Bank of Hawaii ATM** inside the Foodland market in the Ching Young Village shopping center.

The **post office** (*☎ 800-275-8777; 5-5226 Kuhio Hwy; open 7:30am-4pm Mon-Fri, 9am-noon Sat*) is in the village center.

Hanalei has several shops geared to **outdoor sports**. Kayak Kauai specializes in kayak rentals and tours, but also rents bicycles, camping gear, surfboards and snorkel sets. Pedal & Paddle, in the Ching Young Village, rents kayaks, bicycles, camping gear and snorkel sets. Hanalei Surf Company, in the Hanalei Center, rents surfboards, boogie boards and snorkel sets.

Ching Young Village

The old Ching Young Store, the North Shore's main general store since the late 19th century, has evolved into the larger Ching Young Village shopping center. The original Ching Young Store now houses Evolve Love, a gallery with hand-painted silk clothing, jewelry, paintings, woodwork and other handicrafts by local artisans.

Opposite Ching Young Village is the old Hanalei elementary school, which has been renovated and turned into the Hanalei Center complex, with several restaurants and shops. The former school, which is nearly a century old, is on the Hawaii Register of Historic Places.

Waioli Huiia Church

Hanalei's first missionaries, the Reverend and Mrs William Alexander, arrived in 1834 in a double-hulled canoe. Their church, hall and mission house are in the middle of town, set on a huge manicured lawn with a beautiful mountain backdrop. These folks knew how to pick property.

The picturesque Waioli Huiia Church is a favorite subject for local watercolorists. The green wooden church retains an airy Pacific feel, with large windows that open outward and high ceilings. The doors remain open during the day, and visitors are welcome to go inside. A bible printed in Hawaiian and dating to 1868 is on display on top of the old organ. The Waioli Church Choir, the island's best, sings hymns in Hawaiian at the 10am Sunday service.

Waioli Mission Hall, to the right of the church, was built in 1836. The hall, which originally served as the church, was built of coral lime and plaster with a distinctive steeply pitched roof to handle Hanalei's heavy rains. An old church graveyard is beside the hall.

Waioli Mission House Museum

Behind the church and hall is the Waioli Mission House (*☎ 245-3202; admission by*

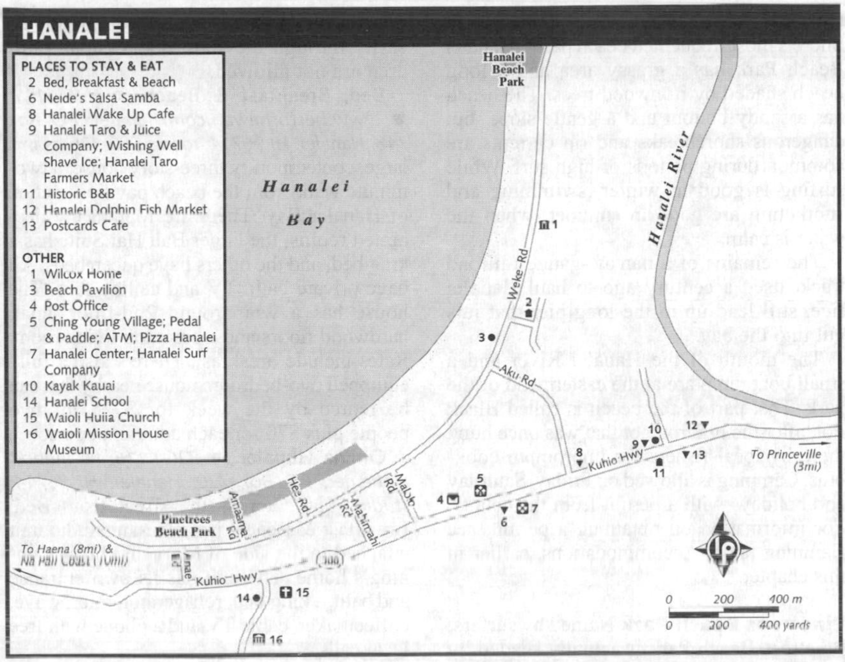

donation; open 9am-3pm Tues, Thur & Sat). The Alexanders spent their first three years living in a grass hut on these grounds, but they couldn't adjust to living Hawaiian-style, so they built this big New England house. It was home to other missionaries over the years, most notably Abner and Lucy Wilcox, whose family became the island's most predominant property holders.

The main part of the house, built in 1837, has period furnishings, including braided rugs, lanterns, a spinning wheel and simple straight-backed chairs.

The house has old wavy glass panes, some nice woodwork and interesting architectural features. For instance, the upstairs porch slopes, not from settling but because it was constructed to allow water to run off during the valley's frequent torrential rains.

The inconspicuous parking lot is just past the church. To get there, turn inland immediately before Hanalei School and then left on the dirt driveway opposite the water hydrant.

Hanalei Bay

Hanalei means 'Crescent Bay,' and that it is – a large, perfectly shaped bay, and one of the most scenic in all Hawaii. Weke Rd, which runs a mile along the bay between Waioli Stream and the Hanalei River, can be reached by turning off Hwy 560 at Aku Rd.

Just after turning right onto Weke Rd from Aku Rd, there's a public beach with a picnic pavilion. The more appealing Hanalei Beach Park is about half a mile farther, at the end of Weke Rd. Pinetrees Beach Park is in the opposite direction.

Each of the three beaches has rest rooms, showers, drinking water, picnic tables and grills. Hanalei Beach Park is the best place for catching the sunset, as you can see Bali Hai from there. It's also a popular summer anchorage for sailboats.

On the opposite side of the road, midway between the pavilion and Hanalei Beach Park, the big brown house with the wraparound porch is the old **Wilcox Home**, which traces its roots to early Hanalei missionaries Abner and Lucy Wilcox.

Incidentally, if the road names sound familiar, it means you're beginning to learn the names of Hawaiian fish – each road along the beach is named after a different one.

Hanalei Beach Park One of the North Shore's most frequented beach parks, Hanalei Beach Park has a grassy area and a long beach shaded by ironwood trees. The beach has a sandy bottom and a gentle slope, but dangerous shorebreaks and rip currents are common during periods of high surf. While surfing is good in winter, swimming and snorkeling are good in summer, when the water is calm.

The remains of a narrow-gauge railroad track, used a century ago to haul Hanalei rice, still lead up to the long pier that juts out into the bay.

The mouth of the Hanalei River and a small boat ramp are at the eastern end of the park. That part of the beach is called Black Pot, after the big iron pot that was once hung there by local fishers for impromptu cook-outs. Camping is allowed on Friday, Saturday and holidays with a permit from the county. For information on obtaining a permit, see Camping under Accommodations, earlier in this chapter.

Pinetrees Beach Park Named by surfers, Pinetrees Beach Park is actually shaded by ironwood trees.

From Weke Rd, turn onto either Hee Rd where there's a bigger parking lot, or Amaama Rd, which has the rest rooms and showers. This section of the beach is also known locally as Toilet Bowls. Pinetrees has some of the bay's highest winter surf and is the site of various surfing contests. One of the most interesting is the Pinetrees Longboard Classic. Held late in April, it features an aging group of surfers on the old-style wooden boards that were used before the advent of fiberglass.

KAUAI

Places to Stay

Historic B&B *(☎ 826-4622; W www.historicbnb.com; PO Box 1684, Hanalei, HI 96714; rooms $80)* occupies the oldest Buddhist temple on Kauai, built in Lihue in 1901 and moved to the center of Hanalei in 1985. Operated by Kelly and Yuchi Sato, this is a pleasant little place, with a serene Japanese decor. There are three rooms with *shoji* sliding doors; two rooms have queen beds and the third has a king bed. Yuchi is a chef by trade, and the rate includes your choice of an American- or Japanese-style breakfast. Guests have use of a refrigerator and microwave oven. Because sound travels easily through the shoji doors, small children are not allowed.

Bed, Breakfast & Beach *(☎ 826-6111; W www.bestofhawaii.com/hanalei; PO Box 748, Hanalei, HI 96714; rooms $80-135)* is in a large, contemporary three-story house, a two-minute walk from the beach pavilion section of Hanalei Bay. There are four nicely decorated rooms; the larger Bali Hai Suite has a king bed, and the others have queen beds. All have private bath, TV and ceiling fans. The house has a wraparound 2nd-floor lanai, hardwood floors and a common living room. Rates include breakfast. There's also a fully equipped two-bedroom house nearby that can be rented by the week for $925 for two people plus $70 for each additional person.

Ohana Hanalei *(☎ 826-4116; e mdbc@aloha.net; PO Box 720, Hanalei, HI 96714; studios $80)*, across the street from Bed, Breakfast & Beach, is a pleasant studio unit attached to the side of Mary and Dave Cunning's home. The unit has its own entrance and bath, a king bed, refrigerator, microwave, coffeemaker, cable TV and a phone with free local calls.

North Shore Properties *(☎ 826-9622, 800-488-3336, fax 826-1188; W www.kauai-vacation-rentals.com; PO Box 607, Hanalei, HI 96714; houses per week $800-5000)* books dozens of houses on the North Shore ranging from small places tucked into the woods to elegant beachfront homes.

Places to Eat

In a van in the parking lot adjacent to Kayak Kauai, **Hanalei Taro & Juice Company** *(open 10am-5pm Tues-Sun)* specializes in products made of Hanalei-grown taro. It's a fun way to try something different while supporting local business, and the food's tasty as well. Vegetarian or turkey sandwiches on taro buns ($6) make a nice meal, and the taro mochi dessert at just 50¢ is a treat not to be missed. There are a couple of picnic tables where you can sit and eat.

There are two other homegrown businesses operating in the same parking lot: **Wishing Well Shave Ice**, which make refreshing shave ice treats in tropical flavors, and **Hanalei Taro Farmers Market**, a produce truck selling fresh fruit and vegetables.

Java Kai *(open 7am-6pm daily)*, in the Hanalei Center, has a casual setting, good fresh-brewed coffee and some tempting pastries to go along with it.

Bubba's *(snacks $2-6; open 10:30am-8pm daily)*, in the Hanalei Center, serves inexpensive hot dogs, hamburgers and fish sandwiches.

Hanalei Wake Up Cafe *(Aku Rd; breakfast $5-7; open from 6am daily)* is popular with surfers and other early risers. The menu features omelettes, pancakes and French toast.

Hanalei Dolphin Fish Market *(open 11am-5pm daily)*, at the east side of the village, behind the Hanalei Dolphin restaurant, sells fresh fish but also has some ready-to-eat take-out items, including big *ahi* sushi rolls ($6) that would make a meal in themselves.

Pizza Hanalei *(☎ 826-9494; open 11am-9pm daily)*, in the Ching Young Village, has good pizza at reasonable prices. A single-topping 10-inch pizza on either traditional white or whole-wheat crust topped with sesame seeds costs $12. The spicy calzone-style 'pizzarittos,' loaded with cheese and vegies, make a good meal for $5.50. At lunchtime, you can also buy slices of cheese or pepperoni pizza for $3.

Hanalei Health Food & Aloha Juice Bar *(open 8:30am-8pm daily)*, in the Ching Young Village next door to Pizza Hanalei, sells fresh-squeezed juices, a few organic vegetables, vitamins and other health food items.

Big Save *(open 7am-9pm daily)* supermarket, in the Ching Young Village, is the area's only grocery store.

Neide's Salsa Samba *(☎ 826-1851; dishes $8-14; open 11:30am-2:30pm & 5:30pm-9pm daily)*, west of the Hanalei Center, has a quiet veranda where diners can linger over excellent Mexican and Brazilian fare. This little owner-run restaurant serves up the real thing. In addition to the usual Mexican dishes like burritos and enchiladas, you can get some delicious Brazilian offerings such as *panquela*, a crepe stuffed with pumpkin. Neide also makes a fantastic passion fruit margarita.

Hanalei Gourmet *(☎ 826-2524; meals $15-23; open 8am-10:30pm daily)*, in the Hanalei Center, offers island-style dishes such as ginger chicken, shrimp scampi and fresh fish, all served with soup or salad. It also makes hearty sandwiches ($7) on your choice of bread. If you want to pick up something for a picnic, there's a deli at the side where you can buy pasta salads, bread and sandwich meats over the counter.

Postcards Cafe *(☎ 826-1191; breakfast $6-10, dinner $15-25; open 8am-11am & 6pm-9:30pm daily)* is a bit pricey but the setting is engaging and the food good. The place emphasizes fresh, healthy ingredients and uses a lot of organic vegetables. It serves seafood dishes but otherwise the menu is vegetarian, with a pleasant blend of Asian and local influences. Breakfast is relatively standard fare, with the likes of omelettes and macadamia nut pancakes. Dinner is chock-full of creative offerings such as Thai coconut curry with tempeh, pineapple-sage fish and seafood pasta in sherry sauce.

Entertainment

Sushi & Blues *(☎ 826-9701)*, in the Ching Young Village, has a dance floor and live blues and jazz music nightly.

Hanalei Gourmet *(☎ 826-2524)*, in the Hanalei Center, has live jazz, rock or other contemporary music nightly.

HANALEI TO WAINIHA

Waikoko Beach

The western part of Hanalei Bay, called Waikoko Beach, has a sandy bottom, is protected by a reef and is shallower and calmer than the middle of the bay. There are beachside places to park under ironwood trees around the 4-mile marker, but there are no facilities.

Winter surfing is sometimes good off Makahoa Point, the western point of the bay, called Waikokos by surfers.

Lumahai Beach

Lumahai is the gorgeous mile-long stretch of beach where Mitzi Gaynor promised to wash that man right out of her hair in the 1958 musical *South Pacific*. It's a broad white-sand beach with lush jungle growth on one side and tempestuous open ocean on the other.

This is a good beach for walking and exploring. Around some of the lava outcrops you can find green sand made of the mineral olivine.

There are two ways onto Lumahai. The first and more scenic is a three-minute walk that begins at a pull-off along a stone retaining wall three-quarters of a mile past the 4-mile marker. Park in the direction of the traffic flow to avoid a ticket. The trail to the beach is marked by a beach access sign and goes down the slope to the left.

The lava point at this eastern end of the beach offers protection from the winds that often blow from the Princeville direction. These rocks are a rather popular place for sunbathing and for being photographed, but size it up carefully, as people have been washed away by high surf and rogue waves.

Lumahai has dangerous shorebreaks and is not a beach to turn your back on. It's particularly treacherous in winter, though there are strong currents year-round. Because of the numerous drownings that have occurred here over the years, Lumahai has been nicknamed Luma*die* by locals.

Back on the road, there are a couple of lookouts with views down onto Lumahai. The first is at the 5-mile marker, though the next one that pops up around the bend has a better angle.

The other access onto Lumahai Beach is along the road at sea level at the western end of the beach, just before crossing the Lumahai River Bridge. The beach at this end is lined with ironwood trees. Across the road is the Lumahai Valley, open and flat with grazing horses.

Wainiha

The village of Wainiha has a tiny **general store** *(open 10am-7pm daily)* that's the last place where you can buy groceries and beer before the end of the road.

Ancient house sites, *heiau* sites and old taro patches reach deep into Wainiha Valley, a narrow valley with steep green walls. This valley is said to have been the last hideout of the *menehune*. In fact, as late as the mid-19th century, 65 people in the valley were officially listed as *menehune* on the government census!

For a glimpse into an older Hawaii, take a side trip up the **Wainiha Powerhouse Rd**, which begins off Hwy 560 shortly before the 7-mile marker and winds up into Wainiha Valley. This narrow road is lined with simple tin-roof homes, old rusting pickup trucks and sleeping dogs. At 1½ miles up, an incongruous manicured estate with a cool blue stream meandering through the property suddenly comes into view. Shortly after, you arrive at the Wainiha hydroelectric plant, built in 1906 by McBryde Sugar Company and still pumping out juice today. Beyond the powerhouse, the road turns to dirt and begins to feel more private.

HAENA

Haena has houses on stilts, little beachfront cottages, a few vacation homes, a YMCA camp, large caves, camp sites and beautiful sandy beaches. It also has the only hotel beyond Hanalei.

Tunnels Beach

Tunnels is a big horseshoe-shaped reef that has great diving and snorkeling when the water is calm, which is generally limited to the summer. There's a current as you head into deeper water. When conditions are right, you can start snorkeling near the east point and let the current carry you westward. It's more adventurous than Kee Beach, and the coral is beautiful.

Tunnels was not named after the caves and other crevices in the underwater walls, but for its tubular winter surf break at the outer corner of the reef. The beach is popular with both windsurfers and board surfers, though the dangerous rip currents that prevail from October to May make it suitable for experts only.

To get there, look for cars parked at the side of the road near phone pole No 144, midway between the 8- and 9-mile markers opposite the beach access road. Or you can park at Haena Beach Park and walk along the beach to Tunnels.

Haena Beach Park

Haena Beach is a beautiful curve of white sand. To the right, you can see the horseshoe shape of Tunnels outlined by breaking waves. To the far left is Cannons, another good dive spot. Haena itself is not protected by reefs and has very strong rip currents and some powerful shorebreaks from October to May.

The county beach park has camp sites, covered picnic tables, rest rooms and showers. Many hikers from the Kalalau Trail camp here, using it as a base before starting the trail. It's a bit over a mile to the trailhead, and this is a safer place to park a car than the end of the road if you're going on to Kalalau.

For information on obtaining a permit to camp, see Camping in the Accommodations section at the front of this chapter.

Maniniholo Dry Cave

Three large sea caves, which were part of the coast thousands of years back, are on the inland side of the road between Haena and

Kee Beach. One is dry, and two are wet with pools of water at their base.

According to legend, the caves were created when the goddess Pele dug into the mountains looking for a place on Kauai's North Shore to call home.

Maniniholo Dry Cave, across the road from Haena Beach Park, is a deep broad cave that you can walk into. Dry is a relative term, as the dripping water that constantly seeps from the cave walls keeps the interior of Maniniholo damp and humid.

Limahuli Garden

Most of Limahuli, the last valley before the start of the Na Pali Coast, is still lush, virgin forest. The National Tropical Botanical Garden, a nonprofit organization that preserves and propagates rare native plants, owns 1000 acres of Limahuli Valley and has opened a section of it to visitors.

Limahuli Garden (*☎ 826-1053; admission $10; open 9:30am-4pm Tues-Fri & Sun*) contains collections of Hawaiian ethnobotanical and medicinal plants and other endangered native species. There are also ancient stone terraces planted with taro. Endemic trees include the endangered *Kokio hauhelcula*, which has a red hibiscus-like blossom, and the equally beautiful but more common *ohia lehua* tree. A three-quarter-mile loop trail winds through the most interesting parts of the garden, and for the cost of admission visitors can make a self-guided walking tour along it.

The garden starts at a concrete driveway on the inland side of the highway, just before the stream that marks the Haena State Park boundary.

Wet Caves

Haena State Park includes the two wet caves as well as Kee Beach. The caves are near each other, less than a quarter mile from the end of the road. The first, Waikapalae Wet Cave, is just a few minutes' walk uphill from the main road along a rutted dirt drive opposite the visitor parking overflow area. The second, Waikanaloa Wet Cave, is easier to spot, as it's right on the south side of the main road.

Both caves are big, deep, dark and dripping, with pools of very cold water. Divers sometimes explore them, but the caves can be dangerous, so it's certainly best to go with an experienced local diver.

Kee Beach

Commonly called 'the beach at the end of the road,' Kee Beach has a picturesque setting and a rich history.

On the left side of the beach is the distinctive 1280ft cliff that marks the start of the Na Pali Coast. Almost everyone calls it Bali Hai, its name in the movie *South Pacific*. To the ancient Hawaiians it was known as Makana, which means 'gift.' A *heiau* and former hula school site are at its base.

Snorkeling is good at Kee Beach, which has a variety of tropical fish. A reef protects the right side of the cove and, except on high surf days, it's usually calm. The left side is open and can have a powerful current, particularly in winter.

When it's really calm – generally only in summer – snorkelers cross the reef to the open ocean where there's great visibility, big fish, large coral heads and the occasional sea turtle. It makes the inside of the bay look like kids' stuff, but check it out carefully because breaking surf and strong currents can create dangerous conditions.

When the tide's at its lowest, you can actually walk a great distance out on the reef without getting your feet wet and peer down into tide pools.

Showers, drinking water, rest rooms and a pay phone are tucked back in the woods behind the parking lot.

North Shore Lore

If you walk down Kee Beach about 15 minutes to the northeast, you'll come to a stream and the site of the former Taylor Camp.

In the late 1960s, a little village of tents and tree houses sprang up on property owned by actress Elizabeth Taylor's brother. Reports of drugs, orgies and pipe-organ music in the middle of the night eventually prompted the authorities to crack down on the camp. When state officials tried to evict everyone on public health grounds, the campers challenged them in court, claiming squatters' rights. The 'squatters' eventually lost, and the property was condemned and incorporated into the state park system. Taylor Camp remains part of North Shore folklore, though there's nothing left to see.

There are several ways to see views down the Na Pali Coast from Kee Beach. One way is to walk the first 30 minutes of the Kalalau Trail (detailed in the following Na Pali Coast section). Another is to take the short walk out around the point at the left side of the beach, toward the *heiau*.

Or, simply walk down the beach to the right for a few minutes and look back as the cliffs unfold, one after the other.

Kaulu Paoa Heiau To make the five-minute walk out to Kaulu Paoa Heiau, take the path on the western side of the beach. The walk is shaded by tropical almond trees, which drop their edible nuts along the trail. Follow the stone wall as it curves uphill, and you'll reach the *heiau* almost immediately.

The overgrown section at the foot of the hill is one of the more intact parts of the *heiau*, but don't stop there. Instead, continue walking up the terraces toward the cliff face. Surf pounding below, vertical cliffs above – what a spectacular place to worship the gods!

Beneath the cliff face, large stones retain a long flat grassy platform. A thatched-roof *halau* (a longhouse used as a hula school) once ran the entire length of the terrace. It was here that dances to Laka, the goddess of hula, were performed. In ancient Hawaii, this was Kauai's most sacred hula school, and students aspiring to learn hula came from all of the Hawaiian islands to Kaulu Paoa.

Fern wreaths, rocks wrapped in ti leaves, leis and other offerings to Laka are still placed into the crevices of the cliff face. The site is sacred to native Hawaiians and should be treated with respect. Night hula dances are still performed here on special occasions.

Lohiau's House Site You'll find Lohiau's house site just a minute's walk above the parking lot at Kee Beach. At the Kalalau Trail sign, go left along the barely discernible dirt path to a vine-covered rock wall. This overgrown level terrace runs back 54ft to the bluff and is said to have been the home of Lohiau, a 16th-century prince.

Legend says that the volcano goddess Pele was napping one day under a *hala* tree on the Big Island when her spirit was awakened by the sound of distant drums. Her spirit rode the wind in the direction of the sound, searching each island in turn until she finally arrived at Kee Beach. Here above the *heiau* she found Lohiau beating a hula drum, surrounded by graceful hula dancers.

Pele took the form of a beautiful woman and captured Lohiau's heart. They became lovers and moved into this house. In time Pele had to go back home to the Big Island, leaving the lovesick Lohiau behind. His longing quickly got the better of him, and on this site he died from his grief.

Places to Stay

Kauai YMCA-Camp Naue (*☎ 826-6419, fax 246-4411; PO Box 1786, Lihue, HI 96766; camp sites per person $10, bunks $12*), in Haena, just before the 8-mile marker on Hwy 560, has simple beachside bunkhouses, each with screened windows, cement floors and six to 14 bunks. The camp is geared to groups but sometimes accepts individual travelers. It has 50 bunks, which have vinyl mattresses but no linen or blankets, or you can pitch a tent. There are hot showers, but the kitchen is reserved for large groups only. The Y doesn't accept reservations, but you should still call ahead, as there are specific check-in policies and on occasion the camp shuts down completely. Also, in summer and some other holiday periods the camp is commonly booked by children's groups, at which times it's closed to individual travelers. The camp is a 10-minute walk from Tunnels Beach.

Hanalei Colony Resort (*☎ 826-6235, 800-628-3004, fax 826-9893; ⓔ aloha@hcr.com; PO Box 206, Hanalei, HI 96714; garden-view rooms low/high season $160/185, oceanfront rooms $230/280*) is an older but renovated low-rise condo complex on the east side of Haena. Each of the 52 units has a full kitchen, a lanai and two bedrooms, although one of the bedrooms is essentially a sitting area with two twin beds that's separated from the rest of the living room by sliding doors. The complex is right on the beach and has a swimming pool and barbecue area. This is a place to listen to the surf: there are no TVs, radios or room phones. The rates are the same for up to four people, and for weekly stays, the seventh night is free.

NA PALI COAST

In Hawaiian, *na pali* means simply 'the cliffs.' Indeed, these are Hawaii's grandest.

The Na Pali Coast is the rugged 22-mile stretch between the end of the road at Kee Beach in the north and the road's opposite end at Polihale State Park in the west. It has the most sharply fluted coastal cliffs in Hawaii.

Kalalau, Honopu, Awaawapuhi, Nualolo and Milolii are the five major valleys on the Na Pali Coast. These deep river valleys once contained sizable settlements.

In the mid-19th century, missionaries established a school in Kalalau, the largest valley, and registered the valley population at about 200. Influenced by Western ways, people gradually began moving to towns, and by the end of the century the valleys were largely abandoned.

The Na Pali valleys, with limited accessibility and abundant fertility, have long been a natural refuge for people wanting to escape one scene or another. While Koolau the Leper is the best known (see the boxed text later in the chapter), there have been scores of others.

Precarious trails once led from the upland Kokee area down to the valley floors along the Na Pali Coast. In some places, footholds were gouged into cliffs, and in others rope ladders were used. These trails no longer exist.

Today, only the Hanakapiai, Hanakoa and Kalalau Valleys can still be reached on foot, solely along the 11 mile Kalalau coastal trail.

Kalalau Trail

Kalalau is Hawaii's premier trail. Here, it's common to come across hikers who have trekked in Nepal or climbed to Machu Picchu. The Na Pali Coast is similarly spectacular, a place of singular beauty.

The Kalalau Trail is basically the same ancient route used by the Hawaiians who once lived in these remote north coast valleys. The trail runs along high sea cliffs and winds up and down across lush valleys before it finally ends below the steep fluted *pali* of Kalalau. The scenery is breathtaking, with sheer green cliffs dropping into brilliant turquoise waters.

While hikers in good shape can walk the 11-mile trail straight through in about seven hours, it's less strenuous to break it up and spend a night camping along the way.

In winter, there are generally only a few people at any one time hiking all the way in to Kalalau Valley, but the trail is heavily trodden in summer. As it's a popular hike for islanders as well as visitors, weekends tend to see the most use.

The hike can be divided into three parts: Kee Beach to Hanakapiai Valley (2 miles); Hanakapiai to Hanakoa Valley (4 miles); and Hanakoa to Kalalau Valley (5 miles).

The first 2 miles of the hike make for a popular day trip, and hiking permits are not required for those going only as far as Hanakapiai Valley.

The trail is within Na Pali Coast State Park. Even if you're not planning to stay overnight, a permit is officially required to continue on the Kalalau Trail beyond Hanakapiai; day-use hiking permits are available free from the **Division of State Parks** *(☎ 274-3444; 3060 Eiwa St, room 306, Lihue, HI 96766)*.

Camping is currently allowed in Hanakapiai and Kalalau valleys and is limited to five nights in total. The trail's third valley, Hanakoa, is currently closed to campers, but it's expected to eventually reopen. State camping permits are required. For details on obtaining permits, see Camping in the Accommodations section earlier in this chapter.

Kee Beach to Hanakapiai The 2 mile trail from Kee Beach to Hanakapiai Valley is a delightfully scenic hike. Morning is a good time to be going west, and the afternoon to be going east, as you have the sun at your back and good light for photography.

The trail weaves through *kukui* and *ohia* trees and then back out to clearings with fine coastal views. There are purple orchids, wildflowers and a couple of tiny Zen-like waterfalls en route. The black nuts embedded in the clay are *kukui*, polished smooth by the scuffing of hundreds of hiking shoes.

Just a quarter mile up the trail, you can catch a fine view of Kee Beach and the surrounding reef. After 30 minutes, you get your first view of the Na Pali Coast. Even if you weren't planning on a hike, it's well worth coming this far.

Hanakapiai has a sandy beach in the summer. In the winter, the sand washes out, and it becomes a beach of boulders, some of them sparkling with tiny olivine crystals. The western side of the beach has a small cave with dripping water and a miniature fern grotto.

The ocean is dangerous here, with unpredictable rip currents year-round. It's particularly treacherous during winter high-surf conditions, but summer trades also bring very powerful currents. Hanakapiai Beach is matched only by Lumahai for the number of drownings on Kauai.

If you're just doing a day hike and want to walk farther, it makes more sense to head up the valley to Hanakapiai Falls than it does to continue another couple of miles on the coastal trail.

Hanakapiai Falls The 2-mile hike from Hanakapiai Beach to Hanakapiai Falls – a side trip off the Kalalau Trail – takes about 2½ hours round-trip. Because of some tricky rock crossings, this trail is rougher than the walk from Kee Beach to Hanakapiai Beach. Due to the possibility of flash floods in the narrow valley, the Hanakapiai Falls hike should only be done in fair weather.

The trail itself is periodically washed out by floodwaters, and sections occasionally get redrawn, but the path is not that difficult to follow, as it basically goes up the side of Hanakapiai Stream. The trail is not well maintained, and in places you may have to scramble over and around tree trunks and branches.

There are trails on both sides of the stream, but the main route heads up the stream's western side. About 50 yards up, there are old stone walls and guava trees. If the guavas are ripe, it's a good place to stock up. There are also some big old mango trees along the way that might have fruit for the picking.

Ten minutes up from the trailhead, you'll find thickets of green bamboo interspersed with eucalyptus. Also along the trail is the site of an old coffee mill, though all that remains is a little of the chimney.

The first of five stream crossings is about 25 minutes up, at a sign that warns: 'Hazardous. Keep away from stream during heavy rainfall. Stream floods suddenly.'

Be particularly careful of your footing on the rocky upper part of the trail. Some of the rocks are covered with a barely visible film of slick algae. It's like walking on glass.

Hanakapiai Falls is spectacular, with a wide pool gentle enough for swimming. Directly under the falls, the cascading water forces you back from the rock face – a warning from nature, as rocks can fall from the top.

This is a very peaceful place to spend a little time meditating. It's a beautiful lush valley, though it's not terribly sunny near the falls because of the incredible steepness.

Hanakapiai to Hanakoa Just 10 minutes up the Kalalau Trail from Hanakapiai Valley on the way to Hanakoa Valley, there's a nice view of Hanakapiai Beach, but from there the trail goes into bush, and the next coastal view is not for another mile. This is the least scenic part of the trail.

The camping site at Hanakoa is tucked into the valley about half a mile inland. Of the three camping areas, Hanakoa is the wettest. It also tends to have the largest number of mosquitoes.

The valley is lovely and Hanakoa Stream has pools perfect for swimming. There's a waterfall about a third of a mile up the valley, but it's rough getting up there as the path is overgrown. The valley was formerly settled by farmers who grew taro and coffee, both of which still grow wild.

Koolau the Leper

Koolau was a *paniolo* (cowhand) who contracted leprosy in 1893. Rather than accept separation from his family and banishment to Molokai's leprosy colony, as was the law at the time, Koolau hiked down into Kalalau Valley, taking along his wife and young son. Shortly after, a sheriff and deputy showed up to clear the valley of renegade lepers. Koolau was the only resister. That night, in the light of a full moon, the sheriff snuck up the valley hoping to take Koolau in his sleep. In self-defense, Koolau shot the sheriff.

When word reached Honolulu, a shipload of soldiers was sent to land on Kalalau Beach. As they marched up the valley, they met Koolau's gunfire. After two of the soldiers were shot off the ridge and a third accidentally killed himself, they switched strategies. Just before dawn, they blasted Koolau's hideaway with cannon fire, not knowing he had slipped through their lines the night before. From a nearby waterfall, Koolau watched as the soldiers loaded up and set sail. They never returned, and Koolau lived the rest of his days in the valley undisturbed.

Eventually the son, and then Koolau, died of leprosy. Both are buried on a valley hillside. When Koolau's wife, Piilani, left the valley, she found Koolau had largely been forgotten. A decade later, a visiting reporter, John Sheldon, recorded her story. Jack London later wrote *Koolau the Leper*, a more fictionalized account.

Hanakoa to Kalalau This is the most difficult part of the trail, although without question the most beautiful. Make sure you have at least three hours of daylight left.

About a mile out of Hanakoa Valley, you'll reach the coast again and begin to get fantastic views of Na Pali's jagged edges. There are some very narrow and steep stretches along this section of the trail, so make sure your gear is properly packed and be cautious of your footing. A little past the halfway mark, you'll get your first view into Kalalau Valley.

The large valley has a beach, a little waterfall, a *heiau* site, some ancient house sites and some interesting caves that are sometimes dry enough to sleep in during the summer.

An easy 2-mile trail leads back into the valley to a pool in Kalalau Stream where there's a natural water slide. If you have a quick hand, you might try your luck at catching some of the prawns that live in the stream.

Valley terraces where Hawaiians cultivated taro until 1920 are now largely overgrown with bitter Java plum and edible guava and passion fruit. Feral goats scurry up and down the crumbly cliffs and drink from the stream.

Kalalau Valley has fruit trees, including mango, papaya, orange, banana, coconut, guava and mountain apple. During the 1960s and '70s, people wanting to get away from it all tried to settle in Kalalau, but forestry rangers eventually routed them out. Even today, rangers occasionally swoop in unexpectedly by helicopter to check camping permits; those without permits are forced to hike back out immediately, and those suspected of being repeat offenders have their gear confiscated.

Warnings & Information The Kalalau Trail is a hike into rugged wilderness and hikers should be well prepared. In places, the trail runs along steep cliffs that can narrow to little more than a foot in width, which some people find unnerving. However, hikers accustomed to high-country trails generally enjoy the hike and don't consider it unduly hazardous. Like other Hawaiian trails, the route can be muddy and slippery if it's been raining – at such times, a walking stick makes a good companion.

Accidents are not unknown. Most casualties along the Kalalau Trail are the result of people trying to ford swollen streams, walking after dark on cliff-edge trails, or swimming in treacherous surf. Keep in mind that the rock the cliffs are composed of is loose and crumbly; don't try to climb the cliffs, and don't camp directly beneath them, as goats commonly dislodge stones that tumble down the cliff walls. Still, for someone who's cautious and aware, this can be a hike into paradise.

There's no shortage of water sources along the trail, but all drinking water must be boiled or treated.

Bring what you need, but travel light. You won't want to have extra shifting weight on stream crossings or along cliff edges. Shoes should have good traction. If you bring a sleeping bag, make it a light one.

The state parks office in Lihue can provide a Kalalau Trail brochure with a map. There is also information posted at the Kee Beach trailhead.

Getting There & Away

There's space for parking at Kee Beach, right at the trailhead. Unfortunately, break-ins to cars left overnight at Kee Beach are all too common. Some people advise leaving cars empty and unlocked to prevent smashed windows. It's generally safer to park at the camping ground at Haena Beach Park. Whatever you do, don't leave valuables in a locked car.

Another possibility is to store everything in Hanalei and take a taxi to the trailhead. **Kayak Kauai** (*☎ 826-9844*) in Hanalei lets hikers park their cars in the shop's lot for $5 a day and stores backpacks or suitcases for $4 a day. **North Shore Cab** (*☎ 639-7829*) charges about $20 for a taxi from Hanalei to Kee Beach.

You might also be able to leave extra luggage at your guest house or wherever you've been staying. Another option for baggage storage is the **Wainiha General Store** (*☎ 826-6251*) in Wainiha, en route to Kee Beach, which stores bags for $3 a day.

In addition to approaching the Na Pali Coast from the North Shore, you can also look down into the Na Pali valleys from Kokee State Park. The park has a drive-up lookout right on the rim of Kalalau Valley, as well as strenuous hikes out to cliff-tops that offer gorgeous views into Awaawapuhi and Nualolo Valleys (for details, see Kokee State Park in the West Side section, later in this chapter).

South Shore

Poipu is Kauai's main beach resort area. It's typically sunny, and for the larger part of the year, including winter, it has calm waters good for swimming and snorkeling. During the summer, the surf kicks up, and it becomes a surfers' haunt.

The village of Koloa, 3 miles inland from Poipu, was the site of Hawaii's first sugar plantation. This sleepy town could have doubled for Dodge City before it got caught up in Poipu's boom. Now most of its shops are geared for tourists, and it catches the overflow from neighboring Poipu.

Poipu and Koloa are about 10 miles south of Lihue. To get there, take Hwy 50 (Kaumualii Hwy) and turn off onto Hwy 520 (Maluhia Rd).

Tree Tunnel

Immediately after turning down Maluhia Rd, you enter the Tree Tunnel, a mile-long stretch of road canopied by swamp mahogany trees, a type of eucalyptus. Originally, the tree tunnel was more than double this length, but when Hwy 50 was rerouted to the south, most of the tunnel was lopped off.

The cinder hill to the right about 2 miles down Maluhia Rd is Puu o Hewa. From its top, the ancient Hawaiians raced wooden *holua* (sleds) down paths covered with oiled *pili* grass. To add even more excitement to this popular spectator sport, the Hawaiians crossed two sled paths near the middle of the hill. The paths were approximately 5ft wide, and if you strain your eyes you might be able to see the X on the hillside where they crossed.

Hewa means 'wrong' or 'mistake.' The hill's original name was lost when a surveyor jotted 'Puu o Hewa' (Wrong Hill) on a map he was making, and it mistakenly went off to the printer like that.

The two grassy hills to the left of the road are known as Mauna Kalika, or Silk Mountain. Two American entrepreneurs introduced Chinese silkworms here in the 1830s in the hopes of developing a Hawaiian silk industry. However, the climate soon proved unsuitable for the silkworms, and so the hills, similar to the rest of the surrounding area, were eventually used to produce sugarcane instead.

KOLOA

Hawaii's first sugar plantation was started in Koloa in 1835. The raw materials had arrived long before; sugarcane came with the original Polynesian settlers, and the earliest Chinese immigrants brought small-scale refinery know-how. However, large-scale production did not begin until William Hooper, an enterprising 24-year-old Bostonian, arrived in Kauai and made inroads with the *alii* (local chiefs).

With financial backing from Honolulu businesspeople, he leased land in Koloa from the king and paid the *alii* a stipend to release commoners from their traditional work obligations. He was then free to hire Hawaiians as wage laborers, and Koloa became Hawaii's first plantation town.

Koloa Rd (Hwy 530), which runs between Koloa and Lawai, is the best way to leave Koloa if you're heading west – it's a pleasant rural drive through pastures and cane fields.

Information

The **First Hawaiian Bank** *(☎ 742-1642; 3506 Waikomo Rd; open 8:30am-4pm Mon-Thur, 8:30am-6pm Fri)* is at the east end of town.

The **post office** *(☎ 800-275-8777; 5485 Koloa Rd; open 9am-4pm Mon-Fri, 9am-11am Sat)* serves both Koloa and Poipu.

Koloa Country Store *(☎ 742-1255; 5356 Koloa Rd; open 8am-8pm Mon-Sat, 9am-5pm Sun)* has computers with Internet access that cost $5 per half hour.

There's a **coin laundry** *(cnr Waikomo Rd & Koloa Rd; open 24hr)* behind the Big Save supermarket.

Sugar Exhibits

Any sugarologists in the crowd? This field, on Koloa Rd opposite Sueoka Store, is for you.

In a tiny garden, you'll find a dozen varieties of **sugarcane** labeled with faded interpretive markers. Some are noted for their high tonnage, others for high sucrose and some for their good ratooning abilities, though the different varieties have all grown to twist and clump together. Who knows, maybe there's a great new hybrid sprouting up among the tangles!

The **stone smokestack** in another corner of the field is a relic from one of Koloa's early mills and dates back to 1841.

KAUAI

KOLOA

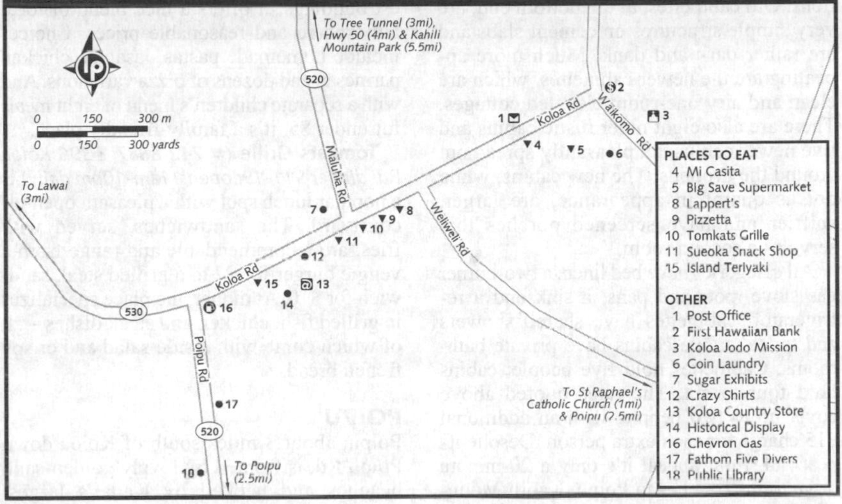

In the center of the field, the principal ethnic groups that worked the plantations are immortalized in a **sculpture**. The Hawaiian wears a *malo* (loincloth) and has a poi dog by his side. The Chinese, Korean, Japanese, Portuguese, Filipino and Puerto Rican groups are likewise in native field dress. You may notice that the plaque on the wall curiously makes reference to a *haole* overseer – present-day islanders found the depiction of this Caucasian plantation boss seated on a high horse so unacceptable that at the last minute he was omitted from the sculpture.

Old Koloa

With its aging wooden buildings and false storefronts, Koloa has the appearance of an Old West town. It was a thriving plantation village and commercial center that largely went bust after WWII.

While its history is sugar, its present is unmistakably tourism. The former fish markets, barber shops, bathhouses and beer halls have become boutiques, galleries and restaurants.

The building that houses **Crazy Shirts** was, until recently, the Yamamoto General Store. Before the theater across the street burned down, moviegoers would line up at Yamamoto's for crack seed (a local snack) and soft drinks. On the sidewalk in front of the store are a couple of wooden sculptures by the late Maui artist Reems Mitchell. In the courtyard behind the store, you'll find the site of the former town hotel, along with a little **historical display** that includes a Japanese bath and some period photos.

At the east side of town is the **Koloa Jodo Mission**, which dates back to 1910. The Buddhist temple on the left is the original, while next to it is a newer and larger temple where services are now held. During services, the smell of incense and the sound of beating drums fills the air.

St Raphael's Catholic Church, the oldest Catholic church on Kauai, is the burial site of some of the first Portuguese immigrants to Hawaii. The original church, built in 1854, was built from lava rock and coral mortar with walls 3ft thick – a type of construction that can be seen in the ruins of the adjacent rectory. When the church was enlarged in 1936, it was all plastered over, and it now has a more typical whitewashed appearance. To get there from Koloa Rd, turn onto Weliweli Rd, then right onto Hapa Rd and proceed half a mile to the church.

Places to Stay

Kahili Mountain Park (*☎ 742-9921; PO Box 298, Koloa, HI 96756; cabinettes $45-55, cabins $65-75*) is a mile up a dirt road just beyond the 7-mile marker on Hwy 50. Run by the Seventh Day Adventist church, it enjoys a beautiful setting beneath Mt Kahili.

There are four categories of accommodations. Old cabinettes, at the bottom end, are very simple structures on cement slabs and are rather dark and dank. Much more appealing are the newer cabinettes, which are clean and airy one-room elevated cottages. There are also eight older rustic cabins and five newer cabins, all pleasantly spread out around the grounds. The new cabins, while not as quaint in appearance, are larger, spiffier and have screened porches that serve as a second room.

All categories have bed linen, a two-burner gas stove, pots and pans, a sink and a refrigerator; cabinettes have shared showers and toilets, while cabins have private bathrooms. Cabinettes hold five people; cabins hold four to six. The rates quoted above cover up to two people, with an additional $15 charge for each extra person. Despite its peaceful, rural appeal it's only a 20-minute drive to the beaches in Poipu. Kahili Mountain Park commonly books up during the high season; make reservations in advance.

Places to Eat

You'll find the following places to eat, as well as a **Lappert's** ice-cream shop, on Koloa Rd (Hwy 530) near its intersection with Maluhia Rd (Hwy 520).

The **Sueoka Snack Shop** *(5358 Koloa Rd; open 9am-3pm Tues-Sun)*, a take-out window at the side of the Sueoka Store, sells burgers, sandwiches and saimin for under $2 and good plate lunches for $4, including a tasty island fish plate.

Island Teriyaki *(5330 Koloa Rd; dishes $4-8; open 7am-9pm daily)* is an unpretentious spot with affordable fare. At breakfast you can order pancakes, omelettes and egg-filled burritos. The rest of the day there's a selection of tortilla-wrap sandwiches, salads and plate lunches.

Mi Casita *(5476 Koloa Rd; meals $8-12; open 11am-9pm Mon-Sat)* is a quaint little family-run restaurant serving home-style Mexican fare. Meals, which are served with rice and beans, include your choice of tacos, *chili rellenos* (green peppers stuffed with cheese) or enchiladas. It's also possible to order à la carte – a tasty chicken burrito costs $5.

Pizzetta *(☎ 742-8881; 5408 Koloa Rd; mains $7-23; open 11am-10pm daily)* is a good little pizzeria that's grown into a full-service Italian restaurant. Occupying one of the town's oldest buildings, it offers a nice blend of local atmosphere and reasonable prices. Choices include homemade pastas, lasagna, chicken parmesan and dozens of pizza variations. And with a separate children's menu of eight meals for under $5, it's a family-friendly place.

Tomkats Grille *(☎ 742-8887; 5396 Koloa Rd; dinner $11-19; open 11am-10pm daily)* is a popular lunch spot with a pleasant open-air courtyard. The sandwiches, served with fries, are recommendable and range from a veggie burger for $7 to a grilled steak sandwich for $10. At dinner, the place specializes in grilled fish, chicken and steak dishes – all of which come with a side salad and crispy french bread.

POIPU

Poipu, about 3 miles south of Koloa down Poipu Rd, is fronted by lovely golden-sand beaches and backed by Kauai's largest collection of hotels and condos. Even if you're not staying here, it's a great place to go if you're looking for a day at the beach.

Other than its beaches, Poipu's most popular attraction is the Spouting Horn blowhole. To get to Spouting Horn, turn right off Poipu Rd onto Lawai Rd, just past Poipu Plaza, and continue for 1¾ miles.

Prince Kuhio Park

This park is about half a mile down Lawai Rd, across from Hoai Bay. Here you'll find **Hoai Heiau** and a monument honoring Prince Jonah Kuhio Kalanianaole, the Territory of Hawaii's first delegate to the US Congress. It was Prince Kuhio who spearheaded the Hawaiian Homes Commission Act, which provided homesteads for native Hawaiians. You'll also find the remains of a fishpond and an ancient Hawaiian house platform.

Baby Beach

A protected swimming area just deep enough for children is off Hoona Rd, east of Prince Kuhio Park. Look for the beach access post that marks the pathway between the road and the beach. Adults may want to walk west down the beach to reach a sandy break with fewer rocks and deeper water.

Lawai Beach

This beach is west of Prince Kuhio Park, opposite Lawai Beach Resort. It's a little rocky,

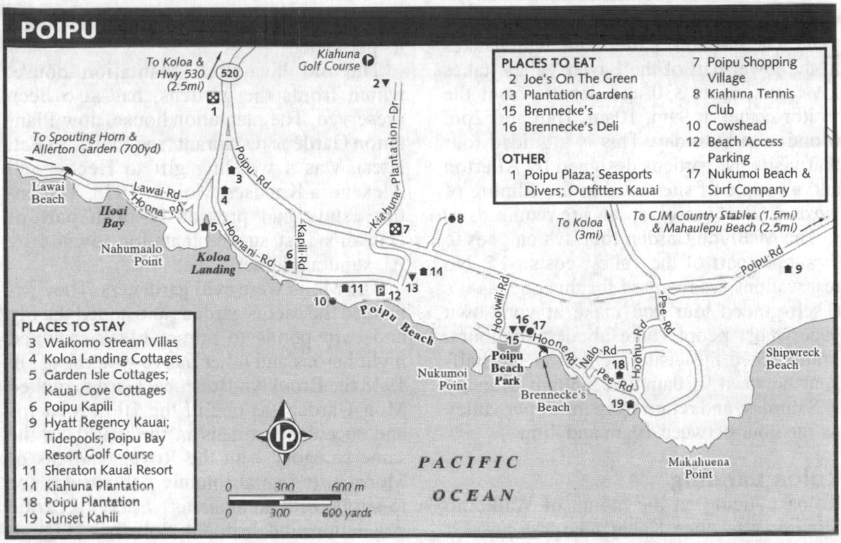

but during winter it's a favorite snorkeling locale. The water is usually quite clear and there's an abundance of tropical fish, including orange-shouldered tangs, rainbow parrotfish, raccoon butterfly fish and white-spotted puffer fish. When the surf's up in summer, the snorkelers leave and the beach is inundated with surfers.

Across from the beach, you'll find rest rooms, a shower and public parking.

Kukuiula Bay

About a half mile east of Spouting Horn, Kukuiula Bay is a small boat harbor maintained by the state and mostly used by fishing and diving boats. The beach itself is rocky and more suitable for pole fishing than other water activities.

Spouting Horn Beach Park

Sometimes Spouting Horn has a fairly impressive spout, while at other times it's simply a nonevent. The waves, the tides and the overall force of the sea rushing into the lava tube decide how much water surges through the spout. Listen for the low whooshing that precedes the rushing water – it sounds like a whale breathing.

During the height of the day, tour buses pull in and out of the parking lot, and there's often a small crowd with cameras clicking away. Jewelry and trinket stalls line the walkway from the parking lot down to the viewing area. You can avoid the tour bus crowd by arriving in the late afternoon, which is also the best time to see rainbows that are sometimes cast in the spray by the sun.

Allerton Garden

The Allerton Garden, in the remote Lawai Valley east of the Spouting Horn area, was started in the 1870s by Queen Emma, who built a summer cottage on the site. Chicago industrialist Robert Allerton bought the property in the late 1930s and significantly expanded the decorative gardens in the 100-acre estate.

In 1971, the site became part of the National Tropical Botanical Garden, which propagates tropical and endangered plant species and does research in ethnobotanical and medicinal plants. The organization, which owns much of the Lawai Valley and allows entrance only via tours, maintains a **visitor center** *(☎ 742-2623; admission free; open 8:30am-5pm Mon-Sat)* opposite Spouting Horn Beach Park.

The visitor center is worth a stop if only to stroll through the exhibition gardens that surround it. One garden is planted with a variety of native Hawaiian plants, and another displays the fruit trees and vegetables typically grown around plantation workers' homes.

The center is also the starting point for two tours. The **Allerton Garden tour**, which takes in the lower part of the Lawai Valley, takes 2½ hours, costs $30 and departs from the visitor center at 9am, 10am, 1pm and 2pm Monday to Saturday. This is a guided tour that visits the gardens designed by Allerton and a couple of sites used in the filming of *Jurassic Park;* reservations are required.

The **McBryde Garden tour**, which goes to the upper part of the valley, costs $15. No reservations are required for this one, as it's a self-guided tour you make at your own pace; most people take about two hours. Trams leave the visitor center on the half-hour between 9:30am and 2:30pm Monday to Saturday, and return from the upper valley on the hour between 10am and 4pm.

Koloa Landing

Koloa Landing, at the mouth of Waikomo Stream, was once Kauai's largest port. It served to ship sugar grown on Koloa Plantation, and whalers called at Koloa Landing to resupply provisions. In the 1850s, farmers used the landing to ship Kauai-grown oranges and sweet potatoes to California gold miners. The landing lost its importance after an island-wide road system was built, and it was abandoned in the 1920s. Other than a small county boat ramp, there's nothing left to see.

Beneath the water, it's another story; Koloa Landing is a popular snorkeling and diving spot. Its protected waters reach depths of about 30ft, and it's generally calm all year, although *kona* winds can sometimes create rough water conditions. The area has some underwater tunnels and a good variety of coral and fish. Sea turtles are commonly seen, and monk seals make occasional appearances as well. For the best sights, swim out to the right after entering the water.

Moir Gardens

Moir Pau a Laka Cactus and Flower Garden *(☎ 742-6411; 2253 Poipu Rd; admission free; open sunrise-sunset daily)* is a beautiful old garden with winding paths, lily ponds and exotic flowers. It dates back nearly a century and was part of the Moir Estate before the estate grounds were absorbed into the Kiahuna Plantation Resort. Fortunately, this mature garden of cactus and other succulents – the finest in all Hawaii – was preserved in its entirely with the condominiums built around its perimeter.

The old lava-stone plantation house, which fronts the gardens, has also been preserved. The plantation house, now Plantation Gardens restaurant (see Places to Eat, later), was a wedding gift to Hector and Alexandra Knudsen Moir in 1933. The entire estate had previously been part of Hawaii's first sugar plantation, owned by Alexandra's father.

The Moirs were avid gardeners. They expanded the cactus gardens and added the lily and carp ponds to attract black-crowned night herons and other native waterbirds. In 1948 the Brooklyn Botanical Garden ranked Moir Gardens as one of the 10 best cactus and succulent gardens in the world, in the same category with the Royal Gardens of Monaco. It's an absolutely delightful place to stroll, with an amazing variety of exotic vegetation and brilliant flowers – though watch out for those prickly thorns!

Poipu Beach

The long stretch of golden sand running from the Sheraton Kauai Resort east to Poipu Beach Park is generally referred to as Poipu Beach. It's actually three attractive crescent beaches separated by narrow rocky points. The turquoise waters are often good for swimming, bodysurfing, windsurfing, board surfing and snorkeling.

Cowshead, the rocky outcropping at the west end of the beach near the Sheraton, has Poipu Beach's best boogie boarding and bodysurfing breaks. Top surfing spots are Waiohai, which is off the east side of Poipu Beach, and First Break, offshore in front of the Sheraton. Slow, gentle waves more suitable for beginners can be found inshore along the beach.

Poipu Beach Park

At the end of Hoowili Rd (off Poipu Rd), Poipu Beach Park is an excellent all-purpose beach. It has a lifeguard station, shallow nearshore waters and safe swimming, making it one of the most popular weekend destinations for families on the South Shore.

Nukumoi Point extends into the water at the western side of the park. At low tide, you can walk out on the point and explore tide pools that shelter small fish and sea urchins. You'll find the best snorkeling at the west side of the point, where there are swarms of near-tame fish.

Beach facilities include rest rooms, showers and picnic tables, and there's a cool playground for kids. Snorkel sets, boogie boards, surfboards, beach chairs and umbrellas can be rented across the street at Nukumoi Beach & Surf Company.

Brennecke's Beach

This beach has a good shorebreak that makes it the South Shore's best spot for bodysurfing and boogie boarding. However, it breaks very close to shore and is suitable only for the experienced. While it's best when surf is highest, which is generally in the summer, there's some respectable action in winter as well. Beware of strong rips that are present with high surf. The beach is only a small pocket of sand and the waters can get crowded. For safety reasons, fins are not allowed and surfboards are prohibited.

Brennecke's is off Hoone Rd, just east of Poipu Beach Park.

Shipwreck Beach

Shipwreck Beach, the pleasant golden-sand beach fronting the Hyatt Regency Kauai, also sees some top bodysurfing and boogie boarding conditions. A couple of challenging nearshore surf breaks attract local board surfers as well. The water conditions here are not for novices, and the pounding shorebreak and high surf make for treacherous swimming conditions along the entire beach.

Mahaulepu Beach

Secluded Mahaulepu Beach *(open 7:30am-6pm winter, 7:30am-7pm summer)*, just a couple of miles beyond Shipwreck Beach, has lovely white sands, sheltered coves, tide pools, petrified sand dunes and sea cliffs. At various times of the year, Mahaulepu is good for surfing, windsurfing, boogie boarding and snorkeling.

Before the arrival of Westerners, the area was heavily settled, and many important historic sites lie buried beneath the cane fields and shifting beach sands. Along the beach, people still claim to see ghost marchers coming in from the sea at night.

The property is owned by Grove Farm, which allows beach access during the aforementioned daylight hours. To get there, drive past the Hyatt Regency Kauai and continue on the cane road for 1½ miles, at which point the road will be blocked by a gate. Turn right, continue past the gravel plant, and after a third of a mile you'll come to a gatehouse; from there, it's half a mile to the beach parking area at the end of the road. A short trail to the beach begins at the right side of the parking area. This will bring you to a popular windsurfing spot and a convenient place from which to explore.

If you walk east along the beach for about 10 minutes you'll reach scenic **Kawailoa Bay**, which is surrounded by sand dunes to the west and protected by jutting sea cliffs to the east. The bay has a lovely beach, and it's not uncommon to find a few Hawaiians net-fishing in the waters along the shore.

Places to Stay – Budget

Accommodations are simple but cheery at **Koloa Landing Cottages** *(☎ 742-1470, 800-779-8773, fax 332-9584; ⓔ dolfin@aloha.net; 2704B Hoonani Rd; studios $70, 2-person/4-person cottages $80/120)*, which comprises five cottages across the street from Koloa Landing. All have TVs, phones and full kitchens. Studio units have queen beds, while the cottages have both a queen bed and two twins. A cleaning fee of $20 for the studios, or $40 to $60 for the cottages, is tagged on to the bill. Reserve as far in advance as possible, as the place is often booked solid.

Poipu Plantation *(☎ 742-6757, 800-634-0263, fax 742-8681; ⓔ plantation@poipubeach.com; 1792 Pee Rd; B&B rooms $100, 1-bedroom/2-bedroom units from $105/150)* consists of nine condo-style units and a 1930s home with three B&B rooms. The best deals are the condos, which are modern and comfortable with tropical rattan furniture, air-con, TVs and full kitchens. While not as spacious, the B&B accommodations are pleasant enough, have private baths and include breakfast. There's a hot tub, a barbecue area and coin-operated washers and dryers.

Kauai Cove Cottages *(☎ 742-2562, 800-624-9945; ⓔ info@kauaicove.com; 2672 Puuholo Rd; units $95)*, near Garden Isle Cottages, consists of three comfortable studio units. Each is pleasant, with hardwood floors, queen bed, TV, CD player, full kitchen, phone, ceiling fans and a little patio with a gas barbecue. The only drawback is that the place is near the road, but it is a relatively quiet street.

Waikomo Stream Villas *(☎ 742-7220, 800-325-5701, fax 742-9093; ⓔ info@grantham-resorts.com; 2721 Poipu Rd; 1-bedroom units $99-119, 2-bedroom $129-159)* is excellent value for a Poipu condominium. The place is on par with many higher-end properties, the grounds have a peaceful stream running across them and the units are modern and spacious. Each of the 60 units has a lanai, a full kitchen, one or two bedrooms and a separate living room with a sofa bed, cable TV, VCR and stereo. There's a pool, tennis court and barbecue area. The minimum stay is four nights.

Garden Isle Cottages *(☎ 742-6717, 800-742-6711, fax 742-1933; ⓔ vacation@oceancottages.com; 2666 Puuholo Rd; studios $122, 1-bedroom apartments $145)*, perched above Koloa Landing, is a friendly place with seven pleasant units. Oceanfront studios have both a double and single bed, refrigerator and coffeemaker. One-bedroom apartments come with ocean-view lanai, queen-size beds, kitchens as well as roomy living rooms. All the units have TVs, ceiling fans and abstract paintings and sculpture by owner and artist Robert Flynn. There are no phones in the units, but a pay phone is out front.

Sunset Kahili *(☎ 742-7434, 800-827-6478, fax 742-6058; ⓔ info@sunsetkahili.com; 1763 Pee Rd; 1-bedroom/2-bedroom units $125/225)* is an older but well-maintained five-story condo. Each of the 36 units has a straight-on ocean view and full amenities, including a washer, dryer, cable TV and lanai. There's a pool. The minimum stay is four nights.

KAUAI

Places to Stay – Top End

A 333-unit condo complex, **Kiahuna Plantation** *(☎ 742-6411, 800-688-7444, fax 742-1698; ⓔ reservations@outrigger.com; 2253 Poipu Rd; 1-bedroom units with garden view $215, oceanfront units $450, 2-bedroom units $345-485)* is spread across acres of quiet, garden-filled grounds between Poipu Rd and Poipu Beach. The units are pleasant, each with a full kitchen, a living room with a sofa bed and a large lanai. Prices mainly reflect the distance from the water. If you book at the lower end, request a 3rd-floor unit, as some have glimpses of the ocean despite being in the garden-view category. The Outrigger chain, which manages the property, offers numerous promotions that can cut the standard rates by as much as half.

Poipu Kapili *(☎ 742-6449, 800-443-7714, fax 742-9162; ⓔ aloha@poipukapili.com; 2221 Kapili Rd; 1-bedroom/2-bedroom units $245/280)* is an upmarket 60-unit condominium complex. The units are large and nicely furnished, with ceiling fans, full kitchens, ocean views and a queen-size sofa bed in the living room. One-bedroom units have either a queen or king bed. The two-bedroom units typically have a king bed in the master bedroom and two twins in the second bedroom. There's a five-day minimum stay. The complex has two tennis courts and a swimming pool.

Gloria's Spouting Horn Bed & Breakfast *(☎ 742-6995; ⓦ www.gloriasbedandbreakfast.com; 4464 Lawai Beach Rd; singles & doubles $250)* is one of those intimate splurges that makes guests feel like a millionaire. This upmarket ocean-side B&B, which is just a few minutes' walk from the Spouting Horn, has a back yard that's literally right on the water. There are three comfortable guest bedrooms, all of which front the ocean. Each room comes with a refrigerator, microwave, phone, TV, VCR, a bath with a deep soaking tub and a seaside balcony. Rates include breakfast; there's a three-day minimum stay.

Sheraton Kauai Resort *(☎ 742-1661, 800-782-9488, fax 742-9777; ⓦ www.sheraton-hawaii.com; 2440 Hoonani Rd; rooms with garden view $300, with ocean view $440)* is a large resort hotel right on Poipu Beach. The 414 rooms have all the expected resort amenities, including lanai. There are two swimming pools, three tennis courts and a couple of restaurants.

Hyatt Regency Kauai *(☎ 742-1234, 800-233-1234, fax 742-1557; ⓦ www.kauai-hyatt.com; 1571 Poipu Rd; rooms with garden view $395, with ocean view $510, suites $1000-3600)* is Poipu's most exclusive hotel. It is a class act, with airy lobbies adorned with antiques and orchids, and its central building nicely incorporates the ocean view into its design. There are also extensive artificial lagoons and waterways spread around the resort grounds. The Hyatt has restaurants, a health spa, tennis courts as well as a golf course.

Vacation Rentals The **Poipu Beach Resort Association** *(☎ 742-7444, fax 742-7887; ⓦ www.poipu-beach.org; PO Box 730,*

Poipu, HI 96756) can mail out a brochure listing most of Poipu's accommodations and also has information online.

The following vacation rental companies book condos and private homes in Poipu:

Grantham Resorts (☎ 742-2000, 800-742-1412, fax 742-9093, ⓔ info@grantham-resorts.com) PO Box 983, Poipu, HI 96756
Kauai Vacation Rentals (☎ 245-8841, 800-367-5025, fax 246-1161, ⓔ aloha@kvrre.com) 3-3311 Kuhio Hwy, Lihue, HI 96766
R&R Realty & Rentals (☎ 742 7555, 800-367-8022, fax 742-1559, ⓔ randr@r7r.com) 1661 Pee Rd, Poipu, HI 96756
Suite Paradise (☎ 742-7400, 800-367-8020, fax 742-9121, ⓔ mail@suite-paradise.com) 1941 Poipu Rd, Poipu, HI 96756

Places to Eat

In the Poipu Plaza, **Taqueria Nortenos** *(open 11am-9pm daily)* has long been popular for its inexpensive take-out Mexican food. The meatless burrito is a good value at $3, while two enchiladas with rice and beans cost $4.50. Don't expect anything fancy, but the food is fine for the price.

Brennecke's Deli *(2100 Hoone Rd; snacks $2-5, open 8am-9pm daily)*, a take-out joint adjacent to Brennecke's restaurant and just opposite Poipu Beach Park, sells standard beachside snacks such as chili dogs, sandwiches and shave ice.

Joe's On The Green *(Kiahuna Golf Course Rd; breakfast $5-8, lunch $7-10; open 11am-5:30pm daily)*, at the Kiahuna Golf Course, is the local favorite for breakfast. You can eat a healthy mix of homemade granola and fresh fruit or choose from a variety of egg dishes such as eggs Benedict, *huevos rancheros* and fluffy omelettes. Lunch is mainly salads, sandwiches and burgers.

In the Poipu Shopping Village, **Keoki's Paradise** *(☎ 742-7535; dinner $15-24; open 5:30pm-10pm daily, bar open 11am-11:30pm)* has an open-air Polynesian motif with artificial waterfalls and lit torches. It's a bit contrived, but it somehow works nicely. The food is reasonably good, and the dishes, which all come with a Caesar salad, include coconut-crusted chicken, teriyaki steak and a half-dozen fresh fish options. A simpler café menu of burgers, sandwiches and snacks, including a nice $5 fish taco, is offered near the bar.

Brennecke's *(☎ 742-7588; 2100 Hoone Rd; lunch $9-14, dinner $17-25; open 11am-10pm daily)*, a touristy restaurant and bar opposite Poipu Beach Park, has an ocean view and good fresh fish dishes. Lunch features fish sandwiches, salads and similar light fare. Dinner dishes, which include a salad bar, range from vegetarian pasta to the catch of day.

Plantation Gardens *(☎ 742-2216; appetizers $8-15, mains $18-27; open 5:30pm-10pm daily)* has a very pleasant setting overlooking the cactus gardens at Kiahuna Plantation. The restaurant features good Pacific Rim cuisine with an emphasis on local seafood dishes. Dishes include the likes of fish wontons in mango-ginger sauce, Kauai shrimp steamed in ti leaves and orange-glazed duck. Be sure to request a table on the veranda, as it really sets the mood.

Roy's Poipu Bar & Grill *(☎ 742-5050; appetizers $7-12, mains $19-25; open 5:30pm-9:30pm daily)*, in the Poipu Shopping Village, has the best food in Poipu, though the shopping center setting is less memorable. A branch of the famed Roy's on Oahu, it has excellent Hawaii regional cuisine, a changing menu of creative dishes and good service. Appetizers include dishes such as shrimp and asparagus crepes and fish satay salad. Popular main dishes are fresh fish with mango-basil sauce, lemongrass chicken and the Asian seared duck. For dessert, the hot chocolate souffle is sinfully indulgent.

Tidepools *(☎ 742-6260; appetizers $9-12, mains $23-30; open 6pm-10pm daily)* is the most interesting restaurant at the Hyatt Regency Kauai. It has a romantic setting with open-air thatched huts overlooking a sprawling carp pond. The menu is heavily weighted to seafood and steak. Appetizers include the likes of crab cakes with passion fruit salsa, *ahi* sashimi and steamed mussels. The signature main dish is macadamia nut-crusted mahimahi in a ginger-butter sauce.

Entertainment

The **Hyatt Regency Kauai** *(☎ 742-1234)* is the main entertainment venue in Poipu. There's live Hawaiian music from 6pm to 8pm nightly in the open-air **Seaview Terrace**, just off the lobby; on Tuesday, Friday and Saturday, the entertainment includes a sunset torch-lighting ceremony and hula dancing. It's all free, though for the price of a drink and an early arrival you can get yourself a front-row table.

There's live jazz from 9pm to 11pm nightly in the Hyatt's **Stevenson's Library** lounge and bar.

The Hyatt also hosts a **luau** *(adult/child over 12/child 6-12 $65/50/33)* from 6pm to 8:30pm on Thursday and Sunday.

Poipu Shopping Village *(☎ 742-2831)* presents a free Polynesian dance show at its center stage from 5pm to 5:45pm on Tuesday and Thursday.

West Side

Kauai's West Side is rural and uncrowded, with a handful of small towns separated from each other by rolling hills of sugarcane and coffee trees. It is this side of Kauai that is best known for the ruggedly spectacular scenery of Waimea Canyon and Kokee State Park, which are must-see sights for all Kauai visitors.

It's 38 miles along the Kaumualii Hwy (Hwy 50) from Lihue to Polihale State Park, the farthest accessible point on the West Side.

KAUAI

KALAHEO

Kalaheo, an old sleepy Portuguese community, is quintessentially local in flavor. Pig hunting remains popular in this town, which accounts for all the hunting dogs in tiny backyard cages.

The town's main shops are clustered around the intersection of Hwy 50 and Papalina Rd. They include a couple of food marts, the post office and Kalaheo's restaurants.

While Kalaheo is off the main tourist track, it has some reasonably priced accommodation options, is within driving distance of Poipu Beach and could make a convenient base for exploring Kauai's West Side sights.

Kukuiolono Park

Kukuiolono Park *(☎ 332-9151; open 6:30am-6:30pm)* is an unassuming little golf course with gardens and scenic views. Kukuiolono means 'light of Lono,' referring to the torches that Hawaiians once placed on this hill to help guide canoes safely to shore.

From Hwy 50, turn left onto Papalina Rd in Kalaheo center. Just short of a mile, turn right onto Puu Rd and then make an immediate right, which takes you through an old stone archway and up into the park. A tidy little Japanese garden is at the far end of the parking lot.

The nine-hole **golf course** is open to the public on a first-come, first-served basis. Greens fees are a mere $7. The little clubhouse has an inexpensive snack shop and a fine view clear down to the coast.

Puu Road Scenic Drive

Puu Rd is a scenic side loop with small ranches, grand mango trees and fine coastal views. It's a winding country road, only one lane with some blind curves, but nothing tricky if you drive slowly. And it's so quiet, you may not even encounter another car.

After leaving Kukuiolono Park, turn right onto Puu Rd to start the drive. It's just over 3 miles back to Hwy 50 this way. About halfway along, you'll look down on Port Allen's oil tanks and the town of Numila, with its old sugar mill (see the Eleele, Numila & Port Allen section later in the chapter).

Down the slope on the west side of the road are coffee trees, part of a total of 4000 acres that have been planted between Koloa and Eleele. The coffee, on McBryde Sugar Company property, is one of that company's grander schemes for diversifying crops on land formerly planted solely in sugarcane.

Places to Stay

Kalaheo Inn *(☎ 332-6023, 888-332-6023; ⓔ chet@aloha.net; 4444 Papalina Rd; small/large doubles $55/65, plus $10 per extra person)* is right in the center of town, adjacent to the Kalaheo Steak House. Chet and Tish Hunt have taken an old local motel and thoroughly renovated it into an inviting, reasonably priced place to stay. There are 15 units; each has a kitchen with microwave, coffeemaker, toaster and refrigerator, a living room with a TV and VCR, a private bath and a bedroom with a queen or two twin beds. Some of the units also have a sofa bed in the living room. For those who plan on staying a month, the rate drops to $40 a day.

Aloha Estates *(☎ 332-7812; ⓔ kalaheo1@gte.net; 4579 Puu Wai Rd; doubles $45-69)* is an attractive B&B within walking distance of the town center. Stained-glass artist James Hargraves and his wife LeeYen have made this 75-year-old plantation home a cheery

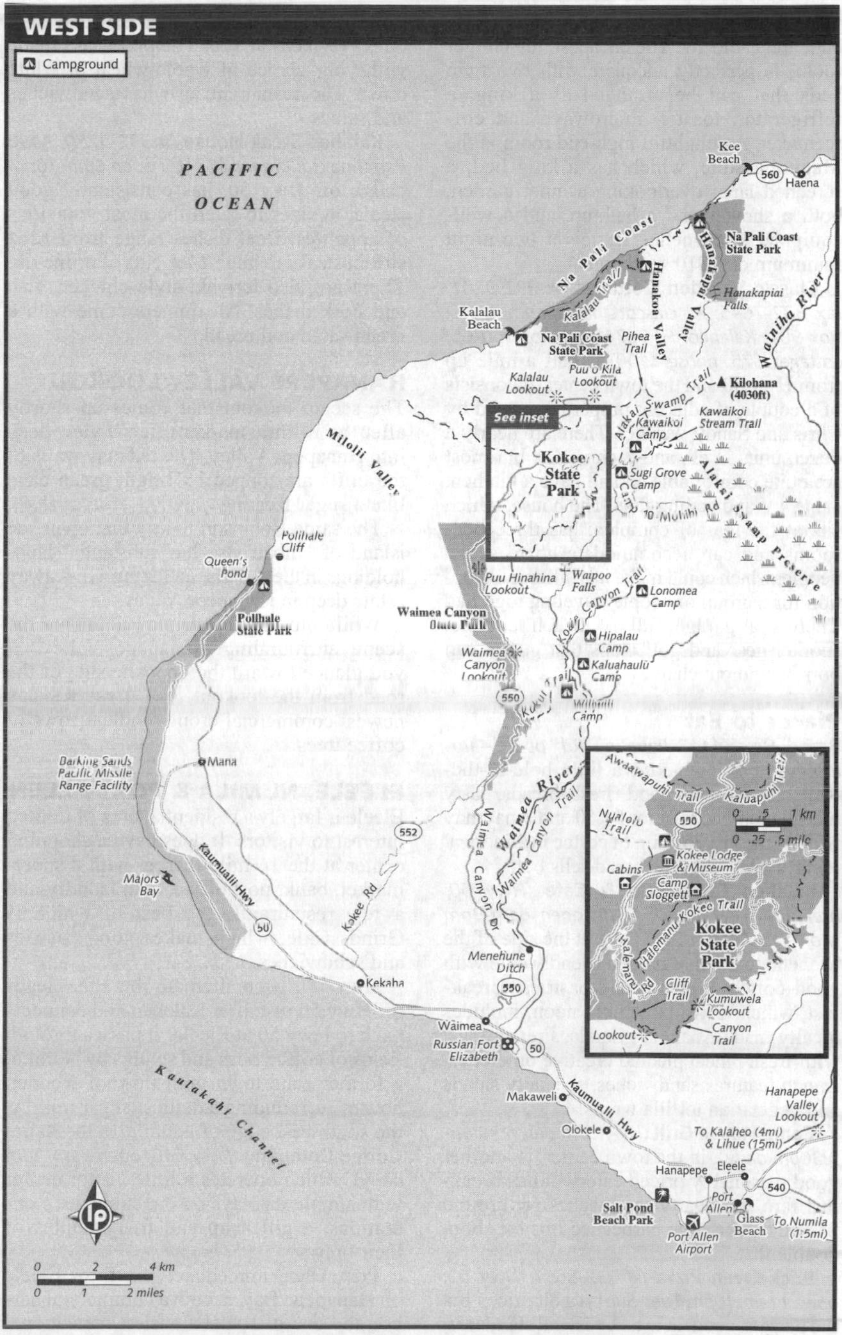
WEST SIDE
Campground
PACIFIC OCEAN
Kee Beach
560
Haena
Na Pali Coast
Na Pali Coast State Park
Hanakapiai Falls
Hanakoa Valley
Hanakapiai Valley
Wainiha River
Kalalau Trail
Kalalau Beach
Na Pali Coast State Park
Pihea Trail
Puu o Kila Lookout
Kalalau Lookout
Alakai Swamp Trail
Kilohana (4030ft)
See inset
Kawaikoi Camp
Kawaikoi Stream Trail
Kokee State Park
Sugi Grove Camp
Camp 10-Mohihi Rd
Alakai Swamp Preserve
Milolii Valley
Polihale Cliff
Queen's Pond
Polihale State Park
Puu Hinahina Lookout
Waipoo Falls
Canyon Trail
Lonomea Camp
Waimea Canyon State Park
Hipalau Camp
Kaluahaulu Camp
Waimea Canyon Lookout
Koaie Trail
Kukui Trail
Wiliwili Camp
550
Barking Sands Pacific Missile Range Facility
Mana
Waimea River
Waimea Canyon Trail
Waimea Canyon Dr
552
Kaumualii Hwy
Majors Bay
50
Kokee Rd
Menehune Ditch
550
Kekaha
Waimea
Russian Fort Elizabeth
50
Kaulakahi Channel
Makaweli
Kaumualii Hwy
Olokele
Hanapepe Valley Lookout
To Kalaheo (4mi) & Lihue (15mi)
Hanapepe
Eleele
540
Salt Pond Beach Park
Port Allen
Glass Beach
To Numila (1.5mi)
Port Allen Airport
0 2 4 km
0 1 2 miles
Awaawapuhi Trail
Kaluapuhi Trail
Nualolo Trail
550
0 .5 1 km
0 .25 .5 mile
Kokee Lodge & Museum
Cabins
Camp Sloggett
Halemanu-Kokee Trail
Kokee State Park
Halemanu Rd
Cliff Trail
Kumuwela Lookout
Lookout
Canyon Trail
KAUAI

place. There are six units, each with private bath and cable TV. The cheapest, the Ginger room, is perfectly adequate with two twin beds that can be arranged as a king, a refrigerator, toaster, microwave and coffeemaker. A delightful high-end room is the Magnolia suite, which has a king bed, a screened lanai overlooking a quiet garden, both a shower and a bathtub, and a well-equipped kitchenette. There's a two-night minimum or a $10 surcharge.

Classic Vacation Cottages *(☎ 332-9201, fax 332-7645; ⓔ clascot@hawaiian.net; PO Box 901, Kalaheo, HI 96741; studios $50-65, cottages $75, house $100)* is half a mile up from Hwy 50 and the town center. It consists of a couple of adjacent properties owned by Chris and Sandy Webster. There are nearly a dozen units in all, and each varies, but most are quite comfortable and all have a kitchen, cable TV and ceiling fans. The house, which sits at the rear of complex, has three bedrooms and can accommodate up to seven people, which could make it an affordable option for a group of people traveling together. There's a garage full of beach coolers, snorkel gear and golf clubs that guests can borrow without charge.

Places to Eat

Bread Box *(4447 Papalina Rd; open 4am-around noon Tues-Sat)*, a little hole-in-the-wall bakery, sells good, fresh breads, tasty macadamia-nut rolls for $1.50 and what may well be the last 25¢ cup of coffee in America. It stays open until the bread sells out.

Kalaheo Coffee Co & Cafe *(Hwy 50; breakfast $4-7, lunch $5-8; open 6am-3pm Mon-Sat, 7:30am-2pm Sun)*, at the side of the Menehune Food Mart, is a friendly café with good coffee, espresso and pastries. Breakfast, which is available until noon, includes locally made Anahola granola, French toast with fresh pineapple and creative omelettes. Lunch features sandwiches, specialty salads and vegetarian tortilla wraps.

Camp House Grill *(Hwy 50; open 6:30am-9:30pm daily)*, in the town center, is another good reasonably priced eatery. It has breakfast fare and hearty sandwiches for around $5 and chicken and barbecued ribs for about double that.

Brick Oven Pizza *(☎ 332-8561; Hwy 50; open 11am-10pm Tues-Sun)* is a bit pricey but the pizza is good, at least by island standards. Small (10-inch) pizzas start at $10, and large ones (15-inch) at $20. The pizzas are made with your choice of whole-wheat or white crust. The restaurant also has sandwiches and salads.

Kalaheo Steak House *(☎ 332-9780; 4440 Papalina Rd; dinner $17-25; open 6pm-10pm daily)*, off Hwy 50, has consistently good steaks in sizes to quell the most voracious of appetites. Beef dishes range from 12oz sirloin steaks to huge 24oz cuts of prime rib. There are also teriyaki-style chicken, fish and pork dishes. All dinners come with a green salad and bread.

HANAPEPE VALLEY LOOKOUT

The scenic lookout that comes up shortly after the 14-mile marker offers a view deep into Hanapepe Valley. The red clay walls of the cliffs are topped by bright green cane like a sugar frosting.

The same Robinson family that owns the island of Niihau also has substantial landholdings in these parts, including a hideaway estate deep in Hanapepe Valley.

While old king sugar may dominate the scene surrounding Hanapepe Valley, if you glance toward the opposite side of the road from the lookout, you'll see Kauai's newest commercial crop – endless rows of coffee trees.

ELEELE, NUMILA & PORT ALLEN

Eleele is largely a residential area of limited interest to visitors. It does have a shopping center at the 16-mile marker with a supermarket, bank, post office, coin laundry and a few restaurants, the best of which is Grinds Cafe, which makes good pastries and sandwiches.

Hwy 540 is an alternate route that leads off Hwy 50 just after Kalaheo and connects back to Hwy 50 at Eleele. It passes through fields of coffee trees and swings by Numila, a former cane town with tin-roof wooden houses surrounding a defunct sugar mill. At the southwest edge of Numila, is the **Kauai Coffee Company** *(Hwy 540; open 9am-5pm daily)*, which operates a little visitor center with simple displays on the company's operations, a gift shop and free samples of their brews.

Port Allen, immediately south of Eleele on Hanapepe Bay, is both a commercial harbor and one of Kauai's busiest recreational boat harbors. The state-run small craft harbor here is protected by breakwaters and has launch ramps, berthing and mooring spaces.

Glass Beach

Just east of Port Allen, Glass Beach is a cove piled high with colorful bits of glass that have been worn into smooth pebble-like pieces. The glass comes from a long abandoned dump site nearby, and its weathering is the result of decades of wave action. At certain times of the year, the glass is deep enough to scoop up by the handful, while at other times it's largely washed out to sea.

To get to the little cove, take Akaula St, the last left before entering the Port Allen commercial harbor, go past the fuel storage tanks and then curve to the right down a rutted dirt road that leads 100 yards to the beach.

HANAPEPE

Before Hurricane Iniki hit, Hanapepe was one of the best-preserved historic towns in Hawaii. Parts of the popular TV miniseries *The Thorn Birds* were filmed here because Hanapepe bore such a close resemblance to the dusty Australian outback of days past.

While the hurricane wreaked havoc on the town's old wooden buildings, claiming about half of them, Hanapepe still has lots of character and a nice unhurried pace that invites lingering.

Hanapepe Rd, the town's main street, retains a decidedly period face, with small local stores and several **art galleries**. Two of the more interesting are Koa Wood Gallery, which occupies the former bowling alley and specializes in wood crafts, and Kauai Fine Arts, which has a collection of antique maps and prints, including some works related to Captain Cook's explorations.

Be sure to take a stroll over the **swinging bridge**, which crosses the Hanapepe River; the path begins opposite the Koa Wood Gallery. Its funky old predecessor fell victim to Iniki, but in a community-wide effort this new bridge was erected in 1996.

The turnoff into Hanapepe is marked by a sign on Hwy 50.

Salt Pond Beach Park

Kauai has long been known for its *alae* salt, a sea salt with a red tint that comes from adding a bit of iron-rich earth. The salt is made by letting seawater into shallow basins called salt pans and allowing it to evaporate. When dry, the salt crystals are scraped off. Native Hawaiians still make salt this way down on the coast south of Hanapepe.

Salt Pond Beach Park is just beyond the salt ponds. It has a sandy beach, camp sites, covered picnic tables, barbecue grills, showers and a lifeguard on duty daily. Water in the cove does get up to 10ft deep and is very good for swimming laps – four times across equals half a mile. Both ends of the cove are shallow and good for kids.

For information on obtaining a permit to camp, see Camping in the Accommodations section, earlier in this chapter.

To get to Salt Pond Beach Park, turn left just past the 17-mile marker onto Lele Rd, then right onto Lokokai Rd; the beach is about a mile from the highway.

Places to Eat

Hanapepe Cafe (*☎ 335-5011; 3830 Hanapepe Rd; breakfast $4-8, lunch $7-10; open 9am-2pm Tues-Sat*), in the town center, is a café-style place specializing in good vegetarian fare. Breakfast, served until 11am, includes multigrain pancakes or waffles topped with macadamia nuts and real maple syrup, as well as mouthwatering scones and pastries made on site. Lunch centers on a selection of hearty salads and creative sandwiches, such as grilled vegetables on focaccia bread.

Green Garden (*☎ 335-5422; 1-3843 Hwy 50; open 10:30am-2pm Mon-Sat, 7:30am-2pm Sun, 5pm-9pm Wed-Mon; meals $6-20, desserts $2.50*) is one of the oldest and best-known restaurants on this side of the island. Its varied menu runs the gamut from standard plate lunches for around $7 to hearty full-course meals of rack of lamb and fresh catch of the day. If you're up for dessert, don't miss the *lilikoi* (passion fruit) chiffon pie – this place has been famous for these pies since the 1950s and that's plenty of time to perfect a recipe!

OLOKELE

Olokele exists only for the Olokele Sugar Company, the last remaining sugar producer on Kauai. Of the company's 220 employees, mostly field laborers, 200 live in Olokele.

The road to the sugar mill, which comes up immediately after the 19-mile marker, is shaded by tall trees and lined with classic, century-old lampposts. Taking this short drive offers a glimpse into real plantation life. Everything is covered with a layer of red dust from the surrounding sugarcane fields and mill. Rather than fight it, many of the houses are painted in beige-red tones.

There's a **visitor center** (*☎ 335-2824; admission free; open 8am-5pm Mon-Fri*) at the end of the road. It's essentially a small gift shop selling T-shirts and sugar products, but it is decorated with period photos and a few simple displays on the company's history.

MAKAWELI

Makaweli is headquarters for Gay & Robinson, Niihau Ranch and Niihau Helicopters, which are all enterprises of the Robinson family, the owners of Niihau. Quite a few native Niihauans live in this area, many of them working for the Robinsons. Once or twice a week, an old military landing craft makes the 17-mile trip between Niihau and Makaweli Landing.

WAIMEA

Waimea (which means 'reddish water') was the site of an ancient Hawaiian settlement. It was at Waimea, on January 19, 1778, that Captain Cook first came ashore on the Hawaiian Islands. In 1820, the first wave of missionaries to Hawaii also selected Waimea as a landing site. In 1884, Waimea Sugar moved in, and so Waimea developed into a plantation town. The old sugar mill, now abandoned, sits along the highway on the west side of town.

Today, Waimea remains the biggest town on this side of the island, while retaining an engaging small-town character. It's an attractive place, with a center comprising small wooden buildings with false fronts. The dominant building by the square is the First Hawaiian Bank, built in 1929 in neoclassical style.

The Waimea Theatre, built in Art Deco style in 1938 and recently renovated, is another lovely building worth a look – or, even better, swing by at night and enjoy a movie.

If you're on your way to Waimea Canyon or out to the coastal beaches on a day trip, and have a looser schedule, Waimea would make a fine place to break for a night or two; use it as a base to explore the West Side.

Waimea Canyon Dr (Hwy 550) heads north from town to Kokee State Park.

Information

The **First Hawaiian Bank** (*☎ 338-1611; 4525 Panako Rd; open 8:30am-4pm Mon-Thur, 8:30am-5pm Fri*) is on the central square in the town center.

The Waimea **post office** (*☎ 800-275-8777; 9911 Waimea Rd; open 9am-4pm Mon-Fri, 9am-noon Sat*) is in the town center near the bank.

Na Pali Explorer (*☎ 338-9999; Hwy 50; open 8am-5:30pm daily*) has a few online computers that you can use for $6 an hour.

Waimea Public Library (*☎ 338-6848; 9750 Hwy 50; open noon-8pm Mon & Wed, 9am-5pm Tues & Thur, 10am-5pm Fri*) has free walking tour maps.

Russian Fort Elizabeth

The remains of Russian Fort Elizabeth stand above the east bank of the Waimea River. Hawaiian laborers started building the fort in 1816 under the direction of Georg Anton Schaeffer, a representative of the Russian-American Company. The alliance between the Russians and Kauai's King Kaumualii proved to be a short-lived one, and the Russians were tossed out in 1817, the same year the fort was completed.

You can take a short walk through this curious period of Kauai's history. The most intact part of the fort is the exterior lava-rock wall, which is 8ft to 10ft high in places and largely overgrown with scrub and colorful wildflowers. The seaward side was designed like the points of a star, but it takes close observation to appreciate the effect.

The fort has a good view of the western bank of the Waimea River, where Captain Cook landed. Bear right down the dirt road that continues past the parking lot and you'll find a vantage point above the river mouth with a view of Waimea Pier and the island of Niihau.

Lucy Wright Park

The Captain Cook landing site is noted with a plaque on a nondescript rock on the western side of the Waimea River. The plaque is on the beach at Lucy Wright Park, on Ala Wai Rd, as soon as you cross the Waimea Bridge. This county park also has a ball field, picnic tables, rest rooms and showers. Camping is allowed on a flat grassy area, but it's at the side of the road in town and does not have much appeal. For information on

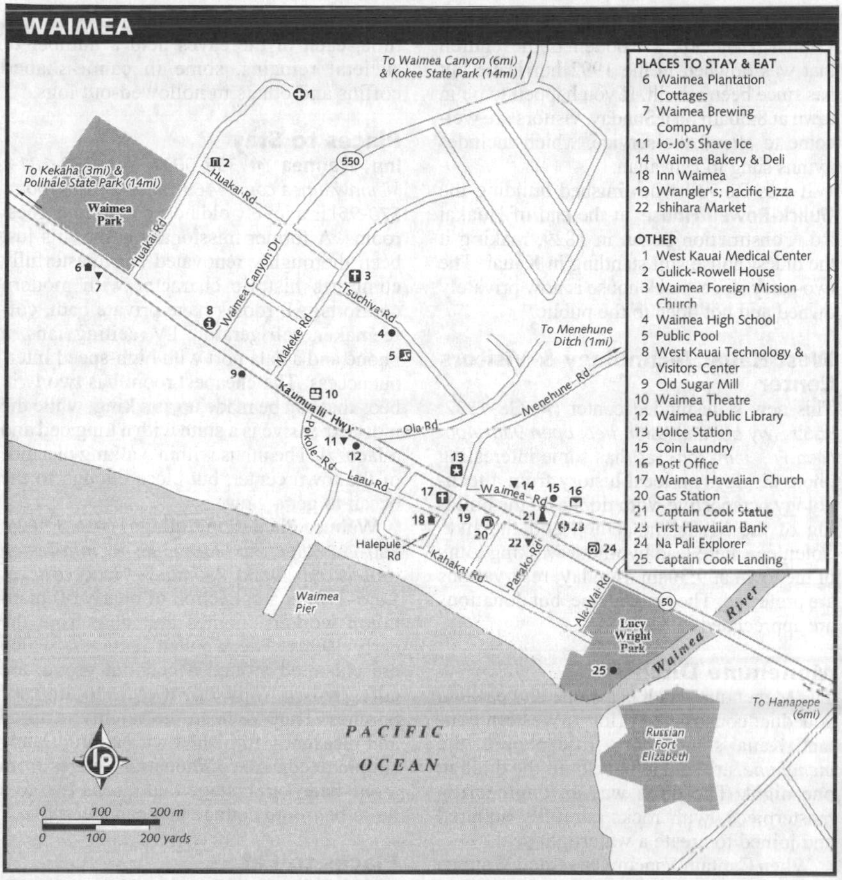

obtaining a permit to camp, see Camping in the Accommodations section, earlier in this chapter.

Captain Cook Statue

The statue of Captain Cook in the center of town is a replica of the original statue by Sir John Tweed that stands in Whitby, England. The Pacific's greatest navigator, clutching his charts and all decked out in his finest captaining finery, now watches over traffic on Hwy 50.

Waimea Pier

Until Port Allen was built, Waimea served as the region's main harbor. It was a major port of call for whalers and traders during the mid-19th century, and plantations started exporting sugar from Waimea later on in the century.

Waimea Pier, off Pokole Rd, is now used primarily for pole fishing, crabbing and picnicking.

Waimea Churches

The **Waimea Foreign Mission Church** *(cnr Huakai & Makeke Rds)* was originally a thatched structure built in 1826 by the Reverend Samuel Whitney, the first missionary to Waimea. Whitney and his wife are buried in the churchyard. The present church was built of sandstone blocks and coral mortar in 1858 by another missionary, the Reverend George Rowell.

In 1865, Reverend Rowell had a spat with some folks in the congregation and went off and built the **Waimea Hawaiian Church** *(Hwy 50)*, a wooden frame church that was downed in the 1992 hurricane but has since been rebuilt. If you happen to be in town at 8:30am on a Sunday, visitors are welcome to attend the service, which includes hymns sung in Hawaiian.

It was Rowell who finished building the **Gulick-Rowell House**, at the end of Huakai Rd. Construction began in 1829, making it the oldest house still standing in Kauai. The two-story stone-block house is now privately owned and not open to the public.

West Kauai Technology & Visitors Center

This new state-funded center *(☎ 338-1332; 9565 Hwy 50; admission free; open 9am-4pm Mon-Fri, 9am-1pm Sat)* has some interesting photo displays on local history from a technology perspective, with tidbits on the building of the Menehune Ditch and the like. Volunteers here lead two-hour walking tours of the town at 9:30am Monday; reservations are preferred. The walk is free, but donations are appreciated.

Menehune Ditch

The Menehune Ditch is a stone and earthen aqueduct constructed prior to Western contact. Kauai's legendary little people, the *menehune*, are said to have built the ditch in one night. The ditch was an engineering masterpiece, with rocks carefully squared and joined to create a watertight seal.

When Captain Vancouver visited Waimea at the close of the 18th century, he walked up the river valley atop the wall of this ditch, which also served as a footpath. He estimated the walls to be a full 24ft high. These days most of the ancient waterway lies buried beneath the road, but one section about 2ft high can still be seen. Even today, the ditch continues to divert water from the Waimea River along, and through, the cliff to irrigate the taro patches below.

To get there, turn at the police station onto Menehune Rd and go almost 1½ miles up the Waimea River. The ditch is along the left side of the road after a very small parking area.

On the drive up to the ditch, notice the scattered holes in the cliffs to the left. These are Hawaiian burial caves. One group of seven caves behind the Waimea Shingon Mission was explored by Wendell Bennett of the Bishop Museum in the 1920s. At that time, each of the caves held a number of skeletal remains, some in canoe-shaped coffins and others in hollowed-out logs.

Places to Stay

Inn Waimea *(☎ 338-0031, fax 338-1814; 🅦 innwaimea.com; 4469 Halepule Rd; rooms $70-95)* is a lovely old house with four guest rooms. A former missionary home, it's just been thoroughly renovated and masterfully combines historic character with modern comforts. All rooms have private bath, coffeemaker, refrigerator, TV, ceiling fans, a phone and a data port with high-speed Internet access. The cheapest room has two twin beds that can be made up as a king, while the most expensive is a suite with a king bed and a Jacuzzi. The inn is within walking distance of the town center, but close enough to the ocean to get a view.

Waimea Plantation Cottages *(☎ 338-1625, 800-992-7866, fax 338-2338; 🅔 info@aston-hotels.com; 9600 Kaumualii Hwy; cottages $205-310)* is a collection of nearly 50 plantation workers' homes that date from the early 1900s. The wooden cottages, which are clustered around a coconut grove, are cutesy-rustic right down to their tin-roof porches. They've been thoroughly restored and pleasantly furnished with appropriately simple decor. Accommodation ranges from a one-bedroom cottage that sleeps two to a three-bedroom cottage that can sleep five.

Places to Eat

Jo-Jo's Shave Ice *(9740 Hwy 50; shave ice $2; open 10am-6pm daily)* makes superb shave ice in 60 tantalizing tropical flavors. You can even opt for a triple flavored version – the *lilikoi*/guava/mango combination is hands-down the local favorite.

Ishihara Market *(9946 Hwy 50; open 6am-8:30pm Mon-Fri, 7am-8:30pm Sat & Sun)* is a grocery store with a good deli selling inexpensive take-out sushi and green salads. It's an ideal place to pick up what you need for a picnic lunch.

Waimea Bakery & Deli *(9875 Waimea Rd; snacks $2-5; open 6:30am-4pm Thur-Tues)* serves inexpensive sandwiches, breakfast burritos and pastries, and makes a decent cup of coffee as well.

Pacific Pizza *(9850 Hwy 50; open 11am-9pm daily)*, adjacent to Wrangler's restaurant, has calzone and sandwiches starting at $5 and pizza for double that.

Waimea Brewing Company *(☎ 338-9733; 9600 Hwy 50; dishes $8-12; open 11am-11pm daily)*, at Waimea Plantation Cottages, lays claim to being the westernmost microbrewery in the USA. The flagship drink at this popular open-air brewpub is Waialeale Ale, a light golden brew with a slightly dry character, but there are always a couple of seasonal ales as well. You can get a 16oz mug for $4 or a taster of four different brews for $5. The place offers pub fare such as fish and chips, sandwiches and quesadillas; there's often live music in the evenings.

Wrangler's *(☎ 338-1218; 9852 Hwy 50; dinner $18-30; open 11am-4pm Mon-Fri, 5pm-9pm Mon-Sat)*, in the center of Waimea, has a varied menu and average food. At lunch you can get a Caesar salad, beef teriyaki plate or burger for under $10. Dinner is a pricier affair with thick steaks and fresh fish shoring up the menu; all dinners come with a salad bar.

KEKAHA

Kekaha has great beaches, or rather it has one long glorious stretch. Hwy 50 follows the beach for about 2 miles, with roadside parking all along the way. This is open ocean, and when the surf is high there can be dangerous currents; when there's no swell, you can usually find swimmers here. Niihau and its offshore island, Lehua, are visible from the beach.

There's a very inconspicuous shower just inland from the highway between Alae Rd and Amakihi Rd; rest rooms and picnic tables are nearby.

A few blocks inland from the beach is Kekaha Rd, which runs parallel to the highway. Modest as it is, it's the main village street, with a post office and a couple of stores. The village's most dominant feature is its old sugar mill, which is visible from the highway.

On its eastern end, Kekaha Rd comes out to Hwy 50 near the Kikiaola Small Boat Harbor, a state harbor with a launch ramp and eight mooring spaces.

Kekaha is Kauai's westernmost town. As you continue on toward Polihale, it's a rural scene, with the inland cliffs getting higher and the ravines deeper. Corn and sunflowers, which are planted for seed production, grow in fields along the road. Cattle and cattle egrets feed in the pastures.

Places to Stay & Eat

Mindy's *(☎ 337-9275; ⓔ mindys@hgea.org; 8842 Kekaha Rd; singles $55)* would make a good base for exploring the Kokee area. Mindy and Dave Heri rent a pleasant 2nd-story apartment above their home, with a large deck, a full kitchen, a bedroom with a double bed and a living room with a double sofa bed. The place is modern and comfortable, with ceiling fans throughout, TV, phone, radio and a shower/tub combination in the bathroom. Add $10 more if you're staying for just one night and $5 for every extra person up to four people. Complimentary fruit and coffee are provided.

Obsessions *(cnr Hwy 552 & Kekaha Rd; snacks $4-7; open 8:30am-6pm daily)* is a great little place in the Waimea Canyon Plaza, Kekaha's main shopping center. Everything is homemade, the salads are homegrown and even the coffee here comes from the owner's 5-acre coffee patch. The menu includes Caesar salad, fish and chips and a delicious Malibu chicken breast sandwich on French bread.

Also in the same center is the **Menehune Food Mart**, which has limited groceries, wrapped sandwiches and a few simple hot items, and **Waimea Canyon Snack Shop**, which sells Lappert's ice cream.

BARKING SANDS

A US Navy base, **Barking Sands Pacific Missile Range Facility** *(☎ 335-4229)* usually has at least one stretch of its beach open to the public. Ring the number above for a recorded message on current access.

On very sunny days, when the wind is blowing off the water just right, the moving sands make sounds similar to barking dogs – hence the area's name.

The road in is at the 'Pacific Missile Range Facility' sign, less than half a mile after the 32-mile marker. At the gate, military personnel will ask to see your driver's license and then explain where you can go, which is usually the beach about 2 miles south of the gate; locals call this beach **Majors Bay** and the military refers to it as RecArea No 3.

This broad, curving sweep of fine golden sand is a good sunbathing and walking beach, though it's open and hot. The scrub brush behind the beach offers no shade, but it hardly matters, as the vegetation line is the DMZ line and you're forbidden to go beyond it anyway.

In winter, Majors Bay is a popular surfing spot although, as with all West Side beaches, the waters can be dangerous. There are no facilities. The purple-tinged island of Niihau can be seen on the horizon.

The missile range facility at Barking Sands provides the above-ground link to a sophisticated sonar network that tracks more than 1000 sq miles of the Pacific. Established during WWII, it's been developed into the world's largest underwater listening device. The equipment is sensitive enough to pick up the songs of wintering humpback whales, and the base has gathered the most comprehensive collection of humpback whale soundtracks ever recorded.

POLIHALE STATE PARK

Polihale is near-desert. When it's raining everywhere else, beachgoers head this way.

The beautiful long white-sand beach here is washed with aqua-colored water that often comes to shore in huge explosive waves. Expert surfers occasionally give Polihale a try, but strong rip currents make the waters treacherous for swimming.

Polihale State Park is about 5 miles from the Barking Sands military base. Turn left three-quarters of a mile north of the base entrance onto a wide dirt road that passes through abandoned sugarcane fields. The road is a bit bumpy but passable. Set your odometer at zero here.

After almost 3½ miles, at a large spreading tree in the middle of the road, a turnoff leads to the only safe swimming spot in the area. To get there, turn left at the tree, and then after a quarter mile, follow the road up the hill to the right to the base of the dunes. Walk a couple of minutes to the north along the beach and you'll come to **Queen's Pond**, where a large semicircle of reef comes almost to shore, creating a protected swimming pool. When the seas are relatively calm, the reef blocks the ocean currents. But when surf breaks over the reef and into the pool, a dangerous rip current runs toward an opening at the southern end of the reef. The rest of the beach is bordered by open sea.

To get to the state park facilities, go back to the tree at the main cane road, turn left and continue another mile. A turnoff on the left leads to a camping area with rest rooms, outdoor showers, drinking water and a picnic pavilion. Farther down, other camping areas are in the dunes just above the beach amid thorny *kiawe* trees. For information on obtaining a permit to camp, see Camping in the Accommodations section, earlier in this chapter.

At the very end of the beach is Polihale Cliff, marking the western end of the Na Pali Coast. Combined with the untamed ocean and vast expansive beach, it's a magnificent sight. Sunsets here can be a meditative experience.

There's a terraced *heiau* toward the base of the cliff. It was originally on the beach, but over the years ever-shifting sands have added a 300ft buffer between the *heiau* and the sea. The *heiau* is so overgrown that even after you tramp into the brush and find it, it's really hard to get a perspective on it. Wasps are another obstacle – if you're allergic to stings, forget about exploring this one.

WAIMEA CANYON

Waimea Canyon is nicknamed the 'Grand Canyon of the Pacific.' This may sound like promotional hype, but it's not a bad description. Although it's smaller and 200 million years younger than the famous Arizona canyon, Waimea Canyon is certainly grand.

The canyon's colorful river-cut gorge is 2785ft deep. The river that runs through it, the Waimea-Poomau, is 19½ miles long, Kauai's longest. All in all, it seems incredible that such an immense canyon could be tucked inside such a small island.

The view of the canyon is usually a bit hazy. The best time to be there is a sunny day after it's been raining heavily – at such times, the earth's a deeper red and waterfalls cascade throughout the canyon, providing unbeatable scenery.

Waimea Canyon Drive

Waimea Canyon Dr (Hwy 550) starts in downtown Waimea. The road is 19 miles long, ending at lookouts with terrific views into Kalalau Valley on the Na Pali Coast.

The views start about a mile up from Waimea and get better and better as the road climbs. There are plenty of little scenic lookouts where you can stop to take it all in. The one at 1¾ miles looks down on the Waimea River and the taro patches that are irrigated by the Menehune Ditch. About 2½ miles up, there are good views out to Kekaha Beach with Niihau in the background. From there on, it's all canyon views.

WAIMEA CANYON STATE PARK

The southern boundary of Waimea Canyon State Park is about 6 miles up the road from Waimea. Waimea Canyon Dr and Kokee Rd merge nearby. Kokee Rd (Hwy 552), which climbs up from Kekaha, also has scenic views, but not of the canyon.

Iliau Nature Loop

The marked trailhead for the Iliau Nature Loop comes up shortly before the 9-mile marker. (This is also the trailhead for the longer Kukui Trail, described in the following Waimea Canyon Trails section.) At the start of the trail, there's a bench with a scenic view, though for the best angle, take a three-minute walk to the left, where you'll be rewarded with a top-notch vista into Waimea Canyon. After heavy rainfall, waterfalls explode down the sheer rock walls across the gorge.

Iliau Loop takes only about 10 minutes to walk. The trail is named for the *iliau*, a plant endemic to the West Side of Kauai, which grows along the trail and produces stalks up to 10ft high. Like its cousin the silversword, *iliau* grows to a ripe old age. Then for a grand finale it bursts open with blossoms and dies.

Scenic Lookouts

The most scenic of the lookout points along this stretch, **Waimea Canyon Lookout** is clearly signposted a third of a mile north of the 10-mile marker. The lookout offers a sweeping view of Waimea Canyon from a perch of 3400ft. The prominent canyon running in an easterly direction off Waimea is Koaie Canyon, which is accessible to backcountry hikers (see the following Waimea Canyon Trails section).

As you continue up the road, the 800ft **Waipoo Falls** can be seen from a couple of small unmarked lookouts before the 12-mile marker and then from a lookout opposite the picnic area shortly before the 13-mile marker. The picnic area has barbecue pits, rest rooms, drinking water, a pay phone and Camp Hale Koa, a Seventh Day Adventist camp.

Puu Hinahina Lookout, at 3640ft, is at a marked turnoff between the 13- and 14-mile markers. There are two lookouts close to the parking lot. One has a fine view down Waimea Canyon clear out to the coast, while the other has a view of Niihau.

Waimea Canyon Trails

For serious hikers, there are trails that lead deep into Waimea Canyon. The trailhead for the **Kukui Trail** is shortly before the 9-mile marker. This trail continues from the Iliau Nature Loop at a sign-in box. From there, the Kukui Trail makes a steep 2000ft descent down the western side of Waimea Canyon, 2½ miles to the Waimea River. Wiliwili Camp is at the end of the trail.

The **Koaie Canyon Trail** begins at Kaluahaulu Camp, half a mile up the Waimea River from the end of the Kukui Trail. From there, it runs east for 3 miles along the southern side of Koaie Canyon. If you'd like to cool off, there are some good swimming holes in the stream along the way and at the end of the trail. This trail should be avoided during stormy weather due to the danger of flash flooding.

The canyon's fertile soil once supported an ancient Hawaiian settlement, and the long-abandoned remains of a *heiau* and some house sites are still discernible. The Koaie Canyon Trail passes Hipalau Camp and ends at Lonomea Camp.

All four camps on these trails are part of the forest reserve system. Although they have simple open-air shelters, there are no facilities, and the stream water needs to be treated before drinking. For information on permits, see Camping under Accommodations, earlier in this chapter.

A third trail in this area is the 8-mile **Waimea Canyon Trail**, which runs south from Wiliwili Camp to the town of Waimea, ending on Menehune Rd. Much of the trail is along a 4WD road that leads to a hydroelectric power station. While there's public access along the route, the trail passes over private property, so no camping is allowed. There are a number of river crossings, making the trail best considered only during periods of dry weather.

During weekends and holidays, all of these trails are fairly heavily used by pig hunters.

KOKEE STATE PARK

This park's boundary starts beyond the Puu Hinahina Lookout. After the 15-mile marker, you'll pass park cabins, Kokee Lodge, a museum and a camping ground one after the other. Kokee Lodge, incidentally, is not an overnight lodge but a restaurant and the concessionaire station for the nearby cabins.

The ranger station in Kokee hasn't been staffed for years, but the helpful people at the Kokee Museum can provide a little assistance, including basic information on current trail conditions. And outside the museum you'll find an information board and a posted trail map.

Kokee Museum

A good place to learn about Kauai's ecology is the Kokee Museum (*☎ 335-9975; admission by donation $1; open 10am-4pm daily*), which features displays of local flora, fauna, climate and geology, along with detailed topographical maps of the area and a glass case of poi pounders, stone adze heads and other historic artifacts. Some good quality handicrafts, an extensive selection of Hawaiiana books and inexpensive trail maps are for sale.

Ask at the museum for the brochure to the short nature trail out back. The brochure, which can be borrowed free or purchased for $1.50, offers interpretive information corresponding to the trail's numbered plants and trees, many of them native Hawaiian species.

By the way, the chickens that congregate in the museum's parking lot are not the common garden variety but *moa*, or jungle fowl. Early Polynesian settlers brought *moa* to Hawaii, and they were once common on all the main islands. Now the *moa* remain solely on Kauai, the only island that's free of the mongoose, an introduced mammal that preys on the eggs of ground-nesting birds.

Meadow Spirits

According to legend, Kanalohuluhulu Meadow, opposite Kokee Museum, was once a forested hideout for an evil *akua* (spirit) who enjoyed harassing people passing through on their way to Kalalau Valley. Distraught travelers appealed to the great god Kanaloa to protect them from the *akua*. Kanaloa responded by ripping out all the trees and declaring that they were never again to grow here, thus destroying the *akua*'s hiding place. These days the meadow is full of good vibes and makes a nice place for kids to play.

Kalalau Lookouts

The Kalalau Valley lookouts, two spectacular coastal viewpoints at the northern end of the road, are not to be missed. The views are among the most breathtaking in all Hawaii.

The first, the **Kalalau Lookout**, is at the 18-mile marker. From a height of 4000ft, you can look deep into the green depths of the valley and straight out to the sea. When the weather is cooperative, late afternoon rainbows sweep so deeply into Kalalau Valley that the bottom part of the bows curve back inward. Bright-red *apapane* birds feed from the flowers of the *ohia lehua* trees near the lookout railings.

Kalalau Valley was once the site of a large settlement and was joined to Kokee by a very steep trail that ran down the cliffs. Today, the only way into the valley is along the coastal Kalalau Trail from Haena on the North Shore.

The cone-shaped pinnacles along the valley walls look rather like a row of sentinels standing at attention. One legend says that rain has sculpted the cliffs into the shapes of the proud chiefs who are buried in the mountains.

The mushroom-shaped white dome and satellite dishes visible on the hill as you walk back to the parking lot are part of the Kokee Air Force station.

The paved road continues another mile to **Puu o Kila Lookout**, where it dead-ends at a parking lot. This is actually the last leg of the aborted Kokee–Haena Hwy, which would have linked Kokee with the North Shore, thus creating a circle-island road. One look at the cliffs at the end of the road, and you'll understand why the scheme was scrapped. The Pihea Trail that climbs the ridge straight ahead runs along what was to be the road.

From this lookout, you can enjoy another grand view into Kalalau Valley and a glance inland toward the Alakai Swamp Preserve. A sign here points to Mt Waialeale, the wettest spot on earth.

Kokee State Park Trails

Kokee State Park is the starting point for about 45 miles of trails, some maintained by the Division of State Parks, others by the Division of Forestry & Wildlife. Pig and goat hunters use some of these trails during the hunting season, so it's a good idea for hikers to wear brightly colored clothing.

Three of the trails – Nualolo, Awaawapuhi and Pihea – offer splendid cliff-top views into valleys on the Na Pali Coast. A couple of trails go into the swampy bogs of Alakai Swamp, while others are easy nature trails.

Halemanu Road Trails The starting point for several scenic hikes, Halemanu Rd is just north of the 14-mile marker. Whether or not the road is passable in a non-4WD vehicle often depends on whether it's been raining recently. Keep in mind that the clay roads provide no traction when wet, and even if you're able to drive a car in, should it begin to rain, driving out can be another matter!

The first hike is **Cliff Trail**, where a short walk leads to an overlook into Waimea Canyon. From there, you can continue on the **Canyon Trail**, a rather strenuous 1¾ miles one way that follows the canyon rim, passes Waipoo Falls and ends at **Kumuwela Lookout** with views down the canyon to the ocean beyond. On both trails, there's a good chance of spotting feral goats scrambling along the canyon walls.

A little farther down Halemanu Rd is the start of **Halemanu-Kokee Trail**. This easy 1¼-mile (each way) nature trail passes through a native forest of koa and *ohia* trees that provide a habitat for native birds, including the *iiwi*, *apapane*, *amakihi* and *elepaio*. One of the common plants found on this trail is banana *poka*, a member of the passion fruit family and a serious invasive pest. It has pretty pink flowers, but it drapes the forest with its vines and chokes out less aggressive native plants.

Nualolo & Awaawapuhi Trails The Nualolo and Awaawapuhi Trails each go out to the very edge of sheer cliffs, allowing you to peer down into valleys that are otherwise accessible only by boat. The valley views are extraordinarily beautiful.

The Nualolo and Awaawapuhi Trails connect via the Nualolo Cliff Trail. You can combine the three trails to make a strenuous day hike of about 10 miles. Then you'll have to either hitch a ride or walk an additional 2 miles back down the road to where you started.

Bring plenty of water, as there's none along the way. Edible plants along the trail include blackberries, thimbleberries, guava and passion fruit.

Wild goats, prolific in the North Shore valleys, are readily spotted along the cliff walls. Capable of breeding at five months of age, the goats have no natural predators in Hawaii, and their unchecked numbers have caused a fair amount of ecological damage.

The 3¾-mile Nualolo Trail starts between the cabins and Kokee Lodge. The trail begins in cool upland forest and descends 1500ft, ending with a fine view from Lolo Vista Point, a lookout on the valley rim. There's a USGS survey marker at the lookout, at an elevation of 2234ft.

The trailhead for the Awaawapuhi Trail begins at a parking area just after the 17-mile marker. The trail descends 1600ft, ending after 3¼ miles at a steep and spectacular *pali* overlooking Awaawapuhi and Nualolo Valleys. The hike starts in an *ohia* forest. About half a mile down the trail, the forest becomes drier, and koa begins to mix in with the *ohia*. Awaawapuhi means 'valley of ginger,' and *kahili*, a pretty yellow ginger, can be seen along the way.

The 2-mile Nualolo Cliff Trail is also very scenic and offers numerous viewpoints into Nualolo Valley. There's even a picnic table where you can break for lunch. The Nualolo Cliff Trail connects at the Nualolo Trail near the 3¼-mile mark and at the Awaawapuhi Trail a little short of the 3-mile mark.

Kawaikoi Stream Trail This trail, a scenic mountain stream trail of about 3 miles round-trip, begins between the Sugi Grove and Kawaikoi camping grounds, off Camp 10-Mohihi Rd. It starts out following the southern side of Kawaikoi Stream, then heads away from the stream and makes a loop, coming down the northern side of the stream before reconnecting with the southern side. If the stream is running high, don't make the crossings.

Kawaikoi Stream is popular for rainbow trout fishing, which is allowed during an annual open season in August and September. Fishing licenses are required.

Camp 10-Mohihi Rd is up past the Kokee Museum on the right. Like many of the dirt roads in Kokee, when it's dry, it can accommodate ordinary cars, at least part way. However, on those occasions when the road is really wet and rutted, even 4WD vehicles can have difficulty.

Pihea Trail The Pihea Trail starts from the Puu o Kila Lookout and combines coastal views with an opportunity to see some of the Alakai wilderness. The beginning of the trail was graded in the 1950s, before plans to make this the last leg of the circle-island road were abandoned.

The first mile of the trail runs along the ridge, offering fine views into Kalalau Valley, before coming to the Pihea Lookout, a viewpoint that requires a steep scramble to reach. The Pihea Trail then turns inland through wetland forest and, at about 1¾ miles, crosses the Alakai Swamp Trail. If you turn left there, you can continue for 2 miles through Alakai Swamp to Kilohana Lookout. If you go straight instead, you'll reach the Kawaikoi Camping ground in about 2 miles.

Alakai Swamp Trail The Alakai Swamp Preserve is inaccessible enough that even invasive plants haven't been able to choke out the endemic swamp vegetation, and native bird species still have a stronghold.

Parts of the swamp receive so little sunlight that moss grows thick and fat on all sides of the trees. Most people that see this swamp see it from a helicopter, but it's possible to walk through a corner of it by taking the Alakai Swamp Trail.

This rough 3½-mile trail starts off Camp 10-Mohihi Rd and goes through rain forest and bogs before reaching Kilohana Lookout, perched on the rim of Wainiha Pali. If it's not overcast – and that is a big 'if' considering this is the wettest place on earth – hikers will be rewarded with a sweeping view of the Wainiha and Hanalei Valleys to the north. While most of the trail has been spanned with boardwalks, this can still be an extremely wet and slippery trail, and in places you can expect to have to slog through mud. It's certainly a trail that's best suited for hiking in the relatively drier summer season.

If your car can't make it down Camp 10-Mohihi Rd, your best bet is to park near the Kalalau Lookout and approach the Alakai Swamp Trail via the Pihea Trail.

Kaluapuhi Trail The Kaluapuhi Trail, a forest trail leading to a plum grove, is about 2 miles long. The trailhead starts at the highway a quarter mile past the 17-mile marker. In midsummer, lots of islanders come to pick the wild plums.

KAUAI

Places to Stay

Camping The most accessible camping area is the Kokee State Park camping ground, which is north of the meadow, just a few minutes' walk from Kokee Lodge. The sites are in an uncrowded grassy area beside the woods and have picnic tables, drinking water, rest rooms and showers. Camping is free and allowed for up to five nights, but state camping permits must be obtained before arriving in Kokee.

Farther off the main track, Kawaikoi and Sugi Grove Camping grounds are about 4 miles east of Kokee Lodge, off the 4WD Camp 10-Mohihi Rd in the forest reserve adjacent to the state park. Each camping ground has pit toilets, picnic shelters and fire pits. You'll need to carry in your own water or treat the stream water before drinking it. These forest reserve camping grounds have a three-night maximum stay and require obtaining camping permits in advance.

The Kokee area camping grounds are at an elevation of almost 4000ft, and nights are crisp and cool. This is sleeping-bag-and-warm-clothing country.

For more information on camping permits, see Camping in the Accommodations section, earlier in this chapter.

Lodges The 12 cabins in Kokee State Park are managed by **Kokee Lodge** *(☎ 335-6061; PO Box 819, Waimea, HI 96796; cabins $35-45)*. The oldest cabins are a little tired and have just one large room but are bargain priced. Newer are the two-bedroom cedar cabins. Each cabin, old and new, has one double and four twin beds and a kitchen with a refrigerator and oven, as well as linens, blankets, a shower and a woodstove. Of the newer cedar cabins, No 2 Lehua is particularly comfortable and has a wheelchair ramp. State park rules limit stays to five days. The cabins are often booked up well in advance, but cancellations do occur, and you can occasionally get a cabin at the last moment.

The YWCA's **Camp Sloggett** *(camp sites per person $10, bunk beds $20)* in Kokee State Park has a lodge that sleeps 10 people, a bunkhouse that holds 40 and a cement-slab platform for tent camping. Guests must provide their own bedding and towels for the bunkhouse, but there are bathrooms with hot showers and a kitchenette. Tent campers have a barbecue pit for cooking and use of the showers and toilets in the bunkhouse. For the bunkhouse and tent sites, call the **caretaker** *(☎ 335-6060)* for availability. The lodge is rented to one group at a time; the per-person rate is $20, with a minimum charge of five people Monday to Friday and eight people on weekends. Bookings for the lodge are made through the **YWCA** *(☎ 245-5959; 3094 Elua St, Lihue, HI 96766)*. Camp Sloggett is about half a mile east of the park museum down a rutted dirt road that's usually passable in an ordinary car.

Places to Eat

Kokee Lodge *(☎ 335-6061; snacks $3-7; open 9am-3:30pm daily)* is the only place to eat north of Waimea. The restaurant serves simple breakfast fare, salads, soup and a variety of sandwiches. In addition the **gift shop** *(open 9am-4pm)* in front of the restaurant sells candy bars, potato chips and a few canned food items.

If you're staying in the cabins or camping grounds, be sure to bring ample provisions, as the nearest stores (and gas station) are in Waimea, 15 miles away.

Niihau

Niihau, which has long been closed to outsiders, has earned itself the nickname 'The Forbidden Island.'

No other place in Hawaii has more successfully turned its back on change than Niihau. It has no paved roads, no airport and no island-wide electricity.

Niihau is a native Hawaiian preserve and the only island in the state where the primary language is still Hawaiian. The entire island, right down to the church, belongs to the Niihau Ranch, which is privately owned by the non-Hawaiian Robinson family. The Robinsons are highly protective of Niihau's isolation.

Most of Niihau's 160 residents live in Puuwai, a settlement on the dry western coast. Each house in the village is surrounded by a stone wall to keep grazing animals out of the gardens. It's a simple life; water is collected in catchments, and the toilets are in outhouses.

Niihauans speak their own melodic dialect of Hawaiian. Business is conducted in Hawaiian, as are the Sunday church services. The two Robinson brothers who manage the ranch speak Hawaiian fluently.

Children learn English as a second language when they go to school. Niihau has a two-room schoolhouse where three teachers hold classes from kindergarten through 12th grade for the island's 50 students. Courses are taught solely in Hawaiian up to the fourth grade.

The island economy has long depended on sheep and cattle ranching, which has always been a marginal operation on windswept Niihau. Major droughts in recent decades have taken a toll on the herds, and consequently Niihau has been through some hard times.

The ranch activities, which once provided most of the work on Niihau, are no longer commercially viable. Consequently, the Robinsons have been looking toward the federal government as a potential source of income and employment. For several years Niihau has leased sites to the government that are used for the placement of unmanned radars, which are linked to missile tracking facilities on Kauai.

In addition, since 1999, military special operations forces have staged periodic training maneuvers on Niihau, using the uninhabited southern end of the island. The operations are small scale, typically with teams of a dozen soldiers practicing a mock rescue operation or the like.

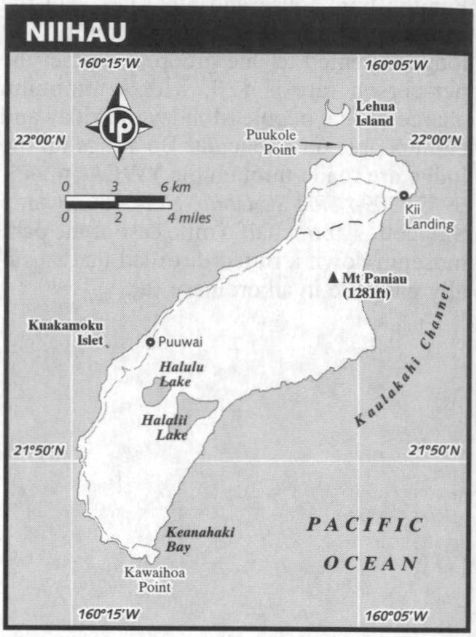

There are ongoing negotiations to use the southern end of Niihau on a more permanent basis, including as a possible launch site for drone target missiles, part of the testing programme for new US ballistic defense systems. The hope is that the military, as a secretive tenant, won't interfere with the rest of Niihau's affairs.

Niihau is 17 miles from Kauai and is connected by a weekly supply boat that travels between the two islands. The boat docks in Kauai at Makaweli, headquarters of Niihau Ranch and the Robinson family. Makaweli is also home to a settlement of Niihauans who prefer to live on Kauai, though many of them still work for the Robinsons.

Niihau is by no means a living-history museum of Hawaiians stuck in time. Although it's got a foot in the past, it takes what it wants from the present. The supply boat brings soda pop as well as poi, and the island has more dirt bikes than outrigger canoes.

Niihau residents are free to go to Kauai to shop, have a few beers (Niihau itself is dry) or just hang out. What they are not free to do is bring friends from other islands back home with them. Those Niihauans who marry people from other islands, as well as those whom the Robinsons come to see as undesirable, are rarely allowed to return.

Still, for the most part, Niihauans to accept that that's the way things are. Some of those who leave are critical, but those who stay don't appear to be looking for any changes.

To outsiders, Niihau really is an enigma. Some romanticize it as a pristine preserve of Hawaiian culture, while others see it as a throwback to feudalism.

The Robinsons view Niihau as a private sanctuary and themselves as the protectors of it all. It's that kind of paternalism that often rubs outside native Hawaiian groups the wrong way, though for the most part Niihauans don't seem to share those sentiments, and they resist outside interference.

HISTORY

Captain Cook anchored off Niihau on January 29, 1778, two weeks after 'discovering' Hawaii. Cook noted in his log that the island was lightly populated and largely barren, a description still true today. His visit was short, but it had a lasting impact.

It was on little Niihau that Cook first introduced two things that would quickly change the face of Hawaii. He left two goats, the first of the grazing animals that would devastate the native flora and fauna. And his men introduced syphilis, the first of the Western diseases that would decimate the Hawaiian people.

In 1864 Elizabeth Sinclair, a Scottish widow who was moving from New Zealand to Vancouver when she got sidetracked in Hawaii, bought Niihau from King Kamehameha V for $10,000 in gold. He originally tried to sell her the 'swampland' of Waikiki, but she passed it up for the 'desert island.' Interestingly, no two places in Hawaii today could be further apart, either culturally or in land value.

Mrs Sinclair brought the first sheep to Niihau from New Zealand and started the ranching operation that her great-grandsons continue today.

GEOGRAPHY

Niihau is the smallest of the inhabited Hawaiian Islands. It is 18 miles long and 6 miles wide, with a total area of 70 sq miles. It has 45 miles of coast, and the highest elevation is 1281ft, at Mt Paniau. The island is semi-arid, in the lee of Kauai.

Niihau's 860-acre Halalii Lake is the largest in Hawaii, though even during the rainy winter season, it's only a few feet deep. In the summer, it sometimes dries up to a mud pond.

FLORA & FAUNA

Of the approximately 50 Hawaiian monk seals that have taken up residence in the populated Hawaiian islands, more than 30 live on Niihau. About half of all Hawaii's endangered coots, the *alae-keokeo*, breed on Niihau.

Introduced creatures also proliferate on Niihau. The island has an estimated 6000 feral pigs, as well as wild sheep, goats and turkeys.

GETTING THERE & AWAY

Although outsiders are not allowed to visit Niihau, the Robinsons have 'opened up' the island – at least to a degree – via expensive helicopter flights.

Niihau Helicopters (*☎ 335-3500*) has no set schedule; tours should be arranged well in advance. The tours, which last about three hours and take off from Port Allen airport in Kauai, cost $280 per person. The helicopter makes a stop at Puukole Point on the northern end of the island, where lunch is provided and passengers can take a swim if they like. The pilot flies over much of Niihau but avoids Puuwai village, where people live.

The helicopter was purchased for emergency medical evacuations, and the tours are given in an effort to help defray costs.

Northwestern Hawaiian Islands

The Northwestern Hawaiian Islands, also called the Leeward Islands, stretch from Kauai nearly 1300 miles across the Pacific in an almost straight northwesterly line.

Volcanic in origin, the islands once jutted up high above sea level as the main Hawaiian Islands do now. However, they are slowly slipping back into the sea as a result of a sagging of the ocean floor and the ongoing forces of erosion. Where the mountains once raised their heads, coral reefs now appear like flower leis left floating on the water.

There are 10 island clusters in all. Together, the clusters encompass 33 islands, all of which are small. They include atolls, each with a number of low sand islands formed on top of coral reefs, as well as some single-rock islands and a reef that is mostly submerged.

Listed from east to west, the clusters are Nihoa Island, Necker Island, French Frigate Shoals, Gardner Pinnacles, Maro Reef, Laysan Island, Lisianski Island, Pearl and Hermes Atoll, Midway Islands and Kure Atoll.

The total land area of all the Northwestern Hawaiian Islands is just under 5 sq miles, though the atoll lagoon areas add up to a hundred times that.

All the islands except Kure Atoll (a state seabird sanctuary) and the Midway Islands are part of the Hawaiian Islands National Wildlife Refuge. Established in 1909 by US president Theodore Roosevelt, it is the oldest and largest of the national wildlife refuges. In 1988, the Midway group was given a separate refuge status as the Midway Atoll National Wildlife Refuge.

With the exception of Midway, visitors aren't allowed on the Northwestern Hawaiian Islands unless they have permits, and these are granted only in the rarest of circumstances. Human activities are simply too disturbing to the fragile ecosystem. The only human habitation in the Hawaiian Islands National Wildlife Refuge is at Tern Island, and that is for wildlife researchers.

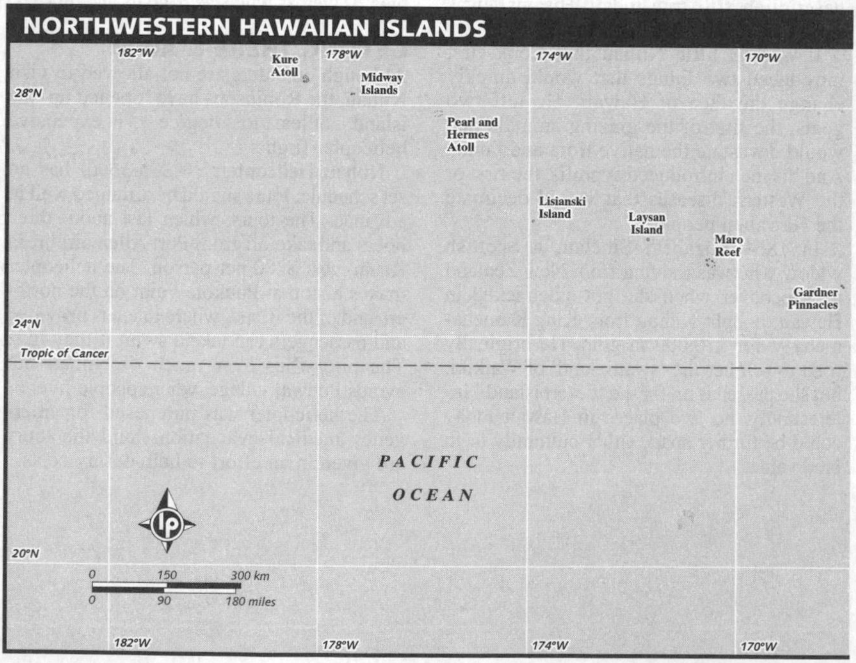

The Northwestern Hawaiian Islands come under the political, though not the practical, jurisdiction of the City & County of Honolulu.

FAUNA

The Northwestern Hawaiian Islands are home to around 15 million seabirds, all of which find room for at least a foothold. Endangered Hawaiian monk seals, green sea turtles and four endemic land birds also live there.

Seabirds

Eighteen seabird species nest on these islands, feeding on the abundant fish that live around the submerged reefs. The avian population includes frigate birds, boobies, albatross, terns, shearwaters, petrels, tropic birds and noddies.

The sooty terns are the most abundant, numbering several million. These screeching black-and-white birds also nest on the offshore islets of Oahu's windward coast.

Shearwaters and petrels lay their eggs in burrows that the birds dig in the sandy soil. The roofs of the burrows can easily collapse under the feet of unobservant walkers, which is one important reason why visitors are discouraged.

Land Birds

The Laysan duck, Laysan finch, Nihoa finch and Nihoa millerbird, endemic to Laysan and Nihoa Islands respectively, are all listed as endangered or threatened species.

This is not because their numbers are declining, but because these species exist in only one place on earth and are therefore susceptible to the introduction of new diseases and predators or the disruption of their habitat. One rat from a shipwrecked boat, weed seed from a hiker's boot or an oil slick washing ashore could mean the end of the species.

Monk Seals

The endangered Hawaiian monk seal, which exists only in Hawaii, uses Kure Atoll, the French Frigate Shoals and Laysan, Lisianski, Nihoa and Necker Islands for its pupping grounds. The seals are easily disturbed by human contact.

In the 19th century the seals were hunted nearly to extinction. Military operations in

NORTHWESTERN HAWAIIAN ISLANDS

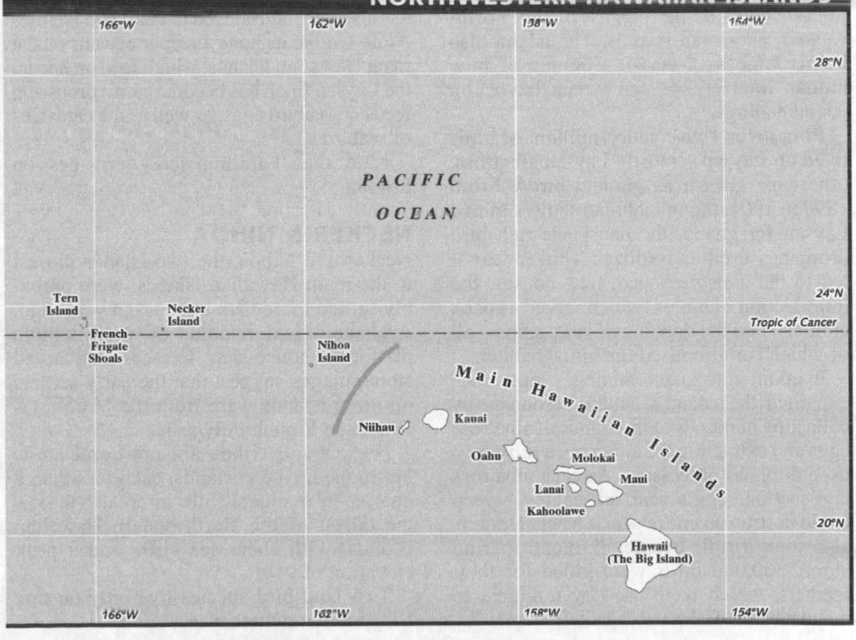

the area during and after WWII also resulted in a decline.

Fewer than 200 seal pups are born each year, many of which die from shark attacks. The total species population is estimated to be about 1300.

THE FRENCH FRIGATE SHOALS

The French Frigate Shoals consist of 13 sand islands and a 135ft rock, La Perouse Pinnacle, named after the French explorer who was almost wrecked on the reef. One of the sand islands, 37-acre Tern Island, is the field headquarters for the Hawaiian Islands National Wildlife Refuge.

Most of Tern Island is covered by an airfield from the days when the US coast guard had a loran (radio navigation system) station there. The old coast guard barracks now house two US Fish & Wildlife Service refuge managers and up to a dozen volunteers.

Tern Island is home to 17 species of seabirds and many Hawaiian monk seals. Ninety percent of the green sea turtles that nest in the Hawaiian Islands nest at the French Frigate Shoals.

LAYSAN ISLAND

Despite its small area (almost 1½ sq miles), Laysan ranks as the biggest of the Northwestern Hawaiian Islands. The island also looms large as a classic example of how human interference can wreak havoc on island ecology.

Prior to the 19th century, millions of birds lived on Laysan – mostly Laysan albatross, otherwise known as gooney birds. From 1890 to 1904, though, human settlers mined Laysan for guano, the phosphate-rich bird droppings used as fertilizer. This endeavor led to the construction of new houses, the introduction of mules (which served as pack animals) and the docking of large ships – all of which compromised the birds' habitat.

In addition to guano mining, people once exploited the island's natural resources by collecting hundreds of thousands of albatross eggs and extracting the albumen, a substance used in photo processing. As each albatross lays just one egg a year, an 'egging' sweep could destroy an entire year's hatch. Hunters also took a toll. In one six-month period alone, 300,000 birds were killed for their feathers, which were used by milliners to make hats for fashionable ladies.

There are now about 160,000 pairs of Laysan albatross on the island, still one of the world's largest colonies. Albatross sometimes court and dance for five annual mating seasons before actually mating. Once they do mate, pairs stay together for life and sometimes live for 30 years.

Rabbits, introduced to Laysan first as pets for the workers' children and later for breeding, virtually destroyed the island's vegetation, and where they left off sandstorms took over. The loss of native food plants spelled the end of the three endemic land birds: the Laysan flightless rail, Laysan honeycreeper and Laysan millerbird. The rabbits were finally exterminated in 1923.

The Laysan duck reached the brink of extinction as a result of the activities of rabbits and hunters. Their numbers were reduced to just six by 1911, but they've since made a modest comeback. Laysan ducks swim in the brackish lagoon in the center of the island, their only habitat. With a current population of about 300, the Laysan ducks rank as one of the rarest kinds of duck in the world.

The Laysan finch, whose population once numbered only 100 (thanks to the rabbits), is once again common on Laysan Island and has also been introduced to Pearl and Hermes Atoll. Unlike its honeycreeper cousins on the main Hawaiian Islands, which feed on nectar, the Laysan finch has become carnivorous and feeds on seabird eggs, as well as the carcasses of seabirds.

More than 1 million sooty terns nest on Laysan.

NECKER & NIHOA

Necker and Nihoa, the two islands closest to the main Hawaiian Islands, were probably settled more than a thousand years ago. Archaeological remains of stone temple platforms, house sites, terraces and carved stone images suggest that the early settlers on these islands were from the Marquesas Islands in French Polynesia.

Necker and Nihoa are not coral atolls but rugged, rocky islands, each less than a quarter of a square mile in area. Nihoa is the tallest of the Northwestern Hawaiian Islands, with sheer sea cliffs and a peak elevation of 910ft.

Two land bird species live only on tiny Nihoa and nowhere else.

The Nihoa finch, which like the Laysan finch is a raider of other birds' eggs, is hanging in there with a population of a few thousand.

In 1967 biologists attempted to develop a backup colony in case something happened to the birds on Nihoa, but the strategy failed when all 42 finches sent to the French Frigate Shoals died.

The gray Nihoa millerbird, related to the Old World warbler family, is rare and secretive. It wasn't even discovered until 1923 and was so named because it eats miller moths. Approximately 400 birds remain.

MIDWAY ISLANDS

The Midway Islands, best known as the site of a pivotal WWII battle between Japanese and American naval forces, is the only place in the Northwestern Hawaiian Islands that allows tourism.

Midway, which in the postwar era served as a naval air facility with some 3000 personnel, was one of several military bases targeted for closing at the end of the Cold War. In 1996 the military transferred jurisdiction of Midway to the US Fish & Wildlife Service and then began an extensive environmental cleanup programme to remove contaminants left over from the military occupation and to rid Midway of non-native plants.

When the Fish & Wildlife Service took over the islands, the agency initiated a unique management policy blending wildlife protection with low-impact tourism. The Fish & Wildlife Service maintained a limited presence on Midway, while a private company handled most of the atoll's operations. This company, Midway Phoenix Corporation, developed the island for ecotourism purposes, renovating the former officers' quarters into a hotel and maintaining Midway's airfield.

Until early 2002 Midway Phoenix Corporation operated tours geared for naturalists and divers. To minimize the impact on the environment, diving and other activities took place only with guides and no more than 100 visitors were allowed on Midway at any one time. Tourism did not significantly disturb the wildlife, and the money generated from tourism helped defray the $4 million cost of operating the refuge.

Unfortunately the operation costs were much higher than expected and Midway Phoenix Corporation pulled out after chalking up huge losses. The Fish & Wildlife Service is now looking for a new vendor to resume operations, but until that happens all public access to Midway has ceased. When, or even if, it will resume is anyone's guess.

More than a million seabirds nest on Midway, including the world's largest colony of Laysan albatross, which are so thick during the months of November to July that they virtually blanket the ground. Fourteen other seabird species pass through Midway, including red-tailed tropic birds, Bonin petrels, wedge-tailed shearwaters, brown noddies and both gray-backed and sooty terns.

Sand Island, the site of the tourist facilities, is the largest island in the three-island Midway Atoll, measuring about 2 miles in length and a mile across. In addition to its dense colonies of seabirds, Sand Island contains a smattering of early 20th-century relics, including the remains of a trans-Pacific cable station that dates to 1903, as well as WWII-era bunkers and antiaircraft guns. The surrounding waters harbor coral gardens, unusual tropical fish and schools of spinner dolphins.

Getting There & Away

When Midway Phoenix Corporation operated tours to Midway, Aloha Airlines provided twice-weekly charter flights from Honolulu. Aloha, or another airline, will likely resume operations on a twice-weekly basis if the island opens to the public again.

If you're interested in finding out whether tourism has started up again on Midway, you can get up-to-date details online from the **US Fish & Wildlife Service** (W *midway.fws.gov*).

Also, the San Francisco–based **Oceanic Society Expeditions** (☎ *415-441-1106*; W *www.oceanic-society.org*) previously led ecology tours to Midway and is likely to do so again if tourism resumes.

Language

The unifying language of Hawaii is English, but it's liberally peppered with Hawaiian phrases, loan words from the various immigrant languages and pidgin slang.

It's not uncommon to hear islanders speaking in other languages, however, as the main language spoken in one out of every four homes in Hawaii is a mother tongue other than English. The Hawaiian language itself is still spoken among family members by about 9000 people, and Hawaiian is, along with English, an official state language.

Closely related to other Polynesian languages, Hawaiian is melodic, phonetically simple and loaded with vowels and repeated syllables.

Some 85% of all place-names in Hawaii are in Hawaiian, and as often as not they have interesting translations and stories behind them.

The Hawaiians had no written language until the 1820s, when Christian missionaries arrived and rendered the spoken language into the Roman alphabet.

Pronunciation

The written Hawaiian language has just 12 letters. Pronunciation is easy and there are few consonant clusters.

There are five vowel sounds, which sound similar to their English equivalents. Each vowel has both a short and a long pronunciation:

a as in 'father'
e as in 'egg'
i as in 'ski'
o as in 'home'
u as the 'ue' in 'blue'

Hawaiian has diphthongs, a combination of two vowels where the two sounds glide into one another. The stress is on the first vowel, although in general if you pronounce each vowel separately, you'll have no trouble being understood.

The consonant **w** is usually pronounced like a soft English 'v' when it follows the letters **i** and **e** (the town Haleiwa is pronounced Halei*v*a) and like the English 'w' when it follows **u** or **o**. When **w** follows **a**, it can be pronounced either 'v' or 'w' – thus you will hear both *Hawaii* and *Havaii*.

The other consonants – **h, k, l, m, n, p** – are pronounced much the same as they are in English.

Glottal Stops & Macrons

Written Hawaiian uses both glottal stops and macrons, although in modern print both are often omitted.

The glottal stop (') indicates a break between two vowels, which produces an effect similar to saying 'oh-oh' in English. A macron – a short straight line over a vowel – indicates that the vowel sound is lengthened.

Glottal stops and macrons not only affect pronunciation, but can give a word a completely different meaning. For example, *ai* can mean 'sexual intercourse' or 'to eat,' depending on the pronunciation.

All this takes on greater significance when you learn to speak Hawaiian in depth. When using Hawaiian words in an English-language context, eg, 'this *poi* (mashed kalo) is *ono* (good),' there shouldn't be much of a problem.

Compounds

Hawaiian may seem more difficult than it is because many proper names are long and look similar. Many begin with *ka*, meaning 'the,' which over time simply became attached to the beginning of the word.

When you break each word down into its composite parts, some of which are repeated, it all becomes much easier. For example, *Kamehameha* consists of the three compounds Ka-meha-meha. *Humuhumunukunukuapuaa*, which is Hawaii's state fish, is broken down into humu-humu-nuku-nuku-a-pu-a-a.

Some words are doubled to emphasize their meaning. For example: *wiki* means 'quick,' while *wikiwiki* means 'very quick.'

There are some easily recognizable compounds repeatedly found in place-names, and it can be fun to learn a few. For instance, *wai* means 'freshwater,' Waikiki means 'spouting water' (so named for the freshwater springs that were once there);

Sharing the *Shaka*

Islanders greet each other with a *shaka* sign, which is made by folding down the three middle fingers to the palm and extending the thumb and little finger. The hand is then usually held out and shaken in greeting. It's as common as waving.

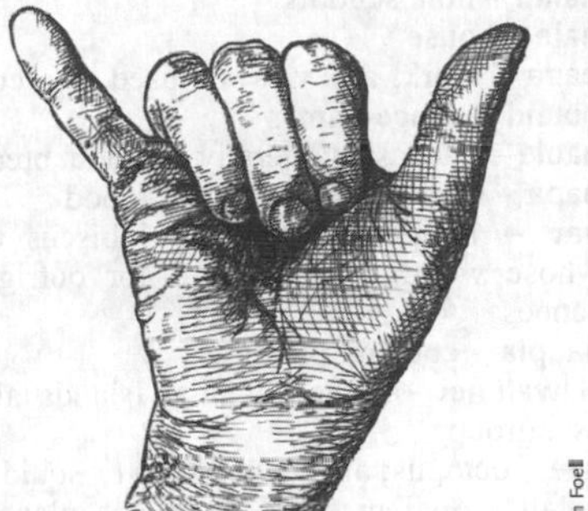

Hayden Foell

kai means 'seawater,' Kailua means 'two seas,' *lani* means 'heavenly,' Lanikai means 'heavenly sea,' *hanu* means 'bay' and Hanalei means 'crescent bay.'

Common Hawaiian Words

Learn these words first: *aloha* (love, welcome, goodbye) and *mahalo* (thank you), which are everyday pleasantries; *makai* (toward the sea) and *mauka* (toward the mountains), commonly used in giving directions; and *kane* (man) and *wahine* (woman), often on bathroom doors.

For more Hawaiian words see the Glossary at the back of the book.

Pidgin

Hawaii's early immigrants communicated with each other in pidgin, a simplified, broken form of English. It was a language born of necessity, stripped of all but the most needed words.

Modern pidgin is better defined as local slang. It is an extensive language, lively and ever changing. Whole conversations can take place in pidgin, or often just a word or two is dropped into a more conventional English sentence.

Even Shakespeare's *Twelfth Night* has been translated (by local comedian James Grant Benton) to *Twelf Nite O Wateva*. Malvolio's line 'My masters, are you mad?' becomes 'You buggahs crazy, o wat?'

Short-term visitors will rarely win friends by trying to speak pidgin. It's more like an insider's code that you're allowed to use only after you've lived in Hawaii long enough to understand the nuances.

Some characteristics of pidgin include a fast staccato rhythm, two-word sentences, dropping the soft 'h' sound from words that start with 'th,' the use of loan words from many languages (often Hawaiian), and double meanings that can easily trip up the uninitiated.

Some of the more common words and expressions include the following:

blalah – big Hawaiian fellow
brah – brother, friend; it's also used for 'hey you'
broke da mouth – delicious
buggah – guy
chicken skin – goose bumps
coconut wireless – word of mouth
cockaroach – steal
da kine – that kind of thing, whatchamacallit etc; used whenever you can't think of the word you want but you know the listener knows what you mean
gee vem – go for it, beat them
grinds – food, eat; *ono grinds* is good food
haolefied – become like a *haole* (Caucasian)
howzit? – hi, how's it going?
how you stay? – how are you?
humbug – a real hassle
like beef? – wanna fight?
mo' bettah – much better, the best
slippahs – flip-flops, thongs
stick – surfboard
stink eye – dirty look, evil eye
talk story – any kind of conversation, tales, gossip
tanks – thanks; more commonly, *tanks brah*
tree – three

Glossary

aa – type of lava that is rough and jagged
ahi – yellowfin tuna
ahinahina – silversword plant with pointed silver leaves
ahu – stone cairns used to mark a trail; or an altar or shrine
ahupuaa – traditional land division, usually in a wedge shape that extends from the mountains to the sea
aikane – friend
aina – land
akala – Hawaiian raspberry
akamai – clever
akepa – endangered crested honeycreeper
aku – skipjack tuna
akua – god, spirit, idol
alae-keokeo – endangered Hawaiian coot
alala – Hawaiian crow
alii – chief, royalty
aloha – the traditional greeting meaning love, welcome, good-bye
aloha aina – love of the land
amaama – mullet
amakihi – small, yellow-green bird; one of the more common native birds
ao – Newell's shearwater (a seabird)
apapane – bright-red native Hawaiian honeycreeper
au – marlin
aumakua – ancestral spirit helper
auwe – Oh my! Alas!
awa – kava, made into an intoxicating brew; milkfish
awapuhi – wild ginger

banh hoi – Vietnamese version of fajitas
banzai – mix of Japanese rice crackers, nuts and dried fish
bento – Japanese boxed lunch

chili rellenos – Mexican dish of green peppers stuffed with cheese
crack seed – snack food, usually dried fruits or seeds; can be sour, salty or sweet

donburi – rice bowls

elepaio – a brownish native bird with a white rump, common to Oahu forests

fuku – Hawaiian-style bonsai trees

gyoza – grilled dumpling made of minced pork and garlic

hala – pandanus plant; the leaves are used in weaving mats and baskets
halau – hula schools
hale – house
hana – work; a bay, when used as a compound in place-names
haole – Caucasian; literally, 'without breath'
hapa – half; person of mixed blood
hau – indigenous lowland hibiscus tree whose wood is often used for outrigger canoes
haupia – coconut pudding
Hawaii nei – all the Hawaiian Islands taken as a group
hee – octopus; also called *tako* or squid
heiau – ancient stone temple; a place of worship in Hawaii before the arrival of Westerners
Hina – Polynesian goddess (wife of Ku, one of the four main gods)
holoholo – to walk, drive or ramble around for pleasure
holoku – a long dress similar to the *muumuu*, but more fitted
holua – sled or sled course
honu – turtle
hoolaulea – celebration, party
hoonanea – to pass the time in ease, peace and pleasure
huhu – angry
hui – group, organization
hukilau – fishing with a seine (a large net), involving a group of people; the word can also refer to the feast that follows
hula – traditional Hawaiian dance
hula kahiko – ancient-style hula
hula halau – *hula* school or troupe
hula ohelo – sensual hula dance
humuhumunukunukuapuaa – rectangular triggerfish

iiwi – bright red forest bird with a curved, salmon-colored beak
iliahi – Hawaiian sandalwood
iliili – stones
ilima – native plant, a ground cover with delicate yellow-orange flowers
ilio holo kai – Hawaiian monk seal
imi – pitlike earthen oven

imu – underground earthen oven used in traditional *luau* cooking
io – Hawaiian hawk

kahili – feathered standard, used as a symbol of royalty
kahuna – wise person in any field; commonly a priest, healer or sorcerer
kahuna nui – high priest
kaiseki ryori – formal Japanese meal consisting of a series of small dishes
kaki mochi – soy-flavored rice crackers; type of *pupu*
kaku – barracuda
kalaipahoa – fire gods who roamed the heavens as shooting stars
kalo – see *taro*
kalua – traditional method of baking in an underground oven *(imu)*
kamaaina – native-born Hawaiian or a long-time resident; literally, 'child of the land'
kanaka – native Hawaiian
Kanaloa – god of the underworld
kane/Kane – man; also the name of one of four main Hawaiian gods
kapa – see *tapa*
kapu – taboo, part of strict ancient Hawaiian social system
katsu – deep-fried fillets of meat
kaunaoa – thin, parasitic vine
kava – mildly narcotic drink made from the roots of *Piper methysticum*, a pepper shrub
keiki – child, children
ki – see *ti*
klawe – relative of the mesquite tree introduced to Hawaii in the 1820s, now very common; its branches are covered with sharp thorns
kii – image, statue
kilau – type of fern
kipuka – an area of land spared when lava flows around it; an oasis
ko – sugarcane
koa – native hardwood tree often used in woodworking of native crafts; fishing shrine
kohola – whale
kokio keokeo – native Hawaiian white hibiscus tree
kokua – help, cooperation
kona – leeward; a leeward wind
konane – a strategy game similar to checkers
koolau – windward side
Ku – Polynesian god of many manifestations, including god of war, farming and fishing (husband of Hina)
kukui – candlenut tree and the official state tree; its oily nuts were once burned in lamps
kuleana – individually held plot of land
kupuna – grandparent, elder
kuula – fishing shrine

Laka – goddess of the hula
lama – native plant in the persimmon family
lanai – veranda
lau – leaves
lauhala – leaves of the *hala* plant used in weaving
laulau – wrapped package; bundles of pork or beef with salted fish that are wrapped in leaves and steamed
lei – garland, usually of flowers, but also of leaves or shells
li hing mui – sour crack seed
lilikoi – passion fruit
limu – seaweed
lio – horse
loco moco – dish of rice topped with a hamburger, fried egg and gravy
lolo – stupid, crazy
lomi – to rub or soften; *lomi* salmon is raw, diced salmon marinated with tomatoes and onions
lomilomi – massage
Lono – Polynesian god of harvest, agriculture, fertility and peace
loulu – native fan palms
luakini – a type of *heiau* (temple) dedicated to the war god Ku and used for human sacrifices
luau – traditional Hawaiian feast

mahalo – thank-you
mahele – to divide; usually refers to the missionary-initiated land divisions of 1848
mahimahi – also called 'dolphin,' but actually a type of fish unrelated to the marine mammal
mai hookaawale – leprosy
maile – native plant with twining habit and fragrant leaves; often used for leis
mai tai – alcoholic drink made from rum, grenadine, and lemon and pineapple juices
makaainana – commoners; literally, 'people who tend the land'
makaha – a sluice gate, used to regulate the level of water in a fishpond
makahiki – ancient annual four-month-long winter harvest festival dedicated to Lono
makai – toward the sea
makaku – creative, artistic *mana*

malasada – a fried dough served warm, similar to a doughnut
malihini – newcomer, visitor
malo – loincloth
mamane – type of fern
mana – spiritual power
manini – convict tang (a reef fish); also used to refer to something small or insignificant
mano – shark
mauka – toward the mountains; inland
mele – song, chant
menehune – the 'little people' who built many of Hawaii's fishponds, *heiau*s and other stonework, according to legend
milo – native shade tree with beautiful hardwood
moa pahee – a game, similar to *ulu maika,* using a large wooden dart
mochi – chewy dessert made from rice
mokihana – type of berry
monja – Japanese custard cakes
mo'o – water spirit, water lizard or dragon
mu – a 'body catcher' who secured sacrificial victims for the *heiau* altar
muumuu – long, loose-fitting dress introduced by the missionaries

naupaka – native shrub with delicate white flowers
Neighbor Islands – the term used to refer to the main Hawaiian Islands outside of Oahu
nene – a native goose; Hawaii's state bird
nisei – people of Japanese descent
niu – coconut palm
noni – Indian mulberry; a small tree with yellow, smelly fruit that is used medicinally
nuku puu – native honeycreeper with a bright yellow underbelly

ohana – family, extended family
ohelo – low-growing native shrub with edible red berries related to cranberries; said to be sacred to the goddess Pele
ohia lehua – native Hawaiian tree with tufted, feathery, pom-pom-like flowers
okole – buttocks
olo – surfboards used by Hawaiian royalty
olopua – olive
onaga – red snapper
one hanau – birth sands in which Hawaiians are buried
ono – delicious; also the name of the wahoo fish
ono grinds – good food
opae – shrimp
opaeula – bright-red shrimp
opah – moonfish
opakapaka – pink snapper
opelu – scad mackerel
opihi – edible limpet

pahoehoe – type of lava that is quick and smooth-flowing
pakalolo – marijuana; literally, 'crazy smoke'
pali – cliff
palila – native honeycreeper
palaka – checked shirt
paniolo – cowboy
panquela – Brazilian crepe stuffed with pumpkin
papio – jackfish; also known as *ulua*
pau – finished, no more
Pele – goddess of fire and volcanoes; she's said to live in Kilauea Caldera
phat thai – rice noodles stir-fried with tofu, vegetables, egg and peanuts
pho – Vietnamese soup of beef broth, noodles and fresh herbs
piko – navel, umbilical cord
pili – a bunchgrass, commonly used for thatching houses
pilikia – trouble
pilo – type of fern
pipikaula – salted, dried beef that is served broiled
poha – gooseberry
pohaku – rock
pohuehue – morning glory
poi – a gooey paste made from *taro* roots; a staple of the Hawaiian diet
poka – member of the passion fruit family; also known as banana *poka*
poke – chopped raw fish marinated in soy sauce, oil and chili pepper
Poliahu – goddess of snow
ponzu – Japanese-style citrus sauce
poouli – endangered native cinnamon-colored bird
pua aloalo – a hibiscus flower
pueo – Hawaiian owl
puhi – moray eel
puka – any kind of hole or opening; small shells that are made into necklaces
pukiawe – native plant with red-and-white berries and evergreen leaves
pulu – the silken clusters encasing the stems of *hapuu* ferns
pupu – snack food, hors d'oeuvres; shells
puu – hill, cinder cone
puuhonua – place of refuge

raku – pottery
rakusen kaiseki – multicourse chef's tasting menu
ryokan – traditional Japanese inn

saimin – a Japanese noodle soup
shaka – Hawaiian hand greeting
soba – Japanese buckwheat noodles

tabi – Japanese reef-walking shoes
talk story – to strike up a conversation, make small talk
tapa – cloth made by pounding the bark of the paper mulberry tree, used for early Hawaiian clothing (*kapa* in Hawaiian)
taro – a plant with green heart-shaped leaves; cultivated in Hawaii for its edible rootstock, which is mashed to make *poi* (*kalo* in Hawaiian)
teishoku – Japanese word for fixed-plate meal
teppanyaki – Japanese style of cooking with an iron grill
ti – common native plant; its long shiny leaves are used for wrapping food and making *hula* skirts (*ki* in Hawaiian)
tiki – image of a god
tsukemono – pickled vegetables
tutu – aunt; used out of respect for any older woman

uau – dark-rumped petrel
uhu – parrotfish
uku – gray snapper
ukulele – a stringed musical instrument derived from the 'braginha,' which was introduced to Hawaii in the 1800s by Portuguese immigrants
ula – spiny lobster
ulu – breadfruit
ulu maika – an ancient Hawaiian game
ume – plums
unagi – eel

wahine – woman
wana – sea urchin
wikiwiki – hurry, quick
wiliwili – the lightest of the native woods

zazen – zen meditation
zendo – communal zen meditation hall

LONELY PLANET

ON THE ROAD

Travel Guides explore cities, regions and countries, and supply information on transport, restaurants and accommodation, covering all budgets. They come with reliable, easy-to-use maps, practical advice, cultural and historical facts and a rundown on attractions both on and off the beaten track. There are over 200 titles in this classic series, covering nearly every country in the world.

Lonely Planet Upgrades extend the shelf life of existing travel guides by detailing any changes that may affect travel in a region since a book has been published. Upgrades can be downloaded for free from **www.lonelyplanet.com/upgrades**

For travellers with more time than money, **Shoestring** guides offer dependable, first-hand information with hundreds of detailed maps, plus insider tips for stretching money as far as possible. Covering entire continents in most cases, the six-volume shoestring guides are known around the world as 'backpackers bibles'.

For the discerning short-term visitor, **Condensed** guides highlight the best a destination has to offer in a full-colour, pocket-sized format designed for quick access. They include everything from top sights and walking tours to opinionated reviews of where to eat, stay, shop and have fun.

CitySync lets travellers use their Palm™ or Visor™ hand-held computers to guide them through a city with handy tips on transport, history, cultural life, major sights, and shopping and entertainment options. It can also quickly search and sort hundreds of reviews of hotels, restaurants and attractions, and pinpoint their location on scrollable street maps. CitySync can be downloaded from **www.citysync.com**

MAPS & ATLASES

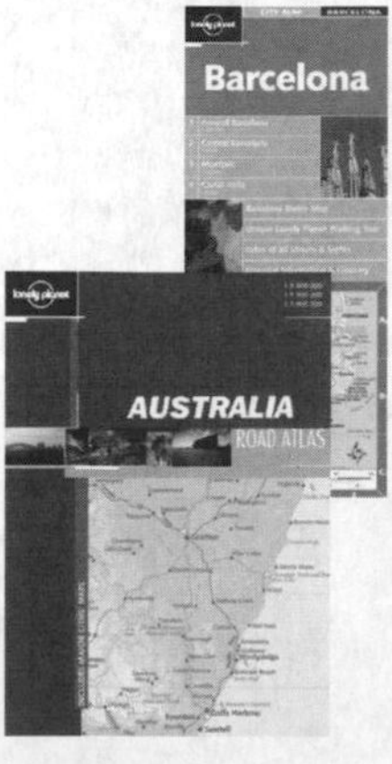

Lonely Planet's **City Maps** feature downtown and metropolitan maps, as well as transit routes and walking tours. The maps come complete with an index of streets, a listing of sights and a plastic coat for extra durability.

Road Atlases are an essential navigation tool for serious travellers. Cross-referenced with the guidebooks, they also feature distance and climate charts and a complete site index.

LONELY PLANET

ESSENTIALS

Read This First books help new travellers to hit the road with confidence. These invaluable predeparture guides give step-by-step advice on preparing for a trip, budgeting, arranging a visa, planning an itinerary and staying safe while still getting off the beaten track.

Healthy Travel pocket guides offer a regional rundown on disease hot spots and practical advice on predeparture health measures, staying well on the road and what to do in emergencies. The guides come with a user-friendly design and helpful diagrams and tables.

Lonely Planet's **Phrasebooks** cover the essential words and phrases travellers need when they're strangers in a strange land. They come in a pocket-sized format with colour tabs for quick reference, extensive vocabulary lists, easy-to-follow pronunciation keys and two-way dictionaries.

Miffed by blurry photos of the Taj Mahal? Tired of the classic 'top of the head cut off' shot? **Travel Photography: A Guide to Taking Better Pictures** will help you turn ordinary holiday snaps into striking images and give you the know-how to capture every scene, from frenetic festivals to peaceful beach sunrises.

Lonely Planet's **Travel Journal** is a lightweight but sturdy travel diary for jotting down all those on-the-road observations and significant travel moments. It comes with a handy time zone wheel, a world map and useful travel information.

Lonely Planet's eKno is an all-in-one communication service developed especially for travellers. It offers low-cost international calls and free email and voicemail so that you can keep in touch while on the road. Check it out on **www.ekno.lonelyplanet.com**

FOOD & RESTAURANT GUIDES

Lonely Planet's **Out to Eat** guides recommend the brightest and best places to eat and drink in top international cities. These gourmet companions are arranged by neighbourhood, packed with dependable maps, garnished with scene-setting photos and served with quirky features.

For people who live to eat, drink and travel, **World Food** guides explore the culinary culture of each country. Entertaining and adventurous, each guide is packed with detail on staples and specialities, regional cuisine and local markets, as well as sumptuous recipes, comprehensive culinary dictionaries and lavish photos good enough to eat.

OUTDOOR GUIDES

For those who believe the best way to see the world is on foot, Lonely Planet's **Walking Guides** detail everything from family strolls to difficult treks, with 'when to go and how to do it' advice supplemented by reliable maps and essential travel information.

Cycling Guides map a destination's best bike tours, long and short, in day-by-day detail. They contain all the information a cyclist needs, including advice on bike maintenance, places to eat and stay, innovative maps with detailed cues to the rides, and elevation charts.

The **Watching Wildlife** series is perfect for travellers who want authoritative information but don't want to tote a heavy field guide. Packed with advice on where, when and how to view a region's wildlife, each title features photos of over 300 species and contains engaging comments on the local flora and fauna.

With underwater colour photos throughout, **Pisces Books** explore the world's best diving and snorkelling areas. Each book contains listings of diving services and dive resorts, detailed information on depth, visibility and difficulty of dives, and a roundup of the marine life you're likely to see through your mask.

OFF THE ROAD

Journeys, the travel literature series written by renowned travel authors, capture the spirit of a place or illuminate a culture with a journalist's attention to detail and a novelist's flair for words. These are tales to soak up while you're actually on the road or dip into as an at-home armchair indulgence.

The range of lavishly illustrated **Pictorial** books is just the ticket for both travellers and dreamers. Off-beat tales and vivid photographs bring the adventure of travel to your doorstep long before the journey begins and long after it is over.

Lonely Planet **Videos** encourage the same independent, tough-minded approach as the guidebooks. Currently airing throughout the world, this award-winning series features innovative footage and an original soundtrack.

Yes, we know, work is tough, so do a little bit of deskside dreaming with the spiral-bound Lonely Planet **Diary** or a Lonely Planet **Wall Calendar**, filled with great photos from around the world.

TRAVELLERS NETWORK

Lonely Planet Online. Lonely Planet's award-winning Web site has insider information on hundreds of destinations, from Amsterdam to Zimbabwe, complete with interactive maps and relevant links. The site also offers the latest travel news, recent reports from travellers on the road, guidebook upgrades, a travel links site, an online book-buying option and a lively travellers bulletin board. It can be viewed at **www.lonelyplanet.com** or AOL keyword: lp.

Planet Talk is a quarterly print newsletter, full of gossip, advice, anecdotes and author articles. It provides an antidote to the being-at-home blues and lets you plan and dream for the next trip. Contact the nearest Lonely Planet office for your free copy.

Comet, the free Lonely Planet newsletter, comes via email once a month. It's loaded with travel news, advice, dispatches from authors, travel competitions and letters from readers. To subscribe, click on the Comet subscription link on the front page of the Web site.

LONELY PLANET

Guides by Region

Lonely Planet is known worldwide for publishing practical, reliable and no-nonsense travel information in our guides and on our Web site. The Lonely Planet list covers just about every accessible part of the world. Currently there are 16 series: Travel guides, Shoestring guides, Condensed guides, Phrasebooks, Read This First, Healthy Travel, Walking guides, Cycling guides, Watching Wildlife guides, Pisces Diving & Snorkeling guides, City Maps, Road Atlases, Out to Eat, World Food, Journeys travel literature and Pictorials.

AFRICA Africa on a shoestring • Botswana • Cairo • Cairo City Map • Cape Town • Cape Town City Map • East Africa • Egypt • Egyptian Arabic phrasebook • Ethiopia, Eritrea & Djibouti • Ethiopian Amharic phrasebook • The Gambia & Senegal • Healthy Travel Africa • Kenya • Malawi • Morocco • Moroccan Arabic phrasebook • Mozambique • Namibia • Read This First: Africa • South Africa, Lesotho & Swaziland • Southern Africa • Southern Africa Road Atlas • Swahili phrasebook • Tanzania, Zanzibar & Pemba • Trekking in East Africa • Tunisia • Watching Wildlife East Africa • Watching Wildlife Southern Africa • West Africa • World Food Morocco • Zambia • Zimbabwe, Botswana & Namibia
Travel Literature: Mali Blues: Traveling to an African Beat • The Rainbird: A Central African Journey • Songs to an African Sunset: A Zimbabwean Story

AUSTRALIA & THE PACIFIC Aboriginal Australia & the Torres Strait Islands •Auckland • Australia • Australian phrasebook • Australia Road Atlas • Cycling Australia • Cycling New Zealand • Fiji • Fijian phrasebook • Healthy Travel Australia, NZ & the Pacific • Islands of Australia's Great Barrier Reef • Melbourne • Melbourne City Map • Micronesia • New Caledonia • New South Wales • New Zealand • Northern Territory • Outback Australia • Out to Eat – Melbourne • Out to Eat – Sydney • Papua New Guinea • Pidgin phrasebook • Queensland • Rarotonga & the Cook Islands • Samoa • Solomon Islands • South Australia • South Pacific • South Pacific phrasebook • Sydney • Sydney City Map • Sydney Condensed • Tahiti & French Polynesia • Tasmania • Tonga • Tramping in New Zealand • Vanuatu • Victoria • Walking in Australia • Watching Wildlife Australia • Western Australia
Travel Literature: Islands in the Clouds: Travels in the Highlands of New Guinea • Kiwi Tracks: A New Zealand Journey • Sean & David's Long Drive

CENTRAL AMERICA & THE CARIBBEAN Bahamas, Turks & Caicos • Baja California • Belize, Guatemala & Yucatán • Bermuda • Central America on a shoestring • Costa Rica • Costa Rica Spanish phrasebook • Cuba • Cycling Cuba • Dominican Republic & Haiti • Eastern Caribbean • Guatemala • Havana • Healthy Travel Central & South America • Jamaica • Mexico • Mexico City • Panama • Puerto Rico • Read This First: Central & South America • Virgin Islands • World Food Caribbean • World Food Mexico • Yucatán
Travel Literature: Green Dreams: Travels in Central America

EUROPE Amsterdam • Amsterdam City Map • Amsterdam Condensed • Andalucía • Athens • Austria • Baltic States phrasebook • Barcelona • Barcelona City Map • Belgium & Luxembourg • Berlin • Berlin City Map • Britain • British phrasebook • Brussels, Bruges & Antwerp • Brussels City Map • Budapest • Budapest City Map • Canary Islands • Catalunya & the Costa Brava • Central Europe • Central Europe phrasebook • Copenhagen • Corfu & the Ionians • Corsica • Crete • Crete Condensed • Croatia • Cycling Britain • Cycling France • Cyprus • Czech & Slovak Republics • Czech phrasebook • Denmark • Dublin • Dublin City Map • Dublin Condensed • Eastern Europe • Eastern Europe phrasebook • Edinburgh • Edinburgh City Map • England • Estonia, Latvia & Lithuania • Europe on a shoestring • Europe phrasebook • Finland • Florence • Florence City Map • France • Frankfurt City Map • Frankfurt Condensed • French phrasebook • Georgia, Armenia & Azerbaijan • Germany • German phrasebook • Greece • Greek Islands • Greek phrasebook • Hungary • Iceland, Greenland & the Faroe Islands • Ireland • Italian phrasebook • Italy • Kraków • Lisbon • The Loire • London • London City Map • London Condensed • Madrid • Madrid City Map • Malta • Mediterranean Europe • Milan, Turin & Genoa • Moscow • Munich • Netherlands • Normandy • Norway • Out to Eat – London • Out to Eat – Paris • Paris • Paris City Map • Paris Condensed • Poland • Polish phrasebook • Portugal • Portuguese phrasebook • Prague • Prague City Map • Provence & the Côte d'Azur • Read This First: Europe • Rhodes & the Dodecanese • Romania & Moldova • Rome • Rome City Map • Rome Condensed • Russia, Ukraine & Belarus • Russian phrasebook • Scandinavian & Baltic Europe • Scandinavian phrasebook • Scotland • Sicily • Slovenia • South-West France • Spain • Spanish phrasebook • Stockholm • St Petersburg • St Petersburg City Map • Sweden • Switzerland • Tuscany • Ukrainian phrasebook • Venice • Vienna • Wales • Walking in Britain • Walking in France • Walking in Ireland • Walking in Italy • Walking in Scotland • Walking in Spain • Walking in Switzerland • Western Europe • World Food France • World Food Greece • World Food Ireland • World Food Italy • World Food Spain **Travel Literature:** After Yugoslavia • Love and War in the Apennines • The Olive Grove: Travels in Greece • On the Shores of the Mediterranean • Round Ireland in Low Gear • A Small Place in Italy

LONELY PLANET

Mail Order

Lonely Planet products are distributed worldwide. They are also available by mail order from Lonely Planet, so if you have difficulty finding a title please write to us. North and South American residents should write to 150 Linden St, Oakland, CA 94607, USA; European and African residents should write to 10a Spring Place, London NW5 3BH, UK; and residents of other countries to Locked Bag 1, Footscray, Victoria 3011, Australia.

INDIAN SUBCONTINENT & THE INDIAN OCEAN Bangladesh • Bengali phrasebook • Bhutan • Delhi • Goa • Healthy Travel Asia & India • Hindi & Urdu phrasebook • India • India & Bangladesh City Map • Indian Himalaya • Karakoram Highway • Kathmandu City Map • Kerala • Madagascar • Maldives • Mauritius, Réunion & Seychelles • Mumbai (Bombay) • Nepal • Nepali phrasebook • North India • Pakistan • Rajasthan • Read This First: Asia & India • South India • Sri Lanka • Sri Lanka phrasebook • Tibet • Tibetan phrasebook • Trekking in the Indian Himalaya • Trekking in the Karakoram & Hindukush • Trekking in the Nepal Himalaya • World Food India **Travel Literature**: The Age of Kali: Indian Travels and Encounters • Hello Goodnight: A Life of Goa • In Rajasthan • Maverick in Madagascar • A Season in Heaven: True Tales from the Road to Kathmandu • Shopping for Buddhas • A Short Walk in the Hindu Kush • Slowly Down the Ganges

MIDDLE EAST & CENTRAL ASIA Bahrain, Kuwait & Qatar • Central Asia • Central Asia phrasebook • Dubai • Farsi (Persian) phrasebook • Hebrew phrasebook • Iran • Israel & the Palestinian Territories • Istanbul • Istanbul City Map • Istanbul to Cairo • Istanbul to Kathmandu • Jerusalem • Jerusalem City Map • Jordan • Lebanon • Middle East • Oman & the United Arab Emirates • Syria • Turkey • Turkish phrasebook • World Food Turkey • Yemen
Travel Literature: Black on Black: Iran Revisited • Breaking Ranks: Turbulent Travels in the Promised Land • The Gates of Damascus • Kingdom of the Film Stars: Journey into Jordan

NORTH AMERICA Alaska • Boston • Boston City Map • Boston Condensed • British Columbia • California & Nevada • California Condensed • Canada • Chicago • Chicago City Map • Chicago Condensed • Florida • Georgia & the Carolinas • Great Lakes • Hawaii • Hiking in Alaska • Hiking in the USA • Honolulu & Oahu City Map • Las Vegas • Los Angeles • Los Angeles City Map • Louisiana & the Deep South • Miami • Miami City Map • Montreal • New England • New Orleans • New Orleans City Map • New York City • New York City City Map • New York City Condensed • New York, New Jersey & Pennsylvania • Oahu • Out to Eat – San Francisco • Pacific Northwest • Rocky Mountains • San Diego & Tijuana • San Francisco • San Francisco City Map • Seattle • Seattle City Map • Southwest • Texas • Toronto • USA • USA phrasebook • Vancouver • Vancouver City Map • Virginia & the Capital Region • Washington, DC • Washington, DC City Map • World Food New Orleans **Travel Literature**: Caught Inside: A Surfer's Year on the California Coast • Drive Thru America

NORTH-EAST ASIA Beijing • Beijing City Map • Cantonese phrasebook • China • Hiking in Japan • Hong Kong & Macau • Hong Kong City Map • Hong Kong Condensed • Japan • Japanese phrasebook • Korea • Korean phrasebook • Kyoto • Mandarin phrasebook • Mongolia • Mongolian phrasebook • Seoul • Shanghai • South-West China • Taiwan • Tokyo • Tokyo Condensed • World Food Hong Kong • World Food Japan
Travel Literature: In Xanadu: A Quest • Lost Japan

SOUTH AMERICA Argentina, Uruguay & Paraguay • Bolivia • Brazil • Brazilian phrasebook • Buenos Aires • Buenos Aires City Map • Chile & Easter Island • Colombia • Ecuador & the Galapagos Islands • Healthy Travel Central & South America • Latin American Spanish phrasebook • Peru • Quechua phrasebook • Read This First: Central & South America • Rio de Janeiro • Rio de Janeiro City Map • Santiago de Chile • South America on a shoestring • Trekking in the Patagonian Andes • Venezuela **Travel Literature**: Full Circle: A South American Journey

SOUTH-EAST ASIA Bali & Lombok • Bangkok • Bangkok City Map • Burmese phrasebook • Cambodia • Cycling Vietnam, Laos & Cambodia • East Timor phrasebook • Hanoi • Healthy Travel Asia & India • Hill Tribes phrasebook • Ho Chi Minh City (Saigon) • Indonesia • Indonesian phrasebook • Indonesia's Eastern Islands • Java • Lao phrasebook • Laos • Malay phrasebook • Malaysia, Singapore & Brunei • Myanmar (Burma) • Philippines • Pilipino (Tagalog) phrasebook • Read This First: Asia & India • Singapore • Singapore City Map • South-East Asia on a shoestring • South-East Asia phrasebook • Thailand • Thailand's Islands & Beaches • Thailand, Vietnam, Laos & Cambodia Road Atlas • Thai phrasebook • Vietnam • Vietnamese phrasebook • World Food Indonesia • World Food Thailand • World Food Vietnam

ALSO AVAILABLE: Antarctica • The Arctic • The Blue Man: Tales of Travel, Love and Coffee • Brief Encounters: Stories of Love, Sex & Travel • Buddhist Stupas in Asia: The Shape of Perfection • Chasing Rickshaws • The Last Grain Race • Lonely Planet ... On the Edge: Adventurous Escapades from Around the World • Lonely Planet Unpacked • Lonely Planet Unpacked Again • Not the Only Planet: Science Fiction Travel Stories • Ports of Call: A Journey by Sea • Sacred India • Travel Photography: A Guide to Taking Better Pictures • Travel with Children • Tuvalu: Portrait of an Island Nation

Index

Abbreviations

BI – The Big Island
K – Kauai
L – Lanai
M – Maui
Mol – Molokai
NHI – Northwestern Hawaiian Islands
O – Oahu

Text

Bold indicates maps.

Bold indicates maps.

I

J

K

Boxed Text

MAP LEGEND

ROUTES

City | Regional

- Freeway
- Tollway
- Primary Road
- Secondary Road
- Tertiary Road
- Dirt Road
- Pedestrian Mall
- Steps
- Tunnel
- Trail
- Walking Tour
- Path

TRANSPORTATION

- Train
- Metro
- Bus Route
- Ferry

HYDROGRAPHY

- River; Creek
- Canal
- Lake
- Spring; Rapids
- Waterfalls
- Dry; Salt Lake

ROUTE SHIELDS

- 80 Interstate Freeway
- 95 State Highway

BOUNDARIES

- International
- State
- County
- Disputed

AREAS

- Beach
- Building
- Campus
- Cemetery
- Forest
- Garden; Zoo
- Golf Course
- Park
- Plaza
- Reservation
- Sports Field
- Swamp; Mangrove

POPULATION SYMBOLS

- **NATIONAL CAPITAL** .... National Capital
- **STATE CAPITAL** .... State Capital
- **Large City** .... Large City
- **Medium City** .... Medium City
- **Small City** .... Small City
- **Town; Village** .... Town; Village

MAP SYMBOLS

- Place to Stay
- Place to Eat
- Point of Interest

- Airfield
- Airport
- Archeological Site; Ruin
- Bank
- Baseball Diamond
- Beach
- Bike Trail
- Bodysurfing
- Buddhist Temple
- Bus Station; Terminal
- Cable Car; Chairlift
- Campground
- Cathedral
- Cave
- Cabin
- Church
- Cinema
- Dive Site
- Ferry Terminal
- Gas Station
- Garden
- Hospital
- Information
- Internet Access
- Kayaking
- Lighthouse
- Lookout
- Mile Marker
- Mission
- Monument
- Mountain
- Museum
- Oasis
- Observatory
- Park
- Parking
- Pass
- Picnic Area
- Police Station
- Pool
- Post Office
- Pub; Bar
- RV Park
- Shipwreck
- Shopping Mall
- Snorkel Site
- Stately Home
- Surfing
- Swamp
- Tao Temple
- Taxi
- Telephone
- Theater
- Toilet - Public
- Trailhead
- Tram Stop
- Transportation
- Volcano
- Whale Watching
- Waterfall

Note: Not all symbols displayed above appear in this book.

LONELY PLANET OFFICES

Australia
Locked Bag 1, Footscray, Victoria 3011
☎ 03 8379 8000 fax 03 8379 8111
email: talk2us@lonelyplanet.com.au

UK
10a Spring Place, London NW5 3BH
☎ 020 7428 4800 fax 020 7428 4828
email: go@lonelyplanet.co.uk

USA
150 Linden St, Oakland, CA 94607
☎ 510 893 8555 TOLL FREE: 800 275 8555
fax 510 893 8572
email: info@lonelyplanet.com

France
1 rue du Dahomey, 75011 Paris
☎ 01 55 25 33 00 fax 01 55 25 33 01
email: bip@lonelyplanet.fr
www.lonelyplanet.fr

World Wide Web: www.lonelyplanet.com *or* AOL keyword: lp
Lonely Planet Images: www.lonelyplanetimages.com